SPORTSOURCE

(Tony Duffy)

(Tony Duffy)

SPORTSOURCE

Edited by Bob Anderson

(Larry Green)

P.O. Box 366, Mountain View, CA 94040
European Address: Box 247, Croydon, Surrey, CR98AQ, England

Library of Congress Catalog Card Number 75-16003
ISBN 0-89037-061-3

**All prices subject to change without notice.*

Cover design and sport illustrations by Micá Quinn

Meet Our Staff

It took a lot of people to put this book together. And we want to thank the many people and organizations that were helpful in making this book possible. Besides myself a team of on-staff World Publications people were involved. And a further team will be involved in promoting and shipping the book. Here are the 16 people that worked many hours with me to produce the **SportSource**.

George Beinhorn is the editor of *Bike World* magazine. He is a vegetarian and lists photography, running, bicycling and outdoor living as his active hobbies.

Hugh Bowen edits *Self-Defense World* magazine and is an omnivorous sports participant. He especially enjoys long distance running, cycling and camping.

Pam Goforth is editor of *Gymnastics World* magazine and assistant editor of *Down River* magazine. She has been running competitively for 13 years and is now sprinting for her fourth year with the San Jose (California) Cindergals. She has taught cheerleading, tumbling and acrobatic stunts for four years and played two seasons of powderpuff football while earning her bachelor's degree at the University of Santa Clara. Pam enjoys a wide variety of sports from archery and badminton to water skiing and rugby.

Joe Henderson, the senior member of the World Publications team after founder-publisher Bob Anderson, came to work as editor of *Runner's World* magazine in 1970. Earlier, he had written for *Track & Field News* and had covered all sports for a daily newspaper in Iowa. Though primarily a runner (active for nearly 20 years, with 600 races behind him), Henderson also participates in bicycling and swimming. He has authored seven books on running and expects to publish three more during 1976.

Teresa Henderson is 19 and was the head typist for the *SportSource*. She enjoys horseback riding, motorcycling and speedboating. She has camped extensively in Texas, Oklahoma, New Mexico, Colorado, Arizona and Northern California. She's played powderpuff football and is currently getting deeply into the game of chess.

Jan Herhold is 24 and is the layout artist for World Publications. An active sportswoman, Jan enjoys tennis, skiing, parachuting, scuba diving, kayaking, and long distance running. Her present goals are to shave down her 3:45 marathon time and to become a yoga instructor. She plans to leave shortly for a year's study at the European Yoga Center in Paris, France.

Ian Jackson is 30 and edits *Soccer World* magazine. He's a former marathoner of near-Olympic caliber. He is a vegetarian and a yoga teacher. Ballet and jazz dancing are his current interests. He wrote the popular book *Yoga and the Athlete.*

Jeff Loughridge is 22 and works as a graphic artist in the layout department. His sedentary hobbies include embroidery and painting, but he keeps busy with physical activities like running, bicycle touring, bicycle racing, autocross, motorcycle road racing and hang gliding.

Dave Prokop is a 34-year-old Canadian transplanted to California where he is editor of *Nordic World* magazine and assistant editor of *Runner's World.* Although he has written about numerous sports, Dave's main interest since his high school days has been track and field. He has wide experience in the sport—as a competitive distance runner, writer, coach, organizer, and historian. He is director of the world-class Springbank International Road Race in London, Ontario, Canada each year, and is founder and director of the Canadian Road Runners Hall of Fame. He has competed in the Boston Marathon on three occasions, finishing as high as 42nd in 1963 with 2:40:15.

Micá Quinn is originally from Southern France. She is 27 years old and has a master's degree in Design and Fine Arts from Stanford University. She's been into classical ballet, modern dance, gymnastics and ballooning, and is currently involved in individual exercise, swimming and running. Micá has illustrated articles for eight sports magazines and designed the covers and illustrated over 25 sports books.

Bill Reynolds is 30 years old and "heavily" into weightlifting. In the past he has participated on a high level in badminton, football and track and field (javelin). He has a M.S. degree from the University of Washington and wrote the authoritative *Complete Weight Training Book,* as well as over 100 articles in weight training publications.

Mike Simes is 18 and recently moved from Massachusetts to set the headlines and assist in layout for World Publications' eight magazines and various book publications. Skiing and tennis are Mike's two passions, but he has a healthy interest in virtually all sports.

Diane Teshima uses the word "perfect" to describe her job at World Publications, since she has always been in love with sports. As managing editor, she is responsible for the entire production of the books and magazines. She handles her job with the same energy and enthusiasm that she plays sports with. Currently her favorites are tennis and swimming, although she's been active in running and golf, and once traveled from Nebraska to California by bicycle.

Sue Turner is 22 and the editor of *Aquatic World* magazine. She has swum and paddled flatwater kayaks in competition, and still works out in both sports. She takes her vacations backpacking in the Sierras and regularly rides her bike 15 miles round trip to work. She has a Water Safety Instructor's certificate and has taught swimming and lifeguarded for many years.

Mark Winitz is 25 and recalls that he was a member of his high school baseball, soccer and football teams. He can even recall getting to play those sports once in a great while. After watching his college baseball team in action from the bench for several years, he decided that a more individual sport might lend him a better opportunity to excell. He took up tennis and became quite proficient at water skiing. He's also dabbled in skiing, snow camping, backpacking, bicycling, chess and training his untrainable dog.

Scott Wiseman is 21 and has lived in Northern California all his life. He writes, is a photographer with a working darkroom, and does light show performances. On the more physical side, he races bicycles, skis downhill and nordic, swims, and plays tennis. Scott chose and edited the book selections at the end of each sport.

Table of Contents

(Cross-references in light print.)

Inside the SportSource

The **SportSource** is not just another sports encyclopedia. True, we have included more sports in one book than any previously have. But we want this to be more than just an information source. We want to turn you on to a sport in an active way. We want to get you *involved* in sport. Or if you already are or have been involved, we want to make sure you know about the magazines and books available, and other contacts to make you more knowledgeable and expand your horizons. Or maybe you are getting bored with your sport and would like to consider something else. Or maybe you just need some inspiration to get back out. If so, this book is for you.

The **SportSource** is one of a kind. Not only is the book different, but so are the people behind the book. Almost without exception, the people involved in writing, editing, typesetting and layout participate regularly in sport and make it an important part of their lives. This is why we feel we can do this book better than any other company.

Our whole company is centered around sport. We publish eight sport magazines, we have published about 50 sport books, have 30 more in production and another 10 on the drawing board. We inventory and sell over 1400 different sport books. In fact, many libraries are ordering all their sport titles from us because they know we have the best selection.

We also do a big mail order business that includes sport shoes, clothing and accessories mainly centered around running. We have a retail sport store called Starting Line Sports. Through eight years of research, we have developed possibly the best athletic drink available. We have presented ideas and research findings in our magazines that have never been presented before.

We not only publish sports magazine but also promote the sports we get involved in. As an example. we put on weekly Fun-Runs that have been going for three years now, drawing an average of 100 runners each week. And we came up with the idea of National Running Week to bring more attention to running nationally. But we feel we have only started. We have so much more we want to do and are going to do.

The **SportSource** is presented by athletes (sometimes this word can sound too official; what we really want to say is "people regularly active in one of the sports listed in this book") for athletes (people already involved or thinking about getting involved). In all sports, we talked with people who have participated in the sport. And in most cases we had them write the essay for us. In looking at our list of contributors, you'll find Olympic, world and national champions. You'll find people with many years of experience and vast knowledge. Our contributors and our entire staff want to present each sport accurately so that you the reader can make a fair decision in picking a sport.

I am interested in getting as many people as possible involved in at least one of the sports listed in this book. We do use the word "sport" loosely. We include magic, frog jumping, card games and checkers. But we feel by covering both the physical and mental sports we can offer enough of a selection to get you started, to find you an additional sport or a new, more enjoyable one. Ideally, at least one of your sports would be "aerobic" (one that develops the heart and lungs) like running, bicycling, handball, or badminton. But certainly there is a lot of value in the other sports, too. You can't expect to be in good physical shape playing checkers, chess, bridge or a similar sport, but any sport is better than none at all.

Dr. Kenneth Cooper explains in good detail in his interview the physical benefits of sports. However, just because you participate doesn't mean you are automatically fit. Watch your weight, have a good diet and do get a check-up regularly.

If you do decide to get into a physically demanding sport, start out slowly. Don't go overboard the first day, week or month. If you are getting into running, for example, start with slow 100-yard runs followed by 100-yard walks. Don't go so hard that you aren't able to talk comfortably. Sport doesn't have to hurt. Sport is fun. Of course, this doesn't mean that once you get "into shape" that you won't push yourself. Just don't start that way.

Here is how this book can be used. Look through and decide which sport looks interesting, then read what we say about it. After that, write away and either get a sample copy of the magazine listed or go ahead and subscribe to it. If there isn't a magazine listed, write the organization or contact noted and ask for information.

A magazine is a good source for information. Upcoming events, equipment sources and general advice can be found. In many sports, you might have to wait until you get additional information before starting.

We have also listed books that offer more detail on the sport. These are available directly from us or you can order through your bookstore. We have listed the publisher after the price for each book.

Knowing about the sport you want to get involved in is very important. The more you know, the more you'll enjoy it. And since we wanted to make things as easy as possible, all books listed are available from one source–World Publications.

World Publications was certainly the company to do this book. Not only did we get the athletes to write up the pieces for the sports; we approached these athletes as fellow athletes. We wanted to present this book to the person who wants to get involved, not just the person who likes to read–even though we think this book provides good reading.

Most of us here already are involved in at least one sport.

Of the 60 people in the company, about 40 regularly are active and the others do something once in awhile. And all have done some sport on a regular basis at one time in their lives.

In December 1975, almost everyone from the office plans to run as a group in a 60-mile relay. I don't think too many companies would have the turnout we will have. We also don't allow smoking in or around the building.

Personally, I (as founder, president, and owner of World Publications) have been running since 1962 and still compete today. I also like to bicycle, raft, cross-country ski and play soccer. And if I had the time, I would like to participate in just about every sport listed here.

I am sold on sport, my company is sold on sport and we hope that we can sell you on sport. It is the most important thing you can do for a long healthy life.

We want to hear from our readers. We want to know what you liked about the book and what we can do differently the next time around. We want to know about any mistakes, any sports we left out and if you would be interested in helping us on our next edition. This book is yours and we want to provide you with the information you want and need.

World Publications is the sport-source and we want to prove it. We have a lot of other ideas that will be announced in our **SportSource Update**. Some are really exciting. But right now we hope that you will pass the word around about this book so we can get it in as many hands as possible. What we do with all sports beyond this rests on the success of this book.

World Publications doesn't want to actively support all of the sports listed. Some we don't enjoy, but we felt we couldn't leave them out. Just because we don't like the sport doesn't mean everyone won't. We also want to stress that you use common sense. For instance, if you get into off-road vehicles or snowmobiling, don't tear up nature. Or if you get into one of the martial arts, don't do it because you want to hurt someone. Do it because you want to learn an art.

Of course we will continue to promote the eight sports in which we publish magazines, but if this book is well received we have plans for newsletters on all of these sports, extensive information sources available to others, books, etc. Do get on our mailing list. The cost is only $1.00 and we'll send you four copies a year of the **SportSource Update** which will include information on the things we will be doing.

One last word: Don't just read this book and then not get involved in the sport you think would be interesting. Everybody has ideas and thinks about doing things but most never take an extra minute to be a "doer." Let us hear from you if this book helped you get started in a sport. We hope we'll be hearing from you soon.

Bob Anderson November, 1975

Bob Anderson, editor of *SportSource,* running with daughter Lisa at the Sunday Morning Fun-Runs that he started three years ago. Bob has been running since 1962 and started his first magazine, *Distance Running News* (now called *Runner's World*) in 1966 while only 17 years old. Today his previous one-man operation for five years has grown to 60. And among the many things that he has done: publishes eight sports magazines (*Runner's World, Bike World, Aquatic World, Nordic World, Down River, Soccer World, Self-Defense World, Gymnastics World);* also is the editor of *Down River;* he has published over 50 sport books including a $10.95 hardback called the *Complete Runner* that has sold over 13,000 copies; sells over 1400 different sport titles gathered from over 200 publishers through his *Sports Book Catalog;* runs tours to the Olympic Games; owns a sport shop called Starting Line Sports that also does a lot of mail order; co-edited a very good book called *Guide to Distance Running;* is the National Director of National Running Week which he started; and most importantly he is very active in sports. He has cross-country skied, taken a 100-mile bike trip, rafted, played soccer, football and baseball and enjoys table tennis, shuffleboard, chess, checkers, etc. He and his wife Rita have two children, Lisa and Michael.

(ABC Sports)

Jim McKay:

Views From the Press Box

Interviewed by Bill Reynolds

During his 14 years as host of ABC Television's *Wide World of Sports,* Jim McKay has won four Emmy awards for excellence in sport telecasting. He has also witnessed a complete metamorphosis in sports television as a result of *Wide World,* from strictly baseball, football, horseracing and boxing telecasts to programming literally 100 sports along a complete spectrum from surfing to skiing, volleyball to wrist wrestling. As an example, ABC's Olympic coverage and subsequent *Wide World* shows have made a tiny Soviet gymnast named Olga Korbut virtually a folk hero in America.

Jim McKay, or Jim McManus as he was then known, was born in Philadelphia in 1921 and spent his youth as a rabid sports fan. It became evident by the time he was in high school, however, that Jim McManus had far more innate talent as a journalist and debater than as an athlete. McManus honed his journalism and dramatics skills at Loyola College in Baltimore, completing a social sciences bachelor's degree in 1943. He served two years in the Navy as a lieutenant aboard a minesweeper, and upon discharge unsuccessfully sought radio work in New York City. With money running low, he was finally hired by the city editor of the *Baltimore Sun,* where he gradually perfected his ability as a newsman by working as a Police Court reporter.

In 1948 the *Sun* began running a television station and Jim worked as a jack of all trades for the fledgling station, singing, reading the news, doing sports and hosting a variety show. Spotted as a rising talent by CBS, he was hired, brought to New York City and had his professional name changed to McKay in 1950. While working at a variety of jobs for CBS, including a three-year stint as the court reporter in the popular drama *The Verdict is Yours,* Jim McKay came to the attention of ABC executives who hired him to host *Wide World* beginning in April of 1961.

Jim McKay labored for 11 years as *Wide World's* host before the true depth of his talent became known, tragically as a result of the 1972 Munich Olympic Games Arab-Israeli incident. With a degree of journalistic professionalism gained from 25 years as a newsman, McKay turned skillfully from sports reporter to news reporter during the 15-hour drama, covered in its entirety by ABC Sports. The sad words of an emotionally spent Jim McKay—"They're all gone"—culminated one of the greatest news reporting efforts of modern journalism. McKay received two Emmy awards for his human treatment of the tragedy and finally reached the position of media superstar that he had merited for so many years.

McKay's technique when reporting events on *Wide World* hinges on a rare ability to make every sport sound interesting and alive to the viewer. He combines a thorough knowledge of sport with a knack for discovering the human element in every story.

Recognized today as the penultimate American sports television commentator, Jim McKay has been in a unique position to view international sports during the past 15 years. He has covered four Olympic Games and his memoir, **My Wide World,** was published in 1973 by MacMillan. He gave this interview to **SportSource's** Bill Reynolds on October 20, 1975.

SSD: Do you feel that sport is a healthy outlet for people? I'm talking about sport at the participant level here.

McKay: I think it is a healthy outlet. Obviously there are many millions more Americans exercising in one way or another than ever before, whether it's riding bikes, jogging, playing tennis, or whatever. It's certainly a way to stay healthy, maybe even get rid of a few aggressions, and have a good time.

Spectator sports, I think, can be a very healthy outlet for people, too, although I'm not sure they are. In England it's not uncommon for people to knock all the windows out of the trains and have riots after soccer games. In South America organizers have to put moats and barbed wire fences around soccer fields to protect the referees. I don't think that's a healthy thing.

SSD: Do you think sport is still healthy for people on a highly organized level?

McKay: It depends on the individual. Anybody who is a competitor in sports has to know his own particular reason for being there. It could be for greed or for total dedication, or it could be for many other things.

I think that the problem in a lot of sports (swimming, for example) is that a lot of very young kids are competing in top world-class competition. It can be a very tough thing for them. Certainly it's more up to their parents to be perceptive enough to see if it's good or bad for them.

SSD: Of course, you're talking about a capitalist form of society, and not about a communist country.

McKay: Yes, I am not talking about the Spartakiade program in East Germany. Some of the other Eastern European countries are doing it, even aside from the Soviet Union. The Rumanians must be doing it to be able to produce an athlete like little Nadia Comaneci who, at 13, is the European women's gymnastics champion. And, at least from what I read, in East Germany they measure kids' hands and feet when they are five and six years old, and they decide what sports the kids are going into.

SSD: Do you personally participate in any sports?

McKay: Yes, I play tennis and golf and I ski. I only discovered skiing five years ago. I don't know what I was doing before then. I probably enjoy skiing more than any of them, although I enjoy golf a tremendous amount, and tennis just a little less.

SSD: Why do you participate in sports? Mostly for health?

"Anybody who is a competitor in sports has to know his own particular reason for being there. It could be for greed or total dedication, or it could be for many other things."

McKay: Well, yes, and because ever since I was a little kid, I wanted to be an athlete and I was never any good at it, and I guess I'm probably still trying to convince myself I never will be [laughing].

But just the idea of concentrating on something, first of all, is totally distracting from any of the problems that I have at the moment, and therefore refreshing. I think that taking three or four hours out to participate in some sport enables you, in a sense, to start again when you finish with it. Exercise is obviously good for you.

SSD: If you had your own choice, and were the Czar over sports in the entire world, what role would you choose for sport?

McKay: It's a complicated thing, in that when you say "the entire world", you bring to mind international relations. Nobody's ever going to be able to pin it down, but I think back to when we first went to the Soviet Union in 1961 for the U.S.-Russia track meet. The atmosphere was one of tremendous tension. It has certainly changed in some way. At least it has not changed for the worse, and we've not had World War III. I think that all of the international contacts since that time in the world of sport, and cultural contacts, have certainly had some effect on the situation – if only because it's really difficult to get people to make war against each other if they are reading every day in the paper about their athletes competing, and in most cases getting along in a pretty sportsmanlike way.

SSD: What about something like the game of ping pong actually opening diplomatic relations between the U.S. and China?

McKay: I think the U.S.-Russia track meet in that day served maybe even in a more important way, but it wasn't publicized in that fashion. The ping pong situation was dramatic because it was the actual first contact between the countries involved after all those years. Sport also can serve as a feeling out process for the government, to see how the other side reacts in an area that is not that politically sensitive. Obviously, that's not the only reason for sport, but international sport – aside from preventing World War III or something – can be a tremendous point of contact among all the people of the world.

SSD: But then maybe if we turn to the Olympic tragedy in '72, that sort of thing can take an opposite trend.

McKay: Well, I feel that the Olympic tragedy had little to do with sport, if anything. The Olympic Games happened to be the world's stage at the moment. It could have been a meeting of the United Nations, an international meeting of scientists, or a packed airplane. These people were simply looking for the world's stage at the moment to draw attention to their cause. In other words, I don't think sport *caused* the situation.

SSD: All that I've read recently in the newspapers indicates that the organizers of the Games are trying to prevent that sort of thing from happening in Montreal, but apparently preparations for the Montreal Olympics are not proceeding exactly according to schedule. A lot of the workers are using the Games as an excuse for their strikes to get more money. Do you think that maybe there is no future for the Olympic Games past 1976?

McKay: I definitely think there will be a Moscow Olympics

"It's really difficult to get people to make war against each other if they are reading every day in the paper about their athletes competing, and in most cases getting along in a pretty sportsmanlike way with competitors from other countries." (Shearman)

in 1980 – that's unless something catastrophic happens. A lot of people have been asking me recently if there *will* be an Olympic Games after 1980. I know people have been writing that 1980 will be the last Olympic Games, or at least that it will be the last Olympics to be held in a large city that has not had them before. And yet when I was in Moscow last month, somebody told me they are already getting feelers for the Olympic Games of 1984, and the person who really wants them is the Shah of Iran. He'd like to have them in Tehran in 1984. Of course, they've built facilities for the Asian Games over there, and he has enough oil money to build whatever he wants anyway. I have a feeling the Games will go on and that they'll probably continue moving to different places, although occasionally they will come back to some places where they've been held before.

SSD: I recall reading that at the last World University Games in Moscow there were quite a few semi-political problems, like discrimination against Jewish competitors. Do you feel that this might be a possibility in 1980?

McKay: Oh, I would think that there would be a lot of problems in Moscow – the sort of thing you mention, finding enough hotel rooms, and so on. But, of course, the political situation could change a lot between now and the Moscow Games.

SSD: Generally, it seems to me that political involvement can present a big problem for sport today. Do you think there is any way around it?

McKay: You know, it is a big problem when you talk about the Olympic Games. I think you can make a very good case for eliminating team sports from the Olympic Games or from other events like the Pan-Am Games. This is where most of the nationalistic and chauvinistic things take place. It's when you literally have the Soviet Union playing the United States, or when you have a situation like that famous water polo game in '56 between the Soviets and Hungary where the blood was actually in the water, that these nationalistic things come to the fore.

Certainly it happens in track, too, and that's where you get to the other problem. People are proposing that athletes just wear white uniforms, that countries not be mentioned nor anthems played. Somehow when I try to picture that in my mind's eye, I think the Games would lose something. I'm not sure exactly what the answer is, and maybe it's just inevitable that the Olympic Games give people a feeling of just what the state of the world is among the various countries. Perhaps it's best to have a realistic situation, rather than one in which we pretend that everybody is from one world, when they are, as of yet, not.

SSD: I personally felt a tremendous nationalistic pride when Dave Wottle beat the Russian Arzhanov in the 800 meters at Munich.

McKay: And that kind of feeling is not necessarily a bad thing. Right? On the other hand, I think that the individual is almost always saluted for the great champion that he is. Look at someone like Uganda's John Aki-Bua, who won the 400-meter hurdles at Munich. I don't think there were a handful of people in that stadium who were fans of Idi Amin, and yet John Aki-Bua got one of the great ovations of the Games when he took an extra victory lap. And that was the pure salute of an athlete. It didn't make any difference where he was from.

SSD: Having been an athlete myself, and still participating in athletics a little bit, I can identify quite readily with the participants. Do announcers feel that same sort of emotion too?

McKay: Oh, of course. Looking back at the '61 US-Russia track meet, I remember when Wilma Rudolph took over the baton a couple of meters behind in the 400 relay, and came down the home stretch. It was one of the great thrills. It actually made the skin tingle. I asked a fellow who was with our party – an ABC executive from Mississippi – how he liked it. He said, "I never thought I would see the day when I would be standing in a stadium in Moscow screaming at a black girl running down a track, "COME ON, BABY!"

SSD: Just for the sake of curiosity, how did you become involved in sports journalism?

McKay: When I was a kid, I was a sports nut. I played every game but was not particularly good at any of them. In school I got involved in being the sports editor of the paper, and actually doing our basketball games on the PA system. Instead of just identifying the name and number, I insisted on doing a play-by-play, which probably drove the people crazy, but it was good practice for me.

I started my professional career in journalism as a city side reporter on the *Baltimore Sun*, and it wasn't until they started a television station that I began doing everything – news, sports, I sang on the show, and I started getting back into sports again with play-by-play. Although I've done a number of things – I was actually brought to New York to do a variety show – at the time I came up I asked to do, and did, a five-minute sports summary every night. So whatever else I have been doing, sports is the thread that has gone through my career. In 1961, I was on the golf course at Augusta covering the Masters Tournament for CBS, when I got the phone call that lead to *Wide World*, which was a summer replacement show.

SSD: Do you get involved very much in the editorial thrust of *Wide World of Sports*, or is that more or less the domain of Roone Arledge, the show's producer?

McKay: I don't know that there is an editorial thrust to *Wide World*. I think that, basically, you have to cover the events and see what is there. And when I'm covering the events I say whatever I think must be said. I've never even discussed with Roone when I'm on location what I'm going to say, any more than I discussed with him what I was going to say on the day of the Munich tragedy when we were on the air for 16 hours. He was in the control room, and he just said to go in the studio and do what we always do, try to cover the story.

SSD: Yes, there was tremendous impact to that telecast. I watched the entire thing.

McKay: Yes, it was some day.

SSD: In all your years with *Wide World of Sports*, what would you consider to be the greatest feat you've seen?

McKay: It's so difficult, when you think of literally 100 sports over a course of almost 15 years. It's so difficult to compare the highlights, but certainly Beamon's long jump from a standpoint of a single explosive performance, has to be the most amazing. And I should think that if any record lasts for 100 years, that would be it – although I noticed that triple jump the other day, in the same pit, was almost in the same class. [Editor: The reference is to Brazil's setting a new world triple jump record of 58' in winning the event at the '75 Pan-Am Games in Mexico City.]

SDD: Do you think that there's any real limit to records in most sports?

McKay: Well, obviously, there has to be a limit. Nobody's going to run a mile in 10 seconds. What is fascinating is that we really don't seem to have gotten close to those limits yet. Don't you have the feeling that somebody is going to run the 100 yards in less than nine seconds, and probably pretty soon? And now that they have the mile down under 3:50, you *know* somebody is going to get it down to 3:45.

SSD: What do you think are the factors that lead to this continual record breaking?

McKay: I guess we all are guessing on that, but it must have something to do with diet to begin with. And then I'm sure that training – which means what we have learned from the past, and moving one step forward from the past – must

"Political involvement is a big problem when you talk about the Olympic Games. I think you can make a very good case for eliminating team sports for the Olympic Games or from other events like the Pan-Am Games. This is where most of the nationalistic and chauvinistic things take place." (Shearman)

have a tremendous amount to do with it. When little girls are swimming distances just to qualify for national championships in times faster than Johnny Weismuller swam to win the Olympics, it is hard to believe that the human being has changed that much. There must be a tremendous amount that has to do with the technique. And then, of course, the old competitive idea, the psychological idea that when somebody else does it, a lot of people suddenly realize they can do something they didn't think they could.

SSD: And, too, there are technological advances like the new artificial surface running tracks and the fiberglass vaulting pole.

McKay: The fiberglass pole has obviously changed the pole vaulting to a different event from the days of the old bamboo pole. But in the others, in swimming, for example, it's hard to see where the pools have changed that much; it's pretty much the human being and the water. So technique and training must be the answer there. I'm sure that the artificial surfaces in track had something to do with the improvement in track records.

SDD: I wanted to ask this question earlier when we were talking about journalism. What do you consider to be the role of sports journalism and broadcasting?

McKay: The job is to be a reporter, which may sound over-simplified, but the job of anybody – whether reporting on sports, or reporting on politics, or reporting of police courts – is to try to communicate what happened as accurately as possible, and I think – particularly in the case of television, although it should be true in print also – to communicate the feeling, and something of the mood, and what it was like to be there at that time.

SSD: I've often wondered how thoroughly you personally prepare for a telecast, particularly in the case of a more unusual sport like wristwrestling, which I know you've covered.

McKay: The wristwrestling is at one end of the pole almost. I did it last year for the first time. I just went out there (to Petaluma, California) and tried to talk to as many of those guys as I could and I found them much more interesting than I thought I would. I thought it would be a kind of a gag, a joke for them. But these guys come from all over the country. And although they are not participating for any money, backstage I found that they were just as psyched up as a guy before the Olympics or anything else.

But generally, I read as much as I can about the particular sport. When we began 15 years ago, I started in on the **Encyclopedia Britannica**, literally, and went on from there. But again, I think it's like any other reporting: try to ask as many questions as possible before going into the event, and read as much as you can about it. Normally, as you know, we do use experts to work with us on different sports.

SSD: What are your feelings about the incidence of drugs in sports? Do you consider that as being a moral issue? Or do

"Obviously there has to be a limit to sports records. Nobody's going to run a mile in 10 seconds. What is fascinating is that we really don't seem to have gotten close to those limits yet." (Duffy)

you simply see it as the type of thing that must be tested for and eliminated?

McKay: I think it is a moral issue, yeah. They seem to be getting closer to conducting tests at the Olympic Games, and competitions like that. It just seems like there's always something new which comes up (that they haven't got a test for at the time). I guess the grayest area I can think of would be the area of blood doping, where you actually can argue that you are not using a narcotic, or anything like that. [Editor: Blood doping is the removal and subsequent re-injection of an athlete's red blood cells to give temporary endurance and strength improvement.]

SSD: In blood doping, apparently it's possible to inject the blood cells into a body wrinkle, so that it's completely undetectable.

McKay: Yes. And you almost have to wonder whether that is morally wrong if it's not an unhealthy thing for the body. The only thing is that it's making the body temporarily stronger than it would be at any other time.

SSD: Apparently, Dr. Roger Bannister – the first four-minute miler – has come up with a test within the last year or so that can determine if a person is on steroids. The problem is that it costs something like $150 to administer the test.

McKay: They might be able to afford it in the Olympics, but when you get down to national and regional competition, it would probably be too costly to get into that.

SSD: And then the trouble is that there are reportedly 75 chemists in the Soviet Union researching new drugs that will be undetectable using the current test.

McKay: Yes, this is a very difficult area in sports. In everything we've said about sports, and how I think sport can be a very good thing, and is a very good thing, for many people, we are always implying, always talking about human beings making the most of the attributes they've been handed. But here, when you get into steroids you are really developing a race of super bodies that are especially trained for this one thing, and for nothing else in life really. Doctors don't know yet if steroids will make one impotent later on, that sort of thing. I think that the use of steroids and drugs in general could eventually, if not destroy, certainly be very bad for sport, more so than the politics and the under-the-table payments (to amateur athletes).

SSD: There has been a lot of controversy in recent years about injuries in sports. In football, for example, the injury rates have been going up rapidly. Do you think that perhaps the human body might have certain limits, and that we may be coming close to exceeding them with the use of drugs, nutrition, and that sort of thing?

McKay: The use of drugs anytime is bad, as I understand it, because it makes your body believe that it can go on at a time when it really isn't prepared to go on.

SSD: And some cyclists have died from amphetamines under such circumstances.

McKay: Exactly. It gives you an illusion. Years ago, I remember, at least one pitcher in the major leagues – he had been shot up in World War II – used to take novocaine in his leg and he couldn't stand up for two days after his pitching turn, although when he was pitching he couldn't feel the leg at all.

"I think that the use of steroids and drugs in general could eventually, if not destroy, certainly be very bad for sport, more so than the politics and the under-the-table payments to amateur athletes."

SSD: I can remember basketball player Gus Johnson of the Baltimore Bullets had a really bad knee, and he complained that he ruined it by playing on it when he couldn't feel any additional pain because of novocaine injections from the team physician.

McKay: That's it, that's what I mean. You're pounding the body and pounding it and you're really destroying it because your body is not able to give you the signals that are built into it.

SSD: I'd like to get your views on the idea of women in sports. Do you think that women can or ever will be able to compete on a par with men?

McKay: I don't think physically women will ever be able to run as fast as men, nor to play muscle sports as well as men. But I think it's basically a great thing that women in school now for the first time are getting their own organized teams and having the chance of making the most of any physical potential. I would hope, and I'm a little bit concerned already on this front, that on the intercollegiate level they would learn from the mistakes that have happened in men's sports, and make sports more for the person than for the overemphasis on winning and getting into the financial big-time.

SSD: In colleges the biggest bone of contention is that the women athletes get most of their revenue from men's sports that bring in fans, like, for example, football. Do you have any comments on this situation?

McKay: This thing is kind of upside down to start with. What really distresses me is when I read about schools that have to cut down the budget and give some of the money to the women. Therefore, they are cutting out golf, tennis, track, swimming – all of the sports that I think are the most important ones. If education is supposed to be the building of the human body – and at the same time it's building the human mind and maturing it – then I think the major sports, if you will, should be the ones I mentioned, and the minor ones should be football, basketball and baseball. First of all, I think the individual sports are better for the body, and they are the ones you can play for the rest of your life.

Obviously football is not a sport that a bunch of guys can play all their lives. I was at a football game the other day, which I seldom have a chance to do, but my son is a junior at Duke University, so we went down for homecoming weekend. It was very exciting – they had the bands and they had the floats and there was great college spirit down there. Duke came from behind in the last minute and a half to win the game. The thought I had was, "Gee, it's so much fun sitting here watching this, that I wish it wasn't a maiming game. But it's a very bad game for the human body."

SSD: I wanted to ask you a couple of questions about the role of professional sports in America. It seems to me that professional sports perhaps serve as a vicarious release for a lot of the spectators.

McKay: Yeah, I don't see anything particularly wrong with that, unless it gets into hooliganism and vandalism, and all that sort of nonsense.

SSD: What about the tremendous escalation of salaries for some of these athletes? For example, basketball player Rick Barry complains because he only makes $250,000 per year.

McKay: I think that if you say you should put a limit on players' salaries, you are really talking about capitalist versus totalitarian form of government. Perhaps you could just as easily say that a corporation president shouldn't make $500,000 a year. But who's going to determine this? Our society long ago was set up so people are free to get as much as they can for their efforts on a supply-and-demand basis. I don't think there's anything morally wrong with a basketball player's making $300,000. You do wonder sometimes, if the amount of effort that comes out of the athlete with a tremendously high salary doesn't go in a reverse ratio, rather than in a positive way. They seem to put out less than the hungry athletes used to. But I guess that's built into the human mind generally, not just the mind of athletes.

SSD: Perhaps the main reason pro athletes want so much money is because they can only look forward to a relatively short career in pro sports. They have to really make it quick before they are banged up and out on the street.

McKay: That's right. And, of course, basically, you do read about the rich guys and not about the 12th guy on the squad. Although in basketball and hockey, I know the salaries are pretty high all the way down the line.

SSD: The reason fans are concerned about player salaries is that ticket prices keep going up as salaries go up, and that the players' salaries go up faster than those of the spectators.

McKay: Yes. Again that's the case in basketball and hockey, and the reason for this is that you still have two other leagues that are basically in competition for the athletes. As soon as you kill the other leagues, as has happened in other sports very effectively . . . You know the salaries in pro football are not nearly as high as they are in basketball and hockey, for example.

SSD: I know you have children. What type of advice did you give them about athletics?

McKay: To use it for their own purposes, as part of their education, as part of their life. I've always encouraged them in the individual sports. When my son was in grammar school, he played football – not too many kids get hurt at that level – but when he went into high school I discouraged him from playing football, although it was his decision. I tried to encourage him in cross-country, which he did for one long, hard, slogging year. Cross-country wasn't for him, but he got interested in tennis and he became quite a good player. I try to encourage them–and my wife does too; she plays tennis four or five times a week – to use physical exercise as a very important physical and health vehicle. It is a very important social occasion and release. From almost every point of view, it's a good thing to do, but the individual sports, again, are the only ones you can take through life with you. I talked to Bill Veeck of baseball once, and he feels that way, too. He said, "What are you going to do the first crisp, clear autumn day after you've graduated from college and want to play football? Call up 21 other guys?"

SSD: What about distance running? Is that good for older people?

McKay: If you have a good heart, and good physical qualities, and if you don't start by running 10 miles the first day, I think it's no doubt a great thing. I think the people who do it get a lot out of it. They are strengthening their heart muscles and their lungs. I think it's terrific! Track, if you think about it – track and field lumped together – is one sport that can provide for almost any kind of a human body, from a tall skinny guy to a short and compact guy to a big shot putter. There is something in track and field for everybody if they find their right slot. In distance running particularly, as I understand it, almost anybody with normal equipment can learn to be a distance runner of some sort – at least recreationally.

SSD: Track and field's decathlon is considered by many to be the ultimate test of athletic ability. Would you agree?

McKay: I don't see how you can disagree. One of our producers – Chet Forte, who was an All-American basketball player at Columbia even though he's only 5'9" – still claims that a basketball player is the ultimate athlete. In the course of a basketball game, you use everything, from long graceful muscles to endurance to hard, charging physical contact. When you put it at the pro level, where players travel back and forth across the country for incredibly long seasons, basketball is the hardest test in sports. But I think that as an event, the decathlon would be it. Football is a game of specialists; although it's a very hard game and it can hurt you a lot, it's for a guy with a great and accurate arm or great running speed and agility or bulk for line play. Basketball does demand it all, so certainly as a team sport, I'd say that it is the ultimate test. But the winner of the decathlon at the Olympics has to be categorized – if anybody can be – as the greatest athlete of that moment.

Dr. Kenneth Cooper:

Views From the Aerobics Center

Interviewed by Dave Prokop

America is a land of latent athletes. Its people know the value of exercise, and feel guilty when told how under-exercised they are. Exercise is something they should start doing more of–tomorrow.

So to get ready for the tomorrow which often remains a day away forever, Americans buy books on how to exercise. The drugstore paperback racks are full of them. The names and the promises on the jackets change every few months as fads come and go, but the books continue to sell.

A trilogy of books on one theme sells better than all the others combined – and it has sold so well for so long that the system it offers has outlived the "fad" label. It's perhaps the most widely accepted fitness program of them all. Fittingly, this system based on endurance training has endured.

Aerobics. Dr. Kenneth Cooper, then an Air Force Medical Officer, wrote this first book in 1968. It did more than any other to change the exercising (or non-exercising) habits of Americans. Later, he added **New Aerobics** and **Aerobics for Women** to the series.

"Aerobics" means "with oxygen" – in this case, continuous exercise of moderate intensity which injects a steady flow of oxygen into the body.

Dr. Cooper says, "The main objective of an Aerobic exercise program is to increase the maximum amount of oxygen that the body can process within a given time. It is called 'aerobic capacity'."

This sounds a bit clinical, but it simply says true fitness begins in the heart and lungs. According to Cooper, "Unless you have good cardiovascular-pulmonary fitness, you're not fit."

Cooper explains that the Aerobics program gives three specific guidelines: (1) types of exercise; (2) how to compare exercise, and (3) how much is necessary.

Types: Any action that is relatively constant. Jogging or running, swimming, bicycling, handball, walking. Choose one or mix them.

Comparisons: Jogging or running gives the most benefit in the least time. Walking is less efficient, timewise, but is safer and more practical.

How much? This is the beauty of Aerobics. Dr. Cooper has worked out a point system which measures the worth of the various exercises. Thirty points per week is "our minimum standard of fitness."

One mile of jogging/running in eight minutes earns five points, so six of these miles a week is a good start. The weekly equivalents in other forms of exercise:

Running in place – 75 minutes.
Swimming – 3000 yards
Bicycling – 30 miles.
Handball – 3½ hours.
Walking – 15 miles

Cooper now has retired from the Air Force, and spends full-time practicing and promoting Aerobics. He manages the Aerobics Center in Dallas, which carries out physical testing training and research. And he is a spellbinding speaker who

"There's been a tremendous shift in attitude toward fitness activities. I've seen physicians who at first were adamantly against me change to the extent that they now come to me as patients and they're now jogging. Why?" (Shearman).

combines the knowledge of a scientist with the missionary fervor of a Baptist preacher.

This combination has made thousands of people realize they can't wait another day to start exercising. And out of this new group of exercisers have grown new groups of athletes.

The following interview with Dr. Cooper was conducted in Monterey, California on October 25, 1975, after he had addressed a group of professional people, including dentists, physicians and physical educators.

SSD: Last night, as you know, the ABC television network aired a one-hour special program called "The Weekend Athletes", which examined the new interest in physical activity and fitness of Americans aged 35 and over. One of the opening remarks made by the host of the show, ABC Science Editor Jules Bergman, was that we're a nation of fitness addicts, that sometimes it seems as if everyone is out running. How does that statement strike you?

Cooper: Well, I don't think we are a nation of fitness addicts – at least not compared to what I've seen in other sections of the world. For example, the enthusiasm we have for fitness and exercise in this country is nowhere comparable to what it is, say in Brazil or Holland. Earlier this summer I was in Holland and I had a chance to see one of the tracks that they have set up there. They have, in their country, over 100 test sites, and what these consist of are 1000-meter course marked off in 100-meter intervals with a big sign at the beginning telling people how to take the Cooper Test, which is known throughout the world. I call it the 12-minute test. In Holland they have provided *Cooperbanns*–or Cooper tracks–for testing. And they've used these tracks since 1971 to give people a means of measuring their fitness and their response.

In Brazil – I've been to Brazil four times – the number of sites they have set up for Cooper testing is just unbelievable. They have them in Porto Alegre, in Sao Poalo, on all the beaches in Rio. Thousands of people are taking the test and are participating in the program. In fact, [my name] has become a colloquial term in Brazil. People ask you if you've done your Cooper. You see, they couldn't translate aerobics into Portuguese, so they nicknamed the program 'The Cooper'. Now it's a colloquial term. Cooper means jogging in Brazil.

So what I'm saying is that the interest we have in fitness in this country doesn't begin to compare with some of the interest that I've seen in other parts of the world.

SSD: Of course, 6 million people have read your books, but that still leaves at least 192 million or so people in this country who haven't read them.

Cooper: That's 6 million sales. If you have 6 million sales, it means that probably three to four times that number of people have actually read the book. But not all of the people who have read my book are American. We have a large number of foreign language translations. There are 15 to 17, somewhere in that range. I can't keep track. And the program just continues to grow and grow. It's just amazing! We will be coming out with a fourth book this next summer ('76). We're working very hard on this at the present time and have compiled new data that supports the Aerobics concept in a most impressive way.

Still there are an awful lot of people in this country who are not involved in exercise programs. I think that the interview surveys conducted by the President's Council on Fitness indicating that 50 to 60 million people are involved in some kind of health related program in this country is probably an enormous exaggeration. I think it's probably more like 10 to 15 million people – probably less. And even these people aren't all exercising regularly.

To the contrary, when I was in Leningrad in June of this year and had dinner with Anatoli Kolesov, who is the vice-president of the Soviet Sports Committee in Moscow, he told me through an interpreter that they had 80 million people involved in competitive sports programs in Russia, out of a population of 200 million. And 48 million of those 80 million people involved in competitive sports programs are over 21 years of age. In Russia they have a very large national, organized, supported sports movement. The Russians believe that the sports movement should be a grass roots movement, and they really emphasize their fitness programs.

Here in the US, many more people are interested in physical fitness than was the case five to 10 years ago. In fact, there's been a physical fitness boom in this country the last few years. But we still have a long way to go before we can compare with some other countries.

SSD: What do you feel has caused the surge of interest in running, jogging and other fitness activities in North America?

Cooper: I don't know. I think it's a self-propagating type thing to the extent that, oh, a member of the family becomes involved in a conditioning type activity, he notices a lot of positive changes in the way he feels, and, as a result, other family members want to get involved. They lose weight, they feel better, they look better, they aren't sick as much.

There's been a tremendous shift in attitude toward fitness activities – not only among people generally, but in the medical profession. I've seen [this run] the whole gamut in the medical profession. I've seen physicians who at first were adamantly against me change to the extent that they now come to me as patients and they're now jogging. I've seen that turnaround. Why?

I've tried to figure this out and the best answer I can come up with is that the physician initially does not want the patient to come to me because I've limited my practice to preventive medicine (working with healthy patients), that I'm not a real physician–I've heard that so many times. But what happens is that the patient comes to me and he's pleased with what he gets. He gets specific individualized instructions as to what he should do from a dietary and exercise standpoint. He gets started, he responds, his blood pressure goes down, his fasting blood sugar goes down, he improves tremendously in many aspects of his life. He improves in the potentially dangerous health areas of his life. Then, as a result of this, when he goes back to his physician, the physician says, "Man, what happened to you?" And the physician starts wondering. That's exactly what's happening now. I've gone from being really severly critiqued to the point where I have a great number of physicians as patients. It's a big change.

But I try to keep things in proper perspective. The great emphasis, yes, is on exercise, on Aerobics, but yet Aerobics is really just one of five basic components to a really good preventive medicine program. Exercise, yes. Proper weight is so extremely important. Proper diet. Avoiding the use of tobacco in *any* form. And then a thorough annual examination for people past 35. The latter is so important. We've picked up so many early cases of malignancies through annual examinations. We've picked up lots of major undiagnosed problems

early, before they cause symptoms. So, again, preventive medicine is a five-fold approach of which exercise is one of the major contributors, but not the only one.

SSD: You said in an interview we carried with you in 1970 in *Runner's World* magazine, that you don't find running particularly enjoyable. An interesting statement coming from a man who's literally started millions of people jogging.

Cooper: Well, as of last month, I've run 15,100 miles plus since 1960, and this month I'll have another 100 miles to add to that. But I don't run for the enjoyment of running. I run because of the tremendous benefit that I get from running. All I have to do is to just lay off for a few days and I can feel the deterioration, both mental and physical.

I ran this evening . . . it's a tremendous way for me to relax after a very hard six-hour session, like the one I had today, where I'm constantly on my feet and talking for six hours with only two breaks during the day. That's awfully hard. Boy, you're just an emotional wreck at the end of that, to the extent that when I came back here (to the hotel), I got my running stuff on, ran for at least three miles up in the hills, and thoroughly enjoyed it. That I enjoyed; that's relaxing. That's taking the pressure off, and that's what I use it for. But I can't say that I personally enjoy just going out day to day for the exhilarating feeling of running. I don't really enjoy that.

"After I'd gone through my internship, served my first year in the military, was way up in weight and down in fitness, I tried to water ski for the first time in years. I could only hold on for just a very few seconds." (Top-Muller, Bottom-Duffy)

"The primary conditioning activities in our books are walking, running, cycling, swimming, stationary running." (Magnay)

I ask patients all the time – people who have been with us for years and have been exercising regularly, running four and five days a week – why do you run? What motivates you to continue running? And most of them say the same thing: "Well, when I got started a few years ago, what motivated me was, well, the death of a loved one of a heart attack; the death of a near friend; an attack of a chest pain that [my doctor] really couldn't diagnose and which really got me thinking about this [running and getting into physical condition]." Lots of people just start running on the basis of that. Now, that starts them, but what motivates them to continue? - because that fear aspect wears off in a hurry. I ask these people the same question all the time and they nearly always give me the same answer: "I've found that it makes me feel so much better." And that's the reason a person continues to run.

We used to think that once a person stops exercising this feeling of deterioration that we get, this feeling lousy, was probably just a psychological feeling that occurs. But there have been some interesting studies recently showing such things as the metabolism of thyroid hormones is different in a person who is exercising, the ability to metabolize that hormone is different in a trained person. There are things that occur that we don't even know yet. The feeling that we have, once we stop exercising, may be the result that the thyroxin is not being metabolized as well. All right, what are the symptoms of a slightly over-active thyroid?–fast heart rate, tension, nervous stress. And that's the way you start feeling after two or three days when you lay off. So it may be a combination of both–the psychological and organic–that causes these changes.

But that's the reason I run. I run because of the great benefits that I get personally. I can't say I thoroughly enjoy runnning. I passed that stage a few years ago.

SSD: In trying to explain the surge of interest we've seen in running, it should be noted that before the jogging movement started the only people who ran were essentially serious competitors. And they were no doubt limited in their ability to influence others to get involved in running simply because they were serious competitors. But the moment the first jogger came on the scene he was immediately in a different relationship with non-runners, because he could talk about running as something he did only for fitness, or enjoyment, or to feel better, etc. I think the whole running-jogging movement probably snowballed from there.

Cooper: That's right. Even in the late '50s, early '60s – when I was running competitively in high school and college – the runner was a very strange person. I mean, you never saw a runner, unless it was somebody who was training. Whenever you saw somebody running on a highway, or on the streets, or anywhere, well, that was always a track man. He was getting in shape for cross-country, track or something.

This concept of the guy going out and running strictly for the health aspect of it didn't really come around until the late '60s, probably in conjunction with the two books – **Jogging** by Harris and Bowerman, in '67 and then **Aerobics** in '68. I think that's what changed the concept, the concept of running per se, from a strictly competitive, high-energy expenditure type activity to one the masses of men and women could participate in as a means of improving their health.

Something else that I think you have to consider very strongly is the desire of people in this country to practice preventive medicine. I'm talking about personal desires. You see, we've kind of gone the whole gamut as far as disease is concerned. We started with, oh, such things as antibiotics, went on to very sophisticated surgery, by-pass surgery, valve replacements, even a heart transplant. And you go to the extreme – last year there were over 50,000 by-pass procedures done in this country at a cost of $800 million. You find that the annual cost of medical care in the United States has risen from $50 billion in 1950 to $115 billion in 1975. Along with it, you look at the statistics and it's quite obvious that we haven't gained that much because our longevity has stayed the same while longevity in other nations of the world has risen. [The average American male dies around 67 years of age, the woman about 72.]

So again, people are much, much more aware of preventive medicine. A statement I use in my presentations frequently is one I borrow from the American Health Foundation, in which they say that ours is a legacy of a medical system that provides too much care too late. And people are aware of that now, that you can do something to make yourself feel better.

Other statements, I think, have a bearing on this interest that we have in exercise at the present time. Statements of Paul Dudley White when he says exercise will help you to add not only years to your life, but life to your years. That's one that I use frequently. Another statement of his is that it's fascinating to know that one can grow healthier as one grows older and not necessarily the reverse.

All these things contribute to the interest in exercise and preventive medicine for better health that we're seeing in this country today.

SSD: You're a proponent of Aerobic exercise – primarily jogging and swimming, I guess . . .

Cooper: Now this is a misconception, because you know

my first book didn't even mention jogging. Jogging was not mentioned once in **Aerobics**. In **The New Aerobics**, it was, of course. Jogging was a coined term in the Harris-Bowerman book.

No, Aerobics is a multitude of exercises. Aerobics is quantification and qualification of exercise. Aerobics is answering the question, what type, how much, how do you compare? That's what we're doing with Aerobics. Aerobics means aerobic-type sports–of which jogging is only one–that can be used to improve your total health picture.

I would, in fact, prefer walking as far as a recommended exercise program for the majority of people. It's safer. It can be equally beneficial. But I know for a fact that people aren't going to do enough of it to do them any good because when walking, you have to increase the distance by at least three fold to get the same benefit that you'd get from jogging. That's the problem. Unlike in Germany, Holland or Russia, people here don't have the time necessary to walk to get fit, so we're almost obligated to use jogging or swimming – something to get more benefit in a shorter period of time.

But the primary conditioning activities in our books are walking, running, cycling, swimming, stationary running. In competitive sports it's handball, basketball, racquetball, squash and sports of that nature. In the women's book (**Aerobics for Women**), we have stationary cycling, stair climbing, rope skipping, things of this nature. This is the total concept of Aerobics. People think Aerobics is strictly jogging. It's not. I probably have as many people on walking programs as I have on jogging programs.

SSD: What is the level of physical fitness – or level of non-fitness – of the average American?

Cooper: I would estimate that during my Air Force days in the '60s), less than 20 percent of the people in the Air Force could meet a minimum level of fitness. I'm talking about the overall Air Force population at an average age of 28 years. I would estimate only about 20 percent at that time could meet the minimum level of fitness, which we considered to be an oxygen consumption of at least 42 milliliters per kilograms per minute for a man under 30. And, of course, this was a select group that would probably rate higher than the average American male less than 30 years of age. So, I would say at that time in the Air Force we were dealing with, basically an unfit group of people.

Then you look at the comparative statistics. The classic example was the article we published in 1970 in which we compared [the fitness level of] Austrian men with American men. We looked at almost 20,000 men – 13,000 Austrians and about 7,000 Americans, ranging in age from 19 to 29 years – and determined the percentage that could run a mile and a half in less than 12 minutes. The Austrians had over 80 percent who passed the test and the Americans had 39 percent pass the same test. So, again, the level of fitness of our young men up to 30 years of age is comparatively low.

SSD: What about the over-35 segment of the U.S. population, both male and female? How does this age group rate in terms of fitness?

Cooper: I don't think it's much better. There's certainly much more of an awareness of physical fitness among people in this age group. I think we're beginning to see some changes but it's too early yet to say there's been any major change in the total aspect of fitness in these people.

SSD: How did you develop the Aerobic program?

Cooper: Oh, it dates back to the early 1960's. I always had an interest in this area, having been a track man in high school and college, and then getting out of shape, terribly so, after leaving school.

SSD: So you know what that's like to be totally out of shape.

Cooper: Yeah. At one time I weighed almost 200 pounds.

SSD: How did you feel when you were that heavy?

Cooper: Oh, sluggish; no energy; tired; fatigued all the time. It all came to a point . . . I loved water skiing, and every summer I spent a lot of time on the water, at least as much time as I could. After I'd gone through my internship, served my first year in the military, was way up in weight and down in fitness, I tried to water ski for the first time in a couple of years. I could only hold on for just a very few seconds before I was really extended to the point where I got nauseated. That scared me. I thought, "Boy, I've really deteriorated terribly." I also had a lot of somatic and psychosomatic type complaints, including difficulty passing my flight physicals because my blood pressure was up.

Once I got myself back in shape, I noticed these things returned to normal. So I started applying those principles to my patients while I was still in the service, and got comparable results. Then I became more interested in this total concept of exercise and the practice of preventive medicine, and I requested permission to spend two years at Harvard working on my Masters in public health, working on my boards (board exams) in aerospace medicine, but also working on my boards in preventive medicine, and on my second doctorate–a doctorate of science in exercise physiology. That gave me a chance to become a little bit more familiar with exercise physiology and exercise programs than most people in the Air Force.

In 1964, I was given the responsibility of working with the Air Force astronaut's program – that was the manned orbiting laboratory program. They wanted us to develop two things. One was the best conditioning program the astronauts could use to build up their cardiovascular reserves prior to going into space. And the other was an in-flight anti-deconditioning device that they could use to keep from deteriorating while they were in space. Well, as you know, the MOL program only lasted for about a year and a half. But during that time I had pretty much of a free hand to develop and work on the programs, and this is where the Aerobics program came from. We actually developed this system of quantifying exercise as a means of giving the MOL astronauts something to work with and use in building and maintaining adequate physical fitness.

It so happened that in 1965 Kevin Brown of *Popular Mechanics* came down to do a story on our bed rest studies that simulated weightlessness. He was interested in the space medicine aspect of the program, but I told him the big breakthrough was the exercise program we had worked out –you know, quantifying exercise, giving it point values, and adjusting it to different age groups. Well, that intrigued him, too, to the extend that he wrote an article that was titled, "Exercise the Astronauts' Way." It was published in January 1966 in *Family Weekly*, and it went around the country into about 15 million papers. The feedback from the article was just unbelievable. Based on that, the publishers of *Family Weekly* a book and have it out in about six weeks. We sat down to work, and it took us two years, almost two and a half years, to complete that first book.

SSD: Is Aerobics the only way to go or could one achieve the recommended level of fitness in other ways, for example, with weight training or using stationary exercising equipment?

Cooper: Well, the general consensus is that Aerobic type exercises are the only exercises that will consistently and safely build up the cardiovascular system if done properly. How much Aerobic conditioning can you get from weight training? I don't think anyone has really answered that question. Now, I'm talking about weight *training* versus weight *lifting*. Weight lifting is a highly resistive type activity that does nothing but build up muscle mass and does very little for the cardiovascular system.

At the present time in Dallas, we have a project going on with the Nautilus and one going on with the Universal Gym, and we're monitoring that right now. We're trying to evaluate the answer to that question you just asked. How much Aerobic type conditioning is indicated by improvement of maximal oxygen consumption? What can you expect in response to a 20-week period of progressive type conditioning on the Nautilus? To 20 weeks of progressive type conditioning on the Universal Gym? My experience in the past has been that I wouldn't expect much in the way of cardiovascular conditioning.

I know the other day I had a fellow come in who exercises twice a week, 55 minutes each time, on the Nautilus (he's been on the program for four years). He's 31 years of age and just as muscular and powerful as can be. We put him on the treadmill, he lasted 16 minutes, maximum heartrate of about 200. That's notoriously poor, yet he really extended himself to last that long. So the Nautilus training by itself is not doing much in building up the Aerobic capacity in that one individual.

But we're not going to make a statement until we complete our studies. My feeling now is that it's going to be very difficult, if not impossible, to build up much in the way of an Aerobic capacity strictly with a weight training type program. I think weight training is a fantastic adjunct to an Aerobic program, to become super conditioned, if you want to call it that, but as far as the basic program to use for total health or preventive medicine, no, I don't think it's the answer.

SSD: What are the dangers of being cardiovascularly unfit?

Cooper: Oh, there are all sorts of dangers. Of course, the big thing that we're trying to do in building up the cardiovascular-pulmonary fitness is to reverse the diseases and problems of those three systems – the lungs, the vascular system and the heart. It's our major health problem, without question, with 55 percent of all deaths occurring from heart and blood vessel disease. So, if the person just ignores his current state of health, ignores the warning signs, you can anticipate that he's going to become one of the millions of people who succumb from one of the degenerative diseases. To the contrary, if he keeps himself in shape, he may be able to delay the onset or, hopefully, prevent some of these degenerative diseases. That's our total objective with the Aerobic program.

SDD: What can you tell us about the Red Chinese fitness program? We've all seen those pictures from Red China showing thousands of people doing exercises simultaneously.

Cooper: Yeah, I use these in my presentations. A quotation I saw when I was traveling in the Orient last February . . . I picked up an Australian newspaper, and there was a big picture of 110,000 youths assembled in Peking, and they were demonstrating their fitness to Chairman Mao. A slogan right under the picture read: "Chairman Mao encourages the youth of China to get fit, keep fit and spur on the Revolution." That's what they think about fitness, and I'm led to believe, from people I have talked to, people from mainland China, that it's a sincere feeling.

To the contrary, we have in this country, of course, a major movement to eliminate any required physical education programs, particularly in our colleges and in our school systems. In view of this, it's particularly encouraging to see what Oral Roberts has done up at Tulsa, Oklahoma. He strongly believes that when a student goes to Oral Roberts University, the student should be spiritually fit, number one, academically fit, number two, and physically fit, number three. And whereas most schools are phasing out any physical education requirement at all, Oral Roberts University has a mandatory four-year requirement. One hour [of Aerobic activity], four times a week for four years.

In 1972 Oral Roberts asked me if I would help them design an Aerobic center on their campus for their 4000 students – which I did. We worked a lot of hours on this. And they now have on their campus a $2½ million Aerobic center second to none anywhere in the world. They have a six-lap to a mile indoor running track. They can handle 150 people on the track at one time. It's fantastic! They have an indoor 50-meter swimming pool, four basketball courts side by side, five handball-raquetball courts, and Aerobic testing facilities. The greatest honor in my life was when I went to Tulsa on the 24th of September, 1974, to dedicate the Kenneth H. Cooper Aerobic Center. He named it after me. It's really a fantastic honor!

SSD: Earlier you mentioned you had visited Russia. Have your books been translated into Russian?

Cooper: They're being translated right now – all three of them. I just got the notification last week. This will be the first time the books have been translated into Russian, but the Russian people are very familiar with the Aerobics program – not because of the Aerobics program in the books, but because of my work with the Brazilian soccer team.

SSD: Was this the Brazilian National team?

Cooper: Yes, I worked with them for a year, prior to their victory in the World Cup in 1970. I worked through their trainer, Claudio Continhuo. We had the team on the Aerobics program for a whole year prior to the World Cup. We kept accurate points on them, what they were doing. They averaged 80-100 points per week for that entire year. We ran them through the 12-minute test for the first time in April '69, and they ran about 3000 meters per man on the average [3000 meters is 1.86 miles, roughly]. And then a year later, in April 1970, three months before the World Cup play started in Mexico City, they averaged 2.2 miles per man. That's about 3550 meters, close to 3600 meters, which was just an amazing improvement.

"The thing we're trying to do in building up the cardio-vascular-pulmonary fitness is to reverse the diseases and problems of those three systems—the lungs, the vascular system and the heart."

Well, they went on to the World Cup and won six consecutive matches. In four of those matches they were tied at the half and in the other two they were only one goal ahead. But in every game they were clearly superior in the second half, usually winning with overwhelming scores, apparently because they were at a very high level of fitness.

UNESCO did some studies on some of the top soccer teams after the World Cup championships in 1970 and by using heart rate recovery techniques, they determined the level of fitness of the Brazilian soccer team players was far superior to any other group. So just overnight the Aerobics program became very successful in Brazil. That's what started it in that country.

SSD: I was unaware that you, in fact, have worked with competitive sports teams.

Cooper: Oh, I work with teams all the time. I have worked with a lot of football clubs.

SSD: I daresay that what you have found is that most professional athletes in the United States, especially in sports such as baseball and football, do need to improve their Aerobic conditioning.

Cooper: For sure. I heard (Dallas Cowboys coach) Tom Laundry talking the other day about the lack of major injuries this year and he attributed it partly to their good off-season conditioning program. I was pleased to hear that since many of the Cowboys work out at theAerobics Center during the off-season.

I've always enjoyed competitive sports, professional football particularly. And I enjoy working with sports teams. That's the reason I've done that.

SSD: To many people in this country, the concept of being in good physical condition means nothing more, unfortunately, than keeping an eye on one's weight and going on a diet when one becomes overweight. From a health standpoint, exactly what do you accomplish when you go on a diet, and get your weight back down from, say, 190 to 160, and that's all you do?

Cooper: Oh, there's all sorts of things – if you get your weight down and keep it down, versus getting it down and then going back up. But if you get it down and keep it down, there is a marked reduction of a lot of things. For example, your triglycerides go down, uric acid usually goes down, frequently your cholesterol drops. If nothing else, your coronary risk factors drop way down once you lose weight. Your ventilatory pattern (breathing) is easier. People who are overweight can't breathe as well. I mean, there's all sorts of documented things that accompany a weight loss program – decrease in kidney problems, decrease in diabetes (there's a great possibility of diabetes in an excessively overweight person). There's no question about the value of losing weight. But how much value is it to lose weight and then gain it all back? And that's why I discourage the fad type diets, the "fasting" or semi-fasting type diets, because the majority of those people put the weight right back on again when they go off the diet.

SSD: You have a number of detractors. One of them is Dr. Meyer Friedman who says that there's no evidence that jogging and other strenuous exercises protect a person from heart disease. Is it, in fact, true that there is *no* evidence that exercise will prevent heart disease?

Cooper: I think that the best evidence to date is going to be our coronary risk factor data versus levels of fitness. That's going to be the first and best quantifiable data anyone has put together. But, as far as preventing or delaying the onset of heart disease, there are very *strong* implications that exercise does have an effect. And a very good prospective study that came from California just recently was published in March, 1975 in the *New England Journal of Medicine*. This study was done on longshoremen. These men were divided into three activity categories – those engaged in high, medium and low level activity. The study, which followed these men for 22 years, showed the instance of heart disease was two times greater in those working in the low-level activity versus those working the high-level activity. So, there are a lot of studies of this type showing that vigorous physical activity does have a protective effect as far as heart disease is concerned, contrary to what Friedman says.

SSD: On the other side of the coin from Dr. Friedman, who is anti-exercise, there's Dr. Tom Bassler. He says you don't call for enough exercise.

Cooper: Based on what? Why does he make that statement? You see, it's strictly a theory. I don't deal with theories, I deal with facts. I'm saying that 30-34 points a week will show a statistically significant lowering of five of the 10 coronary risk factors. Now, that's about as factual as you can get. Bassler can't show you a thing. He's followed a small group for five years. You can't make a statistical study based on that.

I know Tom Bassler quite well. At one time he said that among people who have run 10 miles there's never been anyone to die of a heart attack. Well, when that was proven wrong, he moved it on up to the marathon. But you can't make that statement either. As I told him, don't make the mistake of saying 'never' about anything, particularly running.

Another area in which I disagree with Bassler is in his statement that you have to run six miles six times per week (not 30 points per week, but 140 points). Man, no one would exercise. You've got to be reasonable and practical in this approach, and that's what we've tried to do. We've tried to find the minimum level, the threshold level, to show some protection from a coronary risk standpoint—and that level ends up being about 30-35 points per week. (Dr. Thomas) Cureton used to say much the same thing as Bassler. He'd say you have to exercise an hour a day, five days a week. Based on what? That's all I ask.

SSD: You're not saying you're against people getting 140 points a week.

Cooper: No. I'm not saying that at all. We have people doing that, getting 150-200 points a week all the time. But for someone to make a statement that everyone has to get that amount of exercise to get any protection from coronary disease, I'll say, based on what? No, I'm not against people getting well over 30 points. But I'm trying to work with the level that's reasonable.

SSD: On what are you basing the 30 points as being sufficient?

Cooper: Eighty-five percent of the people who work up to 30 points per week have an oxygen consumption of 42 milliliters per kilogram per minute if they're less than 30 years of age. For those over 50 years of age, the oxygen consumption is age adjusted at 36. I've made this statement for years and I can document it.

SSD: Would 40 points per week be superior to 30?

Cooper: Well, I made a great point of this in my lecture today – that there was no particular benefit of getting more than 30-35 points a week because as you look at these coronary risk factors, you can see a significant statistical difference in fitness categories when you compare the very poor, the poor, the fair with the excellent, but in many cases you can't show any significant difference when you compare the good and the excellent. In other words, there isn't any particular advantage to getting 40-50 points a week as compared to 30 points.

SSD: Therefore, Olympic marathon champion Frank Shorter doesn't necessarily have more protection against a heart attack than the person who gets 30 points a week.

Cooper: We don't know yet. I've been talking about 30 points versus 40-50 points. Frank Shorter probably averages 600 points a week.

SSD: Okay, what about the comparison between 30 points and 600 points?

Cooper: No one has any data on that. My intuitive feeling would be that it's probably offering Frank greater protection – not complete protection as Bassler would make you think, but it's probably offering him much greater protection.

SSD: Is it or is it not true that for exercise to be worthwhile, to have real conditioning value, you have to make it strenuous enough so it hurts?

Cooper: No, you do not. You can train and not strain. The type of exercise depends upon the level of fitness that you are trying to achieve. If you just want to get a training effect, get some benefit from exercise, this can be accomplished without strain.

SSD: You can make it totally painless, is that what you are saying?

Cooper: Yes, I think you could say that it's painless. If you cover three miles in less than 43½ minutes, five days a week, you get 30 points. You get some protection from coronary disease and there's no pain associated with that level of effort.

SSD: You've invited some top competitive runners to visit your Aerobic Center in Dallas. Why have you done this and what have you learned from these athletes?

Cooper: We're trying to learn and study their techniques of training, conditioning. Look at the end results in order to try and adjust our programs, modify our programs. Then maybe make our running more enjoyable for the people, more effective from a training-conditioning standpoint.

Also, we're interested in the competitive runner. We'd like to work with him to see if we can help him reach his maximum performance. We were going to work very closely with Steve Prefontaine and we are working very closely with Frank Shorter. He's visited the center many times. Kenny Moore's done the same thing.

Our interest in exercise physiology goes the whole range from the cardiac patient to the world-class athlete. We have everything in between. And we kind of combine all of this and come up with a whole new concept of the training and conditioning programs.

SSD: If one is going to undertake an Aerobic exercise program, isn't it more convenient – at least somewhere along the line – to become involved in a competitive sport, rather than just exercise for the sake of exercise?

Cooper: Yes, I think it helps. That's why we put up tennis courts and handball-racquetball courts at our center. We have a basketball arena. This spring we're going to be adding a three-acre area which will include a full-sized soccer field, and a football field. We're also putting in a baseball diamond.

SSD: In which direction would you prefer to see a person go – competitive sports or an individual solo exercise program?

Cooper: I don't care what the person does. I had a

40-year-old man in the other day who went 25 minutes on the treadmill, who's in the top 3.5 percent of all the people we stress test, and all he does is play tennis, but he plays 10 hours of singles a week. As I said, I don't care what they do. If they want to do it by competitive sports, fine. I know a lot of people now who are playing racquetball. They're getting nine points per hour for playing racquetball. I'm not adverse to that at all. To the contrary, I encourage people to participate in those sports which they'll continue. If they get involved in a jogging club and it bores them, I say, well, switch to something else that they enjoy.

I try to design programs for people based on their desires, their needs and their availability. If I've got a traveling executive who goes around the country, well, I can't set up a regular jogging program for him because he's going to be embarrassed to leave the hotel in his running gear and work out in the streets. So we try to work out something else. I may have him combine a walking and a jogging program. He jogs at home and he walks when he's on the road. But he has a program and he has to follow it all the time.

SSD: How should a person get started in a fitness program?

Cooper: Slowly and progressively. This is the concept that we had in mind in the second book when we introduced the six-week starter program, which we feel is mandatory. Let me just give you some background on this.

In an article I published in 1970 in the *Journal of the American Medical Association*, I asked physicians to send me documented cases of deaths or problems that occurred as a result of jogging or vigorous activity. Over the years I've probably had about 30 that have come in. I was looking for common denominators in these and this is what I found: they were men in the first six weeks of their conditioning program. They were over 40 years of age. They were jogging and they had no medical clearance. I haven't listed all the factors, but those were the basic common denominators.

Having learned this, what we tried to do in **The New Aerobics** was to overcome some of these problems. We implemented the concept of the six-week starter program which is so slowly progressive that even a person who has an undiagnosed heart disease is not going to kill himself.

Ideally, we'd like to make this recommendation: if you're getting started in a fitness program, you should have a physical examination if you're under 30 years of age – a history and physical within the preceding year is the normal requirement; you should have a history and physical, and a resting ECG within the previous six months if you're 30-40 years of age; and if you are over 40 years of age, a history, a physical, a resting and stress ECG within the previous three months. That would be ideal, but it's also totally impractical because you're not going to have enough treadmills, enough physicians, and not all the people will have enough money to be able to do this. So how do you overcome this?

Of the 6 million joggers in this country, probably 250,000 have had some kind of examination. The majority of people have had nothing. Yet they're getting along pretty well. How?

The answer is the starter program, which is so slowly progressive that it's not going to hurt them even if they have heart disease. Of course, if they develop any symptoms during the starter program–chest pain, discomfort, whatever it may be – then they must seek medical consultation before they go on and really hurt themselves.

SSD: You don't insist that people starting a fitness program see a doctor first before they even take a step? Many doctors seem to insist upon it.

Cooper: Yes, I know. But the majority of evaluations done by doctors are just inadequate. It's not just seeing the doctor – that's what the slogan says, you know, "See your doctor first." The doctor says, "Well, any problems?" "Well, no." "Okay, go ahead and run."

You can't just "see your doctor first." It has to include all those things that I mentioned – the examination, the physical, the resting ECG, the stress ECG, etc. But you have to be practical too. Not all people are going to be able to do this. And that's why I recommend this concept of the starter program. I've gone into great detail explaining it in **The New Aerobics.**

SSD: Last question: what would you like to see happen, or what additional things would you like to see happening, in the fitness area? Further support from the national government? New programs? Better programs in the schools?

Cooper: I'd like to see very sophisticated physical education programs started in the school systems. If I have a pet project, I'd say that's it, because I realize in looking at these young men, 18-20 years of age, 20-22-25 years of age, and the surprising instance of coronary problems among them, that you've got to start a fitness program earlier. That's why I've really worked hard in trying, under the auspices of the Governor's Commission on Fitness in the state of Texas, to upgrade the quality of physical education programs in the school systems, starting at about junior high school, starting at about the seventh grade. That would be my major goal. Another would be teaching the kids ideas and concepts in programs and skills that they could continue once they get out of school. I'm talking about adult-oriented type sports that they will have a desire to continue. I'd like to see the fitness program started in schools, but the concept developed so that people can continue to be active the rest of their lives. I'm not talking about competitive sports necessarily, or vigorous activities. I'm talking about people keeping active by participating in sports that they enjoy.

I'd like to see more effective governor's commissions on fitness. We have a good one in the state of Texas, but we're one of the few states in the country that has that. I'd like to see the President's Council on Physical Fitness having even more of an impact. In the past it's been kind of a negligible type thing, but it's rapidly gaining in momentum. Casey Conrad (the executive director of the Council on Fitness) has done a superb job up there in trying to get this thing on its feet, and it's had an effect. This is one reason there are more people exercising.

I think the contributions of the books and the Aerobics program, the contribution of the President's Council on Fitness – all these things have had a bearing on the level of fitness of the people in our country. But I would like to see more of an awareness of the importance of preventive medicine, of which exercise is one of the major factors.

Books by Dr. Kenneth Cooper

Aerobics, 1968 Hb., 253 pp., $5.95.

The New Aerobics, 1970 Hb., 190 pp., $5.95.

Aerobics for Women, by Mildred & Kenneth Cooper, 1972 Hb., 160 pp., $5.95. (All published by Lippincott).

Abalone Diving

Diving for abalone can be an enjoyable and rewarding sport. This shellfish is considered by many to be among the great delicacies of the sea. Abalone can be found from Baja, Mexico to Alaska in depths ranging from shallow inter-tidal basins to over 200 feet.

Diving for abalone off the California coast is broken into two sports: using scuba and using free diving or snorkel diving. Laws pertaining to abalone diving have been set forth by the California Fish and Game Department: scuba is permissible south of Yankee point in Monterey; north of there, free diving only. Commercial abalone divers are also allowed to work southern California waters (only in areas deeper than 20 feet), but they are forbidden to work northern abalone beds. At present five abalone is the limit a sports diver can have in his possession, and he must carry a valid license from California Fish and Game.

Legal size for abalone varies according to species. The largest is the Red Abalone which must measure a minimum of seven inches across the shell to be legal (some reds have been found to measure up to 11¾ inches). Other known species are the Pink, Green, Black, White, Flat, Pinto and Threaded Abalone.

Abalone can be found tucked in tight places between rocks or under ledges, where they are protected from predators. Because other undersea animals attach themselves to the shell, adding camoflage, spotting this shellfish can present a problem. After gaining a little experience, though, a diver begins to look for the black mantle around the shell of each abalone.

Once a diver spots his quarry, the next step is to pry it off the rocks. Its suction is so great that a man using two hands usually is unable to pull is off, so an ab iron is used. This tool is a long, wide, flat bar, usually with a handle which the diver uses to lever each abalone away from his resting place. Of course, when diving for abalone be sure that it is of legal size before prying it off the rock.

In addition to an ab iron, necessary equipment consists of the diver's mask, fins and snorkel. Depending on the area in which one is diving, additional equipment might include a wet suit, weight belt, hood, gloves, booties, B.C. (buoyancy compensator), tank and regulator, and, of course, a game bag to hold the abalone.

For individuals considering any type of diving, a certification course is a must. This scuba course consists of about 80 hours of instruction, half in the water and half in the classroom. Besides learning safe use of scuba and related equipment, a student is taught about currents, tides, undersea life, and numerous other subjects for safety in and around the sea. Most courses offer a check-out dive under the supervision of an instructor to familiarize students with their equipment in open water.

Several organizations offer diving certification courses through sporting goods stores and dive shops. After certification, additional experience can be obtained through advanced courses. With such proper preparation, diving for abalone can be a safe and exciting sport.

—Jack Stewart

Jack Stewart is a certified skin and scuba diver. He has taught diving at the Jewish Community Centers in San Francisco and at several dive shops. He has also written several articles on the subject including pieces in **Skin Diver Magazine.**

For More Information

There is not an organization or magazine devoted exclusively to abalone diving; however, the Underwater Society of America, 175 W. Jackson, Chicago, Ill. 60604 can provide more information. They also publish the **International Divers Guide** available at the same address. A helpful magazine: *Skin Diver,* 8490 Sunset Blvd., Los Angeles, Calif. 90060, is a monthly that covers skin and scuba diving in detail with articles on abalone diving from time to time. Additional information: see Skin and Scuba Diving.

Acrobatics

Acrobatics usually brings to mind visions of circus performers with pink tights and spangles. Although acrobats are still popular additions to these entertainments, you will find amateur acrobats on the beach, in your local gym, or in great auditoriums and arenas. National and international organizations now extol forms of artistic acrobatics just as they do artistic gymnastics, and acrobats can aspire for titles in competitions that take place in countries all over the world.

Being multi-faceted, acrobatics is one sport that is never dull or limited. You might call it the sport of unlimited physical possibilities since it involves balance and coordination, as well as strength. Chinese acrobats tend to concentrate on balance and can stack objects such as chairs and tables at precarious angles, finally holding a hand-stand on top! Americans prefer the tumbling aspect (also known as acrobatic jumps) called platform tumbling. The world champion acrobatics doubles pair from Russia is known for outstanding teamwork involving balancing, posing, flipping, and dance. Pyramids on the beach that stack acrobats several people high are another form of acrobatics as is the single performer who contorts and twists on a tiny platform.

Acrobatics makes the body supple and flexible, while developing poise and body control. Although many of the movements are easier for younger children, the sport can help improve physical condition regardless of age!

Successful beach pyramids combine qualities of strength, daring, balance, suppleness and steadiness to produce free form creation, perishable except for the eye of the camera and performer's mind. (Acrobat magazine)

The Many Faces of Acrobatics

What is acrobatics? According to the dictionary, it is the art, performance, or activity of an acrobat. It is a spectacular, showy, or startling performance involving great agility and skillful use of the body while performing gymnastic feats. Each unnatural movement performed by the human body is an acrobatic skill if practiced and performed either as an artistic presentation or showcase feat. The art of acrobatics is as old as man himself, a form of acrobatic movement having been used in early ritual dance, and later in the performing arts.

Today, acrobatics is divided into three distinct fields: *pure acrobatics, tumbling,* and *gymnastics.*

Pure acrobatics stresses the ability to bend the body beyond its "natural" range of movement, as in front walkovers, limbers, chest rolls, and splits. The body is used primarily in counterbalance actions to accomplish these movements.

In tumbling, the ability to perform body movements using spring and rebounding action is stressed. In movements like the front handspring or flip-flops and in aerial rotating stunts such as front, side, or back somersaults, the body is used primarily in overbalance actions.

In gymnastics, the athlete executes both tumbling and acrobatic movements with the aid of special apparatus. Free exercise, or the floor portion of a gymnast's training, contains both acrobatics and tumbling combined with dance in order to demonstrate flexibility, balance, control, speed and elevation, as well as the rhythmic ability of the performer. A trapeze, ring, or teeter-board artist in a circus or traveling show is considered a gymnast.

Since most tumbling movements are rooted in a basic acrobatic foundation, it is impossible to learn one field and not the other. Naturally, there is both a correct and incorrect manner to execute the bending and splitting actions incorporated in the movement of the spine and legs. A good teacher is an essential prerequisite for learning acrobatics. He/she should have a thorough knowledge of human anatomy.

The foundation for acrobatic training consists of four basic movements: *rolling,* which takes form in the forward roll; *bending,* as in the backbend; *splitting,* as in the side or front split; and *balancing,* the most common form being a handstand. These basic moves are combined in a series of patterns to build acrobatic combinations. As an example, a walkover is technically a combination of a handstand, a front split, and backbend.

In the performing arts and as pure entertainment, acrobatics has long been favored by the public. In the dance field, acrobatics is often used to enhance a performance, the dancers executing both acrobatic and tumbling movements as part of their routine, in order to heighten the intensity of a number. In a can-can, for example, the dancers do walk-overs and splits for this effect.

The field of acrobatics has grown and prospered through the centuries. New variations and teaching methods are constantly being developed in the field. For practitioners, the rewards are tremendous—they gain a trim, flexible, and controlled body. And for the acrobat interested in a career, opportunities exist in broadway shows, reviews, television, night clubs, and acrobatic dance troops.

—Charles Kelley

Charles Kelley teaches acrobatics and tumbling in New York City and is the author of **Acrobatics from A to Z.**

For More Information

Glenn Sundby has a publishing company that produces *Gymnast* magazine. In early 1975 he formed the United States Sports Acrobatics Federation and started another magazine called *Acrobat.* The Federation is set up to promote the sport and membership runs $10.00 per year which also covers the subscription to the magazine. Write: USSAF, Box 777, Santa Monica, Calif. 90406. Ralph Samuels publishes another magazine called *Acrobatics* which is the official journal of the Association of Acrobats. It is currently being published bi-monthly at $8.00 per year. Write: *Acrobatics,* 23 Victor Road, Brookvale, New South Wales 2100, Australia.

If you need a source of equipment, books, and further information write: Ka-Larks Acro-Supply, 2035 Fremont Ave., Casper, Wyo. 82601. Additional information: see Gymnastics.

There aren't very many good books available but here is one. Available from World Publications, Box 366, Mountain View, Calif. 94040 at the price listed* plus 25 cents postage.

Acrobatics from A to Z, Charles Kelley. A clear manual for all ages and levels of acrobatic skill. Covers the four movements used in most stunts: bending (backbends); splitting (front splits); balancing (hand stands); and rolling (front rolls). Written for those who wish to help foster the art of acrobatics. 1974 Hb., 71 (oversize) pp., ill., $10.00, (Statler Records).

Aerobatics

Aerobatics is the sport of flying an airplane as precisely as you can. It's hard to describe the emotions involved. It seems when you're concentrating intensely you forget about your emotions. It's a little bit like driving a race car. There's an element of danger, and of course for safety you've got to make sure your machine is in good working order, and tuned to the utmost degree. Many pilots treat their planes better than they treat their wives. They all have love affairs with their little airplanes. When you're flying you know there is danger, certainly, but you're concentrating so hard on flying the airplane that it's not uppermost in your mind.

At the World Aerobatics Championships in 1972, the US came out on top, winning the individual championship, the team and women's championships. This effort started with the '68 competition when the US made their first strong, organized bid. In 1970 the team came on stronger, finishing third, leading to their sweep two years later.

The sport started with airshows in the early 1900s. During combat in WWI many maneuvers were invented which are used today. German pilot Max Immelmann, for instance, first used the half-loop with a half-roll on top as an evasive maneuver; later it came to be known as the Immelmann turn. Barnstorming after the war brought airplanes further into the public view. In an age when farm kids would run into the yard to stare at any airplane that passed overhead, adventurous pilots gathered crowds with daredevil stunts and then sold tickets for rides.

By 1958, when I began flying in airshows, there were perhaps 25 such pilots in the whole US. Interest has risen in recent years, though, and while national competitions used to draw 20 pilots this year (1975) 83 entered.

The most commonly flown aerobatic plane is the Pitts Special, and most are home-built. They have a 17-foot wingspan, 15-foot length, and weigh only 750 pounds. With a 180 horsepower engine they have an excellent power to weight ratio. They're sort of the sportscar of the airplane set.

You can buy the plane ready-made, get a kit, or buy plans and gather the parts yourself. The wings are generally constructed with wooden spars and ribs, and covered with dacron fabric, as in the early days. Two wings give more wing area to turn with, and the short wings give a high roll rate since they drag less going over. The planes are light and highly maneuverable, with speed ranging from a maximum of 200 m.p.h. to a stall speed of 60 or 70.

New pilots need to accustom themselves to g-loading, the pressure of centrifugal force that can effectively make your weight four or five times normal when you're climbing. The force tries to push you out the bottom of the airplane, your blood rushes to your feet. When you're flying upside down and climbing the pressure of negative g's tries to push you out the roof of the plane and your blood rushes to your head.

When the plane rolls you shift from positive g's to negative g's, going through a momentary state of weightlessness. It happens so fast that you barely notice it, though.

Orientation is a problem you have to learn how to overcome. The new pilot must learn what to look at, and where to look, to keep from being disoriented.

The tiny Pitts Special aerobatics plane weighs only 750 pounds, so with a 180 horsepower engine it has a superior power to weight ratio. It compares to a giant airliner or cargo plane as a sportscar compares to a semi truck and trailer.

A pilot can fly thousands of combinations of maneuvers. One can choose from slow rolls, hesitation rolls, snap rolls, barrel rolls, outside snap rolls, figure eights, outside loops, square loops, triangular loops, the hammerhead stall turn or the tail slide. In the tail slide the plane is pushed straight up until it quits climbing, the power is cut, and the plane slides toward the earth backward for a few lengths, before slipping over and flying out of it. In a hesitation roll the pilot stops the plane at regular points: every 90 degrees for a four point roll, every 120 degrees for a three point roll, etc. The outside loop, depicted in the movie *The Great Waldo Pepper,* starts with level flight and then you push the stick forward and dive into a circle so you're flying upside down, pulling negative g's all the way.

In competition you make four flights. The first is a set of compulsory figures. The second, a freestyle flight, can include up to 30 maneuvers. Each maneuver has a point coefficient depending on its difficulty, and the total cannot be over 700 points. The flight cannot last over nine minutes. It must fit within an imaginary cube of air 3000 feet long and 3000 feet wide, not below 300 feet and not above 3000 feet. The unknown flight is determined by the judges and given to pilots the morning of the flight. The final flight is again freestyle.

Freestyle flights must include maneuvers from each of the nine categories. Pilots must be versed in all the aerobatic skills. The manual which organizes the maneuvers into nine categories also assigns a point coefficient for difficulty to each. The categories are:

(1) Lines and angles. All rolls possible along vertical, horizontal, and 45-degree angles. 5000 different combinations. (2) Horizontal turn maneuvers. Every kind of turn, 90, 180, 360 degrees, whether upside down or right side up. (3) Vertical turns. Climbing or diving turns. (4) Spin maneuvers. When the engine stalls, and the plane rotates at a high rate of speed, you're in a spin. Include flat, upright, and vertical spins. (5) Wing slide maneuvers. Otherwise known as hammerhead turns. (6) Tail slide maneuvers (described above). (7) Loops, and all figure eights. (8) Several thousand different combinations of rolls. (9) Turnaround maneuvers to change your direction or altitude. Which of these do I prefer? I like them all.

—Charlie Hiller, Jr.

Charlie Hiller took first place in the World Aerobatics Championships in 1972. He lives in Fort Worth, Texas.

For More Information

There are three organizations you should know about. The National Aeronautics Association, 806-15th St. Northwest, Washington D.C; International Aerobatic Club, Box 229, Hales, Corners, Wisc., who publish *Sport Aerobatics;* and the Aerobatic Club of America, Box 11099, Ft. Worth, Texas, who publish *ACA News.*

Here is a good book on the subject. It is available from World Publications, Box 366, Mountain View, Calif. 94040 at the price listed* plus 25 cents postage.

Modern Aerobatics and Precision Flying, Harold Krier. In this unusual book, champion Hal Krier describes in detail all the intricacies of this thrilling sport which has intrigued fliers from earliest flying days. Every important maneuver explained. 1970 Ppb., $3.95, (Crown).

Aikido

Developed after World War II by Morihei Uyeshiba (O'sensei), aikido is the youngest of the Japanese martial arts. Often called the most spiritual of the martial arts, aikido goes beyond the physical aspects and techniques to focus on an individual's development of his internal powers. O'sensei was often able to throw or immobilize an opponent merely with a touch, or by leading his mind in such a way as to use the attacker's strength against himself.

Instead of forcefully pushing back when pushed, aikido teaches one to step aside and pull in the same direction as the attacker is pushing. By directing the pull downward with a subtle motion, the attacker loses his balance and falls forward. Aikido classes consist of two partners practicing a series of prearranged attacks and counters teaching principles of blending, directing energy and immobilizing attacks. Because aikido does not stress the use of physical strength in a head-on confrontation, women are especially successful in grasping the principles of this martial art.

Aikido is the most subtle of the martial arts, relying on technique instead of brute strength. Aikidoists often turn an opponent's own muscular force against him for an easy throw. (Frederick)

Warm-up exercises consist primarily of stretching and limbering to relax and loosen one's muscles. Forward and backward rolls and a steady pace builds endurance and stamina. There are no competitions or tournaments, and partners practice in an atmosphere of mutual development and cooperation that is designed to help each other learn.

Although aikido is an excellent means of self-defense, the ultimate goal is to develop a total discipline for spiritual, moral, mental and physical advancement. Because each person's development proceeds differently, O'sensei allowed a great amount of latitude in instructors' styles. This accounts for the recent schools of Yoshinkan, Tomiki and Ki aikido. Nevertheless, the majority of practicing aikidoists belong to the World Aikido Federation founded by O'sensei and carried on by his son, Kisshomaru Uyeshiba in Tokyo.

–Donald Deed

Don Deed studied goju ryu karate from Gosei Yamaguchi before getting involved in aikido. He liked the soft style and philosophy enough to spend a year in Japan studying under Hikitsuchi Sensei in Shingu. Don was awarded 1st kyu rank in Japan. He currently writes for several martial arts magazines.

Aikido: The Gentle Way

Aikido is a non-fighting martial art. Martial arts are military. They are used in war, but today there is no war, and we don't need martial arts as the samurai in ancient Japan needed them. Today most martial arts have developed into competitive channels: kendo, judo, karate. Aikido, on the other hand, has turned its emphasis to building character.

What use is there in competition? One wins until he loses. When he gets older and his strength diminishes, he loses. You win today and lose tomorrow. And competition is completely different from real life. I could, for example, teach swimming on the mat and you might think you are a good swimmer. You would look good on the mats, but if I put you in the water you might sink. This lesson holds true for many martial arts. Students look good on the mats, but if an occasion arises in which they might need their skill, they do not react so well.

I teach my students to love all of creation. Take the word aikido: *ai* means to combine, *ki* means the universe itself (the power of the mind), and *do* means the path that all can take. This is the meaning of aikido, and if you understand it, how can you fight? Everyone and everything is of the same essence.

I teach students to have a positive attitude, to be centered in the Universe, to unify mind and body, to be able to concentrate all their energies, and to emphasize aikido in daily life. It is not enough to be able to defend oneself or to defeat an opponent; one must also know how to reach and alter another's mind. Aikido teaches one to be in harmony with the laws of nature. If an opponent attacks, he is not in harmony with nature. Since aikido teaches one to be calm and to have a non-fighting mind, it is good that the attacker learns that he only defeats himself in trying to do harm to others. Today more people everywhere are becoming interested in finding the way of harmony rather than discord, so it is also good that the attacker will learn to cease his agressive actions in the face of aikido.

Aikido does not rely on strength, but many people in aikido are learning only strength techniques and entirely forgetting the spiritual aspect. Some teachers say, "use strength," while I say, "relax." If I throw someone and he feels bad about it, I tell my students they can scold me. After I lead your mind, I lead your body, and there must be good feeling. *Ki* (power of the mind) is like water which nourishes the roots of a tree, and a tree must have strong roots and healthy foundation. Thus, it is with aikido.

–Koichi Tohei

Koichi Tohei, 10th degree aikido master, is the founder of the Ki Society International and stresses in his school meditation and the development of ki. He is regarded as one of the foremost practitioners of aikido.

For More Information

There are several magazines that we are not listing here because their coverage of Aikido is limited. Here are some good ones.

Aiki News, c/o Stanley A. Pranin, United-Energy Center, 125 Central Ave., Pacific Grove, Calif. 93950. Published monthly at $6.00 per year. Very small but it has good articles in each issue.

"Often called the most spiritual of the martial arts, aikido goes beyond the physical aspects and techniques to focus on an individual's development of his internal powers." (OM-Photo)

Self-Defense World, Box 366, Mountain View, Calif. 94040. Published bi-monthly at $4.50 per year. Good articles on a regular basis.
Inside Kung-Fu, 7011 Sunset Blvd., Hollywood, Calif. 90028. Published monthly at $8.00 per year. Well-illustrated with good articles on aikido.

There are two major organizations in the United States. American Aikido Federation, 142 W. 18th St., New York, New York 10003. They are associated with the main Hombu dojo in Tokyo.
Ki Society International: Aikido Institute of America, 3302 West Jefferson Blvd., Los Angeles, Calif., or, Bay Area Ki Research Institute, 10035 Austin St., San Francisco, Calif.

The following books cover aikido in good detail. All are available from World Publications, Box 366, Mountain View, Calif. 94040 at the price listed* plus 25 cents each for postage. Write for a complete list.
This is Aikido, Koichi Tohei. A complete, illustrated manual for mastery of the basic techniques of aikido. Over 1000 gravure illustrations. 1975 Hb., 180 (oversize) pp., ill., $18.50, (Japan Publications).
Aikido, Kisshomaru Uyeshiba. A good all-around introduction to the art and sport of aikido. Shows all the basic moves, armed and unarmed. 1974 Hb., 190 (oversize) pp., ill., $12.75 (Japan Publications.)
Traditional Aikido, Morihiro Saito. Three volumes written to lead you to a more vigorous, confident and spirited way of life. Introduces the philosophy, techniques and history of aikido. All 1973-1974, Hardback, ill. and 134 pp. Volume One: Basic Techniques–$12.95, Volume Two: Advanced Techniques–$12.95, Volume Three: Applied Techniques–$12.95, (Japan Publications).

Archery

Archery can certainly be described as "the sport of man since time began." When present-day archers take up the bow and arrow for fun and recreation, their satisfaction comes from a skill that was an inherent part of man's life far beyond recorded history.

Just as the exact date of the discovery of fire or of the invention of the wheel is unknown, so it is with the bow and arrow. Many historians agree, however, these three innovations were the chief factors in man's rise above his fellow creatures. In those early days, and indeed for many centuries, the bow was a tool of grim necessity for obtaining food and winning battles, rather than as a sporting arm.

For more than 5000 years of recorded history the bow has been extremely important in man's legacy. Many nations, in fact whole civilizations–the Egyptians, Sumerians, Greeks, Romans, Babylonians, Syrians, Turks, Persians, Arabians, Mongols, Chinese and Japanese–were largely built or destroyed by flights of humming arrow shafts. After the perfection of firearms made the bow all but obsolete in warfare, it still retained its popularity in many parts of the world as a sporting and hunting arm.

The fact that a bow is made to function through the coordinated muscles of the back, shoulders, arms, and eyes, lends much romance to its use. Legends of stalwart archers permeate history: Odysseus, the Greek Amazons, Genghis Khan, Tamerlane, Sultan Saladin, Robin Hood, and our own Hiawatha, to name but a few.

As a romantic sport of the ages, archery still appeals to man's love of his historic past. It gives him the chance to almost relive the days of his forebears who conquered enemies and sustained life with little else but their bows and arrows.

There are many more practical reasons, however, that explain the lure of the bow for millions of present-day archers. This sport offers an ideal combination of fun, physical fitness and family togetherness. It is of interest to both the individual and to groups to both sexes, and to all ages. It can be as leisurely or competitive as one chooses. Archery is relatively inexpensive, easy to learn, and offers a large variety of games for the beginner and expert alike.

Many sports largely exclude women, but archery imposes no such limitations. Sheer strength is not a prerequisite to success, and women can not only excel in the sport, but find it an excellent builder of poise and posture.

Some archery fans limit their activities to target shooting. They develop skill, and enjoy family outings or competitive shoots. Others use the bow and arrow for hunting, pitting their skill against game on more equal terms than they could using firearms.

A word of caution is needed, though. The archery bug is catching. Chances are great that once you see the fun it offers, you won't be satisfied until you, too, are regularly enjoying the twang of the bowstring and the swish of your own speedy arrows.

–Ernie Lalonde

Ernie Lalonde has been involved in archery for about 10 years. He has written a lot of articles on the subject. He works for the Provincial Fish and Wildlife Agency in Alberta, Canada as a Predator Control Officer.

Exploring Target Archery

Archery is essentially a sport of individual accomplishment. The degree of skill you attain is due primarily to your own efforts. Although archers usually shoot in groups, the sport can be adapted for hours of pleasant individual shooting. It can be enjoyed the year round, indoors and out, and from early youth to advanced age.

Archery can be practiced in your own backyard–a multicolored target even makes an attractive lawn decoration. Target butts of banded hay or excelsior can be cheaply bought, and they give good service. The butt should be placed in a position so the areas behind and to the sides of the target will not be danger spots should your arrows miss. Rising ground behind the butt, or the side of a garage or shed, will keep high

Modern target archery equipment bears little resemblance to Robin Hood's yew longbow and grey goose shafts. Bows are now of laminated wood and synthetics, with elaborate stabilizing weights attached. Arrows are commonly aluminum with virtually no variance in weight or size dimensions from one to another. (Duffy)

arrows from taking off. Two additional bales of hay a few feet behind the target butt will also make a good backstop. Target faces are attached to the butt with large pins which can be made from wire coat hangers. Members of the family can learn and practice with such a setup in their free time. A word of caution here: when youngsters are in the learning stage, do not turn them loose on their own. Proper supervision will keep your neighbors peaceful.

Target archery is the oldest competitive sport for bowmen in the country, having been copied from the classic form dominant in England and the western European countries. The first American target archery group on record were the United Bowmen of Philadelphia, founded in 1828.

Target courses are laid out over level terrain so that shooting is from south to north, when possible. Target butts are spaced equally, from four to six yards apart. At least every third target has a small colored flag, projecting two or three feet above it, serving as a wind indicator. Shooting positions are laid out carefully at measured distances from the targets. The target faces are 48 inches in diameter, with a center gold spot, or bull's eye, which is 9.6 inches in diameter. The bull's eye is surrounded by four concentric bands of red, blue, black and value of the rings from center outward thus become 10, nine, and so forth to one. At FITA shooting distances of 50 and 30 is allowed in target archery, and any kind of sight, point of aim, or other variation of aiming device, may be used.

Arrows are shot in groups, or ends, of six, after which the contestants, upon a given signal, advance to the targets to score the results. Scoring values on standard target faces are Gold-9, Red-7, Blue-5, Black-3, White-1. Thus, a perfect end of six arrows in the gold would score 54 points.

When target archers take part in international meets under the auspices of the FITA (Federation Internationale de Tir a L'Arc), they shoot at the standard 48-inch face, except that each color-band is divided in half by a fine, black line. The value of the rings from center outward thus become 10, 9, 8, 7, 6, 5, 4, 3, 2, 1. At FITA shooting distances of 50 and 30 meters, an 80 centimeter face, divided into similar rings, is used.

—Ernie Lalonde

For More Information

There are many regional publications covering archery and too many to list. But here are the major publications.

Archery World, 534 N. Broadway, Milwaukee, Wisconsin 53202. Published bi-monthly at $4.00 per year. Covers the sport in detail with material for all archers from the beginner to Olympic target shooting.

Bow & Arrow, Box HH, Capistrano Beach, Calif. 92624. Published bi-monthly at $5.00 per year. A well done publication with lots of photos. Good technical articles.

Archery Magazine, Route 2, Box 514, Redlands, Calif. 92373. Published monthly and is the official publication of the NFAA.

There are many organizations, here are the major ones.

National Archery Association, 1951 Geraldson Drive, Lancaster, Penn. 17601. For the amateur archer and is the official representative for Olympic archery and the World Championships.

National Field Archery Association, Route 2, Box 514, Redlands, Calif. 92373. A participants' organization for the field archer which also promotes bow hunting.

Professional Archers Association, P.O. Box 7609, Flint, Mich. 48507. For the professional.

American Archery Council, 618 Chalmers St., Flint, Mich. 48503. The over-all organization that has representatives from all other groups. Dedicated to the support of all kinds of archery.

Most good sports shops have a fine line of archery equipment but if you can't find what you want you might try these.

Anderson Archery Corporation, Grand Ledge, Mich. 48837. They have a free catalog. Have been in the mail order business for over 20 years.

Feline Archery Co. Inc., 220 Willow Crossing Rd., Greensburg, Penn. 15601. They have a giant catalog for $2.00.

Southeast'n, 4718 S. Orange Ave., Orlando, Fla. 32806. Free catalog with a lot of good things in it.

There are lots of books available on archery. These listed are good. All are available from World Publications, Box 366, Mountain View, Calif. 94040 at the price listed* plus 25 cents each for postage. Write for a complete list.

Archery Digest, edited by Jack Lewis. From the editors of *Bow and Arrow* magazine. Its 33 big chapters cover everything about archery from the basics and history of archery to big game bowhunting, how to build your own bow, and how to fletch arrows. 1971 Ppb., 320 (oversize) pp., ill., $5.95 (Digest Books Inc.)

Archery Basic Techniques, Dick Garver, Sr. Good beginner's guide whose author taught archery for 12 years. Seven exercises to develop good archery habits and prevent errors. Details development of archery, how the equipment is made and the principles and safety rules. 1974 Ppb., 68 pp., ill., $1.95, (Shawnee Sports).

Auto Cross

Did you ever have the "Sunday Blues"? Sundays that there just wasn't anything going on? Well here's something that may interest those of you who appreciate cars and driving and also have a competitive urge. Autocross!

Autocross is a fun-filled Sunday affair which tests your ability to drive your car around a closed, flat course composed of pylons (those rubber cones that all the construction companies use) set up in a parking lot. The object is to negotiate the course faster than anyone else. If you can accomplish this feat you will come away with a TTOD trophy (Top Time Of Day). But if your car, like many other cars, is not capable of a TTOD, there are appropriate classes which will allow you to earn a TTOC (Top Time Of Class) award, even if you drive a slug.

Isn't that a better way to spend a Sunday? Right. Maybe you'd like to know more?

Autocross, or slalom as it is sometimes known, became popular in the late 1950's and early 1960's. The cars that were popular in that era had a lot to do with the organization of such a sport. Cars such as Jaguar, MG, Corvette, Triumph, Austin Healy and Lotus made up the ranks of the first Autocrosses.

Basically, autocross came into popularity as a result of the rising costs for competitive cars in regular auto racing. Also, when the typical Sunday afternoon auto race became a three-day event, many racing drivers who had enjoyed competing on the tracks found that they could not afford a whole weekend of competition. To remedy this situation, many drivers turned to autocross.

It was these early drivers who formed clubs with their friends and staged the first autocrosses. Since a well-run event took precise organization even then, only a car club could handle this responsibility. True, their autocrosses were probably a lot different from ours now, but the real significance was that they were open to ALL licensed drivers – a fact which still holds today. There wasn't a lot of money involved either, as in other kinds of racing. And you could race, along with your friend, your wife, son – even your mother!

Today, autocrosses in your area are probably put on by a variety of automobile clubs. Most local foreign auto parts stores can inform you of any autocrossing activity in your area.

Hmmm . . . now you've checked with the parts store and found out that there just happens to be an autocross this coming weekend down in the department store parking lot, put on by the local car club. Now this Sunday won't be the same!

You arrive at eight o'clock in the morning to register. A registration form must be filled out, and for the $2 to $4 entry fee, you get a number for your car for that particular event, and a flashy dash plaque displaying the date and title of the competition.

Following registration, a technical inspection for safety is performed on your car. Safety belts are a must, as is a safety helmet (the helmet is normally supplied at the event). Everything that isn't tied down must be removed from the inside of the car and the hubcaps and wheel trim should be taken off.

As soon as you've passed the inspection, you head down to line your car up in the staging line. From this line you eventually go out onto the course. When the starter gives the green flag you enter the course and take a run of generally three laps–one practice lap and two timed laps. The combined total of the two timed laps plus penalty points, if any, (accumulated for knocking over pylons) is your time for the run. Sometimes you might be able to run your car two or three times in one day, at other times only once; this depends on the number of cars entered in the event. After your run, you can check your time against the other times in your class at the scoring board.

The excitement of racing your own car and pitting your reaction times against other capable drivers is memorable to say the least. And you can bring a picnic, and your friends! How can you beat that for dissolving those "Sunday Blues"?

–Jeff Loughridge

Jeff Loughridge is a veteran autocross driver. He works at World Publications as a graphic artist.

Looking At The Basics

My first autocross was on a very slow course. Courses vary in the top speed that can be reached. On some you might be able to go as fast as 70 m.p.h., but on this one 35 was tops. The turns were closer and tighter than usual, with a lot of 90-degree and hairpin challenges. Due to the slow course, I was able to place third in my first competition despite a slow car. I was hooked!

Course speed varies according to which type of car club is staging an autocross. Since there are no standardized courses, car clubs for Corvettes or Mustangs tend to set up faster courses than would a Volkswagen or Datsun club.

Standardization enters autocross in the form of car classes. These go primarily by engine size, but classes have been formed for sedans, sports cars, and open wheel or closed wheel.

American autocrosses are very different from the English version. English autocross is almost as old as the automobile, and takes place between two cars. They go around an open course, over grassy fields, up and down hills, through mud and dirt, even through the bushes. In response to these natural hazards, English autocross cars use several different kinds of tires and the suspension is adjusted so the cars are up higher off the ground.

In contrast, American autocross is quite new, dating to the late 1950s and early 1960s when English sportscars became popular in the United States. American autocross features timed runs around a paved course by only one car at a time. Cars have their suspension adjusted to ride lowei to the ground, and some even have negative camber (a tilting in of the tops of wheels). With such suspension modifications, American autocross cars tend to handle better than their English cousins.

Safety belts and a crash helmet are mandatory in all autocross events. Roll bars are recommended, but are required only for high-speed autocross competitions sponsored by the Sports Car Club of America and featuring top speeds of up to 120 m.p.h. An additional safety precaution is the inspection of each car's suspension and brakes. Race organizers will not pass any car that fails to meet high mechanical safety standards.

Considerable mental preparation is involved when entering any autocross competition. Basically, it boils down to concentration. It's a good idea to walk the course beforehand to find out where there's gravel or a tight turn. You have to concentrate on how to take the turns, swinging wide and clipping the apex (the inside part of each turn). All of these driving techniques are taught in an autocross school.

I raced in three autocrosses before attending an autocross school. These are put on by regional car clubs and are recommended for anyone interested in the sport. Qualified instructors teach each student exactly how to walk a course, and what to look for. They point out that speeding around turns may not be the fastest way to negotiate a full course. Sometimes going more slowly for two turns will set up the next, allowing for greater acceleration out of the third turn and into a straightaway. If a straightaway is started only two m.p.h. faster than usual, it might result in a peak straightaway speed 10 to 15 m.p.h. faster. These and other little tricks will be revealed by the instructor and will result in marked improvement in autocross times.

Autocross schools usually last a full day. After learning to walk the course, an instructor will take each student slowly around in the student's car, giving detailed instruction on how to take each turn. At the end of the day, an actual autocross is held for the students, with the best receiving trophies for their efforts.

Once a driver has completed an autocross school course, it should be only a matter of time and accumulated experience before he or she is winning trophies regularly. If you enjoy driving and would like a little friendly weekend competition, autocross is for you!

—Jeff Loughridge

For More Information

For information on autocross, contact your local sports car dealer of Sports Car Club of America Solo II, Box 22476, Denver, Colo. 80222. Here is one book on the subject which should prove helpful. It is available from World Publications, Box 366, Mountain View, Calif. 94040 at the price listed* plus 25 cents postage.

How to Win at Slalom and Autocross, Jim Pagel. A definitive, technical, how-to-win book on the fast-growing sports of slalom, autocross, others. Limited supply, Ppb., ill., $3.95, (Crown).

"American autocross is quite new, dating to the late 1950s and early 1960s when English sportscars became popular in the United States. It features timed runs around a paved course by only one car at a time." (F.A.R. Performance)

Auto Road Racing

The huge tires and airfoils of a Formula 500 race car make it look like some futuristic space monster, but both combine for better road traction and handling. (Drennan)

European racing drivers are definitely brought up in a different environment than Americans. In Europe it is all road racing, so young drivers are slanted in this direction. Americans generally start out on oval tracks or in dirt track racing. This doesn't mean, however, that European drivers are better, or vice-versa. It's just that the educations in racing are different.

There are, of course, certain techniques that a driver must learn for each type of racing. The set-up of cars is very important in both forms since a car's performance has an effect on a driver's technique. Personal preference has a lot to do with it, and what one driver does on a road circuit may not suit another.

From a driver's point of view, I think that road courses are more difficult. There is much more to learn and you have more potential problems. At the same time, I think a top oval driver would make a fine road racing driver. The basic requirements for success are the same in both: time and patience. I really haven't concentrated on oval racing, because road racing by itself keeps me busy. Racing Indianapolis, for instance, is something that would take quite a lot of time to learn. In the days when Europeans like Graham Hill and Jim Clark were winning the big oval races, they came with cars that were technically better than the Americans' cars at that time. I don't think their driving skills necessarily were any better.

My favorite type of racing is on long distance road circuits. These courses give you time to settle in and also to look after your car. You have the time to change gears gently and well (when I say "gently" I mean relatively gently). The same thing applies for the brakes and the clutch. I think the Nurburgring is the finest racing circuit in the world. It has 170 corners per 14½ mile lap, and it goes up hills, down dales, through the forests. To me this is the best form of racing, although everyone will have his own opinions.

If you like longer races as I do, your co-driver is a very definite concern. If a driver is looking for a team to race with at the beginning of the season, a team manager might approach him to determine if he is interested in driving. The driver usually will ask in return, "Who will my co-driver be?" and "What kind of car will I be racing?" Thus, in deciding which team he will race for, a driver's two main concerns will be the competitiveness of the car and the co-driver.

I don't necessarily think that it takes an aggressive personality to be a racing driver. You find a lot of road racing drivers who are extremely polite and quiet people. Of course, you do need *a certain amount* of aggressiveness in racing. Quite often you find drivers who are technically quite fast and are able to

Formula Vee road racing cars (Left-Vic Black) differ from Production cars (Above-F.A.R. Performance) in that they are built from the ground up to be racing vehicles. Production cars start as ordinary road vehicles and are modified for racing.

put in fast times, but who don't win races because they're not aggressive enough. They don't take the calculated chances that can make the difference between winning and losing.

The essence of auto racing is calculated risk. You press both yourself and the vehicle as hard as you think is necessary to win the race. If, for instance, you are running in second place and the lead car is obviously pulling away from you, you might take chances in the early stages of the race to try and keep close to that car. As the race goes on and you see that he is still pulling away, you might reduce the element of risk. You would brake a fraction earlier and not rev the engine quite as hard in order to settle for a good second place, rather than blow it up and ruin all chances of winning. There are a few drivers who will still drive absolutely to the limits of themselves and their machines, regardless of the case, but as far as I'm concerned, my tactics depend upon the situation. I try to judge what's happening during the course of the race and treat myself and the car accordingly.

Another very important aspect of racing is concentration. After a few years this just comes by itself. Mentally, you actually become relatively relaxed. You're able to see people at the side of the road and take a general view of what is approaching even though you may be running at speeds up to 170 m.p.h. You still can take a good look at what's going on—have a look at the gauges on the straightaway, look at the tires in the mirrors—without losing your concentration on what is actually happening on the race track.

One of the hardest things in a driver's early racing days is to maintain concentration throughout the race distance, particularly if it's a long race. At first it takes a lot out of you, but after you become more experienced you're able to concentrate without great effort.

The peak age for road racing drivers is getting younger all the time. The top road racing drivers today start in their early teens in go-karts and then move up to Formula I cars later. Today we have a situation where the top 10 or 12 road racing drivers in the world are between the ages of 22 and 26. That's very young. I feel that a particular driver's peak age depends a lot on his personality. They mature at different times, but I think 26 to 34 are probably the peak years for a road racing driver.

Personally, I didn't follow racing with any avid interest in my really young days. I was about 18 or 19 when I went to one or two Grand Prix races and saw Sterling Moss, and some other well-known drivers. Essentially, I got started in racing because I was driving too fast on the ordinary roads and felt that I should try to get onto a track in order to release that spirit.

My biggest thrill in racing was taking part in the very prestigious Targa Florio in Sicily. This is the world's oldest motor race and takes place on a tremendously difficult track. Although it wasn't my best finish, it was the race that I drove most steadily in order to finish.

In my life, auto racing has really given me something to aim for. I wasn't particularly good at school or in business. Racing is something that I can do reasonably well, and it means earning a decent living and a better way of life. It is very much a way of life in itself.

—**Brian Redman**

"A very important aspect of racing is concentration. After a few years this just comes by itself. Mentally you actually become relatively relaxed. You're able to see people at the side of the road and take a general view of what is approaching even though you may be running at speeds up to 170 mph." (Duffy).

The Englishman Brian Redman has made quite a name for himself in road racing since turning pro in 1967. Besides being a member of the World Manufacturers Championship winning team for four years, he was Formula 5000 runnerup in 1973 and champion in 1974 and 1975.

For More Information

For organizations, magazines and equipment check the listing under auto track racing. But here are some books that cover races that are not run on an oval track. All are available from World Publications, Box 366, Mountain View, Calif. 94040 at the price listed* plus 25 cents each postage.

The LeMans 24-Hour Race, Ami Guichard. Over 300 color and black and white photos and a large, complete history of the most famous endurance auto race. Famous duels, victories and defeats, extensive statistics, and the drivers and cars. 1975 Hb., 220 pp., ill., $24.95, (Chilton).

Road Racing in America, Lyle Engel. Covers the Grand Prix, the Indy, NASCAR, Trans-Am, and Formula racing. A chapter on how to learn to race and a glossary of racing terminology rounds out this all-inclusive work. 1971 Hb., 146 pp., ill., $5.95, (Dodd, Mead).

Formula I Racing, Jose Rosinski. Beautifully illustrated with spectacular photos. A complete history of Formula I racing, including portraits of the great drivers. 1974 Hb., 247 (oversize) pp., ill., $14.95, (Grosset & Dunlap).

Francois Cevert—A Contract with Death, Jean-Claude Halle. Jackie Stewart called Francois Cevert "the best French driver of all time" only a few days before Cevert was killed, at the age of 29, during practice. Largely written from Cevert's unfinished autobiography, this book describes his rise from stealing old tires to Grand Prix races worth thousands of dollars. 1975 Hb., 213 pp., ill., $10.95, (Motorbooks International).

Auto Track Racing

If you should ask the elderly lady down the street what automobile racing is she would probably tell you simply, and in two or three lines, that is if you can convince her that you really don't know the difference between a pit crew and a crew cut. "Sonny," she'll say, "An auto race is a competition between two or more mechanically driven cars. The poor young men who drive these cars are half out of their minds. If one of them was my son, I'd snatch his keys away right-off!"

Well, ask a stupid question, you get a . . . Right? So you decide to take the next best alternative and buy a ticket to the Indianapolis 500, the biggest auto race in America. And wouldn't you know it? As you take your place in the grandstand, you find the same elderly lady-friend and her grandson who has decided to treat her with an early Mother's Day gift—a trip to the races.

As the long line of glistening cars circle the track on their preliminary lap, engines revving, you can't help but overhear their conversation. It appears that the elderly lady has come up with a few questions of her own.

Elderly Lady: Sonny, why is it that the road is shaped like an oval?

Grandson: What you call the road, racing people call a track. It is specially-built course, with two long straight sections, two shorter straights, and four curves that have been constructed so the surface tilts at an angle. These banked curves enable the cars to negotiate the turn at great speed, without skidding.

Elderly Lady: But you didn't answer my question . . .

Grandson: In America, a good majority of auto races are held on oval tracks. You remember the first Indianapolis 500, in 1911, don't you? You don't? Well, the oval auto race is a result more of tradition than anything else. The first Indy was held on a track shaped like this, with cars going counterclockwise. Many similar races, with different kinds of cars, are held today.

Elderly Lady Friend: Never mind about the road; look at the cars, Lydia! I've never seen a Kaiser like that!

Grandson: The cars you're looking at are very intricately designed Formula cars, built especially for racing. The streamlined body makes them speedy, and the large tires cling to the course. Actually, there are several different types of Formula racers, grouped into classes according to engine size and other differences. If Kaisers were still around they might be eligible for stock car racing. Stock cars are the same American passenger cars that you see on the highway, except they're finely tuned and modified for efficient performance. In this country, stock car races take place most often on oval tracks. Midget racing also takes place on ovals. Midget cars are smaller and less powerful than the full-sized ones, but they are very popular.

Elderly Lady: What is that driver doing raising his hand like that? "One hand, can't land," Lindbergh said. And why are those men in the fancy workclothes holding up a blackboard?

Grandson: The driver is signaling to his team of helpers, who are called his crew. Their job is to assist their particular driver in all possible ways. They refuel the car when it comes into the pit area for its pit stop. They also change tires, give the driver a drink, and make any quick repairs that are necessary. The blackboards are meant to inform the driver of how well he is doing, by flashing times, and other bits of information.

Elderly Lady Friend: What was that you said about times, Sonny?

Grandson: The object of the race is to finish a predetermined number of laps around the track in the fastest possible time. In this case, the first car and driver to cross the finish line on the 200th lap is the winner. When he does this, he has driven 500 miles.

Elderly Lady: And what good is that? Does he win anything?

Grandson: Yes. A good deal of money, and a kiss from the queen of the race, who you saw earlier. All of the drivers in this race are professionals, as are many others who race on oval tracks. Their winnings help pay their way.

Elderly Lady: My goodness! A kiss from that lovely girl! Maybe those "poor young men" aren't so far out of their minds after all!

"Well, maybe not," you might say to yourself, as the crowd—including you and the elderly lady—rise to your feet in tumultuous applause, as the checkered flag is raised, signifying the winner. "Perhaps there's more meaning in 'Gentlemen, start your engines,' than I thought!"

A Family Affair

When it comes to auto racing, I consider myself to be very fortunate. Ever since I was a boy my whole family has been involved in this sport. All three of my older brothers raced, and just being a part of this atmosphere whet my interests tremedously. Jerry and Louis, who were the oldest, started racing when they were 15 or 16 years old. Then, of course, there was Bobby who began at 14. Since I'm five years younger than Bobby, I was quite young when they were already on the track. Often I worked on the cars with my brothers and went to the races with them. From there, it sort of took its own step. I worked my way up through the ranks, and I finally made it.

Like many kids who eagerly followed the races, the Indianapolis drivers were my idols. Just going there and dreaming of the race was a thrill. I never really thought I would be taking part in the Indy 500 one day. It wasn't a goal that I had set for myself; I never said, "Well, I'm going to go to Indianapolis." I never did think in that manner. I wanted to race, and it just seemed to work out well.

As I was growing in ability, I was lucky enough to get the right breaks at the right time. In 1964, I started racing for Frank Garcia. At first I ran SCCA races with his sports cars all around the country, and by 1965 he decided that he wanted to take me to Indianapolis. I was surprised when he asked me, because it's not easy for a car owner to take a rookie to the speedways. It costs a good deal of money, so he must have some kind of faith in you.

"Auto racing is a dangerous sport. The fact is always there that something might happen to you, and you're always aware of it. The danger is something you learn to face." (Duffy)

The first year at Indy, my car had a Maserati engine, and I blew it in qualifying. Of course, this was a great disappointment, especially since Louis was the chief mechanic. It was sort of a family affair. I did, however, end up getting into A.J. Foyt's backup car, qualified and eventually finished ninth in the race.

Ever since that year, I'm glad to say that I've only missed one Indianapolis, that in 1969 when I broke my leg in a motorcycle fall.

I suppose some people might think that it's rather strange that I was laid up because of a motorcycle accident when my main business is auto racing. Perhaps they're right. After all, auto racing is a dangerous sport. The fact is always there that something might happen to you, and you're always aware of it. Actually, the danger is something you learn to face. You don't plan on having an accident and you don't plan on not having it. It's just a matter of racing the best you can while trying to prevent any mishap as much as possible, and hoping that is doesn't happen to you. When I'm on the track I don't say to myself, "I have to worry about crashing today." When it comes right down to it, it's your actions that count.

One positive aspect that arises out of this peril is that a driver gains tons of respect for the other people involved. Many times in a race he must put his life in somebody else's hands, and because of this, the racing fraternity is very close. While we don't run around in a great bunch, we are still all very friendly, and we know one another quite well. When we race against each other, machine to machine on the same circuit, we become familiar with each other's habits on the race track—our tempers, manners, etc. For this reason, I think we're a very close group.

For most professional racing drivers, our sport is like going to an enjoyable job every day. It's something I personally enjoy very much. While I get tremendous satisfaction out of it, sometimes it can be a strain, since there is quite a bit of mental effort involved. In my earlier days, I used to get myself quite worked up going to a race; my adrenalin would be flowing at an incredible rate. Even today, I have to use something close to reverse psychology on myself a lot of times to keep myself from getting overly excited. When you're upset, you don't do a good job.

A driver has to be thinking constantly, especially driving warm-up laps when he has to make absolutely sure his car runs right and handles properly. Before the actual qualifying, thoughts of what I can do to improve my car are running through my head. A racing driver is always trying to figure out a way to make his car better than the other guy's, how to make it go just a little bit faster. Picking on every corner I can find, so it will run quicker, is an important part of my job. It's a constant thinking game. If you don't have your car figured out by the time qualifying comes around, then you try to come up with the best method of getting around the track, to qualify in the quickest possible time.

When it comes down to the wire, everything is actually very intricately intermeshed: the car, driver, and crew. Since it is a team effort, a driver must develop a good understanding with all the personnel. Actually, winning is a 50-50 proposition. I've never seen a racing driver carry a car alone, nor have I seen a mechanic carry one. It is essential to have a good relationship with every member of the crew–from the chief mechanic all the way down to the guy who pumps the gas. If you don't, things just don't work properly. These people are the ones who get the car ready, and who keep it running. Even if you're an excellent driver, it very seldom happens that you can win with only a fair car. Once in a while this might happen, even with a poor car, but all-in-all it is very rare. The most important element is that the crew is happy. If everything works right, a happy crew is usually a winning crew and the car will record a fast time.

Today speed is the name of the game. For years people have been trying to slow down the sport, but to no avail. Largely, this is due to the fact that even the mechanics compete against each other. When there are totally talented people involved in a sport, then somebody is going to come up with better ideas along the way.

When I first got started, the new trends in racing were just getting into full fling. For instance, the trend at Indianapolis of running rear engine cars was already established. I never did race any of the roadsters, as they called them at that time. Over the years, tires have improved and have become much safer, and the engines have progressively become much more powerful. A big innovation was the introduction of wings. In 1971, we started running these air foils on the cars, and this causes a tremendous improvement in handling. Therefore, the designers had to actually build the car differently, suspension and geometry wise. Everything had to be re-done. The car that a driver was racing in 1971 all of a sudden became obsolete. New ones had to be built. Then when the turbochargers apeared, it changed the whole trend in engines. A normally aspirated engine wasn't even in the ballpark anymore; they simply didn't have enough horsepower. One step after another, this is the way racing is made. It's always an uphill climb and very competitive. For example, when I race against Bobby, I try to beat him, just as if he was anybody else. That's all there is to it. There's no alternative.

This fine competition is part of the reason that auto racing is such a popular spectator sport. The game of football, for instance, is a total team effort. If one player makes a mistake, the whole team might look bad. In racing, when a driver is actually on the track, he's out there all by himself. This appeals to a society where positive individual motivation and action has traditionally been sanctioned. Also, I think people are interested in this sport because they can relate to it merely by driving a car. Cars are an intricate part of our lives; they are living. When people get behind the wheel, they are essentially performing the same ritual as all the racing drivers who ever lived.

This search for individual achievement might also account for the large influx of new drivers into the sport. Just as in any other field, a young driver must work at it diligently in order to learn the required techniques. It takes quite a few miles of racing to become good at it, especially if you want to race on a wide variety of courses. It is essential for a driver to be familiar with a number of driving styles and techniques. For example, on a road course, a driver uses a lot more braking than he would on an oval. Entrances and exits out of the corners are completely different. Learning these techniques takes time–nothing happens overnight.

When I was coming up, I wanted to race everywhere I could. I figured that skill was directly proportional to experience. All over the world races take place year-round. In auto racing you can't get away with the excuse, "Well, I didn't have the opportunity," or "I didn't have the breaks." There's opportunity everywhere. When I was working my way up, there were many drivers who gave me incentive, just by watching their style, their desire to improve and win: A.J. Foyt, Roger Ward, Jim Hertebes– a great bunch of them. As for pure dedication, I think Parnelli Jones was the best example for me.

I feel very fortunate to have been able to reach the same level as these heroes of my younger days. Over the years there have been many good races for me. Of course, when you win on a particular day, that's the race that you're happy about for the moment.

Still, I think the 1970 Indianapolis 500, when I won it for the first time, is the race I can look back on with the most pride. This was the one that I was really wanting. Even so, there are better races to come.

Auto racing has not only been my living, but I can honestly say that it has been my entire life. For me, it's the greatest sport in the world. I have a son, thirteen years old and I'm looking forward to the day when I can watch him race. Like I said, it's a little bit of a family affair. Even so, it's difficult to describe what you really enjoy. Racing has been very good to me. I have no regrets.

–Al Unser

Al Unser has won the Indianapolis 500 race twice, 1970 and 1971. He also was the USAC national champion in 1970 and national dirt track champion in 1973. He has won 27 USAC national championship races. His older brother Bobby, is also a well-known racing driver.

For More Information

By checking the newsstand you will be able to find several good magazines. Here is a sampling of those available. Also check road racing.

National Speed Sport News, Box 608, 30 Oak Street, Ridgewood, N.J. 07451. Published 50 times per year at $9.00. Newspaper format with a lot of news, photos and features.

Area Auto Racing News, 2829 South Broad Street, Trenton, N.J. 08610. Published 50 times per year at $8.75. Newspaper format.

Road and Track, 540 Bond Drive, Marion, Ohio 43302. Published monthly and on newsstands.

Car and Driver, One Park Ave., New York, N.Y. 10016. Published monthly and on newstands.

Since there are so many organizations we are only listing those that can conduct international races.

Automobile Competition Committee for US, FIA Suite 302, 1725 K St. NW, Washington, D.C. 20006. The National sporting authority for international motor racing in US. All following organizations are members of this group.

International Motor Sports Assoc. (IMSA), Box 805, Fairfield, Conn. 06430.

National Association for Stock Car Auto Racing (NASCAR), Box K, Daytona Beach, Fla. 32015.
National Hot Rod Association (NHRA), Box 150, North Hollywood, Calif. 91603.
United States Auto Club (USAC), 4910 W. 16th St., Indianapolis, Ind. 46224.
Sports Car of Club America (SCCA), Box 22476, Denver, Colo. 80222.

There are many places around where you can get equipment for racing. Check your phone book. Or check with these people.
Auto World, 701 N. Keyser Ave., Scranton, Penn. 18508. Has a big catalog with a good selection of specialized goodies.
Specialty Equipment Manufacturers Assn., 11001 E. Valley Mall, Suite 204, El Monte, Calif. 91734. This is not a mail order outfit but most manufacturers of racing equipment belong. Write for a list of members.

There are so many books on the subject that it is hard to decide what to list. Here are a couple that should prove interesting. Available from World Publications, Box 366, Mountain View, Calif. 94040 at the price listed* plus 25 cents each postage. Write for a complete list.

A Guide to American Sports Car Racing, William Stone. All the newest cars, most important race courses, current records and racing regulations are included in this vaulable edition for the racing fan. 1971 (rev.) Hb., ill., $7.50, (Doubleday).

Racing Engine Preparation, Waddell Wilson & Steve Smith. Approaching every part and section with an analytical mind, one of the country's most sought-after engine builders offers a complete mechanic's manual to building and tuning an engine. 1975 Ppb., 144 pp., ill., $7.50, (Steve Smith Autosports).

Backgammon

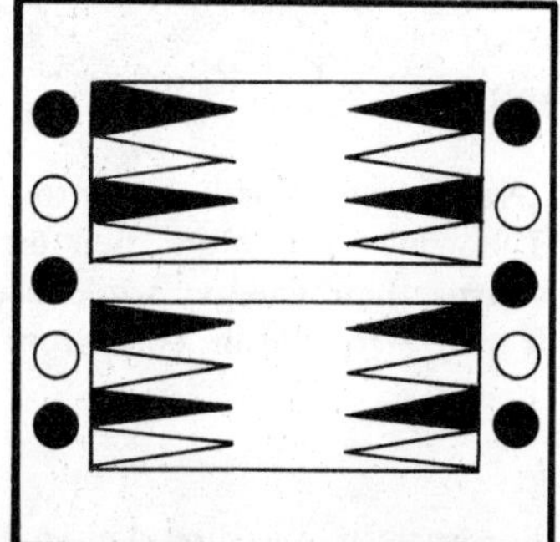

You perhaps remember backgammon as that strange game you never played that was printed on the back of your checker board. The game actually dates back over 5000 years, though, and has gained the respect of time. The ancient Sumerians played an ancestor of backgammon and King Tut's tomb in Egypt contained a gold backgammon board when it was opened. Roman Senators played the game at their baths and Shakespeare wrote about it. Backgammon has even been called the "Game of Kings" since in the days of Arthur's Round Table only royalty were allowed to play by the King's decree.

But how to play it? Each player has 15 men or checkers and they advance around the board by rolls of the dice. One player moves his tokens clockwise and the other counterclockwise. The object of the game is to advance your men to the Home Board or Inner Board and after getting them all there, bear them off the board by rolls of the dice. The first player clearing his men from the board wins. Two or more men resting on the same point during the course of a game is a block, while a lone man on a point is exposed and can be hit and knocked off the board, whereupon he must start over again.

One interesting facet of the game is the *doubler* or *doubling block.* This block doubles the stakes of the game, first to two, then four, then eight, 16, 32, and 64 as the advantage of a player proceeds over the other. Use of this doubling block, however, is optional.

Today, backgammon is tremendously popular throughout the world and is played in many private clubs and homes in this country. Its rise in popularity started about 10 years ago when Prince Alexis Obolensky started the first backgammon tournament in the Grand Bahamas. Thirty-two players convened that year, but by the next it was 100, and succeeding years brought even greater numbers. Popularity can also be traced to the large number of socially prominent people ("jet setters", movie stars and television actors) who play the game. This, of course, leads to greater press coverage and consequent increased interest.

A good backgammon board can be purchased for about $50.00 and two or more players can participate at the same time. The game's blended elements of skill and chance make for exciting matches—lucky rolls of the die are always appreciated.

—Owen Trayner

Owen Trayner founded the first backgammon club in the USA 12 years ago—the Fort Lauderdale Backgammon Club. Ever since, he has been teaching classes, introducing the game to private clubs, and has been the director at major tournaments.

For More Information

There has been a lot of news about backgammon lately. The publisher of *Playboy* magazine, Hugh Hefner, is a player along with a lot of other well known people. And several magazines have carried articles recently on the subject. But if you need more information write the World Backgammon Club, 30 East 68th St., New York, N.Y. 10021.

Here are a few books on the topic. All are available from World Publications, Box 366, Mt. View, Calif. 94040 at the listed* plus 25 cents each postage.

The Backgammon Book, Jacoby and Crawford. How to learn the game and enjoy it. An illustrated history, together with simple, clear writing on play. 1970 Hb., 224 pp., ill., $10.00, (Viking).

Beginning Backgammon, Tim Holland. Written by one of the world's leading players to help the novice player understand and develop his game, this book offers sound advice. 1975 Ppb., 209 pp., ill., $4.00, (Crown).

Backgammon, Don Stern. Fascinating, authoritative, yet uncomplicated introduction to the game sensation of the 1970s —complete with quizzes, diagrams and glossary. Features the Gammon point count. 1974 Ppb., $1.95, (Simon & Schuster).

Playboy's Book of Backgammon, Lewis Deyong. For beginners and experienced players alike, a complete basic and informative guide to the new national craze. 1975, $10.00, (Playboy Press).

Backpacking

A backpacker has often been described as a person with his home on his back, not just a mere dwelling, but a whole home. The reasons for carrying his home with him might be one of several. Often it is used as a means to an end, such as fishing or mountain climbing, but when it is an end in itself, the techniques of backpacking become very sophisticated. Often, this rugged activity becomes a contest between the weight carried and the number of days a person can survive in the wilderness with only his most necessary provisions.

Equipment for backpacking must be carefully chosen, durability and light weight being most important. Each item the backpacker chooses must pass his detailed inspection; imperfect, or bulky objects must be left out.

The most important item is usually the backpack, with its magnesium-aluminum frame, and helium arc-welded joints. A nylon bag is often attached to the frame, to carry the load. Bags come in many models with a multitude of different pockets and convenience attachments to suit almost any taste. A waist band, which helps distribute some of the pack's heavy load onto the hips, is almost universally used.

The next very important element is the sleeping bag. Goose down bags, with either baffles or three layer construction, have gained overwhelming acceptance in recent years. Mummy, or body shaped, bags are preferred over rectangular bags, since this type concentrates the insulation over the sleeper, while rectangular bags distribute the down over a wider area making for much wasted space and extra weight. Many synthetic materials have been produced that can compete with down for warmth, but not for compactability. Unlike down, however, these materials–mainly dacron–can be dried quickly if they get wet. A down bag is useless if it gets soaked and it takes a very long time to dry after a thorough drenching.

Boots for backpacking must also be chosen with great care. The backpacker will be carrying upwards of 30 pounds, and good boots are vitally necessary to support the bones of the foot. Vibram lugs are almost the universal sole material for boots, while uppers are top grain leather, and usually fully lined. Laces are most often secured by hooks or metal loops, with a padded tongue that overlaps the upper. This creates a boot that provides good support for the ankles, firm grip over rough trails and rock, and keeps out small stones and pebbles. Wool socks with cotton liners usually complete a hiker's footwear.

Sometimes the backpacker carries a small tent for protection against mosquitoes and rain, but this usually depends on what area he or she is visiting. A ground cloth, to protect the sleeping bag from ground moisture, is minimum equipment, and a sleeping pad of closed cell foam, or a porous pad covered with coated nylon, is often used.

The remaining equipment is usually variable, depending on the camper and where the backpacking trip will take place.

"Nature's peace will flow into you as sunshine flows into trees. The winds will blow their own freshness into you, and the storms their energy, while cares will drop off like autumn leaves."–John Muir. (Cameron)

For warmth, one should choose wool, as this is the only material that will retain body heat when wet. Sometimes cutoffs or leather shorts are worn, while coated nylon ponchos are necessary to protect the backpacker from rain. In many areas, for both ecological and esthetic reasons, a small kerosene or gas stove is carried.

Food for backpacking is also chosen with care and ingenuity, lightweight, nutritious, easily prepared items being highly preferred. With the advent of quality, freeze-dried foods in recent years, planning meals for a long pack trip is not as difficult as it once was.

Many backpackers have displayed an unusual degree of ingenuity in reducing the weight of their pack. The idea here is that by carrying less gear you can take more hobby equipment and more food to stay longer. Some of the better known weight reducing ideas include removing the handle of your tooth brush (real fanatics have even been known to remove half of the bristles). You can cut your comb in half, or better yet, leave it behind. Also, practice using as little soap as possible. One notorious backpacker went an entire six weeks using only one small motel bar of hand soap. Carry only three socks, washing the spare one every day. Some backpackers use nylon gym shorts as combined underwear and hiking shorts. A large bandana is also a multi-use item, serving as a substitute towel, hat, eyeshade, bead band, pot holder, mosquito swatter, bandage, sling, and friction pad—it is, in fact, much too valuable to be used merely for blowing your nose.

The skills needed by a backpacker are universal, as he is far from the city and its specialized divisions of labor. Backpackers need to be well-trained in medical matters, as they are often forced to remove fish hooks, relieve painful blisters, and recognize situations that might require evacuations to a hospital. They must also be able to treat minor burns and splinters, and definitely should know how to arrest serious bleeding, and perform mouth-to-mouth resuscitation.

Backpackers also must be experts with map and compass. Often it becomes important to travel through the wilderness without benefits of a trail. In order to retain his bearings, the cross-country backpacker needs to be very proficient in orienteering.This skill is not difficult to learn, but cannot be gained exclusively through books. It must also be practiced in the wilderness.

Despite all of this skill and technology, backpackers are really people with their house on their back, gypsys at heart. They carry all they need and go where they please. Simplicity is their byword. They have the attribute of the "pioneer wife" who can do anything, anytime, without fear, panic, or fancy gadgets.

As the wilderness plays the most important role in this activity, minimum impact camping is the only logical answer to eternal backpacking. Trash (particularly aluminum foil which does not burn or decay), inadequately disposed of human wastes, soot-marked rocks, chopped trees and compacted soil all detract from the backpacking experience. For this reason, practical ecology is on the lists of skills for a backpacker. Undoing the damage done by the less astute hiker, as well as minimizing one's own impact, should lead to the eternal perpetuation of the backpacking experience.

Is Backpacking a Fad?

Every day, more and more people take up backpacking. The sales of packs and lightweight camping equipment is literally soaring. The drab colors of ex-Army field gear is being replaced with brilliant blues, greens and day-glow orange. In remote areas, where you would once have met only a few hardy souls, you now see long lines of youth groups, families, and groups of college students. The very popular trails are over-crowded. It is not unlikely, for example, that you could count over 100 people a day, at any given point along the famous John Muir Trail. Is it merely a passing fad, or are these newcomers completely hooked?

If you talk to the people you meet along the trail, you can get a bit of insight into what has caused this exodus into the wilderness. Many of the youth groups go simply to receive a trophy. The act itself is regarded by some as rewarding, but in

Spectacular and rugged scenery can be made timeless for future generations of backpackers only if practical ecology is stressed. If you pack it in, pack it out. (Cameron)

addition to enjoyment, it is deemed necessary to issue a certificate or award to commemorate the event.

Other individuals are certain that they can "get away from it all." I have noticed that this group often brings a small portable radio, usually to little avail, as reception is consistently poor in the mountains. I also tactfully refrain from pointing out that they really brought "it all" with them, in their packs: corn from Kansas, potatoes from Idaho, meat from the West, sugar from Hawaii, nylon from the manufacturer, wool from the sheep ranch, felt hats from the felt hat factory, cheese from the dairy . . . .

Many say they come for the beauty, but there are many beautiful places in the world that have not experienced the same influx, and you can always see beautiful mountains and lakes from the window of your car. In addition, I happen to know that everything is beautiful. I have a set of 35mm slides of highly polluted beaches and skies, but everyone I show them to agrees that they are beautiful, until I tell them what the slides represent.

A large number of individuals come into the wilderness for other activities, like climbing or fishing. I personally do these things, and enjoy them, but I have also noticed that sometimes I don't fish or climb. This does not detract from my experience. When I question the fisherman, and ask if their wilderness backpacking trip is considered a flop if they catch no fish, their answer is inevitably, "No, it's still fun!" The climber, too, still enjoys the wilderness if, for some reason, he does not climb.

Just what is it that makes people put on a heavy pack and hike over mountain passes, endure the rain, strange food (who would eat peanut butter soup at home?), and mosquitoes? Do they pack for a trophy? A fish? A mountain peak? For beauty?

I have no doubt that these things play an important role in motivating a backpacker, but I think my four-year-old daughter also had a more honest, if only partial, answer. We were taking her on her first "official" backpacking trip and had just stopped for lunch. After eating, she wandered off a bit, unrolled her sleeping bag, and set up a "camp" under a tree. Normally, we could never get her to take a nap at home, so I watched eagerly to see what she would do. She took off her boots, unzipped the bag, and climbed in—but she didn't go to sleep. Puzzled, I asked her what was going on, and told her that we couldn't set up camp just yet. With very wide eyes, she firmly said,"Oh no, Daddy, we are backpacking now and I can do what I want to." She was perhaps more aware of her sense of freedom while backpacking than many grownups. The wilderness does provide a freedom and appreciation of space that cannot easily be found in any other place.

I have another theory, too, that is very much like my young daughter's. For many years I have had more than a passing interest in the evolution of man. I have not specialized in the field, but I do know something about the conditions under which *homo sapiens* evolved. He did not evolve in a grime-choked city, but in the wilderness. While I have no proof, it does seem reasonable that at a very early period we were genetically selected to survive in the wilderness. If we were not, then how could we have passed through this evolutionary stage and arrived at the high level of civilization we have today? To me, going into the wilderness is like going home, and I wonder if, way back in my genetic soul, I am saying, "You're home now, so relax and enjoy what you are." Maybe I am, because that is what I observe almost everyone doing in the wilderness.

—Larry Moitozo

Larry Moitozo has spent a lot of his 55 years backpacking. The outdoor is a way of life with him. He is also the technical editor of **Nordic World** *magazine.*

Gourmet backpacking meals may occasionally run to peanut butter soup, but usually dinner never tastes as good as when it is prepared over an open fire after 15 miles of hard trail. (Cameron)

In early Spring before trail crews have been through, backpacking can be a tad rough. Vigilance and care are the best preventions for injuries from trail falls. (Swanson BBM)

For More Information

It wasn't very long ago that it was even hard to find a good article on backpacking let alone a magazine. That isn't true anymore.

Backpacker, 28 West 44th Street, New York, N.Y. 10036. Published bi-monthly at $12.00 per year. By far the best magazine on backpacking. A lot of good technical articles, color photos and enough information to satisfy anyone interested in this activity.

Signpost, 16812 36th Ave. W., Lynnwood, Wa. 98036. Published bi-monthly with a monthly newsletter at $7.50 per year. Newspaper format with a lot of good articles in each issue.

Since backpacking is not really a "sport" but an outdoor activity the organizations involved have a different purpose than a true sport. Here are a couple of very active groups.

Sierra Club, 1050 Mills Tower, 220 Bush St., San Francisco, Calif. 94104. Can be very helpful to the beginner and expert alike. Publishes a lot of useful information.

Appalachian Mountain Club, 5 Joy St., Boston, Mass. 02108. Also publishes information you would be interested in.

Today you can find a lot of stores devoted especially to backpacking. And we suggest that you support these stores. A full-line sport store can be of help but chances are a specialized shop will be more helpful. But if you don't have such a shop in your area we would suggest the following:

L.L. Bean, Inc., 518 Main St., Freeport, Maine 04032. Has a complete catalog with a lot of good stuff in it. Most of the things in their catalog is only available mail order.

Eddie Bauer, 1737 Airport Way S., Seattle, Wash. 98134. They produce one of the best catalogs available. The descriptions are totally complete and it's enjoyable reading.

Ski Hut, Post Office Box 309, 1615 University Ave., Berkeley, Ca. 94701. A good source for equipment.

Sierra Designs, 4th and Addison St., Berkeley, Calif. 94710. Another Berkeley based company that will be able to help you. Has a nice looking catalog.

Frostline Kits, 452 Burbank Street, Broomfield, Colo. 80020. Ten years ago this progressive company was formed. They offer kits so that you can build your own equipment. Very colorful catalog.

Eastern Mountain Sports, 1047 Commonwealth Ave., Boston, Mass. 02215. Thick catalog. A lot of good information in each catalog. Not only backpacking.

Holubar, Box 7, Boulder, Colo. 80302. I really enjoyed the two-page spread they had on their Holubar sleeping bags in the 1975 summer catalog. A lot of good material in their colorful catalog.

Recreational Equipment, Inc., P.O. Box 22090, Seattle, Wash. 98122. In their ads they say "The original outdoor co-op since 1938." Good catalog.

Another tough one. There are a pile of great books. Here are a few of the better ones. All are available from World Publications, Box 366, Mountain View, Calif. 94040 at the price listed* plus 25 cents each for postage. Write for a complete list.

Backpacking with Babies and Small Children, Goldie Silverman. Parents will be pleased with the bountiful information that informs them what to take and what to do when backpacking with children. Clothes, carriers, coping in camp, and much more. Well-photographed. 1975 Ppb., 144 pp., ill., $4.50, (Signpost).

Backpackers Digest, Learn and Tallman. Wherever you are bound, the authors tell you exactly what to expect and how to get the most fun out of your trip. Learn what to take—and what to leave at home. Discover the backpacker's three C's. . . camping, cooking and coping with emergencies. Contains a large catalog section. 1974 Ppb., 268 (oversize) pp., ill., $6.95, (Digest Books).

Hiking the Appalachian Trail, James R. Hare, ed. The absorbing stories of 46 men and women who hiked the 2,023 mile Appalachian Trail. Bound in two big volumes, these day-to-day experiences are packed with hundreds of practical backpacking tips. Also contains beautiful color photos of different eye-openers along the trail, and charts and information. 1975 (2 vol.) Hb. 2004 pp., ill., $39.95, (Rodale).

Badminton

There is more to the game of badminton than first meets the eye. Because of the relatively small court and arching flight of the shuttle (a half-round piece of cork or plastic attached to feathers or a skirt of nylon), the game requires skills and techniques which set it apart from all other court games. A good player learns how to hit the shuttle with a fine precision, keeping it just out of reach of his opponent while retaining a favorable position for the return. Often he must rely upon uncanny patience, for the rallies of skilled players are usually long and they seldom miss any but the most difficult shots. Deception also plays a major factor in the game. The lightness of the racket and shuttle make it possible to send the shuttle in any direction by using a last minute flick of the wrist, perhaps with an eye or body feint. Badminton can be played indoors or out, but outside the smallest wind can change the course of a shuttle. This adds an additional element of excitement. While American badminton is usually restricted to the gymnasium or backyard, some Asian countries have many indoor and outdoor courts. In fact, the Japanese, Indonesians, and Malaysians, because of their enthusiasm, are some of the best players in the world.

Badminton may be played with either one or two players on a team and it is popular with both men and women. A badminton match usually begins with a spin of the racket to decide which team will serve first. This team will continue serving until it loses a rally, at which time the service passes to the opposite side. A point can be scored only by the serving side, and is won by forcing the opposing side to fail to return the shuttle over the net and within the boundaries of the court. In competitive play, the team which wins the best of three games, each of 15 points, wins the match.

The Real Game

Badminton has been a part of most of my life. I loved it even in my early years, as I sat in a wheel chair, having lost the greater part of my right heel to osteomylitis. I used to stand on one foot and bounce an old shuttle off my bedroom wall. Later, I participated in a countless number of tournaments, before I turned pro, at the Winnipeg Winter Club. The joy of coaching my daughters to their great wins has also given me much pleasure. And again now, coaching a group of eager youngsters and keen adults—enough to keep me busy —I feel joy in helping the game.

I'm sure the personal goal of all badminton players once they have become proficient enough to win some important tournaments, is to win the All-England (World) Championships. I still remember my first All-England Singles win in 1925. There had been no National Championships held in Ireland between 1914 and 1922, and when they started again I was living in England. I had won my first All-England doubles in 1922 with a strong Swiss player, but in 1925 I achieved my singles goal. Clearly, I recall my great relief, and a surge of confidence in my own ability that I had never felt previously. On the way up to a great win, to the pinnacle of one's ambition, one loses a great many matches and, I believe, learns from each loss. Stubbornness plays a great part and tenacity keeps one going on through many disappointments. Having gained that coveted number one position I felt that it wasn't all over, but that there was much more to be done. I had to improve and refine my game, until eventually I seemed to know what my opponent would have to do against certain of my shots, and in certain situations which I could create.

It is a feeling difficult to describe. One can "feel" the confines of the court, know exactly where the net tape is, and really never doubt one's accuracy. In this particular game accuracy is measured in fractions of inches. Intense concentration is necessary; one must be oblivious to anything other than the shuttle, with a curious certainty that it is going to fly exactly where you want it to. This sensation must apply to all games, but I have never reached the same heights in other racket sports.

Badminton is more than merely playing a game with a degree of skill, it opens new worlds to the expert player. In my day, it didn't mean wealth, when amateurism was very strict. Rather, for me, it meant two English Team visits to Canada, in 1925 and 1930 (the latter led to teaching in Winnipeg), followed by a trip around the world via New Zealand, Australia and Malaysia while teaching, lecturing and playing exhibition games. In 1957, and again in 1959, I captained a group of badminton players on a "playing tour" of European capitals, and in 1962 we went around the world when I saw the potential of

Good badminton doubles partners are as one. They almost breathe in unison as they concentrate on each shot, and they act as extensions of each other. (Gibbs)

Mixed doubles (next page) court coverage can take two forms. Athletes of equal strength tend to play "sides," while mismatched partners play "up and back," with the strong player in the backcourt. (Badminton)

Japanese women's badminton. A few years later they won the Uber Cup, symbol of world superiority in women's badminton. The cup has been held three times by the United States and, now, has been held four times by Japan.

Unfortunately, badminton suffers from being confused with the game of the same name which is played out-of-doors, with a much heavier racket, much heavier shuttles, and slightly different rules. Played indoors, it is a game requiring great stamina, a game with a wide variety of shots consisting of everything from very hard smashes to delicate net-shots. A good player is capable of using great deception. The rallies are long with each player trying to outplay and outwit the other. While few matches last for more than an hour, one needs to be in excellent physical condition to outlast a three game singles match. Also, a beginner cannot be very accurate, or deceptive, until he learns to use his wrist; thus the rallies are very long. Both juniors and adults enjoy the game, and profit from the exercise.

In my opinion, every player, in any sporting event, must suffer from nerves before the great contest. Being nervous before one plays keys one up and quickens one's perceptions. I know that I was very poor company before, and I suspect during, important tournaments, particularly the All-England Championships. I was always very nervous, impatient, silent, and had difficulty eating. It's natural, but has to be contained or one becomes a nervous wreck before the great event.

Today, badminton is a game played all over the world. There are more than 60 countries who are members of the International Badminton Federation. Unfortunately, it is not as big a game in the US as in many other countries, but one hopes that, in time, it will grow and we can, once more, compete successfully with other nations.

—J. Frank Devlin

J. Frank Devlin, a well-known international badminton champion, is the only player to have won National singles, doubles and mixed doubles championships for two consecutive years and three times in all. He is the author of **Sports Illustrated Badminton.**

For More Information

There is only one magazine devoted exclusively to badminton in the United States. *Badminton USA* is the official publication of the American Badminton Association. It is published five times per year at $3.50. It basically covers news but it does have a lot of photos and feature articles. The address is 333 Saratoga Road, Buffalo, New York 14226. The American Badminton Association's address is c/o Mrs. Virginia Lyon, 1330 Alexandria Drive, San Diego, Calif. 92107. There are 14 regional associations and a total of over 200 clubs.

Quality equipment can be purchased at most good sporting goods stores but if you can't find what you need write: International Sports, Box 883, Hawthorne, Calif. 90250 or Sport Craft, Bergenfield, New Jersey 07621.

We can do better for the book section. Here are some of the best books covering badminton. All are available from World Publications, Box 366, Mountain View, Calif. 94040 at the price listed* plus 25 cents each for postage. Write for a complete list.

Winning Badminton, Kenneth Davidson et al. Whether you play badminton as a pastime or for competitive honors, this book will help you improve your skill and scope of knowledge. 1975 Hb., 150 pp., ill., $8.65, (Ronald Press).

Sports Illustrated Badminton, J. Franklin Devlin et al. A handbook that shows the basics of badminton in clear simple language and illustrations. Rules and laws, grips, serves, clears, the smash, and tactics. 1973 Hb. & Ppb., 96 pp., ill., $4.95/$1.95, (Lippincott).

Badminton, Margaret Bloss. Offers an organized description for both the beginning and advanced player on not only how to execute fundamental techniques, but when and why they should be applied. Also covers techniques, and outlines practice drills. 1971 Ppb., 64 pp., ill., $2.50, (W.C. Brown).

Badminton, Poole. Presents the history, terms, equipment, fundamental to advanced skills, and strategy of this popular game. Includes many line drawings and photos that clearly illustrate all foot, hand, and body positions essential to mastering badminton. 1973 Ppb., 115 pp., ill., $3.95, (Goodyear).

Ballet

Ballet is a theatrical dance presentation involving patterns of ordered movement (choreography) performed by dancers who have been trained in a system of excise, gesture, and vocabulary of steps known as classical ballet technique.

Today's ballet performances and movement tradition have evolved over the last 400 years in a manner closely associated with the development of Western music—from 16th century dance-suites to modern tone-poems, jazz and rock.

The origins of the elegant carriage and imperial gestures of a classical ballet dancer are found in the *balleti,* elaborately figured social dances devised by dancing masters, and performed by the nobility in the Renaissance courts of Italy and France. Lavish entertainments combining dancing, music, poetry, costumes, and scenery reflected the wealth of European aristocracy whose politics, economics, and fashion influenced the evolution of ballet, even into the 20th century.

The first dancing academy for training professional dancers was established by Louis XIV, thus making French the language for ballet terminology. The five positions of the feet, long used in modified form in social dance, became the foundation of all ballet steps.

Performances moved from ballroom floors, where spectators surrounded the dancers, to raised stages with the audience seated only in front. Varieties of turns, and steps of elevation embellished with beats, took the place of the sedate movements of the ballroom. By increasing the turnout of the legs at the hip-joint, the dancers found an easier method of movement, a better base of support, and a clearer design for poses.

Male dancers excelled in this new virtuosity and dominated the ballet stages of the 18th century. But early in the next century, ballerinas rising to the tips of their toes floated to stardom in a wave of Romanticism which swept European theatres, book stores, and art galleries.

What looked effortless was, in fact, the product of more than a century of development of strenuous exercises. These were based on a knowledge of anatomy and physiology, the artists' intuition, and keen observation of the basic ballet instrument—the human body.

For the last 150 years ballet classes have begun with a series of exercises done at a *barre* or hand support. With legs turned outward, dancers bend and straighten their knees, brush their feet along the floor, and lift their legs in high extensions—all carefully timed with music. These movements gradually became larger and more vigorous, the combinations more complex. After 30 to 45 minutes, the dancer may perform a series of stretches, with one leg at a time on the barre, before coming to the center of the room, where the class continues for a similar length of time.

Next are graceful movements of the arms (*port de bras)* and combinations of slow, controlled extensions and balances (*adage*). Many barre exercises are repeated, but without the hand support. Small jumps, intricate patterns of footwork, and turns (*pirouettes)* follow. Finally large jumps (*grand allegro*) bring the class to an exhilarating finish. A courtesy from long ago, the bow, or *reverence,* concludes the class.

Such training, with infinite variety of movement combinations, must take place daily for approximately 10 years before the dancer is prepared to appear on the professional stage.

—Sandra Hammond

Sandra Hammond is a ballet instructor at the University of Tucson, a performer in ballet and modern dance, and author of **Ballet Basics.** *She is also dance editor of* **Gymnastics World** *magazine.*

Ballet Today

A subtle change has occurred in the ballet classroom during the past decade. Before, two categories of student existed: a large number of grade-school-age girls whose mothers wanted them to learn to be graceful, and a small contingent of slightly older (slightly weird according to casual observers) people who professed the desire to be ballet dancers.

The former group—usually white, upper-middle class—would soon tire of the rigors of *plies* and *battements* and would turn their interests to the piano or horseback riding.

Those pursuing a ballet career often suffered social and/or financial ostracism (especially if they were male) from friends and family, in addition to fierce competition with their peers along the ballet barre. Performing jobs were usually scarce and low-paying. Dedication to a dance career generally meant doing without a college education, and often without a "normal life" (marriage, home, family).

Today, the base for ballet has broadened. Learning the rigors of barre work, along with the promise of graceful movement, remains unchanged, however ballet is no longer exclusively for children or aspiring performers. Classes have been added for adult beginners who are flocking in impressive numbers to study ballet in private studios, colleges or universities, and community or art centers.

Greater tolerance for "doing your own thing," plus popular emphasis on exercise and body conditioning, have brought adults to the ballet classroom. There, they find an age-old discipline of movement, allowing no half-way approach, taught by a devoted person who does not hesitate to say, "this is right, that is wrong." Students learn that perfection is seldom achieved, but improvement is always possible.

Changes have also occurred on the ballet stage. An art form, long practiced only by whites, now boasts of such occurrences as The Dance Theatre of Harlem. This all-black, internationally-known professional ballet company is located in an uptown ghetto of New York City, where there thrives an enormous ballet school.

Once theatrical spectacles rarely seen live outside large East or West Coast urban areas, ballets are now produced by resident companies in numerous cities, and by semi-professional or civic companies in many smaller communities.

College curricula have added ballet courses and dance major programs. Graduates are not likely to enter the dozen or so prestigious United States companies (who continue to prefer younger products from the professional ballet schools), but other dance, or dance-related, paths are open to them.

Teaching is a realistic field for many dancers. This is often

"For all who participate in ballet there is the aesthetic satisfaction of a body brought into harmony with itself, of movement, music, and mime fused with painting and sculpture." (Folkedal)

coupled with opportunities to perform and/or choreograph for local companies. A stable, "respectable" profession (for men and women) thus combines with an artistic one. Dance writers, stage designers, costumers, lighting technicians, photographers, notators, therapists, arts administrators—all are professionals whose interest in dance-related activities may have begun in a ballet class.

Genuine respect is slowly replacing skepticism toward male dancers. The media has finally recognized what dancers always knew: ballet training conditions the body as well as most, and better than many, sports. Popular ballet heroes, such as Edward Villella, Rudolf Nureyev, and Mikhail Baryshnikov, command thousands of dollars per performance. Choreography continues to be a profession dominated by men, many of whom work in jet-age style, flying from one international assignment to another.

For all who participate in ballet—in the classroom, backstage, or onstage—there is the aesthetic satisfaction of a body brought into harmony with itself, of movement, music, and mime, fused with painting and sculpture. For the audience, the result may be a valuable insight into their own experiences, a delightful escape via a fanciful story or character, or simply the pleasure of seeing the human body in artistic motion.

Ballet links athletics with aesthetics, and it links the arts with one another. At long last, ballet is reaching a broad section of the public in its classrooms and its theatres. It has been said about music that "tradition is change." Ballet is also enjoying this old truth.

— **Sandra Hammond**

For More Information

There are several good magazines covering dance and ballet is emphasized in most of them. Here are some of the better ones.

Dancemagazine, 10 Columbus Circle, New York, N.Y. 10019. Published monthly at $15.00 per year. This is the world's largest dance publication. Very well done and must reading for anyone who is interested in ballet.

Dance Perspectives, 29 East 9th St., New York, N.Y. 10003. Published quarterly at $10.00 per year. For the serious dancer.

Dance News, 119 W. 57th St., New York, N.Y. 10019. Published monthly. Have not seen this publication but has been published since 1942.

Here are some organizations that should be of help to you: American Dance Guild, 245 West 52nd St., New York, N.Y. 10019; National Dance Association, 1201 16th St., N.W., Washington, D.C. 20036; Association of American Dance Companies, 245 West 52nd St., New York, N.Y. 10019; Dance Masters of America, Inc., 3613 St. Barnabas Rd., Silver Hill, Md. 20023. Many of these groups publish regular newsletters. Also, check your local phone book for dance studios.

A local dance studio should be able to tell you where to get equipment but here are a few companies of interest.

Kling's Theatrical Shoe Co., 218 S. Wabash Ave., Chicago, Ill., 60604. Has a free catalog of shoes, dancewear and accessories.

Taffy's, 701 Beta Drive, Cleveland, Ohio 44143. Produces top quality dance wear. Write for information.

The Ballet Shop, 1887 Broadway, New York, N.Y. 10023. Books, photos, and other interesting art.

F. Randolph Associates, 2300 Delancey Place, Philadelphia, Pa. 19103. This company produces a three times-a-year newsletter devoted to new products, services and personalities in the dance world. And it is free.

International School, Carnegie Hall, New York, N.Y. One of the many well respected schools. They have children's classes.

Books? Here are a few we feel are good. All are available from World Publications, Box 366, Mountain View, Calif. 94040 at the price listed* plus 25 cents each postage.

Nureyev: Aspects of the Dancer, John Percival. The first full biography of Rudolf Nureyev, international celebrity, master choreographer, and the most electrifying dancer since Nijinsky. From his birth to his headline-making "leap to freedom" when the Russian Ballet was touring Paris, here is a candid look at the total man. 1975 Hb., ill., $8.95, (Putnums).

Ballet Basics, Sandra N. Hammond. Ballet at its best, illustrated by Robert Carr. Of great value to any performer. Covers ballet in a relaxed, informative style that will make learning easy. 1974 Hb. & Ppb., 130 pp., ill., $6.95/$3.95, (Mayfield).

The Bolshoi Ballet, photographs by Judy Cameron, introduction & notes by Walter Terry. This stunning collection of nearly 250 photos captures the brilliance and achievement that are uniquely the Bolshoi. Taken during performances and rehearsals, the pictures cover seven ballets, including Giselle, Swan Lake, and Sleeping Beauty. The second part covers 11 dancers in a beautiful visual celebration of an extraordinary ballet company. 1975 Hb. & Ppb., 176 (oversize) pp., ill., $15.00/ $6.95, (Harper & Row).

Ballet Guide, Walter Terry. The dean of dance critics presents a treasury of more than 500 ballets danced around the world. Each is listed alphabetically with choreographic, musical and scenery credit plus the titles of companies which produced them. 1975, 400 pp., ill., $10.00, (Dodd, Mead).

Ballooning

Unlike flying in an airplane, the flying of a hot air balloon is non-directional and this alone is a unique experience. The balloon moves horizontally with the wind and there are no abrupt changes in lateral or vertical altitude or movement. Newcomers to the sport usually attest to the smoothness of the flight and lack of unpleasant sensations caused by rapid change. The closest thing to hot air ballooning might be a flight in a lighter-than-air craft such as a blimp, however, these can be steered and make considerably more noise because of the engines aboard. The balloonist maintains flight and vertical control with use of the burners. Whenever the balloon's internal air temperature elevates to a certain level, the balloon will go up. The rate of ascent is about 1700 feet per minute which is considerably faster than the descent which runs about 800 feet per minute. Horizontal flight is caused by the prevailing wind velocity and direction, and the balloom will almost stand still or hover whenever there is no wind.

Balloonists prefer to fly under the best conditions possible for flying: early in the morning (sometimes at dawn) and when there is little wind to cope with at take-off and in flight. Air sickness is not experienced by the vast majority of flyers. Persons who are prone to air sickness may find ballooning a pleasant way to get into aviation without going through the upset stomachs and nausea. For those readers who are concerned with safety, the Federal Aviation Agency indicates that hot air ballooning is the safest form of aviation. Mishaps of major significance are a rarity.

Today, there are approximately 500 hot air balloon flyers licensed in the US, however, considerably more are enthusiastic about the sport and participate as spectators, or even take-off aides. California leads the nation with the most balloonists registered, about 100. Much interest is being generated in the sport, the balloonist population having doubled in this country each year for the past five years.

Readers who might be interested in going for a trial or a demonstration ride should be aware that there are numerous dealer-school combinations existing, that offer just that—orientation rides to familiarize the novice with ballooning. Costs vary; a deluxe, one hour sample flight for two with a champagne breakfast may cost as much as $100. The riders are often asked to help with the inflation and take-off procedure, which is fun to do.

Almost anybody can fly, and people from all walks of life do. With proper training they can learn to fly without too much difficulty. The Federal Aviation Agency (FAA), the licensing and controlling organization, stipulates that student flyers must be at least 14 years of age and that candidate private balloonists must be a minimum of 16 years of age.

In order to be a licensed balloonist, FAA approved instruction is necessary. The FAA Private License is attainable after 10 hours of formal instruction, successful completion of a test of proficiency, and a check-ride. The training span is usually completed in about a week's time, that is, if the winds are normal and the student progresses adequately throughout the course. The 10 hour private instruction has a tab of $850.

A commercial license, required for any money-making endeavor such as spectator rides or advertising promotion, can be issued after 35 hours of instruction, a test, and two check-rides—plus a standard $50 fee for the FAA. Hot air ballooning, however, is mostly just plain fun and commercial licenses are seldom issued.

There are basically two major designs of balloons available, the AX-6 and AX-7. The smaller AX-6 is the most popular of the models, holds 56,000 cubic feet of air, will fly two people, and is 60 feet high and 55 feet in diameter. The AX-7 is somewhat larger, being 70 feet tall and 60 feet in diameter, holding 70,000 cubic feet of air, and is capable of flying the larger passenger three people load because the AX-7 is obviously capable of more lift, and can carry 1,210 pounds of payload.

Launching a hot air balloon requires more than merely a pilot. Takeoff aids are necessary to help inflate and launch each multi-colored craft. Balloon launches are still novel enough to always draw SRO crowds. (Andrews)

By the way, the fuel used to heat the air is propane or LB gas. With one person aboard, 40 gallons of fuel will provide a four to six hour flight. Hot air balloons operate most efficiently in cold air and can reach altitudes of up to 30,000 feet.

If an interested person approached a hot air balloon dealer to inquire about purchasing one, he or she would be told that they could design their own color/pattern scheme. Sample pictures of various balloons would be offered to the prospective buyer as a guide, suggestions would be made, and then the client would be left to create his own color and style of the balloon.

The basic surface design of the balloon consists of 12 vertically seamed sections that are called gores. Each gore is comprised of 24 to 26 panels. Balloons can be made in a solid color, or in a varied color scheme.

Materials used for the two basic models of hot air balloons are very similar. The AX-6 is made of Rip Stop, which is a lightweight nylon, and the AX-7 is made of taffeta—a heavy nylon that has better structural characteristics, including strength. Both are well suited for the sport, so the choice is simply a matter of individual taste or preference. Average prices for balloons are comparable to average prices for medium priced cars. The AX-6 is about $5500 ready to fly; that is, the balloon, with basket, gas bottles, burners and related apparatus. The AX-7 costs about $6875.

There are great numbers of rallies conducted each year, usually involving socializing and friendly competition. The rally is very popular owing to the informality and the fun that can be enjoyed in the events. After all, hot air balloons cannot be "aimed" and the speed of all participating balloons is the same under the influence of the wind. Mainly, flyers get together purely to enjoy the sport, not to take part in hard competition. The two major ballooning meets are the National Championships at Indianola, Iowa, which attracts 200 balloonists each year, and the World Meet at Albuquerque, New Mexico, with 150 enthusiasts.

The amount of time spent in the air is a matter of personal preference. Some flyers will make a small number of flights each year, others will go up for periods totalling 200 or 300 hours per year.

One can observe hot air balloons at various festivals, carnivals, shows, fairs, and commemorative events. These usually attract large crowds, mainly because balloons are colorful and interesting. Many people have rarely, or never, seen a hot air balloon at close quarters. Advertisers also contract for hot air balloon displays, and often offer rides as an attention-getter.

As you may have begun to notice, hot air ballooning is great fun and can be enjoyed by anyone who has a genuine desire to participate in an exciting sport. Why not get high on a balloon?

—**Orville Andrews**

Orville Andrews is a freelance photographer with a strong interest in ballooning. He lives in Cupertino, Calif.

For More Information

Ballooning is really taking hold in the United States even if it is a very expensive sport. And there is a good publication covering the activity.

Ballooning is published four times per year at $5.00. Besides having many good articles it also has several pages of color photos. Write: *Ballooning,* Box 2592, Columbus, Ohio 43216.

There is only one major organization in the US covering gas and hot air ballooning. The aim of the Balloon Federation of America (Suite 610, 806 15th St. N.W. Washington, D.C. 20005) is to promote sport ballooning and airship flying in the US. It also wants to encourage development of better equipment, assist balloonists in dealings with the Federal Aviation Administration, local regulatory bodies and the general public.

Since you might have a hard time finding sources for equipment, we are listing several addresses that may be of help. All manufacturers listed as US certified.

Don Piccard Balloons, Inc., Box 1902, Newport Beach, Calif. 92663. They make balloons and their advertising says, "fly the best."

Semco Balloon, Rt. 3, Box 514, Aerodrome Way, Griffin, Georgia 30223. Have been in business for 13 years and hold to a promise they once made: "We will produce an outstanding performance balloon at a reasonable cost." One balloon they make costs less than $5000. Write for a free color brochure.

Controlled Airstreams, Inc., Box 1625, Gardena, Calif. 90249. Make inflators that may be worth checking out.

Balloon Loft, Box 12168, Atlanta, Ga. 30305. Make a very interesting gondola. It's roomy (44" x 44"), padded and trimmed in buckskin. Has four 43½ pound capacity fuel tanks, a 7.5 million BTU burner, etc.

Balloons and Things, Inc., 564 W. Washington Blvd., Chicago, Ill. 60606. Has a free catalog listing the many things they have—wall plaques, books, patches, decals, helmet bags, etc.

Raven Industries, Inc., Box 1007, Sioux Falls, S.D. 57101. Their ads say "Raven engineers have pioneered and developed nearly all components now used by hot air balloon manufacturers." Certainly a well respected company. Write them for dealer nearest you.

Cameron Balloons, 3600 Elizabeth Road, Ann Arbor, Mich. 48103. US agent for Cameron Balloons, the balloon that is being used in over 25 countries.

The Balloon Works, Phyne aerodrome RFD 2, Sattesville, N.C., 28677. Ask about the Barnes Fire Fly and the Barnes Dragon Fly.

There have been several books on ballooning over the years but most are now out of print. But here are three that will be of interest. The first two are totally on ballooning and the third one does have a well done chapter on the subject. All are available from World Publications, Box 366, Mountain View, Calif. 94040 for the price listed* plus 25 cents each postage.

Bags Up! Great Ballooning Adventures, Stehling. Daredevils, spies, and scientists are among the hundreds of balloonists whose feats are re-created in this profusely illustrated treasury of balloon lore. 1975, $10.00, (Playboy).

The Complete Book of Ballooning, Will Hayes, ed. The most comprehensive book on hot air ballooning available to pilots and others interested in ballooning. It answers all the most frequently aksed questions about: the theory and practice of ballooning, fuel and burner systems, and the FAA written exam. Feb. 1976 Hb., ill., $6.95, (World Publications).

The Complete Book of Sky Sports, Linn Emrich. Offers a comprehensive look at ballooning for the newcomer. Covers aerodynamics, balloon construction, preflight preparation, landing, navigation, instrumentation, retrieves, organizations, manufacturers and schools. Also contains equally good chapters on parachuting, soaring, gyrocopter, and flying. 1970 Ppb., 208 (oversize) pp., ill., $2.95, (MacMillan).

Ballroom Dancing

Ballroom dance is a highly stylized form of dance that can be called the "ethnic dance" of America and Western Europe. Also called social dance or salon dance, ballroom includes all the couple (two-person) dances that have become popular since the 19th century, particularly in the last few decades. The current rock'n'roll dances are even included in this broad category.

Ballroom dancing is found just about anywhere people relax and socialize: nightclubs, dancing clubs, churches, school gymnasiums, community centers, and private homes. A wide variety of people dance, especially since the "nostalgia craze" has taken a firm hold of the general public. Many young people now learn the dances their grandparents or parents enjoyed; older people return to the steps they knew years ago. What a bridge ballroom dance is between generations!

This form of dance embraces many different ryhthms, kinds of music, and styles of steps, while it provides light recreational activity. The beginner will find variety he never knew existed in the world of dance. Dances like the cha-cha or jitterbug exercise the sense of rhythm, while a waltz requires a straight but relaxed posture. Some of the more contempory dances demand endurance and a good tango helps develop flexibility. All dances enlist an alert mind, quick reflexes, and often a few unwilling muscles!

Since ballroom dance is a highly social activity, one of its major benefits is the bringing together of many different types of people of all ages and life-styles. People share ideas and techniques and make up new steps. Ballroom dance fosters poise and self-confidence, creativity and cooperation. Younger people channel their energies and older people develop new energies as all work together in this most enjoyable physical activity.

"World-wide interest has resulted from the recognition of International Ballroom dancing as a truly great indoor sport and recreation. A movement has even started to get it approved for competition in the Olympic Games." (Photo courtesy of Woodruff Studios, Redwood City, Calif.)

International Ballroom Dancing

Is International Ballroom Dancing all that different from International Folk Dancing? Quite different, in fact it is not the same as American social dancing, either. What is now known as "International" in the United States or "Imperial" in some other countries actually started in England.

Early this century the people there were enjoying their so-called folk dances, such as St. Bernard's Waltz, Eve Three Step, Cumberland Square, and Canadian Barn Dance. Gradually the English dancing public in the cities, especially London, made the change from sequence and set dances to couple dances during the years of the First World War. This was followed by the jazz craze of the 20s and the swinging years of the 30s.

For a number of years fad dances came and went until some English dance teachers decided to standardize a few basic steps and to clarify good technique. Great progress has been made during the last 50 years until today the English style, or International Ballroom Dancing, is regarded as classic throughout the world. For competition purposes it is divided into two categories: Latin, including cha-cha-cha, rhumba, samba, and paso doble; and Modern, including waltz, quickstep, foxtrot, and tango. (Swing and Viennese waltz are sometimes included in competition).

Those wanting to learn this kind of dancing soon find that it is more difficult than ordinary social ballroom or most folk dancing, and that it would take years of study and practice to perfect their form. However, novices can learn the basic steps of most of the different dances in either class or private lessons and soon can enjoy the challenge of participation. Couples practice in large ballrooms of dance studios or private clubs.

World-wide interest has resulted from the recognition of International Ballroom Dancing as a truly great indoor sport and recreation. A movement has started to get it approved for competition in the Olympic Games. As a competitive sport it has already aroused great interest in many countries. Those in the British Commonwealth were originally the most enthusiastic in building dance champions, i.e., Scotland, England, Ireland, South Africa, Australia, New Zealand, and Canada.

In Europe most of the western countries are now involved, such as Germany, Austria, Holland, Denmark, Norway, and Sweden. Interest in ballroom dancing is also increasing in the eastern countries of USSR, Hungary, Czechoslovakia, and Yugoslavia. Participation is high in countries as far away from England as Japan, Ceylon, Indonesia, and Iceland.

Truly international in scope are the world championships which are scheduled every other year in London, while competition is held on alternate years in such leading cities as Berlin, Zurich, Sydney, Tokyo, and New York. The 1975 US Ballroom championships were held on Labor Day weekend at the Waldorf-Astoria Hotel in New York. At the peak of the pryamid of world dance competition is the Blackpool Dance Festival, which includes the World Congress, held every year in May in Blackpool, England, and attended by thousands of participants and observers. This year the festival will celebrate a half century of competition on the highest level of ballroom dancing perfection.

Americans are the most enthusiastic ballroom dancers of all outside of England itself. More than 25 competitions are held each year in the United States in Arizona, California, Florida, Illinois, Michigan, New York, Texas, Utah, Virginia, and Washington, D.C. California heads the list with the most active dancers and the most ballroom studios and private dancing clubs. In northern California the two leading ballroom studios are the Hinton-Pick and Renaissance Ballrooms, and members of the Peninsula International Dance Club have been practicing weekly in Redwood City for 10 years. In southern California there are several ballroom schools, including Cully's, Lexton, Margaret Michaels, Morgan, Sloan, and Webber-Sire, and Westmor.

A large California dance club is called the National Smooth Dancers with 600 members divided into 11 chapters. This popular club originated in Los Angeles about 35 years ago and practiced the "slicker" or smooth style. About 12 years ago they gradually began to learn the International style until most new members have converted.

People like to dance and fortunately they don't have to choose between International Folk Dancing and International Ballroom Dancing. Those with the time and energy can enjoy both!

—**Elizabeth Stevens**

Elizabeth Stevens is a longstanding ballroom and folk dance enthusiast. She works as a journalist and lives in Palo Alto, Calif. This article first appeared in Let's Dance *magazine.*

For More Information

Here are a couple of addresses that should get you started. For more contacts turn to ballet. *Let's Dance,* 1905 Market St., San Francisco, Calif. 94013 is a bi-monthly publication of the Folk Dance Federation of California. Cost is $4.00 per year. The Imperial Society of Teachers of Dancing (Ballroom Branch, Box 90, Vernon, N.H. 07462) also publishes a journal that should be of interest.

Other sources of information: Ballroom Publications, 442 W. 45 St., N.Y., N.Y. 10036 has a free catalog listing books, routines, syllabi and notes. MS Method, Box 636, Manhattan Beach, Calif. 90266 also has a free catalog.

Here is a book that should be of help to you. It is available from World Publications, Box 366, Mountain View, Calif. 94040 at the price listed* plus 25 cents postage.

Ballroom Dancing by Alex Moore. The eighth edition of this popular book. It is considered by many as the basic text for International Style Dancing. Contains over 100 diagrams and photos illustrating the Quick Step, Waltz, Fox Trot, etc. 1974 Hb., 324 pp., ill, $15.95, (Soccer Associates).

Barrel Jumping

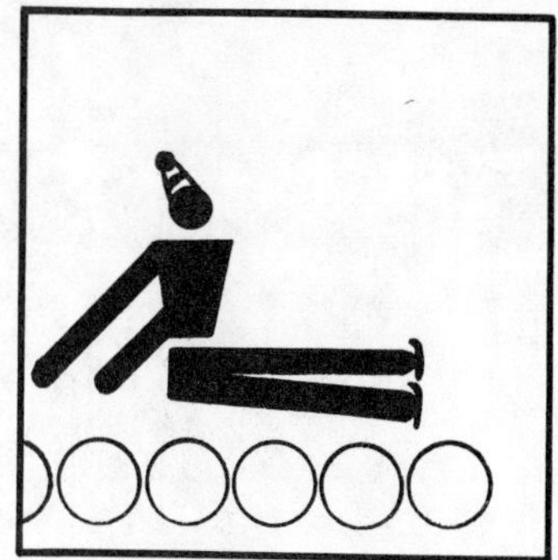

Jumping on skates can be traced back nearly to the origin of ice skating. It probably began a few centuries ago in Holland where skates were a mode of transportation over frozen lakes and canals. Natural obstacles had to be crossed along the way, often by jumping them.

As skills and equipment developed, skating became more popular as a recreational pursuit, and sports such as hockey, speedskating and figure skating evolved. Barrel jumping as we know it today was organized by Irving Jaffee, a former Olympic speedskating champion. The size of the barrel was standardized at 16 inches in diameter, and the initial World's Championship was held at Grossinger, New York in 1951. Terry Browne from Detroit won the event for the first four years, followed by Lake Placid's Leo Le Bel who dominated until 1961. Leo's brother Kenneth established a world record while winning his third title in 1965 with a leap over 17 barrels of 28'8". This record still stands.

Americans ruled the sport until Jacques Favero from Montreal won in 1966. Americans such as Browne, the Le Bels and Richard Widmark of Northbrook, Ill., the 1968 and 1971 winner, were originally speedskaters. Canadian competitors have been primarily hockey oriented.

The present champion is Jim Pappeck, also from Northbrook, who won his second title at Portland, Ore. The world championships for barrel jumping are televised each year by ABC's "Wide World of Sports".

The Greatest Moment

Barrel jumping has always been regarded more as a daredevil stunt than a sport. It is often compared to flying over a row of cars on a motorcycle, but like all other sports on an international level, barrel jumping requires a superb degree of physical conditioning to go with the daring of a cycle jumper. While barrel jumping doesn't have the high death or injury risk factor of cycle jumping, barrel jumpers can be assured of acquiring a number of bumps and bruises during the course of each competition. Talk about the thrill of victory and the agony of defeat!

As a sport, barrel jumping is akin to the long jump in track and field. It has the added handicaps, however, of a slippery ice surface for a runway and a long-bladed pair of speed skates for track shoes. And unlike a comfortable landing in a sand pit, the ice is just as hard as it is slick.

The technique for an approach and take-off closely resembles that of a ski jumper. Speed is built as quickly as possible around the rink, and the body is coiled like a steel spring to build up leg thrust for the take-off.

Despite the profusion of bruises in barrel jumping competitions, protective equipment is kept to a minimum. This keeps a jumper's weight down and results in a longer leap. A helmet and spinal guard, however, are mandatory.

"While barrel jumping doesn't have the high death or injury risk factor of motorcycle jumping, barrel jumpers can be assured of acquiring a number of bumps and bruises during the course of each competition."

At 16 inches in diameter, the barrels are not very large, but a row of them can appear awesome, particularly on a third attempt at a given number. Competitive barrel jumping begins at a "mere" 12 barrels, but this is usually enough to considerably narrow the field. Each competitor is allowed three unsuccessful attempts at any one number of barrels before he is eliminated, and an additional keg is rolled into place after each round.

As contestants are eliminated, remaining men notice that their turn comes up more often, the jumps get longer, the ice seems to hit harder, and the falls begin to take their toll. Attitude becomes an important factor. Champions combine good skating ability with a desire to win and a reckless abandon on each jump, knowing that a painful wipeout is in store at the end of each jump.

When the field finally narrows to two competitors, psychological toughness becomes as important as physical ability. In the 1965 World Championships, for example, Kenneth Le Bel and Jacques Favero were locked in a classic duel after both successfully negotiated 16 barrels. Favero lead at that point, as he had taken less attempts to clear 16. Each contestant failed twice at 17 barrels, and Favero also missed his third attempt. As defending champion, Le Bel had the honor of last attempt, but to retain his title he would be forced to jump a distance never before negotiated. Adding to the tension was the presence of ABC sports television crews. It was late in the day and Le Bel was tired and sore, but like a true champion he vaulted over the 17 barrels, a new world record distance of 28'8".

Le Bel's feat has still not been equalled, and on the basis of its longevity, the jump should be ranked among the greatest single efforts in sport.

—**Richard Widmark**

Richard Widmark is a two-time World Barrel Jumping Champion and an outstanding speed skater.

For More Information

Write National Winter Sports for additional information: National Winter Sports, Inc., 360 East 72nd Street, New York, N.Y. 10021.

Baseball

It is hard to imagine the American tradition of sport not including the game of baseball. Even back in the old colonial days of New York and Boston our forebears were infatuated with the process of hitting a ball with a piece of wood and running for a predetermined goal. Aristocrats spent hours playing and watching games of cricket and rounders – the ancestors of modern baseball. One player would toss the ball slowly to the striker to be sure he would hit it. More than likely he would – a dozen yards to so – and run for a stump or stake before a scout could retrieve the ball, and throw it, attempting to hit him.

Today, pitchers dressed in double-knit, form-fitting uniforms throw a ball at speeds approaching 100 miles an hour towards a batter who might hit it if he's lucky. Aluminum bats have largely taken the place of old wooden versions, and balls are sometimes hit as far as 500 feet. Where the earlier games were restricted to the well-to-do classes, today's baseball has more organized leagues on all levels than any other sport played in this country. Whether baseball is America's national pastime is debatable, but one thing is for sure: Americans love it as their own!

Baseball is played on a field consisting of an infield and an outfield. The infield is made up of four bases, base paths, a pitcher's mound, and two batters boxes – one for right, and one for left-handed batters. The infield and outfield can be composed of either natural or synthetic grass. The farthest limit of the outfield is often fixed by a fence.

There are nine players to a team, the object of the game being to score runs by the batsman hitting the ball into the field of play, circling three bases, and returning to the home base. The batsman-runner scores a run for his team if he succeeds in circling the bases before a member of the opposite team can retrieve the ball and throw it to the base toward which the runner is moving, or can touch the runner with the ball. Each team alternates in taking turns at bat and is allowed three outs. An out is recorded when a batter fails to hit the ball into fair play after three misses with the bat, has his hit ball caught by an opposing player before it hits the ground, or fails to reach a base. The entire game is comprised of the nine innings, an inning consisting of both teams having their turn at bat. In the case of a tie score after the allotted nine innings are completed, successive innings are played until the tie is broken.

While in the field, each player occupies a particular position, the positions being pitcher, catcher, first baseman, second baseman, third baseman, shortstop, left fielder, center fielder, and right fielder.

Baseball has enjoyed considerable resurgence as a spectator sport recently. The one billionth fan to see major league baseball will pass through the turnstiles during America's Bicentennial Year. (Duffy)

From The Top

As the United States approaches its Bicentennial, it is only natural to recall the many events that have contributed to our country's great history.

Sport has played a significant role in the growth of the United States, providing Americans with countless hours of enjoyment. None has provided as many lasting memories as baseball.

As major league baseball joins the country's celebration in 1976 with observances of the National League's Centennial and the American League's 75th anniversary, many nostalgic moments are brought to mind. Such events as Bobby Thomson's pennant-winning home run in the 1951 National League playoffs, Don Larsen's perfect game in the 1956 World Series, and Hank Aaron's record-shattering 715th home run are indelible memories to millions of Americans.

In addition to the great events, the game's illustrious heroes such as Hank Aaron, Ty Cobb, Babe Ruth, Sandy Koufax, Willie Mays, Ted Williams, Tom Seaver, and Johnny Bench have been inspirations to generation after generation of baseball enthusiasts.

Yes, baseball has had a great impact on our country. This is further evidenced by the fact that the one-billionth fan to see major league baseball, in this century alone, will pass through the turnstiles during 1976. Add these fans to the many more who have come in contact with the game through the media or at the minor league level and the impact of baseball is clearly evident.

Since the game of baseball started long before the first major league game was played, it is apparent that the game is one that enjoys prosperity at all levels.

While the major leagues have been enjoying year after year of banner attendance, the latest findings show such youth organizations as Little League, Boys Baseball, Babe Ruth, the American Legion and the American Amateur Baseball Congress reporting impressive increases in number of teams and participants.

The rapid increase in the high schools made baseball one of the fastest growing sports in the National Federation of State High School Associations program. Add to all of this an estimated 450,000 young men involved annually in junior college and college baseball.

Not only do youth programs make a great contribution in the physical education of youngsters, but they serve as a training ground for the Aarons and Seavers of tomorrow. A recent survey, for example, showed that nearly 60 percent of all major league ballplayers had played American Legion.

Baseball serves many purposes. It is an exciting spectator sport which has captured the imagination of untold millions of people all over the world. It is a fun-filled athletic activity which can teach sportsmanship as well as skill to the young and old alike. And, as baseball spreads throughout such countries as Japan, Australia, Holland and Italy, it serves as a game of goodwill between the nations of the world.

It is appropriate that as America and baseball both celebrate significant anniversaries in 1976, today, more than ever before, the game truly serves as our "National Pastime".

—Bowie Kuhn

Bowie Kuhn, formerly a New York attorney, has served as the Commissioner of Baseball since 1969. During his years in office, major league baseball has adopted major changes including the arbitration rule, league expansion, the popular acceptance of synthetic turf, and the designated hitter rule.

For More Information

Baseball gets good coverage in newspapers and mass market magazines and we probably don't have to tell you where to go but we do want to list a couple.

The Sporting News, 1212 North Lindbergh Blvd., St. Louis, Mo. 63166. Newspaper format, published weekly at $17.50 per year. Heavy coverage of baseball during the season.

Bullpen, 1770 Brunswick Ave., Trenton, N.J. 08638. Newspaper format, published four times per year. The official publication of Babe Ruth Baseball.

Baseball Bulletin, 286 Penobscot Bldg., Detroit, Mich. 48226. Published monthly at $6.00 per year. News, views, interviews and features. Many good photos.

For organizations: On the professional side there are two major organizations – the American League, 280 Park Ave., New York, N.Y. 10017 and the National League, 220 Montgomery St., San Francisco, Calif. 94104. Both have twelve clubs each. The commissioner over these leagues can be reached at: Baseball, Office of the Commissioner, 15 West 51st St., Rockefeller Center, New York, N.Y. 10019. On the amateur side there is the American Amateur Baseball Congress, 212 Plaza Bldg., 2855 West Market St., Akron, Ohio 44130: Babe Ruth Baseball, Box 5000, 1700 Brunswick Ave., Trenton, N.J. 18638: Little League Baseball, Williamsport, Penna. 17701; National Amateur Baseball Federation, Rt. 1 Box 280B, Rose City, Michigan, 48654.

As far as equipment is concerned, most good sport shops can help you out totally, but if you do need something special you might check with Wilson Sporting Goods, 2233 West St., River Grove, Ill., 60171 or Spalding, Meadow Street, Chicopee, Mass. 01014. A representative from one of these big companies should be able to help.

There are thousands of books on baseball and here are a few we like. All are available from World Publications, Box 366, Mountain View, Calif. 94040 at the price listed* plus 25 cents each postage.

The Baseball Handbook: Strategies and Techniques for Winning, Walter Alston and Don Weiskopf. The famous manager of the LA Dodgers has condensed his classic larger version and now presents photographs and his interviews with baseball's greats. 1974 Ppb., 504 pp., ill., $14.95, (Allyn & Bacon).

Championship Baseball, Hank Bauer. A former pro player and coach talks about what it takes to master the many basic points of baseball. 1968 Hb., ill., $6.95, (Doubleday).

Baseball Play and Strategy, Ethan Allen. Covers All areas of individual and team offensive and defensive play. More than 500 illustrations supplement the instructions for each playing position on the field, plus sections on team organization. 1969 Hb., 445 pp., ill., $9.95, (Ronald).

Pitching: The Basic Fundamentals and Mechanics of Successful Pitching, Bob Shaw. A great book for all baseball pitchers at all levels of competition, by the pitching coach for the Los Angeles Dodgers. All the skills and mechanics needed to improve a thrower's ERA. 1972 Hb., 224 pp., ill., $10.00, (Viking).

A Century of Baseball Lore, John Thorn. A book of facts, anecdotes, satire and humor from over 100 years of baseball lore, illustrated by Jesse Jacobs. 1974 Hb., 239 pp., ill., (Hart).

Pitching to Win, Raymond L. Hicks. An explosive fast ball these days is not enough. **Pitching to Win** details the proper techniques, training and attitude for the aspiring young pitcher. Contains tips on grips, finger pressure, delivery motions, pitches, and other tricks. 1973 Hb., 106 pp., ill., $5.95 (Barnes).

Charlie O. and the Angry A's, Bill Libby. A no-holds-barred, highly entertaining account of the Oakland A's rise to fame, and Charles O. Finley, one of the most controversial figures in baseball today. 1975 Hb., 324 pp., ill., $7.95, (Doubleday).

Batting, Carl Yastrzemski & Al Hirschberg. The Boston Red Sox star covers the fine points of hitting a baseball for all players from Little League to the majors. 1972 Hb., 118 pp., ill., $4.95, (Viking).

Inside Hitting, Reggie Jackson and Joel Cohen. The story of equipment, attitude, training, teamwork and technique, by one of baseball's greatest hitters. 1975 Hb. and Ppb., 96 (oversize) pp., ill., $7.95/$3.95, (Regnery).

The Science of Hitting, Ted Williams. In a lucid, open style, one of the greatest hitters of the last three decades explains the scientific considerations of hitting: percentages, .400+ strike zones, the bat's degree of upswing and downswing, and many other concepts. 1971 Hb., 95 (oversize) pp., ill., $7.95, (Simon & Schuster).

Baseball: The Golden Age, Harold Seymour. A historical work on the national pastime, covering the emergence of two major leagues and the World Series. Player trades, great rivalries, pennant races, and the great figures of the old days. 1971 Hb., 500 pp., ill., $12.50, (Oxford University Press).

The Official Encyclopedia of Baseball, Turkin and Thompson. Complete information through the 1973 season on all aspects of the game. Statistics, playing hints from the stars, the official rules of play, and more. 1974 (rev.) Hb., 737 pp., ill., $13.95, (Barnes).

Basketball

The United States can take full credit for the origination of basketball since it evolved entirely in this country. In 1891 Dr. James Naismith grabbed a peach basket, nailed it above a gymnasium floor and made a game of trying to throw a soccer ball into it. From this simple beginning sprouted the modern game of basketball–fast, easy to understand, never dull. Today, it is played in every region of the globe. Basketball is a game of speed. Players streak up and down the court as fast as sprinters, frequently making instant stops and starts. They often run as much as five miles during a game. Even though it requires fine coordination and stamina, this game is played by everyone, men, women, and children. And, needless to say, a person doesn't have to be unusually tall to take part. Quickness and jumping ability can often compensate for a lack of height. Only a few pro players have been under six feet tall. While primarily a team sport, basketball easily can be practiced by oneself in a backyard or driveway. It is not only a fine activity in itself, but it is one of the best ways for younger athletes to stay in shape for any other sport while having fun at the same time!

In a regulation game of basketball there are five players to a team who are attired in light shorts, sleeveless jersey and canvas shoes. As they speed up and down the hardwood, rectangular court they attempt to score a goal for their team by gaining possession of the ball and throwing it into the opponent's basket. Players may advance the ball toward the basket either by passing or dribbling it while the opposing team covers them closely, striving to prevent them from scoring. Each goal counts two points, and once a goal is scored the ball is turned over to the team scored upon which is given a chance to score.

You won't find players often coming into physical contact with each other during the course of actual play since basketball is meant to be a "non-contact" sport. Accidental or intentional pushing, shoving or tripping of an opposing player is usually called as a foul by the referee and the inflicted player is allowed one or two free shots at the goal, each of which count as one point if made.

Under the basket is generally the wild and wooly land of giants. Rebounding and tough defense tend to be a big factor in the success of champion teams. A tall and mobile center can plug the middle and bat away shots from smaller guards and forwards as they drive toward the hoop. Good body position after a shot will box out opposing players and make rebounding an easy task. (Duffy)

From the Ghetto to the Boston Celtics

When I was a kid growing up on Long Island, basketball was the whole schmere for many of my friends in the neighborhood. In this respect, I wasn't any different from them–I wanted to play basketball. It wasn't always that way, however. Actually I started playing the game quite late, since I wasn't really exposed to it until I was 13 years old, when I moved to Long Island. Prior to that, I was very busy stealing hub caps in one of the better ghettos of New York City. Once I found out about basketball, though, that was the whole ball of wax. I gave up just about every other sport, including altering cars, and concentrated on basketball.

I'm sure things have not changed drastically, today, in terms of aspiring ball players. Of course, not every kid can reach the pro ranks, or even college ball. Nevertheless, there are several points that a youngster might keep in mind as he goes along. One of them is the fallacy that you have to be tall in order to be successful in basketball. This is absolutely not so. Actually, basketball is similar to many other sports in the basic criterion for success: speed and quickness are essential, rather than height. As far as I know, these are the two main qualities that a scout looking for talent watches for. Of course, if you happen to be 7'4", like Jabbar, and also are fast and quick for your size, then you have an obvious advantage. Still, players like Nate Archibald and Calvin Murphy are successful against men a foot taller than them because of these two main factors. Similarly, in football, a 6'8", 280 pound lineman isn't worth much if he's not as fast and quick as a 6'1", 220 pound lineman. Today, there's a premium on strength and height, but the basic requirement for playing the game on any level is speed and quickness.

The second point I'd like to make is not original, although when I held this idea as a boy, I thought it might have been. I have always felt in respect to basketball and anything else, that it's important to set goals for yourself. The necessity for concentration and dedication toward accomplishing anything is obvious. My particular goal at 14 was to make the high school varsity team, which took me 2½ years to accomplish. Also, I have always set individual goals, in terms of striving to play better, and improve quicker, than my colleagues. Setting goals while working toward an objective is most important, since by doing this a player can get more out of his potential more quickly than if he just takes things as they come. If he sets his sights towards something specific, rather than merely playing the sport, he will be better off. I feel this added incentive is very important.

It is essential for young athletes, regardless of their sport, to build their goals around what I mentioned a moment ago as getting the most out of their potential. This potential isn't something you acquire; rather you thank God for it. You either have mediocre, poor, good, or great talent. I think it is important for youngsters to recognize and assess their potential, and then try to make the most of it.

Two players come to mind who capitalized on their potential excellently. One was Slater Martin, the guard of the old, successful Minneapolis teams—when Mikan, Pollard, and Mikkelsen were there. The other is Larry Costello, who used to play for Syracuse, and now coaches Milwaukee. Both of these players used to give me a very hard time because of their determination and ability to sustain their concentration. They also had the speed and quickness that we talked about earlier.

Specifically, the proper mechanics of a sport should be learned at an early age. Obviously, becoming proficient in a sport takes lots of time spent in pure practice. Kids hear this often from people who are interested in their progress, and sometimes it becomes redundant. For this reason, young athletes, especially the ones with a little better ability, perhaps don't absorb this advice. The point is that you don't wake up one morning and discover that you're an All-American. It is a must to complement proper mechanics, learned at a formative age, with lots of practice, so proper habits are developed early. Then all the work that is done later on—building on this solid foundation—will help to get the most out of one's potential. All I'm saying is that a young player must do the best he can by following this formula. If you've had a bad golf swing for 15 years, for instance, it is just about impossible to break this habit at an older age. Learn to execute properly, and follow this with loads of practice.

For a youngster, it is not difficult to find instruction in basic playing fundamentals. He can go down to the local gym, or almost anyplace where people have been exposed to basketball—and find help. Today, many clinics in all sports are accessible to kids; many of them are inexpensive, and offer excellent instruction. I'm not talking about sophisticated technique, just the very basics that can be added to practice and games. I cannot overemphasize the part that practice plays in reaching one's potential. If a kid is a straight A student, then being a B+ student just isn't good enough. Even if he has the inherent talent to be only a mediocre player, he will never reach that level if he doesn't practice seriously.

For young men and young women I think the benefits of basketball are great from the standpoint of participation—as a team sport—but more so to basketball since I feel it takes more teamwork to play this game successfully than any other. I know I might get many arguments concerning this point, but I think basketball is somewhat unique in the amount of teamwork necessary for a successful team. Growing up in the midst of this team cooperation teaches several lessons that a young man can apply to many of his future endeavors: sacrifice, unselfish play, leadership, and adherence to leadership. I'm not saying that you don't learn these lessons in other sports, only that they are all present in basketball. Obviously, this aspect of the game is very beneficial.

The best example of fine teamwork that I have seen is that which the Boston Celtics have been exemplifying for 17 years. This team has dominated basketball like no other club in any professional sport, and this is not by accident. Many teams have superstars they can rely upon, individuals who are the hub of the team. The Celtics, however, very seldom have a player in the top 10 of any of the statistical categories. This is because they place much emphasis on full participation; everyone works together as a team. Good players are, undeniably, an asset, but when it comes right down to it there are five men out there, playing in a restricted area, all of them interdependent. The Celtics, and I might add UCLA, are as good as any when it comes to taking advantage of team play. UCLA has had players like Jabbar, Walton, and Erickson, but they have only been a cog in the machinery.

While speaking of the team element in basketball, I should not leave out the role of coach. For the young player, the coach's contribution is very significant in terms of teaching the youngster correct fundamentals and teamwork. As you go up the ladder the coach plays less and less of a role. From little league, to high school, to college, the coach's contribution becomes more and more diluted, but nevertheless, his game to game decisions have a great impact on the outcome of the game. On the professional level, this role is even more diluted. The coach has less specific impact on the outcome, game by game, mainly because there are so many games to be played that it is hard to plan for each one individually. When you're playing over 100 games in a seven month span the same situations tend to repeat themselves over and over. The coach doesn't have to make the same preparation as he would if he were coaching 25 college games. Neither does he have the time. As a result, I feel that the coach has less impact, collectively and on individual players, as he goes up the ladder.

Still, a coach can have a significant effect on a higher level team as well. We were very pleased with the results at Boston College. They never had a very successful basketball program, and playing a role in elevating their team was very satisfying. Also, I think the success we had a few years ago in the United States-Russia basketball series was a kick, as a coach. I had always wanted to represent this country in the Olympic Games, and never had the opportunity. Even though this series wasn't the Olympics, Russia was the team that had beaten us a year before in Munich. After that defeat, I was very proud to coach them to a four out of six game win over the Russians.

Although basketball is a great game for building positive attitudes in young men, I wouldn't advise it for the middle-aged athlete looking to stay in shape. Unlike most team sports, basketball is a game that is difficult to stay with as you grow older, unless you do it on a regular basis. I'd caution against the occasional three-on-three, or full court games at the gym because basketball requires constant movement and running. As a person gets older he is most likely not in the proper shape, and his reflexes are not what they once were. Playing a game of basketball requires much effort and stamina, much more than a game of touch football, for instance. It is possible to play a friendly game of football, tennis or golf until you're 80 years old, but basketball is an exception. I don't recommend it to friends who have been away from the game for awhile. Even in the pros and college, injuries generally occur in pre-season when the players are not quite in shape and they try to do things they're not ready for.

Admittedly, for a person who loves basketball, it is hard to give the game up. Everything I've ever been involved in I owe to my participation in basketball, and my relationship with it since. As a kid staying up late to shoot hoops in the dark because it was fun, I could never have realized the opportunities that such a game would open. I thank God for giving me a specific ability in sports–I guess I'm what you might call a "natural athlete." Fortunately, He deposited me in the right place, at the right time. No youngster could hope for better than what I received. I was set in an area of New York which was a basketball hotbed. My ability enabled me to receive notoriety in high school and a four year scholarship education at Holy Cross. If it hadn't been for basketball I never would have been able to go to college at all. By my college education, and play on a fine team, I was able to go on to 13 successful seasons in the pros and to many opportunities that have since stemmed from this. Everything I'm involved in is due to practicing long and hard years ago in a school yard.

—**Bob Cousy**

When one thinks of basketball, Bob Cousy is a name that automatically comes to mind. After joining the famed Boston Celtics in 1951, he helped them win six NBA championships. Following his retirement as a player in 1963, he coached Boston College to an excellent five year record, and served as coach to the Kansas City-Omaha Kings. Bob Cousy is currently the American Soccer League Commissioner. He has authored several books, including **Basketball Concepts and Techniques, The Last Loud Roar,** *and* **Killer Instinct.**

For More Information

Basketball gets good coverage in newspapers and national magazines like *Sports Illustrated* and *Sport* magazines. Both are available on most newsstands. Here are a couple of others that may prove interesting.

Basketball Weekly, 19830 Mack Ave., Grosse Point Woods, Mich. 48236. Published weekly during the season at $6.00 for 18 issues. Newspaper format.

Sporting News, 1212 North Lindbergh Blvd., St. Louis, Mo. 63166. Published weekly at $17.50 per year. Newspaper format and covers all aspects of basketball during season.

Basketball Digest, Box 4564, Des Moines, Ia. 50306. Published six times per year from Nov. to April at $3.50. Personality articles, statistics, team rosters, schedules and more.

Basketball News, 150 East 58th St. 14th Fl., New York, New York 10022. Published monthly at $5.00 per year. Newspaper format covering pro, college, high school and the international scene Extensive statistics with team and personality articles.

Besides the NCAA, NAIA, AAU and National Association of High School Athletics (addresses in appendix) there are two professional league addresses that should be helpful. Write to their public relations departments. National Basketball Assn. (NBA), 2 Pennsylvania Plaza, New York, N.Y. 10001 and American Basketball Assn. (ABA), 1700 Broadway, 42nd Fl., New York, N.Y. 10019. For information on women's basketball write: Mildred Barnes, Women's Physical Education, Central Missouri State University, Warrensburg, Mo. 64093 or Cathy Rush, RD No. 1, Hillsdale Road., West Chester, Penn. 19380. Be sure to include a self-addressed, stamped envelope when writing for information.

Most sport shops have excellent basketball equipment and we aren't going to even list any sources. This is one sport in which good equipment is available readily.

Here are some books on basketball. All are available from World Publications, Box 366, Mountain View, Calif. 94040 at the price listed* plus 25 cents each postage.

Basketball Concepts and Techniques, Bob Cousy and Frank Power, Jr. Two coaches describe the basics and technicalities of basketball. Also included are their own theories about the margin of error. Included are illustrated discussions on offense, defense, and strategy. 1970 Hb., 509 pp., ill., $15.33, (Allyn & Bacon).

The Theory and Science of Basketball, John Cooper & Daryl Siedentop. Basketball coaches of all levels, students of basketball theory, and P.E. students will find a broadened horizon of knowledge from the scientific viewpoint. 1975 Ppb., 253 pp., ill., $8.75, (Lea & Febiger).

Women's Basketball, Stutts. At the turn of the century, only the "daring" women played basketball, and dire predictions were commonplace. This guide presents a vivid picture of those times, then presents the various skills and concepts needed to play and understand the game. Describes in detail offensive and defensive maneuvers. 1973 Ppb., 81 pp., ill., $3.95, (Goodyear).

Basketball: Techniques, Teaching, and Training, Brian Coleman. Officially approved by the English Basketball Association, this book describes in detail every facet of the game. For each subject the author has lucidly described techniques, teaching ideas and training practices. 1975 Hb., 192 pp., ill., $8.95, (Barnes).

How to Play and Teach Basketball, Franklin A. Lindeburg. A complete professional textbook on basketball fundamentals and coaching. Presents basketball in its broader aspects while still covering over 27 team offenses and defenses in clear diagrams and advice on how to choose the best plan. 1967 (rev.) Hb., 368 (oversize) pp., ill., $12.00, (Association).

Baton Twirling

Baton twirling is currently divided into participation for fun, show, or competition. Twirling for fun includes high school majorettes and younger girls who twirl only because they enjoy it. It offers them a chance to excel at something, to develop poise, and to get to know other kids socially.

Show twirling involves an audience and an exhibition routine. You have often seen this type of twirling at half time of a high school, college or professional football game. It is vital in show twirling to do the types of moves that generate wide audience appeal, and not to drop the baton. In show routines, you should never attempt a stunt that you can't do 90 percent of the time, because dropping is death to show twirling. No matter how good you are—even if you are a world champion—you'll always hear the crowd say, "She was good, but she dropped her baton."

In contrast, baton twirling in competition places emphasis on degree of difficulty instead of showy presentation, and it is not that disastrous to drop. Everyone drops occasionally, but to do so is just a half point penalty, the same as for marching out of step. In competition, a drop should be looked at for how many points it takes off your score sheet, and not for the overall effect it gives you as a performer.

In further contrasting show and competition twirling, show tends to repeat movements more. It becomes necessary to do things longer to draw an audience reaction. If you are going to do elbow rolls, for example, you must do many before the audience will clap. It is a proven fact that it usually takes about seven seconds to elicit this response. Audience response is vital to a show routine's success, so less difficult movements repeated often is the key.

It is a natural progression for a girl to move from recreational baton to competition to show. Of all the twirlers in the United States, the vast majority are in recreational twirling, and of the remainder, more are in competition than show. Show twirling lags behind because it requires a high level of proficiency and there are few outlets for this branch of twirling.

As a girl progresses in skill, a variety of different batons can be used, including fire batons, lighted batons, knives, flag batons, and the hoop. The fire and lighted batons used in show twirling are very easy to manage. Any good intermediate twirler can handle them with ease and very little danger. The same stunts can be used with fire as with an ordinary baton, but a little care must be taken not to burn oneself. Relatively easy stunts can be done with the fire baton, as the audience is usually more impressed with the baton being on fire than they would be with a difficult movement.

Knives are not as dangerous as they look, but you do have to be a better twirler to twirl them than a fire baton. Knives are well balanced, but a twirler still must be a high intermediate or advanced to handle them effectively.

The hoop is relatively easy. It limits the number of skills that can be done because of its structure, but once you are used to what you can do with it, the hoop becomes very enjoyable.

Juggling three batons has become popular recently. You can either juggle or twirl three batons at one time. This type of skill is relatively difficult to acquire, but is a real show stopper.

To me competition twirling covers the widest spectrum of skills. In competition you are twirling, juggling, dancing and doing gymnastics. Competitors have a twirling routine, strutting routine, two-baton routine, and three-baton routine. Additional events include solo dance twirl, duets, teams and corps.

A strutting routine demands the most body work. It includes a variety of kicks: fan kicks, illusions (taken from ice skating, this is a movement in which the head goes down and the foot over the top like a cartwheel, but with one foot always on the ground), butterflies, aerial walkovers, and aerial cartwheels. Lunges and ballet moves like *pique* and *arabesque* are common. Since competitors can usually do only part of the total spectrum of possible moves, it is best in competition to hide weak points while emphasizing strengths.

It is best to start twirlers at the age of seven. At this age, teaching must be handled to keep it fun and interesting. The progression of skills should be slow enough not to discourage beginning students. I was seven when I started baton. I took it from the lady across the street who wanted her daughter to twirl. A lot of years were spent working on basics, just getting the fundamentals down and having a good time. At first we did no performing, but later got into the show work by doing parades, lodges and clubs. Our teacher brought in a couple of her friends who taught us a little bit of tap dancing and a hula routine. We did many wild things and had a little variety show. It was really fun and I loved it.

By the time I was 13, I started going into contests. I had six years to build up a foundation of basic skills, and then went to two more advanced teachers to elaborate on that foundation. I competed for five or six years and loved every minute of it. I belonged to a corps that marched in parades during that time, because the high school I went to didn't have a band. I had a lot of good experiences and that's why I'm still around.

I traveled a lot while I was competing, but not until about the age of 15. I was not really a good advanced twirler until about that age. At 15 we took a tour of the Midwest, visiting a different city and competing in a different contest every day for two weeks! It was just great. One town in Wisconsin gave out six foot trophies! It was a tradition with them, and I really felt like part of it.

I was one of those kids who got the *Who's Who in Baton Twirling* and "knew" everyone. I went back East for a contest with my teacher, and I'd say, "Oh, there's Marilyn Champion," (very casually) and my teacher would ask, "How do you know?" Then I'd have to confess, "Well, she looks just like her picture!"

To understand what I have found in baton twirling, you must consider the physical and mental benefits of the activity. It builds coordination and dexterity, makes you stronger, and improves endurance. Twirlers who march learn to use both hands and both sides of the body. Mentally, baton twirling improves concentration and alertness, and has a beneficial effect on the memory. Twirling also improves social graces by enhancing poise in front of an audience. Kids learn to care for their

"Twirlers usually start at about the age of seven, but it must be handled right—fun so they like it and moderately so they don't move too fast." (Glouster)

personal appearance, they learn cleanliness and neatness.

Baton makes kids more creative, a quality that I always try to encourage. When I teach, I always tell them exactly what we are doing and why, so that they can understand and later build on that understanding. This way, the students can easily see progressions and become creative enough to come up with good ideas for routines.

Baton twirlers should always be encouraged to take classes in gymnastics and dance in conjunction with their baton training. Ballet is very much a part of modern competitive baton, because it teaches tremendous technique and body work. Gymnastics is important for body control and straight leg lines, both of which are vital to good twirling. In essence, both activities build the ability to use the body in a graceful way. The better you can use your body, the better you will look.

Every twirler that stays in the activity long enough develops her own unique style, and will look like no other twirler when she is into her exhibition. I've known a few very good performers who have gotten fairly successfully into show business with their twirling. Diane Shelton, for example, performed with Bob Hope in Viet Nam and has been on the Johnny Carson Show.

One final advantage of taking baton lessons is the sense of accomplishment inherent in taking on a task and carrying it through to completion in a competent manner. Success breeds

"Every twirler that stays in the activity long enough develops her own unique style, and will look like no other twirler when she is into her exhibition."

confidence and security, which can make a better world. Dealing with pressure situations like show twirling makes life's little trials more bearable. And the more you do it, the easier it becomes.

—Kathy Comstock

Kathy Comstock teaches baton twirling in Palo Alto, Calif. and is currently vice president of the United States Twirling Association.

For More Information

There is a magazine called *Twirl* (2150 East Rahn Rd., Dayton, Ohio 45440) that is supposed to be good but we haven't seen it. It is published bi-monthly. Organizations you should know about are the United States Twirling Assn., 3550 Briggs Blvd., Grand Rapids, Mich. 49505 and the National Baton Twirling Assn., Box 266, Janesville, Wis. which publishes *Drum Major* magazine. One of several places that have good equipment is Kraskin Baton Co., Box 156, Savage, Minn. 55378.

There is one good book we know about and it is available from World Publications, Box 366, Mountain View, Calif. 94040 at the price listed* plus 25 cents postage.

Baton Twirling, Constance Atwater. "A book addressed to the student and teacher, inclusive, yet written in a succinct style, about a truly American skill. The author, a teacher of baton twirling . . .describes the basics and variations for twirling, marching, poses, strut exercise, etc." -School Library Journal. 1964 Hb., 193 pp., ill., $8.25, (Tuttle).

Beach Combing

There is enchantment for everyone at the ocean's rim. There is the lace edged beauty of the sea, stretching to the horizon and beyond. There is the music of the surf, punctuated by the cries of gulls: the soothing rhythm of quiet waves lapping at the shore or the thrilling thunder of storm hurled waves. There is ocean-fresh air to breathe, and you always seem to have forgotten that fresh air could be more exhilarating than the finest wine. There is therapeutic softness as your bare feet or your whole body sinks into the sand.

From time immemorial people have enjoyed the hours spent by the ever-changing sea, and it is all there, waiting for you now. But there is more; there is an added dimension for the beachcomber.

There's the additional anticipation and excitement in finding seaside treasures. Perhaps a river or creek has sent down twisted wood or roots to be smoothed and bleached by the water, sun and salt. Perhaps valuable flotsam from a shipwreck has floated in or the surf has sent you a graceful sea shell or several shiny beach pebbles. Anything that grows or lives by the sea or is cargo on its surface may be yours to find.

All this, all the enjoyment and anticipation of beachcombing is free. There's no age limit, no expensive equipment to buy. You don't have to be a poet to enjoy this sport. You don't have to put in long years of training. You don't even have to insist on a clear, sunny day. Some of the most exciting beachcombing is when you're bundled up, bent into the wind like the sea birds, savoring the storm's violence, knowing you're there first if the waves deposit something on the shore. Even fog has its own muffled, quiet beauty. Usually, too, fog means that fewer beachcombers will share your shore.

And you will have your day at the beach and be able to return to your home with the memory of its timeless peace.

—Ruth Jackson

Ruth A. Jackson is a freelance writer who "works" as an advertising copywriter for a San Francisco department store. When she isn't off to Japan, Africa or Lapland, Ruth spends most weekends exploring the Pacific Coastal regions south of Half Moon Bay. Her knowledge and love of this area has resulted in her authoritative manual, **Combing the Coast: San Francisco Through Big Sur.**

The Relaxing Sport

Beachcoming is universally loved. One of the many reasons is that whatever you find—even a tiny stone—will remind you of the sight, sound and fresh smell of the sea for long years after.

I spent my entire childhood in an inland city, and the gift I appreciated most in all those years was a box of sea shells my parents brought from a port town. I had never seen the ocean then, but when I looked at those shells and held them in my hands I could imagine the sparkle and stretch of the deep water. When I held them to my ears I could even hear the echoing rhythm of the surf.

Ever since I grew up I have tried to be close to the ocean, and almost every weekend I drive to a lonely beach to comb the shore. It is my therapy, my exercise, my way of surviving a tension ridden job in the concrete city. Even if I don't find beautiful driftwood or something valuable, I have been out in and with nature, and I have deeply enjoyed myself.

That is the main purpose of beachcombing—enjoyment—but there are many more advantages.

Exercise? Horsemen know the value of galloping horses in the sand. It is an excellent way of getting legs and lungs in tone, and you can suit the exercise to your needs. You can race with a joyful dog. You can walk with friends. You can stroll slowly by yourself.

As for finding a gift from the sea, it doesn't have to be a rare sea shell or something worth many dollars. If you use your imagination, you'll almost always have something in your knapsack when you leave the beach.

Shredded pieces of rope? You can use them in macrame or to hang some of the other loot you've found.

Old boxes? Some are sturdy enough to be planters or the base for a table or cabinet.

Flat pieces of wood? Make picture frames. Carve a name plate. Paste a photograph of a seagull or of the ocean on a weathered piece. Glue broken shells to a board in the shape of a fish. Often, too, you'll find the sea has already created murals on the wood with flaking layers of multi-colored paint, lichen and barnacles.

Scooped out pieces of wood will serve as planters.

Tie small pieces of driftwood or gleaming lures with fish lines, hang them from a piece of driftwood and presto—you have a mobile. Chunky pieces of wood make candlestick holders for your own table or for gifts (and you'll find almost everyone appreciates a gift you have made with your own beachcombing loot.)

Long contorted pieces of driftwood make beautiful supports for plants. Some driftwood, of course, is so stunning by itself it needs nothing done, not even oiling or rubbing with stone. These pieces are to be enjoyed on the mantle of your fireplace or in your office to remind you of the sea and free-flying gulls. You'll have fun specializing, too, collecting pieces that resemble animals or people you know, and then thinking up captions to fit.

All you need is imagination . . . and a beach.

Unless you're on the Indian Ocean or a lonely South Sea Island, intact sea shells are rare enough to be appreciated. You can string small shells together as a necklace. You can use big abalone shells as planters or ash trays or serving dishes for

"The big finds are often after shipwrecks. You may be walking the beach on that day when flotsam washes in toys, useable lumber like hatch covers, liquor, cargo of any kind that floats. Perhaps you'll do your bit for history and uncover a memento of an early shipwreck. One man on the beach after a storm discovered a rusted bowsprit band from the *H.W. Seaver*, a ship that disappeared mysteriously from official records about 1887. He searched many months and finally found an account of the shipwreck in a Santa Cruz, California newspaper."

Beachcombing can be an enjoyable experience even for young children, but they should be closely watched. Surf has a tendency toward danger, especially for youngsters. (Drennan)

some seafood feast. Tiny colorfully hued jinglies are perfect for using in wind chimes. Even more prosaic shells look exotic at the bottom of an aquarium or in a jar filled with water on your windowsill.

As for sand dollars, these fragile shells showing the imprint of a star are a pleasure just to look at. Or you can break one carefully open and look at the little white particles in the center. According to one legend, these are small white doves. At least you'll agree that they're white and could be free-form doves. Their purpose is less poetic. They are the sand dollar's alimentary system. Zoologists call them Aristotle's Lanterns.

Probably none of the rocks you find will be valuable, but the quartz and agates will have their own translucent beauty, and the jasper may look like genuine jade. Even "nothing" pebbles may have interesting patterns or an attractive sheen. If you don't want the bother of tumbling rocks for weeks to achieve a permanent shine, put them in a glass bottle or vase with water in a sunny place.

Sometimes you may discover fossil embedded in rocks, although many state parks forbid you to take away these valuable reminders of earlier centuries.

Occasionally you'll find an antique bottle, but many newer bottles have their own graceful shape.

As you're combing the beach you may stumble upon drifters put out to study the ocean currents or bottles holding messages, and you'll read a desperate plea for help or a note from some lonely seaman. One of my most embarrassing finds was a bottle holding a message I had written myself. Evidently it had washed high up on the shore, where it was caught. Years later a storm and high tide lifted it up and carried it out to the beach for me to find again.

Broken pieces of glass in muted purples, greens, brown and white, have their own beauty, especially if they are smoothed by the sea and sand. You can paste them down with epoxy for a stained glass effect. If you don't have enough pieces of glass to cover a window, use a pie plate.

Beachcombing is enjoyable even on days the wind or tide has swept the shore clean, but there's always a chance you'll find a camera or binoculars or knife left by a careless picnicker. I have found enough frisbies to supply all the children of my friends and their friends.

The big finds are often after shipwrecks. You may be walking the beach on that day when flotsam washes in: toys, useable lumber like hatch covers, liquor, cargo of any kind that floats.

There's that old rule about salvage rights. Twice I've been at the ocean when abandoned boats worth thousands of dollars have drifted in, and the first person to report it received salvage rights.

Perhaps you'll do your bit for history and uncover a memento of an early shipwreck. One man on the beach after a storm discovered a rusted bowsprit band from the *H. W. Seaver,* a ship that had disappeared mysteriously from official records about 1887. He searched many months and finally found an account of the shipwreck in a Santa Cruz, Calif. newspaper. paper.

A Japanese watchmaker once encased hundreds of watches in plastic and sent them to sea to prove they were waterproof. Most of them have not washed ashore yet. You may find the next one.

Even empty beer cans and bottles can have their use. Some imaginative conservation minded people hold beach parties for children and award prizes for those collecting the most cans and other non-biodegradable debris. The children, who would have enjoyed their day at the beach anyway, have the added incentive of knowing they have helped keep the beach clean for others to enjoy.

Near the top of the list of prizes for the beachcomber are the green, blue or clear glass fishing floats used to hold up Japanese or Russians fishing nets. These floats have become rare in our era of plastic, but tumultuous storms may bring some in, a few even encased in rope nets.

Right now a storm may be building up far out at sea, and you may be out beachcombing when it deposits booty at your feet.

But be warned. Once you've found seaside treasures you, too, will become addicted to the exciting yet relaxing sport of beachcombing. Head for the nearest beach and find out for yourself.

– **Ruth Jackson**

For More Information

Certainly anyone interested in Beachcombing should know about the Audubon Society (950 Third Ave., New York, N.Y. 10022) and the magazine they put out called *Audubon*. Published bi-monthly at $13.00 per year. Available through the society's address. A lot of beautiful photos and good articles in each issue. A magazine you wouldn't throw away. Here are some books for the beachcomber. All are available from World Publications, Box 366, Mountain View, Calif. 94040 at the price listed* plus 25 cents each postage.

Shells in Color, Sandred and Abbott. Beachcombers and seaside explorers will delight in this magnificent photo book that presents the beauty of the seashell world in full color. 1973 Hb., 112 pp., ill., $12.95, (Viking).

Sea Shells of the World, A. Gordon Melvin. This is a book any shell collector will go wild for! All of the over 1,100 shells are illustrated with those shells in which color is important shown in 27 beautiful color plates. Each shell is identified, briefly described, and its location and price are listed. 1966 Hb., 167 pp., ill., $11.75, (Tuttle).

A Beachcomber's Botany, Loren Petry. An essential reference companion for any visitor to coastal New England, covering all shore plants and seaweeds. 1975 Hb., ill., $6.95, (Chatham).

Guide to Shells, A.P.H. Oviber & James Nichols. A fascinating and informative guide to the shells of the world with examples of all of the major classes and orders. Contains 153 pages of full-color illustrations and over 1,000 species illustrated, making this one of the most complete guides to a field of growing interest. 1975, 320 pp., ill., $9.95, (Harper & Row).

Combing The Coast: San Francisco Through Big Sur, Ruth A. Jackson. A good guide to doing anything along the Pacific coast, from beachcombing for treasure to where to camp and eat. 1972 Ppb., 144 pp., ill., $2.95.

Belly Dancing

As a professional dancer, teacher and editor of the first national news publication devoted to belly dancing (or Oriental dancing as we prefer it to be called in our profession), I am often in a position to be asked the question. "Why is belly dancing so popular in the United States?" This question digs deeper than anticipated. Unfortunately, my own answer is, "I don't know." Even with my experience, it is difficult to know why such dance has grown so rapidly all over the country, even in rather culturally remote areas. It is an exotic and exciting form of recreation, so perhaps no other explanation need be given.

The dance itself is ancient and most likely originated in the Middle East. The most popular theory about this dance form, as derived from studies of other primitive dances, is that is was originally a religious performance specifically related to fertility cult activities. From prehistoric times until the present day, fecundity has been high on the scale of values in the Mediterrean area. The very suggestive movements of a belly dancer's hips, torso, stomach muscles and bosom do seem to bear out this hypothesis. A more modern theory deals with the massive slave trading that took place in that part of the world and suggests that female slaves learned the art as a saleable talent.

But what does all this have to do with the 20th Century American woman? Probably not much, because when I ask my students why they enjoy belly dancing, they usually answer "for the exercise" or "because it makes me feel so feminine."

Let's dwell on the exercise angle for a moment. It is a fine form of exercise because it uses all of the muscles of the body: arms, legs, neck, back, chest, hips, and especially the stomach. Having previously studied and performed more classical forms of dance, I definitely feel that belly dancing uses the muscles in a more natural way. There is no artificial distortion of muscles involved, nor constant training and exercise to maintain that distortion. This is one reason why great belly dancing proficiency can be achieved in a year or less.

Belly dancing is also an individualistic art, because bodies vary so widely in shape, size and proportion. Once one has learned the major steps, dance patterns and finger cymbal rhythms, the opportunity to develop a highly unique dance style becomes apparent. As an example, one dancer may discover that due to the way she is constructed, her stomach flutters are a major asset in her dancing. A second may find that she has an ability to do hip shimmies differently from everyone else, while still another may capitalize on very graceful hands. This is one of the aspects of the dance that I enjoy the most, both in observing and teaching. One's personality surfaces in every dance. It is the antithesis of a chorus line where conformity is the norm.

Many individuals are curious about what possible harmful physical effects belly dancing has on the body. Generally, it

"Belly dancing uses all the muscles of the body: arms, legs, neck, back, chest, hips, and especially the stomach. There is no artificial distortion of muscles involved, nor constant training and exercise to maintain that distortion." (Cunningham)

has none. As I mentioned before, there are no distortions, and no excessive building up of muscles. I have heard from some professional dancers that after years of vigorous abdominal activity, their stomachs develop a slight, but flattering curve. Of course, this is not flab; it is firm muscle and strong abdominal muscles should be no cause for complaint from anyone.

I know of very few injuries. A very small number of knee strains are the only serious problems, and most of these are sustained from doing the "Turkish Drop" (a sudden fall backward to the floor with knees tucked under). This is, however, a step which is not usually taught, and then only to very advanced students.

Of what does an actual belly dance consist? Music is first and foremost. You cannot perform a belly dance without it. Although the dance is often performed to Turkish and Greek music, the essence of it is best brought out by the sensual, subtle and exotic music of the Arabs—the warm sound of the oud (similar to the lute), the harp-like kanoon, the flute and other instruments (including some borrowed from the West.) These are accompanied by the rhythms of hand drums, tambourines and the dancer's finger cymbals. The drum is the heartbeat, setting the pace for both the dancer and her musicians.

A professional performance usually consists of four parts: first, a lively entrance with the dancer covered by a veil or veils; as the music slows, the dancer takes off the veil, dances with it, then discards it; the music quickens again, then slows down to a very intimate portion called the *taksim* where the dancer will descend to the floor and dance on her knees, doing back bends and other sensuous movements; finally, the dancer stands and the music finishes with a fast and exciting crescendo. This is typical of the cabaret style of performance which is found in night clubs.

Some cabaret dancers prefer a more ethnic type of belly dance with traditional folk costumes, as opposed to the chiffon and sequins of most night clubs. These ethnic performances often include sword dancing, performing with snakes, or balancing trays of goblets on the head. In general, it has more of a gypsy flavor. It is in these types of performances that excellent male dancers play a vital role. Although belly dancing is definitely a female-dominated field, all of the musicians are men, so teamwork between the sexes does become essential. In addition, two of the most highly acclaimed teachers, known both nationally and internationally, are men. Belly dancing, then, is a field that is open to all.

—**Sherry Kidwell**

Sherry Kidwell, known as Emira, is a professional dancer, author and the editor/publisher of **Habibi**, *a monthly newsletter on Middle Eastern dance.*

For More Information

There is a good publication that is put out by the author of this section. *Habibi* (726 Sutter Ave., Palo Alto, Calif. 94303) is published monthly at $6.00 per year. Newspaper format with good articles in each issue. Well illustrated with photos.

Roman Balladine (541 Atherton Ave., Novato, Calif. 94947), a nationally known performer, teacher and author is a good contact. Top quality instruction for beginners can usually be found at local community centers, YWCA's and dance studios. Unicorn (73 Virginia Ave., Long Beach, New York 11561) has a free catalog listing books, records, accessories and gift items. Also Silwani & Company, Inc. (6519 Hollywood Blvd., Hollywood, Calif. 90028) has a free catalog listing records and 8-track tapes. Shops that import items from the Middle East will also be able to help you.

Here are a few books covering belly dancing. All are available from World Publications, Box 366, Mountain View, Calif. 94040 at the price listed* plus 25 cents postage.

The New Art of Belly Dancing, Adela Vergara. The art of belly dancing is not only capable of expressing enduring human emotion, it is a discipline whose ultimate demand is the perfect coordination of mind and body. Here is a loving, comprehensive study of the dance in all forms. 1974 Ppb., 127 pp., ill., $3.95, (Celestial).

The Serena Technique of Belly Dancing, Serena & Alan Wilson. Illustrated with over 200 photographs, this book offers ways to keep fit, feel relaxed and expand your creativity. 1973 Ppb., $1.95, (Simon & Schuster).

Slimming: An Oriental Approach, Soraya. This almost academic book by Turkish authoress Soraya is a guide to slimming by belly dancing. Contains dancing knowledge from thousands of years ago. 1975 Hb., 166 pp., ill., $4.95, (Palmetto).

Biathalon

The Biathlon is a winter sport combining cross-country skiing and rifle marksmanship. The competitive event now called Biathlon had its origins in the struggle for winter survival. In order to put meat on the table, Scandanavian men would ski long distances in search of game, stopping to shoot at each likely target. In modern Biathlon competition, wild game has been replaced with paper or glass targets, but the pattern of ski-shoot-ski-shoot remains unchanged.

Biathlon is an Olympic event that includes both individual and team relay races. It was first included on the Olympic program at Squaw Valley in 1960, but competitions combining marksmanship and cross-country skiing have been held in Scandanavia and Europe since well before World War II. The first US competition did not take place until 1956, but American biathletes have progressed rapidly enough to place among the top six teams at the 1972 Olympics.

Marksmanship ability and luck can make or break a biathlon competitor, because penalty minutes are assessed or penalty loops must be skied for excessive misses.

The individual biathlon event consists of skiing a 20 kilometer course, halting four times at a target range to fire five shots for a total of 20 rounds. At least three kilometers skiing distance is set up between each target stop, and the biathlete must carry his own rifle and ammunition throughout the course.

The marksmanship phase of a biathlon can be done in two ways. In the 20 kilo individual race, each competitor fires at paper targets. Penalty minutes are assessed and added to an athlete's final elapsed time for each bullet that lands outside the target area. In team races, breakable glass targets are used. Each competitor must shatter five of these targets within eight shots, or he must ski a penalty loop for each target left intact. Such penalty loops usually take between 30 and 60 seconds to complete. All shooting takes place on a 150 meter target range, with both automatic weapons and optical sights forbidden. A racer's final time score is the complete ski time plus penalty loops or penalty minutes.

Individual event competition commences with each athlete starting at one minute intervals. In order to create more interest for team relay events, however, a massed start is used with all lead-off racers starting at once. Using this method, no doubt can arise over who is in the lead at any one time during the course of a race. That, plus the use of breakable targets, makes team biathlon an exciting spectator event.

The Feasibility of it All

During the fall of 1971, I was training for biathlon somewhat in a vacuum, as I was unable to spend time working with anyone else who was trying to make the '72 Olympic team. I wasn't actually skiing alone, since my schedule during September and October included a number of races for Eastern Nordic skiers, but I felt troubled about putting it all together. In some ways I was confident I would make the team for Japan, but in others I was doubtful. By November, skiing began out West and most of the Biathlon Training Squad was finally together.

While at the training camp, I don't recall ever discussing what might happen at Sapporo. Instead, tension in the air indicated that the major concern of most athletes would be simply making the team. In retrospect, this situation is unfortunate, because an athlete is forced to peak for the trials instead of the major competition. But considering the reality of the nordic athlete as an obscure, yet serious and dedicated individual, making the team was probably the heaviest thought on everyone's mind.

Our skiing workouts rapidly progressed. We had several races, but mostly in cross-country. Finally in December, we had some good biathlon activity at Jackson, Wyo. I came East for Christmas and the cross-country Olympic trials, then I returned to Jackson for the biathlon tryouts. I felt healthy. I wasn't skiing as fast as I wanted (I never do!), but my shooting was very accurate and I was not too worried. I was thinking only about making the team to fulfill my childhood dream. At the trials, I had three good races out of four, but a few seasoned competitors ran into bad luck and finished lower than their talents should have placed them.

Six team members were selected and flew to Sapporo with a team leader, ski coach and rifle coach. With one exception, we all knew each other fairly well, and a team unity soon developed. While training before the races in Sapporo, I gave no thought to how we might do collectively on the relay team, or individually in the 20 kilo race. I do recall mention of our strength in the relay, but only in terms of performing better in that event than in the individual.

Our first race was the 20 kilometer individual, and the best placing was a 14th by Peter Karns, now the National Biathlon Coach. By past standards, he made a great showing, but I wasn't too surprised, for Peter really concentrated on these races.

The team's next event was the relay with four of us competing. The race itself is exciting to watch, but presents horrible pressure for the competitors because bad shooting can cause a disaster for the entire team. Peter Karns started and put the USA in seventh, but still in a very competitive position. Terry Morse, our second man, somehow put his act together and made my heart flutter as he caused the scoreboard to show the United States in third position, bronze medal country. I was the next racer and slipped a notch to fourth. I shot fairly well, but was not fast enough skiing to hold the third place that Terry had gained. I tagged Jay Bowerman, who held his own until he incurred one penalty loop for his standing shooting. He finished an unbelievable—for us and the US—sixth.

I was gratified to leave Japan with an Olympic certificate saying "Sixth Place, Biathlon Relay" tucked safely in my suitcase. Certainly we had some good luck, as final statistics revealed that we had the best shooting results of any team that day. Still, I am not certain that luck was the only reason we did well. Perhaps we were simply capable of winning a medal and never really knew it, or felt it, or believed it. I wish I could pinpoint those areas that would help us do the same again, but I fear there are adverse conditions and policies holding back our sport. These must be overcome before we can take a team to the Olympics or World Championships with full confidence in their ability to win a medal. As evidenced by the relay race in '72, the capacity certainly is there. Perhaps all that is needed is for our athletes to concentrate less on merely making the team, and more on doing well at the important competitions.

I am confident that American Biathlon teams will soon break through and score much higher than our sixth place finish at Sapporo. But for about 35 minutes in '72 we were in third place on the scoreboard, good enough for a medal, and I'll never forget it.

—Dennis Donohue

Dennis Donohue is the American Biathlon Champion and a veteran international competitor. He placed 24th overall in the individual Biathlon event at the 1972 Olympic Games.

Each Biathlete must ski a 20-kilometer course during the individual competition. He must stop four times to fire 20 rounds, and he is required to carry his own rifle and ammunition.

For More Information

This is one of those sports that information is hard to come by. However, there are two organizations you should know about. The United States Modern Pentathlon and Biathlon Assoc. (707 E. Broad St., Falls Church, VA 22046) is the governing body for the sport in the US. Also, there is the US National Biathlon, Box 955, Jackson Hole, Wyoming. They have a booklet that will be of interest. The only other source of information is *Nordic World Magazine* (Box 366, Mountain View, Ca. 94040) which has articles from time to time. The magazine does cover cross-country skiing in detail. Published nine times per year at $6.50.

Bicycle Moto-Cross

Bicycle Moto Cross, or BMX, as it is often called, has grown from a neighborhood vacant-lot pastime to an exciting, widely enjoyed, well-sponsored, and much-disputed form of bicycle racing.

Its deepest roots reach back to the first time a bicycle rider left the beaten track and found that it was fun to go jouncing across an open field. The sport as it exists today began sometime around 1960 with the conversion of small-framed, small-wheeled American bicycles into stripped-down, sturdy, mean-looking machines that could take whatever the vacant lot had to offer in the way of bumps, jumps, and slippery mud. In Southern California, during the period from 1960 to 1965, these bikes became so popular that manufacturers began producing them ready-made, coming out with the "stingray" bike and others similar to it.

While the bicycles were undoubtedly raced in vacant lots all over the country, it wasn't until cross-country motorcycle racing (Moto Cross) became popular in the middle 60s, that well-organized racing of the small yet durable pedal-powered bikes and their young riders got going. With the growth in popularity of daredevil jumping of motorcycles, the jumps in the vacant lots and on the BMX race courses naturally increased in size and number, and dramatic riding styles were developed to live up to the heroic ideal of the two-wheel gladiator.

Many concerned parents and older cyclists have maligned Bicycle Moto Cross because of its similarity to motorcycle racing. They fear that it leads too many young riders away from healthy normal cycling and toward the noisy, nature-ravaging world of the motorcycle.

One need only see the number of larger and older riders participating in BMX, and see the sophistication of their machines and their riding ability to appreciate the great potential value of the sport in and of itself.

Strong, light, resilient frames have been designed for the racing bikes, combining the best of motorcycle and bicycle technology. Shock absorbing frames, though heavier and less energy-efficient, are sometimes valuable on very rough courses. Seats, handlebars, and front forks all have borrowed from their motorcycle antecedents, with design changes added to keep them as light as possible. Extremely strong wheels made with spokes of 100 to 120 gauge thickness and racing bicycle hubs are used by many riders, while others choose harsher but exceptionally rugged magnesium wheels. Wide, strong, nobby-profile tires provide the best possible traction in mud, sand, and dust. The bicycles are often surprisingly light (30 to 35 pounds), considering the punishment they have to undergo.

Official courses for races sanctioned by the National Bicycle Association, the American Bicycle Association, and the National Pedal Sport Association are designed to be punishing to both bikes and riders, without being overly dangerous. The courses rarely call for any extended hill-climbing, but they have every kind of challenging surface from rubber mats (in some indoor events) to mud and water-holes. Berms create banked turns, ramps and dirt-mounds make jumps up to three feet high, and rows of low bumps, known as "Whoop-ti-dos", set up pace breaking vibrations. Riders must learn to jump without flipping forwards (doing an Endo, as it is called) or backwards (known as "looping it"). Controlled sliding is also important, with the front wheel turned into the slide to keep the bicycle headed the right direction, and the maintenance of momentum through all kinds of obstacles, including fallen riders, calls forth great shows of strength and ability from BMX experts.

The result is a race that may be only 500 or 1000 yards in length, but which is packed with action for riders and the audience alike.

—Tom Cuthbertson

Tom Cuthbertson is the author of **Anybody's Bike Book** *and* **Bike Tripping.**

For More Information

There isn't much available on this sport yet, it is too new. However, you might write *BMX Racer*, 9836 Benson Ave., Montclair, Calif. 91763. That is a magazine and they have published at least one issue. Write for a sample copy. For other magazines and organizations, see Bicycle Racing.

There is one book on the topic and it is available from World Publications, Box 366, Mountain View, Calif. 94040 at the price listed* plus 25 cents postage.

How to Win Bicycle Motocross, John Thawley. How to zoom over whoop-de-dos, turns, and jumps and still keep going! Not only a bicycle motocross racing manual, this book also covers how to build your own track, paint your racer, and completely service your bike. 1975 Ppb., 144 (oversize) pp., ill., $4.95, (H.P. Books).

Bicycle Racing

"What goes up must come down," or so the saying goes. To prove that even old familiar sayings can be wrong, though, the sport of cycling is stubbornly refusing to come down. The bicycle racing boom that began in the early 1960s still hasn't boomeranged as cycling has become one of the United States' fastest growing athletic sports.

From the very beginning cycling has had a universal appeal. The kinesthetic sense of coordinated rhythmic movement, the sensation of speed and the freedom of travel afforded by bicycles all combine to quickly create a national pastime. It was only natural that when two riders met on the road they would want to find out which was the fastest. That natural desire to race is now administered by the United States Cycling Federation, the official sanctioning body of all amateur bicycle racing in the US.

Whether you are man or woman, young or old, expert or beginner, the USCF has a suitable program. Age group racing for both men and women now includes competition for Midgets (8-11 years), Intermediates (12-14), Juniors (15-17) and Seniors (18 and older). In addition, men over 40 have their own competition group, Veteran Men. Senior men are further graded by ability and race within categories in order to help each individual realize his own potential. Thus, a novice Senior would be category four and international class riders category one. Occasionally, all riders compete together in handicap races. In these competitions, inexperienced and slower riders are given a head start with faster riders chasing. When done properly, every rider has an equal chance to place and beginners have the added thrill of racing against international class athletes.

Events fall roughly into two types, track races, which require special facilities, and road races held on streets and roadways. Distances run the gamut from violently fast sprints of a few hundred meters to road races up to 120 miles. Criteriums are a very popular form of road races contested over short, closed courses in city streets. These races provide spectators with nearly constant action and allow riders to display skill as well as endurance and sprint ability. Multi-stage races, which consist of several days of racing with the winner chosen by lowest accumulative time, are increasing in popularity. Even during the winter when road and track riding is difficult or impossible, riders can turn to cyclo-cross, a variant of the sport which requires running over obstacles with the bike and then riding smoother portions of the course.

At the extremes of World and Olympic Championships, cycling is one of the most demanding of athletic sports. Success requires equal measures of speed, strength, local muscular stamina, cardio-respiratory endurance and skill. At the opposite end of the spectrum, the novice can enjoyably indulge in the sport with nearly no prior training, instruction, or special abilities. Perhaps this is the real key to cycling's unprecedented and wide spread appeal.

—Vic Black

Vic Black is the Northern California ABL of A representative. He has a diverse background of competition and officiating in bicycle racing.

Looking Back

My earliest memories are of riding in the back seat of an ancient Chevy. During the early '40s my father was a Methodist circuit minister in southern Kentucky. With seven churches to serve, we were on the move most of the time, reaching our starting point again every two months. When Dad decided to go back to school in 1942, we spent the week at college, then drove 150 miles to his church each weekend for four years. Weekends were kind of a bore because I spent most of my time in church, traveling in the back seat of the car or playing in the dirt of a southern pine forest. Back at the college I had more fun, but I was punished more than once for sneaking off and "borrowing" some unsuspecting kid's trike.

When I was old enough to start school we moved to eastern Illinois and my world began to expand a little. Even so, it didn't really extend beyond North Bridge on the north side of town and South Bridge on the south side of town. It was a pretty small world of only about 1000 people until I was eight years old. Then Dad got me my first bike. My initial ride ended in a spectacular crash. It was only the first in a string of them, but by persevering I finally mastered the thing. Suddenly, the world opened up. I could go much farther than ever before, and see lots more in my wanderings.

It was only to last for a couple of years, though. When I was 10 years old, I began to experience severe pains in my right hip and I developed a noticeable limp. Finally, a specialist was called in and a diagnosis made. The head of my femur was deformed by a not uncommon childhood disorder called Legg-Perthe's disease. For the next three to four years I would be on crutches and would be forbidden to place any weight on the diseased joint. Because of the hazards of walking on crutches in snow and ice, the family decided we should move to a friendlier climate. We were going to California. Everything that could fit was packed into a trailer and the rest was sold at auction. That included my only real possession, my beloved Columbia. It was too big for me, it rattled and clanked when I rode it and it was heavy. And it brought only $8 at the auction. I cried all the way to Missouri.

From 10 to 14 I spent my summers learning to fight with my crutches on the way to school. At fourteen I was a skinny, weak-looking little kid, but I was brave and tackled the job of walking again with a sense of purpose. One of my first long walks was to the bank where I applied for a loan to buy a bike. I had already lined up a newspaper job to pay for the bike and as an independent business man I realized the importance of having good business equipment. The job only lasted long enough to pay for the bike. After that I was much too busy riding to spend time on a job.

My friends thought I was really weird. When the 1955 Chevy was introduced it turned on a whole generation to cars. Anyone in his right mind didn't ride a bike. Somehow, though, I think I always knew that someday I'd race bicycles. Since I wasn't allowed to participate in any sports—even during col-

Road races are a popular feature of bicycle racing, with distances up to 200 kilometers. Much longer distances are covered by multi-stage races, which consist of several days of racing with the winner determined by accumulative time. (Mock)

"At the extremes of World and Olympic Championships, cycling is one of the most demanding of athletic sports. Success requires equal measures of speed, strength, local muscular stamina, cardio-respiratory endurance and skill." (Duffy)

lege—and impact loading on my hip was forbidden until I finished growing, my only athletic outlet was cycling. I progressed from casual rider to tourist to fast club rider to racer.

My racing career was not really an illustrious one. In six good racing seasons I barely moved above the novice category. I grew up a lot during those years, though, and I saw the sport grow as well. When I started racing in 1961, my district, Northern California/Northern Nevada, had four clubs, six major races each year and about 60 riders. Things weren't much different in most of the nation. Today we've advanced to one of the nation's leading cycling centers with about 1000 active riders in nearly 40 clubs. It's possible to race several times a week most of the year and the competition is top rate.

I've now made the full tour from club rider to race official and back to club rider. I've never questioned the correctness of any of it. It always seemed that things were supposed to be the way they were. But sometimes I wonder what I would be like today if I hadn't become sick as a youngster. And if I'd spent my childhood learning to drive tractors the way my buddies did in the 40s. And if I'd cruised main street in my Chevy during the 50s. And if I'd learned to hate all physical activity during the 60s.

—Vic Black

For More Information

Bicycle racing is continuing to grow in the United States. And certainly the following publications have helped with that growth.

Velo-News, 140 Elliot St., Brattleboro, Vt. 05301. Published 12 times per year at $3.00. Newspaper format with a lot of news, features, photos and other good information on bicycle racing.

Bicycling, Box 3330, San Rafael, Calif. 94902. Published monthly at $9.50 per year. Most issues have some good racing articles.

Bike World, Box 366, Mountain View, Calif. 94040. Published monthly at $8.50 per year. Certainly a top magazine in the field.

There is one major organization you should know about—Amateur Bicycle League of America (ABLA), Box 699, Wall St. Stn., New York, N.Y. 10005. They are the national organizaton behind bicycle racing.

Even though there have been a lot of books published on bicycling, there haven't been that many on racing but here are a few. All are available from World Publications, Box 366, Mountain View, Calif. 94040 at the price listed* plus 25 cents each postage.

All About Bicycle Racing, editors of *Bike World* magazine. How to train, how to compete, what equipment is needed, plus a section on the training, diet, and ideas of the racers. 1975 Ppb., 96 pp., ill., $2.95, (World Publications).

Bicycle Track Racing. Insights into the high-tension world of track racing—sprints, tandems, pursuit racing and the kilometer time trials. A peek at how the pros train and how to make their tactics work for you. 1976 Ppb., $3.50, (World Publications).

Cycling in the Sixties, David Saunders. Written by Britain's leading cycling correspondent in the national papers, this frank, insightful, often blunt appraisal of a decade of British cycling will provide fascinating reading. 1971 Hb., 148 pp., ill., $4.95, (Pelham).

Bicycle Touring

As President of the International Bicycle Touring Society, I get many letters. These come from people who are about to start on their first bicycle tour, and they want to know how to go about it. The first question is always, how do I go from Point A to Point B? But if you have to ask that question, you have not done your homework. It is a mistake to go on a long tour before you have done a short tour, and a short tour is available right where you live. Start small and learn the basics.

Not long ago I had a visit from a young man who was planning to ride from California to New York. He had studied this project in enough detail to know the average temperature, the annual rainfall, and the mean elevaton of all the states he was going to ride through. However, that was not what he came to ask me. What he came to ask me was, "How do I get to El Cajon?" El Cajon is a suburb of San Diego where this young man lived. Instead of worrying about the annual rainfall in Wisconsin, he should have explored his own neighborhood.

So my answer to these questions is, "Always go on a shakedown cruise." On that trip, which should last at least a weekend, you find out whether your saddle is comfortable, whether your gears are right, and whether you can find your way on the little roads. Even small troubles are hard to correct once your tour has started. I know a young touring cyclist who was forced to return home because of a series of broken spokes.

The bicyclist who is contemplating a long tour has three things to give attention to: his bicycle, his baggage, and his itinerary. Let me say a few words about each.

THE BICYCLE. It is a handicap that touring bicycles are hard to find in America. Usually, it is a matter of converting an existing ten-speed to a reasonable facsimile, a process that can be both expensive and laborious. Here are the principal features of a touring bicycle:

1. Wide-ratio gears with a range of 30 to 90 inches. My favorite combination is a cluster of 14-16-19-23-28, and chainwheels of 30-46 or 32-48. With three chainwheels, my preference is 30-40-50. This avoids the wide jumps. Not all derailleurs will handle wide ratios. Recommended are the Campagnolo Rally, the Shimano Crane GS, and the Suntour VGT Luxe. The most recent model in the Suntour line is the Cyclone GT.

2. Alloy rims with clincher tires. Sew-up tires give a livelier ride but they are a nuisance to fix. Moreover, sew-up tires are not comfortable on a rough road. Comfort is more important than speed.

3. A front fork with enough rake to discourage shimmy at speed and vibration on cobbles.

4. Carriers that are securely fixed to the frame so that they will not sway. Most carriers that are sold in this country fail in this respect.

5. Fenders if you expect rain and dust. Without fenders, your chain will quickly become a mass of dirt, mud and grit, to say nothing of your own body. The front fender is especially important, and it should reach to within five inches of the ground.

6. Lights if you expect to ride after dark. Since there is always the possibility of night rides, I recommend lights. A generator set, however, is no longer necessary. For the occasional night ride of not more than a few hours, I carry a plastic light made by the Wonder Company. It weighs only ten ounces and lasts long enough for anything short of steady use. A plastic strap-on-leg-light can be a useful auxiliary.

YOUR BAGGAGE. Bicycle bags are of three kinds—panniers that you drape over the rear carrier, a handlebar bag that sits on the front carrier, and a saddlebag that hangs from the saddle but gets its support from the rear carrier.

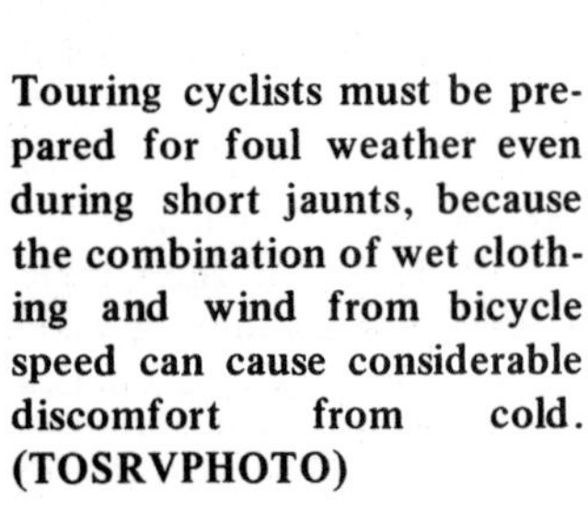

Touring cyclists must be prepared for foul weather even during short jaunts, because the combination of wet clothing and wind from bicycle speed can cause considerable discomfort from cold. (TOSRVPHOTO)

"The handlebar bag is for articles you might need during the day: maps, sunglasses, money, rain cape, camera, film, etc." (TOSRVPHOTO)

These bags come in different sizes and different materials. Canvas is the strongest but also the heaviest. Nylon in its various combinations is the lightest but also the most vulnerable to tears. I prefer canvas.

In packing, you lay out all the articles on a big table and weigh everything. You then discard one thing after another until the weight is under 15 pounds. Campers need more, of course, but even for campers there is a limit—not over 25 pounds. I am not a bicycle camper myself, but I have watched a good many. It is my observation that bicycle campers quickly lose their enthusiasm for outdoor cooking. It takes too long. After all, the idea is to ride your bicycle, not to sit by the side of the road and warm a can of beans over a Primus stove. Cleaning pots and pans is more than the average touring bicyclist has time for. The typical long-distance, self-sufficient bicyclist usually gives up cooking and eats in a restaurant as often as he can afford it.

The handlebar bag is for articles you might need during the day: maps, sunglasses, money, cape, camera, etc. The pannier bags carry a complete change of clothing for the evening, and the saddlebag is for miscellaneous articles. Always leave a little extra space for things you buy along the road, such as picnic food. Wrap each article in its own plastic bag. The following list is a guide only, as every cycle tourist soon works out his own system.

Clothing and grooming

2 riding jerseys, dark
2 pair of riding shorts
2 sets of underwear
2 pair of knee-length hose
1 pair of shoes
1 windbreaker, unlined
1 hat
1 raincape
1 shoeshine kit
4 hankies

Toilet articles

1 plastic leggings
1 pair of sunglasses
2 inflatable hangers

For men

1 sport jacket or
1 sweater
1 pair of slacks
1 shirt
1 tie
1 pair of Pulman slippers

For women

1 dress or
1 suit or
1 blouse and skirt
2 pair of nylon hose
1 sewing kit
1 pajama

Valuables

1 passport
1 driver's license
1 camera & film
travelers checks

For the bicycle

1 tire repair kit
3 spanners
1 spare tube
1 pair of gloves
1 lock
1 pump
2 elastic straps
1 light

YOUR ITINERARY. Choosing the best touring ground is more critical for the bicyclist than for the motorist because escape is more difficult. The cyclist looks for country with little traffic, winding roads, varied terrain, agreeable weather and towns with some character. These can still be found in the U.S., but with increasing difficulty. The enemy is traffic. A cyclist can learn to cope with mountains, weather, flats, loneliness, and adversity of all kinds, but not with traffic. Traffic kills all pleasure.

Admittedly, a dyed-in-the-wool cyclist can enjoy his sport under any conditions (witness the Hemistour expedition). But for the ordinary (and particularly for the beginning) cycle tourist, the vacation is so precious that it should be spent under the best possible conditions.

In the eastern part of the United States the best touring ground is the Appalachian Mountains with their outrunners, from Vermont and New Hampshire in the north to Georgia and Alabama in the south.

In the Midwest, the best areas are more spotty. I would mention especially southern Ohio, northern Michigan, western Wisconsin and the Ozarks.

West of Denver you find areas of singular beauty but also vast stretches of absolutely nothing. I would vote yes on the Colorado Rockies and the Pacific Coast, and no on the Great Basin which lies between. The Bitterroot Mountains in Montana, the Wind River Range in Wyoming, the Black Hills of South Dakota, the Superstition Mountains of Arizona—these are all superb. But don't try to ride from one to the other, be-

Bicycle touring demands meticulous preparation before every long trip, as well as each morning before departure on the next leg of the tour. Equipment must be carefully inspected and stowed on the cycle. (Elms)

cause you will wear yourself out.

The cross-country cyclist should remember that because of prevailing winds it is better to go from west to east than the other way around. If all this leaves you slightly confused, make up your first tour from suggestions in the *American Bicycle Atlas.*

Finally, a word about Europe. I still see too many American cyclists trying to navigate with a road map designed for motorists. Such maps do not show necessary detail. The only way to avoid traffic is on the small roads, and the only way to find these is with a map on a scale of 1 to 200,000, or even bigger. In England, get the Bartholomew half-inch maps (now gradually being replaced with the metricated series). In France, buy the Michelin maps, scale 1 to 200,000. In Germany, Austria and other countries, obtain maps on that same scale. You buy them in bookstores, not at gas stations.

For a European trip, it is not necessary to make out a day-to-day itinerary unless you are planning for a group. Instead, go freelancing. Simply pick a general area and start. If you don't like what you see, you can always take a train to some other spot.

In England, the South Downs, Devon and Cornwall, the Cotswolds, north Wales, Yorkshire, and the Lake District are recommended. In Scotland. the western Highlands. In Ireland, the west. In Holland, everywhere. In Belgium, the German border.

In Luxemburg, everywhere. In Germany, anywhere south of a Cologne-Kassel line. Especially recommended are the Moselle valley and the Black Forest. The Rhine valley is crowded and heavily commercialized, so it is better done by boat. In Denmark, everywhere. In Sweden, the lakes in the south. In Norway, the fjords in the west, starting in Bergen.

In France, everywhere except the northern industrial districts. Especially recommended are the Loire valley, Brittany, the Vosges mountains, Burgundy, the Massif Central, and the south. The Alps have grand scenery, but it is more difficult to escape traffic there. The best part of Switzerland is the Jura mountains in the border region with France. One of the most beautiful areas in Austria is Salzburg, but, in that country you can hardly miss.

Spain, Italy, Yugoslavia and the Balkan countries are not ideal. They lack the extensive network of little roads, and small hotels are more difficult to find. Italy is extremely noisy. In Spain, the coast is heavily commercialized, and the interior is arid. If you must go to Spain or Italy, go in spring or fall, because the summers are very hot.

And now, go to it. The world is your oyster.

—Clifford Graves

Clifford Graves is founder and president of the International Bicycle Touring Society.

For More Information

There are basically three good magazines being published that cover bicycle touring. These have been around for several years and are thus established.

Bike World, Box 366, Mountain View, Calif. 94040. Published monthly at $8.50 per year. Good technical articles in each issue with a lot on touring.

L.A.W. Bulletin, 19 S. Bothwell, Palatine, Ill. 60067. The official publication of the League of American Wheelmen. Published monthly for members.

Bicycling, Box 3330, San Rafael, Ca. 94902. Published monthly at $9.50 per year. The oldest of the bicycle publications.

Here are the organizations active on the touring scene.

League of American Wheelmen, 19 S. Bothwell St., Palatine, Ill. 60067. Very helpful organization that has done a lot for promoting bicycling.

International Bicycle Touring Society, 846 Prospect St., La Jolla, Calif. 92037. This is Clifford Graves' group. If you are interested in taking longer tours or trips abroad, drop them a letter.

American Youth Hostels, Delaplane, Va. 22025. Can be very helpful in many different ways.

Bicycle Institute of America, 1101 15th St., Washington, D.C. 20005. Has a lot of free literature available.

It is very difficult to pick out just a few sources for equipment but we have decided to give you a random cross-section. More sources can be found in the magazines listed. Also, don't forget your local bike shop.

Bell Helmets, 2850 East 29th St., Long Beach, Calif. 90806. Make a good bicycle helmet and is available by mail order.

Bikecology, 3006 Wilshire Blvd., Santa Monica, Calif. 90403. One of the better mail order houses. Has a giant catalog for $1.00.

Bike Warehouse, 6187 W. Blvd., Youngstown, Ohio 44512. Another top mail order house. Their catalog is 35c and it is packed with goodies.

There are many good books on touring and most book stores or bike shops stock some but you might consider these. All are available from World Publications, Box 366, Mountain View, Ca. 94040 at the price listed* plus 25 cents each postage.

The American Bike Atlas and Touring Guide, Sue Browder. The only book of its kind. Contains maps of 150 tours in all 50 states and Canada. Maps detail the main tour, optional side excursions, points of interest, campsites, distances, country stores and bike shops along the way. Perforated pages allow you to tear out one tour at a time. 1974 Ppb., 320 pp., ill., $5.95, (Workman).

Two Wheel Travel: Bicycle Camping and Touring. An omnibus effort by a group of people in love with bicycling. Just about everything on bike riding, touring, and camping, covered in an honest, evaluative style. Lots of hard-to-get info. 1974 Ppb., 192 (oversize) pp., ill., $4.95, (Dell).

Traveling by Bike, staff of *Bike World* magazine. Your bike can be your sole means of transportation—here is information on everything from commuting to work to intercontinental tours, on how to select a good bike, where to go, how to camp. 1974 Ppb., 96 pp., ill., $1.95, (World Publications).

DeLong's Guide to Bicycles and Bicycling, Fred De Long. The most complete book available on cycling—buying, riding, repairing, storying your bicycle, plus hundreds of other ideas on cycling. This guide will be referred to often in the future. 1974 Hb., 278 (oversize) pp., ill., $12.95, (Chilton).

Bicycle Touring in Europe, Karen and Gary Hawkins. An enticing guide to Europe, spiced with anecdotes and stories, all the advice needed, nine outstanding tours, and maps. A guaranteed way of seeing Europe and getting to know the Europeans. 1973 Ppb., 184 pp., ill., $2.95, (Random House).

The New Complete Book of Bicycling, Eugene A. Sloane. An update of the classic Complete Book of Bicycling, with the latest 1974 information. Well illustrated and expertly written, this book successfully covers the total biking experience for all biking enthusiasts. 1974 Hb., 532 pp., ill., $12.95, (Simon & Schuster).

Bike Tripping, Tom Cuthbertson. Another classic by the author of Anybody's Bike Book. Sensible advice on touring, with technical information presented in a very readable style. 1972 Ppb., 178 pp., ill., $3.95, (Ten Speed Press).

International Bicycle Touring. Ever wanted to pedal past the chateaux of the Loire Valley . . .the Norwegian fjords . . .the beaches of Italy's sun-baked coast . . .or the jagged peaks of Spain's Monserrat Range? Here's a guide to inexpensive ways to tour without being sucked into the multi-million dollar tourist industry. Bike Book Quarterly, 1976 Ppb., ill., $2.95, (World Publications).

Billiards

Fluctuations in public taste are not incomprehensible, though they often seem so. Until the early part of this century, billiards was a recreation of the elite. It was a high-class game, an early status symbol. Then, under the prodding of a generation of "rough-and-tumble" writers, the stereotype of the pool-hall bum denigrated one of the finest games of individual skill ever developed.

Stereotypes reflect not reality, but a distorted image of reality. Billiards is simply a group of games played with balls manipulated by sticks over a table. It is a severe test of patience, judgment, concentration, and skill. Billiard players are people who enjoy games which demand qualities everyone has. No one is ever "cut" in billiards because he is too small, or too slow, or black, or Jewish. At the billiard table, all players are equal. Each competes not only with his opponent, but with himself. Each constantly strives for self-improvement. These ingredients make a challenging game enjoyable for all kinds of people.

Now, after years in the doldrums, billiards is rapidly gaining in popularity. The equipment cost has lowered relative to the cost of other forms of recreation. Clean, well-lighted entertainment centers cater to a growing number of players. Where once only the very rich could afford their own table, many homes now sport billiard equipment in the recreation room or basement.

Naturally, I applaud this change in attitude—I love the game. So will you.

As in any field of endeavor, a heavy emphasis on fundamentals is central to the development of a sound game of billiards. I urge the novice to consult one of the excellent books available to develop proper stance, hand bridge, and ball address. My comments will be based on the assumption that the reader knows the rudiments of the game, and is now seeking to improve his play.

Concentrate on making your shots with absolutely no english on the cue ball. This is vital. It is the starting point for the development of a sound game. All english affects the movement of the object ball, and the inadvertant use of english will lead to a puzzling lack of consistency in your shooting. So direct your attention to this problem first. Develop the ability to make your shots with no english.

Practice this. Place one object ball on the head spot and the cue ball directly behind it, half-way to the head rail. Shoot at the center of the foot rail with sufficient force to bring the object ball off the foot rail back to the head of the table. The cue ball should roll slowly to the vicinity of the center spot. Keep practicing this shot until you can consistently bring the object ball back in contact with the cue ball between the center and the head spots.

During this practice, you must concentrate on the precise point at which your cue tip contacts the cue ball. Find that center. Strike it every time.

Now, continuing the same shot, practice keeping your eye on the object of the ball as you stroke the cue ball dead center. The purpose of your hand bridge is to guide the cue tip to the intended point of contact on the cue ball. Develop confidence in your bridge.

As soon as you are confident that you aren't imparting any unintentional spin to the cue ball, start practicing shots into the pockets. Scatter the 15 balls over the table, place the cue ball for an easy shot, and thereafter take the easiest shot you can see from the point the cue ball stops.

Throughout this practice, concentrate on striking the cue ball dead center, while keeping your eye on the object ball as you strike the cue ball. No, it's not impossible.

You've just developed confidence in using your bridge to direct the cue tip to the center of the cue ball. Take a couple of practice strokes to line the cue up, and then direct your attention to the proper aiming point on the object ball.

Watch how you line up a shot when you have to cut an object ball into a pocket. You probably have a tendency to "crib" slightly to one side of the cue ball or the other. Don't! Find the correct aiming point to cut that ball into the pocket without cribbing. Hit the cue ball dead center.

During this practice, don't worry about scratching the cue ball into one of the pockets. We'll tackle that problem later. Right now, concentrate on finding the right aiming point to make your shots.

If you find a particular type of shot that seems difficult for you, take the balls off the table, place the cue ball and one object ball to set up the shot and keep trying until you get it right. With each shot, note whether you are over- or under-cutting, and adjust until you can make the shot with reasonable consistency.

When you feel you are making some progress, start watching the cue ball's action after it strikes the object ball. Which direction does it move? What rails does it strike? The movements are quite logical, aren't they?

Hereafter, before each shot, try to determine where the cue ball in going to stop, and keep practicing until you can adjust the force of your shot to stop the cue ball within a six-inch radius of where you expected it to stop. As I said before, scratching the cue ball into a pocket doesn't matter in this practice, but you should develop the ability to call such a scratch in advance.

Throughout this practice, you will have noticed the thinner you cut each object ball, the further the cue ball rolls after contact with the object ball. Since it is obviously more difficult to predict the stopping point of a fast-rolling cue ball than a slow one, you will begin to prefer, when you have a choice, the most solid contact with an object ball possible.

Now you're starting to think about position, but before we continue, let's deal with a few common complaints: I can't make a long shot! I can't shoot off the rail! I can't shoot over a ball!

These common complaints do not indicate lack of ability. They indicate lack of practice. The only way to develop confidence in your ability to make long shots and shots off the rail is to start with shots you can make, and progressively increase the distance and/or angle. This does not take talent, it takes practice.

The problem of shooting over other balls is slightly different. In the majority of these cases, practice is the only solution. However, you must always consider that touching any

"As in any field of endeavor, a heavy emphasis on fundamentals is central to the development of a sound game of billiards. Concentrate on making your shots with absolutely no english on the cue ball. (Duffy)

ball, or allowing the cue stick to touch any ball other than the cue ball, is a foul. In some of these sticky situations the only practical solution is to make a safety shot. We'll consider these problems later. For now, practice a variety of shots over one or more balls. It's not so hard.

Whenever you play billiards you will be faced with difficult shots. Multiple ball combinations, bank shots, and ultra thin cuts are almost always available for the player who wants to try them. Indeed, skill in making difficult shots is important for those occasional times when there is simply nothing else available. But at this point many beginning players go astray. The ability to make difficult shots, while important, will never make up for the ability to set up easy shots.

The essence of high scoring in billiards is the ability to place the cue ball in a position which allows the player to make the succeeding shot easily, and again position the cue ball for another easy shot. This concept is known as cue ball control, or "playing position".

As we noted earlier, it is easier to predict the final stopping point of a slowly rolling cue ball than one which is speeding across the table. So shoot easy! Take your time, and softly stroke the cue ball to make your shot and leave the cue ball in position for another easy shot.

Several times in each rack you'll have occasion to stroke the ball firmly. Break shots and pocketing balls which have wandered to the head of the table often require a firmer stroke. But don't let it get to be a habit. For the most part: easy. Shoot easy.

—Steve Mizerak

Steve Mizerak, author of **Inside Pocket Billiards,** *has won the US Open Championship four times, the US Masters Championship three times, and numerous other national and international tournaments.*

For More Information

The Billard Congress of America, 20 N. Wacker Dr., Chicago, Ill., 60606 and the Billard Players Association, Box 97, Johnston City, Ill. 62951 can be most helpful. The Congress publishes a bulletin. There is a monthly magazine called *National Billiard News*, 1035 Chestnut St., Philadelphia, Pa. 19107, but we haven't seen it.

Here are a few good books on billiards. All are available from World Publications, Box 366, Mountain View, Calif. 94040 at the price listed* plus 25 cents each postage. Write for a complete list.

Inside Pocket Billiards, Steve Mizerak. A step-by-step guide to becoming an expert, with drawings and photos. Strategy is stressed, and so is a winning attitude. 1973 Hb. & Ppb., 86 (oversize) pp., ill., $7.95/$3.95, (Regnery).

Pocket Billiards with Cue Tips, Edward D. Knuchell. (Also published as "How to Win at Pocket Billiards", Ppb.) One of the prominent masters of the game uses his 35 years of experience in presenting a handbook for both beginner and expert. 1974 Hb. & Ppb., 256 pp., ill., $5.95/$3.00, (Barnes, Wilshire).

Billiards for Everyone, Luthor Lassiter. Learn from a World Billiards Champ all the basics – how to hold the cue, stroking, playing for position – and then go on to master advanced shooting – bank shots, reverse shots and kiss shots. This book teaches entirely by photography – every shot is pictured for practice at the table. 1965 Ppb., 95 (oversize) pp., ill., $1.95, (Grosset & Dunlap).

Billiards As It Should Be Played, Willie Hoppe. A master billards player concentrates on the fundamentals of the game, covering everything from the selection of a cue to the science of the "diamond system" in three-cushion play. 1941 Hb., 78 (oversize) pp., ill., $4.95, (Regnery).

Pocket Billiards, Irving Crane & George Sullivan. The authors offer the easiest and quickest way to learn pocket billiards with a complete step-by-step guide for the beginner and tips on strategy for the more advanced player. Rules and Glossary. Ppb., $1.50 (Simon & Schuster).

Bird Watching

Bird watching is a sport that can be enjoyed by nearly anyone who has an interest in the outdoors. Birds of some sort can be found very near home regardless of where you live, but a few birds are found only in certain regions. Visit your local library to obtain one or two field guides to birds and use them to find out what is in your particular area. Keep in mind, though, that many species are migratory and may only be there at certain times of the year.

A more foolproof and interesting way to learn about birds is to visit an ornithological organization such as the Audubon Society. Undoubtedly there is one near your home which would welcome new members, and there are usually many very experienced birders there who will be anxious to introduce you to their hobby.

Bird watching can be an activity for the whole family. Indeed, it usually becomes a family undertaking after one member becomes immersed in the sport. In addition, it is something which can be done at any season of the year. If you put out a bird feeder, you will be surprised at the variety of species that regularly visit it in search of nourishment. With practice and a knowledge of the kinds of birds in your area, you can even learn to attract certain species to the exclusion of others simply by putting out for them the type of food they prefer.

"Birdwatching can be an activity for the whole family. Indeed, it usually becomes a family undertaking after one member becomes immersed in the sport." (Schell)

"Normally some sort of magnification is needed for watching birds at close range, so a spotting scope or binoculars will eventually be needed. You should obtain the very best you can afford." (Pickrell)

The fact that you can be bird watching while doing other things at the same time is another attraction for many people, especially those whose lives do not allow for a planned schedule of activities. You can bird watch, for example, at the same time you are fishing, hunting, camping or canoeing.

The only prerequisite to taking up the sport is an interest in birds. Later, you might want to buy a pair of binoculars or a spotting scope, but at first these are unnecessary. A check list with which to keep track of what you have seen is a simple way of adding another dimension to an already interesting sport.

There are several excellent bird guides on the market at the present time, as well as many fine books showing the life histories of various species of birds. The Palmer and Fowler **Fieldbook of Natural History** is a very informative work on all types of animals and birds. Also, **The Bird Watcher's Bible**, out in early 1976, promises to be an excellent source material.

Whether you get into it deeply, or confine yourself to a certain family of birds such as predators or water fowl, you will find that bird watching is a most rewarding and informative sport.

–Jerry Pickrell

Jerry Pickrell loves the outdoors and animals. He has a regular column in **Down River** *magazine called "Watching and Wading" covering animals he observes in the wild. Many columns cover birds.*

Techniques and Equipment

The very first essential of bird watching is finding a bird to observe. There are many natural history publications available that can aid you in this endeavor. It would be fruitless, for example, to look for a woodland bird at the seashore, so the first order of business must be to become familiar with the habitat of the particular bird you want to observe.

Just as important as finding him is keeping him around long enough to get a good idea of what he is like, not just in appearance, but also in habits. To do this you must keep him from finding out that you are there watching. There are several tricks to this which you will not find difficult to master.

Most birds are unafraid of automobiles and so will allow you to approach more closely in the car than on foot. If you drive very slowly, you may be able to get within a few feet of birds which would otherwise have flown at the first sight of you.

At a fish hatchery near my home, the ponds are full of very small fish which are easy prey for the wading birds. Consequently, there are hundreds of these birds around, but the only way you can get close to them is by driving around in a hatchery truck. Anyone on foot is quickly spotted and the birds move off to wait for him to leave.

If you happen to be camping, a tent makes a great blind from which to observe birds in the wild. It obscures your movements and allows you to look out at the birds in the area. This technique has the added advantage of letting you observe the early morning birds without even having to get out of bed!

Normally some sort of magnification is needed for watching birds at close range, so a spotting scope or binoculars will eventually be needed. Your spotting scope should be about ten or twelve power, and it can be bought at most stores selling shooters' supplies. If the scope does not come equipped with some sort of tripod or other mounting device, one should be purchased with it, since you will not be able to hold it steady enough by hand to yield satisfactory performance.

Binoculars should be in the 6x30 to 8x50 range of magnification. These numbers tell you two different things. The first is the magnification of the binocular, while the second is the size of the objective lens (the one closest to what you are looking for) expressed in terms of its diameter in millimeters. Thus, a pair of 7x35 binoculars would give you a seven power magnification, and the objective lens would have a diameter of 35 millimeters. This size of the objective lens is important because the wider it is the more light it will admit, and consequently the less light there needs to be in order for you to see.

Whether you get a spotting scope or a pair of binoculars, you should obtain the very best you can afford since some of the less expensive lenses can have aberrations which cause eye strain and headaches when used for any length of time.

If you do not wish to use a blind, and you cannot drive close to where the bird you wish to see is located, you can substitute camoflaged clothing. This gear can be purchased at a shooter's supply house. Keep in mind that it does not make you invisible, just harder to see. It is still very important that you walk slowly and keep behind brush whenever possible. If you need to raise your binoculars to your eyes, for example, do it slowly and behind something if you can.

Essentially, bird watching is hunting. It is a good way to keep sharp on stalking techniques during the off season. If you are not already a hunter, you will be by the time you have mastered the sport of bird watching.

—**Jerry Pickrell**

For More Information

There are many regional publications for the birdwatcher and the National Audubon Society at 950 Third Ave., New York, N.Y. 10022 should be able to supply addresses and other information. And if you are interested in birds at all you should join their society. Their magazine *Audubon* ($13.00 per year for six issues) is super.

To really get into birdwatching you must know your birds. With this in mind, the following books should be helpful. All are available from World Publications, Box 366, Mt. View, Ca. 94040 at the price listed* plus 25 cents each postage.

Bird Watchers America. Olin Sewall Pettingill, Jr., ed. 44 distinguished naturalists write about the best areas for birds in the United States and Canada. 1974 Ppb., 441 pp., ill., $4.50, (T.Y. Crowell).

The Birds of California, Arnold Small. Over 500 birds that are known to inhabit California are comprehensively described in this highly useful study. Explains seasonal movements and the habits of various species. 1974 Hb., 336 pp., ill., $12.50, (Winchester).

Bird Watcher's Book, John Gooders, ed. Describes (with illustrations) the ways to find and watch the seldom-seen species of birds. 1974 Hb., 173 pp., ill., $7.95, (David & Charles).

A Complete Guide to Birdfeeding, John V. Dennis. For those wishing to join the growing ranks of bird enthusiasts, here is a useful fund of information. Besides telling what kinds of foods to offer and describing various feeders, Dennis describes many species of birds, with their preferences in both. 1975, ill., $10.00, (Random House).

Field Guide to Western Birds, Roger T. Peterson. This famous guide is easy to use and interesting, and provides a wealth of information for birdwathcers and naturalists of all ages. 1961 Hb., & Ppb., 309 pp., ill., $6.95/$4.95, (Houghton Mifflin).

The Life and Lore of the Bird, Edward Armstrong. A fascinating look at birds and man's early mythology and beliefs about them. Armstrong has a personal knowledge of legend, mythology, folklore and tribal customs that is woven into these remarkable observations about birds. He describes the role of birds in divination, augury magic, the use of birds in sport, their feathers and finery, and their role in art and literature. 1975, 288 (oversize) pp., ill., $14.95, (Crown).

Bobsledding

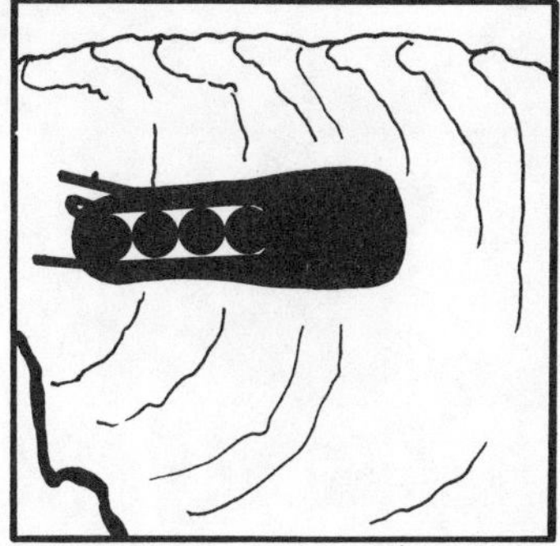

The sport of bobsledding has been called the "Champagne of Thrills" and it's easy to see why when one considers that today's four-man racing sleds shoot down steep, twisting bobruns at speeds of up to 90 miles an hour. Frank G. Menke, author of **The Encyclopedia of Sports,** has described coming down a bobsled course as "an experience combining the thrills of a roller coaster with those of being shot from a cannon."

Bobsled races are held on specially designed courses. Races are decided on the basis of the length of time that different teams take to complete the course. Only one sled is permitted on a course at a time. In championship events each sled makes four trips down the run, the combined time of the four heats constituting the official time for the race. All sleds and crews must conform to certain restrictions set down by the Federation Internationale de Bobsleigh et Tobogganing (F.I.B.T.) For example, the maximum weight of a four man sled and crew cannot exceed 630 Kg. (1389 pounds), or a two man sled 375 Kg. (827 pounds).

The origin of the sport dates back to the 1870s when a group of thrillseeking English and American vacationers conceived and developed the toboggan, with which they went hurtling down a course laid out in the mountains around St. Mortiz. When this thrill became too tame for these daredevils, they added sled-like runners to the toboggans. This produced far greater speeds, but the rudimentary nature of sleds and tracks caused them to go off course easily, causing many accidents and even some deaths.

In 1896 another group of devotees developed much heavier sleds and added ballast to help control them while increasing speeds. The new sleds were called "bob-sleds". This group soon formed its own organization, "The St. Moritz Bobsleigh Club" and mapped a course down the Swiss Alps called the Cresta Run. The big sleighs at the time carried five people and the original racing rules stipulated two of the passengers had to be women. Soon, however, the rules were changed to allow a stout man to replace the two women because there were no females who cared to risk travelling over the treacherous run in bobsleds.

As bobsled enthusiasts gradually developed features on their sleds to increase speeds, the Cresta Run proved too dangerous. A separate run built at St. Moritz in 1904 was the first to be engineered for speed with comparative safety. Others were built soon after, and by the outbreak of the Second World War there were more than 60 runs scattered through the mountains of Italy, Germany, France, Austria, Switzerland and other European countries.

Bobsledding (four-man) was part of the first Winter Olympics held in Chamonix, France in 1924. The US first entered the Olympic bobsled competition in 1928 at St. Moritz, and American crews piloted by Billy Fiske and J. Heaton finished first and second.

"It seems but a moment and the compact, hurtling machine that you and the sled have become is rumbling with an increasing roar and violence over what you thought was smooth ice. It banks and drops off into a new straight with a quickening pace—more noise, speed, higher banks, until you are fairly careening from one vertical ice wall to another, being thrown in all directions simultaneously." (Duffy)

The two-man bobsled competition was added to the Winter Olympic program in 1932 at Lake Placid, N.Y., where the US won both the four-man and two-man events. In succeeding Olympic Games, they have not been so successful, but they have taken scattered world championships.

The mile-and-a-half run built on Mount Van Hoevenburg, near Lake Placid, for the '32 Games, was the first and remains the only international bobrun in the Western Hemisphere. Maintained by the New York State Conservation Department, it is used for both racing and public riding. The Department maintains slower and safer sleds and furnishes experienced drivers for public riding. But the ride down is still a breathtaking experience.

The Exciting Run

Bobsleighing is to the "sliding" sports what Formula No. 1 Auto Racing is to sports on wheels. The most rudimentary of the sliding sports—tobagganing—is practiced on occasion by millions for the sheer enjoyment of feeling the wind and snow on a speedy dash straight down the hill with nothing to do but sit and hang on. In contrast, international bobsleighing is a physically and mentally demanding sport with a variety of dimensions practiced by only a few thousand. The few who overcome the obstacles of cost (both capital and training—a bobsleigh costs from $2,000 to $4,000 and training might require a trip to another country), time, and fear to try bobsleighing often are hooked for life. In spite of the probability of putting less than five minutes on the track on a typical day of bob-sport, they would not trade that five minutes for hours in any other discipline.

Why is this so? As one who has tried most speed sports and competed in several, I believe that it boils down mainly to the multi-dimensional aspects that other sports just cannot duplicate.

Imagine for a moment that you are at the top of a mile long chute, down which you are about to hurtle at speeds of up to 90 miles per hour in a seemingly uncontrolled fashion. The minute or so ahead of you will provide a fantastic variety of sensations, from being literally airborne on occasion to positions more upside down than right side up. Every two or three seconds you will fall off iced curves 10 to 30 feet high and into bouncing straights that batter you from every angle, all in the knowledge that you will have no rails or cable to assure your safe descent.

You have been checking over your metal and fiberglass sled, polishing and alligning its steel runners for maximum speed, checking the axles and steering mechanism for safety, and now your sled is lifted by eager hands into the slot behind the electric starting eye. You and your team-mates take up pushing positions. All is ominously silent as you start rocking the 500 pounds of metal back and forth, developing the rhythm that procedes the countdown to the instant when a roar emits from you and the crowd for that explosion towards the chute. You heave the sled into motion, and with track shoes digging like pistons into the ice, propel it with all your might and speed down the chute. At 15 mph and accelerating rapidly, 20 yards have passed and the sled is about to leave the starting grooves. The pilot pops into his seat, grabs for the steering ropes, and concentrates on the track ahead. The No. 2 man quickly moves in behind him, now it is your turn as No. 3 man to accordion into position after a final lunge at almost maximum speed. The brakeman swings in through the rear push bars, and you all shuffle delicately into racing position, hardly daring to move a muscle for fear of disturbing the equilibrium of the sled at this crucial stage. A skid or a tick into a side wall would destroy the momentum of this initial thrust, and gravity, the only accelerator you have, is just beginning to take hold.

It seems but a moment and the compact, hurtling machine that you and the sled have become is rumbling with an increasing roar and violence over what you thought was smooth ice. It banks and drops off into a new straight with a quickening pace—more noise, speed, higher banks, until you are fairly careening from one vertical ice wall to another, being thrown in all directions simultaneously. The high curves come at you and your head snaps forward as "G" forces push you down into the sled, face and vision distorted. Then you are floating, followed instantaneously by a slam into another wall, off which you ricochet down yet another straight that tears at your grip without let up. It is the longest yet shortest moment of your life. As you brake to a stop, you find that you are gasping for breath, aching and bruised from a pounding that you were totally unaware of on the way down.

To the pure thrill of such a ride, you add the excitement and challenge of competition, with its demands of strength, speed, coordination and concentration right from the 50 yard starting thrust through to the finish curve. If you are the pilot, add the kind of reflexes, judgment and nerves that allow you to find the fine balance between giving the sled its head, and steering the elusive line of maximum speed, flirting at times with a very real danger. Unlike all other dangerous speed sports, however, only bobsleighing does not require you to test your bravery against accelerator and brakes. The runs are designed to allow an all-out descent, and the results are solely determined by the initial thrust and the line of the sled on the way down. During the drive down, the pilot's challenged by the run—its bumpy straights, varied corners, changing ice conditions and incredibly swift changes. Perhaps change is the real key to the excitement in bobsledding. No other sport has such a ration of change. Maybe that is why it is called the King of Sports.

—Victor Emory

Victor Emory piloted Canada's Olympic and World Champion Bobsleigh teams in 1964 and 1965. He was Chef de Mission Adjoint for Canada's 1968 Winter Olympic team, and currently works as an independant consultant in tranportation and leisure fields.

For More Information

Here are a few addresses that may be helpful. Alice Bechel, Manager, Olympic Bobrun, Rt. 73, Lake Placid, N.Y. 12946. Saranac Lake Bobsled Club, Saranac Lake, New York. Keene Valley Bobsled Club, Keene Valley, New York. And the national office is: Bobsled, AAU House, 3400 West 86th St., Indianapolis, Ind. 46268.

Boccie

Boccie is an Italian variation of lawn bowling which is very popular in American communities with a high concentration of immigrants from that Mediterranean country. On almost any sunny afternoon in such communities, scores of Italian men gather around sand box like courts to roll balls, drink good wine and argue incessantly about techniques, games long passed, or whose ball is closest to the jack (often this must be precisely measured). Boccie courts are not standardized, but an average playing area is about 60 feet by 10 feet and enclosed by wooden plank sides a foot or so high. The court is most commonly of hard packed, sandy clay, with a trough about four inches deep at each end to prevent balls bowled too hard from rebounding into play off the end board. Eight balls 4½ inches in diameter are bowled, while a smaller 2¾ inch jack ball is used as a target. The eight larger balls are divided into two colors and in the past have been made of very heavy wood. Today composition balls are more common.

Two, four or eight can play at one time, and when eight compete, two stand at opposite ends of the court for each team and bowl in alternate directions. Once the starting side has been determined, a player from that team tosses out the jack, usually trying to put it near the far end of the court. Then the same player rolls his first ball underhanded as close to the jack as possible. The opposing side then bowls until they succeed in placing a ball closer to the jack. This procedure continues with partners and teams alternating until all the balls have been exhausted. A point is awarded for each ball closer to the jack than the opposing team's best ball. Twelve is a winning score unless the opponent has eleven, in which case the game is continued until one side has a two point advantage.

The Warm Afternoon Game

Near my father's home is a social club. The Italian-Americans who frequent this club call it a tavern, but it has a club license, is non-profit and more or less serves as a community center for the Italian section around Clifton, New Jersey. They have cheap drinks, good food and dances each Saturday night.

My father was nearly sixty when I was born, so by the time I was ten, he had retired and often took me with him to the club. It was dark inside, with amber hued light fighting through shaded windows, or falling weakly from a few bare bulbs high above the floor. There was a bar inside, at which the younger men would congregate, but my father and the other old men preferred to sit at heavy oaken tables near the back. They would nurse a glass of wine for half a day, play cards and swap stories. I'd listen to the colloquial Italian, missing a few words now and then, but enjoying all the tall tales. They could tell lies that would really open a kid's eyes, but it

Boccie is a game of friendship and comradeship in which being a spectator is almost as important as playing in a game. (Drennan)

was always for good fun. They laughed a lot, those old men that I loved.

Every so often a few of them would get up and troop outside to the boccie court in back of the club. Boccie is best played in the sunshine, or maybe with a bit of shade. The court I remember had grapevines growing on an arbor trellis over one end, a few tendrils even groping up the plank sides of the court. Two or four, sometimes even eight men would play at one time. Everybody was a friend, so it was never hard to choose up sides.

After dividing into teams, a few men would be left over and they'd watch and wait for the next game, terrible smelling Dinobili cigars clamped in their teeth. If there were enough spectators, they'd kill time until the next game by singing folk songs from the mountains of Italy. I can still hear the happy notes of *La Violeta* or *Cuel Mazzolin di Fiori.*

Each game started with one side throwing out the *pollina,* or target ball. Then the sides would alternate rolling heavy wooden balls down the court in an effort to come closer and closer to *pollina.* When all of the balls had been exhausted, the team with a ball closest to *pollina* would win and then defend their title against the next challengers. Sometimes two or more balls would be almost exactly the same distance from the *pollina,* causing a torrent of arguments to flood over the court. Even with a measuring rod, it would often be difficult to decide who had won.

After a few leisurely games, all the old men would go back into the tavern and toast victories and defeats. When my father won he would always have a cup of coffee with *grappa* in order to celebrate. When he lost, it would simply be *chianti,* but there would always be good fellowship and the warm feeling of being with friends.

—Dominick Nivioni

Dominick Nivioni is a student at Columbia Law School in New York City. In addition to boccie, he has a passion for translating Japanese short stories.

Bodybuilding

Bodybuilding is probably the least understood of sports, as well as one of the most maligned by the general public. And yet its devotees in the United States alone number in the hundreds of thousands. What attracts them to bodybuilding? Or perhaps more basic, what *is* the sport of bodybuilding?

Weightlifting, bodybuilding's ancestor, dates in the United States from the mid-1800's. In practicing their sport, competitive weightlifters soon found that as strength increased, so did general athletic ability and muscle size. This added muscle mass was considered relatively unimportant, however, until about 1920 when the legendary Bernar McFadden began sponsoring "perfect man" contests with substantial cash prizes. One early winner was an Italian immigrant gardener named Angelo Siciliano who later changed his name to Charles Atlas and became an American folk hero.

Beginning with 1940, the Mr. America contest has been held annually during the month of June under AAU auspices and in conjunction with the Senior National Weightlifting Championships. Winning the Mr. America title virtually insures an athlete of immortality with the bodybuilding public. The best known winner to date was a tall young Californian named Steve Reeves in 1947. Reeves made the Hercules type muscle movie internationally popular during the late 1950's and early 1960's. He still has almost godlike status among bodybuilders despite very infrequent public appearances.

In descending rank from Mr. America, the most coveted domestic titles include Mr. USA, Jr. Mr. America, Jr. Mr. USA, Mr. California (all the best bodybuilders live there) and perhaps Mr. Pacific Coast or Mr. East Coast. Younger bodybuilders compete for teenage versions of these titles. Internationally the Mr. Universe is most sought after, followed by the Mr. World title.

In competition, bodybuilders display their development with a posing routine. Judges rate them on muscle size, definition (absence of fat), symmetry (the proportional relationship between bodyparts), shape and general appearance. The winner usually has the best combination of these five factors. Special awards are given for the Most Muscular Man (this doesn't take into consideration shape, proportion or appearance), Best Arms, Chest, Back, Abdominals and Legs, as well as an occasional Best Poser trophy.

There are a wide variety of rationales for being a bodybuilder. The classic is to look at oneself as a master sculptor, molding a perfect flesh and bone statue. Few bodybuilders subscribe to this theory, though. Many will cite the sport as something they can excell at (due to God-given physical disadvantages, surprisingly few athletes actually can), or they might enjoy the adulation and admiration given them by rabid bodybuilding fans. Most bodybuilders, however, will say that they enjoy training for the sheer physical pleasure of feeling their bodies move under heavy loads. This movement leads to large muscle development, in which case competition becomes an excuse for even harder training and larger muscle gains.

Bodybuilding critics usually deny that it is even a sport. In actuality, though, bodybuilders are fantastically fit and usually are outstanding athletes in a variety of sports. They train harder and longer than most other athletes and also pay very strick attention to diet. Dale Adrian, the 1975 Mr. America, for example, exercised extremely hard five hours a day, seven days a week for several months prior to his victory. Few, if any, other sports can boast of such dedication or heavy training, and that's the reason we are bodybuilders.

—Grant Williams

Grant Williams is a long time commentator on the Iron Game. His articles appear frequently in **Iron Man, Muscular Development, Strength & Health** *and* **Muscle Mag International.**

The Steve Reeves I Know and Remember

Steve Reeves is universally known as the Hercules of the movies. He won Mr. America, Mr. World and Mr. Universe titles, yet few know much about him as a person. Who was he? How did he get started at bodybuilding? How did he train?

My association with Steve goes back over 30 years. In the '40s my Oakland, California gym was located near three high schools: Oakland, Fremont and Castlemont. Reeves attended Castlemont, one of the few schools of that era to offer weight training instruction. He began working out at school and also at home, but spent much of his free time touring local barbell gyms and trying to obtain all possible information about bodybuilding. During this period, he stopped at my gym and decided to train under my supervision, gaining 30 pounds of solid muscle in four months.

For two years Steve worked out with my instruction and encouragement. His progress continued to be outstanding and by the time he was eighteen, Reeves weighed a solid 203 pounds. In the opinion of many experts he could have won the Mr. America contest that year had he entered. His physique was already showing signs of the fine shape and muscularity that would make him the most famous bodybuilder of all time.

Steve graduated from Castlemont in 1944 at the height of World War II and promptly enlisted in the Army. At that time soldiers were being shipped overseas quickly and Reeves was no exception. After six short weeks of basic training he was in on some of the fighting in the Philippines where he earned the Combat Infantryman's Badge and several other awards. While there, however, he contracted a severe case of malaria which required a long period of hospitalization and resulted in a weight loss of over twenty pounds. After several recurrances, Steve was finally transferred from combat duty to the quartermaster corps. He finally ended up in Tokyo with General McArthur's occupation troops.

Steve was still recuperating from his malaria attacks in 1945 and was physically well below par. He had not had a bodybuilding workout in over a year, and with no available equipment, it didn't look like he would be able to train. But in typical Reeves "take the bull by the horns" fashion, he located an interpreter and the two went to a local foundry. With the aid of sketches and much hand waving Steve was able to have a 300 pound barbell set made up. With this crude equipment he began training again and it wasn't long before he had a regular gym set up and a number of other bodybuilders exercising with him. We kept in touch by mail and I was able to monitor his progress that way.

Finally in the fall of 1946, he returned home and was discharged. Without delay he was back in my gym training, but this time he was no longer a pupil. Instead we were workout partners, training diligently three times a week on a routine that included several exercises that Steve had invented. These sessions continued as regularly as clock work and were something we both looked forward to. I was improving and I could see Steve rapidly growing in size and shape. We never missed workouts, so I was surprised that December when Steve didn't show for one of our regular Saturday sessions. I was extremely puzzled because he was in such top condition that he simply could not have been ill. I found out the reason when he showed up for our Tuesday workout and gave me two huge trophies inscribed "Mr. Pacific Coast of 1946" and said, "Merry Christmas, Ed."

Telling only his mother, Steve had secretly flown with one of my other gym members to Portland, Oregon. He left on Friday, won the title and then returned late Monday. I was quite surprised by the unexpected manner in which Reeves entered this major physique contest, but certainly not startled by his victory. He was in great condition! That's how Steve is, though. He never sought publicity and didn't even desire any advance buildup prior to his Mr. America victory.

Early in January of 1947, a Mr. California contest was held. Steve didn't enter, even though he would have had an easy win. Having won the larger Mr. Pacific Coast title a month earlier, he did not think he would be eligible until it was too late to enter. He did, though, retain his Mr. Pacific Coast title and copped trophies at that event for Best Arms, Best Legs and Best Chest. And of course he also won the Mr. America title at Chicago later that year.

Many bodybuilding fans have asked me about Steve Reeves' early years. He was born in Montana on January 21, 1926 and is of Welsh, Irish and German decent. His father died when Steve was a year and a half old, so Reeves attended boarding schools and spent summers on his uncle's ranch in Montana. Steve learned to ride when he was three years old and is an excellent horseman. I believe that the great amount of riding Steve has done is unquestionably a factor that contributed to his small waist and trim hips. These characteristics are found in a majority of active cowboys.

Steve and his mother moved to Oakland, when Reeves was approaching his teens. To do his share in helping out his mother financially, Steve had a newspaper route. He was proud of being the only one among the carriers who could pedal his bike up the steep East Oakland hills with a full load of papers. The rest were obliged to walk and push their loaded bikes up the hills, but Steve always made it a point to pedal up. He gives much credit to this strenuous bike exercise for his early calf shape, and his calves are truly exceptional in size and contour. I would say that even as a boy Steve was physique conscious because he would pedal that bike in a manner designed to provide his calves with the greatest amount of stimulation.

One of Steve's greatest assets was his mother. She was an indispensible and invaluable aid to his bodybuilding progress.

Not only did she encourage his athletic endeavors, but Goldie inevitably cooperated with him in the meals she prepared. They were always wholesome and nourishing. Steve is especially fond of steak, salads, vegetables and fresh fruits. He consumed more than a quart of milk a day when I knew him and he never smoked, drank alcoholic beverages, or ate any products containing devitalized white flour or refined white sugar. He substituted honey for sugar. As a result of this healthy diet, Reeves' teeth are a dental advertisement, totally free of cavities.

Our training program was a very strenuous one. We adhered to a three day per week schedule and had no favorite exercises. Instead, we employed a broad variety of exercises in an effort to arrive at a well balanced program. Steve did not endeavor to specialize in competitive lifts, but the very heavy poundages that he employed in bodybuilding exercises with high repetitions provided plenty of evidence that he was exceptionally powerful.

Steve and I used a very strict type of exercise form in all of our movements. We did each movement from complete extension to complete contraction, no swinging, no bouncing and no cheating of any kind. It did not matter to us if we could only do five or six reps with our heaviest weights, so long as these were done in perfect style. Some of Steve's poundages might seem light to a modern bodybuilder with sloppy form, but in 1947 and with strict style, the weights Steve used were considered phenomenal for his bodyweight.

I will briefly describe one of the routines Steve and I would use. We started with exercises for the deltoids of the shoulders to attain a wide look in that area and followed these with movements for the pectorals of the chest. Then we moved to the latissimus dorsi of the upper back (this gives a "V" shaped and tapered apperance to the torso), the triceps and biceps of the upper arm, the thighs and calves of the legs and even the neck. As mentioned before, we always did a variety of exercises to promote all around development.

Steve and I had many good times together outside the gym, too. During the warm summer months many Bay Area bodybuilders would gather at Sunny Cove Beach in Alameda, just a short distance from Oakland. There we would bask in the sun and swim either in the surf or at an adjacent pool. Jack LaLanne and I handbalanced a lot, while my wife Alyce and many of the local barbell enthusiasts talked and exchanged views on bodybuilding. Steve was always one of the most ardent in all of these discussions.

During the winter months we had an occasional Sunday meeting at the local ice skating rink. Wearing a ski sweater and with his wide shoulders, "V" shape and hips of less than 36 inches, Steve was always the main attraction of our group. The girls did double takes as they passed by him, and after a while they seemed to pass by him quite frequently. He was truly an All-American Boy.

Reeves was always inclined to be a bit modest, but he was also very cooperative, especially in the way he encouraged youngsters in bodybuilding. I knew there would be nothing to stop Steve from going on to bigger and better things, and of course no one was more deserving of this than he. Steve was intelligent and had both high ideals and a conscientious nature. I was confident he would go on to accomplish a tremendous amount of good in behalf of the physical culture movement.

I knew that one day Steve would leave Oakland. The southern beaches had more to offer him. He no longer needed instruction and opportunities in television and the film industry were more plentiful in Los Angeles. I wished him well and he was off to find his fortune.

Regular strenuous exercise with weights will gradually build more and more muscle tissue until one eventually reaches Mr. America proportions. (Duke)

Alyce and I stayed in touch with his folks, and we often saw Steve in later years when he would drop over to his folks' house with many of his friends. He liked to get into the kitchen and help with the broiling of steaks or making of a tossed salad, as these were his favorite foods. I remember how appreciative he was when we gave him a blender to mix high protein health drinks.

Steve went on to win the Mr. Universe, Mr. World and other titles and later toured with the stage play Kismet. His first movie break came in "Athena" with Jane Powell and Debbie Reynolds, and he went on to star in 16 films, his most popular being "Hercules." Steve once had his own bodybuilding studio and later raised Red Angus cattle on his ranch in Oregon. He currently breeds and trains Morgan horses on his ranch near San Diego.

The last direct contact I had with Steve was when I called him and told him our son Bart was driving his way and would stop by his place in Oregon. Bart spent ten days with Steve and his wife and to this day he talks of it as being some experience to stay at Mr. Hercules' place.

I have always said that Steve's physique was much like a drawing of Little Abner, the sort of All-American ideal physique admired by the general public. He had the healthy mind and body that made up the one and only Steve Reeves. We've yet to see another like him, the original Mr. Hercules.

—Ed Yarick

Ed Yarick trained four Mr. Americas and is noted as one of the most knowledgeable authorities of all time in the field of bodybuilding.

For More Information

There are several magazines covering bodybuilding. However, we feel that two stand out ahead of all the others.

Iron Man, Box 10, Alliance, Neb., 69301. Published bi-monthly at $5.00 per year. On the cover it says "The quality magazine for all men interested in physical superiority." The magazine not only shows what the guys look like when they blow themselves up but also how to get there.

Muscular Development, P.O. Box 1707, York, Pa. 17405. Bi-monthly at $4.50 carries authoritative articles and up to date contest results.

Here are eight good books on body building. All books are available from World Publications, Box 366, Mountain View, Calif. 94040 at the price listed* plus 25 cents each postage. Write for a complete list.

Body Building for Everyone, Lou Ravelle. Bodybuilding, says the author, is for everyone – both sexes and all ages. Step by step he explains the mysteries and secrets of physical development, the principles of weight gaining and slimming, muscle building and body contouring. 1965 Hb., 120 pp., ill., $5.95 (Emerson).

Here's Power For You, David Manners. Four complete body building courses with barbells, dumbells, pulleys and calisthenics – including corrective exercises with special instructions for children and adults, the overweight and underweight. 1975 Ppb., 128 (oversize) pp., ill., $3.25 (Arco).

Muscle Building for Beginners, Fallon, Michael, and Sanders. Has good information for beginners as well as advanced body builders. Clear drawings and photos and concise descriptions make this book a sure bet. 1960 Ppb., 110 pp., ill., $.95 (Arco).

Here are some good weight training books

Weight Lifting & Weight Training, George Kirkley. One of the world's foremost competitive lifting coaches covers weight training from its three crucial aspects – as a competitive sport, as a means of improving health and physique, and to improve one's ability at other sports. 1966 Ppb., 160 pp., ill., $1.25 (Arco).

The Complete Book of Weight Training, Bill Reynolds. Acknowledged international authority offers guide for weight training for the athlete or even the man on the street who wants to get in shape for a camping/hiking trip. Covers how to train correctly, all the various training techniques, and then offers training programs for every sport or activity imaginable, from cycling to fencing. 1976 Hb., ill., $5.95 (World Publications).

Weight Training, Dr. Frank Ryan. The fundamental goal of weight training is the development of coordinated power. Power, the ability of a group of muscles to run faster, jump higher, or throw further, is the heart of every sport. Dr. Ryan explains the process of physical development by using weights. Profusely illustrated. 1969. Hb., 84 pp., ill., $8.95 (Viking).

Sports Illustrated Training with Weights, Robert B. Parker and John R. Marsh. Theory of weight training and basic exercises for each muscle group. Designed for the novice weightlifter with minimum equipment. 1974 Hb. & Ppb., 96 pp., ill., $4.95/$1.95 (Lippincott).

Physical Fitness Through Weight Training, Bernard A. Taylor and M.C. Easton. A textbook-like presentation of weight training programs. The author discusses the muscle system, regular workouts and ladder programs for self-improvement. Drawings and photos show the proper exercise positions. 1975 Ppb., 132 pp., ill., $4.95 (Kendell-Hunt).

Body Surfing

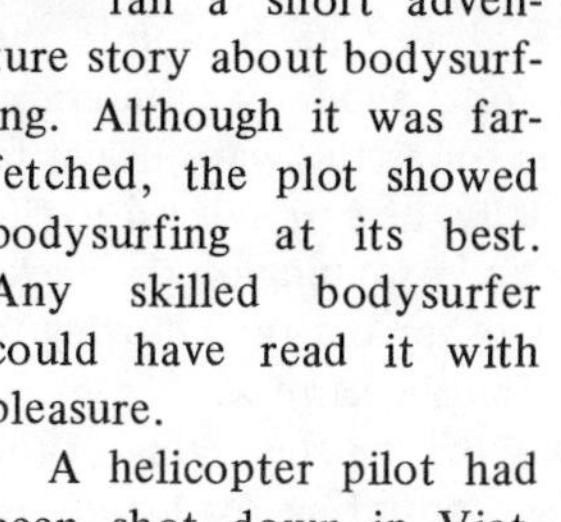

Many years ago, one of the surf magazines ran a short adventure story about bodysurfing. Although it was far-fetched, the plot showed bodysurfing at its best. Any skilled bodysurfer could have read it with pleasure.

A helicopter pilot had been shot down in Vietnam. He had just managed to crash land his crippled chopper at the end of a rocky point, a few hundred yards from a platoon of GIs who were camped near the sandy beach in from the point. Between him and the GIs were some Viet Cong. They knew they had him trapped and they were closing in for the kill.

Fortunately for the pilot, the point was catching a good swell. The waves would break way out on the point and then peel off evenly and powerfully all the way in to the beach. Fortunately, too, the pilot had a pair of swim fins with him for use in ocean rescues.

Seeing his only chance for survival, he stripped down and belly-crawled over the the waters' edge. He waited behind a rock for a good wave, and then dived in and sprinted for a take-off. The water around him was immediately riddled with Viet Cong bullets.

"The first wave is big and clean, but you know there will be bigger and better in the set. So you kick hard out to it and drive up its face, launching yourself high in the air like a leaping salmon." (Surfer magazine)

But when he caught the wave right on the edge of the peeling break, the bullets suddenly stopped. The Viet Cong lowered their rifles and stared in amazement as he flew across the wave like a seal at play.

Initially he rode safety-first, staying high on the wave and passing up chances to play. But half way in to the beach, he faced a steep bowling section that triggered his old instincts. Throwing caution to the winds, he pressed his back into the wave and extended both his arms for a sudden acceleration.

He stalled at the end of the section as the wave began to hollow out for the inside lineup. Finally, he surrendered to the exuberant play of energy, climbing and dropping on the waveface, doing barrel rolls one after the other and then moving to the top and going over the falls into the shorebreak.

He stayed under water as he took off his fins, lying in the shallows. Then he was up on his feet, sprinting for his life to the GIs near the jungle edge. Finally the Viet Cong woke up. Bullets whistled around him and kicked up showers of sand.

Of course, he made it to the cover of the jungle (the hero always has to survive.) As GIs congratulated him, he couldn't tell if his elation was more from relief or from the excitement of the wave. His skill had saved him. He thanked the day that he learned how to really ride a wave instead of just getting pushed along by the white water like the tourists who write home about their "bodysurfing."

The Wedge

The Wedge is a lucky accident. When the jetties at the mouth of the harbor channel at Newport Beach were built, the North jetty was aligned so that it forms a perfect reflecting wall for incoming swells. They pile into the jetty from the north, and peel back off of it at the same angle. The reflected part of the swell crosses the still incoming part of the swell, pushing the water up into a mountainous peak – the Wedge. It pushes higher and steeper on the shallowing bottom, seems to waver momentarily in a delicate balance of enormous weight and power, then pitches forward to pour its thunderous waterfall into its lower slopes. After dropping like a pile-driver, the white water spews up jumbling and explosive, laced with sand stripped from the bottom. The bodysurfer tries to kick into the wave just before it breaks, and fly across the overhanging cliff as far as he can before tucking into it and diving back out into the safety behind the white and brown explosion.

If you don't get clear, if you don't manage to go "out the back door," you can have a rough time. Getting caught in the white water has been compared to getting tumbled in a washing machine, but anyone who has had the experience will tell you that it's nowhere near that tame. You feel like a rag doll shaken by an angry giant. You can get jammed onto the bottom, and held there, rolling and tumbling, until the wave spends its power on the steep beach.

It's even worse if you get stalled at the top of the wave on your takeoff. You get pitched out with the lip of the wave into a helpless freefall. On really big days you might hit the wave face going down, and bounce like a skipping stone, or, if you catch an arm or leg, you'll go down in a bumpy sprawling tumble.

Once you've been caught there's no way out. You might have sprinted out for a take-off, you might have had the air knocked out of you, you might be desperately in need of a lungful of air, but you have to surrender to the power of the wave. If you panic and try fighting for the surface, you just waste precious oxygen and put yourself in greater jeopardy.

Obviously, this is a sport for good swimmers with steady nerves. Few could handle getting mauled and whomped by heavy water and even fewer would want to. What is it about the sport that keeps the dedicated handful coming back for more? Perhaps the best way to answer that is to put on a pair of fins and swim out there on a good day:

You're close enough to the jetty to hear the guttering of the surge in the big black rocks. It's been a long time since the last set. The sun is hot and heavy. It sends shoals of glitters scattering over the blue water. There's a soft feeling in the pit of your stomach, soft and fluttery with fear. Just about when you knew it was due, you hear shouts and whistles from the jetty, you see tanned bodies standing up and pointing. Kicking up out of the water on your fins, craning your neck, you can see a big set moving in. It's time to face the Wedge again.

The first wave is big and clean, but you know there will be bigger and better in the set. So you kick hard out to it, and drive up its face, launching yourself high in the air like a leaping salmon. Before you drop back into the water, you make a mental note that the third looks biggest.

You swim over the second and then size up your wave. It is awesome. You can feel a "What am I doing here?" current of fear interwoven with a fantastic current of desire. You flip over on your back and kick in to where experience tells you to be, timing it so that you're lifted, swooping upward to the peak, just as it starts to throw out. With one powerful scissors kick, and one quick arm stroke, you're in it, with the trough of the wave an incredible depth below you and the open wall to your left–a cavernous glistening bowl. You drop your left arm and shoulder, press your back flat against the face and start planing across the top of the wave, racing like a seal just in front of the peeling break. The juice of the wave, its power and speed, triggers your own juices, flooding your whole being with the luminous intensity of adrenalin.

Just as you sense that you will go over the falls if you stay with it, you duck into the face, and tuck out behind, out the back door. You are breathless with ecstasy. With luck you might be able to get out again for one of the last waves of the set. You put your head down and sprint like mad.

—Ian Jackson

Ian Jackson has bodysurfed for several years at such popular spots as the Wedge at Newport Beach, Boomer Beach in La Jolla, Calif. and the Banzai Pipeline in Hawaii.

For More Information

You won't find very many bodysurfing books at your local bookstore. In fact, you'll be lucky to find any books on the subject. Here is one excellent manual, though. It is available from World Publications, Box 366, Mountain View, Calif. 94040 at the price listed* plus 25 cents postage. Write for a complete list.

The Art of Body Surfing, Robert Gardner. This tough, spirited sport calls for sound skills and technique and good judgment and decision-making ability. This well written guide mixes anecdotes with information to help you ride the waves successfully. History and suggestions on the best surfing beaches. 1972 Ppb., 83 pp., ill., $2.95 (Chilton).

Boomeranging

Boomerang throwing is the skill of throwing a curved piece of wood, designed to amazingly precise aerodynamic characteristics by some unknown genius thousands of years ago, in such a way as to make it go out, up, away, down, back, and to land at your feet. Lorin L. Hawes, Ph.D., of Mudgeeraba, Australia, maker of the famous Hawes Boomerangs, calls it "one of the best time-wasters known to man." It is all of that, and once you've tried it, you'll be hooked forever!

Traceable back over forty centuries and into many lands, boomerang throwing holds the same fascination for today's sportsman as it did for his ancient counterpart. Although modern technology has improved the boomerang by the use of durable materials and mass production, the basic design of this archaic missile remains essentially unaltered and almost universally recognized the world over.

This well-known artifact of early man should not be thought of as requiring great skill or long training to master. In fact, the basics can be acquired by most adults in a short time.

Most failures are based on two errors: 1) The boomerang is not properly made. Be sure you buy (or make) one that is capable of returning. (Any boomerang by Bemco, Gerrish, Hawes, Silady, Timbery, or Urban *can* be made to return, and there is no doubt other good makers of whom I am unaware.) 2) Sailing the Boomerang like a Frisbee. This will result in a steep climb and a precipitous descent, often with fatal (to the Boomerang) consequences.

Here's how to throw it properly: First, grasp the Boomerang rather loosely close to either end, using only three or four fingers of your right hand. Make sure the flat side is toward your palm.

Second, see which way the wind is blowing and plan to throw into the wind but slightly to the right. (If the wind is brisk, put your Boomerangs away and get out your throwing knives or your kite. Most Boomerangs don't perform well in wind much over 5 mph unless they are fairly heavy.)

Third, angle your Boomerang to the right of vertical, about 15 to 30 degrees or so, aim straight at the horizon, and throw the Boomerang. Release it at about shoulder height.

Fourth, give it a flip, sort of like cracking a whip, as it rolls off your index finger. *Spin* is a lot more important than speed, and is a key part of the throw.

If the four ingredients, direction into the wind, angle with respect to vertical, elevation of the throw, and spin, are mixed together in the right proportions, you will be rewarded by a lovely, soaring, swooping flight that brings the Boomerang back to you, descending to the ground in a gentle hover to land at your feet.

—John F. Moe, M.D.

John Moe is actively involved in many sports including boomeranging. He also has a mail order business called Flying Things and is writing **The Boomerang Book.**

About The Flight

In a successful Boomerang flight the missle will swoop forward on a curve to the left. On the outward flight the Boomerang spins in a vertical position and at about its maximum range, gradually tips to the right and finally assumes a horizontal position parallel to the ground for the remainder of its return journey.

Since the Boomerang has an efficient airfoil, a slight wind affects its flight. Always throw the Boomerang into the wind and if it lands to your left, turn to your right slightly for the next throw. Conversely, if the Boomerang lands in front or on your right, make a correction in the direction of throw by turning slightly to the left.

The parabolic flight of the Boomerang is a beautiful thing to witness, as it swerves to the left, and then soars aloft like a bird to come swooping back in a long volplane to land at the thrower's feet. Although the flight of the Boomerang has been generally described, the magic stick can be made to perform a bag full of other antics, such as throwing two at once.

An excellent competitive game to develop accuracy in the point of return is played by the player standing in the center of a target composed of concentric numbered rings marked on the ground of a playing field.

After the return flight has been accomplished, and some proficiency gained, great sport can be had by throwing at targets: another Boomerang in flight, a burlap sack filled with straw, or gas-filled balloons suspended in the air. If you do miss the target, the Boomerang comes back to you like a trained Eagle, wheeling on the breeze ready for another flight.

To hit a target or game close to the ground the Boomerang may be inclined slightly to the left of the vertical plane at the instant of release. This position will cause the Boomerang to swoop low to the ground and then up and around on its return flight.

Almost any object, be it a rabbit hiding behind a stump or a pheasant on the wing, is a fit mark for the flying stick. When you get your Boomerang and have mastered the simple art of throwing it, you will have been introduced to a sport as old as the hills, but still as interesting as the day it was born.

Although the Boomerang is a source of great enjoyment, you must remember that it is not a toy. Initial flights by the inexperienced should not be attempted in an area where injury or damage can result. Under normal conditions, a five ounce Boomerang has a range of about 100 yards in circular flight. A high wind may carry it greater distances and due caution should be exercised in such circumstances.

—John F. Moe, M.D.

For More Information

There isn't an official national boomerang organization, but several people are involved in promoting it. Boomerangs, 4885 S.W. 78th Ave., Portland, Oregon 97225 is run by Col. Gerrish. Since 1920 he has consistently tried to promote boomeranging as a national pastime. Resident Associates, Smithsonian Institution, Washington D.C. 20560 also can provide information. And the Smithsonian does sponsor boomerang-throwing tournaments annually. They are normally held in mid-May and are open to anyone who wants to enter. Flying Things, 3500 Lafayette Road, Indianapolis, Ind., 46222 imports boomerangs from Australia and can send a price list on request.

Very little has been written on the sport of boomeranging. Here are two offerings. Both are available from World Publications, Box 366, Mountain View, Calif. 94040 at the price listed* plus 25 cents each postage.

The Boomerang Book, John Moe, M.D. The fine art of boomeranging is clearly described in this brand new book. With practice, one can expect the boomerang to come back every time. Covers the history, holds, angles, throws, and various boomerangs available. 1976 Ppb., $2.00, (World Publications).

Backyard Games, Nikki Schultz. Contains a section on boomeranging, including how to make your own boomerang, how to throw a boomerang, and different games and boomerang contests. Also describes over 20 other backyard games, from archery to marbleshooting, volleyball to pogo stick and stilt contests. 1975 Ppb., 96 (oversize) pp., ill., $1.95, (Grosset & Dunlap).

Bowfishing

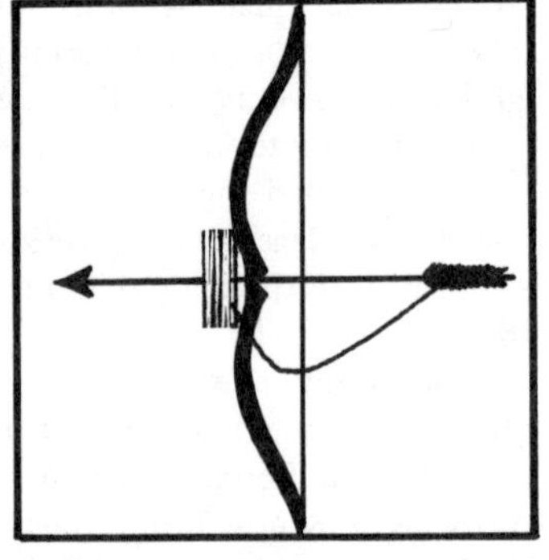

Bowfishing for rough fish is an enjoyable activity, open to the owner of archery equipment. In the past 10 or 12 years, this new fast-growing sport has gained thousands of enthusiasts, who find it a new source of excitement when the regular game seasons are closed. Non-hunting archers also enjoy is as an interesting variation from target and field shooting.

For most archers, big game hunting actually occupies a very small part of the year. Unless a bowman can travel from state to state, the best he can expect, as far as big game, is one or two hits a year. The small game hunter, on the other hand, has something to hunt everyday. Scrap fish are classified as small game, and available species are to be found almost everywhere in the country. In fresh water, carp, suckers, buffalo, squawfish, dogfish and gar are most commonly hunted, while archers who live near salt water have innumerable small food species available, as well as sting rays, skates, barracuda, and small sharks.

Bowfishing is not only easy and exciting, but inexpensive as well. You can obtain a top quality outfit for about $5.00, not counting a bow, of course. Such an outfit consists of a special reel filled with strong line, a weighted bow, and others have a special bracket which allows the reel to be instantly attached or detached from the bow. The reel operates much like a stationary spinning reel, and has a small catch which keeps line from peeling off too soon, when making close shots at a sharp, downward angle.

Large scrap fish can be hunted with bow and arrow in water up to 15 feet in depth, but one must compensate for the effect of light refraction by aiming up to a foot under the fish.

Fish weighing five pounds, or more, often roll when hit and can easily break off wooden, or hollow, glass shafts. For this reason bowfishing arrows are made of solid fiberglass. It takes a hearty fish to break one of these shafts. Another advantage of the solid, glass arrow is its weight, which makes it possible to shoot accurately through 10 to 15 feet of water. These arrows are also usually equipped with rubber or plastic fletching, which saves the archer valuable time that was formerly spent in straightening out matted feathers. Usually, the barbed harpoon head is not fastened permanently to the arrow. The line from the reel is threaded through a small hole in the arrow shaft, just ahead of the nock, run down to the forward end of the arrow, and tied through another hole in the head. This puts the drag of the line on the back-end of the arrow—so, when a hit is made, the loosely fitting point, with line attached, stays in the fish, while the shaft is towed along behind.

Sometimes, bypassing the bow reel provides very good sport, especially when large fish, such as sharks, or alligator gar, are shot, from a boat. Take a fishing rod of the type ordinarily used for the fish to be caught. Pull 15 or 20 yards of line out through the rod guides, and coil it, carefully, in a bucket or on the bottom of the boat. Then attach the end of the line to the harpoon arrow. When a hit is made, the bow is laid aside, the rod is quickly picked up, and the fish is played in the same manner as it if were hooked in the mouth.

Where can you go to bowfish? You'll find hot fishing spots close to your home–the local ponds, streams, bayous, backwaters, lagoons, irrigation canals and bays are good bets. Many such waters, while not containing game fish, harbor a host of rough and ready giants, just waiting to be taken. An important aspect of this sport is that the taking of these trash fish lends a real aid in the conservation of "respectable" game fish–as well as being great fun for the bow fisherman.

Perhaps the species that furnish the most sport, for the inland archer, are the ubiquitous carp and suckers, which are found throughout the States and Canada. When the first warm days of spring and early summer arrive these fish make their spawning runs into shallow marshes and up small streams. Plenty of action awaits the archer who is on the spot when the carp, or suckers, are at the peak of their spawning. For best success with these fish, shooting should be done in the middle of the day, when the sun is high. The fish are nearer the surface during these hours. Also, they cannot see the bowfisher as well, with the sun silvering the surface of the water. Polaroid sunglasses will help the bow fisherman, especially when there is a breeze rippling the water, since they eliminate surface glare.

Bowfishing can be done from almost any type of boat, but wading is also productive. When wading on a fairly calm day, you can see clearly about 30 feet around you.

The arrow must be aimed low, often a foot underneath the fish–to correct the effect of light refraction. This compensation varies with the angle of the shot. A little experience, with a few missed shots, is the best way to gain proper judgment.

One of the most exciting ways to spend an afternoon is with a few friends, your bowfishing tackle, and of course the cooperation of the local carp population. Remember too, that many so-called scrap fish are excellent table fare. Suckers and carp taken from clean waters are very tasty filleted and smoked, and the fish that are not suitable for eating make excellent fertilizer for flower or vegetable plots.

–Ernie Lalonde

Ernie Lalonde has been actively involved in bowfishing for 10 years.

For More Information

All magazines, organizations, and equipment sources are listed under archery and Bowhunting.

There aren't very many bowfishing books around, in fact, you'll be lucky to find just one. But here are some books that have excellent chapters or sections on bowfishing. Both are available from World Publications, Box 366, Mountain View, Calif. 94040 at the price listed* plus 25 cents each postage.

Bowhunter's Digest, C.R. Learn. This is a veritable encyclopedia of bowhunting, and has a good chapter on bowfishing, which explains the how-to's in simple English and includes excellent instructions for making your own bowfishing arrow points. Contains 27 equally good chapters on all facets of bowhunting. 1974 Ppb., 287 (oversize) pp., ill., $6.95, (Digest Books).

Bow Hunter's Guide, Russell Tinsley. An expert bowhunter explores every aspect of this sport, and includes a good chapter on the art of fishing with bow and arrow. 1975 Ppb., 192 (oversize) pp., ill., $5.95, (Follet).

Bow Hunting

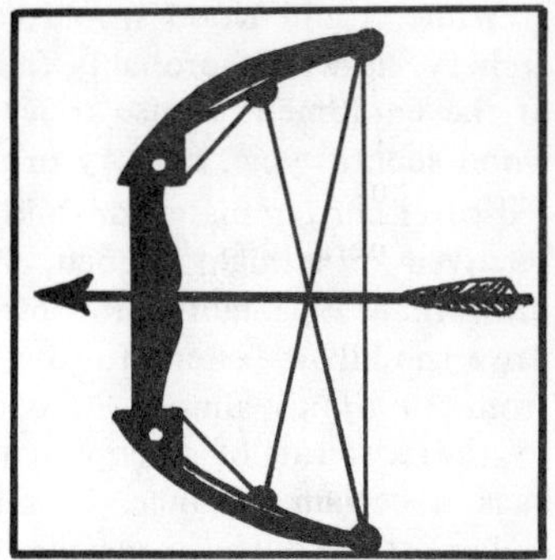

The revival of bowhunting as a popular sport in America was due, in large part, to four men. The first of these were Maurice and Will Thompson, brothers who fought for the South in the Civil War. At the war's end they returned to their Georgia plantation, only to find it in ruins. Maurice had been severely wounded in the fighting and was advised by his doctor to live in the open air, if possible. The brothers had no means of livelihood, and being ex-Confederates, firearms were denied them. They took to the woods, where they lived chiefly on game killed with bows and arrows, which they had learned to make and use in their youth.

In 1877 a collection of Maurice's writings, based on their life in the woods, was published in his book, **The Witchery of Archery**. This fascinating volume proved very popular, and even now it is as interesting and entertaining as when it was written. These writings did a great deal toward awakening an interest in the sport of archery in this country.

The second pair of men to give impetus to American archery hunting were Dr. Saxton Pope and Arthur Young. Pope and Young were certainly influenced by the earlier writings of Maurice and Will Thompson, a fact which Dr. Pope acknowledges in his own writings. In 1911, it became the lot of Dr. Pope to meet and help care for a small, emaciated fellow named Ishi, last survivor of the Yana Indians of California. In turn, Ishi taught his benefactor many of the old Indian skills, not the least of which was the making of bows and arrows, and their use in stalking game.

Arthur Young had learned archery from Will Compton, who in turn had learned it during many years spent among the Sioux Indians. These three, Dr. Pope, Will Compton, and Arthur Young gravitated together, through their mutual interest in archery, and shot with Ishi until his death in 1916.

In the years following, Dr. Pope and Art Young made many hunts together. Notable among these was the taking of five grizzly bears in Wyoming. Three of these bears, the first grizzlies to be killed by modern archers, were mounted, and became a representative group of this species in the California Academy of Science. Young also made two trips to Alaska, where he achieved such feats as bagging the first Kodiak bear, and the first Dall sheep ever to fall to a modern American bowman.

Dr. Pope wrote of their adventures in a volume entitled **Hunting With the Bow and Arrow**. This book, first published in 1923, is probably the finest work yet written on archery hunting, and was unquestionably the single most important inspiration in turning thousands of sportsmen to the use of the bow as a hunting weapon.

Today, bow hunting is an exciting sport that has captured the imagination of a large number of outdoor enthusiasts. Since many game areas are closed to the use of firearms, there is little doubt that archery will become an increasingly popular activity in the years to come. Bows may be used in any hunting season set for firearms. In addition, certain seasons are set for bowhunting, only.

While Robin Hood would certainly approve of interest in archery, he would probably find it difficult to recognize some of the equipment in use today. Bows, traditionally made of wood such as yew, hickory or ash, are, now, usually constructed of either laminated or solid fiberglass. Bows may be either recurved or straight limbed. The recurved bow is easier to draw than a straight limb bow of the same weight, and will drive the arrow faster. Hunting bows come in various weights, from 30 up to almost 80 pounds. The term weight refers to the amount of energy required to draw the bowstring back a certain distance. It is most important that the new archer start with a weight he can handle comfortably. Bowstrings are usually made of dacron, and should be waxed and examined regularly. A bowstring must be heavy enough for the weight of the bow, and an extra string always carried. If a bowstring breaks, the bow may break as well. To keep bows and bowstrings in top condition, store both in an area where the humidity is not too low and the temerpature is fairly constant.

Arrows may be wood, fiberglass, or aluminum. They should be matched, in stiffness, to the weight of the bow. A mismatched set will give poor performance. Arrow length depends on the length of the shooter's bow arm, but they are, generally, 26-28 inches in length. The nock of the arrow is the slotted tip into which the string fits. The fletching is a set of three feathers attached to the shaft just forward of the nock, which spins the arrow, thus making it fly true. A variety of heads are available, according to their use. A wide, two-bladed broadhead is generally the accepted head used in the taking of big game. For small game and birds, a blunt is usually used. It should be noted that broadheads must be razor sharp before being used for big game hunting. When hunting, the bow must have a draw weight of at least 40 pounds, and the arrow must be a broadhead of at least ¾ inch width.

Arrows may be carried in a back quiver, side quiver, or a bow quiver. Most bowhunters use a bow quiver, which carries anywhere from 4 to 12 arrows, and is mounted directly to the bow. Besides being convenient, it eliminates excess arm movement in nocking an arrow on the string.

A wide variety of accessories, such as sights, armguards, and gloves complete the modern archery package. In areas exclusively set aside for bowhunting, camouflage clothing may be worn.

—**Ernie Lalonde**

With 10 years of experience, Ernie Lalonde has a good knowledge of bowhunting.

For More Information

Several magazines of interest to the bowhunter can be found under archery. But there is one publication just on bowhunting. It is the *Bowhunter,* Box 5377, Fort Wayne, Ind. 46805. and is published bi-monthly at $5.00 per year. Very well done publication with a lot of good advice in every issue.

The Professional Bowhunters Society, 901 North 9th, Clinton, Ind. 47842 has one goal—to upgrade, promote and preserve the sport. And they mean it.

Hunting stands are becoming very popular. Woodland Hunting Equipment, Box 5202, Texarkana, Tex. 75501 makes some good ones. Free information on request. Werner Schmiesing, Taxidermist, Box 199, Paris St., Minster, Ohio 45865 has a free illustrated brochure and prices on mounting and tanning, rugs. Rush's Lakeview Ranch, 2905 Harrison Ave., Butte, Mont. 59701 offers some interesting hunting trips for deer and elk. Bowhunting Suppliers, 2227 Lincoln, Cedar Falls, Iowa 50613 has a lot of interesting things in their mail order catalog.

Here are some of the better books on bowhunting. All are available from World Publications, Box 366, Mountain View, Calif. 94040 at the price listed* plus 25 cents postage.

Bowhunter's Digest, D.R. Learn. Probably the most complete book on archery and bowhunting available today. 28 big chapters cover how to hunt, advanced hunting, everything you need to know to build your own bows and arrows, small and big game hunting, hunting calls and practice drills. 1974 Ppb., 288 (oversize) pp., ill., $6.95, (Digest Books).

Hunting with Bow and Arrow, Laycock and Bauer. The definitive work on bow hunting, packed with accurate illustrations and clear explanations of hunting game of all sizes. 1965 Hb., 112 pp., ill., $3.95, (Arco).

Bow Hunter's Guide, Russell Tinsley. An expert bow hunter explores every aspect of this fascinating and challenging sport. The author tells—and shows—the reader how to select equipment, shoot a hunting bow, stalk big game as well as small, how to hunt birds and even how to fish with a bow and arrow. 1975 Ppb., 192 (oversize) pp., ill., $5.95, (Follet).

Bow Hunting for Big Game, Keith Schuyler. Advice for those who already have some experience with the bow, covering effective technique and equipment. 1974 Hb., 256 pp., ill., $8.95, (Stackpole).

Bowling

Rip Van Winkle thought he heard thunder rolling down the valley when the little people played their secret game of bowling in the early 19th century. Today's bowling alleys are still noisy, exciting places filled with the crash of balls and pins and the enthusiastic voices of bowlers. Fortunately, "thunder" need not hinder this game and you do not have to be three feet tall to play! Modern bowling establishments are indoors, designed for all-day, all-weather playing for people of all ages and sizes. Convenient bowling facilities are found in every state in the US, in Canada, Japan, England, and Scandinavia, providing a leisurely activity that people of all ages and sizes can enjoy.

Don Johnson in his book, **Inside Bowling,** reports that over 52 million people enjoy bowling. In annual surveys, bowling is

"Accuracy is essential in achieving a strike. As every bowler knows, there are times when a tricky spare or a horrendous split will result from what looks to be a faultless hit." (Professional Bowlers Association)

outranked only by fishing as America's favorite recreational sport. Since the bowling facilities provide balls, shoes, and lanes as well as scoring apparatus, bowling requires no special expensive equipment (unless, of course, you decide to buy your own ball and shoes) that inhibits very young or older players from participating. Thus, anyone can bowl.

To play you roll the 10- to 16-pound hard rubber or plastic ball down a narrow wood-floor lane, attempting to throw with enough force and spin to knock down the 10 pear-shaped pins set in a triangular formation at the other end of the lane. This requires skill and finesse although more than a few beginners have put the veterans to shame by knocking them all down at once. If all go down on the first roll you have a "strike" or perfect roll. Two tries to knock down the pins get you a "spare." The highest score after 10 "frames" or sets of rolls wins the game. A perfect game is 300!

While professionals spend hours and hours practicing and league players also devote large amounts of time to practice, the casual bowler can take the family to the bowling alley often for a few hours of exercise and enjoyment on a lesser skill level. Good is as good as you want to be in bowling.

—**Ed Lubanski**

Ed Lubanski was the ABC Tournament Champion and the World's Invitational Champion. He has had 11 ABC-sanctioned 300 games. He is a past president of the Professional Bowlers Association.

The Perfect Strike

To just about every bowler, any strike is a perfect one, a thing of sheer beauty. But to any person the least bit technically minded about the game, some strikes are more perfect than others. In the not-so-perfect strike, all the pins go down, but it is more a happy accident than anything else.

Of course it is the flawless strike that you should seek, and to achieve it you must have a strike ball target that is mathematically precise. If you miss such a target by an inch or two, you might get a strike anyway. But if your target is wide, and perhaps a little vague, a miss is going to be costly.

Bowling instruction books tell you that your strike ball target is the one-three pin pocket. This is only partly right. Many bowlers take this advice to mean that they should hit the one and three pins simultaneously. But there is a better way.

What you should try to do is come in high and hit the headpin first. To put it in precise and technical terms, the center of the headpin divides the 20th board from the right-hand side of the lane (actually the center board of the lane). When you hit the headpin on a strike roll, the center of your ball should be on the 17th board, that is, about three inches to the left of the center of the headpin. The ball is hooking at this time, of course.

After the headpin has been toppled, the ball, still hooking, takes out the three pin. The center of the ball has almost reached the 19th board when the three pin is felled.

What happens next follows an unvarying pattern. After toppling the one and three, the ball drives to the left and takes out the five pin. Here you can see the necessity of rolling a hard-driving ball. Not only must the ball take out the one and the three, it must sail in to the five with such force that the five takes out the eight. Often the five pin is called the king pin or the key pin. You must get the five with the ball to earn a strike. After toppling the five, the ball is deflected right and into the nine pin. The other pins are felled in this manner: The one pin, after being struck by the ball, is deflected left into the two pin; the two then carries the four and the four fells the seven. The three pin takes out the six, and the six topples the ten.

Accuracy is essential in achieving a strike. As every bowler knows, there are times when a tricky spare or a horrendous split will result from what looks to be a faultless hit. Sometimes the eight-ten split results from what is a seemingly perfect roll. When this happens it is because your ball did not hit the headpin squarely enough, though perhaps it was off target by no more than a quarter of an inch.

Besides knowing what your target is, and hitting it squarely with an effective hook, your ball has to be rolling properly at the time it hits the pins in order to earn your strike. A ball can roll in one of three ways. Each of these is defined in terms of a track which appears on the surface of the ball after a game or two. The track reveals your ball to be a spinner (the track is near the bottom of the ball), a semi-spinner (the type of roll for which most bowlers strive), or a full roller (ball rolls like a wheel).

Of course there are other factors important in the achievement of strikes. The angle of your hook must be correct, and the ball's speed must be right. (It should take the ball between two and 2½ seconds to reach the pins; it travels about 20 mph). It's impossible to have absolute control over all of these elements. This is evident by the fact that there are so few 300 games. But knowing precisely what your target is, and how to roll for it, gives you some advantage and makes those elusive strikes a bit more attainable.

—**Ed Lubanski**

For More Information

We have a list of 65 publications covering bowling. Many are regional type publications and we are only listing a few to get you started.

Bowling, 5301 S. 76th St., Greendale, Wis. 53129. Published monthly at $4.00 per year. Official publication of the ABC and the leading magazine in the sport since 1934.

Woman Bowler, same address as above. Published ten times per year. The official publication of the Women's International Bowling Congress with over 100,000 circulation.

Junior Bowler, same address as above. Published six times per year at $1.25. The official publication of the American Junior Bowling Congress. Covers all phases of the junior bowling program–bowlers 21 or under.

Bowl Magazine, 6573 Backlick Rd., Suite 207, Springfield, Va. 22150. Have not seen this publication.

Again we find that there are a lot of organizations involved in bowling but these are the more important ones. For more information check with your local bowling alley.

American Bowling Congress, 5301 S. 76th St., Greendale, Wis. 53129. Conducts national tournaments. Write to them for a copy of their booklet "Playing Rules."

American Junior Bowling Congress and the **Women's International Bowling Congress** are housed at the same address. Both have free information available.

American Blind Bowling Association, 135 Vernon Ave., Louisville, Ky. 40206. They publish a publication called *The Blind Bowler* that may be of interest.

National Bowling Association, 1806 Madison Ave., Suite 306, Toledo, Ohio 43624. Formed in 1943 and dedicated to making bowling a truly lifetime family sport.

Professional Bowlers Association, 1720 Merriman Rd., Akron, Ohio 44313. If you are thinking about making a career out of bowling write these people first.

There are many sources for top equipment and probably your top sport shop in town can handle you. Or again, check with your local bowling alley. But if you aren't getting any place write: AMF Inc., Bowling Products Group, Jericho Turnpike, Westbury, N.Y. 11590. I don't know if they will answer your letter but it might be worth a try.

Here are a few books covering bowling. All are available from World Publications, Box 366, Mountain View, Ca. 94040 at the price listed* plus 25 cents each postage.

Inside Bowling, Don Johnson. The nation's top pro bowler explains what it takes to be a good bowler. Instructions are detailed and clear, with explicit photos and diagrams. Personal experiences on the pro tour and entertaining anecdotes lend a light quality. 1973 Hb. & ppb., 87 (oversize) pp., ill., $7.95/$4.95, (Regnery).

Bowling Secrets of the Pros, George Sullivan. The complete scoop from 15 of the world's leading professional bowlers. Stress is on developing an effective and natural personal style. Also includes rules, courtesies of the lanes, keeping score and selection of a ball. 1968 Hb., 168 pp., ill., $5.95, (Doubleday).

Bowling. Showers. Describes the basic techniques and analyzes the fundamentals a student must master in order to become an accomplished bowler. A comprehensive look at how to choose a ball, the proper stance, the pushaway, the approach, type of delivery, and aiming techniques. 1973 Ppb., 104 pp., ill., $3.95, (Goodyear).

The Bowler's Manual, Lou Bellisimo. Here's your chance to improve your score by correcting bowling faults such as balance and control. This step-by-step guide has helped players to improve their bowling by practicing Bellisimo's directions. 1975 Ppb., 134 pp., ill., $3.95, (Prentice-Hall).

Bowling, Joan Martin. Delves into all aspects of bowling for the novice and intermediate, explaining all the skills, equipment and facilities, all with self-evaluation questions to catch errors. Also discusses the values of bowling, early history and development, rules, scoring and etiquette. 1971 Ppb., 61 pp., ill., $2.50, (W.C. Brown).

Boxing

You can knock the man out at the end of the match, but the point isn't to knock him out. It is to hit him and not get hit. As a game, this way, boxing can be fun.

In the newspapers they call me a stylist, which means I box with my brains at least as much as my fists. I would say there are two kinds of boxers, those who rely on style and those who rely on strength. Jose Napoles, for instance, is a stylist who can do many things well. He can pressure you, or he can outbox you. He's been welterweight champ of the world for five years now. Joe Frazier, he can't outbox someone because he doesn't have the basic qualities to do it. So he uses his strength, which is immense. He's only about 5'10" and stocky. When he is fighting someone about 6' or taller, who's good, he's not going to outjazz them.

I'm not that strong physically, so for me winning a fight is thinking faster than my opponent. Sometimes everything just flows and one thing leads to another. If you don't have that edge, that timing and the ability to see the punches coming, you can't do anything.

One of the most important skills, I think, is timing. That's the ability to see a person's punch and react to it. It is a kind of instinct, you can tell what he's going to do. It's a reaction you develop in sparring. If you can't see when a guy's punches are coming, most of the time you are going to get hit.

By outthinking my opponents I can force them to do what I want them to do. I can't grab them and push them and maul them to death for 15 rounds. I've got to outbox them. I like to block and counterpunch, rather than launching an all-out attack. By studying the other man I can predict how he will move, and keep the fight under control.

If he's confident, then he's going to be doing whatever he's good at. So the best thing to do is to take away his confidence, in everything he does. Boxing, if you do it right, is really psychological. Make him uneasy in everything. Don't let him hit you with a solid shot. Slip punches, block some of them, do something different every time. Don't always do one thing, because then you're setting yourself up for a pattern. If you slip it and bang him, if you roll over it and you hit him with a different punch every time, he's going to get frustrated. When some people get frustrated they get excited and they do things they shouldn't do, and that's when you are controlling the situation.

I enjoy my fights (Ray has a 23-1-1 record), and I take satisfaction in fighting as something I can do well. My skill has developed over many years. I'm only 24 now but I started boxing when I was eight. Boxing was always part of my family. My father (Ray Lunney) had a 43-2-3 record and coached for 27 years at Stanford University. He's my manager and coach.

It's a saying in boxing that a fighter may be so-so, but his manager's got plenty of guts. In other words he'll send the boxer into tough fights that he's not ready for. All it takes is a imple state test to be a manager. You see a lot of business ypes, restaurant owners and the like, working in the corners of some fighters. And they are yelling at the guy to do somehing and they don't have the slightest idea what it means. I'm ucky to have my father as my manager.

I've had all these advantages, but the foundation of my ighting is training, just like it is for any boxer.

In training, every individual has a different method. There re several things you do similarly, sparring, hitting the bag nd that type of thing, but the amount of each is based on the ndividual. Just as each individual has his own style, he will ave his own way of training. Now for myself, just before the ight, I'm running three miles a day, maybe four sometimes ut that's all.

I've never done more because my philosophy to get in hape for any type of athletic event is to duplicate that event, hat competition. For boxing I would be in the ring, for tennis lay tennis with someone. But you need basic conditioning. Running and swimming are probably the two best basic conitioners there are. You seem to use all your muscles.

In amateur boxing on an International level, points are scored nerely by the number of scoring punches and not their effect. Thus, a knockdown scores no more than a weak blow to the side of the head. (Duffy)

Right now we only spar two weeks before a fight. Some people spar for a long time before but for us two weeks seems o work out well. The first couple of days I will only do four ounds of sparring, maybe the first week four or five a day. The second week I'm doing six to eight rounds every day.

On an average day I'll do four rounds on the speed bag. I lon't hit it rhythmically, I practice hooks on it and punches ike that so it is not steady pounding. In practice I put the bag a little above head height so what I'm trying to do is duplicate where my opponent's head is going to be.

My opponent might or might not be taller, but the best way o get power out of a punch is to be punching up, not down. If he guy is a little shorter than me, I'll crouch down and then unch up. I might jump rope, a few rounds. Many years ago, when boxing was found in the circuses and side shows, to how people how they trained boxers would skip rope or hit a ag. Just from the history of boxing every fighter figures he has to jump rope to get in shape. I don't feel it really does much for you.

The last part of my workout is to do sit-ups. Usually I'll do sit-ups when I run in the morning and then do them when I work out. I'll do 50 of these each time.

Along with sparring I'll hit the bag. Supposedly hitting a big bag gives you punching power. I don't believe that at all. Apparently some people can be taught to punch, but for the most of us, either you can naturally punch hard or you cannot. I have seen very few guys that have gone in and couldn't break an egg, and in a month's time they can all of a sudden knock you dead. I hit the heavy bag very little.

You can go in the gym and do a lot of sit-ups, and if I walk in and bump you in the belly it's going to hurt. The best way to get your stomach in shape is getting hit in the belly. You learn how to take a punch. A few years ago I worked with a guy who was a contender at the time and his best punch was a left hook to the body. He used it on me and it hurt quite a bit at the time, but over a period of a year he toughened up my stomach. I've never been hurt with a body shot yet.

Combination is a term that's been used to describe, for instance, a jab followed by a right hand punch. I don't think there is any good fighter who can get hit with a combination. A good fighter knows how to block and he's not going to get hit twice in a row. Sometimes the guy in the corner says "throw a combination" and so the guy goes out there and throws a 1-2. You know he's going to throw a 1-2 come hell or high water.

I want to make the other fighter do what I want, so I'll feint. I might send in a few strong hits to the belly, and anybody's natural reaction to that is that they don't want it to happen again. Then I'll exaggerate a punch to the belly, I'll groan like I'm really going to rip one in there. I'll actually start the blow, and his reaction is going to be to block the punch. I'll pull back and as he brings an arm down to block the punch I'll execute a left hook to the jaw. So that's fun.

During the round I can't hear anyone. I've never heard anyone during a round. I can tell a pitch, and I know if the crowd's really going wild. So it influences me some. But if I'm fighting well and really concentrating I won't even know what round it is.

–Ray Lunney

Ray Lunney is a top contender for the junior lightweight (130 lb.) crown.

For More Information

Two magazines do a fairly good job: *Ring*, Pittston, Penn. 18047. Published monthly and mostly on the professional boxers. *Boxing Illustrated*, 225 Roy St., Montreal, Canada. Published monthly at $10 per year.

For the amateur boxer, the AAU is the governing body. For the professional there are two organizations: The World Boxing Council, 1021 O St., Room A153, Sacramento, Calif., and the World Boxing Association, Box 3469, Honolulu, Hawaii. Here are some books that can give you further information. All are available from World Publications, Box 366, Mountain View, Calif. 94040 at the price listed* plus 25 cents each postage. Write for a complete list.

The Greatest–My Own Story, Muhammad Ali with Richard Durham. Brand new autobiography! Now the champ tells the true story of his life–the story no sports announcer, fan, journalist, or biographer ever knew. 1975 Hb., $10.95, (Random).

Better Boxing: An Illustrated Guide, Eddie LaFond. The skills and training techniques presented here are for both beginning and advanced boxers. Includes a wealth of information on ring strategy. 1959 Hb., 118 pp., ill., $8.65, (Ronald).

Boxing Skills, Charles Roy Schroeder. This book is specifically intended to stimulate the inclusion of non-contact boxing skills programs in youth and athletic clubs. Hitting the striking bag, jumping rope, punching the training bag, and using the medicine ball are all demonstrated. 1973 Hb., 121 pp., ill., $9.95, (Regman).

Inside Boxing, Floyd Patterson and Bert Sugar. One of boxing's great fighters shows how to become a winner. He goes beyond the basics and into the strategies and psychological aspects of the sport. 1974 Hb. & Ppb., 78 (oversize) pp., ill., $4.95/$3.95, (Regnery).

Boxing, Edwin Haislet. The information packed into these pages will instruct coaches and boxers in techniques and skills—footwork, attack, defense, training, and more. 1940 Hb., 120 pp., ill., $7.95, (Ronald).

Boxing: An Advanced Coaching Handbook, David James, ed. For the professional or expert. Every coach will benefit from the advice and illustrations. 1972 Hb., ill., $10.00, (Int. Pub. Service).

In This Corner . . . ! Peter Heller. Forty world boxing champions like Jack Dempsey, Mickey Walker, Gunboat Smith, Rocky Graziano, Joe Louis, Floyd Patterson and Sugar Ray Robinson tell their stories, each telling of his championship, his life, his greatest fight, his controversies, and the behind-the-scenes dealings. 1973 Hb., 431 pp., ill., $10.00, (Simon & Schuster).

The Ring: An Illustrated History of Boxing, Harry Carpenter. Three thousand years of boxing are packed into this big, handsomely illustrated book. From the brutal gladiators of ancient Greece and Rome, to the bareknuckled battlers of Britain and the US, to the glory and shame of the 20th century. The greatest boxers, the promoters, the impact of radio and closed-circuit TV, and Olympic boxing. 1975 Hb., 192 (oversize) pp., ill., $15.00, (Regnery).

Muhammad Ali, Wilfrid Sheed. A penetrating look at the world heavyweight champion whose flamboyant personality and lifestyle has earned the admiration and dislike of millions. Sheed's words are combined with the work of over 70 photographers for a look at the public and private image of Ali. 1975, 256 (oversize) pp., ill., $19.95, (T.Y. Cromwell).

The Fight, Norman Mailer. Three champions, Muhammad Ali, George Foreman and Norman Mailer—converge in Zaire, Africa for a fantastic heavyweight title "rumble in the jungle" and the result is a penetrating study. 1975 Hb., 239 pp., $7.95, (Little, Brown & Co.).

Amateur Boxing, Know the Game Series. A good beginner's guide to the basics of boxing. Clear illustrations explain strategy, defensive and offensive positions, and illegal moves. 1952 (rev. 1972) Ppb., 40 pp., ill., $1.50, (E.P. Publishing).

Boxing: The Great Ones, Reg Gutteridge. Here are biographical profiles of the fighting careers of Muhammad Ali, Joe Louis, Sugar Ray Robinson, Jack Dempsey, Jack Johnson, Rocky Marciano, Archie Moore, Ted Kid Lewis, and Jimmy Wilde—a glittering collection of some of the greatest boxers the world has ever known. 1975 Hb., 154 pp., ill., $7.50, (Pelham).

Bridge

Bridge is just a card game to those who have never tried to play it, but it has become an interest, an absorption, a sport, perhaps almost a way of life to people who have had the curiosity and energy to learn to play. Indeed, during the fifty years since contract bridge (the present form of bridge) has been in existence, the number of players has riser to over fifty million in North America alone, plus some milli ons of others in every other part of the world, especially ir Western Europe.

Great Britain has long had many bridge players, some o them converts from ancestral forms of the present game—whist bridge whist, and auction bridge. In the earlier days of Britisl colonialism, the game was transplanted to Britain's dominion and possessions where among civil servants it was an escap from the burdens of governing an Empire. But the game dic not remain the exclusive property of the governing class Today India, South Africa, Australia, Canada and many mor countries have bridge players. The names of their leading ex perts are familiar to bridge fans throughout the world.

Bridge did not long remain confined to English-speakin people. For the last twenty-five years, annual world champ ionship matches have been held. Although players from th United States dominated this competition in its early years relatively small handful of Italians, a group named The Blu Team, won the title year after year following the 1955 champ ionships. When the Blue Team finally retired the American again regained the title. But in 1975 part of the Italian group together with a pair of new recruits, emerged from retiremen and once more won the championship.

South America, Scandinavia, Spain, even war-plagued Israe have many bridge players. Only behind the Iron Curtain i bridge denigrated as a bourgeois or capitalist diversion. Ye even in these Soviet satellites there are pockets of resistance t official policy. Poland now sends teams to international com petitions; Hungary has many players, as well as some bridg writers and theorists of note.

Contract bridge, invented by Cornelius Vanderbilt, bot gained and suffered after its inception. A knowledge of th game actually became a mark of prestige for some, a hallmar of acceptability, a social necessity. As such, it was scorned b others as a passing affectation, a fad like the diabolo or spi curl, soon to pass into oblivion. Cartoonists of the day depict ed bridge players wearing dinner jackets and evening gowns. I was thought of as a game for bored women of the countr club set, a game of innumerable memorized rules and excep tions to those rules. Could this game possibly gain popula rity in the virile America of poker and pinochle. It seemed a unlikely as champagne taking the place of whiskey or beer

Yet the impossible happened. The popularity of bridg never faded, partly through the extraordinary publicity effort of Ely Culbertson, and later through the books of Charles Go ren whose simplified approach to bidding the cards made the game more accessible to Americans.

Today, as always, the game has an intrinsic merit of its own, a fascination for many people so great that other card games seem insipid after they have played bridge. Furthermore, those who try bridge discover that it is not such a difficult game to play as they had previously thought. It is true, of course, that unlike some card games it is difficult to grasp the essentials of bridge with only a few words of explanation, and two or three hands. Knowing the game well takes a bit more than this. But with the help of patient friends, perhaps a book, or a few lessons from a bridge teacher, one can begin actual play. With each game, thereafter, better strategy and technique will be employed by the beginning player.

This quality–that there will always be more to learn–is one of the sources of bridge's fascination. A bridge player never can plumb the depths of the game completely; new aspects, possibilities, always seem to lie beyond. Possibly some expert believes that he has penetrated the game to its extreme limits. In any case, he would be unlikely to admit that any other player could possibly have achieved such understanding, also. Bridge experts tend to harbor great opinions of only their own abilities.

Most bridge games are played right in the homes of Americans. Although it can be a very good game for wagering (if one has sufficient skill), the rewards are usually no more than the score on the board and the pleasures of the game. The game of poker, by contrast, loses its savor and even its basic strategy, without stakes. A professional gambler once remarked that there were only two games he was willing to play for high stakes. He would always choose draw poker as the best test of his ability, and, second, he would choose bridge.

Another way for bridge players to enjoy their favorite game is by playing duplicate bridge, a kind of competition in which players replay the hands of others to see which pairs can achieve the greatest score. Each pair plays against a number of different partnerships in the course of a bridge session, the results are scored, and each pair's ranking is determined at the end of the session. The contestants play seriously, with concentration, and the competition is keen.

Duplicate bridge games are played every day in bridge clubs all over the United States–both afternoon and evening in metropolitan areas. Large duplicate bridge tournaments, of regional and national scope, are held under the auspices of the American Contract Bridge League, an organization which keeps records of the victories in all duplicate bridge games and a lifetime point-record for the players who wish to become members. These players can achieve various ratings, all the way up to the coveted Life Master rating.

Duplicate bridge clubs are open to any bridge player, member or not. For a small table fee he may participate in the duplicate game, each session lasting about three hours. The director of the game can often arrange a partner for the solitary individual immediately, but bringing one's own partner is probably a more comfortable way to be introduced to duplicate bridge. Many clubs conduct a special section for novice duplicate players, allowing those of little or no duplicate experience a chance at winning their first time out. This also gives novice players a chance to overcome the initial awkwardness of playing with strangers for the first time.

A duplicate game is not the place, however, to learn how to play bridge. Although clubs with novice sections sometimes feature pre-game lessons, a thorough knowledge of basic fundamentals is vitally necessary before one can tackle a duplicate game. Once a player is playing regularly, though, improvement often comes quickly. One notices that other players, who are holding cards from the same deck, are able to end up with a fairly decent score. The avid player will be quick to find out why.

At the average duplicate bridge game, the many players are of all ages, from 13 to 93, of all occupations, and races. Physical handicaps do not keep enthusiasts from taking part–for them bridge is a true sport, as evidenced by quickened pulse and tense concentration. No longer is bridge a polite social grace. While sometimes it is played as a kind of duty, or as a substitute for conversation, for most people it is an experience in intellectual partnership that can last a lifetime.

—**Frank Savstrom**

Frank Savstrom has been a duplicate bridge player for the past 25 years, achieving Life Master rating in 1960. He is a certified duplicate bridge director from Palo Alto, California.

For More Information

There are two good magazines which cover bridge.
Popular Bridge, 16250 Ventura Blvd., Encino, Calif. 91316. Published monthly at $7.00 per year. A general bridge magazine.
Bridge World, 39 W. 94th St., New York, N.Y. 10025. Published montly at $12.00 per year. A more technical magazine for the intermediate and advanced players.

If you really are interested in "really" getting into this game, we would recommend writing to these organizations.
American Contract Bridge League, 2200 Democrat Rd., Memphis, Tenn. 38116. With over 180,000 members, it runs over ten tournaments every weekend, publishes a newsletter for members and does other things to promote bridge.
World Bridge Federation, 5400 Jefferson Highway, New Orleans, La. They run many tournaments including many international ones.

There are many fine books on bridge in most book stores but here are a few you might consider. All are available from World Publications, Box 366, Mountain View, Calif. 94040 at the price listed* plus 25 cents each postage.

Goren Settles the Bridge Arguments, Charles Goren. Authoritative answers to knotty problems that are the cause of frequent misunderstandings at the bridge table. 1974 Hb., 429 pp., ill., $12.50, (Hart).

Bridge for Women, Richard Frey, ed. Five of the world's best women players tell how to play bridge with men, understand how men play, and beat them. 1969 Ppb., 224 pp., ill., $1.50, (Crowell).

Improve Your Bridge, H. W. Kelsey. Sound advice for those players who have not been tournament winners but would like to, and for those who would like to change from occasional winners to frequent ones. 1975 Ppb., 192 pp., ill., $2.45, (Hart).

Contract Bridge, Know the Game Series. Ideal beginner's guide that details all the fundamentals of this popular game in simple clear language, leaving all the complications and embellishments for larger books. 1964 Ppb., 36 pp., $1.50, (E.P. Publishing).

Bullfighting

Although bullfighting is most popularly and widely held in Spain, it is practiced in several Central and South American countries, as well as in Portugal and Southern France. Its seed goes back to Paleolithic men who lived in the caves of Northern France and hunted wild cattle for food and clothing. With passions similar to those that prompted these primitive tribes to paint pictures of bulls on the walls of their dwellings, modern bullfighting is held in a sacred and artistic aura among its spectators and participants.

The skilled matador de toros, or killer of the bulls, is as highly regarded as a champion baseball or football player in this country. Certainly he is a decorous sight dressed in his beautifully stylized suit of lights reputedly designed by Goya. Although these men may attain great glory, the grueling risks and hardships they face are unparalleled in sport. The bull is as gentle as a cow in his herd, but he becomes one of the fiercest and bravest of animals when set in the unfamiliar ground of an arena. This dangerous challenge has even attracted a few Americans into the ring, one or two becoming quite well-known matadors.

Actually, the English word bullfighting is inaccurate since it implies a contest where none exists. In the corrida de toros (running of the bulls) there is no match or competition, no winner or loser when a man and a bull confront each other. Therefore, this event technically cannot be called a sport in the traditional sense. Nevertheless, bullfighting is the second most popular spectator sport in the world!

A formal corrida consists of six bulls, one at a time, confronting one of three matadors and his team of assistants in a public arena. Each corrida is rigidly patterned and ritualistic. After a traditional ceremony in which the three matadors and their cuadrilla (assistants) parade into the ring to salute the president (usually a local dignitary who serves as controller of the fight), the actual corrida begins. The banderilleros and mounted picadors, all members of the cuadrilla, play important roles. When the door is flung open and the first bull charges into the arena, he is encouraged and tested by the banderilleros with their working capes. After the bull's fighting characteristics have been revealed in this manner, the matador steps into the ring and accepts several charges from the animal with a capote and muleta, a scarlet cloth on a stick. His goal is to control the bull as much as possible, executing his series of passes in good form, with the bull charging very close to his body. The matador is judged by the aficionados (bullfight enthusiasts) for his grace, style and skill in these maneuvers, and he is greeted either with encouragement or protesting jeers.

After this stage of the fight has been called to a halt by the president, the picadors on their horses enter with the other two matadors. The matadors cape the bull into a position where the picador can thrust his lance into the bull's upper loin. This is necessary because a bull must have his head lowered to reveal the correct killing spot—an area the size of a fist, between the bull's shoulderblades—once the matador is ready to use his sword. A healthy bull will not lower his head long enough for a kill unless his muscles are weakened sufficiently by the picadors. These actions by the picadors are governed by strict regulations, to prevent excessive injury of the bull's faculties.

The next phase of the bullfight features the banderilleros, who expertly attract el toro bravo and place colored, barbed sticks in the hide of his back. This serves to aggravate the animal into fighting well. In the final phase of a bullfight, the matador attempts the killing of the bull, first executing a series of passes, sometimes employing a number of theatrical gestures to show the extent of his mastery over the animal. When the bull is sufficiently prepared, its head low, the matador sights along his sword as the bull charges and then thrusts it over the horns and into an area of its upper back. This may prove fatal, but more than one attempt at this is fairly common. After the bull has been dragged from the ring and the matador received his tokens of reward or failure, the second bull is brought forth and the fight is repeated until the last bull is killed.

The recognized Spanish bullfighting season runs from March to October of each year.

Some Notes on La Fiesta Brava

Contrary to the beliefs of some, Americans can really appreciate the bullfight as an art—some of them far better than their Latin counterparts. Strangely enough, bullfighting has become astonishingly popular in this country with a great many people who seldom, maybe never, see bullfights, but who read about them. There are approximately twenty bullfighting clubs all around America which meet once a month to exchange information and books, look at bullfighting films, and generally participate in the spirit of the Corrida de Toros. Each year these clubs have a large convention in Tijuana at the end of August. Every dav for a week they have bullfights where the members actually take part and try their hand with small bulls. On the first and last Sundays they attend the real bullfights and in between they have lectures discussion groups, and so forth. Many of these clubs have their own publications. In fact, there are approximately fourteen that are published in various parts of this country. The bullfighting club of Chicago, for example, turns out a fine publication every month.

Even though bullfighting holds an uncanny popularity in a country where one cannot attend a bullfight unless he travels out of his locality, the artistry of the ring has yet to be discovered by a majority of Americans. A bullfight is one of the few places in the world where, almost upon order, a person can witness courage and cowardice, skill and daring—in essence, a full range of emotions. Many Americans misinterpret the bullfight as a contest between a man and a bull. This is not true because the bull really hasn't a chance of coming out of the ring alive. In rare cases a bull is pardoned if he is very brave, but usually he is killed. Consequently, bullfighting cannot really be called a sport in the true sense of the word. It is not a contest to win anymore than a ballet is; a person doesn't go to a ballet to see who finishes first. The bullfight is a contest between a man and himself, not a man and a bull. It is essentially about how a man controls himself, not whether he

El Cordobes earns an estimated $3 million per year in the world's toughest profession. For his trouble he has suffered several severe gorings, some of which have put him on the brink of death. El Cordobes is disliked by purist aficionados, who consider his style to be detrimental to the seriousness of bullfighting.

is going to kill the bull, but how he is going to kill the bull. Is he going to do it in a graceful, beautiful brave way, or is he going to be sloppy about it?

I would describe bullfighting more as an art, or as a spectacle, rather than a sport. If it must be associated with a sport then I think it should be likened to diving off a high board. Form is absolutely everything in bullfighting. When you enter the water in a diving contest the position of your feet and hands, how you hold your back, and everything else, is judged just as the matador is judged while handling the bull; in a bullfight you are not judged by points, but by the reactions of the aficionados. (And don't be mistaken; these people really know what they're watching!) This diving comparison might be carried further by pointing out that the size and age of the bull the man is fighting can be compared to the height of the board the man is diving from. Everybody is aware that it is more dangerous to do a triple off a 30- or 40-foot platform than a simple dive off a lower one. Well, the same thing holds—it's obviously going to be a little more dangerous to do a tricky maneuver with an old bull than with a young one.

All this may seem very cruel and heinous to some people. Sometimes you hear arguments in America about the brutality of bullfighting. If, for instance, an enthusiast should point out that the bullfight is no more brutal than football, then his deploring opponent will say, "At least football players go out on the field willing to break each other's necks. They know what they're doing. The poor bull doesn't even have a chance." I think a few things should be brought into focus here. First of all, the "poor bull" lives at least a whole year longer than a bull who goes to the stockyard. Generally he dies a pleasanter death since he does it in hot blood, rather than standing in line waiting to be hit on the head with a baseball bat. But I think the significant thing to remind people is that the fighting bull does live a perfect life. They're not tortured or trained the way some people try to tell you. These bulls never see an unmounted man before they go into the ring, and then it is all over in a fifteen minute contest. If I had the chance to lead my life this way—say, have a perfect life and then go into the prize ring with Muhammad Ali, which would be tantamount to suicide, I think I'd do it.

There is no doubt that bullfighting can be a dangerous activity, and no one should attempt it without expert guidance. Actually, there are quite a few injuries incurred in bullfighting countries, especially by smaller bulls, because many amateurs don't know what they're doing. Also, these small animals have probably fought before, even though it is against the law. It's a crime to fight a bull twice, the main reason being that the bulls learn so quickly. A man can't perform the passes with an animal that knows that the cape is his enemy, therefore, most bullfighters practice with cows. Most matadors fight many more cows in a year than bulls, a fact which most people don't know. Some people tell you that bulls are more dangerous because they charge with their eyes open. This is an old wives' tale, pure poppycock. Both bulls and cows charge with their eyes very wide open. In fact, you want them to charge this way because you want them to see the cape. It is not the red of the cape that they are attracted to, because they are color blind; it is the movement of the cape that a matador wants them to see—and the correct execution of this movement takes practice. For these reasons most bullfighters practice with small bulls because, by law, they can't do this with the big bulls that are going into the ring. They practice with little bulls that are going to end up in the slaughterhouse, or they practice with cows that are never going to go into a real ring. I, myself, was almost killed by a cow, a small cow. I was in the hospital for three weeks and on crutches for six months.

I originally got interested in bullfighting when I went down to study painting at the University of Mexico when I was eighteen. After I saw a fight I became very enthusiastic about it, especially since it looked so easy and since I thought anybody could do it. Well, my friends convinced me to try it since it seemed such a cinch. One day, when I was full of youth and tequila, I jumped down into the arena and found out just how difficult it was—in a hurry! After my period in Mexico I traveled to Spain in the diplomatic service and took it up again, fighting regularly.

Although there have been a great many American bullfighters, they are received with tolerant amusement in the bullfighting countries. The people don't expect the North Americans to be able to do anything in the ring, so even if they can do a little bit the Spaniard is amazed. Actually, there have not been any Americans who have fought well, compared to the Spaniards. John Fulton has probably done better than anyone of this country, having become a senior matador, which is very rare. He is the only American, except for Sidney Franklin, to have done so.

I have been lucky enough to have known most of the great matadors of the modern day. Studying with Juan Belmonte was, of course, a fine experience. Besides being the greatest single matador I have ever known, he is generally regarded as the inventor of modern bullfighting, by giving it its new look through his great style and courage. Then Manolete was also fabulous; and in Mexico, Carlos Arruza, my great friend, was the finest I ever saw in that country. Arruza put on the most impressive performance, as a matador, that I have ever seen.

—Barnaby Conrad

Although an amateur bullfighter, Barnaby Conrad has fought with some of the greatest matadors and is a well-known authority on bullfighting, having written many books and magazine articles. He is the author of **Fiesta Brava, My Life as a Matador,** *and* **Gates of Fear,** *among others.*

For More Information

Bullfighting is not done in the United States, but there are additional sources for information: *Clarin,* 212 Plantation Place, Anaheim, Calif. 92806. Published 10 times per year at $7.50. It is the world's only commercially produced magazine in the English language. Has a lot of good information along with excellent photos. There are two organizations of national interest—National Association of Taurine Clubs, 280 San Antonio Way, Walnut Creek, Calif. This organization is the main body for a number of clubs. It holds a convention each year for interested members. There is also Taurine Bibliophiles of America, 1510 Miramar St., Los Angeles, Ca. 90026. This organization is devoted to the collection of books, posters, prints and other bullfighting memorabilia.

Here are a couple of books that should prove interesting. All are available from World Publications, Box 366, Mountain View, Calif. 94040 at the price listed* plus 25 cents postage.

Bullfighting, John Fulton. This could be retitled the Complete Book of Bullfighting, because it is just that: an extensive look at every facet of bullfighting from the eyes of a premier American matador. A well-illustrated guide to the history, practice and art of the Corrida, from a technical standpoint. 1971 Hb., 197 (oversize) pp., ill., $12.50, (Dial).

The Encyclopedia of Bullfighting, Barnaby Conrad. A profusely illustrated encyclopedia covering all the terms, techniques, personalities arranged alphabetically from Abanico—a two-handed maneuver with a cape—to Zapatillas—the torero's slippers. 1961 Hb., 288 (oversize) pp., ill., $10.00, (Houghton Mifflin).

Death in the Afternoon, Ernest Hemingway. A superb rendering of the fighters and bulls, the emotion and the pageantry, the history and legends. Hemingway at his best in this classic of modern literature. 1932 Ppb., 487 pp., ill., $5.95, (Schribner's).

Camping

When the first man built a house and planted a crop we lost a camper. When man began building groups of houses close together in villages, we not only lost a camper, we gained a suburbanite and began the process of changing from campers to city dwellers. Despite the thousands of years that have passed since this happened, some of us have never completely joined the ranks of "civilized" people. We still camp. We camp for a variety of reasons, but most of us camp simply to be close to nature.

Campers can be compartmentalized to some extent. There are those who camp because it is a means to enjoy some other sport, such as fishing, hunting, four-wheel-drive exploring, trail bike riding, backpacking, snowshoeing, cross country skiing or simply traveling. People engaged in any of these activities have found that camping is an inexpensive way of pursuing their interest. And in the case of those people who travel far away from motels, lodges and other commercial facilities it is the only way they can enjoy their particular sport.

Motorhome campers and those in recreation vehicles are usually travelers rather than campers. Their primary purpose generally is to see the country and they are more apt to stop for the night at a private campground than to seek out a national forest or other "primitive" type campground.

Then there are the gregarious campers, those who enjoy being with people of like interests and doing things together. These campers often belong to one or more clubs such as the National Campers & Hikers Association, the Good Sam Club, and the International Travel and Trailer Clubs of America. Many clubs are affiliated with a manufacturer or other commercial operation such as the Wally Byam Caravan Club (Airstream travel trailer owners), Travco Motorcade (Travco motorhome owners), and the KOA Kampers Klub (affiliated with the KOA campground franchised chain).

And while we can compartmentalize campers they refuse to hold still for this because they cross over categories so often. A motorhome owner who is primarily a traveler may break his routine by spending one or two weeks at a remote campground — just to be away from the hassles of civilization. A tenter, who is the basic camper, may stuff tent and 125 pounds or more of food and other gear into the family station wagon — and take off with wife and kids for a cross country trip to see the Washington Monument, Civil War battlefields and the highly developed Eastern seashore.

U.S. campers think nothing of camping in Canada, Mexico, the far northern state of Alaska or the island of Hawaii. They have found that camping is the least expensive way to see Europe and are continually amazed that Europeans by the thousands camp also. You may even find yourself in a campground in Europe seemingly filled with a thousand native campers. The common policy in European campgrounds is the camp is full only when every bare patch of ground is covered.

The birth of the automobile and construction of roads throughout this country made camping available to more and more people. Henry Ford, Thomas Edison and Harvey Firestone were early campers who used the first recreational vehicles. When the three of them camped they had vehicles equipped for living as well as transportation units. They also were probably among the first of the breed of campers who brought along everything but the kitchen sink. Why bother, because they had their own lightweight sink.

Young camping families have traditionally started with a tent and then moved up to a camping trailer (canvas or solid, fold-out top and sides), then a travel trailer, motorhome or mini motorhome (customarily built on a van chassis).

Today, there is a return to tenting as there is a return to the wilderness. Backpacking has become popular in the past twenty years because of the development of the frame pack and of dehydrated and freeze dried lightweight foods. These developments plus improvement in outdoor clothing, tents, sleeping bags and other lightweight gear have made this type of camping less of a burden and more of a pleasurable experience.

Whatever type of camping is undertaken a beginner can quickly learn the basic skills. Car campers and RV campers need to learn how to operate mechanical equipment. Backpackers need to know map reading and basic survival skills and can get by with little other knowledge.

Today all of these campers rely on an industrialized society for the equipment that they use as well as for the available free time in which to use it. But being continually exposed to nature they are usually aware of the dangers of industrial society polluting that wilderness. They see the need for man to find a niche in a world where he will not destroy the wilderness he continually seeks.

—Bill Shepard

Bill Shepard is a veteran camper and is Editor of **Camping & Trailering Guide** *magazine.*

A Way of Life

When I was seven my parents bought a house and three acres at the edge of town. Surrounding us were trees and brush; a river flowed nearby. Growing up in the woods, observing the changing Midwest seasons, having birds and wildlife nearby and being free to roam river and field all

Campers tend to carry much heavier and more varied gear than will backpackers, because equipment is not carried far from the car or trailer, and space and weight economy are not an object. Dinner, however still tastes best over an open fire. (Krips)

Camping dress tends to be more casual than for backpacking, because with inclement weather a camper will need only a 100-yard dash to the car instead of a 10-mile hike. (Krips)

contributed to my unabating appreciation of the out of doors.

Then came Boy Scouts where my main reason for belonging was to go camping. While many GI's come back from the service vowing never to camp again, camping to me was the most pleasant part of basic training and overseas duty. And traveling in the service was my first exposure to mountains. Today it would be difficult to imagine living away from mountains.

While finishing school, my wife and I began car camping in a seven-passenger, 1938 Packard that was long enough and wide enough to hold a full size double mattress. Camping gear fit under the mattress. We made a trip to Oregon, Washington, and California with a brother-in-law and sister, the four of us sleeping in two pup tents and cooking over wood fires. We weren't pioneers by any means. There were many national forest campgrounds in the West and there were farmers' fields and rural woodlands in the East. Campers seemed to be everywhere in the late 40s and early 50s, some pulling travel trailers, but most in tents as we were. And stowed on car top carriers and in car trunks were tents, Coleman stoves and lanterns, sleeping bags and boxes of food and clothing.

Vacations for us became camping vacations; was there another kind? Most of the time we were traveling campers, on our way to visit relatives or to see places that we hadn't seen before. We did manage to take a few trips where we traveled to a campground and stayed in one place for a week or more at a time. As our family increased so did the amount of camping gear and finally we had to change over from a standard sedan to a station wagon. Until the late 1950's and early 1960's, station wagons still were utilitarian vehicles designed to carry people and cargo.

Somewhere in the process of raising children and taking camping vacations we bought a 4-wheel drive Jeep utility wagon and found that with it we could get ever farther back in the wilderness and find choicer camping places. Then came fishing and hunting as an excuse to get out in the woods and mountains more often. After a few years it became apparent that fishing and hunting were just that – excuses to get out of doors. And once we faced that fact for what it was, the excuse became unnecessary. What better reason is there to be in a forest or on a mountaintop than just to be there? And why bother carrying a gun or fishing tackle when it is more interesting to discover what's over the next hill?

Having hiked in the Scouts and having carried a pack for so many miles in order to pass various tests and to gain a hiking merit badge, backpacking was no new thing. But exposure to frame packs and lightweight gear was. Backpacking became my favorite form of camping and everyone in our family has tried it.

My first exposure to the camping industry came as editor of a magazine for owners of self-propelled recreation vehicles – motorhomes, slide-in truck campers, vans and mini motorhomes. And even though I drove, tested and camped in many of these vehicles, backpacking remains my favorite form of camping. Still I would say every type of camping is pleasant. Campers are friendly people, easy to know and willing to share worldly goods or experiences, whether they ride a Honda 90, tow a small camping trailer, look down from a $30,000 motorhome or tote a raunchy pack on their backs.

There is room for the four-wheel-drive enthusiasts and room for wilderness backpackers. There is room for tenters and room for motorhome owners. Admittedly, they don't mix and shouldn't all be tossed into the same can. A backpacker seeks nature on nature's terms whereas a snowmobiler, trail bike rider or four-wheel-drive operator seeks nature on his own terms. A snowshoer who has given much of himself to get ten miles in from a road resents the roar of a snowmobile amid the quiet of winter. These campers need to be separated and there still is room for both of them as long as there is adequate planning of public backcountry lands.

My camping interests have spanned the gamut of camping units and camping systems. While my own goal is to simplify and carry as little as possible, I see nothing wrong with another camper carrying 10,000 pounds of luxury on a motorhome chassis. If that is the way he wants to experience the out of doors, so be it. Our experiences will be different, but his enjoyment may be just as great as mine. The pleasure he finds in looking out a window at a pine tree could be as great for him as the pleasure I find in looking out over an infinite sea of peaks from a mountaintop.

Camping is a way to return to nature, a way to get back to our roots and above all a way to learn how we fit into the community of earth. Nature has provided checks and balances on every animal species and on all plant life, but man has to provide his own system of checks. We can see some species increasing too rapidly for their range and dying off or becoming undernourished, undersized and disease-ridden. Camping is a way to learn by observing, a way to once again experience land, soil, trees, mountains, deserts and streams. We are a part of all of this. Only we can assure that it will always be that way.

—Bill Shepard

For More Information

There have been a lot of articles on camping in many magazines. Camping also has its own magazines. Here are two of them. For further magazines check backpacking.

Camping and Trailering Guide, Rt. 1, Box 877, McCourtney Rd., Grass Valley, Calif. 95945. Published monthly at $6.45 per year. On the cover it says "The complete magazine of family outdoor fun." I think that sums it up pretty well.

Camping Journal, Box 2600, Greenwich, Ct. 06830. Published eight times per year at $6.95. Well done magazine with many good articles.

Here are some of the major organizations: National Campers and Hikers Association, 7172 Transit Rd., Buffalo, N.Y. 14221. A non-profit camping club. National Camping Association, 353 West 56th St., New York, N.Y. 10019. Cooperative organization of camp owners and directors. American Camping Association, Bradford Woods, Martinsville, Ind. 46151. North American Family Campers Association, Box 552, Newburyport, Me. 01950.

Before leaving home and in fact several months beforehand you should gather information. The following addresses are the regional offices of the Bureau of Outdoor Recreation. These offices can supply maps and other material.

Northwest—United Pacific Building, 1000 Second Ave., Seattle, Wash. 98104; Pacific Southwest—Box 36062, 450 Golden Gate Ave., San Francisco, Calif. 94102; Mid-Continent—P.O. Box 25387, Denver Federal Center, Denver, Colo. 80225; South Central—5000 Marble St. N.E., Room 211, Albuquerque, N.M. 87110; Lake Central—3853 Research Park Drive, Ann Arbor, Mich. 48104; Southeast—810 New Walton Building, 600 Arch St., Philadelphia, Pa. 19106. Here is a list of some of the major private campground chains. Kampgrounds of America, Box 1138, Billings, Mont. 59103; Crazy Horse Campgrounds, 2152 Dupont Drive, Newport Beach, Calif. 92664; Venture Out In America, 3445 Peachtree Ave., N.E., Atlanta, Ga. 30326. By writing these people you should be able to get a list of their campgrounds.

In the backpacking section we list a lot of people that specialize in camping equipment. We also suggest that you seek out a local sport shop that can help you. Further address: Mountain House, Oregon Freeze Dry Foods, Inc., Box 1048, Albany, Ore. 97321. Send a stamped self-addressed envelope for their catalog. They make over 90 different freeze-dry foods.

Here are some books you should be interested in. All are available from World Publications, Box 366, Mountain View, Calif. 94040 for the price listed* plus 25 cents postage.

101 Camping-Out Ideas and Activities, Bruno Knobel. A collection of outdoor lore and projects—how to read animal tracks, construct shelters, navigate by the stars, send smoke signals, use a lasso—enough to keep younger campers amused for hours. 1975 Ppb., 128 pp., ill., $2.00, (Wilshire).

The I Hate to Camp Book, Charmaine Severson. A survival manual for the camping mother. After all, she says, why plan a nightmare? Provides answers to hassles like: "The canvas cave," "your non-wardrobe," eating out with "no faucet, no cupboards, no fridge." 1975 Ppb., 178 pp., ill., $2.95, (Dell).

The Complete Book of Practical Camping, John Jobson. This is the work of a professional outdoorsman drawing from a lifetime's experience in the wilds. With an obvious love for the subject, he discusses authoritatively tents and other shelters, clothing, backpacking, camp food and cooking, vehicles, tools and survival . . . on all kinds of terrain. 1974 Hb., 247 pp., ill., $10.00, (Winchester).

The Family Book of Camping, Leonard Fabian. Places emphasis on the joys and problems of family camping from planning, transportation and making camp to survival, canoeing, and snow camping. 1973 Ppb., 149 pp., ill., $1.50, (Dell).

Camper's Digest, Erwin & Peggy Bauer, eds. Ideal book for the novice who wants to go camping, but doesn't have any idea where, how or when. This book has 45 different articles covering just as many possibilities—from backpacking and camping-fishing to bike camping and snow camping. 1974 Ppb., 288 (oversize) pp., ill., $5.95, (Digest Books).

The Camper's Guide to Alaska, the Yukon, and Northern British Columbia, Raymond Bridge. Beginning with an introduction to Alaska and the Canadian Northwest—the seasons, weather and climate—this book goes on to discuss driving to Alaska, the ferries and the Marine highway, air travel, car camping, backpacking, canoe and kayak travel and ski touring. 1975 Hb. & Ppb., 224 pp., ill., $10.00/$4.95, (Scribner's).

America's Camping Book, Paul Cardwell, Jr. This completely revised edition covers every facet of camping including the most efficient ways to camp, the location and rules of major campsites in the US, Mexico, and Canada; emergency tactics and survival techniques, camp cooking, outfitters and camping organizations. Completely updated. 1976, 590 pp., ill., $17.00, (Scribner's).

Light Weight Camping Equipment and How to Make It, Cunningham & Wanson. Handy with your hands? You won't need to buy all that overpriced camping equipment. With this book—just make it yourself! 1976 Hb. & Ppb., ill., $8.95/ $4.95, (Scribner's).

Alaska by Pickup Camper, P.W. Trout. For those who are planning a trip on the Alcan Highway. Problems have been predicted and dealt with in this book. 1972 Ppb., 138 pp., ill., $3.95, (Trail-R Club of America).

A Pocket Guide to Animal Tracks. Enjoy your next outdoor trip more by gaining a knowledge of wildlife with this clear guide containing lifelike sketches and concise descriptions of the habits, characteristics, paw and hoof prints of 44 North American animals. 1968 Ppb., 57 pp., ill., $2.95, (Stackpole).

Canoeing

Boats and automobiles have a number of similarities: both are forms of transportation, both provide recreation, and both come in a wide variety of models and styles. The boating analog of the luxury sedan is the fancy motor runabout, while a kayak is much like a sports car. The traditional open canoe compares with a family station wagon equipped with four-wheel drive. Like the 4WD wagon the canoe is rugged and versatile. It's a means of getting off the beaten path to find excitement, beauty and solitude.

The recreational aspects of canoeing can be divided into four basic categories: cruising, wilderness, whitewater, and racing. Cruising is nothing more than paddling easily on a lake or river. It may involve camping, or even some mild whitewater, but it's canoeing for canoeing's sake. A cruise may be an hour's paddle down the river that flows through your town, or it may be a week-long trip on a wild and scenic river. Most cruisers camp on their longer trips, but some canoe "white collar": they secure lodging in towns along the way.

Wilderness canoeing is a logical extension of cruising. The canoe is an ideal vehicle for wilderness travel, since it can haul plenty of gear and provisions into places where there are no roads. In a true wilderness there are no motels, cabins, stores, picnic tables, or toilets. The wilderness tripper must be totally self-contained and self-sufficient for the duration of his trip. This challenge eventually proves irresistable to many cruisers.

Whitewater canoeing is the sport of running rapids. The open canoe is well-suited to this activity, although it is less maneuverable and much more prone to swamping out than a covered "whitewater boat", such as a kayak. Running rapids in an open canoe still is thrilling, and those paddlers with fine skill can negotiate awesome water. The beginning canoeist should not attempt to run true white water, since this requires knowledge of a wide variety of paddle strokes, familiarity with the hydrodynamics of the canoe, and the ability to read water. These skills come with time.

Canoe racing takes a combination of skill, stamina, teamwork and the will to practice, practice, practice. The successful racer devotes nearly every spare minute to workouts and practice, striving to shave a few seconds off his time. Races can be held on either white water or flat water, and each requires different skills, techniques, and equipment.

The best place to learn the basics of canoeing is on a pond or small lake, where there are no currents or motorboats. It is best to have an experienced canoeist along as a teacher and critic, since he or she can spot and correct errors in technique before they become habits. If you don't know any experienced canoeists, consider joining a canoe club. They can give instruction, information on lakes and rivers in your area, and tips on buying or renting equipment. In addition, other club members are often good sources for used equipment.

Short of having a teacher, the next best thing is to thoroughly study a good book on canoeing technique before setting out. Re-study it after your first attempts, to see what you did wrong. (Note: don't try to learn to canoe on a windy day). Don't skip the sections on safety. A well-designed canoe is a very safe craft, but canoeists do drown – usually as a result of attempting water beyond their skills.

Canoes can be rented in almost any moderately large town, and nearly everywhere in popular canoeing areas. Many sporting goods dealers who sell canoes also rent them. Your local Chamber of Commerce, or the Yellow Pages ("Boats –

"An experienced canoeists thrills with anticipation at the sight of tumbling whitewater. The stimulating mixture of enthusiasm and apprehension as you approach a good drop, the hellacious fun of your roller coaster ride, and the deep satisfaction afterward are part and parcel of a rare experience." (Yallalee)

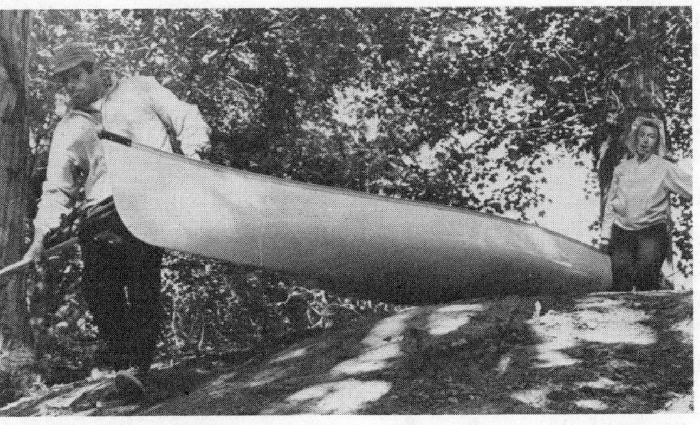

A portage is no fun, but the water on the other side is usually worth carrying a canoe.

rental", and "Rental Agencies"), may be able to help. Depending on the area, canoes rent from $7 to $10 per day.

After you've learned enough to feel comfortable in a canoe, you'll probably start thinking about trips outside your area. Canoeing and exploring seem to go hand-in-hand. Most good canoeing rivers are not suitable for motorboating (one of the reasons canoeists prefer them), so they're little known by the general public. However, nearly every state publishes some sort of canoeing guide, and many of these are remarkably complete. You can obtain them simply by writing the State Department of Natural Resources, Conservation, or Tourism in the capital city. Once you've decided on an area, a letter to the local Chamber of Commerce should put you in touch with some outfitters. Clubs are often good places to find people who've taken the trip themselves.

Most people sooner or later decide to invest in equipment of their own. If you do a fair amount of canoeing, it's cheaper. Hopefully, you will have done enough canoeing with rented or borrowed equipment to have a pretty good idea of what you need – but here are some pointers. The standard length for an open canoe is 17 feet: anything much shorter will draw too much water with a crew of two and gear, and anything much longer will be too heavy to portage comfortably. Traditional wood-and-canvas canoes are like fine pieces of furniture: beautiful, functionally elegant . . . and devilishly expensive. Most modern canoes are made of either aluminum or fiberglass. All things considered, they are probably about equal. The fiberglass manufacturing process does allow for greater freedom of design, leading to canoes with highly developed handling characteristics and some real clunkers. A good aluminum or fiberglass canoe will cost in the neighborhood of $18–$25 per foot of length.

Paddles are like shoes: any old thing will do for casual use, but in serious going the lack of quality soon makes itself known. A good paddle gives increased comfort, control and durability. Good wooden paddles are made of spruce or ash, weighing almost twice as much but being somewhat more durable. Some excellent wood paddles have blades made of strips of wood, laminated edge-to-edge. There are also good paddles made with aluminum shafts and fiberglass blades. Quality spruce or ash paddles run from $15–$20. Laminated wood paddles cost $20–$35. The best aluminum/fiberglass paddles are in the $45 range. As a rough rule-of-thumb, the bowman's paddle should reach his/her chin, while the sternman's should be of nose or forehead height.

Learning to paddle a canoe needn't be more difficult than learning to drive a car. And it can be a lot more rewarding.

—Gary Myers

Gary Myers has done a lot of canoeing and kayaking and is a frequent contributor to **Down River** *Magazine.*

Whitewater Canoeing

A friend of mine who is also an airplane pilot and a skier, when asked to name his most exciting activity, answered immediately: "Whitewater canoeing". He's not alone in his opinion: the experienced canoeist thrills with anticipation at the sight of tumbling whitewater and the roar is a symphony of challenge. The stimulating mixture of enthusiasm and apprehension as you approach a good drop, the exuberant fun of your rollercoaster ride, and the deep satisfaction afterward are part and parcel of a rare experience.

The open canoe is undeniably not the best craft for running rapids – the past decade has seen generations of high-performance rapids boats evolve into maneuverable and virtually unswampable kayaks and covered canoes. But the open canoe lives – it is not a museum piece by a long shot. It has virtues, such as its great cargo-carrying capacity, that covered boats lack. Although the open canoe in some form was one of the earliest modes of water transportation, predating kayaks and rowboats, it can be considered a "compromise" craft. Unlike most compromises, however, it fills its niche comfortably, maneuvering gracefully yet carrying hundreds of pounds of people and gear when necessary.

The paddler who challenges rapids in an open canoe shares the spirit of the artist who shuns the camera in favor of brush and canvas. He works with that which is ancient and painstaking, not that which is modern and precise. Forget your difficult class IV and V drops in water – the open canoe is not made for them. But the medium level II's and III's, there's another story. A class III river may quickly bore a kayaker, but the most experienced open canoeist can find it a continuing challenge.

The class II or III wild river is the open canoe's forte. A wild river is any one that flows through wild country; through land which bears little or no evidence of man's activities. There may be roads nearby, or even an occasional cabin, but there are no towns or dams, and few bridges. The wild river is unspoiled. For safety's sake, it is unwise to run whitewater in a remote wilderness: if help is needed, it may be days away. Experienced open canoeists can safely paddle class II water carrying fifty or sixty pounds of camping gear, making a several days' trip possible. This makes you an independent paddler, free of support personnel.

On an extended trip you can find long stretches of fast-moving but relatively calm water, clear and unpolluted, winding through wild and picturesque country. You can find splendor and solitude in effortlessly gliding past deep forests and meadows. The river is at peace with itself, and the mood is contagious.

At intervals the dozing river stirs like a great beast, dancing in riffles and mild rapids. The canoeists are pulled from their reveries to maneuver their craft through the maze of rocks and shallows.

The beast fully awakens. It stretches in quiet pools, gathering its strength for a headlong rush down one of the rapids

"Canoe racing takes a combination of skill, stamina, teamwork and the will to practice. The successful racer devotes nearly every spare minute to workouts and practice, striving to shave a few seconds off his time."

that make it a whitewater river. It rages and roars as its clear flow turns to sparkling foam, boiling, swirling, and tumbling through chutes and down abrupt drops. It bares its teeth at no one in particular, fierce boulders jutting up through the turbulence. The paddlers approach the rapid alert and wary, with confidence and optimism born of experience. They know that the river is a friendly beast: it means no harm, but its every move must be anticipated. After a run their knowledge and skills are rewarded with exhilaration and a sense of satisfaction that comes from passing a severe test.

The expert canoeist is far from oblivious to the enormous power of the water beneath him. He knows that the river, unaware and dispassionate, is infinitely more powerful than he, that it is foolish to regard the river as an adversary. The paddler who considers the river his opponent is entering a lopsided battle. He can only lose: he may win the "battle", but he definitely has lost the joy of spirit that can accompany him through the snarling peaks of foam. The joy of running whitewater lies in the knowledge that your skills have qualified you to work in alliance with the river, to perform precision ballet with one of the most awesome forces in nature.

When the whitewater canoeist makes camp for the night, he relaxes in a glow of accomplishment. His meal is all the heartier, for he earned it: he has brought his boat and cargo into an area denied to all but those with special skills and knowledge.

And when he finally retires for the night, weary from work and lulled by the sounds of a distant rapid, he can sleep secure knowing tomorrow will be as good as today.

—**Gary Myers**

For More Information

There are two nationally-presented magazines covering canoeing. Besides these, most outdoor magazines do carry articles on the subject.

Down River, Box 366, Mountain View, Calif. 94040. Published monthly at $8.00 per year. The leading publication in the field and the only monthly magazine covering the sport. Excellent articles and photos with most emphasis on how-to rather than news.

Canoe, 1999 Shepard Rd., St. Paul, Minn. 55116. Published bimonthly at $5.00 per year. Has good articles and a lot of ads.

Here are the major organizations involved with canoeing.

American Canoe Association, 4260 E. Evans Ave., Denver, Colo. 80222. The sanctioning organization for all canoe and kayak competition in US.

United States Canoe Association, 1818 Kensington St., Wayne, Ind. 46805.

American River Touring Association, 1016 Jackson St., Oakland, Calif. 94607.

There are many sources for equipment and here are a few to get you started. Check the magazines listed above for more addresses; additional information is listed under kayaking.

Grumman Boats, DR-E, Marathon, N.Y. 13803. Make many different types of canoes. They have a free catalog and will tell you their nearest dealer.

Seda Products, Dept. D, 922 Industrial Blvd., Chula Vista, Calif. 92011. Has a catalog filled with a lot of good stuff, mainly kayaking but also canoeing.

Cannon Products, Inc., 2345 N.W. 8th Ave., Faribault, Minn. 55021. Makes the Power Paddle. Has a free catalog.

Woodlyte, Box 204, Lemont, Penn. 16851. Makes paddles. Free information on request.

Here are some books. All are available from World Publications, Box 366, Mountain View, Calif. 94040 at the price listed* plus 25 cents each for postage.

Pole, Paddle and Portage, Bill Riviere. A complete guide to canoeing for the beginner. Covers everything from the basics of choosing your canoe and loading it in your car through the techniques for any conditions. 1969 Hb., 270 pp. ill., $6.95, (Reinhold).

Introduction to Water Trails in America, Robert Colwell. Practical guides to the best trips throughout the nation, with details on facilities, challenges and things to do and see, 1973 Ppb., 192 pp., ill., $3.95, (Stackpole).

Canoe Camping, Carle Handel. For the serious wilderness canoe camper, the author has given a guide which sets down on paper his vast store of knowledge. 1953 Hb., 196 pp., ill., $7.95, (Ronald).

Canoeing, Michaelson & Ray. Newcomers to canoeing will find comprehensive information on buying canoes, paddles and other equipment, plus instruction on how to paddle and steer. For the more advanced canoer, there are chapters on camping by canoe, reading the rapids, and racing. 1975 Hb. & Ppb. 224 pp., ill., $10.00/$4.95, (Regnery).

Canoeing Wilderness Waters, G. Heberton Evans III. The essentials from handling to portaging, maintenance to selection, plus all the techniques for paddling in the different types of water. 1973 Hb., 256 pp., $15.00, (Barnes).

The Survival of the Bark Canoe, John McPhee. Henri Vailancourt, one of three or four men in America who build bark canoes in the same manner and with the same tools as the Indians did, tells the unique story of the building of birchbark canoes and of a 150-mile canoe trip through the Maine woods. Junior High and up. 1975 Hb., 176 pp., ill., $7.95, (Farrar, Strous & Giroux).

Card Games

Poker, tarot, whist, old maid, slapjack, blackjack, faro, cribbage, solitaire – the roster of card games or games that use cards easily runs into the hundreds. Although the origins of playing cards can probably be traced to ancient China, cards very similar to those in use today were common in Europe during the late 14th century. It is probable that such cards either returned to Europe with wandering China traders, or originated in Europe in something very near their present form.

A 52-card deck divided into four suits of 13 cards each is in standard use through the world. The suits are named hearts, diamonds, clubs or spades. In each suit the cards are numbered two through 10 plus an ace, king, queen and jack. Two jokers are commonly included in each deck, as these cards are actively used in many games.

Before most games, the cards are prepared by shuffling and then cutting. This assures randomness within the deck. A game is commonly started by a dealer handing (or dealing) one card to each player in order, beginning with the player to his left and proceeding clockwise. Cards are dealt until each player has the correct number for the game to be played. It is considered a sin of great gravity to deal cards from the bottom of a deck.

On Poker Odds

The basic idea of poker is to end up with a five-card hand better than those of all other players in your game. Poker tends to expose a wide variety of human weaknesses–greed, inability to quit a loser, fear, hate, bad temper, and even curiosity. Being able to read an opponent's characteristics, while at the same time concealing his own, gives any player an immediate edge. The biggest advantage, however, can be gained by a thorough working knowledge of the odds against drawing or improving various hands.

From a deck of 52 playing cards, slightly less than 2.6 million separate and distinct five-card hands can be dealt. The value of each of these poker hands is ranked by its relative frequency of being drawn pat (on the first deal). Here is a ranking list of the numbers of each hand possible when all combinations are considered: Straight Flushes . . 40, Four of a Kind . . 624, Full House . . 3,744, Flush . . 5,108, Straight . . 10,200, Three of a Kind . . 54,912, Two Pair . . 123,552, One Pair . . 1,098,240.

Making a few mathematical calculations, we can come up with the following table of odds against drawing various pat hands: Straight Flush . . 72,194 to one, Four of a Kind . . 4,164 to one, Full House . . 693 to one, Flush . . 507 to one, Straight . . 254 to one, Three of a Kind . . 46 to one, Two Pair . . 20 to one, One Pair . . 1.3 to one.

From this point, we can determine many other sets of odds for getting some sort of help by drawing after a discard. The odds for helping a hand by drawing three cards against a pair, for example, are as follows: Four of a Kind . . 359 to one, Full House . . 97 to one, Three of a Kind . . eight to one, Two Pair . . five to one.

Probably more valuable, are a few sets of random odds against helping various common incomplete hands. The chances of filling an inside straight by drawing one card, for example, are 11 to one, but completing a straight open at both ends goes down to five to one. Improving a four flush runs 4½ to one, while improving a straight four flush to a straight flush carries 46 to one odds.

Now, keep in mind that the above odds are strictly mathematical. They will increase and decrease according to your discards and what cards might already be showing. By combining the above rough tables with a knowledge of what cards have been already drawn, you can usually roughly calculate the chances of filling an inside straight or turning two pair into a full house. If you do make that big hand, though, be sure to keep a poker face!

–Pete Reeves

Pete Reeves wins often enough at poker to draw interest from the Internal Revenue Service.

For More Information

There are several books that should be of interest. For additional information check Bridge and Gambling. All books are available from World Publications, Box 366, Mountain View, Calif. 94040 at the price listed* plus 25 cents each postage.

Cohen's Complete Book of Gin Rummy, Cohen and Schaff. All aspects of the game in one thorough volume. Terminology, basic play, advanced strategy and tricks, plus a section on gin. 1973 Hb., 346 pp., ill., $6.95, (Grosset & Dunlap).

Play Gin to Win, Irwin Steig. Witty, enjoyable and instructive reading about how to play the percentages and the players, and strategy that piles up the points. 1971 Ppb., $1.95, (Simon & Schuster).

Cribbage is the Name of the Game, Richard Lowder. Despite its popularity, very little has been written about cribbage in books on card games. Here, the author gives you the information you need to play. 1975 Ppb., 60 pp., $1.50, (Harper & Row).

All About Cribbage, Douglas Anderson. The author has been playing cribbage for over 50 years and has collected his own materials on the historical and mathematical aspects of the game. Here he sets down everything about rules based on the six-card game for two to four players. 1971 Hb., 112 pp., $4.95, (Winchester).

How to Win at Stud Poker, James Wickstead. Observing the game as a mathematician, psychologist, and player, the author offers a short history, then delves seriously into luck, probability, rules, mechanics, mathematics, philosophy and ethics of the sport of kings. 1938 Ppb., 116 pp., $2.50, (Gambler's).

Poker to Win, Al Smith. Ever feel you've been cheated but you're not sure how? This is a comprehensive expose of every poker cheater's angles and moves from welshing to false shuffling–of which any serious poker player must be cognizant. 1931 Ppb., 64 pp., $2.00, (Gambler's).

Poker for Fun and Profit, Irwin Steig. The last deal is coming around – you need that ace. Is it still in the deck? Irwin Steig turns his card abilities toward winning play, so you'll know whether that card you just got is the ace. Strategies, tactics, percentages and lots more. 1971 Ppb., $1.95, (Simon & Schuster).

Card Games, Know the Game Series. Here is a good beginner's guide to playing Solo Whist, Black Maria, Cribbage, Newmarket, Skat, Piquet, and Gin Rummy; with rules, tactics and strategy for each game. 1974 Ppb., 36 pp., ill., $1.50 (E.P. Publishing).

Playboy's Book of Games, Edwin Silberstang. This is a thick little pocket book which contains all the information an expert or beginner needs when he sits down to a friendly, or not so friendly game at home or in a casino. Facts and advice range from psychological aspects of winning play to foolproof methods of detecting cheating. 1972 Ppb., 511 pp., ill., $1.95, (Playboy Press).

Win at Poker, Jeff Rubens. There are ways to improve your poker game, and this is one of the best easy-to-follow guides to poker skill and enjoyment. 1968 Ppb., 224 pp., ill., $2.25, (Crowell).

How to Win at Blackjack, Charles Einstein. A professional, yet simplified, method of card counting with variable strategies. This is a great book for every serious blackjack player. 1968. Ppb., $2.00, (Gambler's Book Club)

Common Sense in Poker, Irwin Steig. Draw poker, five-card stud, seven-card stud, high-low split and wild-card variations are all dealt with in a clear, sensible way. The author sets up the situation around the table, then asks you what you would do, explaining what is the correct bid and why. 1963 Ppb., 188 pp., ill., $1.95, (Simon & Schuster).

Poker Strategy and Winning Play, A.D. Livingston. A lively exposition of the strategies of poker, the chances, the statistical odds and nuances necessary to win. 1971 Hb., 227 pp., $5.95, (Lippincott).

Cat Showing

Cat shows are held throughout North America as well as overseas. There are eight cat showing associations in America, and each animal must be registered with the association sanctioning a show. Clubs advertise their shows well in advance through cat magazines, and an entry must be filed prior to the closing date.

At a show, each cat is judged within its own breed and ribbons are awarded for each placing. Finally, the best of each breed is matched against the best of all other breeds in order to determine a Best of Show winner. This is done by comparing each cat to a set standard of excellence, and subtracting points for each judging area not up to standard. A perfect score is 100, but the highest score ever attained was 99 by Nikki Horner's Shawnee Moonflight. Usually a score in the high 90's will take Best of Show.

The ultimate award each year in cat showing is Cat of the Year. Scores are kept for this award by adding up points for the number of cats that a champion defeats in each show. Obviously the larger the show, the more points awarded toward the Cat of the Year. It is possible, however, to pile up a high point total by entering a very large number of smaller cat shows, a situation that gives wealthy owners an advantage. Few animals take Cat of the Year honors more than one time, and only Shawnee Moonflight has taken the award three times, in 1960, 1961 and 1963.

The Babe Ruth of Cat Showing

Nikki Horner of Louisville, Kentucky is the Babe Ruth of cat showing. A former Miss Kentucky, she has bred the only three-time Cat of the Year in Shawnee Moonflight, a male Persian, and has bred more Grand Champions and Best of Shows than anyone ever. Each time she enters a show, she stands a 90 percent chance of carrying off Best of Show. Not a bad batting average in anyone's league.

Nikki became interested in cats at the age of 15 or 16. The Siamese breed appealed to her, and after some deliberation she decided to go after the best she could find. "I talked my parents into buying the very best in the country," Ms. Horner remembers, "but the people who owned him wouldn't sell him to me. So I sent off and bought the father and mother of that champion Siamese. It was the only way around the no-sale obstacle."

These first Siamese were bred and a male sold to another cat breeder. A female sired by this male was then bred with the original male. This father-daughter breeding resulted in Nikki Horner's first Cat of the Year in 1949. It had taken two years of breeding for her to reach the top.

When Ms. Horner began breeding cats in Louisville, she was in a total vacuum, with no one to instruct or advise her. Her early knowledge was accumulated primarily by observation, experience and a certain amount of intuition. After seeing her first cat show in Milwaukee, she returned to Louisville and formed Kentucky's first cat club and staged that state's first cat show.

During her early cat showing years, Nikki supported her hobby by modeling. In recent years, however, cat breeding has become a full-time business. Her Shawnee Cattery employs six people full-time and sells from 150 to 200 pure-bred cats of extremely high quality each year. She sells mostly to breeders and show enthusiasts. Ms. Horner's cats have gained such a reputation for excellence that she can command prices up to $1500 for a particularly good kitten.

Certainly there must be some secret to Nikki Horner's success. "I think it's more or less determination and dedication. First you find out what you want, and figure out where you are going. Then it's just a matter of going out and doing it. Naturally, you have to keep at it and be very, very determined. Never be satisfied with less than perfection. It boils down to perfection, determination and dedication. . .and perhaps pride. I hate to go to a show and not be tops."

A thorough knowledge of breeding and genetics is also important to get the right qualities in a kitten. "If you have a male you have used for two or three years, you soon learn which qualities he throws. Then you have to breed a female for two or three litters and see what she lacks. Finally, it's just a matter of judgment in crossing the two to produce an improved cat."

Is it possible to breed a perfect show cat? Nikki Horner feels that she did in the case of Shawnee Moonflight. "If I ever get another one like that again, I'd consider myself most fortunate. No one else has ever had a cat like that. Cat experts generally agree he was the most perfect show cat ever bred. No cat has ever scored a perfect 100, but Moonflight scored 99. He was the cat I became most attached to. One year I spent six months on the road with him, almost constantly showing. When he died of *nephritis* (kidney failure) seven years ago, I was devastated. He was not a very big Persian, but his conformation was just fantastic."

Ms. Horner has even produced a show cat breed of her own, by crossing a Copper-Eyed Black American shorthair with a Burmese to produce the new Bombay breed. Bombays, which look like miniature black panthers, have been officially sanctioned and can be shown as a championship breed starting May 1, 1976.

At her Shawnee Cattery, Nikki Horner takes very careful measures to provide the best possible nutrition for her cats. "There's no way I'd ever feed them canned or dry cat food like you get in the supermarket. We manufacture our own meat food from chicken, lean beef, kidney and liver. I must keep the exact recipe secret, but these are the ingredients. In the long run it is much cheaper to feed the cats such a quality diet, because canned or dry cat food is only about half as good nutritionally. They would have to eat a considerable amount of that before they got any nutrition out of it.

"Cats don't need variety in their diet; they only need a balanced diet. Humans find it difficult to understand this, because we thrive on variety. A cat's stomach, on the other hand, is simply not geared for variety. They are carnivorous animals and should eat meat as they would in the wild. All they need is a balanced diet of chicken, beef and organ meats.

"For pet owners, the *worst* thing that could ever be done is to feed a cat commercial dry food. It even *kills* Tom cats. I'd say it causes *systitis.* The cat can't urinate, because he gets clogged up from the urinary solids building in his bladder. It plugs up the urethra, killing him almost immediately." Nikki also suggests that pet owners shy away from feeding their cats fish, milk, and anything with pork.

Ms. Horner advises all cat owners to keep their animals inside. "To keep a cat is to keep it in. Let one out just a moment and he will run across a street and under a car's wheels. Outside, dogs will get them, or fleas or ear mites. Cats that live outside have an average life span of three to five years, while an inside cat will live 15."

After 32 years of raising and showing cats, Nikki Horner still receives a thrill from competition. "The excitement is still there. In many cases it's even greater than in my early years, because I can appreciate excellence more. When you know just about everything about something, you can gain more joy from it. I like to win, but the excitement comes more from some judges than others. A few judges' opinions are worth more, and some competition is more stimulating, especially at the bigger shows like Madison Square Garden."

Due to the pressures of running her own cat business, Ms. Horner does not show as often today as she did in the past.

"I exhibit about seven shows a year, and I try to plan them graphically to get to different parts of the country and to new shows each year. I don't necessarily return to the same show each year, but there are a few that I like and I go to them just for the fun of it. I try to go to a few different shows each year, particularly if there's going to be a new club with a first show. I'll go because they are so thrilled to have me.

"I would like to show more often and go for the top awards again, but I don't have that much time. I can't be gone from the cattery as much anymore, because I do a large amount of breeding. I have to be sure I'm there the minute the cats deliver kittens to keep from losing any. Sometimes I'll sit up three nights a week with this, and have gone as much as a month of staying up late every night.

"When I enter cats in a show, I go with my own mobile cattery. I take along all my own cages and set them up in the motel room. I never leave the cats in the show hall overnight, but take them back to the motel. I also take along all their food in a cooler.

"I enter between 10 and 15 cats at a show, but when I show, I can't reveal where I'm going to be showing ahead of time. If showers find out in advance that I'm coming, it cuts entries. The people out for top awards won't show, so it's worthless for me. The people I want to compete with won't come."

Nikki Horner has been raising and showing cats for such a long period and with such intensity that she calls it a way of life. "I started quite young with the idea of having something I could continue to be good at for all my life. It's been so enjoyable that I'll never quit."

—Dave Prokop and Bill Reynolds

Dave and Bill both work at World Publications. Dave owns several cats and has a great interest in cat showing. Dave interviewed Nikki Horner and Bill put it together.

For More Information

Cats Magazine, 2900 Jefferson Ave., Washington, Penn., 15301. Published monthly at $7.95 per year. *Cat World,* 5395 S. Miller St., Littleton, Colo. It is a bi-monthly and costs $5.00 per year. *Cat Fancy,* 248 S. Robertson Blvd., Beverly Hills, Calif. 90211, which is a bi-monthly at $6.95 for eight issues.

The Cat Fanciers Association, 11 Globe Court, Red Bank, N.J. 07701, is the largest organization and sponsors approximately 80 shows a year. The American Cat Fanciers Association, P.O. Box 203, Point Lookout, Maryland, 65726, sponsors approximately 70 shows a year.

Here are two books that were recommended to us. Both are available from World Publications, Box 366, Mountain View, Calif. 94040 at the price listed* plus 25 cents each postage. Write for a complete list.

The Complete Book of Cat Health and Care, J.J. McCoy. In clear, nontechnical language, this book offers comprehensive advice on every aspect of cat health and care during every period of the animal's development from a small kitten to a mature cat. A book not to be passed up by cat lovers. 1968 Hb., 237 pp., ill., $5.95, (Coward, McCann, Geoghegan).

The Complete Cat Encyclopedia, Grace Pond. This is a gigantic book which lists more cats than you ever knew were possible. Every cat is listed, described, and has a picture of it. This is also the best book on breeding, raising and showing cats. Contains two large color sections of cats, cats, cats! 1972 Hb., 384 (oversize) pp., ill., $15.00, (Crown).

Cave Diving

Cave diving is another aspect of man's inquisitive and exploring mind. He is challenged by what can be found in waterfilled passageways and awed by the beauty that surrounds the areas where caves are located.

Why would anyone want to risk the danger of diving in caves? The underwater photographer finds in the natural settings and crystal clear water a rare opportunity to pursue his hobby or profession in the most perfect of situations. The biologist enters a whole new field of study when researching the fauna of underwater caves. Some of his finds may include fossils or mutant strains of fish and crustaceans. But the enjoyment of recreation is by far the biggest reason why so many divers file to the Florida springs each weekend. Where else can you find dive sites with few people, 72 degree water temperature, and unlimited visibility all within a few hours drive of a major metropolis?

Many of the pioneers of cave diving are no longer with us due to diving accidents. Fortunately, other cave divers took the knowledge gained from the accidents and applied it to their own diving procedures, greatly cutting down on the possibilities of an accident.

As in almost every diving venture, the name of Jacques Cousteau surfaces as the individual to do something first. In the first recorded cave dive with Scuba, August 27, 1946, Cousteau and Frederic Dumas explored the Fountain of Valcluse near Avignon, France. The depth of the dive was 200 feet and their penetration was 400 feet into the cave, remarkable for the kind of equipment they used.

Six years after the Cousteau/Dumas dive, underwater cave exploration came to the United States. In 1953 an expedition was formed expressly for cave diving research. The expedition sponsored by the Western Speleogical Institute, included a young man by the name of Jon Lindbergh. Lindbergh, 20 years old at the time, discovered Bower Cave, one of the largest underwater caverns in the western United States.

In the same year, 1953, another research project was attempted, this one to find the source of the hot springs in Devil's Hole in Nevada. The divers were William Brown and Edward Simmons, both members of the Southern California Chapter of the National Speleogical Society. Brown's first dive took him to a depth of 150 feet. Using his high powered light, he let the beam penetrate the darkness another 200 feet . . . still no bottom in sight, and to this day, the bottom at Devil's Hole has not been found.

Over the years, perfected techniques, training, equipment, and increased research have led to a reduction in the accident rate for cave diving. The many thousands of safe cave dives made each year has shown that thorough training, level-headedness, and proper equipment can keep the accident rate low. If an individual would like to become a competent cave diver, it is absolutely essential to receive instruction from an organization such as the National Association for Cave Diving. These instructors will show you the proper methods and techniques that will lead, with experience, to becoming a competent cave diver.

—Bill Eshelman

Bill Eshelman is a veteran Florida cave diver transplanted to California where he enjoys writing, scuba diving and parachuting.

An Impression

Conquest of the unknown and the urge to discover is what brought me to begin scuba diving and what later prompted me to begin cave diving with two of my friends.

Our early attempts in the exploration of caves were marred by incidents that could have been crucial but we fortunately pulled through them. I feel we were a bigger hazard to ourselves than the cave system was. People have accidents in underwater caves primarily because of human error. The cave does not swallow them. The cave will not hurt you unless you compound the hazards that can befall you.

Not planning air consumption and not knowing how much air you have in your tanks may not be fatal mistakes in open water but in caves they are terminal because you have no free access to the surface and life sustaining air. Proper training, proper equipment and common sense will teach you to realize the hazards and prepare you to handle the worst possible situations.

Few cave systems are easily located. Most involve a long walk in the heat toting your gear, with bugs biting and harassing the hell out of you. The beauty of the areas is often overwhelming; the land is unusually rugged as if hewn from a chunk of granite.

On a typical Florida cave dive, the early morning dew lies heavy on the earth as though it's just been watered. Spanish moss hangs from aged Cypress trees. Because of the remote location very few people ever crowd to the springs and sinks for recreation. Only divers.

As you watch the water from shore, the blue hue seems to beckon you with a sensuality known only to those who've experienced the joy of diving in some of the most perfect conditions in the world.

As you return to the van to suit up for the dive, you may find your heart rate has picked up and you are excited about penetrating into the cave. Now comes the worst part—getting dressed. Much like a knight of the deep you always need help with your armor, and your buddies serve as your page and you as theirs.

The equipment is hot, heavy and uncomfortable. First it is on with your wet suit, then the buoyancy compensator, followed by the compass, depth gauge and watch. A small knife is strapped to a forearm of your preference. A communications slate is put in a pocket of your wet suit along with submersible decompression tablets.

Now come the bulky items—the twin 72 cubic foot air tanks with an octopus/quadrapus regulator attached to the manifold. The air is turned on and it's strapped on your back. Last but not least put on your eyes beneath the water, your face mask and primary and secondary lights. This equipment is worn by each member of the dive team. In addition each team has a light safety reel with 500 feet of braided nylon line for marking the progress into and out of the cave system.

The gear is of utmost importance because it is the life support system of the diver and the dive team. In the event of a failure or malfunction of any item, the dive is aborted. The cave diver is much like an astronaut, in that he is totally dependent upon his life support system in an alien environment, and any failure of his equipment leaves him helpless in the hands of the elements.

As you get wet after helping your buddies dress, the cool water bathes your heated body and you begin to relax. You check equipment before leaving the surface and the reel man is the first to surface dive, going down to tie off the line outside the cavern where you can still see and tying it again just before the mouth of the cave.

Your lights are turned on and the brightness permeates the blackness and silouettes many of the formations within your sight, giving them an eerie iridescence. It is arresting to realize that your lights may have been the only illumination in this labyrinth for eons.

The soft melodic sweep of your fins propels you deeper into the cavern and the safety lines vanish behind you as a reminder of your having to return to the surface for survival.

The impression is that you are all suspended like puppets from the ceiling of the cave. You feel like an astronaut in a spacewalk who's orbiting around the earth. Molded like candles in a boutique, with nary a one the same, the limestone formations jut from the ceiling, floor, and walls each displaying a separate personality. Each sweep of your light beam discovers more, a fish swimming upside down or a blind crayfish crawling in a crevice near the bottom of the wall.

One man's air supply is down to his dive termination point and you must return to the surface. From the returning angle the system looks totally different than when entering: it makes you want to thank founding fathers for developing the reel and the techniques and philosophy that make for a safe cave dive.

The dive is over but the memory lingers and will continue to draw individuals whose love for challenge makes cave diving so attractive—and so hazardous for those who are not trained properly. If you would like to learn how to cave dive you should contact an instructor certified by the National Association for Cave Diving.

—Bill Eshelman

For More Information

There are not any magazines devoted exclusively to cave diving but *Skin Diver Magazine* (address under Skin Diving) does have articles from time to time. Newsletters we have been told about but have not seen include: *The Phreatic Diver,* 122 Collins St., San Francosco, Calif. and *NSS Cave Diving Section Newsletter,* RR 14, Box 17, Bloomington, Ind.

The major Cave diving organizations are the National Association for Cave Diving, 2900 NW 29th Ave., Gainesville, Fla. 32601. Also the National Speleological Society, Cave Diving Section, Cave Ave., Huntsville, Ala. 35810 and the California Diving Group, 122 Collins St., San Francisco, Calif. 95916 can supply helpful information.

Most skin and scuba diving shops should be able to supply the equipment that would be needed however these addresses may help: Cave Diving Reel, Bill Schuck, 1453 Highland Ave., Cleveland, Tenn. 37311. For Dry caving gear write Bob and Bob, Box 1187, Alhambra, Calif. 91802. Another good contact is William Cate, PO Drawer 38, Berry Creek, Calif. 95916 who is the leading American authority on cave diving with 20 years of experience. But before venturing any further, you need to read up on cave diving. All of the books listed are available from World Publications, Box 366, Mountain View, Calif. 94040 at the price listed* plus 25 cents postage.

Safe Cafe Diving, Tom Mount, et al. 10 experienced cave divers have banded together to produce this complete manual, offering chapters on different kinds of caves, caving equipment, techniques, the history of cave diving, life support systems, medical aspects, and everything else needed to get started in this exciting sport. 1973 Ppb., 198 pp., ill., $7.50, (NACD).

Mapping Underwater Caves, Exley and Friedman. Two cave diving instructors for the National Association for Cave Diving created this book out of the need for more complete maps of caves. Here are complete instructions for making a systematic record of measured data concerning distance, direction, and depth. 1974 Ppb., 16 (oversize) pp., ill., $2.00, (NACD).

Proceedings of the Fifth Annual Seminar on Cave Diving, Jack Banbury, ed. The basic philosophy of the seminar since its inception in 1968 has been to promote safer cave diving through education and advanced training, and this one was no exception. Lots of relevant information and discussion of new equipment and techniques. 1972 Ppb., 117 pp., ill., $5.00, (NACD).

Proceedings of the Sixth and Seventh Annual N.A.C.D. Seminars and Reserach Papers by N.A.C.D. Instructor Candidates, BIll Schenck, ed. More knowledge of techniques from a multitude of experienced cave divers sharing what they have learned to help make exploring underwater caves safer. 1975 Ppb., 174 pp., ill., $7.00, (NACD).

The Cave Divers, Robert F. Burgess. The author, himself an enthusiastic cave diver, here tells the stories of dozens of explorations in underwater caves and sinkholes, most of which have never appeared in book form. 1975 Hb., 256 pp., ill., $9.95, (Dodd, Mead).

Caving

As the name suggests, caving is the sport-science of exploring caves. The activity, which is also known as *spelunking* (after speleology – the science of studying caves) combines adventure, intellectual and physical challenge and, in varying degrees, danger. As David R. McClury says in his book, **The Amateur's Guide to Caves and Caving:** "To the uninitiated it may seem that caves are only dark, dangerous holes in the ground in which it is all too easy to get lost. But to thousands of dedicated people, they offer a unique challenge, both as a sport and a science . . . Caving is similar to mountain climbing, except that the climber can usually see his ultimate goal above, the top of the mountain. A caver, on the other hand, can't see the end of the cave in which he starts out. At least he hopes he can't. He pushes on in the hopes that the end is not just around the next corner, but many miles further ahead. In the language of the caver, he hopes it goes."

The main organization for cavers in North America is the National Speleological Society (NSS) which has 4000 members in 115 chapters, called grottos, throughout the US. Those interested in trying caving should write the NSS headquarters to obtain the address of the nearest grotto, or contact a local caving club. The reasons for so doing are simple. One of the cardinal rules of caving, for beginner and veteran alike, is never cave alone (in fact, the minimum number of people for a safe caving trip is considered to be four – one to stay with the victim in case of injury and two to go for help). In addition, grottos and other caving clubs know where the caves are located, what equipment is needed, how dangerous the caving operations will be, and almost everything else a beginner might want to know.

Due to the fact that a cave environment is a very closed and delicate system, serious cavers are deeply concerned with cave conservation and opposed to popularization of the activity. The NSS has a simple motto that sums up this concern about conservation: "Take nothing but a picture; leave nothing but footprints; kill nothing but time."

Cavers in the US are fortunate since there are numerous caves around the country, although the numbers and types of caves depend upon the region. As of 1972, there were 170 commercial caves in the US (i.e., caves open to the public through guided tours), with Missouri having no fewer than 30 of these. As of February 1973, the US also had four of the five longest caves in the world. The Flint-Mammoth Cave System in Kentucky is by far the world's longest – 144 miles explored thus far!

Personal Equipment

The ability to conserve and regulate body heat is of great importance to cave explorers. In many areas, considerable physical exertion must be used to negotiate rough areas, and heavy work loads raise the body's temperature. On the other hand, many caves are cold, windy and wet, and can rob you of precious body heat. Thus, cavers' personal equipment inventory should be chosen with these factors in mind.

The value of wool clothing should not be overlooked, because it is the only fiber that will retain insulating qualities while wet. Many undereducated hikers and cavers wear cotton shirts and jeans, which when wet actually cause a faster body heat loss than would bare skin. Similarly, down clothing is also less than satisfactory as an insulator in wet caves. I once spent a frozen night in a wet down sleeping bag and was saved from death only by a knowledgeable comrade who knew the symptoms and treatment of hypothermia.

Coveralls should be worn over the wool layers. These zippered coveralls are the same as those worn by mechanics and heavy laborers, except for several modifications. Since many narrow passages can only be negotiated by wriggling headfirst and face up, the back pockets should be stitched shut to keep out dirt. The trousers should be sprayed with silicone for waterproofing and all zippers should be lightly lubricated. If you are really ambitious, reinforcing patches can also be sewn on the seat, knees and elbows.

Hiking boots or Army surplus combat boots are appropriate footgear. With low-cut shoes or boots, it is advisable to wear canvas gaiters to keep out sand and loose pebbles. Gloves are also essential, both for warmth and protection from sharp rocks. Another valuable protective device is a pair of knee pads for crawling over rough and sharp terrain.

Helmets are next on the list and serve to protect a caver from both loose rocks and headjarring falls while climbing. Suspension helmets are the least expensive, but are generally inferior to rock climbers' helmets. A rock climber's helmet is constructed of a tough shell lined with foam rubber padding. It is specially designed for tight-fitting comfort and safety, so for an extra seven or eight dollars you can't go wrong.

A light source is obviously essential to any cave exploring expedition. A carbide lamp is basic, but should be backed up by a flashlight and candle. Spare carbide and water should be carried for the lamp, as well as spare bulbs and batteries for the flashlight and waterproof matches for lighting your candle. Spare parts and a tip reamer for the carbide lamp will complete your light kit, which should always be transported in a waterproof container. Most cavers have also become conservation minded enough to carry a plastic bag to tote out spent carbide, instead of scattering it all over the cave.

Many cavers carry a first aid kit. Its contents should be adequate to cover any medical expertise you might possess. Certainly it should contain materials for stopping bleeding.

Food should always be taken when going underground, even for very short one- or two-hour trips. Emergencies occasionally arise, and such food can provide a quick energy boost. Drinking water, too, should be carried, because many caves are as dry as the Gobi Desert. Extra dry clothing can come in handy, and should be included in the equipment inventory.

To tote all of this personal gear, you will need a small, light and sturdy rucksack. Steer clear of any pack with snap enclosures, because caves tend to be very dirty and even small amounts of grit can render the most expensive snap fastener useless. Try instead for packs that close with belts and buckles.

There are several other types of specialized gear, including waders, wetsuits and drysuits for wet caves, and vertical ascent equipment for wall climbing. All of these pieces of equipment, however, are a bit out of the scope of the average caver and should be added later when more difficult caves are undertaken. If novice cavers stick to the above essentials, they should have hours of safe and enjoyable cave exploring ahead of them.

—Watson Royce

Watson Royce is a marketing executive from Portland, Maine. His idea of a good weekend is "to escape to the utter peace and quiet of a cave. There I can unwind amid nature's unique sculptures."

For More Information

The National Speleological Society, Cave Ave., Huntsville, Ala. 35810 puts out a lot of literature, including *NSS News*, which is a monthly at $6.00 per year. It is free to members. Another good source for information is the Cave Research Foundation, 206 West 18th Ave., Columbus, Ohio 43210. A couple of sources for gear is Speleo Supply Service, Box 2095, Pasadena, Calif. 91105 and B and B Enterprises, Box 1187, Alhambra, Calif. 91802.

Here are some good books on the subject. All are available from World Publications, Box 366, Mountain View, Calif. 94040 at the price listed* plus 25 cents each postage.

Depths of the Earth, William R. Halliday, M.D. A rich, adventurous history of American caves and their explorers – from the pioneer cave explorations of the young George Washington and Thomas Jefferson to the recent Flint Ridge breakthrough into the mammoth cave system. 1975, 416 pp., ill., $14.95, (Harper & Row).

Cave Exploring, Jennifer Anderson. A veteran of caves on three continents, Ms. Anderson explains authoritatively everything about caving from equipment and how to maintain it, essential knots, belaying, rappelling and prusiking, and cable ladder techniques, with two excellent chapters on emergencies and accidents. 1974 Ppb., 126 pp., ill., $4.95, (Association Press).

The Amateur's Guide to Caves and Caving, David R. McClury. How to find caves and what to do with one once you have. The basic skills and tools are presented with an emphasis throughout on conservation. 1973 Ppb., 191 pp., ill., $3.95, (Stackpole).

American Caves and Caving: Techniques, Pleasures and Safeguards of Modern Cave Exploring, William Halliday. A comprehensive manual on caving dealing with cave types, equipment, medicine and first-aid, and technique. This practical and direct approach helps the cave enthusiast widen his field of exploration. 1974 Hb., 348 pp., ill., $10.00, (Harper & Row).

American Caving Illustrated, Story. A wealth of information about the caving scene. Almost all the practical aspects of caving are at least touched upon in this comprehensive manual. A glossary and reading list are included. 1975 Hb., 302 pp., ill., $9.25, (J. Welborn Storey).

Caves, Dr. A.C. Waltham. Geologist's study of caves all over the world; includes biological adaptations, archaeological surveys, and hydrology in lively readable prose. 75 fine full-color plates, index of caves. 1974, 256 pp., ill., $12.50, (Crown).

Checkers

The late and honorable Sir William Ewart Gladstone, British Prime Minister, once remarked: "Everyone plays checkers, but there are few checker players." This apparent contradiction is quite apt, as the latest Gallup Poll states that there are 17,000,000 individuals in the United States that have played (or do play) the game. Less than 5000 of these, however, have been registered by the American Checker Federation as players who approach the game in a scientific manner, and of that number, only 150 to 200 have gained the exalted level of expert.

Defined in the **Encyclopedia Britannica** as one of the "world's oldest intellectual pastimes", checkers dates back to about 3500 B.C. Recognizable equipment from that era has been unearthed from Egyptian tombs. In Classic Greece, Plato discussed the origin of the game, and Homer described Penelope as playing checkers with her suitors.

The first book devoted entirely to the game was by the Spaniard, Antonio de Torquemeda of Valenciȧ in 1547, while the initial work in English was by the London mathematician William Payne in 1756. The introduction to Payne's book was by Dr. Samuel Johnson, a famous devotee of draughts.

Checkers can be depicted as a simple game, but in that statement lies the reason for many misunderstandings. The object of the game is to take 12 round, flat, pieces of wood or plastic and manipulate them on a board of 64 checkered squares so as to capture or render immobile all of an opponent's pieces. By comparison, tennis might also be termed simple, the object being to hit a ball over a net; or football, the object being to advance a ball down a measured field. However, when faced with an opponent who effectively resists these tactics, the resulting game becomes anything but simple.

Checkers on the highest level has been termed a "battle of ideas" with the contestants' intellectual plans acting as the weapons used. By numbering the checker board's squares from 1 to 32 and coding each move with these numbers, a comprehensive record of the mental gymnastics in each game can be preserved for all time in the literature of checkers. In contrast, a tennis or golf stroke, however fine in technique, execution and result, once made, is lost forever or imperfectly reproduced in only two dimensions on film. With the number of coded records available, an aspiring student of checkers can have as his personal tutors all of the game's great masters.

Checkers is one of the world's oldest intellectual pastimes. There are 17 million checker players in the United States, but a mere 5000 approach the game in a scientific tournament style.

Scientific checkers in grandmaster match or tournament play is a grueling test of mental agility requiring enough physical stamina to combat long 12-hour daily sessions. In addition to fighting his opponent's will to win, a tournament player must contend with the inexorable time clock and its mandatory 30 moves per hour. These factors have often produced mental exhaustion, causing a player to panic when in time trouble and make elementary errors that defy logical explanation.

Sometimes ridiculed by the uninformed as a time-waster, the game of checkers has survived through the ages to charm countless thousands who have reached the portals and have been enfolded in its strange fascination. Many spend entire lifetimes in vain pursuit of total mastery. Present world title holder Dr. Marion F. Tinsley, a mathematics professor at Florida A & M, conservatively estimates that he spent 20,000 hours during the first 12 years after taking up the game and prior to winning the world championship in 1955. Retiring undefeated in 1958 to devote his time to research at Florida State University, Tinsley recently returned to competition and exhibited all of his former prowess by winning the 1970 National Tournament. In 1974 he took the coveted Grand Slam with victories in all four of the major American tourneys. Referring to the "simple beauty and elegance of lines of play", Tinsley now treats the game more as a hobby, while in the past it was an obsession, indeed, his whole life.

The respective merits of chess and checkers have been debated for several centuries. Since both have proven incapable of complete mastery, the issue clearly resolves into a standoff. A wise critic once remarked: "The expert in the game of checkers looks down into a deep, dark, fathomless well, whereas the chess master surveys a vast panorama of countryside."

—Richard Fortman

Richard L. Fortman is a checkers champion of some note and serves as Games Editor for the American Checker Federation.

For More Information

There are two publications that will be of interest to anyone who wants to "really" get into checkers.

Master Checkers, 17304 Lahser Rd., Room 215, Detroit, Mich. 48219. Published monthly at $5.00 per year. Only monthly in the world devoted exclusively to checkers.

ACF Bulletin, 3475 Belmont Ave., Baton Rouge, La. 70808. Published bi-monthly for their membership. Dues are $7.00 per year. News, up-coming events, and blow-by-blow accounts of top games fill each issue.

The only national organization is the American Checker Federation, 3475 Belmont Ave., Baton Rouge, La. 70808. The goal of the organization is to promote checkers from the beginner to the master. Write for a copy of "Basic Rules of Checkers" and "Beginners' Corner". Both are very informative. Membership is $7.00 per year.

For more information we suggest contacting the following: Selchow & Righter Co., 2215 Union Blvd., Bay Shore, New York 11706. They make official boards and pieces in official colors and sizes. Tom Wiswell, 4410 4th Ave., Brooklyn, New York 11220 has written more books on the subject than anyone. Many of his out of print books can be obtained through him. Also, Starr Specialty Co., 4983 Ridgebury Blvd., Lyndhurst, Ohio 44124 has a free catalog with a lot of good stuff in it.

Many of the advanced checkers books are unfortunately out of print, but these books are good for the beginner and intermediate player. All are available from World Publications, Box 366, Mountain View, Calif. 94040 at the price listed* plus 25 cents each postage.

How to Win at Checkers, Fred Reinfeld. Explains how to increase your playing strength by developing fine points and winning methods. Included in the contents are basic rules and variations of the game: traps, shots and star moves, and the theory of oppositions. 1957 Ppb., 185 pp., ill., $2.00, (Wilshire).

The Science of Checkers and Draughts, Tom Wiswell. A hundred and one positions from exhibition play are described in this illustrated book. Diagrams, one to a page, show the problem and solution. The author also relates his experiences from 1951 to 1972. 1974 Hb., 128 pp., ill., $4.95, (Barnes).

Checkers Made Easy, Tom Wiswell. A Free-Style World Champion sets down in ten easy lessons what it takes to win checkers. Chapters include: Checkers basics, standard openings and games, checker traps, a two-move guide, and standard endgames. 1971 Ppb. 126pp., ill., $2.00, (Wilshire).

Learn Checkers Fast, Tom Wiswell. Unrestricted World's Checker Champion Tom Wiswell offers here an excellent textbook for the student of, and the experienced in, scientific checker-playing. Seven basic openings, three-move checkers, traps and shots, basic positions and more. 1946 Ppb., 208 pp., ill., $1.95, (McKay).

Win at Checkers, Millard Hopper. Presents in simple terms a lifetime of checker experience by one of the greatest players of all time and the Unrestricted Checker Champion of the World. All questions are anticipated in more than 100 detailed questions and answers about both specific situations and general principles. 1956 Ppb., 109 pp., ill., $1.25, (Dover).

Cheerleading

Cheerleading probably originated with the overzealous sports fan who encouraged those around him to show their enthusiasm with a little vocalized moral support. You'll find this self-appointed cheerleader today with his banners, air horn, signs, and other paraphernalia at most big sports events, but especially at football, basketball, soccer, and ice hockey games. At college games he's often a father, brother, compatriot, or alumnus. At professional contests he's usually the guy who has been a fan of the home-town team since the franchise was established.

Krazy George is the only professional cheerleader in the United States. Besides his famous "kill" cheer and drum, he is noted for bizzare entrances to the playing field. Have you ever seen anybody else crash land a hang glider into the enemy team? (Ing)

From the top of the stands it looks like a fun and easy job—jumping around, hollering, leading rousing roars from the crowd, indulging in crazy stunts, or generally doing a job that thrusts the "cheerleader" right into the spotlight. During the game it can be rather glamorous, but that superficial gaiety belies hours of thinking and creating, learning what makes people excited and what makes them respond.

If you were a high school or college cheerleader, you probably spent a great deal of time asking many questions about enthusiasm, crowd control, emotion, spirit, involvement, leadership, cooperation, and sportsmanship. To be a good cheerleader you had to like people, like working with people. You had to be organized, be willing to exercise authority, and be responsible for certain cheerleading-related tasks. Actually, you probably spent more time overall working on being a good cheerleader off the field than on it!

Of course, the main responsibility of a cheerleader is to raise morale and spirit in the crowd and athletic team. At pep rallies (assemblies designed to promote athletic endeavors and pride) and athletic contests, the cheerleaders lead songs and cheers (short snappy work-sequences that people can shout in unison). They signal when the crowd should yell with vocal commands and big arm and body motions. For example, the cheerleaders signal a crowd to yell "Defense" with a two-beat (for a two-syllable—de-fense—word) motion. That way everyone yells together for an effective, team-inspiring cheer instead of an unintelligible garble of sound.

Today there is also a much more sophisticated, structured, and stylized form of cheerleading that goes beyond the simplicity of short, big-crowd cheers. Competitive cheerleading is off the field and on stage; thus, it gives cheerleaders a chance to show off their performance skills and the degree of proficiency they have achieved. Large and small groups, boys and girls, use intricate formations, exciting tumbling, pyramid, and arcobatic stunts. In addition, they use mind-boggling body movements and high jumps.

Judges watch to see if the cheerleaders' arms and body motions are well-coordinated. They consider the difficulty of the routine, how precise the group is, if the routine is original in composition and balanced in variety (includes formation changes, jumps, stunts, etc.) Most importantly, the judges look to see that the cheerleaders are enjoying themselves and display confidence. The charisma of the group is very important, with the crowds (or judges') response often dependent on the personality and projection of the group.

Both types of cheerleading, however, on-the-field and competitive, develop coordination, strength, and flexibility from the vigorous exercise. Cheerleaders develop self-confidence along with leadership qualities and decision-making skills.

Krazy George

Hello, all you turkeys out there!!"

If you don't think you would like to be attacked by 10 ice hockey players, chased by the police, mauled by sports fans, crash-landed in a hang glider into the opposing team, or snowmobiled out of control across a football field at 60 miles per hour—then cheerleading is not for you. However, if raising your left hand and having 10,000 people yell "earth" then raising your right hand and having 10,000 people across the stadium yell "quakes," if enjoying being recognized almost everywhere you appear in public, if meeting celebrities such as Pele, Lou Rawls, Jim Plunkett, and Billie Jean King, and (blush), if just possibly having your own female fan club appeals to you, then read on . . .

Why am I able to get such a fanatical response from the crowd when groups of cheerleaders cannot? The main reason is that I'm as violent and aggressive in the stands as the players are on the field. I feel and react to each play as the players would, and the crowds sense the emotion and start to react right along with me. This aggressive approach combined with constant movement through the crowds, from group to group, causes people to react with me. Because of my immediate presence, it's a chain reaction, each group heightening the reaction of the next until they all come together into one large loyal group of fans supporting their team.

"From the top of the stands it looks like a fun and easy job. During the game it can be rather glamorous, but that superficial gaiety belies hours of thinking and creating, learning what makes people excited and what makes them respond." (Drennan)

To me, professional cheerleading has to be rated as an all-time great occupation. First, there is not too much competition. At this time I believe I'm the only professional cheerleader, and since I'm the only one, it makes me the best!

Second, I get a great deal of personal satisfaction out of the way fans react to me. I like the feeling I get when people ask me for my autograph, or ask to have their picture taken with me, or ask me to appear at benefits or public functions. I also like their concern about what I am doing and what I will be doing. All these things make me feel good about being a pro cheerleader.

Professional cheerleading has taken me to many parts of North America, including Canada, Hawaii, and the East Coast to cheer for various teams. I have been able to make many new friends and, in some instances, a few enemies on the opposing teams.

I would like to point out two other reasons for my notoriety, namely my drum and my entrances into sporting events. For the people who have not seen me in action, I would like to explain: as I roam through the stands—and so I won't get lost by the fans—I carry a very loud drum which I pound when the occasion arises, which is often. I beat it with the same ferocity as a football player pounds his opposing man. This gets the fans' attention and also makes me happy.

My other system for getting the fans to notice me is to make an outlandish entrance just before a game starts. Some of these entrances have included driving on-field in a snowmobile, coming in airborne from a hang glider, riding a camel, driving a $30,000 Maserati, on the back of a tiger, in a paddy wagon with a police escort, dressed in a tux and driving a Rolls Royce, and being dropped by a helicopter onto the playing field.

If you take my classic entrances, my mad approach to cheerleading, my roaming through the crowds and add it to the crush of fans at a sporting event—you have me—Krazy George!

—Krazy George Henderson

George Henderson, known as "Krazy George," cheers for the San Jose Earthquakes, the California Seals and the San Jose Spartans. His "Kill" cheer is well known. Krazy George Promotions is the only professional cheerleading company we know about.

For More Information

There are two organizations you should know about: The National Cheerleaders Association, Box 30674, Dallas, Tex. 75230 which publishes *Megaphone* magazine. And the International Cheerleading Foundation, The Neil Building, 7800 Conser Place, Shawnee Mission, Kans. 66202 which publishes *Cheerleader* magazine. A good source for supplies is Cheerleader Supply Company, Box 30175, Dallas, Tex. 75230.

There is one good book. It is available from World Publications, Box 366, Mountain View, Calif. 94040 at the price listed* plus 25 cents postage.

The Complete Book of Cheerleading, Herkimer & ed. This book is jam-packed with practical help for cheerleaders of all ages. Cheers, footwork, gymnastic skills, tips for synchronization, and suggestions for boosting school spirit form the integral part of this vividly illustrated guide. 1975, 285 pp., ill., $7.95, (Doubleday).

Chess

There is a widely-held popular belief that chess is "too deep" for the average person. The idea that one has to be "brainy" to play the game is pure nonsense. No more brains are required to play this fascinating game than are needed to master contract bridge or gin rummy. There are millions of chess players in the world, and most of them are just ordinary people of average intelligence. In Russia—where chess is as popular as baseball in the United States—children play chess almost before they learn to speak. In this country, chess is growing rapidly in popularity and is played by men and women of all ages. Thousands of children are playing the game in their homes and in school clubs. (According to a recent Harris poll, more than one out of ten US residents know how to play chess).

It is true that the chess expert—or master, as he is called—can perform remarkable mental feats on the chessboard, but the same thing could be said of other games and sports. The contract bridge master, for instance, is able to make intricate plays which are far beyond the capacity of the average person—but this does not deter a great host of bridge players from enjoying their favorite indoor sport. Similarly, most chess players are incapable of executing the deep combinations and strategic maneuvers of the chessmaster, but they play their own brand of chess and enjoy it. The ordinary player is able to admire the beauty and art of master play, the amazing tactics and perfect timing displayed by these experts, but he plays with opponents of his own strength and enjoys his own games best of all.

Total shut-out concentration is necessary for successful top level chess. As evidenced by the Fischer-Spassky matches, the loss of this concentration can be a disaster.

We invite you to learn chess because it is by far the best two-handed game in existence. It is an exciting, thrilling game—a lifelong source of interest and amusement. An absorbing hobby, chess will provide you with relaxation and recreation in greater measure than any other home game.

And chess is not a slow game. Most friendly contests last about an hour—and every minute is packed full of interest for both players . . .

Chess is easy to learn . . . you can learn how the chessmen move in a few minutes and master all the rules in one or two evenings.

Excerpted from An Invitation to Chess,
—Irving Chernev and Kenneth Harkness

Analysis or Combat?

Why does chess have such broad appeal? It can be played by enemies and by dear friends, by grandfathers with would-be prodigies, by lovers, by seekers after truth. What is truly remarkable is that such a simple board should have evolved to produce such a durable game! The perfect eight by eight, 64 squares! As Lasker says, you can make a chessboard by halving a square, then halving those squares, then halving those. One piece, the Rook, moves just up and down, across and back. The Bishop slides along diagonals. The Queen is a combination of both. The King is a truncated Queen: just one square in any direction. The Knight, so beloved of Nabokov, makes that queer jump of a dog's leg, black to white at a distance of two squares. And the Pawn, the only man so indentured that he must move only forward, at least has the magic chance of turning himself into a Queen, by reaching the eighth rank! That is the substance of this simple game. Edgar Allen Poe was wrong about the complexity of the pieces and the moves; an eight year old gets over that after several games. The only mystery about the game is the mystery of the interaction of the psyche with logic, of combat with analysis.

"My father was serving as a lieutenant in the cavalry division of the Spanish army stationed at Havana, in Morro Castle. My companions were soldiers; my playground a military fort. Here I delighted to listen to the stories of wars, of strategic battles, of military heroes. Here the glamour of military life made its appeal to me. And here I was made to understand, young as I was, the importance to the soldier of a well-planned attack or defense. As I entered my father's quarters one day the scene that greeted my eyes aroused my interest. In the center of the room sat my father, his cap cupped in the palms of his hands, his eyes staring intently at the table. Opposite him sat a brother officer, in the same attitude. Both seemed to be thinking deeply. Neither uttered a word. I approached closer, and obtained my first view of a chessboard."

In these simple and somewhat forgotten words, Jose Raoul Capablanca, the world champion who was to become known as the "chess machine," described his introduction to chess at the age of four.

As tired as the comparison is, chess really is something like a war, or at least what young boys think war is like. Napoleon was a second-rate player, Lenin a good one. Yet the game is a struggle to seize strong points, to bring one's armor into action rapidly, to capture enemy forces, and thus sooner or later to cause the capitulation of the enemy monarch. The metaphor is compelling.

Nothing is more ineffective in chess, however, than to play

the role of the sabre-rattler at the table. The player who shouts, "Aha, take that!" literally or figuratively, as he rushes about the board brandishing his arms, misses the whole point of a game like chess. It is the interaction between the players that must be taken into account, defense as well as attack. Capablanca, in fact, became the "winningest" player in history more by sensing danger and brushing off his opponents' rash overtures, than by direct assault. The present world champion, Anatoly Karpov, shares this sense of control. Bobby Fischer must be rated as having had all of that and more: a greater ambition to make something out of nothing simply because he is Fischer.

So we must concede that chess is combat, and combat with a lot of ego-investment as well. The domino or backgammon player can complain about blind luck; the gin rummy player about "no brainers." The poker player is necessarily one among many; the bridge player shares his fate with a partner. But the chess player puts his prowess on the line head to head, in perhaps the highest form of mental abstraction in any game.

Such is this sense of abstraction that writers often class chess as mathematical in nature. And the age-old argument begins: is it a science, an art, or a game?

Former world champion Mikhail Botvinnik, the successor of the great players of the '30s and the first strong player to embrace computer chess, wrote: "What is the essence of a chess master's art? In the last resort, whether you are working out variations or estimating an actual position, chess is the art of analysis."

We can deal with the question of whether chess is a game rather easily. When Tigran Petrosian, world champion before Spassky, was asked for his opinion of Bobby Fischer as a person, he replied, "I don't know—I never have had a glass of wine with him." And when Boris Spassky lost to Fischer in Reykjavik in 1972, he confided to reporters that he would now like to play a few games of chess with some friends over a beer. Chess is definitely a game for relaxation, for comraderie, for diversion.

Botvinnik has rather neatly shown the connection between chess as an art and as a science. The correct analysis of a position is everything. And analysis is an art. To bring Capablanca back into the picture, the combat of chess is meaningless unless the combat is properly analyzed.

The beauty of Botvinnik's summation is that it binds together some diverse areas of chess. Some chessplayers cannot abide problems, that is, "studies" in which White is to mate in two or three moves, or win, or even help Black to mate him in a given number of moves. Yet all of the latter is analysis. Great analysts that they were, the world's finest players have also contributed to the abstract world of problems, endgame compositions, and "fairy" chess. Lasker, who yielded his title to Capablanca in 1921, composed an ending with him based on an offhand game they played at a coffee house in Berlin. Lasker's famous Rook and Pawn versus Rook and Pawn ending still ranks among the classics. Paul Keres, perhaps the most successful and best liked of players in the last forty years, never became world champion; but his universality was evident in his work with problems as well as endgames.

Yet in replaying a game (and that is one of the great appeals of chess—all the moves are there for everyone to recreate at his own table), we look less for analysis than for combat. We sense the struggle. We want to know the pressures that each player felt. We want a Billy Jean King face-off with Bobby Riggs every time. We can have them all—art, science, game, struggle.

—**Robert Burger**

Robert Burger's range of chess experience is unusually wide. It includes lecturing on chess to college students, organizing state and national tournaments, and serving as an International Judge of Chess Compositions. A United States Master, he has published several chess magazines. He followed Bobby Fischer's rise to the championship while doing chess reporting and analyzing for TV, radio, and newspapers. He has authored two excellent chess books: **The Chess of Bobby Fischer** *and* **The Chess of Anatoly Karpov.**

For More Information

The only national organization is the United States of America Chess Federation, 479 Broadway, Newburgh, N.Y. 12550. Their purpose: "To broaden and develop chess as an art and recreation, as a significant element of culture in America." Their magazine *Chess Life and Review* is by far the best publication available. It is published monthly at $12.50 per year. Filled with good information including Postal Chess Ratings in each issue. There are many other publications and a full list is available from USCF.

A good source for sets and boards is Wm. F. Druike & Sons, Inc., 601 Third St., NW, Grand Rapids, Mich. 49504. Also the USCF has a mail order catalog with a lot of goodies.

There are a lot of books available on chess. Here are a few you might consider. All are available from World Publications, Box 366, Mountain View, Calif. 94040 at the price listed* plus 25 cents postage.

Modern Ideas in the Chess Openings, I.A. Horowitz. A classic! Three-time U.S. Open Champion covers 12 of the most important modern openings: showing how to strike the first blow and proceed to victory. Each opening has a discussion of its historical and strategical concept followed by move-for-move descriptions. 1953 ppb., 166 pp., ill., $1.50, (Simon & Schuster).

How to Win the Middle Game of Chess, I.A. Horowitz. After the first opening moves, what do you do? How? When? The answers are found in this book, containing the timeless work of one of the world's leading authorities on chess. Some of the tactical plays covered are: pin, knight fork, double attack, overworked piece, removal of the guard, x-ray attack, interference and surprise mating attacks. 1955 Ppb., 190 pp., ill., $1.50,(Simon & Schuster).

How to Beat Bobby Fischer, Edmar Mednis. For chess buffs who want to learn how to outsmart a champion on the chess board. We cannot guarantee that you will—but this book certainly gives you a better chance. 1974 Hb., 282 pp., ill., $7.95, (Harper & Row).

Chess Panorama, Lombardy and Daniels. Explores the world of top-level chess. The tone is light and humorous, the stories entertaining, and the exposes of scandals and blunders make this a fascinating book. 1975 Hb., 176 pp., ill., $6.95, (Chilton).

Beginner's Guide to Winning Chess, Fred Reinfeld. Chess may seem a formidable and difficult game for the beginner, but the author clearly shows the way to becoming a good player in this clear book. 1967 Ppb., 212 pp., ill., $2.00, (Wilshire).

The Chess of Bobby Fischer, Robert Burger. The tactics of this champion's calculating chess game are analyzed in this guide for use by the well-informed amateur. 1975 Hb., 384 pp., ill., $12.50,(Chilton).

Better Chess: How to Play, Fred Reinfeld. Avoiding the sprawling, involved details that often confuse and complicate elementary chess books, this guide gets to the heart of the matter, with precise, simple explanations of the opening play, the middle game, and the end game, making this an ideal book for the average chess player. 1973 Ppb., 120 pp., ill., $2.00, (Wilshire).

Chess Strategy, Fred Reinfeld. Techniques for learning chess strategy from past games and examples. With the basic premise that chess is fun, Reinfeld excites you with composed chess studies, chess problems, a lesson on imagination, and three chapters devoted to Master Chess, including the anatomy of a middle game. 1957 Ppb., 186 pp., ill., $2.00, (Wilshire).

Art and Science of Chess, Robert Robinson, et al. A progressive approach to chess. The basics are covered as early as possible and the final section contains selection of master games, annotated and cross-referenced to appropriate points in the text. 1973 Hb., 137 pp., ill., $7.95, (Harper & Row).

Fischer v. Spassky Reykjavik 1972, C.H.O'D. Alexander. A stirring account of the struggle for the World Chess Championship with illustrated biographies of the players, their previous encounters and an analysis of each game. 1972 Hb., 144 pp., ill., $5.95, (Wildwood House).

Circus Skills

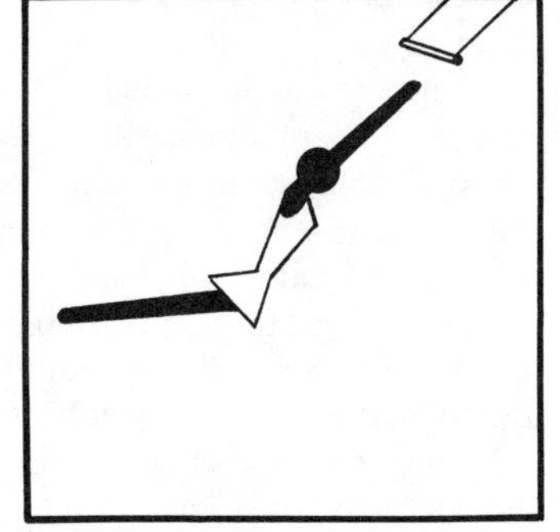

Performing circus skills is becoming a popular recreational activity and sport at the amateur level. I first became interested when in the sixth grade I started learning stunts on a homemade horizontal bar in our back yard. This was followed by stilts, unicycles, pogo sticks, trapeze, trampolines, circus bicycles, tightwire, and juggling. At one point during high school I had what amounted to a complete back-yard circus in our yard. I later taught circus skills in various YMCA programs.

Popular circus activities include juggling, balancing poles and spinning plates, rolling cyclinder board, diabolo, stilts, tightwire, unicycling, circus bicycling, tumbling, gymnastic balancing, pyramids, trampolining, vaulting, Roman ladders, horizontal bar, trapeze, and clowning. A number of schools and colleges now offer classes in circus skills. For example, the University of California at San Diego, New York University, State University College at Purchase, New York, and Nassau Community College, Garden City, New York, have circus arts programs. There are a number of amateur circuses, including the Great Y Circus in Redlands, California, the Florida State University Circus in Tallahassee, Florida, Sailor Circus in Sarasota, Florida, the Hamilton Mini Circus in Hamilton, Ohio, Circus Kingdom in Dover, Pennsylvania, and the Wenatchee Youth Circus in Wenatchee, Washington.

The popularity of circus activities at the amateur level is increasing rapidly, and clubs and groups are forming in many parts of the United States. To date there is no national organization devoted to circus skills at the amateur level.

How does one get started in circus skills? A good source of information is **Basic Circus Skills.** If possible, take a class in circus skills, or join an amateur circus group. While most people won't be interested in every circus activity (there are hundreds of possibilities), there is almost certain to be something of interest to almost everyone. Some activities, such as juggling, require a high degree of skill and coordination, others, such as hand balancing, demand strength. Activities can be selected accordingly.

—**Jack Wiley**

Jack Wiley has really gotten involved with Circus Skills. He has also written a book called **Basic Circus Skills.**

For More Information

Additional information can be found under juggling, but a good source of information is Jack Wiley, 352 Broadway, Box E-3, Chula Vista, Calif. 92010. Or better yet get a copy of his book. It is available from World Publications, Box 366, Mountain View, Calif. 94040 at the price listed* plus 25 cents postage.

Basic Circus Skills, Jack Wiley. Included in this one book is all the information you need to get started. It covers juggling, balancing, spinning, stilts, clowning and everything else. 1975, $6.95, (Stackpole).

Clam Digging

The Pacific razor clam (siliqua patula) is an exceptionally meaty and tasty shellfish that ranges from Pismo Beach, Calif. to as far north as the Aleutian Islands in Alaska. Some of the most popular clam beds on the Pacific Coast are located at Washington beaches not far from where I live.

The average razor clam will reach sexual maturity at two years of age and will spawn between six and 10 million eggs annually. This huge number of eggs is essential because of the very high mortality rate of the young, who spend their first six weeks aimlessly drifting in the surf before finally going underground. Once firmly entrenched in the sand along the surf line, a razor clam grows rapidly until it reaches a harvestable length of four to five inches at two or three years of age.

Only three basic pieces of equipment are necessary to stalk

With good minus tides, clam beaches are flooded with enthusiastic clam diggers burrowing down into the wet sand for their favorite delicacy. (Washington State Department of Fisheries)

a Pacific razor clam. The first of these is a specially designed clamming shovel two or three feet in length. The long and narrow blade of this shovel is set at about a 45-degree angle from the handle. A second means of clam digging is the use of a "pipe" or "tube" to ferret out the tasty little critters. The metal tube is about six inches across and two or three feet in length. The tube is open at the bottom and closed at the top except for a small air hole about a half inch in diameter. Such tubes also have a metal rod or pipe handle welded across the top. Some sort of container (usually a bucket washtub, or game bag) for captured clams will complete your equipment package.

Clams are usually found during minus tides (periods during which low tides are much lower than average). The sandy area just above the waterline is the best place to look for the clam "show" that will tell you where to dig. Although a clam is usually a foot below the surface, he will stretch his neck up to draw in water and microscopic sea life for food. When disturbed, a clam will rapidly draw in his neck, leaving the show, which will be a slightly depressed, oval-shaped hole in the smooth sand. Usually the size of a show will give a good indication of the relative size of the clam, and most experienced clammers will pass by the smaller ones. To find a show, walk very slowly along the edge of the water, keeping your eyes focused two or three feet ahead. As soon as you see a small spurt of water, you'll have a show and with enough digging, a razor clam.

Razor clams must be dug in a hurry, because they can burrow down faster than many people can dig. Using a tube is the easy way. Just center it over the show and work it quickly down into the wet sand. Clams can't move horizontally, so you needn't worry about missing him unless he digs down too fast. Once the tube is deeply set, it's a simple matter to plug the air hole with your thumb and pull out a huge core of sand, usually with the clam still in it. Veteran clammers, however, tend to frown on this method, saying that it kills the sport and makes the whole process too easy.

"Real" clamming is done with a shovel. Its blade is pushed straight into the sand about four inches to seaward of the show. The sand is then removed with a lifting motion, keeping the blade as near vertical as possible. Never pry back on the handle, as this tends to smash the clam's shell, resulting in sharp edges and a finger gash potential when reaching into the hole to extract a clam. Usually after two or three quick scoops the best bet is to plunge your hand in and do the last digging through almost liquid sand with your fingers. As soon as you catch up to the clam, rip him off and throw him into the bucket.

Cleaning a clam is as easy as removing the shell and snipping away with a scissors until the gills and digestive tract (the dark parts of a clam) have been revoved. The best way to cook clams are a chowder, fried like a steak in butter, or cut into strips and French fried.

—**Darrel Martin**

Darrel Martin has been stalking the Pacific razor clam for nearly fifty years. He is a retired logger and lives near Forks, Washington.

For More Information

The state fisheries departments of California, Oregon, Washington and Alaska can supply good information. We got some good information from Washington State Department of Fisheries, Olympia, Wash. 98501. Ask for the booklets they put out on clams. One we really liked was "Washington Razor Clams Regulations." It included information on digging, cleaning and how to prevent wastage.

Conservation

Although many sportsmen may have never considered the important role the earth's environment plays in their favorite sport or activity, nevertheless, conservation is an area that all sports enthusiasts should be aware of.

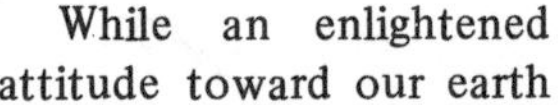

While an enlightened attitude toward our earth is prevalent in some sporting circles more than others, the fact remains that a healthy environment is essential if we are to continue to enjoy our many sports and games. The educated hunter, for instance, is constantly aware of the effect that this hunting has on wildlife populations; the informed camper always makes sure he leaves his campsite exactly as he found it – he might even gather up a can or two that another camper thoughtlessly discarded.

But what about runners, or trail bikers? What do they have to concern themselves with? The 1968 Olympic Games at high altitude Mexico City seemed to educate many sports enthusiasts, whether they knew it or not. Reading and hearing about Olympic athletes training on mountain tops to prepare themselves for the difficult task of competing in a thin atmosphere was a good lesson in the conservation of air – an essential requirement in any human endeavor. Today, many runners ride bicycles not only for transportation and exercise, but also to remove one more air-polluting automobile from the highways. Of course, many bicyclists, whether runners or not, have this same idea in mind as they hop on their bikes and pedal to work.

Environmental responsibility by sportsmen is not to be taken lightly. No matter what your sporting interest, whatever game is your whim, ask yourself questions about the role you play on your planet. Are you a destroyer? Do you "gun" your trail bike over hills, tearing up the earth for thrills? Or do you cycle quietly through the forest, sticking to the trails, and trying your best not to disturb a single twig?

Remember – excessive noise is pollution also! Does your model airplane perform dives and loops with a high-pitched wail? Or does it sail through the air as quietly as a glider?

Conservation cannot be stressed enough, especially where athletes are concerned. What can you do to help preserve our wide world of sports?

A New Ethic

Taming the wilderness and turning nature to man's use has been a fundamental feature of human history. Mankind has behaved as if the earth existed mainly for his benefit, as if its bounty had no limits. Now human might has been magnified by the inventions of technology, and population has increased past all prediction. So the twentieth century sees society facing a crisis of supply, of space, of ethics.

The United States is the prototype of the industrial state, enjoying a standard of living remarkably high, by most measures. Yet a price has been paid – dwindling reserves of petroleum, easily recovered resources used up, air and water befouled, plant and animal species destroyed, land areas laid waste. And these prices will continue to be paid whenever man seeks blindly to better his lot without understanding where he fits in the natural scheme; they will be demanded until poverty and decline replace prosperity.

Numbers increase and needs for space reach out over the land. Mankind needs a new way to relate to his planet, to that little spaceship, Earth. He must be less abusive and more careful. He must moderate his demands and modify his behavior. He must recognize that man is a part of nature, "not man apart".

This new ethic will incorporate the ecological principle that everything is connected with something else, that an action in nature always results in a reaction. Humans will treasure those plant and animal species which presently serve them but will care as well for those which are unrecognized in importance or may some other day be useful. They will want to preserve the predator as well as his prey, the songbird as well as the game animal, the flower and thistle as well as the grain and fruit, the life of the sea and forest and desert. No species will be allowed to be destroyed by man's works; all, including man, will fill their roles in an intricate scheme.

Human behavior will acknowledge that everything must go somewhere, demanding that the technology of prosperity also manage its waste products so that the earth environment remains livable for all life forms. Poisoning and polluting will be unacceptable results of the productive society; recycling will be a regular feature of the industrial process.

Natural communities – unique combinations of plants and animals on a specific land area – will be preserved in designated parks and wilderness, being protected by man's institutions from man's intrusions. These communities then can continue to respond to the processes that brought them thus far. These special places will be valued for their character and quality, not their utility or productivity.

The energy requirements of society will increasingly come from renewable sources so that dwindling reserves of versatile fossil fuels can be saved for other uses. Decisions about use of land will reflect long-term utility over immediate profit; they will emphasize maintenance of soil potential rather than its depletion; they will focus on basic living requirements instead of extravagance. Conservation will demand a moderate statement of human need, and demography will reveal stabilizing populations across the peoples of the world.

The nature ethic here described is not yet fully practiced. But it is a force for some people in some places part of the time. It is no monopoly of nation or creed; it is in the international public domain. It is not yet fully stated or accepted. Yet in its development and implementation is the preservation of the earth.

–Kent Gill

Kent Gill has been a member of the Sierra Club since 1958, serving in various offices. He was elected President of the Club in 1974. Mr. Gill augments his conservation activities with regular backpacking and hiking trips – including major trips in seven western states.

Crew

Crew is among the most demanding of sports. It uses the legs, arms and back in performing varying rates of strokes, each of which requires perfect repeat performance. Cardio-respiratory capabilities are strengthened significantly at all levels of rowing, while the mental demand to train and perform is of the highest level in competitive sport.

Boats are called shells and compete in two general categories, either sculling or sweep events. Sculling comes closest to the average Saturday afternoon recreational row, as every oarsman/woman holds an oar in each hand. Sculling oars are usually about 9'6" in length and oarsmen/women compete in singles, doubles and quads. Some quad events are coxed (steered by a coxswain), but singles and doubles are steered only by careful adjustments in bladework.

In sweep events, each oarsman/woman holds a single sweep oar in both hands. Sweeps are usually about 2½ feet longer than sculls, and sweep competition is held in pairs, fours, and eights. The first two of these events are run both coxed and uncoxed, but an eight–the glamour boat in crew–is always coxed.

All rowing equipment is handmade of wood or synthetics like fiberglass, and is available from various manufacturers in the United States, Germany, Switzerland, Italy and Japan. Racing shells vary in size according to the number of seats that will be rowing, with eights naturally much larger than singles. All are long and very narrow to minimize water drag, and each is constructed with a thin shell of laminated wood or fiberglass stretched over the boat's ribs and braces.

Special oarlocks called riggers are bolted to the sides of each shell, extending upward and outward from the boat. Each member of the crew sits in a moveable slide seat that is mounted on rollers to allow for maximum leg drive with every stroke. For added convenience, each athlete's feet can be secured to the shell by means of laced shoes called boot stretchers. This piece of equipment is vital because power is transfered from the oar in the water to levering the boat forward only through the foot-boat link.

Rowing technique is extremely exacting. Each stroke must be repeated time after time in mirror perfect precision with each other member in the boat. The motion must be smooth and precise, yet powerful and dynamic. Any small stroke irregularity by even a single member of a crew can put a "check" in the boat and reduce speed. It takes constant concentration from every athlete in a boat over many hundreds of miles of training in order to develop the caliber of bladework and physical conditioning necessary for championship performance.

Where an oarsman/woman who rows for fun and recreation finds a relaxing pastime, an athlete who rows for competition will be confronted with challenging workouts. In addition to hundreds of miles actually on the water in a shell, he/she will spend as much as 40% of each two-a-day workout in off-water training. This includes rowing in special tanks, weight training and aerobic workouts in the form of running, cycling, swimming or sprinting up stadium steps.

At major crew competitions—called regattas—tradition plays a large role. The smaller boats begin the competitions, leaving the larger and faster shells until last. Crews usually bet shirts on each race, the loser forfeiting the prize. Many champion oarsmen/women have won enough races that they could work out in a shirt from a different club each day for months without repeating. Coxes are dunked after victories; judges—never questioned—stand with stopwatches and binoculars. All the while coaches and spectators stand on the shore cheering the shells on with shouts of "Stroke! Stroke! Stroke!" in time to the rhythm of the oars. A great celebration usually follows competition.

To get started in crew, one is best advised to contact a local club or university which has the necessary equipment and coaching. Waterwise, nearly any lake or slow running river having a depth of five feet or more is adequate, and many of these will have shell houses.

A Blending of Mind and Body

There exists an almost addictive quality to this sport which lingers for a lifetime. Hence, it is quite common to see men (and likely women) continuing to row into their 80's. Unlike the pounding of a jogger on the track or the monotony of a cyclist, there is a peaceful harmony of man/woman, boat and water which is always exhilarating even in fatigue and exhaustion. Since most oarsmen train year 'round, the beauty of water ways and pastoral settings are never lost as the boats cruise the many miles from one season through to another. The demands of propelling the boat by one's own power, strength, and skill appeal to the most hearty who simply want to achieve something on their own. Since the great American artist Thomas Eakins captured in his paintings the quiet solitude of the oarsmen over 100 years ago, little has changed in the individual style and appreciation thereof.

Today there are categories for competition among men, women, youth (up to 18) and men of both under and over 150 pounds. While those not interested in competing can find recreational or rehabilitational rowing quite rewarding, the basic skills required to balance the boat, and master the art of entering and releasing the water efficiently with rhythmic harmony do require perseverence and time. Yet skills involving motor coordination such as these, once learned, are never forgotten. One can find solitude or camaraderie as he or she sees fit in club or university rowing. For those who seek the competitive lifestyle, rowing remains the second most popular sport worldwide with competition available in the Olympic Games and Pan-American Games, as well as United States, Canadian, and European competition.

One needs only the basic skills of an athlete to learn. Full training will demand running, some strength work such as weight-training, swimming and soccer, but mostly rowing. Today crew remains one of the few "pure" sports as there is no professional circuit. As such, the champion amateur has achieved his success with only the incentives of achieving perfection, skill, grace and poise for his personal satisfaction. This

Crew offers competition for both male and female athletes on the national and international level. Women will compete in crew on an Olympic Games level for the first time in 1976. (The Oarsman)

is the true reward and tends to separate out many athletes who yearn for a different form of satisfaction in a still higher, but briefer level.

Rowing is a "non-contact" sport but most races are won with mere seconds separating competitors. Since visual contact is never lost, tactics of racing are vitally important in a winning effort.

The aesthetic quality of crew is one unparalleled aspect of the sport. Few other athletic endeavors can match the brisk feeling of rowing on a cold, clear morning, or the early morning spectacle of seeing the rising sun glint off water-flecked blades as they leave whirlpools of light in the wake astern each shell. As all arms pull, all legs thrust in unison, the slender boat skims along the water and you can't help but sense the powerful beauty that comes from strong bodies and smooth silent strokes.

—Alan Rosenberg

Alan Rosenberg coxed the eights to a gold medal win in the 1955 Pan American Games. He was the US Olympic Coach in 1964 when the US won a gold medal and also coached American teams at the 1975 World Championships and Pan-Am Games. He will be the US Olympic Coach for the 1976 Olympics.

For More Information

The major organization is the National Association of Amateur Oarsmen, 31552 Waltham Road, Birmingham, Mich. 48009. They also publish *Oarsman* magazine which is issued five times per year. A subscription which also includes a membership is $10 per year. A couple of sources for shells: George Pocock Racing Shells, Inc., Box 111, University Sta., Seattle, Wash. 98105 or Kaschper Racing Shells, Box 40, Lucan, Ont., Can.

Books are hard to find but here are three. All are available from World Publications, Box 366, Mountain View, Calif. 94040 at the price listed* plus 25 cents each postage. For additional information, check rowing.

Ready All, Row!, Karl F. Drlica. Excellent crew manual from the associate professor of physical education and coach of rowing at Oregon State University. Includes chapters on safety precautions, the coxswain, the oarsman, the vernacular and history or rowing, physical conditioning, and racing laws. 1972 Ppb., 43 (oversize) pp., ill., $3.30, (Oregon State Univ.).

How Regattas are Run, William J. Cochrane, et al. This is a complete guide to planning, coordinating, and running your own regatta, a race between two or more crews. Preliminary plans, meeting, rowing courses, entry blanks, even how to plan your rowing dinner. Ppb., 59 pp., $3.00, (NAAD).

Rowing, Know the Game Series. Good beginner's crew book discusses all the fundamentals of crew racing from types of racing boats and oars to discipline, safety, the rowing stroke, sculling, coxing, and training. 1974 Ppb., 40 pp., ill., $1.50, (E.P. Publishing).

Cricket

The game of cricket is supposed to be played on an oval. In the middle of the oval ground, a square area is prepared. This is the playing area, and it should ideally be of fine turf. In the center of the playing area, and lengthwise to the oval, there is a 22 yard pitch, with wickets at each end.

Wickets are set up with three stumps (specially prepared sticks) which are pushed into the ground vertically so that they project 28 inches up. Horizontally, atop the stumps, and balanced in grooves, are placed pieces of wood known as bails. The bails are 4 and 3/8 inches long. Each wicket then presents the bowler with a target 28 inches high and nine inches wide. Should blustery winds constantly displace the bails, they may be dispensed with, provided the Umpire approves.

A bowling crease is marked at each end of the pitch, in line with the wickets. Four feet in front of each bowling crease, and parallel to it, is marked a batting crease. Boundaries, marked flags or lines, are 75 yards from the pitch in all directions. Balls hit to reach the boundary are scored as four runs. A batsman who hits the ball over the boundary is credited with six runs.

In local cricket, six hours of playing time is official. There are usually 11 players on a side. Before the match, the two opposing Captains toss a coin for the right to bat or take the field. Generally speaking, having won the toss, and provided it is a bright and sunny day with a good wicket to bat on, an astute Captain will elect to bat. However, if it happens to be a windy day and the weather is murky with light mist coming from the sea, he may deem it wise to put his opponent to bat.

Two men open the batting. A bowler (pitcher), on hearing the Umpire say "Play," will take a slow or fast run toward the stumps nearest him. As he comes alongside the stumps, he will bowl either an in-swing or out-swing or a straight ball at the batsman 22 yards down the pitch in front of the other wicket. If the batsman hits the ball so as to evade the fielders, and if he thinks he has time, he will run down the pitch to the other wicket while his batting partner exchanges places with him. By exchanging position in this way, the batsmen score one run.

If the batsman misjudges, and a fielder manages to throw the ball back to the bowler before he can cross the batting crease with either his bat or his foot, the bowler will uproot the stumps, and the batsman will be "run out." Either batsman can be "run out" if he fails to reach the batting crease before a fielder has knocked his stumps down. However, there is no such thing as a "double play"; that is, running two men out simultaneously.

On a "big" hit several runs may be scored. If the ball rolls or bounces over the boundary, the batsmen earn four runs without having to move. If it sails completely over the boundary, they earn six runs, again without actually having to move. Batsmen praise this economy of energy, especially those who have been running up and down between the wickets for an hour or more!

Batsmen can be given "Out" for interference if they accidentally or intentionally bump into a fielder who is trying to catch a hit. A batsman can also be given "Out" if his leg obstructs a ball which would otherwise have hit the wicket. This is called "leg-before-wicket." If the batsman misses the ball and it displaces the bails or knocks the stumps down, he is bowled "Out." If he runs out in front of his batting crease to hit a ball, but misses, the wicket-keeper will smartly gather the ball and knock the bails off the stumps before he can get back to his crease. He would be "Out"—stumped.

There are other "eerie" ways of getting "Out," but enough is enough.

If a batsman is hurt, he may leave the wicket and return later to continue his batting. He would be allowed a "runner" while he is not in good repair.

Sporting Captains like to arrange for equality of time at bat. This is an unwritten principle. The very fact that it is not in the news underlines how the sporting attitude is valued above all else in cricket.

It is not unusual for a Captain to declare his team's innings closed at any given point in time if they have scored a good number of runs. For instance, over 200 runs for only four men out would be an almost guaranteed winning score. But the Captain is gambling—it is up to his bowlers and fielders to turn the trick in his favor. Sometimes the underdog team manages to turn the tables.

We veto loud talk, vulgar displays, and obnoxious attitudes toward Umpires. Often a player is not out when the Umpire declares him "Out." He must retain his poise even though he may be boiling like Mount Vesuvius—inside where the eyes can't see. Character and the sporting spirit rise above all else in cricket.

—Dr. Clifford Severn

Cliff Severn is an unsung worker for cricket. In the postwar years, he reintroduced cricket at Stanford, U.C. Berkeley, U.C. Davis, and Texas A and M. In more recent years, he has been coaching youngsters and adults in Thousand Oaks, Newbury Park, and the West Coast generally.

The Spirit of the Game

Trying to convey something of the essence of cricket is like attempting to define an insidious perfume—you know it's there, you can appreciate its heady odor, but it defies definition. Even if you've never heard of cricket, there are terms from the game which have slipped into everyday use: "It's not cricket!" or "batting on a sticky wicket" or being "stumped" for an answer. Cricket is a world wide game. It's even been played in America since 1706 and it survived the Revolution. It even fathered baseball—the two games have many terms in common.

In England the game has been played since at least the thirteenth century. King Edward I legislated against it in favor of archery, and King James I in favor of church attendance, but the game went merrily on. French, German, Russian and Polish aristocracy reacted against the masses: the British aristocracy played cricket with the commoners and perhaps thus saved their heads.

In Victorian days a sort of sickly sentimentality crept into cricket as into most things. Young Englishmen were sternly adjured to "keep a straight bat" with the Lord as well as on the cricket field. The game survived even that.

It was exported to the "colonies" and even after England lost its temporal power, cricket persisted as a British import that was irresistible. India, Pakistan, Barbados, Jamaica, Guyana, Sri Lanka—they have their differences but they are all passionate about cricket.

Australians, for all their seeming similarity to Americans, are devoted to the game, and their avowed object is to "lick the Pommies"—the English. In South Africa, black and white play cricket—unfortunately not yet together although there have been stirrings in that direction. How do you put such a spirit into words—to define the game exactly?

The batsman's duty is to protect the wicket and hit the ball far enough to score runs for his team. A good batsman can make more than 50 runs before he is finally out. (Duffy)

The bowler will take a run toward the batsman and will bowl either an in-swing, out-swing or straight ball a distance of 22 yards down the pitch in an effort to throw the ball past the batsman and displace the bails or stumps of the wicket. (Duffy)

First of all, it is always a game, played on a field absorbing in its drama and sometimes in its boredom. It is a game of infinite variety. Physical skill isn't paramount. Unlike U.S. football, the little man has a chance in this game. Mere brute force gets you nowhere.

Secondly it's a social game. Cricketeers do not abrubtly end the game with the two teams parting not to see each other until the next encounter. Even in the middle of a game there's a "tea interval" in which sometimes stronger brews are quaffed. There's a humanity and a gentility, a social scene that bids entertainment after the long, hot and dusty day in the field. The end of a game means sociability: cricket is a social game.

And perhaps thirdly, in this crowded civilization of ours, it is a chance to mingle on a green field (in some countries!), to feel the good earth beneath our feet, and to enjoy the companionship of men—black, brown, or white, in a form of peaceful war. Cricket is simply absorbing to its devotees: it is drama, life, sociability, meat and drink and companionship. What more can anyone want?

—John Marder

John Marder lives in Beverly Hills, California and is a past president of the United States Cricket Association.

For More Information

There are no magazines published in the US that cover cricket, but there is a good magazine published in England. *The Cricketer International,* Beech Hanger, Ashurst, Tunbridge Wells, Kent TN3 9ST, England, is published monthly at $12.00 per year. The top magazine on the sport.

The United States Cricket Association, Robin McLaren, Secretary, 494 Maymont Drive, Ballwin, Mo. 63011, is the official US group. They are dedicated to promote the game and provide a network of communication between member clubs. Bulletins are published from time to time for members. There are currently 22 states that have cricket clubs and the national office can provide you with their addresses.

Most of the equipment needed for cricket (bats, balls, stumps, gloves and leg-guards) is not available in the United States directly; however, two shops may be able to help you: Magnolia Sports, 10634 Magnolia Blvd., N. Hollywood, Calif. 91601 or Roberts Sporting Goods, 4520 Monticello Ave., Bronx, N.Y. 10466.

You aren't going to find books in book stores but we have a good list to pick from. All are available from World Publications, Box 366, Mountain View, Calif. 94040 at the price listed* plus 25 cents each postage.

Cricket: How to Play, Leonard Hutton, et al. This illustrated guide is perfect for the beginning cricket player or for the enthusiastic spectator. 1969 Ppb., 96 pp., ill., $2.50, (Wehman).

Cricket, Jack Cross, ed. A nostalgic look at the game of cricket and its past—contains 16 specially prepared pamphlets including "Cricket Round the World," "The Laws of Cricket in 1809," "Grand Match" handbill from 1847, plus instruction on bat-building and bowling. 1972 Ppb., 40 (over-size) pp., ill., $3.95, (Viking).

Cricket: More Than a Game, John Sheppard, ed. A celebration of cricket in all its forms. Part one has descriptions of each cricketing country by participants, part two offers instruction on playing the game by nine pro cricketeers, and part three is a miscellany of humor and comment on this age-old game. 1975 Hb., 256 pp., ill., $12.95 (Angus & Robertson).

The Laws of Cricket, Know the Game Series. This clear instruction manual for beginners guides the reader through all the rules, explaining each with official notes and simple-to-follow diagrams. 1951 (rev. 1973) Ppb., 48 pp., ill., $1.50, (E.P. Publishing).

Cricket: How to Become a Champion, John Snow. Writing in a personable, easy-going style, Snow takes the reader through the ins and outs of high-speed cricket on a pro team, showing all the techniques and skills that various pros have developed for championship cricket. 1975 Ppb., 118 pp., ill., $3.95, (William Luscombe).

Barry Richards: Cricket, Barry Richards. Explains the techniques of playing the game, as a batsman, bowler, fielder and captain, as well as giving useful advice on selecting and caring for equipment. Places emphasis on the correct mental attitudes towards playing. 1975 Library Binding, 61 (oversize) pp., ill., $5.95, (Pelham).

Successful Cricket, Greg Chappell. Share the secrets of five of Australia's finest test cricketers. Greg Chappell coaches in batting, Dennis Lilee in fast bowling, Ashley Mallett in spin bowling, Paul Sheahan in fielding and Brian Taber explains Wicketkeeping skills. This manual also covers the finer points of the game for the more advanced player. 1974 Hb., 81 (oversize) pp., ill., $7.50, (Pelham).

Croquet

Although croquet has been extensively identified with the farflung British Empire, its origins were in France, probably in the late 15th century. The term croquet derives from the French *crochet*, a crooked stick, and refers to the type of implement then in use. The game diffused to England during the early 16th century, where written records show that it was played at Pall Mall. Croquet gained little in popularity during the next three centuries, but eventually had its Renaissance in 1857 when rules were codified and the first sets manufactured in England by John Jaques. The croquet craze swept through the British Isles and finally to the United States in the 1870's where it was widely adopted, particularly by high society.

The first Golden Age of croquet in America died at the turn of the century, but enjoyed a revival during the 1930's, spreading from the estates of Long Island to Beverly Hills movie moguls' lawns. After fading during the 40's and early 50's the game is again enjoying a strong resurgence in the East—in New York City, Long Island, Palm Beach, New Jersey, Connecticut and parts of New England—and California.

While croquet is perhaps the most widely played lawn game in the United States, the lack of uniform rules and the relatively low standard of equipment available from domestic manufacturers continues to restrict the growth of the game between players or clubs from different areas. Currently a move is being spearheaded by the recently formed U.S. Croquet Association to organize and standardize competitive croquet in America.

Five basic variations of the game exist. These differ primarily in the various manifestations of rules, equipment used and in Wicket layout pattern:

1. **British Association Croquet**: Evolving for the past 100 years, it is the most highly regulated and organized form of the game and is played throughout the world today. Placing a premium on shotmaking finesse and chess level strategy, Association Croquet is clearly *the* modern day international game. The standard court setting is 28 yards x 35 yards with six 'hoops' (wickets of 5/8 inch cast iron one foot tall and 3¾ inch to 4 inch clearance between uprights) and one center peg (stake). The object of the game is for a player (singles) or players (doubles) to make their two balls score 12 wicket points and final stake point each (for a total of 26 points) before the adversary.

2. **British Golf Croquet**: A simplified version requiring only one ball from each team to score a wicket point before all

"Those who see croquet as a sedentary, polite after-dinner recreation have not played the sport as it is really played. In truth, it is a highly competitive game that requires great skill, concentration and knowledge of strategy."

players contest the next wicket in order. The stake is not played. This is essentially a beginners game.

3. **American (Anglo/American) Croquet**: The U.S. version of the six wicket center stake English game, it is played with long handled mallets (Lignum Vitae or Box Wood) weighing two and a half to four pounds, English Wickets and 3 5/8 inch balls.

4. **The American Double Diamond**: A nine wicket and two stake layout variation most frequently played with the wide mouthed, low wire wickets and lightweight wooden or rubber-headed mallets and smaller striped balls produced in America. (Numbers three and four are both played under the American rules incorporating playing rotation—blue, red, black and yellow balls—and deadness continues until a ball has cleared its next wicket in order, which are the basic rule differences between the English and American games.

5. **Roque**: Is an American offshoot of these variations, formed at the turn of the 20th century in an effort to speed up the game and make it more difficult. Roque features a clay court surface for speed, and narrow wickets which demand far greater accuracy in driving balls. The use of short one handed mallets is most common in Roque.

Even though rules vary widely and are subjected to local interpretation, there are certain aspects that all the above games have in common. In its essence, croquet is played with a mallet of wood and various colored balls of wood, plastic or mixed composition. The balls are driven by the player's mallet through successive wickets in a prescribed order to a finishing stake. Doubles and singles are played, the winner being the side to negotiate the course in the correct order and hit the final stake first.

Getting into croquet is as easy as a trip to your local sporting goods store and a small investment for a set. (American Manufactured sets run from $15.00 to $50.00, English—Jacques of London—from $150 to $450.00). All croquet sets come equipped with a short manual of technique, rules and equipment orientation. From this starting point, you can turn your lawn into the neighborhood tournament site. If you get the croquet bug for real, and aspire to test national or international competition, seek out some of the information available from the associations or clubs below.

—**Jack Osborn**

Jack Osborn is Captain of the New York Croquet Club and serves as Chairman of Osborn/Charles Associates, Inc., a New York City consulting and design firm for marketing communications.

More Than Just a Game

Croquet is a sport that most people have played at one time or another in their lives. Most of us are familiar with the garden variety game, with wire hoops, few rules, and a layout that is as varied as the people who play. In reality, however, croquet is an extremely difficult sport requiring intense concentration and detailed knowledge of strategy. It's just not the same backyard game that most people think it is. Those who have played competitively say it is a combination of chess and billiards played on grass. This analogy is pretty close to the truth.

The rudiments of croquet, like those of chess and billiards, are relatively easy to master. The strategy and play of these games, however, is much more difficult to learn. Darryl Zanuck, one of Hollywood's most fervent players, points out that you can learn to hit the ball very easily, but to learn the strategy of the game takes a minimum of two years. Of course, you can play and enjoy the game almost immediately, without knowing the subtleties and nuances of high level play. But for the interested and serious player there is a wealth of tactics that he can employ to make the sport of croquet the intense and fascinating game that it is. Some of this complexity is reflected in the terminology of the sport, which is larger than that of all other sports, chess included.

There are many qualities that a good croquet player must possess. He must be accurate with his shots, he has to plan several turns ahead, he should always be aware of what possibilities he is leaving his opponent, and, equally important, he must be possessed of a fighting spirit. This aspect of the good croquet player's personality was best described by Moss Hart. Speaking of Zanuck, he said that "he trusts no one but himself; never concedes no matter how far behind he may be—and hates his opponents with an all-enduring hate."

Such strident competitiveness has led to an extraordinary zealotry by many of the sport's devotees. Averell Harriman, a long-time croquet buff, was in the midst of play one Thanksgiving when a snow storm struck. Rather than stop the game, Harriman hired eight men, with shovels, snowplows and a tractor to clear the course. Play was then resumed after this short delay. Once, on the way back to Washington from San Francisco, Harriman made a late-night detour to Palm Springs, where he played croquet with Zanuck on a lighted court until four in the morning. He returned to Washington the next day.

Harpo Marx, another devoted player, recalled a game with newspaperman H.B. Swope, in which Swope kept Governor Al Smith waiting on the phone for some time rather than interrupting the game. Harpo estimated that he and his friends had bought fifty thousand dollars worth of croquet equipment. In order to protect this array of goods, Harpo turned his spare bedroom into a storeroom with accurate temperature and humidity controls. He once spent five hundred dollars to convert the roof of a neighbor's garage into a croquet court. It is said that Zanuck spent fourteen thousand dollars a year simply for the upkeep of his course, and recently, a Palm Beach matron spent thirty thousand dollars to have her court done over in Astro-Turf.

Of course, such devotion as this is not necessary to enjoy the game. It is a game that can be played by people of all ages, sizes and strengths. In fact, it is the only sport in which men and women compete on an equal footing, with no difference in handicap or play. Women have captured several major croquet championships, and the current champion of Australia is a woman.

The game is played world-wide, from the United States to Australia, from England to India (where one viceroy played croquet with an all-ivory mallet). In Australia, where croquet is extremely popular, the sport is offered in high school gym classes. It is a game whose devotees have included Richard Rodgers, Charles II of England, Jackie Gleason, Richard Chamberlain, George S. Kaufman, Dorothy Parker, Louis Jourdan, Tyrone Power and Lewis Carroll. It was even at one time an Olympic sport.

So those who see croquet as a sedentary, polite after-dinner recreation have not played the sport as it is really played. In truth, it is a highly competitive game that requires great skill, concentration and knowledge of strategy. It is often so closely fought that writer Richard Gelman has remarked that "croquet has become as savage a competition as any waged in the National Football League."

—Jim Charton and William Thompson

Adapted by Jim Charton from **Croquet: What It Really Is and How to Play It** *by James Charton and William Thompson, copyright 1976 by Turtle Press, New York City.*

For More Information

The major organization for croquet is the American Croquet and Rogue League, May Alma Lousey, 4205 Briar Creek Lane, Dallas, Texas 75214. Other helpful addresses: New York Cruquet Club, 635 Madison Ave., New York, N.Y. 10021; US Croquet Association, c/o Jack Osborn, New York Croquet Club, New York, N.Y. Palm Beach Croquet Club, 353 Worth Ave., Palm Beach, Fla. 33480. The only place that makes tournament sets is John Jaques & Son, White Heather Works, Thornton Heath, Surrey, England. However, Forster Manufacturing Co., Wilton, Maine 04294 does make family sets.

Here are a couple of books that will be of interest. All are available from World Publications, Box 366, Mountain View, Calif. 94040 at the price listed* plus 25c each postage. Write for a complete list.

Backyard Games, Nikki Shultz. Offers an excellent chapter on the basics of getting started playing Croquet, the equipment you will need, the history of the game, and different variations on the game, 1975 Ppb., 96 (oversize) pp., ill., $1.95, (Grosset & Dunlap).

Croquet: What It Really Is and How To Play It, James Charton and William Thompson. This is the only book on American Croquet available. It is a comprehensive look at the game, covering history with anecdotes, rules and records, strategy, tactics, variations of the game, dress, and the related game of Roque. Contains the newly written US Croquet Rules. To be published March 1976 Hb. & Ppb., 192 (oversize) pp., ill., $9.95/$4.95, (Turtle Press).

Croquet, Dr. G.L. Ormerod. Part of the Know the Game Series, this book details for the beginner everything needed to start playing croquet. Simple illustrations and clear descriptions make this book a winner. 1961 (rev. 1973) Ppb., 36 pp., ill., $1.50 (E. P. Publishing).

Cross-Country Running

In a formal competitive sense, cross-country running refers to footracing over natural terrain, as opposed to man-made tracks or roads. Of course, cross-country running can also refer to long distance training or recreational running over natural terrain—and you don't necessarily have to be a competitive distance runner to do it. Many athletes who participate in shorter track events run "cross-country," as the sport is commonly called in North America, for its conditioning value. So do many athletes from other sports.

Cross-country running can be said to be distance running in its purest form—it's just you and nature, or, if it happens to be a race, you, nature and the other runners. Since cross-country courses vary in terrain, distance, etc., there's far less emphasis on times than there is in track or road running. This frees the runner to concentrate almost entirely on running the course and trying to outrun the opposition.

The origins of cross-country running can be traced back to the early 19th century English sports of Hare and Hounds, and Paper-Chasing. The first English championship was held in 1877. The International Cross-Country Championships, which are recognized by the International Amateur Athletic Federation, were first held in 1903.

At present there are three divisions in the International Cross-Country Championships—Senior Men, Junior Men (under 20) and Women. To date the US has not fared well in the senior division (the third place finish by Bill Rodgers of Massachusetts in 1974 was easily the best ever by an American). But it has done extremely well in both the women's and junior men's divisions. Since the women's competition was added to the International Cross-Country Championships in 1967, an American has finished first six out of the eight years. Doris Brown of Seattle, Washington

accounted for five of those victories, winning five times in a row between 1967 and 1971. Julie Brown (no relation) of Billings, Montana was the women's champion in 1975. The junior men's division was won by Americans in both '73 and '74 (Rich Kimble of California winning in '73 and Bobby Thomas, also of California, winning in '74).

In most parts of the US and Canada cross-country running has become a regular part of the high school, college and university athletic program—for both male and female competitors. Many times, particularly in college and university competition, cross-country races are run on golf courses.

In England, where cross-country running enjoys its greatest popularity and tradition (it's been said that many English distance runners would rather win the British national cross-country championship than an Olympic gold medal), courses tend to be much more rugged and "natural." On a typical English cross-country course, a runner might be called upon to race across plowed wet fields, splash through shallow streams, etc.

In continental Europe, where cross-country running is also very popular (particularly in countries such as Belgium, France and Spain), the courses tend to be flat and grassy, with man-made hurdles situated around the course, much as is the case on steeplechase horse-race tracks.

Cross-country running was once part of the Olympic track and field program. But it was dropped from the program as a result of difficulties encountered by competitors during the 1924 Olympic cross-country race, which was held during a Paris heat wave. Although the heat didn't seem to bother the great Finnish runners Paavo Nurmi and Ville Ritola, who finished one-two, it had a devastating effect on the field in general. Only 15 of the 39 runners were able to complete the 10,000-meter course. One competitor who failed to finish was seriously injured when he became disoriented due to heat and exhaustion and ran into a concrete wall.

The 1924 Olympics were the last to have cross-country running as part of the track and field program. The sport, however, is still represented in the Olympic Games today. It's one of the five events that make up the modern pentathlon.

I Enjoy It

Cross-country too often has been portrayed as the last bastion of the puritan work ethnic, a sport where miles are counted not as units of joy (as are touchdowns or baskets) but of suffering, a sport whose motives are so pure as to be incommunicable. Certainly the runner, at least initially, must have the will to endure. But when he has attained basic fitness, the sense of ordeal ebbs. Through his fatigue he begins to appreciate this most primary of athletic relationships, a man crossing the earth, unaided, as it presents itself to him.

The rewards of cross-country may be unrelated to competitive success. This is not to say that one cannot derive satisfaction from winning, but if competition is the runner's only goal, he is clearly deranged. He would pursue Sophia Loren for her money, order Russian caviar for its protein content.

The two most widely practiced sports that offer virtually no professional opportunities are swimming and track and field. Swimmers are notorious for retiring as teen-agers, but many runners, especially distance runners, carry on for decades (Mamo Wolde of Ethiopia won the Mexico City Olympic marathon at age 35). Elaborate physiological arguments have been put forth as to why this should or should not be so. For the runner the answer is clear: you cannot swim through a forest. The elements of boredom and meaningless pain are present in swimming—with its incessant repetitions and changeless surroundings—to a degree not found in running freely over the

Bunched at the start, the field for a cross-country race will gradually thin out as the fitter runners surge to the front. Cross-country offers a fine competitive outlet during the Autumn for athletes disenchanted with the highly mechanized and brutal nature of football. (Drennan)

Cross-country running appeals to both sexes and to all ages. It is not uncommon to see young female runners outdistance older male athletes over the course of a race. (Johnson)

country. The swimmer continues only so long as his urge to dominate drives him. The runner races one day a week in the autumn. The rest of the time he can indulge his esthetic sense.

New Zealander Jack Foster says, "I run from three to 15 miles five days a week and 20 on Sunday over hilly sheep farming country or through forest, I don't think of running as 'training.' I am not prepared to let it be anything but one of the pleasures of my life."

The longer one runs, in terms of miles or years, the more one savors cross-country. The explanation is simple. There is no better way to know the land, to feel a part of it, than to run across it daily. A morning run through an agricultural area, even if the same route is repeated for a year, evokes increasing involvement. Patterns of frost and fog, the growth and withering of grass, occasionally cataclysmic events such as lambing, induce an awareness of the land's rhythms. The nearness of his own rhythms—of breath and heart and footfall—assures the runner of his place. Such a run offers a chance for self-examination as well, a chance to discover one's sensitivity to poison oak, to find how one reacts to a face full of spider web in a dark glen or stepping on a snake at twilight. (Another effect is to refute the Judeo-Christian concept that man occupies an elevated position in relation to his environment, as if we needed any more disproof of that.)

The significance of the course in racing is such that one's mind is apt to leave out how one finished, retaining only where one went. Who has run the University of Kansas course at Lawrence who can tell you his time? Who can't tell you about the god-awful hill at four miles? Anoxia has burned every tendril of that slope's crabgrass into thousands of collegiate memories.

Cross-country sensitizes the runner not only to the country he crosses but to his own physiology. He becomes a connoisseur of tiredness, distinguishing, for example, the light-headed sensation of a five-mile jog following a series of sprints from the stiff, irritable fatigue near the end of a 20-mile run.

The runner refines his technique. He learns how to carry his hips and arms and head to most easily cover the ground.

—**Kenny Moore**

Kenny Moore, of Eugene, Oregon, is a special contributor to **Sports Illustrated.** *He was a marathoner on the '68 and '72 US Olympic teams, finishing fourth in the Olympic marathon in '72.*

For More Information

More information can be found under road racing, marathoning and track and field. Most of the same organizations are active in all of these. However, there is the International Cross-Country Union, Woodlin, 5 Granta Terr., Stapleford, Cambridge, England. They are responsible for the International Cross-Country Championships. A good magazine which has a lot of coverage is *Runner's World,* Box 366, Mountain View, Calif. 94040. Published monthly at $9.50 per year.

Here is a good book. It is available from World Publications, Box 366, Mountain View, Calif. 94040 at the price listed* plus 25 cents postage. Write for a complete list.

The Varied World of Cross-Country. Shows the unique simplicity, beauty and variety of the sport and suggests ways of protecting and promoting it, plus the stories of some of this country's most famous races. 1971 Ppb., 48 pp., ill., $1.25, (World Publications).

Cross-Country Skiing

To most North Americans, the word skiing is synonymous with schussing rapidly downhill, but the original and most natural form of the sport is Nordic or cross-country skiing. Based on a Stone Age rock carving on the Norwegian island of Rodnoy and on a prehistoric ski unearthed in Sweden, archaeologists can date cross-country skiing back at least 4000 years. Downhill skiing did not evolve from its cross country ancestor until the 19th century.

Cross-country skiing probably originated in Scandanavia in response to a need for travel and hunting in deep snow, gradually evolved there and came to North America with immigrants in the early 19th century. In snowy areas of North America it became the most logical means of snow travel, as it was much faster and less fatiguing than native snowshoeing. The most colorful 19th century cross-country skiing character was Snowshoe Thompson who carried mail across the High Sierra to miners during the California gold fever years.

Today recreational cross-country skiing (also known as ski touring) is growing at a tremendous clip in North America. It is axiomatic among its participants that "if you can walk, you can cross-country ski." Indeed, cross-country skiing can be adapted to very slow speeds and easy degrees of difficulty. This is undoubtedly one factor that has led to the sport's great popularity with families.

On the other hand, competitive cross-country skiing, which is part of the Winter Olympic program, is one of the most strenuous of sports. In Olympic and World Championship competition, men race over 15, 30 and 5C kilometers, as well a having a four x 10 kilo relay. Women's races are five, 10, and four x five kilos. The most famous cross-country ski race in the world is Sweden's Vasaloppet. The race is 83.6 kilos long and draws more than 10,000 participants each year! Little wonder that Nordic skiing is considered an institution in the Scandanavian countries.

The Fastest Growing Ski Sport in the U.S.A.

Born in Scandina thousands of years ago, brought by immigrants to the USA in the 19th century, trail skiing, during the years before the First World War developed into what is best known as Nordic or cross-country skiing for most part the competitive racing that appeals to young athletes. The recreational form of trail skiing—traversing a snow landscape in leisurely pleasure—was almost forgotten by all except a few romantics.

In 1962, inspired by Rudi Mattesich's memories of his youthful touring over Alpine trails, a group of devoted skiers amateurs, ski patrolmen and presidents of ski areas met and decided to revive the sport. They formed a membership committee of volunteers and called it The Ski Touring Council. A few futile attempts to involve the ski clubs quickly revealed that ski touring as a non-competitive, purely recreational acti

vity had the greatest appeal to individualists of all ages who were not very likely to belong to ski clubs, a good proportion of them not yet even skiers. The first Council ski tour at Mad River, sponsored by Roland Palmedo, and the first resultant workshop at Stratton Mountain, organized by Frank Snyder, clearly indicated the characteristics of the potential ski tourer. Of all ages, starting at five, both sexes from many walks of life—the first participants ranged from first time skiers to expert downhillers and cross-country runners. There were families with small children, one family with an infant in a backpack, dropouts from downhill, many professional people who could not risk accidents because of their responsibilities, young people who wanted to start skiing the easy way on the level, photographers after new subjects, outdoor enthusiasts and bird watchers. Even on the first tour, which was upgraded, they all fared well and emerged enthusiasts. Later surveys showed that a large percentage of ski tourers were college graduates and many in higher income brackets; that the large contingent of doctors, lawyers, executives, air line pilots, engineers were almost balanced by white and blue collar workers; that students, hikers, equestrians, bicyclists, backpackers, joggers, other summer outdoor activists and conservationists were heavily represented.

By 1973-74 ski touring had become the fastest growing ski sport in the US and, with tennis, the fastest growing sport overall. The number of ski tourers in the country is estimated at over one million. Although there is no precise way of counting them, the ski import figures issued by the US Department of Commerce do provide a fairly accurate indication, because until two years ago all touring skis came from abroad, chiefly from Scandinavia, with no-wax skis coming from Germany. During the 1974-75 season other countries began to export touring skis—notably Austria and Yugoslavia, exporting chiefly no-wax skis (which are gaining in popularity among amateur skiers). Therefore the figures from 1967 through 1974 are the most helpful in measuring the growth of the sport. In the period '67-68-69 a total of 50,000 pairs of touring skis were imported; in the year 1970 alone, 50,000 pairs were imported; in 1971, more than 157,000; in 1972, more than 300,000; in 1973, 311,000. In 1974, poor snow conditions and the gasoline shortage caused a decline in the import of downhill skis, but the import of touring skis continued to rise. Figures for 1975 are not available, but business reports show satisfaction in the stores selling touring equipment, and an increase in the number of stores specializing in touring skis and backpacking equipment only.

Left-Ski touring is the fastest growing family winter sport in the United States. It offers an opportunity to see Nature's winter wonderland in all its natural glory, free from the noise of snowmobiling. (Johnston) Below-Cross-country ski racing is one of the most strenuous of sports, one demanding year-round conditioning for high-level competition. The sport is an institution in Scandinavian countries, where some races draw up to 10,000 competitors.

Cross-country is the oldest and most natural form of skiing, dating back at least 4000 years. Racing is merely an extension of ski touring.

For this growth The Ski Touring Council does deserve substantial credit—not only for re-introducing the sport and continuing in its guidance and promotion but for initiating the procedures that are now in nationwide use. Because so many beginners mingled with the practiced skiers at its gatherings, it introduced workshops, traded tours, and clearly indicated graded trails. All under the direction of experts, chiefly volunteers, all open to everyone, the Council activities set a standard of procedure that still prevails. In 1963 it launched its Ski Touring Guide, subtitled The Ski Tourer's Manual with information covering all facets of the sport and listing ski touring areas and trails. This same year, it published *The Ski Touring Schedule,* a list of tours and workshops.

From the beginning, the Council concerned itself with trails. The methods of marking trails was covered in workshops. The most widely adopted trail marker was designed and introduced by the Council's Vice President, George Froehlich. Close cooperation developed with the state and federal departments responsible for trails on public lands. The Council is represented on The National Trails Council and advises private landownders on trails. A decisive contribution in this field has been made by the Federal Bureau of Outdoor Recreation which has a plan of the future projecting a transcontinental network. National, State Park, and forest authorities, conservationist and outdoor organizations, and many dedicated individuals have contributed to the Council's work. The early and continuing support of the sports media was also enthusiastic and vital.

Many reasons account for the fast growth of ski touring as recreation. It can be done wherever there is snow—on private lands, golf clubs, meadows, in parks, and requires no organized area. "Anyone in reasonably good health who can walk can ski tour" has become a truism which is basically accurate. The technique is easy to learn, and since it is learned on level or gently rolling ground, it is a good introduction to any kind of skiing. The equipment is inexpensive, a complete new set of skis, bindings, poles and boots costing about $75. If hiking boots and cable bindings are used, the cost is even less. Special children's sets, poles and bindings, sell for about $17.

The frenzied keeping-up-with-ski fashions is totally absent from ski touring circles, whose arbiters generally favor very understated clothes in colors that blend with the environment. In fact, most people have all the pieces of clothes already—wool slacks, knickers, warm underwear, sweaters, mittens, socks. Since ski touring uses many muscles steadily it is a very warming sport, hence requires layers (shirt, sweater, parka) rather than very heavy attire. Darkish shades of green, browns and blues reveal the tourers desire to be part of the scene he frequents, for underlying all the practical attractions is a deep and growing desire to escape from crowds and complex problems into the stimulating beauty of the winter landscape, a desire that ski touring amply satisfies.

Besides the Council Guide and Schedule (obtainable for $3.00 and $2.75 respectively from Rudi Mattesich, President, Ski Touring Council, Troy, Vermont 05868) a rewarding collection of ski touring books and publications is now available. The books usually go into details about technique and so forth, many make fine reading.

Many magazines carry articles on ski touring in season; ski and travel editors of the general press frequently now report on this sport. Many of the stores that carry ski touring equipment also organize tours, as do those in charge of parks and forest areas. In the northern snowbelt hnudreds of privately owned touring areas are opening, some charging a small trail fee, offering instruction and rentals and arranging tours. Citizens' races, competitive only to those who like competition are added attractions.

There is no doubt that if ski touring retains its present simple characters and resists over-commercialization it will continue to grow, become an abiding feature of life in the snow belt. Besides permitting a healthful winter exercise, it will keep the trail into the beautiful winter world open to all at very modest expense.

—Rudy Mattesich

Rudy Mattesich is President of the Ski Touring Council. The 74-year-old Austrian native has authored several books and novels, including **Intrude No More**, *a bestseller during the '40s.*

For More Information

The only magazine that covers cross-country skiing exclusively is *Nordic World,* Box 366, Mountain View, Calif. 94040. Published monthly from September to May at $6.50 per year. Many fine articles covering every aspect of the sport. Well-illustrated.

Some organizations you should know about: Ski Touring Council, 342 Madison Ave., Room 727, New York, N.Y. 10017; Far West Ski Association, 812 Howard St., San Francisco, Calif. 94103; Ski Touring Council, 4437 First Ave. S., Minneapolis, Minn. 55409. For racing, US Ski Association, 1726 Champa Suite 300, Denver, Colo. 80202 can be helpful.

It is much easier to find equipment today and most good backpacking shops are also selling cross-country equipment. But here are two companies that can be of help. Reliable Racing Supply, 624 Glen St., Glens Falls, N.Y. 12801. Their free catalog lists track setting sleds, snow dye & cement, Moon poles, road-ski roller skis, Falk Jumping boots, binding and blocks, Sundins Racing Skis, etc. Miller Ski Co., Orem, Vt. 84057. Has a free catalog with skis, bindings, poles, boots, gloves, etc. listed. Or the best thing is to send $1.50 to *Nordic World* magazine and ask for copies of their September and October 1975 issues. They cover the equipment scene in detail. Address: Box 366, Mountain View, Calif. 94040. Also, additional suppliers are listed under backpacking.

Some books of interest. All are available from World Publications, Box 366, Mountain View, Calif. 94040 at the price listed* plus 25 cents each postage.

Discover Cross-Country Skiing, This brief but complete guide on how to get started in the sport features sections on equipment, technique, waxing and enjoying–all you need to know to make your first tour enjoyable. 1974 Ppb., 48 pp., ill., $1.50, (World Publications).

Nordic Skiing Gear: Skis, Boots, Poles & Bindings. The only book in print devoted exclusively to nordic equipment. A consumer's guide to the selection, purchase, and care of equipment. Complete specifications (including manufacturer's suggested retail price) on most brands and models of nordic equipment. 1974 Ppb., 64 pp., ill., $1.75, (World Publications).

The Cross-Country Ski, Cook, Look and Pleasure Book, Hal Painter. A wild and different look at living in the snow which takes as its motto "Relax–or you won't feel a thing." Sound advice mixed with the story of "Alice in Snowpeople Land." 1973 Ppb., 158 pp., ill., $4.95, (Wilderness).

The Complete Guide to Cross-Country Skiing and Touring, Art Tokle and Martin Luray. The authors, both experienced skiers, detail the basic technique, equipment and conditioning the beginning ski tourer needs. 1973 Hb., 168 pp., ill., $6.95, (Holt, Rinehart & Winston).

Cross-Country Skiing, Chickering, ed. A collection of valuable articles by experienced skiers. Subjects covered include technique, training, equipment, waxing, and emergency tips. 1972 Ppb., 160 pp., ill., $1.95, (Tobey).

The Complete Book of Cross-Country Skiing and Ski Touring, Arthur Liebers. Tired of a five-minute run and a 20-minute wait in line? No such thing as a line in cross country skiing, and this is a good book for newcomers to the sport. Includes chapters on basic intermediate and advanced skills, cold-weather camping and touring areas. 1974 Hb., 284 pp., ill., $8.95, (Coward, McCann & Geoghegan).

Cross-Country Skiing, David Rees. An excellent "first" book, it anticipates and answers all the questions regarding basic equipment, waxing, and techniques. The advanced skier is provided with complete information on competition, training condition, racing know-how, and race organizations. 1975 Hb. & Ppb., 207 pp., ill., $9.95/$5.95, (Chilton).

Training for Nordic Skiing, Dave Prokop, ed. Here are the latest training techniques of top racers and their coaches. The only book of its kind on the market. Contributors include Bob Gray, Rolk Kjaernsli, John Caldwell, Marty Hall and others. 1975 Ppb., 96 pp., ill., $2.95, (World Publications).

All About Winter Safety. Be prepared for any snow emergency: broken ski, sudden storm, mountain accident of just about anything else that could happen. Just published. 1975 Ppb., 100 pp., ill., $1.95, (World Publications).

Ski Cross Country, Brady & Skjemstad. An Olympic skier and the nordic editor of *Ski Magazine* collaborate to bring you the authoritative book on ski touring and nordic racing. The latest information on technique, exercise, equipment, waxing and racing. 1974 Hb. & Ppb., 261 pp., ill., $10.00/$5.95, (Dial).

Caldwell on Cross-Country, John Caldwell. The dean of cross-country skiing writers takes up where his best-selling *New Cross-Country Ski Book* left off–with an advanced manual of methods and conditioning for the enthuiast aspiring to top expertise. 1975 Hb., $8.95, (Stephen Greene).

Curling

Curling has sometimes been called "shuffleboard on ice". It isn't. Not by any stretch of the imagination. It has been called a lot of other things, too, but usually by devotees of the game who have just missed an apparently easy shot. Originally, a stone (any size or shape would do) was slid along a stretch of ice towards a visible mark – a piece of wood or cloth. Later, the stones became standardized in shape and weight. Brooms were required to keep the ice clear of snow. Teams could be of any number up to 12 per side. Today, teams are standardized at four players on each side.

The game had its origins in Scotland, although there are some people who claim – with very little proof – that it began in Holland. Most curlers couldn't care less where it began; they do know, however, that Scotland was the country that brought it to the attention of the world, and it was Scotland that provided the history, the original rules and the traditions that surround the game.

But it wasn't until the Scots brought curling to Canada that it found its real home. Canada, where curling has found its greatest popularity, has close to a million curlers. The game is also popular in many of the northern states of the U.S. and in many parts of Europe. It is also played in New Zealand.

The game is played on a sheet of ice approximately 145 feet in length and about 15 feet in width. At either end of the ice is a bullseye of concentric circles, known as the house. A foothold (curlers call them hacks) behind each house provides a launching position for curlers to deliver the stones to the house at the far end of the ice. Each player on the team delivers two stones alternately with a player on the opposite team. When all 16 stones have been delivered, a count is made.

Since the object of the game is to place as many stones nearer the center of the house than any of the opposition stones, one shot (point) is scored for every stone which is closer to the center than any stone of the opposing team. Measurements are taken from the center tee to the nearest part of the stone and only stones which lie within the boundaries of a house are eligible for counting. All games are decided by a majority of shots, and the game is played for eight, 10, or 12 ends, by agreement.

The stone is specially quarried microgranite (usually from the Scottish Island of Ailsa Craig, where the hardest granite in the world is found), approximately 42 pounds in weight, and has a concave bottom so that only a small part of the granite (a circle of stone about ¼" wide) actually is in contact with the ice. Thus the friction between stone and ice is minimal. To make that minimal friction even less, the ice is "pebbled" prior to the start of the game by sprinkling the ice gently with warm water so the droplets of water, when they hit the ice, form a pebbled surface. This raises the stone minutely above the general plane of the ice.

The four players on each side are known as the Lead (he

throws the first two stones), the Second, the Third and the Skip (who throws the last two stones). The Skip also provides the strategy for the team by standing in the house and giving signals to the curler delivering at the other end of the ice. The other two members of the team use long, straw brooms to sweep the path in front of the moving stone – when required. Most people, upon viewing curling for the first time, wonder about all the excitement of sweeping. Does sweeping really make a difference?

Actually, sweeping not only makes a significant difference in the distance the stone will travel, but it also serves to keep the other two members of the rink (i.e., the sweepers) intent on the game and to keep them warm when the temperature drops lower than normal.

What distinguishes curling from "shuffleboard on ice" (or the German sport of Eistockschiesson) is the distinctive action of the stone as it proceeds down the ice. As the rock is released from the curler's hand, a turn is imparted to the stone, either clockwise or counterclockwise. This clockwise turn (for a right-handed curler) is called an in-turn, for the obvious reason that the hand turns the stone in towards the body. The out-turn is the counterclockwise rotation. As the stone's momentum decreases, the stone curls in an arc from its original path. It is this fact that gives the game its strategy. Skillful players can curl a stone behind another rock so that it is completely hidden to the opposition by the front stone. Or they can watch a stone that appears to be headed directly for its target suddenly curl too much and miss the opposition's rock completely.

The two basic shots in the curler's arsenal (there are a number of others but they all stem from these two) are the draw and the take-out. A draw shot is one which has just enough momentum (curlers say "weight") so it comes to rest exactly where the skip wants it. A take-out shot is one delivered with much greater force, so it "knocks out" an opposition stone. Thus a team with possession of the last rock will try to place its stones so that it can count more than one on that end. On the other hand, a team that does not have the last rock is on the defensive and will try to ensure that the opposition does not count more than the last stone of the end. The simplest way to ensure this is to use a lot of take-out shots to keep the house clear.

Obviously, with the curling action of the rock and the length of the sheet of ice, it's not difficult for a curler to be short or long on a draw shot, or to miss completely with a take-out shot. A further complicating element is the fact that as the game progresses and the curlers move up and down the ice the pebble wears off and the action of the stone in one end may not be quite the same as the action two or four ends before. Thus the skip's ability to "read the ice" becomes a key factor in the success of the team.

But all of this tells only the technicalities and the facts of curling. What sets the game apart from most other sports is an element of its Scottish heritage. Unlike most other games, curling has few rules, and these are simple ones.

Rather than try to legislate on every eventuality, the Scots preferred to leave the major decisions to the sense of fair play and sportsmanship of the competitors. Thus, while an umpire is a part of the game, by common consent and etiquette he never renders a decision until he has been invited to do so by the two competing sides. In practice, this means that he is usually called on to measure stones at the conclusion of an end, where the competitors are uncertain which is closest to the center. Otherwise, the players settle all matters themselves.

This attitude of sportsmanship and etiquette is one of the most cherished ideals of the sport, and adds a dimension that is, unhappily, missing from most other games. It means that curlers do not strive to beat the umpire, but to beat each other in fair play. Curlers would rather lose a game than lose face by winning unfairly, or by a subterfuge. It means that curlers can be tough opponents on the ice while remaining close friends before and after a game. Indeed, another of the cherished Scottish traditions is the one that calls for the winners to buy a drink (or its equivalent) for the losers after the game is over. The sociability of two teams gathering at the conclusion of a game is a cherished hallmark of curling.

Curling is a game that appeals to all ages. While many curlers start in their early teens (and continue until they are 90), there are others who may not start until age 50 or later.

Women find that they can compete on equal terms with men. The only instance where men may have a slight edge over women is in the one facet of curling that requires muscular strength, namely sweeping. This advantage is minimized, however, since many shots do not require this sweeping at all. Indeed, mixed curling (two men and two women on a team) is increasing in popularity all the time.

Curling is also a spectator sport where nothing is hidden from the audience: spectators can second-guess the competitors continually, applaud excellent shots or groan over missed shots. It's a colorful game with its Scottish heritage and background. Also, it is a game that novices can learn easily and quickly. Curling has even attracted handicapped people, who compete on equal terms with the non-handicapped.

Little equipment is required for curling. The stones are invariably the property of the curling club and are provided to the playing members. The brooms are sometimes provided by the club, but more often are purchased by the players. No special clothing is required, although it is obvious that a warm sweater and warm footwear is essential. Special curling boots or shoes are manufactured which combine warmth with good footing on the slippery ice.

Curling season usually starts in October and runs through the winter months, until Easter. During this time there are club games (against your neighbor), regional bonspiels (competitions against curlers from other parts of the area) and national championships (for men, ladies, mixed teams, schoolboys, schoolgirls, police, firemen, Rotarians, Elks . . . you name the organization and you will find that they have a bonspiel sometime during the winter). At the top of the competitive ladder there is the World Curling Championship for the Air Canada Silver Broom.

Air Canada, which assumed sponsorship of the World Championship in 1968, has watched the event grow until the present, when 10 or so countries compete for the coveted Silver Broom. The World Championship has been held in Scotland, Canada, United States, France, Germany and Switzerland. In 1976 the U.S.A. will host the Silver Broom at Duluth, Minnesota. In 1977, Sweden will act as host for the first time, when the Silver Broom competition travels to Karlstad, Varmland.

Play in the World Championship is limited to the national champions of each of the 10 competing countries. The 10 champion teams play a round-robin preliminary series with the top three or four teams proceeding to a sudden death playoff

Vigorous sweeping before the stone will smoothe the ice enough to cause it to travel a greater distance. It also serves to keep the sweepers intent on the game and warm in cold weather. (North American Curling News)

series to determine the world winners. After the round-robin series, if the first place team is undefeated, it receives a bye to the finals, while the second and third place teams meet in a sudden-death semi-final. If the first place team has been defeated, then the playoffs involve the top four teams in sudden-death semi-finals and finals.

Prior to the Air Canada Silver Broom, there had been an unofficial World Championship sponsored by the Scotch Whisky Association. This event grew from an invitational series in 1959 (Scotland vs Canada) to an eight-nation series by 1967. In 1973, Italy and Denmark joined Scotland, Canada, U.S.A. Sweden, Switzerland, Norway, France and Germany to make the Silver Broom a 10-nation event.

Since 1959, Canada has won the world title on 12 occasions. The United States has won twice, Scotland once, Sweden once, and Switzerland once.

Thanks to the success of the Air Canada Silver Broom, a World Junior Championship has been established, and there is little doubt that further world championships, (ladies? mixed rinks? seniors?) will be established.

—Doug Maxwell

An acknowledged curling expert, Doug Maxwell of Toronto, Ontario, is a well-known curling commentator for the CBC television network in Canada and has organized the World Curling Championships.

For More Information

There is only one magazine being published in the U.S. on curling. *North American Curling*, 723 Milwaukee Ave., South Milwaukee, Wisc. 53172 is published bi-monthly at $2.50 per year. It is the official magazine for the United States Men's Curling Association and the United States Women's Curling Association. The men's group can be contacted through the magazine and the women's through Mrs. Forrest McConnell, 1826 Knollwood Rd., Lake Forest, Ill. 60045. Another magazine of interest, *Curler Magazine*, 56 Esplanade St. E., Suite 401, Toronto, Ontario, Canada. The Readers' Service Bureau, The Curling News, Box 365, South Milwaukee, Wisc. 53172 can take care of all your equipment needs.

Curling books are not the easiest thing to find. But here are two good books that should help satisfy your desire for more curling information. These are available from World Publications, Box 366, Mountain View, Calif. 94040 at the price listed* plus 25 cents each postage. Write for a complete list.

Beginner's Guide to Curling, Robin Welsh. Curling enthusiasts will love this complete guide that covers the paraphernalia, terminology, history of the sport, and then details in clear photos how to curl, from the sliding delivery and take-out technique to the art of sweeping. 1969 Hb., 184 pp., ill., $4.95, (Pelham).

Sports Illustrated Curling, Mark Mulvay & Ernie Robinson. The Scottish game of hockey is played on ice and is vividly portrayed by the editors of *Sports Illustrated*. Deals with the game on a pro level. 1973 Hb. & Ppb., 107 (oversize) pp., $6.50/$2.95, (Lippincott).

Cyclo-Cross

Cross-country bicycle racing began its bumpy and mud-smirched existence in the early part of the 20th century as a winter diversion for European cyclists who raced on the roads during spring and summer months. It has since become a unique and important sport in its own right. World Championships have been held since the 20s, and since 1950 the sport has had the recognition of the international cycling union (UCI).

Cyclo-cross racing up and down steep hillsides, across roaring creeks, and over tricky, rock-strewn pathways creates a terrific feeling of speed. It does so without most of the dangers inherent in other high-velocity sports because the average speeds rarely exceed 15 miles per hour. To be competitive, however, the riders must have the ability to do sprint-like accelerations over and over for the entire 15 to 20 kilometer race, and to react with lightning-fast reflexes to avoid and/or scramble over the many obstacles encountered.

Because of the high probability that a cyclo-cross racer will hit some of the many obstacles in his path, the equipment used in the sport must be designed and built for extra strength. High-carbon or chrome molybdenum steel tubes, either heavy gauge or heavily butted, are brazed into longer than usual frames, frames with less critical head and seat tube angles than those on road-racing bikes. Long top tubes and high bottom brackets are often employed as well to improve clearances. The wheels must be of the strongest and most resilient construction possible, and the rear wheel is always mounted with a highly sculpted tubular tire for traction. Special cycling/running shoes with soccer cleats mounted to the rear of the pedal-contact area are used for traction while the racer is on foot. Wide pedals and double-strength toe-clips are used on the bicycles to facilitate quick mounting and placing of the feet after a run.

Special cantilever brakes are often mounted to the bike frame to provide extra clearance around the mud that often gathers on the tires, and double chain-guard rings are sometimes mounted on a single chainwheel to prevent chain throwing. Gears used for cyclo-cross are relatively low to fit the slow speeds and steep terrain.

To use so special a bike on a tough course, the rider must be in top shape, and must be able to dismount, carry the machine, and remount smoothly at full speed. Running and long-distance rides are often used by racers to build endurance, and exhaustive mounting and dismounting drills are repeated many times before the racing season.

The reward to a cyclo-cross enthusiast who trains sufficiently comes not only from successful competition, but also from meeting the challenge of any rugged terrain that he is confronted with.

—Tom Cuthbertson

Over particularly difficult terrain, cyclo-cross competito must dismount and carry their bicycles. Occasionally this wi mean climbing up a nearly vertical cliff with a bike slung acro the back. (Lacey)

Tom Cuthbertson is the author of **Anybody's Bike Book** *and* **Bike Tripping.**

An Easy Cyclo-Cross Course

The start of one cyclo-cross course is at the bottom of a long sloping lawn, which at the time of the race eacl year, just after the heavy December rains, is always ap proximately the consistency of a peat bog. At the top of th lawn there is a narrowing to a steep path with ditches on botl sides. The steep path can only be negotiated by doing a sprin on the bike, or by dismounting and running. Riders have nc room here to pass runners, so many take to the ditches, whicl are just deep enough to stop a front wheel.

After a short flat stretch there is a steep descent into a muddy, leaf-and-eucalyptus-bark-strewn right turn. On the outer side of this turn there is a large wild berry bush. After close examination, many riders have reported that the berries are not ripe at race-time, but they say the thorns are always in prime condition.

Another short flat stretch follows, marred only by a slightly protruding root (it is six inches high) on the left. Then comes a drop down a rocky pathway into a rockier stream-bed. The stream is different every year. Sometimes it trickles, other times it roars. It is never quite negotiable in the saddle, though, nor is the bank beyond it, which gets progressively more slippery as the race continues and more and more entrants slosh their way up to it.

In the backstretch following the first creek crossing, there is nothing more challenging than a bone-shaking section of cobble-size stones and an area of soft dirt which becomes deeply rutted before the third or fourth lap. After the fast stretch, though, the course drops abruptly into a second creek crossing. The creek at this point is often quite placid, but always muddy enough to make pedalling up the far bank a supreme challenge to man and machine. Just after the second crossing, the riders emerge onto a bit of pavement, which would be a source of great relief if it weren't tipped up at such an unreasonable angle.

Just at the top of the paved hill, the course turns to the left and begins another leaf-and-eucalyptus-bark-strewn hill leading into a sharp right turn. There is no berry bush at this turn, but two tree stumps make out-of-control slides unpleasant.

A narrow trail leads from this turn on through a grove of stately eucalyptus trees, which obligingly shed their bark each year to guarantee poor traction. The slipping and sliding which ensues lasts until the riders begin the impossibly slippery and slick descent to the third crossing of the creek. Most entrants, at some point in the race, take this descent on their chamois.

The final climb out of the creek is up a small cliff. Some years the race promoters put a rope up the cliff, and some years they cut a few steps into the slippery embankment. Often they leave it for the intrepid rider-carrier-crawler to figure out for himself.

A wide, smooth road covers the bulk of the remainder of the distance back to the start-finish area, but before the riders can sink back into the peat bog, they must pass through a narrow, often-rutted gate with two wicked iron gate-posts looming up from the sides. Just past this gate, and immediately before the starting line, there is a dirt area which turns into a swamp on particularly wet days. Mud fights have been known to break out spontaneously in this wallow during warm-up laps.

After passing the swamp and beginning the uphill peat-bog grind, the rider is into the second of eight care-free laps. It makes for a colorful sport, but the colors tend to be more earthy and less synthetic than those in many other athletic events.

—Tom Cuthbertson

For More Information

Additional information can be found under racing and touring. *Bike World* magazine, Box 366, Mountain View, Calif. 94040, published monthly at $8.50 per year, does have articles on the sport from time to time.

Darts

Warlike tribes commonly used darts of various forms as weapons, but these implements were not used as a game until about 1100 A.D., during the reign of King Henry II of England. The original game was called butts and was played at inns across the country. English bowmen in searching for pleasurable diversions, adapted light flight arrows and threw these shortened arrows or darts at the rounded end, or butt of an ordinary ale cask. This cask butt gradually evolved in to our contemporary cork or composition dart board.

The rules for playing butts were simple. Each soldier had three arrows to throw at the cask, upon which five concentric circles were laid out as scoring areas. The total score per game was determined after throwing three arrows five times or a total of 15 times per game. As years went by, the game of butts became very popular and the shortened arrows evolved into implements more closely resembling present day darts. It is known that Anne Boleyn, Henry VIII's second wife, once gave him richly appointed darts to use in games at court.

Darts came early to America: the Pilgrims played the game aboard the Mayflower in an effort to dispell boredom.

As it is played in the US today, darts uses a target board set on a wall with its center 5'3" from the floor. A foul line is marked on the floor, 7'3" from the target. The dart board is numbered, and divided into sections of various graduated scores. A player is given three darts to throw and must remain behind the foul line at all times. Each player alternates throwing, so only one player's darts are on the board at one time. Scores are determined by what area of the board has been hit by each dart.

The American Dart Association was formed to administer the sport in 1933. There are over eight million dart players in the world and the game is steadily gaining in popularity.

—Edmund Hady

Edmund Hady is very involved in the dart world. He also authored the book **American and English Dart Games.**

For More Information

The United States Darting Association, 516 Fifth Ave., New York, N.Y. 10035 is the official group in the United States. They publish a lot of good information including a quarterly called *Dart News.* Another good contact is Darts Unlimited, 30 E. 20th St., New York, N.Y. 10003. They have available professional English darts, boards and accessories. Even signature darts are available through them. There is the Conrad Daniels dart referred to as the 10202 Daniels. If you didn't know Daniels was the 1975 US Champion and winner of England's 1975 TV-Times Champion of Champions Tournament where 15 the world's best players competed. Rules of the games are accompanied by each set that this company sells. Very well-respected company and an excellent source for top equipment.

A good book and available from World Publications, Box 366, Mountain View, Calif. 94040 at the price listed* plus 25 cents postage is **American and English Dart Game**, Edmund Carl Hady. Most people have played darts at one time or another but have been confused by variances in the rules. This book will clear up the confusion, since it not only teaches how to throw the darts correctly, but contains the rules for both American and English games. 1973 Ppb., 50 pp., ill., $3.00 (Mayflower Graphics).

Decathlon

The greatest all-round test of athletic ability in sports is track and field's decathlon. And ever since the legendary Jim Thorpe won the event in the 1912 Olympics (the first time the decathlon was contested in the Games), the press has invariably acclaimed the Olympic decathlon winner the world's greatest athlete—and for good reason.

The decathlon is a two-day test in which participants compete in 10 separate track and field events (five the first day, five the second day). The events, which are always run off in the same order, are: (first day) 100-meter dash, long jump, shot put, high jump and 400-meter dash; (second day) 110-meter hurdles, discus throw, pole vault, javelin throw, and 1500-meter run. Clearly, to become a decathlon champion, an athlete must possess speed, strength, spring, agility, coordination, poise, endurance and mental toughness—in other words, just about every primary athletic quality one could ever want in an athlete.

Performances in the decathlon are rated on a points-scoring system—a 25-foot long jump, for instance, is worth 945 points, a 24-foot, six-inch long jump is worth 915 points, etc. The official points table, which is set up relative to the existing world records in the various events, is periodically revised in every event and the winner is the one who accumulates the highest number of points. The athlete's actual placement in each event has no bearing on the points he received; only the relative merit of his performance wins points.

In women's competition, the counterpart of the decathlon is the pentathlon, a two-day event in which competitors participate in the 100-meter hurdles, shot putt, high jump, long jump and 200-meter dash. The women's pentathlon, which is also scored on a points system, is part of the Olympic track and field program.

Anatomy of A World Record

The current world record holder in the decathlon—and the world's number one ranked athlete the last two years—is 26-year-old, 6'2", 195-pound Bruce Jenner of San Jose, California. Bruce, who's an insurance representative, was raised in Connecticut and went to college in Iowa. It was while in college that he took up the decathlon and also met his wife, Chrystie. The Jenners moved to San Jose, Chrystie's hometown, in 1973 so Bruce could train alongside such single events specialists from the San Jose area as world recordholders Al Feuerbach (shot put) and John Powell (discus). Chrystie, who's a stewardess with United Airlines, is easily Bruce's number one fan. The main reason she became a stewardess, she says, is so she could fly free of charge to all of his meets. Since they were married shortly before the Munich Olympics, Chrystie has been to every meet in which Bruce has competed. Here Bruce talks about the decathlon and gives an event-by-event rundown of his .8524-point record effort in Eugene, Oregon, August 9-10, 1975 . . .

The first event of the decathlon is the 100-meter dash. Bruce Jenner started his World Record point total of 8524 at Eugene, Oregon in August, 1975 by breaking his personal record with 10.7 seconds. Running events in the decathlon include the 100-, 400-, and 1500-meter distances.

The decathlon is the all-round championship in track and field. That's one way of describing it. And I guess I have to agree with those who say that the Olympic decathlon champion is the world's greatest athlete. I mean, in the decathlon you have to throw three different implements, you have to high jump, long jump, pole vault, run the hurdles, run a sprint race (the 100 meters), a sprint-endurance race (the 400 meters) and an endurance race (the 1500 meters). So it's obviously a very, very good test of somebody's athletic ability.

There have been many great decathlon men over the years. With the exception of Nikolai Avilov, who won the decathlon in the '72 Olympics and who held the world record until I broke it in Eugene, I've never seen any of them in action. For instance, I never saw Bill Toomey, the '68 Olympic champion, compete. He retired in 1969 and my first year was 1970. But I have heard a lot about these past decathlon greats. From what I've heard I would have to say Rafer Johnson was the best of them all. He was tremendously talented. He was big (6'3", 200 lbs), had beautiful speed, spring, and co-ordination. In 1956 he made the US Olympic team in the long jump as well as the decathlon. He was just a fantastic athlete!

But you have different styles of decathlon men. Bill Toomey wasn't anywhere near as naturally talented an athlete as Rafer, in my opinion, but Bill was an extremely hard worker. He probably had about half the talent of Rafer Johnson, but worked twice as hard. As a result, he won an Olympic gold medal and set a world record in the decathlon.

Rafer, for all his great ability, ran a lousy 1500 meters by today's standards. But in his day (1954-1960), you didn't have to run a good 1500 meters to win, so the competitors—even the best ones—never really trained that hard for the event. When Rafer won the gold medal in the 1960 Olympics in Rome by hanging on the shoulder of his closest rival, C. K. Yang, in that unforgettable 1500, he ran only 4:49, and that was easily his best ever in the event. Now I have to go out and run 4:10 to 4:15 to win the meet. Things have changed.

If I were to put guys like Rafer Johnson and Bill Toomey in categories, I guess I would fit in somewhere between them. I think I have more natural talent than Toomey, though not the talent that Johnson had. But I work very hard at the decathlon. I train very hard. I've been able to produce the results that I have through hard work, because I was never supremely talented. I was a 13-foot pole vaulter and 6'2" high jumper in high school, but it's only when I started working seriously the decathlon that my overall performances started coming up.

"The press has traditionally portrayed the decathlon as being a gruelling two-day test of guts and stamina. I find the hardest thing about the decathlon is not the actual competition, but training for it."

What I did have was versatility. In high school I played football, basketball, and ran several events in track. As soon as track season was over I would start competitive water skiing (I competed in four national championships in water skiing). I used to be a swimmer and I was a diver, so I've done just about every sport.

When I graduated from high school in Sandy Hook, Connecticut (you'll have to look awfully close at the map to find Sandy Hook), I decided football was going to be my game at college. With that in mind, I enrolled at Graceland College in Lamoni, Iowa. I lasted through about a month of football before I tore up my knee. I had surgery done on the knee on New Year's Day of 1969. I didn't know whether my athletic career was over or not, but I was lucky. By working on the knee, I rehabilitated it to the point where I could run or jump on it.

In my sophomore year I played basketball at Graceland. At the end of that year I decided I was going to compete in a decathlon. My coach, L.D. Weldon, had been a decathlon man, and my roommate in my freshman year was also a decathlon man. All of us had talked about it and it sounded like a lot of fun. Besides, it was right up my alley since I enjoyed competing in a lot of different track events. I scored 6,991 points that first time out—this was in the summer of 1970—and I loved it. I just found the decathlon tremendously challenging. That's when I decided that this was the event for me. I essentially quit every other sport and began training solely for the decathlon. In '71 I scored 7,531 points. In '72 I made the Olympic team with 7,846 points (I was 10th in Munich). Since then my training has been so totally geared to the decathlon that I don't even walk fast up stairs anymore—too much chance of getting injured.

Due to the number of separate events involved, of course, the decathlon takes a tremendous amount of training. I average about six hours of training a day, 365 days a yar. I usually do about an hour of running and stretching in the morning. Then I go to the office for about three or four hours. After that it's out to the practice field. I train all afternoon, until about six or seven o'clock. If I have a business appointment in the evening, I go to that. Then it's back home and bed. Next morning I get up to do the whole thing over again. I'm lucky to be in the insurance field where I'm more or less my own boss. Even so, if I don't sell I don't get paid, as I work on strict commission basis. Actually, there's no way in the world I'd be able to follow this training routine of mine if my wife wasn't working.

The press has traditionally portrayed the decathlon as being a gruelling two-day test of guts and stamina. I find the hardest thing about the decathlon is not the actual competition, but training for it. Not only does the training take a tremendous amount of time, as I said, but it's almost impossible to train to be a very fast sprinter and also a distance man. They just don't mix. How do you train to be a good long jumper and also a shot putter? To make matters worse, there aren't too many decathlon coaches in the U.S. who know what they're talking about. There are a lot of coaches who know how to coach maybe six or seven events, but few of them know how to train you for a decathlon, how to tailor the training so you can get the most out of yourself and the 10 events.

In my own case I don't have a coach. I'm self-coached. I do almost all my running workouts with Fred Samara, another decathlon man here in San Jose. Fred, who was the U.S. AAU decathlon champion for 1975, lives three doors down the hall from me, so there's no difficulty for us to get together. We plan the workouts together and do them together. Sometimes I'll time him, then he times me. Or else we may run together, one of us carrying a stopwatch to get our times.

All my technique work is done with athletes in this area who are specalists. If I'm going to pole vault I can get together with Bob Slover, who's done 17'7" and lives just across the street. Dan Ripley, the world indoor recordholder in the pole vault (18'1"), also lives here in San Jose. If I want to throw the discus, I can work out with John Powell, the world recordholder. John lives only two miles away. If I want to throw the shot, I can train with Al Feuerbach, who still holds the world amateur shot put record. I do all my weight training with Feuerbach and a bunch of other guys who are very involved in Olympic type lifting. In just about every event we have in the decathlon, there's someone in this area who's very, very proficient. For a decathlon man, it's almost a perfect situation. The decathlon has become so competitive in the last five to 10 years that you have to be proficient in every event to win in major competition. You cannot get by–people did in years past–by being exceptionally good in some events and relatively mediocre in others. Today, if a guy is slow in the 1500 meters, for instance, I can pick up 300 points on him in that one event–and I've done it in a lot of cases. So you're getting a more rounded decathlon performer today. Russia's Nikolai Avilov, the defending Olympic champion, is an example. He's proficient in every event. So am I. I'm not outstanding in any one event, but at the same time I'm not weak in any event either. Balance is the key.

In striving to achieve this all-round proficiency, however, you have to sacrifice a little bit on at least some of your individual events. That's why I don't think you'll ever again see a decathlon champion who's also of world record caliber in an individual event. The kind of training needed to excel in one event simply takes too much away from the other nine. To be a world class long jumper, for example, you have to do a lot of quick, short sprints and technique work. Your legs have to be fresh all the time. You can't go out, run 10 miles, then come back and do 26 feet in the long jump. It just takes too much out of you. Today's decathlon man has to do distance work along with all the rest of his training. In other words, you can't be a long jumper who does the decathlon, or a pole vaulter who does the decathlon. You have to be a 100 percent decathlon man and train accordingly.

My world record decathlon in Eugene, Oregon, August 9-10 in the U.S.–U.S.S.R.–Poland meet was an example of the all-round proficiency I spoke about earlier. I won only two of the 10 events–the discus, in which I was only one centimeter ahead of the second-place man, and the 1500 meters. But I was in the second to fifth range in all the other events, with 25 athletes competing.

The Eugene meet was one of those instances where everything fell beautifully into place for me. A month earlier in the AAU Decathlon Championships I had failed to clear a height in the pole vault and was knocked out of the competition. It was the first meet I'd lost in two years, and it really upset me. After that decathlon I changed my whole mental outlook. I had sort of had it in my mind that I would like to go undeafeated right through to the Olympic Games in Montreal–that would have been three years without losing a meet!–and then crown it all with a gold medal. But with thoughts of an undefeated string now out of the way, I could concentrate simply on winning meets and scoring well.

In the month before Eugene I changed a lot of technique points around, and I took it very easy in my running workouts (I'd been training without a break for a whole year and if you're not in shape by then, you're not going to get in shape that last month). I wanted to stay fresh for that entire month. In the weight events, I spaced the workouts further apart and made them shorter. Instead of taking 20 throws in the shot put, I'd take only five–but make them hard and as technically perfect as I could. As a result, I was achieving better marks in practice in the throwing events than ever before.

So I went up to Eugene feeling really ready and determined to prove to myself that I could come back after that AAU defeat. Eugene has always been a very good place for me. That's where I got my international start, so to speak, by qualifying for the '72 Olympic team. The facilities in Eugene are excellent, the competition in the meet was great–Avilov, Leonid Litvinyenko of the U.S.S.R. and Ryszard Katus of Poland (the top three in the '72 Olympics) were all there. My family had come all the way from Connecticut to see the meet. My sister and brother-in-law from Miami were there. Cousins I hadn't seen for 12 years were there. In most of my decathlons during the previous year I had had difficulty getting psyched up for the competition. I guess the reason was that winning had become almost commonplace. But when I went out there in Eugene, I could just feel the old adrenalin pumping. I was "hungry" again.

In the first event, the 100 meters, I jumped the gun on the first two starts (before the meet I fugured, "I'm going to jump the gun twice if I have to because if I guess right, I'm going to be gone." Sometimes you catch it and sometimes you don't. Those two times I didn't. On the third start I had to sit back in the starting blocks to make sure I didn't false start (you're allowed only two false starts in international competition). Consequently, at the gun I was last out of the blocks. The track was fast, there was a 3.8 mile-per-hour trailing wind. Usually my first 60 meters of the 100 are my strongest–I have a tendency to tighten up in the last 40, but this time I accelerated right through that last 40 meters, finishing with the rest of the field at the tape.

Afterwards, there was this extraordinary delay of about 20 minutes before they announced the times from my heat. The reason was that someone had failed to turn on the electrical timing device that was to be used to time all the races. The result was that they would have to use hand times for everyone, a break for all the competitors since electrical timing is always slower than hand timing. Finally the winner of my heat was announced as having run 10.6 and I went, "ooooh," because I knew I had been right behind the guy. The second guy also ran 10.6 and I was 10.7–2/10ths faster than I'd ever run before! At 26 points per tenth, that meant I was already 52 points up on myself. More importantly, before the 100 I knew that if I wanted to break the world record–which had been on my

"In the javelin my first throw was nice and relaxed–boom!–214'11", only one inch off my goal. At that moment I knew I was going to go over 8500 points easily. My other two throws weren't as good. I was trying to "muscle" them, and when you do that the javelin doesn't go as far–although sometimes you figure that once in a while you're really going to 'hit it' on a throw like that and the javelin is going to go out of sight."

mind from the beginning–I would have to do at least 10.8. Having done 10.7, I was on my way.

In the next event, the long jump, I felt I had to do 23'6" to stay on pace for a world record (when you've competed in the decathlon as much as I have, and are as familiar with the scoring tables as I am, you know exactly where you have to be at the end of every event to reach a certain point total). My first jump was 22'3" or thereabouts. My next jump was 22'9" and my last jump was 23'6"–exactly what I wanted. After the 10.7 100 meters, I knew I was going after the world record. That 23'6" long jump just sort of proved it. Everything was perfect: the crowd was good; the wind conditions were perfect; the competition was excellent. I knew this was the time. (Editor: Bruce Jenner has done 24'1" in the long jump using the forward flip style, but this style has been ruled illegal by the International Amateur Athletic Federation, although it's used in professional track.)

We next went to the shot put. My best ever in the event was 47'10", but in practice two weeks before, I threw 49'4", so I knew I'd be going for a personal best in Eugene. The warm-up throws felt beautiful and I knew I was ready for a big one. Sure enough, I came up for my first throw and–boom!–50'¼"! A personal best by more than two feet! In my other two throws I was also over 49 feet. I was just "on." My technique felt absolutely perfect.

We moved to the high jump. I felt I had to go at least 6'6" and I wanted to make 6'7". The best I'd ever done before was 6'6¾". I cleared 6'6" on my first attempt. I missed my first two tries at 6'7", but on the last attempt I was really psyched and–boom!–I went over the bar with a good two inches to spare. Again, it was another personal best, my fourth one in four events.

The last event of the first day in the decathlon is the 400 meters. I hadn't been running the event as well as I should have this year. I had only run 48.8, while last year I had run 48.2. I figured I had to at least get under 49 seconds in Eugene. In the race I ran a real solid pace all the way around the track and felt good at the end, which is the way you always seem to feel at the end of your better races. My time was 48.7. I was pleased with that. It gave me a total of 4,268 points for the first day, 120 points better than I'd ever done.

The only competitor ahead of me at that point was my American teammate Fred Dixon, who had 4,330 points. But that didn't bother me one bit, since I knew that if I kept up the pace I would pass him in total points the second day. Even if Fred had an unbelievable day (for him) I would still pass him, because almost all of my strongest events are on the second day. So I wasn't concerned with Fred or anyone else, nor with how they were doing event to event. (Editor: In fact, Fred Dixon did have an excellent second day at Eugene, but Bruce outscored him by more than 300 points to win 8524 to 8277, Avilov finishing third with 8211).

What I was concerned about was the world record. I would still have to total 4200 points the second day to set a new mark, no mean feat considering that the second day record, which I held, was only 4,181. In view of my mental attitude, the conditions and the way my events were going, however, I felt it should be easy to score 4200 points the next day.

We started off the second day with the 110-meter high hurdles. I wanted to do at least 14.7. I ran 14.6, but it wasn't a good race. From about the third to the seventh hurdle I couldn't get back up on my toes; I was running flat-footed, just sort of stumbling along. But at least I had the momentum going again. "Now just keep it going," I thought.

Next came the discus. As with the shot, I had been throwing the discus extremely well in practice in the weeks before. I had changed my style to the one John Powell uses, had worked on the technique quite a bit and before Eugene I was throwing so well it was almost ridiculous. I knew it was almost automatic that I would improve on my personal best of 161'-1". When I threw 160' in the warm-up, I was even more certain I was ready for a big one.

On the first official throw, I didn't "hit it" right, and the distance was only 154'. But my second throw was solid as a rock—164'0" and another personal best. I walked out of the circle thinking, "I knew it! I just knew I was going to do it!" On my last throw I tried for a good one, but I ploughed the discus out a little bit. The tip of the discus was a bit high and it just didn't go. The distance was only 157' or 158'. But I didn't care. I had thrown 164'0" and that's all I wanted.

We moved to the pole vault, the event that had been my undoing at the AAU. The runway was fast, we had a nice little breeze going with us. I thought, "Heck, everthing's right. I'll start out with my heaviest (fiberglass) pole instead of working from a light pole to a heavier one." But on my first vault at 14'0", the pole pushed right out and I missed the height badly. There was just no snap to the pole. In 90 percent of the cases the pole would have been stiff enough. In fact, I had used it successfully on several occasions. But my run-up was so good (due to the fast runway and the following breeze) and my pole plant so aggressive that I guess I was getting too much in the pole, and it just wasn't holding me. In addition, it was a warm day, which meant that the pole was bending easier. I made 14'0" on my second attempt, but I knew I'd better find a heavier pole or I was in trouble.

I asked Craig Brigham, one of the other competitors, if he knew whether there were any heavier poles around. Craig, who's from the University of Oregon and was therefore competing on his home field, said he didn't think so. I then checked with some of the other decathlon men to see if any of them had a heavier pole. Nothing. Craig finally suggested that I check the equipment shed beside the track on the off-chance that there was a heavy pole left over from a previous meet. I went over to the shed and started looking through a bunch of poles. All of them were light. Then I pulled out this one pole—it was a 6.7 flex, the very same flex as my heaviest pole. I thought, "Ooooh, that's awful close to the flex that I need" (I wanted a 6.6 flex). There was another pole in the box. I pulled it out—it was a 6.6, and just the right length! It even had the tape wrapped at the level of my hand hold, just as if the pole had been made for me! It was unbelieveable!

I brought the pole back to the vault area and started playing around with it to see how it felt compared to my heaviest pole. It felt pretty good, but the differences in flex are so slight that you can't really tell how a pole will feel just by bending it. You actually have to vault with the pole to see what happens.

I had wanted to pass until 15'0" after clearing the opening height. But now that I had this new pole in hand, I thought I'd better try it out at 14'9". If the pole didn't feel good I would take the other two attempts with my own pole. On my first attempt with the new pole I missed the height, but the pole felt much better. So I thought, "What the heck, I'm going to stick with it." On my second attempt I just bombed up over the bar.

My original plan had been to go from 14'0" to 15'0" to 15'5" to 15'9". But having vaulted at 14'9", I thought I'd better pass 15'0". Otherwise, I'd tire myself out with too many vaults. Of course, by passing 15'0" and going straight up to 15'5", my best vault would only be 14'9" if I missed. But I thought, "What the heck. I'm going to clear 15'5" anyway; I'm jumping well. Forget about it."

On my first attempt at 15'5", I cleared with no problems. So the gamble had worked out alright. And at 15'9" I just nicked the bar twice on the way up. On my last attempt I moved the standards back two inches. Then I went straight up the pole and came down on the bar. It was a little discouraging because I knew I had been way over the bar (and I do have a personal best of 16'1" in the pole vault). But still, I knew that all I needed to do in the first place was clear 15'0" or even 14'9", and I would still have been going on world record pace. Having done 15'5" I knew the world record was a certainty. But now I wanted to get over 8500 points—8500 being another milestone, so to speak. Chrystie, who was in the stands, figured out that if I threw the javelin 215' and ran the 1500 meters in 4:15 I would score 8537 points, so I decided to shoot for those two marks.

In the javelin my first throw was nice and relaxed—boom!—214'11", only one inch off my goal! At that moment I knew I was going to go over 8500 points easily. My other two throws weren't as good. I was trying to "muscle" them, and when you do that the javelin doesn't go as far—although sometimes you figure that once in a while you're really going to 'hit it' on a throw like that and the javelin is going to go out of sight.

Finally we came to the 1500 meters. The announcer explained over the P.A. system that all I had to run to break the world record was 4:26. The slowest time I'd ever done in the 1500 is 4:26. My best time is 4:13; I had to run 4:20.

Even before the gun went I knew I'd be under 4:20. Not only was there a world record waiting for me at the end of the race, but the hollering of the crowd–they were shouting "Go Jenner" as I was warming up–really got me psyched.

As I expected, the race turned out to be a good one. I went out a little bit slow–my first lap was 72 seconds; I wanted to go through in 69 or 70 (I always try to run as even a pace as possible). In the second lap I picked up the pace to 68, coming through the 800 meters in 2:20. I did the third lap in 70 seconds (exactly as I wanted), and sprinted the last 300 in 46 seconds to finish in 4:16.6. As I came across the finish line the crowd was going crazy. They were cheering, chanting my name. Those beautiful people! It was 8:30 at night, they had been there ever since we started competing at 12 noon and there they were shouting their heads off for me. My total was 8524, beating Avilov's old mark by 70 points. The world record which I had wanted for so long was mine.

—Bruce Jenner

—as told to Dave Prokop

Dave Prokop is the assistant editor of **Runner's World** *magazine and is keenly interested in track and field, including the decathlon.*

For More Information

See Track and Field for more information about the decathlon.

"The diver must achieve a kinesthetic sense of where he is located in free fall and at the same time, develop a conditioned reflex as he does multiple spinning and twisting dives." (Duffy)

Diving

Diving is more closely related to gymnastics than to swimming, since the water of the diving pool serves in a similar manner as a mat—primarily as a landing medium. Performing intricate movements through the air is the challenge for divers.

The main parts of the dive are the starting position, the take-off, the flight through the air, and the entry into the water. Dives are categorized by their starting and finishing positions (forward, back, reverse, and inward) and body positions during flight (straight, pike or tuck). The number of somersaults and twists is also considered when assigning a particular dive its degree of difficulty.

International competitions are conducted for both men and women on the three meter springboard and the 10 meter platform. National contests also include the one meter springboard.

Competitors are expected to perform both required and optional dives in different groups. A list of dives, their order of execution and their assigned degree of difficulty must be submitted prior to the opening round. In competition each dive is judged solely on its execution. The judges' scores are then multiplied by the degree of difficulty to get an accurate score.

It takes many years of hard work and good coaching to become an international-class diver. Coordination, timing and flexibility need constant work to be perfected, and there is a long list of dives to be learned and mastered. Most top divers are in their late 20s. The few who are rather young have generally started intensive training earlier and have worked an equally long time.

Cliff diving, particularly in Acapulco, and high tower diving are other facets of the sport which afford excitement and entertainment. Cliff diving demands precision timing to avoid being smashed on the rocks. High tower diving usually features the ability to land safely in 10 feet of water from a height of up to 100 feet.

As I See Diving

Diving is a precise, technical sport that combines exact mechanical action with smooth and graceful movements. The diver must achieve a kinesthetic sense of where he is located in free fall and at the same time, develop a conditioned reflex as he does multiple spinning and twisting dives.

Divers consistently display a grace and suppleness unmatched in any athletic endeavor. This is combined with the strength and courage necessary to dive from 10-meter towers, or from the cliffs at Acapulco. (OMPhoto)

To accomplish the strength, timing, reflexes and beauty of a dive, the diver must over-learn his mechanics until they are automatic to him. Consistency is the goal. When he stands ready on the board, a diver must know that he will do the dive exactly as he has practiced it for months and years. Since it is a technique sport, the longer one dives the more mature and precise are his moves. Age and experience, then, are an asset.

The fact that I dove in the Mexico Olympics and several other international contests was definitely in my favor as I started the long four years from '68 to the '72 Games. As a college student training for the '68 Games I was able to put in the necessary 4 to 5 hours a day practice. I logged the time necessary to perfect not only my required list, but also to pioneer several new dives never done by women. My coach, Dick Kimball, knew the price we each had to pay to be a winner. because each five-hour workout found us both there. And so with his unselfish guidance I drilled and repeated and learned and overlearned until I reached Mexico and the peak of several years' training.

A freak accident, a miscalculation, an error in judgment, fate . . . whatever; I missed a medal, I was only fourth. And for months I nursed an injury for which I condemned myself regularly. Not only had I cheated myself, but I cheated my coach. My decision to make a comeback was to satisfy both of us.

No longer a college student, I had an Air Force job to fulfill. I no longer trained with the Michigan team, my alma mater; I could no longer practice five hours a day; and most significantly, I had no coach. I trained nightly for two hours after work, driving 40 miles round trip. My weekends and vacations were spent at poolside too, as I tried to train properly. I took leave to train at the University of Michigan, but ultimately I depended on the years I spent training for Mexico as my background during the years I prepared for Munich. Together the repetition and resulting consistency, the experience and resulting maturity paid the dividend.

I look back on my 18 years as a diver with fond memories of the great people, fun trips and exciting competitions. It is an audience sport . . . the kind of athletic event people can enjoy without understanding the rules or the intricate moves involved. When you see a dive you like, you know it. You simply watch and enjoy the beauty and the art as the diver performs. I couldn't be more proud to have been an athlete involved in such a great sport.

—Micki King

Micki King was leading in the finals at Mexico City when, on her next to last dive, she hit the board and broke her arm. The pain kept her from maximum performance on her final dive, and she finished fourth. Four years later, she came back to win the gold medal at Munich. She is now the diving coach at the U.S. Air Force Academy.

For More Information

For more information turn to swimming. The magazines *Swimming World* and *Aquatic World* have many articles during the year on diving. As far as books are concerned, we are listing two that are totally about diving. Many others only have chapters on it. These books are available from World Publications, 366, Mountain View, Calif. 94040 at the price listed* plus 25 25 cents each postage.

Inside Diving, Dick Smith. A comprehensive guide to competitive diving by a two-time Olympic diving coach. Begins with basic conditioning and technique and progresses to the competition stages. Explains all required dives. 1973 Hb. & Ppb. 96 (oversize) pp., ill., $7.95/$3.95 (Regnery).

Diving. Know the Game Series. Good introductory book on diving which covers all the dives in a progressive program. Every dive is well illustrated and explained clearly. 1973 Ppb., 40 pp., ill., $1.50, (E.P. Publishing).

Dog Field Trials

Dog Field Trials are competitions between gun dogs in which they are judged for desirable hunting traits such as scenting, pointing, flushing, and retrieving. Events take place both on water and on land and the dogs which take part are usually purebreds like Labrador, Chesapeake and Golden Retrievers, Spring and Cocker Spaniels, and the pointing breeds. Practically every section of the country holds trials at least once a year, and there are upwards of 10,000 canine competitors appearing annually.

Dogs, their owners, and trainers take part in different classes of competition and stakes according to the age of the dog. Professional and amateur classes are differentiated. In the most common type of Field Trial game birds are shot, and also planted, and the dogs are set to seek them out. Other types find Beagles seeking rabbits, and Fox and Coonhound meets have gained in popularity.

Trials are most often run in two series of heats. Unless the winners stand out unquestionably at the end of the first series, the dogs that have given the most brilliant performances are picked as second-series contenders.

Some of the most important persons involved in a Field Trial are the bird throwers. There is considerable skill involved in throwing a bird so it will fly in the exact direction, and the young men who perform this duty must be sure that their throwing does not lend an advantage to one dog over another. In the same way, the official guns must be the finest wing shots in the territory. A bird must be shot just at the right distance to give nearly equal falls for all dogs. If the bird flies just slightly out of range it may only be crippled by the shot, making it considerably more difficult for the dog to retrieve.

One of the values, and sources of satisfaction, derived from this sport is the fine interrelation that develops between a man and his dog. The best handler in the world can't win with a poorly trained dog; neither can the world's best dog win with a poor trainer!

Trials and Tribulations

The first official Field Trial for non-slip Retrievers in the United States was put on by the Labrador Retriever Club, in 1931, on the East Coast. Since then, they have grown steadily in popularity, evolving into the sophisticated sport we have today. Field Trials are one of the few sports in which men and women can compete equally. It is highly competitive without rivalry, because it can't be done alone. A dog owner must have others to help him: shooters, and organizers of the tests. In this sport, you find professional handlers and amateurs helping each other equally; there is a genuine feeling of goodwill.

Retriever Field Trials are open to Labrador Retrievers, Golden Retrievers, Chesapeake Bay Retrievers, Flatcoated Retrievers, Curlycoated Retrievers and Irish Water Spaniels. Labs, Goldens and Chesapeakes are the principal breeds; the others are seldom seen competing today.

The Labrador Retriever, which is the most popular, is an affectionate, even-tempered dog with a short, dense coat. The majority of Labs are black; however there are also yellow Labs which range from cream to dark gold, and chocolate Labs which are dark brown.

The Golden Retriever is also an affectionate, good-natured dog. The Golden has a medium length coat which is soft to the touch, but very dense underneath. Their colors range from cream to dark red-gold.

The Chesapeake Bay Retriever is usually a slightly larger dog than the Lab or Golden. They tend to be more of a one person dog than the other two. The coat is short and wavy with an oily, dense undercoat. The color can be straw-colored (deadgrass) to reddish brown or dark brown.

All three of these breeds are extremely intelligent, with a strong desire to please. They are good water dogs and have good marking ability, an essential for a good Trial dog. In addition, the better Trial dogs have an exceptional desire to retrieve, and are very stylish. A fast dog is far more exciting to watch than a dog who trots out to the bird and walks back.

In all stakes of a Field Trial, the dogs are tested individually on both land and water and are judged solely on their performance. The winners are chosen by process of elimination by the judges. Each stake usually has four series.

The Derby Stake is open to dogs from six months to two years. The tests consist of single retrieves, double retrieves and occasionally triple retrieves.

The Qualifying Stake is open to any dog over six months of age providing he has not won two Qualifying or placed in a championship stake. The tests range from double and triples to beginning blind retrieves. A blind retrieve is when the handler knows where the bird is and the dog does not. The dog is sent in the direction of the bird and must be directed to it by the use of hand signals. A Qualifying blind is usually not over 125 yards in length.

The Open All-Age Stake is again open to dogs over six months; although it is quite rare to see a dog under two years in this stake. This is a championship stake and the dogs accumulate points toward their Field Championship. The tests are very exacting and include extremely difficult doubles, triples, and blinds up to 300 yards.

The Amateur All-Age Stake is comparable to the Open All-Age in that it also carries championship points and the tests are quire similar. The basic difference is that it is the only stake for amateur handlers only. A dog can achieve his Field Trial Championship being handled by an amateur or professional; but can achieve his Amateur Field Trial Championship while being handled by an amateur only.

These last two stakes, or major stakes as they are often called, offer the opportunity to qualify for the Nationals. Qualification for either the Open National or Amateur National requires a win in the given stake plus two points in any given year. The Amateur National Championship Stake is held each year in June, and the Open National Championship Stake is held in November. The Nationals bring together the best retrievers in the country in order to determine the champion for that year. There are no places in a National, only a winner. To win the National is the highest honor a dog and handler can achieve. It is the culmination of years of time, training and dedication, and never comes easily. It is a coveted honor and is always well earned.

Retriever Field Trials are very difficult to train for in that the trials are always in different locations, and there are as many ways to set up tests as there are judges. The dogs begin their training at about eight weeks of age and continue throughout their trial careers. Most good dogs compete through their ninth and 10th year, going through quite a bit of training in their lifetime.

From a personal standpoint, I enjoy training as much as the trials. I like being outside working with the dogs and the learning process is very gratifying.

We start with our little puppies at birth. They are handled gently and petted, so they are always aware of people. We try to keep a radio on low volume 24 hours a day so, as their hearing develops, they become accustomed to voices and other sounds. Puppies require a great deal of personal attention in order to develop into well adjusted adult animals – not smothering attention, but attention to develop their awareness.

At about three or four weeks, as soon as they are walking well and their eyes are completely open, they are introduced to bird wings to acquaint them with the scent and texture of feathers. It's very interesting how instinctively they try to pick them up and carry them, even at this early age. After their first immunization at six weeks, they see the outside world for the first time. After their initial excitement wears off, we give them dead pigeons to carry and retrieve and they love it. Within a few days, they are carrying live, clipped-wing pigeons and feeling very proud of themselves. By the time they leave for their new homes at seven or eight weeks, they have had a thorough introduction to birds.

As soon as a pup gets his second immunization, off we go to the water. For the first swim, I try to pick an area with a firm, gradually sloping bottom. In the summertime, which is best, I walk out into the water and let the pup follow. If the water is not really warm, I use hip boots. I do not feel that a pup should be introduced to ice cold water in cold weather. For winter puppies, I try to select a day when the air is warm, even if it's raining, and make the water initiation short. We never allow our puppies (or adult dogs for that matter) to get chilled or overtired. They are always towelled dry before going back to their crate in the car.

Some pups take to the water immediately while others are a bit more hesitant. The aggresive puppy isn't necessarily the best one; give the hesitant one a few opportunities to build his confidence, and he may surpass the others.

I definitely do not believe in throwing puppies into the water to "sink or swim" any more than I feel it should be done with children. They don't swim automatically; they have to learn. For example, several years ago, a woman called and asked us if we would have a look at her dog to evaluate his potential as a field dog. We agreed and she arrived with the dog, who was about a year and a half old. We threw several dummies on land and he retrieved them nicely, with great style. Then I threw one into the water for him. He made a spectacular leap from the bank out over the water – and sank like a rock. Since it was mid-November, it was a bit chilly. Needless to say, I had to go in fully dressed to rescue him. I had assumed, by his age, that he had been in the water before, and hadn't even thought to ask the owner. My assumption was wrong. As a token of apology, we spent the next several hours teaching him to swim. Today, he is not only a beautiful swimmer, but a fine trial dog.

In early training, I like to see a bold, alert puppy who investigates new situations. To me, curiosity indicates intelligence in an animal. We take our puppies to shopping centers and walk them on a leash, encouraging people to pat them. It's a great place to expose them to noise and hubbub. We also take them for walks in the fields and woods, always exposing them to different situations: over ditches and dirt roads, from plowed ground to high grass, any kind of change we can find. When we start throwing dummies for them on land, we always throw them where the pup must run varied terrain. At this point, it is very important to always make everything fun for the pup; it is teaching without him realizing he is being taught.

When the pup gets older the real training starts. None of the preceding can be considered actual training for field trials. Rather, it is conditioning and preparation for the serious field work that comes later on. A lot of time and effort go into getting ready for beginning work, but if you enjoy it, the time is well spent.

Field Trials are not a sport for everyone. If a person is willing to give his dogs kindness and correct attention, it can be a lifelong hobby – and one of the most rewarding sports I know of.

—Sandra Akers

Sandra Akers began training field trial dogs as a youngster with her parents. Today, she and her husband are kept quite busy training Golden Retrievers, hunting and attending trials.

For More Information

Many dog magazines cover field trialing, among their many topics. However, for exclusive coverage, see *The American Field*, American Field Publishing Co., 222 West Adams Street, Chicago, Ill. 60606, a weekly which carries schedules of field trials and reports their results. Amateur Field Trial Clubs of America, Hernando, Miss. 38632, is the only organization dealing exclusively with open breed field trials. Additional information can be found in the other dog categories.

Here are some excellent books on field training. All are available from World Publications, Box 366, Mountain View, Calif. 94040 at the price listed* plus 25 cents each postage. Write for a complete list.

Field Trials: History, Management, and Judging Standards, William F. Brown. Not only of great value to the sportsman who is involved with trails, but also the average bird hunter who wants to select a good hunting dog will find this book useful. 1975, 320 pp., ill., $12.00, (A.S. Barnes).

Training Your Own Bird Dog, Henry P. Davis. Written for the man who is starting out with his first bird dog, and is designed to help prepare himself for the problems ahead by showing him how to understand his dog, and easily teach the dog the essentials to be learned. 1969 Hb., 176 pp., ill., $6.95, (Putnums).

Training Your Retreiver, James Lamb Free. A classic guide, unanimously regarded by experts as the definitive book about retrievers and how to select, train and care for them. Every step of training is carefully set down, from simple citizenship, obedience, and housebreaking to retrieving and advanced work on blind retrievers. 1949 (rev.) Hb., 336 pp., ill., $7.95, (Coward, McCann, and Geoghegan).

Practical Pointer Training, Sherman Webb. Here's a step-by-step guide to a tested procedure, from the start of training with an eight-month-old pup to the polishing of a finished pointer dog. Includes what to do about the classic problems of training: the bolter, self-hunter, flusher, chaser, blinker or gun-shy dog. 1974 Hb., 178 pp., ill., $6.95, (Winchester).

Hunting Dog Know-How, David Duffey. Information useful for the beginning dog man or expert trainer alike. 1972 Hb., 192 pp., ill., $6.95, (Winchester).

The Practical Hunter's Dog Book, John Falk. Hunters who want to know more about their canine comrades will find this an excellent and well-written book. 1971 Hb., 320 pp., ill., $8.95, (Winchester).

Dog Showing

In simple terms, a dog show is an exhibit of pedigreed show dogs which compete against each other in pursuit of the first prize: the coveted blue ribbon. Actually, many ribbons are awarded, sometimes with financial reward, and silver trophies are often presented.

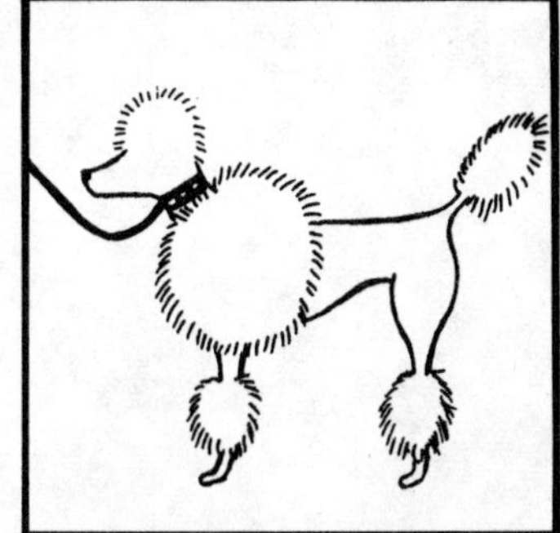

Show dogs can be divided into two groups: (1) house pets that are entered in important competitions, (2) dogs that are used only for show purposes, and which rarely lead the life of a pet. For some owners showing dogs is a business, and they leave their dogs in the care of professional handlers. For others it is an enjoyable way of showing their pride in their pets, training and caring for themselves, and showing them at their leisure.

The American Kennel Club now recognizes over 100 distinct breeds of dogs, each belonging to one of six major classifications: Hound, Working, Terrier, Toy, Sporting, and Non-Sporting. The number of standard breeds is not actually fixed, however, since new breeds may be formed by cross-breeding, where blooded ancestry on both sides develops. Many of today's breeds were unknown 150 years ago, although as many as 60 distinct species are known to have roamed the Crazy Mountain region of Montana millions of years ago.

The first dog show in the United States took place in New York in 1877 and lasted three days. It was so successful that many shows were held thereafter. In a show, dogs are judged in their particular breed class first, and then they are judged in the broader classifications mentioned above. The dog judged best of the six classification winners is the winner of the show. Dogs are judged mainly on appearance, on a point basis, but they may be judged for conduct also. In a show, each breed is judged by an authority on that breed and each breed has its conformation rules for judging.

All in a Day's Work

Versatility has to be an important key to the success of a professional dog handler. The public sees him in the ring, smoothly putting one dog after another through its paces, nattily dressed, confident and unruffled. And, so they think, getting extremely well paid for a few minutes of easy work.

Of course what they do not see is the hours of work with the dog before the show. . .teaching that dog to help him hide his faults and make the most of his better qualities. . .and to do so in a manner that looks unstudied. The trimming, conditioning and training that go into making a dog into "show-dog" all appear so natural that no one thinks about it much, except the handler. "It all looks so easy when he does it."

And, after playing the roles of trainer, nutritionalist, groomer, psychologist, and even bookkeeper (most handlers spend long hours completing hundreds of dog show entry forms and keep elaborate records of all dogs shown and the points and placements of them all) the handler now dons the final role: truck-driver!

Most professionals enter between 50 and 100 shows a year. It might be California one weekend and Texas the next, and that represents a lot of driving in a year. On circuits, you show all day and then load up and drive to the next town or state that night. For every hour he spends in the ring the handler probably spends another five on the road! Unlike the regular truck driver who hauls cotton or oil, the handler carries a cargo that requires all kinds of special care, and even, sometimes, a share of understanding and imagination. Take, for instance, the following incident:

Grass and shade trees beckoned as I wheeled the motor-home into the roadside rest stop. I was on my way to a show in Oregon and it was time to give my load of dogs a break. We quickly put up the portable exercising pens and filled them with about a dozen dogs of various breeds. The dogs were soon snorting happily around in the pine needles; one of the Corgis was playing with a pine cone and we were all enjoying the balmy weather when I noticed something amiss out of the corner of my eye. But too late!

It was a new Airedale Terrier that I had never shown before, and the owner had neglected to tell me that she was a fence jumper. Before I could even get to my feet she had bolted the four foot fence and was off down the road at a dead run!

The first terrible thought was of the six-lane highway and its heavy traffic. But she veered and shot up a steep hillside. I went crashing behind through the heavy brush and rough pines. Finally at the crest of the hill she vanished. I looked through a gap in the woods to see a flash of bronze and black dart through a meadow a half a mile away and took off after her again.

This went on for hours. Up and down hills and meadows, back and forth across the highway as my anxieties mounted. Finally I staggered onto some tourists who had her spotted but could not approach her. She had figured out just how close she could allow anyone to approach and still make a safe getaway, and was playing the game to the hilt. I was exhausted, my clothes in tatters, covered with scrapes and scratches. It was obvious that I would never get her back this way. But a handler just doesn't lose dogs, no matter what. I had to get her

"Of course what they do not see is the hours of work with the dog before the show . . . teaching the dog to help him hide his faults and make the most of his better qualities . . . and to do so in a manner that looks unstudied. The trimming, conditioning and training that go into making a dog into a 'showdog' all appear so natural that no one thinks about it much, except the handler."

back!!! And to complicate things I was running out of driving time to get the rest of my dogs to the show!

Strolling casually into the woods, I made a great effort to be completely disinterested and never look at her. I got as close as I dared and plunked myself down on the ground and started looking through the carpet of pine needles. Suddenly I found a tiny twig and snatched it up as though I had made some great discovery. Fascinated with it, I turned it over and over, playing with it and making sounds of excitement. From the corner of my eye I could see her curiousity was aroused, and I started to find other objects on the ground with even more excitement. She inched closer and closer at each new discovery as I resisted every temptation to lunge for her. Closer and closer she came until I could finally feel her warm breath as she peeked over my shoulder, totally absorbed in my "game." I quietly slipped my arm around her and the chase was over.

Even though I was a shambles from the afternoon's pursuit, she was fit and happy when I got her back to the motorhome. It's no trick at all for a dog to travel 10 miles an hour so I can't even guess how far she had been that day.

At the show the next day she showed beautifully, won her class, then Winners Bitch and finally Best Airedale. When the photographer was taking the picture of the win the judge confided, "Y'know, Doug, this is a great bitch and deserved the win today. But let me give you a little bit of advice. I'd like to see her in a little harder condition. Why don't you take her out once in a while and give her a good run!"

I didn't even answer. Tomorrow is always another day and another show. And whatever happens, you know it will be different.

It is partially this constant new challenge and variety that keeps handlers putting in long hours of demanding work. And the rewards come from both the sense of accomplishment and despair that result from a one-to-one type of competition. When you are finally in the ring, win or lose, it's just you and the dog. There is no team to back you and no second string to call on.

Your only real teammate in this game is the dog and he will share either win or loss with unaltered affection. That's hard to beat!

—**Douglas Bundock**

Douglas Bundock is a licensed (AKC) professional dog handler and trainer who has been showing dogs for almost 20 years. He has guided the careers of a number of well-known best in show dogs and has trained several dogs for Walt Disney films. His kennels are located in Sepastopol, California where he breeds Pembroke Welsh Corgis.

For More Information

There are several dog magazines but here are a few that are certainly good: *Dog Fancy Magazine,* 11760 Sorrento Valley Rd., San Diego, Calif. 92121. Published bi-monthly and the largest of the dog magazines. *Dog World,* 10060 W. Roosevelt Rd., Westchester, Ill. 60153. Published monthly at $10.00 per year. The largest monthly and a very well done publication. Each issue is well over 100 pages. *Dogs,* 257 Park Ave. South, New York, N.Y. 10010. Published bi-monthly at $7.50 per year. Their slogan on the cover is "The magazine for everyone who enjoys them (dogs)." Not as big as the other publications. *Bloodlines,* 321 W. Cedar St., Kalamazoo, Mich. 49006. Published bi-monthly and is the official magazine of the United Kennel Club at the same address. Other magazines we haven't seen: *Dog News,* 205 West 4th St.,Cincinnati, Ohio 45202; *Popular Dogs,* 2009 Ranstead St., Philadelphia, Pa. 19103; *Kennel Review,* 3626 Potsi Road, North Hollywood, Calif. 91604.

The American Kennel Club, 51 Madison Ave., New York, N.Y. 10010 and the United Kennel Club (address above) can both be helpful. Also check other dog listings.

Most good pet stores can take care of your supply needs. However here are a few companies that may be of interest: Animal Specialties, Box 531, Camden, N.J. 08101 publishes a free catalog. They have everything for your dog and at discount prices. New York School of Dog Grooming, 248 East 34th St., New York, N.Y. 10016. They teach dog grooming as do several other people. Check your phone book or write for their brochure. G & H Pet Supplies, Box 4474, Panorama City, Calif. 91412. Grooming sling, dog bath tub, air dryers, clippers, etc. are all in their free catalog. Vets Company, Drawer C, Temple, Texas 75601. They have a big free catalog which offers grooming supplies, small animal health products, accessories, kennel supplies, etc.

Here is one book we've found on dog showing. It is available from World Publications, Box 366, Mountain View, Calif. 94040 at the price listed* plus 25 cents postage.

Dog Digest, Susan Bernstein, ed. Offers an excellent chapter on dog showing which covers showing, understanding a dog show, judging, obedience training, obedience training regulations, and listings of the top bench show winners. This book also contains equally good chapters on all facets of owning and bringing up a dog. 1975 Ppb., 320 (oversize) pp., ill., $7.95, (Digest Books).

Dog Sledding

Sled dog racing is perhaps the most complex running sport. In order to participate in a maximum of eight to nine races during a winter, a sled dog driver must care for and feed year-round a number of 40- to 55-pound canine athletes. A firm understanding of how to condition and train each one of these individuals within a team for the intensive two months of competitive racing is demanded.

Sled dog racing originated in Alaska nearly 70 years ago for the purpose of improving the care of the dogs and their breeding/working characteristics, which were being used to explore and develop the Arctic north. Today the sport of sled dog racing fullfills a similar role for the modern day sled dog population, a small segment of which contains the finest running athletes alive today.

The sport offers individuals and families who enjoy sled dogs a wide range of recreational and winter sports. On the racing scene, both the serious driver and the weekend pleasure driver have race events they can participate in. For the three dog class enthusiast, there are three to four mile distances; for the unlimited class professional, driving up to 15 dog teams, there are 20 to 30 mile events. And for the ultimate test, there is Iditarod Trail Race, 1024 miles of running through the Alaskan interior.

Look at Them as Athletes

For 27 of my 41 years I have been a runner, and have become emotionally dependent upon the anticipation which precedes competition and the tranquility which follows. Having no desire to spend my remaining winters in a state of athletic depression, I decided to tie together three separate things, all of which I am very fond: running, cold weather and dogs. The integration led to my first sled dog racing team, five Siberian Huskies. Despite our inexperience, that team, with me running behind, was good enough to win the Maine state five-dog racing championship in our first year of competition. Since then my wife and I have added new dogs and new titles, including the Laconia, N.H. World Championship Sled Dog Derby.

I prefer small, easily manageable teams as my light weight and running style do not require the power of a large team. Heats range from 10-30 miles per day, with the combined time for the two (sometimes three) heats on consecutive days determining the winner. A good team on a packed trail can finish 30 miles in under two hours while pulling a sled. The pace can get much faster in shorter races.

The sense of pace which most distance runners acquire is invaluable when driving a sled dog team. The dogs must be kept from over-extending, particularly during the first heat of a three-day race. Siberian and Alaskan Huskies are easy to pace, whereas Hounds (which are sometimes used in this sport), tend to burn themselves out with too fast an early pace which their drivers do not seem to be able to reduce.

Year-round conditioning is essential for best performance from man or dog. With this conviction, my wife and I train our dogs throughout the summer. We jog with the puppies as soon as they are weaned. As they mature, they adopt me as the pack leader and are conditioned to stay near me when I run. This allows me to let from 10-15 dogs loose simultaneously and know that they will accompany me as I run through the hundreds of acres of woods behind our farm in Gorham, Maine. Two such runs each day takes care of the summer conditioning. This non-stress "fun running" will last from 20 minutes to one hour. Summer is also the time to teach promising young lead dogs the necessary verbal commands, which include: gee (turn right); haw (turn left); woah (stop); go ahead (start running or pass a team); no (whatever you're doing, don't), and a few others. "Mush" is no longer used as a command.

During the winter racing season, dogs can sour in a manner akin to a stale road runner. It is emotional, not physical. A break of several days usually rekindles enthusiasm. Running the dogs loose rather than making them work in harness has much the same rejuvenating effect as a fartlek type workout has on a souring distance runner.

For the most part, sled dog drivers tend to be rugged individuals, as the sport is physically very demanding. Only the tough endure. Seldom are dog drivers fast of foot. This is where a road runner gains a tremendous advantage in the sport. It is my opinion that a fit runner can increase the speed of his or her team by 1-2 miles per hour. My own technique is to run hard when I feel the pace is dropping below what it should be. The team immediately accelerates when they realize I am off the sled and running with them. I also run hard up all hills, and peddle (scooter fashion) whenever I am not running. The only running rule which must be observed is that the driver may not run ahead of the front part of the sled. This is considered pacing, which is illegal.

My major problem is staying warm while training several teams. Like most runners, I carry very little excess fat. Consequently, four hours on a training sled at temperatures as low as 30 below can get to me. It's no problem in a race because I constantly run or pedal and thus sweat freely. But I prefer to

"The sport offers individuals and families who enjoy sled dogs a wide range of recreational and winter sports. On the racing scene, both the serious driver and the weekend pleasure driver have race events they can participate in. For the three dog class enthusiast, there are three to four mile distances; for the unlimited class professional, driving up to 15 dog teams, there are 20 to 30 mile events. And for the ultimate test, there is Iditarod Trail Race, 1024 miles of running through Alaskan interior."

stand on the sled in practice and teach the dogs how to work. Then the races seem easy to them. Practice runs vary from 10-20 miles per day, five days a week or as the weather permits.

A few words of advice for any runner considering this sport. Buy the best female you can and get her bred to the best running male available. Twelve months later you should have a class A team. Remember it costs as much to feed and care for a poor dog as it does for a good one. Bargain dogs are seldom that in racing. Good team dogs cost from $300-$500, and top leaders now bring $1500 if you can find one for sale. When a dog is that good, its owner usually does not want to part with it at any price.

Unlike road racing, the prizes for sled dog racing are in cash rather than inventory clearing merchandise. Although most races pay under $1500, there are at least eight races in the US and Canada with purses between $5000 and $10,000 (one pays $50,000), with the winner receiving about one-third of this amount for a weekend of racing. However, kennel expenses and time demands are high, and I strongly advise against entering this sport with any illusion of making a financial killing. Those who manage to cover expenses are a fortunate minority.

—Lloyd Slocum

Lloyd Slocum is a marathoner of 2:30 class and a champion sled dog racer. He is considered a pioneer because he trains his dogs the same way he trains himself.

For More Information

The official organization in the United States is the International Sled Dog Racing Association, Center Harbor, N.H. 03226. They do put out a publication called *Team and Trail.* Another publication covering the sport is *Northern Dog News,* Box 310, Snohomish, Wa. 98290.

Dog sledding books are a little uncommon, but here are some good ones. All are available from World Publications, Box 366, Mountain View, Calif. 94040 at the price listed* plus 25 cents postage.

Training and Racing Sled Dogs, George Attla. In the first comprehensive book ever written about sled dog racing, one of the world's top ranking mushers passes on all the secrets he has learned in a lifetime devoted to this highly competitive sport. He tells everything he knows from breeding, feeding, equipment and training, right up to the strategy of winning a race, all in an easy, informal style, sprinkled with anecdotes and home-spun philosophy. 1974 Hb., 230 pp., ill., $9.95, (Arper).

Mush! A Beginner's Manual of Sled Dog Racing, Bella Lavorsen. The author trains and races a team herself and gives a step-by-step description of how a person with one to three pet dogs can get started. This looks like the best book to date. To be published Feb. 1976. Hb., 260 pp., ill., $9.95, (Arper).

Sled Dog Encyclopedia, Raymond Thompson. The definitive work on dog sledding, with the history of the business/sport all over the world, breeds and breeding of dogs, choosing a dog, and coverage of the all the major races all over the world. Vol I: Alaska Sled Dogs, 1970 Ppb., 64 pp., ill., $2.75. Vol. II: Canadian and US Sled Dogs,1973 Ppb., 56 pp., ill., $2.75. Vol. III: Sled Dog Breeds, 1973 Ppb., 55 pp., ill., $2.70, (Raymond Thompson).

Dog Training

Whether you want a dog for hunting showing, guarding your store, as a soulful companion or family addition, in order to have a worthy, well-kept canine you're going to have to know the basics of dog training and keeping. Although teaching your floppy-eared friend to obey may not traditionally come under the heading of a sport, it can easily become a rough-and-tumble activity as you wrestle him down to a sitting position, or struggle to get him off your best couch. A new puppy in a home can present a never ending battle, or it can mean pleasure and companionship for all who are involved. Dog training can also be fun and rewarding.

There's nothing quite like the sense of accomplishment that comes with a well-trained dog. Not only is it an engrossing activity for adults, but it is also a healthy outlet for children. The child who shows no interest in the usual games and sports might take well to tending his small furry comrad. The contribution to the child's self-confidence, should he be a successful teacher, will not be a meager one. Man's best friend? Yes. But don't forget the women and children!

Usually, formal obedience training is not begun until a puppy is about six months old since their coordination is not well developed before this age. When you do begin actual training, the only equipment you will need is a six foot, leather leash and a chain "choke" collar. The first basic command you will teach him is "Sit!", a relatively simple task if you go about it correctly. After this, you and your dog will rapidly progress to "Heel," "Stay," "Down," "Come," and "Fetch." If your dog continues to show promise after this training, and your patience has not run out, you may want to progress to more important tasks such as jumping and scent discrimination.

But don't forget the three most important rules of training: (1) speak commands with authority and don't jumble them up with a lot of other chatter. Excess wordage will only confuse your animal, (2) correct your canine immediately when he makes an error with a firm "No!" or a tug at his leash, and (3) praise your dog highly after he successfully carries out a command. Your enthusiasm will help him learn the difference between right and wrong quickly.

Dog Training as a Sport

The dog population has increased to the degree that to own a dog it is essential that you train him. Dogs are irrational creatures unless trained to obey, causing anguish and difficulties to well-meaning owners. The owner's personal interrelationship and personality will have a definite effect on dog behavior. Dogs who are given fond attention and are treated as a member of the family will manifest a better degree of respect and love for their masters, families and surrounding community.

If your dog is a family dog and you are interested in competing in field trials, breed shows or obedience trails, you, as trainer, must teach your household the proper approach to having a well-mannered and happy dog. The same is true for the household pet. A dog who works for you and still is an asset to his home, family and community is a joy. Although an owner can train the dog, that dog can also teach his master. Canines teach companionship and faithfulness to the family—something they rely upon as they meet uncertain situations in life.

Love and affection that is engendered between some masters and their dogs goes far beyond many human sympathies. A dog fills a void in a person's emotional needs, and in providing these needs, the dog should be accorded the same respect and love from his master. He is truly man's best friend. He is the only animal in the world who loves you more than he loves himself.

However, love and respect are not enough. As in all of life, one must earn the dog's love and gain respect through good training and caring for its needs. Your dog may be a pleasure or a concern, and it will not be the dog who decides this—it will be you. Nothing in life is as pleasurable if you make it a labor.

A good dog is good just as far as its temperament and disposition pleases you, his owner. What one person may desire, another may not care for. His love and respect for you will grow as soon as you select it, provide a good home, food and water—and through good training.

All dogs can be trained but not all dogs will attain the same high degree of proficiency in their training—this is where dog training becomes a sport. A dog's training depends upon the knowledge and understanding of his trainer. Dogs possess an innate instinct tendency to please. Although they possess this quality in lesser or greater degrees, the normal dog desires to please the person it loves.

No dog is well trained if it performs through fear. A dog should perform out of respect. A dog appears to be stubborn when he actually is confused. Sometimes you may think he doesn't understand, when really you haven't made yourself understood.

But don't let all this talk intimidate you. Dog training is a sport! It is sport whether training for field, breed, or obedience trails, or for unsoiled carpets. Did you ever think of dog training as a family sport, or as personal accomplishment? Teaching a child dog training is very rewarding and can bring lasting and beneficial effects.

Time to the child is eternal but patience is quite finite. Working persistently in training a dog to heel (meaning to walk quietly at the side), the youngster gains something which time and fortune cannot buy! The talent for persistence, and the patience necessary to attain a goal.

Youngsters discovering the bright new world around them soon learn to stop at each curb before crossing the street. Allowing the child to train the dog to sit in one spot while distractions prevail around it, gives the young one an added sense of respect to parental cautions.

The personalities and physical attributes of children are as varied as the shapes of snow flakes. Still, all of us enjoy success. Many youngsters cannot achieve this on the playing fields of baseball or football, but all can gain satisfaction through personally improving the behavior of their pets. Learning to give commands to a pet is often the easiest path on what can be a long journey to graciously carrying out orders.

I have to admit that I have been in the business long enough to have seen many of the children to whom I have taught dog training, returning as responsible citizens—bringing their own children and dogs to me for training.

Yes, dog training is a sport, and a very rewarding one.

—John Kellogg

As a professional dog trainer, John Kellogg has participated in obedience trials, and given many obedience demonstrations, while training both dogs and their owners for many years. He has also operated a dog training school in his hometown, near Philadelphia, where he lives with his wife and their West Highland White Terriers.

For More Information

Here is one dog training magazine that is circulated nationally: *Off Lead Magazine,* Arner Publications, 8140 Coronado Lane, Rome, N.Y. 13440. Here are a few organizations you should know about: United Kennel Club, 321 W. Cedar St., Kalamazoo, Mich. 49906—licenses and registers full-blooded dogs and sponsors events and shows; American Kennel Club, 51 Madison Ave., New York, N.Y. 10010; Professional Handlers Association, Box 207, Huntington, N.Y. 11743—provides information to those who show purebred dogs at shows as a profession; Owner Handler Association of America, 16 Cliff Way, Port Washington, N.Y. 11050—chapters conduct breed handling and obedience classes among other things; **Dog** Obedience Instructors and Trainers Association, 11351 Montgomery Ave., Granada Hills, Calif. 91344.

Here are some books to make dog training easier for you. All are available from World Publications, Box 366, Mountain View, Calif. 94040 at the price listed* plus 25c each postage. Write for a complete list.

John Kellog's Book of Dog Training, John Kellogg. A definite must for dog owners who appreciate the enjoyment and the rewards of a well-trained dog. How to do it step by step with many line drawings. 1970 Hb., 160 pp., ill., $8.50, (Viking).

Sports Illustrated Dog Training, editors of *Sports Illustrated.* Introduction to basic dog training: first commands, discipline, and tricks. Sections on field dogs, spaniels, hounds, retrievers and pointers. 1972 Hb. & Ppb., 98 pp., ill., $4.95/$1.95, (Lippincott).

Dog Training Made Easy and Fun, John W. Kellogg. Training your dog doesn't have to be a chore: it can be a rich and rewarding experience. 1974 Ppb., 141 pp., ill., $2.00, (Wilshire).

Puppy Training & Care, Maxwell Riddle. Practical guide to puppy training and care covering every area of dog-ownership from selection of the puppy to obedience, health care, grooming—everything you need to know presented in a wise, unorthodox, but practical way. 1963 (rev.) Hb., 187 pp., $6.95, (Coward, McCann and Geoghegan).

How to Train a Watchdog, Bruce Sessions. With 20 years of watchdog training under his belt, the author sets down in clear language what it takes to train an alarm dog, threat dog, manstopper; how to choose the perfect dog for what you need; and how to detect common diseases. 1975 Ppb., 224 pp., ill., $5.95, (Tab Books).

Drag Racing

Speed, Speed, Speed! That's the name of the game when it comes to the thrilling auto sport of drag racing. Hot rod fans jam the grandstands along the busy strips to experience a mirage of blinking lights, roaring engines, screeching tires, orange engine flames and smoke-hidden cars that emerge at the finish line, parachutes popping to slow them down – all within 10 seconds from start to finish.

In a drag race, cars sprint, usually two at a time, over a quarter-mile course, beginning from a standing start. The races are usually run on special drag strips – straight-line paved runways (sometimes airfield strips are used) with adjacent lanes, one for each of the two cars. Runs are timed by electronic devices, and beyond the finish line lies a shutdown area which gives the cars room to decelerate safely. Service roads are connected to the main strip, providing a means for return to the area behind the starting line.

In the most popular type of drag race meeting, a series of races are held on an eliminating basis, in a number of car classes and eliminator brackets. Various factors are considered in the classification of cars: whether they are modified or specially built models, the modifications of the engine, and the type of fuel they use. Everyday pump gasoline is designated as the gas category, whereas a special methanol-type fuel is simply called the fuel category.

Generally, the car classes specified by the National Hot Rod Association are now accepted internationally, with the sport being most firmly established in the US. To a lesser degree, drag racing is seen in countries such as Australia, Canada, England, Germany, Italy, Japan, New Zealand and Sweden.

By far, the fastest cars are the Top Fuelers which comprise the sport's ultimate vehicle: the high horsepower, rear engine dragster using a supercharged engine. The Top Fuel dragster is capable of covering the quarter mile in less than six seconds, with speeds of 250 miles per hour. The sophisticated Top Fuel car features an engine mounted behind the driver but in front of the large rear tires, called slicks.

Besides Top Fuel, other eliminator brackets include Funny Car (a short-wheelbased fuel dragster hidden by a fiberglass replica of a late model American production car body), Pro Stock (modified production line automobiles from Detroit which serve as showcase models), Pro Comp (six different classes of cars which are equalized through fuel and weight restrictions and allowable modifications), Competition (comprised of mixed classes of vehicles while making use of a handicap starting system to equalize competition), Modified (mixed classes of cars that are equipped with equipment required for legal street use), Super Stock (stock production American passenger cars with restricted modifications) and Stock (stock passenger cars with very few modifications).

If all this seems a bit confusing, a little clarification might be found by likening a major drag race to a tennis tournament. In tennis, there are men's singles, men's doubles, women's singles, women's doubles, mixed doubles . . . plus a wide variety of age group categories. Drag racing has corresponding divisions – called Eliminators – which begin with Top Fuel and progress downward to Super Stock and Stock.

In tournament tennis, competitors in each category are placed on the draw sheet according to their abilities. Such a process is called "seeding" and, ideally, the No. 1 and No. 2 seeded players will oppose one another in the finals.

Drag racing competition progresses in an almost identical manner. The major exception is that instead of being arbitrarily "seeded" by a tournament committee, race cars qualify for their positions by establishing qualifying ETs, or elapsed times.

The ET is the time required for a drag racing car to complete a quarter mile, straight line course from a standing start. The quicker the car accomplishes the task, the higher it qualifies in its particular "draw". As in tennis, the No. 1 and No. 2 qualifiers are so situated that, barring an upset, they will meet in the final round.

Each Eliminator champion earns his crown by eliminating opponents, one at a time, until only he remains. The original starting fields vary – from as few as eight qualifiers to as many as 64.

Since even starts from standstill are of utmost importance in this sport, a complex electronic system has been developed over the years to ensure this. A vertical series of lights signalling the countdown for each lane's start is called the Christmas Tree. When both cars have moved into their proper staged position at the starting line, the official starter depresses a hand-held button that activates the tree. Green signals "go" in each lane, but when one car jumps the gun, a big red light says "foul", and the race's offending driver is thus disqualified from further competition.

Some classes use only the amber-to-green starting system, while other classes utilize the tree's full countdown of five ambers at half-second intervals, then green. In either case, it is the driver who best anticipates the green's action and coordinates his move accordingly who usually wins the race. Driver reaction and a car's traction are two most important assets for winning in drag racing.

In 1955, the NHRAs first national championship meeting was held at Great Bend, Kansas and thereafter was held annually. Today a number of NHRA sponsored national events are held each year.

Of course, drag racing is not only restricted to male competitors. Women are welcome to try for licenses, which are required for the top five racing classifications, and are encouraged to compete in the lower three, which require no license.

—Thanks to the NHRA

The Progression of Drag Racing

Having been involved in drag racing for many years, I've seen many innovations, breakthroughs, and improvements in the sport. In many of them I played an important role; others I simply accepted gratefully.

One problem that we came across in the early years of drag racing – one which is still with us to a certain extent – is that of traction. The original dragsters were essentially roadsters. They had little bodies on them and the drivers sat ahead of the rear axle. As engines got more and more powerful, however, a new design had to be improvised. This resulted in the streamlined, low-slung "slingshot", with the driver sitting in back of the rear axle. With this improvement, cars immediately moved up to 140 m.p.h. and traction was quite a bit better.

The next high-point in drag racing came when the Cook and Bedwell California-based car ran with the first high-gear, direct-drive dragster. This brought speeds up to 160 m.p.h. In 1957, I managed to hit 176 m.p.h. utilizing the new Chrysler hemi of that era – a 392 cubic inch engine slung to a high-gear slingshot. That was a big breakthrough.

After that, everything progressed very smoothly with speeds moving slowly toward 200 m.p.h. When the "slipper" clutches came into use, that was another big improvement. Tires ceased to smoke as the cars sped down the strip slipping the clutch. This kept everything on more-or-less a steady plane until the next innovation, the rear engine car, came into existence in 1970. The slingshot had served its purpose for 16 years until this new design came along. With engines getting still more powerful this change was inevitable. With the driver directly over the transmission in the old powerhouses, there were many accidents. Usually when there was one – an engine or power train failure – it injured the driver severely, sometimes even killing him. I, myself, had a very bad accident in 1970, when I lost part of my foot. All this brought on the advent of the rear engine car, which moved the driver out in front of all this.

Today we're still faced with traction problems to a certain extent, but we're overcoming them with bigger tires and a sticky substance called VHT which they spray the tracks with. These improvements have brought on the sub-five second times, and of course my 250 m.p.h. run.

Safety has, obviously, been a major concern in the progression of drag racing. The first really big breakthrough in safety devices was the fire suits that the driver is now required to wear. In 1959, I had a serious accident in Chester, South Carolina; prior to that there were no fire suits, gloves of any type, or face masks required. The fire in Chester was really the first one they had in drag racing. I was hospitalized for eight weeks. That incident brought on all the safety devices that are now worn.

Still another alteration for safety's sake was the introduction of the full 360-degree bell housing which enclosed the clutch assembly completely. This contains the clutch should it explode.

When M and H tire company developed their drag racing slick in 1957, it was the first tire produced especially for this type of racing. Prior to this we were running on recapped passenger car tires – which were somewhat of a safety hazard. With the M and H breakthrough we finally had a tire available that was big and strong enough for drag racing. This was also a big factor in putting us up to the 180 m.p.h. mark.

Also, the adoption of the on-board fire extinguisher, later on, was a big step for safety. Of course, with the newer rear engine cars we aren't required to carry them anymore since we don't have a fire problem up-front. They're still in good use in the funny cars, however.

While talking about the progression of drag racing, it would be impossible to leave out the widespread use of the "Christmas Tree". Prior to the invention of this device, we started at the line on a wave of the flag, although there were a few tracks who used a red and green light. Both of these early methods were unsatisfactory. The green light came on too abruptly and the driver usually wasn't ready. The flags were even worse in many respects. When the Christmas Tree was introduced in 1963, it was immediately accepted widely. This new starting method gave the flashing lights which came down the tree, warning the driver that the green was about to come on. When it did, he started to break. There were problems with it at first, however – the frequency of the light, the guys jumping ahead before the green actually came on. These defects were improved upon just the same, and the system is a pretty good one now. It is an integral part of the quarter and everybody likes it.

One great advantage of the Christmas Tree is that it allows for handicap races. Since each driver has his own set of lights which he watches, the green on one set can be made to come on before the other set. While in the professional categories the lights might come on at the same time, in the handicaps one car can start ahead of the other. This is an excellent way to run cars of different classes against each other.

Of course, higher purses for winners of drag racing events have contributed to the sport greatly. At first we ran strictly for nothing; it was a purely amateur sport. As costs rose it became impossible to continue on this basis and small purses were offered, which gradually increased. When the Professional Racers Association was formed in 1972, we successfully made a bid for reasonable prize money for each of the pro categories.

Today, the top fuelers in drag racing are an unlimited class. The only restrictions we have are concerned with safety. Obviously, there is a limit on speed but I'm not quite sure what it is. With the equipment we have available today, it is probably up around 265 m.p.h., with ET's around 5.50 seconds. But who knows what products, new metals and so forth, will be brought into use? These might negate the present limitations.

Generally speaking, drag racing has meant everything for me. I always say that I kind of started my life right along with drag racing. When I came out of high school I had no real ambitions. I only knew that I was interested in cars; it was fun, a hobby for me. In Tampa, Fla. in 1949, there wasn't much organized drag racing going on. This was the situation in most of the country. The guys had cars that they tinkered around with and tested against each other, usually on vacant country roads. Like many young racers, they committed the usual faults – running through stop signals, etc. Many of these guys got in a lot of trouble as a result, but one thing was for sure: they wanted to race.

As a solution to this problem, we secured an old, abandoned World War II airport in Zephyr Hills. With the blessings of the city administrators of Zephyr Hills, we held our first legal drag race there. This is basically how I got started in drag racing; I was involved in this movement and grew up with the sport. Of course, my first car back in those days was a 1944 coupe with a little Mercury motor that turned the quarter in 19 seconds.

To date, my biggest satisfaction in drag racing came in the recent 1975 Supernationals at Ontario, Calif. Not only did I have the top time – a new world record, 250.9 m.p.h. with an elapsed time of 5.637 seconds – but I also won the event and the World Championship all in the same day. This was a tremendous achievement for me, and was very gratifying. Prior to this, the most outstanding meet of my career came in 1967 at Indianapolis. At the time I was having a

The "burn out" is a feature of the preparation for each run down the track. Liquid is poured under the rear wheels and the engine gunned to make the wheels spin and smoke. This procedure warms the tires, bringing them up to a temperature that will result in maximum grip on the track. (Gatornationals)

slump; I hadn't won any events, didn't hardly qualify. Then I came to Indy sporting a beard and I vowed I wouldn't shave until I ran in the sixes. Luckily, I won the event, running a 6.77 in the final – all before the cameras of ABC's Wide World of Sports. This was the high point of my career up to then.

All in all, drag racing has given me a life that could never have been so interesting and satisfying had I not had it. In the upcoming years I plan to continue with it. I enjoy it very much.

–Don Garlits

Over the years, Don Garlits has earned his reputation as the "Big Daddy" of drag racing. He has been involved in most of the milestones in the sport, setting many speed records. Besides being the first man to clock 200 m.p.h. on the drag strip, he holds the current record of 250.9 m.p.h. He is also author of **King of The Dragsters** *with Brock Yates.*

For More Information

Large newsstands are filled with publications dealing with drag racing. We recommend *Hot Rod Magazine, Car Craft Magazine, Popular Hot Rodding, Super Stock and Drag Illustrated, Cars Magazine, Rodder* and *Super Stock Magazine.*

The grand daddy of drag racing organizations is the National Hot Rod Association, 10639 Riverside Drive, North Hollywood, Calif. 91602. They provide rules and regulations governing drag racing. They sanction races and race tracks, produce national drag racing circuit competitions, and promote racing in general. A new organization with the same goals is the International Hot Rod Association, Box 3029, Bristol, Tenn. 37260.

Here are three good books on drag racing. All are available from World Publications, Box 366, Mountain View, Calif. 94040 at the price listed* plus 25 cents each postage.

The Sox & Martin Book of Drag Racing, Ronnie Sox & Buddy Martin. This large book is the work of one of the most respected teams in drag history. In it, they not only tell the stories of their introduction to drag and their successes and failures, but they make this book the most complete book on drag racing by covering the history of drag and covering every racer there has been . Goes beyond the glitter of the sport to really show what it takes to get started. Many color photos. 1974 Hb., 227 (oversize) pp., ill., $17.95, (Chilton).

King of the Dragsters: The Story of Big Daddy (Don) Garlits, Garlits & Yates. "More than just autobiography it's the history of a sport, drag-racing. . .Don tells of his victories and how they were attained; he also describes the races which he lost, and analyzes the reasons for and causes of his having lost. . . .boys interested in this type of racing (aren't they all?) will love it."–School Library Journal. 1970 Hb., 246 pp., ill., $5.50, (Chilton).

Six Seconds to Glory, Hal Higdon. The true, thrilling story of Don Prudhomme's valiant effort to become the first driver to win a fourth victory in the most important drag championship of the year, the 1973 National in Indianapolis. 1975 Hb., 159 pp., ill., $6.95, (Putnum's).

The blend of horse and rider over a jump is a classic image dating to Greek and Etruscan antiquity. In watching a show jumping horse and rider, one almost has a feeling that the two were born that way, attached, moulded into one form. (Duffy)

Dressage & Jumping

Today, the equestrian art truly flourishes on an international scale. Horse trials and competitions take place worldwide, on a variety of levels. The equestrian competition for world championships and the Olympic Games are broken up into three main events: 1) The Prix des Nations, which is concerned with show jumping; 2) The Three-Day Event, which includes dressage, cross-country, steeplechase, and stadium jumping; and 3) Individual Dressage Competition, which is judged solely on individual performances. Each of these events communicates a unique aesthetic that involves the total harmonization of movements between two very different creatures: horse and man.

In show jumping, a horse and rider jump a course composed of fences which are especially designed for the particular contest. There are three categories of competition here: in one, jumping ability is tested according to the time it takes horse and rider to reach a destination; in the second, jumping ability is alone considered; the third puts the emphasis on speed and agility.

In the Three-Day Event, horse and rider are tested for all-around ability. The name of this competition comes from the fact that the various phases of the event take place on three separate days. The dressage portion of the event consists of a number of movements at the walk, trot, and canter. Each movement is carefully marked by the judges. The testing of speed, endurance, and jumping ability in cross-country horsemanship is the aim of the second phase of the event, and is the most important and toughest part of the competition (see "Steeplechasing and Hurdle Racing" section). The object of the final phase is to prove that a horse can still continue in service after a difficult test of endurance. Therefore, the last day's course is not a difficult one.

Dressage is a word derived from the French word "dresser," meaning to train. Dressage is practiced by all good horsemen. Competitive dressage's object is to show that the horse's training is successful. Successful dressage training involves both horse and rider. They must work together in harmony, performing movements that enhance the natural movements of the horse. Dressage can be an art form, and it can also relate to many areas of horse activity.

On Show Jumping

There is one very major difference in horse sports as opposed to other sports—the equipment. This alone can be a limiting factor. To buy, maintain, and transport a horse, or horses, and everything that goes with him is obviously quite different than doing the same with a swim suit, track shoes, etc.

Most equestrians who participate in show jumping start out because of their general interest in horses rather than their interest in sport. A few of them might be sports enthusiasts, but, by-and-large, they have a love for horses. In this respect, I would have to say that I became involved in jumping in much the same way as the majority of riders.

Although I could not afford a horse in my early days, I had a great passion for them, and a strong desire to ride. This interest led me to horse dealers, not only for employment, but for the opportunity to pursue the joy of riding. I gained a tremendous amount of initial experience by riding and showing the horses there. Then, later on, I started riding for people who owned horses, but who were not riders themselves. Soon I gained enough knowledge to be able to select horses for owners, school them, and then show them.

Like everybody who has been around horses for awhile, I learned the different ways that each horse is an individual, in the same way people are. They each have their own unique habits and temperament. As a trainer, it was my job to be able to appraise a horse for its potential as a good show jumper. Riders, owners, and trainers are always on the lookout for young, green horses that look promising. Actually, looking for horses sometimes borders on "the impossible dream." You're constantly looking for the really top horse, but they are very few and far between.

So, very slowly, step-by-step, I learned about show jumping–from the standpoint of riding technique, and knowledge of the horse themselves. This education is a long process, besides the fact that one must have access to the very good horses that are needed. If a rider doesn't have the money to start out with, then it can be hard in that he will most likely have to work for other people–but that's a wonderful education. One might file it all under "where there's a will there's a way," but by the same token, it doesn't mean there's always a way. Just because a rider puts out his utmost effort, it doesn't mean that there's a guarantee. Only those with the greatest desire, the most talent and with fortunate circumstances make it to the top. This is a normal situation in all our lives, and is what makes life interesting–looking forward to the unknown.

Even if you are able to afford your own horses, it is still just as essential to develop your abilities so that you can use horses wisely and well. If a rider can't afford a very expensive horse then he must rely on his knowledge for picking out horses that are not expensive but have some potential if they are well schooled. For jumping, it is essential to have the right kind of horse, or it's not going to work.

Once a person is really involved in show jumping he'll find that there are many people, already involved, who are willing to contribute to the learning process. Riders are generally very helpful to each other, and are generous in giving suggestions. This is fortunate, since riders never rid themselves of problems. As he improves, the problems he faces are just on a higher plane. This aspect of the sport makes it continually interesting, and experiments are always in the making.

No matter how a person is introduced to jumping, though, and no matter how far he or she gets, there can be great satisfaction involved – whether the initial interest was in horses, or in sports, is no matter. It's one of life's good facets – very interesting, very rewarding. It was a long jump to the top, but well worth it.

–Kathy Kusner

Kathy Kusner started riding with the U.S. Equestrian Team in 1961. Since then she's participated in the Olympic Games at Tokyo, Mexico and Munich, riding in the equestrian jumping events. In 1967 she was Ladies European Champion, and she also has won numerous events such as the U.S. President's Cup, Grand Prix of Ireland, and Embassy Grand Prix of England.

On Eventing

Another jumping sport designed to test the stamina, fitness, training and ability of the rider is known as Eventing, Combined Training or Three Day Eventing.

To be a winning Event horse, a horse must compete successfully in three distinct phases – dressage, cross-country, and show jumping. The dressage test used in eventing, even at Olympic level, is not nearly so demanding as the tests used for "pure" dressage. It is designed to show simply that the horse is supple, obedient, and has reached a certain level of training. This test, however, is performed by horses fit enough to complete the most gruelling cross-country jumping test covering 20 miles or more the very next day! On the third day of the event, to prove that the horse is still fit, sound, and full of go, he performs a show jumping course of intermediate difficulty.

Eventing started in England, the cradle of hunting and racing, in the early 1950's. The first big Three Day Events were held on huge, privately owned country estates in England where they are still held each year.

For me, eventing is the most exhilarating and rewarding of the jumping sports. The cross-country day is the highlight of the competition. At a three day event the cross-country day will begin with a section of perhaps five miles of roads and tracks ridden at nine miles per hour, a good brisk trot with an occasional canter. This is a "warm-up" for the steeplechase which follows. Phase "A" (roads and tracks) is carefully timed, with just a few minutes break before phase "B" (steeplechase). The steeplechase is approximately three miles and is to be performed at a racing gallop. The course has eight or 10 full-size steeplechase fences, often including an open ditch (a big brush jump with a gaping ditch on the take-off side) and a water jump where the water is on the landing side of the fence. Each competitor performs alone and is timed.

As soon as the steeplechase is completed the horse and rider commence phase "C", a second roads and tracks at nine m.p.h.–longer this time – around seven miles. There are no jumps on the roads and tracks phases but they are designed as a test of stamina and fitness before the final most gruelling phase – phase "D", the cross-country.

The compulsory 10-minute break between phases "C" and "D" is used to cool the horse, check him and his equipment, and go through a final vet-check to ensure all is well. The cross-country is the most exciting, both to ride and watch. It can be up to 5½ miles at the big events, over all sorts of country with approximately 30 enormous, solid fences to be jumped. The maximum height for advanced level is 3'11", which may not sound too big until you find a fence with a 6-foot spread placed on the edge of an 8-foot drop; or with the landing in a river; or down a quarry; or immediately followed by a steep slide with an upright fence at the bottom! There are no penalties for hitting a fence but there are heavy penalties for falls or refusals. Judges are placed at each fence to watch the competitors carefully. An event horse (and rider) must be very bold, as well as being well trained and a superb gymnast at peak fitness.

Eventing in the U.S. is a very young sport indeed. It really only started in the late 1960's but it is growing very rapidly now. Despite the fact that England and Ireland have dominated the sport world-wide since its inception, the U.S. sent a team to the 1974 World Championships at Burghley, England and ended up winning them. Since the winner always hosts the next championships the 1978 World Championships will be held in the United States.

What makes eventing so exciting for me is that it requires not only a bold, fit, and well-trained horse but also a trained, capable, intelligent rider who knows how to get the best from the horse in the confines of the dressage arena and around a twisty show jumping course and who has the guts, drive and determination to go boldly across country. There is enormous satisfaction for a trainer in knowing at the end that you have fully developed and produced an all-round horse and an all-round rider.

—**Mary Rose**

Mary Rose started riding at age five in England, where later she showed her own horses in jumping, hunter trials and eventing. After becoming a well-known professional instructor in England, she moved to Denver where she opened her own school. Today she shows successfully, is a recognized judge, gives clinics all over the country, and is the author of **The Horseman's Notebook.**

Focusing In On Dressage

Dressage training involves both a mental and physical approach to schooling. The horse develops understanding, willing obedience, and rapport with his rider, as well as physique, which improves suppleness, flexibility, balance with forward impulsion, smoothness, and regularity at all gaits. In short, dressage training produces a horse that is a pleasure to ride.

Competitive dressage (participation in dressage tests) enables the horseman to judge the progress of his horse's training, from Training Level tests to F.E.I. competition (Federation Equestre Internationale). Competition stimulates the interest of riders and improves the training of horses. The American Horse Shows Association (AHSA) tests are arranged as stepping stones stones from one level to the next, culminating in the elegant Grand Prix de Dressage. The tests are performed in a marked arena before an AHSA judge. The many horse shows that sponsor these competitions encourage the development of harmony between man and horse.

Dressage as a living art has been nurtured and given worldwide fame by the Spanish Riding School of Vienna, Austria. At the school, this classical art form features Lipizzan horses and the training is based on the horse's natural movements. The horse learns to perform some of these movements both in hand (without a rider) and under saddle. The dressage horse must be willing and able to lighten his forehand and to engage his hindquarters. This is the principle upon which dressage is founded. He is collected, "on the bit", and responds with brilliant precision to the aids (cues given by his rider through weight, hands, and legs). The voice is considered an aid when training.

Hunters, show jumpers, police horses, polo horses, gymkhana horses, and western horses all benefit from dressage training, as do their riders. The trained horse can extend and collect, bend and flex, and make smooth transitions in gait, even though he may not go on to haute ecole. Dressage principles need not be executed in a manege or arena, but can be practiced, wherever knowledgeable, sensitive horsemen perform.

—**Eleanor Prince**

Eleanor Prince lives with her husband on Sodergreen Ranch in Wyoming. Besides raising and training Arabian horses, she manages Sodergreen Horsemanship School and teaches equitation at the University of Wyoming. She is co-author of **Basic Horsemanship: English and Western.**

The object of competitive dressage is to demonstrate the de gree to which a horse has mastered his training. It can be an ar form and it can also relate to many areas of horse activity

For More Information

Additional information can be found in the other horse sec tions. But here are some important addresses. Eventing is reg ulated by the United States Combined Training Association 1 Winthrop Square, Boston, Mass. 02110. Membership cost $15.00 per year and includes a subscription to their newslette which is full of information including pictures of eventing i the US and around the world.

Dressage's major organization is the United States Dressag Federation, Box 80668, Lincoln, Neb. 68501. There are abou 40 local and regional dressage clubs and organizations who ar members of the USDF. Addresses and other information ca be obtained by writing the Federation. The best magazin covering the sport is *Dressage,* Box 2460, Cleveland, Ohi 44112. The magazine also has articles on eventing. Beside technical articles on various aspects of the rider and hors training, the magazine deals with people in the field and keep you up to date both on the national and international leve Another source for information is the American Dressage In stitute, Box 3257, Darien, Conn. 06820. And for mail orde you might try these people: Libertyville Saddle Shop, 30 Peterson Road, Hwy 21, Libertyville, Ill. 60048; Millers, 13 Varick St., New York, N.Y. 10013; H. Kauffman & Son 139-141 East 24th St., New York, N.Y. 10010. But as one pe son says "equipment is seldom ordered by mail since it ofte must be fitted and modified to suit a particular horse or ride You are better off going to a tack shop."

"An event horse must be very bold, as well as being well trained and a superb gymnast at peak fitness. The cross-country is the most exciting part of eventing, both the ride and watch. It can be up to 5½ miles at the big events, over all sorts of country with approximately 30 enormous solid fences to be jumped. The maximum height for advanced level is 3'11", which may not sound too big until you come down a steep slide with an upright fence at the bottom!" (Duffy)

There are two organizations that can give you more information on horse jumping: The American Horse Shows Association, 527 Madison Ave., New York, N.Y., 10022 is a large general organization, and The United States Equestrian Team, Gladstone, New Jersey, 07934 is an organization for those who wish to become riders.

Here are a few excellent books on dressage and horse jumping. All are available from World Publications, Box 366, Mountain View, Calif. 94040 at the price listed* plus 25 cents each postage.

An Expert's Guide to Basic Dressage, Jean Froissard. Covers how to choose your horse, understanding the aids, balance, and how to use your legs and arms. Teaches you how to ride a horse competently in elementary tests. 1971 Ppb., 100 pp., ill., $2.00, (Wilshire).

The Olympic Dressage Test in Pictures, Gregor deRemaszkan. Translated from the German, this book provides the best graphic presentation available on the difficult Olympic dressage test. 1967 Hb., 146 pp., ill., $6.95, (Stephen Greene).

Dressage, Henry Wynmalen. A unique study, the first of its kind in English, exploring the interplay of mental and physical factors on which the training of a horse is based. 1975 Hb., 288 pp., ill., $7.95, (Arco).

Basic Horsemanship—English and Western, Eleanor E. Prince and G.M. Collier. Clear, easy prose highlights a step-by-step guide for riders and instructors. Lessons proceed from first mounting to intermediate levels and participation in competitive events. 1974 Hb., 353 pp., ill., $8.95, (Doubleday).

Complete Training of Horse and Rider in the Principles of Classical Horsemanship, Alois Podhajsky. All the principles and techniques are set forth by this accomplished master. 1957 Hb., $8.95, (Doubleday).

Jumping: Learning and Teaching, Jean Froissard. This extraordinarily comprehensive guide to jumping emphasizes the importance of basic training, training on the ground, and of course the traditional training over fences. 1971 Hb., 169 (overisze) pp., ill., $10.00, (Arco).

Riding and Jumping, William Steinkraus. US Olympic Equestrian Team Captain discusses the whole range of horsemanship—from first mounting to international competition. The numerous photos show today's top riders in action and illustrate his points strikingly and explicitly. 1969 Hb., 131 pp., ill., $6.95, (Doubleday).

Teaching Your Horse to Jump, J. Froud. From the first stages of training to 2- and 3-day events, this helpful, thoughtful manual emphasizes establishing a happy relationship between horse and trainer. Clear step-by-step progression of training. 1971 (rev. 1974) Ppb., 104 pp., ill., $2.00, (Wilshire).

The Complete Book of Show Jumping, Michael Clayton, ed. Written by a group of experts, this complete book covers jumping types, how to break a horse in and start it on early jumping lessons, care and protection plus more. 1975 Hb., 288 (oversize) pp., ill., $14.95, (Crown).

Show Jumping. Know the Game Series. Good beginners' guide to horse jumping in competition. Clearly discusses the course and all of the obstacles, classification and awards, rules, history, administration, and the horse and rider when jumping. 1974 Ppb., 40 pp., ill., $1.50, (E.P. Publishing).

Duckpins

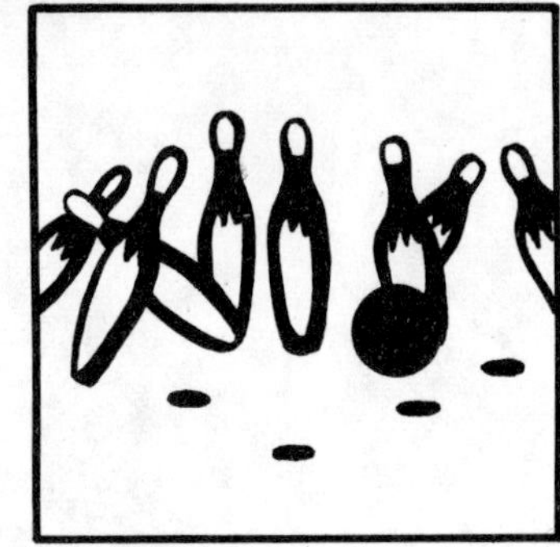

Duckpins is the bowling game of bowling games. It doesn't require speed nor is a hook an absolute necessity. Accuracy is the name of this game.

The pins used in duckpins stand less than nine and one-half inches high and weigh between 23¼ and 24½ ounces. This makes them a much smaller target than the conventional tenpin, which stands 15 inches high and may weigh from 46 to 58 ounces.

The ball can be no more than 5 inches in diameter or 3 pounds, 12 ounces in weight. These are supplied free by those alleys featuring Duckpins. Due to its size, no holes are required.

The alleys are identical to tenpin alleys, 41-42 inches wide, 60 feet from the center of the Head (No.1) pin to the foul line behind which the bowler must release the ball. The approach must be clean and level and not less than 15 feet in length. Pin spots, upon which the pins are placed, are spaced 12 inches from the center of each spot to the center of each adjacent spot and there must be 34 3/16 inches from the center of the No. 1 pin spot to the pit.

The pin action is very limited and as a result, a 300 game is an impossibility, and the highest game ever bowled was 246. A 130 average is tantamount to a tenpin average of over 200. This is regardless of the fact that a third ball is rolled per frame, if required. Yes, three balls as opposed to two in tenpins, or conventional bowling. If all the pins are knocked down on the first ball, a strike is scored. If two balls are required to knock down all 10 pins, a spare is given. When the third ball is used only the total pins are scored and no mark earned.

Due to the size of the ball, newcomers to the game find it easy to handle, although the smallness of the ball increased the need for accuracy. This ball can fit through the space between adjacent pins. Hitting "the pocket" can result in a split, taking out only the 1, 3, and the 5 pins. These are a few of the hazards that contribute to the high incidence of low scores.

A three step approach is adequate, and it will tend to keep the bowler from veering left or right. Begin with the left foot and finish with the left in a slide. You should stop a few inches before the foul line.

The ball should start moving with your first step, out from the body, down and back. A short backswing will suffice and should occur simultaneously with the second step. The third step (slide) and the release of the ball at the bottom of the swing finish the delivery. The right arm should be straight and continue on, finishing above the head.

Rubberband Duckpins differs in that a thick, black band of rubber is set into a groove around the girth of the pin. This imparts much more "pin action" and only two balls are used per frame. The space between the pins is somewhat decreased by the bank of rubber, though the ball can still fit between adjacent pins and a split through the center is possible with only the 1 pin and 5 pin knocked out.

The ball weighs 3 pounds, 8 ounces. 300 games are rolled every year and a 175 is considered a high average while 135 to 150 is the norm. Scorekeeping is exactly the same as in tenpins.

Bowling of any kind is a challenge. It gives the individual a chance to excel in competition with others and in league bowling this is coupled with team effort. It brings together people from all walks of life on a common ground with no sexual or racial barriers.

—**Dante Liberatore**

Dante Liberatore used to play a lot of duckpins when he lived on the East Coast.

For More Information

We have not seen it but there is one magazine devoted to duckpins. *Duckpin World,* 711 14th St. N.W., Washington, D.C. 20005. This is the official magazine of the National Duckpin Bowling Congress at the same address.

Falconry

Originally, our great ancestors were creatures of the outdoors. Like the primitive birds and beasts that he lived among, he depended entirely upon the natural environment for all his basic needs. His gregarious nature and search for resources led man to the slow conquest of much of the untamed wilderness. Unfortunately, the animals that were once his living-mates were domesticated, or driven to extinction by his carelessness; many species were lost to future generations.

Thanks to dedicated falconers, one creature, at least, has escapted the tyranny of mankind. The magnificent falcon has even become man's companion.

Many people think that falconers, or those who engage in the sport of falconry, are "outlaws," enemies of the animals that they capture. On the contrary, the people who study these wild predatory birds are probably some of the staunchest conservationists in the US. They never kill the hawks and falcons they use, they merely capture them for a time—more or less "borrowing them from Nature"—before returning them again to the high cliffs and trees and brush of their natural habitat. In fact, it is well known that falconers have kept certain species from dying out through care and breeding.

To become involved in falconry, one needs to appreciate the freedom of these wild predatory birds while harboring an utmost respect for their kind. The falconer must learn all he can about the bird he plans to capture: its feeding and nesting habits, growth patterns, temperament. He must be able to act as veterinarian if the bird becomes ill or injured; and, most of all, he must be a friend to the hawk or falcon, releasing him at the end of the season. The bird's training and care is a full-time job that necessitates enormous amounts of time and energy—it should never be taken lightly.

Once the novice falconer has become familiar with the needs and habits of predatory birds, he can either buy a young falcon from a breeder, or more likely, capture his own from the wilds. While never actually taming the falcon or hawk, he will train it to strike a bait, perch and release to find its prey, and return when called. Without negating the bird's natural instincts, he will teach the bird to channel its natural abilities to his request.

Falconry is a sport with a long and honorable ancestry. Its tradition includes emperors and kinds who hawked for fun and food. At one time, in the 13th century, hawks were protected by Canute the Danish king, but by the beginning of the 18th century firearms supplanted falconry as a means of catching game for food and the sport nearly died out.

Modern falconers are still an exculsive "royal" clan which takes pride in its work. Falcons are cherished and it is well-known that falconers keep a keen eye out for poor work or bad advice about their sport. Most falconers make their own mews (cages), perches, jesses, bags, and so forth; however, the equipment can be bought from reputable dealers both in the US and abroad.

A Little History

The word "falconry" has an ancient ring about it. Like a peal of medieval bells, the note comes down the centuries of man's activities. Four thousand years ago, sportsmen of China and the Far East cast trained falcons off their fists at birds and animals, often for the pot as well as for sport.

Throughout the ages, the fascination of a working alliance between man and hawk has never lost its appeal. The grandest birds, the most spectacular, were reserved for Kings and Emperors. Only they could afford the time and money needed to seek out and train the rarer and more magnificent birds of prey most suited to the purpose. Kubla Khan kept 200 gyrfalcons and 300 other kinds. He had on call an army of 10,000 beaters armed with whistles for his hawking expeditions. But lesser hawks of all descriptions have long been employed by humbler folk to keep their larders filled.

As travel and trade between East and West gradually developed, so the art became wider known in Asia and Europe. By the third or fourth century A.D., falconry was well understood in central Europe, but at least two centuries more elapsed before its introduction into Britain.

By the 13th century severe laws protecting hawks (originated by Canute, the Danish king) were slightly reduced, and more common people were able to take up the sport. It reached its peak in the 16th century as the most widespread and popular sport in Britain.

By the end of the 17th century, portable firearms which could readily be fired at moving birds and animals superceded the attraction of hawking as a means of filling the larder. The sportsman also turned to this gun for amusement.

By the beginning of the 18th century, a trained falcon was a rarity. It was not until Colonel Thornton of Thornville Royal appeared in the latter half of the century that the interest was revived. A hawking club was formed around 1775 which led to others in the years later.

In 1954, hawking was made a lawful sport again in France, after a prohibition of nearly 100 years and in Spain and Italy there are a few enthusiasts. In the US there are many highly skilled falconers.

Falconry cannot regain the universal appeal which it enjoyed in the 17th century: modern conditions make this almost impossible. But the art has never died out and there are many expert falconers in Britain and the US today, enough to ensure continuity of the traditional skill.

For More Information

Two addresses should be useful, North American Falconers Association, 310 Hanks Hill Rd., Storrs, Conn. 06268 and North American Falconry and Hunting Hawks, Box 1484, Denver, Colo. 80201. Another source of information is William Hecht, Box 67, Scottsdale, Ariz. 85252. Here are some books on the subject. All are available from World Publications, Box 366, Mountain View, Calif. 94040 at the price listed* plus 25 cents each postage.

Falconry Today, Jack Samson. The history of hunting with birds of prey, plus care and training, natural history, the law and more, 1976 Hb., Ill., $7.95, (McKay).

Art and Practice of Hawking, E.B. Mitchell. A practical treatise (originally printed in 1900) which explains best methods of training, care and selection of birds, furniture and fittings. 1959 (3rd printing) Hb., 291 pp., ill., $8.50, (Branford).

The Art of Falconry, Gerald Lasscelles. A reprint of the classic 1895 edition that will be useful for all falconers. 1971 Hb., ill., 172 pp., $7.25, (Branford).

Falconry, Gilbert Blaine. A practical, personal guide from a man who practiced the sport for over 40 years. Covers species of falcons and hawks, education, hooking, feeding, game hawking, and ailments and remedies. 1936 Hb., 253 pp., ill., $6.50, (Branford).

A Manual of Falconry, M.H. Woodford. This authoritative text covers all aspects of falconry: choice of hawk for training, proper furniture, health and disease, lost hawks and the moult. Special chapter on game hawking. 1960 (rev.) Hb., 194 pp., ill., $9.25, (Branford).

Harting's Hints on Hawks, James E. Harting. Explains simple and practical points of hawking to the beginner. This manual was originally written in 1898, and is now a collector's item. 1971 Hb., 269 pp., ill., $12.50, (Branford).

Falconry for You, Humphrey Ap Evans. Written in an easy and readable style for those with a general interest in falconry. Covers background, which hawks to use, equipment, flying a hawk, diet, health and hunting. 1960 Hb., 206 pp., ill., $5.95, (Branford).

Falconry: An Illustrated Introduction, Humphrey Ap Evans. One of the world's great falconers explains every aspect of owning and training a hawk from obtaining a bird and using the hawking apparatus—hood, glove, bells and jess—to feeding and training. 1974 Hb., 160 pp., ill., $12.95, (Arco).

The Life and Lore of the Bird, Edward Armstrong. A fascinating look at birds and man's early mythology and beliefs about them. Armstrong has a personal knowledge of legend, mythology, folklore, and tribal customs that is woven into these remarkable observations.The role of birds in divination, augury magic, the use of birds in sport and their role in art are all described. 1975, 288 (oversize) pp., ill., $14.95, (Crown).

Fast Draw

Fast Draw is a fast moving, growing sport which carries on the traditions of our Western Heritage. It is a test of speed, dexterity, reactions, and accuracy. It is exciting and safe!

Fast Draw competition involves an attempt to draw a single action revolver from a holster at a given signal, fire, and hit a target, stopping a timer in the least possible time.

Contestants must conform to a set pattern of rules governing distances, types of charges, guns and holsters so that everyone competes under the same conditions.

Strict safety measures are set up and enforced at all times. No live ammunition is ever used and is not permitted in or near the shooting area. All shooting is done with either wax bullets against a silhouette target, or with blank cartridges (black powder) at a balloon. Impact switches for the "wax target," and micro-switches for the balloons are used to stop a timer. The timer is capable of measuring the draw in hundredths of a second and some of the newer timers can even measure in thousandths.

Fast Draw is considered a family sport and there are competitors ranging from 10 years old to 60 years and older. In fact, the oldest competitor in Fast Draw is over 80 years of age and travels extensively around the United States and Canada to shoot any place there is a gathering of fast guns.

—Cal Eilrich

Cal Eilrich says of himself, "I am in love with Fast Draw and the people in it. Nowhere in the world have I found more contentment and excitement than in this sport." Mr. Eilrich is presently the treasurer of the SFDA and was the 1972 World Fast Draw Champion.

Gil Guerra, Jr. is the World Champion for Fast Draw. As a modern day Wyatt Earp, he can draw and hit a target in .25 of a second.

Records and Stars

The fastest shot ever recorded in sanctioned WFDA competition is .20 of a second. Stan Sweet of West Covina, California holds this record in Standing Reaction Balloons at 8 feet. This event involves reacting to a signal, drawing a single action revolver, firing, and hitting the target. Among the many ways to shoot Fast Draw are events in which the shooter walks, while waiting for the signal to draw. The record for walking balloons in .23 of a second which is held by Joe Benson of Buena Park, California.

Balloon events record the fastest times, the reason being that these targets are a little easier to hit. Wax events demand more accuracy since the shooter must hit a FBI style silhouette target at 15 feet with a single wax projectile. The World Record for standing wax at 15 feet is .25 of a second, which is held by Gil Guerra, Jr., the "1975 World Champion" from Upland, California. The record for Walking Wax is .28 of a second, which is held by Cal Eilrich, the "1972 World Champion" from Manteca, California.

Fast Draw is usually scored in five shot series. When a shooter misses the target he received a standard 1.00 (one second) score for that shot. The record for the five shot Standing Balloons series is 1.25 seconds—an average of under .25 of a second for each shot. This record is held by Gil Guerra Jr. Mel Stockwell, the "1974 World's Champion" from Bothell, Washington, holds the five shot Standing Wax series record with 1.46 seconds—a .29 second average per shot.

Many well-known movie personalities have been active in Fast Draw at one time or another. In the early 1960's, when our sport had an annual contest in Last Vegas, among the competing celebrities was Clint Eastwood. Many other stars simply practice in the privacy of their own homes for "professional purposes"—so they know how to look effective with a gun when acting a part in a movie.

Sammy Davis, Jr. and Jerry Lewis are both very handy with six-guns. They are about the best celebrity shooters that we know of, but they are no match for professional "Top Guns" competing in various contest throughout the country.

Glenn Ford, Johnny Cash, Kirk Douglas, Robert Redford, and James Stewart are also fairly fast with revolvers.

With Hollywood's uncanny talent for speeding cameras, it takes a trained eye to tell who's actually good and who isn't. Still, many competing "Fast Guns" undoubtedly first became interested in the sport by watching their favorite Western actor outdrawing every outlaw in sight!

—Cal Eilrich

For More Information

The World Fast Draw Association, 961 Springfield, Upland, Calif. 91786, is the organization behind the sport. They publish a monthly newspetter which goes out to all members. Cost of membership is $15.00 per year and this includes a patch, rule book and the newsletter. Other addresses are Jim Dyer, Chairman of WFDA, 4495 Candee Lane, Fallon, Nev. 89405 and Cal Eilrich, Box 84-89, Reno, Nev. 85907. These people can help you acquire the equipment you need and tell you about your local club.

Fencing

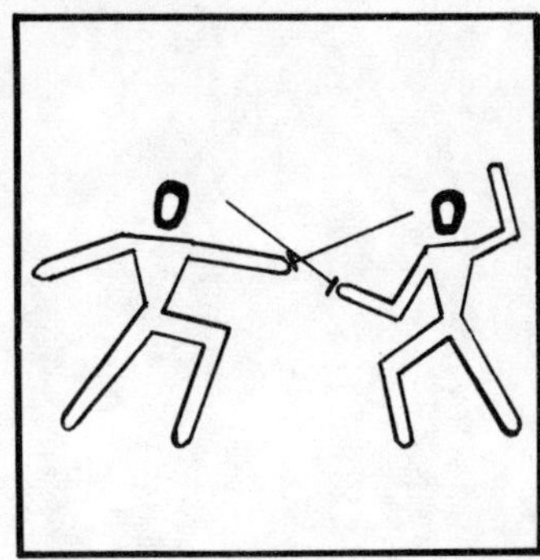

Fencing has a long and fascinating history. Stories of Cyrano de Bergerac, The Three Musketeers, and The Knights of the Round Table have flourished for years. In the early days, the sword was used mainly as a weapon but with the invention of gunpowder and firearms it lost its supremacy as a death dealing device. Swordsmen, however, continued to practice their skills in a more cordial manner, and in 1780 the mask to protect the face was introduced and the game of fencing was firmly established.

Today, while preserving much of the romantic background and history, fencing is a thoroughly modern and athletic sport. Protection is provided by a glove worn on the sword hand, with a padded cuff that extends over the sleeve of the padded fencing jacket. Also, a heavy wire-mesh mask is worn with padded bib and trim. Full length trousers or knickers and knee hose are generally worn. The official dress of a competitive fencer is all white.

The three types of swords used in fencing are the *sabre, epee,* and *foil.* While the sabre is used for both cutting and thrusting, the epee and foil are used only for thrusting. The sabre has a flattened v-shaped blade, with a blunt cutting edge and the point is folded over to form a button. It also has a half-circular guard to protect the hand. The valid target for sabre (an area where, theoretically, a hit would be fatal) consists of the head, arms, and trunk reaching to just below the waist.

The epee, or dueling sword, is the closest to what would be used in a real duel, with a tapered triangular blade. The target, here, consists of the entire body, and valid hits must be made with the point of the weapon.

The foil is the lightest of these three weapons with a small bell-shaped guard. The target for foil includes the entire front torso and back torso down to the waist. Since it is a thrusting weapon, scores must be made with the point.

Of the three weapons, the foil is considered to be the most basic, and is usually taken up first by beginners. Women are able to compete in foil fencing, whereas only men are able to cope with all three blades.

Fencing competitions take place on a rectangular mat called a *piste,* which is marked with lines that indicate the initial "on guard" position, and others which warn the competitor when he is nearing the rear limit of the piste. A bout between men is fenced for five hits, thus the fencer who receives five hits loses the bout. In women's foil a bout is fenced for four hits. Time limits for bouts are six minutes for men, five minutes for women, and if five hits by one fencer are not scored by the end of this period, the competitor who is leading is the winner. In senior foil and epee competitions, hits are registered exactly, by an electrical judging apparatus.

Currently, fencing is a truly worldwide sport with international contests, including the Olympic Games. The universal appeal of the sport can be due to its being a perfect form of relaxation. Within the short space of time of this concentrated exercise, it is impossible to fence and think about anything else at the same time. No particular physique is required for fencing, and it develops coordination of mind and body while exercising every muscle of the body.

A Case for Fencing

One may be motivated to learn fencing for a variety of reasons. The majority of fencers find fencing an excellent and interesting way in which to develop and maintain overall physical fitness. Others find the competitive aspects of fencing a challenge which offers the chance to compete on the highest levels through national and international events. Still others are drawn intellectually to fencing through the fascination of its methodology and conventions that have been developed over a period of centuries, and which offer a rich tradition, revealing in microcosm an evolution of western man's codes of behavior and competitive development. As the only western "martial art", fencing has something to offer everyone regardless of sexual, physical, or mental predisposition.

While fencing is a highly athletic game, it is difficult to find a physiological prototype among its champions. Because of the essentially mental demands made by fencing, a purely physical advantage over a skilled adversary is impossible to maintain. Fencers come in all sizes and shapes, employing diverse approaches to fencing strength. Whether one is short or tall, fast or slow, fencing success depends on how each individual develops and employs his or her own particular physical predisposition. In essence, fencing requires only that one discover and nurture his or her own best assets and use them to advantage.

Whatever one's motivation, fencing offers an exciting and interesting recreational or competitive experience to anyone who is able to expend the necessary time and energy required to form a solid game. One need not defend the beneficial effects of physical exercise and few sports offer as balanced and interesting an approach to fitness as does fencing. Instruction relates directly to techniques of relaxation, control of energy and mental predisposition, hand-eye coordination, physical movement, fighting psychology, and mind-body harmony. The only prerequisite to fencing strength is a healthy body and that is developed in the process of learning the game.

As with tennis or golf, it takes from three to five years for one to develop a sound game. Needless to say, it is a wonderful luxury to start young and children love the excitement of fencing. In my own case, I started late, relative to other sports, enrolling in my very first fencing class when I was 24 years old. As one who has fenced on both the recreational and competitive levels for over 20 years it is still surprising to observe that my game continues to undergo changes, refinements, and improvement. I know many men and women in the fencing world whose ages range from the pre-teens to the 60s and 70s. As a lifetime activity in which one may continue to improve and sustain sound health in a fun and most interesting way, fencing is highly recommended.

The learning process, as it relates to fencing, is not unlike that of tennis, golf or other individual skill sports. The most favorable place in which to begin instruction is the class situation. Here one may learn the theory and practice of fencing while gaining the proper physical conditioning which enables one to meet the purely physical demands encountered in sparring practice. At first the methodology of fencing will seem difficult and exhausting. The physical movements and postures of fencing are not natural, and one needs to work toward strength gradually, until muscles have adjusted and developed to withstand the particular stresses imposed by the requirements of effective attack and defensive techniques. In a short time difficulties disappear as the body strengthens and the mind adjusts to the uncommon speed of the modern game.

When one has gained his or her "fencing legs" it is time for more advanced methodology to supplement basic skills. Here again, one can compare training to golf or tennis, where an occasional individual lesson can produce startling results. For the serious competitive fencer, individual lessons from a competent teacher are mandatory if one is to prepare properly for the lightning fast interaction of high-level competition. The game is literally measured in split seconds. Errors in technique at this level are readily exposed and one's training procedures are crucial to success. There are no "natural fencers," and there are no champions who have neglected proper training procedures. Skill development and conditioning are realized only through individual lessons. Like all sports, "you get out of it what you put into it."

In the years that I have fenced the pleasure and rewards of fencing, which are intrinsic to the game, have been worth every big of the effort and time I have given. Fencing is exciting and pleasurable and the healthful physical and mental dividends which are a by-product of participation are worth more than money can buy. I urge anyone who is interested in healthful recreation of highly spirited competition to take advantage of the splendid opportunities that fencing offers in return for a little energy and time.

—Charles Selberg

Charles Selberg represented the United States in the World Masters' Fencing Championships in 1970 and was a member of the three-man US Foil Team. This team placed first, thus giving the US its first Gold Medal in fencing.

For More Information

The major organization for fencing is the Amateur Fencers League of America, 249 Eton Pl., Westfield, N.J. 07090. They publish a bi-monthly called *American Fencing*. Cathy Taylor, 18 Pleasant Place, Kearny, N.J. 07032 is a good source for information for women. She is the executive secretary for the National Intercollegiate Women's Fencing Association at the same address. Some good sources for equipment include: Fencers Equipment, 348 N. Vermont Ave., Los Angeles, Calif. 99004; Frederick Rohdes, 169 E. 86th St., New York, N.Y. 10028; The Kings Armourer, 6317 Clayton Rd., St. Louis, Mo.; Costello, 836 Broadway, New York, N.Y. 10003;

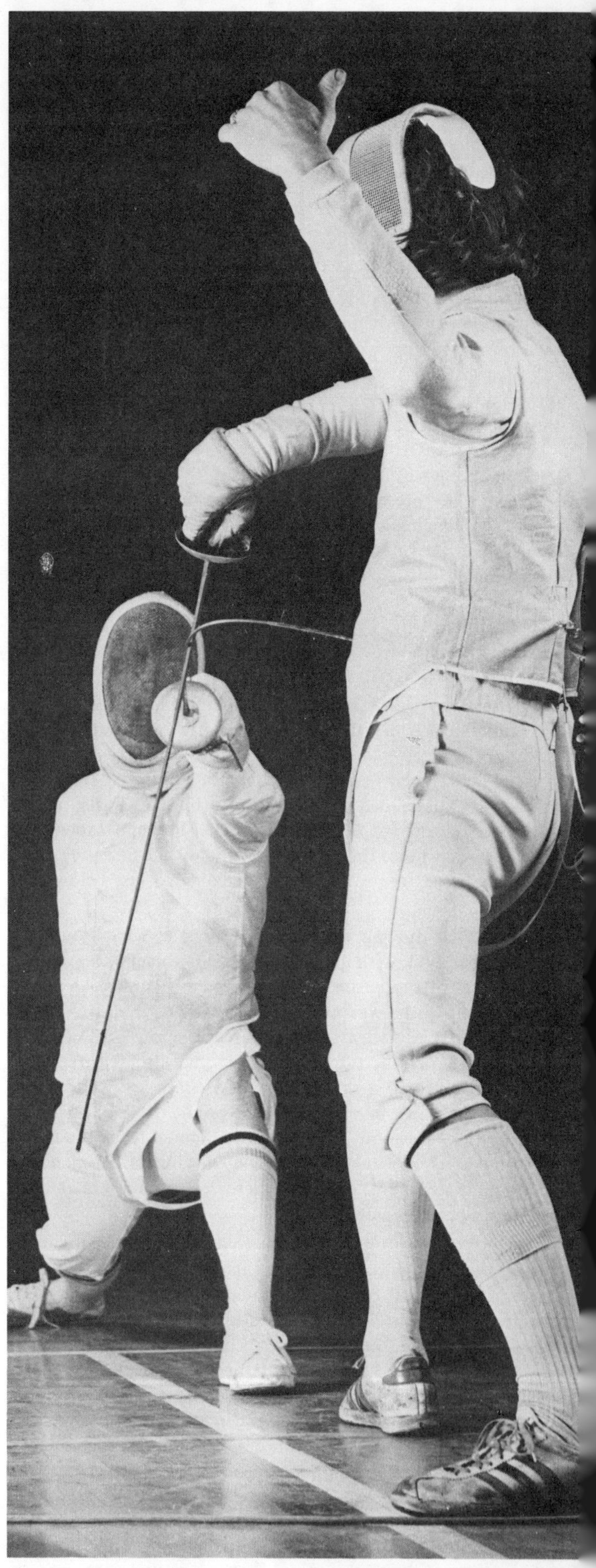

Foil is the most basic of the three forms of fencing. The foil target is the entire front and back torso above the waist and touches can only be recorded with the tip of the foil. To avoid judging errors, touches are recorded electronically through wires from the tip of the foil out the back of the fencer. (Duffy)

Joseph Vince Co., 15316 S. Crenshaw Blvd., Gardena Calif. 90249; George Santelli, Inc., 412 Sixth Ave., New York, N.Y. 10011; Sudre Equipment Co., 5 Westwood Knoll, Ithaca, N.Y. 14850; and American Fencer's Supply, 2122 Fillmore St., San Francisco, Calif. 94115.

Here are some good books on fencing that will help you get started. All books listed are available from World Publications, Box 366, Mountain View, Calif. 94040 at the price listed* plus 25 cents each postage.

Modern Fencing, Clovis Deladrier. Here is a comprehensive manual for students of one of the most demanding competitive sports and most historic. Covers in detail foil, epee, and sabre. 1948 Ppb., 289 pp., ill., $4.95, (Arco).

Fencing, Maxwell R. Garret and Mary F. Heinecke. The concepts and strategies of fencing are explained, as well as the use of equipment and rules for competition. Provides references and information about technique. 1971 Ppb., 107 pp., $2.75, (Allyn & Bacon).

Modern Fencing, Michel Alaux. The late international fencing expert and U.S. Olympic Fencing Coach shares his special knowledge and skill in a comprehensive guide to fencing from initiation to competition. Discusses and illustrates the equipment and skills required for each weapon, all with an emphasis on instant analysis that every fencer needs to win. 1975 Hb., 190 pp., ill., $12.50, (Scribner).

Winning Fencing, Marvin Nelson. The author begins with necessary equipment – and how to buy it – and proceeds to the basic stance, movements, and blade work. To help the fencer improve his game, the author discusses how to combine beginning movements with swift, efficient attacks, parries, ripostes, and defensive moves. 1975 Hb. & Ppb., 144 pp., ill., $8.95/$4.95, (Regnery).

Fencing: Ancient Art and Modern Sport, C.L. deBeaumont. A textbook for the modern fencer from the beginner to the expert. Numerous photographs and illustrations help explain technique and tactics for foil, epee and sabre. The advantages and disadvantages of different schools and methods of fencing are discussed in precise, practical terms. 1970 Hb., 274 pp., ill., $8.95, (Barnes).

Fencing, Curry. Systematically analyzes the basic techniques that the student must master in order to become an accomplished fencer. Covers the history of fencing, equipment (sabre and epee), techniques of foil fencing, rules, and bouting strategy. 1969 Ppb., 79 pp., ill., $3.95, (W.C. Brown).

Fencing, Castello. A systematic instruction method designed to offer beginners a valuable reference guide. Includes conditioning exercises, electrical foil principles and maintenance, and dozens of sequence photos. 1962 Hb., 116 pp., ill., $8.75, (Ronald).

All About Fencing, Bob Anderson. The fundamentals of foil fencing are fully explained and illustrated with the aid of over 400 unique photos, written by one of the world's leading fencing coaches. 1970 Ppb., 100 pp., ill., $1.65, (Arco).

Modern Foil, Charles Allen Selberg. Written by an American fencing master, this is a how-to text that steers away from the romanticism which too often detracts from similar works and relates the material directly to the recreational or competitive fencer who wishes to improve his game. Points out the advantages of each approach, with special emphasis on the all-important study of tactics and psychology. Jan. 1976 Ppb., 224 pp., ill., $4.95, (Addison-Wesley).

Field Hockey

Field hockey is a fast-moving and exciting sport played by both men and women. Men's teams dominate the international scene with India, Pakistan, and Germany displaying the most skill. More women's teams play in the US, however, thereby attesting to the popularity and adaptability of the game. In fact, field hockey is probably the most popular US outdoor sport played by women today. It is a good primary school, secondary school, and college game with the many who learn to play continuing throughout their adult lives.

Modern field hockey originated in England in the mid-1800s and came to the US soon after. It was a "men-only" sport until 1887 when women took over the hockey scene in America. Hockey was introduced here by Constance Applebee and Harriet I. Ballintine who saw it through its early stages of growth in private schools and colleges on the East Coast. The US Field Hockey Association (women) formed in 1922, and the Field Hockey Association of America (men) followed in 1930 to prepare for the 1932 Olympics. Although field hockey became an Olympic event for men's teams in 1908, the US did not participate until 1932, then continued to compete in the 1936, 1948 and 1956 Olympics with limited success. The Olympics along with the recently established World Cup is the ultimate in competition in the sport, as no professional teams exist.

Rules for men and women are nearly identical: the field is 100 yards long by 60 yards wide (smaller fields are accepted for junior play) with a netted seven-foot-high goal at either end. A striking circle forms the area where one-point goals are set up. Obstructing blocking is penalized in field hockey due to the hitting force of the sticks and the potential danger of colliding with a newly-struck ball. Goalkeepers are padded and many players wear shin guards.

The object of the game is for one team of 11 players to score goals on the other team, completing two 35-minute halves of play with the higher score. Players hit, dribble, and pass a hard plastic or leather ball with curved wooden sticks that are flat on the left side (striking surface). A "bully" starts the game with two opposing players striking the ground then sticks before playing the ball.

Although field hockey is played year-round in various parts of the world, it is mostly a spring and fall sport in the United States. Some teams will play field hockey in the fall and lacrosse, another fast-moving stick-and-ball game, in the spring.

Game of Opportunity

Field hockey is virtually unknown as a man's sport in the United States, but for Lee Yoder of Ambler, Pennsylvania it has provided a ticket to international competition and travel that has spanned more than a dozen years.

Lee, an Industrial Arts teacher in Springfield Township, has

In many countries of the world men's field hockey is second in popularity only to soccer. It is essentially a non-contact sport in which speed and quickness are far more important than brute strength and huge bulk. The sport requires speed, agility, stamina and a high degree of skill and fitness. (Duffy)

an impressive record of athletic achievement. Before becoming interested in field hockey he was an outstanding track star, setting two American records for the 400 meter hurdles and earning a place on the US track team which took part in the XV Olympiad in Helsinki, Finland.

It was at Helsinki that Lee was introduced to hockey as he watched the game played by teams from other countries. But when he expressed curiosity about the sport he was told that the US team had not qualified for the Olympics that year. Indeed, it had never qualified for the Olympics.

It was at not until 1957 that he was able to revive his initial interest when he learned by chance that the Philadelphia Men's Field Hockey Club was holding tryouts at the Merion Cricket Club. He tried out, made halfback, and has played for the team continuously since that day.

In 1963 he qualified for the US Olympic trial team which competed in Lyon, France for a spot in the 1964 Olympics. (Out of 70 countries competing, only 16 are chosen for Olympic participation, and only one of those 16 is invited from the Western Hemisphere.) The team was defeated at Lyon, but in 1967 Lee accompanied it to the Pan Am Games in Winnipeg, Canada and returned home with a bronze medal—the highest award the US men's field hockey team has ever received in international competition.

When questioned about the US team's lack of success and popularity compared to other team sports in this country, Lee answered by suggesting that the sport has too few participants from which to attract team members, and that many of those who play regularly on the club level are not American citizens and therefore ineligible to represent this country internationally. He feels that this demanding sport requiring speed, agility, stamina and a high degree of skill and finesse should be developed and encouraged in the high schools and colleges, much as is women's field hockey. Without this early training, it is almost impossible to effectively compete with other countries of the world where men's field hockey enjoys the status of being the second most popular team sport, surpassed only by soccer.

An exciting spectator sport as well as a stimulating participatory sport, men's field hockey has not grown as rapidly as its counterpart played by thousands of women in the US. So

More than 50,000 women play field hockey in the United States. The game was introduced to women in this country by Constance Applebee and Harriet I. Ballintine in 1887 where it was played initially in private schools and colleges in the East. (McDaniel)

well known is women's field hockey that most people think of the sport as belonging exclusively to women and therefore not requiring rigorous physical effort. Nothing could be further from the truth. Field hockey, whether played by men or women, is a challenging and exhausting activity. The principal reason that the sport can be enjoyed by both sexes is simply that it is not essentially a contact sport limited by size and brute strength . . . it involves much more than these factors and could offer a whole new area of athletic competition and pleasure to countless young men like Lee Yoder, if only the opportunity to learn and participate was more readily available.

Women's field hockey player, 28-year-old Joan Moser of Glenside, Pennsylvania is one of the most extraordinary sportswomen on the hockey field today.

In a sport where competition is keen (There are more than 50,000 players in the United States) Joan, a 1968 honors graduate of Ursinus College, a school noted for its victorious hockey teams, has been an Ursinus Varsity player–only losing two games in four seasons, a member of the Philadelphia (First) Team, and in her junior year was chosen as an All-American and earned a position on the US team . . . a position she has kept every year but one for the past eight years.

Some of the most spectacular action in field hockey occurs around the goal mouth, where leaping and diving stops are common. (Duffy)

Joan's expertise in hockey has given her the opportunity to travel to four World Conferences held in Germany, New Zealand, Holland and last year Scotland where she competed in the first World Championships.

Though Joan says she enjoys hockey because of the skills involved and the opportunities for a skilled player to go on national and international tours, she has had to divide her time between field hockey and softball. A member of the 1974 World Champion Raybestos Brakettes (a "fast pitch" team whose home is in Stratford, Connecticut), Joan was required to commute between Philadelphia and Stratford each week during the summer of '75 when training for the Women's Field Hockey World Championships and league competition for softball's national championships overlapped.

In spite of her crowded schedule, she still finds time to play tennis, basketball and lacrosse. And, incidently, while preparing for the 1973 field hockey season she was selected to represent this country on the National Lacrosse Squad.

When Joan isn't competing, she's teaching physical education at North Penn High School where she also coaches hockey in her "spare" time.

–Tom Lingenfelter

Tom Lingenfelter is in advertising public relations in Pennsylvania. He is quite active in promoting field hockey in the US.

For More Information

There are two major field hockey organizations in the United States. The Field Hockey Association of America, 1160 Third Ave., New York, N.Y. 10021 and the United States Field Hockey Assn., 107 School House Lane, Philadelphia, Penn. 19144.

There aren't any magazines published in the US but there is one from England. It is called *Hockey Field*, Whitemilnes, Kencot, Lechlade, Glos. GL7 3QT. We have not seen it but it is supposed to be a good one.

Some sources for equipment: Cran Barry Inc., 2 Lincoln Ave., Marblehead, Mass. 01945; Sauk Valley Farms, Brooklyn, Mich. 49230; and Towers Associates, 266 Wilde Ave., Drexel Hill, Pa. Another good source for information is Gertrude Hooper, 369 Atlantic Ave., Cohasset, Mass. 02025.

Here are some good books covering the sport. All are available from World Publications, Box 366, Mountain View, Calif. 94040 at the price listed* plus 25 cents postage.

Field Hockey, Ann Lee Delano. Written for the student with little or no experience in field hockey. Techniques and rules are described, strategies, practice suggestions, positional play and more. 1966 Ppb., 69 pp., ill., $2.50, (W.C. Brown).

Field Hockey for Players, Coaches and Umpires, Individual and team techniques and tactics, with a brief history of field hockey in the United States and chapters on umpiring, equipment, and hockey terms. 1969 Hb., 152 pp., ill., $9.30, (Ronald).

Field Hockey, Caroline Haussermann. The elements of the game from the first fundamentals and drills to game situations and rules. Different strategic concepts are also covered. 1970 Ppb., 70 pp., ill., $1.95, (Allyn & Bacon).

Field Hockey; The Coach and Player, Mildred Barnes, ed. Articles by members of the 1969 US Team and 151 sequential photo series describe strategy and play. Drills, bad weather techniques, and much more. 1969 Hb., 262 pp., ill., $13.25, (Allyn & Bacon).

Figure Skating

Figure skating is quite rightly referred to as one of the most beautiful, if not *the* most beautiful of sports. The French call it *Patinage d'Artistique*, artistic skating. It is also one of the most physically demanding sports, requiring the agility of a gymnast, the stamina of a long distance runner and the grace of a dancer.

Skating began on the frozen canals of Holland in the 16th century. From there it spread and gradually evolved into a free form style of drawing patterns on the ice. By the mid-19th century, the English had disciplined and developed the art of skating school figures. An American, Jackson Haines, was the inventor of the popular freestyle. He swept Europe off its feet in the latter part of the 19th century with his freeflowing ease of movement. In addition to bringing elements of ballet and dance to the ice, Haines fathered pair skating.

The competitive sport of figure skating began in 1896 with the first World Championships for men. Ladies joined the scene 10 years later, pairs in 1908 and ice dance in 1952. Figure skating has even been featured in two summer Olympic Games, 1908 and 1920, and it has been a popular fixture of the winter Olympics since its inception in 1928.

There are many athletic and artistic elements in figure skating. Initial skills include the all important basic stroking forward, backward and in both directions. Jumps are so predominant in modern figure skating thtat we could say that this is the "jump era." There are seven preliminary jumps that can be rotated in the air. Since their inception towards the beginning of the century, these jumps have been doubled and now quite commonly trebled by both men and women. Spins tend to hold a fascination for the general public, but to the practiced and knowledgeable eye this is not a difficult move.

The lifting of the lady by her male partner in numerous and inventive positions is the one area reserved for pairs competition. Artistically choreographed, all these movements, along with imaginative footwork to music of a required length, produces the most spectacular and dominating factor in figure skating–freestyle.

Our sport is divided into four events: men's singles, ladies'

"The most successful competitive skaters are those who have kept the sport a normal side of their lives. They have good social lives and continue on to college while involved with demanding training hours. They learn to budget their available hours to allow enough time for practice. A majority of competitive skaters improve their school grades considerably from the discipline of budgeting time." (Duffy)

singles, pairs, and dance. Singles have three categories to skate for a total mark. School figures, recently reduced to 30 percent from its long dominant 60 percent of the total score, is the tracing of numerous regimented geometric patterns, all based on the figure eight. Recently added is the compulsory freestyle, in which a previously determined pattern of jumps, spins and footwork is set to two minutes of music. This comprises 20 percent. The remaining 50 percent is for the rapidly rising area of the pure athletic and artistic freestyle.

Pair skating, of all the events, has made the most unbelievable advances in technical difficulty over the last two decades. They skate in competition a compulsory freestyle for 20 percent of their total score, and a freestyle program for the remaining 80 percent. Pairs today do most of the jumps and spins of the singles in addition to their own pair lifts and spins. This must all be performed in perfect unison, making for the most attractive and popular event in the eye of the public.

In ice dancing, very similar to ballroom dancing, competition is divided into three categories; compulsory set-pattern dances like the tango or waltz, an original set-pattern dance, and a free dance.

Figure skating has caught the public's fancy, and little wonder. These lithe and graceful gazelle-like athletes, on their steel blades, flying like the wind across the ice with seemingly effortless energy, makes figure skating one of the most unique, difficult and beautiful sports in the world.

—**Bob Paul**

Pair skater Bob Paul and his partner Barbara Wagner took two North American, four World Championship and one Olympic (1960) gold medal back to Canada. He currently lives in California where he is a choreographer for Olympic team members and for Peggy Fleming's television and personal appearances.

Behind the Scenes

Figure skating is one of the most misunderstood of sports. It has been considered an art with a "Tinker Bell" image, yet for those who participate avidly it is physically grueling. A senior competitive program is easily equivalent to a Marine Corps obstacle course for toughness and endurance. Why this difference of opinion? Why such a wide range of attitudes?

Skating can be different things to different people. A great deal can be gained from participating in it, but often beginners are discouraged before they start. I often see children on ice for the first time dressed with fur muffs and hats in a costume so encumbered with maribou that they can hardly stand up let alone move, struggling all the while on ill-fitted boots with bells tied to the laces. Little wonder that so many potentially good skaters give up and hate the sport forever! And many don't even try, because they hesitate to be associated with the stigma of this "show-biz" sport. What satisfaction could they possibly gain from it? Their prejudice does not allow them to discover that there are many sides to the idea of being able to skate, or how and why they should skate.

Skating is not all show business oriented. In fact, I would consider that to be the very smallest part of its enjoyment potential.

Sunday skaters have so much fun just being with their friends or being alone but with lots of people. There is an excitement found nowhere else, a challenge to be met just getting around the rink standing up. The cold is invigorating and nothing feels better than the next time they are finally warm. And doing all of this to *music*!

In the past I've heard people remark how parents "make a skater." This is a great misconception, because figure skating is one sport that you can't be forced to do if *you* don't like it. If a youngster wants to go on to become a competitive skater,

"School figures, recently reduced to 30 percent from its long dominant 60 percent of the total score, is the tracing of numerous regimented geometric patterns, all based on the figure eight." (Williamson)

90 percent of ultimate success comes from the child and 10 percent from the teaching professional (this is nevertheless an invaluable 10 percent).

The most successful competitive skaters are those who have kept the sport a normal side of their lives. They have good social lives and continue on to college while involved with demanding training hours. They learn to budget their available time to allow enough time for practice. A majority of competitive skaters improve their school grades considerably from the discipline of budgeting time.

Valuable self-confidence is developed in most skaters as they learn sportsmanship and how to work with others to achieve goals. In my daughter Peggy's case, it was a bigger than expected victory for me personally whenever she won a medal, because she was a very shy girl who had overcome her introverted personality through skating. That she was able to master enough nerve to perform in front of many thousands of spectators with confidence was a victory greater than any gold medal.

The cost of training a skater can be monumental, but not althogether impossible to manage. Economy involves making the most of opportunities like using public session ice time (because it's cheaper), making self-designed costumes (instead of costly ready-mades), and learning to cut your own records for music to skate by. There are many ways that overall costs can be kept within limits to give more youngsters an opportunity to develop their skills.

In our household of four children, my daughter's skating was geared to what we could afford to do. Limits needed to be set, and Peggy got lessons when we were able to squeeze it from the budget. She occasionally went as much as three months at a time without lessons and made do on what she had already learned, concentrating on practicing each skill more thoroughly. She knew that each lesson was important and that she needed to make the most of it. She was never lazy about practicing what she had been taught and was so eager for the next lesson that it was a joy to see her work and absorb like a sponge all the new things she had yet to learn. She never complained and always treated her professionals with the utmost respect for their knowledge. I feel that this part of her makeup was a reason why she was later able to cope so well with the tremendous stress of high level competition.

At no time did our family feel that we *wanted* Peggy to become a champion. In her case it was something that just happened, and it was enjoyable. She was definitely not so dedicated that she could not develop as a well-rounded and normal girl, and this is what I feel is important to understand for those just learning about Figure Skating. There is so much offered in enjoying this marvelous sport that everyone has something to gain. It is all up to you and how big a challenge you wish to accept.

—Doris Fleming

Doris Fleming is the mother of Olympic figure skating champion Peggy Fleming.

For More Information

Figure skating has one magazine, *Skating,* Sears Crescent, Suite 500, City Hall Plaza, Boston, Mass. 02108, which seems to be very well done. It is published eight times a year and is the official magazine of the United States Figure Skating Association, at the same address. The USFSA sanctions all competitions and exhibitions, certifies judges, and is responsible to the international governing body.

There isn't a multitude of figure skating books, but here are a few of the better ones. All are available from World Publications, Box 366, Mountain View, Calif. 94040 at the price listed* plus 25 cents postage.

Figure Skating, Marion Proctor. Elementary figure skating—the basic movements, a brief history, rules, advice on equipment, school figures, jumps and spins, pairs and dance. 1969 Ppb., 70 pp., ill., $2.50, (W.C. Brown).

The Fun of Figure Skating, Maribel Owen. One of the country's foremost skating teachers and coaches presents a complete beginner's guide to the sport. From the first shaky steps on ice to the mastering of competition's demanding stunts, this book can be your constant guide. 1960 Hb., 172 pp., ill., $8.95, (Harper & Row).

I Can Teach You to Figure Skate, Tina Noyes with Freda Alexander. An illustrated guide for the beginner, bringing you the essentials of proper form. 1973 Hb. & Ppb., 178 pp., ill., $6.95/$2.95, (Hawthorne).

Fishing- Fresh Water

Freshwater fishing goes back perhaps as far as 1300 A.D. A painting of a Chinese angler, carp fishing from a high-bowed skiff with a rod and reel has been preserved. According to Dr. John T. Bonner of Princeton University's Department of Biology, the painting is attributed to Ma Yaun who lived sometime in the first half of the 14th century.

Initial written words on fishing reels date to England in 1651, two years before the first edition of the world famous **Compleat Angler** written by Izaak Walton, the father of fishing.

The most sought-after and most coveted of all freshwater fish is the stream trout. From fireside chats to poetic verse, this timid to bite and hard to fight fish, with its many hued and bespeckled body, has held the angling spotlight for most of recorded fishing history.

To spend a day on a gin-clear, free-flowing stream with rod and reel is one of the ultimate experiences of a lifetime. To watch a wild trout rise to the freshly hatched midge, or witness the spawning ritual in a gentle riffle are bonus benefits afforded the streamside angler.

To challenge a fast flowing mountain rill with no more than a wading staff and felt-soled boots is also a part of the stream fisherman's world. In this case, safety is paramount and must be observed constantly along the boulder strewn, sometimes moss covered banks.

No fisherman could be blinded to the beauty that surrounds a typical brawling trout stream. (Green)

The most popular fishing techniques used by stream trout anglers include artificial lures—spinners, spoons and feathered flies—or baits, either natural or manufactured. Artifical baits come in different shapes and odors. Some are like salmon eggs and others resemble paste which can be molded on the hook. These are cheese, garlic or blood flavored and very effective.

Natural bait, however, is always the most effective and is generally found in a stream or along its banks. Natural baits include helgramites, stoneflies, cadis fly larva and salmonflies, to name a few.

A streamside angler must know where to find and how to gather natural bait. He must know how to place such bait on a hook to keep it most natural looking, and how to present the bait to one of the most finicky of fish.

Presentation of the lure to a fish is only one phase of trout fishing which an angler must master. He must also be able to read the waters in which he fishes.

Trout are basically lazy and will tend to hold in those portions of the stream where the water eddies or gently swirls. Smooth areas behind rocks in a stream's course, and areas where the water reverses its flow at the side portions of holes are holding areas. Feeding areas tend to be in fast flowing riffles or at the slick tailrace at the bottom ends of holes, just before they spill into the next rapid. White water generally is a poor place to fish.

The angler must also remember that any fish he can see, can see him and usually will not be the least bit interested in his hook, regardless of how nicely garnished it might be.

With all the enjoyment of fresh water angling, however, comes a single irony. Once an angler has fully mastered the skills mentioned here, and then put in another 20 to 30 years on the streams with rod in hand, he will, as this writer has, come to the realization of just how little he really knows about the ways of the fish called trout.

—Phil Ford

As a freelance writer, Phil Ford doesn't have as much time as he would like for fishing.

For More Information

Almost any newsstand is going to have some magazines on fishing. *Outdoor Life, Field & Stream,* and *Sports Afield* are the big ones. One you might not find there is *Fishing World,* 51 Atlantic Ave., Floral Park, N.Y. 11001. Published bi-monthly at $4.00 per year. The publication is the official publication of the Fishing Club of America. A good source of information is the Sport Fishing Institute, 608 Thirteenth St. N.W, Washington, D.C. 20005. They issue monthly bulletins. For the female angler, the International Women's Fishing Association, Box 2025, Palm Beach, Fla. 33480 can provide information. Most good sport shops can supply you with all the equipment you need. Here is one mail order source: Netcraft Co., Box 5510, Toledo, Ohio 43613. They have a free catalog that lists over 5000 fishing items.

Here are some books on fishing. All are available from World Publications, Box 366, Mountain View, Calif. 94040 at the price listed* plus 25 cents postage. Write for a complete list.

Angler's Bible, Kenneth Lane, ed. A reliable source on nearly all types of sports fishing equipment. It includes complete descriptions, specifications and illustrations on all types of gear, tackle and accessories. 1975 Ppb., (oversize), $7.95, (Follet).

Why Fish Bite and Why They Don't, James Westman. An insightful look into this author's scientific methods of knowing fish and catching them. In a style rich with anecdotes, Westman describes the techniques of fishing in different water and explains lures, lines and baits. 1974 Ppb., 211 pp., ill., $2.00, (Wilshire).

Introduction to Bait Fishing, Ray Ovington. Solid how-to facts on presenting fish with the food they naturally food on. From first catch to netting and landing, this guide reviews the basics of fishing with natural bait in fresh and salt water under all conditions wherever fish are found. 1971 Ppb., 192 pp., ill., $3.95, (Stackpole).

How to Find Fish and Make Them Strike, Joseph D. Bates, Jr. By learning to spot telltale currents, calms, ripple patterns and other surface features, anyone can soon know more about the bottom structure of a lake or stream. The idea is to spend more time fishing where the fish are instead of over empty water, and this new book tells how to do it. 1975 Hb., 216 pp., ill., $8.95, (Harper & Row).

Steelhead, Mel Marshall. To give you the savvy you need to match wits and skill with this classic game fish, the author has provided this book, for the novice and the veteran, packed with practical information. Covers habits of the fish, use of bait, lure and flies; tips on tackle and equipment; and the best streams in both the Midwest and the Northwest including seasons. 1973 Hb., 208 pp., ill., $6.95, (Winchester).

Wilderness Fishing for Salmon and Steelhead, Roy McInturff. Covers all the techniques and the author's experience working the Klamath River for salmon and steelhead. 1974 Hb., 224 pp., ill., $8.95, (Barnes).

Trout Fishing, Joe Brooks. Abounds in color photos. Concentrates on the principles and subtleties of fly fishing, especially the handling of the rod. 1972 Hb., 302 pp., ill., $10.00, (Olson).

Where to Fish and Hunt in North America: Jerome Knap. The Complete Sportsman's Guide. This book is devoted to providing the latest and most up-to-date information on fishing, hunting, and where to go for best results. Hb., 192 pp., ill., $8.95, (Arco).

The Expert's Book of Freshwater Fishing, Steve Netherby, ed. The continent's greatest fishing authors, many of them legendary for their knowledge reveal all to the reader: the secrets of tackle and technique that they themselves took long years to discover or develop. Steam trout, mountain trout, lake trout, atlantic and pacific trout, and more. 1974 Hb., 317 pp., ill., $9.95, (Simon & Schuster).

Lure Fishing, A.C. Decker, Jr. A book for the beginner who wants to know how to be a successful lure fisherman. The author goes beyond methods of proper lure presentation to treat such topics as the importance of sight and sound qualities in a fish and the types of lures available for fresh and salt water fishing. 1970 Hb., 189 pp., ill., $8.50, (Barnes).

Through the Fish's Eye, Mark Sosit and John Clark. A really different and unusual fishing book. You will discover here how fish live, think and react. Learn to predict and outwit them. 1973 Hb., 256 pp., ill., $8.95, (Harper & Row).

The Complete Book of Casting, Rex Gerlach. The techniques for all types of fishing rod casts. Includes a history of tackle and other methods. 1975 Hb., 224 pp., ill., $10.00, (Winchester).

Fishing- Salt Water

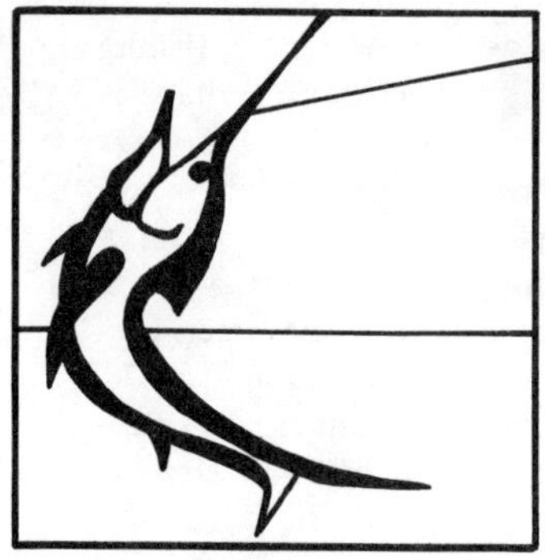

Saltwater fishing covers a much broader scope than its freshwater cousin, because the angler must also be a navigator, oceanographer and meteorologist. Ocean angling sometimes is done under cover of fog and in heavy seas, many times out of the sight of land.

Trolling and bottom fishing are a part of ocean angling and schools of migratory fish must be located, as well as subsurface reefs along the continental shelf where bottom fish congregate. Gamefish spawning cycles must be studied to know when inshore waters might carry the heaviest concentrations of what would normally be deep water fish. At these times the saltwater angler must know where and how to catch those fish from shore.

Saltwater angling requires the ability to cut and prepare bait, and correctly rig it on the proper sized hook. It requires a knowledge of live bait rigging, and the skill to tie a multitude of intricate angling knots, and a thorough understanding of deep sea fishing gear.

On long hauls or overnight trips, the angler must know how to preserve his catch. With any amount of heat, fish tend to spoil rapidly, so icing or refrigeration is often required.

Saltwater fish tend to be of the toothy variety and an angler must know how to handle these much larger and more ferocious types of fish safely and efficiently. One slip and "Ye Compleat Angler" might not be so compleat.

A Deeper Look

Saltwater fishing is a sport which has many faces. It requires the development of a large number of angling skills, such as tying myriad high-strength fishing knots, using the proper rigging and baiting techniques for countless numbers of sportfish, and navigating safe passage from port to sea and return. Saltwater fishing also requires the stamina and intestinal fortitude to withstand the incessant yawing, rolling, and pitching of an ocean going vessel.

Saltwater fishing can be adjusted to cover a wide range of angling expertise. A bout with bottom fishing, for example, requires little skill. All the angler must do is use the proper size weight on a heavy test line, fit it with a gang of baited hooks or feather jigs, lower it to the rocky bottom, jig it up and down a few times, and reel in the fish—sometimes two or more at a time!

Drifting live bait is also a form of bottom fishing. Here the angler must keep his offering on the bottom, but drifting across it. The trick to this type of fishing is to keep the line free by "feeling" the bottom. This is accomplished by tapping the bottom with the sinker and not allowing it to rest. If the bottom goes away, let out more line. If it comes up, wind in rapidly for a few turns to avoid a snagged sinker and lost tackle.

This technique will keep the angler quite busy, and he must learn to recognize a bite when he gets one. In this case, exper-

Salt water fish tend to be larger than their fresh water cousins, and more curiously shaped. (Saltwater Sportsman)

ience is by far the best teacher as the bite can be extremely subtle.

Undoubtedly, the most popular form of saltwater fishing is trolling. This technique is employed by commercial party boats and private anglers alike. Albacore, striped bass, salmon, bonito, jack mackrel and spotted sea bass are consistently taken on trolling gear.

More affluent anglers can pit their skills against larger and more exotic species like the mighty marlin, swordfish and bluefin tuna. These fish are harder to catch, as they have weight, stamina and cunning in their favor. The angler and boat captain must work together as a team to control the direction of a hooked fish in relation to the boat, and not allowing the catch to run off too much line. An empty reel means a lost fish, to say nothing of several dollars worth of equipment.

Tournaments are held on a yearly basis around the world. Off the fabled Kona Coast of Hawaii, tournament billfish catches of well over 1000 pounds are often recorded by winning anglers.

Ocean or saltwater angling does not always require the use of a boat. Surf casters with long rods and spinning reels may be found casting from sandy beaches and rocky points along coastal shorelines. Perch, flounder, halibut and small rock cod are their general fare.

Pier angling is sometimes most appropriate, because the whole family may participate without exposing younger members to sometimes turbulent shoreline hazards. Pier angling requires no special equipment, only a rod, reel and bait.

There are a number of saltwater species for which rod and reel are not needed. Poke poles, for example, are used to catch rock blennies, monkeyface eels and rockfish in tidepools along the shoreline. Throw nets, "A" frame nets and two-man seins are used by surf smelt anglers. A long-tined rake is the fishing tool of the pismo clammer, while a flat leaf spring is used by abalone pickers who grope the rocky sub-surface grottos for these succulent shellfish.

Enough can never be said for saltwater angling. It is one man's frustration and another's salvation. It can be restful or extremely exciting. It can bring the care-worn angler utopian pleasure and peace from within.

–Phil Ford

Phil Ford lives in Mountain View, Calif. and is a free lance writer. He has done a lot of saltwater fishing.

For More Information

There is one good magazine covering this sport exclusively. *Salt Water Sportsman,* 10 High Street, Boston, Mass. 02110 is published monthly at $6.00 per year. I like their description of "voice of the coastal sport fisherman." It is very clear that these people are very much into saltwater fishing. There is coverage in other fishing magazines from time to time and these are listed under freshwater fishing.

The only national organization devoted to the preservation of oceanic gamefish in the National Coalition for Marine Conservation, Box 5131, Savannah, Ga. 31403. Another organization that might be helpful is the Salt Water Fly Rodders of America, Box 304, Cape May Court House, N.J. 08210.

Here are some mail order houses that specialize in saltwater fishing. The Salt Water Lure Co., Box 258, Woods-Hold, Ma. 02543 has a catalog (25 cents) filled with fishing tackle and related accessories. Stans Custom Rods, 20 Haig Ave., Milltown, N.J. 08850 will build the rod you want. Write for information. The Salt Water Tackle Box, Box 263, East Falmouth, Mass. 02536 has a catalog (25 cents) with hundreds of salt water lures, rods, reels and accessories listed. F 'n' P Sales, Box 126, Milford, Conn. 06460 has a free catalog.

Some books to help you out. All are available from World Publications, Box 366, Mountain View, Calif. at the price listed* plus 25 cents postage. Write for a complete list.

How to Catch Salt Water Fish, Bill Wisner. A thorough study of the technical aspects of fishing. For 21 different species the author notes geographic distribution, feeding habits, seasonal migrations, and then goes on to describe how to rig your line and present your bait. 1973 Hb., 581 pp., ill., $8.95, (Doubleday).

Fishing the Pacific, Don Holm. A complete and up-to-date manual on fishing the western saltwater areas and marine fishes. 1972 Hb., 256 pp., ill., $6.95, (Winchester).

The Complete Book of Striped Bass Fishing, Henry Lyman and Frank Woolner. Techniques for catching striped bass on the Atlantic, Pacific, or Gulf. 1954 Hb., 384 pp., ill., $5.95, (Barnes).

Salt-water Game Fishing, Joe Brooks. America's most celebrated light-tackle fisherman reveals his angling secrets for taking the major game fish from boat or beach. Catch everything from perch to black marlin, 1968 Hb., 380 pp., ill., $10.95, (Harper & Row).

The Complete Book of Striped Bass, Nicholas Karas. Here's the book with everything the recreational angler needs—a complete description of the fish, its environment, its behavior, all the methods used to take it, tackle, boats, accessories and even cooking methods. 1974 Hb., 365 pp., ill., $10.00, (Winchester).

Flag Football

The rules of flag football are almost exactly the same as the rules of football as played by teams in the National Collegiate Athletic Association. The major difference is that in the former game the ballcarrier is stopped when one of his flags is detached. The ballcarrier may not in any way shield his flags from the opponents. Although blocking is permitted, the primary is to limit the amount of contact.

A flag football field is usually 40 yards wide, and 60 or 80 yards long. Often, lines are drawn across the width of the field at 10 yard intervals. A team is awarded a first down each time it crosses one of these lines. Teams usually consist of seven players. The quarterback cannot run with the ball (i.e., advance it across the line of scrimmage). A player can advance the ball only after receiving it via pass or hand-off from the quarterback. Every offensive player is eligible to catch a pass, regardless of his position. (Note: many rules are flexible—the number of players per team, the size of the field, etc., can be adapted as circumstance requires.)

Powderpuff

Picture a long, twisting broken-field run—the halfback continually eludes the defenders, and seems to traverse the width of the field at least three times before arriving at the goal line. Such pictures have a habit of lingering in the memory. I still remember every move O.J. Simpson made in his run which beat UCLA in 1967. In the past few years I have seen a number of these memorable runs, and the unusual fact is that some of the finest were executed by women.

Women's flag football is enjoying a tremendous boom on high school and college campuses. This type of football is widely known by the label "powderpuff," but the name may no longer be appropriate. Women's football is often anything but the dainty diversion which "powderpuff" suggests it to be. What was once laughable has become a serious and quite vigorous activity as women have improved the caliber of their play.

Until recent years the game of football was an exclusively male pastime. Most people thought women too weak and fragile to play such a rough game; it was thought that women would suffer numerous serious injuries. While this reasoning is doubtful, what is certain is that flag football has allowed women to play a game which is the closest approximation of tackle football. In flag football as in tackle football, a running attack can be as important as a passing attack. Touch football, however, is almost entirely a passing game as it is easy to touch a person who is running with the ball. But pulling a player's flag is almost as difficult as making a tackle.

Women's flag football continues to get more sophisticated each year. The players have shown that all they were lacking was an opportunity to play the game.

For additional information see touch football.

—**Steve Skolnik**

Steve Skolnik is involved in the intramural sports program at the University of California at Berkeley.

For More Information

One fine book is available on flag football. It is available from World Publications, Box 366, Mountain View, Calif. 94040 at the price listed* plus 25 cents postage.

Touch and Flag Football, Louis M. Marciani. Kids play touch and flag football all the time, and here is that missing ingredient—a practical, thoughtful guide for players and officials. 1975, 160 pp., ill., $8.95, (Barnes).

Fly Fishing

A brawling trout stream, rumbling over and around moss covered boulders, holds challenge for a fly fisherman. There lurk trout that feed on flying insects, nymphs, grubs and caterpillars that fall into the stream. A fly fisherman's challenge is to present the correct artificial fly in the right position and at an appropriate time to create enough deception to convince a trout that it is real and edible. Add to this the very light tackle used, the difficult conditions for landing a fish, plus one of nature's greatest fighters, and you have a fishing sport that gives brother trout a better than even break. Boiled down, this consistently adds up to the toughest form of fishing and presents new challenges with every stream.

Artificial replicas of a trout's natural food are tied on small hooks using feathers, various animal furs, synthetic yarns and threads, all of various hues. A skillful fly tyer, and most avid fly fishermen tie their own custom artificials, can use these materials to reproduce almost any kind of food that would interest a trout. From there it's a matter of depositing your Sulphur Dur, Light Cahill or Quill Gordon in the right part of the stream. In addition to the sport incurred from fly fishing, you will be one with nature, sharing intimately with flora, river, trout, water fowl and deer.

Why Fly Fish?

Catching a trout with an artificial fly is undoubtedly the most difficult form of angling. As a result, it is pursued by a group of purists that shun other forms of freshwater fishing. They prefer to be known as environmentalists, as well as fishermen. Why?

Millions of anglers clog the available fishing streams, but with proper conservation techniques there could be enough fish for millions more. Obviously, stream pollution has reduced both the fish population and the number of fishing streams, but overharvesting has resulted in the largest loss of trout.

Fly fishing enthusiasts tend to release all but a few of the trout they hook. While beginners are often carried away by the number of fish they can catch, experienced fly fishermen become enamored with technique and challenge. To them, the size of a fish matters little when compared to the difficulty of hooking and landing it, so keeping a trophy becomes irrelevant to most "real" fly anglers. Only one or two fish are kept each day for food.

Releasing a hooked trout is a delicate business, which if bungled will result in a dying fish better kept for food than released. Fish should never be handled if they are intended for release, because even light finger pressure will damage the sensitive and slick mucous membrane that covers a trout's body. Once the integrity of this defense system is breached, the trout is open to invasion from both aquatic parasites and disease bearing organisms. Usually this results in death within a few weeks, and brother trout will never again rise to a fly.

The only way to effectively release a trout without handling it is to grasp the base of a lightly barbed hook and gently twist it free while the fish is still in the water. This can be easily done with fly fishing gear while causing minimal damage to the mouth tissues of a trout. Unfortunately, other forms of freshwater angling are not so gentle.

Spinning presents one or more brutal treble hooks to a fish, each of which can tear away irreplaceable mouth tissue. When firmly implanted, these three pronged hooks are impossible to extract without a pair of pliers and a firm grasp on the doomed trout's body. It might be a better practice for spinning devotess to use only lures with a single hook, but unfortunately most are after a limit of fish instead of sport or challenge.

Bait fishing is an even bigger offender of the "release 'em" code. Trout tend to immediately swallow any sort of organic bait, and a hook deep in the fish's throat can never be extracted without fatal injury. An additional environmental hazard is presented by those anglers who use live minnows to lure in trout. These minnows are usually rough fish like carp, crappies or bullheads. If they fall off the hook and survive, this type of fish will quickly multiply and provide vigorous competition for sport fish. Tragically, I've even seen many thoughtless anglers dump unused live minnows into a lake or stream at the end of a day's fishing. It is little wonder that many formerly good trout fishing waters are now clogged with rough fish slowly killing off the trout population.

Most "real" fly fishermen keep only one or two fish each day for food. (Green)

Due to the fly fisherman's habit of safely releasing fish, there will be some trout for his descendants for generations to come. Perhaps if every freshwater angler could be converted over to fly fishing, there could be a multitude of trout for all time!

—Jeff Stephens

Jeff Stephens is a self-described "fishing bum" from Denver. To support his habit he works at ski resorts during the winter, employment which indulges his second passion, hotdog skiing.

For More Information

There is one bi-monthly magazine dealing specifically with fly fishing, but we haven't seen it. *Fly Fisherman*, Manchester, Vt. 05254. The Federation of Fly Fishermen, 4500 Beach Dr. S.W., Seattle, Wash. 98116, is devoted to the promotion of fly fishing as the most enjoyable and sportsmanlike method of fishing. For other information, see Freshwater Fishing, Saltwater Fishing, and Tournament Casting.

Here are some good books on fly fishing. All are available from World Publications, Box 366, Mountain View, Calif. 94040 at the price listed* plus 25 cents each postage.

Fly Fishing for Trout, Richard Talleur. A beautiful book for the adult beginner. Equally valuable as a practical guide or for at-home reading. 1974 Hb., 272 pp., ill., $10.00, (Winchester).

Simplified Fly Fishing, S.R. Slaymaker. Guaranteed to have the beginner on the water and fishing with flies in half an hour. Covers everything from the basics to using advanced equipment. 1969 Hb., 160 pp., ill., $7.95, (Harper & Row).

Sports Illustrated Fly Fishing, Vernon S. Hidy and eds. of *Sports Illustrated.* Straightforward, factual guide to the fundamentals of fly fishing. Describes the nature of a trout's diet, then discusses stream characteristics, fundamentals of casting, tackle, and the techniques of fly fishing. 1972 Hb. & Ppb., 93 pp., ill., $4.95/$1.95, (Lippincott).

Fly Fishing Digest, Bill Wallace. The complete, modern, useful guide to fly fishing. Full discussion of new methods, equipment and tackle, in plain and simple language, backed up by over 300 photos and drawings, show the average fisherman just how easy and interesting it is to learn. 1973 Ppb., 256 (oversize) pp., ill., $4.95, (Digest Books).

Art Flick's Master Fly-Tying Guide, Art Flick, et al. Nine masters of fly-tying disclose in precise and easy-to-understand directions and photographs how to tie their patterns. "A book that belongs in every fly-tyer's library."—Sports Illustrated. 1972 Ppb., 200 (oversize) pp., ill., $5.95, (Crown).

Hatches: A Complete Guide to Fishing the Hatches of North American Trout Streams, Caucci & Nastasi. Incredibly comprehensive guide to dealing with the hatch in all kinds of situations, dusk, different seasons, when the waters are high, or when they recede—and knowing all the insects that breed in these areas—basically how to deal with the hatch in the quickest manner, and go on to the catching. 1975 Hb., 320 (oversize) pp., ill., $15.95, (Compara-Hutch).

Fly Fishing Strategy, Richards & Swisher. Concentrates on the strategies of fly fishing across the country, east and west, and for lake and salt water fishing as well as stream fishing. 1975, 200 (oversize) pp., ill., $10.00, (Crown).

Flying

What in hell am I doing here? Why didn't I study those books? What if the engine quits? I need more practice! The ground looks so far away!

With great effort I force myself to concentrate on the task at hand – to utilize what I've been taught and do whatever it takes to get my feet on solid ground again with my body intact. Wiggling the controls produces results! But if I move them too far the wrong way, I'll fall like a stone to the unyielding earth 500 feet below and end up a smoldering heap.

These memories of my first solo flight when, with a mere seven or eight hours total flight experience, I wrestled a helicopter in mid-air and brought it down both safely and unassisted. (For additional information on helicopters, see Rotorcraft.)

Sharing the feeling won't be easy but I'll try. It's not unlike what you might feel if you were sealed up in a huge Mason jar, suspended by a piano wire from a cable stretching across the Grand Canyon, and all you need to do to ensure a soft touchdown on the distant ground is maintain a headstand on a beachball for a mere 20 minutes, while performing a juggling act.

In the years since, I've flown airplanes and gliders in addition to the helicopter and, having gained some experience and understanding, find myself much more comfortable in the air. However, the sense of achievement I felt then after the study and struggle still satisfies, despite much ego abuse suffered from the harsh words of my flight instructor.

Basically, whether one is involved in flying for sport or business, there is only pleasure flying, because it is a pleasurable and gratifying way to spend one's time. Everyone who flies does it for the enjoyment it brings. Even the airline pilot or instructor began by spending his own time and money for the rewards it offered long before there was any possibility of financial return.

However one defines the love of flying, some of the sensations felt are similar to those provided by other sports. There is the thrill of trying something new and ever challenging. The freedom of escape from the nine to five workday into a world with different confines, where total concentration and involvement with something we thoroughly enjoy become reality. There are demands upon both mind and body as one applies his knowledge to changing circumstances.

Competitive individuals can attempt to set new world's records, participate in air races, powderpuff derbies, or simply work to perfect a particular maneuver. Others spend their time restoring antique aircraft and entering them in shows, or joining in club activities. There is a fraternal nature to the aviation world; those with more experience are always happy to explain things to a novice.

On a strictly practical basis, flying not only provides the advantages of quick transportation, but can be a sport offering a means to an end—namely financial gain. Employment runs the gamut from aerial photography to passenger transport to helicopter usage in rescue or logging operations, and, of course, the most rewarding – passing on one's knowledge to students.

Like most other sports, flying requires coordination. Few of the others, however, allow so narrow a margin for error, with such rapid and irreversible consequences resulting from mistakes. Also, consider that the pilot has ultimate responsibility for, and control over, not only his own destiny, but perhaps the lives of many others – whether they be passengers or people on the ground below. It is for this reason that flying is the only federally licensed and controlled sport. It has rigid requirements for the physical condition of both machine and operator, and high standards for the knowledge and experience levels of the pilot.

I mentioned earlier that some of the sensations flying affords might be like those of other sports. It supplies some benefits, though, that nothing else can duplicate, and which make it unique. Among these are: the strange and almost indescribable experience of flight, the unequaled feeling of actually hanging upon the air, the conscious perception that one is viewing earth's crinkled face from above – almost god-like, and controlling gravity – defying forces with one's thoughts and limbs in a manner considered absolutely impossible at the turn of the century. And there is more. Sharing with one you love a warm Sunday afternoon of golden hills, billowing clouds, softly buffeting winds, and visits "to far off lands and distant shores – so many friends to meet." There is nothing else like it.

There are antique fly-ins at Merced and Watsonville, Calif., and many other small airports around the country The city of Oshkosh, Wisc., just hosted its 23rd annua Experimental Aircraft Association convention in July anc August. In early December each year you can attend the Bahamas Flying Treasure Hunt at Nassau. Prizes include a $10,000-half-acre home site at San Andros! And if you wan to stay closer to home, the Reno Air Races are fantastic

The "flying bug" is highly contagious. Orville and Wilbu Wright started it in December of 1903 when they made th first manned flight in a self-powered, heavier-than-air machine That particular "flight" lasted 12 seconds and covered 120 feet There have been countless changes in airplane constructio since then and we have witnessed amazing technologica progress. Since that first flight, only one average life span ha elapsed and we have seen manned spacecraft place a human (o unchanged basic construction from the Wrights) on the moon Flying could almost be considered a yardstick of man' progress.

Upon witnessing one of the Wright brothers' early flights Maj. B.F.S. Baden-Powell, president of the Aeronautica Society of Great Britain said: "That Wilbur Wright is in posses sion of a power which controls the fate of nations is beyon dispute." The ensuing World Wars have obviously proved tha but the Wrights were into flying for the love of it.

When offered funding for research, Wilbur refused i writing: "For the present we would prefer not to accept it fo the reason that if we did not feel that the time spent in thi work was a dead loss in a financial sense, we would be unab to resist the temptation to devote more time than our [b cycle] business."

We cannot know precisely what Orville was thinking as h

The goal of man since the time of Icarus has been to fly like the birds. With modern technology, he can fly better. (Air Progress Magazine)

launched his 605-pound craft into the air and manipulated the controls for 12 seconds of flight into history. But we can share his feelings on his first solo flight, during which he was alone among all men who ever lived on this planet. I shared some of them on my first solo and so can you. Give it a try!

–Jonathan Walker

Jonathan Walker is a pilot with SFO Airlines, Inc. of San Francisco and a member of the Air Line Pilot Association. He was a combat helicopter pilot and taught student pilots at the Army Primary Helicopter School in Texas.

For More Information

There are several magazines covering flying. Here are a few we have seen followed by a few others we haven't seen. We still are leaving out several others but these should get your started and these listed are the bigger ones.

Private Pilot, 248 S. Robertson Blvd., Beverly Hills, Ca. 90211. Published monthly at $7.95 per year. They say, "For the aircraft owner and pilot who does his flying both for fun and business."

Plane & Pilot, 631 Wilshire Blvd., Santa Monica, Ca. 90401. Published monthly at $9.95 per year. A recent issue carried articles like "Tips on Cross-Country Flying," "Flying Higher and Faster," and "Where to Fly in Winter."

Here are the ones we have not seen but probably should be listed.

Sport Flying, 7950 Deering Ave., Canoga Park. Ca. 91304. Published monthly at $7.98 per year.

AOPA Pilot, Air Rights Bldg., 7315 Wisconsin Ave., Washington D.C. 20014. Published monthly.

Sport Aviation, Box 229, Hales Corners, Wisc. 53130. Published monthly.

Some of the major organizations and clubs include:

National Pilots Association, 806 15th St., N.W., Washington, D.C. 20005.

Aircraft Owners and Pilots Association, same address as AOPA Pilot Magazine.

Experimental Aircraft Association, 11311 West Forest Home Ave., Franklin, Wisc. 53132.

National Business Aircraft Association, 425 13th Street N.W., Suite 401, Washington D.C. 20004

The best place to find out about equipment is at your local community airport, but you might write: Sporty's Pilot Shop, Clermont Country Airport, Batavia, Ohio 45103. Their free catalog includes plotters, chart cases, study guides, books, charts, radios and watches plus more. Ask for their free flight test guide. They say they are the "world's largest Pilot shop." Or if you are looking for skis for your plane write FluiDyne Engineering Corp., 5916 Olson Highway, Mpls., Minn. 55422. Free literature is available on request. The Stevens Company, 631 Wilshire Blvd., Suite 202, Santa Monica, Ca. 90401 makes 3-D aero relief maps. As they say, "gives a preview in miniature of the sight you'll see from aloft."

Here are some books that will be of interest. For additional information turn to Soaring or Ballooning. All books are available from World Publications, Box 366, Mountain View, Calif. 94040 at the price listed* plus 25 cents each postage.

Anyone Can Fly, Jules Bergman. If you always wanted to learn how to fly an airplane but never really got started, then this book might help you get up in the air faster than you thought possible. 1964 Hb., 225 pp., ill., $7.95, (Doubleday).

Instrument Flying Guide, Robert T. Smith. Under present F.A.A. rules, every student pilot must learn to maintain control of his plane while flying blind. This book explains instrument flying as a relatively simple skill that can be learned with sound instruction and a few hours practice. 1974 Ppb., $3.95, (Crown).

Pilot's Weather Guide, Lindy Boyes. A fuzzy subject made clear in few words and lots of illustrations. Fronts and air masses; significance of cloud and wind sequences, isobars, dew points, lapse rates; meaning of wind gradients; how to read teletype sequences and weather maps; making your own forecasts. Boyes reduces the complex to its simplest terms. Ppb. $3.95, (Crown).

Racing Planes Guide, Joe Christy. A must for the racing plane enthusiast! Covers all planes available, which are more suitable to racing, priming your plane, techniques and strategies. 1963 Ppb., 140 pp., ill., $3.95, (Crown).

Wager with the Wind, James Greiner. The incredible feats of a veteran Alaskan bush pilot (Don Sheldon) will thrill readers who enjoy true adventure. The true story of one of the few pilots who can safely transport climbers and their gear to high glaciers from which they launch their attacks on the summits. Recommended for young adults. 1974 Hb., 256 pp., ill., $8.95, (Rand McNally).

The Skyracers: Speed Kings of Aviation's Golden Age, Joseph F. Hood. Fascinating stories and photos of the speedsters of the '20s and '30s who pushed the airplanes of that period to the limit of their performance, thus paving the way for commercial aircraft of the future. 1969 Hb., 160 pp., ill., $4.95, (Grosset & Dunlap).

Stick and Rudder: An Explanation of the Art of Flying. Wolfgang Langewiesche. A former test pilot for Cessna Aircraft Co., Langewiesche goes beyond textbookish "theories of flight" and introduces the novice pilot to the art of flying, or how to feel what the plane is doing with clear illustrations of "what really goes on" when he flies. 1944 Hb., 389 pp., ill., $9.95, (McGraw-Hill).

Folk Dancing

Folk dancing as a recreational or participation physical activity is within the reach of almost everyone. Along with swimming it is considered to be one of the most evenly balanced of all physical activities. In most sports a particular group of muscles will be exercised more than others. With a good variety of folk dances all muscular activity will be distributed equally to the general needs of most human daily activity.

Over the years the rhythmic interpretation of daily life in the form of body movements has developed into what we now call folk dancing. In most cases this activity is accompanied by music. In almost all cases it has been accompanied by some form of rhythm producing aid such as the voice, clapping of the hands, sticks clapped together, drums, cymbals, castanets or any noise-making device as well as instrumental music.

The history of folk dancing goes back beyond the recollection of modern man. Undoubtedly any form of pre-human that existed carried on some form of rhythmic activity that would be the precursor of folk dancing. It has been noted among animals that there are ritualistic "dances" performed in many instances, such as courtship rituals, food gathering rituals and simply rhythmic response to a happy occasion such as a colt gamboling in a field.

Today folk dancing is for some a refined stage art and for many it is simply a fulfilling recreational activity. To all who participate it is both interesting and fun to do as well as an extremely good way to keep physically fit.

—**Max Horn**

Max Horn has for 30 years been a teacher of folk dancing. Together with his wife June, he teaches in the San Francisco Bay Area.

Folk Dancing Today

Folk dancing can be divided into several levels of authenticity or ethnic quality. Each level of authenticity will have its protagonists (there are good and bad points to be considered for each of these lines of reasoning). In general, we can say all forms of the dance are good physical activity. It therefore becomes a matter of choice to the individual what they may prefer to do.

- *Ethnic Folk Dancing* is best defined as any form of dance following the form of any one particular range or group of peoples. Many clubs will limit themselves to a particular type of ethnic dance: Israeli, Greek, Slavic, German, etc.

- *International Folk Dancing* is usually thought of as dances from all nations. In practice most of these dances will be ethnic dances but there will be a few "round" dances and some "ballroom" dances included in most international folk dance programs.

- *Square Dancing* has become a well-defined group of dances done in square formation to the prompting of a caller. There seems to be a trend in recent months for the square dance clubs to also include a few "contra" dances in their programs.

- *Round Dancing* has been staging an upsurge in popularity. These are dances recently choreographed to good beat music from the '30s and '40s or any other catchy tune. These are simply a large number of steps and patterns put to the music and often repeated in various forms throughout the dance or from dance to dance. Round dances originally were a part of the square dance program but have evolved into a major part of some programs.

Ethnic or international folk dancing can be broken down into the type of dance by the area or region of its origin. To divide the dances simply by nationality would require a very large library of historical documents to authenticate who belongs to what nation, or when that nation existed. A simpler way is to divide the dances into regional forms. Each region may represent some easily identifiable nation but as often as not the regional boundaries will cross national lines as we know them today. An example of this would be the Basque dances. These people span the border areas of France and Spain and even into Portugal. Conversely, Rumanian dances can be divided into three general types or main divisions, all within the boundaries of Rumania as we know it today.

Body movements and actions in folk dancing can be identified in many different ways for teaching purposes. With finite study of movement and action it is possible to classify any movement as it may occur in several different situations. Thus we may have a movement or action in French dancing that is also common to Russian dancing except that it may take a slightly different form. The simple act of placing the hand on the hip will have many different forms. In Central Europe (Germany, Holland, etc.) it will be found usually as a fist on the hip. In Eastern Europe this same action may be a loose fist on the hip. As you proceed toward Russian and down into Rumania it will appear more often as a hand on the hip–fingers forward. The reasons for these regional changes in stance, action and gesture is ingrained into the people of that region. It is all part of who they are and what they are. In folk dancing for the avid participant these things become interesting subjects for study.

Today folk dancing takes many forms. Ethnic folk dancing as such is being rapidly diluted with modern interpretations. With the advent of the stage production of folk dancing many choreographers are creating new dances, some using the old steps and music but all too many creating completely new dances and music to suit their own whims. The best example of this would be the hundreds of Israeli "folk dances." There are many dances of the Israeli or Jewish people from all over the world, but very few would be indigenous to the land we now call Israel. The current fad for new Israeli dances has produced several new choreographers who have selected music and developed dances, fun to do, good rhythms, and with a distinctly Israeli flavor. These could hardly be called "folk dances" in the truest sense of the word but they are nevertheless "folk dances" in that they represent the feeling of a particular group of people.

Each nation or race of people has their own folk dance. We here in the United States even have ours, commonly called "square dancing." Square dancing as it is done today has but little resemblance to the original square dancing of our early settlers of the Blue Ridge Mountains and the hills of

"Over the years the rhythmic interpretation of daily life in the form of body movements has developed into what we now call folk dancing. In most cases this activity is accompanied by music. Today it is for some a refined stage art and for many a fulfilling recreational activity." (Linscotts)

Kentucky. In those historical settings the square dance was a recreational activity carried on in someone's parlor or in the church social hall, usually to the tune of one or more instruments such as the fiddle or the banjo. It consisted of some 35 to 50 basic movements that were repeated in many different combinations. In many cases the square was used only one or times in the evening of fun and parlor games and most of the evening was taken up with quadrilles, round dances and simple ballroom dancing. The highlight of the evening was usually the grand march in which a simple dance or marching rhythm was played while the party goers marched around to patterns on the floor and exchanged partners in geometric regularity or to the prompting or calls of the leader or musician.

The work of compiling folk dancing materials has continued over the years but only in the past 30 years can we say there has been concerted effort expended. During the depression years the US government put forth some effort in their cultural programs to foster the study of folk arts, including folk dancing. At about the same time Henry Ford created a commission to study folk dancing to preserve some of the dances for future generations. There were many small groups started during the late '30s and immediately following World War II for the purpose of preserving and learning folk dances. One of those groups was Changs International Folk Dancers in San Francisco. Some of the people active in Changs were also exhibition dancers at the Worlds Fair on Treasure Island in the San Francisco Bay in 1930. From these beginnings a need for uniform dancing materials was realized. An organization was eventually developed to research the dances and choreograph them so that they could be done by anyone wishing to learn and so that large groups of people could join in a dance together, all doing the same dance.

Through the years there have always been those who were proficient at doing the dances we now call folk dances. From these people who have remembered these dances or written down notes on how to do them there has developed the nucleus of our libraries of folk dances. There are thousands of individual dances with their recorded music available from various sources. For the folk dance teacher one of the most difficult tasks is to decide to what limits they should work.

Eventually the Folk Dance Federation of California was born. This organization is dedicated to the research, preservation and publication of folk dances and the furthering of the folk dancing movement in California. It is probably the most closely knit group of folk dance clubs in the United States at this time. There are larger groups, ethnic groups, square dance groups, modern dance clubs, and too many forms of dance associations to mention but none that stick more closely to the purpose of preserving international folk dances.

Today many nations foster the preservation of their own heritage of the dance. We here in the United States are fortunate in that we have many organizations interested in preserving the dances of their forebearers from all over the world. Unfortunately, except for local recreation departments, there is little effort being expended by our government toward this end. Many individual clubs working alone or in groups throughout the US are performing this task. We can only hope that the interest of these people will continue and that our heritage which is really the heritage of the entire world will be at least partly preserved in these activities.

—Max Horn

For More Information

There are no commercial magazines devoted exclusively to folk dancing but a number of folklore and folkarts magazines do exist. One of the best is *Viltis,* Box 1226, Denver, Colo. 80201, published bi-monthly at $5.00 per year. A couple of other regional publications are *Folk Dance Scene,* 13250 Ida Ave., Los Angeles, Calif. 90066 published monthly at $3.00 per year. *New York Folk Dance News,* 777 Foster Ave., Brooklyn, N.Y. 11230 which is published bi-monthly at $3.50 per year. *The Dancer,* 12505 N.E. Fremont St., Portland, Ore. 97230 does not just cover folk dancing but each issue has some good information in it. Published monthly at $2.00 per year. A helpful organization is the National Dance Association, 1201 Sixteenth St., N.W., Washington D.C., 20036. They have a lot of information available through their offices.

Football

Football requires two teams and an inflated ball that is oblong and narrow at the ends. The team that controls the ball is called the offense: it tries to score. The other team is the defense: it defends the goal. A kickoff starts the game and the receiving team becomes the offense. It tries to gain 10 yards in four tries by running or passing the ball, forward or laterally. If it fails to gain the 10 yards, the ball is turned over to the other team who gets four tries, or downs. When the ball crosses the opponents' goal line a team scores a touchdown, which is worth six points. The scoring team gets an extra chance to earn one or two more points by a conversion: one point for kicking the ball over the crossbar and between the goalposts; two points for running or passing the ball over the goal line. A field goal (kicked from the playing field) is worth three points and a safety (when a team tackles an opponent behind his own goal line) is worth two points.

Teams set up in various formations and run intricate patterns designed to surprise or confuse the opposition. For the offense, formations like the wishbone, I, pro, or shotgun are common; many defenses use colors or numbers to designate their formations. While the casual Sunday afternoon game may appear more like a mad dash and rumble, the pro and college players execute highly sophisticated and guarded plays that each and every player must memorize.

For information on a more recreational game, check the flag and touch football sections in this book.

A Word from Gale Sayers

My rise to success in football was the result of a gradual progression. While at the high school level it was mostly fun, when I got to college I found that there was quite a bit more work involved. Still, after I adapted to the higher level of play and learned the more complicated technicalities, I found that I enjoyed it even more. At that time my ultimate

Winning football teams can consistently gain five or six yards each first down to keep a scoring drive alive. There are far more offensive possibilities with second and five than with second and nine, a situation that virtually dictates a pass. To get good first down yardage, a skillful quarterback will mix his plays in an effort to keep the defense guessing. (Johnson).

"One of the great advantages of football is that it builds an ability to try and do one's best—something that will be of use an entire lifetime. When you lose very badly it takes a lot of character to say, 'I did my best. This is only one ball game. I'll try equally hard the next time.' More importantly, football teaches you how to get along with people. It is a team sport, and cooperation is a must." (Drennan)

goal was to play professional football, and when I finally made it to the pro ranks I was quite overwhelmed at first. All of a sudden I was playing against some of the top stars – Johnny Unitas, Lenny Moore, and Sam Hunt – players whom I admired very much.

All through my successful football career I've been able to say that I've been very lucky. I've always had a good line in front of me and I have to say that 60 percent of the credit for a running back's success should be given to his linemen. No matter how good a running back is there's no way he could ever make it past the line of scrimmage without someone in front of him. Even if he has a bad line he must have somebody between him and the defensive players to provide a little daylight, a hole he can get through. After that the running back is more or less on his own, but from his position five yards deep in the backfield to a point three yards on the other side of the line he depends almost entirely on his blocking to provide him with the opportunity to use all the speed, feints and great moves he is known for. Honestly, I must give a lot of credit to the line.

The traits that make for a great running back are all God-given. Of course, I always tried to get myself in the best possible condition; but as for running, I never had had to practice any of my moves, it's all natural. I always knew instinctively what to do while carrying the ball. I was blessed with excellent peripheral vision and was aware of where the other players were when I was running down the field. Somehow, I just knew the right move to make; it wasn't something I could improve upon with practice. Before a game, I never considered what I would do. It just happened at the moment I met an opposing player. This is why I insist that my ability is God-given.

From my own experience, I would say that the only person on a football team who must have natural ability is the running back. I think a receiver, if he has a fair amount of speed, can practice his moves – catching the ball in his hands, and keeping his eye on the ball. With practice, he can become very proficient at these skills. A lineman can practice taking drop-steps while going back for pass protection. In the same way, a defensive back or linebacker can practice backpeddling. Throwing the ball through a tire is great practice for the quarterback. On the other hand, it's difficult for a running back to practice faking a man out; in fact, it's impossible. You either have it or you don't.

In general, I would urge all football players to practice their skills, but it might be very difficult for the running back who doesn't have this natural ability. He might be a good running back if he has speed; if he's tough he can be good. It is impossible, though, to be a great running back if you don't have the innate ability.

Football can make a fine career, but for the aspiring professional, I have a few words of advice. Top football, like any pro sport, is not a long-term proposition. The average playing life of professional football players is only 4.5 years. For this reason it is important to take advantage of the opportunities that come along with big-league sports: be considerate toward the business contacts that you meet; the money that you might eventually make – invest it wisely. While being involved in sport, try to get a second job that you can make into your life's work. Probably your studies in college will determine the type of work, so take them seriously. If you make it to the top ranks in football in the meantime, then that's icing on the cake.

Try to remember that football can be the means to an end, but never the end itself. Don't plan on playing professional football for 20 years at the top because it doesn't happen that way. Take advantage of every opportunity that comes along.

One of the great advantages of football is that it builds an ability to try and do one's best – something that will be of use an entire lifetime. When you lose very badly it takes a lot of character to say, "I did my best. This is only one ball game. I'll try equally hard the next time." More importantly, football teaches you how to get along with people. It is a team sport, and cooperation is a must.

I can honestly say that my biggest thrill in life has been my involvement in football. For many years I played the game at a variety of levels, and I enjoyed every minute of it. I loved everything about it – the pain, the injury, the victory and the defeat. I doubt if many people can say they did something for 20 years of their life while feeling every moment was worthwhile. I'm very lucky to be able to say that I have.

–Gale Sayers

After becoming a two-time All-American halfback at the University of Kansas, Gale Sayers went on to play seven successful years for the Chicago Bears. Known for his swift running style, as a rookie he scored 22 touchdowns for an NFL season record and tied the record for the most touchdowns in one game with six. Gale was selected to the NFL All-League team five times before he retired in 1971 because of knee ailments.

For More Information

Football is covered very well in newspapers and many general magazines. *Sports Illustrated* and *Sport* magazine do a very good job on the sport. Also, *Sporting News* (address in baseball section) does a good job. All three of these magazines can be found on most newsstands.

There are several others but the one we really like is *Pro Football Weekly*, 5606 N. Western Ave., Chicago, Ill. 60659. Published weekly during the season and monthly the rest of the year for a total of 32 issues. The cost is $15.00 per year. Newspaper format with complete coverage of all aspects of professional football. A couple of others are *Football News*, 19830 Mack Ave., Grosse Point, Mi. 48236 and *Football Digest*, 1020 Church St., Evanston, Ill. 60201.

For professional football there is one major organization: The National Football League, 410 Park Ave., New York, N.Y. 10022. Within the League there is the the National Football Conference and the American Football Conference. Each conference is broken up into an eastern, central and western division. For the younger player there is Pop Warner Junior League Football, 1315 Walnut St., Ste. 606, Philadelphia, Pa. 19107.

Equipment can be very easily obtained by visiting your local sport shop. And if you are playing on a team, equipment will probably be supplied.

Here are a few books that will be of interest. All are available from World Publications, Box 366, Mountain View, Calif. 94040 at the price listed* plus 25 cents each postage.

Inside Defensive Football, Dick Butkus. The greatest linebacker of modern football has written this guide for beginning linemen and linebackers. 1971 Hb. & Ppb., 96 (oversize) pp., ill., $7.95/$3.95, (Regnery).

Quarterbacking, Joe Theismann. "This is the most complete quarterbacking book I have ever read." Ted Marchibroda, Head Coach, The Baltimore Colts. Written by the Notre Dame All-American quarterback, it analyzes and instructs as only a champion can. 1975 Hb. & Ppb., 108 (oversize) pp., ill., $8.95/ $4.95, (St. Martins).

Football Rules in Pictures, Schiffer & Duroska, eds. Devoted to interpreting and clarifying the fundamental rules of football, this is an important aid to the player who is learning the game. Through illustrations and explanations, he learns what can and cannot be done eliminating the chance of a needless penalty. 1964 (rev. 1974) Ppb., 80 (oversize) pp., ill., $1.95, (Grosset & Dunlap).

Pro Football, U.S.A., Hal Higdon. Forty of the country's outstanding football player's from the NFL talk with candor on the fine points of playing their positions and the strategy of the game, including Johnny Unitas, Joe Namath, and more. 1968 Hb., 312 pp., ill., $6.95, (Putnam).

Football Coaching, John H. McKay. The head football coach of the University of Southern California reveals football philosophy and techniques, from practice to plays of USC that helped his team win ten games without a loss, and go on to win the Rose Bowl. Covers every facet of football with the understanding of a man who knows and loves it. 1966 Hb., 239 pp., ill., $10.60, (Ronald).

Coaching Youth League Football, John Friend, et al. Ideal coaching manual for the volunteer coach who has been away from the game for a while and, naturally, has forgotten some details of the game. This book covers everything with a multitude of clear pictures and factual, down-to-earth instruction for teaching kids to have fun playing football right. 1974 Ppb. 128 pp., ill., $1.95, (Ath. Inst.).

Youth League Football: Player's Edition, John Friend, et al. Directed towards the first-time football leaguer, this guide is a thoughtful, clear look at all the fundamentals of football jammed with excellent pictures and detailed instruction geared for the young football player. 1975 Ppb., 114 pp., ill., $1.50, (Ath. Inst.).

How to Coach Football's Attacking Defenses, Drew Tallman. This "encyclopedia of defensive strategy" as one coach put it, explains all the defensive movements through the necessary alignments fundamentals, techniques, angles, secondary adjustments with every point and maneuver explained in complete detail. 1973 Hb., 242 pp., ill., $9.95, (Prentice Hall).

Explosive Muscular Power for Championship Football, John

Jesse. Excellent pre, during and post-season training manual for players who wish to develop the three physical qualifications for football: strength, explosive power, and muscular bulk. 1968 Ppb., 94 pp., ill., $1.95, (Athletic Press).

Pro Football's Kicking Game, Goerge Sullivan. In recent years the place-kicker or punter has gained an increasing prominence in pro football, and this new book examines this phenomenon. Explains in depth why kicking has taken over, what it takes to be an outstanding punter, techniques of blocking kicks, and kick returning. Great place-kickers and punters of the past and present are profiled. 1973 Hb., 144 pp., ill., $4.50, (Dodd Mead).

Pro Football's Passing Game, George Sullivan. The forward pass is football's most electrifying play. Here is a discussion of the forward pass – when it became a part of the game, the passers who use it and how, what defense there is against it. Noted passing plays are analyzed and diagrammed, the strategies of each explained. 1972 Hb., 140 pp., ill., $4.50, (Dodd Mead).

Linebacker, George Sullivan. Presents the inside story of pro football's linebackers. This illustrated history captures the tensions and trials of modern defense in action. 1974 Hb., 124 pp., ill., $4.95, (Dodd, Mead).

Offensive Football, Gale Sayers. One of the greatest running backs in collegiate and professional football discusses the intricacies and strategies of effective football offenses. 1972 Hb., ill., $8.95, (Atheneum).

The Official Encyclopedia of Football, Roger Treat. This volume brings the fan and player every fact and figure and personality in football. 1974 (rev.) Hb., 723 pp., ill., $13.95, (Barnes).

Inside Quarterbacking, Len Dawson. Written especially for the young players, with all basics of playing the position expertly covered. 1972 Hb. & Ppb., 88 (oversize) pp., ill., $7.95/$3.95, (Regnery).

George Allen's New Handbook of Football Drills, George Allen. One of the nation's greatest coaches shows over 300 of the greatest drills for building and strengthening your body for better football. 1974 Hb., 240 pp., ill., $10.95, (Prentice Hall).

I Am Third, Gale Sayers. The autobiography of the great running back of the Chicago Bears. Well illustrated with photos of the author's private and professional lives. 1970 Hb., 256 pp. ill., $6.95, (Viking).

Namath: My Son Joe, Rose Namath Szolnoki & Bill Kushner. This is the kind of biography only a loving mother could write; it's different and it's fun. Here's Joe Namath – boy, youth, man, superman – seen through the affectionate but undazzled eyes of his mother. 1975 Hb., 192 pp., ill., $7.95, (Oxmore).

The First 50 Years: The Story of the NFL, Bob Oates, et al. A beautiful celebration of the first 50 years of the National Football League and football in general, in incredible color and black and white shots with moving descriptions. Features all the players, strategies, records and uniforms that made up the last 50 years. 1969 Hb., 256 (oversize) pp., ill., $15.95, (Simon & Schuster).

I'll Always Get Up, Larry Brown with William Gildea. From childhood and school days to college and pro football recruiting, this is the dramatic and sometimes touching story of Larry Brown, the star running back of the Washington Redskins, and of his emergence from a Pittsburgh ghetto to become the idol of football. 1973 Hb., 192 pp., ill., $6.95, (Simon & Schuster).

Foraging

Foraging is the oldest sport for it is nearly as old as life itself. It began more than a billion years ago when the first mobile living organisms appeared on earth and moved about searching for the best living conditions. From this ancient beginning foraging habits evolved as organisms, mainly animals, evolved. As the animal body and brain became ever more sophisticated and specialized, so did foraging change from trial and error behavior to the highly organized, purposeful hunt of the cougar or the eagle.

Even the activities of the grazing and browsing animals, much less mindful than those of the hunter, are organized. To the human eye, a deer may appear to be wandering aimlessly about, nibbling at various plants here and there. The deer is actually following a previously established broad pathway through its home range—a pathway for foraging that the deer knows will lead to food. This pathway varies with the seasons because of the seasonal influence on the availability of preferred foods. It may also vary due to increasing or decreasing browsing competition from other deer or grazing animals. Since the plant eaters are the food supply for the meat eaters, the cougar's pathway for foraging will coincide and change with that of the deer, and if all goes well, all of the foragers will feed.

To survive at foraging, these animals have highly developed sensory perception. They are all alert, have enormous patience, can be silent when necessary, are instinctively methodical, are keenly observant, can listen to the sounds of nature, are instinctively willing to expend great amounts of effort to satisfy their needs, and they are all curious.

Over the eons of foraging history humans have also highly developed these abilities, but they have developed most highly something else, something that helps set them apart from other animals. Humans have developed a fund of knowledge about nature which could be passed on from generation to generation. Because of this knowledge humans could reasonabily predict the future from the events of the past. With an air of detachment, humans could remove themselves from the present and prepare beforehand for the foraging venture. As a result, humans have carried the sport of foraging to its highest development, having devised tools (including weapons) for specific foraging tasks—digging sticks for collecting edible roots and bulbs; baskets for collecting seeds; waterproof skins, bladders and pottery for collecting water; nets, wires, traps, spears, arrows and other tools for collecting game.

With the advent of agriculture 10 or 12 thousand years ago the survival need for foraging diminished, but the instinctive need did not. Now, instead of using our enormous ability of detachment for foraging, we used it to separate ourselves from nature, the result being the situation in which most humans find themselves today.

Knowledgeable foraging is immensely pleasurable, satisfying

the drive of one of life's most ancient instincts. Most of us know what fun it is to gather pine cones, collect different leaf specimens, or to pick wildflowers. Such activities are meager attempts to satisfy the drive to forage. Leave the wildflowers unpicked, for they look much better on their natural stalks than stuffed, wilted, into a vase. Leave the pine cones on the ground, for they are needed there as a part of the natural cycle of forest life. Let the leaves remain on the tree, for they provide its very sustenance. Develop once again your age old sensory perceptions, now almost forgotten under the crush of social pressures. Start living in nature—it can be done almost anywhere—learn what it is you are looking at, for nothing is more satisfying than walking down a trail, seeing things you know are edible, and knowing that here you could not only survive, but live.

—**Don Kirk**

Don Kirk is the author of **Wild Edible Plants.** *His "Eat 'Em Wild" column is a regular feature of* **Down River** *magazine.*

Behind the Myths

Myths and false ideas, all of them dangerous, abound about eating off the wild. Much of this fiction is merely personally damaging, but at least one misconception held by many people, and dangerous to all, is that one has the right, perhaps even the moral obligation, to eat the wild things to effect a return to the earth, to rebuild one's primal relationship with the land, now lost forever beneath asphalt and concrete. Nothing could by further from the truth.

It is this writer's opinion that humans have a moral obligation to not live off the fat of the land. The land is not fat. Once there were sufficiently few people that the wild edibles, plant and animal, could provide support. That day is long gone. Now there are far too many people, everywhere, for even one person to live in clear conscience entirely on nature's produce. Nature needs help, not hindrance, understanding, not ravaging.

With the dubious exception of the insects, which most people refuse to eat anyway, no wild edible, plant or animal, should be harvested wholesale anytime, anywhere. Subsistence harvesting of wild edibles, especially plants, should be done only in emergency, when one is in the position of needing the wild foods to maintain reasonably normal levels of health and strength. Besides, any good outdoorsman knows that when lost in the wilds, food is of no immediate importance. Shelter from exposure, and water are the primary needs. In most cases, even the need for water is not as pressing as the need for shelter.

If you are newly lost, food should be the last thing on your mind. Your stomach will, of course, clearly remind you of your normal eating schedule, and you may experience actual stomach pain as that organ more or less tries to digest a nonexistent meal. You are in no immediate danger of starvation for the average American has enough extra fat in his body to sustain him through many days of no food at all.

While the foregoing is designed to discourage the ripoff of nature, it is not to say that nature is a museum piece, to be left on display only. We humans are as much a part of nature as prairie dogs, and in some ways similar. We have needs that nature can satisfy, and to have extensive knowledge of edible plants is to make oneself feel very much at home in wild places, nowhere a stranger.

Is it edible? Or will it poison me? These are questions that a forager must carefully research before setting out to stalk the wild stalk. (Cameron)

The road to wilderness intimacy must begin in the explosion of a few more myths. One of the most common fables suggests that to know what is poisonous makes everything else edible. If we take the 11 western states as an example we shall see that this idea is very foolish. There are more than 1000 known poisonous plants in the West. It is probable that nobody can recognize all of these under all conditions. I have compiled a list of slightly more than 2000 species known edible. That totals some 3000 western plants that are known to be edible or poisonous. There are 12,000 to 14,000 species of plants found in the West. Subtract 3000 from this and we come up with 9000 to 11,000 plants that are unknown as to these qualities. Conclusion: know specifically what is edible, and when in doubt, don't eat it.

Another old tale asks you to watch what the animals eat, meaning that if they can do it, so can you. Don't try it. Most rodents, for instance, are able to eat the deadliest of the Amanita mushrooms with no ill-effects. Even if you survive you will have sustained considerable physical and physiological damage. Another example is the baneberry (Actaea spp.) whose beautiful berries are safely eaten by some birds, but are poisonous to humans.

Still another yarn insists that you eat a small piece, wait a reasonable length of time for bad effects to appear, and if none do, you may assume the plant to be edible. Two things are wrong with this advice. First, what is a small piece? Tablespoon size? Thumbnail size? A piece of water hemlock root (Cicuta spp.) the size of a peanut may kill you. This archaic advice is especially dangerous to the river boater, canoeist and other down river travelers, for the favorite habitat of this abundant weed is in fairly good soil right at the water's edge. Water hemlock is considered by many to be the most poisonous plant in the Northern Hemisphere. Secondly, what is a reasonable length of time to wait for ill effects? Water hemlock may kill you within 30 minutes, whereas after eating some Amanita mushroom species, symptoms of fatal poisoning may not appear for 10 hours or more.

A summer boy's camp leader whom I used to know would tell the boys that if you tasted a plant and it tasted "good," it was safe to eat. The problem here is that what tastes good to some people does not to others. I happen to like parsnips, and it is said that the root of water-hemlock tastes like parsnips. Red Elderberries have a sweet-sour, pleasant taste, but are poisonous to most, perhaps all, people.

Even when you are certain of your plant identification, common sense is needed in the use of the plant. Only moderate amounts of any wild edible should be eaten until you are sure of its compatibility with your body. Never eat more of a wild edible than you would of a comparable domestic plant. It is vastly surprising to most folks to hear that parsley, turnips, rhubarb, peas, onions, kale, cabbage, apple seeds, peach pits, and many other domestic plant products can be dangerously, even deadly, poisonous when used improperly.

For those who want to train themselves in edible plant recognition here is a simple game that preserves the landscape and saves the wild edible palnts for those who are in real need. Go on a survival hike of enough days so that wild goods become necessary, but carry normal backpack rations and a notebook. As you hike along, jot down the edible plants you see that you could have gathered, but didn't. For each edible plant you identify you may remove a commensurate amount of food from your pack and enjoy it.

Chances are you will be hungry! You will also discover interesting things about your intellectual honesty and mental discipline.

—**Don Kirk**

For More Information

These are all good foraging books. All are available from World Publications, Box 366, Mountain View, Calif. 94040 at the price listed* plus 25 cents each postage.

Feasting Free on Wild Edibles, Bradford Angier. A one-volume edition of Free for the Eating and More Free for the Eating, with more than 500 ways to banquet on nature's bounty. Illustrated with line drawings to aid in identification. 1973 Ppb., 288 pp., ill., $4.95, (Stackpole).

The Outdoorsman's Guide to Edible Wild Plants of North America, Knap and Knap. Over 130 wild plants, trees and shrubs that provide edible food. Includes recipes that were originally used by pioneers, early settlers and Indians. Completely illustrated. Hb., 192 pp., ill., $8.95, (Arco).

From Euell Gibbons. Learn how to find, recognize and prepare wild plants, useful herbs, and sea creatures throughout North America. Good eating awaits you through the guidance of these illustrated pages. **Stalking the Wild Asparagus,** 1970 Hb. & Ppb., 303 pp., ill., $7.95/$2.95. **Stalking the Blue Eyed Scallop,** 1964 Hb. & Ppb., 332 pp., ill., $7.95/$3.95, **Stalking the Healthful Herbs,**1970 Hb. & Ppb., 295 pp., ill., $9.75/ $2.95, (McKay).

Edible Wild Plants, Oliver Perry Medsger. A guide to the identification and preparation of North American wild edible plants. Over 150 species described with detailed illustrations and clear text. The classic work on the subject. 1939 Ppb., 323 pp., ill., $3.95, (MacMillan).

Fox Hunting

In one popular version of fox hunting, a number of mounted horsemen follow their pack of fox hounds over fences, rocky walls, ditches, and often through thick woods in pursuit of a fox that has been let loose by the hunters. Fox hunting has been most often practiced in Britain, Ireland, the United States and France ever since the first organized hunt for fox, as a sport, in 1730.

The head organizer and leader of the hunt is the elected Master of Fox Hounds. He is assisted by the first whipper-in who cares for and trains the pack, the second whipper-in who keeps the pack together, and the earth stopper whose job is to plug up the holes in which the fox might take refuge.

Both the horses and hounds used by fox hunters are especially bred for this fast-paced sport. The horses are called hunters and the pack in comprised of a variable number of hounds who rely upon scent in tracking. A fundamental rule for hunters is never to cross the pack or ride through it once the hounds have given tongue.

Often bystanders take an interest, and usually stop to watch the field ride by. Invariably they get a thrill from a good jump as the riders negotiate the obstacles with speed and decision.

In another version of the sport, hunters, either by themselves or in a group, take their pack of hounds out on foot and let them loose for the chase. This usually takes place at night, with the hunters sitting around a campfire waiting for their dogs to pick up a scent, or running after them if they locate a fox, coyote or bobcat.

Night Fox Hunting On Foot

If you read this on a week night, chances are somewhere between 5000 and 25,000 fox and wolf hunters are loading dogs, turning them loose, listening to them run, and attempting to follow them as you read these words. They're the successors of those colonial Englishmen who brought over hounds and firmly established fox hunting in what became the United States. George Washington, for example, was an avid fox hunter. If tonight is a Friday or Saturday, you may more than double the figures above. If you consider manhours and effort spent fox and wolf hunting, it is certainly one of America's major sports because it takes place year-round, two and three nights a week on the part of thousands of fox hunters.

Fox hunting in America has taken two directions. One is the organized hunt—red coats and all that—where some hunt to ride and some ride to hunt, usually after English hounds, and always in the daytime. This style of hunting may be found across the country, but predominately on the Eastern seaboard. It is not of this which I am concerned with here. Instead, I write of the single owner who keeps a pack of hounds, as few as two or three or as many as forty or more, turns them loose,

"Both the horses and hounds used by fox hunters are especially bred for this fast-paced sport. The horses are called hunters and the pack is a number of hounds who rely upon scent in tracking. A fundamental rule for hunters is never to cross the pack or ride through it once the hounds have given tongue." (Shearman)

usually at night, to seek and chase the fox or coyote (hunters call them wolves, buy coyotes are what they are). After eight to 12 hours, much of it spent running if his luck is good, his dogs drift back to be returned to the pen only to repeat in a few days. He may go alone or with others. He may spend the evening around the fire or drive 50 miles to catch the hounds as they cross the road, so he can see what hound is in the lead—and he will listen, for the cry of the pack is the thing. His hounds will be American foxhounds, smaller than the English breed, more musical, with better sense of smell and more endurance.

The American foxhound is the outgrowth of the needs of American night hunters. A combination of English hound and native hound evolved in the era before and after the Civil War by a good number of enthusiastic hunting families. Faster hounds were needed for the less than ideal hunting conditions of the United States, and to meet the increased demand caused by the Red Fox having been imported from England, becoming established in the eastern United States alongside the native Grey.

The night hunter generally does not expect to catch his quarry, although he expects the pack will press it hard enough to send it to earth, if a Red Fox, or to a tree, if a Grey. The chase is the thing. A dead fox cannot run again. So a fox not caught is a cause for rejoicing, especially if he runs well.

Coyotes and bobcats run the same way with the same hounds, but are something else again. The hound that can catch and kill these animals is prized, and the game does not so often get away. But it is still a contest since the quarry still has an excellent chance to survive—where the hunter hopes he does, so he may run again.

Three things threaten fox hunting: the increase in deer, urbanization, and more and more roads and automobiles. There is nowhere near the good running country there once was, and in some states good places for the hundreds of field trials held each year across the country are getting nearly impossible to find.

For the present, thousands of night hunters pursue this peculiarly American sport, in which the chase and its music are the thing, every night of the week, all across our land.

—Ed Everett

Ed Everett is editor of the **Hunter's Horn**, *a fox hunting magazine founded by his father in 1928. "Obviously, I grew up around the sport," he says.*

For More Information

There are two publications: the *Hunter's Horn*, Box 426, Sand Springs, Okla. 74063 and *The Chase*, 1140 Industry Rd., Lexington, Ky. 40505. Both are devoted to the sport of running foxes and coyotes with American foxhounds. The major organization is the National Fox Hunters Association, Box 1806, Jackson, Tenn. 38301. Some mail-order suppliers: Happy Jack, Snow Hill, N.C. 28580; Vet Vax, Box 13304, Edwardsville Station, Kansas City, Kansas 66113; The Slip Check, Box 132, Centralia, Mo. 65240; Nite Lite Co., Box 1, Clarksville, Ark. 72830. Some of the things you need are a pack of American foxhounds (four to 20 or more), a dog trailer, dog collar and leads, and veterinary supplies.

Here is one good book about fox hunting. It is available from World Publications, Box 366, Moutain View, Calif. 94040 at the price listed* plus 25 cents postage.

The History of Foxhunting, Roger Longrigg. Sport hunting has reached its zenith with the color, pomp, and formality of fox hunting. In this well-illustrated book the author covers the US, Britain, and Ireland, describing hunts such as the Meadow Brook and the Middleburg, as well as beagling and Irish Stag Hunting. 1975 Hb., 272 (oversize) pp., ill., $29.95, (Crown

Frisbee

If the ball evolved from primitive man's playing with rocks, then the Frisbee* was fashioned to fulfill his greatest dream . . . to fly. Although it appears to be an innocent and wafty thing, Frisbee is more than just another game or sport. It is an aerodynamic advancement in form, the ball of the 21st century come early and shed of the encumbrance of gravity and greed. For as surely as the flying disc flies, it also defies organization into a spectator sport squeezed dry of playfulness.

Although there has been some form of flying disc tossed around for hundreds of years, the first plastic version appeared in 1947 when California's Walter Frederick Morrison and Warren Francioni, ex-World War II pilots, carved a crude prototype from a solid block of plastic. They called it the Flyin' Saucer, for the world was just then dazzled with UFO's and stories of visitors from outer space. The idea was then sold to Wham-O Manufacturing Company in 1955.

The name Frisbee was gathered from the East Coast and a century-old student tradition on Yale University's campus of tossing the empty pie plates of the Frisbie Pie Company of Bridgeport, Conn. Although there are other names, Frisbee is by far the most popular, but among serious enthusiasts, the term "flying disc" is gaining acceptance. Purists prefer the term "discus plasticus".

The Frisbee was first viewed as only a novel toy, a curious phenomenon and a fad soon to fade. But the toy discus plasticus refused to leave us. Like Pinochio, Frisbee yearned to be more real than it appeared to be. In 1965, the first Professional Sport Disc appeared and today, disc sport promises to become a major international pursuit. A dedicated band of disc enthusiasts is even seeking its inclusion in the Olympic games.

The past 10 years have seen an incredible surge in Frisbee play. Frisbee tournaments and games have sprung up all across the United States and Canada, even in Great Britain and on the European Continent. It was ping pong that thawed the cold war between China and the US, but it was Frisbee that dazzled the Chinese and stopped traffic in their streets when American students visited Mainland China. American world travelers have learned that Frisbee speaks a universal language wherever they go. Some, such as Peter Jennings of ABC News, always take a flying disc on their travels.

Sport theorists have called Frisbee the modern yoga of super sport, but for most people it is a simple toss and catch activity. Actually it is a more challenging object to master than a ball, requiring determination and coordination, yet surprisingly little effort and time to enjoy. Disc play is egalitarian; the best can play with the newest novice, to the enjoyment of both. Mass, brawn, and speed contribute little to expertise. In whatever version of the game, players of both sexes and all sizes share the only common denominators: determination, coordination and practice.

There are two camps of players: grass and beach, called grass-bees and beach-bees. Each have their favorite versions of play but both agree on basic techniques of throwing and catching.

Grips and Throws

There are five basic grips beginning with the common grip for backhand with the thumb on top of the plate (convex surface) and the four fingers curling gently across the under surface. The sidearm and thumb grip are thrown from the forehand side and are excellent power throws in a game such as Guts. The overhand wrist fling grip is also a forehand throw and is the reverse grip of the common type. The thumb is now on the undersurface and fingers one through four spread lightly over the upper surface of the disc. The overhand wrist fling resembles the ancient discus hurl. The fifth basic grip is the least important of the five. It's a modified overhand wrist fling, thrown from the backhand side and is called the hooked thumb grip.

There is no official Frisbee game, but the flying disc can substitute for the ball in many ball games, often to better effect. (Ultimate)

Catching

Frisbee catching is divided into basic and simple forms. Catching should always be accomplished one-handed with the thumb up or thumb down style. Experts argue on the respective merits of each, but most great Frisbee catchers favor the thumbs down style. Advanced catching techniques employ varying styles of retarding the catch by tips, deflects, and roll-arounds of the disc off, along and across the body of the catcher. These advanced catching techniques form the nucleus of the popular Frisbee contest known as Freestyle.

The Disc

For many people any flying disc is a Frisbee, but of course only Wham-O discs can claim that name. Disc sizes vary from nine to nearly 40 centimeters in diameter and from 15 to almost 300 grams in weight. Models of 23 to 25 cm. diameter and weights of 108 to 150 grams are the favorites and best flyers. Design, streamlining and quality of plastic are equally important performance factors. Frisbee freaks and students of the sport seek certain plates from specific molds of particular batches of plastic. Wham-O's split digit mold No. 14 (identi-

* Frisbee is the trademark of the Wham-O Manufacturing Co. of San Gabriel, Calif.

fiable as a small number in the center of the underside) especially in the glowing Moonlighter Pro model of 1968 vintage, may be the most fabulous of all. For others the Wham-O Super Pro mold No. 50 in yellow, made especially for the 1975 International Frisbee Tournament is numero uno.

Games

There is no official Frisbee game. The flying disc can substitute for the ball in many ball games, and in fact perform better, more interestingly and with greater sophistication.

The most popular Frisbee games, aside from simple toss and catch, are Guts and Ultimate. In Guts, teams of up to five players line along respective goal lines drawn 15 yards apart. The game's object is to pass an accurate throw through the opponent's goal space uncaught by all opponents attempting one-handed catches. This is the Frisbee game of incredibly high-speed throws. Velocities of up to 110 miles an hour have been recorded! Uncaught throws register a point for the throwing team; badly placed throws – too high, too low or too wide – award a point for the receivers. The game is played to 21 points.

Ultimate Frisbee is a soccer-like game played on a 60-yard field with two teams. The object is to move the disc into the opponent's goal space with quick, accurate throws between teammates. Possession of the disc changes with dropped throws, interceptions and out-of-bounds tosses. The game is usually played within a prescribed time limit. Ultimate boasts an intercollegiate league of over 20 US colleges. Rutgers is the perennial champion. The Guts championship is determined annually at the International Frisbee Tournament held in or around Hancock-Houghton, Michigan in early July. The Air Aces of Detroit most recently won the fabled Julius T. Nachazel Cup emblematic of World's Guts Frisbee supremacy.

Frisbee also adapts to golf very successfully, creating a more sophisticated and complicated game. Frisbee baseball and football are more exciting, graceful versions of these time-honored ball sports. Frisbee golf, or Folf, can be played without upsetting the ecology. Trees, buildings, tables and wee animals add zest and challenge.

Tournaments

Frisbee tournaments usually include a distance contest – the current world's record for distance is held by Dave Johnson of Boston, Massachusetts, who executed a throw of 126 yards in 1974 at the Octad Tournament in New Brunswick, New Jersey. The accuracy event can be tested for not only straight flights but even curves and skips. Other tournament events can include Maximum Time Aloft where the thrower attempts to keep the disc in the air longer than any other competitor and still make a successful one-handed catch. The world's record is 11.2 seconds, set by Steve Sewall in 1973 at the International Frisbee Tournament. Other tournament events have included Frisbee golf, Discathon (a combination of cross-country running and accurate throwing), and Throw-Run-and-Catch where a competitor catches his own throw. Distances of 60 yards have been recorded in TRC.

Frisbee Freaks and "Froupies" (Frisbee followers) have organized into several international organizations and many local groups. Jim Palmeri of Rochester, New York opened the first flying disc store. John Kirkland and Vic Malafronte toured the U.S.A. this past year with the Harlem Globetrotters and put even the Trotters' talented basketball to shame with their incredible freestyle disc play. There are even Frisbee stars in the canine world. Ashley Whippett of Southern California has appeared as a halftime performer on numerous pro sport TV shows displaying his nine-foot-high aerial catches!

What is the future of Frisbee? Hopefully it is not to take its place alongside other over-televised, under-played, over-watched, non-fun modern sports. Frisbee is still fun.

–Stan Johnson

Dr. Johnson is a psychiatrist in Pacific Grove, California. His authoritative book **Frisbee** *is the Bible of the sport.*

"Frisbee catching is divided into basic forms. Catching should always be accomplished one handed with the thumb up or thumb down style. " (Corea)

For More Information

The International Frisbee Association, Box 4578, North Hollywood, Calif. 91607 and the Olympic Frisbee Federation, Box 5396, Carmel, Calif. 93921, are the official organizations. the IFA puts out a publication called *Frisbee World*, Box 664, Alhambra, Calif. 91802. A good source for equipment is the Flying Disc Shop, 102 Commercial West, E. Rochester, N.Y. Also the New York Flying Disc Institute, 235 West 76th St., 3B, New York, N.Y. can be of help. There is one book. It is available from World Publications, Box 366, Mountain View, Calif. 94040 for the price listed* plus 25 cents postage.

Frisbee, Stancil E.D. Johnson, M.D. Incredibly complete treatise and manual all rolled into one by the world's recognized authorities on Frisbee. Includes history, lore, disc anatomies, tricks, organizations, and much more, 1975 Ppb., 221 pp., ill., $4.95 (Workman).

Frog Jumping

In the summer of 1863, Angels Camp became the home of the first Jumping Frog Jubilee. Angeles Camp was then Calaveras County, California's most thriving city, filled to overflowing with miners who on working days sought the elusive yellow metal and on weekends, any kind of amusement.

Saloons, dance halls, and gambling dens were numerous, but funseeking miners demanded—and found—still more entertainment. Frog racing or jumping became popular. Several miners had their own frog ponds or stables where they spent many days training their jumpers. At regular intervals a frog jumping event was held, in which large sums of money were won and lost by the hop of a frog.

Jim Smiley, a local gambler, was the owner of the best jumper in Calaveras County—a frog named "Dan'l Webster." Smiley used to parade around the streets with the frog in a basket under his arm, boasting of the amphibian's jumping ability.

It was the antics of old Dan'l Webster that caused Mark Twain to write his immortal story, "The Jumping Frog of Calaveras."

The citizens of Calaveras County re-enacted "The Celebrated Jumping Frog of Calaveras County" to celebrate the paving of the streets in Angels Camp, May 21, 1928. With 5000 people in attendance and 51 frogs jumping, the Jubilee was reborn.

Jumping frog contests must be held in warm weather (the one in Calaveras County is always the third weekend in May), when frogs have come out of hibernation. The best jumpers are those picked from a pond or stream and brought directly to the jumping pad. They do not have time to become dormant and will be willing to jump.

Frogs are jumped on a carpet or tarp about 20 feet by 20 feet. The frog is placed in the center of a 12-inch circle about six feet from the back of the carpet or tarp. A frog will not jump backward, only forward or to the side.

Each contestant presents an entry blank with his name, the name of the frog, and states whether he or she will jump the frog or whether they prefer to have a jockey jump it. The entry blank also states whether the contestant has a frog or wants a frog provided (yes, you can rent a frog!)

Two judges with canes determine the length of the jump by placing the cane where the frog landed on the third jump—like hop, skip, and jump. The length is measured with a tape measure in a straight line. If the frog jumps forward once, sideways once and then forward again, the second jump is not counted—it must be measured in a straight line from the center of the circle to the spot where he landed on the third jump. This distance is recorded on the entry blank, and after the contest is over, the judges are able to determine the winner.

If you jump your own frog, he must measure four inches from nose to base of tail. He will be allowed 15 seconds on each jump. He will be disqualified if he does not jump within the allotted time.

After a frog is placed on the starting pad, he may not be touched although the contestant may jump up and down, shout, blow on him or do anything else to get him to jump. The wild antics of the jockeys are almost as amusing as the unpredictable frogs as they urge their croakers on to victory with kicks, stomps, and yells. Frog jockeys range in age and talent from toddlers like 18-month-old Kristin Walther of Pacific Palisades, Calif., who was the youngest frog jockey in the 1974 International Grand Finals, to entrants in the Senior division who must be at least 65 years old.

In 1966 Bill Proctor and Leonard Hall of Lafayette, Calif. entered a frog named "Ripple" which set the world's record of 19 feet 3-1/8 inches. They're still trying to break the record in jumps all over the US and at the grand-daddy Jubilee in Calaveras County. "Ripple," however, has yet to be as famous as the original jumper described by Mark Twain. And the frog, according to Mark Twain, never even jumped:

"Coleman with his jumping frog—bet stranger \$50—stranger had no frog and C got him one—in the meantime stranger filled C's frog full of shot and he couldn't jump. The stranger's frog won."

The success and celebration of the Calaveras County Jumping Frog Jubilee has inspired similar jumps all over the United States. The fun of catching and jumping frogs knows no age barrier or skill level, and only requires a frog, a circle, and a "jockey" with enthusiasm.

Qualifying jumps are held until all frogs entered are jumped. The 30 frogs with the longest jumps are announced as the finalists for the jump-off, the International Grand Finals. Winners of preliminary jumps held throughouth the United States also jump in the finals.

—Charon Scott

Charon Scott is the publicity director and researcher of the Calaveras County Jumping Frog Jubilee.

For More Information

If you want to get your frog into competition more information about the International Frog Jumping Championships can be obtained from Calaveras County Fair, P.O. Box 96, Angels Camp, Calif. 95222.

Gambling

Based on the dictionary definition—"to take a risk in order to gain advantage"—most of life's uncertain endeavors are gambling in one way or another. *Homo sapiens* seems innately endowed with an urge to take risks on almost any uncertain phenomenon. If he doesn't bet on his ability at shooting pool or playing cards, he might wager on his skill at guessing—will a horse win a race, a team win a race, or the dice crap out?

Recognizing man's penchant for staking things of value on uncertain outcomes, some individuals have organized a framework for speculation so that men and women could more easily participate in testing their skills. These gambling organizers have precisely calculated the risks of each betting venture on a probability model, and they reward the winner with a little less than the degree of risk should imply. This "take" is what keeps organized gambling alive, but despite the inherent minus expectancy of such gambling, some people still successfully defy the odds and win. Usually they attribute their windfall to skill and/or luck.

Gambling is as old as man. In the Book of Genesis, Adam took a calculated risk when he scarfed a bite out of Eve's apple. The payoff would have been womanly rewards from Eve, but the penalty was loss of Paradise. Gambling artifacts dating to 3000 B.C. have been recovered from Egyptian tombs; dice games and wagering were popular in India and China at least 3500 years ago. Greek and Roman citizens enjoyed a variety of gambling forms. Indeed, all of the basic forms of gambling were in existence long before the birth of Christ. Gambling has flourished even during periods of great Church dominance and survives today as one of man's most popular diversions.

Many of society's most staid institutions are based on gambling. During the 16th and 17th centuries, wealthy English shipowners speculated with one another on the probability of success or failure of cargo-laden cruises from the New World. During that era, one ship in 16 simple disappeared during the long voyage, victims of weather or privateers. Since lost ships could be ruinous, the owners would bet with each other on every sailing so that a lost ship would at least be compensated by a winner wager. This was the forerunner of our modern insurance industry, in which each premium is essentially a bet against adversity.

Approximately 80 million—over half the adult population of this country—are gamblers. More than 20 million annually trek to Las Vegas alone. Over 14,000 arrive by chartered airliner each day to play the tables, attend spectacular shows and generally revel in the total comfort of the many hotels. Of course most lose their stake at the casinos, but the brief wallow in luxury can leave pleasureful memories for a lifetime.

Even with the present economic down trend, gambling has soared in popularity. This upswing has been attested to by the Gambler's Book Club of Las Vegas. They have noticed that sales graphs are diametrically opposed to those of the Gross National Product. Overall, their indicators show that gambling is here to stay and is rapidly growing. Twenty-one, anyone?

How to Bet on Football Games

Hey, Sandy! I'll give you the Steelers and a touchdown for a fin," my friend Larry said as he popped into my office Raiders-Steelers, 1975 Super Bowl. I thought it over for only a few seconds before accepting. The rest is history. The Steelers walked all over Oakland, and I collected an easy $5.0(bet. Why easy? Well, my friend had made several basic errors that any experienced bettor would avoid like the plague

For starters, never make an emotional bet. Larry was from Oakland and he went unthinkingly with the home team. It' easy to get carried away with what the local papers say abou your team. If you believed the reporters in the Bay Area, the Raiders were ready to beat any team that ever punted a pig skin. But I'd go two to one that the Pittsburgh papers were building up the Steelers the same way. The secret is to forge about the emotional choice and get away from home tow journalism. Seek the best form of objectivity available, usuall in the form of a neutral out of town newspaper, or nationa radio and television network broadcasts.

Larry also failed to take into consideration, as did man writers and broadcasters, the relative weight of the previou week's playoff games. The Steelers had a relatively easy rout to the Super Bowl, but the Raiders had been in a dog figh with Miami the week before, winning by the narrowest o margins in a very physical game. To a sensible bettor, thi should suggest several things. Just the sheer physical wear an tear of a tough game can leave a team flat for the next oppo nent. And, momentum going into a championship game i vital. In this case, the Steelers were cruising, and the Raider were almost dead in their tracks. Add to this my impressio that Oakland was taking Pittsburgh too lightly, and I conside ed the Steelers a sure thing, especially with six points throw in.

There are a few other miscellaneous football betting tip that you should learn if you want to win more than you los The most basic is to stick to mano a mano bets with friend You'll see a lot of parlay cards floating around from bookie but stay clear of them. Aside from the fact that they are ill gal, even the world's greatest football handicapper can't consi tently beat a parlay card, especially if more than three or fo games must be picked.

Check into the number of key injuries on each team, ar try to keep tabs on how each one does under different we ther conditions or at home and away. With a lot of rain, f example, a good running team can usually shade a passi team. The quarterback is the key position for injuries. Tean seldom win with a backup at the helm, and a first string playing hurt usually reduces the offensive efficiency of ar team.

One simple football handicapping method is so obvious th most bettors totally overlook it. Rate the coaches and team and see who usually wins. I can always find a sucker who bet against Ohio State, USC, or a George Allen team. A secor pretty easy method is to check out first down efficiency f each team. One that can consistently crack for four, five, s yards on the first pop is going to win. This type of efficiency indicative of a good ground game, and a second and five situation opens up a whole lot more play options than second and nine.

A final hint is to always be prepared for a bet. Somebody's going to come up to you with a proposition if you're a betting man. If you don't know the teams, beg off, or maybe stall for time until you've collected enough data to judge objectively. But if you know the teams ahead of time, you can nail down a sure bet before your adversary changes his mind. And, don't be shy about taking his money.

—**Sandy Coleman**

Sandy Coleman is an avid sports fan and will bet on almost anything. He works as an insurance salesman in Northern California.

For More Information

Here are some books on gambling. Also check card games. All are available from World Publications, Box 366, Mountain View, Calif. 94040 at the price listed* plus 25 cents postage.

Gambler's Digest, Clement McQuaid. A complete treatment of the entire subject of gambling with full rules, tactics and winning ploys on every type of wager from the kitchen table to Vegas. Sprinkled with classic gambling stories. 1971 Ppb., 320 (oversize) pp., ill., $5.95, (Follet).

Beating the Bookie, Huey Mahl. Brand new book that thoroughly describes the sports betting structure presently in use throughout the nation. Learn how to create your own odds or pointspread line to spot overlays for profit. Appendix provides simple math primer on figuring probabilites and odds. 1975 Ppb., 64 pp., $2.00, (Gamblers).

How to Win at Roulette, Norman Squire. Covers both European and American styles, and contains one of the finest, most comprehensive collections of systems, which can be played on blackjack, craps and baccarat. 1968 Ppb., 221 pp., ill., $2.50, (Gamblers).

The Winner's Guide to Dice, John Savage. A book written to help turn the losing craps player into a winner. The author discusses how to receive free junkets to gambling casinos, how to know the odds and how to place bets that give you the best chance of winning. 1974 Hb., 143 pp., ill., $7.95, (Grosset & Dunlap).

Complete Book of Dice Games, Skip Frey. Thorough guide to the world of dice games. 39 games, with simple rules and tips. Craps, Chuck-a-Luck, and other casino games are listed here. 1975 Ppb., 160 pp., ill., $1.50, (Hart).

Oswald Jacoby on Gambling, Oswald Jacoby. The noted card player and mathematician tells in clear language how to get the best odds at any casino. Also contains basketball, baseball, football and horse racing odds. 1975 Ppb., 288 pp., ill., $2.45, (Hart).

Playboy's Book of Games, Edwin Silberstang. This is a thick little pocket book which contains all the information an expert or beginner needs when he sits down to a friendly, or not so friendly game at home or in a casino. Facts and advice range from psychological aspects of winning play to foolproof methods of cheating. 1972 Ppb., 511 pp., ill., $1.95, (Playboy Press).

Golf

Nearly every city in America has its golf courses, long green rolling hills and flat fairways with sculptured trees and groomed putting greens, rimmed with the unkempt grounds. Early morning golfers walk along, bags on shoulder trying to get in a few holes before work; evening players roll along in carts on the back of the course hurrying to finish before sundown. In most places these are familiar sights.

It is somewhat overwhelming to think that people have been participating in golf since 1413 in St. Andrew's, Scotland. For hundreds of years golfing societies and clubs have built courses and groomed links for the elite who could take the great amount of time to play golf. Organizations in Scotland and England received land grants to develop facilities for growing memberships confined to a privileged and prestigious group called the "gentlemen golfers."

In most hitting sports, the follow through is vital for developing maximum power. Jan Stephenson, playing in the Colgate Women's Open, shows how it is done. (Duffy)

In a very few years, Johnny Miller has established himself as one of the best professional golfers in the world. He has been the top money winner on the pro tour, but still finds his ball lodged, on occasion, in a sand trap. Proper concentration and keeping the head down are keys to blasting out of a bunker and on the green close enough to salvage par. (Drennan)

According to Nevin Gibson in *A Pictorial History of Golf,* the game became so popular that it was actually prohibited at one time by King James II of Scotland. It seems that golf interfered with the compulsory archery training to such an extent that King James had to ban it for the common defense of Scotland. Later, with the advent of gunpowder, the golf prohibitions became obsolete and once again people enjoyed it as a recreational pastime.

Today exclusive golf clubs still exist; however, the average athlete or golf buff can still swing his clubs once or twice a week for a reasonable fee at one of the many beautiful public courses. This is also a sport that the family can enjoy together, a leisurely skill that is quite conducive to casual talk and technical play.

An actual game of golf is called a round and is composed of 18 holes of play. Matches such as tournaments may require several rounds to determine the winner. Golfers try to hit a small, hard ball with long sticks "clubbed" at one end. These are usually made of metal or wood. The object is to hit the ball into each hole with as few strokes as possible; the player with the lowest score is the winner.

Golf courses will evaluate the individual holes to determine the minimum number of strokes needed to put the ball into the cup. This number is called the *par* for the hole. The total minimum strokes for the 18 holes is the par for the course. A good golfer will try to score as close – if not below – to the par as possible. Courses will vary, depending on the length of the fairway, the terrain, and the layout of the course, and will therefore have different pars: the longer or more difficult the course, the higher the par.

In addition to regular 18-hole courses, you can improve your skills at a driving range that tests your hard-hitting strengths. Or, if you need improvement in your putting, strokes, you can practice those last delicate shots at a putting green.

Unfortunately, all golf shots are not played on a level fairway with short cut grass. Thus, in practice shots should be taken in various grass depths and on the sides of hills, as well as level ground. (Duffy)

Silverado Gold

Having been an avid golfer since age 11 and having harbored sporadic aspirations toward becoming a professional, I am always keenly interested in seeing the pros in action. There is always an aura of the fantasy world at rich American tournaments – the lush immaculately groomed verdant course; the inevitable warm, cloudless, dry day (these tournaments are scheduled as to have resort climates at every stop on the tour); and the crackling whoosh of drive after pure drive that goes so high and far that you wonder if it will ever come down. Indeed, every time I see a pro tournament, I can't help recalling my father telling me, "You've got to see the pros. You can't believe how well they hit."

I was not disappointed in the least when I witnessed the final day of the $175,000 1975 Kaiser Invitational at Silverado Golf Club in Napa, Calif. Here were the ultimate in golfers – each one a hometown champion and tournament winner in his own right. Now they were all in the toughest tour in the world, where one stroke out of 280 can affect their income by $15,000; where just qualifying for the tournament is an achievement, and where even par frequently just makes the 36-hole cut. However, for those who can produce, the rewards can be lucrative. Confident Lanny Wadkins quit college after only three years to turn pro and won $120,000 his rookie year. People like Jack Nicklaus and Johnny Miller win $300,000 a year in prize money alone.

I followed Miller for the entire back nine of the Kaiser. Although not having as good a year as 1974, Miller was very much in his element on his home course, leading the tournament after 54 holes with rounds of 68, 67 and 68. After a par 36 on the front side, his lead was one stroke, and he was not exactly running away with the tournament.

On the 10th, a 415-yard par four. Miller's high straight drive was out about 270 yards. His nine-iron second shot was so directly on line that from where he stood the ball was indistinguishable from the pin! He sunk the 12-foot birdie putt. The 11th is a 181-yard par three with two traps in back of the green and a large lake covering most of the approach to the green. Had I been playing a casual round the water wouldn't have bothered me, but under tournament pressure some pessimistic thought would have come to mind. Miller looked like he didn't even see the lake, however, as he hit a high, pure five iron right at the flag. He missed his 10-foot birdie putt.

On the 12th, a 365-yard par four, his high far drive had about a five yard fade as it landed in the middle of the fairway. An easy wedge again covered the flag, but ended up 20 feet past the hole. He two putted for a par. Miller's long drive on the 13th (412 yards, par four) just caught the right rough. This caused him a minor inconvenience in that the green had a trap right in front. Thus, he could not afford to hit short, although he knew the rough would make the ball run once it hit the green. True to form, his eight-iron hit near the cup but rolled 30 feet by. His charging putt rolled halfway around the hole before coming back at Miller. Had I been in Miller's shoes, a bogey would likely have been the result. But he almost got a birdie!

On the 395-yard 14th, Miller hit another straight 270-yard drive which he seems to be able to manufacture at will. A smooth wedge put him five feet from the hole, but his birdie putt lipped the cup and missed. On the well-protected 205-yard 15th, Miller's three or four iron was six feet from the hole, and he made the birdie.

On the 526-yard par-five 16th, two big woods with slight fades put the blonde leader in a greenside trap about 40 feet from the pin. Next came his first bad shot of the back nine. He caught very little sand and went 30 feet past the hole. Although sand shots are my weakest area, I would have often done as well or better. Miller promptly knocked his putt in for his second straight birdie – something that wouldn't have entered my mind.

The 345-yard 17th was a routine par four, but the eighteenth was interesting. By now Miller was leading by three strokes. His drive on the 545-yard par five was a slice into the heavy right rough – his second bad shot of the nine. About 50 yards from his ball, blocking his path back to the fairway, were several thick, tall trees. As I waited for him to arrive, I thought of what I would do. First, I thought of putting a four wood over the trees, but then I noticed his lie. The ball was too deep for me to get at it with a four wood. Then I thought of slicing a four iron around the trees (which would have required at least a 50-yard slice to avoid going into the trees on the other side of the fairway). Finally a low-punched two iron through the trees flashed through a five-yard opening in my mind and out again. (Miraculous accuracy would have been required.) I wasn't at all sure what he would do.

When Miller arrived he had the marshalls clear the crowds from his line. Then he looked at his ball for a few seconds and quickly announced, "Well, I'll just hit a seven iron." Without so much as a practice swing, he smoothly knocked it over the tall trees safely into the fairway. After all, why risk losing the tournament by trying anything harder. Miller proved his point by putting another seven iron 20 feet from the hole and two-putting for a par.

This hole illustrates one of the major differences between a six-handicapper like me and a tournament winner – poise and a positive mental attitude. To gain this a player must have much experience under tournament pressure and have absolute confidence in his golfing ability.

Of course, to have such confidence, the golfer must be able to consistently hit 250- to 270-yard drives within 10 to 15 yards of where he aims; irons, within five yards of center, and so on. Miller's back nine is a perfect example of consistency. He hit six super woods, one just off line (hole 13) and one bad one (hole 18). All nine of his irons were dead straight. I have the ability to hit a given shot as straight and maybe even as far as Miller, but I would never be as consistent.

The final difference that I noticed was that Miller putts in the 10- to 30-foot range often enough (twice in nine holes) that it is not just luck. Unfortunately, I probably three putt from those distances more than I one putt. This is a very important difference, as it brings birdies to the scoreboard.

In short, my visit to Silverado showed me again that the five to 10 strokes that separate thousands of golfers like me from touring pros is a giant chasm which can be scaled only with large amounts of desire and ability.

–Jim Simmons

Jim Simmons was a six-handicap golfer until one year ago when he began working for an electronics firm in California. His handicap is now eight. Jim was second in the Southern California Athletic Conference Championship in 1972 with a score of 153 and third in the NAIA District V Championships with a 148.

For More Information

There are over 13 magazines exclusively devoted to golf and of course most of the general sport magazines give it good coverage. Most newsstands have at least one of them available. Here are the two biggest ones.

Golf Digest, 1255 Portland Place, Boulder, Colo. 80302. Published monthly at $7.50 per year. With over 600,000 subscriptions this magazine is the biggest golf magazine in the world. Very well done and anyone who golfs should have a subscription.

Golf Magazine, Box 2757, Boulder, Colo. 80302. Published monthly at $7.00 per year. With over 500,000 subscribers this is the second largest golf magazine. Not nearly as good as the digest but another good one.

There are many organizations which would be expected but the following could at least start you off in the right direction. United States Golf Association, Golf House, Far Hills, N.J. 07931; United States Seniors Golf Association, 60 East 42nd St., New York, N.Y. 10017; Ladies Professional Golf Association, 1776 Peachtree St., Suite 515, Atlanta, Ga. 30309; International Golf Association, Time-Life Bldg., New York, N.Y. 10020.

Finding good golf equipment isn't hard. Most good sport shops, golf shops or pro shops can be of great help. Or check the ads in the magazines for those specialized items.

Here are a few books of interest. All are available from World Publications, Box 366, Mountain View, Calif. 94040 at the price listed* plus 25 cents each postage.

A Pictorial History of Golf, Nevin Gibson. An outstanding array of almost 400 color and black and white photos illustrating over 400 years of golfing history. Practically every major golfer—past and present—is pictured here. The major tournaments and clubs are shown. Informative text answers many questions about the sport. 1968 (rev.) Hb., 282 (oversize) pp., ill., $15.00, (Barnes).

Golfer's Digest, Earl Puckett, ed. An all-inclusive collection of wisdom that any golfer will find rewarding as well as stroke-saving. The entire game is taken apart, analyzed and put together again with helpful advice on play, strategy, and equipment. 1974 Ppb., (oversize) pp., ill., $6.95, (Digest Books).

Sports Illustrated Golf, Charles Price et al. Here, a complicated game is presented in understandable terms. Describes development of the game, the course, and golf etiquette. 1972 Hb. & Ppb., 93 pp., ill., $4.95/$1.95, (Lippincott).

My 55 Ways to Lower Your Golf Score, Jack Nicklaus. One of the greatest golf superstars of all time explains in 55 simple, concise lessons, one point at a time, all the important fundamentals and unusual tips that only a pro can give. 1964 Hb., 125 pp., ill., $8.95, (Simon & Schuster).

Golf: How to Become a Champion. Nicholas Tremayne. Analyzes the strengths of the great players, past and present, discusses the methods they use, and recalls occasions in major championships when those strengths were crucial to the final outcome. 1975 Ppb., 126 pp., ill., $3.95, (William Luscombe).

Tips from the Teaching Pros, Golf Magazine. A rich treasury of stroke-saving advice written by the professionals who are trained to analyze the golf swing, spot faults land suggest remedies. Some aspects covered are: fundamentals, the swing, the long game, the short game, putting, practice and proper equipment. 1969 Hb., 228 pp., ill., $9.95, (Harper & Row).

Jack Nicklaus is noted as one of the longest drivers on the professional tour. (Duffy)

Golf, Virginia Nance, et al. Written to serve as a supplement to golf instruction. Illustrates, describes, explains and emphasizes the fundamentals of golf to help the player achieve more consistent success. 1966 (rev.) Ppb., 66 pp., ill., $2.50, (W.C. Brown).

All About Putting, eds. of *Golf Digest* Magazine. A definitive guide to putting, the shortest and most crucial of all golf strokes. This book explains the secrets of golfing's greatest putters, who reveal their methods and ideas with concise text and clear photos and illustrations. 1973 Hb., 191 pp., ill., $7.95, (Coward, McCann & Geoghegan).

My Game and Yours, Arnold Palmer. A golf instruction book by the master; a loving testimonial to the game. Starts by saying that golf is essentially a simple game and that the only difficult thing about it is the way it's taught. Can make all the difference in your game. 1963 Hb., 156 pp., ill., $8.95, (Simon & Schuster).

Golf, Ellen Griffin, et al. Clear, simple guide to the fundamentals of golf, covers how to hold a club, take aim and swing with effortless power, exercises on critical movements in the swing, what equipment is necessary and how to use it with authority. Over 100 illustrations. 1972 Ppb., 44 pp., ill., $1.50, (Athletic Institute).

The Perfect Putting Method, Paul Trevillion. The story and secrets of a man who has experimented, improvised and tested various styles of putting, and finally come up with one that will help you lower your score a few crucial strokes. 1971 Hb., 128 pp., ill., $6.95, (Winchester).

Greyhound Racing

Dog racing, sometimes called *coursing*, originated many centuries ago as a form of hunting when hares, deer, and foxes were pursued by dogs. Later, when hares were set loose and chased by greyhounds the sport turned into a true race.

Today, the most popular form of the sport is called greyhound racing, in which five to eight dogs chase a dummy "mechanical rabbit" around an oval track that varies in distance from under a quarter of a mile to over a half. This practical rabbit device was invented in 1919 and works well since greyhounds depend on sight for chasing their prey and have little sense of smell. The rabbit is usually given a 25-foot head start as the muzzled dogs are released from their starting stalls and, in most cases, maintains its lead as it is chased over the finish line.

Greyhound racing is one of the most popular sports of the British Isles, and there are tracks in South Africa, New Zealand, Australia, China, France, and Italy. In the United States it is legally sanctioned in 11 states, with Florida having the greatest number of enthusiasts. There is a great deal of betting on greyhound races.

The greyhound goes back into history over 70 centuries. The name has nothing to do with the color. Rather it may be a derivation of the early Gallic "Greek-hound." Actually the colorings of greyhounds are black, blue, brindle, fawn, red and white, with combined colorings common.

Before the start of a race the dogs, which wear variously colored jackets with numbers attached, are taken from the kennels, checked for identity, and examined by a veterinarian for fitness to race. The color of the jacket indicates the position which the dogs will take at the starting line.

The Road to Excellence

The most extraordinary achievement that proved for me the greatest thrill of my professional career is found in my participation in transforming the sport of greyhound racing from its early mediocre colorless presentation as a daylight spectator sport in Florida (where it could not be permitted Pari-Mutuel wagering) to a thrilling colorful nighttime entertainment in spacious, luxurious facilities. Today's greyhound racing offers comfort, good food, a good environment, and wagering where the bettor is king, his money beyond the vicissitudes of fraud.

In the 50 years from 1925 to 1975 greyhound racing has risen gloriously to the position of fifth most popular spectator sport in America while boasting of its $1,166,466,967 in pari-mutuel handle and 16,274,471 spectators. Only thoroughbred and harness racing, football, baseball, and hockey can presently claim a greater number of spectators.

How and why did I become interested in this sport? It was to again prove to myself my ability to begin with nothing and rise to the lofty levels of success for myself and others. In 1928 everybody in Florida was without money and praying for the return of prosperity and plenty.

In 1928 my past encompassed service in the US senate as Assistant Sergeant At Arms, night classes student at Georgetown University Law School, US Navy World War I, LLB degree Georgetown University 1919, Florida Bar 1920, later all levels of Federal judiciary, and eight years of prosperity in law practice. The economic crash took me off the roster of prosperous people.

1928 was the year of the financial panic that was to last until 1936. It was the time Roosevelt took us off the gold standard, closed all banks, cashed in all gold-backed currency and gave us the present naked promise-to-pay US currency. It was the period of gloom everywhere. It was a time needing new ideas, new industries, new types of entertainment, and much new thinking. It was a time tourist-oriented Florida needed badly a good diversified sports program to attract and entertain visitors each winter.

In 1928 the greyhound racetrack dream property of Tex Rickard (then deceased) was involved in several law suits based on unpaid contractor's and materialmen's liens, and also unpaid ground rental. For potential buyers I handled the purchase of this property, the disposition of the mass of litigation, the rehabilitation of the racetrack facilities, and ultimately the legalization of pari-mutuel wagering on all types of racing.

In those early days I could see a great future for the sport as a part of the winter sports program of Florida. Its popularity, its value to the community and the Senate could be in the years ahead advanced to the respected high rank as a spectator sport it so richly deserved. It would take time, patience, innovations, development of electrical and mechanical devices to eliminate to a great extent the human element so prevalent in other sports. On the road to excellence came the first ele-

Greyhound racing is very popular with the betting fraternity, who examine the dog's sires, as well as his past performance on the track. Each dog must be examined closely during the course of the race to see not only how fast he runs, but how tightly he takes corners. A fast dog that swings wide can often be defeated by a slower dog that runs tighter corners. (Duffy)

tric timing of races, the first photo finish camera, the race starting box (forerunners of the starting gate), grading system based on actual performance, established weight maintenance system, past performances in the daily official racetrack programs, etc.

All this adds up to a maximum appreciation of the sport by the fan: he is entitled to, and must have, maximum protection in every area against any avenue of fraud. No other pari-mutuel wagering sport affords the better so much protection and honesty of operation, in such pleasant, comfortable facilities for so little comparative cost. This is evidenced in the fact that the sport of greyhound racing has spread from Florida, its legalized birthplace, to 10 other states.

While greyhound racing is not my sole interest, it is for me a most pleasant and thrilling form of entertainment. Ever present in my mind is the satisfaction that comes from participation in the development and progress of greyhound racing, America's fastest growing sport.

My dreams of yesteryear about the future of the sport, are today the attained goals in a constant march onward and upward to the high level of respect and popularity Greyhound racing enjoys today.

Looking back today over the years of my past I am both thrilled and amazed to see so many difficult challenges accepted and successfully handled, bringing some measure of happiness and benefit to others. Therein lies the measure of success of mankind. I am happy I played a part in the development of Greyhound racing.

—Carl Hoffman

Carl Hoffman has worked continuously since 1928 in the legalization, promotion, expansion and public acceptance of greyhound racing. His is the author of **Greyhound Racing—America's Fastest Growing Sport.**

For More Information

The Greyhound Review, Box 543, Abilene, Kansas 67410. Published monthly at $10.00 per year. This is the official publication of the National Greyhound Association at the same address. There is also the American Greyhound Track Operators Association, 139 S.E. 14th Lane, Miami, Fla. 33131. If you want to know if there are any tracks near by, just drop them a note. The *Greyhound Racing Record,* Box 520-217, Miami, Fla. 33152 is a weekly newspaper. The cost is $36.00 per year.

If you are looking for suppliers, here are some addresses: Clement Feed Mill, Box 1367, Waco, Texas 76703 can supply Sport Club. This is a dog food that is formulated especially for the greyhound. If you are looking for prints, or jewelry you might check with Nevin & Kathy Lyon, Box 1122, Burbank, Calif. 91505. Custom Fiberglass Coaches, Box 1306, Homosassa Springs, Fla. 32647 can help you out with that special trailer. And Tony Lupo Specialty, Box 382, Titusville, Fla. 32780 specializes in leather and muzzle supplies.

We only have one book now but should have more later. This book is available from World Publications, Box 366, Mountain View, Calif. 94040 at the price listed* plus 25 cents postage. **Greyhound Racing—America's Fastest Growing Sport**, Carl Hoffman. Acquaints the reader with the history of the racing greyhound, the breeding, training and life of the greyhound, and the development of greyhound racing today. 1974 Hb., 112 pp., ill., $4.50, (Carl T. Hoffman).

Gymnastics

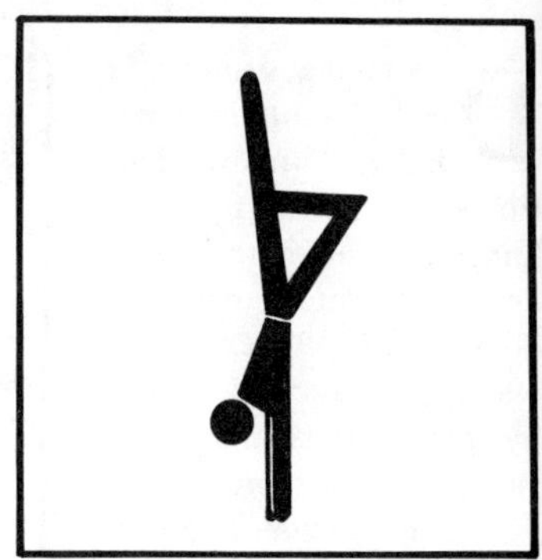

Gymnastics is one of the fastest growing sports in the United States and ranks high in popularity on a worldwide basis. It demands a great variety of physical qualities; it requires a great amount of courage.

Gymnastics is not tumbling, although tumbling is an important part of gymnastics, nor is it acrobatics. Gymnastics is a competitive sport just like football, basketball and baseball, and it is made up of many different events like track and field and swimming.

In the 1800s when physical education was becoming established as a part of the school curriculum in countries such as Germany and Sweden, the term "gymnastics" was used to refer to all activities that took place in the gymnasium. Later, as the physical education program developed and was broadened to include a wide variety of different activities, the scope of the term "gymnastics" was narrowed although it still was used for all the formal activities of the program such as marching, calisthenics and the heavy apparatus work. A more modern definition of gymnastics describes it as sport in which men or women compete both as individuals and teams by performing routines (either prescribed or optional) in a specified number of events: six for men, four for women. Men perform floor exercise, sidehorse, rings, vault, parallel bars and horizontal bar. Women perform on balance beam, uneven parallel bars, floor exercise, and vault.

In the last four Olympic Games the Japanese have won the men's gymnastics competition with the USSR close behind. The USSR has dominated the women's competition. The fact that Mr. Takashi Ono, a gymnastic gold medal winner for Japan in the 1967 and 1960 Olympics, was selected to represent all competitors and take the athletes' oath during the opening ceremonies of the 1964 Olympics is an indication of the status of gymnastics in Japan. Czechoslovakia, Romania, Germany and Poland also consistently have produced strong international gymnastics teams.

The United States is becoming a team leader in international gymnastics although we have not produced an individual winner in any Olympic gymnastics event since 1932. Out highest team finish has been fourth. Although our performers are improving greatly so are the other teams. The two leaders, Japan for men and the USSR for women, are by far the outstanding international teams.

Gymnastics is one of the fastest growing American sports. We now have volume participation and from large numbers usually comes quality. It seems logical that within the next four or five years the United States will produce better gymnastic teams that could move up the international ladder and challenge the leaders.

In our society, we depend on the high schools and colleges to produce our top athletes. Fifteen years ago there were fewer than 20 universities with an active competitive intercollegiate gymnastic program. Now the number is over 100. Before World War II there were only a few small "pockets" of high school gymnastics activity in the country such as Los Angeles, Minneapolis, Chicago and Philadelphia. The emphasis on physical fitness during the war and in the early 1950s, however, resulted in increased gymnastics participation in school programs. There are now gymnastic teams in almost all, if not every state in the US. About half the states have some type of state high school association that promotes gymnastics and many hold a state championship meet.

Gymnastics is a demanding sport that requires a great variety of physical qualities. Strength and flexibility which are the most important ones we usually think of opposing each other. However, a person can be—and must be—both strong and flexible to be a good gymnast. Other important qualities are balance, agility, power, and grace in movement. A gymnast must also be rugged and tough to stand frequent poor landings and falls during the learning process and to withstand considerable "contact." Not body contact as in football, but contact with the equipment and the floor! Above all a gymnast must possess a great amount of courage. There are only a few sports such as ski jumping and platform diving that demand as much in this respect as gymnastics.

A gymnast reaches his or her peak in the mid-20s. Because there are so many different skills to be learned in gymnastics it takes longer to become a top performer than in other sports. A high jumper, for example, has one skill to perfect. A swimmer uses from three to 12 skills depending on how many strokes the athlete swims. Team sport players seldom have more than 10 or 12 skills to learn. An all-around gymnast, on the other hand, has hundreds of skills to perfect.

Moreover, in most sports the skills the beginners uses are identical or very similar to the skills of the expert. The expert merely learns to perform the same skills more effectively. In gymnastics the beginner must learn 50 or more skills for his routines. The intermediate may use these 50 skills as a background, but to progress must learn others more difficult skills and compose new routines. This is a never-ending process. To progress a gymnast must keep learning new and more difficult stunts. An Olympic gymnast may have learned 400 or 500 skills during his career. This takes time and it is very difficult for a gymnast to reach the top while still a teenager.

In international gymnastics there are six members on a team and each competitor must participate in all events. In the United States the rules permit specialization in one or more events although many of our competitors compete in all events and are referred to as all-around performers.

Each competitor is scored by four judges. The high and low judge scores are eliminated and the middle two scores are totaled and then divided by two to give the individual's score in the event. The routine performed is allotted points for such things as difficulty, composition, combination, amplitude, execution and general impression. Men's and women's judging have slightly different categories for evaulation of performances. Every competitor starts with 10 points and the judges deduct points for errors or omissions as specified in the rules.

Team winners are determined in international competition by totaling the five best scores obtained by the six competitors in each event. That is, the lowest score of the six is eliminated in determining the team total for each event. There are many different methods used for determining a team champion in various states in the United States. It is becoming very common however, to use a system similar to the international method.

Confronted with a four inch beam, the average person on the street would have difficulty walking its length without tumbling off, but an experienced gymnast can do back flips, walkovers, aerials and other jumping moves in rock steady precision. (Duffy)

Gymnastics is an enjoyable sport and yet a demanding one. It is popular on a world-wide basis and growing in popularity in the United States. I hope this article will stimulate many readers to join the ever-increasing number of gymnastics participants in the United States.

—**Eric Hughes**

Dr. Eric Hughes is the University of Washington gymnastics coach and served as the 1972 Olympic gymnastics team manager. He is the author of **Gymnastics for Men** *and* **Gymnastics for Women.**

For More Information

There are two good magazines that cover gymnastics exclusively. *Gymnastics World,* Box 366, Mountain View, Calif. 94040. Published bi-monthly at $4.50 per year. A new publication that is really coming along. Good articles and well illustrated. *Gymnast,* 410 Broadway, Santa Monica, Calif. 90401. Published monthly at $12.00 per year. Very good magazine that keeps you up-to-date on what is happening in the sport.

The two major organizations are: International Gymnastics Federation, c/o AAU, 231 West 58th St., New York, N.Y. and US Gymnastics Federation, Box 4699, Tucson, Ariz. 85217.

Gymnastics supplies and equipment may be hard to find. Sidlinger Trampoline Co., Box 2, Garland, Texas 75040 has a free catalog listing trampoline equipment and supplies. Zwickel, Box 309, Jenkintown, Pa. 19046 has a free catalog showing men's and women's uniforms. Olympic Spieth Anderson, Box 40, Orilla, Ontario, Canada makes all sorts of equipment. Crons Gymnastic Specialties, 41-14 Broadway, Astoria, Long Island, N.Y. 11103 has a free brochure listing pants, shirts, slippers, handguards, leotards, equipment, etc. A/C Gymnastics Etc., Suite 110, 2 Mack Rd., Woburn, Ma. 01801 has good equipment. Gibson Gymnastic Supplies, 5734 Shasta Circle, Littleton, Colo. 80123. They make a beam that is less than $100. Something to consider for your home or gym. Taffy's, 1571 Golden Gate Plaza, Cleveland, Ohio 44124. Free catalog listing uniforms. Frank Endo, 12200 South Berendo Ave., Los Angeles, Ca. 90044. Has wooden rings, shoes, pants, suspenders, chalk, shirts, travel bags, films, etc.

There are many good books on gymnastics to choose from. Here is a small selection. All are available from World Publications, Box 366, Mountain View, Calif. 94040 at the price listed* plus 25c each postage.

Gymnastics Illustrated, Don Tonry. Profuse illustrations and concise language make this one of the best guides to gymnastic terms and nomenclature in print. An easy reference key for coaches, and performers. 1974 Ppb., 236 pp., ill., $9.50, (Gymnastics Aids).

Gymnastics Handbook, Sam Fogel. Complete gymnastics program, taking you all the way from teaching the most basic skills to coaching champion-caliber routines. 1975 Ppb., ill., $10.95, (Prentice-Hall).

The Tumbler's Manual, William LaPorte and Al Renner. Still one of the basic books on tumbling, with all the popular stunts progressively illustrated and discussed. Both individual and group stunts. 1938 Hb., 128 pp., ill., $8.50, (Prentice-Hall).

Complete Book of Gymnastics, Newton Loken & Robert Willoughby. Illustrated by hundreds of photographs of champion collegiate gymnasts in action, this book offers explicit instruction for the simplest and most difficult gymnastic movements. 1967 Hb., 284 pp., ill., $13.50, (Prentice-Hall).

Olympic Gymnastics, Bruce Taylor, et al. A logical approach to training for all Olympic gymnastic events, written by international experts. 1972 Hb., 236 pp., ill., $14.50, (Prentice-Hall).

Gymnastics Routines for Men, William Vincent. Covers everything—background information, terminology, simple moves, series of skills and complete routines—all from the specialized point of view of the male gymnast. 1972 Ppb., 124 pp., ill., $3.95, (Saunders).

Gymnastics for Men, Eric Hughes, M.D. Well-thought-out book for beginners and intermediate gymnasts, and coaches alike. Crammed with photographs, many of them shot in progression for easy comprehension. Covers all facets of gymnastics with clear descriptions. Written by 1972 Olympic Games Gymnastics Team Manager. 1973 (rev.) Hb., 477 pp., ill., $11.95, (Ronald).

Feminine Gymnastics, Phyllis Cooper. Written as a guide for teachers and coaches of gymnastics. It includes methods of teaching and evaluating, skill analysis, spotting tehcniques and a guide to common beginners' errors. 1973 Ppb., 250 (oversize) pp., ill., $6.95, (Burgess).

Introduction to Women's Gymnastics, Drury & Schmid. Primarily for the beginning student who would like to develop basic gymnastic skills, good condition, and knowledge about the world of competitive gymnastics. 1973 Ppb., 112 pp., ill., $2.50, (National Press Books).

Gymnastics for Women, Drury, Schmid & Thompson. Extensive information on history, equipment, techniques, teaching curricula and judging, plus warmup programs. 1970 (rev.) Ppb., 275 pp., ill., $6.95, (National Press Books).

Men's floor exercise includes movements demonstrating tumbling ability, balance, strength and flexibility. These elements are skillfully interwoven with dance-like grace to arrive at a public presentation that is both powerful and visually pleasing. (Indiana State University)

Tumbling & Trampolining, Newton Loken. Every step in tumbling and trampolining stunts, from preparatory positions and mid air jumps to landing, is covered in addition to the more difficult stunts. 1961 (rev. 1971) Hb., 128 pp., ill., $3.95, (Sterling).

Olga, Justin Beecham. Filled with vivid photos, this biography dramatically describes Soviet Olympic star Olga Korbut's life, challenges and triumphs in training, at school, on tour, at home, and in international competition. 1974 Ppb., 128 pp., ill., $2.95, (Two Continents).

"Sports Techniques" Gymnastics Series, The Athletic Institute. This series of booklets describes specifically the individual men's and women's events, going into greater detail than is possible in a more general work. Each is an illustrated paperback and is priced at $1.50. The following titles are available:

Floor Exercise, 75 pp., **Floor Exercise and Vaulting for Women**, 81 pp., **Rings**, 62 pp., **Horizontal Bar**, 79 pp., **Parallel Bars**, 70 pp., **Uneven Parallel Bars**, 51 pp., **Balance Beam**, 64 pp., **Side Horse and Long Horse Vaulting**, 68 pp., (Athletic Institute).

Handball

Handball is thought to be the oldest of all games played with a ball. The game began in about the 10th century and is of Celtic origin.

The only items that are really necessary for play are a ball made of black rubber, tennis shoes, and a court – either of one, three, or four walls. Four-wall handball is the most popular, although it really is a five-wall game since the ceiling plays an important part in game strategy.

The game is very similar to squash, paddleball, and racquetball, except in this case the ball is hit with the hands (leather gloves are necessary) instead of a racket. Two, three or four players may participate at once.

To win a point in handball the server must place a shot off the front wall that the receiver cannot return before the ball has bounced twice on the floor. The whole idea of handball is to keep returning the ball to the front wall while utilizing the side walls and ceiling for ricochet shots. The first player to score 21 points wins the game.

Handball exercises all the body systems, and a game or two can give the player an excellent short, intensive workout.

The Big Challenge

Handball is more than a game – it is a way of life. The man-to-man competition and the complete release from the tensions of our everyday business and living trials and tribulations make it extremely popular. We call handball the "chess" of the court sports, the never-ending challenge of seeking perfection. Not only is it good mental exercise, but is also offers benefits for the body. By the time many of us solve those four walls and ceiling the spirit is still there, but the flesh is weakening.

In handball there is a comeraderie among the players that is unique. A handball buff, seeking a game in a strange area, will invariably get the red carpet treatment by his fellow players. Such is the sum and substance of the United States Handball Association, aptly named the "Players' Fraternity".

My own personal introduction to handball came after a short fling as a professional baseball player, and the usual dosages of basketball, swimming, golf, and bowling. Nothing has ever compared to the enjoyment and self-satisfaction gained from playing what the late Avery Brundage, who headed the International Olympic Committee, tabbed as "The Perfect Game".

Over the past 20 years, I have lived with handball, both as a vocation and avocation: organizing tournaments, publishing the official magazine for the Association, running two seasons of the pro tour, playing the game regularly – even gaining some measure of recognition as Canadian national doubles champion (I had the legendary US six-time singles and six-time doubles national titlist, Jim Jacobs, as a partner). Handball has made the last two decades of my life not only very enjoyable, but also immensely satisfying.

Handball offers a real challenge in learning to play a half-way decent brand of ball. The necessity of utilizing two hands and the strenuous stop and go action dissuade many young men from staying with the game. Often they migrate to raquetball, played on the same court and with practically the same rules but a game in which it is much easier to acquire the basic fundamental skills. Only those who have perseverance and dedication reap the benefits after learning the angles, positioning, offensive and defensive shots of handball.

For physical wellbeing, there can be no equal in obtaining satisfying results in such a short period of time. A one-hour session, several times a week, is the best health insurance any man could acquire. Handball is the fun way to maintain peak condition.

Handball has enjoyed a steady growth in the past 25 years, the biggest surge coming after World War II with so many new facilities erected. Also, because of the meteoric growth of racquetball, handball gets the fringe benefit of many new courts in private clubs, condominium and high-rise apartment complexes, office buildings, schools, park districts, and even in some homes. While racquetball growth zooms upwards, handball also continues on a steady rise. It is there to offer the big challenge to whoever will take it.

—Mort Leve

Mort Leve is Executive Secretary of the United States Handball Association and editor of **Handball** *magazine. He has been involved in the game for over 20 years, organizing, playing and writing. He is also the co-author of* **Inside Handball.**

For More Information

The United States Handball Association, 4101 Dempster St., Skokie, Ill. 60076 is the official national organization for handball. And their magazine *Handball* is the "official voice". The magazine is published by-monthly at $3.00 per year.

The main specialized equipment you need for handball is balls, gloves and shoes. Two glove manufacturers, Champion, 2200 E. Ovid, Des Moines, Iowa 50313 and Saranac Glove Co., Box 786, Green Bay, Wisc. 54305, are the leaders in the field. Seamco and Spalding both make good balls. And Adidas makes a good shoe. Kem Sports, 2632 N. Goyette Ave., Tucson, Ariz. 85712 offer a full line of handball equipment by mail order.

There aren't very many books on handball yet, but the number is increasing. All are available from World Publications, Box 366, Mountain View, Calif. 94040 at the price listed* plus 25 cents each postage. Write for a complete list.

Handball, Tyson. A former handball champion presents the challenge, fun, and excitement of this furiously paced game. Details the strategies of singles and doubles play, outlines a program for the beginner, and gives the practice methods used to learn the various offensive and defensive shots. 1971 Ppb. 117 pp., ill., $3.95, (Goodyear).

Handball, Nelson and Berger. Breaks the game down into its important segments – the serve, various shots, body and court positioning, anticipating, and singles and doubles strategy – and treats these in simple terms for the player in this fast and furious sport. 1971 Hb. & Ppb., 66 pp., ill., $6.50/$3.00, (Prentice Hall).

Handball, Michael Yessis. Designed for the intermediate student who wishes to improve his game. Emphasizes the thinking process as the secret of success. 1970 Ppb., 58 pp., ill., $2.50, (W.C. Brown).

Handball, Thomas Yukic. A beginner's introduction, well-illustrated with excellent line drawings, which includes a few chapters on strategies for experts. 1972 Ppb., 128 pp., ill., $3.95, (Saunders).

Inside Handball, Paul Haber. By the U.S. Handball singles champion. 1970 Hb. & Ppb., 96 (oversize) pp., ill., $7.95/ $3.95, (Regnery).

Handball. Part of the Sport Techniques series, shows all the moves and techniques of winning handball. Ppb., $1.50, (Athletic Inst.).

Hang Gliding

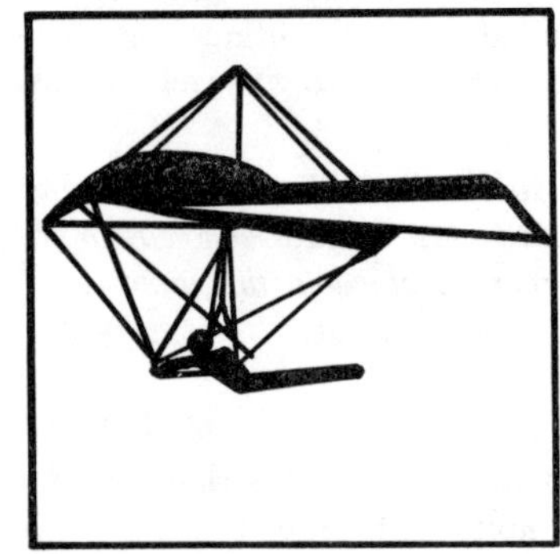

Man's age old dream of flight has at last been realized, and birds are no longer sole occupants of the skies in powerless flight.

The true feeling of flight, as experienced by the natural inhabitants of the skies, is now shared by men who fly not by instruments and engines, but whose sole means of support in the air is the air itself. Their flight pattern is not controlled by computors, but by their own sense of "feeling" the wind. It is truly as close to being a bird as one can ever imagine.

Developed from a Delta Wing Ski Kite as first introduced to the United States by an Austrialian, Bill Bennett in 1966, hang gliding has developed in great leaps and bounds and is fast becoming a major new sport.

Although the term Hang Gliding belongs in the 19th century, when it was first coined by gliding pioneers, Montgomery, Lillianthall and compatriots, it has had a fantastic revival, particularly in Southern California in the last four years.

There on any weekend, one can see strange, but beautiful and breathtaking sights, as young and old, male and female enthusiasts of this latest craze defy the laws of gravity. They step off hills and mountain tops to soar like giant condors from their God-made launching pads, to glide smoothly to its base for a beautiful bird-like landing. This is how the fledgeling birdmen begin to learn their art. They quickly develop their skills to the point where, with a sufficiently strong breeze for their weight and particular size kite or glider, they are able to soar like their little brothers, the eagles and hawks. And to the almost speechless first-time observer, it appears that they do it just as effortlessly as the birds.

Perhaps one of the most gratifying aspects of this new super sport can be revealed in the words of pioneer flyer Bill Bennett: "They are the perfect ecology vehicle – they make no noise, emit no exhaust fumes, no smoke. They do not destroy the terrain or foliage, pollute or contaminate man or the elements in any way – they hardly even disturb the air they fly in."

Enthusiasts usually begin their flight training by running off small hills about 50 to 100 feet in height. They learn rapidly and graduate to bigger and better hills. It is not unusual to find a flyer with only six to ten flights from a 100-foot hill stepping off a 3,000 to 4,000-foot vertical drop.

The transition from being low and slow to high and soaring is remarkably quick, much to the dismay and anguish of the flyers' wives and sweethearts, who watch with bated breath as their loved ones seemingly step off into eternity. But they are the same women and sweethearts who race forward to greet their hero as he floats in for a landing to cries of "Beautiful, darling – just beautiful."

Bill Bennett was the first man to step off a mountain more than a mile high, when he flew from Dante's View to Badwater in Death Valley, a vertical drop of 5,757 feet.

There are now many members of Bennett's Mile High Club, and before long there are sure to be many more, as flyers are always looking for bigger and better mountains from which to launch.

Several are even planning to fly from Mt. Kilamanjaro. They are planning 30,000-foot balloon drops, 24-hour flights in Hawaii, 500-mile soars around the Great Lakes. The list goes on and will probably not be complete until all the mountains, hills and waterways of the world have been flown.

According to Bill Bennett, there are Delta Wing Kites being flown from water, snow slopes and hilltops, in more than 20 countries. Competition is being held more and more often, including annual international meets.

Built of aircraft aluminum or stainless steel and dacron, modern kites vary in weight from 30 to 55 pounds. They are very highly maneuverable and responsive to control, and can be landed in a very small area with relatively little experience. With such ease of flight, it is little wonder that hang gliding has become so popular.

Here To Stay

Flying is a sport no longer just for birds, but one to be enjoyed by man with an ecologically perfect vehicle in an environmentally conscious world.

Hang gliding is not a sport in which man sets out to defy the elements, but rather one where he sets out to use to great advantage the freedom of the wind, the vastness of the sky and the majestic heights of the mountains.

From a very inconspicuous beginning, this beautiful sport has grown to where it is now enjoyed by thousands of participants and millions of spectators around the world. With the modern advent of aluminum, dacron, mylar and stainless steel, man has at last achieved his goal of unpowered flight, but this is still only the beginning.

Unlike most new sports, hang gliding has advanced so rapidly that the flyers themselves can hardly keep pace with the new and improved kites which appear almost daily. These new gliders are constantly adding performance, safety and ease of handling to accommodate an ever increasing number of enthusiasts.

Why do people do it? No one knows until they have tried it, and even then it is hard to explain. Maybe it is simply exhilarating and like absolutely nothing else. You are completely

"The true feeling of flight, as experienced by the natural inhabitants of the skies, is now shared by men who fly not by instruments and engines, but whose sole means of support in the air is the air itself. Their flight pattern is not controlled by computers, but by their own sense of 'feeling' the wind. It is truly as close to being a bird as one can ever imagine." (Drennan)

free and alone to go where you please in a completely new world where one can soar and roam like the birds.

In the early days of hang gliding, it was easy to hold one or more records and be a champion, because almost any unusual flight was a first, a longest, or a highest. Now with so many young athletes getting into the sport, we will see a new breed of champion emerge – one day we might even see hang gliding in the Olympic Games.

Hang gliding is so versatile that it can be done in any climate or season. It can be done over water, on snow, mountains, cliffs, deserts – in almost any terrain one can use some method or another to become airborne and fly. It is achieved by towing, ridge soaring thermals, on foot, snow skis, water skis, hot air balloons, helicopters – all a means to the same end of obtaining enough altitude to soar and remain in the air as long as possible.

As with all thrill sports, hang gliding has its dangers, but statistically it has been proven that 99.9 percent of all accidents are caused by pilot error.

The strangest thing is that the majority of flyers who have crashed were those with one or two years' experience. They appear to reach a point where they become over-confident and go beyond the limits of their ability. Hang gliding is, however, at least as safe as all other thrill sports if safety rules are followed.

It is significant that at least 20 national and international meets have been held with an average of 1000 flights each competition, and that in these 20,000 flights there have been no fatalities, only very minor accidents. The important point is that if flying is conducted under closed, regulated conditions, it is completely safe.

Nature has provided some beautiful sites for hang gliding in national parks, along miles of oceanside cliffs, and in the vast desert regions, but already a move is afoot to close some of these sites to hang gliders. Surely this is another bureaucratic blunder by those who should know better!

But despite bureaucratic hassles, hang gliding is here to stay now that man has found his wings.

–Bill Bennett

Bill Bennett introduced water ski kites to the United States and was the first to hang glide in excess of 5000 feet of vertical descent. He is the designer/owner of Delta Wing Kites.

For More Information

The only national organization is the United States Hang Gliding Assoc., Box 66306, Los Angeles, Calif. 90066. They publish a magazine called *Ground Skimmer* which is included with membership dues. When a sport is still as new as this one is you will have to keep your eyes open for new magazines. We will just list names and addresses of publications and before you do anything, write for a sample copy. *Hang Glider*, 246 North Fries, Wilmington, Calif. 90744; *Wings Unlimited*, 4155 E. Jewell, Suite 301, Denver, Colo. 80222; and *Hanging In There*, 6301 Knox Ave. S., Richfield, Minn. 55423.

An interesting catalog is available for $1.00 from Man-Flight Systems, Box 872, Worcester, Mass. 01613. Filled with everything the hang glider would need. Also, Delta Wing Kites and Gliders, Inc., Box 483, Van Nuys, Calif. 91408 is a good contact for top equipment. Other manufacturers are: Eipper-Formance, Box 246, Lomita, Calif. 90717; Seagull Aircraft, 3021 Airport Ave., Santa Monica, Calif. 90405; Sport Kites, 1208H E. Walnut, Santa Ana, Calif. 92701; Sky Sports, Box 441, Whitman, Mass. 02382; and Zephyr, 27 Mill St., Glastonbury, Ct. 06033. Keep this in mind, some manufacturers produce "advanced rogallos" which should not be purchased by the beginner, due to control sensitivity.

Here are some of the better books on hang gliding. All are available from World Publications, Box 366, Mountain View, Calif. 94040 at the price listed* plus 25 cents each postage. Write for a complete list.

Skysurfing: A Guide to Hang Gliding, Eddie Pual. A witty, comprehensive look at all the angles of this skysport explosion. Explains the history of powerless flight, how to fly a glider, winds and turbulence, designing and constructing your own hang glider, and the golden rule of hang gliding, "Never fly higher than you want to fall." 1975 Ppb., 120 pp., ill., $3.95, (Crown).

Fly: The Complete Book of Sky Sailing, Rick Carrier. A uniquely illustrated book presenting the basic techniques of hang gliding, including launching and landing. Information regarding all standard types of sky sails, clubs and manufacturers. 1974 Hb., 128 (oversize) pp., ill., $7.95, (McGraw-Hill).

Hang Gliding: The Flyingest Flying, Don Dedera & Stephen McCarroll. Incredible book. With 137 wild, screaming color plates and exhilarating text, you are swept off your feet onto the current of the wind and feel the excitement of one of the newest explosive sports in the world. This is a beautiful celebration of flight, wind, people and courage. 1975 Ppb., 140 (oversize) pp., ill., $9.95, (Northland).

Hang Gliding: The Basic Handbook of Skysurfing, Dan Poynter. Includes history, how to get started, glider design, launching and soaring, and the law. Exact diagrams for construction and reference tables leave nothing to chance. 1974 Ppb., 198 pp., ill., $5.95, (Parachuting Publ.).

The Complete Book of Hang Gliding, D.S. Halacy, Jr. A comprehensive history and modern guide to one of today's most exciting sports that covers everything from types of fliers and launch techniques to safety rules, clubs and publications. 1975, $6.95, (Hawthorn).

Hang Gliding Handbook: Fly Like a Bird. A book of basic information on hang gliding, covering launching and flight techniques, glider construction, design principles, and the history and traditions of the people who fly. 1975 Hb. & Ppb., $8.95/$5.95, (Tab).

Kiting, Dan Poynter. The only book devoted to launched hang gliding. Since much of the world lacks mountainous terrain or finds its hills covered with trees, towing is the only launch method open to gliders. Goes into great detail on towing equipment, but also includes chapters on para-sailing and gyrocopters. 1975 Ppb., ill., $3.95, (Parachuting Publ.).

Harness Racing

The sport of harness racing can be traced back in history to its early Roman ancestor of chariot racing. While both thoroughbred and harness races are held on tracks, harness racing differs from thoroughbred racing in that harness horses have to maintain a specified gait and are guided by a driver seated on a sulky instead of a jockey in a saddle. A sulky is a light seat with bicycle type tires which the horses pull.

Horses that participate in a harness race are known as standardbreds, all of which have long pedigrees. They are further differentiated as either trotters or pacers, names derived from the two separate gait styles which horses are trained to use when running.

The trotter has a diagonal gait, a high knee movement, and a left-to-right nodding of its head.

The pacer has a lateral gait, moving its legs in a piston-like action, while swaying from side to side. Most pacers wear hobbles, leather or plastic straps connecting front and rear legs on the same side.

Harness races are held individually for trotting and pacing classes; the usual distance of a race is one mile, and races are usually contested at speeds averaging 25-30 miles per hour. They take place at over 60 pari-mutual tracks all over the country, where fans may wager on horses and drivers. Also you can watch trotters and pacers in action at many fairs, and at tracks in Canada, almost every European country, and many other lands.

Harness racing is a colorful sport; each driver wears his own brightly-hued riding clothes called colors. Most of the drivers are professionals yet some of the best ones are amateurs.

The Farmers In My Family

The sport of harness racing probably began when two farmers both thought they had the faster horse. The only way to determine this for sure was a race—with the horses hooked to the lightest buggy the farmers had.

Harness racing has changed dramatically from those days when only the farmers cared who had the fastest horse. The advent of pari-mutuel wagering produced a funding mechanism for greater purses and broadened the appeal to include millions of harness horse enthusiasts.

My career in harness racing has spanned much of the old and the new in the sport. I was born and raised in the small town of Logan, Ohio. My father owned and operated a business that used horse-drawn wagons to deliver groceries from the many independent grocers in town. This was before the major grocery chains had taken over the business and it seemed like every neighborhood had its own market. My uncle was a rural mail carrier. He also used a horse and buggy on his mail route. He had a spare horse quartered half way along his route and would change horses at that point.

Much like the farmers of earlier times, the time came when

the Brandt brothers thought they had a faster horse than anyone else. At that time the place to prove it was at the many county fairs across the Midwest.

At first I was the driver of the truck that transported the horse (at that time the law did not concern itself that I was under 16). Later I was to become the harness driver and I drove my first race at Pennsboro, West Virginia at the age of 13. Other diversions interfered with my racing, however, but after graduating from high school and trying college, professional baseball, and the Navy in World War II, I returned to the harness horses. In the years since then I have won over 500 races and the earnings of the horses I drove is approaching one million dollars.

I have been fortunate to have been able to purchase top caliber colts for my patrons (the owners of the horses I train and drive) for modest prices. The first two minute horse (a horse winning a mile race in a time of two minutes or faster) was a mare named Chet Lynn Hayes, which I purchased for Mr. I. J. Collins for $4000. That was in 1958. Now Mr. Collins is 100 years old and is still active in the stable.

From the start, my participation in the harness horse business has been a family affair. I think that this is the one aspect of the sport that draws many people to participate in it. Now my wife, Betty, is the stable bookkeeper and schedules all of my transportation from track to track. During the course of the summer I may find myself competing in five different cities in as many nights. My son, Dick, although working in industry in labor relations, also drives horses for me when he can. My father-in-law is also one of my major patrons.

Although we now race harness horses at elaborate raceways in metropolitan areas, instead of on the dirt country roads which the farmers used, the reason for racing is still the same. We still like to see who has the best horse. This basic competition insures that harness racing will continue to grow as a major sport.

—Dick Brandt

Dick Brandt has been involved with harness racing for many years as a successful driver, raiser, and trainer of harness horses. Today he continues to race and spend time at his stables in Ohio.

Random Thoughts on Harness

Ever since I can remember I've been raised in harness racing. My father and five of his brothers were all harness horse trainers and drivers. I got started when I was a very small child, working in the barn, and a few years later I started training horses. At the age of 17 I drove my first race, and ever since—for 28 years—I've been driving steadily. During this time I've raced in most of the major stakes throughout the country.

Although I've never operated a large stable, I've owned some excellent stake horses that have appeared in outstanding races. Presently, my home is located close to both Hollywood Park and Los Alamitos Raceway, where I race often.

Actually, there is only one avenue to take for those who want to become harness drivers. First of all, you've got to come to the track and find employment, or else get a job with a trainer. You've got to start at the bottom and work your way up—even if it means starting as a stable hand. It takes quite a while to learn all that is necessary to even take a horse out on the track for light exercise. This is the only approach that an aspiring driver can take, other than going out and buying his own horse. In this case he would still have to spend a great deal of time working in the barns, just learning about the horses, before he could even attempt participating in a race.

The horses in this sport have been bred for this type of racing for well over 100 years. Of course, down through the years the horses developed and improved. They became faster, easier to train and drive as time went on.

Horses are really just like people. Each one has a different personality—sometimes bad habits which must be overcome before they become good runners. At the barest minimum it takes six months to train a young colt for harness racing, and most probably the better part of a year. After this initial training they have a harness racing life of about three or four years, on the average. In certain cases a horse might race until he is 14 years old, at which point he is not allowed to race on US tracks anymore.

Perhaps it need not be said, but speed is the factor which makes one horse better than another. There are a number of elements that make for speed. Drivers, owners, and trainers look for the best bred horse they possibly can find; this is an advantage where speed in concerned. Secondly, we like a horse that has good manners and is easy to handle. This makes our job a lot easier. Thirdly, a horse must be in sound physical condition in order to race, let alone to win. He can't have any legs or hoofs that hurt him because this will take away from hs performance.

As far as drivers are concerned, they are all athletes, just the same as boxers, golfers, hockey players, or anyone else. The driver with the fastest reflexes, who is the most alert, and who takes best advantage of the various situations that arise will be the winner.

I really don't know how to explain my feeling toward harness racing other than it's just home to me. I've never really known anything else. It's been my whole life so-to-speak.

—Ted Dennis

Ted Dennis was the leading percentage-winning harness driver at Los Alamitos Raceway in California last year.

Progression of a Harness Driver

Almost all harness racing drivers are athletes. When I was in high school I played basketball and baseball, was the most valuable player in football, and set a shot-put record in track. So, I was very athletically inclined.

I also started racing horses when I was in high school. I owned a cheap horse and did what I could with him. After I graduated I went to New York with Larry Gregory, a friend of mine, whom I worked for—no wages, I just wanted to learn how to take care of horses and train them. After two years I bought my own horse for $1000. I cared for him myself and Larry would hob him until I was capable of handling him on my own.

After two years of training and hard work I decided I wanted a license to drive in harness races. At first I went to the races at the fairs, got my fair license and drove in the lesser competitions where I couldn't hurt anybody.

Drivers usually start out at the fairs and after taking part in those races for awhile they go to a major track where they drive in the qualifiers for awhile. It takes 15 races as a qualifying driver before one is able to drive in an extended parimutuel meet. He must appear before a board who observes his capabilities as a driver. If he passes their inspection he'll be given a provisional license for one year. In that period of time he must drive satisfactorily in 25 races. If he does that he will advance to top class–where he can drive anywhere in the US and Canada.

There is always an element of risk while driving in a harness race. Personally, I've been in several accidents. Sometimes a horse will act up and kick you with his hind legs; other times a competitor's horse will break right in front of you so you have nowhere to go except into him. For these reasons a driver has to be constantly alert, looking in front of him, being aware that a horse might break.

So far, last year was my biggest. The most races I had ever won before then was 51. Then, all of a sudden, I won 174 races and the horses I drove accumulated $471,000 in winnings. This was in California races only. Nobody had ever done that in this state before. As a result I was rated 18th in the nation overall, second in percentage.

In California, harness racing started long before thoroughbred racing,–100 years ago, in fact. For awhile it died away, but now there is a resurgence and it's really coming into its own. People are becoming more interested in harness racing. There's a lot of action involved and this draws the fans. It is a sport that is surging forward.

–Gerry Longo

Gerry Longo is one of the better known harness drivers in California. Last year he rode his own horse, Cachuma Chief, to a 1:59 mile–the biggest thrill of his career.

For More Information

Many of the mass marketed horse magazines cover harness racing from time to time but the following publications cover it exclusively. *The Harness Horse,* Box 1831, Harrisburg, Pa. 17105. Published weekly at $20.00 per year. *Harness World,* Box 100, Cote Des Neiges, Montreal, Que., Can. H3S 2S4. Published semi-monthly at $10.00 per year. *Hub Rail,* 6649 North High St., Worthington, Ohio 43085. Published quarterly at $5.00 per year. For organizations: US Trotting Association, 750 Michigan Ave., Columbus, Ohio 43215; National Association of Harness Drivers, 580 Willis Ave., Suite 4A, Williston Park, N.Y. 11594; Harness Tracks of America, 333 North Michigan Ave., Chicago, Ill. 60601; Hall of Fame of the Trotter, Goshen, N.Y. 10924; American Harness Racing Secretaries, Vernon Downs, Vernon, N.Y. 13476. The USTA does publish an official monthly magazine. It is for their members and membership is $6.00 per year.

For equipment: Pearson's Harness Horse Equipment Co., 2260 N. Walnut St., Muncie, Indiana; Greenville Tire & Wheel Supply, 33 S. Race St., Greenville, Pa. 16125; Rich and Riegle, 951 Wayne Ave., Box 5, Greenville, Ohio 45331–driving colors and racing apparel; Sulky Sales and Service, 159 Jackson St., Saratoga Springs, N.Y. 12866.

Harness racing is another sport with very few books written on the subject. Here are two good ones. Both are available from World Publications, Box 366, Mountain View, Calif. 94040 at the price listed* plus 25 cents postage.

Adios: The Big Daddy of Harness Racing, Marie Hill. The life and racing record of the supreme sire of Standardbred Horses–Adios, a horse whose offspring have earned more than $15 million in purses, and whose stamina, speed and heart led to seven world pacing championships–retold with skill and accuracy by a long-time racing devotee. 1971 Hb., 204 (oversize) pp., ill., $8.95, (Arco).

Harness Racing, A general introduction to the exciting world of harness racing. Sections include information on all of the basics: gaits, training methods, sulkies, drivers and driving techniques. Ppb., $1.95, (Simon & Schuster).

Highland Games

The sound of bagpipes is whining melodiously from all corners of the park and drums are beating an accompaniment. Robed in colorful costumes, dancers are emulating the wild antics of a stag back in the old country. And in the main attraction down on the stadium floor, athletes are alternately tossing around small telephone poles as if they were broomsticks.

Imported from Scotland and virtually untouched by a group of enthusiasts who do not practice the American habit of tinkering with things already beautiful, the Scottish Highland Games are both unique and intriguing.

For those unfamiliar with the ancient forms of Scottish athletics, or for those unaware of the Highland Games which are annual occurances across America and abroad, these activities might seem like an alien version of international track and field, with a lot of exotic fanfare thrown in. The fact is that many sports events practiced internationally could very well have had their humble origins in the highlands of Scotland. The Scots who immigrated to America in the late 18th and early 19th century greatly influenced the formation of sports in America. And of course this country helped shape international athletics as they are today.

Perhaps the most spectacular event in the Scottish Games is the caber toss. Participants in this event hurl into the air large pieces of rounded timber. But tossing the caber carries with it far more subtle qualities than a mere test of brute strength. It is a sport where balance, dexterity, strength, even speed, are important factors. It is not a sport restricted to musclemen.

The most widely used cabers are the McClure Caber, measuring 17 feet and weighing about 100 pounds, and the Ballantine Caber, a 19-foot pole sculptured from Caledonian fir and weighing about 120 pounds. The caber toss participant, with the aid of another person, lifts the caber to an upright position. Without any further help, the contestant picks the piece of wood up and balances it in an upright position, grasping the thinner end of the caber in his hands and allowing some of its weight to rest against his chest. Believe it or not, he then begins to run with it.

Once the contestant believes he has gained sufficient momentum, he comes to a quick and complete halt. He then flips the caber into the air. Hopefully, the pole turns 180 degrees in flight, its thicker end hitting the ground. And then, if all goes well, the pole will fall directly away from the tosser and land

A feature of each Highland Games gathering is the caber toss, an event in which an unwieldly log nearly the size of a telephone pole is flung into the air in an effort to turn it 180 degrees in flight. Some cabers are nearly 20 feet in length and weigh over 100 pounds. To keep the weight standard cabers are often buried in the mud of creek beds between contests to be removed and dried off only hours before they will be thrown by brawny Highland athletes. (MacPhail)

on the ground in a line pointing directly away from him.

Imagine a large clock, with the caber tosser standing at six o'clock. If he perfectly executes the throw, the large end of the caber will be pointing to the 12 as the small end hits the ground. Points are deducted if the caber is pointing to the left or right. A perfect throw is called a "12 o'clock" toss. A "one o'clock" toss is better than a "two o'clock" toss, and an "11 o'clock" throw is better than a "10 o'clock" throw.

If a caber is not successfully flipped over, that is, when its larger end lands on the ground and it falls backward towards the participant, no points are scored. There are, however, a few Highland games where second or third place are decided by how close the caber comes to being in a vertical position before it falls back. In other Highland gatherings, it is permitted to saw the caber shorter and shorter until an athlete finally manages a successful toss.

Among the lingering theories as to how the sport came about, probably the most widely accepted is one which makes ancient Scottish lumberjacks the sport's pioneers. During their leisure moments, they would compete against each other, inventing various games of skill as they went along. Eventually the caber toss developed, and slowly became a national pasttime.

A large number of Caledonian societies all over the United States conduct annual Scottish Gatherings and Games. The two most popular events are held in Santa Rosa, Calif. where the National Championships are staged and in North Carolina, where the famed Grandfather Mountain Games are held.

Other "heavy events" at these gatherings, and other similar contests held all over the country, include:

Putting the stone: Very similar to the conventional shot put, but a 17-pound river stone is used instead of a steel ball.

Scottish hammer: The contestant, without moving his feet, must throw a 16-pound weight attached to a 50-inch wooden shaft and with his back to the line of flight.

Twenty-eight-pound weight for distance: a weight attached to a short chain and ring is hurled in the discus style. The contestant grasps the ring and throws it with one hand.

Fifty-six-pound weight for height: the contestant swings this giant weight between his knees to gain momentum and then hurls the weight over a bar above him using one hand. Similar to pole vaulting, a participant can "pass" until the bar reaches a desired height. After three misses at the same height, he is eliminated. The athlete with the fewest misses at a lower height is victorious in the event of a tie.

–Rich Mellott

Rich Mellott is a sports reporter and freelance writer from Santa Rosa, Calif., where he annually covers the Highland Games National Championships.

Hiking

Hiking is one of modern man's encounters with nature. The sport is popular and enjoyed by all participants. And, it can be participated in by anyone possessing the capacity to walk. Hiking is inexpensive and shuns the fetish of having a line of elite scientific paraphernalia; nor does it demand a new vocabulary. In short, it is not the sport for those crying to be heroes in our time. Hiking is a universal activity used by man to achieve peace, exercise, and knowledge in a simple, uncomplicated and enjoyable manner.

Here is a sport for all ages. To be a hiker does not require superhuman acts of strength, gymnastics, and endurance. Comfortable clothes and good shoes or boots are the basics required.

Just a short simple excursion anywhere; a hike takes on a new meaning when asphalt and concrete are left behind. Americans are limited in the number of places to walk. Either distance, barbed wire, or crime keep Americans away from the majority of potential trail areas. A more complex society will demand more free trails to roam.

Densely populated European countries have popular hiking trails outside of many towns. Sunday afternoons can mean a walk with relatives of all ages through half a dozen farms, woods, meadows, streams, and valleys.

Deep within the jagged cliffs, I was dwarfed by the glaciers of the Swiss Alps. Honored as the Continental parent of all

"Hiking is not abrasive. A hiker's senses are not subjected to extremes, and a gentle to vigorous hike gives a peace and wonderment lost to the hero too busy trying to find himself. Hikes are for exercise, an education in the ways of nature, achieving the goal of reaching a destination. Hiking is exploration. Childlike eyes search out new sights: strewn driftwood on the beach, patterns in water and clouds, a snake, a mineral spring, lizard, hawk. Associated with experiences, these words can recall deep feelings of joy." (Krips)

mountains, my reverence of the Alps was soon to be broken. Up the trail, sometimes steep and very rocky, and past my resting spot, hiked several people in street clothes; the women in dresses, the men in white shirts and street shoes. Sure, we were only several thousand feet up and two hours away from the resort village of Grindelwald, but did that justify the irreverence of street clothes? My image of a hiker had been cultivated in the Western United States. Much to my chagrin, these people did not fit the hiker concept. Or did they?

Hiking is tame. Compared to the big boy sports that have people staggering over glaciers at 15,000 feet or clamoring spider-like up every sheer virgin slab of rock, hiking becomes civilized. True, people have to hike to the rock and to the mountain, but as a sport in itself, it moves slowly along well-defined routes quite removed from the immediate dangers that provide psychological thrills.

Hiking can have danger. Once while returning across a densely forested hillside, a storm set in. The thunder rolled right over the treetops. I could not see the lightning, but the thunder was so loud, it forced me to the ground. I did not panic, but my legs just could not hold me because of fear.

Hiking requires practice and knowledge. First aid, weather, and topographical map reading are all subjects to become acquainted with. Hypothermia, heat exhaustion, and altitude need study. Water, food, clothing, maps, and matches are some of the inexpensive necessities. Hiking is tame only when indulged in wisely. Trekking through a wilderness area, we came upon an abandoned campfire. Its flames were only feet from a packed tinder dry forest. Extinquishing it, we knew that due to man it can all be destroyed.

Hiking is not abrasive. A hiker's senses are not subjected to extremes. And a gentle to vigorous hike gives a peace and wonderment lost to the hero too busy trying to find himself. Hikes are for exercise, an education in the ways of nature, achieving the goal of reaching a destination.

Hiking is exploration. Childlike eyes search out new sights: strewn driftwood on the beach, patterns in water and clouds, a snake, a mineral spring, lizard, hawk. Associated with experiences, these words can recall deep feelings of joy.

—**Bruce Neuschwander**

Bruce Neuschwander has hiked the better trails of Europe and the Western United States. He is assistant editor of **Soccer World.**

For More Information

Additional information can be found under backpacking and camping. Here are two books. Both are available from World Publications, Box 366, Mountain View, Calif. 94040 at the price listed* plus 25 cents postage.

Introduction to Foot Trails in America, Robert Colwell. A good beginner's guide for those who want to spend a day to a week "somewhere" but aren't exactly sure of where or how to get there. Contains a useful City-Trail index listing trails three hours driving-time away from over 100 cities in the US. 1972 Ppb., 221 pp., ill., $3.95, (Stackpole).

Trail Country, Robert L. Wood. Describes every Olympic National park trail, its condition, points of interest, flora and fauna. Also presents the park's ocean beach strip, its geological history, botanical life zones, living creatures, primitive Indian inhabitants, early-day explorers, and subsequent development as a park. Hb., 298 pp., ill., $6.95, (Mountaineers).

Hitchhiking

Just as travel is a dramatization of life, so hitchhiking is a dramatization of travel. It breaks down even deeper norms and releases even more energy. Hitchhikers, like all adventurers, vibrate with this energy. It makes them sensitive and alive to their experiences, and attracts others to them. Of course, handling this energy is difficult: the more that things are random and unexpected, the more you need to improvise, the more fully use all of yourself in the business of being. But then one day on the road, you suddenly realize you're having the time of your life. You feel the energy of the universe flowing right through you. It's the dream come true.

The dream of hitching goes something like this: "With my dusty pack on my trusty back, I travel for free across the wide spaces of my native land. I think people are beautiful, and I trust them. As a result, I meet many friendly folks who give me rides and food and places to stay. But I also give and share the little I have. I help the drivers I meet by taking the wheel, telling my tales and listening to theirs. I honor Nature and the land by not polluting as I go. As a hitchhiker I see America with clear eyes, its good and bad, and I listen closely to its rhythms. Finally, I arrive at my destination wiser for my experiences, knowledgeable from my travels, warmed by the new friends I made. I am the dream hitchhiker." Believe it or not, more hitchhikers are pretty well described by this dream—young, idealistic, friendly, openminded, interesting.

Hitchhiking as practiced today is a healthy mass-reaction to America's current preoccupations with safety and security, money and materialism, police and paranoia. Today's travelers are saying no way to these soulshrinking forces, and they're putting their faith on the line and their packs on the road to prove it. They want freedom and adventure, and traveling by thumb is made to order—it's unpredictable, it's cheap, and it's about people. The widespread notions of its danger and illegality only make it more attractive.

—**Ed Buryn**

Ed Buryn is to hitchhiking what Mozart was to music. He authored **Vagabonding in America,** *the most complete book ever written on hitchhiking and traveling.*

Requirements

What does it actually take to go hitchhiking? Who should do it and who ought to shun it? Here's a profile of a modern American hitchhiker.

Character. A hitchhiker should be a character with character, because hitchhiking is a test of who we are. Character has something to do with deliberately choosing the better way over the easy way. To do that and make it, you may have to pull out all the stops. Being on the road is a challenge to become a whole person . . . you should be confident in the face of doubt, tolerant when victimized by the weakness of others, tough in order to endure the physical hardships, flexible enough to go with the changing fortunes of the road. You also need a sense of humor to ward off the ever-threatening cynicism.

Hitching is a test of humanity, because you'll see people at their best and their worst. It means opening yourself to people in the face of frequently damaging evidence. Some people will dump on you and laugh. Somehow you must live it and forget it. Most people will simply ignore you, and that can be even harder.

Being on the road means learning to "be here now," taking each moment and extracting whatever it has to offer. You'll stand countless hours in dozens of places, struggling with the mysteries and miseries of reality. Gradually a feeling of contentment and fullness can be reached, no matter how forsaken and weird your situation may be. If it's a skill you want to acquire, then hitchhiking may be for you.

Shortage of Money. Lack of cash may open your heart to hitchhiking where spiritual arguments fail. Dig this: Even in the plutocratic USA, you can travel just about anywhere on $1 to $5 a day. The cost variation depends mostly on your style of travel—that is, comfort requirements, traveling companions, and such. You save money directly, of course, by getting transportation for nothing; but you also save money because hitchhiking is a lifestyle in which finding inexpensive food and lodging becomes second nature. It's based mostly on meeting people, so you also invariably undergo great social adventures as well. All this comes from the advantage of not having too much money to start with.

Abundance of Time. The more time you have, the stonier it gets. A few weeks hitching on the road gives you a heavy charge and can get you across country or over a short tour. But a summer's tour will really do it to you, and you can't possibly come back the same person you left. No way. Serendipity is the hallmark of hitchhiking, and it takes time for that—to get itself together in the right sequences. Why not take time before it takes you? Remember, time is always there; it's we that pass.

Health is Wealth. Or, to render the wisdom in its homey fullness, "Good Health is the Only Real Wealth." Amen and thank you, Dr. Bronner. Yet, it's true. Hitchhiking requires you to be physically tough and resilient, again to an extent depending on your particular traveling motif. Tarzan need not step forward; he isn't called for. But the uncertainty and irregularity of hitchhiking is at times disturbing or unsettling. You'll get rained on occasionally, wind-blown a lot, sand-blasted and smogged-on, sun-burned and frozen. You'll be stiff from sleeping two hours, then stiff from standing three hours. On the credit side, you intensely experience the weather and the spaces around you. It's heavenly to feel gusts and puffs of zephyrs lightly stroke your skin; to watch tall clouds fall slowly by.

Your chronological age has some importance, but the limit is at the lower end, not the upper. Older hitchhikers are seen far less than young 'uns, but it's not a matter of ability so much as life style and enthusiasm. Not many older people (like, over 40) hitchhike, but it just isn't their style anymore. It could be, though, for older people get rides without extraordinary difficulty.

Stuff. A certain minimum amount of good-quality stuff is necessary: A light pack, sleeping bag, canteen, extra clothes, boots, etc. Beyond the practical, you'll need some political baggage: ID especially, and other paperwork like money and maps. The police around the country will want to inspect your papers carefully.

"As a hitchhiker I see America with clear eyes, it's good and bad, and I listen closely to its rhythms." (Buryn)

And that's what you'll need.

—Ed Buryn

For More Information

Here are some books of interest. All are available from World Publications, Box 366, Mountain View, Calif. 94040 at the price listed* plus 25 cents postage. Write for a complete list.

Vagabonding in America, Ed Buryn. There is no other hitchhiking/traveling book we recommend higher than this one. Complete in every way, it is a massive book describing every form of travel, with 100s of photos by the author on his trips through America. 1973 Ppb., 354 (oversize) pp., ill., $4.95, (Random House).

Hitchhiker's Handbook, Tom Grimm. This book details most of the situations that can occur when hitchhiking, and tells you what to do about them. Will easily save you the price of the book with its hints on living cheaply. 1972 Ppb., 176 pp., $2.95, (New American Library).

Hitchhiker's Field Manual, Paul DiMaggio. For the professional hitchhiker on tour, this book is a must to take along. A basic guide to survival in urban and rural America. 1974 Hb. & Ppb., 335 pp., ill., $6.00/$1.95, (MacMillan).

Horseback Riding

Eohippus, or the "dawn - horse", an early ancestor of the modern horse, evolved in the Rocky Mountain region about 45 million years ago. He had a short neck, padded feet, small teeth, and wasn't much bigger than a good-sized tom cat. After Eohippus, the horse disappeared from the North American continent for 25 million years, only to reappear again larger than before. This was the beginning of several disappearances and reappearances of the horse, who grew larger all the time, until the invader Hernando Cortez brought the animal to North America from Spain and Mexico in the 16th century. Since then, this muscular, good-natured animal has served in many capacities—as both a sporting and work animal.

Of course, trail riding is one of the better known marriages between horse and man, an activity highly romanticized in tales of our cowboys who roamed the great midwestern plains. Actually, "riding the trail" is a phrase that, today, might be used in connection with taking your horse for a stroll in Central, or Golden Gate Park, trotting along a wilderness path, or in an open field—even riding along a busy city street.

Anyone who has the desire can learn to ride a horse. It only takes a few lessons for a person to be able to ride comfortably at a walk, trot, or canter. Experience breeds confidence, and the better your form and the greater your understanding of your horse, the more readily he will respond to your commands.

In horseback riding there are three different riding styles, or seats, in popular use. Each style is best suited to a certain type of horse; each has a special set of disciplines with a distinct variety of *tack* (equipment used in riding). Although the stock seat, which requires the western saddle, is a very popular style for trail riding, the English saddle seat also finds popularity with the pleasure rider.

Riding Western calls for the use of the comparatively heavy saddle that the cowboys used and western clothing (jeans, western hat, boots, etc.).

The English style tack used in riding the saddle seat has the cut-back show saddle as the main piece, and apparel is composed of Kentucky jodhpurs (pants), boots, and a simple riding shirt or sweater.

A third riding style, known as the hunt seat, is suitable for cross-country jaunts, where there are many obstacles. This group of riders can be seen dashing along at a fast gallop, while jumping everything in sight.

Once a rider has ridden for awhile, he probably will grow to prefer one riding style over another, although many fine horsemen are familiar with two, or all three of the seats. Several factors should be considered when choosing a particular seat. The kind of riding you plan to do, the particular terrain you will be riding over, and the type of horse, should all be taken into account.

A popular form of sport today is the competitive trail ride and endurance race. In a competitive ride the horse and rider are not pushed to the limits of stress, while the endurance ride is a more grueling affair. In 1936, the Green Mountain Horse Association held its first endurance ride, and today various contests are held throughout the country.

A Little History

Before there were roads, man rode the trails on horseback. His horse was his closest—sometimes his only—companion, carrying him across the steppes and through the forests and into the mountains. Man discovered that when he cared well for his horse, the mount would carry him far and serve him well.

The earliest riders quickly appreciated the advantages of riding over walking, and this gave new dimensions to war. Mounted warriors could sweep in on the enemy, stun him in devastating attack, and be gone faster than they could be followed. But there were endless hours on the trail for every hour of combat.

In some cases, whole tribes and groups became horse nations—the Assyrians, the Mongols, the American Indians—building their culture around the horse and developing their own master brand of horsemanship. For these peoples, the valued mount was not necessarily the fleetest nor the prettiest—he was the one who endured, the one who took his rider there, performed whatever duties were required of him, and brought him all the way home.

Imprinting the trails of history are exceptional feats of travel and endurance. Bucephalus carried Alexander the Great from Macedonia to the borders of India. Napoleon's Vizir, an Arabian stallion, took the Emperor from Paris to Moscow and back again through the fierce Russian winter. The Chinese, the Russians, the Turks, the Spanish in their exploration of the New World—all have tales of staggering distances traveled and incredible hardships endured.

Among the grandest of these is the 10,000-mile ride made by A. F. Tschiffely, a Swiss who wanted to prove the toughness and endurance of the Argentine Criollo. With Mancha and Gato, ages 15 and 16, he left Buenos Aires in 1925. Two and a half years later, after traveling through jungles, over mountain ranges, and even across a hanging bridge, they arrived in Washington, D.C. Both horses were in excellent condition and lived to a ripe old age. This was truly the trail ride of all time.

The American West grew on a gridwork of Indian, cattle, and pioneer trails, criss-crossed all over by the myriad marches of the U.S. Cavalry. It was the Army that began looking more closely at what went into making a good cavalry—or trail—horse. It had become evident that in man's tinkering with breeds to produce speed for racing, strength for pulling, or style for showing, endurance in many cases had become secondary. What breed makes the best trail horse? What kind of feed, care, and conditioning best promote good health and staying ability?

The Army held grueling endurance trials in the 1920's, hoping to find the answers to these questions. Although the tests were inconclusive because of few participants, they did indicate that high endurance depended less on breed than on proper feed, conditioning, and training. Perhaps even more important, the Army rides sparked new interest in trail riding as a sport.

In 1936, the Green Mountain Horse Association organized its first 100-mile trail ride, and planned it to be a competitive, but popular, event promoting good horsemanship, thoughtful conditioning and care of the horse, and pleasurable sport and companionship. The ride became an annual institution. From these beginnings, other trail riding organizations have blossomed and many annual rides, such as the California 100-miles-in-24-hours Tevis Cup ride, are well-known throughout the country. Many of these are under the auspices of the North American Trail Rides Conference.

Competitive rides are divided into two categories. An *endurance ride* is a race that approaches the limits of stress for both horse and rider. A *competitive trail ride* is timed but is not a race; emphasis is placed on horsemanship, safety, and sportsmanship, and the ride is less exhausting. Both require conditioning, good riding, and sound management practices. Most trail riders find that Western gear and dress are most practical and comfortable for both horse and rider.

All of these rides have helped to pin down the characteristics of a good trail horse. He should be a mature, sound horse that has a calm, dependable disposition, easy gaits, good conformation, and good sense.

Of course, not every rider is enthusiastic about competing or testing his mount's endurance, and not every horse is capable of pressured long-distance riding. Informal trail riding is enjoyed today by increasing thousands, whether on dude ranch pack trips, highly organized social rides, club treks, or Sunday get-togethers. Trail Riders of the Wilderness, a division of the American Forestry Association, holds annual pack trips in many wilderness areas of the United States. And like so many of his ancestors, the working cowhorse still trails the cattle to and from summer ranges throughout the West.

All forms of horsemanship create a companionship and harmony between two creatures. This is part of the tremendous enjoyment and challenge of equestrian sports. But the trail rider and his horse can't always choose the weather or conditions through which they must travel together. While moving stock, Rex and I have been caught by darkness, downpours, and blizzards. We've had sleet and hailstones build up in the creases of saddle and clothing, melt in the body warmth, and then freeze hard in bitter wind, making an ice-sheathed armor of my levis, daggered icicles of his mane. But misery shared is better endured, and there's good comfort in the steadiness and warmth of a home-bound horse.

Tschiffely told about detouring through the mountains because landslides and swollen rivers blocked the road. High on a mountain trail at dusk, his Indian guide deserted him, taking with him all the food. There was no grass for the horses, and all he could find in his saddle bags was a small piece of sugar. The three waited out the night, and in the morning Tschiffely cut the sugar into three pieces and shared it with his equine friends. This companionship is the essence of trail riding.

—Gaydell Collier

While Gaydell Collier has written and edited works in a variety of fields, one of her greatest loves is horses. Living with her husband and four children on a farm in Vermont, and later on a Wyoming ranch, has given her ample opportunity for riding. She is co-author of **Basic Horsemanship—English and Western.**

For More Information

It seems that more horse magazines are coming out every year. There are loads of publications and most newsstands have one of them. There are over 50 publications that we know about and we simply don't have the space to list them all. That is why we are listing just a few. For other magazines, check the other horse listings. Here are some of the bigger horse magazines: *Horse & Rider,* 145 Rowland Ave., Covina, Calif. 91723. *Western Horseman,* Box 7980, Colorado Springs, Colo. 80933. *American Horseman,* 257 Park Ave. South, New York, N.Y. 10010. *The Horseman,* 5314 Bingle Rd., Houston, Texas 77018. *Horse Lover's National Magazine,* 9420 Activity Rd., Suite D, San Diego, Calif. 92126.

Here are some good books on the subject. All are available from World Publications, Box 366, Mountain View, Calif. 94040 at the price listed* plus 25 cents each postage.

Horseback Vacation Guide, Steven D. Price. For the first time a a single-volume guide to all the places, events, arrangements, facilities, and money-saving tips one needs to know to plan an exciting vacation in the saddle—across North America and beyond. 1975 Hb. & Ppb., 160 pp., ill., $7.95/$4.95, (Stephen Greene).

Trail Horses and Trail Riding, Anne & Perry Westbrook. A well-written, comprehensive, and illustrated handbook on how to cover considerable distances on horseback in a pleasurable manner. Hb., 117 pp., ill., $4.95, (Arco).

Basic Horsemanship—English & Western, Eleanor E. Prince and G.M. Collier. Clear, easy prose highlights a step-by-step guide for riders and instructors. Lessons proceed from first mounting to intermediate levels and participation in competitive events. 1974 Hb., 353 pp., ill., $8.95, (Doubleday).

Horse Racing

Horse Racing, popularly known as "The Sport of Kings", bears little resemblance to the sport that was reserved only for those of royal blood in the days of England's Charles II. Today horse racing includes the wealthy Thoroughbred owners of Kentucky and Maryland down to the unnoticed stable hand. Its popularity is well-illustrated by the fact that it is the most-attended paid spectator sport in the world. Of course, this popularity stems largely from the opportunity to gamble.

While horse racing is looked upon as a large money-making industry in America, it is regarded with different attitudes in other parts of the world. The English take their racing very seriously and in France it is more of an art form than a sport. Modern painters such as Toulouse-Lautrec and Degas have found great inspiration at the racetrack.

Actually, organized horse racing is divided into two main types: flat racing and steeplechase and hurdle racing. (See Horse Steeplechasing section.) Presently, the most popular form in America, however, is flat racing.

"While horse racing is looked upon as a large money-making industry in America, it is regarded with different attitudes in other parts of the world. The English take their racing very seriously and in France it is more of an art form than a sport." (Duffy)

Most flat races are held on oval dirt tracks which are specially prepared or skinned. Racing distances vary from the short quarter-mile sprints to some of over two miles in the big Cup races in Britain. Starting stalls, or gates, have replaced the dropping of a flag used long ago to start the race. These mechanical devices insure that all horses and their jockeys are started equally.

Besides the longer races, in which Thoroughbred racing horses compete, many tracks include races for Quarter Horses. A regulation quarter track is a straightaway course of 440 yards in length.

The Kentucky Derby

The Kentucky Derby is America's greatest horse race. Nearly every breeder, trainer, owner, jockey and groom would rather win this one race than all the other big stakes combined. The Derby ranks in glamor with the World Series, the Indianapolis 500 and the Super Bowl.

Stardust, riches, and a measure of immortality attend the Derby winner. The instant the winning colt flashes under the wire – only one filly, Regret, ever won – his value reaches at least one million dollars for stud purposes. Even before the 1973 Derby, in which he was the favorite, Secretariat was syndicated for $6,080,000.

Now in its second century, the mile and one-quarter race for three-year-olds is run on the first Saturday in May at Churchill Downs in Louisville. Its history teems with excitement, humor, pathos, and a good deal of delightful schmaltz! Colonel E.R. Bradley offered to bet his Kentucky home, his land, and his horses on the 1926 Derby. Ben Jones trained five of Calumet Farm's eight Derby winners and liked nothing better than a good fist fight. Isaac Murphy, the gentle black jockey, liked to frighten his owners by winning his races by a nose.

Glorious thoroughbreds – Aristides, Old Rosebud, Exterminator, Count Fleet, Whirlaway, Citation, Canonero II – and famous jockeys such as Earl Sande, Eddie Arcaro, Willie Shoemaker, and Bill Hartack – have all contributed to the Derby legend.

The Kentucky Derby is a triumph of the business and promotional talents of the late Colonel Matt J. Winn, an attractive and popular figure who first concerned himself with management of an ailing Churchill Downs in 1902. Winn transformed the event into a race of national importance. He did it by courting the big New York owners, and by wooing big-time sportswriters.

The Derby is not without its faults as an intelligent test of three-year-olds, and as a sorts spectacle. Many trainers and owners believe the race comes too early, for most of the animals have just turned three, and their bones are still soft and growing. This is the first time many of them have been called upon to run one mile and one-quarter and tote as much as 126 pounds, the scale weight for colts, and 121 for fillies. For some horses, the race proves a crippler.

From the spectator's standpoint, the crowds are too big and unruly, the race too commercialized.

But having said all that, there is still only one Kentucky Derby. The late Joe A. Estes, onetime editor of *The Blood-Horse* magazine, once explained the spell it casts over horsemen:

"They watch the Derby with almost hypnotic concentration because it is, to breeders of thoroughbreds, the most important race of all. For it is racing which reveals good horses and good mares, first through their own performance, and second, through the performances of their produce.

"The most important single race in America for this purpose is the Kentucky Derby because, with fewer exceptions than must be made for any other race, it brings together for a test of their racing class, and hence a test of their breeding class, the best horses from every crop of foals."

–Peter Chew

Peter Chew is a freelance writer whose articles on horse racing have won many awards. In his youth he became interested in horses when he exercised race horses and schooled steeplechasers. He is the author of **The Kentucky Derby, the First 100 Years.**

For More Information

There are many horse magazines but most don't cover racing regularly. Those listed here, however, only cover racing.

Turf and Sport Digest, 511 Oakland Ave., Baltimore, Md. 21212. Published monthly at $9.00 per year. The magazine is for the Thoroughbred horse racing fan. It covers jockeys, trainers, horse tracks and other facets of the racing scene. They also publish a weekly tabloid which gives ratings to all the horses running in the country.

The Blood-Horse, Box 4038, Lexington, Ky. 40504. Published weekly at $25.00 per year. For a weekly it is really thick. The copy we have is over 100 pages. This magazine will totally keep you current on what is happening in the horse racing scene.

Also, you might check out *The Backstretch*, 19363 James Couzens Hwy., Detroit, Mich. 48235 and *Thoroughbred Record*, Box 11788, Lexington, Ky. 40511.

The Jockey Club, 300 Park Ave., New York, N.Y. 10022 is the registry office for all Thoroughbred horses foaled in the U.S. They register over 28,000 foals each year. There is also the Thoroughbred Racing Association, 220 East 42nd St., New York, N.Y. 10017; Thoroughbred Owners and Breeders Association, Box 36, Ozone Park, Jamaica, N.Y. 11417; National Association of State Racing Commissioners, Box 4216, Lexington, Ky. 40504; and The Quarter Horse Racing Guild, 801 S. Anaheim Blvd., Anaheim, Calif. 92805.

The best source for equipment is to visit your local track and saddlery shops. However, one place of many that does offer mail order is H. Kauffman & Sons, 139 E. 24th St., New York, N.Y. 10010. Additional information can also be found in the other horse sections.

Here are some good horse racing books. All are available from World Publications, Box 366, Mountain View, Calif. 94040 at the price listed* plus 25 cents each postage. Write for a complete list.

The Kentucky Derby: The First 100 Years, Peter Chew. Illustrated with scores of nostalgic and dramatic photos, this big, oversize book is a fascinating commemorative volume of 100 years of Derby history. 1974 Hb., 303 (oversize) pp., ill., $15.00 (Houghton Mifflin).

Secretariat, Raymond Woolfe, Jr. The story of the first Triple Crown winner in a quarter of a century – a big, golden-red colt who could run in front, come from behind, carry weight and fascinate millions of Americans by his captivating style. 1974 Hb., 187 (oversize) pp., ill., $15.00 (Chilton).

Run for the Roses, Jim Bolus. This is an exciting chronicle in words and pictures of every Kentucky Derby since 1875. Not a dry history, the book covers the fizzles, stretch runs, and long shot winners. Many color photos. 1974 Hb., 209 (oversize) pp., ill., $14.95 (Hawthorn)

The Lady is a Jock. Lynn Haney. There are approximately 50 women jockeys in the U.S. today, and this book plunges into the gypsy life of some of the top women riders in the world. They're just as horse crazy and willing to take on grubby jobs as the drifters who are traditionally part of the racing world. 1973 Hb., 180 pp., ill., $5.95 (Dodd Mead).

America's Quarter Horses, Paul Laune. A complete guide to the spunky little American favorite. Covers history, use, care, training and showing and racing. 1973 Hb., ill., $14.95 (Doubleday).

They're Off! Regal Murray. How to win on the horses at the racetrack. This book is definitely a good bet. 1974 Hb., 45 pp., $9.95 (Naylor).

Horseshoe Pitching

One of the most popular athletic activities in Classic Greece was discus throwing. The discus was a 10 to 12 inch circular plate made of metal or stone. Tradition has it that camp followers of the Greek army who could not afford the discus picked up horseshoes instead, and began throwing them at stakes in the earth.

In between this ancient game and modern horseshoes came quoits, in which a circle of iron or loop of heavy rope was thrown at a peg. Englishmen in 1869 established rules for quoits, setting the distance between pegs at 19 yards. The player stood level with the quoit and threw it on his first step. There was no weight restriction but the outside diameter had to be eight inches or less. The ground around the stakes was clay and all measurements for points were taken between the peg and the part of the quoit closest to it.

The US adopted English quoits rules to horseshoe pitching, but no tournaments were held or records kept until 1909. The game appears to have been a favorite among soldiers returning from wars. Coming home, these men interested others in the sport and hundreds of pitching courts in the US were laid out in cities, villages and farming communities.

The first world horseshoe pitching contest was held in Bronson, Kansas during the summer of 1909. Frank Jackson was awarded a World Championship belt with horseshoes attached. Jackson had never heard of holding a shoe so it would open toward the peg. He had been practicing holding his fingers around the heel calk (a ¾ inch nub) so he could pitch ringers. That initial tourney was played on dirt courts with pegs two inches high and 38½ feet apart. Jackson was able to put two rings on the stake time after time so his opponents' shoes would slide off.

Rules, by laws and a constitution were established by the Grand League of the American Horseshoe Pitchers Association (now known as the National Horseshoe Pitchers Association of America) in 1914. They raised the peg height to eight inches, which was met by approval by most pitchers, and de-

"The game appears to have been a favorite among soldiers coming home from the Spanish-American War. They interested others in the sport and hundreds of pitching courts in the US were laid out in cities, villages and farming communities."

clared that tie throws cancel. Shoes were to weigh between two pounds and two pounds three ounces. Leaners would count three points, ringers five points, and no points were given for shoes more than six inches from the peg. The pitcher's box reached three feet each side of the peg and six feet back, while 38½ feet separated the stakes. These rules were contained in the book *Horseshoe Guide.*

Today horseshoe pitching competition is divided into groups for men, junior boys, women, junior girls, intermediates and seniors. Most of these categories are covered in the Ray Williams family of Auburn, California. Everyone in the family pitches horseshoes. Between the seven children and Ray they hold 20 state and national titles. The father is the promoter. Ray is national secretary for the Horseshoe Pitchers Association, and actively spreads the word about the game.

Walter Ray, one of their 16-year-old boys, is the current national junior champ. It takes "a little bit of patience and a lot of practice" to throw well, he says. In the qualifying round for the world tourney he set a record of 96%, hitting ringers 48 out of 50 shoes. During the one-day competition he threw 670 shoes and average 86.6% ringers.

Walter's 15-year-old brother Jeffrey, who finished second at the world tournament, keeps the pressure on. A recent match between them lasted 130 shoes. When each threw two ringers, there was no score. Time after time they'd each throw twice, walk to the other stake and throw back. Jeffrey led through most of the long match, until the score was 45 to 40. The first one to 50 wins. At that point "I decided to close the game," his older brother says. He did.

The 10-year-old twins in the family, John and Nathan, keep the older boys hopping.

Esther, the mother, Cynthia (20), Debbie (21), and Barbara (18) have all held the California state title. Still, Walter is the most serious pitcher of the group. He steps out with his left foot. He's right handed and holds the shoe with the opening toward the left. On its trip to the stake it spins one and a quarter clockwise turns, where usually it will land a ringer.

Beginning players, Walter Ray says, usually hold the middle of the shoe and throw so it flips over and over. Only one person has mastered this "unorthodox" technique and been able to win with it in high-level competition. Most experienced players spin the shoe to the right or left ¾, 1¼, or 1¾ turns.

The open men's tournament at the nationals this year spanned five days. Playing time lasted up to seven hours per day. Elmer Hohl of Wellesley, Ontario, this year's men's champion, says he got tired chiefly from walking back and forth. So long as both players keep throwing ringers the game goes on.

The men throw at stakes 40 feet away. Juniors and women throw 30 feet. There are many different styles of play, not only in grip, stance, and which foot is used to lead, but in pace. Some throw immediately, others dally around.

In such an intense and precise sport, it's easy to get rattled. Elmer Hohl rates an ability "not to get riled easily" as one of his most important attributes. Psyching requires that a player stay calm, and not lose concentration, even if an opponent suddenly starts playing much better.

It's not that easy to "throw a show properly," says Walter Ray. "While it can be learned from a book it would be easier to get in touch with a local club."

What is the value here? The Williams family likes it. "Not only is it fun," Esther says, but "it gives you good exercise walking back and forth, out in the fresh air. There's a lot in it."

"And you get a little dirty," Walter Ray adds.

For More Information

The National Horseshoe Pitchers' Association, Box 1702, Auburn, Calif. 95603 is the national organization and they publish a monthly magazine called *The Horseshoe Pitcher's News Digest.* Cost is $5.00 per year. Some companies that can supply official tournament pitching shoes and supplies: Diamont Tool and Horseshoe Co., Box 6246, Duluth, Minn. 55806; Ted Allen Horseshoes, 1045 Linden Ave., Boulder, Colo. 80302–Ted Allen is a 10-time world champion and has designed a very good professional shoe; The Queen City Forging Co., 233 Tennyson St., Cincinnati, Ohio 45226.

Here is a book that should be of interest. It is available from World Publications, Box 366, Mountain View, Calif. 94040 at the price listed* plus 25 cents postage.

Pitching Championship Horseshoes, Orrie Reno. Whether in your own backyard or in a tournament, you will appreciate all the information covered in this book. Complete playing and scoring rules, instructions for laying out a backyard court. Top players give their own tips on pitching. 1973 Hb. & Ppb., 350 pp., ill., $6.95/$2.95, (Barnes).

Horse Showing

In 1883, the first horse show was held, largely as a result of horse owners' eager interests in displaying and matching their animals against those of others. This show, in New York City's Gilmore Gardens, was sponsored by the newly organized National Horse Show Association of America and was open to anyone who wanted to participate. As a result, a great variety of equine species were shown: thoroughbreds, trotters, delivery-wagon horses, farm horses, even a few donkeys!

In the years following this first event, the horse show became increasingly popular, especially as a social gathering place for wealthy aristocrats. The show became an annual affair in New York, and was moved to Madison Square Garden in 1890.

In 1913, a significant change was incorporated into the New York show. Events that had been exclusively for work horses were discontinued, since motorized vehicles had largely replaced the need for this type of horse. In their place were substituted events designed for the new breed of show horses. This trend continued, making it possible, eventually, only for a horse bred especially for a certain task, or a carefully trained thoroughbred or standardbred horse, to win.

Largely because of the success of the early New York shows, other events were established in the U.S.–although much less elaborate. With an increasing number of shows, the American Horse Shows Association was formed as the supervising body.

Today, horse shows are held year-round, indoors and out. Ribbons and cups are offered the winners and, in larger shows, cash is awarded in addition. Even so, these prizes do not nearly equal the expense that a horse owner might put into training and maintenance of his animals. Thus, horse showing remains, in most instances, a rich man's sport.

The days of buggy horse entries and "all comer" shows are over. Today's horses are specially bred for show purposes–hackney and saddle horses, thoroughbred jumpers and interbred hunters. Much emphasis has been put on the horse's gait; the three-gaited and the five-gaited horse are especially favored. These horses may be shipped around the nation from one show to another during the peak of their careers, competing for rich prizes.

The American Saddle Bred Horse

The American Saddle Bred Horse has not only been acknowledged by his admirers as "The World's Most Beautiful Horse," but also as "The Horse That America Made."

A versatile individual, his development came from the early pioneers of this country who wanted a horse of easy gait, utility and beauty, plus excellent disposition, quality and stamina.

The ideal specimen of this breed is quite beautiful and, naturally, has much quality and fineness. He stands approximately 15 to 16 hands (a hand is four inches) and will weigh from 900 to 1200 pounds. He must have a well-shaped and finely chiseled head, large bright eyes and small ears that are sharp and used with alertness. His neck should be long, fitting onto the head with a small throat latch and into a sloping shoulder. He should have prominent withers, a short, level back, clean flat-boned legs, long sloping pasterns and well-formed feet.

The American Saddle Bred Horse is shown in three major divisions of a horse show: *three and five-gaited,* and *fine harness.* He is also shown as a *Pleasure Horse* and makes an excellent *Hunter/Jumper* entrant. However, his basic use is three- and five-gaited, fine harness and Pleasure.

The Five-Gaited Horse: This is the aristocrat of the entire breed, and is considered by many as the most spectacular and exciting in any horse show. He wears a full mane and tail and is shown wearing *Quarter Boots* that protect the front feet of the horse when he is performing his gaits.

This horse is shown at the three gaits which are natural to all horses regardless of their breed (*walk, trot* and *canter*) and then at the two man-made gaits (*slow-gait* and *rack*). He is judged on performance at these gaits, plus soundness, animation, manners and conformation.

The trot is actually a two-beat affair that must be square and bold, with a natural action that is high. Speed is desirable if done in form, but too much speed may throw off his form.

The canter should be a slow and rhythmic sort of thing, accomplished with something akin to a rocking chair smoothness and motion and executed on the correct *leads* (left lead when going to the left, right lead when going to the right).

The slow-gait must be a rather high yet methodical gait, done very slowly and with high frontal action.

The rack is a four-beat gait, free from any lateral motion or pacing. The knee and hock action should be snappy and speed is desired if done in form.

Form is particularly important in showing. If a gaited horse is pushed too rapidly he will fall out of his gait, drag his hocks, and look like anything but a true show horse.

The walk must be done in an elastic step, prompt, primpy and in an alert manner, while being a true, flat-foot walk.

Classes for five-gaited horses are separated as to sex, age, amateur, juvenile, open, ladies, and Stake or Championship events.

The Three-Gaited Horse: Required to perform all three of the natural gaits: walk, trot and canter, he must go both ways of the ring and is judged on his action, conformation, animation, manners and soundness.

The three-gaited horse is shown with a clipped mane and tail, and is often referred to as a *walk-trot.* His gaits must be executed in a slow, collected manner and with very high action, carrying his head high, and having alert ears and over-all airs of brilliance.

His walk should be prompt, showy, done cheerfully in perfect form and at about a speed of four miles per hour without any fretting, dancing or side-ways motion.

The trot is the gait most emphasized and must be true, high in action and very well collected without any leg dragging (hocks) in the rear, and without excessive speed.

The canter should be slow, rhythmic, and done on correct leads, depending on which way the horse is going in the ring.

Classes for this type of horse are designated by size (Over 15.2 and Under 15.2), also their age (a junior if four-year-old or under). His events (amateur, juvenile, Open, Stake Championships and ladies events are the same as the five-gaited horse).

The Fine Harness Horse: Unquestionably one of the most beautiful of events in any show ring, particularly in the ladies division, the fine harness horse must be shown at two gaits—the walk and trot—and both ways of the show ring. Judging is done on performance, conformation, animation, manners and soundness.

He is shown harnessed to an appropriate four-wheeled vehicle and has a full mane and tail.

A fine harness horse should be exactly as the name implies: beautiful, fine, and showing exceptional brilliance and personality in the ring.

He is shown at an animated walk and an airy park trot, which should show lots of motion both front and behind. Extreme speed is penalized, for the simple reason that he would then be stretched out without form. The slower and loftier the gait, the prettier he is.

Classes for the fine harness horse are made up for sex (mare, stallion, gelding, with often the mare class alone and the stallion/gelding class together), age, amateur, ladies, Open and Stake or Championships.

—Melvin Peavey

Melvin Peavey describes himself as a "crusty, cranky old redhead," who has worked with **The National Horseman** *and* **Saddle and Bridle,** *among other publications. Presently he is Publisher/Editor of* **Horse World** *magazine.*

For More Information

For additional information see horseback riding or check with the American Horse Shows Association, 527 Madison Ave., New York, N.Y. 10022.

Here is a book that has an excellent chapter on horse showing. It is available from World Publications, Box 366, Mountain View, Calif. 94040 at the price listed* plus 25 cents postage. **The Horseman's Book,** Barbara Van Tuyl. The complete dictionary of the horse world. Thorough and easy-to-find definitions of terms relating to the various aspects of horsemanship. A collection of 13 mini-dictionaries, covering specific fields such as harness racing, horse shows, fox hunting, breeding, etc. 1973 Hb., 262 pp., ill., $9.95, (Prentice Hall).

Horse Steeplechase

A steeplechase race is one in which horses and riders race over obstructed countryside, usually over hedges, water jumps, banks, fences, etc., with the purpose of testing the horse for its qualifications as a hunter. Thus the horses are usually of the hunter type, with strong builds, and the riders prefer a modified forward seat rather than the jockey seat.

The term steeplechase comes from the fact that in early races the horsemen used church steeples as bearing points while racing over the course.

Another version of countryside racing is the cross-country race which takes place under the natural conditions of open terrain, with little or no obstacles. Both steeplechasing and cross-country are included in the Olympic equestrian Three Day Event which is designed to test the all-around ability of horse and rider.

Still another form of the sport, called hurdle racing, is different from steeplechasing in that the course is usually over a short track, often inside a race track, and over hurdles which are not solid.

The most famous steeplechase is the Grand National at Aintree, England, over a distance of more than four miles. It is undoubtedly the toughest of all courses with many more horses starting the competition than finishing. In 1928 forty-two started and only one finished, demonstrating that manners and obedience are just as important as stamina and speed in this special race!

Behind the Scenes

A few years ago, a young trainer who had managed to save a few dollars decided it might be fun to buy a cheap yearling himself—to race in his own name and colors. A large breeding establishment was having a dispersal sale in Saratoga that year and a friend had told this trainer that there might be some bargains there. Accordingly, with little more forethought than is normally given to buying a new pair of socks, the man decided to buy the first reasonably sound-looking colt that sold for less than $5000. For an outlay of only $2,200, he therefore became the owner of the second yearling to be auctioned.

The colt was sent to the trainer's farm in the country for breaking, and, being rather small and particularly kind and gentle, the little fellow became something of a pet among the employees on the farm. When the trainer returned from Saratoga a few weeks later he found that the colt had proved an apt pupil: besides the usual breaking routine, he had been taught how to kneel down, to bow, to count by nodding his head, and also how to jump small fences.

By the end of his year as a two year old the colt had not shown much ability as a flat racer, so he was gelded and schooled seriously as a steeplechaser. He made his debut in a jumping race at Saratoga as a three year old and far exceeded everyone's expectations by finishing first. Although he was later disqualified, and was placed third for causing some interference in the late stages of the race, he had shown enough ability to be considered more seriously by his owner-trainer.

Not much later the little horse was entered in a hurdle stakes race at Belmont Park. Unfortunately, he fell at the second fence, broke a bone in his hind leg, and was returned to his owner's farm where he was put out to pasture for more than a year.

In the spring of his fifth year the horse was put back into training, a half share was sold to one of the trainer's patrons, and the game little horse went on to win six races including a $25,000 stakes race.

That winter the trainer and his partner flew to Florida to receive an Eclipse award for the outstanding steeplechase horse of the year. It seemed that their wildest dreams had been realized–the $2,200 colt, who had been so small as a yearling that he was considered more as a pet than a racing prospect, had been ridden bareback by the trainer's infant daughter, had broken a leg as a three year old, had defied the laws of nature and statistics, and finally had become a champion.

Little did they realize, as they laid ambitious plans for the following year, that in only his second race as a six year old, a freak jumping accident would cost their little hero his life.

This true story seems to illustrate the things that make steeplechasing such an extraordinary sport. Although the major part of my training stable is comprised of flat race horses–which themselves obviously present a great challenge, and at times can be very rewarding–it is the jumpers that capture the imagination and affection. In many cases jumpers continue racing for one owner until they are nine or ten years old, whereas the turnover is far greater in flat horses. I once claimed a flat horse on a Sunday and lost it in a claiming race the following Saturday–exactly six days later.

More than flat racing, steeplechasing offers a release for one's emotions, encompassing all levels, from the depths of despair and frustration to the highest peak of human and equine achievement. It is natural for a thoroughbred horse to want to run as fast as he can for as far as he can, but to accomplish this while simultaneously negotiating a series of four or five feet high obstacles requires a degree of discipline and training that is not necessary on the flat. A steeplechase trainer, therefore, looks at his job as something more creative and feels that he has put more of himself into the finished product. This naturally makes his job more rewarding when he meets with success.

Curiously, it is the very factors which make jumping racing so unique that have also prevented its growth. The nature of the sport naturally causes it to be looked upon as flat racing's "little-brother." It is not an attractive betting medium because it is an action sport that is filled with chance and danger. It deters all but the most dedicated owners, trainers and jockeys because of the great risk of injury to horse and rider.

In spite of these negative factors there is still a surprisingly large number of devotees for whom steeplechasing seems to offer a welcome contrast to the mundane, regimented day-to-day lives that the vast majority of Americans are forced to lead. It is a sport that was developed in another age, that has not lent itself easily to the commercial, business and machine orientated period of history in which we live.

As a trainer, I consider myself fortunate to be able to make a living working at something I enjoy so much.

–Jonathan Sheppard

A native Englishman, Jonathan Sheppard learned from his father the techniques in judging racehorses at an early age. In 1961 he came to America to study racing and in 1973 and 1974 held the distinction of being number one in his profession as a steeplechase horse trainer.

For More Information

For additional information see Dressage and the other horse sections, or write the National Steeplechase and Hunt Association, Box 308, Elmont, New York, 11003. They also print an annual called **Steeplechasing in America** which can be obtained through the same address. It costs $12.50.

There aren't too many good books on steeplechasing but here is one that caught our eye. It is available from World Publications, Box 366, Mountain View, Calif. 94040 at the price listed* plus 25 cents postage.

The Secret of Successful Steeplechasing, Tony Pearn M.F.H. The author puts on paper the lessons he has learned about every aspect of steeplechasing from qualifying and training a thoroughbred, point-to-points and hunter-chases to breeding, breaking, and schooling a potential "winner of the Grand National." 1972 Hb., 121 pp., ill., $4.95, (Pelham).

Houseboating

As most people know, a houseboat is a floating structure that has been designed for livability. In essence, it might be called a modest apartment afloat with space utilized to best advantage. Houseboats come in many sizes and shapes, from the inexpensive owner-built boats made from materials at hand to a $70,000 plush, customized craft. Since most houseboats have a low draft, and ride high, they can travel in a very few feet of water, which lets them go into the stingiest of water areas. Since the 1940's and 1950's when all houseboats were custom built look-alikes, and very expensive, manufacturers have developed a variety of hull types, stylized interiors and exteriors, and comparatively lower price tags. Today, the modern houseboat has one or two powerful engines, comfortable sleeping quarters, and is self-contained with running water, oven, refrigerator, and much more.

Besides complementing and contributing to the enjoyment of many water sports and activities, a houseboat is a convenient and comfortable way of observing the entire aqueous habitat. Feeling the crisp salt air over a cold, gray sea, or reflecting the subtle ripples lapping the shore of a clear lake, one can't help but feel the sensitive interaction with the rhythms of nature while aboard a houseboat. For many people this sort of life provides a necessary means of escape from traffic jams, bothers at the office, and sooty air. For others it has become an economical alternative to living ashore. Families with a love for the wilderness make their floating homes along secluded waterways; those with an attraction for the city set up houseboatkeeping on the waters near Chicago, New York, and San Francisco, commuting to work by bicycle or public transportation.

The possibilities of recreation, entertainment, and just-plain living aboard a houseboat are infinite. Even wedding receptions aboard are possible, and have been held, with 30 guests hardly affecting the houseboat's trim!

Many houseboaters are introduced to the sport via rental houseboats. These craft can be procured for a weekend or several weeks, and provide a comparatively inexpensive vacation. Rental boats are available in most parts of North America.

Home in the Water

Houseboating is a sport enjoyed by water lovers around the world. You see houseboats tucked away in the gentle canals of Amsterdam, and drifting with the current of the river Seine in downtown Paris. You see them blanketed in London fog on the Thames, and basking in the Adriatic sun in that hodgepodge of islands that hug the coast of Yugoslavia. Mostly though, you see them in ever increasing numbers in the rivers, lakes and protected ocean waters of North America.

Although I can find a sort of Huck Finn happiness aboard a houseboat in most any waters that will keep it afloat, I have to confess a preference for the Delta formed by the waters of California's San Joaquin and Sacramento rivers. It offers over 1,000 miles of navigable waterways in a fairly compact network of rivers, sloughs, cuts and even lakes. Even the neophyte skipper can find his way without getting lost too often, or for too long.

It's in these waters that I use my houseboat *Delta Dawdler*.

Lolling away hours along the shore is one of the primary pleasures of houseboating. In a recent survey, more than half of all houseboaters did not know the correct day of the week. (Schell)

It's not really a fancy boat (some say it bears a faint resemblance to Bogart's *African Queen*). She's a sturdy 34-foot-long vessel powered by a 55 horsepower outboard engine, and good for maybe 10 mph on a clear day. I purchased her for $1800. About $1200 and a lot of elbow grease later I had a nifty little craft that would sleep six in comfort. A craft that sported the most modern of toilets (head) and a kitchen (galley) with refrigerator and a 4-burner stove with an oven large enough to accommodate the Thanksgiving bird.

My investment of time and effort was well worth it.

But you may wonder just what one does on a houseboat after the initial novelty has worn off. Well, for many of us this may never happen. For one full summer I cruised with my teenage sons and their friends as crew. Toward evening we'd nuzzle the bow into the tules on some secluded slough and drop a stern anchor. Out came the fishing poles and with luck we'd soon catch the evening meal of catfish or striped bass. You can drop baited traps over the side to lure in delectable crayfish that will rival any you get in the expensive restaurants of New Orleans.

The shores of the Delta are profuse with wild blackberry bushes. We would merely poke the bow of the boat into the bushes and pick a pailful right from the deck. They are excellent tossed into pancake batter or eaten with milk.

Sometimes we'd find a peaceful spot to our liking and remain there for a few days. Other times we'd poke along, exploring, perhaps only traveling a few miles to our next anchoring spot. The waters of the Delta are tidal waters and low tide reveals many fine sandy beaches. When on the move, we'd always watch for these. When we would find a good one, we'd drive the bow of the boat onto the beach and swim and sunbathe for hours.

The tides also introduce an element of adventure into Delta houseboating. Many a skipper has tied fast to shore at high tide only to find his vessel high and dry at low tide! There's little one can do but settle back with a good book and wait for the arrival of the next high tide. Tides affect the clearance under bridges too, and the wise skipper charts his course with this in mind if there are bridges that don't open on his route. Although it is a great thrill to sound a few toots of the horn and watch a giant bridge rumble, groan, and finally yawn open to let your little houseboat through.

Still, houseboating is considered a low-key sport. Houseboaters aren't supposed to be in a hurry. Our credo is "if we don't get there today, maybe we will tomorrow–or next week, anyway!"

You shouldn't get the idea that we houseboaters are waterborne hermits because we sometimes seek the seclusion of a remote anchorage. For the most part we are a gregarious bunch. Here in the Delta there are dozens of marinas where we tie up side by side and entertain one another on our floating apartments. We have potluck dinners together and we gather for group cruises to interesting spots.

Many of the boats are equipped with marine radio with channels that are commonly monitored by other boats in the area. A lonesome houseboater need but make a radio plea to get company steaming on its way. Too, some of those "secluded anchorages" aren't all that secluded. Some reach surprising levels of popularity. It is not unusual to find 50 to 100 boats bowed into the tules of such popular Delta "remote" areas as *The Meadows* and *Mandeville Tip*.

When we want action "city style", we can tie our houseboats to docks in downtown Stockton or Sacramento, dress up a mite, and do the town. There are also dozens of fine restaurants at water's edge where boaters can tie up and partake of gourmet fare. Not a bad life.

In the summer months, clothes don't present much of a problem. Cut-offs or bathing suits are my typical garb. My feet get toughened and tend to resist the confinement of shoes. The skin takes on an enviable hue of tan. The calendar is of little importance. In fact, a local television station was doing a show on houseboating some time ago. The T.V. crew was aboard a boat and they interviewed houseboaters out on the water. One standard question was, "What day is it?" *Over half the houseboaters answered it incorrectly!*

Although our boating season is long here in California's Delta, we do get some foul winter weather. It gets cold, heavy rains blow in, we get smothered by damp thick tule fogs, heavy winds buffet us about. Many houseboaters forsake their crafts during this season. The true river rats don't give up though. I weathered the winter aboard the *Delta Dawdler* at the Hemingwayesque 52-acre island called *Lost Isle*. Thermal blankets and an extra catalytic heater kept me snug and warm. A portable T.V. kept me company when the fog was too thick for visitors to find the isle.

The island children left for school by boat. The mailman brought letters by swift runabout, the sheriff guarded us by cruiser, supplies were barged in. I watched giant ocean-going freighters of foreign flag loom out of the fog on their way to the port of Stockton. I saw and heard tens of thousands of migrating birds. I became more aware of the sounds, sights and smells around me. Developed an inner peace.

And that, I believe, is part of what houseboating is all about.

—Hal Schell

Hal Schell is a writer-photographer who lived for over a year aboard his houseboat mentioned in this essay. His houseboating articles have appeared in numerous national magazines. He still spends most of his summers, weekends and holidays aboard the houseboat at Lost Isle, commuting by fast runabout kept at the river just a few minutes from his Stockton apartment. He describes himself as a "river rat."

For More Information

For additional information see motorboating. A helpful organization: Houseboat Association of America, Box 7285, Asheville, N.C. 28807. They offer chartering for trips, insurance programs, discount on rentals and information to those that are interested. There was a magazine covering the activity called Family Houseboating but it is no longer being published. However, you might see if they have any back issues available. Write: Trailer Life Publishing Co., 23945 Calabasas Rd., Calabasas, Calif. 91302.

Here is the one good book we found on houseboating. It is available from World Publications, Box 366, Mountain View, Calif. 94040 at the price listed* plus 25 cents postage.

The Complete Guide to Houseboating, John W. Malo. The joys, pitfalls and technicalities of this fast-growing leisure activity is thoroughly presented in this well-illustrated volume. 1974 Hb., 182 pp., ill., $8.95, (MacMillan).

Many larger cabin cruisers can be considered houseboats, because their crews live on the boats for long periods. One drawback to such craft, however, is that they are much deeper draft than most houseboats and most commonly must be moored in marinas. (Schell)

Hunting-Big Game

The famed Ernest Hemingway, who knew something about big game hunting as well as writing, once wrote, "There is much mystic nonsense written about hunting but it is something that is probably much older than religion. Some are hunters and some are not." When one takes into account the fact that, to early man, hunting was not only a means of providing food, but also clothing and tools, Hemingway's words become even more significant. While hunting, for primitive man, was a necessity, today it has evolved into something quite different. Despite the "mystic nonsense", the search for game is practiced by many adherents, largely as a pleasurable pastime.

The term *big game* is applied to animals such as deer, bear, elk, moose, the big cats, antelope, sheep, goats, and other large species. Often in big game hunting (as opposed to small game) the pursuit is executed at great risk to the hunter.

In North America, this type of hunting is largely restricted to deer simply because they seem to outnumber the other types of large game. Deer forage all across the continent and are readily accessible to hunters who possess the patience and know-how.

Generally speaking, a rifle is used for big game, rather than the shotgun that is often seen in the hands of small game hunters. A hunter of large animals most always needs a high-powered weapon that he can use at relatively long range, if necessary. Of course, the specific game being hunted and the type of terrain are to be considered when it comes to choosing the rifle and the method of hunting.

In open country, where both the animal and the hunter can be seen from afar, the stalking technique is the most useful. Here the hunter quietly and stealthily approaches the quarry, using every manner of concealment available – rocks, stumps, high grass, etc. – while paying close attention to the direction of the wind.

Still hunting is the term used for hunting while walking slowly and cautiously through dense brush or shrub, where game is most likely to be discovered suddenly.

Some animals, who cannot be stalked or still hunted are found by a method called tracking. Big animals that herd together, like elephants, leave noticeable tracks in soft ground, and skillful hunters can even follow their trails on hard terrain.

One of the oldest European hunting techniques, referred to as calling, is commonly practiced in the pursuit of deer. Here the hunter hides and makes noises, imitating the call of a female, or the challenge of a male. When the male answers, he will gradually come right up to the sportsman.

In general, the magnum small caliber rifle is the best for stalking, since it gives the bullet a flat trajectory – a great help in overcoming the difficulties of distance. A rifle that does not fire a fairly heavy bullet should be avoided since these bullets are liable to only wound the animal, necessitating a sometimes long pursuit. In cases where the game is not killed immediately, it is an unwritten rule that the hunter continue the hunt until the animal is killed.

It is advisable that a heavy-barreled rifle of rather large caliber be used for dangerous game shot at close quarters, as in still hunting. Small caliber should be used only by experienced hunters. In addition, the beginning huntsman should inquire of the conservation departments of the big game territories for advice on conditions, technical matters, and for procuring a mandatory license.

It is also a good idea to hire a reputable professional hunting guide, or to join an established public or private safari group. Many hunters, with years of experience, will hire a local guide who has hunted a particular region frequently, when venturing into new or unfamiliar territories. Generally covered in the fee are the cost of camping equipment, gun bearers, trackers, skinners, and other services.

Big game hunters may travel either by foot, horseback, jeep or other motor vehicle. Airplanes are often used to reach wilderness areas. Game animals, however, should never be shot from moving vehicles. Not only is this practice dangerous and unreliable, but most hunters consider this to be an act of heresy against the true art of the hunt.

One special breed unique to big game hunting is the *trophy hunter*. These hunters seek out the biggest and finest of the species that they can find – usually older bucks and bulls. While some of these sportsmen are constantly on the lookout for record trophies, many are content with finding animals with fine heads for mounting. In order to make the fine judgments required in trophy hunting, a hunter must be able to make a fair comparison of antler and horn size using another part of the animal's anatomy as a yardstick. In many cases, the trophy hunter has a reliable guide in his company whose judgment is relied upon.

The Great Game

The sport of big game hunting, "The Great Game", as we used to call it in the old days, is fast coming to an end. In Africa many of the big game hunting companies have closed their doors forever, and in Asia there is little or no hunting left for the true sportsman. The reasons for this are basically twofold: 1) the general decline of the larger species of wildlife due to poaching, increasing human populations, and, in India – the principal big game hunting field in Asia – the ruthless extermination of trophy animals by the professional Indian hunting companies; and (2) the wave of international concern that has swept across the world during the last two decades for the great wild beasts of the mountains, plains and forests – a wave of solicitude, particularly among the younger generations, based on new insights and knowledge of the total ecology of our sphere and the vital part that animals play in it.

These factors – the lack of game and the new thinking – have greatly affected the hunting of large wild animals to the point where the popularity of the sport has decreased and big game hunting is beginning to be looked upon as old fashioned, cruel and pointless.

But a few years ago it was all different. In the days of plentiful wildlife, big game hunting, when conducted in a sporting and gentlemanly fashion, was a grand and glorious pastime in which any young man considered himself indeed fortunate to have the smallest part. I was one of these fortunate young men.

I served my apprenticeship in big game hunting when I was a young tea planter in the wild, game-filled jungles on the Bhutan border in north Bengal. I started as a rank amateur with the larger game animals. I did, however, have the advantage of the background of an Irish hunting, fishing and shooting family.

In 1954 I applied for, and was granted, a safari concession in the Kingdom of Nepal, the tiny Himalayan country that lies to the north of India. In those days, the jungles of Nepal teemed with wildlife. There were plentiful tiger, leopard, elephant, rhinoceros, buffalo, bison, wild boar, six kinds of deer and ample game bird shooting and fishing. In the mountains to the north lived wild goat, goat antelope, musk deer, snow leopard and bear. It was a sportsman's paradise.

My professional safari company, Nepal Safaris, Inc., was based in Kathmandu, the capital of Nepal, and my clients were mostly Americans. They came in all shapes and sizes and over the years they provided me with a veritable kaleidoscope of unforgettable experiences. I remember Ennis, from San Antonio, in many ways a typical client.

Chuck Ennis, as he liked to be called, was a tall, gangling Texan who wanted to try and collect a tiger trophy. As a client, he had two points in his favor before he arrived. One was the word, passed to me on the professional grapevine from Africa, that he was a hard hunter and a good sportsman. The other, his own letter to me, stated that he wanted to hunt in the most sporting manner available – on foot and on the ground.

Chuck flew into New Delhi in India, and from there I and John Bonney, a young Englishman who was my partner at that time, collected him and drove him the 300 miles to the Terai jungles of southwest Nepal. Chuck wanted a good hunt so we decided to let him have a try for the Dumillia Cat, a big tigress that had successfully eluded several previous clients of mine. She was now getting old and dangerous.

Dumillia is a tiny Taru village set deep in the southern jungles of Nepal. It has a population of 30 souls and it is supported by about ten acres of rice fields that lie to the south of the village. The rice fields are bordered by a series of deep ravines filled with tangled thorn jungle and brush. This is where the Dumillia Cat lived, as several men of Dumillia knew well.

She was an old tigress with an extremely cantankerous disposition; twice within the last few years she had attacked and mauled men of the village. One man had been pounced on and badly bitten in the back and buttocks as he cut grass on the edge of the rice fields. The other was attacked and bitten in the face. His nose and jaw were broken and he was permanently disfigured. The cat was not a maneater, but she was dangerous. And now, in the clear cold days of the Nepal jungle winter, we would stalk and try to kill her.

We started Chuck with the usual walking and instruction. He fired a few target shots and took some small game. Then we got down to the serious business of the Dumillia Cat. Chuck would hunt with me and John would be in charge of logistics, men, movements, beaters if they were to be used, etc. Chuck armed himself with a popular .375 rifle. I carried, on this hunt and on all of my hunts for many years, my own custom-made rifle. We both loaded with 300 grain expanding ammunition. Neither of us used telescopic sights, preferring to depend on open sights for the quick, short-range shooting that foot stalking often requires.

The first day we spent in a reconnaissance of the area, walking quietly and steadily around the whole terrain of the ravines. My instructions to Chuck were simple: absolute quiet, stay alert and watch for my signals.

On that first day we found the pug marks of the cat twice but we were unable to determine where she had a lair. She had not killed any cattle in recent weeks and there were no kill sites that might indicate a lair and no killing area on which to zero the search. We could bait her, later, but that would come if foot stalking failed.

On the second day we started just before dawn and after about three hours, moving very quietly and slowly through the forest that bordered the ravines, we came into an area of dense elephant grass. Suddenly I smelled decaying meat. Sure enough there was a kill – a big Axis buck. Scattered bones and hair indicated a temporary lair. We watched the area from the concealment of the grass for several hours but the cat did not appear.

On the third day we were out again in the first light of dawn and as we entered the forest at the edge of the rice fields I detected the faint but definite odor of a tiger. I motioned to Chuck to wait and we stood and listened for awhile. The cat had been there, of this there was not doubt, perhaps watching us as we came down across the rice fields. We crouched in silence while I examined with great care the jungle ahead and to the right and left of us. I had a nasty feeling that the cat was close. Suddenly the air was shattered by the staccato barking of a big male langur monkey, the heavy six note call that denotes the presence of a carnivore. Immediately, half a dozen peacocks took up the signal and sent their wails echoing through the dawn forest. The tigress was on the move.

We started searching in the dripping gloom of the early morning forest and soon I picked up the pugs of the cat and we began to follow them. But though we followed them, lost them, found them and lost them again – all through the day – when evening came we still had not seen the cat.

I was pleased with Chuck's endurance. He was not a young man and the going was rough in the ravines. Much of our progress was under dense brush that required going on hands and knees; the tracks of the tigress took us up and down the ravine walls themselves a dozen times. But now the evening was closing in and we were both tired. It was time to turn and head for camp.

The sun was slowly setting into the trees, a huge red ball that signalled the end of another day. Flights of bright green Alexandrine parrakeets darted like sparks through the evening light on the way to their roosting spots and brown monkeys chattered and quarreled in the tops of the giant simuls, the younger ones complaining loudly of their secondary positions on the outer branches. From far away a jackal howled; his cry was taken up by other packs, deep in the forest. A hyena cackled his hideous laugh and then for a while it was very quiet.

We were squatting together, whispering quietly about starting back for camp. Directly in front of us was the mouth of a small dark ravine, its entrance choked with dense brush and tall dry grass. Suddenly a barking deer gave a short, sharp bark and came bounding out of the ravine in a rush. The bark was a warning cry to the jungle folk, telling them a carnivore was on the move. The deer looked back towards the entrance of the small dark ravine and barked again, twice, indicating that it could see the cat. Then it turned and leapt into the brush and disappeared.

Suddenly it was very quiet. I looked at Chuck. He was tense and watching me for a signal. I had a short piece of grass in my mouth and without any other movement I inclined it towards the mouth of the ravine. There was little doubt in my mind that the Dumillia Cat was in there, that she was moving – coming directly toward us.

Except for the night birds which had now started to call, there was very little sound. From far away I heard the tinkle of cattle bells as the villagers took in their cattle for the night. Close-by some tiny rodent was busy in the bole of a tree. Then, so faintly that it was almost not there, I heard the distinctive rustling that grass makes when it is pressed back and runs against the coat of a big cat. The sound was followed almost instantly by a long, deep growl followed by a series of short, heavy grunts.

After that things happened very quickly. I whispered to Chuck to stand and be ready to fire. I moved swiftly to his left and away from him to give him good cover. As I slid the safety off my rifle the cat came out of the ravine directly in front of us, moving fast and coming straight towards us. There was no time for argument or error. Chuck raised his .375 and with one clean shot drilled the big tigress, killing it instantly. It flopped into the short grass at the mouth of the ravine and lay still.

We stood for a moment or two and then I followed normal professional procedure, walking up to it with loaded and cocked rifle, making absolutely sure that it was dead. Chuck, quite speechless at this point, joined me, and then turned and fired his rifle in the air three times – a signal that soon brought a torchlight procession of men from the camp and the village.

Later, skinning the old cat, we found that she had three broken canines. Two, snapped off at the roots, were filled with festering pus and she must have lived in great pain through those last years of her life. This is probably what made her so short tempered and dangerous.

Very few of my clients through the years hunted tiger on foot. But even those who did not use Kipling's method, as we used to call it, often enjoyed great hunting. The safari was what counted and the hunt embraced many things.

There was Ron Rosner, of New York, who, despite his Wall Street broker looks, his puffing pipe and his old India sahib's hat, was one of the most determined hunters that I have ever met. I can see Rosner now, all these years later, on the morning that he took his record Swamp Deer.

We were in the Sukla Phanta grassland of southwest Nepal. The swamp deer were, naturally enough, in the swamp areas of the grassland. 500 yards of deep, miserably cold, black swamp water separated Rosner from the only place that would give him a vantage point for a shot. Without hesitation he plunged in up to his armpits and, holding his trusty 30.06 over his head, waded all the way to the little island of mud that gave him his trophy shot.

There was Sally McConnell, a quiet lady from Red Bluff, California, who drilled a peacock through the head at 200 yards with a .300. There were thousands of them in the jungle in those days and we used them for camp meat all the time.

There was Mary Jane from South Carolina who suffered from hallucinations, who caused my little camp man, Tashi Sherpa, to murmur, "Very dangerous memsahib." To this her husband, Ken, quietly agreed.

There was Colonel Bingham, from Nashville, Tennessee, a 65-year-old tobacco chewing, spitting, cussing, cantankerous old southern gentleman who successfully drilled holes in trees, anthills, stumps, rocks, termite mounds, everything in fact except that which he aimed at.

There was Manuela Fuller, the fiery little Sabra wife of an American diplomat who came down to the jungle to kill animals but who, when confronted with her first trophy – a fine young Sambhur whose big brown eyes glistened moistly at her through the telescopic sight of her rifle – dropped said rifle, burst into tears, and never fired another shot for the whole safari.

Unfortunately, there was also a sadder side to big game hunting. Its essence lay in the old saying, "All gentlemen are hunters, but not all hunters are gentlemen." There was Gil Boldretta from Los Angeles, who, accompanied by a photographer, wanted to gut-shoot a tiger so that he could get what he called "good action shots" as it charged around. Mr. Boldretta, naturally enough, planned to be in a tree during the photography.

There were Harold and Claudia from Texas, who were drunk from the minute they arrived on the safari to the minute they left. Later they wondered why they did not get any trophies, and later still they complained loudly that their professional hunter took their rifles away from them whenever they wanted to have just a little drink or two.

There was Bennet, from St. Louis, who shot at every single thing that moved and once there was Mrs. Martell who liked guns and who left camp alone–without the permission or knowledge of her pro–and shot a porcupine, several song birds, and a village dog.

There was Conroy from West Virginia who fired at and missed the same leopard three times. Eventually, in sheer rage and frustration, he had a nervous breakdown and had to be shipped home.

Of course there was Mr. Francis, from St. Louis, a large red-faced gentleman with a very mean streak, who shot an old, rather harmless male tiger and later claimed that it was a maneater. He even had a ghost writer do a book about it, which told of his courageous hunting of this vicious and terrible beast!

There was also, for the professional, and often for the client, the humerous side of big game hunting. I recall David, from Pennsylvania, who got lost every time he left camp and had to be watched like a hawk every minute of the day and night. Of course, Clark Henry, from Chicago, was terrified of snakes and insects and arrived in camp in a huge pair of solid leather, near hip-high snake boots that must have weight 20 lbs. He never took them off for the whole safari. For all I know he slept in them.

A memorable personage was Mr. Lawrence who was frightened of elephants but who eventually came to know and understand our camp elephants – our seven domestic elephants that were used for hunting. One day, walking out of camp, he saw one of our elephants that had wandered into a patch of native corn. He walked up to it and shooed it out with his handkerchief. It turned and trotted off into the jungle. Later, anxious about our "lost" elephant, he told us about the incident. We did a quick count. There were none of ours missing. Lawrence's elephant had been a wild young tusker that had chased several people in that area and was generally regarded as dangerous. The poor fellow's mental state concerning elephants promptly reverted to square one after that incident and he gave even our camp pets a wide berth.

Melvin McDay, from New York, quite frequently raised his rifle and fired into the totally empty jungle. "An enormous tiger," he would whisper dramatically, "biggest tiger that I ever saw."

There was Carter, whose heavy recoil rifle knocked him off a high bank and twenty feet down into a pleasant little river pool that was the home of three large mugger crocodiles. He emerged unscathed but we had to shoo the three crocs out of the pool before we could dive for his rifle. And finally, there was Bill Brenard who dearly wanted to prove himself a hunter, and who nearly caused his professional hunter to rupture himself with laughter, when, confronted with his first tiger, he rammed a bullet-shaped piece of soft candy into the firing chamber of his .468 rifle.

Heroes, cowards and comedians aside, it has still been my privilege through the years to know some of the great sportsmen in the world of big game hunting. Among them are men like Karl Jonas, of Washington D.C., Jay Mellon, of New York, Neal McLanahan, of Elberton, Georgia, and David Hasinger, of Philadelphia, Pennsylvania, who took one of the largest tigers ever to come out of Asia and the biggest carnivore ever collected in modern times.

The great days of big game hunting are dead and gone and they can never be brought back. But it might come as a surprise to the avid conservationist to know what big game hunting really meant to so many hunters, both professional and amateur. It was certainly not the killing of animals. It was hardly, in many cases, the hunting of them, or even the trophies that were collected. It was something entirely different. For those who lived it, and loved it, it was things like the sight of an elephant, standing gold in the morning sun, Kilimanjaro in the background. It was a herd of checkered Black Buck antelope, bounding with 20-foot leaps against the harsh brown plains of northern India. The sawing cough of a leopard from a deep ravine. The first scotch at the campfire after a long, hard day in the open, bodies bone weary, and a hundred miles of jeep dust in the teeth. The warmth and companionship of the safari camp and the intimate and enduring friendships that it created. The smell of canvas and the thin light of the stars coming through the wall of the tent from an indigo sky that was a million miles across. It was the jungle and its almost prehistoric atmosphere, never changing, always intriguing. And the long sad moan of the tiger as he wound his burning way through the forests of the night.

—**Peter Byrne**

Since retiring from professional hunting in 1968, Peter Byrne has helped to found the International Wildlife Conservation Society and has planned and created the Sukla Phanta Tiger Sanctuary in southwest Nepal. He has led four expeditions into the Himalayas in search of the abominable snowman and is presently head of the Boston Academy of Applied Science-sponsored Bigfoot Investigation Project in the U.S. Pacific northwest. His new book is entitled, **The Search for Bigfoot**.

For More Information

Several magazines do a good job with big game hunting. These nationally distributed magazines, *Field & Stream, Outdoor Life,* and *Sports Afield,* all have articles covering this sport frequently. Another magazine, *American Rifleman,* 1600 Rhode Island Ave., Washington D.C. 20036 has over one million circulation. The magazine is for members of the National Rifle Association at the same address. The magazine is not only on hunting but should be of interest to anyone that owns a gun.

A good source of information is the Fish and Wildlife Service, c/o United States Department of the Interior, Washington, D.C. 20240. They will supply addresses of individual State fish and game departments which will be able to fill you in on all the laws of the area, etc. You also might write African Safari Club of Philadelphia, c/o David Hasinger, Paul & Beekman, Inc. 1801 Courtland St., Philadelphia, Pa. 19140 for information about going on a safari.

Now, on to some books on big game hunting. More books are listed under small game hunting. All are available from World Publications, Box 366, Mountain View, Calif. 94040 at the price listed* plus 25 cents postage.

African Hunter, James Mellon. One of the world's greatest hunters has taken 10 years to produce the bible of African safari. A book that will captivate all sportsmen and naturalists who thrill to reading about adventures in some of the wildest regions left on earth. 1975 Hb., 544 (oversize) pp., ill., (18 maps), $39.95, (Harcourt, Brace & Javonovich).

Hunter's Digest, Edwin A. Bauer, ed. 52 exceptional features by leading outdoorsmen tell the best ways, times, and places to hunt large and small game in North America. Learn how to develop hunting skills, become a better shot. Which guns to use when and how to choose, train and use hunting dogs. 1975 Ppb., 320 (oversize) pp., $6.95, (Digest Books).

Sheep and Sheep Hunting, Jack O'Connor. The author thoroughly covers all aspects of the game and hunting methods in every kind of sheep country, from parched Mexican deserts to the mountain pastures of the Yukon. Full of hunting suspense, high wilderness vistas, and the skills of a master outdoorsman. 1974 Hb., 308 pp., ill., $10.00, (Winchester).

The Complete Book of Deer Hunting, Byron W. Dalrymple. A book based on the philosophy that hunting depends on understanding the animal. It tells you almost everything you need to know about all the North American species, including all their habitats, their senses and their limitations. 1973 Ppb., 247 pp., ill., $5.95, (Follet).

Hunting- Small Game

Small game hunting and "varminting" have really come into their own only within the last 30 or 40 years. In the not-so-distant past, shooting for squirrels, woodchucks, rabbits, and skunks was looked down upon as "sissy stuff". But with the development of high-intensity .22 cartridges in the 1930's, and the decline of many big game species, hunting for these smaller fellows became increasingly popular.

Today there are rifles, cartridges, and riflemen with capabilities for picking off critters at 400 yards.

While stalking and shooting racoons and ruffled grouse may not offer the same sense of danger or accomplishment as the larger species, still small game hunting can improve many big game hunting skills. From mounting of the rifle to trigger squeeze, there is every element of a big game shot when a small animal is poised for flight. In addition, a wider variety of hunting weapons can be used for scurrying, winging creatures. Alongside the rifle, handguns and shotguns are often favorites of many hunters in search of this type of quarry.

Some other animals that are classified as small game are foxes, wolverines, badgers, porcupines, crows and owls, and gamebirds such as duck, goose and quail.

A Landowner's Friend

Bows and arrows, rifles, shotguns – small game hunting has something to offer all sportsmen who find it hard to remain indoors when autumn touches the maples with its magic. Now, when the quail are calling lonesomely for the lost summer, and the squirrels are busy storing their winter supply of nuts and cones, is a time to be afield, as all small game hunters know.

Fortunately, there is usually small game hunting within reasonable distance of the average hunter. After all, it only takes an acre or so of cover for good squirrel hunting, with maybe an occasional rabbit turned up as an extra dividend. Practically all small game hunting is done on private property, and it begins by getting permission from the landowner.

Hunting on private lands must be given plenty of consideration, both in the inquiry and in the conduct during the hunting. When you get permission, inquire about restricted areas where the landowner doesn't want any hunting done. These areas may be sections of a farm where harvesting operations are in progress. They may be sections where livestock are presently grazing. Know these restricted areas before you start your hunt. Ask about the proper place to park your car so it will not be in the way of the farmer's activities. All this is in addition to the basic courtesy of refraining from hunting immediately around the farm buildings.

Usually, if you show the landowner that you understand his side of the fence, permission to hunt will be given as a matter of course. But there is still another consideration. Suppose you are given permission to hunt certain fields where woodchucks are a problem. On your way to these fields you notice an open gate between an unharvested field and some cattle. You know, without being a farmer, that the landowner doesn't want cattle in unharvested crops. You close the gate and go on. Then you discover three other hunters in another field beyond this unharvested one. You notice that they have left another gate open. What should you do?

Several courses are open to you: you can forge ahead to the fields where the farmer gave you permission to shoot woodchuck, and disregard the obvious problem of trespass. You can close all the gates behind these inconsiderate hunters. You can close the gates and report back to the landowner.

This last course is the proper one. Not only should you report to the landowner, but you should go with him when he orders these trespassers out. After they leave, go with the landowner while he checks on the gates and fences; he may need some further help.

If you show enough interest in the landowner's property rights in this fashion, you may rest assured that you have made yourself a private small game hunting preserve that will always be open to you. Not only will you always be welcome on this particular farm, but on adjoining farms as well. Word gets around; other farmers will hear about your consideration and will welcome you on their property.

As for the rest, contact your state game commission about the type of small game hunting found in your area. Study the possibilities before the season opens. Contact land owners. You'll not only turn up plenty of small game hunting, but in addition you'll meet a lot of fine people.

–Francis Sell

Francis Sell, a foremost hunter and gun authority, lives in rural Oregon where he often takes to the field when not free-lance writing. He is the author of **Art of Small Game Hunting.**

For More Information

For magazines on small game hunting check the Big Game Hunting section. Here are two important organizations: American Coon Hunters Association, Box 30, Ingraham, Ill. 72434; Ducks Unlimited, Box 66300, Chicago, Ill. 60666.

Here are some good books. All are available from World Publications, Box 366, Mountain View, Calif. 94040 at the price listed* plus 25 cents each postage.

Art of Small Game Hunting, Francis E. Sell. One of America's foremost hunters and gun authorities imports the wisdom of many decades on the selection of rifles, sights and small handguns for the purpose of hunting small game. Good advice on care of the shotgun. 1973 Ppb., 190 pp., ill., $3.95, (Stackpole).

Game Bird Hunting, Philip Rice and John Dahl. Identification, habitats, distribution and characteristics of many species of birds. Also includes sections on dogs and techniques. 1965 Ppb., 190 pp., ill., $3.95, (Olson).

Ice Boating

Since the dawn of civilization, man has been fascinated by sailboats for pleasure and commerce. As machine powered vessels gradually replaced sail power trade ships, sailing for pleasure not only survived, but increased in popularity. In a few places in the world, frozen lakes, rivers, and estuaries remain more or less snow-free for a few months each year. It is here that we find a clique of sportsman hopeless addicted to ice sailing.

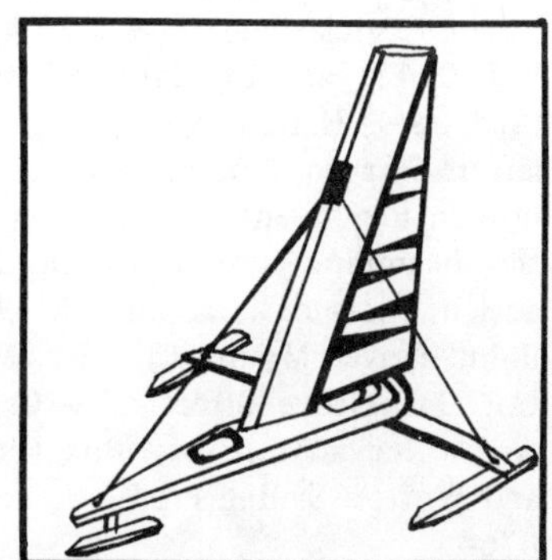

Whether on skates while shouldering a half-held sail, or slouching down in the cramped cockpit of a stiletto shaped, raked mast, competition ice yacht, ice sailors are seeking the uncomparable thrill of using wind power to create speeds of travel normally associated with fast motor cars. The coincidence of good ice and wind justifies to them their frozen fingered labor of assembling the dozens of items that go to make up these strong, light craft.

Dressed like an arctic explorer, the ice boat skipper pushes his craft to a reluctant start, climbs aboard, tightens the line to the sail, and is suddenly accelerated in a few breath-taking seconds to mile-a-minute speeds.

Thin ice may be a deterent to onlookers but it rarely discourages a dedicated ice sailor. Cold baths occasionally reward the winter season's early birds and spring diehards, but rescues are always successful.

There is a compelling challenge in controlling your craft as it heels over and rises up on two of the three skate-like runners as you whisk along with the frigid wind in your teeth. Passengers scream with a combination of fear and delight usually associated with roller coasters. At speeds of 60 to 90 mph, an ice boat is not inclined to turn sharply. When turning is made mandatory by the approach of shoreline, obstacle, or another iceboat, centrifugal forces on runners and rigging can be tremendous. It's a well documented adage that says, "An iceboat reaches its top speed just before it falls apart."

Although many "soft water" seamen are inducted into "hard water" sailing ranks, the sailing skills are very different. For example, tacking upward separates the men from the boys during aquatic regattas, while on the frozen mirror of a lake the real test comes when trying to get downwind fast. Sailboats at their best can go only a fraction of wind speed downwind. An iceboat can go four times as fast as wind speed when travelling crosswind. An iceboat can coast a half mile on inertia alone, while a watercraft quickly slows when its driving force is lost.

Enough of words and hyperbole! There's no way to understand what keeps the fanatics working so hard at an improbable, bone chilling, weather dependent sport until you try it.

—Jack Andresen

Jack Andresen lives in the Bahamas, but goes north each winter go get in as much ice boating as possible. He is the author of **Sailing on Ice.**

For More Information

Two organizations are active in ice boating: the Eastern Ice Yacht Association, c/o Mrs. P. Angrick, Awosting Rd., Hewitt, N.J. 07421 and the International Skeeter Association, Rt. 1 Box 389, Harland, Wis. 53029 which publishes a newsletter. For equipment, the fastest hulls are custom built or homemade based on other successful designs, but, at least in the beginning, use a proven design. Manufacturers of one design boats or boat kits are: William Sarnes, 38101 Huron Point Drive, Mount Clemens, Mich.; Lockley Manufacturing Co., 310 Grove Street, New Castle, Pa. 16103; International Arrow Iceyacht Assoc., Box 126, Mt. Clemens, Mich. 48043; and Wotton Sailing Products, Box 218, Montvale, New Jersey 07645.

There is only one book available. It is available from World Publications, Box 366, Mountain View, Calif. at the price listed* plus 25 cents postage.

Sailing on Ice, Jack Andresen. The skills and nuances of the sport of iceboating. Packed with information on safety, dress, racing, and sailing techniques. 1974 Hb., 161 pp., ill., $8.95, (Barnes).

Ice Fishing

The first ice fishermen sought their prey merely for survival. Eskimos and Arctic Indians fished through holes bored in the ice of lakes in an effort to obtain fresh food during the winter. Undoubtedly, many trappers in the North Country learned from the natives, and were able to sustain life by fishing through the ice when supplies ran low.

Fish tend to change their habits and become more canny during the winter, but they can still be caught by any enthusiastic ice angler with good equipment, the right bait or lure, and appropriate knowledge. Warm clothing is the first essential, as temperatures can reach well below zero on good ice fishing days. In past years, it would require so many layers of woolen clothes to stay warm that an ice fisherman would tend to look and walk like a penguin. More recently, however, the widespread use of goose down and synthetic materials has resulted in both superior warmth and greater mobility.

A standard ice fishing rod should be next on the list. This rod is usually about two feet long and is often equipped with a reel. Related tackle includes two- to four-pound test monofilament line, appropriate hooks and lures, and a small bobber to reveal when a fish nibbles on the bait. Some type of tool for cutting through the ice is also necessary, be it an axe, ice auger, chisel or ice spud. Luxury equipment includes wind shelters, warming devices and ice sleds to help transport equipment to the fishing area.

Once a fisherman is properly equipped, the next problem is to find the fish. In general, a lake with good summer fishing will also provide plenty of winter action. Inquiring at a bait shop is another good way to locate the hot spots, as is merely driving around a lake until a cluster of fishermen is spotted. While most summer anglers are very secretive about their favorite fishin' holes and lures, ice fishermen tend to welcome company, often with a steaming thermos of hot chocolate.

Both live and artifical baits can be used. Live bait usually takes the form of corn borers, wood borers, or goldenrod gall worms; as backups, meal worms or earthworms can be used. A bit more difficult to obtain, but nonetheless the best all-around live bait, is a minnow. These can be hooked in such a way as to remain alive and swimming naturally for long periods of time. And if a large fish happens to be hungry, it's hard for him to resist lunging at a tasty minnow. The most common artificials include specially made ice jigs, ice spoons and ice flies.

Don't be too disappointed if you fail to catch fish the first time or two out on the ice. There are so many factors working on a fish's appetite during the winter, that even experienced ice anglers will have a dry spell or two. But for every dry spell you'll hit a hot streak, and it is well worth waiting for!

—Clint Crawford

Clint Crawford is an ice fishing enthusiast from Madison, Wisconsin. He contributes occasional articles to various outdoor journals and works as a high school teacher.

For More Information

Additional information can be found under Fishing. Here is a book of interest. It is available from World Publications, Box 366, Mountain View, Calif. 94040 at the price listed* plus 25 cents postage.

Ice Fishing, Gene Little. Every person's guide to fishing through ice. Begins with a thorough discussion of equipment, and the chapters that follow describe how to use the equipment to best advantage in capturing fish, which lures or baits to use for which fish, what depth to fish, and where to ice fish in the US and Canada. 1975 Hb. & Ppb., 224 pp., ill., $10.00/ $4.95, (Regnery).

Protective equipment for hockey goalies has undergone considerable improvement in recent years, much of it despite heated objections from hockey purists. The face mask, for example, was scorned as un-masculine when first introduced in the National Hockey League by Jacques Plante, but it is now standard equipment. (Duffy)

Ice Hockey

Spawned on harbor ice in Canadian garrison towns of the mid-19th century, ice hockey is thought to be an adaptation of European "hurling" and "shinty" which is field hockey played on skates. Montreal, Quebec and Halifax, Nova Scotia share claims as the birth places of the organized game. Writers Bruce Kidd and John MacFarlane capture this fact best in these words: "Hockey is the Canadian metaphor – some people call it our national religion. In a land so inescapably and inhospitably cold, hockey is the dance of life, an affirmation that despite the deathly chill of winter, we are alive."

Modern amateur hockey is controlled by associations like the USAHA and the CAHA which in turn are members of the International Ice Hockey Federation. The IIHF administers international competition, including the World and Olympic Championships. School hockey thrives in Canada and the northern States and is organized by college and high school associations.

The blazing speed of the game (about double that of the fastest runners) and the unprogrammed creativity in play execution, combine with tough physical contact to make hockey an exciting spectator sport. Professionally, 18 teams in three Canadian and 15 American cities compete for the National Hockey League's Stanley Cup. The newer World Hockey League has franchises in five Canadian and nine U.S. cities.

Played on rinks of approximately 200 feet by 90 feet, the game lasts for three periods of 20 minutes each. The object is to score a goal by shooting a hard rubber puck into a net (4 feet by 6 feet) using a hockey stick. Players with a strong shot have been known to blast the puck at a velocity of 150 feet per second. Only six players from each of the two teams are on the ice at any one time – a well-padded goal tender, two defensemen and three forwards. So fast is the pace of the game that substitutions are made every 60 seconds or so with or without play stoppages. Any rule infractions result in penalties in which offending players leave the ice for two or five minutes, during which time their teams must play short-handed.

The world-wide development of the sport has been so swift it can be predicted that open World Cup competition will soon appear. Russia, in particular, having no more worlds to conquer in IIHF play, is ready to test the best of the North American professionals. The 1972 and 1974 exhibition series between the U.S.S.R. and Canada's best professional players gave dramatic testimony of the high excitement, the gripping drama, and brilliant spectacle of games which lie in store when hockey is played by the most skilled specialists in the world.

Bill L'Heureux

Dr. L'Heureux has been connected with ice hockey as a player and coach for the better part of 40 years. He has both conducted clinics and served on hockey committees in Canada.

More Than Just Entertainment

It is February, and in Toronto the days are short and grey, the snow dirty and cheerless. Maybe it will be better in Winnipeg. You have business there, and the air traffic controllers are on strike so you are taking the train. It is nine o'clock at night, and the train has stopped in a small town in northwestern Ontario. The wood frame station is the only building larger than a house. Not many people live here, probably fewer this year than last, and from the train window you can see houses boarded up. It is below zero outside, a blizzard has dumped four feet of clean snow, and the town probably has never looked better than it does now through the darkness and the snow and the steam that drifts up from the train past your window. It is quiet. There are only two signs of life, only one if you do not count the presence of the train which will be somewhere else in 15 minutes. A few hundred yards from the tracks, on the town side of the tracks, cleared of snow and lit up like a smalltown used car lot, there is a hockey rink – old boards carefully nailed together to form a wooden rectangle around a sheet of natural ice. A dozen men and boys, oblivious to the cold and the town and the train, are playing hockey.

Hockey is the Canadian metaphor, the rink a symbol of this country's vast stretches of water and wilderness, its extremes of climate, the player a symbol of our struggle to civilize such a land. Some people call it our national religion. Well, what better? Like the ball games of the Mayan Indians of Mexico, worshipped because the arc of the kicked ball was thought to imitate the flight of the sun and moon across the heavens, hockey captures the essence of the Canadian experience in the New World. In a land so inescapably and inhospitably cold, hockey is the dance of life, an affirmation that despite the deathly chill of winter we are alive.

Hockey is something most of us share almost from birth. From the frost of October to the thaws of April, in the outposts of Newfoundland, the rural villages of Quebec and the manufacturing cities of Ontario, in the prairie towns of Saskatchewan and the trailer camps of northern British Columbia, boys learn to skate propped up by hockey sticks. Canadian fathers brag that their sons learn to skate before they walk, a revealing lie, and it is the deprived Canadian boy who does not once get a hockey stick for Christmas. The game is a national puberty rite, performed by wobbly-legged kids for congregations of rink-side parents. What is Canada? A country of 250,000 kids getting up at seven o'clock on Saturday morning for a game in a dingy concrete block arena, dreaming of the day when their red, white and blue Canadiens hockey socks will be real instead of the kind anyone can buy out of Eaton's catalogue.

A boy learns more than stickhandling at the community arena. Hockey, as a unique expression of our culture, is also a vessel for its values, passing them father-to-son from one generation to the next. In the corners and along the boards, in the dressing rooms and on the bench, in the clash of body against body, wood and ice, a boy learns our attitudes towards team play, fair play and dirty play, towards winning and losing, tolerance and prejudice, success and failure. "Break the rules and you'll get a penalty – if you're caught." It is through hockey that a Canadian boy first perceives his geographic horizons. He knows there is another part of town because he has played hockey there, and that Canada stretches across the Prairies and the Rocky Mountains to the Pacific because that is where Vancouver is, and Vancouver has Dale Tallon. And it is through hockey, through the encouragement of his family and friends and the entreaties of his coaches, that he learns that apart from his own desires and ambitions he must live with the expectations of others. Hockey also teaches him the difference between boys and girls. In 1956 nine-year-old Abigail Hoffman, who went on to become one of Canada's greatest Olympic athletes, played defense for the St. Catharines Teepees in the Little Toronto Hockey League. When it was discovered she was a girl she was immediately dropped from the team. Playing hockey is for boys. Girls are permitted only to watch. In school a boy learns what we profess to believe. In hockey he learns what we really believe.

All this is to show that for Canadians, hockey is more than just entertainment. It has a significance here it has nowhere else in the world, like bullfighting in Spain or cooking in France. But it is not for its significance that we love the game. We love it because it is one of the most beautiful games in the world. The exhilaration of rink-long rushes in the chilling air. The satisfaction of a well-delivered body check. The special elation of scoring a goal, that thrilling culmination of physical and mental reflex, wit, discipline – and sometimes luck.

International amateur hockey has changed from a Canadian monopoly to a situation in which many national teams are vying equally for honors. The international game has become so free-wheeling and explosive that National Hockey League play was considerably modified following the Canada-USSR series several years ago. (Duffy)

Hockey is all of these things, but it is first the sheer pleasure of skating. Eric Nesterenko, who played 21 years in the National Hockey League, rhapsodized: "Some nights you just go. You can't stop. The rhythm gets to you, or the speed. You're moving, man, moving and that's all." You do not have to play hockey professionally to experience that feeling. Novelist Hugh Hood, who plays once a week in a Montreal industrial league, describes it like this: "Once or twice a season I'll hit a point where my skating comes together. There is no physical feeling I know of that is quite like that, and only one that's better. When my skating finally comes right, it isn't a short intense pleasure, it's a long slow one spread over my whole body, a sense of great health and well-being. My legs seem to be swinging loose from the hip in a long stride that eats up ink space, and my breathing is close to what it would be if I had the guts to give up smoking. Making love is even better, but next to it comes the feeling of skating freely, as if you could go on for hours and never feel fatigue."

Skating makes hockey one of the most sensual of sports, which is why so many of us play it. But it is also among the most creative. Not as programmed as baseball or football, where offenses and defenses are carefully worked out in dvance, so that the game becomes largely a question of xecution. Faster than those other wonderfully spontaneous ames, soccer, rugger and basketball (a man can skate almost wice as fast as he can run, and a puck can be shot at more han 150 feet per second). In hockey, plays are conceived and xecuted instantly, almost instinctively. "When I carry the puck across the blueline," says Dave Keon, "I've got less than a second to choose from any of a hundred plays I could make to try and get by the opposing defensemen." Rushing, stickhandling, backchecking, diving, rushing, passing, backchecking, rushing – the basic plays are obvious and simple and they are repeated endlessly, but never in the same way or in the same sequence. So when the puck is dropped for a faceoff, whether it is the Canadiens in the Montreal Forum or the neighborhood kids on the street, something different happens every time.

That is the magic of hockey, its unlimited dramatic possibilities. And that is what makes it almost as exciting a game to watch as it is to play. The spectator cannot experience the game the way the players do. And maybe it is true, as some pro hockey players insist, that anyone who has not played the game professionally sees only half of what takes place on the ice. But there are compensations. The spectator sees the game as a whole, like someone watching a game of two-handed poker, knowing each player's cards. The spectator experiences more fully the subtleties of physical expression different players bring to the game – the grace of Frank Mahovlich, turning in his own end, starting up the ice with long flowing strides; the self-assurance of Bobby Orr, whose command of the game's basic skills is so sure that he can do anything it occurs to him to do at the instant it occurs to him to do it; the speed and flair of Yvan Cournoyer, racing into the clear between two helpless defensemen; the bravado of a Jacques Plante, who can make even the easiest saves seem dramatic. Only the spectator can appreciate the abstract beauty of the

To a goalie, there is no more fearsome sight than an enemy right winger broken past the defensemen and stickhandling in toward the net for a one on one confrontation. With a deft feint or two, a completely open man can usually leave the goalie sprawling helplessly on the ice, lifting the puck easily over him. (Duffy)

game – the ebb and flow of bodies drawn this way and that by the puck, like iron filings arranging and rearranging themselves around an elusive black magnet.

More Canadians watch hockey – in the streets, at rinks and on television – than engage in any other single public activity. More Canadians watch hockey now than go to church. *Hockey Night in Canada* really *is* hockey night in Canada. We schedule our lives around it. During elections, Canadian political parties tell their canvassers not to knock on doors during hockey games, because to interrupt a hockey fan at his pleasure is almost certainly to lose his vote. At playoff time, Canadian churches hold their services early so their congregations can get home in time for the Sunday afternoon game. And at Canadian universities, where final examinations and playoffs have a tendency to coincide, there is an inevitable exodus from libraries and study halls just before game time, even scholarly discipline having its limits. How many Canadians watch the Saturday night hockey telecast? The CBC says 6 million, 10 million during the playoffs. A Montreal taxi driver will tell you that on Saturday nights he can practically set his watch by the slack period that begins with the opening faceoff at eight o'clock and ends when the game is over around 10:30. It is said of virtually every Canadian city that during a hockey telecast its consumption of water increases perceptibly between periods.

It was the same in the beginning. Old-timers tell stories about how they used to bundle themselves up to stand in sub-zero winds watching hockey on outdoor rinks. It was not until 1911, when Frank and Lester Patrick introduced artificial ice to Vancouver and Victoria, where natural ice is a sometimes thing, that hockey fans were afforded shelter from the elements. Even in the covered arenas, symbols of community prosperity, doors and windows were left wide open to keep the ice good and frozen. Likewise, of course, the fans. And in those days, years before radio and television, getting the results of an out-of-town series was not the easy thing it is today. When the Toronto Wellingtons went to Winnipeg for the 1902 Stanley Cup series against the Winnipeg Victorias, thousands of fans stood in the cold outside the King Street offices of the Toronto *Globe* where a running account of each game was relayed by CPR telegraph. And when each game was over, *The Globe* sent a courier to the Toronto street railway powerhouse, where the name of the winner was relayed to the waiting city by a prearranged signal – two whistles signifying a Toronto victory, three whistles a Toronto defeat.

To this day, hockey remains a universally understood language in a country where the English do not speak French and the French do not speak much English, in which Britain is still referred to as "the old country" and Maritimers call people in Ontario "Upper Canadians". Hockey spans the distances, cultural and topographical, that separate the 22 million people who inhabit these 3,851,809 square miles of land and fresh water. If it was the Canadian Pacific Railroad and the wheat economy that encouraged culture to flow east and west instead of north and south during the first 70 years of Canada's existence, *Hockey Night in Canada* has played much the same role ever since. Foster Hewitt began broadcasting the Toronto Maple Leafs Saturday night hockey games to Canadian Broadcasting Corporation listeners across the country in 1931. During one such broadcast in 1937, his audience was estimated at more than 6 million – which, if true means that more than half the people in the country, men, women and children, were for a few hours that night united around their radios. The popularity of those Saturday night broadcasts was astonishing. There was one year when Hewitt received 90,000 fan letters. "They streamed in from all across the country," he has recalled. "From a lighthouse on the Bay of Fundy, a trawler on the North Atlantic fishing banks, a dormitory in a Maritime ladies college, a Hudson's Bay trading post far north of Churchill, a theatre in a French Canadian community in North Alberta, a construction camp many miles from rail in Northern Ontario, a barber shop in a small Saskatchewan village, an isolated British Columbia home where mail arrived only once a month." It did not matter that Hewitt described the game in a verbal shorthand because his listeners knew hockey so well they could fill in the detail for themselves. It was the Saturday night hockey audience that launched Canadian television, providing CBC-TV, not otherwise notably successful in developing popular Canadian programming, with a ready-made national audience. Hockey came to television in 1954, when a TV set was a community resource, like a newspaper during the Depression and a backyard swimming pool today. If you were a boy in those days, you really worked at your friendship with the kid whose parents were the first on the block with TV. To offend him was to risk not being invited into his living room on Saturday night to watch the hockey game. The Montreal Canadiens were emerging as the golden team of hockey back then, with Rocket Richard, Elmer Lach, Boom Boom Geoffrion, Bert Olmstead, Doug Harvey and young stars like Jean Beliveau and Jacques Plante. And in Montreal, even on the coldest and snowiest of winter nights, people would stand outside appliance store windows watching the Rocket, Boom Boom and Le Gros Bill on TV. Sometimes a thoughtful store owner would provide benches of barrels and old boards.

It was only natural that hockey players should have become our national folk heroes. Hockey, after all, was the only popular culture we did not import. Lacking the initiative and self-confidence to create alternatives to Broadway, Hollywood and Tin Pan Alley, Canadians assumed until very recently that all the great actors, film stars and popular singers were Americans (or Canadians who became Americans). Of the handful of celebrities Canadian television has produced, the majority have been, not artists, but journalists. So it is not surprising that compared to hockey players like Syl Apps, Maurice Richard and Gordie Howe, our artists and intellectuals have lived in relative obscurity. It is doubtful that any Canadian, including the Prime Minister, would be recognized by more people on the main street of a Canadian town or city than Gordie Howe. Although he was born and raised in Floral, Saskatchewan, for more than 20 years he has lived in Detroit, where he was a star with the Detroit Red Wings. But in Moncton and Lennoxville, Sault St. Marie and North Battleford, Red Deer and Powell River, Gordie Howe is still regarded as one of our own. Howe tells a story about a fishing trip he made a few years ago to a place north of Edmonton called Moose Lake. He was driving across a bridge and rolled down the car window to talk to a man fishing over the side. "How are they biting?" he asked. The man turned, and as if he and Howe were next-door neighbors, replied, "Pretty good, Gord."

Hockey players like Howe are for Canadians everything that actors like Paul Newman, television stars like Johnny Carson, and athletes like Joe Namath, Muhammad Ali, Johnny Bench and Arnold Palmer are for Americans. We revere them not only for their mastery of hockey, but also for the wealth and acclaim that go with it. We begrudge our Members of Parliament $28,000 a year, we balk at giving a $9,000-a-year teacher a $500 increase, but when Bobby Hull negotiates a $2.8 million contract we are delighted, because Hull, after all, is one of us, only better, and his success symbolizes the possibility, however remote, that wealth and acclaim might be ours too. Later on, perhaps, a Canadian boy with ambition sees himself as a doctor, lawyer, chairman of the board, maybe even prime minister, but while he is still a boy and can still make the team, he sees himself as a hockey star, because a hockey star is the one true Canadian celebrity . . .

Bruce Kidd and John MacFarlane

Adapted from **Death of Hockey**

For More Information

American magazines are scarce in this sport, but Canada does its best to make up. *Hockey Digest,* 1020 Church St., Evanston, Ill. 60201, puts out eight issues a year for $4.50. It carries many good stories on the current stars and teams. *Hockey Pictorial,* 1434 St. Catherine Street West, Suite 217, Montreal, Canada H3G 1R6, covers the NHL, WHA and Canadian games. Seven issues a year for $5.25. *Hockey News,* same address as above, is a newsprint weekly which covers all the games in Canadian and American professional leagues. $10.50 per year.

There are two major professional leagues and an amateur governing body: National Hockey League, 920 Sun Life Building, Montreal, Canada, is the largest and oldest (founded 1917) league in America. It has franchises in many American and Canadian cities. World Hockey Association, 1010 North Main St., Santa Ana, Calif. 92701, is a new professional league which has gotten off to a good start. Amateur Hockey Association of the United States, 7901 Cedar Ave., Bloomington, Minn. 55420, promotes amateur hockey in the US and maintains relations between the US and international teams.

Here are some good hockey books. All are available from World Publications, Box 366, Mountain View, Calif. 94040 at the price listed* plus 25 cents postage. Write for a complete list.

The Ice Men, Gary Ronberg. An inside glimpse at the men of hockey, the goaltenders, referees, superstars, bad guys and managers. The action-packed color photographs which highlight almost every page give an emotional and informative look into a hidden world. 1973 Hb., 256 pp., ill., $15.95, (Crown).

Inside Hockey, Stan Mikita. A step-by-step hockey guide for beginners, by one of ice hockey's brightest stars. All subjects—equipment, skills, and more—are covered. 1971 Hb. & Ppb., 106 pp., ill., $7.95/$3.95, (Regnery).

Pocket Hockey Encyclopedia, B.V.B. Research. An extremely complete book which gives you an alphabetical guide to hockey's rules, history and other facts necessary for informed appreciation of the game. 1972 Ppb., 254 pp., ill., $3.50, (Scribner's).

The Mad Men of Ice Hockey, Trent Frayne. A look at ice hockey's licensed madmen—the players, managers, coaches and owners whose styles have sustained hockey's high level of eccentricity from the turn of the century. 1974 Hb., 191 pp., ill., $8.95, (Dodd,Mead).

Playing Hockey the Professional Way, Rod Gilbert and Brad Park. Two of hockey's top players tell and show how professionals play. How to handle every position, well-illustrated with photos and diagrams. 1972 Hb., 276 pp., ill., $9.95, (Harper & Row).

Sports Illustrated Ice Hockey, Mark Mulvog et al. Basics of ice hockey covered in a concise, easy-to-follow text. Rules, penalties, stick handling, passing, tactics of defense, and goal tending are all covered and illustrated with excellent action drawings. 1971 Hb. & Ppb., 95 pp., ill., $4.95/$1.95, (Lippincott).

The Hockey Handbook, Lloyd Percival. Of all the hockey books we've seen, this is by far the most comprehensive. Intended as much for ready reference as for detailed study, this manual deals with every aspect of the game for player, coach, and spectator. Covers training, practice organization and coaching technique, goalkeeping, skating, scoring goals, offensive and defensive strategy and tactics, carrying the puck, and more. 1960 (rev.) Hb., 321 pp., ill., $7.95, (Barnes).

Jai-Alai

Jai-Alai (pronounced hi-li) is the fastest, most dangerous sport ever devised by man, with its origins extending back to ancient Egypt and Greece. Modern jai-alai was invented during the 17th century by the Basques in the Pyrenees Mountains of France and Spain, and eventually spread throughout Spain, on to Mexico, the Philippines, then to Cuba in 1901. The game was permanently established in the United States in 1924 by the firm that founded Miami Jai-Alai, and legalized pari-mutuel wagering followed in 1931.

The thrilling sport experienced rapid growth in Florida, and frontons (jai-alai establishments) are operated by World Jai-Alai, Inc. in Miami, Tampa, Ocala, and Ft. Pierce; other facilities are located in Dania, West Palm Beach, Melbourne, Daytona Beach and Orlando. The game was recently introduced in Las Vegas, and three frontons are scheduled to open in 1976 in Bridgeport and Milford Connecticut, and a World Jai-Alai facility in Hartford. Construction is also underway on a fronton in Newport, Rhode Island.

Most peltaris (professional jai-alai players) have traditionally been Basque, but with the advent of amateur jai-alai courts in Florida, more and more Americans are becoming involved in this tough, demanding sport.

Jai-Alai resembles handball, but is far more difficult and challenging. Players begin training as children to reach professional status by the age of 17 or 18 although the exacting nature of the game places men in their prime between 25 and 30 years old. Jai-Alai is played on a three-walled court, 176 feet long and 50 feet wide. Each player uses a cesta, or crescent-shaped straw basket, strapped to his wrist to throw and retrieve a rock-hard ball called a pelota. The pelota is comprised of hand-wound virgin de Para rubber covered with a layer of nylon thread and two coats of specially hardened goat skin.

The players wear no protective padding or equipment, except a helmet, to insure safety against the riccocheting pelota, which travels at speeds exceeding 150 miles per hour.

The game proceeds in a round robin manner, with the winning player or team remaining on the court until defeated. The object is to field and throw the pelota in one fluid motion, catching it on the fly off the front wall, or after only one bounce. The player will throw the pelota against the front wall causing it to bounce back into the "fair" area. The opponent scoops it up in his cesta before the second bounce and throws it–in one motion–to the "fair" area on the wall. When the pelota returns it must land in the playing area again.

When a player misses the ball, misses a serve, or throws the ball into a foul area such as the overhead screen, a point is scored for the opponent. The player in violation must leave the court while the player who wins the point continues until he either loses a point or wins a game, which usually is seven points.

Each match lasts between 12 and 20 minutes, and both singles and doubles competitions are featured. Each fronton carries about 46 players on the roster, equally divided between front court and back court men.

The jai-alai frontons are unlike other sports centers. Most offer theater-style seats, restaurants, snack bars, cocktail lounges, and closed-circuit TV viewing rooms for patrons.

—Milt Roth

Milt Roth is the Public Relations Director of World Jai-Alai, Inc.

For More Information

Additional information can be obtained by writing World Jai-Alai, Inc., Milton Roth, 1175 N.E. 125th St., Miami, Fla. 33161. Also you might look up the article in *Sports Illustrated* about the game. It was in their July 23, 1975 issue.

Jai-Alai features acrobatic play and some of the fastest action in the world of sport. Players must begin training during childhood and seldom reach their potential in the sport in less than 15 years. (Roth)

Jazz Dance

Versatility is the main quality to distinguish the jazz dancer of today. Desire for constant change and refusal to be categorized into a specific performing style is what makes jazz dance unique and exciting.

A dedicated jazz dancer/teacher/choreographer is on a never-ending search for new ways to express with his body what the musician expresses with his instrument. A true jazz dancer is totally involved with the music and is therefore continually adapting and improvising.

As much as you may respect disciples who spend a lifetime mastering one person's style (i.e. the Martha Graham Method), they become locked into a movement and time period which no longer truthfully can be called "modern dance".

Ballet companies experimenting with contemporary music all too often suffer from a credibility gap, as the movements of a classically trained ballerina are not easily identifiable with the sounds of Freddie Hubbard or Santana, for example. These are obvious classifications, but the same comments apply to flamenco dancers, ballroom dancers, tap dancers or any other isolated area of study.

More than ever, it is necessary for an aspiring jazz dancer to absorb as quickly as possibly techniques which will free the body from regimentation. There are already jazz styles that are passe, and nothing is more archaic than a teacher/choreographer who becomes locked into a dance style equivalent of the 50's rock-and-roll era.

Aside from not relaxing into stylized cliches, the jazz dancer continually must adapt and blend techniques to complement the similar adaptation and blending which take place in today's music.

We have, for example, Santana and his blend of Rock, Latin and Indian music; Chuck Mangione who uses symphonic orchestrations as a framework for his small jazz combos; Herbie Hancock, an innovator who contrasts electronic effects and primitive rhythms; and Earth, Wind and Fire who combine double-time bossa novas and sambas to create the basis of many popular social dances.

As there are techniques, steps, and styles that are dance counterparts to all of the foregoing, it becomes evident that the truly contemporary jazz dancer can't begin early enough to learn the tools of his trade – while constantly reminding himself that there are many "correct" ways to do the same thing.

Turns provide the classic example. There are pirouettes, chaines, fuetes, attitudes, step-up turns, touch turns, Spanish turns, barrel turns and many others. Once the placement and basic techniques of turning are mastered, the jazz dancer can fit the turn to the style expressed in the music since he has open to him as many choices as his background and imagination permit.

To be justified in referring to his classes as jazz techniques, a teacher should be continually exposing his students to movements that complement and fit music styles that include lyrical jazz, Afro jazz, rock jazz, Latin jazz, blues and swing. One should not be qualified as a jazz teacher because he uses "Luigi" warm-up exercises.

Illustrative of the range of music styles with equally varied dance styles is the work of The Dancers' Synectics Group of San Francisco, California. In the past two years the Group has choreographed and performed professionally to music by Santana, Boz Scaggs, Quincy Jones, Chicago, Dr. John, James Brown, M.F.S.B., and Scott Joplin.

In addition the jazz dancer may perform character dances which tell a story or describe a way of life. Musical comedy relies almost exclusively on these "situation" dances. As this medium provides one of the few outlets for full-time working professionals, a conscientious teacher includes combinations in this art form in his classes.

One reality of jazz dance is the difficulty in obtaining recognition as a legitimate artist in the jazz dance world. As we are dependent on the musicians for inspiration, we also seem to be destined to follow in their arduous struggle for recognition as legitimate artists. (For an insight on the life style of a jazz musician in the '40s, read **Bird Lives!** by Ross Russell.)

Unfortunately it is still the '40s for a serious jazz dancer today. Choreography in musicals is too frequently only background setting for the main action. Television specials such as those featuring The Goldiggers behind Dean Martin are hardly inspirational; nightclub dancers are indiscriminately labeled chorus girls with the usual knee-jerk responses.

On the brighter side, we have musicals that do say something worthwhile to the public. We can start with "West Side Story" and continue with "Cabaret", "Chorus Line" and "The Whiz". Ben Vereen's recent television series contained certain sections where the dancers were choreographed excitingly and the Ann Margaret and Shirley MacLaine nightclub acts are outlets for some of the best pure jazz dance being performed anywhere today. These are indications that jazz dance is moving upward to its rightful position as an art form.

Hopefully in the near future we will see a jazz concert company formed which will tour colleges and theatres, providing exposure necessary for this art form to become an accepted part of the culture.

Ideally we would have the dance equivalent of the Newport/Monterey Jazz Festivals where companies from various geographic and ethnic backgrounds would appear and present their works. This has been accomplished by ballet enthusiasts in every major city in the United States; therefore it would be logical enough to expect the jazz community to be involved in a similar pursuit.

A performing company, however, has to have repertory; this takes time and repetition to establish. Conversely, for most jazz dancers the idea of performing anything for longer than the music remains relevant is antithetical; thus, the concept of permanent repertory becomes a contradiction in terms.

We who love jazz dance and live for it will continue to do so – as it always has been with those who care. Musicians found their way and maintained their integrity. I'm sure we jazz dancers will find a way to do the same.

—Anne Marie Garvin

Ann Marie Garvin is the coordinator of Dancers' Synectics Group of San Francisco and teaches jazz, tap and Afro-jazz.

For More Information

The American Dance Guild, 245 W. 52nd St., New York, N.Y. 10019 can supply further information. They also put out a newsletter that should be of interest. Also, Baum's, 106 S. 11th St., Philadelphia, Pa. 19107 is a good source for equipment.

Jiu-Jitsu

Jiu-jitsu is a product of the Japanese martial arts systems (which probably came from China), and was adapted, then molded, into the modern discipline. Jiu-jitsu means "the Art of Gentleness" and as Donald Angier has explained in *Self Defense World* magazine, "the gentleness is expressed in the application of the art, not the effect upon the attacker."

Like its offspring, judo, jiu-jitsu employs throwing arts, but it also includes striking, kicking, locking the joints, dislocating and bone-breaking arts, tying and escaping arts, and strangulation techniques. To temper these violent-sounding techniques, jiu-jitsu is based on a philosophy of nonviolence. Advance jiu-jitsu-ka (practitioners) resort to action only when nothing else can be done. As a further tempering, students are taught to use only enough force to neutralize the situation. If a jiu-jitsu-ka can subdue his attacker painlessly with one simple technique, that is all he will do. If he must resort to injury or intense pain, however, he will do so with no reservation.

There are many different types of jiu-jitsu (feudal Japan acknowledged over 700 systems according to Angier), but the purest type is "soft" or yielding in its te-waza form (hand techniques). Since students must learn hand-to-hand, hand-to-weapon, and weapon-to-weapon techniques, te-waza builds a solid foundation for further sophistication, and helps develop the non-aggressive aspects of the art, its traditions and etiquette.

The study of pure jiu-jitsu requires many years of research and practice. The student must learn to open his mind to the development of ki (positive mental and physical energy), perfect the body movements and techniques of te-waza, and then, as he becomes more proficient, work to master the sword and other weapons as well.

Jiu-jitsu can be very dangerous if taught as a technique alone. It is for this reason that so much emphasis has been placed on the mental aspect, on having an open and free but aware mind. When the student can master the principle of mizo no kukuro ("mind like water") he practices aiki-ju-jitsu, the purest form of jiu-jitsu where he is perpetually relaxed but also ever ready to react when the situation arises.

Jiu-jitsu, aside from providing a means of self-defense, trains the student to have a calm, absorbing mind, good physical reflexes and muscle tone, and a confident, healthy, and positive attitude toward life.

Jiu-Jitsu Is My Life

I was raised during the World War II era, and was therefore subjected to an avalanche of propaganda relating to the Japanese. Needless to say, none of it was favorable.

From the day of the bombing of Pearl Harbor, the words "sneak attack" and "Jap" became synonymous. Motion pictures began showing Japanese soldiers bayonetting babies and grandmothers. Their planes came out of the sun to shoot down the clean-cut "boy next door" and riddled helpless pilots descending in parachutes. But my young mind couldn't understand the sudden change because up until Pearl Harbor, my hero had been a Japanese detective named "Mr. Moto". I used to sit through the movies two or three times to figure out how my hero tossed the bad guys around with a flick of the wrist. And so, jiu-jitsu was in my blood to stay. I couldn't be convinced he had now become a disreputable character. Jiu-jitsu had become an obsession with me, but I had nowhere to go. It was rare for a non-Japanese to be proficient in the martial arts in those days, and all of the Japanese in America were in concentration camps. But luck – or fate – was with me. In 1949 I met Mr. Yoshida Kenji, master of Shidare

Jiu-Jitsu practioners become adept at controlling opponents by putting pressure on key nerve points throughout the body. In this case a knife wielding attacker is made peaceful with pressure on a neck nerve. (Kirby)

Yanagi Ryu Aiki Jiu-Jitsu (Weeping Willow Style of the Mind Blending Art of Gentleness), a man who has been the most powerful influence on my mind and my life.

Mr. Yoshida was the first Japanese I had ever seen in person. Without wanting to admit it, the anti-Japanese propaganda from the war had made some impression on me. So to say that I had mixed emotions on that day I approached him in the playground where he had been watching us play, is a gross understatement. But my "need-to-know" won out.

After Yoshida "sensei" (an honorific title) accepted me as a student, a process that took over two months, I began to learn many things. Not only concerning self-defense, but life itself. One lesson that is still especially vivid in my memory and that gave me an insight as to just how great a man he really was, and how much he understood life, was this:

One Saturday I was helping Yoshida sensei as he made his round cutting lawns, cleaning out cellars, attics, etc. The occupant of the house where we were clearing weeds came to us and stated, "Hey, Jap! If you clean out that old shed I'll give you a couple of bucks extra. My kid wants to use it for a clubhouse, so don't get any Jap-smell on it."

I was enraged, and told Mr. Yoshida to tell him where to go and we'd punch his lights out. Instead, Yoshida sensei just turned around and said, "I'll do my best." Not only did we clean out the refuse from the shed, we cleaned the walls, floors, windows, and aired the place out. I still couldn't understand Yoshida sensei's attitude.

Later he explained that he had done the extra work for the son and his future enjoyment of our work, not for the father. Furthermore, there is no such thing as menial labor. If a task is necessary, it is honorable. As far as the father's attitude, it should be understood because of the recent war years and besides, he had seen Americans treated much worse in Japan. To have opposed him would lead to conflict. To accept and understand leads to success. The father is happy with my work, the son is happy with the father, and I am happy within myself.

We apply the same principles to the art of jiu-jitsu. From then on I realized that the study of jiu-jitsu went beyond self-defense. The principles which allow the art to work in defense also allow you to win at life.

During the years of study to follow, I not only learned devastating throws, bone breaking, joint dislocation, and the ability to wield and defend against weapons, I also learned to appreciate the delicate color of a dragonfly wing, the stateliness of a redwood, and to respect everything that lives and breathes. I learned to appreciate architecture, painting, sculpture, and the beauty, craftsmanship, and deadly utility of a samurai sword. I learned history, tradition, Japanese language, and self-reliance. All from a man whom I was, according to my peers, supposed to reject and detest as unprincipled, and who came from a land I was told was barbaric and cultureless.

These lessons, not preached to me but demonstrated by example, have enabled me to get through many difficult periods in my life where I know I would have otherwise resigned myself to my fate, wallowed in self-pity, or rationalized my plight.

Now I try to impart these lessons to my students and hope that what I have learned from Yoshida sensei and the lifestyles of those martial artists before him will someday enable someone else (rewriting Shakespeare) to, "Take arms against this sea of troubles, and by blending, end them."

Jiu-jitsu will remain my life. In it I feel useful. It has taught me self-reliance, confidence, how to live in harmony with my fellow man, to be my own man rather than to follow the crowd, and of course, the ability to defend myself and those I love.

—Donald Angier

Donald Angier studied under Yoshida Kenji from 1949 to 1954. At Mr. Yoshida's death in 1954, he fell successor to the art of Shidare Yanagi Ryu Aiki Jiu-Jitsu, the Weeping Willow Style of Mind Blending Art of Gentleness. Angier has taught and lectured since 1955 in the Los Angeles area and is a frequent contributor to martial arts periodicals.

For More Information

There are no magazines or organizations in the US that cover Jiu-Jitsu exclusively. However, magazines like *Black Belt, Self-Defense World* and *Official Karate* give coverage from time to time. Check karate for addresses. Jiu-Jitsu is not widespread and does not hold public events except on special occasions. However, a good contact is Donald Angier, 11057 S. Atlantic Ave., Lynwood, Calif. Or call a local dojo and ask if they can get you started. Here is a book of interest. It is available from World Publications, Box 366, Mountain View, Calif. 94040 at the price listed* plus 25 cents each postage.

The Complete Kano Jiu-Jitsu, H. Irving Hancock and Katsukuma Higashi. An unusually well-illustrated book of the original tricks of the early Judo Kano system. The book begins with the simplest of combat tricks and progresses by degrees to tricks that can cause bodily harm. 1905 Ppb., 500 pp., ill., $3.50, (Dover).

Jousting

Jousting, the medieval combat between knights on horseback who charged each other with lances, is demanding and rigorous like American rodeo. Getting knocked off a horse at full gallop is no fun, but some people are drawn to the excitement and thrill of this difficult and often strenuous sport. Although different tournaments have different rules, universally the lances are blunted, a contestant is disqualified for striking a horse and competitors aim at the shield rather than the man. The contestants usually have three chances to strike the shield of the opponent and some contests allow for dismounting and continuing with blunted swords. Many jousting societies are attempting to get the sport, with all its excitement and gay spectacle, admitted to the Olympics.

To begin a jousting tournament, the Knight Marshall proclaims the rules and declares the tourney open; a fanfare of trumpets sound, calling the knights before the Royal Box, enacting a medieval custom. Each knight returns to his respective pavillion to await the start of the jousting.

The knights start at opposite ends, one on each side of the tilt, or barrier, and at a sign they gallop at each other, lances high at first, couching as they get closer. For one it usually ends in a spill on the ground!

In addition to the individual tilting, either between individual knights or different houses, the knights compete at catching a hanging ring on the end of their lances while their horses run at a full gallop.

The quintain, or shield, is likewise tilted with and the purpose is to strike the pivoting shield without getting hit by the dangling iron-spiked ball which spins as the quintain is hit. The object is to score more points than the other side, thus winning the tournament.

Whether the handkerchiefs tied to the arms of the knights by women from the audience have anything to do with bringing luck to the winner is anybody's guess!

Jousting began to die out in the 16th century when the effectiveness of the heavily-armoured knight was antiquated by the longbow which could pierce armor at 800 feet with its iron-tipped arrow. Occasionally, tournaments were held in the 17th and 18th centuries in Germany, Italy, Sweden, Denmark, Austria, Spain, Malta, and America. Today, many jousting societies are reviving their ancient heritage; others are attracted to the pageantry and glamor of the past. Still others do exacting research on manners, costumes and history to simply show the ancient knights in a modern, living context.

—Don Deed

Don Deed is a freelance writer who has a special interest in unusual sports.

Modern knights meet in jousting tournaments that attempt to recreate the historic era of King Arthur's Round Table. They preserve the traditions, equipment and excitement of a jousting tournament that might have been attended by Sir Lancelot or King Richard the Lion Hearted. (White)

A Bit of Tradition

Jousting isn't in the same context today as it was in the past. In medieval times it was chivalry. A man on a horse riding in the forest would see another man riding on a horse and they would naturally want to be friends or fight. For some reason, women or something, this really used to happen. Men used to die for women.

England was feudal then. There was a king, and dukes who were even more powerful than kings. Dukes used to make and break kings and they had a sufficient force of men to back them up. Those were bad days, one could be killed very easily. But then, too, people marched against the kings and killed many of them.

Today, the weapons we use are replicas of the originals which now hang in the Tower of London. We try to be as authentic as we can but the swords are made of an alloy and fortunately aren't sharp. The originals were made of iron, were quite sharp, and weighed three or four times as much as the replicas we use. Our costumes are copies, too. The ones in the Tower of London are 500 or 600 years old and many of them are made of gold. The chain mail weighed a lot but we've cut this down by using woven cord in the place of the chain and alloys instead of the original armour.

The horses are very important in jousting but because of health regulations we can't bring our draft horses when the Tourney of the Knights comes to America. We trained with quarter horses for about a month before coming to the US, taking them down the chutes at each other. Believe me, it was a lot of hard work. Sometimes people don't appreciate the time and energy that goes into the horses. Each of the horses and the knights are different and they just won't do the same thing every night.

We can't train too much because it's harder than it actually looks. We've all been trained by stunt men who learned the trade but there are just too many ways to get injured to practice a lot. About the only thing we can practice is the rings; as for the quintain and shield, you can leave them out. All of our people are athletic and keep in good shape lifting weights and running. We have to have our wrists taped up before a tournament because when you hit something with your lance, your wrists can't take the shock and get sprung.

Of course, we have set routines worked out—we use leg cuts, belly cuts, head cuts and back cuts in our sword work. They've been carried down from the past. These swords aren't thrusting swords, they are to cut. I think the actual aim in medieval times was to keep at it till you got so tired you couldn't parry, and the other knight cut through your armor. With the rapier, it's the man with the brains that wins, but here it's the man that's the biggest, the strongest and has the most stamina. It doesn't matter how smart you are. If the other guy was bigger and stronger, you'd die.

Jousting is like American rodeos; it's a bit of tradition. In England, people think back to the times of their great-great grandfathers and it appeals to them. At home in England we do lots of T.V. programs and play the county fairs. It's a sensible show; the people who come to see us love it. I hope they like it here in this country.

—Dinny Powell

Dinny Powell is a professional jouster who jousts with the Tourney of the Knights, a jousting show from England.

For More Information

The National Jousting Association, 1701 Stockton Rd., Joppa, Md. 21085 can provide more information. Or you might check with the Maryland Jousting Tournament Association, Box 14, Jessup, Md. 20794.

Judo

Kodokan Judo is probably the only Oriental martial art whose object is to neutralize an opponent without hurting him. The defender uses the assailant's motion and energy to his own advantage, capitalizing on the assailant's aggression while conserving his own energies. The practical background described by Kano Jigoro, the sport's originator, explains why he felt its development was necessary. He wrote: "Many jujutsu ryu often indulged in such dangerous practices as throwing by rather unfair means, or by wrenching limbs. This led not a few people who had occasion to witness those wild exercises to deprecate jujutsu as being dangerous and harmful to the body. Moreover, there were some ill-disciplined jujutsu ryu, the disciples of which made themselves obnoxious to the public by willfully throwing down innocent people or by seeking quarrels . . . . Hence my desire was to show that my teaching, in marked contrast to jujutsu teachings . . . was quite free from danger and was not to be used as a means for reckless aggressiveness . . . ."

It took Kano eight years to develop his first series of eight throws. There are now five series of eight throws each and Anton Geesink, international kodokan judo champion, predicts a sixth series soon. Modern judoists use throws like osotogari, haraigoshi and seoinage in contests, keeping in mind that techniques must be scientific and noninjurious. Judoists must also work to achieve maximum result from the minimum mental and physical effort – energy is conserved as much as possible whether practicing or performing.

Judo practitioners wear a judogi which is composed of a white jacket, loose-fitting white trousers and a colored belt. (Women can wear a leotard or undergarment under the jacket, also.) The colored belt indicates the level of proficiency of the wearer: novices wear a white belt while only experts wear the coveted black belt.

Beginning with the stance and holds, the novice spends much time on the basics of balance and movement before ever attempting a judo throw. One of the major parts of judo, for

"Only a novice tries to overcome an opponent's strength with his own. The one with the greatest strength and energy will win, but true judo promises the maximum results with the minimum strength. Men are naturally stronger than women, and they train more to build up their strength. I don't think it is necessary for women to train this way. My motto is 'be strong, be gentle, be beautiful.' " (Duffy)

example, is falling properly, learning to land in various positions without injury. The beginner may spend many sessions learning just a few simple techniques. Then, very slowly, the throwing techniques are introduced and perfected until the student is a master of hand, hip, foot and leg, back-on-ground, and side-on-ground throws.

Modern judo can be learned at a local dojo, and competitions take place on a local, national, and international level, and include Olympic competition.

The Art of Gentleness

Thinking of judo, many people envision a pair of six-foot heavyweights strongly grasping each other's judo gis. Their intensity locks them into a closed circle of muscle – grunting, pushing, pulling, and jerking, they sweat, each trying to throw the other to the mats. A crushing choke-hold will finish one or the other, declare the winner and the loser.

Keiko Fukuda is a breath of fresh air, dispersing these visions of a Roman spectacle and clearly explaining the origins and meanings of judo for the uninitiated. "Only the novice tries to overcome the opponent's strength with their own," she explains. "The one with the most strength and energy will win. But true judo promises the maximum results with the minimum strength."

Although she modestly says she speaks only out of her experience, Keiko Fukuda has been studying judo for 40 years, obtaining the rank of 6th dan (the highest rank awarded to women in judo) from the Kodokan Judo Headquarters in Tokyo. She is the highest ranking woman judoist in the United States and the second highest ranking woman in the world (another woman has seniority). Beginning training in 1935 at the invitation of Professor Jigoro Kano (the originator of judo who studied jujitsu from her grandfather), Ms. Fukuda decided by the time she was a brown belt to devote herself to spreading judo throughout the world.

After traveling to the Philippines, Australia, and Canada to teach she settled in San Francisco in 1967. Now she is a full-time judo instructor at Mills College for Women in Oakland, S.F. City College and at the Sokoju Zen Buddhist temple in S.F.'s Japantown. In addition she finds herself busy traveling to such places as New York, Chicago, Seattle, and Santa Barbara giving workshops for summer training camps.

Although she originally taught men's and boys' classes in addition to women's classes, she now feels she will devote all her energies to teaching and spreading women's judo. And women's judo or joshi judo is different.

"Men are naturally stronger physically than women," she relates. "Men train more to build up their strength, lifting weights and such. I want to teach good, strong judo but too many places are teaching stiff judo. If you teach too much of the strength kind, they can't learn the techniques. Too much thinking of strength and just fighting, fighting, fighting.

"I don't think it is necessary for women to train this way. Women's bodies are different. My motto is 'be strong, be gentle, be beautiful.' If when we work with men, they can't throw us, that is being strong. Then when we get a chance, we throw them.

"But many women complain that if they don't train with men they won't be able to train strongly. If training for self-defense, men will be the ones to attack them. In training for competition, the real money, awards and emphasis is on men's competition. A woman needs extraordinary strength or outstanding technique to compete with a man but it isn't impossible.

"My experience is that women who want to compete can compete very well with men. Mostly we don't go out of the dojo to practice with men but sometimes we need to practice with men for the experience. It takes a long time the way I teach but the body grows up correctly."

For the newcomers who think of judo as just pulling on a gi, Ms. Fukuda's joshi judo opens up entirely new vistas. In her book, **Born for the Mat: A Kodokan Kata Textbook for Women**, she explains that kata (prearranged practice done with a partner but without throwing and with an emphasis on correct form) is usually reserved for men in the higher ranks. Women practice kata from the beginning.

Joshi judo is divided into three major parts: throwing, grappling, and striking techniques. Kneeling and standing techniques are studied as well as dagger and sword counters, methods of escape where the attacker is left uninjured, aggressive defense methods and ju-no-kata, a form of slow kata practice which allows the uke to get a maximum stretch.

Combining her knowledge and applying it to self-defense classes has been a new experience and a problem for Ms. Fukuda. "When I teach self-defense, the students don't change into a judo gi, they just wear street clothes, and they don't understand the spiritual side when they study. They just want to learn if someone grabs them how they can break the grip, that's all. They only want to learn the technique.

"When we practice we must be serious and concentrate our minds. The mind works with the body. Often they don't concentrate and listen to my form. When they strike, I show them how to strike strongly with a Kiai. Then they practice very weakly with a high voiced squeak."

Given this narrowly practical attitude in her students, Ms. Fukuda now feels, "The most important thing for women to learn is that judo is not something to study quickly. It's not instant. It takes a great amount of practice to actually become applicable. We have mind training and body training. They need patience, then go to the dojo and train."

For those who only see the techniques of judo, she tries to explain, "The principle of true judo is how effectively one defends oneself against an attacking opponent by training one's body and mind rather than merely defeating an opponent."

At the same time she says people who attain a high degree in kata may reach satori (or enlightenment, as in zen), and she believes hard training goes hand in hand with the spiritual side. It is extremely important for her students to work hard without over-stressing their physical capabilities.

"I am very careful to teach the correct form," she adds. Form is very important. If the form is not correct, one cannot throw the opponent. The movement of unbalancing the opponent is as important as the initial correct form. One should try to take the opponent off guard and lead them into an unbalanced position, by turning the body to the right and to the left and in big circles.

"One must learn to follow the opponent's form too, in movement – if they pull, I push more. I use my partner's strength plus my own strength, therefore I save some of my strength all the time. Nowadays, everyone is too stiff and muscle-bound.

"I teach good posture. You have to have strength to throw your partner but you need good posture too. We don't drop our weight when someone tries to throw but just keep natural balance and posture. Then when we get a chance we can throw them when their technique doesn't work."

To become good one must learn to be aware, alert and relaxed, all qualities beneficial for daily life. Dojo training, through the constant pressure of dealing with an opponent on the mat, leads to the unconscious acquiring of these traits.

Randorai (sparring) demands these qualities, as does kata. "In Randorai, it is important to hold lightly without letting the other person be aware of any resistance, to remain calm and in a natural position. Of course you must watch the whole body. Watch everything and you can see all their movements, which foot goes forward, which goes backward. Just have good posture and you can see everything.

"I watch in my mind too. Your mind can relax. If you are fighting in your mind, thinking, 'She is coming, I must throw her', you are working too hard. If a partner attacks, I escape; if they make a weak attack, I make them unbalanced and throw."

When she speaks of being relaxed, she doesn't mean "dead" relaxation. Ms. Fukuda stresses that the mind must be ready for action. "If your partner is tense," she relates, "we must be somewhat balanced and hold tense or they will throw you. If you are too relaxed you will have no energy to throw them. My body is small and I must watch her movement in my mind too."

After watching Ms. Fukuda's classes, it's obvious that she is an excellent instructor. She devotes time and energy to instructing every student in the proper form. Although she doesn't feel it is necessary for all women to study self-defense, she does have strong feelings on the subject. "It is essential to learn how to protect ourselves effectively without weapons. During a lifetime we encounter many unexpected incidents, including robbery and even murder.

"For women who aren't motivated by the need to defend themselves, they unconsciously obtain composure and are able to make swift decisions in case of emergency."

Feeling that too many women in college leave just as they improve after two or three years, Keiko Fukuda is devoting her time to establishing a women's judo association so women can continue in judo. She is particularly pleased that women stay in judo after marriage. In Japan, a woman drops out as soon as she marries. "It's the traditional way. But here with wives training it is a much better feeling. I think after two or three years there is a marked change in my students, I think they are happier and more serious people."

—Don Deed

Don Deed has been a martial arts enthusiast for several years, having studied both in the U.S. and Japan. He is also a free-lance writer and photographer, a regular contributor to several martial arts magazines.

For More Information

There are several magazines that give good coverage to Judo: *American Judoman,* 4944 Date Ave., Sacramento, Calif. 95841. They say "We are the only periodical devoted solely to American and international Judo technical features and news information." Over 20,000 people subscribe. *Judo Illustrated,* 3445 N. Broadway, Chicago, Ill. 60657. Published bi-monthly. A lot of results. *Black Belt,* 5650 W. Washington Blvd., Los Angeles, Calif. 90016. Published monthly and has over 100,000 circulation. A full martial arts magazine with good judo coverage. *Self-Defense World,* Box 366, Mountain View, Calif. 94040. Published bi-monthly at $4.50 per year. Considered by many as the best martial arts magazine being published.

The major organization is the US Judo Association, 3921 Ella St., Bossier City, La. 71010. Their official magazine is *American Judoman* listed above. This organization has over 1200 clubs throughout the United States and will send you a list upon request.

Two good sources for judo uniforms and supplies are: Mutual Judo Supply, 1090 Sansome St., San Francisco, Calif. 94111 or S & P Imports, 1501 Hertel Ave., Buffalo, N.Y. 14216. Or ask at your local dojo.

Some of the books available. All are available from World Publications, Box 366, Mountain View, Calif. 94040 at the price listed* plus 25 cents each postage. Write for a complete list.

Judo Principles: Ne Waza, Anton Geesink. Discusses the ground techniques and uses hundreds of photographs to demonstrate the correct execution. For intermediate and advanced students. 1967 Hb., 95 pp., ill., $4.95, (Arco).

Judo Principles: GoKyo, Anton Geesink. A presentation of the famous Five Series techniques originally used in Japan. The moves and nuances of each are thoroughly discussed. 1974 Hb., 96 pp., ill., $8.95, (Arco).

The Techniques of Judo, Shinzo Takagaki and Harold Sharp. A fully-illustrated and authoritative manual giving step-by-step explanations, practical pointers, and thorough analyses of all the most commonly used techniques (wazas) of judo. Over 550 illustrations. 1957 Ppb., 148 pp., ill., $6.25, (Tuttle).

Illustrated Kodokan Judo, A well-illustrated introduction to the basics and general aspects of Judo. It is a manual for the beginner unable to obtain the assistance of an instructor, and for the advanced student and teacher. 1955 Hb., 293 (oversize) pp., ill., $22.50, (Wehman).

Judo, Daeshik Kim. A good introduction to judo as a hobby. Ten judo throws and nine grappling techniques are described in addition to history, philosophy, rules, belt requirements, terminology and much more. 1969 Ppb., 64 pp., ill., $2.50, (W.C. Brown).

Judo for the Gentle Woman, Ruth Gardner. A guide to the art and practice of judo for the so-called weaker sex. Written by one of the few Western women to gain a black belt. 1971 Ppb., 152 pp., ill., $3.25, (Tuttle).

The Secrets of Judo, Jiichi Watanabe and Lindy Avakian. An excellent basic technique text, but the real importance is its emphasis on the dynamics of judo, its physical and psychological stresses, and the relationship between judo and Zen. 1960 Hb., 190 pp., ill., $7.50, (Tuttle).

The Sport of Judo, Kiyoski Kobayashi and Harold E. Sharp. Judo as practiced at Japan's famous Kodokan, the original judo institute. Emphasizes development of the popular throwing holds. Especially good are its complete instructions on judo matches. 1956 Ppb., 104 pp., ill., $5.75, (Tuttle).

Judo: How to Become a Champion, John Goodbody. The British judo "heavies"—Brian Jacks, Dave Starbrook, Angelo Parasi and Keith Remfry—discuss with the author the moves which they have found efficient in competition. The secrets of their throws, grappling techniques and contest tactics are revealed. 1974 Ppb., 127 pp., ill., $3.95 (Wm. Luscombe).

Juggling

If you have ever seen a good juggler in action then you've probably noticed the personal pride that they take in their ability, and in entertaining others. And well they might, since expert juggling requires years and years of involvement and practice. You might think that keeping two or more objects going in symmetrical patterns through the air with only two hands is only a matter of dexterity, but take a look at a juggler's eye movements sometime. If you can, leave off your concentration on his hands and take in the excellent coordination and discipline of the other moving parts of his body. An expert juggler is not only an excellent entertainer, but most often he is a fine athlete. In fact, many athletes, musicians, dancers and actors take up juggling to provide regular exercise and relaxation.

The history of juggling can be traced back to ancient Egypt, but it probably started much earlier. In ancient ruins carvings of jugglers have been found.

Traditionally, juggling has been more of an entertainment than a sport. However, this activity started evolving into a sport in the US in the early 1970s. Today, it is taught in high schools and colleges. It's being taught in both amateur and professional drama groups. In turn, these individuals–students, actors, and actresses–are teaching it to their friends, relatives, and audience. This new mass of people is approaching it, not as a circus entertainment, but as a recreational sport.

The three basic patterns of juggling are known as the Cascade, One-Handed, and Shower. Any number of different objects may be used–easy-to-handle balls are usually the preference of beginners; clubs and rings are often seen; and the more spectacular jugglers have knives, hatchets, fire batons, and basketballs flying about.

In the Cascade pattern three balls cross back and forth between the hands; in One-Handed two or more balls are tossed side by side or in circles in one hand; in the Shower all the balls are tossed with one hand and caught with the other, and then thrown sideways back to the original hand. Watch for these patterns the next time you see a juggler. Better yet, get yourself a few colored balls, a teacher, or a good book, and try them yourself!

You Too Can Juggle

Many people have certain false preconceptions about learning to juggle. As any of us begin any new activity, we bring certain mental preconceptions to bear on our effort in learning that activity. These preconceptions can be valid and therefore helpful, or they can be false and detrimental. If you are thinking of possibly giving juggling a try, I'd like to shed some light on the following three false preconceptions most people have:

1. Juggling is a circus skill that takes years of practice to learn.
2. Juggling requires an outstanding sense of coordination.
3. One must learn to juggle at a very early age.

All of these statements are false! However, let me develop further each of these points, so you may decide for yourself if you should try juggling.

First, throughout the world there are many thousands of individuals who have had the desire to try juggling. For those who have gone to the trouble of locating someone who juggles, read a book or attended a class on juggling, most have found that basic juggling was much much easier than they had imagined. With good qualified personal instruction, a person with average learning ability can learn to juggle three balls in 30 to 60 minutes. Of course, if you are attempting to learn from a book, or from an unqualified instructor, it will take longer. The main point is that thousands of people without any juggling background have already found that basic three ball juggling is easy to learn.

Secondly – regarding the myth that basic juggling requires an outstanding sense of co-ordination – this is simply not true. If you can throw and catch a ball you can learn three ball juggling. It is true that if you haphazardly throw objects in the air, "juggling" will seem very difficult. On the other hand, if you mentally understand the throwing and catching patterns involved, basic juggling is as simple as throwing and catching a ball, walking, jumping rope, or riding a bike. However, as you become more and more involved in juggling, it will help improve your coordination, self-confidence, dexterity, alertness, reaction time, and eye and hand coordination. But, to learn basic juggling you do not need any unique coordination or skills.

Finally, to learn basic juggling you do not have to start learning when you are young. Yes, it is true that youth is an advantage if you are trying to become an outstanding traditional circus juggler, but that is not what the sport is about to the majority of people involved in it. Juggling patterns and moves are basically unlimited and these different patterns and moves require different degrees of physical body involvement. For this reason, an elderly juggler can work on moves that require less physical exertion, while the youthful juggler can work on moves that require a great deal of physical body movement. In other words, the huge gamut of juggling moves allows the individual to become physically involved as much, or as little, as he wants, or can. Also, the satisfaction of juggling as a sport for a person of any age, is the mental satisfaction one gains when learning each new move or pattern. Someone who learns to do five very easy moves at age 65 can gain as much, if not more, mental satisfaction as someone who learns five extremely difficult moves at age 15. So, the overall point is that age is not a factor in your becoming involved in, or deriving pleasure and exercise from the sport of juggling.

This again brings us to the point of my whole article: If you have had the interest to read this far, you should now be questioning the false preconceptions which most people allow to get in their way while thinking about taking up juggling. If you are questioning these false preconceptions, you are ready to learn to juggle.

–Ken Benge

Ken Benge has been a professional juggler since the age of 17. In addition to being a former president of the I.J.A., he was a multi-medal winner in the 1971 World Juggling Championships, and has juggled on many national television shows and commercials. He is the author of **Three Ball Juggling**, *and has another book in the works.*

For More Information

The International Jugglers Association, 129 Fourth Ave., Bartlett, Ill. 60103 publishes several newsletters of interest. They also have a yearly convention that features shows, movies, contests and loads of just plain juggling. A couple of books available from World Publications, Box 366, Mountain View, Calif. 94040 at the price listed* plus 25 cents each postage, are:

Juggling for Fun and Entertainment, Ron Humphrey. This accomplished juggler takes the beginner through the most basic steps and includes some advanced show techniques. 1967 Ppb., ill., $2.50 (Tuttle).

The Juggling Book, Carlo. A handbook on the fundamentals of juggling with particular attention given to exercises meant to develop and enhance coordination. Includes juggling patterns and variations for both the beginning and advanced student. 1974 (oversize) Ppb., $2.95, (Random House).

Karate

Karate literally means "empty hand" and has been widely developed by the Japanese since being imported from Okinawa in the early 1900's. There are still Okinawan schools that developed after the country was annexed by Japan and all weapons confiscated. Korea also developed a form of karate called tae kwon do which today stands as the hardest or most muscular of all karate systems. Besides sharing the basic movements of kicking, punching and blocking, all of these systems could be traced back to the many forms of Chinese boxing which go back to 100 B.C. but were imported and developed indigenously in Okinawa and Korea.

Most karate classes last two hours and begin with stamina building exercises such as push ups, deep knee squats, sit ups and other toughening exercises. Next are series of basic blocks, punches and kicks which are learned for form before being used in set exercises where two people face each other and spar only by set pattern. Finally comes ju-kumite where the practioner puts together all the basics he has learned and uses it to do mock battle with another opponent. Punches and kicks are "pulled" to prevent serious injury to the partner, yet full speed and full force is difficult to control within an inch of the target!

Kata and competition represent the other two sides of the triangle. Kata are performed by more traditional schools. They are like dance being practiced solo for coordination, timing, balance and concentration. On the other hand, competition provides the sports minded with an outlet to try the skills he has so faithfully studied. There is now a movement to get karate accepted for the Olympic program.

Weapons systems are taught by many schools but usually reserved for the most technically and psychically advanced. Although many people will not stay with karate over many years, anyone who has trained even for a short period of time feels he has had a good physical workout and learned some basic things about both karate technique and self.

—Don Deed

Donald Deed is a frequent contributor to martial arts magazines.

Many Faces of Karate

From my experience I think if 100 people start karate today, in five years, ten will remain. Half of these people last six months and only one quarter last several years. Those who are interested in the romantic or sensationalist ideas of fighting, like the Bruce Lee movies, last about two months. Even though they have this kind of motive, their ideas can change in one month during participation in our dojo. During our exercises we emphasize several aspects and they soon learn a different approach. They soon realize the difference between the movies and reality, then they either quit or do it the way it is supposed to be if they can switch their motivations and become interested in another goal.

I try to give many faces to this art, instead of emphasizing only one aspect. One such face is coordinating the mental and physical, the mind and the body, the reflexes. A second is emphasizing the artistic aspects as they do in dance. Third is discipline, both physical and mental. People have to come and practice everyday, not merely in the mental or artistic aspect, but working out and exercising hard. Fourth is my idea of coordinating all the aspects—the fighting aspect, the actual combative aspect and the psychological aspect. When you are fighting you have to get involved in emotional conflict. A person has to overcome his fear. This is very important because although a person might be six feet tall, weigh 200 pounds, do exercises for ten years, and be very strong, he is not necessarily good in fighting, because of his experience and emotions. He may freak out after one blow or from seeing someone doing breathing because he knows nothing about fighting. Actually fighting is the study of human beings, and how they act and react in a certain physical or mental environment. Studying the nature of fighting is related to a basic study of human beings, of their most primitive desires and instincts. See how people fight, why they fight, why they enjoy fighting and why they fear fighting. To learn about people is the ultimate goal of my art. It comes very late and is very difficult, but it is my final goal.

Free fighting exercises will bring people's personalities out. Some complain when they get hit. In other words, they are reacting too emotionally. Some are always aggressive and always pushing—not necessarily because they are good fighters, but because they are afraid. A good fighter can see what fear causes him to do. We can learn through fighting and then we can apply this to anything. Because you understand it and can control it, you can overcome and control it when it happens in real life. I teach a beginner to first win confidence. He has to win it before he can lose it and get a realistic view of the world.

—Gosei Yamaguchi

Gosei Yamaguchi is the 7th dan director of Goju-kai Karate-

Breaking bricks and boards with karate kicks and blows is a means of demonstrating ability in the sport. It is, however, a flashy public presentation that has little to do with the true philosophy of karate. (Muller)

do. He is the eldest son of the famous Gogen Yamaguchi and has been studying karate for over 30 years. Arriving in the United States in 1964, Yamaguchi is headquartered in San Francisco where he maintains his own dojo.

For More Information

Good magazine coverage is available. In addition to these, check our listing under Judo. *Official Karate,* Charlton Building, Derby, Conn. 06418. Published monthly. Complete coverage of karate including personalities, events, and happenings. *Karate Illustrated,* 5650 W. Washington Blvd., Los Angeles, Calif. 90016. Published monthly and the largest of the karate magazines. *Self-Defense World,* Box 366, Mountain View, Calif. 94040. Published bi-monthly at $4.50 per year. Covers all martial arts with good coverage on karate.

The largest organization is the United States Karate Association, Phoenix, Ariz. which has a lot of regional groups.

A couple of good sources for equipment: Martial Arts Supply Co., 10711 Venice Blvd., Los Angeles, Calif. 90054 and Honda Associates, 485 5th Ave., New York, N.Y. 10017.

Many good books have been published and here are some of the better ones. All are available from World Publications, Box 366, Mountain View, Calif. 94040 at the price listed* plus 25 cents postage.

Gojo-Ryu Karate, Gosei Yamaguchi. More than 400 diagrams and photographs are used with accompanying text to introduce the reader to the concepts of the "hard-soft" system of one of Japan's most popular styles of karate. 1972 Ppb., 175 pp., ill., $5.95, (Wehman).

The Way of Karate, George Mattson. A fully-illustrated explanation of Okinawan-style karate. Places special emphasis on karate's value as a system of training body amd mind. Special chapter on training equipment, classes, and schedules. 1963 Hb., 200 pp., ill., $10.00, (Tuttle).

Advanced Karate, Masutatsu Oyama. A complete explanation of the scientific principles behind karate techniques, freestyle fighting, and stone-smashing. Oyama discusses how to embrace the karate warrior code in today's complex world. 1500 gravure illustrations. 1970 Hb., 256 pp., ill., $19.95, (Japan).

Black Belt Karate, Jordan Roth. A comprehensive handbook on the fundamentals of modern karate. Hundreds of photographs serve as excellent teaching devices for students unable to receive competent private instruction. 1974 Hb., 379 (oversize) pp., ill., $27.50, (Tuttle).

The Karate Dojo, Peter Urban. A book that goes beyond karate as a means of self-defense and explains its other important aspects, as a sport and a philosophy. Interesting sections discuss the schools of the dojo where karate is taught and the belt system. 1967 Hb., 145 pp., ill., $5.95, (Tuttle).

Korean Karate: Free Fighting Techniques, Sihak Henry Cho. A systematic, scientific approach to the study of karate using over 1000 photos, by one of the world's top karate experts. Sections of the book cover the history of karate, calisthenics and stances and free fighting positions and moves. 1968 Hb., 249 (oversize) pp., ill., $13.50, (Tuttle).

Modern Karate, Arneil & Dowler. Indispensable guide to the ancient art of karate. Not only does the book show correct procedure and form, it includes chapters on breathing, calisthenics, techniques. Photos demonstrate proper form. 1974 Hb. & Ppb., 192 pp., ill., $8.95/$4.95, (Regnery).

Karate and Personal Defense, Kim and Leland. An introduction to the basic techniques of Japanese and Korean karate. Covers history, traditions, philosophy, supplemental readings, and a section on climbing from various forms of self-defense. 1971 Ppb., 64 pp., ill., $2.50, (W.C. Brown).

Karting

In the past 18 years, karting has evolved from a simple weekend pastime, to a nationally organized, competitive form of motor-sport. Yet, a great deal of the original appeal of karting remains today. Karts are still the most inexpensive way to enjoy the thrills and excitement of auto racing. Whether you're male or female, looking for family fun or downright serious competition, the versatility of karting provides it all.

In less than 20 years, karting has spread to every country in the world and taken its place as a truly international sport. The popularity of karting stems from the fact that it offers so much, to so many different types of people. Karting can be an inexpensive hobby in which the whole family participates. Karting can be a sport in which the young learn the safe use of motor vehicles and rewards of competition. Karting can be for the Walter Mitty in each of us, who wants to share the experiences of A.J. Foyt without the cost or risk. Karting can be for the mechanically minded who like the challenge of extracting every ounce of performance from a race car. Karting can be a stepping stone for the driver who wants to gain experience before moving into other forms of auto racing. Karting is fun, competitive and challenging.

The first look at a kart is usually deceptive. It's hard to take anything so little, seriously. Yet, closer scrutiny reveals that while a kart is simple in construction, it is quite sophisticated in design and theory. Some karts have small engines for the young or the timid, but there are also 140 mph, fire breathing monsters, which steal lap records from all but the most expensive race cars. A kart combines all of the latest technological advancements of its larger counterparts, in one small package. A kart is a pure, basic, no frills race car.

The original parking lot play toy, the "Go-Kart" has evolved into two unique types of racing cars: the Sprint kart and the Enduro kart. Sprint karts are characterized by their sit-up driving position. They are raced on short road courses of a half mile or less in length. One sprint race is usually broken down into three heat races combined. Sprint kart racing is also an excellent starting point for the beginner. It gives him an opportunity to learn the basics of karting, at speeds somewhat slower than those found in Enduro racing.

Enduro kart racing came into being when sprint karts began racing on longer sport car tracks. It was found that by laying the driver down, out of the windstream, aerodynamics and top speed were greatly improved. As the length of the races increased, there became a need for large capacity, side mounted fuel tanks. Soon the Enduro kart had its own distinctive look and purpose.

Enduro kart races are usually one hour in length. They are staged at some of the finest motorsport complexes in the United States. Ontario Motor Speedway, Indianapolis Raceway Park, Watkins Glen and Riverside International Raceway are only a few of the tracks an Enduro karter can enjoy, at a fraction of the cost incurred by the professional race driver.

"I'm sure my feelings are the same as those most drivers have before a race—whether it's Indy or go-karts. I get nervous and find myself keeping my mind busy by plotting moves for the race." (Knapp).

There are a number of different competition classes for both Sprint and Enduro karts. Age, weight, number and size of engines, are all factors for establishing class structure.

Children can begin sprint kart racing, on the local level, at eight years of age. They are able to compete in National caliber events at nine. At 12 years of age, the young karter is allowed to participate in small engined, enduro classes. The majority of spint and enduro classes, however, have a minimum age of 16. The remaining classes, the wild and wooly dual engined karts, require drivers to be over 18.

No matter how old you are, how much you weigh or how fast you want to go, karting has a class to suit your needs.

—International Kart Federation

The Nationals

The first question people ask me is "Why go-karts?" They think of karts as a vacant lot plaything, but that's not the way it is. Karting is super-competitive. At a relatively low cost, I can take part in head to head competition at speeds up to 125 miles an hour.

My racing season starts in October with a series of Northern California championship races, winter national and divisional events. When I go to these races, it is with one thing in mind: to get prepared for the Nationals in August. Since I've been around for over 10 years, starting when I was eight, and have won a good share of championship races and national events, I don't get as excited as I used to over the smaller races.

During these races, we spend our time testing different motors and karts with different handling procedures on the various tracks. The reason for all the testing is that we manufacture all our own karts in our kart shop. With so much new equipment coming out all the time, we have to keep trying new things to stay on top. Through all this testing we have come up with a kart that has won more national championships in the last two years than any other. It has also taken first place in the all-important Pro Race two years in a row.

Finally, the Nationals come around. When we go to this event, which is held in a different state every year, anywhere from New York to California, we drive a motorhome, and the chief mechanic, Rich Burton, transports the karts in a van. We usually take two karts ready-to-race, and a spare frame, an assortment of motors, tires, and lots of spare parts. We go about 10 days early to start practicing on the track and get everything dialled—in for the Pro Expert race.

In our crew we usually have three or four drivers running for our kart shop, in different classes, and we all work to help each other out. Rich does all the modification on the motors and handles all the work on my karts. If he has any time left over he helps the rest of the crew. I'm strictly a driver, but I do have to tell him how the kart performs on that particular track, especially if it lacks power, and he makes the final decision concerning our equipment.

The first race is the Pro Expert race. Not only is this the only race for money sanctioned by the International Kart Federation, but all the best drivers compete in it. Fifty of the best, cut to 30 after semi-main events, makes for some pretty fierce competition. The top 15 could be within two-tenths of a second of each other on a curvy, three-quarter mile track – and that's close. The winner of this race is considered to be the best driver in the United States. This is only the second year for this pro event, and last year I was lucky enough to win it. It was, by-far, the greatest thrill I've had in karting. Even though I won the prize money, the thought of beating the best in karting makes it worthwhile.

The morning after the pro event, which is held in conjunction with the Nationals, we immediately start getting ready for the National events. Usually we get two or three days of practice before time trials start, then after a day off the races begin.

In national events there are 16 different classes you can run, depending on the weight of the kart, the driver's age and weight, and on the bore and stroke of the motor. In the Nationals, you can run any number of classes that you can keep up with. Three's my limit; that keeps my mechanic and pit crew hopping all the time. In sprints each class runs three heats and the winner is determined by a point system, the winner having the most points at the end of the day. A heat usually consists of 10 to 12 laps. Starting position is determined by qualifying time in the first heat. In the second and third heats, you start where you finished in the previous one. This year in the three classes I ran, I won two of them and took third in the other. The wins were my 11th and 12th national titles.

Although there is no prize money involved in these events there are many prizes awarded to the top five finishers in each class. These are mostly in the form of merchandise awards from karting manufacturers. Our shop awarded a kart to the highest finisher running our product. We also gave other merchandise awards to top finishers.

I'm sure my feelings are the same as those most drivers have before a race – whether it's Indy cars or go-karts. I get nervous and find myself keeping my mind busy by plotting moves for the race. I've usually run against the competition in practice, so I know how I'm doing compared to them, and where my best chance of passing them might be. The funny part of it is that once the race starts, I usually forget all about my plotting because it doesn't work anyway. Nobody seems to do what they're supposed to. Experienced drivers act by instinct, depending on the situation, and don't have time to think about the moves; they just make them.

At the moment, it's only September, and already we're starting on next year's karts. Karting is a great way to start a racing career. Hopefully, for me, it will lead to bigger and better things.

—Dave Knapp

Dave Knapp started kart racing when he was eight years old. He has won 12 National Championships.

For More Information

The International Kart Federation 444 W. Foothill Blvd., Glendora, Calif. 91740 is the major organization. They publish *Karter News* which is printed monthly at $8.00 per year at the same address. Excellent magazine with a lot of photos and a color cover. There is also the World Karting Federation, 5825 Jackman Rd., Suite 209, Toledo, Ohio 43613. Good sources for everything are: Russell Karting Specialties, Box 9669, Kansas City, Mo. 64134; Michiana Midget Motors, 19819 Orchard St., South Bend, Ind. 46637: Wiseco Piston Co., 7201 Industrial Park Blvd., Mentor, Ohio 44060. All these have catalogs which cost $2.00.

If you would like to get information on ice racing (karting on ice) write: Williams Lake Go-Kart Club, Box 4243, Williams Lake, B.C. Canada V2G-2V8.

Kayaking

Henry David Thoreau once wrote that rivers are a constant lure to the adventurous instinct in mankind. Whitewater kayaking provides an outlet for this instinct in modern society. These outlets can be realized by slow paddling on a quiet, nearby stream, by running the hardest rapids of the Arkansas River, or by testing oneself in a whitewater slalom race. Among active Americans kayaking has assumed a popular niche alongside other individual, participatory sports such as running, bicycling, and cross-country skiing. The sport has also grown due to television's coverage of the whitewater slalom event at the 1972 Olympics and the movie "Deliverance".

Although kayaking had its origins in the Arctic where Eskimos used these fragile, skin-covered boats for hunting and transportation purposes, it was in the alpine countries of Europe that kayaks emerged as sporting craft. In Germany the folbot, or folding kayak, made of canvas and wood became very popular in the 1930's and 1940's. Soon after, the sport came to this country, and people took to the rivers of Colorado, California, and the East Coast in ever increasing numbers. In the late 1950's, the sport was revolutionized when the use of fiberglass became commonplace in the construction process. Kayaks could then be made more durable than the old wood-canvas models, and the weight was also greatly reduced. Today a standard kayak weighs only 25 pounds while being 13' long and 22" wide at the broadest point. There are several companies which manufacture kayaks and accessories, although many people prefer to build their own equipment. A kayak enthusiast can be completely outfitted for approximately $150.

River touring remains the basis of the sport, for the thrill of successfully negotiating a tricky rapid, or maneuvering through a boulder strewn river is unique and unforgetable. Sparkling water and fresh air combine with the excitement of the river to captivate the enthusiasm of outdoor oriented people. Due to this beauty, an important issue for all kayakists has become the preservation of our free-flowing rivers. Many boaters are currently leading the fight to clean up the country's waterways and keep our other beautiful streams from being dammed. In addition to river touring, many people have discovered kayak surfing and are just as 'hooked' as their counterparts with surf boards.

The competitive branch of the sport also came to us from Europe where the first whitewater World Championships were held in 1949 at Geneva, Switzerland. Over the years two forms of whitewater racing have developed: slalom and wildwater. Whitewater slalom is similar to ski slalom in that each competitor must pass through a series of gates in the shortest time possible. Each gate consists of two poles at least 1.2 meters apart between which the paddler must pass without touching either pole. These gates are hung from wires over an 800-yard stretch of rapids, are numbered and must be negotiated in order. The final score is a combination of the time from start to finish plus penalty seconds which are assessed for touching poles or missing gates. Slalom racing demands precise boat control in difficult water as well as speed, coordination, and conditioning.

Wildwater racing can be compared to cross-country ski racing in that racers are started one at a time at set intervals. The racer arriving at the finish line several miles downstream in the shortest time is the winner. Wildwater racing boats are longer and less maneuverable than slalom boats, yet are much faster while going forward. This type of racing demands good stamina and the ability to find and follow the fastest route through the rapids.

World Championships are held every two years, with the 14th Slalom and 9th Wildwater World Championships held in 1975 at Skopje, Yugoslavia. These international competitions have been dominated by the Eastern European countries, particularly by athletes from East Germany. A high point for the sport was the appearance of whitewater slalom in the 1972

"River touring is the basis of the sport, for the thrill of successfully negotiating a tricky rapid, or maneuvering through a boulder strewn river is unique and unforgettable. Sparkling water and fresh air combine with the excitement of the river to captivate the enthusiasm of outdoor oriented people." (Bauer)

Olympic Games at Munich where millions of television viewers were exposed to the event for the first time. In the mid-1950's there were only three or four major slalom races in this country. Today there are well over 150 major slalom and wild-water competitions in the course of a year. Success in white-water racing now demands year-round preparation. During the winter months, the use of indoor swimming pools for the development of proper technique has become a standard procedure throughout the country. Many racers engage in weight training and are involved in a cardiovascularly taxing sport in the off season.

With the growth of kayaking has come a greater need and concern for safety. For safe boating the following rules should be observed:

1. Learn the basic fundamentals through an established club or school.
2. In white water always wear a helmet and a lifejacket, and a wetsuit when the conditions are cold.
3. Never paddle alone in white water.
4. Do not attempt to run a rapid that is above your ability.

It is usually the foolhardy who ignore the basic safety rules, hurting both themselves and the sport by getting into trouble on the river.

Participant sports like kayaking are the wave of the future for many Americans who have a burning desire for self-expression and the leisure time in which to realize it.

—Eric Evans

Eric Evans is a many times National Champion in whitewater slalom. He has placed as high as third in the World Championships.

White water slalom has grown in popularity since the American public was first exposed to it during the televised Munich Olympics. Slalom racing demands precise boat control in difficult water, as well as speed and conditioning. (Stowe)

For More Information

Three magazines give good coverage to kayaking. None exclusively, however. Check canoeing and rafting for further information. *Down River,* Box 366, Mountain View, Calif. 94040. Published monthly at $8.00 per year. Good coverage with feature articles on kayaking in each issue. *American Whitewater,* Box 1584, San Bruno, Calif. 94066. Published bi-monthly at $5.00 per year. A well done publication. *Canoe,* 1999 Shepard Rd., St. Paul, Minn. 55116. Published bi-monthly at $5.00 per year. Some good articles.

Two organizations you should know about: American Canoe Association, 4260 E. Evans Ave., Denver, Colo. 80222 and Olympic Canoe & Kayak Committee, Box 99, Wasco, Ill. 60183.

Here are some good sources of equipment and supplies: Wildwater Designs Kits, Box D, Penllyn, Pa. 19422. Neoprene Sprayskirt Kit, Hi Float Life Vest Kit, Paddle Jacket Kit, are just three kits they have available. Free brochure on request. Whitewater West, 727 S. 33rd, Richmond, Calif. 94804. Good source for kayaks, paddles and other accessories. Seda Products, 922 Industrial Blvd., Chula Vista, Calif. 92011. Their catalog is very complete. An excellent source for good equipment. Whitewater Boats, Box 483, Cedar City, Utah 84720. Makes some good kayaks. Free brochure on request. Hyperform, 25 Industrial Park Rd., Hingham, Ma. 02043. Manufacturers of Lettmann and Prijon boats and a major supporter of kayaking. Boat Technology, 310 Curtin Ave., Pittsburgh, Pa. 15210. Offer a complete boat building kit. Their kit and a mold is all you need to build a kayak. Phoenix Products, Box 1075, Ryner, Ky. 40486. They have a free Phoenix buyers guide which answers many questions about kayaks. Brownline, 2539 Bitters Rd., San Antonio, Texas 78217. Makes canoes and kayaks.

There are many good kayaking books. They are available from World Publications, Box 366, Mountain View, Calif. 94040 at the price listed* plus 25 cents each postage. Write for a complete list.

Kayaking, Jay Evans & Robert Anderson. One of the newest and most complete books on kayaking. Written by the US national kayaking coach, it deals with history of kayaking, how to get started, equipment, technique, training and more. Both recreation and competition are given equal attention. 1975 Hb. & Ppb., 192 pp., ill., $8.95/$4.95, (Stephen Greene).

Whitewater Coaching Manual, Jay Evans. A US Olympic coach's indispensible work on whitewater competition. Covers training, techniques and mental preparation. 1973 Ppb., 56 (overisze) pp., ill., $6.95, (Evans).

Kayak Canoeing, The British Canoe Union. This small but complete book is intended to start you on your way in using a kayak. Covers handling, safety, equipment and advanced skills. 1973 Ppb., 48 pp., ill., $1.50, (E.P. Publishing).

Whitewater Handbook for Canoe and Kayak, John T. Urban. The Appalachian Mountain Club's concise, no-nonsense guide to rough-water boating. Hard-to-find, expertly compiled technique and safety tips for canoeists and kayakers. 1965 Ppb., 86 pp., ill., $2.50, (Appalachian Mtn. Club).

Kendo

The smooth graceful motions of Toshiro Mifune, Japan's leading samurai actor, lead many to become interested in the art and sport of kendo. Tracing its origins to the days of individual matches between swordsmen, kendo today develops patience, stamina, personality and spirit, all at same time.

The beginning kendo student attends the dojo (practice hall) and begins the arduous task of making a coordinated attack with a shinai (fencing sword made of strips of bamboo). After learning correct hand positions and how to move the body as one unit, the beginner advances to wearing the kendo armor which includes padded gloves (kote), breast plate (do), a padded body protector (tare) and a visored helmet (men). Hours of practice teach the correct striking areas.

Years can be spent mastering these techniques and in the course of time a kendoist will begin to do kata (prearranged moves practiced alone) with the boken (wooden sword) and katana (live blade). Tournaments are a means of testing one's skill gained through months of practice. All practioners are given an opportunity to compete in the exciting rush of the barefoot, yelling kendo attacks.

Whether in annual or semi-annual tournaments, daily dojo practice or self-practice, kendo is a process both of mastering the weapon and of mastering the self. The do or way of kendo is a ritual and traditional means to focus upon the development of inward self.

—Donald Deed

Donald Deed is a prolific freelance writer on martial arts subjects. He lives and trains on the West Coast.

A Form of Exercise

The popularity of Bruce Lee hasn't swelled over into kendo. A few people came in from Zen but most come from interest in the samurai films such as "The Seven Samurai," "Under the Banner of the Samurai," "Yojimbo" and "Sanjuro." But the staying power is less than for other sports. We have an attrition rate of around 90 percent. Most people don't see that kendo requires a great deal of self-discipline. While kendo may look easy, one very quickly finds he cannot master the skill in a day, a month or even two or three years. After the first three months the attendance rapidly falls off and we see who will stay with it.

For the people who stay with kendo, there are many different and diverse motivations. Some see in it a self-discipline that is gone out of modern society, or as a physical conditioner. I conduct practice in my dojo with an emphasis on controlling oneself as well as mastering the weapon. One of the things we do after each class is to recite a 10-word guide toward values: etiquette, courage, knowledge, group unity and harmony within the dojo—the first five are character traits. The second five deal with the weapon—exploit opportunity, keii or a vocal expression of feeling (shout isn't really a proper

The sport and art of kendo has survived from the Samurai days of feudal Japan when wandering warriors lived and died by the sword. To modern practitioners, kendo is both a sport and a disciplined way of life that focuses on developing the physical self, as well as the inner self. (Duffy)

"Most people don't see that kendo requires a great deal of self-discipline. While kendo may look easy, one very quickly finds he cannot master the skill in a day, a month or even two or three years. After the first three months of instruction, attendance rapidly falls off and we see who will stay with it." (Duffy)

description, it's an explosion of feeling vocalized), posture, token which literally means using the proper portion of the sword and finally zanshen, that is, don't let down after an attack but be ready to continue and to counterattack.

I tend to agree with Donald Draeger that much of the feeling is gone out of the modern budo. I've written about this in Japanese. I also have a lot of technical disagreements with Draeger but I do agree there is too much emphasis on winning. This comes from the large Japanese universities, but I noticed in Japan last year that there was a real tightening up of slack discipline, especially in the high schools.

I don't place a great deal of emphasis on competition; it's incidental, although our dojo does well when people do compete both on the kyu or grade level and the dan or black belt level. Up to the rank of 2nd and 3rd black belts, spectators are very impressed. They are very active rushing at each other. But the better one gets the less they move. If an untrained person watches someone of 6th degree or higher in a match the action usually is so fast, it's over before it begins. Competitors just stand there and then move lightning fast.

For me kendo is a form of exercise, although I didn't approach it for exercise. It develops stamina and co-ordination which I find to be a nice counter-balance to the rather sedentary occupation of teaching. It is a way to vent frustrations, as well as a physically and emotionally stabilizing element.

—Dr. Hazard

Dr. Hazard is a professor of history at San Jose State College and a Kendo 6th dan. He began Kendo in 1948 while serving as a translator in Tokyo. In 1967 and 1970, he participated in the World Kendo Tournament in Japan.

For More Information

The major organization is the Kendo Federation of US, 1715 W. 256th St., Lomita, Calif. 90717. For information on magazines, supplies and other organizations, see karate, judo, aikido and other martial arts. Here is a book just on Kendo. It is available from World Publications, Box 366, Mountain View, Calif. 94040 at the price listed* plus 25 cents postage.

Fundamental Kendo, All-Japan Kendo Federation. The oldest of all Japanese martial arts is presented here, arranged to make self-teaching possible for the novice. 1974 Hb., 179 (oversize) pp., $13.95, (Japan).

Knee Boarding

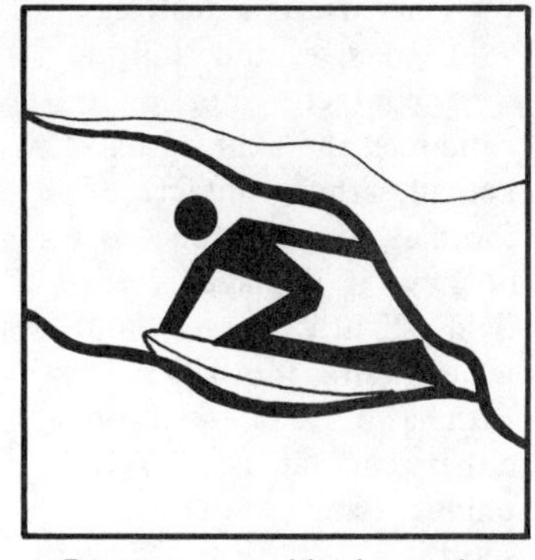

There are a lot of ways to ride ocean waves. You can sit in a kayak or surfski, stand on a surfboard or catamaran, lie on a bellyboard, or use nothing but your own body. Another way is on your knees.

Kneeboarding is sort of like bodysurfing, and sort of like stand-up surfing, and sort of a unique experience. Because you ride down there on your knees, underneath all but the smallest waves, you get a feeling for the energy of the wave that is almost as intense as the feeling you get bodysurfing. But because you ride on a smooth planing surface instead of a lumpy chest and belly, you have as much speed as board surfers and even more maneuverability.

Like surfboards made to stand on, kneeboards consist of a polyurethane foam core covered with fiberglass and resin. Some manufacturers make both kneeboards and surfboards.

Kneeboards are shaped a lot like a surfboard, except that they're shorter–4'6" to 5'6" compared with 6' to 8' for surfboards–and often a bit wider to make up for some of the flotation lost with the shortened length.

Still, they don't float as well as a surfboard, and most kneeboarders find it necessary to wear swimfins and paddle out to the waves by kicking their feet instead of paddling with their arms like stand-up surfers.

The shorter length makes kneeboards more portable than surfboards. They'll fit inside most cars. They also cost less than a surfboard–$95 or so compared with $130 and up.

Kneeboarders and stand-up surfers pick up on riding styles and board design ideas from one another. If an innovation works on a kneeboard, it will often work on a surfboard, and vice versa. A kneeboarder from Santa Barbara, California named George Greenough was a strong influence in the massive changes stand-up surfing went through in the late '60s when surfboard lengths dropped from 10 feet to near-kneeboard sizes and riding styles changed from more or less just planing across the face of a wave to kneeboard-like sweeping turns with an emphasis on riding in and about the curl.

A compromise board that can be ridden on the knees or standing has been developed, but most people still prefer to go one way or the other. Stand-up boards do seem to work better than kneeboards in small, less powerful waves in which the kneeboard's inferior flotation is a hindrance. Medium (4'10") waves like those often found in California and Australia are ideal for kneeboarding, and it is in those places that it has taken its strongest hold.

The worldwide ratio of erect surfers to kneeboarders is probably about 10 to one, but the heavily-surfed Huntington Beach to San Diego area of Southern California seems to have as many kneeboarders as stand-up riders. A little further north Jacobs Surfboards, a Hermosa Beach manufacturer of kneeboards and surfboards reports that about 25% of their sales are kneeboards.

"A kneeboarder walks to the beach when the morning is still new and quiet. His dog romps ahead and seeks out secret smells among the flowers in the field. His board is underarm, swimfins in hand, and he is barefoot on the asphalt." (Ramuno)

Kneeboarding is certainly easier to learn than erect surfing. You don't have the balance problem to contend with. Down on your knees, you have a lower center of gravity and you're much more stable. The comparative ease with which it is learned is one reason kneeboarders used to encounter flak from some erect-riding surfers. "Babies crawl; adults stand," was their line of thinking.

Then kneeboarders began to show that they can do things that can't be done standing up on a surfboard—or can't be done as often. Their stability enables them to pull off radical turns and maneuvers more easily than an erect surfer can. They don't lose their balance and fall off in the attempt. By being lower and able to maneuver better, kneeboarders are more often able to ride inside the curl of a wave—and that's the most exciting place to ride.

—Hal Humphrey

Hal Humphrey began riding waves in 1967 after his mother won a surfboard in a dairy company sweepstakes. His new book about the formation of ocean waves, their prediction, and the variables which affect them will be published soon by **Surfing** *magazine.*

Another Kind of Surfing

A kneeboarder walks to the beach when the morning is still new and quiet. His dog romps ahead and seeks out secret smells among the flowers in the field. His board is underarm, swimfins in hand, and he is barefoot on the asphalt.

At the beach, dark blue lines glide silent from sea to shore, early sunlight glinting silver on their crests. There are surfers in the water. Some ride standing and some ride on their knees. He watches for a while, sitting on the sand, and then he walks down to the water, straps on his fins and backs into the ocean with his board.

He paddles into the center of the peak but lets the first wave pass because someone else was going to catch it. As the swell lifts him up and out to sea he can view the approaching lines of other waves in the set.

He turns and paddles toward shore. He feels the wave catch him, and he pulls himself to his knees as he begins to drop. He sweeps into a turn at the bottom of the wave, and it is walled up steep and hollow far in front of him.

His body remembers all the waves he has ridden before, the hundreds of similar positions he has experienced. It reacts with subtle movements to place his board on the fastest track and give him the greatest pleasure.

He rises into the curl, then down again. The top of the wave loops over him, and he is surrounded by the water. There is a roar from the wave breaking and a sensation of the water sweeping around him, and he is speeding along in a shadow. This is the best feeling of riding a wave. The circle of light before him shrinks, then grows, and he flies out of the curl, onto the shoulder of the wave.

When the ride is over, he paddles back out to the lineup, finned feet chugging like a motorboat. There is within him the satisfaction of a good ride and an anticipation of more to come.

—Hal Humphrey

For More Information

More information can be found under the surfing section.

Lacrosse

Lacrosse is a fast, aggressive, and skillful contact sport. It combines the skill of basketball, the contact of football, and the speed of hockey. It is played on a field slightly longer and wider than a football field with a 6' x 6' goal on either end. It is a truly unique and interesting sport.

Lacrosse was first played by North American Indians. They used a ball fashioned from wood and played with two small sticks in each hand which were used for catching and throwing the ball. Contests were played between entire tribes and usually lasted for days. French settlers became interested in these contests and named the game "La Crosse" meaning "the stick." The game was first played by the white man in the early 1800s in Canada, and was played in the U.S. for the first time in 1877 when inter-collegiate lacrosse was introduced in New York.

Many sports require a specific body size in order for an athlete to be successful. In basketball the height of the athlete is important. In football, size is also a factor at most positions. In Lacrosse, however, the size of the athlete has very little bearing on his success as a player. The short as well as the tall, the heavy as well as the light can participate in this sport without giving up any advantage to an opposing player of a differing stature. The only natural skill needed is the ability to run. This enhances the universal appeal of the game.

Lacrosse is a great spectator sport due to its continuous action, contact, skill, and speed. It is the only contact sport played in the spring, which makes it very appealing to both the participants and the spectators. The sport enjoys a fanatical following of fans wherever it is played and large crowds are not uncommon in the Eastern section of the country where the sport is most popular.

Lacrosse has steadily grown in popularity during this century, with over 150 colleges and universities now participating on a varsity level, over 400 high schools playing, and numerous club teams competing. In 1971, lacrosse was included in the NCAA program and National Collegiate Championship Tournaments are held on two levels, Division I and Division II.

The sport is currently played extensively in four nations in the world: Australia, Canada, England, and the United States. A World Championship Series is held every four years with the next to be played in Manchester, England in 1978. The United States has won the first two championships, the last one having been played in Melbourne, Australia in 1974.

—Skeet Chadwick

S.H. "Skeet" Chadwick was a two time first team All-American goalie at Washington and Lee University and was named the nation's outstanding goalie in 1974. He represented the United States in the 1974 World Championships and is currently the Executive Director of the Lacrosse Foundation, Inc.

Originally a Canadian Indian game, lacrosse has become popular on the club, high school and collegiate levels. It features continuous action and plenty of physical contact. (Wagner)

Every Shot is a Personal Battle

The thing I remember about lacrosse is how I became involved in the game. My father had been a professional football player from Notre Dame and an All-American. He was six feet tall and weighed 230 pounds. When I was in high school I was 5-foot-one and weighed 110 pounds. I was the smartest in my class but not exactly the best athlete around. I wasn't a bad athlete, but just too small.

I went off to a small college in upstate New York called Union College in Schenectady. By then I had grown up a little bit and had gone out for freshman football. When Spring rolled around they didn't have a freshman baseball team because the school was so small. A bunch of us who played football together decided to start rugby. The athletic director had a fit because there were 13 varsity sports and less than 1000 men in the school already. He didn't want another sport started, so he suggested we play lacrosse.

We all scratched our heads and said, "What's lacrosse?" We had never seen it before. After he described the game we decided it had a significant amount of mayhem and we were willing to try it.

I will never forget the first game that I ever played in – it was the first I had ever seen! It left an absolutely indelible impression on my mind. We went to play our first freshman game at Cornell University (Cornell was probably 10 times the size of Union). They had a lot of experienced prep school players and as we were coming off the bus on a cold, rainy, windy, stormy March day in Ithaca, New York, the Cornell varsity was about to engage the Yale University varisity. The Yale kids had shaved their heads in Mohican haircuts, and they all came off the bus roaring. I think half our team was ready to quit and go back to Schenectady!

We did play, however, and got beat 21-1. It was an absolutely disastrous day, but from that point on I think all of us were hooked on the game.

From that freshman group, a nucleus of seven stayed on and we took the varsity team from a 1-10 record (which they had that year) to a 10-2 record and a league championship by the time we were seniors. My senior year I gained some national recognition as I played in the All-Star game. Coming from a small school like Union, it's pretty rare to have someone make the All-Star team.

It was a thrill for me to play in the North-South game. Things went very well for me in the game, and even though we lost, I had a fairly good day–a very important day. My father having been a professional athlete, this was my way of finally being able to play in front of thousands of people and to say, "Dad, I can do it, too!"

The degree of devotion I had to the game is best illustrated after my graduation from college. The summer before I went to graduate school at Lehigh University, I worked in Rochester New York. Every weekend I drove 450 miles from Rochester to Long Island to play summer lacrosse.

I'd leave work about 4:30 on a Friday afternoon, drive down to Long Island, and get to bed about 1:30 on Friday night. I'd get up the next morning, play a lacrosse game and spend the evening with my folks, then Sunday play another game. I'd get back in the car about five o'clock on the afternoon and take off back to Rochester to work for the week.

When I started my graduate work at Lehigh I had a teaching assistantship at a neighboring university, Lafayette College in Easton, Pennsylvaina. My department chairman at Lafayette had been on record many times before as being against "orgainzed sport"–he was not against sport, he was against "Organized Sport."

The first staff meeting he introduced me: "I would like you to know that the physics department is not really biased against athletes. I want to introduce Mr. Riffle to you, who comes to us from Union College with a Bachelor's Degree in physics, has a teaching assistantship, and will be doing his graduate work at Lehigh. To prove my point I want you to know that he is a devotee of lacrosse and has had national recognition." He thought this was just neat because he was able to say that he wasn't really that biased after all.

No sooner was the meeting over than the athletic director came over to me and said, "We don't have a lacrosse coach this year. How would you like to coach?" Because Professor Kick had just trapped himself with this policy statement, there was no way he could say no! So I became the lacrosse coach.

While I was at Lafayette, I was young (21), coaching guys who were older than I. Lafayette didn't have the best of talent—we usually struggled to a record of 5-6 or 6-6 or 6-4—we were never outstanding as we played in some pretty tough leagues. But it was a worthwhile experience.

Later on I played club lacrosse, with the Long Island Lacrosse Club and now with the Palo Alto Lacrosse Club. I feel like I'm a better goalie now than I ever was when I was 21 years old. In respect to overall play, and especially in reference to playing the goal, I feel I get the job done better than 10 years ago. I may not be as quick anymore, but I'm smarter, my judgment is better and I think I play position better, play the percentages better, and play the angles better. I don't want to say that I play more conservatively because I still take a lot of chances, but I choose my spot better. I can remember doing some pretty dumb things in my senior year in school. I think age can really make a contribution but it's the classical maturity that makes the real contribution.

One problem you can have with a club lacrosse team made of post-college players is that you can have guys out there for recreation and others out there for the competition. The problem playing the goal on a club team is that you have some guys who are doing both!

In the goal you can't. To illustrate, imagine somebody throwing at you a hard rubber ball that weighs about a quarter of a pound. You're the goalie and that thing is coming at you in excess of 100 miles per hour at anywhere from five to 50 feet away. You can't play the goal recreationally—you have to play competitively, otherwise you get hurt. I've been hit in the Adam's apple; I've had my nose broken when the ball came through my face mask. I've made saves with my head where the ball has come through the mask and I find myself looking at the ball crosseyed because it's resting between my nose and the mask!

You have to be able to force yourself into unnatural reflexes. A guy is on the side and coming around; you have to be right on the spot. The goal is six feet tall, and he's shooting from shoulder high at about five or six feet, so his tendency is going to be to shoot high and wide. You've got your stick there but that only covers part of the goal so what else do you use? You use your head. Can you imagine the reflex training it takes to be able not to dodge but to go for the ball? (You've got a face mask on and it's not going to hurt very much.) Or what if the ball is shot at your head? The tendency is to pull your head away and duck, let the ball go in the goal. But you've got to marshall your concentration to the point where you can put your head in the way of a ball approaching at speeds close to 100 mph.

It has always been a frustration for me, when a guy plays recreationally and he lets his man free. This attacker is bearing down on the goal, only 15 feet away, and he's about to let loose with a hard one and I don't know where the damn thing is going. More than likely when it hits me it's going to hurt because the only padding I wear is a helmet, mask, and a very small chest protector which is thin and covers the front chest area.

When a defensive midfielder gets beat, and the offensive man comes in and shoots, I'm not going to be able to make a stick save. I'm not going to be able to react to where he's shooting and get the stick on it. What I've got to do is try to cut down the angle, play the position, come out, cut off his angle and more or less hope that he hits me. It means that I'm going to get hurt. It is very frustrating for a goalie to whom being competitive is a necessity to have "recreational" people on his team. If the goalie doesn't play competitively he's only going to get hurt even more!

You might ask what kind of person it is that always likes to play defense. Well, I like being in control; it says something about my personality. I like to control the situation I'm in. Goalie is a position where you are the last line of defense; goalie is probably more dangerous than any other position on the field. It is the position that requires most concentration.

Lacrosse goalie is probably a more difficult position than a hockey goalie. The hockey goal is only four feet high and six feet wide compared to the lacrosse goal which is six feet high and six wide. The hockey goalie stays down low, has a lot more padding, a lot more equipment. He doesn't have to worry about the high shots. In lacrosse you have to stand up straight because the goal is high as well as wide. The ball can come from all different directions. In hockey the puck always slides along the ice. In lacrosse a guy can shoot from from two feet over his head or two inches off the ground or he can flip the ball behind his back. It requires a much greater degree of concentration.

The point I want to make about playing the goal is that there is probably a degree of masochism involved. You reach a point where you get so psyched playing the goal that when you get hit by a shot it feels good. You become so intense that the only thing that matters is stopping the ball from going in the goal. When it hits you—it feels good. I've done it! You don't really feel the pain—until the next day when you get up and you've got that big lump on your arm. But that feeling, it is a terrific high.

I remember that for the All-Star game I played in up at Lake Placid, New York, the NCAA had the book they put out every year with the rules and a picture of one of the expected-to-be-good players that year. An attack man for the South was the guy on the cover and he was supposed to have the meanest shot in the world, always going for the upper left-hand corner. After I stopped three shots of his in a row I was so high, so psyched, they were not going to get another goal for the rest of the game. It was just that kind of feeling from this tremendously "psyche" position.

Another example I can cite is last year when I ran into Norm Webb, a goalie down at the All-Star game, who had been All-American at Army in 1964. He was in the military academy and came out to the post-graduate school down in Monterey. I had a super day down at the All-Star game last year, won MVP. Their attacks were all All-Americans in college that I had played against for 15 years and I knew them from back East—Johnny Valestra, Al Kardiff, Jimmy Lewis. I really had a hot day; I knew them so well that I knew where they were going to shoot and I shut them down, I got lucky. We were in a situation twice where we had three men out on penalties: they had us outnumbered six to three. We called a time out, came back on the field. I walked out to their attacking guys and said, "You guys aren't going to score." They didn't. They were so frustrated, but when you get your mind made up, you get psyched. It's just amazing how fast you can move.

I was very cocky and afterward Norm said to me, "You haven't changed a bit. You're still one of the most cocky, arrogant people I've ever met!" And I said, "Norm, on the field I don't have any other intention!"

When I was in college I used to walk down to the other team's goal while they were warming up. I'd watch them shoot and I'd say, "That's not good enough." At the beginning of the game my crease defensemen used to introduce me as "Guardo, the Invisible Shield." A goalie has to believe he can stop every shot and every shot is a personal battle. A good goalie is a person who has that kind of intense drive of wanting to be the best, wanting to meet that "ultimate challenge." There's nothing there but you and the ball: can you get to it, can you beat it?

The goal is usually referred to as "the cage." Perhaps it's because the goalie is a crazy enough animal that you've got to keep him locked up.

—Bill Riffle

Bill Riffle played lacrosse for Union College in New York where he was an All-American goalie. He was the MVP in the California State All-Star game in 1975.

For More Information

The best source for information is the Lacrosse Hall of Fame, Newton White Athletic Center, Homewood, Baltimore, Maryland 21218. They also publish a quarterly newsletter of interest. Also, the United States Intercollegiate Lacrosse Association, University of Virginia, Charlottesville, Va. 22204 can supply information. One company that has done a lot and can provide a lot of information is Stx, Inc., 9 West Aylesbury Road, Timonium, Maryland 21093. They have a complete line of equipment and the people that run the company are lacrosse players themselves.

For more detailed information, check out these books. All are available from World Publications, Box 366, Mountain View, Calif. 94040 at the price listed* plus 25 cents each postage.

Box Lacrosse: The Fastest Game on Two Feet, Jim Hinkson. An authoritative instruction manual. The fundamentals of the game are taught utilizing detailed photos and diagrams and a clear and simple text. 1974 Hb. and Ppb., 120 pp., ill., $8.95/$3.95, (Chilton).

Lacrosse, W. Kelson Morrill. A detailed description of this fast-growing game, designed to serve as an introduction for spectators and players. 1966 Hb., 177 pp., ill., $9.25, (Ronald).

Lacrosse: Playing and Coaching, Margaret Boyd. The author is well-known as an outstanding player and coach. This is not only a volume on technique and play, it is the best source available on the obscure origins and history of the game. 1971 Hb., 126 pp., ill., $5.95, (Barnes).

Lacrosse Fundamentals, Evans & Anderson. Covers attack and defense patterns, stick work fundamentals, goalie skills, and general tactics. Particularly valuable for the coach. 1966 Hb., 432 pp., ill., $8.95, (Barnes).

Lacrosse for Girls and Women, Ann Lee Delano. Directed toward the female beginner, it shows necessary techniques, requirements of each position, rules, and strategies are included. Added attractions are the questions and suggestions for practice. 1970 Ppb., 76 pp., ill., $2.50, (Brown).

Lawn Bowls

Lawn Bowls is a sport blessed with two extremes—it is highly competitive and extremely skillful, and yet it is still a game that may be enjoyed merely for the sake of fun, exercise and fresh air.

Different from the indoor alley game of bowling, lawn bowls is played out of doors in the fresh air and sunshine on a velvet smooth grass surface. The balls used—bowls as they are called—are not round but slightly irregular in shape or "biased." This irregularity is where the fun begins, as it allows one to deliver each bowl with a curved path.

The playing area is 120 feet long and bowls are rolled towards a small target ball called the *jack.* Skill comes into play in determining the correct amount of width of grass to be given each bowl as it is rolled, and at the same time, the correct distance in order for the bowl to reach the target ball. Getting as close as possible is the object of the game, so a "touch" or "feel" of distance must gradually be developed over long hours of practice.

The usual compact playing area of 120 feet square can accommodate six to eight individual games at one time. With eight players to a game, this affords 48 to 64 individuals the opportunity of close contact, good fellowship and friendly competition.

Other games that may be played include singles, pairs and triples or one, two or three players to a side. Games usually take about two hours to complete and a pre-determined number of ends (like innings) constitute a game. Singles is almost always played by points.

Major tournaments are conducted annually in various sections of the country, and these include two top level events. The United States Championships begins at the club level and proceeds through various sectional playdowns. This event is limited to US citizens. The second top-flight competition is the American Lawn Bowl's Association National Open which draws bowlers from all over the world. In addition, Canada and the US have very close bowling ties and matches are frequently arranged between these two countries.

Two World Championships have been held, the first at Sydney, Australia in 1966 and the second at Worthing, England in 1972. A third is scheduled for Johannesburg, South Africa in 1976. About 20 countries participate in these world championships.

Bowling tours have been organized in many countries to go to overseas bowling centers for both official and unofficial matches. These tours consistently provide both good competition and a host of pleasant memories of each country visited.

Lawn Bowls is a game where men and women can compete and often do on an equal basis. Extreme concentration, the easy flowing, smooth delivery of the bowl add up to making it both a fascinating sport and one in which women can successfully compete against men.

"Skill comes into play in determining the correct amount or width of grass to be given each ball as it is rolled, and at the same time, the correct distance in order for the bowl to reach the target ball. Getting as close as possible is the object of the game, so a 'touch' or 'feel' of distance must gradually be developed over long hours of practice." (Shearman).

Sports enthusiasts who have played all types of games throughout their lives have expressed overwhelming enthusiasm for bowls when introduced to the game. They call it the most challenging and rewarding sport they've ever participated in.

Lawn bowls has been a fascinating part of my life for many years. With my father a successful and enthusiastic lawn bowler, I more or less grew up in the game and I've never regretted it.

The highlight or perhaps most memorable experience had to be in 1966 when I was selected on a five-man team to represent the United States in the First World Bowls Championships in Sydney, Australia.

The trip in itself was a thrill, but to represent your country in two weeks of top flight competitive bowls involving 16 countries was a never-to-be-forgotten experience.

To get us in the right mood we were accompanied by over 90 enthusiastic American bowlers to help root our side home winners. With stops in Hawaii, Fiji and New Zealand we were really primed for the wonderful reception by the Australians. The friendliness and hospitality of our hosts, the pagentry, the parades and parties, the friends we made and will never forget, all add up to one huge mountain of memories that can never again be equalled.

To participate in the "first" of anything is a thrill in itself. World Championship Bowls provided that thrill for me down under in Australia.

—**Harold L. Esch**

Harold Esch has been the ALBA singles and doubles champion as well as US doubles champion. In 1966 he was selected for the American World Lawn Bowls team.

For More Information

The American Lawn Bowls Association, 10337 Cheryl Drive, Sun City, Ariz. 85351 is the official organization for the US. They are sanctioned by the International Bowling Board. Also there is the American Women's Lawn Bowls Association, 2029 Ptarmigan Dr. No. 1, Walnut Creek, Calif. 94595. The only publication is *ALBA Bowls,* 30 Covina Ave., Long Beach, Calif. 90803. It is published quarterly. Some sources for equipment: John Harold, 244 Chiquita St., Laguna Beach, Calif. 94618 and Harold Esch, Box 6141-C, Orlando, Fla. 32803. Equipment includes a set of four bowls. We have one book for lawn bowls, available from World Publications, Box 366, Mountain View, Calif. 94040 at the price listed* plus 25 cents postage.

Lawn Bowls, KTG Series. Good beginner's guide to bowls. Covers everything needed to begin playing: grip, delivery, choosing your bowls, basic shots, duties of the umpire, and more are all explained for both Flat Green Bowls and Crown Green Bowls. 1972 Ppb., 40 pp., ill., $1.50, (E.P. Publishing).

Lawn Tennis

Quite a few people aren't aware that the official name designated for the game of tennis is actually lawn tennis, even though today's game is often played on other surfaces than grass. Since the first game of tennis was played—on grass, of course—this name has survived, and grass has remained the traditional surface in three of the largest tennis countries: Great Britain, Australia, and the US. While clay, asphalt, shale, sand, wood, and gravel courts are common, especially in the US, grass has been the surface used in the major championships at Wimbledon, Paris, Forest Hills, and Australia.

While a grass court encourages an aggressive game because of the low bounce the ball tends to take, the disadvantages of keeping up such a surface makes it one rarely seen at the local club. Maintaining a grass court takes considerable time, skill, and money, and it recovers slowly from rain, whereas another surface may be ready for play in a couple of hours.

While grass has been the source for particular strategies and playing styles (plenty of spin and slice, played with patience and accuracy), popular cement surfaces require a "service and volley" game, played by those with strength and quick reflexes.

For the first time, in 1975, the US Championships at Forest Hills were played on a clay surface, while for years grass has been used. Thus it might be a wise bit of advice to those who have a chance to play on the greener substance to take it, since in years ahead there may be no opportunity to do so.

Whether tennis is played on a lawn, synthetic surface, or on piled ant heaps, as the South Africans sometimes do, the rules of the game are the same. For a description of these rules, equipment, etc., see Tennis.

Recollections in Tennis Politics

I feel that my tennis career has been extremely fortunate since I have personally been involved in the greatest changes that tennis had made in its over 100 year history. Perhaps to illustrate the changes more clearly I can briefly give a backtrack of my tennis history:

Sydney, December 26, 1953, Age 10—Sitting in the living room of my parent's home in Sydney, Australia, with my ear glued to the radio, 600 miles away in Melbourne, Lew Hoad and Ken Rosewall—Australia's whiz kids—are beating America's more experienced Tony Trabert and Vic Seixas in the Davis Cup Challenge Round. Every man, woman and child throughout Australia is in a similar position. Already various coaches have cried my tennis talents, and I declare silently to myself that at 16 I, too, will be travelling the world with a tennis racquet.

Sydney, April 1961—I depart on my first official overseas trip with the Australian men's team with all my expenses paid plus $4.00 per day for pocket money. Our trip lasts six months; my only concern is playing tennis but momentous decisions are being made in tennis politics that will affect my life. Open Tennis is voted on by the International Lawn Tennis Association and it misses by four votes.

London, July 1967—I wake up with a terrible hangover but with the dreamy knowledge that I became Wimbledon Champion the day before.

Forest Hills, New York, Stepember 1967—I am top seed in the US Championships and it is half way through the tournament. The phone rings in my room—it is Tony Roche, my doubles partner and close friend. We have already won every major doubles title and are considered the top two of the new breed. Tony's opening sentence was, "Hey Newk, do you want to become a millionaire?"—to which I replied "Is the Pope a Catholic?" World Championship Tennis, known today as WCT, was making its first move on the tennis world. I won Forest Hills, in December we won the Davis Cup, and in January Tony and I turned pro. My contract was $45,000 for 40 weeks of play a year for three years, with two option years. At the time of turning, I was probably worth from 10 to 20

John Newcombe of Australia is noted for his booming serve and overall power game. Newk won Wimbledon singles titles in 1970 and 1971, as well as doubles with Tony Roche in 1965.

thousand dollars. We never thought we would play Wimbledon, Davis Cup, etc., again.

Bournemouth, England, 1968–The ILTF, forced by pressure from Wimbledon and the WCT signing of eight top amateur players, agrees to open tennis. The pros play against the amateurs (who were now referred to as "just players") for the first time ever.

Briston, England, 1969–Charlie Pasarell and myself put together the first Players' Association, and in two weeks have 100 members. However, we have a giant by the tail, and no idea of what to do next. Our main problem was that 32 players were still under contract to WCT and so could not legally give allegiance to a Players' Association. By 1970 the Association was no longer viable.

Wimbledon, July, 1972–Wimbledon decides to ban all players under contract to WCT and I am really disappointed as I won the title in '70 and '71 and had my sights set on three years in a row. However, rumblings for a new players' association are very evident. A lot of WCT contracts were to terminate at the end of 1972 and we WCT players had organized ourselves into a loose association. The independent players had done likewise, and since I was going to Wimbledon to do TV commentary I was chosen to be the emissary to get the other guys to join with us in forming one association.

Forest Hills, September, 1972–We form the Association of Tennis Professionals, known as ATP.

Wimbledon, July, 1973–I don't get to play Wimbledon, again, because the ATP is boycotting. The reason–Nikki Pilic has been suspended by the Yugoslav Tennis Association for not playing a Davis Cup match. The ILTF backed them up despite our warning that we would not compete in any tournament that Nikki was not allowed to enter. As history shows, we lost the battle at Wimbledon but we won the war. Only three members out of 90 broke the boycott–Nastase, Kodes and Keldie.

September, 1975–As of now, the ATP is the dominant force in world tennis. Ninety-nine percent of the top players are members and we try as best we can to fashion the game in a way that will be appreciated by the public and players alike. It is not an easy job because prize money tennis is really only eight years old. There is a tremendous amount of cash involved and many factions are straining to get a piece. We, the players, are now in control of our destiny, and I, like Ashe, Drysdale, Pasarell and many others, am proud that we played a significant role in helping shape this new game of Open Tennis which reaches into every corner of the globe.

–John Newcombe

Although John Newcombe's tennis victories have provided him with much satisfaction, he believes that "the family is probably the most important aspect of a person's life." His wife and children are also tennis enthusiasts and play significant roles in his recent **Family Tennis Book**, *which he authors. "Newk" also runs the T Bar M Tennis Ranch in New Braunfels, Texas.*

For More Information

For additional information check tennis. Here is one book, however, which covers lawn tennis specifically. It is available from World Publications, Box 366, Mountain View, Calif. 94040 at the price listed* plus 25 cents postage.

Lawn Tennis, Mike Davies. A pro gives tips on the techniques and tactics of lawn tennis. 1962 Hb., ill., $3.50, (Arco).

Log Rolling

Log rolling began when logging began. During the Spring log drives the lumberjacks became rivermen, and had to know how to keep their balance working on the floating carpet of logs. Wearing woolen shirts, "stagged" overalls of light material which dried quickly, and high topped boots that dug into the bark of the turning logs, they leaped from one log to another while they pushed, prodded and unjammed them. Log drivers moved the timber on the river from the forest lands to the mill. Probably the first contest took place in front of the cook house after the men had finished their evening meal.

From these early days in the northern New England states and the eastern Canadian provinces of Nova Scotia and New Brunswick this profession moved with logging westward through Michigan, Wisconsin and Minnesota on into Idaho, Washington, Oregon and Northern California. The very first prefessional log rolling contest was held in 1898 in Omaha, Neb. Rivers in Wisconsin and Minnesota saw official contests among lumberjacks in the early 1900s, and contests spread to the Northwest, to Port Townsend, Wash., in 1935 and '36.

During the last decade, the logging industry has shifted away from river transportation and storage of logs. Now it is common that mills are built inland where the logs can be trucked in and stored on the ground. While the profession of log driver has passed, the sport of log rolling has grown.

The International Log Rolling Association hosts a world tournament yearly. The last 16 have been held at Hayward, Wisc. Each meeting is a lumberjack affair, its spirit coming directly from those legendary log drivers who developed the timing and coordination to propel huge fleets of timber. It takes as much agility to dance on a tree trunk in the water as it takes strength to saw it in the forest.

The diameter of a log determines how hard it is to stay on top of it. A practice or "slow log" is 20 inches in diameter. and 13 feet long (as are all competition logs). A "medium log" of 15 inches is used in competition under a three to five minute time limit. For the smaller logs the time limit can vary. The "fast log" is 15 inches in diameter. The treacherous "faster log" has a diameter of 14 inches and is known as "the killer." The "finisher" is only 13 inches through. Each log is painted with a six-inch red center band, serving as a neutral zone. Birlers can step on the band, but if they cross it they forfeit a fall. Two falls out of three decide a match. A fall is constituted by going in the water above your waist. A six-inch blue band an inch from either end serves as a warning. Logs are numbered on the ends.

When the referee starts a match, competing birlers grasp their pike poles and get on the log which is pushed away from the referee's platform. When the birlers have equal control the referee calls "throw your poles" and the match starts at the whistle. It continues to a fall or the end of the time limit. Cuffing (starting the roll), spinning, or snubbing (digging in the calks on your boots to abruptly stop the log) and reversing are common techniques. The cardinal rule is, "Never take your eyes off your opponent's feet."

Male birlers wear "stag" pants cut off just below the knees, and lumberjack shirts. Female birlers wear "stag" pants and shirts, or bathing suits. All wear caulked boots.

This sport can truly be called All-American. It grew up in the eastern United States and has long been the favorite of American lumberjacks.

—**Jocko Burks**

Jocko Burks is a forester with Weyerhaeuser and a former Western Logrolling Champion.

For More Information

The International Log Rolling Association, George Mathison, President, 5855 N. Sheridan Rd. Apt. 5-J, Chicago, Ill. 60660 runs the world championships each year and can provide you with information. On their letterhead it reads, "formed to perpetuate and promote birling—the outdoor sport of America's lumberjack." A vice president and a good source for information is Judy Scheer, Box 311, Hayward, Wisc. 54843.

Luge and Tobagganing

Luge is a winter sport in which competitors ride small sleds down a narrow, twisting, trough-like track called a run. The luge sled's origins can be seen in the ordinary "Flexible Flyer" that appears in the northern United States soon after winter's first snowfall. It is typically about 50 inches long and weighs 45 to 47 pounds. Most of this weight is located in the runners which are constructed of laminated wood capped with a high grade steel running edge. The rider lies on his/her back on a lightweight fiberglass seat located between the runners and supported by the sled's cross members.

A luge sled is steered by shifts in body position, and by means of a leather strap connected to the top of the upturned runners and held in the rider's hand. The rider's legs extend forward on the outside of each of the runners and pressure can also be exerted with the ankles to turn the sled. So flexible is a luge sled that even a slight turn of the rider's head can produce a swift change in direction.

A typical luge run is located on a hillside and has grades varying between one and 17 percent. Each run has up to 15 curves of varying radius and duration. As an example, at the site of the 1976 Winter Olympics in Innsbruck, Austria, there is a murderous 270 degree curve with a radius of 50 meters. Historically, the surface of luge runs was of glass smooth ice over ice blocks or a hard snow pack. Such a run was limited to winter use, however, and newer runs are being built from refrigerated cement over which a relatively thin film of ice can, if necessary, be retained year round.

There are three classifications for luge races: men's singles, women's singles and men's doubles. Men's singles competition takes place over runs of approximately 1200 meters in length, while women's and doubles events are conducted on runs of approximately 800 meters.

In formal competition, an elapsed time is taken for each rider to complete the run. Usually the smallest total time from four runs determines final placings. Very high speeds are attained during these competitions, with women completing their 800 meter ride in less than 40 seconds and men completing their longer ride in less than 50 seconds. In the final total elapsed time, very small fractions of a second may often separate several competitors.

Geographically, luge is primarily a European activity, with the strongest competitors coming from East and West Germany, Poland and Italy. In the United States, competitive sledding was not introduced until 1966, and the only training site is the bobsled run near Lake Placid, N.Y. Since luge is such a new sport in the United States, it is still in an embryonic state of development. The American team has nevertheless established itself as a contender on the international circuit. The best performance to date is an eighth place finish by myself during the 1970 World Championships at Konigsee, West Germany.

Luge has been an Olympic sport since 1964, with three events contested—men's single seat, women's single seat, and men's doubles. Speeds in excess of 80 miles per hour can be achieved during a luge run.

Prospects for the future of American luge teams is beginning to look up, though. An Olympic developmental program is in full swing, with the purpose of building future champions at the grassroots gradeschool level. Each year, more and more young athletes appear at the Mr. Van Hovenburg Bobsled/Luge Run, intrigued with the thought of competing in this thrilling sport of courage and skill. As luge becomes better known in our country, we should be able to both attract and train at an early age the high quality type of athletes that can compete on an equal basis with the fine European lugers that currently dominate the sport.

—**Kathleen Homstad**

Kathleen Homstad is a veteran international luger. Her eighth place finish at the 1970 World Championships is the highest ever by an American.

For More Information

Fred Hushla, 141 Church St., Victor, N.Y. 14564 is the president of the American Luge Association at the same address. He is also the chairman of the National AAU Luge Committee. Fred did a booklet called **The Sport of Luge.** It is available by writing him. There are no other books available.

Magic

A rabbit produced from a tall silk hat, a woman being sawed in half, or a human body levitated and made to float unsupported above a couch – all are part of the modern image of that popular pastime called magic. It is practiced throughout the world, and has been a standard part of society since long before recorded time.

Primitive tribal priests gradually learned a few tricks, a magic incantation, perhaps a secret powder that would cause a campfire to dramatically flare up and punctuate a priest's opinion about wealth distribution. Each trick was passed on to an experienced priest's younger apprentice, and over generations a large body of magic knowledge was accumulated. These primitive witch doctors easily capitalized on the superstitions of their followers, usually gaining positions of considerable prestige and power within the social structure of each tribe. Parallels can be seen in the American Indian medicine man of a century ago, or more recently in Caribbean Voodoo practioners.

Perhaps the most famous magician of all time was King Arthur's sorcerer, Merlin. Having supposedly learned his art from the ancient Druids, Merlin was able to dominate the very direction of life at Arthur's court. He is usually depicted in popular literature as a long-bearded and wizened old man, sequestering himself in some lofty castle tower to research through hundreds of mystic manuscripts for an appropriate spell or incantation.

Modern magicians draw upon ancient skills to deceive and thrill an audience, but their art is tame when compared to ancient priests dominating entire civilizations. Today's magician seeks only to entertain an audience with various sleight of hand skills or manipulations. The audience clearly knows of his trickery, and much of their enjoyment comes from vainly trying to discover the secret behind each stunt. Undoubtedly, this is one reason behind the timeless popularity of magic.

An "Amaze Your Friends" Card Trick

Here's an easy to learn card trick for anyone from nine to 90. With just a little practice, you should be able to amaze friends at parties, business associates at the club, or kids at school. It involves predicting a card, writing the prediction on a piece of paper so everyone will be sure you're not cheating, and then guiding a member of your audience through the deck until he finds it for you. Here's how to do it . . . .

Have someone from the audience shuffle through a deck of cards several times to assure spectators that the deck isn't stacked. Take the shuffled deck and surreptitiously glimpse at the bottom card. One easy way to do this is hold the deck against your forehead to "concentrate" on the order of the cards. Anyone who can't decide what card is on the bottom either while the deck is on its way up to his forehead or on its way back to the table needs a seeing eye dog.

As soon as you have "concentrated" and know the bottom card, place the deck face down on a table. Take out a pad and pencil, write down the name of the bottom card, fold the paper into a tight ball and place in on the table. Choose a new member of the audience and ask that person to cut the deck into two equal piles. You will still know which pile has the "hot" card on the bottom. Ask the audience member to choose one of the stacks. If he picks the pile with the hot card on the bottom, tell him to discard the other pile and cut the remaining cards into two groups. If he happens to pick the "cold" pile, merely tell him to discard it.

By keeping in mind the location of the hot card, this process of cutting the decks can be continued until plenty of suspense has been built up and only a few cards remain. At this point have him turn the remainder of the deck face up to reveal the original bottom card. Then have him read off your prediction, which will obviously be the same as the bottom card.

This simple trick sounds too easy to put over on anyone, but you will be surprised how few people listen closely enough to catch the secret. Try it and see. Did I hear anyone applaud?

—**Carol Sundberg**

Carol Sundberg is a San Francisco housewife who enjoys entertaining her four children and all their young friends with impromptu magic tricks.

For More Information

Two organizations are active in this activity. The Society of American Magicians, 711 Cantebury Lane, Hursham, Pa 19044 and International Brotherhood of Magicians, 112 N Detroit St., Kenton, Ohio 43326. A good magazine covering magic is *The Magic Magazine*, 381 Park Ave. S., New York, N.Y. 10016. Published monthly at $10.00 per year. A really good source for information and supplies is Magic Limited, 4064 39th Ave., Oakland, Ca., 94619. Lloyd Jones who runs the company also does a monthly newsletter called *Son of the Bat* which costs $7.00 per year.

Here are some books that will interest you. All are available from World Publications, Box 366 Mountain View, Calif. 94040 at the price listed* plus 25 cents each postage. Write for a complete list.

Card Tricks, Geoffrey Lamb. Twenty easy-to-learn and perform card tricks bring the novice magician instructions for a variety of tricks that will give his performance the diversity of a professional show. The author also reveals the secrets of misdirection, which is the secret of all good conjuring. 1972 Hb., 88 pp., ill., $5.95, (Nelson).

Mental Magic Tricks, Geoffrey Lamb. The art of "sleight of mind" as opposed to "sleight of hand" is offered here in beginner's terms. Mental magic can be performed anywhere, anytime. Includes 17 tricks. Ideal for novices. 1972 Hb., 89 pp., ill., $5.95, (Nelson).

Magic Digest, George Anderson. Hundreds of tricks that require no special apparatus and can be performed with simple common objects. Tricks with ropes, cards, etc., 1972 Ppb., 256 (oversize) pp., ill., $5.95, (Digest).

Magic With Cards, Garcia & Schindler. 113 easy-to-perform card tricks with an ordinary deck clearly explained and fully illustrated. Hb., ill., $7.95, (McKay).

141 Magic Tricks Ripley & Spina. 37 selected card tricks, 27 tricks with billiard balls, 23 professional coin tricks, 25 mystifying tricks with vanishing silks, and 15 mysterious stage tricks with linking rings, Chinese rice bowls, goldfish bowls, tubes and wands. 100 step-by-step illustrations show you how to perform like an expert. 1975 Ppb., 128 pp., ill., $1.95, (Arco).

Marathoning

The most historic and demanding of all Olympic events is the 26-mile, 385-yard marathon run. As almost everyone knows, the marathon derives its name from the feat of the Greek soldier-messenger Phidippides, who in 494 B.C. ran from Marathon to Athens, a distance of about 25 miles, to bring news of the Greek victory over the Persians. "Rejoice! We conquer!" Phidippides is supposed to have said on his arrival in Athens; then he fell dead.

Although the marathon was not part of the ancient Olympics, it was included in the revived Olympics in Athens in 1896 on the suggestion of the French professor, Michael Breal. The first Olympic marathon, run more or less over the same course Pheidippides had run, was won, fittingly enough, by an unknown Greek shepherd named Spiridon Loues. Since that time, the marathon has become the longest standard racing distance in the sport of track and field, although there are road races (called ultra-marathons) which are longer.

The early miles of a marathon can be relatively enjoyable. As miles accumulate, however, the body's energy reserves diminish until many runners "hit the wall" a few miles from the finish. (OMPhoto)

The massed start of a marathon is an exciting moment for runner and spectator alike. It can also cause headaches for race organizers, particularly in an event as large as the Boston Marathon which attracts more than 2000 competitors. (Johnson)

The 26-mile, 385-yard marathon distance became standardized as a result of the 1908 Olympic marathon in London, England. As a courtesy to the English royal family, the race was started in the courtyard of Windsor Castle and finished in front of the Royal Box at White City Stadium. The distance between these points was precisely 26 miles, 385 yards (42,195 meters), and this has been the official distance ever since.

The most famous marathon race in the world, outside the Olympic event, is undoubtedly the Boston Marathon, run each April from Hopkinton, Massachusetts to Boston. This race is also the oldest annual marathon event in the world. It was first held in 1897.

Ever since the first modern Olympics, the marathon has captured the imagination of the public as almost no other event – at least this is the case with the Olympic marathon (many local marathons held in the US and abroad often attract fewer spectators than runners). And no Olympic champion takes on quite the same stature in the eyes of the public as the Olympic marathon winner – men like the late Abebe Bikila of Ethiopia, who is the only one ever to win two Olympic marathons, and Frank Shorter of the US, winner of the event in the Munich Olympics (*see essay*).

In at least two ways – speed and number of competitors – the marathon has changed drastically over the years. What was once a plodding endurance test has become a *race*. When Spiridon Loues won in Athens, he was timed in 2 hours, 58 minutes, 50 seconds – an average pace of approximately seven minutes per mile. Today's highly trained champion marathon runners are able to average five minutes per mile or faster for the entire distance! The current world record is 2 hours, 8 minutes, 33 seconds, set by Derek Clayton of Australia in 1967. Clayton, now retired, averaged 4 minutes, 53 seconds per mile during his record run. Several runners, including Frank Shorter, have run within two minutes of Clayton's record.

Likewise, this long, lonely race which was once considered a frightening physical ordeal (even by runners themselves) has become an exciting, attractive challenge to a growing number of runners. In North America particularly, the number of marathon runners and marathon races has mushroomed in the last few years – no doubt because of the increased interest and participation in running and jogging generally. In 1970, there were 46 marathons in the US. By 1975 the number had almost tripled. The entry list in the Boston Marathon has seen a similar explosion. In 1969, the entry at Boston was about 1100. Since then it has climbed steadily, despite the fact that race organizers instituted a four-hour qualifying standard in 1970 – a first for the race – and a 3½-hour qualification standard in 1971. The entry at Boston this year, 1975, was an all-time high of 2041 runners, including 49 women.

—Dave Prokop

Dave Prokop is the assistant editor of **Runner's World** *magazine. Besides that, he has run a 2:38 marathon and regularly runs today.*

The Frank Shorter Marathon Philosophy

At Munich in 1972, Frank Shorter became the first American Olympic marathon champion since Johnny Hayes had won in 1908 at London. What type of person does it take to win an Olympic marathon?

Frank Shorter was born on October 31, 1947 at Munich, West Germany, where his father was stationed with the US Army following World War II. He grew up in New York state and began running at the age of 15. Frank attended Yale University and began his national level running career with an inconspicuous 19th place finish in the 1968 NCAA Cross-Country Championships. As a senior a year and a half later, he took the NCAA outdoor six-mile title in 29:00.

Shorter didn't run his first marathon until 1971, by which time he was already well established as an international caliber 5000-10,000 meter man. Why would such a successful track runner turn to the marathon? "I just decided to give it a try 'cause I thought I'd always run well over longer distances. I always enjoyed running very long in training, and I always seemed to be able to last a lot longer than most runners. All the way through school I was the one who ran the longest event, so it just seemed natural to give the marathon a go. And it turned out that I did alright. The first one didn't go that well and I finished second (in 2:17, to Kenny Moore at the 1971 AAU Championships), but I had this feeling when I finished that I was going to do a lot better the next time I ran.

Frank Shorter's next marathon outing won him a Pan American Games gold medal at Cali, Columbia in August of 1971. His 2:22 was good, considering an emergency "pit stop" half-way through the race occasioned probably by the local drinking water. Despite the public's conception of the grueling nature of marathoning, Frank found he liked the distance.

"I was a little apprehensive because I never run that far in training. Running 26 miles is just something I go out and do every time the race comes around, so initially, I wasn't really sure I could go that far and still be competitive. But as soon as I'd done it once or twice, I really knew how I had to go about training for it. Everything sort of fell into place and I felt very comfortable with the distance. I think that it was mostly a mental thing, knowing that mentally you can get through it."

Even an Olympic champion, however, feels the physical drain of 26 miles 385 yards. "It's a very strange feeling of having everything drain out of you and just having to push yourself very hard mentally. I think that's precisely what it is. Everything sort of leaves. You can almost feel it draining away – strength, speed and awareness. You begin to get a little fuzzy, and you're just trying to push yourself to keep going. It becomes a battle to maintain a certain effort and pace."

Frank feels this drain very differently in a marathon than in a 10,000-meter track race. "You have longer to think about it in a marathon. You slow down so much that you can actually make yourself run a little faster using your mind to push yourself. By contrast in the 10,000, if you're trained right for it, you're just gonna run as fast as you can the whole way. It's more like your body is doing what it was trained to do and your mind isn't that important a factor. In the marathon fatigue comes much more slowly, while in the 10,000 it comes on pretty fast (towards the end). In the marathon, it comes on and stays with you for six or seven or eight miles, whereas in the 10,000 you may get it for one or two or three laps, and that's all. It's infinitesimal compared to the amount of time you have to deal with it in running a marathon."

Despite his consistent success in marathons, Frank Shorter still trains basically as a track runner. "I think I'd become terribly bored if all I did was run marathons. I just like competing in other events, even if I do not do as well as in the marathon. I couldn't stand all that marathon type training – that long, long kind of training – if I didn't have the other kinds of competition to look forward to. In training, I just go out and run no matter how I feel. Anyone who wants to run 2:10 has to be a compulsive runner to some extent.

"Prior to Munich, I hadn't been under 100 miles a week for something like three years. I think consistency is more important than total effort. I don't kill myself every day, but I go fairly near my limit. I feel I'm pretty good at consistently training hard, at playing with the fine line of what I can do. There's no secret. You just go out and do it all the time."

Shorter's training program is a model of simplicity. He runs twice a day, the morning run always being an easy seven to 10 miles. The afternoon workouts are really the heart of his training. "I run intervals three times a week and I run long once a week, and that's about it. The long run is in the 20-mile range, and I count race days as one of the interval workouts. The other three days I run however I want to. Some days I run a really hard long distance run up a mountain or something, but other days I just run easily, and I think that's why I like it. I don't have build-ups and cross-country seasons and winter seasons and speed seasons. Maybe it's to my detriment, but it seems that I function best when I do it this way. I don't really vary it very much. I work on variables within the intervals – the number and the speed and the recovery on the intervals. It's a very simple theory, but there are infinite variations."

With thousands of miles and scores of worn out track shoes behind him, Frank Shorter was ready at Munich. "I felt pretty bad at the start. I don't know why, but I just felt tight. Maybe it was because the pace was so slow, because sometimes you can feel worse when you're going slowly at 5:30 a mile than at a 5:00 pace. At about nine miles, everybody slowed up to almost six minutes a mile and suddenly I was in front. I said to myself, 'Okay, here goes,' and just ran like hell. From the nine-mile point, I guess I ran 14:05 and 15:15 for the next two five-kilometer segments. Between 15 and 25 kilometers, I ran about half an hour.

"After this burst, I settled into pace, but by that time I was ahead of everybody and actually kept gaining over the rest of the race. Once I got ahead, it was just a question of keeping it going with the same effort all the way to the finish, just staying relaxed and just running. You have to hang on, because you can feel things slipping away. I sat there and told myself that everybody else was doing the same thing I was and that they couldn't be feeling much better.

"Towards the last two or three miles I began to tell myself, 'Well, you've come this far and this is what you really have to do. You have to get through this last part here.' And then when I entered the stadium everything was suddenly worthwhile. I had already decided early that I wasn't going to sprint in. It was going to be pace to the end. Even after I was in the stadium and saw that I could have gotten the Olympic record by running hard, I didn't want to do that. I figure it's bush league to sprint. The last half mile is not the race. It isn't demonstrative of anything to sprint there, because the real race is out there between 15 and 40 kilometers. Sprinting during the last lap of a marathon would be tantamount to picking it up during the last stride of an 800-meter run. It's all over by that point."

A commonly held theory in running is that a runner can only handle four or five years of the kind of training needed to stay at or near the top. But Shorter has been an international-caliber runner for six years and he's still improving his times. "I enjoy training and competing, and I'll keep doing it until I stop improving. Once I'm not getting any better, I'll probably just stop. But that's where I've been lucky. I've been s-l-o-w-l-y getting better and better. It's not like I've peaked out and have had subsequent years of bad performance. Even the year after Munich I ran relatively well. I got hurt, but I ran well early on. And then last year I ran fairly well. And this year (1975) has probably been the best I've had."

In view of this steady improvement, Frank Shorter's chances of repeating as Olympic Marathon champion next year in Montreal must be rated promising indeed.

—Bill Reynolds and Dave Prokop

Bill Reynolds has done a lot of running, but has yet to run a marathon. He works at World Publications.

For More Information

Runner's World Magazine, Box 366, Mountain View, Calif. 94040, is the best source for more information. Published monthly at $9.50 per year. Each year they have a special marathon issue which is super. For additional information, check Road Running.

Here are some books of interest. All are available at World Publications, Box 366, Mountain View, Calif. 94040 at the price listed* plus 25 cents each postage. Write for a complete list.

The Complete Runner, *RW* Staff. The only book in print to cover every aspect of running in such great detail. Articles by the experts on distance training, sprinting techniques, diet, shoes, racing psychology and many more subjects – picked and assembled in one volume by the staff of *Runner's World* magazine. 1974 Hb., 398 pp., ill., $10.95, (World Publications).

1975 Marathon Handbook. A complete list of the marathons scheduled to be run in the U.S. and Canada during 1975 . . . a listing of all sub-3:00 men and sub-4:00 women from 1974 . . . articles on top marathoners, the race walking scene, the 24-hour relay and much more. 1975 Ppb., 116 pp., ill., $1.95, (World Publications).

The Boston Marathon. This book looks at the classic race from a variety of angles – history, legends, course, organization, and – most of all – people. 1972 Ppb., (RMB 10) 48 pp., ill., $1.00, (World Publications).

Tale of the Ancient Marathoner, Jack Foster. A delightful, low-keyed individual, the 41-year-old 2:11 marathoner tells how he improved so much, so late, mixing the story of his career with advice for runners of every age. 1974 Ppb. (RMB 41), 48 pp., ill., $1.50 (World Publications).

Run Gently, Run Long, Joe Henderson. In his sequel to **LSD**, Henderson brings readers up to date on the "state of the art" in gently paced distance running. A book for thoughful runners. 1974 Ppb. (RMB 37), 96 pp., ill., $2.50, (World Publications).

The Frank Shorter Story, John Parker. Articulate and philosophical, the winner of the '72 Olympic Games marathon tells his story to a close friend and teammate. 1972 Ppb. (RMB 18), 48 pp., ill., $1.00, (World Publications).

Marble Shooting

Marble shooting seems as much a part of our heritage as our feelings about Mother Country and apple pie. For generations, well-known personalities (e.g. Pee Wee Reese and Thomas Jefferson) and not-so-well-known figures have "knuckled down" to a game of "Potsies" on a lazy Sunday afternoon.

But marbles predates our country's founding. In fact, it predates most other countries' foundings too, though, we don't know by how much. The literature and lore of marbles is scant and imprecise, but accounts have surfaced from time to time to provide a sort of historical framework.

According to Fred Ferretti, author of **The Great American Marble Book**, undocumented reports have the suitors of Penelope rolling marbles for her hand in Ithaca as Odysseus wandered among the Lotus Eaters. Marble lovers insist David felled Goliath with his truest of marbles, not a stone.

Taw, a game in which players attempt to shoot marbles out of a ring, has been played in the Sussex village of Tinsley Green since Elizabethan times, says Ferretti. Traditionally, no team member is under 50 years old and one past star was nicknamed "Hydrogen Thumb."

No matter how different the cultures, however, marble games have generally fallen into three categories: hole games, in which players must progress through a series of holes dug at irregular intervals; chase games, where two players take turns shooting at each other's marble; and enclosure games, in which prearranged marbles are shot at with other marbles within a marked-off area. Over 50 variations of these three basic styles of play exist today.

Perhaps the best known game is Ringer, or Tournament Marbles. It is played in a ring 10 feet in diameter with 13 marbled arranged in the center in the shape of a cross. The object is to shoot these marbles out of the ring. The player shooting the most marbles out of the ring wins the game. In tournament matches, only two play, though up to six may play under normal rules.

Tournament marbles has been played in the United States since the first National Marbles Tournament was held in Atlantic City in 1922. In 1976, the Tournament will be held during the second week in June in Wildwood-By-The-Sea, New Jersey.

The first marbles were fashioned out of nearly any available material, including flint, stone, clay, polished nuts and wood. Over time other materials came to be used, such as brass, iron, steel, porcelain, glass, precious gems and plastic.

Today, equipment rules state that "the standard size marble shall be five-eighths inch in diameter. Shooters shall be round and made of any substance except metal and shall not be less than one-half inch nor more than six-eighths in diameter, as determined by the referee." Only five dedicated firms remain today to stock marbles in America.

Due to the advent of concrete and asphalt, the nature of marble shooting is changing. Hole games are being replaced by surface marble games. Some experts see this as a step to the eventual disappearance of traditional marble games and their replacement by a more standardized, formal game.

But for now, at least, the future of marbles is secure. And generations of shooters, young and old alike, continue to hone their competitive edge in hopes of someday becoming the local, worrisome "sharp shooter."

For More Information

For more information on marble shooting write: Mr. Oka Heston or Mr. Roger Howdyshell, c/o Marble King, Paden City, West Virginia 26159. We have one book on Marble Shooting. It is available from World Publications, Box 366, Mountain View, Calif. 94040 at the price listed* plus 25 cents postage. **The Great American Marble Book**, Fred Ferretti. A complete compedium of marble lore and marble games. A fun-to-read book including information on how to play marbles—and how to play marbles better. For former, present and future marbles players. 1973 Ppb., 160 pp., ill., $2.50, (Workmans).

Marksmanship

International target shooting is a sport which receives very little publicity in the United States although it is one of the Olympic and Pan American sports. A note on its background and its development in the United States is necessary before relating phenomenal expeience pertaining to the sport.

The United States shooting team, made up of rifle, pistol and shotgun shooters, participates in a major shooting competition each year. The Olympics, held every four years, is the most prestigious event for the shooting sport, but contains only individual competition. The largest event is the World Shooting Championships which are also conducted every four years, at two year intervals with the Olympic Games. They are sponsored by the International Shooting Union (ISU) which governs international shooting world-wide and has 104 member nations. These championships have events for men and women, in rifle, pistol and shotgun—for teams as well as individuals. In the remaining two years of this four-year cycle, U.S. shooters compete in the Pan American Games and Championships of the Americas which limits entries to countries in the western hemisphere. The marksmen from the rest of the world compete in the European Championships and Asian Games during their two off years. These competitions form the nucleus for international shooting and are the only events where the ISU recognizes world records.

Although we are often referred to as a nation of marksmen, our international shooting teams fared very poorly in world competition in the '40s and early '50s. Due to the efforts of the armed forces, primarily the US Army, our teams began making strides forward in the mid-'50s, after marksmanship units were formed in the various military services. Most of our top international shooters received years of training in these military units.

By the 1962 World Championships, the US team was recognized as a world power in marksmanship but still was not considered in the class of the well-trained and highly disciplined Soviet marksmen.

Continued improvement by US shooters helped realize a goal during the 1964 Olympics when American marksmen dominated the shooting events at the expense of the world's best, including the Russians. They proved this performance was no fluke when they again outshot the Russian team in the 1966 World Championships. The success was short lived, however. The Russian shooting team rebounded and posted slight overall team victories during the 1968 Olympics and 1970 World Championships—due, primarily, to the poor performance of our pistol and shotgun shooters. Pistol and shotgun shooting continued to decline in the '70s while rifle shooting showed steady improvement. This resulted in complete dominance of rifle events by US shooters in the 1972 Olympic Games and 1974 World Championships although the Russian shooters posted overall team victories due to their strong pistol and shotgun shooters.

Having been a competitive target shooter for 25 years, many significant highlights stand out in my mind. The two Olympic gold medals I won in 1964 and 1972 rank very high because of tremendous personal satisfaction and achievement of lifelong goals. The complete dominance of the Russian rifle shooters by the United States rifle shooters—where I played a significant role during the 41st World Championships in Thun, Switzerland when we won 15 gold medals to their six—was extremely gratifying for our whole team. This was a tremendous accomplishment for a sporting team from a "free-world" country.

In my opinion, however, the performance of the United States four man team in the smallbore rifle three position Caliber 22 event in Mexico City during the Championships of the Americas, October 1973, stands out as the most significant accomplishment ever made by a United States shooting team, and possibly in the history of all sports. I'm proud to say that I was a member of this team. The phenomenal performances and results of the four shooters in this event is the experience I want to relate.

Entries in the Championships of the Americas were limited to countries from the western hemisphere. Although competition was keen for the United States in the pistol and shotgun events, the outcome of the rifle events was fairly well conceded to our nation's strong rifle shooters. Since winning was relegated for the most part to our shooters, our efforts were pointed more toward individual performance and attainment of the world records which belonged to the Russians.

The smallbore rifle three position event, considered the most prestigious of all rifle events consists of 40 record shots fired from each of three positions: prone, standing and kneeling at 50 meters with iron or open sights. Even though all rifle events are conducted from a shooter protected area, good scores are in direct proportion to good weather. The wind plays a big factor in determining the outcome of the strike of the bullet during its flight toward the target since it is exposed to the elements after leaving the muzzle.

Our team in this event was made up of veteran shooters, all of which were US Army trained, including Margaret Thompson Murdock, world champion 1966 and 1970, and considered the best woman shooter in the world; John R. Writer, Olympic silver medalist in 1968, World Champion in 1970, and Olympic gold medalist and world record holder in this event in 1972, and considered by most as the best smallbore rifleman in the world; Lanny R. Bassham, Olympic silver medalist 1972 (second to Writer) and later to be a three time world champion in 1974; and myself. I was the oldest and most experienced, but was considered the weakest member due to inconsistent practice scores prior to the match.

Our goal of breaking the world records depended on two things: an outstanding individual performance by each team member and good weather on match day. All members of the team, except myself, were in a peak state of training and consistently shooting scores in practice near the world record level of 1166/1200, established by John Writer the year before in Munich.

The weather on match day, slightly overcast with virtually no wind, was almost ideal when the match started. It remained this way until mid-day. The first stage of the match was fired from the prone position and had a time limit of 1½ hours for the 40 record shots. Each shot had a maximum value of 10 points provided it hit the dime-size ten ring in the center of the target. The targets are graduated into scoring rings, with values of 10, nine, eight, seven, etc. A score of 395/400 is considered very good.

We all got off to a good start by posting excellent scores. Writer, Bassham and I had 399's while Margaret shot a 398. The team total was an astounding 1595, a new world record by eight points! The previous record had been set by the United States team in 1966 during the World Championships at Wiesbaden, West Germany, and later tied by the host Czechoslovakian team at Pilsen during the European Championships.

The second stage was fired from the standing position, which had a two hour time limit for the 40 record shots. Standing is the most difficult position and is actually the key to good three position scores. Scores over 370/400 are considered excellent. All four shooters performed extremely well and shot scores over 370. I tried to put extra effort into each shot, utilized most of my allowable time, and was the last shooter on the firing line to finish. My extra effort paid off with a near record breaking score of 378–three points less than the individual world record for standing. Bassham also had an outstanding performance with a 376. Writer and Murdock shot high enough to normally win the standing match with identical 372's. The team total of 1498 set the second world team record of the day, surpassing the Russian record, which was established in Pilsen in 1969, by four points.

Our outstanding performance, coupled with the prone scores, caused a stir in the crowd. They realized they were seeing history in the making. We were re-writing the record books at the expense of the Russians and they loved it. Any of the four of us was in a position to win the match and with an outstanding kneeling score all had a chance at Writer's individual record. The records in the two remaining team matches were also definitely within reach.

It was mid-day by now, and as the temperature became warmer the wind started to pick up, indicating conditions were going to deteriorate. The kneeling position would be more difficult than expected.

Writer, an excellent kneeling shooter, decided to shoot fast before wind conditions worsened. He finished his 40 shot record string in 30 minutes, even though the allowed time limit was one hour and 45 minutes. His gamble paid off with an excellent score of 393/400. (A score of 390 is considered outstanding.) He totaled 1164, two points less than his gold medal and world record performance at Munich in 1972. This tied the third highest score ever recorded in this course of fire.

Bassham, also an excellent kneeling shooter, used the same strategy as Writer and finished a few minutes later. His gamble did not pay off, however. He ran into wind problems during his last 10 shots and finished with a 91–almost double the points lost during the previous 30. His poor finish cost him his chance at Writer's record. His kneeling total of 386 gave him a three position aggregate of 1161, which was still a very respectable score, and his best performance in a major match.

Margaret and I had never been known for our kneeling scores. We were always much slower and more deliberate kneeling shooters, therefore unable to take advantage of the better wind conditions. She, however, managed to combat the poor conditions and shot a remarkable score of 394 which won the individual kneeling match. Her outstanding kneeling performance gave her a total of 1164 which tied Writer for the match lead.This was also by far her best match performance in this course of fire.

I realized I needed a 390 kneeling to break Writer's individual record of 1166 by one point. I also knew even if I broke the record I might still lose the match to a teammate. I wanted to win the match and even more, I wanted the World record. Perhaps I had added incentive. Before the match I was considered the underdog and not much of a threat to win. I wanted to prove myself. I had held the individual record for this event for five years after I shot 1164 in the Olympic Games in Tokyo in 1964. A Russian, Oleg Lapkin, shot 1165 in Pilsen in 1969 and held the record for three years until Writer brought it back to the United States in 1972.

All of these things were running through my mind as I started shooting in the kneeling position. Perhaps the pressure, or maybe lack of concentration, caused me to shoot nines on the first four shots. Anyway, this significantly reduced my chances of winning. I slowed down, became more cautious and deliberate, and began to concentrate on performance. I was very careful, making sure wind conditions were just right before I shot, sometimes waiting five minutes between shots, and finally began to shoot tens. I lost only three points during the next 28 shots. By this time the other shooters had finished.

I was again the only shooter on the range still shooting and wind conditions were worsening. Everyone on the range had gathered behind my firing point to watch. I was extremely tired, began to lose my concentration and let my mind drift. I wondered how my teammates had finished. Maybe I was already beat. I started thinking about my score and the record and what I needed for a 390. I knew I could lose only three points in the remaining eight shots. The lack of concentration caused a let-down and I dropped two points in the next four shots.

Now I was in trouble again. I could only lose one point in the last four shots. The pressure began to bother me and ten-

Thousands of hours of shooting goes into producing a champion like these Americans who set five world records in winning the Confederation of the Americas Shooting Championships at Mexico City. (NRA)

sion mounted. Somehow I managed to regain my concentration and thought about one shot at a time. Each shot was agonizing but I put every ounce of know-how and effort into the next three shots and someway was able to shoot 10s. I knew my goal was now almost a certainty. All I needed was a nine. However, there was a possibility I might need a 10 to win, not knowing the other scores. I had lost my concentration again by now, and that, coupled with a slight misjudgment of the wind on the last shot, resulted in a nine.

Pandemonium ensued! The range erupted in cheering and clapping. I was immediately mobbed and congratulated for setting the world record and winning the match. (As of September 1975, this three position world record of 1167 still stands). I was so mentally and physically exhausted (six hours since we had begun) and relieved that it was finally over, it took several minutes for everything to sink in. I was more elated than I had ever been. I couldn't believe it. I kept asking "Are you sure?" "What did the others shoot?" It was a tremendous personal satisfaction for me because I wasn't supposed to win.

I then learned of the scores of my teammates and was told we had set team records, kneeling, by six points–1563, and overall by 24 points–4656. Both records had previously been held by the Russians. It was a clean sweep! Four new world team records–and for me, the best of all, the three position individual record.

The performance that day by the US Rifle Team was one of those "once in a lifetime" happenings and I was extremely proud to be a part of it. All the variables–luck, weather, equipment and shooters (three fired their best scores while one had his second best in major competition) had to be just right for this to happen. No shooting team before, or since, has ever approached this phenomenal accomplishment. It could well be the greatest achievement in the history of all amateur sport.

—**Major Lones W. Wigger, Jr.**

Among Major Lones Wigger, Jr.'s long list of accomplishments as one of the world's best rifle marksmen, you'll find 18 world records–more than any other shooter. He is a member of the US Army Marksmanship Unit.

For More Information

There are several magazines covering marksmanship and listed here are the better ones.

The American Rifleman, 1600 Rhode Island Ave. N.W., Washington, D.C. 20036. Published monthly at $10.00 per year for members. This magazine is the official publication of the National Rifle Association which has over one million members.

Precision Shooting, Box 6, Athens, Pa. 18810. Published monthly. Official publication of the International Benchrest Shooters and publishes their match results and information. "Accuracy is the main objective of our material," they say.

Shooting Times, News Plaza, Peoria, Ill. 61601. Published monthly. Have not seen the magazine but they have over 100,000 subscribers.

For organizations: besides the two mentioned above there is also the United States Revolver Association, 59 Alvin St., Springfield, Mass., 01140 and the United States Army Marksmanship Training Unit, Fort Benning, Ga. 31905.

Additional information can be found under hunting and shooting.

Here are two books we recommend. Both are available from World Publications, Box 366, Mountain View, Calif. 94040 at the price listed* plus 25 cents each postage.

Marksmanship, Gary L. Anderson. The definitive guide to target shooting for the beginner and the would-be expert alike, in which a distinguished marksman provides the subtleties of the sport in simple terms. Covers sport shooting, competitions, equipment, the 10 secrets of adapting them to four shooting positions. 1972 Hb., 79 pp., ill., $5.95, (Simon & Schuster).

Position Rifle Shooting, Bill Pullum and Frank T. Hanendrat. A complete, authoritative analysis of rifle-shooting psychology and technique. All elements of shooting skill are covered, most basic to the most advanced. 1973 Hb., 288 pp., ill., $10.00, (Winchester).

Model Aircraft

Whole families enjoy their favorite sport of flying model airplanes. They fly on vacant lots, at ball parks, and at other sites designated for model aviation during holidays and on weekends.

He could be 60, the gray-headed fellow standing there, radio-control transmitter in hand, putting his model airplane through its paces on the ground. Rudder, elevator, aileron, flaps–all respond to his touch. He can't check the retractable landing gear until the bird leaves the ground, but you can bet he will then.

Locking the brakes, he opens the throttle, and like Liberace running the scales, takes the engine from low to high-speed settings and back again. Once satisfied that "all systems are go," he releases the brakes, a gray-white cloud billowing from the exhaust swirls behind the plane as he taxies it slowly out to the take-off strip.

About 100 yards away, an excited kid in ragged cut-offs, T-shirt, and tennis shoes is standing in the center of a large circle painted on the asphalt. His arm is outstretched, and in his hand is a handle connected to a control-line airplane model by two dacron lines. An older man crouching at the edge of the circle holds the plane until the boy calls out, "Let 'er go." His father/helper releases the craft which wobbles slowly forward, uncertainly picking up speed until it finally leaps into the air.

While the free-flight flier checks and re-connects the battery to her model engine, the timer looks down at his watch. He thinks, she has one more minute to start that engine.

Inside the flier's head, a clock is thumping . . . Checked the battery . . . checked the plug . . . checked the wiring . . . It must be flooded . . . Don't prime! Don't prime! Don't prime!

Sweating hard, she grips the propeller and swings it sharply through its arc . . . grins as the engine fires, sputters, then breaks into a steady rumble. Holding the plane nose high, silhouetted against the sky, she tunes the carburetor until the engine screams with life.

She flicks a lever which will regulate the length of time the engine can run, then tosses the model into the air. As the plane spirals upward ever faster, she climbs on the small Honda used for retrieving her model; it may glide for miles before coming down.

What do modelers see in the hobby?

Many of them fly radio control as a less expensive substitute for flying the real thing. Others take pleasure from remotely controlling the antics of their planes, in many cases doing maneuvers which are impossible on a full-sized aircraft.

Control-line fliers love the feeling of positive control, getting great satisfaction from well-executed maneuvers.

Ask any free-flight flier and he'll tell you that free flight is the ultimate in modeling skill. Whether the model flies or crashes, and how well it flies depends upon how well it is balanced and adjusted before flight. And there is the thrill of competing with other fliers; you win only if your model stays up longer than the other guy's.

In general, while model aviation enthusiasts differ in their preference among the facets of the hobby, they do agree that building and flying model airplanes is challenging and fun.

—**Jerry Litwak**

Jerry Litwak is an enthusiastic model airplane hobbyist who frequently contributes articles to **Model Airplane News** *and several other model magazines. He lives in Santa Ana, California.*

Something I Really Enjoy

In many sports and hobbies, the biggest reward is the satisfaction of accomplishment. And this is really true of model airplanes. There's a special thrill to making something yourself and having it fly. To make something that not only flies but is also competitive with the best that other modelers can do is like nitro in your tank.

My main interest is competition. I guess there's the same thrill in competition with all sports, but competing with a model airplane I have made myself adds something special to it.

I used to compete in control line combat. You use 60-foot control lines from combat, and the two guys match their planes and skills by chasing each other all over the sky. Each plane has a streamer of ribbons attached to the tail. The idea is to come up behind the other guy's plane and chew off his streamer with your prop.

Now I compete in pylon radio control. I find Formula One pylon more challenging because there are fewer variables. It's less a matter of luck. Marked out with three pylons, the full course is two and a half miles. The two base pylons are 150 feet apart and the far pylon is 610 feet away. Ten laps make two and a half miles.

The idea is to fly your plane around that course just as fast as you can. It's head-to-head competition, just like control line combat, but you're flying against three other planes rather than just one. The planes take off at one second intervals, signalled by a guy with a checkered flag. You fly until you have completed the 10 laps.

It's fast and exciting. The planes are going upwards of 200 miles an hour going down the chutes. The record for the two and a half miles is one minute and 15 seconds. Imagine what it's like to jockey model airplanes at that speed! Occasionally we have midair collisions.

You have to make the turns around the pylons as tight as you can without coming inside. Ideally, you bring your plane right over the poles or just outside them. This takes really fine handling of the control surfaces and the engines.

We use .4 cubic inch engines. There are only two that are competitive: one is made by K and D of Los Angeles; the other is made by Super Tiger in Italy. They cost around $90.

With the radio systems, you have complete control over your plane. Except for the fact that you're not actually sitting in the airplane, you're in all ways the pilot. You're flying from the ground. What we find surprising is that some real pilots have big problems with radio control flying because they don't have their familiar cockpit orientation anymore.

We all take pride in our planes. We pay attention to fine details—the little things that we hope will give us an edge over our competitors. We want our planes to be a little cleaner. We want to have a better propeller. We want to have a better engine. We try to run as much nitro as we can. Like in any racing, it isn't any one thing that makes you win, it's a combination of a lot of little things.

The model airplane competitors are an interesting bunch. Every one of us thinks he has something special inside. Every one of us has his own little ego thing. That's part of the excitement—bringing these together in competition.

Some people who are interested hold back because they think you need to know a lot about aerodynamics to build and fly model airplanes, but all you need is a little common sense. For instance, you want to keep all the surfaces straight and true, you want a minimum of deflection, and of course you want to keep the weight down. A strong engine makes up for a lot of things, and so does a better prop.

The pitch and area and diameter of the prop are all important. You try to juggle with all three, and you play around with the wood flex. You want to find a prop that flexes just right, and really pulls well in the air. It's partly a matter of intuition but mainly a process of elimination. When you hit on a top prop, you put it aside for races.

Anyone who wants to get into model airplanes should start with freeflight, and then progress into control line and then radio control. This is not a hard and fast rule, though. Some people are interested in radio control and don't want to be bothered with the others. But if you do start with free flight, you learn a lot about aerodynamics—common sense things like building a plane straight. It costs about $500 to get an RC plane in the air. You can get a good free flight plane in the air for about $20. For a control line plane, you'd figure on about $50-$55. It's not really more expensive than most other sports and hobbies.

The sport is growing all the time. A conservative estimate of the number of modellers in the country would be 200,000 to 300,000. And it's really an international sport. The US took first in the most recent international RC meet, held in Switzerland. The US has traditionally been very strong in international competition, especially in the RC events. The Russians seem to dominate in control line and free flight, but then their teams are subsidized by the state. That state support makes a difference.

—Ron Sheldon

Ron Sheldon has been a model airplane enthusiast for 15 years. The hobby is a major part of his life. If you happen to visit Ron's place (Sheldon's Hobby Shop in San Jose, Calif.), and if you happen to ask him about it, he'll tell you: "I can't think of anything I'd rather be doing."

For More Information

Three magazines stand out in this field. *Flying Models,* Box 700, Newton, New Jersey 07860. Published monthly at $7.00 per year. Mostly on airplanes but does have information on other types of models. *Model Airplane News,* 1 North Broadway, White Plains, New York 10601. Published monthly at $10.00 per year. Has been in publication for 45 years. Well-illustrated with a lot of good news in each issue. *Scale Modeler,* 7950 Deering Ave., Canoga Park, Ca. 91304. Published monthly at $18.00 per year. Just on airplane models. On the cover it says, "The world's largest modeling magazine."

An organization you should know about is the Academy of Model Aeronautics, 806 15th St., N.W., Washington D.C. 20005.

There are many places to get supplies and here are a few. Tower Hobbies, Box 778, Champaign, Ill. 61820 has a 116-page catalog ($1.50) featuring over 2300 items. Some of the things they have are fuel filters, stick-on weights, electric starters, epoxy brushes, etc. Austin-Craft Co., Box 207, Kingman, Ariz. has a free catalog. Some of the things they have are battery holders, fuel pumps, A-C timers, needle valves, glue guns, etc. Hobby Center, 146 West 22nd St., New York, N.Y. 10011 has a 160 page catalog for $1.00 But a good place to start is your local hobby shop. They can probably help you.

Here are some books that will be of interest. All are available from World Publications, Box 366, Mountain View, Calif. 94040 at the price listed* plus 25 cents postage.

How to Make Model Aircraft, Chris Ellis. A complete guide to building and flying every type of model airplane imaginable—and when to duck! Hb., $5.95, (Arco).

Model Making, Herbert Lozier. Suitable to all ages of modelers and hobbyists, this book is for those interested in making models of planes, miniature cars, gliders, trucks, boats, and the like. ". . . a model among modelmaking books . . . good enough for even the youngest beginner"—*Library Journal.* 1967 Hb., 165 pp., ill., $7.50, (Chilton).

Aeromodeling, R.H. Warring. How to build and fly all types of model planes, including gliders, rubber-powered models, free-flight models, and radio-control models. 1966 Hb. & Ppb., 168 pp., ill., $4.50/$1.45, (Arco).

Modern Dance

Dancing! None of us can say what dancing is, and yet from early childhood each of us knows what dancing is. To say this is not a contradiction. *What* and *is* clearly refer to two different kinds of knowing – the one to definitions of more or less concrete and measurable elements, the other to experiences in being. That there are two kinds of knowing which pertain to the same phenomenon, but which are not at odds with each other, is especially evident in our physical activities, our games, recreations and dancing, whether they are spontaneous or planned. Bowling is not its peculiar set of rules and regulations. If it were, we should be quite satisfied to pay admission to sit in a sports arena and read a program outlining those rules.

Like any other physical activity which we allow, or will, to capture our full attention, dancing is a state of being aware of self, organic and whole. It escapes definition, just as the experience of bowling escapes the definition of its rules. It is certainly not lesser knowledge for being indefinable. The self that comes to know itself is not a collection of so many calculable atoms arranged in such and such an order. Rather that self is change, growth, feeling, motivation – in short, all that is implied by organic wholeness: alive and therefore changing, yet whole and complete.

Dance is unique among the many activities we have contrived for our pleasure and knowledge in that its rules are particularly plastic. The rules in folk forms, tap, go-go, chorus line, square and round, concert modern and ballet are all arbitrary. They are stylistic rules and although there is undeniable pleasure to be gained in the perfecting of one's technique in accordance with those rules, far greater than those rules is the wit, imagination, ingenuity that one may practice in developing fresh and personal stylistic ideas. Who can say that I am not bowling if I am doing so under water? For my own purposes I might be bowling with more flair, fun (and a considerably better score) than I have ever experienced according to terrestrial rules.

No, rules of style should not be confused with the act of dancing. Rules of style provide a formalized discipline that is essential to one who wishes to give the greater part of his life's attention over to dancing. Rules of style organized into techniques may also aid us in increasing stretch, strength and coordination as we prepare our bodies for dancing. And rules of styles may give us insights into the self images which our race has cultivated for itself socially and historically. This is all of great value to us as we explore the resources which made us human.

But the most engaging and charming rules to explore are those which nature has endowed unto our race through careful genetic progression. We are a most articulate species. We are articulate in how we think and speak and write, in how we feel, react, adapt and design, in how we move, express and communicate for our own pleasure and edification, and for that of others. For many of us, dancing is an activity which best fulfills all the promise of nature's endowment. Dancing constricts us least with rules, yet demands most that we discover the rules that define the self, organic and whole.

As a performer, choreographer, and most importantly as a teacher, I strongly advocate cultivation of the amateur spirit, regardless of how "professionally" the dancer might regiment his or her training. It is the amateur spirit which leaves one open and vulnerable to the astonishment of a widening knowledge of the self. It is the amateur spirit which keeps one engaged with nature's inexhaustible endowment. When the body exhausts, the imagination is still free to soar and prepare for the return of physical vigor. The most graceful self knowledge one can gain is when one receives the accolades of a "professional" while sustaining in one's heart the spirit of the amateur.

I do not teach my students to love dance; that is cold and dry as a recruiter's slogan which promises Honor, Respect, or Manhood if one will submit to rules – never mind being honorable, respectful (and therefore respected), or manly (and therefore human). Rather, through dancing, my students and I engage in the art of being human.

—**John Wilson**

John M. Wilson is a professor of modern dance and adjunct professor of theatre at the University of Utah. He was coordinator, choreographer and performer for four years with the Wisconsin Dance Theatre. He is currently preparing a book on dance education.

For More Information

Additional information can be found under ballet. In addition, you might check out the magazine *Dance News,* 119 W. 57th St., New York, N.Y. 10019. A good source for dance wear is Danskin Inc., 1114 Ave. of the Americas, New York, N.Y. 10036.

Modern Pentathlon

In ancient times the Spartans complained that the Olympic Games did not have an all-around event for warriors. The pentathlon, competition in five events, filled this gap and was instituted in 708 B.C. It was tailored to the soldier-athlete, and contestants were gradually eliminated in each of the five events: the broad jump, javelin throw, 200-yard sprint the length of a stadium, the discus throw, and a final wrestling match between the remaining two men to determine the victor.

The pentathlon was made part of the modern Olympics in 1912. It is sometimes called the "military pentathlon" since it is based on the exploits of couriers from the Napoleonic era whose duty it was to carry across battlefields messages that might determine victory or defeat. The courier had to ride strange horses over unfamiliar terrain. When his horse was exhausted or shot from under him, he then ran cross-country. If he came to a stream or river he swam. Encountering an enemy he would shoot his way through, and fight with his sword at close quarters if necessary to finally deliver the message.

The modern pentathlete must be an all-around athlete skilled in five events: riding 1000 meters against time and over 20 obstacles; fencing; pistol shooting, swimming 300 meters, and running a 4000-meter cross-country course.

The US Army maintains a pentathlon training center at Fort Sam Houston, Texas, and their intensive workouts give a good idea of how to prepare for this event.

At Ft. Sam Houston beginners in riding learn first how to post, and how to go over small jumps in fair style. They progress to the point at which they can ride a strange horse over a jump course of 600-1200 meters with double and triple jumps in the way, interspersed with ditches, water obstacles, and fences about four feet high.

Candidates train much as cavalrymen did in the last century. Some days they ride without a saddle, go through a chute or over small jumps without reins, or go without either while the instructor longes the horse. A rider must acquaint himself with various horses. It takes a sense of pace and planning to make the jumps.

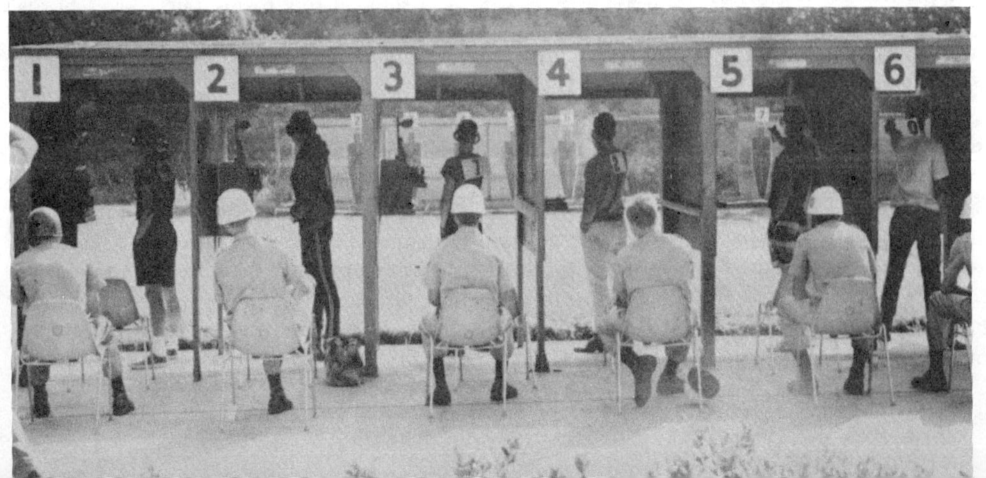

Pistol shooting at a turning international rapid fire target from 25 meters is an integral part of the modern pentathlon. This event symbolizes one of the five skills that a military courier during the early 19th century would need to deliver a message through enemy lines—horse riding, running, swimming, fencing and shooting.

The course is 1000 meters long and requires stadium-type jumping. Riding cleanly at 400 meters per minute earns 1000 points, considered a par score for each event. For each second over 2:30 five points are deducted, while for each second under, five points are added, up to 100 additional points. Points are also deducted for poor form.

In fencing the pentathlete must coordinate his footwork, develop his reflexes, and perfect the fundamental hand-arm movements.

Each competitor must fence every other. One touch decides the bouts. The electrified epee is the modern counterpart of the duelling sword, and the bout corresponds to a duel. The epee can be fixed with an orthopedic or conventional grip. Any part of the anatomy may be struck. The epee is wired to a light and buzzer which go off when a hit is made.

The time of each bout is three minutes. If no conclusion has been reached, a double loss is declared. Any contestant winning 70 percent or more of his matches receives 1000 points.

The skills essential in pentathlon shooting are the same ones needed in all pistol shooting: proper stance, position, grip, breath control, sight alignment, and trigger control. These should be studied with both live and dry firing. The pentathlete fires at a turning, international rapid-fire target at a distance of 25 meters. Twenty shots are fired for score. Three seconds are allowed for each shot and then the marksman turns away for seven seconds. When the target turns toward the shooter he must raise his arm and bring it down to shoot. A target score of 194 out of 200 merits 1000 points. (Lieutenant Charles F. Leonard of the US shot a never equalled 200 out of 200 at the 1936 Berlin Olympics.) For each point above or below this mark 22 points are added or subtracted. All contestants use a .22 caliber revolver or automatic pistol with open front and rear sights.

Pentathletes must also swim 300 meters for time. Heats are drawn by lot. This event draws on strength, speed, and a background of rigorous training. A typical workout for senior pentathletes at the Sam Houston center covers 2600 meters in the pool. This is far from the quantity common for international class swimmers, but each athlete's resources must be rationed among the five activities. At the center they do: warmup, 10 x 100m swimming, kicking and pulling; swim 500m; swim 6 x 150m at three minute intervals; swim 300m; swim 10 x 50m at one minute intervals. Training is designed for athletes to "peak" at the major competitions. A time of three minutes 54 seconds harvests 1000 points. For each second faster or slower the score goes up or down eight points.

The 4000-meter foot race is run over two and one-half miles of terrain more rugged than most cross-country courses. Stamina and strength in running are called for, as well as the ability to read terrain and plan a route. It is advisable to build strength gradually through long runs, and not to start with sprinting or interval work on the track.

Training moves through three phases at the Sam Houston center. At first daily workouts are at least six miles bolstered by two long runs per week of 30 minutes to an hour in length.

The second phase shifts to more quality, and includes repeat 440s on the track and some speed work such as 20 to 40 times 110 yards run in "sets."

In the final phase distance is further shortened and speed sharpened. A time of 14:15 merits 1000 points, with three points more or less being given for each second above or below that time.

The US has never won an Olympic gold medal in modern pentathlon but has been steadily gaining strength in recent years.

For More Information

Additional information can be obtained by writing the US Modern Pentathlon Association, 707 East Broad St., Falls Church, Va. 22046.

We have one good book on modern pentathlon. It is available from World Publications, Box 366, Mountain View, Calif. 94040 at the price listed* plus 25 cents postage.

Modern Pentathlon, Frigyes Hegedus. A comprehensive study of a complex Olympic sport. Chapters discuss the history and development of the sport along with more specialized information regarding training and preparation for competition. 1968 Hb., 225 pp., ill., $12.25, (Imported Publications).

Motorboating

If you haven't gotten your feet wet in motorboating, then you're really missing out on something! Not only is this popular activity a pleasurable pastime in itself, but it also goes hand-in-hand with many sports that take place in and around the water. Outdoor exercise is the byword when it comes to motorboating – and that means for every member of the family. Skindiving, fishing, waterskiing, swimming, beachcombing, exploring and camping by boat are just some of the worlds that can be enjoyed and enhanced once you step into a motorboat.

There are almost as many types and sizes of powerboats as there are fish in the sea. They range from the plush, seagoing yacht to the small outboard-powered aluminum canoe (see Yachting, Canoeing, etc.). If speed is your desire, there are the sleek hydroplanes and new jet boats; for outdoor living a cabin cruiser will fit your needs; if ease and tranquility are your goals, then the small, low-powered skiff is just right. But no matter what you choose, one of the benefits of boating is that you'll be exploring new areas and learning new skills as you go along. Once you go motorboating, you'll want to tie different knots, learn about buoys and markers, and watch for weather signs – to name a few. Also, the possibility of trailering your boat to different lakes, rivers, and other water areas will lend itself nicely to the discovery of new sections of the country.

To really understand a motorboat, the first thing you must know about is her hull – the most important part of any boat. Hulls are shaped to the specific purpose of the boat. For example, a flat-bottom hull will carry a lot of weight for the boat's size, but it will pound badly in choppy seas. A V-shaped hull provides more stability and will throw spray downward,

"Outdoor exercise is the byword when it comes to motorboating—and that means for every member of the family. Skindiving, fishing, waterskiing, swimming, beachcombing, exploring and camping by boat are some of the worlds that can be enjoyed and enhanced once you step into a motorboat." (Baum)

keeping the boat dry. The deep V hull fosters a soft ride and speed, but it is somewhat inefficient at low speeds. Then there are the hulls that are shaped like a gull's wing spread. These have good stability and are efficient at all speeds.

Of course, each hull has its corresponding price, as do the various types of engines available. Whether you choose the removable outboard engine, the automobile-like inboard, or a combination of the two in an inboard/outboard engine, you'll want to consider carefully which type best suits your needs.

And keep in mind the advice from the expert boatsmen: Once you have your boat for awhile, you'll probably be looking toward another one – perhaps bigger, faster, or with a more elaborate design. But don't let this stop you!

An Education in Sinking

Boats are supposed to stay afloat. Most of them do, fortunately for the millions of Americans who enjoy powerboating. But sometimes they don't. Sinking is a traumatic experience, but it does offer some advantages. It is highly educational. Sink once and you learn enough to write a book.

I sank a boat in 1964. It was a 40-foot raceboat, which requires some explanation. Ocean powerboat racing was at its peak in the early 1960s, with many manufacturers involved. It amounted to "research on the run", as builders tested hulls, engines and accessories. It was not unusual for boats to sink in the early days of offshore racing. Fires were also fairly common, radios turned into junk in the severe pounding, compasses were almost useless.

There was a period, in the youth of the gruelling game, when more than half the boats might fail to finish a race. Now, in its mature years, most boats complete the course.

Along the way, American boats have all become tougher and more seaworthy; radios can take more of a beating than once was the case; engines are improved; and compasses have been built that will help you hold on a steady course without the card gyrating all over the place.

These lessons were learned in the laboratory of ocean racing. They have benefitted American boatmen immensely.

But we were still learning when I sank. Here's how it happened – and a few of the lessons I learned are included:

We were leading in the 1964 Miami-Nassau Race, a 180-mile run across the Gulf Stream to the Bahamas. It was somewhat rough, which is why I could put the 40-footer in front. She was large enough to take the punishment of the steep, short seas. And it was rough. The navigator was briefly knocked out when we thudded into a sea with such force that he was slammed into a bulkhead.

We were almost across the Gulf Stream, and I could see the lighthouse on Gun Cay, one of the Bahama islands nearest to Miami. Suddenly the steering went sour. The boat wouldn't turn to starboard.

The engineer pointed aft. A jet of water was shooting up through the lazarette hatch aft. He dove below and checked, came up shaking his head.

To condense things, we got out a "Mayday" call on the radio, inflated our life raft, and clambered aboard as the 40-footer went down.

We were picked up within 30 minutes, and no one was injured. But we lost the boat. Apparently, we had struck some floating object under the port propeller shaft, which opened the planking on the port side of the bottom, aft. At the near 40-knot speed, in four- to five-foot seas, there were brutal shocks every few seconds, so we hadn't felt it.

We learned much. For one thing, when water rises over your batteries, your radio may not work (it failed after our Mayday call). For another thing, a sinking hull can "work" and twist; the locker in which we kept our emergency kit – signal flares and the like – was jammed shut. Luckily, our inflatable raft had been on deck.

But most of all, we learned that emergencies aren't something that happen to the other fellow. They can happen to you. And if you prepare for them, they are no longer emergencies.

It was easy, then, to sink a boat in a race – especially a wooden hull. It's more difficult now, and sinking is rare in offshore racing. But we learned it can happen to anyone.

I've never gone to sea since without first carefully checking the inventory of safety gear. The practice is recommended to all hands.

When you are properly equipped, sinking becomes just another adventure.

–Jim Martenhoff

Jim Martenhoff has been a boating enthusiast for many years. He has written countless articles on the subject for major outdoor and boating magazines in addition to authoring **The Powerboat Handbook.**

For More Information

There are over 40 magazines that cover boating. We can't list all of them but we'll give a good cross-section of those available.

Motorboat, 38 Commercial Wharf, Boston, Mass. 02110. Published bi-monthly at $9.50 for 12 issues. Good features with many good regular columns including navigation and piloting, seamanship, engines, small boats, weather and maintenance. *Sea,* 1499 Monrovia Ave., Newport Beach, Calif. 92663. Published monthly. Each issue has good information which will inform and entertain the recreational boater. *Boating Magazine,* One Park Ave., New York, N.Y. 10016. Published monthly. This magazine is edited for the knowledgeable, dedicated boatman, both power and sail. An average issue contains a cruising story, how-to-do-it articles, a boat test report on a power boat, a sailboat evaluation, design section, news, an electronics column, plus more. The biggest of boat publications. *Rudder,* 67 West 44th St., New York, N.Y. 10036. Published monthly. The seccond largest boat publication that is another good one.

Again, there are several organizations. Here are enough to get you started in the right direction. National Boating Federation, 629 Waverly Lane, Bryn Athyn, Pa. 19009. With over one million members they want to improve and strengthen amateur boating. United States Power Squadrons, Box 345, 50 Craig Rd., Montvale, N.J. 07645. These people teach basic boating. United States Coast Guard, Commandant (B-AU), U.S. Coast Guard, Washington, D.C. 20590. Involved with safety along with a lot of other things.

There are a lot of good sources for equipment. However, *Motorboat* magazine puts out a publication called Motorboat and Equipment Directory. It is filled with a lot of helpful information. You can order it through the magazine at $3.00 a copy. It is well worth it. Or for $2.00 you can get a copy of Goldberg's catalog which has over 6500 items listed. Write Goldberg's Marine, 202 Market St., Phila., Pa. 19106.

The number of books that have been written on boating is really large. Here are just a few of them. All are available from World Publications, Box 366, Mountain View, Calif. 94040 at the price listed* plus 25 cents postage. Write for a complete list.

The Complete Book of Boat Trailering, Tom Bottomley. Provides the reader with all the information needed to take advantage of the flexibility provided by the boat trailer. Major sections deal with how to select a boat and trailer and how to modify your automobile to accommodate your boat. 1974 Hb., 96 pp., ill., $6.95, (Association Press).

The Family Book of Boating, Mike Kaplan. An "everything" guide to family boating, including care and handling of all types of pleasure boats, safety rules in all waters, competitive do's and don't and hints for buying and selling boats. 1973 Ppb., 159 pp., ill., $1.50, (Dell).

Self-Taught Navigation, Robert Y. Kittredge. Here at last–simplified step-by-step instructions to enable the most inexperienced beginner to teach himself celestial navigation. In 10 easy steps the author gives precise instructions, from the first move of picking up your sextant to the last move needed for position from any celestial body. 1970 Hb., 81 pp., maps & charts, $5.95, (Naval Institute).

The Complete Book of Outboard Boating, Lyle Engel. Here is accurate and highly detailed information on all types of power–everything from finding a dealer, choosing a model and motor to useful accessories. 1975 Ppb., 16 pp., ill., $3.95, (Arco).

Piloting, Seamanship and Small Boat Handling, Charles F. Chapman. This is still the leading book in the field of boating and seamanship. Year after year this large volume has been improved and expanded, so that nothing can approach it in scope, completeness and authority. 1972 (rev.) Hb., 640 pp., ill., $9.95, (Hearst).

Basic Boating, Piloting and Seamanship, Andrews & Russell. Information for skippers. Covers piloting, navigation, first aid, sea law, weather forecasting. Recommended by the US Power Squadrons. 1974 (rev.) Hb., 381 pp., ill., $8.95, (Prentice Hall).

The Complete Book of Boating, Ernest A. Zadig. Hundreds of illustrations, photographs, and an uncomplicated text highlight this well-detailed handbook for boatmen. Boat handling, repair, furnishing, safety, trailering, and more. 1972 Hb., 640 pp., ill., $12.95, (Prentice Hall).

The Powerboat Handbook, Jim Martenhoff. A handbook for beginning boaters. The clear, non-technical text contains everything the novice needs to know about selecting, maintaining and operating powerboats. 1974 Hb., 262 pp., ill., $8.95, (Winchester).

The New Cruising Cookbook, Russell K. Jones and C. Norton. Loads of information and recipes for cooking aboard the small cruising boat. Every galley cook will delight in the cooking resulting from this great book. 1960 Hb., 320 pp., ill., $7.95, (W.W. Norton).

Dutton's Navigation and Piloting, G.D. Dunlap, et al. Widely recognized as the standard authority in the field, this is the basic text for the US Naval Academy and others. Suitable for home study and for use as a reference, it emphasizes celestial navigation, which remains the basic backup system for sophisticated electronic methods. 1972 Hb., 734 pp., ill., $18.65, (Naval Institute).

Sports Illustrated Powerboating, Tony Gibbs. Complete beginner's guide to powerboating. Stressing safe, smooth operation of boats in tranquil and rough waters. Good advice about choosing a boat, safety rules, handling, and all equipment. 1973 Hb. & Ppb., 93 pp., ill., $4.95/$1.95, (Lippencott).

Powerboat Maintenance, Eric Jorgenson. This extensive "how-to" book covers virtually every area of powerboat maintenance and offers clear instruction on hull and interior structures, electrical systems, the galley, plumbing and heads, basic engine maintenance, corrosion protection, and far more. 1975 Ppb., 280 (oversize) pp., ill., $9.00, (Clymer).

Motorcycle Racing

Today's motorcycle competitions are held in a number of different forms, using specialized machines and according to varied sets of rules. In moto-cross competition, motorcycle riders scramble over rough terrain, from steep hills to creek beds, at speeds approaching 60 m.p.h. Motorcycles are also raced on formal tracks which are varied as to shape and composition. Cinder, shale, grass, boards, sand, ice, as well as asphalt are used on tracks. Some are large ovals, others have a series of turns, switchbacks, etc. Motorcycle racing implies, however, road racing on ordinary public roads or on artificial tracks.

Today, the sport flourishes in places such as Britain, Germany, Italy, Spain, and other European countries, as well as Malayasia, South Africa, the USSR, Japan and North and South America.

Motorcycles most often race in classes which are usually determined by engine size. Since, theoretically, all motorcycles in a race should be fairly equal on a competitive basis, the race is begun with all participants beginning en masse. American races are begun with engines already started, clutch in, and gears engaged. In other countries races are started with engines dead – production machines can be started with a kick or electric starter; all-out racers have to be push-started. Needless to say, the starting grid is usually fairly crowded, with riders lined up in two or more rows. The winner of the race is usually the first to complete the given number of laps around the circuit. There are, however, road races where the competitor who has covered the furthest distance in a certain length of time is declared the winner. In other types, participants race against the clock, which signifies a time trial.

The motorcycle competitor must have a knowledge of a number of riding skills. He must also possess a sense of courage and strategy. Good coordination is a must since fast acceleration depends greatly upon the fast execution of gear changing. Good cornering is a result of correct down-shifting and sensitive braking. Of course, a practical mechanical knowledge by the rider is much to be desired, as he can often assist his crew in repairs and maintenance while in the pits.

Of course, protective clothing is required in races: helmet, goggles or visor, gloves, boots, and leather overalls. These are inspected before the start of the race and riders who do not meet standards are disqualified. A number of other measures for safety are employed, such as straw bales, sandbanks, or other protective barriers at suitable points on the track.

Other types of motorcycle events not mentioned above are sprints, acceleration contests over a quarter of a mile distance; and motorcycle rallies, where riders must proceed to a number of pre-determined checkpoints.

"If you're planning to race it's a good idea to be in shape. Moto-cross is very physically demanding so you should do some running and weight lifting for your arms. For the hands you might use spring-loaded squeeze grips."

Setting Up for Moto-Cross

Imagine flying over jumps, hills, and all sorts of rough terrain at speeds of up to 80 m.p.h. You're moving so fast that you miss every other bump and you feel as if you're on top of the world – in a sense you are. This is moto-cross.

Moto-cross originally came from Europe and was called scrambles. After seeing this sport overseas, American military men brought it to the US upon their return to this country after World War II. It remained fairly obscure in America, however, until the late 1960s and early 1970s when motorcyclists caught sight of this very special motorcycle competition. In 1967, a California promoter invited a group of professional European racers to ride against the Americans. Even though our inexperienced riders were no match for them, they learned many new techniques which enabled them to improve on the quality of their riding.

A moto-cross "bike" is a very specialized piece of equipment. The frame should have a lot of rake by the neck to enable the bike to steer slower. This keeps you out of trouble at high speeds. The swing arm should be made of square tubing for strength, and should be several inches longer than a conventional arm, for more travel in the rear suspension. This also helps keep the rear wheel from hopping and losing power. Your forks and rear shocks should have six to eight inches of travel for high speed jumps.

Most importantly, a moto-cross bike should be equipped with "knobbys", deep-cut rubber tires which enable the bike to get traction in slick mud. A 21-inch front wheel is also used; its large diameter helps it to go over rocks and ruts, rather than colliding with them. Very wide handle bars are used to give you leverage in turning in deep mud.

It is very important to make your bike as light as possible. Aluminum wheels and conical hubs are helpful. I think the

best wheels of this type are the DID type, which do not clog with mud. Aluminum engine cases have been used for many years and magnesium engine mounts are used for the same purposes. It is very important to keep the center of gravity down low. For this reason many bikes carry aluminum gas tanks that are big enough just to hold the gas needed for the race.

Moto-cross bike engines vary from 75 cubic centimeters to the large 500 cc. types. Depending on what class you want to run in, you will choose an appropriate engine.

Several years ago an unbreakable fender was developed, and remains the best way to go.

Seat height is also very important. If you're tall, it's a good idea to put extra padding in the seat so your legs won't be too cramped. This padding will also serve to absorb the shock of running over rough terrain.

If you're planning to race it's a good idea to be in shape. Moto-cross is very physically demanding so you should do some running and weight lifting for your arms. For exercise for the hands, you might use spring-loaded squeeze grips. Practice is also a must; you have to know your machine and how to handle it.

Many moto-cross events are sponsored by the American Motorcycle Association. Fees for participation are $10 per year, which also covers your insurance. Also, a Sportsman Card must be obtained for $2 a year.

There are three riding ability classes in moto-cross: novice, junior and expert. These classes are obtained by the accumulation of points, according to Olympic scoring.

—**Terry Dickson**

Terry Dickson has harbored an interest in motorcycles for many years. Besides racing and street and trail riding, he owns an impressive stable of motorcycles.

For More Information

There are about nine zillion motorcycle magazines on the news stands, most of which cover competition motorcycling in one manner or another. We checked these out and recommend six. *AMA News,* Box 141, Westerville, Ohio 43081. Published monthly at $5.00 per year. Official journal of the AMA covering all phases of the sport from competition, to legislation, to touring and road riding. *Cycle Magazine,* One Park Avenue, New York, N.Y. 10016. Published monthly at $8.00 per year. This is the largest cycle mag in the United States. Coverage is mainly road tests, but race coverage always find its way into the book. *Cycle World,* 1499 Monrovia Ave., Newport Beach, Calif. 92663. Published monthly at $5.00 per year. This is the second largest magazine, and coverage features road tests, competition and features on special bikes. *Motorcyclist,* 8490 Sunset Blvd., Los Angeles, Calif. 90069. Published monthly at $6.00 per year. A good all-around publication with better than average photography and layout. *Motorcross Action Magazine,* 16200 Ventura Blvd., Encino, Calif. 91486. Published for motorcross competitors and fans at $9.00 per 12 issues. There is a major national motorcycle association in the United States and it is the American Motorcycle Association, Box 141, Westerville, Ohio 43081. The AMA is the national sanctioning body for all major motorcycle activity, including road riding, touring, motocross, flat track, enduros and all other forms of the sport. Competition is sanctioned on both the professional and amateur level.

Three pretty good cycle mail order houses have catalogs out: Try Florida Cycle Supply, Box 5245. Jacksonville, Fla; KK Motorcycle Supply, 431 E. Third, Dayton, Ohio 45402; and Hap Jones Distributing, Box 3068, San Francisco, Calif. 94119. Each of these houses carries all types of motorcycle products for the serious competition rider as well as the road rider.

Here is a selection of good books. All are available from World Publications, Box 366, Mountain View, Calif. 94040 at the price listed* plus 25 cents each postage. Write for a complete list.

How to Win Motocross, Gary Baily with Carl Shipman. Written by America's leading instructor of motorcross technique, this big book covers everything taught at his schools. Solid advice on your equipment, maintenance, and more. When you see this book, you won't lend it to your competitors! 1974 Ppb., 190 (oversize) pp., ill., $5.95, (H.P. Books).

Motorcycle Racing in America, Spence & Brown. A complete prose and photo essay on all types of motorbike racing, containing information on history, equipment, rules and tracks. 1974 Ppb., 135 pp., ill., $4.95, (Olson).

Enduro, Thomas Firth Jones. "An enduro is a motorcycle race run against time and terrain and in company with several hundred hearty cyclists on special machines built to ford streams, leap logs, and drive through sand . . . packed with the kind of sound practical advice that will take the novice through the purchase . . . up to, hopefully, his first win . . . Recommended."—Library Journal. 1970 Hb. & Ppb., 155 pp., ill., $5.50/ $2.95, (Chilton).

The Cycle Jumpers, Marshall Speigel. A short, easy-to-read narrative of the lives of the two top cycle jumpers in the world, Evel Knievel and Gary Wells. 1973 Ppb., 174 pp., ill., 95c, (Berkley).

Motorcycling-Off Road

Off-road motorcycling generally entails big excursions into the wilderness – State and National Forests, desert areas, privately owned motorcycle parks, or even a local vacant lot. The machines used for off-road riding, trail bikes, have features suited to the task of moving a rider over unpaved ground. "Knobby" tires, high ground clearance and lightweight are helpful in keeping the machine from becoming mired or high-centered. Other features include a skid plate under the engine, uplifted exhaust pipe, small headlight and taillight units, headlight lens protectors, and flexible non-metal fenders – all intended to minimize damage to the motorcycle.

Many excellent trail bikes are available from Japanese and European manufacturers. The most popular have single cylinder engines, 150 to 350 cubic centimeters in displacement.

Preparation of a trail bike for a day's ride includes checking oil levels and tire pressure and making sure all nuts and bolts are tightened. Other routine maintenance operations will be described in the owner's manual.

The rider's personal equipment should include a helmet, eye protection, gloves, boots, long sleeves and other appropriate dress for the particular weather conditions. Faced with potential hazards from rocks, large trees, water and sand, even the most carefully prepared machine will develop minor malfunctions. Therefore, one would be well advised to carry a basic tool kit, electrical tape, bailing wire, and a few spare parts such as extra cables, light bulbs and drive chain links. Many hours of sightseeing and practicing of riding skills await the off-road motorcyclist. Experience will reveal the best methods of preparation and what equipment to carry along.

With the mass production of ready-to-ride trail bikes, there has been great concern about this sport by environmentally concerned folks. Each year the possibilities of more air and noise pollution and destruction of the land increases with growing numbers of trail bikes and trail riders. Machines fitted with mufflers and spark arresters along with riders who have a bit of common sense and a respect for Mother Nature should keep these problems at a minimum, however.

—**Richard McCarey, Jr.**

Richard McCarey, Jr. has been involved in off-road motorcycle riding and racing for many of his 30 years. In 1974, he was ranked third in Colorado motorcycle road racing and he works as a service manager for a Honda dealer in Denver.

"Trail bikes have features suited to the task of moving a rider over unpaved ground. "Knobby" tires, high ground clearance and lightweight are helpful in keeping the machine from becoming mired or high-centered..'

For More Information

There's one fine magazine for off-road bikers. It's *Dirt Bike*, 16200 Ventura Blvd., Encino, Calif. 91436. It is published irregularly at $9.00 per 12 issues. Covers competitive dirt bike riding and plenty on trail bikes. Nice technical articles.

For additional magazines, supply houses and organizations, see the section on Motorcycles–Competition.

Here are some good trailbike guides to get you started. All are available from World Publications, Box 366, Mountain View, Calif. 94040 at the price listed* plus 25 cents each postage. Write for a complete list.

California Trailbike Guide, Joe Driscoll. A guide to some of the nation's best motorbike trails, with a strong ecology-minded stance. Problems of trail preservationand the impact of biking on the environment, a score of detailed maps, the politics of trailriding, and much more. 1973 Ppb., 124 pp., ill., $5.95, (Ten Speed Press).

How to Select, Ride and Maintain Your Trail Bike, Doug Richmond. A well-illustrated manual encompassing nearly every aspect of trail bike riding. Tips include how to select a bike, ride it properly and set it up for dirt. 1972 Ppb., 160 pp., ill., $5.95, (H.P. Books).

The Woods Rider: The Guide to Off-The-Road Motorcycling, Robin Perry. The first book-length guide to off the road motorcycling. Shows how to buy and maintain these machines and gives complete instructions on riding under all weather and terrain conditions. Recommended by Library Journal. 1973 Hb. & Ppb., 128 pp., ill., $4.95/$2.95, (Crown).

Riding the Dirt, Bob Sanford. Trail biking and off-road motorcycle racing—intermediate and advanced techniques dealing with every aspect of dirt riding. 1972 Hb., 221 pp., ill., $6.95, (Bond-Parkhurst).

Motorcycling-Street

The world of street motorcycling is one of special appeal for individuals possessing a high degree of self-reliance, a sense of appreciation for fine machinery and exquisite engineering, and a dislike for the routine, comfort-controlled pampering that life in a modern industrialized society has become. Obviously, the cycles of today wouldn't exist without industry and technological progress. In fact, neither would roads and gasoline. But sometimes it all gets to be a bit too much, and using a motorcycle for getting to work or for a fun weekend trip is about as close as we can get to the good old days of open spaces and clean air, when one's quickest mode of transportation was also probably the most constant of companions – a horse.

On-road motorcycling offers advantages and challenges quite different from those of dirt riding. It's a quick, cheap (in terms of fuel consumption) personal conveyance with no parking problems and a refreshing closeness to the sights and smells of nature. And a ride in the mountains or to the beach makes a fun date, not to mention the refreshing closeness (again).

Coordination and traffic dodging offer plenty of challenge. Indeed, the extreme vulnerability of both rider and driver is the only serious drawback of street riding. It requires constant anticipation of other motorists' actions and the allowance of a comfortable safety margin, as they often seem to do the worst things from a cyclist's point of view.

Motorcyclists generally get involved with their machines, tinkering and adding accessories, sometimes identifying with a particular brand. Maintaining a bike can be a lot of fun, and getting the right combination of tires, suspension and shock damping rates is essential for safety and comfort whether you intend to push your bike to its handling limits or not. There are some fine accessories on the market that allow personalization of any machine from a mini-bike or mo-ped to a big tourer. If you are interested in touring and tripping there are many items for reducing fatigue on long trips, and keeping bugs and raindrops at arms length. Among them are fairings and windshields. Fairings provide lots of storage space for food, tools and a jacket, and route the wind up and over, making all-day rides a lot less tiring.

To get started in the joys of motorcycling is easy enough. There are lots of dealers around and ads in the papers. Prices can range from about $100 for a used 90 cc Honda or a minibike to $4500 for a new BMW R90S (a few brands are priced even higher). If you've never owned a motorcycle, reading a few of the cycle magazines should help you decide which one will be best for you. They road test and comment on faults and desirable traits of almost every brand.

–**Jonathan Arnold Walker**

Jonathan Arnold Walker is a commercial pilot from Palo Alto. He enjoys recreational flying and motorcycling.

Bike Tripping

I started out at the age of 12 with a Solex. It was a sort of bicycle with a 50 cc two-stroke engine mounted above the front wheel. It was of French manufacture, and required pedalling to get the engine started. It would then putt along at about 15 or 20 miles per hour. At that tender age, I got a taste of the thrills of competition by racing the mailman in his little Cushman cart up and down our small street. I won sometimes, but of course I never told him we were racing.

Since those early days, I have owned 13 bikes – a few Hondas, a Jawa, a Kawasaki 500, and now a BMW. I must admit that the BMW is vastly superior to all the others and I don't feel I would want anything else. The engineering is superb and inspires a kind of confidence and oneness with a machine that I'd never felt before. It's sort of the Porsche/ Mercedes of motorcycles.

To enjoy a bike, one really has to believe that getting there is half the fun, or maybe even all of it. The sheer adventure of throwing a pack on the back of your mount and zipping over roller coaster-like roads with steep banked curves – bathed in warm sunshine, surrounded by animals and trees, and feeling the breeze – is unattainable in any other way. And the magic of twisting one's wrist and varying the rate at which the world rushes by, to finally arrive at some new and exciting place, is almost like a time machine.

My favorite trip is one from the Bay Area to Yosemite in the summer or early fall. Taking the country roads rather than the freeway is well worth the extra time. The temperature is usually in the 80s or 90s, which feels great as long as you keep moving. And the smells of alfalfa, onions, and even manure let you really feel the experience of a ride through the country more than in a car, even if the windows are down. If you like, you can stop and watch the cows or a big harvester, or drop by the local cafe and get a feeling for the area.

About 45 minutes out of Yosemite on Highway 20 is a small restaurant called The Lighthouse and the owner's wife makes the best apple pie I've ever run across. It's a good place to fill up the bikes, too, so you won't have to worry about gas once you get into Yosemite Valley. Yosemite is a cyclist's paradise, with sheer cliffs as high as one can look up, mountains all around, winding roads to test one's skill, and breathtaking views around almost every turn. In the autumn a rider is literally bathed in golds, reds and browns as leaves swirl in the breeze. The rushing air feels cool and crisp on the face and this effect awakens the senses. The world is a beautiful place and it's great to be alive.

It gets pretty hard to think of my bike as just a machine, classed with furnaces and lawnmowers, when it can bring such distant places near and transport me anywhere I wish to be, as fast as anything known to man, save traveling by air.

–**Jonathan Arnold Walker**

For More Information

There's a good magazine for street and road riders . . . *Road Rider,* Box 678, South Laguna, Calif. 92677. It is published monthly at $10.00 per year. Written and edited by one of America's foremost road riders especially for road and street riders.

For additional magazines, supply houses and organizations, see the section on Motorcycles–Competition.

Here are several books we recommend. All are available from World Publications, Box 366, Mountain View, Calif. 94040 at the price listed* plus 25 cents each postage. Write for a complete list.

Motorcycling for Beginners, I.G. Edmonds. An introduction for the novice. Emphasis is on safety and conditioning the rider to react quickly to traffic and trial situations. 1972 Ppb., 156 pp., ill., $2.00, (Wilshire).

Chilton's Motorcycle Repair Guide. This new addition to Chilton's line of repair manuals is a complete guide to the tune-up, maintenance, and general repair of all component systems of the most popular motorcycles now sold in the US. Covers from the date indicated to 1973: BMW (1960); BSA singles, twins and triples (1963); Bultaco (1963); Harley Davidson singles and twins (1947); Honda singles, twins and fours including the XL250 and the MT125 and MT250 (1963); Kawasaki single, twins and triples, and the 900 Z-1 (1966); Montesa (1966); Moto Guzzi (1966); Norton 750 and 850 (1966); Ossa (1968); Suzuki singles, twins and triples (1963); Triumph singles, twins and triples (1963); and all Yamaha street and dirt bikes, including the TX500, TX650, and TX750 (1964). 1974 Hb., 1370 (oversize) pp., ill., $22.95, (Chilton).

The Road Rider: A guide to On-The-Road Motorcycling, Robin Perry. For beginners who have just bought their first motorcycle or are contemplating buying one. Provides all fundamentals for riding in safety and comfort with pleasure and economy. 1974 Hb. & Ppb., 128 pp., ill., $5.95/$2.95, (Crown).

Motorcycle Tuning for Performance, Carl Shipman. Street or dirt, performance is important. This is the book with everything you need to get maximum performance from your bike. Contains clear explanations and photos of operation and adjusment of carburetion, ignition, and gearing. 1973 (rev. 1975) Ppb., 174 (oversize) pp., ill., $5.95, (H.P. Books).

Chilton's Complete Guide to Motorcycles and Motorcycling, Koch. How to buy a road or dirt bike, responsibilities of the owner, maintenance, racing, touring, accessories, and more. Special chapter on ecology for bikers. 1974 Ppb., 197 pp., ill., $5.95, (Chilton).

The Motorcycle, Lacombe and Beltoise. A beautifully illustrated history of the motorcycle, presented in an exciting and eye-pleasing manner. Complete sections on riding advice, bike design, accessories, and racing. Color photos. 1974 Hb., 235 pp., ill., $14.95, (Grosset & Dunlap).

Motor Rallying

The point of rallying is to find your way over an unknown open route at a prescribed average speed, neither slow nor fast. High speed is penalized in the scoring.

Rallying is a fascinating, demanding, competitive game of navigational skill. It has been called a parlor game for adults, played outdoors on the open road, with cars. One wag described it as a drive in the country to grandmother's house, only you don't know where she lives, and you don't know how to get there, but you have to arrive exactly on time. You might think of it as a kind of organized shunpiking, with a party after.

Essentially, there are two aspects of a typical rally. First, you must follow the route instructions, sometimes rather cryptic and abbreviated to keep the game interesting; second, you must come as close as you can to the prescribed average speeds (by club regulations these are below the posted speed limit), so that you will arrive at the secret checkpoint locations at the right time.

Route instructions might look something like this:

1. First possible Right. Maintain 32.5 m.p.h.
2. Left on second paved road.
3. Right after Gulf Station.
4. Left on Dry Fork Road.
5. Right at stop sign. (and so forth)

Note that no mileages are given between these points. The only way to find the mileage is to record the reading on your car's odometer at each point. (The odometer is the mileage-measuring part of your speedometer—the part you look at when buying a used car or when you're wondering if it's time to change the oil.) Knowing the distance you have driven enables you to calculate, with pencil and paper, how close you have come to maintaining the average speed. At this point one of the quick students in the back of the room points out that you will always be behind in your calculations, as you have to drive the distance before you can figure the time. Exactly. This is where the skill enters the picture. An experienced rally driver can maintain a speed very close to that 32.5 m.p.h. (or whatever) for several miles while his navigator calculates their average speed to the last decimal point. It takes practice, but like any skill, it can be learned in time.

What kinds of people are rallyists? All kinds and all ages, from 18 year olds with shiny new licenses up to and often including their parents. Rallying is a game of mental as well as driving ability—distance measurement to the one-hundredth of a mile and timing to the second put a premium on people who enjoy doing precision work.

But high math ability is not necessary since the arithmetic involved is not above the eighth grade level. In fact, many rallyists simply drive "by the seat-of-the-pants," guess at the average speeds, enjoy the scenery—and often beat the more mathematically inclined types.

In short, if you like a drive in the country on a Sunday afternoon, and take pleasure in competitive games of skill and precision, you will enjoy rallying. If you're the sociable type, remember there's almost always some kind of social affair after the rally—to the extent that some people think of a rally as an excuse for a party.

The equipment needed to get started in rallying is pretty simple. A car, of course, is kind of obvious. And it must be in safe condition, with seatbelts. But what kind of car? The game is usually called sports car rallying, so is a sports car necessary? Not at all. You'll see many sports cars on every rally but you won't feel a bit out of place in your old family bus. Rallies have been run by just about everything from the tiniest of imported two-seaters to the most capacious American station wagons as well as jeeps and pick-up trucks. Once, on an economy run (a type of rally in which the point is to follow the route and get the best gas mileage) one thoughtful chap entered a gargantuan ready-mix concrete truck! The gas mileage calculations for scoring the event took into account the vehicle weight (in order not to give too much advantage to the little imports) so, though he only averaged about 10 or 12 miles to the gallon, his enormous gross weight gave him top honors in terms of "ton-miles" per gallon. He called it a "sports mixer" on the entry form.

About the only guidelines that can be given on vehicle type are that motorcycles are out (rallying alone is too dangerous—you must have a navigator to help you follow the route instructions). Also, since the emphasis in choice of routes is winding back roads rather than superhighways, your Fleetwood or Continental may prove a trifle ponderous for a lighthearted tour down country lanes. Rallies are run in all kinds of weather, and the modest weather protection of some of the more sporting sports cars may prove too limited for you. Having to brush snow off the clipboard so as to read the next route instruction can dampen even the most ardent enthusiasm.

Generally, the larger and better appointed sports cars come off well, as do the middle-size imported sedans, and the smaller (and sportier) domestics. Commonly seen on local rallies are Mustangs, Cougars, Porsches, VWs, Volvos, Mercedes-Benz, Camaros, Triumphs, Corvettes and Datsuns.

And don't worry about a rally being hard on the car. A properly set-up local rally will not require you to abuse your car in any way. Do think about starting out with the car in safe condition. Rally organizers are a safety-conscious bunch, and may preface a rally with a safety check that would rival an official state inspection. Seat belts are almost universally required.

Optional equipment will depend on tastes, abilities, and interests. As I mentioned, you must be a navigator—it's required by the rules, and the rules also usually say only two people per car. If you're single here's a good place for a Sunday afternoon date. But if you are married, you have a choice. You can rally with your spouse, and many top-rated rally teams are husband and wife; or you can split up. On a number of local rally teams the wives join up against their husbands—and the girls have been known to come in first.

Clipboards are a big help for holding route instructions where they can be read and for keeping track of such things as check point cards and special notes. Extra pencils are recommended, since you usually drop one under the seat just when the route gets complicated. Slide rules are a help in doing arithmetic, if you know how to use them. If you don't there are special rallying slide rules marked off in minutes and miles. These are available from sports car specialty houses, and they come complete with instructions. You'll need a watch of some sort with a sweep-second hand if possible. Stop watches are very useful. Finally, pads of paper in a convenient size are an absolute must.

As in any sport or hobby, how far you want to go in the equipment line depends on the depth of your pocket and your personal taste for gadgets. There are lots of trinkets you can buy for rallying, up to and including electronic computers costing hundreds of dollars. The best way to find out what you want is to try a rally or two and see how tings go. If you turn out to be happy as a carefree seat-of-the-pants rallyist, you won't need to spend your money on anything more than a tune-up for the buckboard.

—Sports Car Club of America

For More Information

Write the Sports Car Club of America, P.O. Box 22476, Denver, Colo. 80222. Also check our other auto racing sections.

Considerable care must be taken in crossing glaciers, especially early in the season when crevasses can be covered by a thin bridge of snow. Three person rope teams are most commonly used, because two can more easily effect a rescue if one team member breaks through. (Rowell)

Mountain Climbing

Mountaineering is not for everyone. Many people just can't handle the dangers involved. It is risky. Many of the dangers can be controlled by knowledge and experience. Some cannot. If you're the type of person who buys a lot of life insurance, or you think that the 55 m.p.h. speed limit is a good thing for safety, then you probably won't make a serious mountain climber.

If you want to learn to climb, try walking or scrambling up easy peaks first. Many people start right out on technical stuff, which is sort of like learning how to drive a race car before you pass your driver's test.

Mountain climbing began as the final stage of terrestrial exploration. Mountains were the leftover spots after valleys, deserts, rivers, and oceans became known quantities. The first mountaineers were explorers. They had to climb in order to go places in rugged, mountainous terrain.

Today, mountaineering has become a sport in itself. Climbers have become specialists. Some prefer expedition climbing on big-snow mountains, while others become rock climbers

Some very difficult climbs will challenge all a climber's abilities. Near vertical rock walls demanding the use of various mountaineering hardware will be interspersed with difficult snow and ice pitches. Combining this with the fact that many mountains can only be climbed in winter—because they are subject to massive rock falls during warmer months—we arrive at the challenge that is the Eiger and a few other "super" mountains. (Rowell)

(see "Rock Climbing" section), perhaps never setting foot on snow. These specialized niches often seem to have little relation to one another. Some climbers can do them all, and it is this select group who do the most severe alpine climbing—where all their talents may be needed on a single route.

For some, mountaineering has become much more than a sport. It becomes a way of life, almost a religion of sorts. Their lives revolve around personal interactions with nature. Others merely play in the mountains as they would play tennis or golf. Mountaineers do agree universally on one thing: the activity must be kept free from highly technological or motorized equipment.

The so-called *Golden Age* of mountaineering lasted about 100 years from 1860 to 1960. During this period most of the important high peaks of the world were scaled for the first time. Gone forever is the ethos of the early mountain explorer, traveling without trails, maps, or contact with the civilized world. But something has been gained. Today's mountaineers can reach the most remote places on earth in a fraction of the time required by past generations.

It used to be that only rich gentlemen could afford to go on six-month expeditions to the Himalayas. Today many working people go to the same places during their holidays. There are many plums to be picked in the world of mountaineering besides being the first one to climb a peak. The first ascent is only the beginning. Infinite variations remain, each of them a new human endeavor: new routes, solo climbs, winter ascents, all-free ascents, pitonless ascents, and alpine-style climbs of mountains previously climbed only by big expeditionary seiges. Just this year a two-man party climbed 26,470-foot Gasherbrum I, one of the world's dozen highest peaks, by a new route, in alpine style. Their entire expedition consisted of the two of them!

—Galen Rowell

Why Cimb Mountains?

Whole volumes have been written without explaining the eternal question: why do men climb mountains? George Leigh Mallory, of Everest fame, uttered his famous words, "Because it is there," quite facetiously to a bunch of newsmen who were bugging him. No short answer can possibly uncover the complex reasons why people climb mountains.

Much of the lure is something rooted in the human psyche. An urge to search out the unknown. A desire to interact with the world, not just with other men. Raw adventure with a few classic tools. Perhaps the best short answer to the question was passed on to me by an eastern European climber. "Do you know what the Russians say," he told me with a grin. "They say alpinism is like sodomy with a goat: it's funny and dreadful and no use at all!"

Western culture has a strange penchant for usefulness. Lives, activities, tools—everything must be useful. A strict interpretation of evolution makes many people think they can discover nature's logic in everything. I'll be the first to admit that I can't find much usefulness in mountaineering.

Once I spent a day watching the antics of the world's greatest natural climber, a mountain goat. I thought I had a clear comprehension of what made goats climb. They avoided predators and sought food among the lush alpine vegetation. I was wrong. If any reader has a useful explanation after reading the following account, I'd like to hear it.

The events began when my actions in a remote meadow in Canada's Northwest Territories frightened a mountain goat onto a steep cliff. I watched it run across a headwall on which I had used ropes and pitons only a few days earlier. In fact, our climb had failed slightly higher up the cliff. With almost cruel pleasure, I approached the cliff and guarded the only possible descent from the bulging, 2000-foot wall. The goat tried every conceivable way of climbing down, but instead of stopping at a point where he began to feel uneasy, he pushed himself, as a climber would when trying something one grade above his standard. I nervously watched him pivot on a narrow stance, leap for a distant hold, and attempt a traverse that eventually ended in flawless granite. While wandering around the base I made a discovery: the broken, mummified body of another goat which evidently had fallen while climbing on the same cliff.

This shattered my foregone conclusion that animals have an innate sense of where to stop. I had watched dogs and cats who followed their masters into the mountains. They seemed to have good judgment, but this goat was carrying on in what seemed a manner foreign to nature. Most non-climbers would have called the goat crazy. I looked at the goat, up there taking chances, and I looked again at the broken body below the cliff. I realized that here was an animal that takes risks, just like human mountaineers. His reward was an aggressive alpine life. He was an animal counterpart of a timberline tree—pushing the fine edge of the limits of existence.

After several hours of watching the goat, I returned to camp, still in sight of the animal, but half a mile away. Instead of immediately descending and continuing in the direction he was originally headed, the goat stayed on the wall for quite some time. When he did come down, he looked to see if I was still watching. Just being cautious for once, I thought to myself. Wrong again!

My position now offered no threat to his passage, but he followed the base of the cliff in the opposite direction. At the first crack system he began to climb again, this time a flashy, 300-foot romp. At the top of the pedestal he pivoted a full circle, like a fashion model, then bounded down the cliff again. He repeated his antics in other spots, seeming to always make sure that I was watching. Finally, he headed casually in the direction he was originally going. Where was the instinctive animal prudence I had assumed?

The goat's antics appeared to have no survival value. If anything, I thought they merely seemed to be the dangerous frolockings of an alpine show-off, but on further reflection I realized my response to the goat's climbing was similar to the public's reaction to mountaineering. Products of the technological age, we are quick to condemn as frivolous any activity whose purpose we cannot explain with reason and logic. I realized that the goat's actions were like my own: funny and dreadful and no use at all.

—Galen Rowell

Galen Rowell is a well-known mountaineer who has scaled many peaks in his lifetime, including Yosemite's Half-Dome a dozen times. He is the editor of the fine book, ***The Vertical World of Yosemite.***

For More Information

There are four good mountain climbing publications. All cover rock climbing, too. *Climbing,* Box E, Aspen, Colo. 81611. Published bi-monthly at $5.50 per year. Beautiful color cover and well-illustrated on the inside. *Mountain Gazette,* 2025 York St., Denver, Colo. 80205. Published monthly at $6.00 per year. Not just on climbing but many issues carry excellent articles on the subject. Large format printed on newsprint. *Off-Belay,* 12416-169 Ave. S.E., Renton, Wash. 98055. Published bi-monthly at $7.50 per year. Outstanding photographers and a well put together magazine. *Summit,* P.O. Box 1889, Big Bear Lake, Calif. 92315. Published 10 times per year at $7.00. Each issue has a lot of color and good articles. Oldest of the magazines listed.

There are a lot of clubs and organizations but only three major ones. Alpine Club of Canada, Box 1026, Banff, Alberta, TOL OCO Canada. Puts out an excellent publication called The Canadian Alpine Journal. American Alpine Club, 113 E. 90th St., New York, N.Y. 10028. Only national organization. Publishes American Alpine Journal annually and more regularly the AAC News. Sierra Club, 530 Bush St., San Francisco, Calif. 94108. The club is not only involved with climbing. Published *Ascent* annually.

Equipment can be hard to find but here are a few addresses to get you started. Mountain Paraphernalia, Box 4536, Modesto, Calif. 95352. Equipment, books, etc. A total climbing shop run by well-known author/climber Royal Robbins. Climb High, 227 Main, Burlington, Vt. 05401. Distributor and manufacturer of quality equipment. Forrest Mountaineering, Ltd., 1517 Platte St., Denver, Colo. 80202. They publish a catalog full of climbing equipment. Eastern Mountain Sports, Box 626, Boston, Mass. 02215. Publish a really nice catalog for $1.00 that is full of climbing equipment and supplies. The North Face, 1234 5th St., Berkeley, Calif. 94710. Their catalog will be most interesting to you. The Great Pacific Iron Works, Box 150, Ventura, Calif. 93001. A good source for a lot of good equipment. One of the best. Gibbs Products, 854 Padley St., Salt Lake City, Utah 84108. Has a free catalog and gives a 20 percent discount with orders of over $90.

There are lots of books available on climbing. Here are a few. All are available from World Publications, Box 366, Mountain View, Calif. 94040 at the price listed* plus 25 cents each for postage. Write for a complete list.

Big Wall Climbing by Doug Scott. History of mountain climbing on all the major faces of the world. Nicely illustrated, 1974 Hb., 348 pp., ill., $12.50, (Oxford).

Field Book of Mountaineering and Rock Climbing, Lyman and Riviere. Covers the author's climbing experiences and techniques in clean and precise description. Gives an awareness of the conservation of alpine areas with the finer points of equipment, rope handling and more intertwined. 1975 Hb., 256 pp., $8.95, (Winchester).

Icecraft, Norman Kingsley. Probably the best coverage of climbing over ice. Well-illustrated with both photos and drawings. Cramponing, belaying, and more. 1975 Ppb., $3.95, (La-Siesta).

Medicine for Mountaineering, James A. Wilderson, M.D. Detailed examination of accidents and illnesses encountered at high altitude. 1967 Hb., 350 pp., $7.50, (Mountaineers).

Mountaineering Freedom of the Hills. This textbook is standard reading for every climber. All aspects from weather to equipment are well covered, with special attention to ice, snow, and routefinding. 3rd edition, Hb., 478 pp., $9.95, (Mountaineers).

Muzzle Loading

Muzzle loading, or black powder shooting, as it is often called, is the sport of shooting muzzle-loaders – rifles of the early American revolutionary and civil war eras. The name attached to this activity is derived from the fact that the rifle must be loaded through the muzzle. First, a charge of black powder is poured into the muzzle, followed by a projectile (or projectiles) which is rammed far down the barrel with the ramrod. Sometimes cloth patches are placed both beneath and over the projectile. The most common type of projectiles used are round balls, or minie bullets. The role of the patch is very important since, when properly lubricated and wrapped around the ball, it transmits spin to the ball, which is very important in successful shooting. When the ball leaves the rifle, the patch drops away, leaving the projectile freely propelled toward its destination.

The loading of this type of gun is, of course, very important, and is usually done according to the particular ideas of the individual. When a shooter hits, or comes close, to the bullseye on the target he can rest assured his method of loading is right. But if he misses often, he most likely will change loading methods. Usually the best accuracy and performance is obtained when there is a more-or-less tight fit between the patched ball and the bore.

The muzzle-loaders used by pioneers, revolutionary and civil war soldiers, and present-day black powder enthusiasts employ either the flintlock or percussion lock for ignition of the powder. In the flintlock system, a piece of flint, which is attached to the hammer of the rifle, strikes an upright piece of metal, showering sparks into a small charge of primary powder which, in turn, ignites the main charge. The key to the percussion system is the percussion cap, a small cup of copper into which is pressed a pellet of detonating compound. The black powder, or "gunpowder", is actually a brown material made from charcoal, sulphur and saltpeter. When graphite is added to this mix, the black (slate-grey) color results.

Today, muzzle-loading guns have been placed back into production, and many of these guns are sold each year. This type of shooting has become very popular, and the actual shooting competitions are often accompanied by a close study of the period of history of the particular rifle chosen. Often black powder shooters dress in the full costume of pioneers and historic soldiers when they get together. For example, twice a year over 2000 shooters assemble with their families at Fort Shenandoah, Va. to join over 150 teams or "regiments" that represent major civil war units from the various states. Attired in blue and grey, they take part in friendly, but determined marksmanship competition.

Black Powder Shooting Today

The use of muzzle-loading guns for hunting, target work and just plain pleasure shooting has never died out in our country, not even in the 20th century, long after the muzzle-loading system was obsolete. In fact, the sport not only held on but began a major rally around 1960. Today, black powder shooting ranks as the fastest growing segment of the shooting sports.

Why this resurgence? I don't think it can be attributed to one single factor. It is, instead, a combination of the proximity of the Civil War centennial, Revolutionary War bicentennial, an increased awareness and enjoyment of nature, and the need for the hunter or target shooter to sharpen his skills beyond those of his modern peer. Finally, there are now plenty of modern muzzle-loaders on the market to service the interested shooter.

I enjoy the sport because it is so relaxing. No matter whether one is hunting or target shooting, he cannot avoid slowing down and concentrating on the step-by-step tasks so vital to a successful, well-aimed shot.

People from all walks of life hunt and shoot with muzzle-loaders. Many people make their weekend shoots a family affair and take along their tents and campers. All in all, this sport is more family-oriented than any other function of the shooting sports.

Another boost for the sport lies in the fact that costly and elaborate equipment is not needed. Expensive guns are seen, of course, but these tend to be much less costly than their centerfire counterparts. In fact, many of the muzzle-loading guns are made by their owners, adding another measure of satisfaction to the sport. Typically, the guns themselves are very durable with barrels lasting many thousands of rounds beyond those of their centerfire high-velocity peers.

Hunting is perhaps the most visible growth area. Only a handful of states do not offer special muzzle-loading seasons and hunting areas. There are no more than one or two states, if that many, which do not permit big game hunting with a muzzle-loader during the regular firearms season.

The hunter is strongly challenged by the need to completely master his gun and the necessity of getting sufficiently close to his quarry to make the one shot count. Broadly speaking, only those who hunt with the handgun and bow face similar challenges.

—**Ken Ramage**

Ken Ramage has been shooting and hunting with a variety of black powder firearms for years. Presently, he works for Lyman Shooting Products, Middlefield, Ct., as publications manager and handbook editor. He is the editor of Lyman's **Black Powder Handbook** *and* **Black Powder Basics.**

For More Information

Two of the best publications are *The Muzzleloader,* Box 6072, Texarkana, Texas 75501. *Muzzle Blasts,* Box 67, Friendship, Ind. 47021. Both magazines have good information for muzzle loaders. *Muzzle Blasts* is the official magazine of the National Muzzle Loading Rifle Association at the same address. There is also the North-South Skirmish Association, 3062 N. 54th St., Milwaukee, Wis. 53210. This organization promotes marksmanship competition with the small arms and artillery of the Civil War era. Specifically, eight-man musket matches, five-man carbine team matches, five-man crew matches and standard individual matches with small arms. A bi-monthly publication called *The Skirmish Line* is their official publication and is available from Charles Hunter, 6214 29th St., N.W., Washington D.C. 20015. A good source for equipment is Golden Age Arms, 14 Winter St., Box 283, Delaware, Ohio 43015. Or Dixie Gun Works, Sun Powder Lane, Union City, Tenn. 38261 is supposed to have the most extensive muzzle-loading catalog available.

Here is a book on the sport. It is available from World Publications, Box 366, Mountain View, Calif. 94040 at the price listed* plus 25 cents postage.

Home Guide to Muzzle Loaders, George C. Nonte, Jr. A comprehensive study of muzzle-loading guns. Contains basic information for the new black-powder user as well as technical material for the experienced enthusiast. A directory of the dealers and suppliers is included. 1974 Ppb., 219 pp., ill., $6.95, (Stackpole).

Off-Road Vehicles

Everything is taxed when you're racing. Parts can come off. Traction is intermittent. You're in the air. You're coming down on one wheel. Going over boulders. Things are trying to put holes in your tires." That's what it is to race off-road, according to Steve Ellsworth, who's raced over the past dozen years with his brothers Doug and Sheldon. They won the Mint race in '68, the desert classic sponsored by the Mint Hotel in Las Vegas. Several times at Baja they've been up in the money, taking two thirds.

If you only want to chop down a $500 VW bug for non-competitive, off-road rambling, it doesn't take much. Take off the fenders and put on extra shocks and you're ready. The Volkswagen is especially suited for driving that takes you over rough terrain. It won't go far hauling logs, but it's lightweight, the short wheelbase keeps it from hanging up on rocks, and the rear engine adds weight and traction to the back wheels. A dune buggy can be further trimmed down so it consists of little more than two seats, framework, transmission, engine and tires. And it looks like it's all tires.

There are many other vehicles to choose from: Land Cruisers, Broncos, Scouts, Blazers, Chargers and more. Four-wheel drive pick-ups and jeeps are generally heavier and higher than the buggies, and hence more likely to roll.

You have to be careful because off-roading can take you into incredible places. For instance, if the vehicle is fitted with independent brakes, by locking the uphill rear wheel, and keeping power to the other rear wheel, you can stay upright while driving sideways on quite steep slopes.

Steve and his brothers race a Baja bug, and they see some of its advantages as the low gear ratio, full belly pan skid plate that protects it from below, and the trailing arm suspension that allows each wheel to get up and over rocks independently.

Much can be done, of course, to get a car ready to race hundreds of miles over a demanding desert course. The Ellsworth's Baja bug has 14 shocks. Steve estimates its total worth at $7-10,000. And more than powerful, the car is tough. Reliability is the key. Every part must be tight and right if it is to withstand hours or hurtling over rocks, streams, roads and lake beds. Bigger tires, 33" high, take some of the shock.

The engine, of course, is beefed up. Displacement on the Ellsworth's bug was pushed up from 1.6 to 2.2, the horsepower is tripled. They put on a modified cam, bigger valves, and ported heads. Compression is increased. An outside cooler and full-flow oil system keep the oil from overheating. All tolerances in the engine are closer than stock. The crank shaft is fully counterbalanced.

For driving in the dark at high speeds six lights are mounted at the front and at the sides. Like aircraft landing lights they light up the area in front and below, to show where the car will be landing when it's airborne.

For most racers a roll cage is not enough. They start with a complete chassis made of strong tubing and build a car around it.

The minimum safety requirement for races calls for a full roll cage built of tubing of a minimum thickness, held up by the proper triangular supports. It is required that gas tanks be strengthened so they don't puncture, and anti-drain valves be placed on the battery so it won't empty if the car turns upside down.

In an average field of 400 cars, Steve says, 25 will roll. Good preparation in no way ensures that you'll finish. It's an unusual race if half the cars finish. Experience teaches you how to minimize unexpected emergencies, though, such as when you fly off course. In that situation keeping your wheels straight will help keep you from flipping. "The desert always wins," Steve says. "All it takes is one mistake, and you've bought it."

You should carry tools for "whatever might happen." You can leave things such as your timing light at home, though. It won't slow you too much, or stop you, if the timing is jarred half a degree off one way or the other. More likely you'll need a big hammer to persuade your front wheels back into appropriate alignment. You'll need tire changing equipment, vice grips, tape and wire to jury rig whatever comes apart.

"You've got to be an excellent race driver, and be able to read terrain," Steve thinks. It takes a specific skill that's different than just knowing how to handle corners on the road. You have to be able to read bumps, an ability that might be developed downhill skiing or riding a motorcycle.

The average speed for a race is close to cruising speed on the freeway. But it's not a steady pace. The car might be tooling along at 5 mph in a streambed, then going over 100 on a lake bed. At that speed the dust finds its way under the best goggles. It flies up like bagfuls of fine flour, slapping your face and sifting through your clothes. And there's constant battering. You have to be "in shape" to make it through hours of such punishment.

To keep the car moving under these conditions takes a "good seat of the pants feel for the car," Steve says. How it sounds and how it drives can tell you when a breakdown is coming. If the car won't stay on the ground you know the shocks are probably wearing. If you know when something is going to give, you can slow down enough to finish.

"The sport used to be made up of a lot of backyard people. They'd get together a race and put up $10 for the winner," Steve remembers. He also remembers driving freely over 30 miles of mountain roads between his house in Mountain View, Calif., and the ocean. Most of those roads are now blocked off. Farmers are bothered by so many people seeking out the backroads.

Increasing numbers of people in the sport have made it more professional, especially in the last five or six years. It costs from $250 to $400 to enter many races now. To get a car ready can take $5000. The competition is keener for the bigger purses.

Despite these changes, the sport stays the same: churning around boulders and high-tailing it through the dust.

—Hugh Bowen

Hugh Bowen is an editor at World Publications. He has driven to Alaska and back in a jeep.

Fear and Loathing at Pismo Beach

There I was, sitting in my beloved bug that wouldn't start on a sand dune in the middle of the night at Pismo Beach. I was beginning to wonder if I would ever get out of that place at all. Every 15 or 20 minutes or so, I would brave the cold winds and rain and venture outside to see if I could figure why my loyal, trustworthy, faithful '64 Baja Bug did not want to move very much.

Since the weather was getting ominous, we decided we would forgo our planned campout and brave the coming storm in a motel. We started back when my car quit. Upon quick inspection, I discovered a broken distributor rotor. Luckily I carried a spare which I hastily installed. After a brief spurt of life, the engine died again. Another distributor rotor. In my haste I had not gotten the distributor cap fully seated. This was my last rotor. Putting the distributor rotor and cap on carefully, I expected the engine to bubble to life once more—but it was not to be. Steve tried to tow me with a rope, but the line broke ("the monkey got choked, and we all went to heaven in a little rowboat. Clap clap.")

I decided to stay with my bug through the night. The others went to town to a motel, saying they would be back for me first thing in the morning. All alone on the beach, I alternated between sitting in the lame bug trying to figure out why the engine wouldn't start and going outside each time I thought I had the answer (which was over and over and over . . .). Even though the wind was considerable and it was raining, I could see the lights of dune buggies zooming around on the dunes. Since I had come to rest at the bottom of a short, steep hill, I was in constant fear that some jeep or dune buggy would come bounding over the crest, rendering me unable to write this article. Then, in a blinding flash of light, that was right out of the movies, the truth, with a capital "T" came to me. If the rotor caught on the cap with enough force to break it, then it probably had enough force to move the distributor enough to change the timing. After a few minutes of furious fiddling, the wonderful beast was running. It was dawn by that time, and I waited for Steve and Scotty to show up. Hours passed and they didn't come. Finally they arrived, and after various adventures that involved crossing a creek, water gushing from our exhaust pipes, and coming to the stunning realization that we were lost, and sliding down unexpected slopes—we made it back to the hotel.

The next day the weather was beautiful. We went out to the beach and had the times of our lives. No mechanical problems at all. There were dune buggies all over the place, and everyone was having fun. About midday, we packed up and went home. The last few hours made the entire trip worthwhile, and we vowed to return (with a new distributor, of course!).

—Eric Norris

Eric Norris is experienced off-road, both in cars and on motorcycles. He is a political science major and is also vice-president of the Flat Earth Marching Band and Chowder Society.

For More Information

There are two publications of interest. *Off-Road,* 131 S. Barrington Place, Los Angeles, Calif. 90049. Published monthly at $9.00 per year. Oriented toward pick-ups, jeeps and campers. *Dune Buggies and Hot VWs,* Box 1757, 1499 Monrovia Ave., Newport Beach, Calif. 92663. Published monthly at $7.50 per year.

There are several organizations involved: The National All-Terrain Vehicle Association, 342 Broad St., New Bethelem, Penn. 16242 and Short Course Off-Road Enterprises, 2701 E. Anaheim, Wilmington, Calif. 90744 the group that standardized the rules for racing.

Here are some books of interest. All are available from World Publications, Box 366, Mountain View, Calif. 94040 at the price listed* plus 25 cents each postage. Write for a complete list.

Off-Road Racing, Monty Norris. Head for the Boondocks! In off-road racing, survival and finishing the course are as important as winning, and after reading this book, you'll know why. 1974 Hb., 148 pp., ill., $5.95, (Dodd, Mead).

Racing Engine Preparation, Waddell Wilson & Steve Smith. Approaching every part and section with an analytical mind, one of the country's most sought-after engine builders offers a complete mechanic's manual to building and tuning an engine. 1975 Ppb., 144 pp., ill., $7.50, (Steve Smith Autosports).

Orienteering

"Hey, let's go orienteering."

"Orien-what?"

"Orienteering. You know, kind of like a car rally only you're on foot."

"Yeh? How does it work?"

"Well, you use a map and compass. They give you a map at the meet site, and you can rent a compass there too. Wanna go?"

"Naw, I don't know anything about it."

"Nonsense, it's easy. The map they give you is a topographical map. It shows all the roads and streams and contours too. The course is marked on the map by a series of circles showing the places you have to go. All you have to do is go to the center of each circle, using any route you want. And the one to find them all in the quickest time is the winner."

"Really? Well how do you know when you're in the center of the cricle?"

"There's a marker there, a red and white marker with three sides about a foot square. If you're in the right place you can see it easily. And they got a little code letter on them so you know you're at the right marker."

"Sounds like fun. But how do they know if you went to all the markers?"

"Easy. There is a little punch that looks something like a clothespin at each marker. Each one has a different code and you just punch the code into a little card you carry with you. Then when you finish you turn the card into the officials and they check up on you."

"Great, but all you'd have to do is follow the guy in the lead and then sprint by him at the finish."

"Not so! They start you at two minute intervals and you're on your own with just a map and compass to guide you. If you do happen to meet someone in the woods you sure don't want to follow them. If they started ahead of you then they already goofed somewhere. And if they started behind you they'll be minutes ahead if you finish together. And who says the person you're following isn't completely lost? Besides, the real sense of accomplishment in this sport comes in just finishing a course the best way you can."

"I can understand that. But who wants to go out and get shown up by all those studs who go blitzen by so fast?"

"That's one of the beauties of it. Those fast guys can't always think as fast as they can run. And it doesn't make any difference how fast you can run if you're going the wrong way. Besides, they always have easier courses for beginners and longer courses for experienced orienteers. You just start at the beginning level and have fun working your way up. You'll be surprised how fast you learn. They even have way-faring courses that grandparents can walk through together. It's just fun getting in the outdoors and navigating in the woods. How about it? Wanna go try it this weekend?"

—Steve Andresen

Steve Andresen is Chairman of the Competition Committee of the United States Orienteering Federation. In 1973 he was the All-Marine and Quebec Orienteering champion.

"Of course no orienteering meet is complete without the classic 180 degree azimuth error. It is a simple task to align your compass to the South instead of North when placing it on the map." (Andresen)

Smile, It's Frustrating

Larry Long, twice North American Orienteering champion, once said that the most important aspect of orienteering was the ability to smile. And it is true that much of the fun and excitment of orienteering comes from the frustrating and comical experiences that inevitably arise at every orienteering meet. Without the ability to laugh at yourself and with others you may find orienteering too challenging to try.

For instance, the 1971 All-Marine Orienteering team ran into trouble before they even warmed up. They left Quantico, Virginia in a pick-up camper early one morning to go to Carbondale, Illinois for the Southern Illinois University Orienteering meet. The team captain slept in the camper until hunger caused him to look out the window for a place to eat. Imagine his surprise when he saw the sign that said, 'Pittsburgh, Right Lane.' They were far off their route and rightly embarrassed. Of course they didn't tell anyone at the meet. In fact it was a military secret until this ex-Marine (not on the '71 team) decided to tell.

Since orienteering is such a young sport in America, many people are curious and skeptical about what is going on. Dick Adams, then an aspiring young orienteer, can verify that it is not always easy to explain orienteering. Dick was searching for a control marker located on top of a big forested hill. At the bottom of the hill was a large field with one corner right below the point where the control marker was supposed to be. Since the field would be easy to find, it was a logical route choice to go to the field and then shoot a compass azimuth uphill to the control. Dick did just that. But his azimuth was slightly off and after looking vainly for the control, Dick went back to the corner of the field to try again. Just as he was set to head back into the woods again he heard a loud 'click,' and turned to face the business end of a big double-barrelled shotgun.

"Whatcha doin' here, Sonny?" asked the old Virginia farmer.

There was Dick clad in a tight fitting, brightly colored nylon orienteering suit. He was covered with sweat and had scratches all over his hands and face. The only things he had in his hands were his map and compass. Imagine trying to convince that farmer that he was just playing a game.

And you can't blame the famer for being upset. He had been seeing all these weirdos charging up the hill after stopping in the corner of his field. He just wanted to check things out.

Well, it took Dick five minutes to convince the man to put the shotgun down and another five minutes for a quick lecture on orienteering. To top it all off, the meet director refused to deduct the time from Dick's total. He just walked away mumbling something about natural course hazards.

It is a frustrating experience to be lost. But no orienteer was ever quite as frustrated as one young American on his first orienteering experience in Canada. He had missed the marker and not realizing where he was he ended up running off the map. Frustration was growing stronger after many attempts to find himself and it was with great relief that he heard traffic not too far away. He ran to the road and flagged down a passing motorist. That was no easy task because orienteering is fairly new in Canada too. But finally someone stopped and he climbed in and explained his situation. Imagine his dismay when the answer came back in French. The man knew no English at all. Finally the unlucky orienteer talked him into a ride to the city where he called for help. The next day he laughed off the whole episode and placed high in the second race.

And of course no orienteering meet is complete without the classic 180 degree azimuth error. It is a simple task to align your compass to the South instead of North when placing the compass on the map. Then when the orienteer takes off it is the exact opposite direction from where he wants to go. In the excitement of competition it is easy to make that simple mistake, and the frustration that follows is sometimes unbearable. The most important thing is not to let anyone know you made such a dumb mistake.

I had orienteered many times and had never made a 180 degree error. This day the competition was really stiff and I was nervous even as I approached the fourth control. Don Davis, one of the best orienteers in the country, was right behind me. That made me feel even more nervous and pressed for time. I punched the control, set my compass, and took off. The compass pointed straight up a large hill. I really pushed hard because Davis was a super runner and I didn't want him to pass me. About three quarters of the way up the hill I took a look over my shoulder. Davis wasn't following. He was standing at the control laughing so loud I thought everyone in the woods would hear. He had stood at the control for nearly three full minutes watching me run uphill. Then he hollered "180" real loud and loped off through the woods. I was far behind him, dead tired, and frustrated, but my biggest worry was what Davis would be telling everyone at the finish.

Then there are the personal mistakes a person likes to keep to himself. I was taught to pace-count constantly while orienteering. That way you can always tell how far you have gone. I was counting my paces very well at the beginning of a race. But as fatigue set in, my mind started playing tricks. I had just covered a long distance at a face pace and stopped to check my map. After a few seconds I realized I was still counting. But it wasn't my paces, it was my breaths. I had no idea how long I had been doing that, and therefore no idea how far I had come.

It is an unwritten rule in orienteering to give the wrong information if someone asks where they are. In the levels of high competition this deception is an art. Runners turn and run the wrong direction just to fool others nearby. This writer was the biggest fool in orienteering. I had reached the area of the first control in a big race and found the marker there to have the wrong code letter on it. I checked the description sheet again and finally located the correct marker hanging over the edge of a big cliff. Just as I was ready to leave another orienteer appeared. It was Bob Turbyfill, the toughest competitor I had in that race.

"Did you find it?" he asked.

"Nope, wrong code. I've leaving for number two." I was hoping he'd punch the wrong one and leave with me. But he played it cool and checked everything out. I knew he would find it but I was still in the lead. Later I saw him again. He was coming down a large valley just as I was starting up. Now it really seemed strange because if the marker was up in the valley he shouldn't be running down but up.

"It's in the wrong place!" he said as he swept by me. "Must be in the next one."

Little did I know he was telling the truth. But I was sure he had found it and was just doubling back to screw me up. And he knew that is what I would think so he wasn't surprised at all when I started up the valley anyway. He found it in the next little valley and ended up winning the race by two minutes. We are still very good freinds, though, because we can both smile at our orienteering.

It should be mentioned that it isn't all cut-throat competition and frustrating mistakes. In my first big orienteering competition I met a guy from the West Coast named Kip Sturdevan. We met at the second control of the All-Marine Championships, and then both took off on different routes to the third control. We met again there. He then plunged through a waist deep stream so I followed. We ran similar routes to number four and met again. Number five had a very long run through an open field and we matched each other stride for stride for nearly a mile. Then it was over a barbed wire fence and 200 meters to the control. I reached the fence first and tried to scramble my 6'2" frame over it. Short little Kip just popped underneath and was off into the woods. I was caught by one leg and one arm, hanging precariously over the fence, my map blowing away in the breeze. Suddenly Kip stopped and ran back to the fence. He helped me get unhooked and we were off again, trying to beat each other any way we could think of. We ended up a mere two minutes apart after a week long competition and over nine hours of total orienteering time. We both made the team and I made a friend, the best trophy an athlete ever won. Somehow all the frustration seems worth it. As a matter of fact all those frustrations were fun. I think I'll do it again.

—Steve Andresen

For More Information

The United States Orienteering Federation, Box 1081, Athens, Ohio 45701 is the major organization in the US. They have over 35 clubs throughout the United States. The Federation issues a newsletter called *Control Point* and a journal called

Orienteering - USA. Both can be obtained by sending $5.00 to the Federation. The only regularly issued magazine (in English) is *The Orienteer,* British Orienteering Federation, Lea Green, Matlock, Derby DE4 5GJ England. Published bimonthly at $4.50 per year.

Here are some sources for equipment: George Harris, American Orienteering Service, Box 547, LaPorte, Ind. 46350, general equipment; Sports Inc., 12 S. Court St., Athens, Ohio 45701, general equipment; Bill Rusin, American Orienteering Service, 308 W. Fillmore, Colorado Springs, Co. 80907, training films; Abar Plastic Inc., 10801 Tucker St., Beltsville, Md. 20705, plastic bags; and Silva Co., Box 547, LaPorte, Indiana 46350, compasses which are the best you can buy and used around the world.

Steve Andresen is working on a book and it will be published soon. When you write for a complete list of books, we'll include this new one. All books listed are available from World Publications, Box 366, Mountain View, Calif. 94040 at the price listed* plus 25 cents postage.

Orienteering, John Disley. This new-to-America sport (a sort of auto rally without the automobile for cross-country runners or skiers) calls for speed, stamina and intelligence. This book is a complete guide to the history, traditions, rules and techniques of the sport. 1973 Ppb., 170 pp., ill., $3.95, (Stackpole).

Be an Expert with Map and Compass, Bjorn Kjellstrom. The author teaches orienteering and many other map and compass games as a means of learning accurate land navigation. Once you have mastered the information in this book, it will be difficult to ever be lost again. Includes practice map and compass. 1967 Ppb., 136 pp., ill., $3.95, (Scribner's).

Know the Game Series. Good beginner's guide to the skills of orienteering. Describes clearly types of maps, the event itself, how to prepare for competition, map making, and how to train for orienteering. 1975 Ppb., 47 pp., ill., $1.50, (E.P. Publishing).

Outdoor Photography

Outdoor photography is a special branch of the graphic arts, a special part of outdoor activity, an attempt to extend an experience or suspend a moment.

Why do people take pictures? For many reasons, but basically they boil down to an attempt to capture on film a time, a place, an especially beautiful scene, a face or body, form or texture, perhaps a group or mood. It is a way of perpetuating the present, of solidifying a moment in time, of replacing the mind's eyes.

Ancient Greeks talked about the dead as shades, likely because as memory fades with time, the faces of the departed became less distinct, gradually fading into shadow.

But with a camera you can capture that face and preserve it for as long as the picture lasts and thereby—through shades and shadow—extend the duration of that special face or form or scene.

Photography can be aptly described as the eye's mind. Not only does the camera (from the Greek *kamara,* which means vaulted chamber, like the brain cavity of the human body) capture images of the present and store them for future use like our mind, but it can also create through the lens or in the darkroom. This creation, no matter how unique and apparently different from any actual image, is only a reproduction of an object, even though it may have been filtered, enlarged, reversed or reduced to produce a new creation.

"Subjects for outdoor photographers warrant special comment. Too many aspiring photographers just take pictures. They see a lovely scene, open the camera and fire away with little or no thought to composition or to subject matter. Good pictures require thought and care if the eye's mind is to be put to use effectively." (TOSRVPHOTO)

On the mantle of a log cabin near Moose, Wyo. is engraved: "The wonder of the world, the beauty and the power, the shapes of things, their colours, lights, and shades: these I saw. Look ye also while life lasts." This inscription was originally found on an old gravestone in a Cumberland, England cemetery. As an outdoor photographer I harken to these words again and again. Perhaps what we are trying to do is help others see "the beauty and the power, the shapes of things, their colours, lights and shades."

Successful outdoor photographers—amateur or professional—will disagree on many aspects of the art: the best camera, the proper film, the appropriate format, the right kind of lighting, the best time of day or year to shoot photos, but a few rules become almost standard. You need good equipment and film.

But beyond the camera and film, an outdoor photographer needs knowledge, experience and a subject. Knowledge—both of your equipment and your subject—and experience comprise technique. As you use your camera and try different film, you gain knowledge and experience. It's a good idea to keep records of your subjects and the kind of film used, the light information (f-stop and shutter speed) so that you can learn a lot more quickly from your mistakes and successes.

Subjects for outdoor photographers warrent special comment. Too many aspiring photographers just take pictures. They see a lovely scene, open the camera and fire away with little or no thought to composition or to subject matter. Good pictures require thought and care if the eye's mind is to be put to use effectively.

Just what are you shooting at? What do you really want to capture here? Perhaps it's too far away for a meaningful picture. Perhaps the light isn't right. Will the background distract from or enhance the picture? Is this the right moment or should I wait a minute for that cloud to pass (or an hour for the sun to hit that rock wall)? If you expect to function as the eye's mind, you must be constantly thinking and applying your technique.

As a final suggestion, create the picture in your view finder. If what you see doesn't look like what you want, don't shoot. What you see is usually what you get. Make use of sunlight and shadow, of color, of back lighting, of different speeds (to give running water that blurred look of movement or to stop a raft in mid-rapid), and of different f-stops to diffuse the background. In a word experiment! Enjoy yourself and your pictures, and learn as you gain experience and improve your technique.

—**Verne Huser**

Verne Huser is a regular contributor to **Down River** *and he supplies his own photos with each article.*

"Photographers can be likened to artists who paint with light. Whether you use black and white or color film, the only thing that will make a picture is light. Because of the ever changing qualities of it, there are many tricks to learn about its angle, its intensity, and its degree of diffusion." (Huser)

In the Beginning

In the 16th century, Giovanni Battista Della Porta described the first camera. It was a remarkable instrument, but was thought to be of little practical use since the thing was so large it could not be moved once it had been constructed. It was more like a small building than the camera we know today. The "photographer" sat inside of this affair and drew the image that was projected through a pinhole in one side and onto the back wall. Since the camera was invented long before film, a photographer needed to be something of an artist. The image was large and was reproduced by tracing in great detail. Della Porta was accused of sorcery for his trouble, but photography was on its way.

First came the moveable sedan camera, then smaller models which allowed the photographer to remain outside the camera itself. Soon, various people began to experiment with different kinds of emulsions, which later became plates, and then film. But still the art of photography was reserved for a few, mostly the very rich.

This remained the state of the art with minor improvements until recently. Even 40 years ago an instrument with which you could make a consistently sharp, clear photograph was very expensive, and quite large.

Today, thanks to technical improvements in both the equipment and its method of manufacture, almost anyone can afford a camera which is capable of producing fine photographs. In addition, these modern cameras are small enough to be carried in one hand by even the youngest child.

Not only has the camera itself undergone a transformation, but the corollary equipment has as well. Film has been improved to the point of being able to handle almost any light condition, even the total absence of light as in the case of infra-red film.

Lenses are so refined as to be almost unbelieveable. There is a story of one lens on a satellite that took a photograph so sharp you could read the time on a man's wristwatch from more than a hundred miles out in space.

The outdoor photographer has never had so much technology at his immediate disposal as today. Whether you use an inexpensive drugstore camera or a $2000 Hasselblad, you can expect to get quality reproductions at a reasonable cost.

—**Jerry Pickrell**

Jerry Pickrell writes "Watching and Wading," a column on wild animals, for **Down River** *magazine. He supplies his own photos of each animal.*

Using the Light

An outdoor photographer often faces problems which a studio photographer cannot understand. When a studio man needs a different light angle, he simply changes the position of his floodlights. In contrast, an outdoor photographer may have to run halfway around a mountain to change his light angle. Not only that, but after setting up his camera, focusing to precision, making all the light adjustments and tripping the shut'ter, he may look up to find that the bird he was trying to photograph just took off! My own files are full of photographs of birds feet seemingly suspended from the sky.

Outdoor photography, especially wildlife work, is a lot like hunting, only more difficult. Not only do you have to get close to the animal, but you must do it in a favorable light condition and in such a way as to not alarm the subject. No one enjoys seeing pictures of a deer that is scared to death and only an instant from headlong flight into the woods.

Photographers can be likened to artists who paint with light. Whether you use black and white or color film, the only thing that will make a picture is light. Because of the ever changing qualities of light, there are many tricks to learn about its angle, its intensity, and its degree of diffusion.

Many light factors come into play and, with experience, can be used to great advantage.

Landscapes, for example are greatly enhanced by being shot early in the morning or late in the afternoon. During these hours of the day, the sun angle is very low, deepening shadow and lending depth to the photograph. This technique can also be applied to animals to add detail to the skin of an alligator or the shell of a turtle. Shooting with the sun directly overhead will fill in the shadows and make an alligator look smooth, so wait until the light angle is more favorable in the afternoon.

Direct sunlight seldom adds to the effect of a photograph, so low angle and diffuse light is nearly always preferable. A lightly overcast day is an especially good time to make color pictures, particularly close-up shots. Overcast tends to spread light and give an even appearance that enhances color. In addition, color film tends to be high contrast and subdued light will soften it.

If you wish to make pictures showing the clouds you will, of course, not want to choose an overcast day. Usually color film can handle this assignment well without any extra equipment, but a polarizing filter will make the clouds stand out better without adding or subtracting colors. When using black and white film, the additional of a yellow filter along with the polarizer will result in a more dramatic sky. A red filter will change the skin tones of any people in a black and white photo, but it will make the clouds stand out very dramatically, almost as if they were set in a black sky. Manufacturers' labels on filters should be read carefully to determine what effect their use will have on the proper exposure since some filters will reduce light entering a camera by a factor of two. If your camera has an internal light meter, this will be no

Beautiful subjects abound in nature. For shots like this we recommend an SLR with Plus-X and f-11 at 1/125th. You might even consider using a yellow filter to make a subject stand out from the background. (Krips)

problem, but for those who use a hand held meter it will be necessary to make final adjustment after the reading has been taken.

Getting a proper exposure with the film you are using is critical to obtaining a workable negative. The use of a light meter is always advisable, but occasionally this is not possible. A good rule of thumb for these occasions is to set your exposure for a bright sunny day with a lens opening of f11 and a shutter speed of one over the ASA of the film you are using. For example, a film with an ASA rating of 125 should be shot at f11 and 1/125th of a second on a bright day. If the day is less than bright, or if you are particularly interested in some shadow or detail, the exposure can be adjusted from there. This rule of thumb applies equally to black and white and color films, and may prove to be very handy for the outdoor photographer who often has so little time to set up his shots.

With practice you will learn to always be conscious of minute changes in light conditions and automatically adjust your habits and camera to suit them. Once this happens, you will surprise yourself at how quickly you can respond to shoot a fine picture when others are still fumbling with assorted gadgets. The key to this ability is volume. Shoot as many photos as you possibly can to get used to the way in which your equipment responds. When you know your camera and the way it will function under a number of different conditions, you will be ready for even the toughest situation.

—Jerry Pickrell

Selecting the Camera

There are two basic groups of cameras being used by both indoor and outdoor photographers–the range finder or reflex types. Reflex cameras are further subdivided into the twin lens and the single lens reflex.

When using a range finder camera, the photographer looks through a view finder which operates independently of the lens taking the picture. He focuses this view finder, which in turn focuses the lens automatically by means of a linkage. Usually the viewfinder shows a split image, the halves of which must be aligned to result in a single clear image. When this has been done, the camera is in focus and the photograph is ready to be made.

Twin lens reflex types are usually "boxy" in appearance, and are focused by looking through a view finder mounted on the top of the camera. As their name implies, they are equipped with two lenses. One is sighted through to compose and focus the photograph, while the other admits light to the film and is the operable portion of the camera's lens system. One must be careful when using this type of camera especially for outdoor work, since the sighting lens is not seeing exactly what the camera will see. The angle of difference, called *parallax,* is generally negligible, but can be dangerous to picture composition. You might have set your camera beautifully, composed the picture well through its view finder, and tripped the shutter with a good steady hand, only to find that the picture taking lens was obscured by a leaf which wasn't visible through the focusing lens.

Of all the types of cameras available, a single lens reflex is the most versatile and desirable for outdoor photography. With this camera you can compose and form a picture by looking directly through the lens of the camera. In essence, "What you see is what you get." In addition to this, single lens reflex cameras are normally the only ones with interchangable lenses. With a shorter focal length lens for wide angle viewing, a longer one for telephoto shots, and the standard lens that comes with the camera, an outdoor photographer is equipped for virtually any photography situation. For died in the wool camera bugs, there are many graduations of long and short lenses, but a wide angle, a standard length, and a telephoto are all that most of us will ever need.

Unless you are a professional, it will take surprisingly little cash to equip yourself. It always pays to buy the best camera you can afford, but never avoid making pictures with whatever is at hand. Many very fine photos have been made with only a drugstore camera. The most important thing is the photographer, not the camera. Learn to use it well, and almost any camera will give you fine service.

—Jerry Pickrell

For More Information

Four magazines, all available on the newsstand, can be very useful for the outdoor photographer. They are, *Popular Photography, Modern Photography, Petersen's Photographic Magazine* and *Camera 35.* And *Consumer Guide* just recently published *Photo '76* which gives information on cameras and photographic equipment. The Photographic Society of America, 20005 Walnut St., Philadelphia, Pa. 19103 and the Associated Photographers International, 9426 Santa Monica Blvd., Beverly Hills, Ca. 90210 can both be of help. Here are a few books of interest. All are available from World Publications, Box 366, Mountain View, Calif. 94040 at the price listed* plus 25 cents each postage. Write for a complete list.

The Writer-Photographer, John Milton. How to put a story together and how to illustrate it with a camera are the essence of this book by a writer-photographer whose work has appeared in many publications. 1972 Ppb., 196 pp., ill., $4.95, (Chilton).

Taking Pictures From the Air, Don Downie. Widen your photographic perspective by getting high on aerial photography. This book has everything about the basics of aerial photography for still or movie camera. What to shoot and when, use of black and white or color film. Ppb., $3.95, (Crown).

How to Call Wildlife, Byron Dalrymple. The book reveals field-proven techniques for getting wildlife into range of gun or camera, illustrated with 125 photos of equipment techniques, and callers in action. 1975 Hb. & Ppb., 192 pp., ill., $7.50/ $4.50, (Crowell).

The Craft of Photography, David Vestal. This is becoming the comprehensive guide to black-and-white photography. Written by one of the country's most famous photographers, it includes detailed discussions of equipment; step-by-step instruction and techniques. 1975, 384 pp., ill., $12.50, (Harper & Row).

Outdoor Photographer's Digest, Erwin & Peggy Bauer. Learn which is the best equipment to take along on hunting, fishing, camping, hiking, boating and skiing trips. Covers lenses, filters, camera and carrying cases. Even gives tips on how to shoot action that will sell. 1975 Ppb., 288 (oversize) pp., ill., $7.95, (Digest Books).

Hunting With a Camera, Erwin A. Bauer. A world guide to wildlife photography. "Hunting With a Camera should become a textbook for anyone involved in taking pictures of wildlife, be he beginner or pro."—Dayton Daily News. 1974 Hb., 352 (oversize) pp., ill., $12.95, (Winchester).

Over The Line

What is Over-the-Line? The rules are simple. You need two teams of three people each, a ball and a bat. Your own teammate pitches the ball and you bat it over a line (hence the name) located 55-feet away down a 60-foot corridor without the opponents catching it. Sounds easy—anyone can do it, that is true—but, like any sport, some people become very proficient at it.

What makes it unique is that there are no special physical restrictions except coordination. You do not have to be big and strong, tall, muscular, gutsy, or even very intelligent.

The game is very popular these days in Southern California with interest spreading across the country and inquiries increasing.

Over-The-Line has many variations. It can be played on dirt, grass, playgrounds, or the beach. The center and home-ground of the sport is in San Diego, Calif., where each summer tournaments are sponsored by the Old Mission Beach Athletic Club (OMBAC).

In 1975, 600 three-man teams played 1200 games in the "22nd Annual World Championship Over-The-Line Tournament." The tournament is played on beach sand under official tournament rules established by OMBAC. These rules are accepted as the official guidelines for all Over-The-Line tournaments played today. The "World Championship Tournament" has three divisions—Open, Women and Century (accumulative ages add to 100 or more)—and is played over two weekends in July on 18 playing courts.

Over-The-Line started on the beach years ago in Mission Beach, Calif. Mission Beach is a small peninsula of sand which at that time did not have many residents. It was difficult to find enough kids to field a team of any size so Over-The-Line was the answer. It has progressed from a local beach boy game to today, where many people of all ages play.

The rules are described below. After reading them you can see they are fairly loose as far as method and individual play are concerned. Because of this, different styles and strategies are common. For instance, your teammate can pitch from anywhere in front of "the line." Some stand back 10-15 feet and pitch a soft liner. Others kneel right next to the batter and just lob the ball up like you would pitch to yourself. Batters will hit the ball on the way up, on the way down or switch from one method to another. Some hit the ball when it is only a few inches off the ground with a "golf" swing (which is more difficult and takes more practice).

The fielders adapt to the batter's style with different defenses. The standard defense has the three fielders in a row—front man, middle man, and back. This will change if you face a batter who is basically a "place hitter" by playing a two man front or a staggered defense. Facing a long ball hitter, naturally you play back further. Obviously, there are many combinations.

In addition to the "World Championship Tournament," OMBAC sponsors a Junior Tournament in August for kids, with four divisions—boys and girls 8-12 years old and boys and girls 13-15 years old. Over 100 teams played in 1975. The rules are the same for everyone, except girls may wear gloves and the courts are smaller for the mini-people.

The membership of OMBAC is a myriad of people, most of whom are connected to the beach by residence, birthplace, or love of the beach, surf, and fun. The membership is comprised of gardeners, tradesmen, blimp pilots, and other professions, all having one common interest—the sun and OMBAC's sporting activities.

These activities include the volume of Over-The-Line tournaments mentioned above and also lob ball, a basketball tournament, golfing, snow skiing, water skiing, tubing (floating down the Colorado River), a women's and men's volleyball team and a women's and men's rugby team.

—**Michael Curren**

Michael Curren is not only a director of the Old Mission Beach Athletic Club but also carries the distinction of being one of the original founders of Over-The-Line and a five-time winner of the OTL tournament. Of his favorite game he says, "We're not a bunch of buffoons conducting an orgy. This is an athletic event!"

The Official Rules

The only things you need for an invigorating game of Over-The-Line is six players (three players to a team), a softball or Little League bat, a regulation size football, and a fairly open, unobstructed flat area (a flat section of the beach is perfect). Set up a playing field, marking the lines accurately. Home doesn't have to be marked with an "iron cross" (if you want to play "regulation" it should be, though)—a shirt or other marker will do. The same goes for the foul lines. The line, however, should be clearly marked in its entirety. On the beach, it is easy to etch it in the sand.

Once the field is in order you can begin the actual game. One team takes their place at bat, the other in the field. The first batsman takes his position at home while a teammate pitches to him from anywhere in front of the line or its extensions. Players on the fielding team may take positions anywhere past the line.

Unlike baseball, there are only two kinds of "hits" in Over-The-Line: a hit and a home run. Any ball hit into fair territory on the fly without being caught by fielders is a hit, as is any ball that is touched and dropped by fielders. A hit is also scored for the team at bat if a fielder crosses the line or its extensions when attempting to catch a ball. Thus, at no time should fielders cross from one side of the line or its extensions to the other when catching or attempting to catch a hit ball. To avoid penalty (a hit scored for the team at bat) a fielder must make a definite stop before crossing the line. If he catches the ball and his momentum carries him across the line, it is a penalty (hit). A home run is counted as any ball hit past the last man in fair territory, on the fly without him touching it. It only has to go past him, not necessarily over his head.

As in baseball, a team is allowed three outs while at bat before taking its turn in the field. The following are counted as outs: (1) two foul balls, (2) one strike, (3) fly balls caught by fielder, (4) ball hitting line(s) around out area, (5) ball touched or dropped by batter or pitcher (a ball caught on the fly by either the batter or pitcher counts as a "no pitch." Foul tips that hit the batter and land in foul territory are foul), (6) pitcher crossing the line after a hit ball. Fouls are counted as any ball landing outside the "out" or "fair" areas on a fly. Foul line "liners" are foul.

But how do you score, and how long is the game? Three hits in an inning scores one run. Each additional hit in the same inning scores one more run. Home runs "clear the bases." Intentional throwing of the bat is a three run penalty. Games last for five innings unless the score is tied at the end of five, when an additional inning to break the tie is played. If tied after six, play one more. If the game is still tied after seven innings, the team with the most hits is the winner. If a tie exists in hits, play additional innings until the tie is broken, either by hits or by runs. Runs take preference over hits in this situation. If at the end of an inning, a team has an 11 or more run lead, the game is over.

O.K. You're ready to play, except for a few small details. No gloves can be used for fielding (except by the girls). In official competition, taping of hands and fingers is permissible if padding is used. Golf gloves may be used while batting. Also, you must have a full (three man) team to start a game. There is no warming up allowed on playing courts. Games are to be begun immediately.

If more than two teams are involved in an Over-The-Line tournament then the winning team of a game (all three members) will serve as officials for the next game on the same court. The captain of the winning team will be responsible for keeping track of the game ball. Any team not ready to play within five minutes after the completion of the previous game will forfeit.

There you have it! As you can see, Over-The-Line is no variation of hop-scotch. If you can convince your friends of this fact, then a ball and a bat might open up new possibilities on your next trip to the beach or the park. Oh—don't forget to bring the rules along!

—Michael Curren

For More Information

Additional information can be obtained from the Over-The-Line Committee, Old Mission Beach Athletic Club, San Diego, Calif. 92109.

Paddleball

In 1930, Earl Risky of the University of Michigan got the idea for paddleball while watching tennis players using the handball courts to practice their strokes. Actually the playing court, rules and equipment of the game are basically the same as those of another offshoot of handball, racquetball (see Racquetball), with one important difference: instead of a strung racket, paddleball is played with either a solid paddle or one with small holes bored into it, made of wood, steel, or plastic. With this solid paddle, a player is not able to impart as much spin on the ball, or hit it as hard as he might with a strung racket. Thus paddleball may offer an advantage for some people who are seeking a slower game and a less complicated one due to less ball spin. It might be best to try both games and see which one you like best. Remember that each game offers the same opportunities for exercise and enjoyment.

Like handball, paddleball may be played either in the one-three- or four-wall versions. Most outdoor courts are of the one-wall or three-wall type, while four-wall is played, of course, in an enclosed room.

Although the growth of paddleball is evident mostly in the East, especially in New York City, it is gaining in popularity nationwide.

One-Wall Paddleball

One-wall paddleball is among the fastest growing games in the northeastern United States. There are over 100,000 enthusiasts in the metropolitan New York area alone, and the popularity of the game is spreading to the south and midwest.

The reason for this rapid growth is basically the ease of learning the game and the attraction of "instant participation" with which the game can be learned. Another important reason behind the game's acceptance is that the equipment required is truly minimal, and the cost of the equipment is affordable to almost everybody. A wooden paddle ($4 to $20), a rubber ball (pink hi-bounce 40 cents, or a black handball – $1.25), and a pair of sneakers (tennis or basketball – which almost everybody owns), comprise the totality of the requirements.

The game is played on a standard one-wall handball court to be found in most schoolyards, many parks, and some indoor gymnasia. The objective and rules of the game are the same as for one-wall handball; the only difference being that the ball is struck with the paddle rather than the palm of the the bare hand.

The two basic forms of the one-wall paddleball game are: singles—one player versus one opponent; and doubles—team of two players versus two opponents.

In either type of play, the player (or team) serving is the only one that can score a point. When the defensive player (or team) wins the rally being played, he wins the serve but does not score a point. In doubles, both partners on a team must lose their serve before the defensive team takes over the service. The first player or team to score 21 points wins the game, which must be won by a minimum 2-point margin.

The server must stand behind the short line and no further back than the service line. The service is accomplished by bouncing the ball on the ground once, hitting the ball upon the rebound from the ground against the front wall from which it must bounce between the short and long lines. At this point, the opponent must return it to the front wall on the fly after it has bounced not more than once. A serve landing in front of the short line or behind the long line is a fault. Two faults result in loss of service. When two opposing teams are well matched, service will change hands many times.

The game ends when one player or team has won 21 points. Generally, the best two out of three games constitutes a match.

Players who rise to tournament competition invariably play with either hand; that is, they switch the paddle from hand to hand during the course of play. At this level of competition a player does not rely exclusively on sheer power. He will utilize the lob, deep and passing shots, drop shots and a great deal of finesse. At its best, one-wall paddleball is a fast, graceful, exciting game that provides great satisfaction to the player and spectator alike.

—**Howard Hammer**

Howard Hammer is a three-time national singles paddleball champion and was twice on the USPA doubles championship team. He is the author of **Paddleball – How to Play the Game.**

For More Information

There are two organizations active in paddleball: American Paddleball Association, 197 Fulton St., Massapequa, N.Y. 11758 and the United States Paddleball Association, 243 E. 27th St., New York, N.Y. 10010. They can supply you with good information. There are no magazines yet just on paddleball but *Tennis* magazine which can be found on most newsstands has a regular column on the sport.

Here are a couple of books on the subject. Check racquetball for more books. All are available from World Publications, Box 366, Mountain, View, Calif. 94040 at the price listed* plus 25 cents each postage. Write for a complete list.

Paddleball: How to Play the Game, Howard Hammer. A step-by-step method teaching the essentials of this fast-growing sport. Complete information for players, officials, and fans. 1972 Ppb., 96 pp., ill., $2.95, (Grosset & Dunlap).

Paddleball & Racquetball, Fleming and Bloom. This fast-moving game, first developed in the 1930s, is completely explained by this guide, which analyzes the rules of the game, strategy, and all basic strokes. 1973 Ppb., 97 pp., ill., $3.95, (Goodyear).

Paddle Tennis

Paddle tennis was originated more than 75 years ago by Frank Peer Beal as a playground game for children. Reverend Beal simply halved the dimensions of a regular tennis court, making the court 39 feet by 18 feet—exactly one-fourth the area of a tennis court. All of the rules of tennis were retained except that short-handled wooden paddles and hard rubber balls were used instead of strung tennis rackets and tennis balls. The game was especially attractive to young players, since the short-handled paddle made it easy to control the ball, and learning the basic skills was simple. In addition, it required less space and was cheaper to play than tennis.

The game was first introduced in New York City where Reverend Beal was Associate Minister of Judson Memorial Church in Greenwich Village. In 1922, Washington Square Park was the site of the first city-wide paddle tennis tournament conducted by the New York City Department of Parks and Recreation. The sport soon spread to other cities across the country, notably Los Angeles and its suburbs, attaining wide popularity in the late 1920s and early 1930s.

The high point was attained during the Great Depression on the wings of a massive work program sponsored by the federal government which poured hundreds of millions of dollars into the nation's municipalities for the construction and maintenance of playgrounds.

"The game is a natural. It can be played on any flat surface. The required area is comparatively small. Paddles are inexpensive, long-lasting and you never have to worry about stringing. Although the beginner can enjoy paddle tennis, it takes a real athlete to play in tournament competition."

More than 1000 39 feet by 18 feet paddle tennis courts were constructed in New York City Park and Recreation Department playgrounds, including four to eight courts painted on the bottom cement surface of each of the expansive outdoor municipal swimming pools for use during the fall and winter months. The more than 100 playgrounds constructed in Los Angeles each had from two to six paddle tennis courts. Jones Beach, the showplace of the Long Island State Park Commission, had 24 courts, and Jacob Riis Park in Queens had six courts.

With the passage of time, interest in the children's game waned. The original court and rules had built-in weaknesses which inevitably led to the virtual demise of the 39 feet by 18 feet court. As players improved their overhead serves and rushed the net, it was almost impossible to lob against these "net rushers" on the short court. There were hardly any rallies; it was essentially a game of slamming. Nearly all the courts in the New York City and Los Angeles Park and Recreation Departments' playgrounds eventually fell into disuse and disrepair.

The exciting paddle tennis renaissance began in January 1959, with the nationwide publication of the radical, contemporary United States Paddle Tennis Association rules, court dimensions and unique court markings. The adoption of the one overhead serve, tennis ball punctured to deaden its bounce, 2'7" taut net, three-foot lob area rule, larger court (to 50' by 20'), the one-bounce rule for singles, etc. has made contemporary paddle tennis a fast, furious and spectacular sport with prolonged rallies and a premium on agility. Paddle tennis is no longer a children's game, although it's a great game for children.

New York City and Los Angeles suburbia have, to date, developed the highest class players, with Florida, New Jersey, Virginia, Colorado, Seattle, Vancouver and Quebec on the upbeat. Requests for USPTA rules, court plans and specifications have been received from Sweden, Japan, Australia and Luxembourg. Although paddle tennis is essentially an outdoor sport, Seattle's world's largest indoor tennis complex, scheduled to open in November 1975, includes a court for paddle tennis addicts. The sport is flourishing on all fronts.

How can it miss? The game is a natural. It can be played on any flat surface. The required area is comparatively small. Paddles are inexpensive, long-lasting and you never ever have to worry about stringing. The short-handled wooden paddle enables anyone with fairly ordinary reflexes to enjoy a rally the very first time he or she steps onto a court. The low, pulled-taut net permits hard flat drives, and the 50-foot court makes the lob an effective defensive or offensive stroke. Although the beginner can enjoy paddle tennis, it takes a real athlete to play in tournament competition.

Whether played by neophytes or champions, paddle tennis is a fun game, especially in doubles where long, exciting rallies are the order of the day. Night too: an increasing number of courts are installing lights for nocturnal paddling. The fascination of this lifetime sport is so profound that zealous converts in turn feel impelled to proselytize their friends, who gratefully inquire, "Where has paddle tennis been all these years?"

Three categories of sportspersons love paddle tennis:

(1) those who play the game all year round and make it their main sport;

(2) tennis players who have found in paddle tennis the perfect off-season activity, although really, with the proliferation of perfectly illuminated and surfaced indoor facilities, tennis no longer has an "off" season. Veteran tennis players get hooked on paddle tennis with its fast returns, smashes, accent on net play and lightning footwork. Although my friends and I are avid regular tennis buffs, we save our fall and winter weekends for the sheer exhilaration and fun of outdoor paddle tennis – without regard for freezing temperatures or high winds. Nothing but a blizzard or heavy rain drives us indoors. Paddle tennis zealots are a strange and hardy lot;

(3) children, for whom paddle tennis is an excellent stepping stone to tennis. The grips, strokes and strategy are essentially the same, and there is no better introduction to the joys of tennis. Althea Gibson first attracted the attention of her tennis patrons with her prodigious feats on the public paddle tennis courts of Harlem, and Bobby Riggs was boys' paddle tennis champ of Los Angeles where his brother was a playground director in the Department of Parks and Recreation. Pancho Gonzales is another superstar who got started in tennis wielding a wooden paddle. Any tennis player will find paddle tennis ludicrously easy to play. It takes about 10 minutes to make the adjustment to the short-handled paddle, after which he can fit right into a fast game of doubles – although it takes a little longer to compete on even terms with experienced paddle tennis players.

—Murray Geller

Murray Geller is President of the USPTA. In 1941, he was national open singles paddle tennis champion. Since retiring from his position in the New York State Supreme Court in 1973, he has devoted most of his time to the promotion of paddle tennis.

For More Information

The best source of information is Murray Geller, President of the United States Paddle Tennis Association, 189 Seeley St., Brooklyn, N.Y. 11218. He has done a handbook which will give you all the official rules.

Parachuting

To be forced to jump from an airplane in an emergency, pull the ripcord of a parachute, have the parachute open and lower you safely to the ground – that's parachuting. To willfully jump from an airplane, do maneuvers while falling toward the earth, pull the ripcord at a predetermined altitude, have the parachute open and to be able to land on a predetermined spot – that's sport parachuting.

In the last 10 years, sport parachuting has evolved into a complicated sport of accurate landings, quickness and skilled horizontal movement across the sky.

The sport got its beginning when barnstorming was the big rage and something new was needed to thrill the crowd. Not

Sport parachutes bear little resemblance to their military ancestors of World War II. Scientifically designed vents and panels have been added for the greater maneuverability demands of sport parachuting. (Shearman)

many precautions were taken and a lot of thrill-seeking parachute jumpers met their fate when a parachute didn't open. The general public's attitude that present-day skydivers are still thrill-seekers, trying to escape death by a hair, is left over from the barnstorming days.

Today, a skydiver (or parachutist) goes through a basic training, giving him all the fundamentals to make his first jump. After that initial jump, it is up to the individual's perseverance as to how far he will pursue the sport of parachuting.

A student is taught how to deal with emergencies; the process of entering the plane on the ground and leaving it in the air; how to maneuver his parachute through the air; and how to land properly. The student's parachute is opened for him until he proves capable of opening it himself. When a skydiver jumps from the plane, opening his own parachute, he has stepped into *freefall*.

After a parachutist becomes more proficient at freefalling, that is, after he has displayed the ability to make turns, backloops and dives, he begins jumping from the airplane with other skydivers. The jumpers fly horizontally across the sky to link hands and form a "star". The largest "star" ever made, with all jumpers leaving the same airplane, was put together by 31 skydivers.

Competition is inevitable as in most American sports. The National Parachuting Championships are held each year with hundreds of skydivers competing. Competition is broken down into three categories – accuracy, style, and relative work.

Accuracy, as the name indicates, is the landing of the parachutist on a five-inch target. It is not unusual for a jumper to land on the target 10 or more consecutive times.

Style is when the jumper falls from a height of about 7000 feet, spinning four 360-degree turns and backlooping as he falls – doing all maneuvers as fast as he can. The best competitors "turn style" in seven seconds or less.

Relative work is the forming of "stars" as jumpers leave the airplane, fly across the sky and join hands. Relative work is judged on how fast 10 skydivers can leave the airplane and form a "star". Fifteen seconds is an excellent time.

In the past few years, competitive parachuting has reached the international level, with the United States Parachute Team, chosen for their performances at the National Parachuting Championships, competing against teams from around the globe.

Parachuting has evolved from a thrill-seeker's sport to one for dedicated and sophisticated athletes. There are many skills you must perfect to become a good parachutist and as in all sports, it takes time and effort to become a top-notch skydiver.

—Tim Davis

Tim Davis has made nearly 200 jumps and is looking forward to making many more. He currently is working at World Publications in the marketing department.

The Big Jump

I'm sure the public sees sport parachuting as a daring, but very limited, sport. A jumper is stereotyped as a fool who straps on a parachute "that may not open", climbs aboard a small aircraft, and hurls himself into the sky at some dizzy altitude. From then, people think, the jumper struggles to breathe as the ground rushes up to meet him. Then, at the last minute, he pulls the ripcord and his parachute snaps open (painfully). He then spends the next few minutes drifting aimlessly with the wind until he makes a bone-crushing landing in some field. If he's still in one piece after all this, he carefully repacks his parachute, steels up his courage, and does it again. This process is repeated until he runs out of courage, or gets injured (or worse) or realizes how stupid the whole game is. Dangerously thrilling, they think, but almost monstrous.

I'm happy to report, however, that the public has some very misguided impressions about the sport. Yes, it's exciting and, like all action sports, it can be painful at times, but it's mostly challenging, fun, and rewarding.

It's an unfortunate fact that a person's first introduction to the sport is scary. His ignorance is fed by frightening stories he's read in the newspapers about tragic accidents. The equipment is heavy, bulky, and somewhat uncomfortable. The airplane is noisy as the door is open, and the ground is very far away.

Only a few of the people who make their first jump will decide to make another. Only a few of these will make it to freefall. Those that do, however, find a sport that has no equal.

What is it like to freefall? A typical freefall lasts about 45 seconds, and during that 45 seconds you are more aware, more alert and, well, more alive than you can imagine. Psychologists have called sport parachutists "stimulus addicts" – a term that, I think, is not really true. Parachutists don't jump because they revel in the feeling that "there's nothing between me and eternity but my ripcord" and that each jump is a flirt with death. There might be a little of that involved, but there is much more. Can you imagine sitting at 3000 feet under a parachute at dawn in early summer? It's incredibly quiet, the air is cool and moist and the sun is a golden disc that makes small lakes look like pools of shimmering mercury. I guess I'm saying that I've never appreciated dawn until I jumped into it for the first time. I would need poetry to really describe the beauty.

Or how about a jump from 12,500 feet with 15 other parachutists. In this case, the aircraft would be an older, but airworthy, twin-engined aircraft such as a DC-3 or a Lodestar. You're sitting on the floor, with the rest of your friends packed around you. The big radial engines are throbbing confidently and the cabin is a bit chilly from the thin air that is blowing through the open door. Periodically a jumper sticks his head into the slipstream to check the aircraft's position over the ground – his face distorts in the 100-mile-per-hour windblast. The plane makes a final bank, levels out, we're almost there. The parachutists stand up, make final adjustments to straps, helmets and goggles. Some people clap their hands and stomp their feet to limber themselves up after the 20-minute climb to altitude. The jumper by the door sticks his head out, and yells corrections to help guide the aircraft over the drop zone. The corrections are relayed to the pilot, who responds with quick rudder movements. Finally, the command is given to "Line it up!", and the jumpers form a tight line that winds from the door to the front of the aircraft.

"Three – two – one – Go!" Things happen fast now. The idea is to exit as fast as possible to keep the group together as much as possible. Each jumper dives through the door in a blur of color. You're hustling up to the door, the man in front of you jumps through, and you're out!

It's bright outside. For a few seconds you're diving with your arms out in front of you, riding the slipstream of the aircraft much like a body surfer. Down below you, strung out over hundreds of feet, are your friends, each diving down to the first two people who left the aircraft first. Your hands are pulled to your sides and your chin is tucked to your chest to give you a head-down attitude for the fastest possible acceleration down. The wind noise is a steady shriek in your ears, your jumpsuit flaps in the wind, and you can feel yourself picking up speed. After several seconds you glance up. A small "star" is building below as the jumpers glide toward each other to form a circle by holding hands.

The star seems to be coming up fast now; it is falling slowly, about 120 m.p.h. while you've built up a dive speed of nearly 200 m.p.h. Up come your head and arms as you assume a big spread-eagle position to slow down to the speed of the star. The wind feels like a big mattress, pushing mightily on your body. The star is still building as jumpers move in and join the circle or "star". You pick a slot and maintain a forward glide to the wrists: grab, shake and pull the grip open – you're in! Across the star someone is grinning like a banshee. The star wallows gently as you feel someone dock on your wrists and break in. The world is spread out below. You seem suspended above it, lying on this big, noisy cushion of air. Other jumpers continue to dock, the star gets bigger and grins keep popping out. Finally, less than a minute from when you dove out into the bright sun from the aircraft door, the star disintegrates as jumpers let go, turn and dive away from each other. A look at the ground or a check of your altimeter, a quick look around, and you pull your ripcord. The parachute sits you up, snaps open noisily but gently, and freefall is over.

Your friends do the same and, in a few seconds, gaudy parachutes are turning and rocking around you. The silence is punctuated by a few whoops and whistles that can't be contained.

The next two minutes are spent maneuvering your canopy to the ground. It has both forward speed and turning ability. Landing on target is easy. A stand-up landing makes you earthbound again. You pause for a few moments to remember what happened up there – things happen so fast that the jump is usually a parade of images that will be sorted out and assembled later, usually with the help of others on the load.

That's a normal jump for an experienced parachutist. Scary? No. Painful? No. Exciting? You bet! Even if you take those same people and go up 15 minutes later to do the same thing, it will be a completely different jump. You challenge yourself to do a better job, get in the star faster and smoother. Mistakes are made. A star is fragile and can be easily torn apart by an overanxious jumper who doesn't concentrate on his motion. A jumper in freefall can dive to go down faster, flare out to fall slower to float above the star, slide backwards, forwards, and sideways, turn, loop and roll. It sounds difficult, but it's quite easy to do adequately, although, like any sport, it takes a lot of dedication to do it superbly.

I have tried to give you an idea of what it's like to skydive. As I stated before, it's something that I cannot adequately put into words, it has to be experienced to be appreciated. More and more people these days are climbing aboard sailplanes, hangliders, or powered airplanes and discovering that the sky is a magnificent place to play and compete, or just relax. If you really want to experience the sky first hand, without artificial wings, you'll have to join our ranks and become a sport parachutist.

—Michael F. Truffer

Michael F. Truffer is the Assistant Director of the United States Parachute Association. He began jumping about five years ago and has logged over 1000 jumps. You can find him in the sky over California on any given weekend.

For More Information

The United States Parachute Association, Box 109, Monterey, Calif. 93940 is the organization for parachuting. They publish a magazine called *Parachutist* which is very good. It is published monthly at $7.00 per year. If you are thinking about getting into this sport, you should join this organization.

Here are some exciting equipment sources. The Chute Shop, Highway 202, Flemington, N.J. 08822 has a catalog ($1.00) which offers a complete line of equipment and supplies. Para-Gear Equipment Co., 3839 W. Oakton, Skokie, Ill. 60076 has a big catalog ($1.00) with over 800 items pictured. A handy reference book for all makes of sport parachuting equipment and accessories. Or do you want a custom jump suit? RW Equipment Sales, Rt. 13, Brookline, N.H. 03033 has some interesting suits. They say, "don't settle for anything off a shelf, create your own flying machine, you deserve it."

Some good books. All are available from World Publications, Box 366, Mountain View, Calif. 94040 at the price listed* plus 25 cents each postage. Write for a complete list.

Sport Parachuting, Charles W. Ryan. This fully illustrated instructional manual contains nearly everything that potential beginners need to know about instruction, equipment, and costs. Safety and first aid are also given thorough and careful treatment. For the advanced parachutist, there are sections on competition–accuracy, style and information. 1975 Hb. & Ppb., 208 pp., ill., $10.00/$4.95, (Regenry).

Parachuting for Sport, Jim Greenwood. All about sky diving told by a real expert–its history, modern applications, including wartime uses, equipment construction and operation, packing and rigging, 'jumping, types of craft most suitable, advanced jumping, unexpected landings, competition, and much more. 1962 Ppb., 128 pp., ill., $3.95, (Crown).

Sport Parachuting, R.A. Gunby. Covers everything about sky diving in the simplest of terms, inevitably infecting the reader with the author's own basic love of the sport. 1971 Ppb., 162 pp., ill., $4.95, (Para Gear).

Parachutes and Parachuting: A Modern Guide to the Sport, Bud Sellick. Dispels a lot of the myths about skydiving nuts. Covers every aspect of the sport from its history to how to do it. 1971 Hb., ill., $7.95, (Prentice Hall).

Towing parasails and kites is usually done with a boat, but automobiles, skimobiles and even aircraft have been used. Being towed over water, however, is considered the safest practice. (Poynter)

Para-Sailing & Kiting

Manned kiting is the riding of a kite type vehicle which is either tethered in a strong wind or, in the absence of wind, one that is under tow. In some forms of these aviation sports, one has the election once aloft to disconnect the tow rope for a free-flight back to earth. Generally, there are three types of man kited craft: the flat kite, the Rogallo (hang glider) kite and the Para-Sail.

Manned kiting is quite old since kites themselves go back a long way – some 3000 years. Man has wanted to imitate the birds, to rise aloft for an aerial view, probably since the first man enviously watched the first bird soaring effortlessly above him. Now through kiting, his dreams may be fulfilled. While there are a number of accounts of people hoisting themselves up to tethered kites in the 1800s and early 1900s, manned kiting didn't catch hold until the early 1950s with the towing of kites behind water ski boats. These flat kites did not have harnesses to support the flyer's weight; he simply hung bare handed to the crossbar while the altitude of the kite was controlled by the speed of the boat. This required a certain measure of strength and daring. Later, a harness was developed which allowed the rider to fly "hands-off" or to control the lateral movement of the kite by moving the bar in front of him. A boat-end quick release, or pin, also came into use and allowed the pin man (observer) to jettison the airborne cargo should it get into trouble. Once the kite is pinned, it reacts as an air brake and settles into the water. Flat kite flying became fairly easy and relatively safe.

The water skiers continued to fly under the tow and soon adapted the flat kite to their slalom course; they would swing the bar to tilt the kite and fly around the buoys on each side of the course. Then certain gymnastic routines performed on the bar developed into another event called "tricks" and competition began. The American Water Ski Association began to sanction kiting tournaments.

Flat kite flying is a natural extension of water skiing; it's exciting and great recreation.

Hang gliding, which captured the imagination of millions in the early 1970s, like snow skiing, simply was not available to those without mountains. But there are many ways to get up there and the kite launch is filling the bill for thousands who would never have the opportunity to fly otherwise. The flat land, water borne outdoorsman is now taking to the air. Tow launching, or "kiting", has many advantages over the standard foot launch; water is softer than dirt and very forgiving, there is no need to hike back up the steep hill carrying some 50 pounds of bulky gear; launching is simple (almost guaranteed); control is easy to learn and easy to instruct. Once up and released into free-flight, all hang gliding is the same and in some areas, enthusiasts are towing up several hundred feet and releasing to "thermal" (ride the uprising hot air currents) to remain aloft an hour or more.

The Rogallo wing was developed by NASA engineer Francis Rogallo in the late 1940s as a tethered kite, so towing it is nothing new. Later it was flown free as a hang glider and unstiffened models were tried as gliding parachutes. While the Rogallo design was never adopted for the landing of spacecraft, it has become the most popular form of hang glider and with good reason: it's lightweight, inexpensive, simple, folds quickly, flies well and will "parachute" to earth in a stall. Under tow, the Rogallo rises higher than the flat kite and the view is incredible. In free-flight, it provides an inexpensive and relatively safe introduction to aviation. Hang gliding is true flying as you find yourself out in the open with the breeze in your face, silently gliding along with the birds.

Para-sailing is similar to kiting and kite launched gliding except that a parachute-like canopy is used. It may be towed or kited and the pilot may release himself at altitude for a parachute type return to terra firma. Military surplus canopies have been modified and used as para-sails but they are rarely as successful as the new one made for the purpose by Pioneer Parachute Company of Manchester, Conn. The canopy consists of 24 gores and suspension lines, and two center lines which serve to retract the apex. Air slots in the rear of the canopy create aerodynamic lift, and the left and right stabilizer panels provide directional stability under tow. The front of the nylon canopy is attached to left and right front (upper) risers, and the rear portion, identified by the solid V-shaped coloring, is attached to rear (lower) risers. These risers are connected to a tow rope by means of a yoke. In flight, the para-sailist's harness is suspended from lower left and right risers by large snaps which attach to D-rings located on the shoulders of the harness.

The Para-Sail is an ascending or lifting parachute that may be towed aloft in much the same manner as a kite. As speed increases, the parachute ascends. When towing slows or when it stops, the para-sail descends gently to earth, just like a conventional parachute. By controlling the speed of the tow vehicle, it is possible to fly the para-sail at any altitude permitted by the length of the tow rope.

Para-sailing is a healthy, safe outdoor water sport which can be terribly exciting, particularly when you release at altitude for a normal parachute descent back to earth. It allows you to experience the thrill of parachuting without jumping from an airplane and suffering anxiety during the opening process.

The towing of kites and para-sails may be done with a boat but automobiles, skimobiles and even aircraft have been used. Only tows over water are recommended, however.

Towing can be more dangerous than free-flight because the flight vehicle is a "kite", not a glider and as such it is subject to forces other than those contributed by the pilot. Every child has seen his toy kite affected by changing winds which cause it to change from steady flight to darting and terminate in a crash. The kite is tethered to the ground and can get into positions from which only an experienced pilot can recover and this experience takes time to acquire. The high speeds and hard landings are what make towing over land dangerous. The answer is to fly over water, progress slowly, and get proper instruction.

One excited kite flyer decided the easiest way to para-sail would be to wait for a high wind and then to tie the rope to a stationary object. He ventured out alone, firmly tied the rope, inflated the canopy and rose upwards quickly. The next problem became obvious once the thrill of his accomplishment wore off – how to get down!

—**Dan Poynter**

Dan Poynter is on the Board of Directors of both the US Hang Gliding Association and the US Parachute Association and is the author of **The Parachute Manual, Hang Gliding,** *and* **Kiting.**

For More Information

Additional information can be found under hang gliding and parachuting. However, the American Kitefliers Association, Box 1511, Silver City, N.M. 88061 or the American Water Ski Association, Box 191, Winter Haven, Fla. 33880 can supply information. And Water Ski Kite Flying, Raven Industries, Box 1007, Sioux Falls, S.D. 57101 can be helpful.

Pigeon Racing

Pigeon racing is without a doubt one of the most fascinating and challenging hobbies of today. Our feathered racers, similar to thoroughbred race horses and greyhound dogs are the fulfillment of man's endeavors. They are the aristocracy of the pigeon world and should never be compared with the species that infests city buildings or church steeples. This latter variety is known as commies and is useless for sporting purposes. The racing homer of today is fully pedigreed and one of the most spectacular performers for its size and weight in the world. Racing homers when in top condition should weigh no more than 16 ounces as too much weight only hampers them in flight.

They are definitely a sporting breed and can remain on the wing or in flight when competing from distances of 600 to 700 miles from sunup to sundown. Very often they fly into the dark hours of the evening so that they can complete their journey and get home. Their courage and determination has no equal.

The initial culture of the racing homer commenced in Europe during the turn of the century. The Belgians were most conspicuous in the experimental purpose. These were the days when telegraph and telephone were thought of, but not perfected by any means. The Belgians used many varieties of birds that were gifted with the homing instinct. Some of the larger birds used in the experiment were imported from foreign areas: the carrier, the horseman, the dragoon. These birds were endowed with good structures, raw-boned with good wing spread. These were then interbred with small birds, the smerles, the culumets, and the Blue Rock doves, all well known for their high flying and maneuvering abilities in the skies.

In the early part of the 19th century racing homers were used extensively in many Belgian cities. They were the very important message carriers of news from the stock exchanges; many fortunes were accumulated through this communication service. The racing homer also gave valuable assistance to communications in World Wars I and II resulting in some of the birds being decorated with the Dickens Medal for outstanding service. During some of the terrific battles the homing pigeon saved many lives, and when all other means of communication failed, the racing homer carried on.

The entire scheme of pigeon racing is based upon the racing homer's undying desire to return to its home as quickly as possible. Its mysterious ability to navigate the uncharted skies is certainly a feat that has not yet been explained.

The racing pigeon sport is unionized throughout the world. Rigid rules govern all the competitions and all racing homers are banded with seamless aluminum bands that are slipped onto their legs when they are about five days old. The leg at that time is quite flexible and the band is easily slipped over the toes of the subject. After it gets a little older, the leg grows with the band and cannot be extracted unless cut. The band itself contains the year of birth, also the union from which the bird is issued. The letters and numbers are a definition that can be identified in any part of the world.

Two series of races are flown each year, one of which is for the old birds and the other for young birds that are bred that particular year. The old bird races usually commence in the month of April, and the young bird races in the month of August or September. The races start at a distance of 100 miles and are increased progressively each week to 200, 300, 400, 500 or more miles in many areas. Five hundred- to 700-mile races can be accomplished by the racing homer on the day of liberation.

The loft or coop of the racing homer is its castle, no matter how humble the structure is, just as long as the bird is happy in its environment. This is definitely one of the keys to success. The coop must be kept dry at all times and cleaned each day. Homers will not thrive in dirty and wet coops. In fittings, the loft must be made safe from intruding predatory vermin and especially cats. There must be a separate box for each pair so they can have privacy for their romance and the raising of their babies. Homers will defend the breeding boxes until their strength gives out. Homers generally keep the same breeding boxes, the same mate and the same perch year after year. The hen lays her eggs 10 days after mating takes place. The cock and hen take their own turns sitting on the eggs; the hen will sit all night and the cock during the day. The period of incubation is 18 days with the hen normally laying two eggs. Both parents feed the babies a milk-like substance that forms in their crops for this particular purpose, and are possibly the only birds known to man that are capable of this particular feeding of their young. This milk-like substance disappears after 10 days, at which time the babies are pumped with the actual food the parents eat after it's been masticated in the parents' crop. Pigeons are the only birds known to man that can drink like a horse. They insert the beaks into the water troughs and just drink until they've had enough. The baby birds are usually educated enough to be moved from their parents and into their own quarters at 25 to 30 days old. They have watched their parents eat and drink and they follow likewise.

The young homer will soon find its way out of the pigeon coop when given the chance. It's a truly gifted bird with plenty of brain power, but one must always remember, it's a baby and needs care and understanding, as in the case with everything that lives. Its qualities develop with growth and there's always the stage where it cannot employ all of its faculties. It's always best to allow the young homer its own way, never scare it from the coop in order to see it fly. In its own time, it will take care of itself. The young homer must have both mental and physical potentials; they must be trained carefully for the first 50-60 miles, then they seem to take themselves.

Racing homers are fed various grains that help sustain their health and working power. When engaged in the races, they need the best and cleanest grains possible. Usually a good comcommercial mixture does the trick. These mixtures contain field peas, dent corn, milo corn, hard red wheat, and if possible to secure, common vetch and maple peas. The usual amount of protein necessary for good health in about 18 percent with certain amounts of fats, fiber and ash to make up the perfect diet. Fattening grains are not conducive to the health of homers competing in races.

Since all pigeon races are conducted under specific rules and the birds themselves released in group form (many times in the thousands) from the selected race points, each member's coop location must be officially measured. The surveyor is an expert approved by the various clubs and federations. Surveys for each member from the different race points are made in miles and fractions thereof. These are afterwards recomputed into yards-per-minute by the simple equations of yards in the mile (1760) by the minutes in the hour. The amount of time taken by the racing homer to fly from the race point to his home is then reduced into seconds and divided into the yards-per-minute to ascertain the speed velocities. Many race decisions are won and lost by the difference on the last decimal point.

Fanciers who engage their birds in the races must complete an entry form which shows the bird's color, its sex and also all the identifications shown on its seamless aluminum band. They cannot compete unless the band is authentic. Each pigeon is afterward countermarked with a rubber band called the race band. It has two numbers, one inside and the other outside. These numbers must correspond to the slip of paper that accompanies the band. The secretary records the countermark number against the entry of the bird, places the slip of paper in an envelope with the name of the fancier and seals it. The pigeon is then placed in the racing baskets or panniers with other member's entries; this is done so that each member will have a certain number of birds in each race basket.

In order to engage in the actual racing homer races, provisions must be made for a continuous running timer. These clocks are made, of course, especially for the purpose of clocking the birds from the races. The clock is synchronized with the club's master timer so that provisions will be made in the event it gains or loses time. A part of the mechanism is a movable paper tape, on which, at the turn of the crank, the exact time is stamped that the bird arrived home. The clock is always sealed by the secretary prior to the release of the birds at the race point. Each pigeon as it arrives home is more or less coaxed by its owner to drop from the air and onto the pitch boards or into the pigeon coop directly. The rubber countermark is then removed from its leg, placed in a brass capsule, and dropped into a slot or hole provided on top of the the sealed clock for this purpose. The crank is then turned and the bird's time recorded. The sealed clocks are then returned to the club house and compared with other competitors.

The racing homer sport is a fascinating and healthy sport for all members of the family. It offers good clean recreation for everyone, especially since a partnership is usually the going thing. What could be better for the younger generation of today? It's a definite curb on delinquency. When parents can see their children with their birds on the family property, there's little worry about unsupervised idleness.

The initial outlay for potential fanciers is possibly not quite as expensive as other sports, especially horses, dogs and automobiles. Young people of today that wish to race homers are given every opportunity by the local fanciers and the officers of the national unions. The annual dues for juniors are absolutely minimal. The sport in itself teaches high principles of sportsmanship and the preservation of health and sanitation. The tuition of figuring racing speeds and time calculations are subjects worth knowing for future education.

For the senior citizen, what could be better than the racing homer hobby? Keeping your mind active is certainly a necessity for longevity. The affinity between man and the racing homer sport is a definite challenge offered in many various ways. The breeding theories are without doubt a complex project. To breed the elusive champion by the process of mating a male and female is no easy task. Eye sign theories have helped many fanciers in their breeding programs; it creates a yardstick for potential winners. Balance of body and suppleness of wing also demand a great deal of attention, and that wonderful thing called "homing instinct" and determination all play important parts in the breeding programs.

Local ordinance laws are sometimes prohibitive to the retaining of racing homers in certain areas. It's always best, before having any notions of becoming a racing homer fancier to check out the local zoning laws of your city. Disappointment can be averted by checking this matter out thoroughly. These people that look down their noses at the word "pigeon" please remember, pigeons are like people – they come in assorted kinds.

—**James Lewis**

James Lewis, originally of Wales, has been "racing homers" for over 45 years in the US. He is an official in the California State Racing Pigeon Organization and the Northern California and American Racing Pigeon Unions. He was awarded the National Hall of Fame award in 1974 for his contributions to the sport.

For More Information

There are four major organizations. The American Racing Pigeon Union, Charles Herin, Box 26, Maineville, Ohio 45039; International Federation of Homing Pigeon Fanciers, Inc., Nona Feuerbach, 474 Wilson Blvd., Central Islip, N.Y. 11722; the United States Racing Pigeon Assoc., 6129 S.E. Insley, Portland, Ore. 97206; and the National Pigeon Assoc., Box 83, Watertown, Wisc. 53094.

For magazines:

American Racing Pigeon News, 2421 Old Arch Road, Norristown, Pa. 19401. Published 11 times per year at $7.00

American Pigeon Journal, Warrenton, Mo. 63383.

Poultry Press, The Fancier's Newspaper, Box 947, York. Pa. 17405. Write for a free sample.

The big one is *British Homing World*, 26 High Street, Welshpool Powys SY21 7JP, Wales, England. It is published weekly at $20.00 per year and has a circulation of over 50,000.

We have several sources for supplies: Chas. Siegel & Son, 866 St. Charles St., Elgin, Ill. 60120 has a large free catalog showing perches, traps, feeders, twin fountains, scrapers, nest fronts, address bands, bobs, nest bowls, dummy eggs, exhibition coops and much more. Gerry Leberman, Box 342, Fort Dodge, Iowa 50501 has a complete line of health products for pigeons. Tramisol wormer for hair worms, vitamins, Emtryl water treatment for canker, etc. Foy's Pigeon Supplies, Clinton, Iowa 52732 has a free catalog with a lot of items for the pigeon raiser. And if you are looking for birds, try Dan Bellitto, 738 E. Marshall St., Norristown, Pa. 19401.

Here are three good books. We'll be adding to our list shortly. All are available from World Publications, Box 366, Mountain View, Calif. 94040 at the price listed* plus 25 cents each postage. Write for a complete list.

Racing Pigeons, Colin Osman. The essential facts that a newcomer to the sport needs to know. In compact and readable form the author carefully handles breeding, feeding, racing, housing, and the biological make-up of the pigeon itself. 1971 Hb., 192 pp., ill., $4.95, (Faber & Faber).

Pigeon Racing, Herbert R. Axelrod & Edwin C. Welty, Jr. A book describing the sport of pigeon racing, written by an authority on several kinds of semi-domestic animals, from tropical fish to rabbits. 1973 Library binding, 208 pp., ill., $7.95, (Sterling).

How to Raise and Train Pigeons, William H. Allen. A book for the beginning and advanced pigeon raising enthusiast. This handbook goes through all the steps, from selecting the birds to training and racing them. 1974 Ppb., 127 pp., ill., $2.00, (Wilshire).

Platform Tennis

Platform tennis is a younger brother to both paddle tennis and tennis since it is played on a court with a net using a racquet and ball. It is a comparatively recent addition to the sports scene, getting its start in 1928 by two snowbound tennis players who wanted an outdoor game they could play in winter months.

At one time platform tennis was popular only in states of the northwestern seaboard but now it is growing by leaps and bounds, and courts are springing up in many other parts of the country. Since it originated in an area of snowy winters the court is raised off the ground and enclosed by wire-fence screens. Courts are equipped with hinged snowboards to facilitate rapid clearing, and a sanded surface assures good traction.

A rather large-faced, short-handled paddle made of perforated plywood is used for play, together with an orange-colored unpressurized sponge-rubber ball. When you climb up to the elevated court don't expect to see players decked out in fancy athletic suits. Dress is informal for platform tennis and often participants choose sweaters, parkas and other types of clothing which can be taken off layer-by-layer as they warm up.

The rules of the game and scoring are basically the same as those of tennis (see tennis), except for one major difference that adds an extra element of excitement and additional skill: if the ball hits the deck and then touches any part of the back or side screens it can be played as long as it doesn't hit the deck a second time. Also, platform tennis is always played with two people on a team.

There are always a variety of tournaments open to enthusiasts of all ages and abilities; in fact, Dick Squires, in his *Complete Book of Platform Tennis,* estimates that approximately 3,000 courts used by over 150,000 devotees presently exist. Quite a count for a fine game that the majority of West Coast sportmen have never discovered!

The All-Weather Racket Sport

We can predict that platform tennis is destined to become America's next participation sport to explode. And for many good reasons.

The courts occupy only one-fourth the area (30 feet by 60 feet) of tennis, and as they are usually built up in the air on concrete piers, they can be installed on practically any type of terrain no matter how sloped or rough. Since only doubles is played, the square-foot usage is important where land is at a premium. Sixteen people (on four paddle courts) can be enjoying themselves in the same area whereas only two people can play singles on a terrain court.

The tremendous boom in tennis during the past five years has rubbed off onto its kin, platform tennis. The number of paddle courts constructed since 1971 has doubled. Currently estimates show that there are over 3,000, and the present rate of growth is a healthy 25 percent per annum. Scoring and strokes are identical to tennis; even the tie-breaker at six-all has been adopted by the sport's amateur governing body, the American Platform Tennis Association.

The game is far easier to learn for the beginner than tennis. Because of its built-in equalizers–the smaller court, the single serve, and, the essence of the game, the wires off which the ball may be returned–platform tennis does not require the skill, court coverage, stamina or power that regular tennis does. Most people, male or female, young and old alike, can, therefore, start having fun and realize self-satisfaction from the first moment they step onto a platform tennis court. You don't have to be a great natural athlete. At the same time, the sport challenges the superior racquet-wielder and most ardent, combative competitor. It is also difficult to master.

No other racquet and ball sport can be played outdoors in almost any kind of weather. Platform's heritage is that it is the perfect form of recreation and fun for people living in northern climates "between seasons." The traditional season, therefore, is from early October through early April. There is no reason, however, why platform tennis cannot be played and enjoyed the year 'round. Impregnated in the surface of the deck is an abrasive substance which provides a sure bounce for the ball and firm footing for the players in the wettest weather. As the equipment consists of a solid, plywood paddle with perforated holes and a solid, sponge-rubber ball, there is no logical reason for being dependent upon a capricious Mother Nature. Adverse weather conditions are seldom cause for cancelling a platform tennis match.

There is a sociability related to the game that is not as prevalent in other racquet sports. This conviviality and good fellowship "make" platform tennis for many of its participants. Apres' platform tennis activities in the "warming hut" or clubhouse are just as much fun as the competition on the courts. Most paddlers consider their pastime more than just a sport–it's a way of life.

Despite being 48 years old, platform tennis is still pretty much a game played by the upper class, Country Club Set. The majority of courts are located at tennis and golf clubs and in well-to-do individuals' backyards. Approximately 80 percent of all courts are to be found between the Boston to Washington, D.C. corridor. The game is spreading, however, and rapidly. It is now played in 34 states and in over 400 cities and towns across the U.S. Recently courts have been installed in foreign countries such as France, Germany, Spain, Bermuda, Canada, Italy, Indonesia, Japan, Poland, and, yes, even Russia (at the American Embassy).

Because of the many broad appeals of platform tennis, there is no question that its continued–perhaps even accererated–growth is assured. More national television coverage of a few top tournaments, more publicity and exposure will inevitably make platform tennis *the* sport of the '80s–or sooner.

–Dick Squires

Dick Squires, a former national platform tennis champion, is known as the top authority in the game. He has authored **How to Play Platform Tennis, and The Complete Book of Platform Tennis,** *and also has the distinction of having won US titles in three different racquet sports–tennis, squash racquets, and platform tennis.*

For More Information

Some of the tennis magazines cover platform tennis from time to time. And we have been told that there is a magazine in the makings but the first issue has not appeared yet. The American Platform Tennis Association, 152 Upper Montclair Plaza, Upper Montclair, N.J. 07043 and the U.S. Platform Tennis Clubs, Inc., Box 235, Rowayton, Conn. can both supply information. Also, Century Sports, 400 Park Ave., Plainfield, N.Y. 07061 is a good source of equipment. There are some good books on the sport. All are available from World Publications, Box 366, Mountain View, Calif. 94040 at the price listed* plus 25 cents postage.

Paddle: The Beginner's Guide to Platform Tennis, George Sullivan. The most up-to-date and comprehensive guide to suburbia's fast-growing fall and winter sport–complete with rules and strategies. 1975, ill., \$8.95, (Coward, McCann, Goegeghan)

The Complete Book of Platform Tennis, Dick Squires, ed. The details of this fast-growing sport are gathered together in a complete book, by one of the national champions of platform tennis. Whether you are just starting out or want to perfect your game, all the chapters will be of value. 1974 Hb., 202 pp. pp., ill., \$9.95, (Houghton Mifflin)

The Official Guide to Platform Tennis, Oliver Durrell. Called the nation's newest sport, platform tennis is played on a wooden platform with paddles. This book describes the origin, rules, and competitions of this fast moving and easy-to-learn sport. 1967 Ppb., 79 pp., ill., \$1.95, (Grosset & Dunlap)

How to Play Platform Tennis, Dick Squires. Ideal book for beginners, this book introduces the novice to the equipment and then explains everything from the history and rules of the game to strategy, swings, serves, and practical game psychology. 1969 Hb., 113 pp., ill., \$6.95, (Derin-Adair).

Polo

Polo is an ancient game that was played by the Persians about 600 B.C. in almost the same form as it is today. The game came to the United States via India and England in 1878.

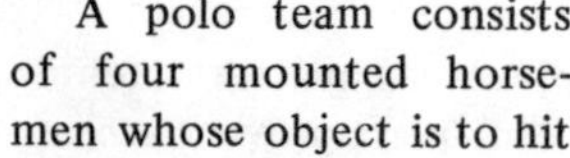

A polo team consists of four mounted horsemen whose object is to hit a small wooden ball with a wooden mallet through goal posts at each end of a turf field. The field is 300 yards long and 180 yards wide and is enclosed on each side by wooden sideboards.

Each player on a side is identified by a number on his shirt. Numbers one and two are offensive players, number three is the pivot man, and four is the defensive player. Each player wears a hard hat lined with sponge rubber to protect his head from a fall or blow. It is traditional to wear white breeches, brown leather boots, and a jersey of the team color. The polo ball, slightly larger than a baseball and painted white, is usually made of willow root. The game is divided into four to eight chukkers of seven-and-one-half minutes each. Each goal scored counts one point.

Two variations of regulation polo are paddock polo and arena polo. Both games are played on smaller fields, three players to a team, and the ball is made of inflated leather.

Teamwork is an essential aspect of good polo, with accurate passing between teammates common. In many casual pickup games, however, the players often adopts a selfish type of polo in which an individual may take more of an initiative.

Polo is played on a handicap system so that bad players can often compete against good ones. Each player on a team is given a handicap rating from minus two (minimum) to plus 10 (maximum). In most countries not more than 10 percent of the players attain a handicap of more than plus three.

After a decline following World War II, polo is again gaining widespread popularity in the United States.

Advice For Beginners

Polo is played in more places than ever before. It is a fine sport for many individuals because you can start in and play at practically any level. There are expanding opportunities to participate, and if a person becomes a good rider he can become a good polo player. However, you must have a good horse to participate on a high level. The horse is a player's transportation in the game and because of the large size of the polo field, he must be an exceptional animal.

Knowing your horse is one of the most important aspects of polo. A player shouldn't consider a polo team as having only four players. Each time you go out on a new horse it's a new game and that makes eight. Playing on a strange horse is very difficult and for this reason the best players coach their own. Your horse is like your dancing partner and the better you know him the better you can play. You need to know, for example, the way he banks into the turn and how much speed he has. It's a little like driving a car for the first time. As a result, a player might want to start out on a new horse carefully to avoid "wrecks" while ironing out the wrinkles.

I personally started by playing other people's horses before I got my own. Now I have a fine string of horses and am always recruiting new ones that have potential, but for the beginner, the average saddle horse is usually the starting place for polo. He will be quiet enough to just sit and allow you to push the ball around.

I became interested in the game through my father who helped coach the old Stanford polo team. Playing and scrimmage against Stanford was great experience for me at that time, because a person must take up a game when he is young in order to become really proficient at it.

The best thing a beginner can do today if he wants to get involved is to contact the US Polo Association to find out where polo is played in his area. Many clubs and teams have training sessions and they usually welcome new players. The better players will want to play with each other, so be prepared to work your way up through the ranks. Initially, if you can ride, and if you're a good sport, you can bring your horse and start hitting the ball. And when you get better, you will be given a chance to work into a game to test your skill.

A player must count on accumulated experience if he wants to play well. A good polo player is one who scouts horses and players, and who is used to fast competition. The player who can ride the fastest, consistently hit the ball the farthest, and see the pattern of a game usually becomes the best polo player.

As you get older you lose some hitting ability, but you will have enough experience in placing yourself in a game to compensate for the lost strength. A few players are good at an early age, but most of the better players are between 30 and 40 years of age. There are even many fine players around 50 playing in international competition.

My thrills in polo have come from traveling to play the game with people around the world. I've been lucky enough to play in countries like China, Japan, Guatemala, El Salvador and Hawaii. Playing three times in the English Coronation was very pleasant, and it is always exciting to take part in the trophy ceremony with Queen Elizabeth and Prince Philip.

My biggest polo thrill took place in 1966 when I played in the Argentine Open where the world's best polo is played. The Argentines are the best and the fastest players in the world, and polo is their national game. The English are also very good, as are the Australians, New Zealanders and Spanish, but none can match the Argentines. And I'm happy to say the US now ranks second in world polo competition.

I've been playing on American teams for a great number of years, and the time and efffort has been well worth it. You might say my life has been centered around polo, coaching and being with horses. It has been so enjoyable that I'll continue in this manner as long as I can.

—Billy Linfoot

Dr. Billy Linfoot is generally known as the best American polo player of his day. For 11 years he played in international competition while being rated nine goal on a scale of 10. He is also an accomplished veternarian and respected authority on horses.

For More Information

The United States Polo Association, 1301 West 22nd St., Suite 706, Oak Brook, Ill. 60521 is the official governing body. *Polo*

News, Box 855, Middleburg, Va. 22117 is their official publication. It is a new publication with only a few issues out. Published monthly at $10.00 per year. Also, the United States Pony Clubs, Inc., 303 South High Street, West Chester, Pa. 19380 can provide information.

For equipment you might check with these people: H. Kaufman & Sons, 139 East 24th St., New York, N.Y. 10010; Miller's, 123 East 24th St., New York, N.Y. 10010; or Gray's of Westbury, Inc., 251 Post Ave., Westbury, L.I., New York 11590.

As far as books are concerned, we have one. It is available from World Publications, Box 366, Mountain View, Calif. 94040 at the price listed* plus 25 cents postage.

Beginning Polo, Harry Disson. A concise introduction to the sport with basic rules and playing procedures. Comments on the schooling of the polo pony, the basic polo strokes, and the handicap system. 1973 Hb., 200 pp., ill., $6.95, (Barnes).

Power Boat Racing

Powerboat racing in the United States dates back to before the turn of the century when a few "Iron Men" and their "Wooden Ships" did battle in the waters off Long Island Sound. Although interest in racing in those early days was limited, due in part to the reliability of the equipment, with the refinement of the internal combustion engine, interest increased accordingly. By 1902 there were sufficient craft putt-putting around to stimulate interest in organized racing.

These early crafts were of many varieties and capabilities, so it was agreed that a system of handicapping all craft equally must be divined. In 1903, the American Power Boat Association was born at a meeting attended by 20 yachting clubs.

Although limited in its scope in those early days, today powerboat racing offers something for everyone, with competition in nine facets that see speeds ranging from 30 mph to over 160 mph.

Powerboat racing takes place on either inland or offshore waters and the boats are propelled either by outboard or inboard motors. Many of the fastest craft, hydroplanes, are designed so the boat rises partially out of the water and skims over the surface. An even more spectacular advancement is the hydrofoil. At high speeds, this type of boat literally flies over the surface of the water, touching it at three points only. Two wing-like foils extend into the water on either side of the boat, and along with the propellers, lift the craft out of the water.

In drag boat racing, another form of powerboat racing, two boats at a time race over a straight stretch of water, ¼ of a mile in length. These boats, from 16 to 23 feet in length, may reach speeds of 190 mph in the last 50 yards of the race. This sport is recognized as one of the most hazardous, since the tiniest piece of debris, or the merest wave on the water can cause the speeding boat to upset, or the driver to lose control.

—Rusty Rae

Rusty Rae has been a boat racing enthusiast for many years. Although he is presently employed as photo editor for the American Motorcycle Association's official journal, he notes that "around the office I feel like a duck out of water." He is also the author of **Speed and Spray**.

A Word on Safety

Powerboat racing is one of the oldest motor sports in the United States and I feel lucky to have become involved in it. The sport has a long and colorful tradition, but I enjoy boat racing primarily because it is one of the cleanest and safest of all motor sports. Most drivers pride themselves on their sportsmanship as much as their driving skill, and the American Power Boat Association has set high standard for safety equipment.

The APBA safety rules require that certain precautions

The danger of powerboat racing lies in occasional spills, but modern safety measures prevent injuries so effectively that rescue crews are usually concerned only with getting the boat back to the pit area and ready for the next race.

must be taken before a boat is allowed out on the course, either for a race or practice. Drivers must wear helmets and life jackets when in the boat, and each craft must be equipped with fire prevention devices and automatic shut off throttles in case a driver is thrown out. Just imagine how hard it would be to run down a powerboat capable of 150 mph speed, and you'll see the wisdom of this throttle arrangement. And, the shut off keeps an out of control boat from going around in circles and running over a dunked driver.

APBA safety rules require an ambulance and physician to be present whenever a boat is on the course. Crash boats must also be stationed in strategic locations to swoop in and rescue drivers in trouble. Qualified first-aid personnel are often carried in each crash boat.

Although spills are not uncommon in powerboat racing, the above safety precautions have virtually eliminated serious mishaps. Injuries of any kind are few, and usually the biggest concern is to get a flipped boat back in shape for the next race.

When I won my first race at the age of 11, power boat racing was not as safe, but in the intervening 23 years it has become a thrilling motor sport with a very low risk coefficient. And along the way, I've been fortunate enough to win 41 national and world titles in four different racing classes.

Had powerboat racing not been so safe, I certainly could not have been able to experience the hundreds of thrills that have come my way. I could point to being selected a member of the APBA Honor Squadron as a high point in my racing career, but the happiest moment of my life was when I won a world championship race in St. Louis in front of my hometown fans.

—Bill Seebold, Jr

Bill Seebold, Jr. is a Mercury factory driver and has been a participant in boat racing since he was old enough to squeeze a throttle.

For More Information

Two excellent magazines exist for powerboat racing enthusiasts. *Propeller,* 22811 Greater Mack, St. Clair Shores, Mich. 48080. Published monthly at $5.00 per year. This magazine comes with an APBA membership (see below). It covers all phases of the sport and has complete schedule information. *Powerboat,* Nordco Publishing Co., 15917 Strathern St., Van Nuys, Calif. 91406. Published monthly at $9.00 per year. Covers all types of racing, as well as waterskiing and pleasure boating.

There's only one national organization for powerboat racing, the American Power Boat Association, 22811 Greater Mack, St. Clair Shores, Michigan 48080. Sanctions competition in nine different types of boats.

A couple of trillion equipment manufactuers and distributors exist for boating supplies. We have only been able to find one that has any sort of complete inventory of racing hardware for all classes of racing boats. Try Williams Manufacturing Co., 6450 Olympic Avenue, Bremerton, Wash. 98310.

Here is a book we recommend. It is available from World Publications, Box 366, Mountain View, Calif. 94040 at the price listed* plus 25 cents postage.

Speed and Spray, Rae and Blackburn. Powerboat racing in the United States. History of boat racing from the beginnings to the powerful machines of today's world. 1975 Ppb., 176 pp., ill., $5.95, (Stackpole).

Quarter Midget Races

Quarter midget racing is basically a little brother sport to big-time auto racing. Drivers of the specially built quarter midgets (scaled) down replicas of the full-size racing machines) are all youngsters. As a competitive sport for children, it started during the late 1930s in the Los Angeles area. Its popularity grew and spread into almost every state of the US, reaching a leveling off point during the late 1950s.

Quarter midget racing is a pastime for the whole family. The racing is limited to youngsters (both boys and girls) between the ages of 5 and 15, but the father, as crew chief, and mother as the timer/scorer/tower also play a very important role. The rules and specifications are extremely strict so that no competitor can have a distinct mechanical advantage over the other racers.

All drivers have attended and completed a required driving course, usually staffed and conducted by their parent club. Everything is safety oriented: first aid kit, track fire extinguishers, corner men, flagman, control lights, seat and shoulder belts, leather jackets, gloves, a helmet, goggles and/or race shield, naturally all QMA approved. One rule, for example, requires that an ignition cut-off switch be located outside of the cowl area so that the engine can be "killed" by someone other than the driver in case of an emergency.

Quarter midget clubs often participate in car shows, shopping center displays and driving demonstrations at the "big" tracks in their local area. During these activities, nationwide, the most frequently asked questions are: "Do they ever get hurt?" "How fast do they run?" "Are the drivers safe?"

In regard to the questions, "Do they ever get hurt?" and "Are they safe?" Quarter midget racing is very proud of its safety record. Yes, they do have "pile-ups", bumps and flips just about as often as the "big" tracks. However, no driver has received more than a few bruises or scratches. Falling off a bicycle usually produces more serious injuries. This enviable safety record is the result of a comprehensive safety program that stresses both safety procedures and equipment. In over 30 years there has never been a fatality in quarter midget racing—that's why a lot of people consider it safer than riding a bike these days.

In answering the "speed" question —this depends on the individual track and engine class. Quarter midget tracks, both dirt and asphalt, are designed specifically for quarter midget racing. Most of the tracks are banked, 1/20th mile around the inside, and 25-32 feet wide. The average pattern that a driver takes is approximately 366 feet long, and a fast stock class car will take 7.9 seconds to complete one lap, averaging 30 m.p.h. and reaching peak speeds of about 36 m.p.h. on the straights. As the drivers grow older and driving skills improve, they have the opportunity to advance to more powerful and faster cars.

Quarter midget racing is not a training ground for future race drivers. Though some of the competitors do go on to other forms of racing after they are over the age for quarter midgets, most do not. The emphasis of the sport is on sportsmanship and a family working together, rather than simply on winning. One of the most outstanding examples of the sportsmanship aspect of this sport can be seen in the fact that the prizes for the winners at all local and national races are never monetary awards. Trophies are the only physical recognition given in honor of a racing victory. The true prize in this sport, however, is the intangible one–the benefits garnered by a family that spends its time together in the pursuit of an ideal.

What is quarter midget racing doing for the youngsters? As close as can be determined, 99 out of 100 will never step into racing equipment after they leave quarter midgets. Most participants in this sport are here for much more than that. They develop a parent/son or parent/daughter "team" comradeship that is unequaled in any other sport. They gain the experience and meaning of sportsmanship, of knowledge and an appreciation of things mechanical.

Each August a Grand National Championship race is held. Drivers must qualify in sanctioned events and states races to be eligible to compete for national championship in each of 18 classes. Each registrant receives a participant plaque, and trophies are awarded to winners in the consolation, semi-main and main events. It is often noted that some of these trophies are taller than their proud recipients. A program is printed by the host club just for this event, and any driver, whether or not he attends, may have his picture and racing history printed in this official yearbook.

Clubs having suitable facilities bid for the privilege of hosting this event. The location is alternated between clubs east and west of the Mississippi River, thereby giving all members an equal opportunity to participate in a Grand National Race.

–Thanks to QMA for this introduction

History of Quarter Midgets

Miniature auto racing has been with us almost as long as auto car racing itself. Although it is nearly impossible to date the start of the sport, I'm sure the early 1930s were the real spawning years. Children have always copied their elders, so it was not uncommon for them to turn to "soap-box" racers as soon as the first big cars stripped down and began to race one another. It didn't take long before fathers began to attach washing machine or similar engines to the wooden boards and toy wagon wheels, so their children could drive on country lanes and in backyards, in imitation of the race cars of those days.

The first notice of an organized meet was a two day event called the "Children's Speed Classic" staged on May 26-27, 1934 at the famed Indianapolis Motor Speedway. The cars

"All drivers have attended and completed a required driving course, usually staffed and conducted by their parent club. Everything is safety oriented: First-aid kit, track fire extinguishers, corner men, flagman, control lights, seat and shoulder belts, leather jackets, gloves, helmet, and goggles." (Guilford)

were built by Floyd "Pop" Dreyer, who worked for the Duesenberg Brothers, Indianapolis race car builders. Oil drums were placed on a section of the main straightaway to mark out a small oval where the cars reached the fantastic speed of 20 m.p.h. Pop's three-year-old son was one of the drivers.

Prior to this, in 1932, the Winston Corporation of Joliet, Ill., manufactured a "Winston Racer" which was large enough to hold either a child or an adult. By 1934 the Maytag Washing Machine Company of Newton, Iowa was turning out a somewhat similar car. Both cars had the engine mounted behind the driver and drove the wheels by a "V-belt" arrangement. The engine in this case was the same one cylinder "Multi-Motor" used by Maytag to power their washing machines. During the years from 1934 to 1940, Maytag sold over 500 of these little "Maytag Racers".

By 1938 a group of fathers had banded together in the small Los Angeles community of San Marino, and under the guidance of a local service station operator, Coyle Tracy, formed the Junior Midgets of America, Chapter One, more to keep the little motorized cars off the street than to promote racing. Some cars were the aforementioned Winston and Maytag Racers, but most were home built. Very few had any form of a body, only wooden frames. Power came from a variety of sources, including ex-washing machine engines, lawn mower and pipe threading engines. One car used an electric battery powered auto starter.

Ages of the drivers ranged from six to 14 and included girls. Speeds up to 30 m.p.h. were reached on the 1/10th of a mile flat, dirt oval during the weekly races. Of the 21 cars, in the club, costs varied from $65 up to $1200. Anything was raceable as long as it had four wheels and an engine under two horsepower–no body, no floor board, no seat belt. Safety equipment, as such, was not required, with the exception of goggles to protect the eyes from the dirt. By winning the "Helmet Dash" several weeks in a row, a youngster could win a driving helmet. A unique aspect of membership in the Junior Midgets included the drivers' school grades provision–failing grades and no racing that week. Nation-wide attention was given this group of racers by articles in major magazines and newspapers as well as in newsreels and films.

A big boost to the sport of miniature car racing came with the formation of the Junior Midget Motor Car Company by a Los Angeles auto parts dealer, Joe Lucus, and Lou Faegol, the son of the owner of the Faegol Truck Company. They began making a hand-made production model racer styled after the "big" midgets of those days. The engine was mounted in front of the driver and used a chain drive to the rear axle. Without a body, it was called a "Midget-Midget" and looked like the first go-cart. The appearance of these cars brought a standardization to the cars and a few safety features.

After World War II, various groups across the nation formed local Junior Midget clubs to resume racing the small cars. A couple of kids driving their cars on the street were invited to a vacant lot to participate with other youngsters in some informal races. One of these boys was Jimmy Caruthers, now a Indianapolis 500 race car driver. Jimmy was nine years old and brother Danny only four. The skill and enthusiasm of the youngsters inspired Jimmy's father, Doug Carruthers, to build a track for them on the grounds of his Viking Trailer Company. Dubbed the "Jelly Bean Bowl" it was a 1/20th of a mile, banked, dirt oval.

Having had prior racing experience racing dragsters on the dry lakes of Southern California, Doug Caruthers saw the need for some form of organization to the races, and thus formed the Quarter Roadster Association, styled after the big time URA (United Racing Association), using many of the same rules and regulations. Caruthers also saw the need for a standardization of cars and engines and soon began the manufacture of a rear engine, one-fourth scale midget–a true quarter midget. Many of these cars were sold through a large department store, and soon after many clubs across the country adopted similar engine and car specifications as those of the Quarter Roadster Association.

Within a few short years, there were more than a dozen companies turning out hundreds of these little Quarter Midgets. The hand-formed sheet metal bodies were replaced by the light weight fiberglass style that were easier to produce. Safety standards were raised, with the introduction of mandatory driving helmets, roll bars and seat belts.

National growth came in leaps and bounds to the sport. In Northern California, alone, there were 17 tracks and almost 3000 drivers in 1957. During this period there were 35-40 companies mass producing quarters as well as hundreds of smaller garages turning out custom made cars.

The popularity of the little speedsters also caused an event in 1957 that was to give the sport a major turn. While country-wide National Competitions were being held in such cities as Phoenix, Tulsa, Portland and Las Vegas, and attended by hundreds of drivers from almost every state, Art Ingles, a worker in the Kurtis Kraft shops of Frank Kurtis (famed Indy 500 race car builder and quarter midget manufacturer), originated the idea for a small economical form of miniature race car–the Go-Kart. By eliminating the suspension and body of a quarter midget and adding to the horsepower of the power unit, Art was soon the envy of every passerby on the parking lots where he ran. Others soon joined him in this pastime, and tracks similar to those used by sports cars were built for the karts. Costs for the karts were less than one-fourth those of the quarters and had the added advantage that not only the kids, but Mom and Dad could drive them on any nearby parking lot. The low price of purchase was a good reason why it only took two years before there were more than 60 brand names of karts being sold in this country alone. The parking lot at the Pasadena Rose Bowl held the first organized race meet. The go-kart held the answer to the desire by many that wanted to compete in the expensive sport of sports car racing, but were prevented by the cost.

At the same time the karts made an inroad into the ranks of the quarter midgets, there appeared a larger version of the quarter–the half-midget. Large enough for the older members of the family as well, it too stole many of the supporters of the smaller cars that limited its drivers to ages five to 12.

Realizing the strength in a national organization, another attempt was made to nationalize the sport by the formation of a single association to be the governing body for all races. These races were to be run under a program of standard car and engine specifications and a uniform set of racing and safety rules. From these efforts was born the Quarter Midgets of America, a nationally recognized sanctioning body for quarter and half midget races in this country and Canada. Since its birth, the organization has been responsible for setting uniform engine, car, racing and safety rules. Coordinating and sanctioning racing events, providing insurance for tracks and drivers, and publishing an Annual Directory and a bi-monthly newsletter–

The QuarteReporter– all came into the realm of the Association. Annual meetings of National Officers and Directors are now held at the yearly Grand Nationals.

Since the formation of QMA, membership growth has not been rapid, but nevertheless it has been constant. In 1964 the first "QMA Grand National Championships" were held in Hayward, Calif., with 150 entries. By 1975, and the running of the 12th Annual "Grand", attendance has grown to well over 500 participants.

A recently added region in Florida has brought the Quarter Midgets of America into 13 regional areas, including a club in Canada. Governed by elected national officers and a board of directors, QMA has taken steps recently to gain more national recognition, including the entry of a float in the Indianapolis 500 Festival Parade. Many of the regional States Races and the Grand National have had a financial assist from major auto parts companies.

Still one of the very few children's sports activities that makes no distinction between girl and boy participants, the present age requirements are from five to 15 years old, with an opportunity to move up to the half-midgets when they reach 16 years old. The half-midgets allow the children to continue to race with QMA.

There has never been a recorded fatality in the more than 35 years of miniature race car competition, an enviable safety record shared by few children's competitive sports. Although not designed as a training ground for big-car drivers, many of the drivers have gone on to fame on the race tracks of this country. Many have joined regional racing associations and quite a few have joined the ranks of USAC (United States Auto Club). Five have made it to the biggest of them all–the Indianapolis 500 Race: Swede Savage, Bruce Walkup, and three drivers that raced together as quarter midgeteers–Jimmy Caruthers, Duane "Pancho" Carter, Jr., and Johnny Parson, Jr. The latter two also had racing fathers that competed at the famous "Indiana brickyard".

As to the future of quarter midget racing: it will continue to grow and make changes the same as the sport it imitates. Already the past 10 years have seen several innovations, such as mandatory safety roll cages, quick release seat and shoulder harnesses, new style fiberglass bodies with such added strength that it replaces the need for bumpers and nerf bars. In addition, better performance from the small engines has in turn lowered track records with increasing regularity.

So it looks as though quarter midgets will be with us as long as there are girls and boys looking for a safe, exciting, motorized recreational sport that enables the entire family to participate, and at the same time develops a closer relationship between children and their parents.

–Ernie St. Germain

Ernie St. Germain has been a QMA member for 10 years, and had two of his children drive quarter and half midgets. He initiated, and is the producer of, nine color/sound films for the QMA Film Library. Currently he has three films in production, including a history of miniature and quarter midget cars.

For More Information

The best source of information is from Quarter Midgets of America, Edward Wyatt, Rt. 2, Box 177, Landenberg, Pa. 19350. They put out a regular newsletter that will be of interest. There are 61 clubs throughout the US and one in Canada.

Quoits

The game of quoits was brought to America by English colonists and was popularly played in the British Isles as long ago as the early 14th century.

Quoits consists of pitching a heavy metal ring at an iron peg driven into the ground, much like horseshoe pitching. The quoit to be pitched is usually between six and nine pounds in weight, with a diameter of 8½ inches or less. The doughnut hole in the center is usually narrower than 3½ inches, the smaller the hole the more difficult it is to throw the quoit over the peg. A quoit is shaped very much like an upside down saucer with a hole in the middle of it.

When playing, ringers count for two points, and if no ringers are scored, the nearest quoit to the pin (called a hob) counts one point. Upside down quoits do not count, and games are played to an arbitrarily pre-arranged score.

Deck quoits was once played on ocean liners with wooden pegs and quoits made from rings of rope. Today the game is played with hard rubber or plastic quoits and sets can be found in children's toy stores.

Race Walking

As a specialized and even esoteric offspring of the parent sport of track and field, race walking has often been a misunderstood and neglected stepchild. Yet, despite lack of public acceptance, the sport survives and manages to draw a dedicated group of competitors and officials, who defend their sport as one equally challenging as any in athletics.

Organized walking competition had its start in mid-19th century England, when town-to-town walking events drew large and enthusiastic crowds of both spectators and competitors. Race walking as we know it today, however, had its start in the early Olympic Games, where international competitions with standardized rules first were held.

The modern rules of race walking state that one foot must be on the ground at all times, with the heel of the advancing foot striking the ground first, and the toe of the trailing foot leaving the ground last. In addition, the knee of the supporting

To the casual observer, race walkers look like some weird combination of stork and penguin as they amble down the track. Genuine track fans, however, admire the dedicated training of these athletes. Anyone who can maintain a walker's blistering pace for 30 miles combines hard training with a superior degree of will power. (Shearman).

leg must be straightened as it passes under the body's center. To walk legally at a high speed, the walker turns his hips with his stride and drives the arms for power and balance.

These rules place unusual demands on the body, and keep race walking distinct from running . . . requiring a different set of muscles and a different breed of athlete.

The ideal walker must combine the endurance of a distance runner, the strength of a weightlifter, and the flexibility of a gymnast. The top walkers of today do in fact possess these qualities.

International walking competitions are held as a regular part of such contests as the Olympic Games, the Pan-American Games, and the European Track and Field Championships. In addition, walking has its own unofficial world championship, the Lugano Cup 20- and 50-kilometer walks, held every two years in Europe.

The existence of race walking as an international sport has often been a tenuous one, but it has a long history and a dedicated group of enthusiasts behind it. Doubtlessly it will continue, attracting a particularly gifted and tenacious type of athlete, and the support of those who appreciate the unique demands of competitive walking.

—Martin Rudow

Martin Rudow was the alternate to the 1968 U.S. Olympic team in the 20-kilometer walk. He is the author of the book **Race Walking.**

A Great Walker

The sport of race walking has, with some justification, been termed "the sport of the intellectuals and eccentrics." And the one individual who probably more than anyone else represented the struggles of the race walker could truly be said to fit both categories.

Beatnik (this was before the "hippy" era), itinerant house-painter, University of Chicago graduate student, and apparently hopeless non-athlete, Chris McCarthy nonetheless propelled himself to the top of the US distance walking scene in the early 1960s, and pointed the way to a whole generation of walkers to follow.

In early 1962, McCarthy, writing in his own *American Race Walker* magazine, stated that no American athlete was doing the training necessary for distance walking, and that anyone so doing would guarantee himself a place on the 1964 50-kilometer Olympic walking team. Evidently inspired by his own prose, McCarthy undertook the rigorous training necessary to turn an unnatural athlete, in his own words a "scrub", into a competent 50-kilometer walker.

The physical and mental demands of a 50 kilometer are, to say the least, extensive. The 31-mile event requires considerable overall body strength, a strong constitution, a tremendous background of training, and far more than the usual amount of will power. McCarthy lacked all but the latter ingredient.

As he undertook 50-kilo training, readers of the *American Race Walker* followed his progress. Injuries, Chicago's horrendous weather, threats of physical violence by onlookers – nothing stopped McCarthy's training program. And slowly, painfully, it began to pay off.

By 1963 McCarthy was established as the top distance walker in the country – to the amazement of all who had known him throughout his largely unsuccessful athletic career. But he was still far below the form of his European counterparts, and even another year of training couldn't change this. In the 1964 Games, McCarthy walked to a lifetime best, the fastest time ever turned in by an American walker under international conditions. But this 4:35 effort earned him only 19th place, over two miles behind the first place finisher.

The Games over, McCarthy abruptly retired, and hasn't walked seriously since. But his contribution to the sport cannot be overlooked. He "showed the way" to a whole generation of American walkers, demonstrating that hard work alone could still bring successes in distance athletics.

His example has been well taken, for since his era, other Americans have walked far faster times than his 4:35. Larry Young even won two Olympic bronze medals in the "50". But McCarthy, more than anyone before or since, epitomizes the spirit of the race walker. The intellectual/eccentric, the unnatural athlete, training and sacrificing for an ever-so-small spot in the athletic limelight.

—Martin Rudow

For More Information

The best single source for information is John Boitano, AAU Race Walking Chairman, Fairfield University, Fairfield, Conn. 04630. And *Runner's World* magazine, Box 366, Mountain View, Calif. 94040 does the best job in covering the sport. Not every issue has an article on race walking but most do. Published monthly at $9.50. Here are a couple of books of interest. Both are available from World Publications, Box 366, Mountain View, Calif. 94040 at the price listed* plus 25 cents each postage. Write for a complete list.

Race Walking, Martin Rudow. Introduces beginning walkers and would-be walking coaches to the sport. Features articles on training for distance, tips on establishing a proper walking style, special strength for walkers and more. 1974 Ppb., 48 pp., ill., $1.50, (World Publications).

Competitive Race Walking, Ron Laird. A guide to technique, training and judging by one of America's top walkers. Sequential photo-illustration of all facets of technique, as well as pictures of many world-class walkers. 1972 Ppb., 64 (oversize) pp., ill., $3.95, (Track & Field News).

Rackets

The game of rackets (sometimes spelled *racquets*), played in the U.S.A., England and Canada, is widely held as the fastest of all traditional court games. The playing of rackets is very similar to that of its popular offshoot, *squash racquets.* Two or four players play this historic game on a court which is enclosed by four walls.

The equipment for rackets consists of a strung racket, a hard ball built around a moulded polythene core, light clothing including coverups for colder weather, and light athletic shoes with gripping soles. The hard ball is one of the distinguishing traits that separates rackets from squash racquets. A rackets player would do well to avoid being hit by this ball which can travel at high speeds.

As far as rules of play, they are similar to those of squash (see Squash Racquets), with one exception: In rackets, the first player to score 15 *aces* wins the game, excepting a 13-all or 14-all score, when the winning point is reset by the players.

Rackets, in its modern form, was first played by jail inmates in England in the 19th century, although its true origins can be traced all the way back to its ancestor, handball, which was played in the middle ages. In England, the backyards of taverns and inns in many towns sported racket courts, as well as in Fleet prison—a court which is described in Dickens' *Pickwick Papers*:

"The area formed by the wall in that part of the Fleet in which Mr. Pickwick stood was just wide enough to make a good racket-court; one side being formed, of course, by the wall itself and the other by that portion of the prison which looked (or rather would have looked, but for the wall) towards St. Paul's Cathedral. . .Lolling from the windows which commanded a view if this promenade were a number of persons. . . looking on at the racket-players, or watching the boys as they cried the game".

Due to the influence of the British Army and Navy, rackets spread to other parts of the world. After growing popularity in Canada the game spread to the US, where racket clubs were set up in New York, Boston, Chicago, Detroit, and Philadelphia.

The world's racket championships, the most coveted event in the sport, dates back to 1820. Clarence C. Pell is known as one of the greatest American rackets players of all time. Not only did he win 12 national singles titles, but he won Canadian singles championships nine times and Canadian doubles six times. Still, the standard of play is higher in England than anywhere else, mainly because of its early seeds in the game and its skilled coaches.

For More Information

Additional information is available from: Steve Colhoun, 270 Park Ave, New York, N.Y. 10017 and George Hendrick, 111 West Monroe, Room 1700, Chicago, Ill. 60603. Both head up the North American Rackets Association. Another good contact is Racquet and Tennis Club, Park Ave., New York, N.Y. 10017.

Racquetball

Racquetball is a relatively new sport on the American scene, having been introduced in organized form in 1968. The game has grown with great strides—so much so, as to have now outgrown its three primary parents: handball, paddleball and squash. Racquetball is played indoors on a standard four-walled handball court measuring 20 feet wide, 20 feet high and 40 feet long. The mandatory back wall must be at least 12 feet high. The game is played with virtually the same rules as handball—a game is 21; points can be scored by the server only. The ball must be returned to the front wall on one bounce, or on the fly. Two games out of three is a match. Racquetball is played with a short, strung racquet measuring a maximum of 18 inches in length and nine inches in width. To non-players it looks like a miniature tennis racquet. Most racquets are strung with nylon filament in a frame of wood, plastic, aluminum, steel, or fiberglass.

The origins of racquetball are difficult to pinpoint. Nobody is sure exactly when the first handball player took his tennis racquet and began playing the new game on the tennis courts. Perhaps it was a squash player widening and shortening his racquet and moving to a slightly larger handball court. But whoever it was, that person touched off a growth process that continues to amaze North American sports enthusiasts.

What is the secret of racquetball's success? The first reason is the simplicity of learning the sport: racquetball's short racquet, lively ball and enclosed court all make for easier play. The racquet gives more control than the longer, heavier tennis racquet. The ball is lively enough to stay in the air longer, permitting more retrieves. And the walls make the ball bounce back toward the players, instead of out away from them, as in most other racquet sports; thus more time is spent playing, and less time retrieving poor shots.

Racquetball, because of its ease of play, is a family sport. Married couples, sweethearts, boys and girls, can all be seen at almost any time of the day in mixed doubles play. Ten-year-olds are commonplace on the courts; all ages can and do enjoy racquetball.

Another key to racquetball's success is physical fitness. Racquetball is a body-builder, a cardiovascular aid, a fun way to get in and maintain your health. The vigorous exercises afforded in an hour of racquetball can keep physically fit bodies that way: tone muscles, expand lung capacity, increase circulation, and release built-up tensions. Racquetball is also competitive. Numerous organizations have sponsored and hosted hundreds of tournaments, clinics and exhibitions over the last eight years. There are tournaments for all age groups from 15 to 65. There is even a professional tour, first organized by Kendler's National Racquetball Club, in which over $50,000 in prize money and awards were won by players. The national championship tournament is held annually, with players from the United States and Canada competing for top prize in a multitude of age classes. Of course, the real plum is the professional championship, held annually and won in 1975 by San Diego attorney Charles Brumfield. The 26-year-old Brumfield, a two-time winner in the years prior to professionalism, dethroned defending champ Bill Schmidtke from Minneapolis, also a two-time winner.

—**Chuck Leve**

Chuck Leve is National Director of the USRA and editor of **National Racquetball** *magazine. He is also author of* **Inside Racquetball.**

For More Information

The two major organizations are the International Racquetball Association, Box 1016, Stillwater, Oklahoma 74074, and the United States Racquetball Association, 4101 Dempster St., Skokie, Ill. 60076 who publish *National Racquetball.* For additional information check out these books. They are available from World Publications, Box 366, Mountain View, Calif. 94040 at the price listed* plus 25 cents each postage. Write for a complete list.

Inside Racquetball, Chuck Leve. The authorized International Racquetball Association player's manual and rule book. Shows you why racquetball is rapidly rising in popularity, and how to play to win. 1973 Hb. & Ppb., 96 (oversize) pp., ill., $7.95/ $3.95, (Regnery).

Racquetball/Paddleball, Allsen and Witback. A book which provides the beginner with an easy to follow sequence of playing techniques. Basic skills strategy. Practice drills are presented in a clear, logical manner. 1972 Ppb., 52 pp., ill., $2.50, (W.C. Brown).

Rafting

Rafting was hardly a new activity when Mark Twain created *Huckleberry Finn* nearly a hundred years ago (1884), and it has become one of America's fastest-growing sports. From a history of bullboats and log rafts grew inflatable boats roughly 50 years ago. Commonly known as river rafts today, these crafts developed out of the Second World War.

Initially they were military surplus bridge pontoons, life rafts and assault boats, but as the activity became more popular, various crafts designed specifically for river running were developed, to a limited extent by American companies and to a much larger degree by companies in England, France, Japan and China. Today virtually no inflatable rafts are manufactured in the United States, and with the massive increase in the activity throughout America, there is a growing market for quality crafts.

Rafting consists primarily of floating along the surface of a river or stream using paddles, oars, sweeps or a motor to control the craft. The flowing water that supports the craft also provides the power, for the most part, while the means of control keeps the craft on the water and off obstacles that might damage it or cause it to upset or be held subject to the power of the current without being able to move. That is a dangerous situation that could have serious implications for the passengers.

Rafting trips may be simple short trips on lakes or reservoirs that require little or no experience and additional equipment, ocean-going crafts run by high-powered motors, or extended trips on river that require extensive overnight camping and cooking equipment and elaborate planning. Usually, however, they involve—in addition to the craft itself and the means of propulsion—at least a personal flotation device for safety. Waterproof bags, boxes, cans or containers of some sort to keep things dry—cameras, food, clothing, other equipment—become important if you take anything along but the bare necessities. It is possible to purchase flimsy one- or two-person crafts that are more playthings than boats for less than $50, but a quality craft for four or more people will cost several hundred dollars. Avon (British) and Campways (made in Japan) boats are among the most readily-available rafts; inflatable canoe-kayak types of craft made in Taiwan and France are sometimes considered "rafts," but do not really fit the pattern.

The means of control, paddles, oars, sweeps, motor—constitute an additional expense. You can buy cheap paddles for as little as $10, but the better ones start at more than twice that and range to well over $100. Oars are more expensive and require an oar-lock plus, in most situations, a rowing frame as do sweeps. Soon you're into a few hundred more before you're ready for the river. Motors require some kind of motor mount plus the price of an engine, plus the fuel. I never use

"Why do I run rivers? For many lesser reasons that seem important to me: seeing a herd of 80 elk on the upper Snake, the cows abandoning the calves to the river in their rush for the shore and the calves drifting down to land on gravel bars, crying like so many seagulls. Feeling the spray on my face, the rhythm of the rapid, the pulse of nature." (Krips)

them myself because I don't like the noise nor the fuss and fumes, but they are used extensively for river trips in some areas.

One-day or even trips of a few hours' duration are among the most popular rafting experiences like those on the Upper Snake in Jackson Hole, Wyo.; the Stanislaus in California; the Rogue in Oregon; the Youghiogheny in Pennsylvania; the Cheat and the New in West Virginia; the Chattooga on the Georgia-South Carolina stateline; perhaps the Flambeau in Wisconsin.

Extended trips have become highly popular on many western rivers in the past decade—so much so that many of the western rivers and even a few eastern rivers are not highly regulated: the Colorado River through Grand Canyon and Catacart Canyon in Canyonlands National Park; the Yampa and the Green in Dinosaur National Monument; the Snake in Hells Canyon; the Wild Middle Fork of the Salmon in Idaho and the Main Salmon itself; the Rogue; the Snake; the Chattooga; and others.

But depending upon the size of your raft and the season, the water level and your knowledge and experience, a great many rivers throughout these United States can be rafted with ease and pleasure. Rivers that have been considered the domain of the kayaker and canoeist are possible rafting streams. Check them out before you commit yourself, and if you're new to the sport, start gradually, using an intelligent progression.

The first time, go with someone who knows the sport. Perhaps take a commercial trip or two. Practice the skills on quiet water, even on lakes and reservoirs (many kayakers begin their training in swimming pools). Test your knowledge and ability before you try anything tough, and learn from others and from watching what flowing water does to objects on its surface—it could save your life.

—**Verne Huser**

Verne Huser is the author of **River Running** *and also contributes regularly to* **Down River** *magazine.*

Please Don't Ask

Riding the back eddy upstream, we pull gently on the oars as Indian warriors run their horses before a battle to enter the fight on second wind. Pulling harder, we cross the eddy line and edge into the strong main current flowing 40,000 cubic feet per second. Now the big effort to catch the full force of the narrow chute: pull, pull, pull! The river is too strong for us and we swing around in a quick 360, pulling back into the lessening current where the river widens just above the rapid, Wild Shee—rated a nine (great to extreme difficulty and hazard) on the American Canyon and Rapid Rating System. We approach the head of the rapid still too far left—pull! The right bank is Idaho; pull Idaho, pull hard! Now she's coming in. Straighten her out, bow downstream, steady.

Down the sharp initial drop of the smooth tongue, up and over the first wave. Wow, what a hole! Into the vortex of the rapid where all hell breaks loose with a mad dashing of waves against each other and against the boat, roostertails breaking high over the boat and smashing into braced bodies and shocked faces. The boat, taking on water, dives into huge holes, riding them out in a froth of white water to climb the next wave, and the next as the rubber pontoon bucks like a wild bronc. Exhilarated yelling now that the fear of the first big rapid is all but over, and we're through and afloat, wet as dunked donuts and still battling the tailwaves. Man the bailing buckets and pull hard once more, this time for the Oregon side to land and put the party ashore to watch the other boats run the rapid.

Hell's Canyon: deepest gorge on the North American continent, a special place of green velvet walls and secret places,

Down river rafting can have its quieter moments, and it can be a sport for family involvement. River rafts were initially military surplus bridge pontoons, life rafts and assault boats, but as the activity became more popular crafts were specifically designed for running rivers. (Krips)

but only one of many rivers I've run, and each is special in its own way.

Why do people raft?—run the wild rivers with nothing but a bit of inflated nylon-and-neoprene fabric between them and the roaring rapids? The best answer I've heard is simply "You can't explain it to people who have to ask."

John Wesley Powell, Gustav Doane, and Lewis and Clark were explorers. Why do I run rivers? For many lesser reasons that seem important to me: seeing the herd of 80 elk on the Upper Snake, the cows abandoning the calves to the river in their rush for the shore and the calves drifting down to land on gravel bars, crying like so many seagulls. Feeling the spray on my face, the rhythm of the rapid, the pulse of nature. The cool springs on the Cheat on a hot day in late July.

Elves Chasm, Redwall Cavern, Vasey's Paradise in the Grand Canyon. The Middle Fork in May with Rick Petrillo and no passengers, high water in the Impassable Canyon . . . blackberries on the Rogue in late August, autumn color on the Skagit in the North Cascades . . . water ouzel on the Hoback, beaver on nearly ever river I've ever run from the Inner Gorge of Grand Canyon to the Dolores in western Colorado where they seem to prefer sagebrush to box elder . . . .

Cross-bedded sandstone on the Cheat, on the Dolores, on the Colorado, on the Green . . . canyon wrens in Grand Canyon . . . green heron on the Rogue—and one at the head of Horn Creek Rapid in Grand Canyon, believe it or not . . . young owls in the woods at Granite Creek Campsite in Hells Canyon—and miners' lettuce to add to our salad . . . the petroglyphs at Pittsburg Landing and at Buffalo Eddy.

The carnival atmosphere on the Youghiogheny on a busy day in mid-summer . . . the dream of running the Chattooga. My first run on the Middle Fork with Hank and Sharon, Earl and another Sharon, following Cort Conley, and blowing it at Redside—and running Redside right the next time. Forty eagles, both bald and golden, on the Snake in Idaho in April—just below Palisades Dam . . . flipping in Big Mallard with Rod Nash at the oars, my first and only dunking to date. You learn from every experience that you store in your quickening mind.

Why raft a river? If you have to ask, you'd better try it.

—**Verne Huser**

For More Information

Check kayaking and canoeing for additional information. The best magazine covering the sport on a regular basis is *Down River*, Box 366, Mountain View, Calif. 94040. Published monthly at $8.00 per year. Here are some good books. All are available from World Publications, Box 366, Mountain View, Calif. 94040 at the price listed* plus 25 cents postage.

River Running, Verne Huser. A comprehensive guidebook on river running in inflatable rafts. The explanations on equipment, routines of rafting expeditions, safety procedures, and specific information on wild rivers in the US and Canada will make your river trips more fascinating and comfortable. 1975 Hb. & Ppb., 294 pp., ill., $10.00/$4.95, (Regnery).

A Guide to Paddle Adventure, Rick Kemmer. An invaluable book for those who are or want to be involved in the exciting and inexpensive hobby of paddle travel. Provides a comprehensive discussion of the craft available, and the author's observations on capacity, depth, weight, construction and approximate price. 1975 Hb. & Ppb., 295 pp., ill., $10.00/$6.95, (Vanguard).

Whitewater Rafting, Bill McGinnis. In addition to a complete treatment of the subject of river rafting, this book presents camping, cooking, photography and many other pursuits from a river runner's point of view. 1975 Hb., 361 pp., $12.50, (Harper & Row).

Recreational Vehicles

Use of a recreational vehicle is a means by which to better enjoy a sport, rather than a sport itself. But if the prime qualification for classification as a sport is possession of a huge, devoted following, RV usage truly is up there with the best of them.

More than five million Americans own RVs of all sizes and shapes and ownership of such a vehicle can become so engrossing as to represent a life style all its own. Many RV owners are out in their vehicles pursuing their diverse interests at least two weekends a month; many do it even more often. Of course, annual vacations are invariably taken in the RV.

What the RV represents is a special kind of freedom, a special kind of mobility. Take, for instance, a ski trip of ours last year to Yosemite. When we arrived in the park, it was snowing heavily but as yet there weren't any problems getting around. In Yosemite, the snow tends to be wet and heavy. It continued to pile up for three days until the power lines were down and the roads were closed in all directions. The snowplows couldn't keep up with it and one of them had hit a tree felled across the road by the heavy snow.

It was a heavy weekend for skiers, both alpine and cross-country, and many simply were up for the day, with no lodging. It was a miserable wait for many of them in service stations, and sitting in their cars.

For us, it wasn't even an inconvenience. Many RVs are equipped for what we call self-containment – that is, they need no outside connections other than the usual necessity to periodically take on gasoline for propulsion, propane for cooking and refrigeration, water and food. We were snowed-in for two days but we hiked on snowshoes, used our cross-country skis, and were quite comfortable.

This incident is an example of the versatility which the RV offers, although certainly not everyone would choose to venture into the high mountains in winter. In fact, most RV owners are sun seekers, and the RV comes in for its prime use during warm months. A lot of owners are out there purely for the enjoyment of RVing, but others use the RV as a base station for sports such as hiking or backpacking. For others it's fishing, rock hunting, spelunking, motorcycling, boating and other such activities. The "sport" of RVing simply is to enjoy yourself, regardless of the activity . . . or lack of it. Many owners like to find a quiet spot and simply sit for a weekend, reading and relaxing.

Preferences for specific kinds of camping spots vary as widely as the RV owners themselves. Many like the commercial parks where activities and a high degree of socializing are offered. Others head for the back woods and get as far away from congestion as possible. The ultimate for this kind of RV owner is to find a spectacularly beautiful spot and be the only one there.

Four-wheel-drive vehicles are used by many RV owners, mostly as tow vehicles for travel trailers. Also, there are a few four-wheel-drive vans and mini-motorhomes. The classifications of RVs tend to be a bit confusing to one who hasn't studied the vehicles but the categories are fairly simple. Most popular is the travel trailer, towed by anything from the family passenger car to a jeep-style vehicle. Travel trailers vary in length from 13 to 32 feet. Fifth-wheel trailers are similar in usage but are connected to the tow vehicle (a pickup truck) differently. They overhang the truck much as a commercial semi-trailer overhangs a diesel tractor. The hitching principle is similar, even though the appearance is different. Another trailer classification is the camping trailer, a unit which has folding sides allowing it to collapse to a considerably smaller size for travel than when extended.

Motorhomes vary in size from 15 to 32 feet, with some converted passenger buses going to 35 feet. Campers hauled by pickup trucks range from eight to 10 feet in the sections which actually occupy the pickup bed and overhang it in the rear, plus what is called the cabover section (sleeping section) above the truck cab, for another five feet.

Still another category is the van conversion – a van in which there are installed living accommodations.

These categories indicate a tremendous amount of variety in what the RV offers, in what the owner can do with it, and in what it costs. The price range varies from $1500 for a small travel trailer to $50,000 and above for luxury motorhomes.

The attitudes RV owners have toward their vehicles are diverse. Many consider the RV merely a means to an end -- transportation and accommodations leading to the events to come. Others, myself included, are intensely involved with the vehicle as a hobby in itself. Much as the performance car enthusiast or backpacker can while away hours working on his equipment, the RV owner's involvement ranges from routine maintenance to installation of new devices and systems designed to improve comfort, convenience, vehicle stability, performance or appearance. The list of possibilities is endless. The real RV enthusiast's coach may have been "built" before he bought it, but it is never "finished".

When the two ingredients – the destination activities and the continual involvement with the vehicle – are combined, they can provide a very high level of enjoyment and satisfaction.

Still another factor is the social angle. To many owners, the RV is the hub of their social lives. They belong to clubs such as the 150,000-member Good Sam Club, sponsored by Trailer Life Publishing Co. of Calabasas, Calif., in whose local chapters they plan outings, caravans, meetings, banquets and whatever else they choose.

A growing number of retirees are selling their homes and moving into the larger motorhomes and trailers full-time. National magazines such as *Trailer Life* and *Motorhome Life/ Camper Coachman* are devoted exclusively to telling these and all other RV owners about new places to go, interesting things to do, and how to make their RVs more comfortable, more economical, and safer.

Many owners must save for years to buy the vehicle of their choice and they regard it as their escape route from the pressures and frustrations of daily living. The RV, in short, is a way of life to an increasing number of Americans. In view of the new horizons it opens, it isn't any wonder.

—Bill Estes

Bill Estes is a long-time RV enthusiast. He is Editor of **Motorhome Life & Camper Coachman** *and Technical Editor of* **Trailer Life** *magazine.*

For More Information

There are two excellent magazines for the RV enthusiast: *Trailer Life* gives camper and motorhome evaluations, new equipment reports, how-to articles and describes motorcamping areas. *Motorhome Life and Camper Coachman* deals along similar lines. Both magazines are put together by Trailer Life Publishing Co., 23945 Craftsman Rd., Calabasas, Calif. 91302. They also sponsor the Good Sam Club, the largest RV club in existence. Local chapters plan outings, caravans, meetings and other activities.

Many RV dealers are located throughout the continent who are prepared to answer any questions you might have. Of course, equipment and accessories are also available through them.

"Races, as a rule, are open to anyone and everyone. Rarely are there any age, sex or ability barriers. Because of this, several US events now draw a thousand runners or more. The largest, the Bay-to-Breakers in San Francisco, has topped 5000." (Frederick)

Road Running

Road running is making the best of a bad situation. Automobiles have put wheels under us and threatened to turn our legs into dead stumps. The concrete and asphalt over which the cars roll have buried the natural environment at an alarming pace.

Yet the same roads are putting a growing number of people back on their feet, and back in touch with what's left of nature. Streets and roads are the most available places to race, so road running is the fastest growing sport under the umbrella of track and field athletics.

Since the late 1960s, road running has matured. It had been a small band of marathoners, noticed only once every four years at the Olympics and for one day each April at Boston. Two movements changed this in a hurry.

The first was road training. Arthur Lydiard, a coach from New Zealand, changed the direction of training when his athletes won four gold medals at the Rome and Tokyo Olympics. Most of Peter Snell's and Murray Halberg's running was on the streets and highways. Runners everywhere began imitating them in the mid-'60s. And their road training soon led to road racing.

The second movement was even more important. Call it the "Aerobics Revolution." Dr. Kenneth Cooper set it off with a book proclaiming the values of jogging for health. Joggers by the thousands took to the streets in their neighborhoods. Jogging became running, and running became racing for many of them.

The trackmen and graduated joggers joined the old marathoners at the family-picnic-like road races. There was room for everyone, and the number and size of events exploded.

In 1968, for instance, US runners supported 38 marathon races. By 1975, there were four times that many events. The latest *Marathon Handbook* lists nearly 2500 runners under three hours for 1974. That's almost 10 times more than ran that fast before the twin revolutions of the 1960s.

The 26-mile 385-yard marathon has been and probably always will be the focus in road running. It has the Olympic tradition. However, this is only one stop on a continuum starting at a few miles and ending at 100.

The standard distances are five, 10, 15, 20, 30, 40, 50 and 100 miles, and 10, 15, 20, 25, 30, 50 and 100 kilometers. The Amateur Athletic Union of the United States (which along with the Road Runners Club of America sponsors most of the races) promotes regional and national championships at the marathon and metric distances.

Races, as a rule, are open to anyone and everyone. Rarely are there any age, sex or ability barriers. Because of this, several US events now draw a thousand runners or more. The largest, the Bay-to-Breakers in San Francisco, topped 5000 last year.

But there are a couple of ironies here. Even as the number of road specialists booms, the track people do most of the winning. The race upfront is fast–generally under five minutes a mile for distances as long as the marathon–and the road-trained trackmen have speed to go along with their endurance . For example, Frank Shorter, Kenny Moore and Jack Bacheler–the US marathoners in the 1972 Olympics– all raced quite well on the track before and during their road careers. Shorter, the Olympic champion, placed in the Munich 10,000 meters as well.

The second irony involves the slower runners. Road running is having growing pains, and some races are now limiting their size. The Boston Marathon is the main example. Men over 40 and all women must run 3½ hours to get in. Everyone else needs a sub-three-hour qualifying time. And the runners who've made the race big enough to need limits are the first to be eliminated.

So far, Boston hasn't inspired many imitators. But if it does, a sport which takes pride in its something-for-everyone tradition will lose a flavor that is already rare enough in sports.

—Joe Henderson

Joe Henderson has been running since 1958, competing in hundreds of road races since then. He is and has been the editor of **Runner's World** *Magazine since 1970, and is the author of several running books including* **Run Gently Run Long.**

My Own Story

If ever there was a candidate for "least likely to succeed", I was it. When I started running as a freshman in high school, there was no sign that I had any business in the sport or would stay in it for long.

My high school was small. We had no track, unless you stretched a point and called the 220-yard chalk line around the football field a "track". We did have a track team, but in name only. The coach coached everything. Football, boys' and girls' basketball, track. He was tiring by spring, and was ready to coast instead of coach.

He felt this way about track: "If you want to run, fine. I'll come out with my stopwatch and time you. But if you don't want to run, that's fine too. I can stay inside and drink coffee and grade papers. If you want to go to meets, I'll be glad to take care of the paperwork for you and to see that you get there and back. But if you don't want to do, I won't force you. I won't mind having my nights and weekends free."

Occasionally, the school would accidentally win a place in one of the natural-ability events. But never in anything that took training. For the few runners with any interest in preparing for races, the coach's method was quite basic. Run two or three time-trials a week. If you were a quarter-miler, you'd dash off a quarter. If you were a miler, you'd go a mile. Nothing more, nothing less. No warmup. No repeats. No warmdown.

I ran my first race on no training. And I dropped out of it after one lap of a mile. I decided then I'd rather be a half-miler. I started the coach's time-trials. Always half-miles.

I got to like running and wanted to do more of it. So I added several easy miles on the roads, some before and some after the daily trial, some more on weekends. By the end of the season, I was in the state meet in the two-mile relay. The next year, I did more miles and fewer trials and placed in the state in the mile.

As a junior and senior, I went to a new school in a new town, eight miles from home. I usually ran home from school because I could beat the bus that way. That distance plus a few races gave me six state championships in cross-country and track.

I'm not straining to pat myself on the back. None of that is intended or deserved. Remember, this was among the small-class schools in a rather backward track state, and it was almost 15 years ago. The times I ran then wouldn't win most dual meets now.

But the point I'm making is that I instinctively hit upon a simple and enjoyable way of running which at the same time took me about as far as I could go with my limited talent. Most importantly, I was anxious to keep running, not looking for a stopping place as so many high school graduates are.

So I went away to college. I signed on with a coach who knew just about everything about training methods. He gave me workouts so complicated that I couldn't figure out where I'd been and where they were leading me. No more easy miles on the roads combined with a few races and trials. That was too primitive. It may have worked in high school, but it wasn't good enough for the big-time.

Maybe not. But I didn't belong in the big-time, either, and I needed something more "primitive". In the first year of college, my mile time went from 4:20 to 4:50, my three-mile from about 15 minutes to over 16.

Earlier, I'd stumbled onto the right combination of endurance and speed – a torrent of distance and a dribble of fast stuff. I didn't know what the combination was, so I stumbled in and out of it a half-dozen more times until I finally broke the code a couple of years ago.

I relaxed after the first year of college racing – dropping pretenses of becoming an Olympic champion and settling again on lots of miles and a few races. My times went back down, to faster than they'd ever been.

I got ambitious again, sped more and got hurt.

I relaxed, turned to a kind of running that came to be known as LSD (long slow distance) and was able to go long and fast again in my rare distance races.

I raced more often. Performances leveled off and then slowed. I was tired most of the time. And sore. I ignored the tiredness and soreness, and it developed into illness and injury. I couldn't race any more. And then I couldn't run any more.

I was in the sorriest mental-physical shape of my life. Only then, out of desperation, did I figure out the formula I'd been on during every successful, healthy happy running period since the start – and off of during the down times.

It's as simple as this:

Goal: Keep moving

Means: (1) Keep healthy; (2) Keep fresh. (3) Keep loose. (4) Keep hungry.

Recipe: At least 10 parts of any easy running to one part hard.

The only valid test of a running method is, "Can I keep running with it?" If not, no coach, no German physiologist can make it work. Throw away the schedule if it won't pass your road test.

The way to keep going is to eliminate the negatives. If you want to run tomorrow morning and the next day and as many days into the future as you can imagine, and if you are able to do it, you've already won.

Keep healthy. Any method or running which hurts can't be helping much. What have you gained if you run 150 miles this week and are too sore to run at all for the next month?

Keep fresh. Chronic fatigue leads to injuries and, worse, the feeling that you can't face the next morning. What have you gained if you run five-minute miles today but can't run 10-minute pace for the next week?

Keep loose. Run your running, don't let it run you. A schedule is a guide, not a holy order chiseled in stone. Slavery to a pre-set routine causes you to run too much when you don't feel like it, and not enough when you feel ready for more. Trust your feelings.

Stay hungry. Hungry in the psychological sense, meaning that something is always left unexplored. Keep an appetite for tomorrow. Don't stuff yourself so much on running that it makes you sick.

The key to all of this – avoiding injuries and nagging fatigue, inflexibility and disinterest – may be the ratio of easy to hard runs, slow to fast ones.

I had no idea what it might be until two wiser men tipped me off. Independently, Arthur Lydiard and Ernst Van Aaken came to much the same formula. They discovered it years before I realized what they meant.

Lydiard, in New Zealand, said that endurance miles should outnumber speed miles 10-1. Van Aaken, a German medical doctor and coach, was even more conservative. His ratio was "20:1 or even 50:1."

I'd listed every race and every run in a loose-leaf, diary-type binder. Since 1966, all of my running had been one extreme or the other – easy or all-out. So my own running-racing balance was easy to figure out. Two patterns jumped out of the mass of statistics:

1. I raced best when I raced 5 percent of my miles.
2. I raced worst, was tired, sick and hurt most often when I raced 10 percent or more of the total.

There may have been a point down around 2 percent or less where I lost sharpness from not racing enough. I couldn't tell. I'd never been down that low. My problem had always been in the other direction.

It was a problem of recovery. I seem to need 10-20 recovery miles for every all-out one. Think of it as money in the bank. Gentle endurance running adds to the account, and hard speed work drains it.

Anyone who has balanced a checkbook knows that money flows out a lot faster than it comes in. The same is true in running. Endurance builds slowly. Speed takes away quickly. So the trick is to keep a large reserve account built up – to have enough endurance on hand to meet emergencies, and then to make up all deficits before withdrawing again.

This is the reason for running no more than one fast mile in every 10. It takes the easy 10 to replace what was lost in the one.

How fast is "easy"? I can't say. It's something you have to feel. It's set by an internal clock which is quite delicate.

Yoga uses the concept of "playing the edges". Stretch slowly to the border between comfort and discomfort, then hold that position. You can't improve flexibility without maximum stretch. But improvement stops and strain begins if you push on into pain.

This happens with running, too. You run along the edge between comfort and discomfort. Run at a pace which feels right. Stretch but don't strain. Trust your instincts to tell you what's right.

How far to go? Trust your feelings there, too, but with two qualifications:

First, go a minimum of 20-30 minutes on each run. This is psychological and physiological. Neither the head nor the legs get in gear and start humming along smoothly until you've gone that long. Before 20 minutes, you run as poorly as an old car on a winter morning.

The other qualification has to do with racing distances. Run enough to handle the longest one. How much is "enough"? The minimum is one-third of the racing distance (or time, if you keep records as I do, by time instead of distance) per day. Not necessarily every day, but at least averaging that one-third.

For instance, I typically average a little less than one hour a day. That puts my upper limit at about 2½ hours. I should be able then to handle any race through 20 miles, but my marathon – which takes me all of three hours – might fall apart at 22-23 miles.

This upper limit of distance is called the "collapse point". Beyond it lies pain and disappointment. I know. I've been there many times. Since I don't care to go again, I now make sure I have enough distance background for any race I run.

The best way to prepare for racing is to race. Racing calls out hidden abilities you can't get out of yourself any other way. You can't duplicate in normal speedwork the effort of racing because the excitement and shot of adrenalin aren't there. People like me who dread and despise interval work, time-trials, that kind of thing, and will have nothing to do with them, still look ahead eagerly to races.

I get so worked up about them, in fact, that I'm tempted to run too many – to race the next time before I'm completely over the last one. This isn't much of a problem for a miler, who recovers quickly and needs to race one, two or even three times a week at peak season. But it's an increasing threat to a long-distance man like me who has the chance to race twice a weekend but shouldn't do it more than once or twice a month.

As recently as a few years ago, I wasn't satisfied to do a few races well. I had to try them all. On consecutive weekends, I raced a marathon, 20 miles and 30 kilometers. I hurt my foot badly enough in the marathon to pull out after 15 miles. It still hurt the next week, but I raced anyway. It hurt worse the Sunday after that, but I ran again. It was the better part of two years before I raced normally again.

Since then, I've found and used my recovery-rebuilding timetable. I've learned that 10 easy miles after every hard one is a bare minimum. I'm hung-over from the race for at least that long. So I multiply the race distance or time by 10 and refuse to let myself go hard again until that quota is reached.

Racing 10 percent of the time is enough for me, and I suspect for anyone. And good racing, like all good running, is knowing how to hug the border between enough and too much. "Enough" keeps you going. "Too much" breaks you down.

—**Joe Henderson**

For More Information

This is an easy one. The best source for information is from *Runner's World* magazine, Box 366, Mountain View, Calif. 94040. Published monthly at $9.50 per year. With over 40,000 subscribers it is the bible of the sport. A must for any serious runner. Other good contacts: Bob DeCelle, National Long Distance Running Chairman (AAU), Box 1605, Alameda, Calif. 94501. Or Gar Williams, President, Road Runner's Club, Box 454, Star Route, Morrison, Colo. 80465. Most big cities have races each weekend. In the San Francisco Bay area we sponsor fun-runs each week. These are races from a quarter mile up to six miles. There is no entry fee. Just come and run. Several thousand runners have competed during the first two years of the program. Write Bob Anderson at *Runner's World* for more details.

A good source of equipment is Starting Line Sports, Box 8, Mountain View, Calif. 94040. Or you might try the Athletic Department, Box 743, Beaverton, Oregon 97005; The Athletic

Attic, 2415 N. Monroe St., Unit 203, Tallahassee, Fla. 32301; The Athlete's Foot, 217 Locust Trafficway, Kansas City, Mo. 64106; Carlsen Import Shoe Corp., 524 Broadway, New York, N.Y. 10012.

Here are some good books covering the sport. All are available from World Publications, Box 366, Mountain View, Calif. 94040 at the price listed* plus 25 cents each postage. Write for a complete list.

The Complete Runner, Runner's World staff. The only book in print to cover every aspect of running in such great detail. Articles by the experts on distance training, sprinting technique, diet, shoes, racing phychology and many more subjects—picked and assembled in one volume by the staff of *Runner's World* magazine. 1974 Hb., 398 pp., ill., $10.95, (World Publications).

The Young Runner. The most heavily populated field in running is the "junior" or under-20 age group. This book centers on these runners and their special concerns. Includes profiles of top young runners. 1973 Ppb. (RMB 24), 48 pp., ill., $1.00, (World Publications).

Exercises for Runners. The latest information on strength and flexibility training. Shows you how to use yoga and weights to prevent crippling injuries. 1973 Ppb., (RMB 29), 80 pp., ill., $1.95, (World Publications).

Athlete's Feet. Proper running starts—and often ends—at ground level. Podiatrists offer valuable tips on diagnosing and treating your own injuries and preventing them from recurring. Evaluations of 30 popular distance running flats. 1974 Ppb. (RMB 42), 48 pp., ill., $1.75, (World Publications).

Age of the Runner. The specifics of how a runner's age affects his performance, with charts (all distances, half mile and up) for evaluation times on an age-adjusted basis. Also documents the effect of running on the aging process. 1974 Ppb. (RMB 39), 56 pp., ill., $1.75, (World Publications).

First Steps to Fitness. This book concentrates on the problems and pains that prevent a runner from establishing the running habit. Takes the place of running friends and coaches when none are available. 1974 Ppb. (RMB 40), 68 pp., ill., $1.50, (World Publications).

Beginning Running, Joe Henderson's classic on how to start running and why. Inspiring (but very practical) reading about the foundation that will determine your future in running. 1972 Ppb., (RMB 15), 32 pp., ill., $1.00, (World Publications).

Runner's Training Guide. This book doesn't push any one method. Instead, it describes principles that underlie all methods, giving you the knowledge necessary to construct your own best program. 1973 Ppb., (RMB 23), 96 pp., ill., $2.95, (World Publications).

The Runner's Diet. A guide to the feeding and watering of runners. Covers proper eating and drinking habits, fasting, carbohydrate loading, hot weather liquid intake, vitamin supplements and other vital subjects. Based on the latest scientific data and tested by runners themselves. 1972 Ppb., (RMB 14), 80 pp., ill., $1.95, (World Publications).

Running With Style. Running is more than simply putting one foot in front of the other. It's putting them down properly. This well-illustrated guide gives you the information you need about proper running technique. 1975 Ppb. (RMB 47), 52 pp., ill., $1.50, (World Publications).

Rock Climbing

Rock climbing is a branch of mountaineering. Although Everest climbers encounter rock high on that peak, the term *rock climbing* is usually reserved for technically difficult rock, free from ice or snow. *Alpine climbing* is the term used to describe steep climbs with mixed rock, snow, and ice.

Unlike most other outdoor sports, climbing is not fundamentally dependent on equipment. A skier can't ski without his skis, but a climber *can* climb without ropes, pitons, or other special gear. Beginners can climb only very easy places without a rope, but some climbers, after years of intense experience, have done extremely difficult cliffs climbing unroped and solo. I'm not recommending that others should climb unroped, but it does illustrate a fact that the public fails to grasp from exposure to Hollywood distortions of climbing: equipment is normally used for safety, not for direct assists. Gawking tourists always ask climbers, "How does the rope get up the cliff so that you can climb it?" The answer is, "It's tied to the leader's waist."

In the old days, leaders followed the philosophy of Geoffrey Winthrop Young: "The leader must not fall." Today's climbers often fall without injury or accident. A fall is not an accident unless a person is hurt. It is a normal part of attempting problems that are close to one's limits. The extreme solo climbers that I mentioned earlier maintain their relative safety by having precise technique and precise knowledge of their own limits. Protection from injury to the leader is usually accomplished by placing anchors in the rock every 10 or 20 feet and attaching the rope to them by means of a large aluminum snap-link called a *carabiner.* One end of the rope is tied to the leader, while the other end is fed out in a *running belay* by a well-anchored climber below. If the leader falls, he will go twice the distance between himself and his last anchor in the rock. Since the cliff is usually steep, and the rope is made of flexible nylon, the sudden stop rarely causes injury.

Rock climbers used to employ pitons exclusively for anchors in the rock. This worked fine while only a few people climbed. It was soon discovered that the act of placing and removing pitons hundreds of times on popular climbs made them look like worn granite peg boards. Modern climbers try to use *nuts*—artificial chockstones—wherever possible. They can be slipped in and out of constrictions in natural cracks with just your fingers.

Style in climbing emphasizes the interaction of man in a natural setting. Just a few classic tools are used. Climbing by mechanical means is not in the same league as free climbing, where mechanical gear is used only for safety, like a net beneath an acrobat. Most climbers are a bit secretive about their sport. They don't want their favorite spots to be overcrowded. Many say this is a selfish attitude, but the fact remains that climbing is unlike most other sports: the play-

ing field cannot be renewed in the off season and the number of cliffs and mountains is finite.

If you are interested in trying rock clmbing, read the warnings under *Mountaineering* in this book. It's not for everyone. Be sure you fully understand the sport before you try anything difficult. And leave Mother's clothesline at home.

–Galen Rowell

Galen Rowell is very well known in the rock climbing circles. He has made many difficult climbs including Half Dome.

Climbing Half Dome

I am under Half Dome's spell. I have climbed it more than a dozen times, from all four sides, and in all seasons of the year. No one has, nor ever will conquer Half Dome. Climbing it is an extension of man's greatest natural gift: his adaptability. Man is being reminded that in order for a species to survive, it must adapt not only physical characteristics but also behavior to its surroundings. Man has turned the tables: he is trying to adapt his surroundings to himself. Climbing is an activity in which man works in surroundings far less adaptable than normal. Is the climber trying to adapt them to his needs? . . .to conquer them? I think not. Possibly he finds something unconsciously satisfying about returning to a biologically proven situation where it is he who becomes adapted. A climber finds his personal dignity in a struggle with natural forces, not with other men.

The first visitors to the valley envisioned that Half Dome must once have been a whole dome, one side of which was sheared away in some ancient colossal disaster. One early theory was that the bottom had suddenly dropped out of the valley, leaving the steep cliffs of El Capitan and Half Dome. Later, John Muir found evidence of extensive glaciation and theorized that a glacier had cleanly chopped away the front of the dome. Modern geologists have concluded that the upper part of Half Dome was never glaciated.

Although man finds it strangely satisfying to explain his surroundings by cataclysmic events, it appears that the dome is the result of slow geological processes that were well on their way before the coming of the ice ages. Without a doubt the ice was responsible for the present clean appearance and lack of debris at the base of Half Dome's cliffs, but the superb natural architecture of the dome cannot be attributed to any single geological event.

The two major faces of Half Dome are as different as one could possible imagine. The northwest face, which fronts on the valley floor is the product of vertical joints, cast into the granite as it cooled under the surface of the earth. The south face is the result of the total absence of these joints. The northwest face is streaked with lichens and usually in the shade. The south face bakes all day in the summer sun.

"The father of modern Yosemite climbing is John Salathe, a Swiss blacksmith who forged his own pitons from the hard steel of old Model A Ford axles. This made it possible for his pitons to be hammered back and forth by the last man in the party until they were loose enough to be removed and used again. In this way, a climb requiring 100 piton placements could be accomplished with a selection of only 20 or 30." (Rowell)

When climbing on the northwest face, as I have on three occasions, a person becomes quite aware of current geological processes at work–so aware, in fact, that some climbers choose to protect themselves from rockfall by wearing crash helmets. In contrast, the south face is a timeless vertical desert where natural rockfall of any kind may not have occurred in the past century.

The first ascent of Half Dome was made in 1875 by a Scotsman named George Anderson. He laboriously drilled his way for 700 feet on the 40-degree slabs of the northeast side of the dome. A month later, John Muir made an ascent following Anderson's bolts. This is the shortest and most gently sloping route to the top, and in 1919 the National Park Service constructed a trail to the summit by placing hand cables up the steepest section.

Half Dome is now climbed by thousands of tourists who possess enough energy to hike the eight miles to its base and enough coolness to ascend the easy but airy cable system. The summit subsequently has become littered with bottle tops, gum wrappers, and other human paraphernalia. If John Muir was alive today, I doubt that he would have written the words he penned a century ago: "The dome. . .would hardly be more conquered or spoiled should man be added to her list of visitors. His louder scream and heavier scrambling would not stir a line of her countenance."

In the early 1930s a group of Sierra Club climbers began use ropes and pitons in Yosemite for the first time. The sport burgeoned until today Yosemite is considered to have the most highly developed rock climbing in the world. Although its cliffs are among the sheerest in the world, technical skills were developed more quickly in Yosemite because, in many ways, the environment lacks the harshness of the higher mountains. A climber is much more apt to push himself and try something new in Yosemite, at 4000 feet elevation, a short distance from the road, on fresh firm granite, than is his alpine counterpart who has lugged himself and his equipment to 10 or even 20,000 feet, many days' walk from a highway, in a region of unpredictable weather and friable rock. Mountain climbs, such as Everest, take much stamina and knowledge of alpine terrain, but they never have the continuous technical difficulty of the sheer granite walls of Yosemite.

For many years, climbing in Yosemite was confined to routes that could be completed in a single day. European pitons made from soft iron were left in place on most climbs, since trying to remove them would distort or destroy them.

The father of modern Yosemite climbing is John Salathe, a Swiss blacksmith who forged his own pitons from the hard steel of old Model A Ford axles. This made it possible for his pitons to be hammered back and forth by the last man in the party until they were loose enough to be removed and used again. In this way, a climb requiring 100 piton placements could be accomplished with a selection of only 20 or 30 pitons.

In the postwar years, Salathe pioneered several of the first multi-day climbs in Yosemite. Among these was a two-day ascent of the southwest face of Half Dome, the curving, somewhat less than vertical cliff just to the right of the sheer northwest face. This climb, with Anton Nelson, was the first new route up Half Dome since Anderson's original ascent in 1874.

Many of Salathe's hardest climbs were made when he was past the age of 50. They were always accomplished with a minimum amount of food, water, equipment, and publicity. His name is still little known beyond the circle of climbers who have gained strength and inspiration from his bold, yet humble, achievements.

In the 1950s, climbers turned their eyes toward the vertical northwest face. Several exploratory attempts were made by parties including such names as Royal Robbins and Warren Harding. In June 1957, Harding arrived in the valleys to make an all-out attempt on the face. He found a party led by Robbins, who is often considered to be the most skilled rock climber on this continent, already high on the wall. Robbin's party spent five days on the Half Dome face, reaching the summit to shake hands with Harding, who had climbed the cables to greet them on top. (As an alternative, Harding began an attempt on the unclimbed face of El Capitan, reaching the top a year later after several attempts and 47 days of climbing).

The northwest face has now been climbed many times by mountaineers from all over the world, usually in two or three days now that the route is known. The original route lies near the left-hand side of the face. In recent years Robbins has pioneered three new routes on the same face.

In the spring of 1963, I was part of an attempt to climb a a new route up the middle of the northwest face. The climb was a failure but it left an indelible imprint on my memory. Several hundred feet above the base, the narrow crack which I was following suddenly widened from a few inches to a "chimney" several feet wide. I was able to crawl inside and to climb upward by cross pressure between my back and feet. After about 50 feet I stopped to place a piton for safety in a crack at the back of the chimney. Resting briefly, I gazed in wonder at the geometry of nature.

At either side of the back wall of the chimney was a three-inch-wide crack, continuing out of sight for hundreds of feet overhead. The back wall itself was flat, parallel to the main cliff, and about eight feet behind its present surface. The three-inch cracks completely separated the outer rock on which I was climbing from the back wall of the chimney. Here was the northwest face of the future, fully cleaved and waiting patiently, be it one or 100,000 years before it gleams for a geological moment in the noonday sun.

In 1964, when I climbed the usual route on the northwest face, I chimneyed behind a 60-foot-high granite block at the 1,500-foot level, which had been named "Psyche Flake" by previous climbers, owing to its precarious position. In the winter of 1967 it disappeared. The forces of wind and frost had far exceeded the diminutive exertions of men.

The south face presents a stark contrast to the dynamic action taking place on the northwest face. The extreme age of the present surface is made obvious by grooves up to a foot deep, worn into the gem-hard granite by water draining from the summit over tens of thousands of years. In some places, leisurely but long-continued weathering has left rounded knobs of more resistant rock jutting outward nearly a foot from the surrounding rock.

Until 1966 no one even attempted the mile-wide south face. It was the last major cliff in Yosemite to remain unclimbed by any route. In June of that year I joined Warren Harding and two others in an unsuccessful bid on the face. It was the first in a yearly tradition of storms and defeats. We spent five days on the cliff, three of them waiting out storms. Each year we got a little higher.

In 1968 we were caught by an unpredicted fall snow storm

high on the wall. Even the cabled tourist route was essentially unclimbable with several feet of avalanche-prone snow sitting on the steep slabs. After three days in the storm we were rescued by a group of climbers who were landed on the summit by a helicopter. They lowered Royal Robbins 750 feet on ropes to our position. He brought us hot soup, dry parkas, gloves, and equipment to ascend the fixed rope to the summit.

Eleven years earlier the roles had been reversed. It had been Harding who met Robbins on the opposite face of Half Dome after a successful climb. Now both the parts they played and the faces they climbed were reversed. At first, Warren didn't recognize Royal under all the paraphernalia in the dark of night. He leaned over and said, "Who are you, anyway?"

After a good laugh, I used Jumar ascenders to climb the rope in 40 minutes. Warren had a much harder time. He had been shivering in a fetal position for three days, curled up in a wet hammock. His down-filled pants were frozen in that position. He finally had to take a knife to them in order to get enough leg movement to climb the rope.

In 1970 we failed again. Storms and lightning turned us back. On a clear July day we began yet another attempt. In a matter of hours it was raining. We stuck it out, as we had previous times, sleeping in hammocks covered with sheets of plastic. But this time the rain stopped. For five days we climbed in hot sunny weather, passing our previous high point and inching toward the summit at less than 10 feet per hour. The sixth day dawned cloudy. Inky black clouds gathered ever more ominously with each hour. By noon, we were climbing in a light drizzle. Our hammocks were out and waiting in case the storm became more intense.

We reached what we thought from below would be a wide crack. It proved to be a rounded, flawless groove, worn by eons of drainage from the summit plateau. We had to drill holes for expansion bolts in the center of the groove.

All afternoon the storm threatened, but the expected heavy rain never came. Near dusk, the drilling stopped and I heard a cry from above. "I'm up!"

We had faltered our way through the defenses of the last unclimbed side of Half Dome.

—Galen Rowell

For More Information

Additional information on magazines, organizations, and equipment can be found under Mountain Climbing. But here are some books. All are available from World Publications, Box 366, Mountain View, Calif. 94040 at the price listed* plus 25 cents each postage.

Basic Rockcraft, Royal Robbins. This book covers the basic techniques of rock climbing—ropes and knots, other climbing equipment, belays, grips and holds. Carries the reader through all of the techniques needed for most, high-angle climbs. 1971 Ppb., 72 pp., ill., $1.95, (La Siesta).

Advanced Rockcraft, Royal Robbins. Takes up where *Basic Rockcraft* left off. Covers soloing and the philosophy of climbing. 1973 Ppb., 96 pp., ill., $2.95, (LaSiesta).

Ropes, Knots and Slings for Climbers, Walt Wheelock and Royal Robbins. An excellent book describing the basic knots needed for climbing. Very well illustrated with easy-to-follow diagrams of all knots. Also includes useful information on rope care and selection. 1967 Ppb., 36 pp., ill., $1.00, (La Siesta).

The Vertical World of Yosemite, Galen Rowell, ed. Seventeen climbers describe their exhilarating and harrowing experiences climbing from the bottom to the top of the various walls in Yosemite. Each article contains the information and insights that will enrich your climbs in this popular area. 1974 Hb., 207 pp., ill., $16.95, (Wilderness Press).

Climbing, James Bunting. An illustrated guide to rock climbing and mountaineering for the beginner. Gives you all the information you need to get started—safely. 1973 Hb., 92 pp., ill., $2.95, (Crowell).

On Ice and Snow Rock, Gaston Rebuffat. Very up-to-date advice on the various aspects of climbing, including information on equipment, bivouacking, and climbing techniques under different conditions. 247 plates including 58 in color. Translated from the French. 1971 Hb., 192 pp., ill., $19.50, (Oxford).

Introduction to Rock and Mountain Climbing, Mendenhall. All the basics for the beginner. Explicit step-by-step directions about what the novice needs to know, have, do and take. 1969 Hb., 192 pp., ill., $6.95, (Stackpole).

Climber's Guide to the Yosemite Valley. A Sierra Club Totebook. Guide to the most popular climbing area in the US, with over 500 different ascents in Yosemite, plus a history of the geological formations, flora and fauna of the valley. 1971 Ppb., 306 pp., ill., $6.95, (Scribner's).

Downward Bound: A Mad Guide to Rock Climbing, Harding. A celebrated mountaineer writes a fantastic conglomeration of personal confessions, accounts of his most famous climbs, a somewhat distorted view of climbing history, plus first rate advice for both beginning and expert climber. Illustrated with wild cartoons. 1975 Hb. & Ppb., 256 pp., ill., $7.95/$4.95, (Prentice Hall).

Beginner's Guide to Rock and Mountain Climbing, Ruth and John Mendenhall. Complete in every way, this book covers all the basics of climbing rocks and mountains safely. Well illustrated, with useful information on ropes, usage, which to take and when to use them. Ppb., $3.95, (Stackpole).

Rodeo

The word "rodeo" immediately brings to mind images of the Great American West—of tall men in boots and wide-brimmed hats, stirring action, drama, and romance. And it should, for rodeo is the only sport to have been truly conceived by American tradition.

In the past, the cowboy's work day began before daylight and often ended after dark. He worked outdoors in the dust, the rain, the heat, and the cold. For recreation, the working cowboys turned to games of friendly competition. They challenged each other to contests in riding and roping; there were no rules and no awards.

For competing rodeo cowgirls, the barrel race is a favorite. In this event the purpose is to run a highly trained quarter horse around three barrels in a clover leaf pattern and back to the starting line in as short a time as possible. Barrel racing is a championship event in the International Rodeo Association championships. (Gloucester)

In 1882, Buffalo Bill Cody was asked to help stage a Fourth of July celebration in North Platte, Neb. Rodeo events were included in his "Old Glory Blow-Out" and prizes were given to the winners.

The town of Pecos, Tex., turned main street into an arena and cowboy contests were held in 1883. Prizes were also given then.

By 1897, rodeo had been turned into a spectator sport, as the famed Cheyenne Frontier Days celebration was organized. Admissions were charged and prizes were given.

Although many cowboy contestants were making a living "rodeoing" early in the 20th century, there was no real organization for them until 1936 when the Cowboys Turtle Association was started in Boston. Prior to that date attempts had been made to get the cowboys together, but it was difficult due to the problem of assembling a large group of contestants at one time and place.

A large assembly was finally achieved when the cowboys went on strike at the famed Boston Garden Rodeo, primarily to get an increase in purse money. While together, they established rules and guidelines for their sport.

In 1945, the association was reorganized and the name was changed to Rodeo Cowboys Association. Then in 1959, the first National Finals Rodeo was staged at Dallas, Tex. This rodeo which is now an annual event, is comparable to the World Series of baseball and the Super Bowl for football. Only the world's top 15 cowboys in each event are eligible to compete. The toughest bucking stock of all the PRCA stock contractors is acquired. The bulls and broncs are voted into the finals by the cowboys, thus pitting the nation's top cowboys against the country's best bucking stock.

Oklahoma City was selected as the site for the National Rodeo Finals in 1965 and it has been held there since then. The purse for the 1975 finals rodeo will be more than $175,000.

Since its organization in 1936, the Professional Rodeo Cowboys Association has grown steadily. Today there are over 3500 cowboys competing at more than 600 professional rodeos in 44 states and four Canadian provinces. Cowboys vie for close to six million dollars in prize money annually. The all-around champion of the world wins in the neighborhood of $100,000 per year.

—Bob Ragsdale

Bob Ragsdale is serving his third term as President of the Professional Rodeo Cowboys Association. He is also Western wear, tack and accessories advisor for Sears. During his 15 years of professional rodeo participation, Bob's winnings have grown to over $300,000.

How to Score For Yourself

Even if you're an experienced cowboy, judging is tough. You stand out in the arena, with thousands of dollars at stake, scoring the ride the way you see it, and the rider on the way he rode. The pressure's always on.

The Rodeo Cowboys Association has a program for judging that helps clarify the problem areas. It helps the individuals that judge to know exactly what they are looking for and exactly what their job is. And that is not only knowing how to flag a steer but everything involved including drawing stock clear through setting up the barrier for the roping and dogging events and then final posting of the books and scores.

More than 3500 professional cowboys compete each year in 600 pro rodeos covering 44 states and four Canadian provinces. Total prize money is now up to $6 million annually and the all-round champion wins in the neighborhood of $100,000 each year. (M.J. Baum)

Any member of the RCA in good standing is qualified to judge. This doesn't necessarily mean they can do it. Judges are often pulled from the ranks of injured cowboys, but they must have contested within the previous 12 months. Each rodeo has two judges, and each scores an animal from one to 25 points on how hard the bronc or bull bucks, and the rider also one to 25, on how well he spurs and his degree of control. Often the word "spur" is misconstrued.

To give the animal every advantage, the cowboy is required to do something in addition to hanging on for dear life. His spurring stroke—the lick—is exquisitely timed to the bucking rhythm. Spurs are dulled by association rules. The cause of many a rider's abrupt departure from his mount has been caused by a spur hanging up in the saddle or becoming entangled in the horses' mane. For this reason the riders use a short-shanked spur with rowels no sharper than the edge of a nickel.

Judges stand on either side of the chute, and the first thing they look for in bronc and bareback riding is whether the rider's feet are over the point of the horse's shoulders when the animal's front feet hit the ground on the first jump out of the chute. If this doesn't occur, the rider is disqualified. Rider is also disqualified for being bucked off, touching the animal with the free hand, using sharp spurs or placing spurs or chaps under the rope when rope is being tightened. If a horse stalls in the chute, or hits a cowboy while still in the chute, that cowboy does not have to spur the horse out. In that instance the horse is taking advantage of the cowboy so that particular rule is waivered.

If a horse or bull doesn't buck, and the cowboy therefore has no real chance, the judges watch for toes turned out, spurs on the neck of the horse, being up on the rigging, straight and not tipped over the side, length of lick, and a wide gap. In bronc riding, spurring is important. Watch the cowboy's feet, and the free arm that moves in time with the bronc. The same rules apply for bronc as for bareback riding, except to lose a stirrup also means disqualification.

In bull riding, judges mark on control, body position, spurring. A loose rope is used and riding must be done with one hand, as in bareback and bronc riding. A bull rider doesn't have to spur the animal, it would be almost impossible and much too dangerous, but spurring could be to a cowboy's advantage once the bull's out of the chute. The cowboy should, however, be almost sitting on his rope.

The timed events—roping and steer wrestling—require two men. One is at the starting scoreline, and notes whether the contestant "breaks the barrier, the other is on horseback." The latter drops his flag, stopping the timers' watches, on completion of the run. Unnecessary roughness is not allowed. If a cowboy's horse drags a calf after he's tied, a judge can penalize with disqualification.

In calf roping, a legal tie is one or more wraps and a half hitch and there is a 35 second maximum elapsed time in this event.

In team roping, even though there are two riders, three loops are allowed. Legal head catch is shown on this page, a five-second penalty is added to time if only one hind foot is caught. There's no time if no heels are caught. In steer wrestling, animal must be caught from a horse, and steer will be considered down only if it is lying flat on its side, or on its back with all four feet and head straight. In bull dogging if the hazer touches the steer, the dogger is disqualified.

But judges have to look at the stock as well as the cowboys. In the riding events they are looking for power, speed, high kicking, twisting, changing direction. A rank animal makes for a tough ride and a high score (70s are very good) a sorry horse means few points for the animal, and inevitably a losing day for the cowboy.

At your next rodeo, why not judge for yourself.

—From the RCA

For More Information

There are many horse magazines that have articles once in awhile on rodeo but we are listing a few of the better exclusively rodeo publications. *Rodeo News,* 703 North Cedar, Box 587, Pauls Valley, Okla. 73035. Published 11 times per year at $7.00. This is the official publication of the International Rodeo Association, Box 615, Pauls Valley, Okla. 93075. They say on their masthead "dedicated to the betterment and promotion of professional rodeos regardless of size and the establishment." *Rodeo Sports News,* 2929 W. 19th Ave., Denver, Colo. 80204. Published twice monthly except one issue during December and January at $6.00 per year. Official publication of the Professional Rodeo Cowboys Assn. at the same address. Newspaper format. Other publications we have not seen but certainly worth checking out are *Hoof & Horn,* Box 2000, Evergreen, Colo. 80439; *Little Britches Rodeo News,* 2160 S. Holly No. 105, Denver Co. 80222; and *Western Horseman,* Box 280, Colorado Springs, Co. 80901.

Another organization you should know about is the National Intercollegiate Rodeo Assn., Box 2088, SHSU Station, Huntsville, Texas 77340. They promote rodeos at the university and college level. There is also a Girls Rodeo Assn. but we don't have their address.

Saddles, bareback riggings, bull ropes, lariats, spurs, chaps, trailers, are some of the equipment you need. Here are a couple of sources: Rodeo & Riding Equipment, 300 Public Square, Franklin, Tenn. 37064 has tailored chaps as well as other things. Dub Grant, Rt. No. 2, Box 359, Benton, Ark. 72015 has lariats, "Hand-sewn leather or rawhide burners." Or maybe you want to get a rodeo game called "Hoolihan." Write Rodeo News, Box 8160, Nashville, Tenn. 37207. For hats write: American Hat Co., Box 2468, Houston, Texas 77001. Maybe you would like to go to a rodeo clown school, if so write T. Sheffield, Box 144, Rankin, Texas 79778.

Here are a couple of books. All are available from World Publications, Box 366, Mountain View, Calif. 94040 at the price listed* plus 25 cents postage.

Fast Horses and Short Ropes, Williard H. Porter. The exciting, fast-paced story of the world of roping and riding. In this book we are telling tales of the rodeo circuit, as well as how-to information for anyone interested in participating in this thrilling, dangerous sport. 1975, 256 pp., ill., $9.95, (Barnes).

Rodeo—Standard Guide to the Cowboy Sport, M.S. Robertson. For every rodeo enthusiast or newcomer here is an excellent guide to present-day rodeo and its rugged history. Hb., 164 (oversize) pp., ill., $6.95, (Howell North).

Rodeo: The Suicide Circuit, Fred Schnell. A pictorial essay following prominent riders on the circuit. Highlighted by pictures. 1971 Hb., ill., $12.95, (Rand McNally).

Roller Skating

Joseph F. Shevelson, in the introduction to O'Neill's **Roller Skating** calls the sport "the ideal bridge between active athletics and more sedate, inactive pastimes. It helps the young to grow up and the older persons to retain their youth."

Nothing could be more true! Children on metal or hard plastic street skates, band-aids on knees, have been a common sight for decades. Roller skates are as much of being a child in America as peanut butter sandwiches! Worn-out they become wheels for soap box racers and bicycle trailers, castoffs in favor of shiny new wheels.

Many older persons, past the stage of band-aid knees, also roller skate for pleasant exercise at the local roller rink. Relaxing but recreational, roller skating gives Mom and Dad a sport that they can share with the family and each other for hours with little cost for the enjoyment and exercise they gain.

Nearly 20 million Americans roller skate at local rinks, schools, colleges, assembly halls and recreation centers. While you can purchase your own skates, stops, skating costumes, and other skating paraphernalia from manufacturers or the shop at the local rink, most casual skaters just wear comfortable clothes and rent skates for a nominal fee from the skating establishment.

Metal or hard rubber skates that fit over street shoes are fine for sidewalks and streets; however, the best skates for rinks and indoor skating are composite-wheel skates with rubber toe stops for braking. These are screwed into the skating boot at the sole by means of a metal plate. The skating boot is very like the ice skating boot that fits tightly over the ankle for support. Female skaters prefer short skating skirts that leave the legs free, and the new stretch materials make excellent costumes for both men and women.

There are several types of competition for roller skaters, most based on ice skating. Speed skating is done on outdoor ovals or on the open road, although indoor competition with restrictions on speed are also held. Figure skating is like ice figure skating, utilizing the same figures, rules, judging, etc. Roller dancing is also like ice dancing with the same techniques and judging. Roller hockey is an indoor game derived from field and ice hockey. The players use shorter skates than ice hockey players, but the object of scoring the highest number of goals to win is the same.

Skating gives a person a wonderful feeling of freedom whether he is racing, tracing figures, dancing, or just striding along. Like dance or gymnastics, roller skating develops grace and balance and a poised performer. It helps develop leg and arm coordination, basic body strength, and good posture. Vigorous skating stiumlates the cardiovascular systems, also.

Roller skating is undoubtedly one of the fastest growing sports in the US. As more and more people skate, new rinks are built and equipment becomes safer and even more readily available. More teachers and trainers are teaching with better

knowledge and more advanced facilities for those interested in competitive or advanced skating.

What better time than now is there to become involved in roller skating?

Believing in Myself

This was the 13th year I competed in the National Championships. But this was different, something changed, instead of feeling like a loser, I felt like a winner. In previous years, I always felt like I was just lucky to be skating in National competitions, and felt satisfied to place fifth or sixth. I guess I didn't feel as I was as good as the other competitors. I think I was just defeating myself with that attitude. Not this year, though. Maybe, at age 21, I've matured. At last I wanted to win and thought I could. I skated because of myself, not in spite of myself. I wanted to make the other skaters have to beat me.

"Skating gives a person a wonderful feeling of freedom whether he is racing, tracing figures, dancing, or just striding along. Like dance or gymnastics, roller skating develops grace and balance and a poised performer. It helps develop leg and arm coordination, basic body strength, and good posture. Vigorous skating stimulates the cardiovascular system, also." (Tony Duffy)

The night I won the American Senior Ladies Championship was the first time in my life that I instinctively felt like smiling when I was on the floor. Instead of skating to please my teacher, or the judges, I was skating to please myself. I was enjoying myself and it showed. I was smiling on the inside and the outside, and proud to be doing my routine.

The event I won is Senior Ladies Singles. Contrary to Dance or Pairs, in Singles you perform alone on the skating floor; all eyes are on you. It is a tremendous challenge to be able to please the audience.

After I performed my double axel without a flaw, I had a strong happy feeling that at last I might win; really win this time, not come in fifth or sixth, but win. It had taken me three years to perfect the jump, all the years of practice had finally paid off.

Skating, like everything, takes a lot of practice and discipline to do well. Practice is important, but in quality not quantity. In skating my practice hours are valuable to me according not to how long I skate, but how much I push myself while I'm there. I spend at least 12 hours a week practicing.

I wonder sometimes if spending so much time skating hasn't made me miss a lot in life, like swimming, camping, things other kids do. But, when I think of all the friends I have, all the travel and experiences roller skating has brought me, I can't regret it. I haven't missed life, I've just had a different kind of life.

I started skating at the age of three. There was a roller rink in San Diego four blocks from where I lived. My parents were skaters and I have always enjoyed sports and creativity. I liked roller skating from the start because I found that here I could mix the two.

Some people think that now that I've won the Senior event, I've reached the top and can retire. That is hard for me to imagine. I wouldn't want to get away from skating. Next year, there is still much growing and developing as a skater I would like to do. For instance, if only I could spin faster, my jumps would be better.

Even after I'm done skating competitively, I want to become a skating teacher. I'll advice my students to practice hard, try more than what they think they would be able to achieve and, most important, I'll tell them to believe in themselves.

My skating teacher, Elmer Ringeisen, has been like a father to me since my own father died. He gave me a firm foundation in the fundamentals of skating which I would want to pass on to my students when I teach.

But for now, I want to compete. Like most Americans, I am a competitive person. In school I competed for good grades and top standing in my class. I graduated fourth in my high school class. Now I am in college and still competing for grades. The hardest part has been convincing myself that I can do it. Now, at long last I have found the confidence in myself and my skating, and the freedom which that confidence brings. It is no time to quit. Rather, it is a good time to begin.

—Moana Brigham

Moana Brigham is the 1975 American Senior Ladies Singles Roller Skating Champion.

For More Information

The US Amateur Roller Skating Assn., 152 W 42nd St., New York, N.Y. 10036 and United States of America Confederation, 7700 A St., Lincoln, Neb. 68510 are the two major organizations. At the same address as the Confederation is the Roller Skaters of America which puts out a magazine called *Skate*. These people should be able to help you get going on the right track.

Rope Jumping

There's a whole lot more to skipping rope than three 10 year old girls playing "Double Dutch" on the PS336 playground. It can also be a fine mode of exercise for adults, a nostalgic trip back to the good old days, or a vital part of off-season conditioning for athletes in any sport.

For more, first exposure comes in the form of the scores of jump rope games and rhymes abounding on any playground. It's not very hard to learn. If you're alone, you jump by yourself, concentrating on footwork and crossing or double turning the rope. In pairs, a longer rope can be used for dual jumping feats, but the real action starts with three or more participants. Two can turn one or two ropes at a time, while one or more jumpers can go at once or alternate according to a chanted rhyme.

When used for fitness or athletic training, solitary rope jumping will tone up leg muscles and sharpen foot-eye coordination. Just skip along at 80-90 jumps per minute for 10 minutes and you'll be breathing hard enough to tell it's doing some good!

How to Get In Shape by Jumping Rope

A person is only as young as his or her legs. In actuality, the legs serve as an excellent barometer of the entire body's health and physical fitness. I have a couple of neighbors—a man and his wife, both in their late 70s—who walk everywhere. They must wear out a pair of shoes a month walking to the market, to the movies, to their dance class, or just out for an after dinner stroll. You should see the color in their faces and the spring in their step—it's a perfect testimony for lifelong leg exercise.

More and more physicians are recommending walking, running and cycling as the fountain of youth. George Sheehan, M.D., author of **Dr. Sheehan on Running**, is one of the formost advocates of regular leg exercise for continued mental and physical health. Unfortunately, walking, cycling and running are not easily or safely undertaken by many. Poor weather, heavy automobile traffic, the threat of muggers, and lack of equipment combine to close each of these doors to many aspiring fitness converts.

Fortunately, a fine alternative exists for leg and total body fitness, and it requires minimal equipment and little space. It's rope jumping and it can easily be done with a length of clothesline in the privacy of your own bedroom. But is it good for you? Definitely! In 1968 a researcher at Arizona State University concluded that 10 minutes of rope skipping provided physical fitness improvement in unfit individuals equal to that from 30 minutes of jogging.

Okay, so you've rounded up a hunk of rope, donned loose fitting clothing and a pair of sneaks, and are itching to get at it. Well, slow down and don't get too carried away. If you're over 40, get a physical with an EKG before you start any improvement program. Next, keep in mind that you can get carried away, overexercise the first session and end up sore enough to scrap the program. Your best bet, then, is to start easy and progress slowly for lifelong fitness involvement.

Stay relaxed when you jump, and spring only high enough to make it over the rope. Keep your arm movement under control and land on the balls of your feet to prevent stress injuries to your lower extremities. Start out with 100 skips, jumping both feet at a time. Add 20 every other session until 200 is relatively easy. Drop back to 100, but jump the rope one foot in front of the other as though you were running. Work up again to 200. Once at this point, start working on speed, aiming at a slightly breathless state. Add more skips each week and go faster until you can do 500 jumps in five minutes or less. Maintaining this work level on a daily basis will maintain physical fitness at a high level for as long as you jump rope.

—**Gordon Gardner**

Gordon Gardner coaches high school football in Los Angeles. He has long recommended regular rope jumping for everyone from out of shape mothers to professional athletes.

For More Information

For additional information write: Lifeline Production, 1803 Regent St., Madison, Wisc., 53705. Ask for their informational kit on rope jumping.

Here are some good books covering rope jumping. All are available from World Publications, Box 366, Mountain View, Calif. 94040 at the price listed* plus 25 cents each postage. Write for a complete list.

Jump Rope, Peter L. Skolnik. A fun, easy-to-understand study written for youngsters and oldsters alike. Includes sections on rope lore and technique, as well as a more serious discussion regarding physical fitness. Incredible collection of jump rope rhymes from all over the world. 1974 Ppb., 157 pp., ill., $2.95, (Workman's).

Skipping the Rope for Fun and Fitness, Frank Prentup. Rope skipping is a great conditioning exercise, and this book details all the routines you did as a kid plus some new ones. 1963 Ppb., 36 pp., ill., $2.25, (Pruett).

The Perfect Exercise—The Hop, Skip and Jump Your Way to Health, Curtis Mitchell. The reader learns how, in five minutes a day, he can get all the exercises needed to tone muscles, rejuvenate a tired body,and release tensions. Contains carefully planned programs for men and women (and children) of all ages. 1976, $6.95, (Simon & Schuster).

Rotorcraft

What kind of flying machine weighs only 250 pounds, can top Pike's Peak in a single bound, and is cheaper to own than a new economy car? If you said, "A homebuilt rotarywing aircraft" – congratulations. You guessed right.

An explosion is taking place today in the homebuilt rotorcraft movement. Over 2000 amateur-made whirlybirds are currently flying in the US, with new additions popping up everywhere like toadstools after a rainstorm. A

network of dealers and distributors stretches from Atlantic to Pacific. The 13,000-member Popular Rotorcraft Association, which was organized in 1962 for the sole purpose of uniting and educating sport rotorcraft builders, has grown by 10 percent per year for a decade and shows no sign of slowing down. For hover lovers everywhere, the millenium may just have arrived.

What's behind the boom in popularity of this novel sport? Flying has always been a challenging and rewarding endeavor for those whom the sky and the wind and the clouds have captivated. More than this, there is (and will always be) a fascination in human beings for what Richard Bach calls "that strange distant mystique of machines that carry men through the air." For some, this mystique is frozen in the sleek, graceful lines of a sailplane; others find it in the brilliant colored canopies of hot-air balloons; still others prefer miniature biplanes. So as increasing numbers of pilots begin to seek fresh alternatives to conventional fixed-wing flight, perhaps it is only natural that rotarywing aircraft – the homebuilt kind, in particular – have come under scrutiny.

Shortly after World War II, myriad small companies came into existence practically overnight, each with the goal of making the "copter in every garage" dream come true. Governmental restrictions on the manufacture and sale of aircraft components, and the formidable complexity of existing helicopter designs, prevented these small companies from making any progress. But today, under "Experimental" Category licensing laws, manufacturers are allowed to sell one- and two-man rotorcraft in kit form, to be assembled by the buyer as he would a ham radio or a set of bookshelves. As a result, the "copter in every garage" dream is now closer to becoming a reality than ever before.

—**Kas Thomas**

Kas Thomas is by now a familiar name to a majority of rotorcraft enthusiasts. In addition to contributing a column to Popular Rotorcraft Flying, *his articles have appeared in numerous aviation magazines and he has recently written a book entitled* **Guide to Homebuilt Rotorcraft.**

Some More Facts

The father of sport rotorcraft, if there is one, is Russian-born engineer Igor Bensen, an inventor who, having test-flown man-carrying rotarywing kites for General Electric after the war, pooled his resources in 1953 to go into business for himself. The upshot of Dr. Bensen's experimentation was a device which came to be called the gyrocopter. Today, well over 10,000 sets of plans later, the Bensen B-8M ranks as the most widely built do-it-yourself aircraft (fixed or rotarywing) of all time. Bensen Aircraft Corporation counts among its past customers not only the three branches of the US military, but NASA, Ford Motor Company, Goodyear Tire & Rubber Company, Cessna Aircraft, Lockheed, Westinghouse Corporation and many others.

The B-8M gyrocopter is perhaps the simplest of all powered rotorcraft to fly. It is not a helicopter. Look carefully and you will see that the machine's engine turns a small propeller – producing thrust in the same way as an airplane – which is in no way coupled to the main rotor. The main, or overhead, rotor is completely freewheeling and tilted back in flight so as to catch air and keep it turning (much in the way a child's pinwheel turns in the wind). Accordingly, the only controls a gyrocopter has are: (1) throttle, to increase or decrease forward propulsion; (2) rudder pedals, to control yaw; and (3) a center-mounted control stick which acts to tilt the rotor in the desired direction of flight. Since the main rotor is not powered, hovering is impossible (except in a strong wind).

Air must always be passed through the rotor to keep it spinning, and for this reason a rolling airplane-like takeoff is used. The average gyrocopter, powered by a 90-horsepower McCulloch two-stroke engine, requires several hundred feet for takeoff, breaking ground at about 30 m.p.h. The initial rate of climb of 1200 feet per minute is often startling to newcomers, and at first the controls seem sensitive. Experienced pilots, however, find the gyrocopter to have a surprisingly "natural" feel and, in fact, the gyrocopter is one of few rotarywing aircraft in existence that can be flown hands-off.

Pushed to the extremes of its performance "envelope", the gyrocopter will achieve speeds of close to 100 m.p.h. and heights of over 15,000 feet; conversely, it can be flown at extremely low speeds without fear of stalling. At zero miles per hour forward speed, the gyrocopter enters a 1000 foot per minute vertical let-down. That's about 17 feet per second, which is too fast for normal landings, but not so fast that it could cause serious injury. A normal procedure for landing is to approach the runway at 45 m.p.h., ease the throttle back to idle, and touch down nose high as airspeed decays. Any rollout of more than 25 feet can be considered unusually poor – that rotor helps slow the machine down in a hurry.

If true VTOL (Vertical Take-Off and Landing) performance is desired, obviously a gyrocopter will not do. In this case, the amateur builder has but to avail himself of one of several homebuilt helicopter designs on the market. Generally, these birds require much more time to construct and are considerably more difficult to learn to fly than a gyrocopter; also, price takes a quantum jump, the average homebuilt heli running about $7000 to the gyrocopter's 3000. Still, that's a far cry from spending the $60,000 that's being asked now for new store-bought (commercially produced) two-passenger helicopters. And for the ultimate in elan, dash, pride, and personal mobility, nothing beats having one's very own private helicopter . . . as F. Lee Bailey (and others) will attest.

The question inevitably crops up: Do I need a pilot's license to fly one of these things? The answer is yes, you do. Pilots who have already obtained a private pilot's certificate in airplanes can, according to regulations, fly any aircraft other than jets or heavies, solo. This means that anyone holding a private license or better in any category of machine, can solo a homebuilt gyrocopter or helicopter. (If a passenger is to be taken,

It's almost literally like flying on the seat of your pants. The main rotor is not powered: the gyrocraft's engine turns a small propellor so as to produce thrust in the same way as a conventional aircraft propeller. The overhead rotor is tilted back so that it catches air and turns much as a child's pinwheel does. In spite of its rather precarious appearance, the gyrocopter is one of the few rotary wing aircraft that can be flown hands off. (Century Studios)

the pilot's certificate must carry a special rating appropriate to the type of aircraft being flown.) Those who lack certification may begin to learn to fly at any time and need only possess a student pilot's license in order to go up alone. Under present regulations, the student license is easy to obtain.

Young or old, affluent or indigent, there's something for (almost) everybody in homebuilt rotorcraft.

—**Kas Thomas**

For More Information

The official organ is the Popular Rotorcraft Association, Box 3896, S. El Monte, Calif. 91733. They print a magazine called *Popular Rotorcraft Flying* for their members. Published six times per year and included with membership dues which are $13 per year. The magazine has good information on construction, flying, safety topics, etc. Nothing but rotarywing. There is also the Experimental Aircraft Association, Box 229, Hales Corners, Wisc. 53130 which publishes *Sport Aviation* monthly. The organization is for the sport aircraft builders. Their magazine is primarily fixed-wing oriented, although there is rotarywing representation. Magazine comes with $18 membership.

Although there are many smaller dealerships across the country, the following represent the largest and oldest homebuilt rotorcraft suppliers.

Bensen Aircraft Corp., P.O. Box 2746, Raleigh NC 27602. $5 information kit is well worth the money, with the price refundable on future orders. The granddaddy of them all.

Ken Brock Manufacturing, 3087 Ball Road, Anaheim, Calif. 92804. Oldest and largest Bensen Distributor, famous for custom gyro accessories. Catalog $1.00.

Barnett Rotorcraft, 14307 Oliverhurst Ave., Olivehurst, Calif. 95961. J-3/J-4 series gyros feature enclosed cockpit, welded steel construction. Information pack $5; for PRA members, $4.

Rotordyne Co., 1208 Chestnut St., Burbank, Calif. 91502. Gyrocopter components, specializing in bonded aluminum blades. Catalog 25 cents.

Helicom, Inc., 4411 Calle de Carlos, Palm Springs, Calif. 92262. Offers plans, kits, components for Helicom Commuter series helicopters. $10 info pack is, as the ads say, "an education in helicopters."

RotorWay, Inc., 14805 S. Interstate 10, Tempe, Ariz. 85281. Kits, components, educational program for construction and flying of two-place Scorpion helicopters. $6 buys a very professionally done information kit.

Unfortunately, an acute shortage exists in the area of books on rotorcraft. The following titles should prove helpful to those novices seeking detailed information on the building or flying of rotorcraft. All are available from World Publications, Box 366, Mountain View, Calif. 94040 at the price listed* plus 25 cents each postage.

The Complete Book of Sky Sports by Linn Emrich. One lengthy chapter of this 1970 book discusses the building and flying of gyrocopters in some detail. Photos and diagrams. 1970 Ppb., 208 (oversized) pp., ill., $2.95 (Collier).

Guide to Homebuilt Rotorcraft by Kas Thomas. To date, the *only* book dealing exclusively with homebuilt gyrocopters and helicopters. Authoritative, down-to-earth presentation. Ppb., ill., $3.95, (Crown).

Rowing

Rowing, moving a vessel across water by using oars, was once only a means of conveyance, a way to transport people and goods across bodies of water. It has progressed, however, to include pleasure rowing and rowing in competition. (See Crew for competitive rowing.)

Pleasure rowers are those who engage in rowing for healthful or recreational purposes, in an old rowboat or sleek racing scull. William J. Cochran in his book, **Rowing, Competitive and for Pleasure,** explains that the pleasure rower moves with an easier stroke and less force. He usually rows longer distances, stroking steadily for an hour or more.

After placing his boat in the water and securing the oars to the craft's oarlocks—possibly a comfortable racing scull—the oarsman laces his feet into wooden soles designed to hold the feet steady and increase the push. These "boot stretchers" must be adjusted so that the rower does not hit the track of the movable seat as he slides back with the oar. He gently pushes away from the dock and pulls through the stroke a couple of times to get clear and establish direction. From there he merely moves ahead, enjoying the scenery and outdoors.

Casual oarsmen, who are involved in competition, may take out rowboats that are much sturdier than the one-man shell used in college competition. These recreational boats are made to handle rougher waters in bays or on the open ocean, while the one-man shell is designed for the waters of rivers or lakes. The recreational boats are sturdier, heavier, and have a higher freeboard, though they may still have foot stretchers and a sliding seat.

Persons of all ages and both sexes can row, provided they swim and can learn the rules of the waterways. This is an excellent sport to begin as a young person and continue into old age. It releases the abundant energy of youth but relieves tensions and invigorates the lassitude of old age with fresh air, open space, and wholesome activity.

Rowing clubs appear anywhere there is water! For a small membership fee, the clubs provide boats, oars, and boathouse; coaching, training, and instruction; sponsor competitors and publicize races; and manage team or peripheral events.

For More Information

There are very few rowing books on the market, but here is one that we've found. It is available from World Publications, Box 366, Mountain View, Calif. 94040 at the price listed* plus 25 cents postage.

Rowing, William J. Cochrane. A descriptive study of both competitive and pleasure rowing methods. Chapters concern such aspects as the psychology of racing, where to buy boats and information regarding rowing associations. 1971 Ppb., 67 pp., $3.00, (Cochrane).

Rugby

It was once suggested that rugby football was so popular in the tough mining towns of South Wales because manslaughter was illegal. To the casual spectator it looks as if it is manslaughter! There is, however, a good degree of method behind what seems to be madness.

The game looks rather like football without pads or helmets – it is! Football has been played in different parts of the world with all sorts of rules for centuries. It is known that the soldiers of the Roman legions played a form of football, and from medieval times until the middle of the last century, various types of football were played, mainly in the British Isles, where Gaelic football, soccer and rugby became the three best known varieties. Rugby football takes it name from Rugby School – an exclusive boys' academy in the English Midlands – where the game is said to have been "invented" in 1823.

A few Ivy League colleges were introduced to rugby towards the end of the last century and from these beginnings American and Canadian football was born.

The development of rugby had gone its own way, mostly in the British Commonwealth countries, before the post-war explosion of popularity. The game is now played nearly everywhere in the world and although the best exponents of the game are still to be found in the British Isles, France, South Africa and Australia, rugby is to be found in a very healthy state in the South Pacific, Japan, Soviet Union (the taxi drivers' team was recently named as Moscow's champions!) all over Europe, South America and Southeast Asia.

With a very real need for competitive recreational sport in the United States, rugby has become the main growth sport nationwide with some 900 clubs scattered across the land.

The appeal is obvious. Rugby combines all that is best in football – teamwork, fitness, speed and agility – but it is a more fluid game. Play only stops for an infringement, or when the ball goes out of bounds. The aim is the same as in football – to carry the ball over the line – although to score a "try" (worth four points) the ball must actually be touched down. A successful kick at goal following a try is worth two points, a drop-kick from broken play is worth three, and a penalty kick, awarded after some infringement of the laws, is also worth three points.

Forward passing is prohibited, but football's line of scrimmage was once rugby's "scrumdown". The scrum is one of the best known but more confusing features of rugby. After a minor infringement (serious breaches of the law carry the penalty of a free kick at goal) the non-offending team lobs the ball between the two "packs" – tightly bound combinations of eight men from each team who push against each other to win possession of the ball. "Pack" is the right word! The largest and most fearsome men on the team normally contest the scrums. The same men take part in the "lineout" which occurs when the ball has gone out of bounds – play is restarted by throwing the ball between two rows of players, eight from each team.

There are no "downs" in rugby, no platoons for set plays and no time-outs. The 15 players on each side throw the ball to one another, trying to find a way past their opponents. If a man is tackled, then he must release the ball, and both teams, through a combination of power and trickery will battle to get possession.

Rugby is certainly a tough and bruising game, but any rugby player will tell you that it is the social aspect which makes it all worthwhile. Win or lose it is a rugby tradition that players from both sides fraternize afterwards, and as the post-match atmosphere relaxes, the players will be seen chatting and buying each other drinks, forgetting the dreadful things they did to each other during the game!

Singing is an important feature of the rugby evening. A team is judged as much by its hospitality as by its playing strength, and becomes known by its vocal repertoir. In Wales, a small country, but one which consistently produces an excellent national team, international contests take place in front of 65,000 spectators, singing hymns and battle songs, willing their heroes to victory.

Rugby is a strictly amateur game – a refreshing change in a world where the quest for the dollar is all-important. The young men who play rugby do so simply because they enjoy the game and the conviviality and camaraderie it produces. No one cares about their teammates' politics, race or social standing. Stockbrokers play alongside construction workers; giants from the local mines team up with bank managers, opera singers "scrumdown" with neighborhood toughs. Prince Charles and Richard Burton proudly relate their rugby exploits – so do sheep farmers in New Zealand, boatmen in Fiji, and ski bums in Utah.

If you've never seen rugby played, ask the young men singing in the corner of the bar. They'll buy you a beer and fix you up with a game!

–Steve Pooley

Steve Pooley is a rugby enthusiast with a special interest in the history of the game.

On Club Rugby

Consider the club rugby player.

There he is, this strange breed of cat. He is progressing – all too rapidly, he often feels–toward middle age, or he's just out of college or occasionally he's still a beardless youth. He's struggling to make a career, or he's footloose; he's a carefree bachelor or a bridegroom or the father of five kids; he's a doctor, an attorney, a student, a teacher, a truck driver; he's rich, poor, famous, anonymous, infamous, rowdy and profane, quiet and studious . . .

And every Saturday, for about four months during the winter and spring of each year, he is crazy. Absolutely crazy.

He endures cracked bones and concussions and separations, cold showers and rain and mud and snow, all for the love of what has been called "a barbarian's game played by gentlemen."

And he pays money to do it.

Most American rugby players have never played, rarely seen and sometimes not even heard of the sport until they reach college, where it is a "minor" sport, a springtime diversion for football players that does, after all, keep them in shape during the off-season. But something gets in the blood . . .

Even when the spacious training quarters with the whirlpool is replaced by a drafty shack with a too-small hot water tank for the showers, and the trainer is an obliging teammate with a roll of adhesive tape, and the coach is a teammate who gets half the team – if the weather is nice – for one practice a week and begs them please to run by themselves occasionally; and even then the football scholarship is replaced by a dun of $25 or $50 dues or a few bucks to buy beer for the visiting team; even then, that spark somehow remains.

In fact, while other club sports are fighting to survive, rugby is growing all over the United States. New clubs spring up every year and the old ones get better and the result is a natural upward spiral – more and better teams resulting in better competition, which raises the level of play, which draws more touring international teams, which further raises the level of play, and so on toward the day when the United States will be competing on a true international level.

But there is more to it than that. Or maybe we should say, less to it. The importance of the sport can be found just as easily in a Saturday afternoon third-team slugfest as at the prestigious Monterey Tournament, and this is what makes club rugby. Here is an outlet, social and physical, for the athlete who has nowhere else to go – pro football chooses so very few, nor would all choose pro football, and what they have instead is rugby, the most social, and one of the most physical, sports in the world.

California plays the best rugby in the United States. That is not a provincial outlook, simply a statement of fact, supported by virtually all of the too-few inter-area matches that are played. And one of the best club teams in California, and an illustration of what club rugby is all about, is the Bay Area Touring Side, the BATS of San Francisco, which takes on the best opposition available and has yet to have a losing year.

Of course, the BATS' history is not yet a long one, but as was pointed out, this is a growing sport. The club was formed out of an Olympic Club tour of Europe in 1967, at that time about as ambitious and successful a trip as had yet been undertaken by an American rugby team. Upon their return, many of the players decided, for a variety of reasons, that they might be happier playing under their own banner. Most of the touring players went with the BATS; a few remained to rebuild the Olympic Club into another powerful team. (Ironically, that group too left the Olympic Club a few years later and now campaigns as the XO Club, the BATS' greatest rival as Northern California's top club team.)

The BATS originally drew largely from the University of California, and specifically from its great team of 1964-65, but now have a heavy Stanford representation and players from perhaps a dozen other colleges. The team runs heavily, for some reason, toward attorneys, from flamboyant "dope lawyer" Michael Stepanian to such as Mike Gridley, an assistant district attorney in Marin County. But there's a psychiatrist and a dentist and a carpenter and teachers and students and all manner of other types. And all ages, too – from Jim Waste, the coach who still plays with the second team and is 45 years old, through several other over-35s and on down to a second team forward who joined the team in 1973 at age 16. And it is possible that in the next year or two Waste's son, a fine high school athlete who is rugby-bent, will be in the same lineup with his father. (This would be unusual, but not unique. Eddie Marr, a scrum half who also is a

Wembley Stadium, the Rugby League Cup Final, Widnes vs. Warrington. Like football, rugby is a tough and bruising game. Unlike football, the players wear no pads or helmets, and there is no forward passing. Unlike football too, is the tradition of a friendly beer between the opposing teams after the game. (Duffy)

national-caliber squash racquets player, still referees rugby and has vowed to play in one game with his son, who already is a member of San Francisco Rugby Club.)

The BATS' captain, Jerry Mosher, the former Cal All-American football player, is an investment counselor; the executive end of the team is handled by a sportswriter and an antique dealer; Dan Hickey, the team's personal touch judge who was presented a plaque for his work in that department by the Northern California Rugby Football Union at Monterey last year, is a politically and socially active teacher; Dick Markson, the trainer (the BATS are one of the few club teams lucky enough to have a professional trainer) is a physical therapist.

Rugby, like politics, makes strange bedfellows, united by nothing more common than a love of the game.

The BATS, born out of a tour, lived up to their name again in 1972 with another precedent-setting tour. This time they became the first American rugby team to travel behind the Iron Curtain with two games against Romania's top teams (a trip which inspired someone to note the irony in the BATS playing in what once was Transylvania, for you Count Dracula fans). Then they went to France, England and Wales to play the toughest schedule yet attempted by a US side–teams like Ebbw Vale, London Irish, Paris Universite Club and Newport. The BATS lost more than they won, but only one loss was by more than three points and that to Newport, which three months before had beaten the New Zealand All-Blacks (their national team).

"We were determined to find out whether a good American team could play with teams of that caliber, the best teams we could schedule," Waste says. "I think they were dubious about out ability – we got a letter from the Welsh Rugby Union giving us permission to contact these teams but with the notation, 'I think you're being too ambitious, but go ahead.'

"But we proved that we belonged on the same field with them. If we played in a league with those teams, we might not win it – at least not for awhile – but we wouldn't be disgraced. I think it proved something for all of American rugby."

It proved enough to open the door for other United States teams which have toured there since then, and to bring Ebbw Vale, one of the better Welsh teams, to the West Coast for a return visit in 1973. In 1974, California hosted two Australian club teams, Sydney University, a strong New Zealand side, two of Argentina's top clubs and, in April, the Welsh national champion, Bridgend. And against this, California teams have held their own.

The BATS also were involved in two of the more convincing demonstrations of California superiority within the country. In 1968, the Old Blues of New York were unbeaten and being proclaimed "national champion" in a complimentary piece in *Sports Illustrated* Magazine. They asked for a game in the Boston Tournament against the Olympic Club/BATS (then in the transition period) because of the San Francisco team's publicity from the 1967 European tour.

The BATS won, 27-3

And last September, the BATS won the Aspen (Colorado) Tournament, one of the nation's more enjoyable rugby-fests, against the top teams from the Rocky Mountain area. The BATS didn't allow a try in four games – although playing with virtually their second team, bolstered by no more than half a dozen first-team regulars.

Waste has played and coached rugby for 25 years, in Northern and Southern California, Canada and Wales. He has seen a lot of good rugby. And when he says, without equivocation, "We are one of the 20 or so best rugby club teams in the world," he is not just showing fatherly pride in his own club. He's stating the case for American rugby.

You've come a long way, baby.

–Al Moss

Al Moss, a sportswriter for the San Francisco Chronicle, *is an avid supporter of rugby. Rugby, he feels, is a rarity in this country, where winning is everything. Rugby is a social sport. It is great fun. It is the essence of what amateur sports should be – a chance to get together for a game and a beer.*

For More Information

The publication for and about Rugby is *Scrumdown,* 157 E. 86th St., New York, N.Y. 10028. Published eight times a year at $5.00. Newspaper format. Information articles and news. The major organization is the United States of America Rugby Football Union, c/o Odyssey Travel, 6260 South Lake Drive, Cuadahy, Wisc. 53110. There are three major areas: Eastern Rugby Union, 123 South Broad St., Philadelphia, Pa. 19109; Midwest Rugby Football Union, c/o Bane Northwest, 1 First National Plaza, Chicago, Ill. 60670; Pacific Coast Rugby Football Union, 700 S. Flower St., Suite 1702, Los Angeles, Calif. 90017.

Finding rugby equipment and supplies can be very difficult but the following people should be able to offer some assistance. US Rugby Soccer Supply, 4308 Wakonda Parkway, Des Moines, Iowa 50315. Their free catalog offers jerseys, socks, shorts, scrum caps, jackets and books. Doss Rugby Supply Ins., 1668 First Ave., New York, N.Y. 10028. Balls, pants, shorts, jerseys, stockings, all available in their free catalog. Leather Balls, Box 6035, Arlington, Va. 22206. Complete rugby supplier. Write for free catalog. Rugby American, 115 D. Street, S.E. No. 108, Washington, D.C. 20003. Noted by many as one of the more prominent mail order houses. Irish-Thai Company, Box 2, Arlington, Mass. 02175. Another good supplier. Rugby Imports, 144 Catlin Ave., Rumford, R.I. 02916. Complete line of equipment. Mostly imported from England.

Here are some good books that cover rugby. All are available from World Publications, Box 366, Mountain View, Calif. 94040 at the price listed* plus 25 cents postage. Write for a complete list.

Rugby Football, F.N.S. Creek. Designed to give both players and coaches a thorough knowledge of the principles of the game, its laws, and the main tactical points. Covers the fascinating history of the game, then lists complete laws, and finally shows the player what he must practice to improve his kicking, catching, tackling, passing, and dribbling skills. 1968 Hb., 208 pp., ill., $4.95, (Crowell).

John Dawes: **Rugby Union**. Former captain of Wales and British Lions, and now the Welsh National Coach, Dawes deals with every aspect of Rugby in detail, from passing to scrummaging, and explains the role of each individual player. Illustrated with many action photographs taken in match situations. 1975 Library Binding, 64 (oversize) pp., ill., $5.95, (Pelham).

Sail Boat Racing

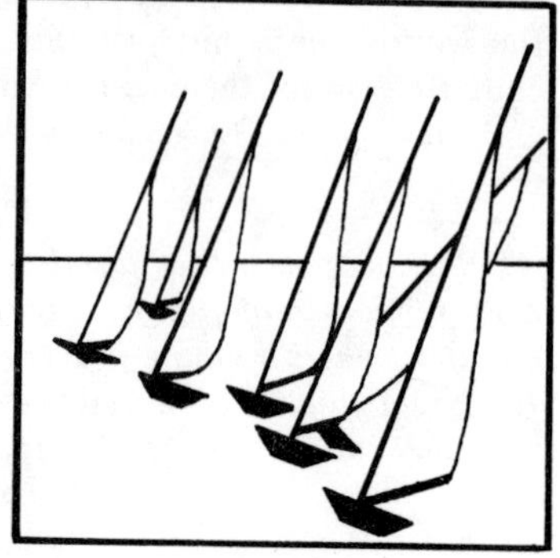

Sailboat racing is a sport that requires the patience of a Job, the stamina of a mountain climber, the coordination of a ballet dancer, the strength of a football player, the tactical ability of a chess master, the sensitivity to wind and weather of a meteorologist and in some cases, the bankroll of a Rockefeller. But since few of us have any, far less all, of these attributes, it is a sport enjoyed by thousands on various levels around the world.

It is a rather strange sport in that everyone is so obsessed with speed and yet the fastest sailboats – probably the high-bred, C-Class Catamaran – rarely exceed the speed that the family automobile does when driving through a residential area. The fastest sailboats go about 25 miles per hour, while most racing is conducted at speeds well below 10 and in some cases below one. So, the reason that the participants play the game is not for pure speed – although at times the speeds seem breakneck – but for optimum or relative speed under all wind and weather conditions.

Boats come in all sizes, from the small seven-foot racing prams built at home and raced by school kids on lakes and rivers around the world to huge, 79-foot ocean racers that literally race around the world and carry crews of 20 men.

There are two types or competition: around the buoys and offshore racing. Open boats, like dinghies, race most often around the buoys with the competition lasting for hours, while offshore racing is conducted in enclosed boats equipped to go offshore (out of the sight of land) and the length of the competition may vary from overnight to several long weeks.

There are two types of dinghies that race around the buoys: strict one-design and development classes. In strict, one-design racing, the boats and sails are kept as identical as man and machines can make them, so the emphasis is on the skill of the sailor, rather than any advantages provided by slight differences in the boats, sails or equipment. Expenses are kept down as there is no pressure to keep up with the Joneses because Jones can't make major changes to his boat.

A class which has capitalized on this type of tight control is the Laser, a 14-foot, off-the-beach board boat. The producer has given quality control special attention and consequently the boats and sails – no matter if they are built in Australia or in the States – are as equal as can be. Consequently older boats can still compete on a par with the newer ones. Testimony to the success of this approach is that in just four years, since the boat was designed, about 25,000 have been sold worldwide, the equivalent of a boating hula hoop.

The other type of dinghy racing is developmental, where the class rules permit some experimentation in equipment. The most exotic example of this type of class would have to be the C-Class catamarans, where class rules permit almost unlimited variation on a three-or-four-rule theme. Some of the sailors have even eliminated cloth sails and are now using rigid, articulating wing sections, which are exactly identical to airplane wings.

Proponents of this type of racing should enjoy tinkering and experimenting with equipment as there's a technological test as well as a test of men. They also must be willing to spend extra money and time to try out new approaches or to copy things that are currently working on Jones' boat.

Offshore racing is something of a different game that requires, if nothing else, more money to participate in, as everything is more expensive. This type of racing is conducted in boats that must have at least minimal cruising equipment to make an offshore passage, such things as an enclosed cabin, bunks, a head (marine toilet) and some facility to cook and store food.

There is some overlap in the types of courses that dinghies and offshore boats sail, as much of the racing done by offshore boats occurs on around-the-buoys courses. But these boats can and often do make race passages well offshore, such as from Chicago to Mackinac Island, Los Angeles to Hawaii or Newport to Bermuda. And although offshore boats and dinghies are concerned with the same elements, wind, waves, current and weather, offshore boats must in addition be concerned with seamanship as they make much longer passages during which all these elements may change several times. A dinghy race is often called off when things get too rough, but offshore racers must be prepared to handle themselves and their boat in all conditions. In addition to knowing how these elements are behaving now, the offshore racer must take a longer view of the wind and weather because at times he is out racing for days or even weeks.

Stamina is even more important in offshore racing than in dinghies. A successful dinghy sailor needs the stamina of a miler; while the offshore racer requires the stamina of a marathon runner. Also important to success offshore is a competent navigator as much of the racing is done out of the sight of land.

It is easier to learn how to sail than it is to learn how to race. Usually people start racing after they know the fundamentals of handling a sailboat. Basic sailing is taught by such organizations as the American Youth Hostel, parks and recreation departments, and by some school systems and at yacht clubs. Some of these organizations feature racing instruction in their advanced course. There are some commercial schools in the country that do teach both sailing and racing. These schools advertise extensively in local newspapers, as well as regional or national boating magazines.

What is becoming popular in this sport, like in tennis or skiing, is the weekend or even week-long racing school where a vacation is combined with learning a skill, in this case how to race.

Another road into the sport is to learn the basics of sailing and then put up advertisements around yacht clubs or in the local marina saying how a "fast learner, with the Patience of Job, the coordination of a prima ballerina . . ." ad nauseum, desires a crew position. This approach works well.

—Michael Levitt

Michael Levitt is the Senior Editor of **Yacht Racing** *magazine and a frequent racer on circuits such as the Southern Ocean Racing Circuit.*

"There are two types of competition: around the buoys and offshore racing. Open boats, like dinghies, race most often around the buoys with the competition lasting for hours, while offshore racing is conducted in enclosed boats equipped to go offshore (out of sight of land) and the length of the competition may vary from overnight to weeks." (M.J. Baum)

Ocean Racing, The Way It Is

Before a race, there is planning, organization and execution. Myriad details scream at various levels for attention, people are recruited to assume the various positions on the boat from the athletes on the bow who handle all sails to the more cerebral types in the cockpit, who make all the decisions. Back home, bosses are manipulated for some "time off" or the desperate decision is made that this might be a good time to have the wife call in sick for you.

Menus are made up and then ripped up when it is discovered that one crewmember "just can't stand brisket." Then crew members, wives, girlfriends and secretaries are pressed into service cooking casseroles and baking cookies, and then quickly freezing all of this so it will be fresh when racing.

Every piece of rigging must be checked, cleaned, replaced, if necessary, sprayed with ounces of silicone and then taped if there is anything sharp that might cut a sail on its way up or down.

The wood is oiled and the deck cleaned, in spite of the fact that the raft of racing boats that you are part of comes complete with a parade of sailors, friends and camp followers who cross your deck with dirty shoes, leaving footprints. The bottom of the boat is wiped clean by a scuba diver so that the salad of algae that has begun to flourish there won't slow the boat's progress.

Finally, you have cornered the electronics guy, who comes to adjust your wind and navigational instruments and leaves with the stuff still not right. Your sailmaker has begun to duck your frantic calls about how the storm trisail needs one inch removed from the leech – "the whole race could depend upon it."

Mountains of food and beverages are carried down the dock to the boat in such quantities that it looks like you could feed an army for weeks – and this is only a three-day race. Places are found, somehow, for all this food and now the boat is floating two inches below its waterline, but "an ocean racer travels on its stomach." First aid kits are checked and replenished with pills and ointments ranging from Dramamine to aspirin and sunburn lotion – two kinds – one to prevent it and the other to soothe it after you have it.

Those who work the sails add telltales of ribbon to the luffs and also to the leeches to identify areas of flow or stall. All sails are folded and stowed. Spinnakers are stopped in rubberbands, including the light-air one which, when hoisted in the dying breeze, will require six guys tugging on its sides to break it free from the rubberband trap.

The navigator checks his charts and courses. He listens to weather reports and tries to remember if the flow is clockwise or counterclockwise around a low-pressure area. The navigator worries about the deviation table (that identifies magnetic disturbances) he had been meaning to do for the radio direction finder but never got around to. He is also in an absolute panic about whether the 1.3 multiple for the log – figured two years ago – is still viable. He turns on the Loran to work a fix that places him around Cedar Rapids, Iowa then mumbles something cryptic about the interference caused by the forest of masts. Then he takes a sunline or two, while the boat and the ladies are still at the dock to reacquaint himself with HO 214 and his sextant and besides, it looks so sexy to the lovelies who watch this performance.

The owner of the boat flits around in a thousand and one activities, showing the troops that he is one of them, a regular guy, not even above swabbing the deck, but rarely the whole deck because so many other things really do demand his attention. The local chandler is wise enough to present his bill before the race starts for all the gear that the owner has bought, because otherwise they might not meet again until next year's race. Even with all his collection work, the chandler finds himself still with many unpaid bills in hand, and goes home entirely drained and laments to his wife about how "they are so rich and yet such slow payers . . . ." And the owner must remember to register for the race and get his rating certificate in (it is amazing how often these details are forgotten), and check to be certain that all the ORC safety equipment is aboard.

And then, ready or not, there is the pre-race celebration where everyone catches his breath. And there the liquor and camaraderie flow free. And there in alcohol and bravado, bets that have no business being bet, are . . . .

Then comes the hangover, the morning after, and the race, which is often an anticlimax compared to the hysteria of the preparation. After motoring out to the start, sails are hoisted and tacked so the crew and helmsmen get loose and into it. Lead positions are checked for optimum sail trim. The starting line is run again and again to find which end is most advantageous. Then finally just before the crew has started to breathe some under their exertion, the head sails are dropped so as not to wear the guys out before the racing really starts. If it is meal time or close to it, food is brought out because this is the calm before the storm of activity. And then during this hiatus, the spectator fleet is perused for girls in bikinis, and greetings are exchanged from boat to boat.

Suddenly the skipper gets anxious and the head canvas is hoisted again and the clowning of the crew stops. This seriousness tends to ripple through the fleet as other boats respond and the maneuvering starts in earnest. With a boom the white flag signifying 10 minutes until the start is hoisted and the navigator starts the stop watch. "Eight minutes and 30 seconds," he calls softly but distinctly.

"Ready about, Hard alee!" shouts the skipper and he spins the boat through the wind and the jib sheet is tossed free and the tailer grabs for feet of sheet and then under load for inches.

"Five minutes and 30 seconds," says the navigator as the white shape drops. The skipper jams the boat off the wind and away from the line.

"We'll try a timed run," says the skipper hoping to hit the line exactly five minutes and 30 seconds later. "Trim for speed."

"Two minutes and 40 seconds . . ."

"Let's tack because the air will be chewed up plenty . . . Hard alee! Trim fast! Come on, get it in . . . dammit get it in!

"One minute and five seconds . . ."

"We are too early," says the skipper with growing panic in his voice. "Ease the sails out. Let's slow down."

"Come up," shouts a guy on the boat to leeward who, in keeping with the rules, has rights to control the weather boat.

"My helm is all the way over," the skipper shouts back. "Give me some sail trim to get up," he whispers to his crew. With more speed, the boat breaks away from the luff. "Good, OK. Let's go. Trim for speed. We are going for the line. Call the time now every five seconds."

Twenty. Go for it! Fifteen. See the boat trying to sneak in. Ten. No room up there! Five seconds. We're racing." Bam! And the red starting flag is hoisted on the committee boat.

"We weren't over early!" says the skipper. "Were we over early? Check the radio," he orders the navigator. "We weren't; Good! Let's do it . . . . "

Then the race establishes a rhythm, usually an individual rhythm, as waterline length tends to spread the fleet out and miles and horizons separate the boats, and they are sailing in different weather conditions. Myriad sails are hoisted and then dropped to stay in harmony with wind systems that seem to have no consistency. And the talk varies little from hour to hour or day to day: either about boats or women.

Skin is tanned or burned furiously or else clothes are soaked, and finally the decision is made that you will put the wet ones back on because you are running out and they only stay dry for a few minutes anyway. But the pain of putting on wet pants or a soaking sweater for a two a.m. watch is unbelievable. It is a very lonely moment.

Meals are cooked in a galley that hasn't seen level in days and the cook has to strap himself in to work. Meals are eaten and pills are taken, and often both are seen again as sickness walks slowly around the boat.

And then, at last, the destination. And every muscle hurts and you are spent. Had this been a three-week race rather than three days, you wouldn't hurt this much. But you pace yourself differently, both mentally and physically.

And yet, in some way, it has been fun. And if someone asked whether you'd do it again, without much thought, you would say, "yes!"

Often, even more interesting than the preparation or the race is the destination: places like Isla Mujeres (Mexico), Bermuda, Hawaii, England, Nassau or Mackinac Island. Among other things, ocean racing is a tremendous excuse to see out-of-the-way places, including foreign countries, where the post-race celebration is legendary, not just for the winners, but for everyone who plays the game.

These are places where you lose/win at the casino – with the emphasis on the lose; where you meet people from different cultures; where the diving is superior on the reefs. Places where there are horses to rent and motorbikes to play "Wild Ones" with. Places where there are native dishes and drinks – "island drinks" – to try and try again. Food like Nassau's conch chowder, served in the real native bars – not the ones with the signs on the outside describing them as "real native bars" – that can reduce the strongest of men to tears, or worse. And, places like Isla Mujeres in Mexico where there are ancient ruins to explore and the amigos race, where the Mexican kids are brought aboard the racing boats in incredible number to "help" race the yachts.

—Michael Levitt

For More Information

There are over 20 magazines that cover sail boat (some time called yacht) racing. Here are the bigger and better ones. *Yacht Racing,* 143 Rowayton Ave., Rowayton, Conn. 06853. Published monthly at $12.00 per year. For the one-design and offshore yachtsman. *Yachting,* 50 W. 44th St., New York, N.Y. 10036. Published monthly at $10 per year. Presents complete coverage of the sport including race results. *Sail,* 38 Commercial Wharf, Boston, Mass. 02110. Published monthly at $12 per year. Emphasizes racing techniques, sail trim and hull design. A lot of how-to-do-it and not much on what is happening. *Rudder,* Fawcett Building, Greenwich, Ct. 06830. Published monthly at $8.00 per year. Covers the modern small boat and cruising scene. *Sailing,* 125 E. Main St., Port Washington, Wisc. 53074. Monthly at $7.50 per year. Very well illustrated showing the beauty of the sport.

A good source for information is the Offshore Racing Club of America, Box 14, Rowayton, Conn. 06853. They are a member organization of the Offshore Racing Council and the United States Yacht Racing Union, 1133 Avenue of the Americas, New York, N.Y. 10036. Also the Inter-Collegiate Yacht Racing Association, 8893 Melinda Ct., Milan, Mich. 48160 is a good contact.

This is a good crossection of books. All are available from World Publications, Box 366, Mountain View, Calif. 94040 at the price listed* plus 25 cents postage. Write for a complete list.

Race Your Boat Right, Arthur Knapp, Jr. An updated, revised edition of one of the classics on sailboat racing. Information regarding preaseason preparation to what to do after crossing the finish line is presented to the reader in a precise, detailed manner. A book for the neophyte and expert alike. 1973 (rev.) Hb., 396 pp., Il., $8.95, (Grosset & Dunlap).

Invitation to Sailboat Racing, Alan Brown. A book that brings the art of sailboat racing to both the beginning and advanced student in structured visual lessons. The reader is taken from the fundamentals of racing tactics to the complexities of racing strategy. 1972 Hb., 255 pp., ill., $9.95, (Simon & Schuster).

Sailing Solo To America, Frank Page. The dramatic story of the 1972 Observer Singlehanded Transatlantic Race. Each entry sailed alone across the Atlantic, risking violent weather, capsizing, going off course while asleep, and many other dangers. 1972 Hb., 91 pp., ill., $10.00, (Quadrangle).

Cornelius Shields on Sailing, Cornelius Shields. An expert on sailing shares the opinions and techniques which made him the famed racing sailor he is. A manual for racers, written from a personal and authoritative viewpoint. 1970 Hb., 240 pp., ill., $9.65, (Prentice Hall).

The Longest Race, Cook & Fisher. The complete story of the most adventurous yacht race of all time—a round-the-would race by 14 ocean-sailing yachts in 1973. Includes technical information to satisfy the most demanding nautical buff, and a great book for all lovers of an adventure story. 1975 Hb., ill., $14.95, (McKay).

Tactics and Strategy in Yacht Racing, Joachim Schult. Racing sailors find the greatest part of their pleasure is derived from the cut and thrust of tactical battles. This book covers the basics of the subject. 1971 Hb., ill., $9.95, (Dodd, Mead).

Wind and Strategy, Stuart Walker. The effects of wind and its changes on sailboat racing strategy, by one of the world's foremost sailboat racers. How to predict, live with, and benefit from the wind. 1973 Hb., 416 pp., ill., $9.95, (W.W. Norton).

Dinghy Team Racing, Eric Twiname. The first and only book on sailboat racing in the dinghy class. Includes rules and their interpretation, as well as complete information on tactics and teamwork. 1971 Hb., 139 pp., ill., $6.95, (Quadrangle).

Sailing- Recr.

Sailing for pleasure probably originated in Holland. The people of this hearty country have long been celebrated seamen, and were the first to develop whale and herring fisheries. Since they were living in a country intersected by waterways and canals, it was natural for them to use the jaght or yacht for transportation, and eventually recreation.

Charles II, who had been exiled from England to Holland during the 17th century, took yachting back to England on his restoration to the throne. English nobility was quick to follow his royal example and were soon enthusiastically sailing small boats. Within a short time, recreational sailing spread to the other European countries.

During the 19th century, small boat sailing in America was not as popular as in Europe, but it eventually spread to include most of the wealthier families on the East Coast. It was natural for American recreational yacht owners to band together and form what eventually became a vast network of yacht clubs. The members of these clubs started challenging one another to races called regattas over prescribed courses. One of the best known regattas handed down to us is that of the Hundred Guineas Cup, or as it is better known, the Americas Cup.

Spurred by American success in racing, advances were made in this country in the types of boats and equipment used to sail. These advances brought sailing within the reach of more people, to the point where most modern Americans can indulge in the sport.

Choosing a Boat

When an individual attempts to select a boat, he/she comes face to face with over 1000 different designs. It is little wonder that some people take years sifting through dealers, magazines and friendly advice to find a boat that satisfies their own particular need.

Initially, one must consider who will use the boat. If you intend to sail alone, you need only to please yourself. If other people will be involved, however, their desires should be accommodated to prevent many potentially miserable days sailing.

Three basic types of boats are available: day sailers, cruisers, and multihulled boats. With the first two types, enough sail can be applied to each hull to convert them to racers. And, most regattas offer handicap programs so cruising boats will not be excluded from competition.

Day sailors are the most popular and least expensive of sailing craft. These boats are usually under 30 feet in length and are primarily designed for afternoons of fun, not for extended cruising. Cruising sailboats are usually 30 feet and over. Depending on the design, they can be comfortable enough for extended voyages. Multihulled craft range from small catamarans to large trimarans, and are fast becoming popular with yachting enthusiasts.

The notable success of American racing sailboats has encouraged advances in boat and equipment design. The spinoff benefits to the more casual recreational sailors have been considerable. The sport is now open to many more Americans than ever before. (M.J. Baum)

Sailors usually obtain their craft in one of four ways: (1) buy a new boat that is ready to sail; (2) buy a second-hand or used boat; (3) build one from a kit; or (4) build one from plans and raw materials. Building a boat offers the pride of constructing and sailing your own craft, along with a savings of one third to three quarters of potential cost.

Second hand boats are usually purchased through a broker or private party. Most small yachts are generally obtained through private parties, though, because brokers prefer handling large yachts with their correspondingly higher commissions. If a buyer is in any doubt about a craft, marine surveyors are available to inspect and evaluate a boat. Surveyors usually deal with the larger craft, because it is usually an easy task for buyers to personally inspect smaller boats.

Buying a new sailboat is the easiest, safest, and probably the most expensive way to acquire your craft. If you cannot find a dealer that carries the particular type of boat that you desire, it is possible to order it by mail directly from the manufacturer.

Any way you cut the deck, sailing is going to cost money, demand time, and involve effort. But it does give pleasure and a sense of achievement that is difficult to measure. The unparelled freedom of beating into the wind, spray whipping across your face, is a sensation you will not want to trade, once you experience it.

—Joshua Bigelow

Joshua Bigelow has been involved in aquatic activities all of his life, with special emphasis on sailing for the past six years. He is a former sailing instructor at the Univeristy of California at Berkeley.

For More Information

For magazines and organizations check sail boat racing. Here is a selection of sailing books. All are available from World Publications, Box 366, Mountain View, Calif. 94040 at the price listed* plus 25 cents each postage.

Introduction to Sailing, Leeds Mitchell, Jr. A skill-starting primer written for the beginner. Step-by-step instruction takes the reader from picking the right boat to handling working jibs. Discussions of fundamentals and boat hardware and rigging are simple and complete. 1971 Ppb., 192 pp., ill., $3.95, (Stackpole).

The Beginning Guide to Sailing, Donald Law. A book designed for the beginning sailor who knows nothing about sailing or about boats. Simple language and numerous diagrams make the book easy to understand. Emphasizes boat safety. 1975 Hb., 169 pp., ill., $7.95, (Drake).

Starting Sailing, James Moore and Alan Turvey. This is a step-by-step approach to how to sail, designed specifically for newcomers. Over 400 extremely clear and accurate drawings of all the maneuvers involved in getting a sailing craft to perform safely and correctly on all points of the wind. 1974 Hb., 112 pp., ill., $5.95, (Doubleday).

The Mariner's Catalog, Volume 2, David Getchell, ed. This is an incredible catalog along the lines of the Whole Earth Catalog, only completely devoted to boating information. Every page is filled with info, good photos and diagrams, with an emphasis on small boats, boatbuilding, tool sources, and boats of design and type not normally found in boating publications. 1974 Ppb., 179 (oversize) pp., ill., $4.95, (International Marine Publishing).

Encyclopedia of Sailing. Covers all phases of sailing, from history to techniques, and answers hundreds of questions in its many fact-filled pages. 1971 Hb., 484 pp., ill., $16.95, (Harper & Row).

This is Sailing, Creagh-Osborne. A fresh, new approach that creates a "feel" for the on-board experience. 300 detailed full-color drawings to illustrate the techniques of sailing. 1972 Hb., 220 pp., ill., $12.95, (W.W. Norton).

Sports Illustrated Small Boat Sailing, the editors of *Sports Illustrated*. Everything the novice needs to know to become a competent small boat sailor. Detailed illustrations show the construction, rigging, and classes of boats. 1972 Hb. & Ppb., 93 pp., ill., $4.95/$1.95, (Lippincott).

Heavy Weather Sailing, K. Adlard Coles. A rare book for the yachtsman. Examples of the various heavy weather conditions are presented and dealt with in 22 chapters. 1972 Hb., 305 pp., ill., $12.50, (De Graff).

Sailing Step by Step, Jack R. Knights. Britain's leading sailing expert discusses every aspect of sailing, from the basics to racing strategy. A great instructional manual. 1961 Ppb., 150 pp., ill., $1.45, (Arco).

Sand Yachting

In its simplest form, a sand or land yacht consists of a sail boat mounted on wheels so that it can be propelled along by the wind on any reasonably flat and hard surface. In early days this is indeed what the craft looked like. On land, the sailing dynamics and sail use are very similar to those employed in sailing on water, and the thrills of racing quickly along before the wind heeled over on two wheels are also similar.

Modern sand and land yachts are usually of light materials, with fiberglass commonly used. They sport three wheels, two mounted wide apart in the rear and the other one forward and amidships, much like a child's tricycle. Cockpits for a pilot and sometimes a small crew are mounted aft. American yachts typically are single seated, about 10 feet long, and carry approximately 45 square feet of sail. Some European yachts may be crewed by three, are 25 feet long and carry as much as 400 square feet of canvas.

The first world championships were held in Lancashire, England in 1970 with more than 100 competitors.

For more information write International Federation of Sand and Land Yacht Clubs, 100 Avenue de Statuares, Brussels 18, Belgium.

Scuba Diving

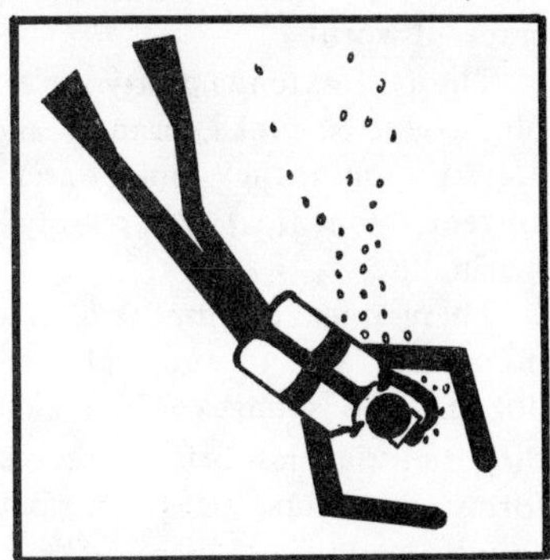

Man's interest in the underwater world is not just a recent occurrence. Records of the Romans, Greeks and even the earlier Persians show man's attempts at various underwater exploits. Leonardo da Vinci, an insatiable explorer of the world of art and flying machines, was also fascinated with underwater research.

While history tells us of many interested men throughout the years, diving's real breakthrough came with the Cousteau-Gagnan invention. Though an Englishman, W. H. James must be credited with the first scuba operation in 1825 via a belt designed for carrying air, the Frenchmen's Aqua Lung and demand regulator mark the beginning of the sport of scuba diving. The rig was inexpensive and allowed divers to stay underwater for longer periods of time.

The 1950s brought the advent of the wet suit. This allowed more divers in less temperate parts of the world to participate in this relatively new sport. Changes from this period of time began to occur rapidly.

Approximately one million people joined the ranks of divers from 1950 to 1970. Between 1970 and 1974 there were one million more. Diving has proven to be the last frontier, an ecological attraction being explored and appreciated more each year.

The diver's experience of weightlessness can perhaps be somewhat duplicated in outer space journeys; not too many men have access to such travel. Participating in this new world of adventure – spearfishing, photographing or just sightseeing – is challenging, interesting, and absorbing. Trade in your pinstriped suit for a neoprene rubber suit and try it!

—**Nancy Ackerman**

Nancy Ackerman is presently the Associate Editor of **Skin Diver** *magazine. She is currently pursuing ocean research and photography along with her literary endeavors.*

The Diving Experience

All eyes are focused on your intrusive body as you float by. Your strange appearance startles and fascinates them. Your size, skin, appendages and incredible train of bubbles that seem to follow you everywhere are totally unusual.

Where did you come from? How did you get here? What are you doing here? Do you intend the inhabitants any harm? Some choose to flee your appearance, others seem to be attracted, mysteriously, to it.

With Self-Contained-Underwater-Breathing-Apparatus (SCUBA) the diver can hover in the silent world. The experience of weightlessness is magnetic in itself, but when you add the attraction of exploring or spearfishing, scuba diving becomes quite compelling. (Skin Diver Magazine)

You are an outsider in their magnificently beautiful, liquid universe. Only a few minutes before, you donned your scuba gear and decided to explore this new reef, their home. Now an intruder, you respect and appreciate their colorful, fluid and graceful world.

The reef extends past your vision. It is a patchwork of vivid blues, greens, pinks, oranges and startling whites. The colors are so intense, they almost seem unreal. Being carried by the current, you float effortlessly over this living tapestry of marine life.

There must be hundreds of different forms of life in the immediate area of the reef you are hovering over. At least a dozen or so sponges. These alone are worth coming to see – their rich purples, bright oranges and crimsons. Their unusual forms and diverse sizes contribute a great deal to this exciting aquatic garden.

You drift over the edge of the reef and down a vertical wall which offers still more for your mind to absorb. A mass of schooling grunts sweep across the top of the reef. Moving slowly, there are hundreds of individuals in this group, including several obviously different species.

Turning your attention back to the wall, you see an arrow crab peeking from behind a sea fan. You move to pick him up and he attempts to elude you on his long, exaggerated, spindly legs. You find him incredibly light and fragile. You release him and he folds back his legs, streamlining his body. He plummets to the bottom and finds refuge in a basket sponge.

What makes you return to Neptune's aquatic wonderland? What does this world, in which you are the curiosity, the outsider, hold for you? How can you explain to someone who has never tried it, the quiet excitement a dive holds for you?

Maybe it is your weightlessness, the feeling you get soaring above the ocean floor being carried effortlessly by a current. Or maybe the thrill of being underwater comes from knowing that you are exploring man's last ecological frontier here on earth.

Does the aquatic world help you forget your worries from the anhydrous world topside?

Perhaps the remembrance of the kaleidoscopic garden filled with an infinite crossection of marine life–in a multitude of colors, shapes, textures – draws you back to diving like the fabled sirens. For some it is underwater photography, for some exploring and communing with the underwater inhabitants. The hunt, or spearfishing entices others. The Lloyd Bridges syndrome appears in many.

Why bother trying to figure it out? Break another sea urchin open and feed the fish. They've finished with the last urchin you broke for them and will lose interest and swim away if you don't supply them with more. You blow bubbles at a passing turtle and completely forget your earlier enigma.

—Nancy Ackerman

For More Information

See skin diving and cave diving for additional information.

The strange shapes and elaborate coloring of the fish that teem in tropical waters may be satisfying to the eye, but don't try to satisfy your palate with one. They're nice to look at, but not good to eat. (Skin Diver Magazine)

Shooting–Handgun

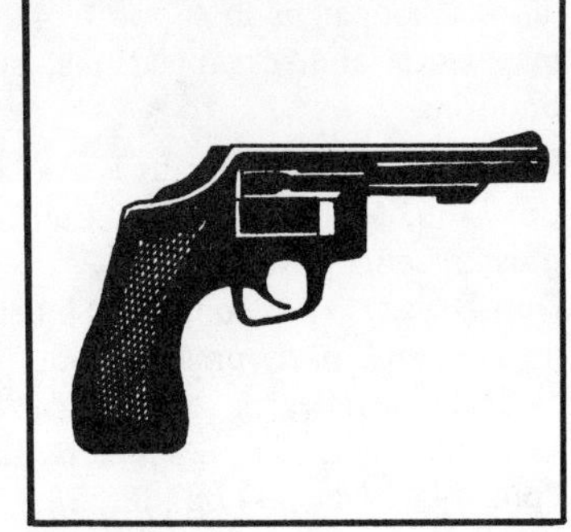

A handgun, as most people know, is a firearm that is designed to be fired with one hand. Originally, the term pistol was used to denote all handguns, but today it is more-or-less used to refer only to single-shot and autoloading designs.

In 1540, Caminello Vitelli invented the first pistol in Italy, which continued to be the only hand weapon until Samuel Colt of the United States improved on this crude design and developed the revolver. Whereas the pistol could only fire one shot, the revolver could fire from five to seven bullets in one loading, by means of a revolving chamber.

Following Vitelli, the English became aware of the value of the pistol and developed it to where it could be of use to soldiers. Later, in the early frontier days of America, the pistol was an invaluable tool for those who could use it adeptly – deadly accuracy was needed since it only fired one shot at a time. By the time gunslingers in the American West – the Wyatt Earps and Jesse Jameses – became well-known, the revolver had become widely accepted.

Today, the handgun plays an important role in a number of sports and activities (see Hunting, Fast Draw and Marksmanship).

In comparison to the rifle, handguns are of comparatively limited range and accuracy.

The Gun and I

Looking back on more than 14 years of competitive pistol shooting, I have many warm and happy memories. There are some bitter moments, but their taste is more than lost in the sweetness of success. Many of my warmest recollections are of people, some superstars such as Bill Blankenship and Harry Reeves, and others of lesser or equal fame that shall be mentioned later. Other memories are of particular moments in the sport when an event of some significance occurred.

Although many people do not associate shooting with the word sport, competitive shooting is clearly in that category. Any person who has fired in a match would be quick to define shooting as a sport, citing that it has the same physical and mental requirements for success by a participant. One needs coordination, mental discipline, a certain amount of physical ability, the determination to succeed, and good equipment. Each of these must come together in a competitive atmosphere, at some levels so fierce that the weaker falter no less than runners or swimmers or any other athletic participant. At the same time, it is a sport enjoyed by thousands of people only for the sake of the sport itself. They shoot to see how small a hole they can put five shots into, or just to be afield, without giving thought to being a champion or a member of a winning team. They simply enjoy themselves, liking the tall tales that inevitably follow the matches, and the unique comradeship that exists among shooters of all ages, abilities and backgrounds.

My own start came during the summer of 1961, following a year of graduate study in biology at the Pennsylvania State University. Several friends introduced me to their hobby, showed me their pistols, and I was hooked. I began accumulating equipment, read every book I could get my hands on, and felt with the raw newness of the rookie that I could conquer the shooting world. My first match was in the fall of that year at a local club in the Massachusetts Outdoor Pistol Championship. With my homemade pistol box and my K-22 revolver, I sallied forth determined to place my name atop the list of current sports heroes. After a few comments from my new friends: "Your name is Colt and you shoot a Smith and Wesson pistol? Tch, Tch, Tch . . .", and several caustic comments from the chief range officer about that clown trying to load the wheelgun: "My God, who would shoot a wheelgun in the .22 matches . . .?" I was beginning to wonder if I had made a bad choice.

But that inauspicious beginning lead to better days. As time passed and more practice rounds went down range I began to pick trophies here and there. I met men who have shaped and guided my talents and built my character in the game. These men taught me not only fundamentals of the sport, but also made me understand the moral code by which all reputable sportsmen must abide. Bob Baxter, an early and still very close friend, helped me immensely in those early days, and his only demand was that in my turn I must help those on the way up. With Bob's friendship came membership in the Sharon Fish and Game Club, and in later years its presidency for four years.

The Sharon Club became my home away from home. I joined its pistol team, a team which has posted as many as 70 straight wins without a loss. My three eldest children have been through its excellent junior riflery program, each in turn became Club Junior Rifle Champion, between them holding that title for five consecutive times. My eldest son, David, went on to win two letters on the varsity rifle team at Navy, Steve became a pistol shooter and of this writing is burning up the Sharpshooter category in such matches. Jean has gone to the University of Maine and will shoot on the rifle team there.

Outside of the club activities, I also remember my first state championship. It was the gallery title, and the match was fired at the Norco Club in Worcester. I carried the immense trophy, more than three feet tall, home in my lap in the car. I'd have walked home with it, as proud of the day as I was.

About that time I met two other men. One was Don Hamilton, later three time National Pistol Champion and member of the 1960 Olympic Team. The other was Tom McLennan, then Marksmanship Instructor at Hanscom Airfield in nearby Bedford, Mass., and now Pistol Coach at the Massachusetts Institute of Technology. Through the years since those early days, the friendship of these two fine men has been a strong guide in both my personal achievements in shooting and in my role as a coach. Both are superb technicians in the field of shooting, and both have always been ready to help when it was needed.

As time went on I won more and more. I picked up the New England Gallery Title in 1966. My first Massachusetts State Outdoor Title in 1968, and my first Regional Pistol Championship in 1970. Each has very special memories, if only because each represented the culmination of long hours of work and the determination to succeed. Yet, in those years the test of the shooter was his entry into the select National Rifle Association 2600 Club. Our conventional pistol matches are fired in individual matches with each of three guns, the .22, the centerfire, and the .45. Each has a possible point total of 900 points, and the full match aggregate is 2700. A high level of achievement has been reached by any shooter who drops 100 or fewer points during such an aggregate match.

I do not remember all of the match details, but I'll never forget the last 10 points. The match was the Maine State Championships in 1967. With only 10 rounds to go we prepared for the final stage. It consisted of two series of five shots, each to be fired in 10 seconds. The target was at a distance of 25 yards and the pistol was a .45 caliber government automatic that had been rebuilt by Al Dinan. I fired my first string and had three 10s and two nines. In the second string I fired two nines, then during the recoil of the second shot bent my wrist, a No-No, and the gun then malfunctioned, trapping a case. So I had to fire an alibi string. This I did, posting four 10s and one nine, giving me a 95 of a possible 100 in that stage of fire. When I checked the target through my scope and saw the score I knew I had posted a 2602 for the day, my first such 2600 score. I threw my baseball cap downrange and yelled like a wild man, such was the feeling that the score brought out in me. A very good friend of those days, the late Hugh Gorton, made me a special trophy commemorating that event in my career.

Another memorable event of those early days was my first trip to the Mecca for all shooters, Camp Perry, Ohio, the site of the National Shooting Championships each year. I went as a member of the Massachusetts State Pistol Team. We did not win anything of significance, but there I learned that all pistol shooters were human beings. Anyone coming up through the levels of skill of any sport has to learn that those on top are just as human as those on the bottom, they put on their trousers the same way and so on. Then you begin to learn just what you are supposed to be doing on the range.

I have returned to Perry many times since then, and now in 1975 have just completed my second tour of duty as The Challenge Referee for the Smallbore Championship Phase of the National Matches. I think that I am one of the youngest ever to serve in that capacity, so my selection for that post has been a moment of satisfaction for me.

In most recent years, I joined the shooting program of the Connecticut National Guard and was immediately placed on the All-National Guard Team. We travel a great deal, putting on clinics, shooting, helping others to learn the game. This team is ranked number two nationally, right behind the Army team (for the moment), and to be part of such a team is an ego-building experience. We won the All-Army Championship in this year of 1975, and swept the team matches. Those gold medals hold a special place in my trophy list.

—Le Baron Colt

LeBaron Colt, Jr. is presently a professor of biology and varsity coach at Boston State College. He has served as President of the State Rifle and Pistol Association of Massachusetts.

For More Information

The magazine specifically on pistols and revolvers is the *US Hand-Gunner*, 59 Alvin Street, Springfield, Mass. 01104. It is bi-monthly, and costs $5 with a membership to the United States Revolver Association, at the same address. The USRA is devoted to developing interest and competition in handgun shooting. The Shooters Club of America, 8150 N. Central Park Ave., Skokie, Ill. 60076, conducts educational and public relations campaigns in support of pro-gun legislation. For other magazines and organizations, see Marksmanship and Rifle Shooting.

Here is one good book. It is available from World Publications, Box 366, Mountain View, Calif. 94040 at the price listed * plus 25 cents postage.

Gun Digest 1976, John T. Amber, ed. The absolute authority on firearms, past, present and future featuring authoritative, exclusive articles on every facet of guns and shooting. Noted authorities writing on subjects that made them famous. 1975 Ppb., 448 (oversize) pp., ill., $8.95, (Digest Books).

Shooting-Rifle

There is no doubt that rifle shooting is as much a part of the American tradition as the Davy Crocketts and Daniel Boones of our early heritage. Rarely will you find a picture of Old Davy without his trusty "Betsy" planted firmly to the ground, as if this beloved object were a root drawing sustenance from the American soil. Not only was the early musket an important piece of equipment in the frontier days, providing individuals and families with food and clothing, but it also encouraged sport, in the form of marksmanship, within the early settlements.

Today, the continuance of this sporting arms tradition is evident in the large numbers of people who use firearms for sporting purposes – a right guaranteed in the Constitution. This "Right to Keep and Bear Arms" is second only to the right of free speech. While recently there has been much objection to this basic law, the majority of arms bearers are law-abiding, informed persons. With the many shooting associations and groups in existence today that give instructional programs in the proper handling, firing and maintenance of firearms, mishaps are rarely the cause of shooting accidents.

When one realizes the many sports and activities in which rifles play a part today (to get an idea, see Marksmanship, Skeet and Trap, Hunting, Muzzle Loading, and Biathlon), it is hard to imagine that man was once without this tool. Actually, it all began in the ninth century when the Chinese invented gunpowder. When it was learned that this power could be harnessed, the Asiatic tribes constructed wooden tubes to shoot stones, and later, bits of metal, at their enemies. These were, in essence, the first rifles known to man. Thereafter, the development toward the modern day rifle progressed steadily.

In simplest terms, a rifle works by means of a spark which is produced by the striking of metal surfaces, which in turn ignites a cartridge containing primer, explosive powder, and a metal projectile. This projectile, or bullet, is forced through a cylindrical metal tube (barrel), and out into the open. Another type of rifle, called an air or pellet rifle, works on the principle of air pressure created by pulling a lever, which rushes down the barrel, propelling the pellet.

In actuality, there are many different variations, sizes, and styles of "lead-throwers". Each rifle is matched to the specific purpose it will be used for. For example, the beginning target shooter will probably want to select a single-shot .22 caliber rifle. This is also an appropriate choice for small game hunting. The shotgun is designed to emit a package full of many projectiles, and is used by gamebird hunters, and skeet and trap shooters. The last word for the serious shooter is the class A rifle, which includes adjustable sights, specially designed stock, and other features incorporated for accuracy and efficiency.

Some of the things that should be considered when selecting a rifle are age, physical structure, amount of experience you have, how serious you intend to be, and, of course, how much you can afford.

For More Information

Magazines in this area include: *Rifle,* P.O. Box 3030, Prescott, Ariz. 86301. The official publication of the National Bench Rest Shooters Association. Bi-monthly, $6.50 per year. *Handloader,* same address and price as above, is the Journal of Ammunition Reloading, and deals mainly with the merits of various cartridges. For other magazines and organizations, see Marksmanship and Pistol Shooting.

Here are two good books. Both are available from World Publications, Box 366, Mountain View, Calif. 94040 at the price listed* plus 25 cents each postage.

John Olson's Book of the Rifle, John Olson. Every phase of using the rifle is covered in detail. Design, manufacture, performance and more, plus an appendix of shooting organizations and manufacturers. 1974 Ppb., 255 pp., ill., $5.95, (Olson).

Gun Digest 1976, John T. Amber, ed. The absolute authority on firearms, past present and future featuring authoritative, exclusive articles on every facet of guns and shooting. Noted authorites writing on subjects that made them famous. 1975 Ppb., 448 (oversize) pp., ill., $8.95, (Digest).

Shuffleboard

We usually think of shuffleboard as a mild game played by senior citizens in recreation centers, but the tournament game is challenging, hard hitting, and highly skilled.

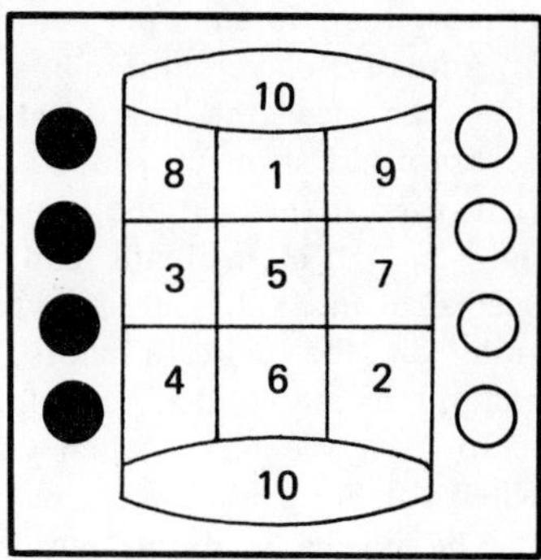

Years ago, weightlifting was the most unknown and unappreciated of sports. That position, today, is perhaps occupied by shuffleboard. In describing shuffleboard, one must take the game as it is played, and has been played for many years in Florida, North Carolina, Ohio, Michigan, and New Jersey. And one must take the game as it is played by the leading shufflers in statewide tournaments, not as it is played by elderly men and women for recreation. The tournament game is very different from the game played by most people whom you will see on a shuffleboard court.

Shuffleboard is played with eight discs, four black and four yellow. Red was used for years, but its relative lack of contrast with black makes it unsuitable for serious play; the word "red" is still often found in instructional material. Discs are shot alternately by the opposing two players, and it is an advantage to have the last shot in any round. Black has the last shot in the first round of the first game and, if there is one, the third game. Choice of color is determined by a single shot before playing. If both players execute perfectly, black must necessarily win. On the other hand, courts are not perfectly level, and this causes a drift of the discs that might favor yellow. For both these reasons, the fairest method of playing is that adopted by California and Arizona, with each individual or team playing a certain number of rounds on yellow and then the same number on black. Many students of the game hope that this method will eventually be adopted in other states.

The court has a triangle at each end which is divided into spaces scoring 10, eight, seven, or minus-10 for discs remaining in them at the end of each round. Many students of the game believe that it can and should be made more athletic by reducing the value of the kitchen area (minus-10) to minus-five. This would increase the value of fast shots (clearing the board), and decrease the value of the slow shots of kitchen play. It would also speed up tournament play when point-games are used.

Basically, the objects in shuffleboard are to score as many points as possible as quickly as possible, prevent the opponent from scoring points, prevent your own disc from being put in the kitchen by your opponent or by overshooting on your part, and put any exposed disc of your opponent in the kitchen. The way this is done follows gambits and tactics that cannot be briefly explained.

Let me quote here what I wrote for David Willoughby's book **The Super Athletes**:

"Shuffleboard is probably the least appreciated of all outdoor sports, in its genuine tournament form. Like golf and bowling, it is non-athletic in the sense of not requiring agility, speed of foot, or unusual strength. However, besides the physical skills involved in making the spectacular caroms and angled combinations that the leading players make, the game includes a great deal of hard hitting, which taxes the endurance of a tournament player in singles competition. It is estimated that, in clearing the board, shuffleboard discs travel at more than 60 miles per hour."

Actually, players differ in style. Some are so accurate that they can clear the board with moderate speed. Others, less accurate but stronger, shoot as fast as they can, on the theory that, even if they hit the enemy disc too close to the center, a hard enough hit will still send both discs flying. Some players specialize in "knocking everything off" while others concentrate on the delicate shots of "kitchen play". The real champions are good at both, for the basic strategy of the game is to clear the board when you are ahead and play kitchen when you are behind in the score.

The novice is always puzzled by the fact that an expert player does not just shoot his discs onto a scoring area in the triangle. Instead he shoots first for places outside the scoring triangle. These discs are guards behind which he later hopes to hide supporting discs that his opponent cannot remove. One of the skills of shuffleboard is the ability of "pick off" such an enemy disc when only a tiny bit of it protrudes from the protection of the guarding disc. This is one of the most accurate and also one of the fastest shots in the game.

Another outstanding skill of shuffleboard is that of making caroms or angled combinations. This is similar to what one sees in billiards (the earliest shuffleboard champions were youthful pocket-billiard players working in Florida hotels).

The interesting thing about shuffleboard, and the thing that makes it far more interesting than golf or bowling to those who know it, is that it is a game of strategic complexity. Choice of tactics depends entirely on the score and open possibilities (which with eight discs are infinite). It seems shuffleboard combines many elements of golf, bowling, billiards, and chess.

Shuffleboard is an ideal sport for women as well as men. Men and women compete together in recreational games. Corecreational participation was formerly true in Florida doubles tournaments, but a female player found that a women's team had won only about three times in 40 years of play, and she campaigned successfully for a separate women's division in doubles. A women's doubles team has often defeated a men's team, but apparently the women's teams lack enough endurance to successfully complete a tournament. Mixed teams, however, have often won tournaments.

Tournament matches usually consist of winning two games of 75 points each, or in consolation events, one game of 100 points. An alternate method sometimes used in club tournaments in Florida and adopted as the regular tournament in California, is to play a certain number of rounds, at the end of which the player or teams with the higher score wins.

Serious tournament shuffleboard started in Florida about 1928 and the first national singles championship was held there in 1931. It is naturally the major event of the sport and has been held in Florida ever since. Players come from all parts of the country to spend the winter in Florida and play in its winter season.

—**George R. Weaver**

George R. Weaver was for years the shuffleboard writer on the **St. Petersburg Independent.** *As a player, he has won the amateur division of the Full Moon Singles at Lakeland, and placed third in the Senior National Championship. He wrote the chapters on tennis and baseball in David Willoughby's book,* **The Super Athletes.**

For More Information

The official organization is the National Shuffleboard Association, 10418 N.E. 2nd Ave., Miami, Fla. 33138. There are no magazines but Jane and Karl Van Schuler, 730 14th Ave. N., St. Petersburg, Fla. have done up a little newsletter called "Beginners Digest of Shuffleboard." Just send a 10 cents stamp for a copy. Other contacts: Craig Leers, 364 Chapin Court, Oreadell, New Jersey 07649; Fairfax Saunders, 12361 Fourth St., Yucaipa, Calif. 92399.

A good source for equipment is Allen R. Shuffleboard Co., 6585 Seminole Blvd., Seminole, Fla. 33542. They have official tournament discs, shuffleboard clubs, scoreboards, etc. Another good source is Cosom., Div. of ITT/Thermotech, Minneapolis, Minn. 55416. They make the free glide discs and cues.

Here are some books of interest. All are available from World Publications, Box 366, Mountain View, Calif. 94040 at the price listed* plus 25 cents each postage.

Let's All Play Shuffleboard, Karl von Schuler. This brand new book contains complete playing instruction and explains clearly all winning strategy and tactics. 1975 Ppb., ill., $3.95, (Von Schuler).

Secrets of Shuffleboard Strategy, Omero Catan. This is the second revised edition of a book which is considered the standard reference book on shuffleboard. Offers a beginner's guide, league play, rules, scoring, court maintenance, tournament charting, history, and much more. 1973 Ppb., 224 pp., ill., $3.00, (Omero Catan).

Backyard Games, Nicci Schultz. Contains a good chapter on shuffleboard for beginners which covers the game, equipment, scoring, how to play, and penalties. Offers equally good chapters on over 30 different backyard games. 1975 Ppb., 96 (oversize) pp., ill., $1.95, (Grosset & Dunlap).

Skate Boarding

The center of skateboarding activity is Southern California, in the Los Angeles and San Diego regions. It is here that the advances in equipment are being made, and this gives Southern California skateboarders an advantage over the rest of the country. The most recent major breakthrough is the polyurethane wheel, which is much closer to being perfectly round than anything up to this time, and has more traction and greater durability. Other areas of the country have to play catch-up where these equipment advances are concerned.

A skateboard is a cross between a roller skate and a surfboard. Usually about two to two and a half feet long, a skateboard has four wheels in two pairs, mounted at the ends of the board on trucks which allow them to turn as the rider shifts his weight.

The basic part, the board itself, used to be made of wood, but many manufacturers are now bringing in laminated fiberglass boards, which add to performance capabilities because they flex. A skateboarder can choose a rigid board, an extremely flexible board, or one somewhere in between, depending on his requirements. Most claim that the flexing boards are more controllable than the stiff boards. Yet several professional skateboard teams still use the rigid wood boards exclusively. I personally prefer the flex boards for downhill and wood boards for flat ground tricks.

The skateboard trucks are the secret of their great maneuverability. They are available in many styles, but they all basically work the same, with a thick rubber bushing to allow the pairs of wheels to turn in different directions according to the way the rider weights and unweights on the deck of the board.

The wheels are made of a rubber-like polyurethane plastic, which gives excellent traction on the cement and asphalt surfaces. The safety value of this is considerable, because falls can cost a lot in abraded and lacerated skin.

The art of skateboarding is a combination of many sports. The board can be maneuvered with weight shifts and body movements much like surfing and snow-skiing. In combination with these movements, tricks can be done which interweave gymnastics and ballet so that playing on the board looks like an athletic dance form. A good skateboarder can put on a show of muscular coordination that borders on the surrealistic.

The beginner should be warned, though, to stay away from travelled streets where there is a danger from passing cars. It would be a shame to lose the enjoyment of skateboarding through a collision with a heavier machine.

—**Chris Yandall**

Chris Yandall combines a love of skateboarding with a love of surfing. With 10 years of surfing behind him, he won the 1975 National Skateboarding Championship. He rides for Gordon and Smith.

Freestyle Skateboarding

A few years ago, when skateboards first came out, most people thought of them as a sideline diversion for when the surf was flat or as a different way of getting around. But things have changed since then. Now, freestyle skateboarding has become a true art form. A small number of elite skateboarders has developed myriad tricks and organized competition has inspired them to keep pushing back the barriers of "impossibility." As ingenuity and inventiveness keep expanding the limits of skill, more and more beginning skateboarders are exploring the more basic tricks.

A novice skateboarder might discover a basic trick quite by accident. For instance, when he finds his way blocked by an obstacle, such as a curb or a garden hose, he might see that he can get over it by lifting first the front wheels and then the back wheels. He can lift the front wheels by shifting his weight behind the back wheels, and when the front wheels are over the obstacle he can bring the back wheels over too, by shifting his weight forward of the front wheels.

Advances in the skateboard suspension system—the trucks—and in materials for the wheels, have given the sport a new lease on life. Skateboards are everywhere nowadays. (M.J. Baum)

This may seem difficult at first, but with a little practice it can be done with ease. A well coordinated skateboarder can advance with this basic trick. If he practices with determination, he will eventually be able to climb a flight of stairs without removing his feet from the board.

Other beginning tricks involve maneuvers on the board such as squatting, sitting, riding backwards, or walking in circles while the board is in motion. A little more advanced is the "wheelie," which is done by riding the board on either the back of the front set of wheels. It takes very fine balance and coordination to ride in this way.

The higher levels of the art involve the airborne or acrobatic tricks. Besides a highly developed level of skill, these tricks demand a great deal of self-confidence and a complete lack of fear.

The aerial tricks can be dangerous even for the experienced and confident rider. If your body is not perfectly perpendicular to the board when you land, or if your feet do not distribute your weight evenly on the wheelbase, you can take quite a violent tumble. For this reason, I advise the use of protective gear when learning these tricks. A helmet, and elbow and knee pads, can save you from cuts, scrapes, and bruises.

Once learned, though, the aerial tricks are spectacular to watch and a great satisfaction to do. An example is the jump spinner, which is done by jumping up into the air, spinning 360 degrees, and landing on the board facing the same direction. Another aerial trick, this one using props, is the high jump.

The high jump is done with a crossbar, just as in the field event. The jumper must take off from a moving skateboard, clear the bar, and land on the board. Timing is of the utmost importance. If the rider jumps too soon he will beat his board to the other side. If he jumps too late, the board will beat him to the other side. In either case, he might hit the crossbar. A good high jump competition is an exciting spectacle to watch. I have personally cleared four foot jumps and over with a safe landing, and I know others who have done the same.

Riders with long, gripping toes can do aerial tricks by wrapping their toes around the ends of the board and taking it up into the air with them. Some are using straps on the board, to keep it connected to the feet, but many feel that this is more an extension of roller skating than a skateboarding variation.

Some of the other advanced tricks are highly gymnastic. For instance, most professional skateboarders will ride doing handstands, headstands, forearm stands and other gymnastic maneuvers as part of their routine. In competition, the best scores are given to riders who accomplish their tricks without coming off their boards or losing their momentum.

Skateboarding has come a long way since the days when kids were a hazard to themselves and others, riding out of control on public streets. If you really want to see some breathtaking action, come to a major contest and watch some skateboard magic.

—Bob Mohr

Bob Mohr, now 26 years old, has been skateboarding since he was 15. He has written for **Skateboarder** *magazine. A top competitor, he has placed in every contest he has entered.*

For More Information

There are two magazines that cover skateboarding: *Skateboarder Magazine,* Box 1028, Dana Point, Calif. 92629 and *Skateboard Magazine,* 246 Fries Ave., Wilmington, Calif. 90744. The United States Skateboard Association, 2236 Pacific Ave., San Pedro, Calif. 90731 is the official organization.

Skate Sailing

The sport of skate sailing is probably almost as old as ice skating itself. Sketches show early sails in use in Denmark as long ago as 1879. These initial efforts employed sails that enabled one to cruise downwind only, requiring the sailor to struggle upwind with sail dismantled or colsapsed. Later versions provided the ability to ride crosswind and upwind just as sailboats do.

The basic requirements for skate sailing include a large body of snow-free frozen water, either a lake or river, and a good wind. Safe ice is at least four inches thick. Some sailors do venture out on ice as thin as 1½ inches, but it is not recommended to go out under such risky conditions. Snow covers cracks and holes, making sailing too dangerous, and when sticking to the surface, it also makes turning very difficult. One should sail through small patches of snow with extreme caution.

The above requirements narrow down the areas where sailing can be practiced to the latitudes below where snow falls early in the season, covering the ice, and remaining all winter long, and above the latitudes where lakes don't freeze to a safe thickness. In the eastern part of the United States this includes New Jersey, Pennsylvania, New York, and Connecticut. In the Midwest, Ohio, Wisconsin, Michigan, Illinois, and Minnesota provide good conditions. When there isn't too much snow, the more northern states and Canada can also have good sailing.

Sails come in many different shapes and sizes, from a bed sheet stretched on a simple wooden frame, to the most popular shape, known as "the Hopatcong Racing Sail," named after the New Jersey lake where the design was developed. This sail is aerodynamically designed to balance properly on the shoulder, with the center of pressure directly against the body preventing a twisting and unbalancing of the sailor. It is made in various sizes for use according to the sailors' height and weight, and the wind velocity.

The design of the Hopatcong Racing Sail was conceived in 1917 by the late W.Van B. Claussen; it has undergone very little change since that time. Wind tunnel tests in the 1930s scientifically proved the design to be sound, and any great variation of the dimensions usually results in a sail that proves difficult to handle. Modern materials have replaced the Wamsutta sailcloth and spruce spars of the original design, resulting in less maintainence after sailing.

A properly constructed sail is effortless to hold and easy to control. It is sewn from nylon or dacron sailcloth with the top and bottom edges parallel to the warp or selvage of the material. Depending on the number of square feet desired, the sail is from eight to 10 feet high in front, and tapers to four or five feet in the rear. Both front and rear edges of the sail have pockets sewn in them the entire width of the sail to receive jib and tail bows made of a springy material, usually rattan or fiberglass.

Stretching the sail is accomplished by attaching a boom to the center of the jib bow, and with a lashing cord of nylon or dacron, pulling the tail bow towards the opposite end of the boom. The boom is about one foot longer than the sail itself, but some early sails had very long booms which were allowed to drag on the ice. With a properly designed sail, the boom will balance on the shoulder. The mast serves to stretch the sail in the vertical direction, and provides a means of holding it. The mast length should be such that it clears the ice when the boom is resting on the shoulder while wearing skates. Spars are usually made in sections, joined by ferrules, to enable one to disassemble the sail and pack it into a car.

Skate sailing is an exhilarating experience. In "Waiting For the Morning Train," Bruce Catton describes his experiences as a youth during an attempt at sailing: ". . . the sun was a friendly weight on our shoulders, the wind was blowing harder and we were going faster than ever, and there was hardly a sound anywhere. I do not believe I have ever felt more completely in tune with the universe than I felt that morning on Crystal Lake. It was friendly. All of its secrets were good."

Catton expresses beautifully the feeling one gets while being propelled silently across the frozen surface, the only sound being the wind rushing by, or an occasional clatter as you traverse rough ice. Early in the season the ice is smoothest and

The only sounds you hear are the rushing of the wind and the occasional clatter of your skates as you go over rough ice. (Kamener)

black in color, so sometimes it is difficult to ascertain whether you are coming upon good ice or smooth water. Extreme caution should be used until the safety of the ice has been checked out. Later in the season, air released by underwater plants, and melted, refrozen snow give the ice a gray color and it is easier to spot open areas.

As the season gets along pressure ridges and cracks develop from the expansion of water as it freezes. Sometimes a ridge will form along a weak line, thrusting slabs of ice 2 or 3 feet above the lake's surface. Some ridges are actually valleys, with the ice buckling under, and several feet of water on top of solid ice. In either case, keep away from ridges.

To start sailing, you should stand with your back to the wind and pick up the sail by the jib bow, the mast and boom on the underside. Grasping the mast with one hand on each side of the boom and facing into the wind, turn slightly in the direction you wish to sail, and lower the boom onto your windward shoulder. At the same time, rotate the sail to a vertical position. Away you go!

The mast should be held with one or both hands below the boom in a comfortable position. By sliding the boom forward or backward on your shoulder, the proper balance point can be found. The boom should slope down towards the rear so that the lower edge of the sail is parallel to the ice.

To change direction, grasp the mast with one hand on each side of the boom and raise the sail to a horizontal position. Then, gliding in a smooth curve into the wind, come about, lower the boom on the opposite shoulder, and continue sailing in the direction from which you just came.

The sail is always held between you and the wind, offering protection from exposure. Some Norwegians sail on the windward side of the sail, but this is very tiring on the arms, as the sail is always pulling away from you. A properly held sail will actually support part of a sailor's weight as he leans into the wind. It takes practice and confidence to attain this form, but by leaning into the wind, more air is trapped by the sail and you go faster.

Downward turns, or jibing, can be done if the tail of the sail is held low to prevent it from being blown overhead. When sailing on a downwind tack, speeds greater than twice the wind velocity are possible, while sailing directly downwind decreases speed due to frictional losses. If speed becomes too great and your legs feel like they are made out of rubber, you can slow down by turning into the wind and dumping wind from the sail. If all else fails, let go of the sail; it can take lots of abuse.

Most sailors own several sails of different sizes so that the appropriate one can be chosen for the conditions of the day. On a gusty day with 30-m.p.h. winds, for example, a 25-square-foot sail might be more than enough to handle, while on a mild day 65 can be handled with ease.

Skates used for sailing are similar to outdoor racing skates, but are longer. The blades are from 18 to 22 inches long with a slight "rock" or curve at the rear to enable one to lean back slightly and raise the tips when rough ice is encountered. When the blades of a pair of skates are held edge to edge, they should be in contact only at the center, under the shoe, and gradually separate to about ¼ inch at the ends. If the blades are absolutely straight or flat, it becomes very difficult to turn. Figure and hockey skates are generally unsatisfactory due to their short length and resulting instability in the direction of travel. The long blade of the sailing skate glides over small cracks and smooths out the bumps on the ice, so that ice too rough for pleasure skating, can frequently be sailed across with no difficulty.

Clothing for skate sailing is similar to that which a skier or snowmobiler wears. Some wear a flotation jacket, and each year more sailors are turning to protective head hear. Hockey helmets are very popular, as they can be made to accommodate a warm hat underneath. Ice awls are also carried by most sailors in case of an unexpected dip into open water. As an additional precaution lengths of rope and perhaps an old inflated inner tube should be kept nearby to help rescue any sailors or fishermen that go through the ice. Skate sailors follow the rules of most other sports where there is some danger involved—never sail alone.

The Skate Sailing Association of America, organized in 1922 to promote the sport, holds races whenever conditions permit. Competitions are held on a triangular course with each leg about ½-mile long. A handicap system is established to give the heavier and slower sailor a chance to win. Sails used in competition are limited in size to one square foot for each two and a half pounds of the sailor's weight.

—Basil Kamener

Basil Kamener is the Secretary of the Skate Sailing Association of America and is very active in the sport.

For More Information

The Skate Sailing Association of America, Basil Kamener, Secretary, 4 Manor Road, Livingston, New Jersey 07039, is the official organization. They have a lot of good information including a booklet on skate sailing. Racing type skates are preferred for skate sailing with a light, strong kite-like sail. Sails can be homemade or purchased. Waterfun, Inc., Box 3442, Ridgeway, Stamford, Conn. 06905 manufactures sails.

Additional information can also be found under ice boating. There is one book in print on the subject and only one chapter is devoted to skate sailing. It is available from World Publications, Box 366, Mountain View, Calif. 94040 at the price listed* plus 25 cents postage.

Sailing on Ice, Jack Anderson. The skills and nuances of the sport of ice boating. Packed with information on safety, dress, racing, and sailing techniques. Also, it includes an excellent chapter concerning skate sailing. 1974 Hb., 161 pp., ill., $8.95, (Barnes).

Skeet/Trapshooting

Trapshooting is a precision-accuracy sport in which clay "pigeons" are thrown into the air as moving targets for keen-eyed marksmen. The "pigeons" are actually 4½-inch disks discharged by traps, mechanical devices that eject the clay pigeons into the air. The shooters use 12-gauge shotguns from a distance of 16 yards from the trap and try to score by breaking these clay disks as they skim across the sky.

Skeet is actually a specialized form of trapshooting. The shooting area consists of two trap houses, spaced 40 yards apart, from which pigeons are released. These houses are located on the opposite sides of a semicircle whose diameter is equally divided into shooting stations with another station located midway between the two houses. The shooter stands at each station in turn and successively shoots at the pigeons from different angles. Two clay pigeons are sometimes released at the same time and the shooter tries to break them both.

The name trapshooting goes back to the original trapshooters in early England who imprisoned live birds in a series of traps, let them go and fired upon them. Skeet, which is an old Scandinavian form of the word "shoot", is of more recent origin. It got its start in the early 1900s by a group of wild fowl hunters who wanted to improve their field shooting.

"The name trapshooting goes back to the original trapshooters in early England who imprisoned live birds in a series of traps, let them go and then fired upon them. Skeet, which is an old Scandinavian form of the word "shoot," is of more recent origin. (Shearman)

Shooting Trap

When I first started trapshooting, I was in the process of transferring from a junior college to San Jose State. I had to lay out for one semester because of a football eligibility requirement, so I was home in Los Banos with nothing to do.

Some friends and I started going out to the local club, just shooting at night, practicing, messing around. Then we got five guys together and joined a league that shot every Wednesday night. I shot pretty well and somebody said, "Why don't you go to a registered trap shoot?" Well, I said okey and I did very well at the first one I went to and I made 60 bucks. The following week I went to another shoot in San Jose, won two handicaps, and made some more money. So I started wondering where in the hell did this sport come from? I shot pretty well there for awhile, but I didn't shoot too many targets.

I shot for two years then I laid off for a couple of years. I didn't have too many bucks – I was going to school. Then I started working for the Santa Clara County Juvenile Probation Department. I finished my football so I just quit school because it wasn't interesting me that much. I started working full-time and going to the shoots. About three years ago I started shooting a lot, going just about every week. Things progressed right along and a couple of years ago I gave up my job and just started shooting. I've been traveling around the country ever since.

I don't practice at all for the competitions. Usually when I'm shooting – like right now for the summer stuff – we shoot five days a week and the only time I will shoot a practice is if I'm feeling a little bit rough. I go out and look at it like calisthenics – miss or hit the damn thing. I just have to warm up. Or else I go to a new club where I haven't shot before and I can check out the background.

I don't trapshoot for hunting practice. You can use it for hunting practice but I think skeet actually would be better for hunting practice. You get them flying right over.

Trapshooting is all a skill game between hand and eye coordination. I think a guy has got to have a lot of patience. As long as he doesn't set his goals too high and he's satisfied with a little bit of progress. The game is set up on a 100-target program and of course 100 straight is the ultimate. You have to figure out where your ability lies. You can't expect to break 100 straight – nobody has – every time you walk out on the line. You have to figure it out on an average how well you're going to shoot or how well you are capable of shooting. Some guys go out and they're not capable of breaking 100 straight and they get thoroughly frustrated when they never do. I've seen guys lose their tempers, throw their guns on the ground and do all kinds of things. Really, I wouldn't know the percentages on it, but we've had over 80,000 registered shooters last year and a really small percentage – maybe five or 10 percent – would even break 100 straight and they've been shooting for years and years.

I think you must be patient, must practice and should shoot in as many different places as you can. If you are going to travel and shoot you can't be a very tough competitor if you can only shoot at one club. Each club is very different background, color of targets and so forth.

There are a lot of guys who don't hunt any game at all who shoot trap. You know, the majority of them are sportsmen – they've been out in the field a little bit and they've shot trap somewhere, hand-thrown or something like that along the line. But you don't have to have any other special experience with a shotgun for trap. I think if you're going to learn to shoot trap I think it would be easier to teach guys who haven't gone out and made a lot of mistakes. You just start them from scratch. I think it would be easier that way.

The one great thing about the game of trap shooting is that it invites everybody, from the littlest kid up to the oldest man and the lady, and the handicapped. People shoot out of wheelchairs and we have kids that run around seven, eight years old. As long as they teach them the gun safety and they can handle it, there's no problem at all.

If you join the Amateur Trapshooting Association and subscribe to *Trap and Field* magazine, they send you a yearly average book. It will have the names of the clubs in your area, phone numbers, how to get there, when the shoots are going to be held and other information. It's pretty helpful.

There's an impossible dream in trapshooting, that you can break them all in a program. I think I'd like to win the main handicap at the World Championships. Nobody has ever won it from the 27-yard line in Van Day, Ohio, where they hold more or less the world championships of trap shooting. If anything, that would be my goal. Between me and a couple of other guys we've won just about everything else in the country at least once, but that's the one thing that has escaped all of us.

The one thing about trap shooting is that it is something that you personally achieve. There's no team status to it at all. It's just you and that's it and if you fail there's nobody to blame but yourself. Then when you do achieve it, it makes you feel good: you beat the best in the whole world!

The biggest thrill I've had so far is having the highest average in the nation last year. Of course that has to rate among one of a shooter's better achievements: finishing over 90 percent on the doubles last year. Not many, perhaps four or five people, have ever done it. And with the number of targets that I shot to do it, it was good. I enjoyed it. Some of the wins around the country – I can't say that some are better than others – have been really good. I've won the all-around and overall championship for four years straight in Reno. I take a personal pride when I go there, probably exert myself a little bit more when I go to that club.

I'm sure confidence and natural ability play a part in trapshooting. There's no doubt that if I had gone out and lost 40 bucks the first day I would have been a little reluctant to go back. But when I went out and had a good time and made a few bucks, it gave me confidence. This is definitely the way to do it.

I think there are more people involved in trapshooting, that I can see, than the other shooting sports. The sport is very accessible since there are so many clubs around the nation. You can make money at it – enough to cover your expenses. It's a sport that will pay for itself if you achieve any kind of marksmanship at all, whereas in skeet it's all money out. You just pay and shoot. All they get is trophies. There's no money in it. Same thing in marksmanship; you're really quite limited in rifle. There aren't that many tournaments.

When you travel in trapshooting and go to the big shoots, you meet more or less the same people. You have a regular core of people who travel around, say 50 to 60 people, and you meet these people all the time. I can go anywhere in the United States to a trapground and know somebody. If it weren't for trapshooting, that wouldn't be possible at all.

–Dan Bonillas

Dan Bonillas, 28 years old, has been one of the top trap shooters in the nation for the last several years. In 1974, he led the nation in all-around averages, and the ATA in doubles.

For More Information

There are two good magazines: *Trap & Field,* 1100 Waterway Blvd., Indianapolis, Ind. 46202. Published monthly with two issues in March at $10.00 per year. This magazine is the official publication of the Amateur Trapshooting Association at the same address. *Skeet Shooting Review,* Box 28188, San Antonio, Texas 78228 is the official publication of the National Skeet Association at the same address. Published monthly at $10.00 per year. Some good sources for special equipment: Decot Hy-Wyd, 3530 E. Indian School Rd., Phoenix, Ariz. 85064 for quality sport glasses. Ed and Nancy Place, Box 10553, Phoenix, Ariz. 85064 make custom fitted jackets.

Here are a couple of books covering the sport. Both are available from World Publications, Box 366, Mountain View, Calif. 94040 at the price listed* plus 25 cents each postage.

Score Better at Skeet, Fred Missildine. The author's vast experience, both teaching and shooting, enables him to diagnose faults and give corrective measures. 1972 Ppb., 162 pp., ill., $2.95, (Winchester).

Field, Skeet and Trapshooting, Charles Chapel. A book about the shotgun, written for the beginner and intermediate marksman. Presents step-by-step information needed to achieve success in trapshooting, skeet shooting, or hunting. Details gun safety and handling, plus methods of hitting waterfowl and upland game. 1949 (rev. 1962) Hb. & Ppb., 291 pp., ill., $7.95/ $2.50, (Barnes).

Skibobbing

Skibobbing is a popular European winter sport that is rapidly gaining enthusiastic support in American ski areas. A skibob (the word denotes its combination of skiing and bobsledding) resembles a springy bicycle frame with short skis attached in place of the usual wheels. Skibobbers also wear short miniskis called patinettes for balance and to use as brakes. In general, any ski slope is suitable for skibobbing, but many winter recreation areas set aside runs exclusively for skibobbers who tend to travel down the slope more slowly than skiers. Speeds of 25 to 50 miles per hour can be attained on a skibob, while the world record for a downhill speed run is in excess of 100 m.p.h.

Skibobbing originated in Austria at the turn of the 20th century, but did not attain any acceptable degree of technical and performance perfection until after World War II. The current manifestation of a skibob grew from the efforts of several badly wounded Austrian soldiers who could no longer ski but who still wished to careen down the slopes. The first modern skibob was produced by Gefaller corporation during 1948 in Germany. Today skibobs average about seven feet in length and weigh about 22 pounds for men's and 20 pounds for women's models.

The Federation Internationale de Skibob (FISB) was formed in 1961 to administrate competitive skibobbing. Events are similar to skiing, with both downhill and slalom contested. A steeply descending run about three minutes in length and with speeds of about 50 m.p.h. is featured for the downhill. Slalom skibobbers zigzag between gates set a minimum of 20 feet apart. Scoring in both events is based on elapsed time and not on technique.

Skibobbing for recreation can take many forms, from the madcap downhill fun of the Beatles in "Help" to organized or informal skibob touring. Such touring demands a knowledge of techniques, with various steps of the patinettes used to climb up slopes in order to make an exhilarating run down the far side.

For More Information

The United States Skibob Federation, 5711 S. Nevada St., Littleton, Colo. 80120 can supply more information. They publish a bi-monthly newsletter called *Skibob Times.*

Skiers are finding their slopes sporting skibobbers of late. Skibobs are like springy bicycle frames with short skis instead of wheels. Since they generally travel slower than skiers, skibobbers are assigned special runs by many recreational areas. (Williamson)

Skiing-Alpine

Because snow has been collecting on mountain slopes longer than man has recorded history, early accounts of skiing are sketchy and it is difficult to accurately trace the history of this now internationally popular sport. The sport's mysterious past can be loosely outlined, however.

Norse hunters, approximately 3000 B.C., pursued wild game on rudimentary skis and are apparently responsible for conceiving the first techniques for sliding over the snow. Changes came slowly. Until the 1700s, a pair of skis were of mismatched lengths – one was considerably shorter than the other and was used for steering, while the longer ski provided a sliding platform. Skis of this type were used in both hunting and military forays, but hardly for recreation. Since turning was a yet undeveloped skill, sliding downhill was more for the temerous than the timid.

Later, a drag pole was introduced to aid in turning, maintaining balance in a descent and propelling the skier like a gondolier's pole on the flat. Still, this means of winter locomotion was limited primarily to the Norse peoples.

Major developments in skiing occurred in the 1800s when Scandinavian miners journeyed to California and the Sierra mountains in pursuit of gold. Interestingly, this jump bypassed central Europe, generally considered the cradle of modern skiing. But once in the Sierra, skiing began to develop a sporting side and antique photographs record skiing 49ers racing down the mountainsides for cash prizes.

Probably best known of early American skiers is Snowshoe Thompson, a mail carrier who, from 1856 to 1876, transported letters and parcels in a backpack 90 miles over the Sierras from Genoa to Hangtown. A heroic figure of the time, Thompson accomplished his feat on cumbersome and quite primitive 12-foot skis with toe strap and heel-lock bindings. The widely accepted pole-drag system was Snowshoe's means of turning and, hopefully, stopping.

The early developments in skiing are quickly summed up in **The Book of American Skiing** by Ezra Bowen: "If you are a Norwegian, it is satisfying to know that the first skis seen in the Alps were brought there in 1883 by a Norwegian expedition to the Monastery of St. Bernard. If you are an Austrian, it is comforting to think that an Austrian inventor named Mathias Zdarsky was the first great promoter of skiing as an Alpine sport, circa 1900. And if you are English, you can ponder with pride the fact that when Sir Henry Lunn persuaded some of his British friends to spend a few winter days in Chamonix, France, in 1898, he started the entire business of winter-sport tourism."

Since these primitive beginnings, skiing has experienced a continuing evolution of techniques and equipment. From the drag pole turn on 12-foot-long turned-up boards to the telemark (a daredevil turn popular up till World War I), to the Arlberg system (introduced and perfected by Austrian Hannes Schneider during the 1920s and '30s) to modern-day Graduated Length Method of instruction, skiing has continually advanced and spread as a sport. Wood skis were replaced by metal, which gave way to fiberglass. Now some skis even contain rubber cores. Bindings are nearly failsafe.

Concurrent with technique and equipment advances, has come an evolution in the type of individual skiing in the United States. What was once the property of a particular ethnic group, and was later an outlet for the affluent, has become a sport for virtually all snow and outdoor loving Americans.

World Pro Skiing 1970–76

The emergence in America of competitive skiing as a spectator sport parallels the development of the unique, dual-challenge format of the World Pro Skiing tour. More exciting than man-against-the-clock racing, dual challenge competition matches man against man on twin courses.

This type of competition first came to the attention of the American sports fan via a telecast of the French-American Team Races from Aspen, Colo. in 1968. Racing head-to-head against another skier was as new to most of the racers as it was to the television audience, and at the time it would have been difficult to decide which of the two groups was more turned on by the new style of competition. Stimulated by this format, the American National Team raced to victory over the powerful French.

Seeing the acceptance of this new style of competition by both spectator and racer, Bob Beattie, then coach of the American Team, was convinced the future of American ski racing lay in this direction. When he left the amateur ranks and joined the group of professional racers to direct their own organization, the International Ski Racers Association, he pushed for exclusive use of head-to-head racing.

He didn't have to push hard.

From the racers' viewpoint this is the only way to compete. When racing man-against-man, you know where you stand all the time. Abilities are tested and strained to the edge of tolerance . . . and beyond.

Technical lessons also abound in dual challenge. When your opponent pulls ahead in a turn, it is painfully obvious what you did wrong . . . and what he did right. Today, coaches marvel at what happens to youngsters racing in dual slalom matches. Mental blocks disappear and the results often surprise coach and racers alike.

And for the spectator, the benefit of dual challenge racing is obvious: the fans can tell which racer is winning without using a pocket calculator.

Not only did Beattie employ the dual-challenge format, but he also flavored his events for American taste buds. Knowing that ski racing man-against-the-clock has always enjoyed its greatest popularity in Europe, Beattie appreciated the need to modify the sport. So, not only do the pros race man against man, they start their event from behind horse-race type starting gates (like those at Churchill Downs), and they race over three built-in bumps, ranging in height from three to seven feet, depending on terrain.

Now, a spectator is able to watch a thrilling start, see the race from top to bottom, watch top skiers zoom over imperiling jumps, and observe as the pros sprint to the finish line where the first man across is the winner. And winners advance

Austrian Franz Klammer, racing in the amateur World Cup tour. This tour added head to head dual-challenge for its final event last year.

and race again, much like a tennis tournament, making it possible for spectators to see their favorites in as many as five runs (two in the opening round, quarter-finals, semi-finals and finals) during a single afternoon.

At first, of course, there were skeptics of this innovative format. But World Pro Skiing fought for acceptance. The first season, the spring of 1970, Beattie and his band of racers scheduled three events, each consisting of a slalom and giant slalom (the standard pro meet format). Two were held in Europe and the Lange Cup took place at Vail, Colo. American Billy Kidd, who only days before the pro circuit opened had won the combined gold medal at the amateur World Championships in Val Gardena, Italy, emerged also as the World Pro Skiing champion that winter.

In 1970-72, nine racers and greater total prize money – $127,000 – attracted more name racers, among them a young American named Spider Sabich. For two seasons, 1971 and 1972, Sabich paced the tour, winning six of 18 events the first season and nine of 18 the second. As World Pro Skiing champ in 1971, he banked a total of $21,188, inflating that to $50,650 the following year. Sabich was fast becoming the most famous American ski racer of all time.

France's Jean-Claud Killy interrupted the American's dreams of a third title in 1973. Killy, who came out of a five-year retirement to race on the World Pro Skiing tour, outlasted Sabich in 12 meets to win the title. Injured in the final meet while only a few points behind Killy, Sabich might have won the title for an unprecedented third time had he not been hurt. Killy banked $68,625, a figure which reflects the rapid growth of pro ski racing.

Veteran Austrian Hugo Nindl, twice second to Sabich in 1971 and 1972, emerged a rich champion in 1974. The 32-year-old Nindl, a compact and stern Austrian, won the opening slalom of the season and maintained the circuit lead throughout the winter. Overall, Nindl dazzled the ski world by winning six of 28 events (14 meets) and $93,200. World Pro Skiing had established itself as a big-league sport. By 1972, the tour had gone to Canada, Europe and the US, with crowds of more than 10,000 witnessing some events.

Last season, American Hank Kashiwa, a half-Japanese, half-Irish 24-year-old from Steamboat, Colo., grabbed the top honors and pro title from the Europeans. Counting in his endorsement bonuses, this former US Olympian banked over $100,000, again proving that World Pro Skiing is big business. As an indication of the popularity of the World Pro Skiing format, last season the amateur World Cup tour, stronghold of man-against-the-clock racing, borrowed the dual-challenge

A supremely conditioned athlete, with speed and power etched into the body lines, racing against the clock.

format for its final event. Head-to-head professional ski racing has come of age.

—Greg Lewis

Greg Lewis is the public relations director for World Wide Ski Corporation.

For More Information

Skiing is now one of the most popular sports in America and it has the magazines to prove it. *Ski*, 380 Madison Ave., New York, N.Y. 10017. Published seven times a year (September to March) at $5.94. Good articles on ski areas, techniques and keeping in shape. Originated Nastar concept (citizen races). *Skiing*, One Park Avenue, New York, N.Y. 10016. Published seven times a year (September to Spring) at $6.98. Informative articles on travel, fashions, equipment and new techniques. Ski Racing, 1801 York Street, Denver, Colo. 80206. Published 27 times a year, at $12.00. A newsweekly which reports international and national racing results, amateur, professional and hotdogging.

The main organization is the United States Ski Association, 1726 Champa St., Suite 300, Denver, Colo. 80202. The USSA regulates alpine racing, oversees fund raising, membership, and ski promotion. Local and regional organizations are usually USSA affiliated. The National Ski Patrol System, 2901 Sheridan Blvd., Denver, Colo. 80214 promotes safety by providing patrols at ski areas. It teaches survival, first aid, and rescue. Skis, boots, poles and fashions are easy to find in most areas.

With skiing so widespread throughout the world, it is not surprising that there are many books on the subject. Here are some of the better ones. All are available from World Publications, Box 366, Mountain View, Calif. 94040 at the price listed* plus 25 cents each postage. Write for a complete list.

The Ski Better Book, Auran & Winter. Exciting changes in equipment call for a new approach to skiing—a focus on perfecting turns. This how-to book is unique in its emphasis on basic skills, and getting mileage as the surest way of improving on skill. 1975 Hb. & Ppb., $8.95/$5.95, (Dell)

Ski Magazine's Complete Book of Ski Technique, Mort Lund & the editors of *Ski* Magazine. Here is an all-inclusive manual providing expert instruction and advice on every phase of ski technique. Emphasizes stance, simple traversing and turning for the beginner and more complicated maneuvers, such as acrobatics, racing, difficult powder skiing, and ice conditions. 1975, 256 pp., ill., $9.95, (Harper & Row).

Winning Skiing, Billy Kidd. Presents a learning plan for the beginner designed to promote mastery of the important skiing skills in just six days, by one of the best-known skiers in the US. 1975 Hb & Ppb., 160 pp., ill., $8.95/$4.95, (Regnery).

Ski With the Big Boys, Stu Campbell. A description of the various techniques that the best skiers use, with clear language, detailed drawings, by well-known ski photographers. 1974 Hb., 192 pp., ill., $10.00, (Winchester).

Sports Illustrated Skiing, John Jerome and *Sports Illustrated* eds. Sound advice for beginners on such basics as balance, edge control, traversing and snowplowing. Progresses to stem christies and more advanced skills. Special advice on negotiating different terrains and conditions. 1971 Hb. & Ppb., 96 pp., ill., $4.95/$1.95, (Lippincott).

The Skier's Handbook, editors of *Ski* magazine. Hundreds of downhill ski tips from the world's finest instructors and racers. Over 130 sequential photos and action line drawings, featuring a complete illustrated rundown on the "American technique." 1965 Hb., 262 pp., ill., $7.95, (Harper & Row).

We Learned to Ski, Evans, Jackman & Ottaway. According to experts and critics alike, this is the best book written about skiing. Seven staff members of the London Sunday Times staff not only learned to ski, but travelled across the world talking to experts and assessing new techniques. Vivid lessons, supported by brilliant illustrations from the graphic design department. 1975 Hb., 255 pp., ill., $12.95, (St. Martins).

Skiing, Leonard H. Kalakian and Cheryl L. Wayne. An instructional guide for beginners and experts alike. The book goes beyond skiing skills to discuss equipment, courtesy, safety and how to ride various lift devices. 1971 Ppb., 107 pp., ill., $1.95, (Allyn & Bacon).

Skiing Simplified, Doug Pfeiffer. A book that covers the entire range of the skiing experience from the first attempts at control to the most advanced techniques. Numerous drawings neatly illustrate each step. 1966 Hb., 200 pp., ill., $7.95, (Grosset & Dunlap).

Skier's Exercise Manual, Paul Davidson and Robert Fuller. A complete guide to ski exercise programs. It offers series of exercises for both the recreational and competitive skier, starting with the basics and leading up to advanced techniques. 1968 Hb., 99 pp., ill., $4.95, (Barnes).

How the Racers Ski, Warren Witherell. The techniques common to all the world's greatest skiers, presented here for the recreational skier or racer alike. Offers a more natural and effective way to ski than that is taught in most schools. 1972 Hb., 206 pp., ill., $7.45, (W.W. Norton).

Ski America Cheap, Mokres. Tells you how to ski, eat and sleep for less in 49 popular downhill ski areas in all parts of the country. An incomparable guide to getting the maximum return for your money. 1973 Ppb., 305 pp., ill., maps, $3.95, (Little, Brown & Co).

Skiing- Freestyle

The style of skiing known as freestyle or "hot dog" dates back farther than many realize. As long ago as 1915, a skier named Carl Paulson did a single front flip on skis at the First American Intercollegiate Ski Meet at Hanover, New Hampshire. The modern era of freestyle, however, began in the mid-50s. In 1957, Olympic great Stein Eriksen appeared on the cover of *Ski* magazine doing his famous flip. In 1960, Art Furrer, a Swiss, began teaching tricks while working as a ski instructor in the US. He did much to popularize skiing acrobatics through demonstrations, films and articles during the 1960s.

In 1971, ski cinematographer and freestyle innovator Dick Barrymore and the K2 Ski Company sponsored the world's first hot dog contest in Aspen, Colo. Barrymore's concept was that the winner should be the skier who made the hottest, fastest, most exciting run down the toughest slope.

Three days later, in Waterville Valley, N.H., *Skiing Magazine* and Chevrolet sponsored the first true freestyle event, and called it the National Championships of Exhibition Skiing. It was won by Hermann Goellner. This event gave points for technique and skill as well as speed and excitement. Also, the contest was divided for the first time into three events—moguls, or bump skiing, ballet and aerials. Freestyle contests continue to use the same three events today. One other contest was held that season, the Rocky Mountain Professional Freestyle Skiing Championships in Vail, Colo. The total purse for the first season was $20,000.

Since that initial season, professional freestyle skiing has advanced rapidly. There were three contests with a combined purse of $26,000 in 1971-72, eight meets offering prize money of $60,000 the following season, and in 1973-74 the pot rose to $74,000 for six big meets. Last season's circuit consisted of 12 contests, six for men and six for women. Midas International was the major men's circuit sponsor with continued support from Chevrolet and *Skiing Magazine.* Colgate Palmolive was the sole sponsor for the women's tour. The women's purse was $90,000 for the season, making freestyle skiing one of the most lucrative professional sports for women. Professional Freestyle Associates organized and produced the 1974-75 freestyle tour that totaled $272,500 in prize money. During 1976, the Colgate women will divide a $220,000 purse, and the men a similar pot. The total prize money for this year's international PFA tour will approach an incredible $500,000.

The classic freestyle competition is divided into three distinct events: moguls, aerials and ballet. Although each one-day event is conducted separately, with separate prize purses, the combined result of all three events determines the overall winner.

The mogul event challenges the ability of competitors to maneuver over steep, moguled slopes. It is held on a course 50 feet wide and 1000 feet long with an average gradient of 30 percent. Competitors are scored by judges for their speed, quality and number of turns, and air (jumps). The mogul event is considered to be the most prestigious by many of today's competitors.

The aerial event, often the most spectacular for onlookers, is conducted on a manicured course made up of three jumps in sequence. Each competitor performs a predetermined routine of aerial acrobatic maneuvers. Score is determined by the quality of form, degree of difficulty, height/distance of the moves, and landing. Maneuvers such as double somersaults, moebius flips and 720 helicopters, once considered impossible, have become standard for the top ski aerialists. The event is closely monitored, and competitors must be thoroughly qualified for any difficult maneuvers they wish to attempt.

The ballet event is often likened to figure skating. The competitor puts together a routine of unique steps, spins and jumps performed to selected music. The ballet course is 650 to 800 feet long, usually smooth and of medium gradient. Judges look for technical merit, difficulty and variety of moves, composition, and harmony between the moves and the music. Ballet has become the showcase event for many innovative skiers.

At the end of the professional freestyle season overall winners in each of the disciplines and the combined overall champion are determined according to total money winnings.

Mark Steigemeier was named the 1975 Freestyler of the Year. He finished first in both point standings and earnings, winning $28,890 in six meets during the 1975 season. He finished first overall in contests at Crested Butte, Colo. and Bogus Basin, Idaho and won three ballet events last winter. Though ballet is his forte, he is also strong in moguls and aerials. Originally from Washington, Mo., Mark is 22. He began skiing at age 12, raced at 15, and has been a freestyle competitor since 1973. He coaches at a number of freestyle camps during the summer.

Genia Fuller, 21, originally from Framingham, Mass., has shown herself to be the best woman freestyle skier in the world. She had dominated the women's skiing circuit for the last two years and has earned from *Skiing Magazine* the title of Female Freestyle Skier of the Year for the past two seasons. She also won the women's World Freestyle Skiing Championship both years. In 1974-75, she was first overall at five out of six meets and third at the other. She topped all women with earnings of $20,912 and finished first in Grand Prix points. She also finished first overall in aerials, and second overall in ballet and moguls. Genia competed formerly as a figure skater, which she says particularly aided her ballet skiing. A certified ski instructor, she has coached at summer freestyle camps, appeared in numerous ski films, and is slated to compete in the Superstars competition.

—Skeeter Zoberski

Skeeter Zoberski was a freestyle skier in the early days of the sport, taking second place at the World Championships in 1971 and '72. Currently he is vice-president in charge of publicity for Professional Freestyle Associates.

For More Information

There are two active organizations: Professional Freestyle Competitors Association, 300A Kearns Building, Salt Lake City, Utah 84101 and the Professional Freestyle Associates at the same address. The first group is for the competitors and the second is the organization involved in the production of professional events. For additional information see skiing.

Ski Jumping

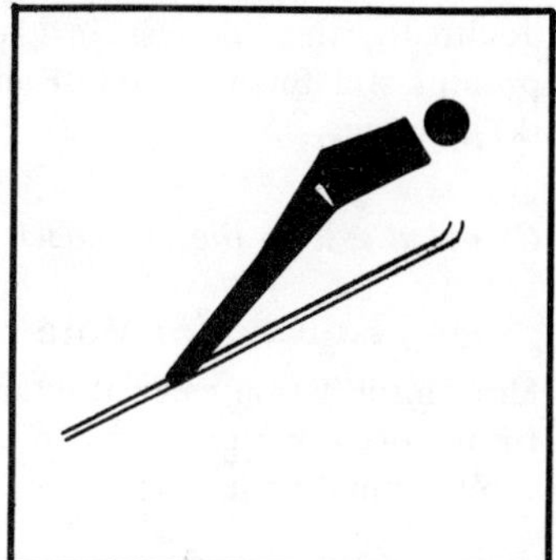

It was once said, "All skiers can jump but some are born to be great jumpers. They are the boys who ride the wind and lean out on their luck."

In the early 1800s, Sondre Norheim from Telemark, Norway invented a ski binding and thus became the father of modern skiing. Norheim was one of the first to practice ski jumping. In 1850 he jumped 60 feet, which is the first known world's ski jumping record.

Ski jumping was brought to the United States in the late 1850s by the Norwegians. They settled in Northern New England, the Midwest, and Pacific Northwest.

In 1891 at Redwing, Minnestoa, Mikkel Hennm established an American jumping record of 102 feet. His brother, Jorjus, exceeded that record by jumping one foot farther in 1893. Both of these men were taught to ski by Sondre Norheim.

Nearly all jumping skis today are made of synthetic materials. They are much wider and longer than recreational skis; they are over four inches wide and approximately eight feet two inches long. The bottom of the ski is made of a plastic called Kofax or P-tex. Five grooves are in the bottom, giving the jumper more stability during the in-run and when he lands.

Ski jumping is a very brief sport, lasting only 15 to 20 seconds from the time the skier leaves the top of the jump until he stops at the bottom. The actual time that he is in the air is only about three to five seconds, depending on the size of the jump. Ski jumping looks like it is very dangerous, but in reality is safe if certain precautions are taken.

The size of a ski jump is determined by the distance a ski jumper can travel through the air safely. If a jump is 70 meters in size, a jumper can travel 70 meters from the take-off for the jump to a point on the landing hill where it is safe to land. A ski jumper can travel over 70 meters through the air but he may go over the critical point of the landing hill and this can be dangerous.

The four phases of ski jumping are: (1) the in-run; a low crouched body position that the jumper assumes directly after the start; (2) the take-off; the point when the jumper launches himself into the air; (3) the flight; the position when the jumper extends himself almost flat on his skis, riding the air as if he were a glider (he must stay extended over the skis until he has come within three feet of the landing surface); and (4) the landing; in which the jumper assumes a telemark position to absorb the shock when landing on the hill.

The scoring of ski jumping is relatively easy to understand. The object of every competitive ski jumper is to acquire as many points as possible during two rounds of competition. The jumper can earn these points by both the distance and the style of the jump.

Ski jumping today is one of the most spectacular events in the Winter Olympics, having a greater attendance than any other single event. Many of the United States high schools and colleges often participate in ski jumps, as a part of their interscholastic ski programs.

Ski flying, where jumpers exceed distances of 500 feet, draws huge crowds and tremendous spectator interest. Undoubtedly this interest in the sport on the big hills will prompt still further interest and development in the sport of ski jumping.

—**Chip LaCasse**

Chip LaCasse is the ski coach at the University of Vermont.

For More Information

More information can be obtained form the US Ski Team and from *Nordic World, Skiing, Ski,* and *Ski Racing.* All addresses can be found under skiing and cross-country skiing.

It's no wonder that ski jumping has a greater attendance than any other event in the Winter Olympics. Spectacular, exhilarating, and breathtaking, it is always a crowd pleaser. (Skiers Gazette, Manley)

Skin Diving

Skin diving is a sport that allows a diver to experience the underwater world with only a minimum of equipment. The basics of gear used are: mask, snorkel, fins and possibly wet suit. While the experiences may be similar between the two sports, differences in skin and scuba diving may best be seen in their equipment.

The scuba diver generally spends hundreds of dollars on gear, is faced with a growing sport and rapidly improving equipment. The scuba diver also carries his own air on his back (not just oxygen). Because of this, the scuba diver also has an advantage in being able to participate in underwater salvage work, underwater still photography, some scientific studies, and spearfishing for large species of fish like the giant black sea bass.

While these activities are important and enjoyable, the skin diver, or free diver, can also participate in varied underwater activities unencumbered with all the scuba equipment. The free diver is truly free. Preparing for a dive is less time consuming; there is less equipment and less expense. The skin diver also does not have the complicated decompression worries scuba divers have—staying under different atmospheres of pressure.

A mentally relaxing, though physically challenging activity, skin diving is a unique sport unto its own. Used too often as only an insignificant facet of scuba diving, skin diving is a quietly beautiful experience that should not be overlooked.

—**Nancy Ackerman**

Nancy Ackerman is presently the Associate Editor of **Skin Diver** *magazine. She is currently pursuing ocean research and photography along with her literary endeavors.*

Diving Free

Hovering over a bed of kelp, a snorkeler swoops down to pry loose a few abalones. These single-shelled gastropods, found in nearly all oceans, cling to rocks, hide in cracks and look very much like their environs. One marine biologist claims to have identified over 150 different organisms growing on the shell of one red abalone.

While it may not sound like much of a challenge, free diving to 20 or 25 feet or more, trying to locate these elusive mollusks and prying them loose can really be work! The gripping power of the abalone's foot is tremendous. And many divers only skin dive, not scuba dive, for them.

Many divers feel that the sport of getting abalones and spearfishing is a great challenge, when skin diving methods are used. While this would be difficult and maybe even physically impossible for some, there are free diving advocates that can make several successive dives to 60 feet and more. With surface intervals of one minute, and dive times to one minute, two hours in the water would give a free diver one hour of underwater time.

The beauty of free diving, of swimming unencumbered with only mask, snorkel, fins and possibly wet suit, is exhilarating. While only allowing a diver to become a momentary visitor in the aquatic world, snorkeling is still a very fulfilling experience.

Skin diving requires more physical stamina than does scuba diving. Swimming along the top of the water, a free diver meets much more resistance than the scuba diver who moves underwater. Acquiring the technique and timing for breath-hold diving takes practice and control.

While free diving can be categorized as good physical activity, it also can be incredibly relaxing for the mind and soothing for the soul. Communing so intimately with nature in such a free, relaxed state is tremendous therapy. Moving in the three-dimensional aquatic world, full of brilliant colors, new and interesting shapes, is always fascinating and absorbing.

Since the mastery of snorkeling skills is an important prerequisite to scuba diving, most scuba divers have had a few occasions to snorkel. But many have completely forgotten this more invigorating sport. In this age of machinery and technical data, more people might benefit by slowing down and enjoying the quiet beauty of the underwater universe offered by free diving.

—**Nancy Ackerman**

For More Information

The best magazine is *Skin Diver,* 8490 Sunset Blvd., Los Angeles, Calif. 90060. Published monthly at $9.00 per year. These people are very involved in this sport and will be very helpful. An organization you should know about is the National Association of Underwater Instructors, 22809 Barton Rd., Colton, Calif. 92324. Also, there is the Underwater Society of America whose address can be found along with others under cave diving. For equipment you'll need a wet suit, tank, fins, mask and snorkel, weight belt, regulator, etc. Two of the largest mail-order houses are New England Divers, Inc., Tozer Rd., Beverly, Mass. 01915 and Aqua-Craft, 3280 Kurtz St., San Diego, Calif. 92110. Knowing what the sport is all about is important. These books are available from World Publications, Box 366, Mountain View, Calif. 94040 at the price listed* plus 25 cents each postage.

Great Diving I, May. Describes the best inland, river, coastal, and open-sea underwater attractions of the eastern United States and Gulf Coast. Dive sites are grouped according to locality with listings of diving shops, recompression chamber locations, and charter boat operators. 1974 Ppb., 256 pp., ill., $3.95, (Stackpole).

Skin and Scuba Diving, Albert Tillsman. A book for both beginner and intermediate diver. Emphasis on "why" as well as "how". Covers history, language, skills, and much more. 1966 Ppb., 67 pp., ill., $2.50, (W.C. Brown).

Scuba Divers Guide to Underwater Ventures, Judy Gail May. This book is a treasure chest of fascinating things to do after basic diving skills are mastered. Underwater photography, fishwatching and catching, shell collecting, and treasure hunting. 1973 Ppb., 222 pp., ill., $3.95, (Stackpole).

Practical Diving, Mount and Skahara. Covers every aspect of compressed air diving. The YMCA has adopted this book as its text for advanced scuba diving classes. 1975 Hb., 191 pp., ill., $10.00, (Univ. Miami).

Diver Below! The Complete Guide to Skin and Scuba Diving, Hank and Shaney Frey. A clear, self-instructional guide to the techniques of skin and scuba diving, with expert advice on equipment, cave exploration, diving in wrecks, spear-fishing, underwater photography, and what boats to use for diving. Safety is stressed, with decompression tables, first-aid instruction, and advice on the underwater environment. 1969 Ppb., 182 (oversize) pp., ill., $2.95, (MacMillan).

The New Science of Skin and Scuba Diving, Council for National Cooperation in Aquatics. Full coverage of skin diving, including technique, medical aspects, safety procedures, and many more subjects, plus an excellent glossary. 1974 (rev.) Ppb., 288 pp., ill., $4.95, (Association Press).

Invitation to Skin and Scuba Diving, John D. Craig and Morgan Degn. A book for both the beginning and experienced diving enthusiast. The authors cover every aspect of diving, from pre-diving training and basic equipment to special activities for the advanced diver such as underwater photography and spear-fishing. 1965 Hb., 192 pp., ill., $7.95, (Simon & Schuster).

Diving for Fun, Joe Strykowski. A complete textbook on skin and scuba diving. Gives vital information for safety and enjoyment underwater. 1969 Ppb., 132 pp., ill., $5.25, (Docor).

Sports Illustrated Skin Diving and Snorkeling, *Sports Illustrated* editors & Barry Allen. Everything needed to dive safely is covered with clear explanations and great illustrations. 1973 Hb. & Ppb., 96 pp., ill., $4.95/$1.95, (Lippincott).

Scuba Safe and Simple, John Resack, Jr. From your first step in fins to exploring undersea caves—all essential skills, principles and techniques are covered in a light, lively way with special emphasis on development of proper attitude. 1975 Hb., 240 pp., ill., $8.95, (Prentice Hall).

Skin and Scuba Diver, Borgeson and Speirs. This definitive book on skin and scuba diving includes sections on the latest diving equipment, what boats to use, underwater navigation, diving for treasure, and underwater photography. 1962 Hb., 148 pp., ill., $3.95, (Arco).

Skin & Scuba Diver's Digest, Robert R. Springer. Well-detailed book on diving, snorkeling and scuba diving. A complete guide to planning, equipment, techniques, diving physics, and psychology, spearfishing, and more. Ppb., 288 (oversize) pp., ill., $7.95, (Digest).

Dive: The Complete Book of Diving, Rick & Barbara Carrier. "One of the most comprehensive and lavishly illustrated of recent skin-diving handbooks. . .the writers cover the underwater world and its creatures, the physiological hazards of diving, equipment, techniques of spearfishing and underwater photography, and desirable diving locations."-the Booklist. 1975 Ppb., 304 pp., ill., $4.95, (T.Y. Crowell).

Free Diving, Jacques Delacrois and Eric Multhaup. A general discussion of diving, including the different types of diving, diving equipment, places to dive, what to look for and catch and how to dive safely. 1975 Ppb., 96 pp., ill., $4.95, (Chronical).

Adventures in Marine Collecting, Robert P. Straughan. This book acts as a window to the mysteries of the sea. Written by a well-known marine collector and skin diver, it is the story of his diving exploits and his encounters with sharks, eels and other dangerous creatures that roam the ocean floor. 1973 Hb., 237 pp., ill., $6.95, (Barnes).

The Complete Illustrated Guide to Snorkel and Deep Diving, Owen Lee. A guidebook on technique, equipment and safety for snorkel and salvage diving, and how to make money at these hobbies. 1963 Hb., ill., $8.95, (Doubleday).

Skittles

Skittles is an indoor bowling game popular in Great Britain and Western Europe. Rules for the game differ widely, but each version is based on a diamond shaped configuration of nine pins (skittles) placed at the end of an alley. Skittles are variously shaped, but are usually about 12 inches high and six inches in diameter. Hard rubber balls five inches in diameter are pitched at the pins, or in some cases a "cheese" is used in place of the ball. Cheeses are typically flat slabs of heavy wood very similar to the discus used in track and field. They are about nine inches in diameter and weigh 10 to 12 pounds.

Skittles is played with even sides, usually five players each. Every player is allowed three tries to knock down the nine skittles, and each time all the pins have been toppled before a player's turn has been exhausted, they are reset. Thus a perfect turn can score 27, or three times nine skittles. A game ends as soon as both teams have gone through a predescribed number of turns (called chalks), the highest aggregate score winning.

Snow Camping

Perhaps no other camping term is as descriptive as "snow camping", and that's exactly what it is – camping on the snow. Eskimos have something like 100 different words to describe the various conditions of snow, and meteorologists have at least 10 different classifications. While it is true that winter provides brilliant, sunny, calm days, there are also fierce and intensely cold stormy days, and everything else in between. In order to be a complete snow camper then, you must be prepared to deal with a multiplicity of situations. Having the skill, knowledge and equipment to deal with whatever arises is essential, and having the creativity to improvise with what you have at hand is equally important.

Snow camping is usually done in areas more isolated than summer backpacking areas. Ranger stations are often abandoned and meeting another snow camping party is usually an infrequent event. Assistance in times of need is, therefore, not as easily obtained as in the summer. This means the camping party should be much more self-reliant than the usual summer expedition.

The top priority piece of equipment is most likely your shelter, which is probably a tent or snow cave. To be useful as snow shelters, tents need special construction features like water-tight floors and adequate pole supports. They must be designed to withstand heavy winds and snowfall. Some provision for cooking and using a gas or kerosene stove while providing shelter for the cook is also quite important. Some tents solve this problem by using a vestibule, while others are constructed with high centers or ends using adjustable ports or windows for adequate ventilation.

Snow caves have many attractive features and also some hidden flaws. True, they have no weight, are very durable when properly built, and are very easy on the environment, but they also take considerable time to build, and require deep snow for their construction. Wet snow and dry powdery snow present engineering problems that are very difficult to solve. Selection of a snow shelter site is also critically important. The direction of the wind, depth of the snow, and configuration of the surface as well as the digging tools available may considerably reduce or increase the amount of time and energy necessary to construct an inhabitable snow structure.

It is highly recommended that the necessary skill to build a good cave or house be obtained before going deep into the wilderness and really needing one to provide your shelter. Spending an afternoon or two building models to see what your skill and inventive powers can produce might be a very profitable venture indeed!

Hypothermia, the reduction of core temperature of the human body, is a prominent threat to the snow camper. Thus, the selection of clothing may be as important as the selection of shelter. Wool is often the best choice for socks, shirts, trousers and head wear. Outer body wear should keep the insulation layer dry. Moisture simply causes heat to be conducted away from the body much more rapidly than when the clothing is dry. It makes little difference if the moisture is from perspiration or melted snow (even expert skiers fall and snowshoers can work up quite a head of steam), wet clothing should be avoided, particularly as the sun leaves the sky. Snow campers cannot carry excessive loads, so remaining dry should be a matter of technique, not accomplished by carrying several changes of clothes.

Providing for sufficient sleep is also a high priority item in snow camping. Essentially, this means adequate insulation from the snow and a sleeping bag designed for snow use. Full-length closed-cell foam sleeping bag pads are the popular way to insulate the sleeper from the snow. Down sleeping bags with sufficient loft to deal with below-freezing temperatures are also the usual way to sleep comfortably on the snow. The down must, however, by kept dry! Any down item will be useless if it becomes wet enough to mat the down. Several kinds of synthetic materials are less subject to the wetting problems but they are somewhat bulkier to pack into pack sacks.

Snow camping is much like backpacking. The notable difference is the necessary precision of the snow camping techniques. A wetting in the summertime is a mere mishap, but in the winter might easily result in a tragedy.

Careful planning of meals as to quantity and quality, precise route finding, with map and compass (most trail signs are covered) and a thorough knowledge of the capabilities of

"Snow camping is much like backpacking. The notable difference is the necessary precision of the snow camping techniques. A wetting in the summertime is a mere mishap, but in the winter might easily result in a tragedy." (Johnston)

the group are all important considerations.

Perhaps the most attractive aspects of snow camping are the solitude and beauty . . . you find the world exactly as it was made. Man's intrusions are easily covered by snow. Even the storms are truly beautiful. Graying skies, driven snow and howling winds should be experienced at least once in a lifetime. It really emphasizes that the root word of wilderness is "wild".

—Larry Moitozo

Larry Moitozo, chief contributor and technical editor of **All About Winter Safety**, *has hiked, climbed, backpacked, cross-country skied and kayaked from Hawaii to Switzerland. He's a certified cross-country ski instructor, developed the Youth Science Institute wilderness program in California, and teaches a wilderness ecology summer course at the University of California in Santa Cruz.*

On A Trip

March is the month I like to ski across the Sierra. The driving force of winter is mostly over and you can expect the weather to be at least cooperative. The sheer beauty of the Sierra Nevada in the winter and the ecological impact of snow and ice stimulated me to plan a winter crossing as part of an ecology class emanating from the University of California at Santa Cruz. Eight of us, four of each sex, set out for Reno, then went south to June Lake on the Greyhound bus. We planned to trek back to Yosemite Valley and five days later be picked up by friends and returned to our usual pursuits.

Because we didn't want to carry any extra weight, we rode the bus in our ski clothes. Regardless of how immune we were to quizzical stares, none of us was ready for the reception we got from our fellow bus riders. We were quickly relegated to the condition of crazy, stupid, suicidal . . . "no one could possibly sleep in the snow." One friendly old soul couldn't understand why we would ride all the way across just to go back again . . . why didn't we just stay on the other side of the Sierra? We soon grew tired of explaining and merely smiled or feigned sleep.

Finally we arrived at the eastern side of the Sierra and camped for the first night at the road head. After a quick breakfast and last minute distribution of food and supplies, we set off for our exciting adventure.

From a geological point of view, the main Sierra Block is sharply tilted upward with the easternmost edge being the steeper angle. This meant that the first part of the trip would be a steep, steady climb with the promise of less rugged terrain to follow. After an hour or so it became very obvious that, in spite of the good weather promised by the weather person, we were in for a good storm. The sky was getting progressively grayer, with scudding clouds. The winds were increasing as the temperature dropped. I knew of a protected valley just beyond the next ridge and we headed for it with haste motivated by the impending storm. We arrived with plenty of time to spare and carefully pitched our tents. The few existing dwarfed trees were used to anchor our nylon "houses". Where no tree was available we stamped the snow and purposely froze our metal stakes into the snow. Later they could be dug free using the ice axe we had brought. Soon our "tent city" sprouted firmly and securely against the approaching storm. Our reliable kerosene stove was soon busy making a pot of deliciously aromatic soup. With our gear and skis safely secured we settled down to enjoy our soup and wait out the storm. And wait we did – for 30 hours!

Except for several biologically motivated trips we remained in those tents for 30 hours! We finally emerged to find that the storm had presented us with about two feet of new snow. The 30 hours had given us enough sleep and boredom to last forever.

Now we had a grave problem. The new snow had stacked up on the ridges of our protected valley so as to necessitate changing our route. We had to climb up at an awkward and steep angle to avoid potential avalanches, but finally we reached the top of the ridge. Before we skied down, I looked back into our valley – just in time to see the snow sag and then flow downward with a soft muted "clump", into the valley from which we had come. The avalanche was hundreds of feet from our camp and we were never in any danger, but it did reinforce in me the importance of not getting caught in the path of such destruction. Quickly and with caution borne of the recent snow slide, we replanned our whole day's route to avoid the possibility of being buried by an avalanche. It also became quickly apparent that with the delay by the storm and the necessity of changing our route, we would need more than the three days we had left to complete our trip. We knew that we would have to stretch our food supplies and humorously speculated what our employers and professors would say about our being tardy. Nonetheless, we happily continued and enjoyed the marvelous weather. Several of us went topless and were chided by the others with "How are you going to get away with your caught-in-a-storm story if you go back with a suntan?"

The new route selection made it very important to accurately use our maps and compass. Several times we miscalculated and went a quarter mile or so out of our way. But finally we reached the main pass into Yosemite National Park, Donahue Pass and there decided to take the short route to the canyon floor. It was after we reached the point of no return that we discovered the slope too wind-blown to hold the new snow and consequently too icy to ski down. With the ice axe and rope, we worked our way down about three pitches, 500 feet, before we could ski again.

By now the snow had changed and the beautiful powder was transformed into a consistency of freshly mixed Portland cement. After cussing and a wax change, we reached the floor of Lyell Canyon. Again we set out on what we light-heartedly knew was the last leg of our journey to Yosemite Valley. We whizzed on to Tuolumne Meadows and briefly chatted with the wilderness rangers there. Now we headed toward Tenaya Lake, keeping clear of the canyon walls that presented a considerable avalanche hazard. We all felt perfectly superior and competent as we watched several avalanches mutedly roar to a stop a few hundred yards off to our right. On our left we would watch in awe as repeated avalanches descended from the sides of Clouds Rest, a huge peak we were using as a landmark.

Even though our food was getting low, we "knew" we would be eating steak the next evening in one of the Valley restaurants. We confidently proceeded on our way. Finally we started down a canyon which everyone thought would lead to the floor of Yosemite Valley. I felt uneasy about the route, but in addition to ecology discussions on the way, we also decided that everyone should share the responsibility for routefinding. As we progressed, I knew we had blown it! The route was clogged with brush and carrying a pack and skis was about as sensible as putting the skin back on a piece of bologna . . . and about as frustrating as well. Scratched, frustrated and hungry – but safe – we reached a flat place where we could rest. All agreed we would have to put off our steak until another day. In front of a small fire we nibbled at our now meager food supply and that night we slept fitfully.

Arising early the next morning we discovered that this was not the way to the valley and the only way out was either back up the brushy "hell" canyon or up a clearer canyon next to it. This canyon had an uncertain head wall and an even more uncertain snowpile that had been deposited by an earlier avalanche. What's more, there was water running out from under the snowpile and the pile had to be crossed before we could reach the head wall.

This called for a conference. Most of the group voted to be rescued by a helicopter. With strong but carefully chosen words I reassured the group that it wasn't necessary. No one was injured, it was well established that humans could do without food for many days, and it would do us good to fast. Then, with a few silent prayers I began to lead the group up the least brushy part of the canyon. As we got closer to the snowpile, it really began to look like it might not go. It might even be possible to get around it. Silently repeating the few prayers I did know well, I continued. Reassuring the group by looking backward at the distance we had already covered was quite helpful.

After three hours of continuous and sometimes quite exposed climbing, we reached the horrendous snowpile. Carefully I roped up, worked my way across the small stream that flowed from it and reached its base. It was sturdy and safe even if somewhat exposed! I climbed up a complete rope's length, anchored the end to a well placed ice axe and left the rope to be used as a hand line for the rest of the group. They easily made it up and by the time I had recovered the rope and ice axe they had proceeded over the head wall and were waiting at the top. When I arrived the four ladies were hugging each other as well as the male members of the group. The ladies also gleefully rewarded themselves with a few pent-up and salty tears. After we had settled down a bit, I candidly pointed out that if it were really necessary we could turn right around and duplicate the feat we had just done . . . and a few hours before they were ready to call a helicopter. They sheepishly agreed. We lit our stove, drank some hot water with a bit of sugar (which was all we had left) and postponed our steak dinner for another evening. We slept again in our snow tents, but very peacefully this time.

The next day we found the right canyon down and turned our attention once more to the signs of bear, porcupine and to the booming of the Blue Grouse.

We reached the valley floor, had our steak and headed for home very tired but with the satisfaction that we had done it – not in five days but nine. Occasionally we still get together and immediately get the feeling of closeness that people have when they know they have shared, cooperated, and endured a firsthand hardship.

–Larry Moitozo

For More Information

Several books can provide the additional information you need. All are available from World Publications, Box 366, Mountain View, Calif. 94040 at the price listed* plus 25 cents each postage.

Snow Camping. A how-to book for the beginning cold weather wilderness traveler. It deals with the techniques of exploring the white wilderness on skis or snowshoes and of living there while traveling. 1974 Ppb., 128 pp., ill., $2.50, (World Publications).

Winter Hiking and Camping, John A. Danielsen. An Adirondack Mountain Club book. Serves as a basic manual to wilderness expeditions under winter conditions. Full index and small size make it perfect to take along on all your trips. 1972 Ppb., 192 pp., ill., $5.00, (Mtn. Club Adirondack).

The Complete Snow Camper's Guide, Raymond Bridge. Written for the lightweight winter camper–discusses the techniques and equipment needed to make winter wandering as safe, comfortable, and rewarding as possible. Special emphasis is given to protecting the fragile beauty of the winter landscape. 1973 Ppb., 390 pp., ill., $5.95, (Scribners).

Paradise Below Zero, Calvin Rutstrum. A complete handbook on how to camp in winter by one of the foremost writers on the America wilderness. Shows you how to enjoy the invigorating challenges of winter camping by accepting and adjusting to the natural hazards rather than fighting them. 1968 Ppb., 244 pp., ill., $2.45, (MacMillan).

Snow Camping & Mountaineering, Edward A. Rossit. Everything you need to know to meet the challenge of living outdoors under the most rigorous winter conditions in the highest altitudes. 1974 Ppb., 288 pp., ill., $2.95, (T.Y. Crowell).

Cold-Weather Camping, Ray Stebbins. A complete and fully illustrated guide for both experienced and novice campers to camping in winter. From the first thoughts of a trip through enjoying the experience to a safe return, every aspect of this exciting sport is thoroughly discussed by a veteran of many winter-camping seasons. 1975 Hb. & Ppb., 256 pp., ill., $10.00/$4.95, (Regnery).

Snowmobiling

Snowmobiling is a convenient means of escape from the tedium of long winter months indoors to the great, white and wonderful out of doors! It is a way of having family fun for dads, moms, children and even a growing number of snowmobiling grandparents.

Those who have lived for years above the North American snowbelt and not experienced winter – cold, crisp, and clean – now have reliable snowmobiles to take them over the great winter trails. From their snowmobiles, these winter tourists will be able to see and experience the beautiful scenery and tranquility all around them – the snow-laden trees, frozen lakes, long open spaces. In short, they can be a part of all Nature's beauty.

Snowmobiles are not only for fun, however. For many, they are a means of transportation to other outdoor winter activities, like ice fishing, hunting, cookouts, camping, cross-country skiing and a host of other recreational pursuits. For forest rangers, a snowmobile can even be a work vehicle.

Despite the fact that snowmobiles have been in existence for many years, they did not gain great public popularity until the advent of snowmobiling competition. This did not occur until the late 1960s and early 1970s. Many snowmobiling race formats have been tried over the years. Oval track racing is most popular with spectators, but long distance races (like the 500-miler from Winnipeg, Canada to St. Paul, Minnesota), rib jarring cross-country events, drag races, hill climbs and Grand Prix races are included in snowmobiling competition. All of this adds up to a sport that's just as exciting for the spectators as for the contestants.

With the rise of snowmobile racing has come the United States Snowmobile Association (USSA) to administer the sport. In addition to sanctioning races, the USSA formed racing classes based on total engine displacement, including any engine modifications. The standard snowmobiling classes are currently for 250 cc, 340 cc, 440 cc and 650 cc displacement engines.

One factor that seems to keep snowmobile races exciting is the possibility of breakdown. This can happen to a factory sponsored professional, as well as an amateur racer, opening the possibility of a win for even complete darkhorses.

In conclusion, I am convinced that snowmobiling easily provides one of the best possible ways to enjoy winter. All you need to do is hop on one and cruise far away from civilization's cares.

–Mike Trapp

Mike Trapp won World Snowmobiling titles in 1971 and 1972, and was runner up in 1973. He was off the pro circuit from 1973 to 1975, but is making a full-fledged return to racing during the 1975-76 season. He lives in Woodruff, Wis.

Oval track snowmobile racing is the most popular form of the sport with spectators. A 340 cc snowmobile like this—piloted by world champion Mike Trapp—will develop dazzling speeds around the oval track, but the possibility of breakdown always lurks in the background. Even factory sponsored snowmobiles are susceptible to breakdowns, opening the door of victory to a darkhorse.

Snowmobile Safety

Several safety rules should be observed to help keep snowmobiling as enjoyable and safe as it should be. Occasionally a careless few can produce grief for large numbers of other happy snowmobilers. So, the first rule of safe snowmobiling should be to know and observe all municipal, county, state, provincial and federal regulations.

Learning to ride correctly is the next important safety consideration. It is vital that you never put your feet under the machine's running board support bars. These bars look like inviting stirrups, but if you have a spill while your feet are imprisoned by the support bars, you could be very seriously injured.

Once out on the trail, it is important to know the trails and operate your snowmobile at safe speeds for each type of terrain. Be alert for guy wires and barbed wire fences, as well as low branches and other overhangs. It is also important to watch for rocks, stumps and other partially hidden obstructions in the path of your machine. Hitting one of these at high speed can catapult you for quite a distance over the handlebars. Since most serious accidents occur after dark, it is best to be extremely cautious during these hours, or better yet, you can refrain from riding after dark.

You should always wear a helmet and appropriate warm clothing while snowmobiling. Never wear loose-fitting apparel like long scarves, as they can be caught up in a snowmobile's machinery and cause serious injury or death.

Be especially careful near roads, as auto accidents can be deadly. It is equally foolish to drive on railroad tracks. Not only is this private property, but an unexpected train can put quite a dent in your equipment. I also caution snowmobilers to refrain from jumping snow banks. It can be dangerous to the rider, and one never knows when a small child might be playing unseen on the other side of a bank. Other hidden dangers can include thin lake ice, so never snowmobile on a frozen lake without first checking the ice thickness.

If the above simple rules of safety and courtesy are followed, you should have no trouble enjoying a day in the great white outdoors. Maybe I'll see you there!

—**Mike Trapp**

For More Information

Several good magazines have developed in the sport of snowmobiling. Ones which have been recommended to us include: *Snotrack,*, 534 North Broadway, Milwaukee, Wis. 53202. $4 for six issues (during winter). Official publication of the United States Snowmobile Association. *Snow Goer*, 1999 Shepard Road, S. Paul, Minn. 55116. $4.00 for five issues. *Snow Sports,* 1500 East 79th Street, Minneapolis, Minn. 55420. A publication for snowmobile families. $3.50 per year. The major organization is the United States Snowmobile Association, P.O. Box Snowmobile, Rhinelander, Wis. 54501. They do most of the work in organizing and sanctioning races, among other duties. Other organizations are the American Snowmobile Association, P.O. Box 4403, Columbia Heights, Minneapolis, Minn. 55421, and the North American Snowmobile Federation, Box 368, Anoka, Minn. 55303.

Here are some excellent snowmobile books. All are available from World Publications, Box 366, Mountain View, Calif. 94040 at the price listed* plus 25 cents postage.

Snowmobiling: The Guide, John Malo. A comprehensive coverage of this fast-growing sport. Buying and renting a snowmobile, safety and overnight expeditions, plus much more. A valuable manual with lots of photos for interesting browsing or informative instruction. 1971 Ppb., 185 pp., ill., $3.95, (MacMillan).

Snowmobilers Bible, Morten Lund and Bea Williams. A complete handbook on snowmobiles, from purchasing one to snowmobile exploits such as exploration, rescue, and racing. 1974 Ppb., 179 (oversize) pp., ill., $2.50, (Doubleday).

Chilton's Repair & Tune-Up Guide for Snowmobiles. Fun and safety in snowmobiling depends on a snowmobile being in good running condition. This guide will help the average owner, as well as the skilled mechanic, keep it that way. 1972 Hb. & Ppb., 243 (oversize) pp., ill., $6.95/$4.95, (Chilton).

Snowmobile Trails, Mike Michaelson. An introduction to snowmobile trails with a complete discussion of the top 100 trails throughout the seven northern states. A special section deals with snow-chowing—the art of trailside cookery. 1974 Ppb., 288 pp., ill., $4.95, (Great Lakes Living Press).

Safe Snowmobiling, James L. Thomas. A book for the beginner or experienced driver. The author introduces the reader to the snowmobile and how to operate it, then goes on to discuss riding safety, accessories and how to keep a sled in top condition. 1971 Library Binding, 120 pp., ill., $4.59, (Sterling).

Snowshoeing

The dictionary defines a snowshoe as "a light oval frame strung like a tennis racket and worn under the shoe to enable the wearer to walk on snow without sinking." To be classified as a sport, it must be used in a voluntary activity in leisure time, seldom for pay or profit."

The snowshoe frame is commonly made of wood (usually ash), and strips of animal hide are used as webbing weaved across the frames. The complete shoe is varnished to make it waterproof. A complete pair of snowshoes weighs an average of 4½ to 5½ pounds. Recently synthetics have become more common. These include metal alloy frames, aluminum frames, neoprene lacings and bindings, and metal hinged bindings with heel control. A variety of shapes are available: shoes without tails, shoes with turned up noses, flat noses, wide shoes and narrow trail shoes, ladies' and children's snowshoes and wide loadbearing shoes for backpackers and heavyweights.

For a purist, most outdoor recreation in snow country needs to be ecologically sound. This demands either the ski or the snowshoe be used for travel, not a snowmobile.

Born of necessity by herdsmen and hunters of Central Asia 400 years or so BC, snowshoeing eventually developed through the ingenuity of American Indians. It was recoged and adopted by trappers, hunters and settlers of North

America. In America, it was even used in warfare by the French, Indians, and Americans during colonial wars. For many who make a living in the snow belt it is still a necessity.

The snowshoe can be used purely for the pleasure of walking in snow at one's own pace, up or down hills in brush country, thick woods, or open fields. With the addition of serrated strips of metal or wood, the shoe can even be used for climbing steep hard-packed snow slopes.

As a sport, snowshoeing is used by hikers ana climbers to continue their activities in deep snow. Showshoes enable anyone who can walk and hike in summer to continue their activities in the winter, and it is most effective after the snow cover is at least 10 inches or more in depth.

Competition on snowshoes for the most part has been confined to Canadian and American showshoe clubs conducting races. The 50, 100 and 440 dashes and low hurdles are performed on a packed snow track. Marathon races of the same distances as foot races are also popular. Simple games can be conducted on snowshoes in deep snow and add considerable fun for young and old alike. Fox and Geese, Tag Games, Dodge Ball, Softball, Potato Relays, and Three-Legged Races can all be played with minor modifications.

—Leslie J. Hurley

Leslie Hurley is on the physical education faculty at Norwich University. He is the co-author of **The Snowshoe Book.**

Snowshoeing, like ski touring, allows the participant to experience Nature's winter wonderland first-hand and in the soundest possible ecological manner. Where noisy and fume spewing snowmobiles tend to degrade the spectacular winter landscape, snowshoers live in harmony with it. (Above-Park; Right-Cameron)

For More Information

The American Snowshoe Union, 138 Bartlett St., Lewiston, Me. 04240. Promotes snowshoe racing in the United States. Additional information can be found under cross-country skiing. Here are some books. All are available from World Publications, Box 366, Mountain View, Calif. 94040 at the price listed* plus 25 cents each postage. Write for a complete list.

Snowshoeing, Gene Prater. An expert Northwest snowshoer provides information on technique, selection, care for and use of snowshoes. Travel on all types of terrain and in all types of weather plus a chapter on snow camping. 1974 Ppb., 120 pp., ill., $3.95, (Mountaineering).

The Snowshoe Book, William Osgood and Leslie Hurley. Everything about walking on snow: history, equipment, technique, competition and safety. An excellent introduction to a little-known sport. 1971 Ppb., 128 pp., ill., $4.50, (Stephen Greene).

Cross-Country Skiing & Snowshoeing, Edward Bauer. Cross-country skiing and snowshoeing combine the invigorating pleasure of outdoor exercise with the awesome beauty and serenity of the winter landscape, and this ideal guide covers techniques, tips on equipment, clothing, and accessories, finding and building trails, camping in the snow, how to cope with winter emergencies, wildlife watching, and photography. 1975 Hb., 210 pp., ill., $8.95, (Winchester).

Soaring

Soaring is the only true form of sporting aviation in the world today. Because piloting ability and knowledge play such a large part in the distance and speed performance of a sailplane, it is possible to hold organized contests and competitions. Many regional meets are held, plus an annual national contest and a biannual World Championships. Even with weekend sport soaring, there is an ever-present challenge to stay aloft that draws soaring enthusiasts back again and again to experience the thrill of flight.

The difference between gliding and soaring can be explained as follows: gliding is coasting downhill on an inclined plane of air, while soaring is maintaining or gaining altitude on upcurrents of air. Upcurrents occur for a variety of reasons, the most common being uneven heating of the ground by the sun. This results in rising columns or bubbles of hot air called thermals. Such thermals are common everywhere, regardless of the terrain. Wind being deflected upward on the face of a ridge, or downward and then upward in the lee of a ridge, can also provide soarable upcurrents.

A sailplane is generally launched by an airplane tow to approximately 2000 feet, but autos and winches can be used for economy when take-off space is available. The average altitude obtained on a winch or auto tow is 1000 feet.

Cross-country flights in medium-performance sailplanes can exceed 100 miles, with the world's record currently at 908 miles. Altitude flights are generally limited to the cumulus cloudbase, unless actual cloud flying is indulged in. The soaring altitude record was set at 46,267 feet in the lee "wave" of the Sierra Nevada Mountains, and was limited only by the oxygen equipment available. Including spiralling time cross-country speeds average 40 mph in upcurrents. Without including spiralling, typical cross-country cruising speeds are around 70 mph, although top speeds of more than 100 mph have been recorded around a triangular course.

Soaring is a very safe sport because most sailplanes land at a speed of between 40 and 50 mph and have a low center of gravity. This gives great landing stability. In addition, the excellent flying judgment developed from soaring training results in all-around piloting ability.

Because it is easier to land and does not have the added complication of an engine, the sailplane is an excellent machine for teaching basic flying skills. Less flight time is generally required before soloing than in powered planes, and power pilots find little difficulty in checking out in sailplanes once the few limitations of powerless flight are understood.

Going For a World Record

Soaring is a self-descriptive sport because you literally soar through the air on rising columns of air. These "thermals" are detected by sensitive instruments in the sailplane and can usually be found over parking lots, roads, fields, or anywhere that the sun is most likely to warm the earth and cause heat to rise. A second way to soar is to utilize ridge lift, which occurs when wind blows against a ridge of mountains and causes the air to rise vertically. With ridge lift, sailplanes can fly along, above or beside the ridge to maintain a definite altitude, or they can go back and forth to gain altitude. On a good soaring day a pilot can take advantage of both of these types of lift, while on a poor day he/she must make do with any lift. Of course, in non-mountainous areas, ridge-lift does not exist and a pilot must rely totally on thermal activity.

During the last four or five years, ridge-lift has been used to set several world records, for distance flight in sailplanes. By flying along the Appalachian Mountains, for example, long distances can be achieved by staying close to the ridge and taking advantage of available ridgelift. On a record setting day this will exist along most of the mountain range. The present world goal and return record, where a pilot flies to a predetermined goal and back to his point of origin, is held by myself and was achieved on May 4, 1973 along the Appalachians.

In order for a world record to be set in any sport, everything has to be perfect: weather (most importantly), pilot, instruments, sailplane, ground crew, and radio communications. The ground crew prepares the sailplane for the pilot, assembling it, washing it, and making sure all necessary equipment is in the craft. They also retrieve the sailplane and pilot in case of an off field landing. The crew cannot act as a witness to any record attempt, however, so an official witness must be obtained to observe the takeoff and landing.

In order to prove that the declared flight was actually accomplished, the pilot must carry a barograph to measure and record both altitude and distance flown. He/she must also carry two cameras fixed inside the canopy to photograph a designated point, such as the goal in a goal and return flight. At the end of a flight, baragraph and camera data are sent to a committee which approves, certifies and records the flights.

In order to set my world record, I followed a pattern similar to that of former world record holder, Karl Streideck, who pioneered the use of the Appalachian ridges as a means to achieve record flights. The secret of successful ridge flying is to stay close to the ridge and fly one that has few gaps from one range to the next, so as not to lose your source of lift. Karl had set his record from State College, Penn to southern West Virginia and back to State College. This flight was over one of the longest sections of the Appalachians, with only two or three gaps.

The first time I attempted a record, Karl and I flew together. Near the end of our flight he got a little ahead of me and because of his better knowledge of the terrain and the quickly setting sun, he made his goal of 680 miles. I landed 23 miles short of Karl, and my barograph had run out of ink six hours before that. So, even though I learned alot and it was the farthest I had ever flown in a sailplane, my effort did not count. This must be the most frustrating of all soaring lessons. It happens to everyone once, but only once.

Karl Streideck was the teacher and I was the student on that first flight. It taught me to be prepared, so when the next perfect world record day rolled around on May 4, 1973, I had been ready for months. On the 3rd we drove up to Lock Haven, Pennsylvania, which is further up the ridge than Karl and I had started the last time. We prepared for a 6:00 am take off on Friday the 4th, and this time the sailplane would carry two barographs along with its two cameras.

After quickly assembling my Libelle H301-B fiberglass sailplane, I took off at 6:02 am and released from tow at 6:07 am. (Sailplanes are towed aloft by a small airplane, usually to around 2000 feet). The flight was to be from Lock Haven, Penn. to Hansonville, Virginia and back, making a total of 783.5 miles and breaking the old record by 103 miles. At approximately 70 mph around speed, it would take about 12 hours to complete the flight. This accounts for my early take-off and a late landing at sunset. Sailplanes cannot fly at night due to the fact that, as the sun goes down, the earth cools and thermal activity becomes either weak or non-existent.

Everything went perfectly. The weather was exactly as forecast, and sometimes even better. Ridge lift was interspersed with thermal activity. I reached Hansonville at 12:07 pm, took the required pictures, and turned north for the return trip to Lock Haven. The day was still "booming" and it looked as if I would make it. At 6:03 pm I touched down at the Lock Haven airport to receive enthusiastic congratulations from my wife, number one crew chief Sophie, and a few friends who had heard of my attempted flight and gathered to greet me. It was not quite the reception that Lindberg received in Paris, but the inner satisfaction and feeling of accomplishment was tremendous.

Soaring is not just a sport for competing or setting records. There are hundreds of soaring pilots who receive just as much satisfaction from flying close to home, or on short and/or long cross-country flights. Like any sport, there are both competitors and non-competitors who enjoy the soaring for the personal challenge. And soaring is always a challenge. Whether competing or flying for fun, it is a continued contest between you, your sailplane, and the weather.

—**William C. Holbrook**

William C. Holbrook is the co-author of **Soaring Cross-Country**, *co-founder of Soaring Symposia, an organization devoted to improving competitive techniques, and holder of a world record goal and return flight of 783.5 miles.*

For More Information

The organization for soaring is The Soaring Society of America, Box 66071, Los Angeles, Ca. 90066. Their magazine *Soaring* is very good and available to their members. An associate membership is $12 per year. The society is a nonprofit organization founded in 1932. They have published several books and also issue several other publications such as *Motorgliding and Technical Soaring.* Also, they issue numerous local and regional newsletters. If you want to get started right in this sport, write to them first.

Here are some interesting contacts for equipment, and other things. The National Soaring Museum, Harris Hill, Elmira, N.Y. 14903 has a free catalog listing over 100 available films. An example is titled, "Soaring the Hummingbird Over the Sierra." Skysailing, Inc., 1871 Severn Drive, Salt Lake City, Utah 84117 has an easy-to-build trailer kit. They have kits to fit your sailplane. Or how about radio-controlled soaring? Hobie Model Co., 2026 McGaw Ave., Irvine, Ca. 92705 makes the Hobie Hawk which comes completely ready to fly. They can send you more information. If you are looking for a good variometer write Ball Engineering Co., 2140 Kohler, Boulder, Colo. 80303. Their variometers were used by the first place winners in the 1975 US Open Class Nationals. Glider Aero, Inc., 2680 E. Wardlow Rd., Long Beach Municipal Airport, Long Beach, Calif. 90807 has a lot of good stuff available by mail order. Soaring Symposia, 408 Washington St., Cumberland, Md. 21502 holds an annual symposium on competitive soaring. Two of the best manufacturers are Graham Thomson Ltd., 3200 Airport Ave., Santa Monica, Ca. 90405 and Schweizer Aircraft Corp., 1 Airport Road, Elmira, N.Y. 14902.

Here are some good books on soaring. All are available from World Publications, Box 366, Mountain View, Ca. 94040 at the price listed* plus 25 cents postage. Write for a complete list.

Soaring Cross-Country, Ed Byars and Bill Holbrook. A technical book for sailplane pilots wanting to learn good cross-country techniques. Sections cover proper preparation, in-flight decisions, crewing and instruments and equipment. 1974 Hb., 201 pp., ill., $6.95, (Soaring Symposia).

Sailplanes and Soaring, James Mrazek. An easy-to-read guide about sailplanes and how to sail them. Also included is information regarding soaring schools and instructors, using winds and clouds and how to buy a sailplane. 1973 Hb. & Ppb., 159 pp., ill., $6.95/$2.95, (Stackpole).

Soaring On the Wind, Joseph Colville Lincoln. A photographic essay on silent flight. A selection of 80 of the best photos of soaring, depicting some of the most dramatic moments in the history of flight—from the earliest attempts in primitive machines to the streamlined sailplanes of today. Spiced with quotations from a variety of sources. 1973 Hb., 130 (oversize) pp., ill., $15.00, (Northland).

Soaring Guide, Peter M. Bowers. Intensive discussion on all planes of gliding and soaring movement in this sport of great challenge—art of flying without power. 1966 Ppb., $3.95, (Crown).

The Joy of Soaring: A Training Manual, Carle Conway. This large guide is devoted to teaching the beginner to fly a glider, and the rated power pilot to learn the differences between gliding and powered flight. Then goes on telling how to use this knowledge to master the art of soaring. 1969 Hb., 134 (oversize) pp., ill., $7.95, (Aviation Books).

The Art and Technique of Soaring, Richard A. Wolters. A complete manual of soaring, designed primarily to instruct the person with no previous experience as he progresses through the first year of active soaring. Gives the practical information needed to master the risks involved. Profusely illustrated with specially prepared photos that show what the pilot sees and what the sailplane is doing during training maneuvers. 1971 Hb., 197 (oversize) pp., ill., $14.95, (McGraw-Hill).

Soccer

We have records of games much like soccer being played in ancient China and Egypt, and in Greece and Rome, but the modern game is most immediately rooted in England. At one time royal proclamations were issued banning the game because it kept the English yeomen from their archery practice, thus threatening the security of the realm. Edward II, Richard II, Henry IV, and Elizabeth I were among the royal foes of soccer.

But the game persisted despite official disapproval, growing into massive contests in which whole villages were pitted against one another, each trying to force an inflated animal bladder into the opposing village. Teams sometimes consisted of hundreds of men, and the games were extremely rough; as far as we know, any and all means of play were legal.

In the modern game, the goal is no longer an opposing village, but rather a frame eight feet high and eight yards across. The goals are at each end of a field, which can vary between 100 and 130 yards in length, and 50 and 100 yards in width. The old "anything goes" rule has been replaced with the present Laws of the Game (17 of them), the most remark-

"In parks and playgrounds, in cities and suburbs, you can see that the game is taking hold at the grass roots level. Young boys and girls are having fun kicking that black and white ball. Youth soccer programs are springing up all over the country. They are growing so fast in some areas—like Miami, Dallas, San Diego, San Francisco and Seattle—that there are more youngsters in organized soccer than in Little League Baseball and Pop Warner football combined." (Frederick)

able of which is that only the goalkeepers can handle the ball. Field players can use only their feet, foreheads, chests, and thighs to move the ball. Unlike American football, the game is continuous and flowing, bringing both players and fans to a high intensity of involvement.

Soccer is the international game. It is estimated that over 800 million fans watched the last World Cup, in which West Germany won the highest international honors.

The Soccer Explosion

Until quite recently, soccer was out of the mainstream of American sports. Most people, if they thought of soccer at all, would dismiss it as an ethnic sport. Soccer clubs were for immigrants who wanted to keep in touch with the sports culture of their homeland. But in the last few years, the situation has changed radically. Soccer is exploding all over the United States.

In parks and playgrounds, in cities and suburbs, you can see that the game is taking hold at the grass roots level. Young boys and girls are having fun kicking that black and white ball. Youth soccer programs are springing up all over the country. They are growing so rapidly in some areas (like Miami, Dallas, San Diego, San Francisco and Seattle), that there are more youngsters in organized soccer than in Little League Baseball and Pop Warner football combined.

The boom started back in the mid '60s when CBS introduced professional soccer to the American public with weekly TV coverage. But at that time the first professional leagues, the National Professional Soccer League and the United Soccer Association, were not grounded in the widespread youth participation of today. As a result, they lacked fan support and ran into financial difficulties.

Despite the setback, soccer's broad and strong appeal assured its survival. In the last pro soccer season, the North American Soccer League boasted 20 franchises, which makes it the third largest professional sports league in the country.

In the rest of the world, where soccer is known as football, it is by far the most popular sport. More than 20 million players participate in organized competition, and several times that number participate in recreational games.

Baseball has its World Series, but baseball is hardly played outside the United States, so it is a World Series in name only. Soccer is a truly international sport. The world governing body of soccer is FIFA (Federation Internationale de Football Association). The membership of FIFA exceeds the membership of the United Nations, so soccer brings the people of the world together more than any other sport and perhaps more than any political organization. The 1974 World Cup was watched by almost a billion people throughout the world.

There are good reasons for soccer's world-wide appeal and for the mushrooming American interest in the game. It is a very simple game, easy to learn and easy to enjoy as a spectator. Unlike football, it is a continuously flowing game in which the excitement of the action can develop to an incredible pitch of intensity. And unlike football, the action is out in the open, the ball can always be seen, the display of skill can be appreciated by all. Each player has a great deal of room for individual expression, spontaneity, creativity and improvisation. In good soccer, surprising developments and unexpected turns occur frequently. Since there are no set plays, the demands on the players' alertness and intelligence are far greater than in American football, and since there are no time outs or substitutions, the demands on their physical fitness are also greater.

Soccer is a democratic sport: anyone can play, including those not tall enough or heavy enough for football or basketball. It has an appeal for everyone, players and fans, young and old. According to the President's Council on Physical Fitness, soccer "is one of the best all-around activities for the development of physical fitness, sportsmanship, teamwork, and all the other intrinsic values of sports competition . . . These facts, combined with the relatively low incidence of serious injury to participants, make soccer worthy of major support by all people interested in the promotion of physical fitness and sports among the American people."

—Ian Jackson

Ian Jackson is the editor of **Soccer World** *and author of* **Yoga and the Athlete.**

For More Information

The number of soccer publications is expanding alongside the growth of the sport. The major ones are: *Soccer Monthly,* 350 Fifth Avenue, New York, N.Y. 10001. Published monthly at $7.50 per year. The official magazine of the United States Soccer Association. *Soccer World,* Box 366, Mountain View, Calif. 94040. Published monthly at $8.00 per year. Interviews and articles by and on coaches, players, and referees.

Organizations can be found in nearly every state, but the major ones are: United States Soccer Federation, 350 Fifth Ave., Rm. 4010, New York, N.Y. 10001. The USSF provides standard rules, sanctions tournaments and promotes the sport on all levels. They also have a youth program, the United States Soccer Association. American Youth Soccer Association, 4015 Pacific Coast Highway, Suite 202, Torrance, Calif. 90505, is primarily Californian, but has one of the largest youth programs in the country. Also, the Catholic Youth Organization runs fine programs in many parts of the country. Check your local group.

Soccer equipment is becoming more available. One good source for the proper clothing and other items is: Tullyco, Dept. 125, P.O. Box 306, River Forest, Ill. 60305.

These are all good soccer books. All are available from World Publications, Box 366, Mountain View, Calif. 94040 at the price listed* plus 25 cents postage. Write for a complete list.

Winning Soccer, Al Miller. A nicely-illustrated introduction to the game of soccer. The author gives the reader insights into getting in shape, ball control techniques and strategy. 1975 Hb. & Ppb., 149 pp., ill., $8.95/$4.95, (Regnery).

Goal!, Paul E. Harris. A soccer handbook especially written for young players. Filled with drawings and photographs, the book discusses the skills involved in soccer, the positions, the equipment, keeping in shape and soccer for girls. 1975 Ppb., 88 pp., ill., $3.95, (Soccer for Americans).

Soccer: Guide to Training and Coaching, Alan Wade. An important contribution to the growing need for teaching and coaching aids in America. The principles, systems and tactics of soccer are outlined for both coach and player, as are playing requirements, methods and a program for acquiring needed skills. 1967 Hb., 259 pp., ill., $7.95, (Crowell).

Goalkeeping, Bob Wilson. An All-Star goalkeeper gives his theories on the techniques and approach to training needed to achieve championship-level goaltending ability. A book for all goalies. 1970 Hb., 114 pp., ill., $5.95, (Pelham).

Soccer Techniques and Tactics, Jimmy Greaves. Greaves takes a hefty kick at some of the sacred cows of soccer coaching, offering a fresh approach to soccer technique and strategy. 1966 Hb., 139 pp., ill., $4.95, (Pelham).

The Book of Soccer, Enzo Domini. A photograph- and diagram-packed primer expressly telling how to kick, head, and, generally, control a soccer ball. Ideal for beginning soccer enthusiasts. 1972 Hb., 127 pp., ill., $8.95, (Van Nostrand Reinhold).

The Basic Soccer Guide, Bobby Moffat. Brand-new soccer guide, written with special understanding of the problems of coaches who have grown up in a football/baseball-oriented society. Innovative format stresses learning one skill at a time through exercises which can be done by two boys or 200. 1975 Ppb., 144 pp., ill., $3.50, (World Publications).

History of the Soccer World Cup, Brian Glanville. The only comprehensive history of the most important soccer competition—chronicles the game in the 40-year history of the soccer World Cup. 1973 Ppb., 260 pp., ill., $4.95, (MacMillan).

So You'd Like to Know More About Soccer: A Guide for Parents, Paul Harris, Jr. For the parent as a spectator, assistant coach, and supportive friend to the youthful soccer player. 1974 Ppb., 133 pp., ill., $2.95, (Soccer for America).

Teaching Soccer to Boys, Alan Gibbon and John Cartwright. An excellent guide to the teaching to boys in the 9 to 13 age group, written for teachers, youth group leaders, parents and coaches. Great drills, activities, and practice games. 1972 Ppb., 121 pp., ill., $3.50, (Cedars).

Soccer, 42 Programmed Principles, Bob Cheney. Young adults can teach themselves the basics of soccer technique and strategy with this simple, interesting guide. Makes use of many modern programmed learning techniques to ensure comprehension. 1972, 73 pp., ill., $2.50, (Bear).

The Challenge of Soccer, Hubert Vogelsinger. An omnibus work covering all aspects of the game, especially written for the American audience. As complete a guide to the game as can be found anywhere. Well-illustrated. 1973 Hb., 382 pp., ill., $13.95, (Allyn & Bacon).

Playing Soccer the Professional Way, Gordon Bradley & Clive Toye. Players and fans alike will enjoy this book by the coach and general manager of the New York Cosmos. Packed with information on rules, equipment, strategy and technique, plus the complete "Official Laws of the Game." 1973 Hb., 218 pp., ill., $8.95, (Harper & Row).

Sports Illustrated Soccer, Phil Woosnam and Paul Gardner. Designed especially for an American audience, with emphasis on the points of the game domestic players need special help with. An important special feature is the special exercises to improve soccer agility and endurance. 1972 Hb. & Ppb., 96 pp., ill., $4.95/$1.95, (Lippincott).

Bob Wilson: Soccer, Bob Wilson. A former Scotland goalkeeper deals clearly and lucidly with all aspects of the game—forward, midfield and back play, and, of course with an excellent section on goalkeeping. Action photos from competition illustrate the arts of passing, dribbling and fielding the ball, with tips from Wilson to the youngster who has set his sights on a pro career. 1975 Library Binding, 61 (oversize) pp., ill., $5.95, (Pelham).

Soccer: How to Become a Champion, Allen Clarke. Writing in a personable, easygoing style, Clarke takes the reader through the ins and outs of high-speed soccer on a pro team, showing the techniques and skills that make him the gifted striker that he is. 1975 Ppb., 124 pp., ill., $3.95, (William Luscombe).

Softball

The game of softball is played on a field similar in shape to a baseball field, but with smaller dimensions. Like baseball, there are nine players to a team, the object of the game being to score runs by the batsman hitting the ball into the field of play, circling the three bases and returning to the home base. The batsman-runner scores a run for his team if he succeeds in circling the bases before a member of the opposite team can retrieve the ball and throw it to the base toward which the runner is running, or can tag the runner with the ball.

Each team alternates in taking turns at bat and is allowed three outs. An out is recorded when a batter fails to hit the ball into fair play after three misses with the bat, has his hit ball caught by an opposing player before it hits the ground, or fails to reach a base.

The entire game is comprised of seven innings, an inning consisting of both teams having their turns at bat.

While in the field, each player occupies a particular position, the positions being pitcher, catcher, first-baseman, second-baseman, third-baseman, shortstop, left fielder, center fielder, right fielder.

In the U.S., two variations of the game are played: the fast-pitch game in which the pitcher tries determinedly to strike the batter out, and slow-pitch where the pitch is required to be thrown so that it can be hit.

Softball: A Game for Everyone

Softball is the game for everyone! Many companies advertise their product is made for everyone – nine to 90.

Softball makes that same claim and has the figures to back it up:

This year, nearly 600,000 youngsters, boys and girls, ages nine through 18, are competing in the ASA Junior Program. They are learning a sport that will remain with them throughout their lives. As long as a person can walk up to home plate, he or she can play softball.

To substantiate this point, one need only look at St. Petersburg, Florida's Three-Quarter Century Softball Club. To be eligible for the team, a man must have reached the age of 75. The catcher on this year's team is 92; the shortstop is 85; an outfielder is 88; one member plays with a pacemaker in his heart. A pitcher for the Three-Quarter Century Club retired

More than 26 million Americans enjoy playing softball, and the sport is especially popular among women. It can literally be played by anyone nine to 90; more than 600,000 youngsters from age nine are playing as well as a host of old timers. Florida's Three-Quarter Century Softball Club boasts a catcher who's 92, an outfielder of 88 and an 85 year old shortstop. (Gloucester)

two years ago at the age of 96, after playing 21 years with the club.

When you have a game that appeals to nine-year-olds as well as 96-year-olds, then you really do have a game for everyone.

The A.C. Nielsen Company indicated through surveys that over 26 million people are playing softball in the United States. It was also revealed that softball is the largest team participation sport in the U.S.

The 26 million Americans who play softball come from all walks of life. It would not be uncommon to find a doctor, school teacher, factory worker and store owner all playing on the same team or against each other.

Credit for the rise in softball popularity must be given to the Amateur Softball Association of America. The ASA is one of the fastest growing amateur sports associations in America today. Its membership is composed of adults and youngsters who are dedicated to amateur sports.

Softball is not a new sport; in fact, its beginning came in 1887 at Chicago.

Softball is not even limited to the United States: 36 million people in fifty countries are playing the game.

Slow pitch continues to be the dominant factor behind the tremendous growth of softball in this country. At present, seventy-nine percent of softball is of the slow pitch variety. That figure may go even higher as thousands and even millions discover this fun-filled, competitive game.

Softball players enjoy their sport, but as happens in any sport, some achieve greatness. At present, 51 men and women are enshrined in the National Softball Hall of Fame in Oklahoma City.

But each day, men, women, boys and girls, aged nine to 90, prove that softball is a game for everyone!

—Dave Hill

Dave Hill is Public Relations Director of the Amateur Softball Association of America. Before becoming associated with the ASA, he was a television sports director and for four consecutive years he was named winner of the Softball Writers and Broadcasters Association Television Award.

For More Information

There are two magazines we know about. *The National Slowpitch News,* Wirt Gammon St., Rossville, Ga. 30741 which is published monthly and *Balls and Strike,* 2801 N.E. 50th, Oklahoma City, Okla. 73111 which is the official publication of the Amateur Softball Association, Box 11437, Oklahoma City. Another organization is the International Softball Congress, 2523 W. 14th St. Rd., Greeley, Colo. 80631.

Here are three books. All are available from World Publications, Box 366, Mountain View, Calif. 94040 at the price listed* plus 25 cents each postage.

Softball, Kneer and McCord. Emphasis on the values of softball and its place in our culture, as well as on the techniques and special skills required for playing. 1966 Ppb., 73 pp., ill., $2.50, (W.C. Brown).

Winning Softball, Joan Joyce and John Anquillare. A complete, fully illustrated guide for recreational and competitive softball players, as well as for spectators, by two of the top softball players in the US. 1975 Hb. & Ppb., 109 pp., ill., $8.95/$4.95, (Regnery).

Women's Softball. Part of the Sports Techniques series, this guide explains all the techniques and strategies of winning softball. 1974 Ppb., $1.50, (Athletic Inst.).

Spaceball

Spaceball? Sounds like some futuristic, far-out game played by people in metal-alloy suits. Actually, it *is* somewhat futuristic in that it combines the modern sports of volleyball and basketball—and *trampoline*? Spaceball is a new ball game played while jumping on a trampoline!

The object of the game is to volley the ball back and forth through a basket in the middle of the center *gantry* or divider of a specially-made trampoline. The trampoline has backstops players can bounce off as well as the regular bed, and the gantry is designed to rebound also. One player, the server, initiates action by throwing the ball through the basket, and the players continue volleying until one misses. This results in a score for the other player. A game is seven points; a set, two out of three games. Spaceball can be played as single, double, or team competition with up to four players on a team.

Spaceball is a fast-moving game as complicated as your skill level allows it to be. Practically anyone can play with a minimum amount of training and the variations on the basic game are infinite. You can engage in a leisurely game of bounce-on-the-tramp-and-catch-through-the-gantry or you can work on skills that will take you to the World Spaceball Championships.

The proponents of spaceball list the benefits other than the recreational as "control in the air, dexterity, reactions, and timing. Most of all, spaceball is a fast, continuous action sport which greatly contributes to a person's general physical condition."

It's true—very few sports can pack so much activity into such a small space in a short time as spaceball.

For More Information

Additional information is available from George Nissen, Nissen Corporation, 930 27th Ave., SW, Cedar Rapids, Iowa. Mr. Nissen is the inventor of the trampoline and promotes new and varied trampoline games such as spaceball. Or you might try contacting Ron Munn with the United States Trampoline and Tumbling Association, 1333 Bloor St., East, Apt. 2307, Mississauga, Ontario, Canada. See also the section on Trampoline and Tumbling.

Spear Fishing

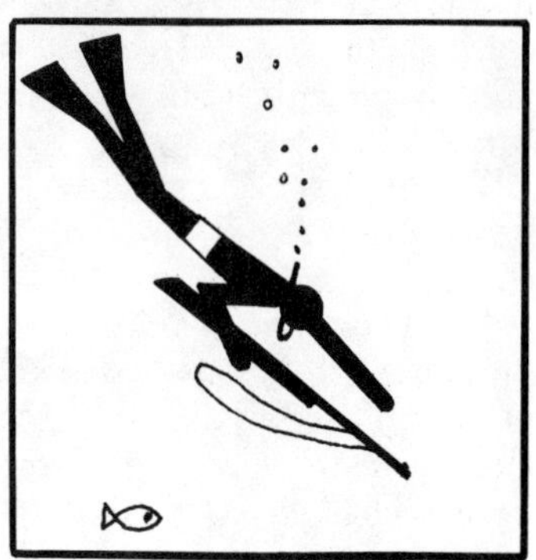

The spearfish, a marine animal related to the swordfish and the sailfish, got his name from the spearlike growth on his upper jaw. Man does not come equipped with a built-in spear, so he must carry one when he goes hunting under water.

Man's spearfishing originated over two thousand years ago when a South Pacific native attached a sharp point to the end of a bamboo pole, dove into the water and attempted to spear a fish while holding his breath. Today, over 2,000,000 people in the United States hunt a wide variety of sea game, ranging from perch weighing less than a pound to giant seabass as heavy as 600 pounds.

And today the equipment is much more sophisticated. With the convenience of scuba gear, we no longer need to hold our breath, although many free divers still use this method.

There are six basic types of spears and spearguns to choose from. Handspears and Hawaiian slings are the most primitive and require the most strength and skill because they have no moving parts.

The four types of guns are classified according to the way they are powered. The gas gun, almost obsolete, uses a CO_2 cartridge. It cannot be used in recognized spearfishing competitions because no power is derived from the diver, either to load or to fire it. It also makes a lot of noise and has no safety features to prevent it from going off at an inopportune time.

Pneumatic guns are powered with compressed air pumped by the diver. Spring guns contain a metal spring which is compressed inside the barrel when the spear is inserted. One disadvantage common to both these guns is that the barrel and the spear must both be completely clean and free of dents, or the gun will be useless.

The rubber gun has become the most popular with spearfishermen. Rubber slings are looped through a retainer on the muzzle to provide power. These guns are safe because they are not loaded until the rubbers have been stretched and cocked. And since the spear does not fit inside the barrel, they will still function if there are a few small dents.

In general, the longer the rubber gun, the greater the range. The length of the gun used, however, always depends on the visibility. The poorer the visibility the shorter the gun should be, since you must be able to see the end of the gun at all times.

The type of game hunted depends on the environment and the terrain, just as on land. Bill Barada, a 40-year diving veteran and author of **Spearfishing: How and Where**, quotes an old-timer's view of the sport: "It's just a question of being at the right spot at the right time, and knowing what to do when it happens."

Not all spots are the right ones, the productive ones. Reefs, wrecks, oil rigs, and rocks with an underwater kelp forest are some of the best places to hunt.

Fish, like land animals, must be stalked. It's a game of hide and seek. The fish hide, and you seek. Fish have a sense organ in their lateral line that awakens them to danger, and since fish reactions are about four times faster than yours, the trick is to convince the fish that you aren't dangerous. Your movements must be in slow motion to make no ripples, either above or below the surface.

Getting a good shot at the fish requires the type of skill and knowledge that comes only from experience. Some fish can be enticed to come within range. The Pacific Jewfish, for example, will come closer if you bang two pieces of metal together. Strumming the gun rubbers and flashing the crystal reflection of your diver's watch are two more tricks that will entice fish closer. The White Seabass, however, is too wise for any of this. Even Scuba bubbles will chase him away, so free diving is the only way to land this species.

Most fish should be shot behind the gills in line with the eye. The fish's head is usually solid bone, so if you hit it there, you will only injure and not kill it. An injured fish will charge in the direction it is facing, so getting in the way of a large injured fish could cause you injury.

Randy Seitz, a diving instructor with 18 years of spearfishing ("sticking", he calls it) experience, cites several other dangers.

"The biggest danger is other people. If they don't know what they're doing, they may stick you instead of a fish," he says. Randy strongly recommends that you take the fish to the surface as soon as you hit it, too, because blood in the water can attract sharks and seals. During mating season, male seals consider you a threat and they will bite.

Your local dive shop is the best source of spearfishing information – including dangers specific to your area. Some shops give spearfishing classes in which you can learn the right spots, the right times, and the proper techniques for landing fish.

As a final note, Randy Seitz adds a rule of ethics to the sport of spearfishing: "If you shoot it, you eat it."

–Jan Riddle

Jan Riddle has done a lot of spearfishing and, being from California, she has a lot of opportunities to practice the sport.

For More Information

There is one organization, the International Underwater Spearfishing Association, at the Los Angeles County Museum, Exposition Park, Los Angeles, Calif. 90007, which encourages underwater spearfishing as recreation and a potential source of scientific knowledge and sponsors several contests. For others, see Scuba Diving and Skin Diving.

Here is the only book we know of. It is available from World Publications, Box 366, Mountain View, Calif. 94040 at the price listed* plus 25 cents each postage.

Modern Spearfishing, Vane Ivanovic. A veteran spearfisherman with over 25 years of experience offers sound basic instruction and discusses equipment and underwater safety. Special section is devoted to spearfishing areas throughout the world. 1954 (rev. 1974) Hb. and Ppb., 208 pp., ill., $8.95/$4.95, (Regnery).

Speed Skating

If you see a person running sideways up a hill, chances are it's a speedskater. By crossing the right foot in front of the left foot going uphill they can simulate the skating motion, for training in the summer months when ice is not available. With a smooth, fluid motion skaters are now able to move around a 400 meter oval at speeds approaching 30 m.p.h. It is the world's fastest self-propelled sport.

Distances raced at the Olympics range from 500 meters to 10,000 meters. It is only the rare individual who can excel at both the sprint and endurance distances. Ard Schenk of the Netherlands showed this breadth of talent at the '72 winter Games in Sapporo, Japan, winning the 10,000, 5,000 and 1500 meter events. His pace in the 10,000 meter race was just slightly slower than the winning time for the 500 meters at the Olympics eight years earlier.

To achieve such consistent speed and form coaches watch for smoothness, rhythm, and extension of the pushing leg. The depth of the knee bend must be just right, and it will vary for the individual. A shorter person will probably bend less. Maximum power is developed on the corners by pushing with both feet, using the cross-over technique.

To skate forward pressure is applied at the rear of the skate. Like a slippery bar of soap, if it is pressed on the back it will scoot forward. Skaters balance to keep their body weight over the rear portion of the skate.

The skates move in a side to side motion, not from front to back. Top speed skaters generally have fast reflexes and are able to move their legs at a high tempo. Sprinters generally are not taller than 5'8" or 9".

Training for speed skating begins as soon as the competitive season ends. This dry training runs from March to October or November. Artificial skating is practiced on a door covered with formica, with bumpers at either end. Wearing thick socks the skater simulates the skating motion slipping from side to side along the board. It is sprayed with silicon or other similar substances to keep it smooth. Hill running, going up sideways, strengthens the corner stroke motion, through severe training on ski hills that tax the leg muscles to the extreme. Cycling is an excellent conditioner since it most closely resembles the speed and steady rhythm of speed skating. Often racers bike 50 to 100 miles per day in the off season. The Norwegian training manual advises that on Sunday, for a day of relaxation, racers take a leisurely 100 mile bicycle ride through hilly country. Weight training develops power in the legs and upper body. When skating the back is bent forward, so strengthening the back muscles keeps them from tiring in that position.

On the ice in the fall skaters work on the distance that is their specialty. They generally work with a teammate, timing each other's laps and offering advice on technique. Many US skaters unfortunately have to train in Europe, because there is only one Olympic 400 meter oval in the United States, in West Allis, Wisconsin. In Japan, for instance, there are 11 such tracks, four in Germany, etc. Due to limited funds the one US track cannot open until late November, just one month before our Olympic team trials. Our best skaters, at their own expense, make an annual pilgrimage to Norway, Holland, Germany and Austria for the ice and coaching that will prepare them for international competition.

The total budget to support our speed skaters is about $40,000 per year, with some more money available during the Olympic year. The governments of Norway, Sweden and Holland will spend $200,000 to $350,000 for their speed skating programs. In the US funds come from the Olympic committee and other private sources—none from the federal government.

Facing all these hardships, our skaters have done an outstanding job. In 1968 Terry McDermott, Jeanne Fish and Mary Myers each brought home one medal, and Dianne Holum two, for a total of five out of the seven medals won by our winter Olympic team. In 1972 American speed skaters won four of the eight medals taken by our winter Olympic team. At the Games Anne Henning set an Olympic record for the 500 meter event.

In world's competition Sheila Young won the 1973 sprint event and in '74, Leah Poulas won the overall championship.

Due to the diverse climate in the US, the numerous hockey rinks and the lack of official Olympic size tracks, speed skating is conducted on many different size tracks.

Indoor events are conducted on a 16 lap safety track, each lap a distance of 110 yards or 100 meters. This oval will fit within a hockey rink 85 feet wide and 185 to 200 feet long.

Outdoor tracks in areas where you can expect a deep winter freeze are the largest. The smallest outdoor track is usually eight laps to the mile, and often six laps to the mile. The American Skating Union recognizes only the four lap track for the National Championships.

Because of the different cornering styles required for these different sized tracks, a skater may use two or three different pairs of skates each season.

On the short tracks of 16 and 12 laps to the mile the blade of the skate will be very short and a little higher than the outdoor models. The blades will usually be offset to the left side of each foot. This allows the skater to lean harder into the turns with less fear of falling.

On the longer outdoor track the blade is usually longer to give a better glide with each stroke. As the lean is lessened the blade is mounted more in the center of the boot.

—**Einar Jonland**

Einar Jonland is the immediate past president of the Amateur Skating Union of the US, director of the US International Skating Association, and is planning the first indoor speed skating championship to be held in Champaign, Ill. in April, 1976. He is a former midwestern figure skating champion.

For More Information

We found one good magazine on speed skating. *The Racing Blade,* c/o Dorothy and Milan Novak, editors, 1231 Sobre Lomas, Tucson, Ariz. 85718. Published in six issues from Sept. to spring at $5.00 per year.

Here are two speed skating organizations. United States International Skating Assn., c/o President, George Howie, Beggs Isle, Oconomowoc, Wisc. 53066. Amateur Skating Union of the United States, Secretary, Lawrence Ralston, 4423 W. Deming Place, Chicago, Ill. 60639.

Squash Racquets

The game of squash racquets is one in which a rubber ball is hit with a racket (in construction it falls somewhere between a badminton and tennis racket) onto a hard-surfaced wall made of either wood or cement. Cement walls, however, are not regulation.

A squash court consists of an enclosed rectangle that has four of these walls, any of which the ball may be played off of.

During a game, the ball is returned alternately by the two (or four in doubles) players. In order for a shot to be good it must hit the front wall between the telltale and the topmost red line before hitting the floor. The ball has to be hit on the fly and it can hit the side walls or back wall before reaching the front wall. A player can score while being the server or receiver and a player continues to serve as long as he wins points. The winner is the first player to receive 15 points. However, if the score reaches 13-all or 14-all the number of points needed to win is reset and the game continued.

Courtesy toward the opponent is an important feature of squash. A player must give his adversary room to swing in this relatively small enclosure – even if it means placing himself at a disadvantage. Failure to observe this unwritten rule may result in a serious accident. In essence, this is a unique principle that applies to few other sports: to do your best to keep your opponent from hitting the ball at one moment and in the next making equally sure that you do not interfere with his right to do so. If the players are playing a game of doubles, this aspect of the game becomes even more important.

A fact, which is not unusual in many sports, is that serious squash players are very devoted to their game, perhaps even a trifle more so than participants in other activities. Whereas professional tennis players, for instance, may win large sums of money in major tournaments, in squash this is impossible because of the necessarily small spectator areas which are considered large if they seat 50 people. The best squash players do not make much by competing, but with the development of tough, clear plastic walls that can be set up in large arenas this may change in the future.

Squash, What?

Squash Racquets – there is history in the name. Like thoroughbred race horses, racquet sports have bloodlines that converge to a narrow point. It all began in the 16th century with court tennis, a stately exercise contested in a fenestrated, high-ceilinged gallery across a slack net with lopsided racquets, to the accompaniment of a medieval French lexicon.

By the 19th century, English schoolboys were playing a souped-up derivative of court tennis called, simply, rackets. Along with the French spelling, the net had been dispensed with. Play was made by belting a small rock-hard ball off the front, side and back walls, while the opponents maneuvered in

Squash is a game which demands intense concentration and well planned split-second movements. Not only does a player have to be constantly aware of the position of the rebounding ball and his opponent, but he must adapt quickly from a position of hitting the ball to retrieving the shot made by the player. The small playing area also makes courtesy between players extremely important. (Duffy)

the same court. It was – and still is in the few places where courts remain – one heck of a game. The racquet, longer by 3 inches than a conventional squash racquet, moves the projectile at great speeds. A blow in the head is likely to be fatal. Despite that fact – or possibly because of it – lads at Eaton and Harrow lined up to play. To bide their time and to warm up while waiting for the court, someone devised a soft, inflated India rubber ball that could be knocked up against the outside wall – the 19th century equivalent of the plastic golf ball that suburban gents whack around their back yards today.

Compared to the rifle crack of the solid racket ball (wound and bound like a modern baseball), the new rubber ball made a soft, squashy sound. And, surprisingly, it presented a special kind of challenge. A new racquet sport was born. The original game of rackets became known as hard rackets. The new game was squash rackets – or now that it has all but eclipsed its progenitor, simply squash.

Because the rubber ball moved more slowly, squash could be played in a smaller room. The walls could be lined in hard wood instead of the slate required for hard rackets. The expensive racquets did not break so frequently. The rallies were longer. Altogether, squash proved more suitable to the pace and economy of the 20th century.

The game of squash entered the U.S. via Canada around the turn of the present century. St. Paul's, a boys' prep-school in Concord, N.H., takes credit for the first court. From there it spread to other schools and colleges and into country clubs and men's clubs in the major East Coast cities. People who played tennis in the summer outdoors, played squash in the winter indoors.

As the game developed on this side of the Atlantic, American taste modified it back in the direction of hard rackets. The English ball was thought to be too squashy. A harder, thicker-walled and heavier ball was designed. The pace of the game speeded up. As a result, two versions of squash exist today: the English game, played in Britain and in former crown colonies around the world with a truly squashy ball that can be mashed between thumb and forefinger; and the American game, played in Canada, the U.S. and Mexico, with a hard black rubber ball that barely bounces when dropped, but moves like black lightning around the court.

As with most players, my introduction to squash came at college. As a youth I had played some tennis, with only moderate success. Although I liked the game I had been put off by the fact that if I were not hitting properly, or if my opponent were not, if we netted the ball or hit it out of bounds, play stopped. We were continually picking up balls, walking about, taking position for the next point – in short, spending more time getting ready to play than playing. By contrast, play in a squash court is contained within four walls. It takes some doing to put the ball out of bounds or even below the 17-inch-high tell-tale mounted on the front wall.

The first time I tried squash at college – it was with a player equally callow as I – we had plenty of rousing, if inept rallies. I was encouraged to take the next step, to go into the court by myself and hit the ball. A few hours spent in the court alone goes a surprisingly long way to nail down the rudiments of the game. And, after that I was hooked for life.

It is inevitable when describing the attraction of squash to compare it to tennis. Both require the same hand-eye coordination, the same fierce concentration and attention to stroke production (though the strokes differ markedly).

The difference? There is no question that tennis, because it requires greater ball control, is the more difficult game to master – which, depending on one's point of view, is either a plus or a minus. And tennis is played out of doors—a plus in anyone's book. But squash demands a player to be quicker on his feet; it provides more concentrated exercise. A half hour of squash is equal to at least twice the time on a tennis court. But the greatest difference between the two games is that squash puts opposing players in the same court. The battle is more intimately joined, more physical. This almost-body-contact, the electric speed and the condensed nature of the game make squash, for this player at least, the ultimate racquet sport.

—**Peter Wood**

Peter Wood has played squash for more than two decades. Besides being the author of **The Book of Squash** *he has been a high-ranked national veteran player.*

For More Information

One magazine covers the sport: *Squash Racquets U.S.A.*, Box 11051, Salt Lake City, Utah 84111. There are several organizations and the main one is the United States Squash Racquets Association, 211 Ford Rd., Bala-Cynwyd, Pa. 19004. This organization runs regional and national amateur tournaments and in conjunction with Canada runs the North American Open. It is the central organization for establishing playing rules and court and equipment specifications.

There aren't too many books available now on squash, but the number is growing with its popularity. Here are some good ones. All are available from World Publications, Box 366, Mountain View, Calif. 94040 at the price listed* plus 25 cents each postage. Write for a complete list.

Sports Illustrated Squash, staff of *Sports Illustrated*. This fast-moving court game is taught with SI's usual tradition of photos and drawings. A good guide for the beginner embellished by tips from champions. 1971 Hb. & Ppb., 96 pp., ill., $4.95/$1.95, (Lippincott).

The Book of Squash, Peter Wood. Squash, once the game of wealthy players and exclusive colleges, is sweeping the nation. Here in one enthusiastic guide are the rules, history and instructions on how to develop your swing, serve, return and volley. Extensive photographs. 1972 Hb. & Ppb., 127 pp., ill., $8.95/$3.95, (Van Nostrand Reinhold/Little, Brown & Co.)

Squash Racquets, John Skillman. An outstanding coach and player presents all the basic strokes and plays, discusses selection of equipment, training and the official playing rules and court specifications. 1964 Hb., 86 pp., ill., $8.65, (Ronald).

Richard Hawkey: Squash Rackets, Richard Hawkey. The famous Director of Coaching for the Squash Rackets Association explains how to play the sport, describing training methods and equipment, tactics and all the British rules of play. 1975 Library Binding, 62 (oversize) pp., ill., $5.95, (Pelham).

The Science and Strategy of Squash, John Truby, Jr. Covers all the strokes and strategies with a scientific and systematic approach. 1975 Hb., 260 pp., ill., $12.50, (Scribner's).

Squash Racquets: The Khan Game. Hashim Khan. Professionals and amateurs agree that Hashim Khan is the world's greatest squash racquets player, and this is his own story, told verbally to player and writer Richard Randall. A wealth of squash experience, anecdotes and game strategy and technique. 1967 Ppb., 160 pp., ill., $3.95, (Wayne University Press).

Sumo Wrestling

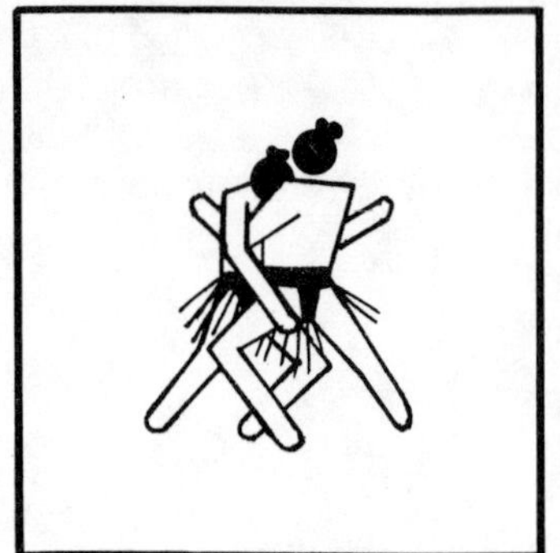

Sumo is the time-honored traditional sport of Japan that dates back to pre-Christian times. "The Sport of Emperors" as it was called, engaged particularly large and strong men in wrestling matches in sacred temples and imperial palaces. Young men throughout Japan would grapple in sumo rings, developing reputations in hopes that they, too, would one day be invited to train and be champions.

Although professional sumo began long ago in the 16th century, the sport continues much the same today. You can find sumo rings in many of the rural parts of Japan, from which nearly all modern sumo wrestlers still come. The everyday physical labors of farming and fishing seem to develop boys to a larger, sturdier size at an earlier age. Very few city-bred sumo wrestlers ever gain success.

Sumos apprentice at a very young age, about 13 to 14 years, but must meet size requirements: five-foot-six-inches in height and 160 pounds in weight. (The requirements become higher and higher as modern nutrition builds bigger and bigger aspirants.) Once invited, an apprentice sumo joins up to 100 others who train for competition, novices and veterans together, all men.

The novice will rise very early (five or six a.m.) to clean the practice area and begin his warm-up exercises. Without breakfast he must practice four hours under the supervision of the elders who are gentle but very demanding. He will serve the mid-day meal to the elders then leave to soak his exhausted body in a hot tub before he ever indulges in the common stew, chanko.

The young boy will grow in size and strength, participating in tournaments judged by boy officials who also must begin their training as youngsters. It will be a long time, however, before the sumo boys are part of the maku-uchi group of champions. It will take years of learning before they develop the thick, strong stomach characteristic of the sumo, develop the low balance point, increase hip flexibility, and solidify the strong, sturdy legs that sumo requires. They also must grow as large in proportions as possible to gain weight advantage for leverage. Sumos can be over six feet in height and over 300 pounds in weight. One 17th century behemoth was reported to be 7'5" tall and over 400 pounds in weight!

Sumo wrestlers participate regularly in tournaments. Six are held each year in Japan under the jurisdiction of the Japan Sumo Association. Tournaments were once five day affairs; however, as competition became tougher, they were extended to 15 days with the novices competing earlier in the day and the older, more skilled sumos wrestling in the afternoon.

"Ranked" sumo wrestlers are listed on an official roster still written in Chinese characters. As a competitor is successful, his rank is raised; if he is unsuccessful, it is lowered. Only a *yokozuna* or grand champion can never have his title revoked. Scores or win-loss records sound like batting averages in baseball, with the most successful sumos averaging .920 or .948.

The actual competition matches are partly brute strength, partly good technique and partly mental preparation. Most Westerners fail to comprehend the significance of the former two components of sumo, thereby losing a real appreciation of the sport. The clapping, stomping, and salt throwing are all forms of invocation and mental preparation. The four-minute *shikiri-naoshi,* or stare down, that *seems* to be comparable to the psyche job that professional wrestlers put into their "act" is really the wrestler's time to "read" the opponent, size him up, and show him he is aggressive and ready to wrestle.

The wrestlers meet at the end of this preliminary period in the *tach-ai* or first encounter. They pull, push, slap, throw, and trip the opponent out of the 18-foot ring to win. Most matches last only a few seconds and rarely, if ever, go over one minute. The big man who is aggressive and clever in the ring usually wins.

Although the matches are exciting they are but one part of the pageantry and tradition that surrounds sumo wrestling. In one of the six yearly tournaments it is not just the competition that prevails. The atmosphere of ceremony and dignity, sportsmanship with humility, the mixture of modernity and antiquity touches everyone in the arena. Participating or watching sumo wrestling is really participating in the cultural heritage of Japan.

For More Information

We have one book covering sumo. It is available from World Publications, Box 366, Mountain View, Calif. 94040 at the price listed* plus 25 cents postage.

Sumo: The Sport and the Tradition, J.A. Sargeant. Sumo, "The Sport of Emperors" in Japan, dates back before the Christian era. The only English language work on the subject, this book explains the exciting sport, its history, its pagenatry, its nomenclature, its techniques and its charm. 1959 Ppb., 96 pp., ill., $3.25, (Tuttle).

Surfing (Board)

Surfing could be defined as the art of sliding down the face of a wave in a controlled manner." Steve Pezman, *Surfer* magazine.

It is thought that the sport originated in Polynesia, although primitive forms of wave riding can also be found in the Carribean and along the western coast of Africa.

It was in Hawaii, however, that the sport flourished, and was first described by Captain Cook and later by such notable romantics as Mark Twain and Jack London, who were captivated by its grace and poetic beauty. In those early days of surfing, it was primarily the Hawaiian Alii, or royalty, that were allowed to practice the sport, riding 150-pound olo boards, as a demonstration of their favorable relationship with the sea gods. As the true Hawaiian culture began to diminish in the 1800s, surfing also subsided, only to reappear in the early 1900s in the Waikiki area from whence it developed as one of the trademarks of a flourishing Hawaiian tourist industry.

In 1914, a Hawaiian beach boy named George Freeth introduced surfing to the US mainland, and later, emissaries such as Olympic swimming champion Duke Kahanamoku took it with them to Australia and other oceanfront countries.

It was in the late 1940's and 1950's that surfing, through the adaptation of modern technology applied to surfboards (making them lighter and more maneuverable), really caught on as an expressive and widely popular form of recreation. By 1965, there were over 1,000,000 surfers in the US, another 1,000,000 in Australia, and yet another 500,000 practicing the joys of riding ocean waves in such far-flung corners of the earth as France, England, South Africa, New Zealand, Brazil, Peru, Samoa, Japan, and even the chilly shores of Lake Michigan (no foolin'). At present, the sport is more widely practiced and in greater numbers than ever before, as surfers discover that our ocean-covered globe has potentially many thousands of suitable surf breaks yet to be discovered and ridden for the first time.

—Steve Pezman

Steve Pezman is the editor and publisher of **Surfer** *magazine.*

This Great Sport

The art of wave riding is an intensely personal and magically gratifying experience. Perhaps it is man's age-old urge to fly, manifested in soaring and gliding across a wave, that is the secret of its pleasure. Surfing takes many forms, from sliding down the front of a wave using only one's body as a planing surface, to the use of belly (paipo) boards, kneeboards (slightly longer than paipos), and the conventional longer "stand-up" surfboard. Up until the late 1950's, stand-up surfing was primarily based on catching a cresting wave before it broke, and coasting straight towards shore with a wall of pounding white water pushing you in. However, a new era of surfing began as boards grew lighter and shorter, with the addition of a rear-mounted fin or skeg (for directional control). Surfing turned into a game of racing *across* the wall of a wave, staying right in the curl (the hook of the wave as it pitches over), and maneuvering both board and body in the most graceful and elegant manner possible.

Surfers compared themselves to a matador "dancing within the circle of death" (the range of a bull's horns at any given moment), and were given to a search for breaks that provided an evenly curling wave of good size, with a long, clean wall to carve and arch across. Such classic breaks as Malibu and Rincon Point in California, Sunset Beach, the Banzai Pipeline, and Waimea Bay in Hawaii, and comparable waves in other countries became famous for the rides they offered, and for the various surfers who became known as masters of those unique breaks.

Every surf break, indeed, every set of waves, has a character all its own, with no two rides being exactly alike, and with no two waves presenting the same challenge. And while the waves are infinitely varied, the surfers who ride them are the same. Some surfers feel that riding a wave is like looking at one's self in a mirror. It's a chance to blend and flow with an incredible and dazzling natural force which allows you to taste, for an instant, its innermost secrets, or to be roughly chided if you fail to sync yourself with its power. Once you experience the widely exotic sensations of a tube ride (inside the curl), or a successful set of maneuvers executed at high speed (surfing speeds vary from 5 to 35 mph), it becomes a feeling that you will have the urge to find time and time again.

Surfing combines the athletic grace of a dancer/gymnast with a deep knowledge of the sea in all its variety of conditions, and the art of creating sculptured surfboards (much like fine musical instruments) that allow you to impose your own individual style and form of attack.

Surfing is something that no one has ever truly been able to describe in mere words; it's something you have to feel for yourself. Phil Edwards, considered to be the greatest surfer of the last 20 years, puts it this way:

"It's an adventure to get on a surfboard and paddle out. Something is going to happen to you."

—**Steve Pezman**

It's like being born again. Terry Fitzgerald way back in the green room at Velzyland on the North Shore of Oahu. You can almost feel the whitewater pouring down across your back on this fast, hollow, hard-breaking wave. (Weaver, courtesy of *Surfer* magazine)

For More Information

There are two major surfing publications: *Surfing*, 27635Q Forbes Rd., Laguna Niguel, Calif. 91677. Published bi-monthly at $6.50 per year. And *Surfer,* Box 1028, Dana Point. Calif. 92629. Published bi-monthly at $6.00 per year. Both are good magazines. There is one organization we know about: Western Surfing Association, 2024 West Cliff Dr., Santa Cruz, Calif. 95060. They sponsor surfing competition. The magazines are filled with contacts for equipment.

Before you grab that board you might want to check out these books. All are available from World Publications, Box 366, Mountain View, Calif. 94040 at the price listed* plus 25 cents each postage. Write for a complete list.

How to Surf, James Wagenvoord and Lynn Bailey. A famous outdoor sports author gives a quick but comprehensive overview of the proper techniques for surfing. 1968 Ppb., 96 (oversize) pp., ill., $2.95, (MacMillan).

The Surfing Life, Midget Farrelly. A book on the techniques of surf riding, and on the surf and surfing champions. Valuable advice on the world's best surfing areas, how to make your own board, and body surfing. 1967 Hb., 196 pp., ill., $4.95, (Arco).

Surfing: A Handbook, William Desmond Nelson. Talks to the beginning surfer, although the intermediate or expert can still learn from it. Included are basic how-tos, buying, techniques, where to go, physics of surfing, and special chapters on the woman surfer and surfers over 30. 1973 Hb., 237 pp., ill., $12.50, (Auerbach).

Survival

Considering the way most people act when lost in the wilderness, it's a wonder the human race survived at all. Modern life seems to have short-circuited our survival instincts. We continually venture into the wilderness looking for peace and quiet, or excitement and adventure. Often we end up with nothing but misery and discomfort.

As more and more people have responded to the appeal of the great outdoors, there have been greater and greater demands on Search and Rescue (SAR) organizations and volunteers. In just the opening weekend of the hunting season in Washington state this year, there were 12 SAR missions for lost hunters.

Most of these emergency situations are easily avoidable and would be little more than minor inconveniences if we were properly prepared and used a little common sense. The old adage, "survival of the fittest", is a little out of date in the modern world. Fitness helps, of course, but preparation and common sense are more important.

We are bombarded with so many erroneous tidbits of information in newspapers and magazines and movies that it is hard to approach any emergency sensibly. As we read "she ate toothpaste and chewed on a belt" or "they ate snow to stay alive," what are we expected to believe? As we watch a movie of people working in the heat of the desert day trying to get their aircraft flying and to clear a runway for takeoff, losing two gallons of precious body water through sweat in the process, is it any wonder that we develop a false set of survival priorities? Is it any wonder that we try to walk back to civilization when the best thing to do would be to get shelter and wait for rescue?

Have you ever noticed a person carrying a huge "hero" knife just in case he ever ends up in a survival situation? Most of these people end up needing their knives because of the energy they burn carrying them around. And since we are supposed to carry a compass when heading for the wilds, most hikers buy the readily available import that points to Japan, or if they buy the better quality one it is with the idea that the rescuers who come looking for him may know how to use it. The what-we-think-we-are-going-to-need syndrome, based on the idea of "survival by fighting against the elements" is really inappropriate.

Wilderness survival, or survival anywhere for that matter, really boils down to maintaining as high a degree of mental alertness and competence as is possible for as long as possible. When we become mentally inefficient for any reason at all, we begin to make mistakes, and once that starts to happen the outcome of the situation may rest upon luck. If some of the mistakes are made on critical decisions, the consequences could be devastating. If you spend a little time pondering what it really takes in order to survive and how you can prepare for that unexpected emergency situation, you will have an excellent opportunity of turning the odds for survival in a favorable direction.

Life's necessities are a PMA (Positive Mental Attitude), oxygen, shelter, rest, water and food. These are the basic elements of life. They are needed daily as well as in survival situations. The only difference is that we become responsible for furnishing these needs if we are faced with a survival emergency. In order to get some understanding of which of these needs must be satisfied during survival, take this article out into the chilly night. After sitting there until you have cooled down a little, try to visualize which necessity you need to take care of first. If you don't have a PMA you really won't be able to think correctly and the rest wouldn't matter. Since air seems to be in sufficient quantity and we aren't at a high altitude or suffering from a medical emergency, it is not a concern. Out of the remaining (shelter, rest, water and food), what do you think is next in importance?

We probably would desire a little better shelter – clothing is a type of shelter – before we need a snack or a nap. Try sleeping in your yard tonight dressed in fairly warm clothing and you will probably do a lot of star or weather gazing. After shelter usually comes the need for rejuvenation, which can be accomplished through rest. After rest comes water. We can survive 3 days without water in the hot desert if we conserve the water already in our system by obtaining shaded shelter and minimizing our activity during the hotter daylight hours.

Now comes food. As far as I know, the record for fasting is held by a lady who went for 249 days without eating, under the scrutiny of a doctor. That's a little better than eight months. If she can go that long, we should be able to go at least 30 days. It is really sad to see people so obsessed with food that they load their survival kit with snare wire and fishing gear and leave out shelter material.

When we really analyze survival situations, we find that most are over within 24 hours. With a degree of bad luck, the longer ones are almost always over in 72 hours. In that period of time, which of the needs don't deserve much worry? Food and water are the first removed from immediate needs. Rest will only be effective when we obtain the proper shelter and air is usually in abundance. That leaves PMA and shelter from the elements.

Here is one possible approach to a wilderness emergency. When you are in doubt about the outcome of your situation, you should stop and start considering some options. Now that you have stopped, even if you had to hug a tree to do so, start thinking in terms of keeping your mind about yourself. This can be accomplished if you think about the real dangers of the situation (these are probably few, if any) and the resources that you have to work with. Most problems we face can be reduced to minor inconveniences at worst, if we simply take the time to think them through.

You might immediately signal by yelling loudly or blowing a whistle in the hopes someone may be in the area and can offer assistance. If that brings no immediate results, consider finding proper shelter from the elements. If the weather is good, the situation is probably not very serious. If you have good weather, what problems do you really face?

Bears? Bears don't eat people or they would live in cities where they could eat anytime they wanted to. The only real problem you will face will be yourself and giving in to panic or confused thinking.

After you have taken care of shelter, if you can drink some

warm fluids for morale and internal heat, it would be quite a bonus. Signalling should be a high priority. Making yourself contrast with the surrounding environment is the key. Disturbing the vegetation in the area, green evergreen boughs (used only during emergencies) tossed onto a hot fire, or any number of ingenious approaches will do the trick. Adding a few of the boughs to the floor of your shelter will help to insulate you from the cold ground.

You may find that once you stop and regain full mental composure, you will be able to handle the survival circumstances very easily. You may even be able to start working with SAR by telling people about your experience. The key to any emergency is to obtain and maintain that positive air about yourself, that PMA. It will pay off in many ways in everyday life as well as during a survival emergency.

—**Tim Kneeland**

Tim Kneeland is a former U.S. Air Force survival instructor. He founded and currently directs the Institute for Survival Education in Seattle, Washington.

For More Information

Two good sources for information: Council for Survival Education, Box 13117, Ft. Carson, Colo. 80913 and Survival Education Association, c/o Gene Fear, 9035 Golden Given Rd., Tacoma, Wash. 98445. Also the United States Air Force Survival School, Fairchild AFB, Washington 99011 will send out information and let you know of other resources. The Aviation Seminars on Survival, Box 1296, Ventura, Calif. 93001 is a new organization establishing seminars for pilots. Additional information can be obtained from these books. All are available from World Publications, Box 366, Mountain View, Calif. 94040 at the price listed* plus 25 cents postage. Write for a complete list.

Outdoor Survival Skills, Larry Olsen. How to survive in the wilderness with nothing but the shirt on your back. Advice on making natural shelters, locating and obtaining water, the gathering and preparation of wild foods and tool-making. Numerous color plates identify various plants that can be used or eaten. 1973 Hb. & Ppb., 188 pp., ill., $7.95/$4.95, (Brigham Young University).

The Survival Book, Paul Nesbitt, et al. "This book is highly recommended . . . for all who might possibly find themselves stranded some day . . . " San Francisco Chronicle. Incredibly comprehensive book that covers so many situations that can happen anywhere . . . a veritable encyclopedia of survival. Ppb., 352 pp., ill., $1.95, (Crowell).

Survival with Style, Bradford Angier. Sensible and entertaining tips on how to keep body and soul together in the wilderness—how to find drinking water, how to understand weather indicators, how to stay warm . . . build a shelter . . . live off the earth. 1972 Ppb., 320 pp., ill., $2.45, (Random House).

How to Survive in the Wilderness, Prepared by the US Air Force. This manual provides a complete course in survival training covering fatigue, hunger, thirst, sleep, shelters, fire making, tool improvisation, trapping and hunting, fishing and foraging, orientation, forests and deserts, digging for water, and rescue. 1975, 256 (oversize) pp., $5.95, (Drake).

Bushcraft, Richard Graves. An encyclopedic guide to subsistence-level survival for long periods in inhospitable environments, by the leader of the Australian Jungle Rescue Detachment. 1972 Hb. & Ppb., 346 pp., ill., $10.00/$3.95, (Schocken).

The Survival Handbook, Bill Merrill. Drawing on his 36 years with the US Forest and Park Services, the author not only explains how to avoid trouble in all kinds of terrain and weather, but also provides detailed advice on shelter, food and first aid for those caught unexpectedly in emergency situations. 1972 Hb., 312 pp., ill., $5.95, (Winchester).

Alive: The Story of the Andes Survivors, Piers Paul Reed. The story of a Uruguayan rugby team's struggle for survival in the rugged Andes, following the crash of their plane in 1972. An unforgettable book on survival. 1974 Hb. & Ppb., 318 pp., ill., $8.95/$1.95, (Avon).

Wilderness Survival, Berndt Berglund. How to survive with what's there in the North American wilds. Ideas are from the author's experience living with Eskimo and Indian guides. 1974 Ppb., 175 pp., ill., $3.50, (Scribner's).

Frostbite, B. Washburn. A highly recommended guide to the cause, prevention and treatment of frostbite. 1963 Ppb., 25 pp., $1.50, (Museum of Science).

Swimming

Swimming is one of the most ancient sports known to man. The Greeks and Romans swam regularly and swimming competitions were recorded as early as 36 B.C. in Japan. Modern organized swimming began in the early 1800's in England and three events were held in the first modern Olympic Games in Athens, 1896. The world governing body, Federation Internationale de Natation Amateur (F.I.N.A.) was founded 12 years later in 1908, and designated the first list of official world records.

Today, F.I.N.A. recognizes only records set in 50-meter pools. The following are official events: 100, 200, 400, 800 (women) and 1500 (men) meters freestyle; 100, 200 m. backstroke; 100, 200 m. breaststroke; 100, 200 m. butterfly; and 200 and 400 m. individual medley (equal distances of each of the four competitive strokes); 400 and 800 (men)m. freestyle relay and 400 m. medley relay, which are all contested in the World Aquatic Championships. Records are also recognized in the men's 800 m. freestyle, women's 1500 m. freestyle, and women's 800 m. freestyle relay. Due to economy measures, fewer events are swum in the Olympic Games.

Although swimming as a competitive sport takes place primarily in pools, marathon swims also have their challenges. Attempted crossings in lakes, oceans and channels are frequent, with the English Channel being the most famous. Long distance swims are also the only area in which there is any professionalism in the sport. There is a World Professional

"I always reasoned that the more I hurt in workout the less it would hurt in a meet. When I think back on it I really don't know how I made my body do it, except that I wanted to go to the Olympics more than anything else and I was going to give myself the best chance that I could." (Duffy)

Marathon Association, which sponsors a series of races in the U.S., Canada, South America, and Egypt. These races range from 10 miles in length to an unlimited distance to be swum within a time limit, for example, of 24 hours. Prizes of one or several thousand dollars may sound glamorous, but often barely cover expenses. Only the hardiest survive for long in this branch of swimming.

We are probably most familiar, however, with those who merely paddle around to keep cool on hot summer days. Or you may know one of the hundreds of thousands of children and teenagers who participate in age group swimming programs with competitions at local, state, regional and national levels. This extensive base has produced perhaps the best group of swimmers in the world. Members of the elite train from four to five hours a day, nearly all year round. The U.S. also boasts a growing masters program, which offers opportunities for training and competition to those over 25.

A Dream Come True

Swimming was the greatest time of my life. I had a special group of friends, something to do to keep me busy, and above all something that I had to do on my own. Sure, you have all the help that others can give, but you are the one that has to get up at 6:30 a.m. for morning workout, knowing that it is 34 degrees outside, and you have to swim outdoors no less! The roughest part is to keep your arms going when you are hurting so much that your stomach has turned inside out.

When I was training for the Olympic Games my life was very simple. It consisted mainly of two things: swimming and school. That was the toughest year that I ever went through while I was competing, but I was lucky enough to have one of the greatest coaches in the world to help get me through the ordeal. Above all, I could not do it without the backing of my family. Your family has to give you support when you need it and refrain from undue pressure or push.

It is funny how your mind reacts in the year leading up to the Olympics. You cannot do anything that would have any chance of injury. You could have a hangnail and all of a sudden your mind has you in a hospital room dying of it. And it is not the dying that tears you up, but the idea that you won't be able to swim any more that year and you blew your chances for the Olympic Team. You take scrupulous care of yourself. Naps, good food, no junk, and no other activity than swimming.

Now, the training was not so easy either! I always reasoned that the more I hurt in workout the less it would hurt in a meet. There were a couple of times that I worked so hard that the meal I ate before workout would find itself in the bathroom toilet. Then I would go back for more laps. When I think back on it I really don't know how I made my body do it, except that I wanted to go to the Olympics more than anything else and I was going to give myself the best chance that I could. I was spending five hours a day in the water and no way was I going to waste that much time or effort. To keep myself going I would sing to myself while I was swimming laps. Swimming can be boring to spectators but imagine us going up and down the pool 1400 times. That is in only one workout! Believe me, the bottom of the pool does look the same the whole way, although maybe you would run across a clump of hair or even some leftover money from recreation swimming.

The best part of swimming was the trips. The Olympics was

"If you are lucky enough to have won, the joy you feel is indescribable. You really don't have a chance to ponder the subject 'til they give you your medal and start the National Anthem. You are happy, sad, excited, and filled with so many emotions at the same time it is difficult to separate them. It is one of the most beautiful moments of your life, one that you can pull out for years, look at, and feel the goosebumps all over again." (Duffy)

the most fun, most thrilling, and the most horrible experience I have ever had. I have never been so scared in all my life! I lived on three hours of sleep every night, lost 10 pounds (while eating a tray of food for every meal), and swam my races a million times before I even got in the water for the real thing. Funny though, when you are swimming your races it is just another meet. But when you finish you realize that this is the race that you have waited years for. If you are lucky enough to have won, the joy you feel is indescribable. You really don't have a chance to ponder the subject till they give you your medal and start the National Anthem. You are happy, sad, excited, and filled with so many emotions at the same time it is difficult to separate them. It is one of the most beautiful moments of your life. One that you can pull out for years, look at, and feel the goose bumps all over again. I loved my swimming; it wasn't easy but it was so well worth it.

—Keena Rothhammer

Keena Rothhammer was the gold medalist in the 800 m. freestyle at the 1972 Olympic Games. She is now retired but is involved in broadcasting with CBS.

For More Information

Almost every country has its own swimming magazine or newsletter. In the US, we have *Aquatic World,* Box 366, Mountain View, Calif. 94040, which carries feature articles on top athletes, training methods, psychology, and all phases of the sport. Bi-monthly, for $4.50 per year. *Swimming World,* 8622 Bellanca Avenue, Los Angeles, Calif. 90045, has articles and extensive results from competitions around the country and the world. Monthly, $9.00 per year. Amateur competitive swimming is governed by the Amateur Athletic Union, 3400 West 86th Street, Indianapolis, Ind. 46268. Under its auspices is the Masters Swim Program, 5340 N.E. 17th Ave., Ft. Lauderdale, Fla. 33308, which offers recreational and competitive swimming to those over 25 years. The United States Swimming Foundation, Reed & Washington Streets, Reading, Penn. 19601, is a new organization which will promote all phases of aquatic sport and programs.

Swimming books are easy to find, but here are some of the better ones. All are available from World Publications, Box 366, Mountain View, Calif. 94040 at the price listed* plus 25 cents each postage. Write for a complete list.

Inside Swimming, Don Schollander. A guide by one of the finest Olympic swimmers of the past decade. In addition to valuable commentary on swimming basics, the many amusing anecdotes of Schollander's career make it "must" reading for swimmers. 1974 Hb. & Ppb., 90 (oversize) pp., ill., $7.95/$3.95, (Regnery).

The Basic Swimming Guide, Joseph Groscost. A book about teaching children to swim. It gives the benefits of the author's experience teaching 3000 youngsters to swim in the last 12 years. Each skill is treated as a separate unit, with suggested teaching methods and an analysis. 1975, 100 pp., ill., $2.50, (World Publications).

Cecil Colwin on Swimming. South Africa's great coach has explained competitive swimming with masterful word pictures, diagrams and photos. 1969 Hb., 262 pp., ill., $6.50, (Pelham).

Swimming and Diving, Higgins, Barr & Grady. A complete treatise of swimming and diving for the newcomer as well as the experienced swimmer, including instructions on mouth-to-mouth resuscitation. 1962 Ppb., 345 pp., ill., $4.95, (Arco).

The 50-Meter Jungle, Sherman Chavoor and Bill Davidson. A controversial, hard-hitting book which exposes the phony amateurism, the pain, the behind-the-scenes squabbling of officials, coaches and parents, and all the other realities of big time "amateur" swimming competition. Written by a winning swim coach who's seen it all. 1973 Hb., 224 pp., ill., $6.95, (Coward, McCann & Geogheghan).

The Science of Swimming, James "Doc" Counsilman. A classic in its own time, this book by the Olympic men's coach is an outstanding study of training and theory that should be in every swimming library. 1968 Hb., 457 pp., ill., $13.95, (Prentice Hall).

Medical Aspects of Competitive Swimming for Coaches, Parents, and Swimmers, James T. Allardice. Covers all the physical and psychological problems encountered by swimmers and is a useful and valuable addition to the library of every swimming coach and family. 1972 Hb., 123 pp., ill., $5.95, (Pelham).

Forbes Carlile on Swimming. Marked by a refreshingly original style, good common sense and a deep understanding of swimming and swimmers, this book is a good companion fot the aspiring swimmer. 1963 Hb., 125 pp., ill., $4.95, (Pelham).

Land Conditioning for Competitive Swimming, J. M. Hogg. Exercises are listed under three main headings: strength, endurance and flexibility training. Numerous illustrations make this book easy to use. 1972 Hb., 260 pp., ill., $6.50, (E.P. Publishing).

Swimming, Don Gambril. An assistant coach for the US Men's Olympic team presents a scientific analysis of each type of swimming stroke, turn and start. Includes drills, exercises, and sequence drawings showing exact positioning of arms, legs, torso and head. 1969 Ppb., 88 pp., ill., $3.95, (Goodyear).

Sports Illustrated Swimming & Diving, Eds. of *SI.* Basic instruction in three swimming strokes and diving. Special advice for helping a child feel at home in the water. 1973 Hb. & Ppb., 95 pp., ill., $4.95/$1.95, (Lippincott).

Swim-Nastics, Sidney Shapiro. A guide to water exercises for better health. Gives sets of in-pool exercises to develop strength, stamina, flexibiliby and coordination. For competitive swimmers and fitness enthusiasts alike. 1971 Ppb., 76 pp., ill., $2.95, (Athletic Press).

Synchro Swimming

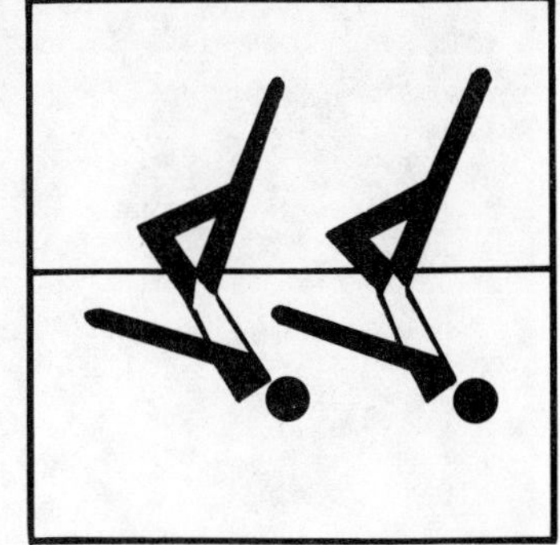

Few sports combine athletic skill and artistic ability to the degree found in synchronized swimming. Stationary poses, swimming movements and acrobatics in the water are pleasingly combined and synchronized to thematic music.

Synchronized swimming had its beginnings in the lavishly produced water shows of the 1930's. Then a spectacle of simple tricks and floating formations with a musical background, it has grown increasingly more complex and sophisticated up to the present. Routines are composed of difficult stunts and intricate swimming strokes, choreographed to theme music, and performed in synchronization to the music's beat and other swimmers.

National championships have been held since 1945. Synchronized swimming is recognized and controlled by the international swimming organization, F.I.N.A., and is included in the Pan American Games and the World Aquatic Championships while striving to become part of the Olympics.

The sport actually can take several different forms, depending on the aspirations and skill levels of the participants. At its most competitive, synchro swimmers are graded on the perfection of their stunts, and the originality and synchronization of their routines, whether solo, duet or team. The International Academy of Aquatic Art emphasizes the creativeness and artistic expression over technical skill and gives performers a critique. Members of the National Institute for Creative Aquatics use the technical skill of synchro and the artistic choreography from aquatic art to present aquatic compositions. Each develops many facets in its participants: ease in the water, coordination, endurance, strength, grace, creativity and appreciation for design and music.

Swimming's Precision Elite

Synchronized swimming – the poor relation in the aquatic kingdom, long scorned as easy by the swimmers, divers and water polo players, denied its status as sport by the Olympic organizers – still manages to attract new and talented swimmers. Participation in the World Aquatic Championships in 1973 and 1975 gave needed exposure to the swimming public, but synchro still suffers from a general lack of recognition and understanding.

Synchro combines many aspects of the other aquatic sports, but the synthesis leads to an aesthetic form not seen in the rest. Using swimming strokes, precisely judged body positions as in diving and making heavy use of water polo's 'egg beater' kick, synchro competitions end up like nothing so much as figure skating. And like figure skating, synchro has earned a reputation for long, exacting workouts.

Girls do not choose synchronized swimming solely on the basis of all that hard work. Rather, they are attracted by its graceful, feminine image combined with the opportunity to be active and compete in international sport.

"Synchro combines many aspects of the other aquatic sports, but the synthesis leads to an aethetic form not seen in the rest. Using swimming strokes, precisely judged body positions as in diving and making heavy use of water polo's 'egg beater' kick, synchro competitions end up like nothing so much as figure skating. And like figure skating, synchro has earned a reputation for long, exacting workouts." (Aquatic World)

The girls themselves are an interesting mixture of charm and competitiveness. Coming out for practice, they look much the same as the competitive swimmers, wearing tank suits, caps and goggles. Perhaps they are no prettier than other girls, but they move more gracefully and smile more quickly.

And they have dedication. To reach the top level on one of the better teams – synonymous with becoming a national-caliber competitor – takes five to six years of hard work. There are an incredible number of things to learn. For instance, on the Santa Clara Aquamaids, current national champions, girls from eight to about 12 or 13 try out for the team twice a year. If they are judged acceptable in their basic swimming skills (they are required to be at the intermediate level), and to have some athletic ability, they are accepted into a six month trainee program. The trainees come to practice twice a week, for an hour each time. They work on perfecting their strokes, learning simple stunts, and do lots of sculling – a very important method of propulsion and balance. At the end of the six-month trial period, the girls with the best mastery of skills are invited to join the club.

Providing she is still enthusiastic after what she has seen and experienced, and isn't afraid of hard work, a girl will join the club at the B team level. This level encompasses all the age groups and ability levels up to the A team. These girls train an average of two hours a day, four times a week. The striving for perfection begins here. They learn the five groups of stunts – Ballet Leg, Dolphin Feet First, Dolphin Head First, Somersaults and Diverse – and begin to attempt and master the simpler stunts in each group. They begin to synchronize the stunts to music and to coordinate their movements to other girls', one of the most difficult things to master. In a team routine, up to eight girls must move at the same speed and with the same degree of each movement. This is complicated by the fact that each individual has her own buoyancy level, and therefore her own adaptations in sculling and kicking. Stunts which appear beautiful and graceful on the surface require strenuous exertion below the surface. Ballet legs require sculling and breath holding for long periods of time. And when surfacing, it is not considered good form to take a big gulp of air. The egg-beater kick is used for support when making arm movements above the water and there are many more of these than in the past, when synchro often became a ballet of legs.

Moving up through the B team means increasingly difficult stunts and routines. Only the best eight girls are on the A team (enough for a team routine), and therefore vacancies occur rarely. But once a girl is on the A team, she is involved in an even more demanding schedule. The senior group trains six days a week, for up to five hours a day. A girl in this ability level is expected to be proficient at all 114 stunts she may be required to perform in competition. Beyond that, she will be able to do optionals (non-standard stunts) and hybrids (combinations of stunts) and create new ones; synchronize herself to the music and her teammates; and do interpretations and choreography of music on her own. An easy sport?

Synchronized swimming, like diving, requires the close and constant supervision of an enthusiastic and capable coach to attain superior skill. Constant criticism and constructive suggestions lead the girls to progressive refinements in individual stunts. The coach must see each stunt through the eyes of the judges and pick out everything that might be judged negatively. Of course, she can't just point out what is wrong, but must also advise on how to correct the fault. This can include the minutest details, such as using smaller, quicker sculling movements or not rolling a hip so much, details most observers would find impossible to see.

A coach with a new club has to allow time for her teaching to soak in and her swimmers to develop to a national level. The Aquamaids, for example, were begun as a synchro group by a local high school teacher. A parents' group was organized when they saw the virtues of the sport and they began to look for a year-round coach. They selected Mrs. Kay Vilen, who had just coached Paso Robles to a national championship. It took seven years before Santa Clara produced its first national champions, but they have been consistent at it since.

Creating and mastering a routine for competition requires mental exertion equal to the physical labor put in. The coach, or in the case of the A team, the girls themselves, must listen to hours and hours of music to find the bits to fit together for a piece. Sometimes only a few bars will be used from a record. Then four or five required stunts must be included, with no more than two from the same group. The basic stunts are linked together with optionals and swimming movements. The choreography is based more on the sound of the music than the theme. A strong, stirring passage of music may call for a strong, uplifting movement. Music with a swirling effect will call for a swirling, or circular motion.

The music's difficulty varies with the abilities of the performers. Younger swimmers require music with a simple strong beat. Senior girls often use more complex, classical pieces. Duets and teams, because of their numbers and the problem of synchronization to each other, generally use simpler music than solos. Whatever the difficulty, the music usually conveys an emotion to the listener and the girls do their best to enhance that emotion.

Competition in the Senior AAU Nationals consists of stunt, solo, duet and team events. The stunt competition is not exactly a separate event; rather it is a judging of technique and form and the score is carried over into the other events. There are different groups of stunts which may be called. One list is selected the night before the meet starts. The girls have the night to think them over, but very little practice time. In stunt competition, the girls are required to wear dark, solid-colored suits so nothing distracts the judges' eyes. The stunts are judged solely on their technical perfection. Routine competition begins the next day, with preliminaries for unseeded entries. The highest scorers then proceed through the semi-finals and finals. At each level the routine score is added to the stunt score for the final placings. In duets and teams, the members' stunt scores are averaged. So it is very important for every member of a team to be competent in the stunts. Routines are judged on perfection of the required stunts, quality of optionals, synchronization to the music and each other, and artistic impression. The girls who master all these aspects to the degree required to win at nationals truly deserve the title of champion.

—Sue Turner

Sue Turner is the editor of **Aquatic World** *magazine and a swimmer herself.*

For More Information

Two organizations are active: National Institute for Creative Aquatics, c/o Doris Dannenhirsh, 7015 Crittenden St., Philadelphia, Pa. 19119 and the Synchronized Swimming Committee, AAU, 3400 W. 86th St., Indianapolis, Ind. 46268. There is a bi-monthly publication called *Synchro-Info,* 11902 Red Hill Ave., Santa Ana, Calif. 92705. Also, *Aquatic World* and *Swimming World* have good coverage from time to time. For their addresses and other information see swimming.

You won't find many books on synchronized swimming, but here are some that we recommend. All are available from World Publications, Box 366, Mountain View, Calif. 94040 at the price listed* plus 25 cents each postage. Write for a complete list.

Synchronized Swimming, George Rackham. A full-length guide intended for instructor and student alike, this book covers both the vital basic preparatory work and more complicated techniques for the advanced pupil. Teaching methods are fully covered. Special chapter on the mechanics of buoyancy and balance throws new light on these subjects. 1968 Hb., 228 pp., ill., $5.95, (Faber and Faber).

The Components of Synchronized Swimming, Francis L. Jones and Joyce I. Lindeman. From conditioning muscles, through developing skills and activities, to putting together and producing a complete show, this is a reliable guide to every aspect of synchronized swimming. Profusely illustrated with over 250 sequence pictures of national champion performers illustrating 70 transitions. 1975 Hb., 270 pp., ill., $15.00, (Prentice Hall).

Progressive Synchronized Swimming, Helen M. Coryell, ed. A step-by-step approach to synchronized swimming from the beginning stages to the advanced. Illustrations help to explain body positions and strokes. 1972 Ppb., 80 pp., ill., $3.95, (Association Press).

Teaching Sunchronized Swimming, Betty Vickers. A guidebook for developing and training beginners through the fundamentals and creative processes of synchronized swimming. Written by an experienced teacher and coach, the basics are all clearly presented here. 1965 Ppb., 180 pp., ill., $10.00, (Prentice Hall).

Synchronized Swimming, Yates & Anderson. For the teacher and coach, this is a practical and comprehensive book on the sport, illustrated with clear line drawings. 1958 Hb., 164 pp., ill., $11.30, (Ronald).

Table Games

Probably everybody has, at one time or another, rummaged through the top shelf of their closet in search of their own favorite rainy day standby: Monopoly, Club, Scrabble, Dominoes, Aggravation, Chinese Checkers, or one of the myriad of other table-top games. When an unexpected summer shower ruins your plans for an afternoon of tennis or golf, or when the local gym has closed for the evening, a casual game with dice, markers, card decks, and an unobtrusive cardboard playing board can turn an otherwise dull hour or two into a few moments of leisurely enterprise, or into a tumultous scramble-and-race competition, depending upon your mood.

While millions of people are casual table game participants, there are many enthusiasts who play their games seriously and regularly, join clubs, hold tournaments, and herald their champion players. Some buffs go to even greater extremes (or heights). In 1974 two University of Michigan students played a four hour Monopoly game on a board drawn on the ceiling of their dormitory room!

Table games can generally be divided into three broad categories: (1) games involving luck, (2) games involving skill, and (3) games involving both luck and skill. Most adult table games fall into that last category, since even in a game such as Parcheesi, where movement is controlled by throws of the dice, a certain amount of room is allowed for skillful maneuvering of pieces. Essentially, there are table games catering to many interests and aspects of life: stock and business games, family games, race games, sports games, and battle games, to name a few.

By far, the most popular and well-known of commercial table games in America over the last several decades has been the famous Atlantic City game of wealth, Monopoly. Since Charles Darrow first laid out the now familiar places of Boardwalk and Park Place on his kitchen table during the Depression, Monopoly has sold over 80 million copies.

Another old favorite is Clue, a detective game where players move from one room to another in a large mansion, picking up clues to the murder of a certain Mrs. Peacock, Colonel Mustard, and a variety of other characters.

Of course, there's always dominoes, the old standby. The object here is to lay out on the table rectangular tiles which represent faces of a pair of dice.

More than likely you've tried all three of these games, but don't forget about the others you might have temporarily forgotten, gathering dust in the attic or basement. Or is it in the Conservatory?

Boardwalk Goes Underwater

Monopoly had been the world's best selling proprietary board game for nearly 30 years when, in 1961, a fraternity at the University of Pittsburgh informed Parker Brothers, publisher of the real estate trading game, that its members wanted to establish a record for the longest continuous Monopoly game. No recorded standard existed, so the students' 120-hour marathon became the first officially sanctioned event of the newly formed Monopoly Marathon Records Documentation Committee.

The MMRDC, based in the New York offices of Parker Brothers' public relations firm, has subsequently sanctioned records in more than a dozen different categories, including unlimited player, three-player, four-player, underwater, underground, treehouse, elevator, balance beam and bathtub. The original 120-hour unlimited player record has been broken 17 times, most recently by a group of youngsters in Dix Hills, N.Y. who played from 2 p.m. on June 27, 1975 until 9:30 p.m. on August 10—a total of 1,063½ hours.

The motivation that drives Monopoly players to such feats is the opportunity for immortality between the covers of the *Guinness Book of World Records.* After several years of negotiation and correspondence, the Guiness editors recognized the MMRDC as the only organization authorized to sanction Monopoly playing records. The eventual amicable agreement prevented further international controversies such as those that occurred when the 1973 and 1974 editions of the book listed Monopoly records set in England that fell far below MMRDC standards.

Rules and regulations of the MMRDC for establishing an officially sanctioned record state that a non-participating witness must sign a log every hour attesting that there were no breaks in the game. On some occasions, I have served as witness to these historic events. My most memorable experience was witnessing the world's first underwater Monopoly marathon in Beverly, Massachusetts in 1967. A high school fraternity asked Parker Brothers for assistance in constructing a special set. Working full time for three weeks, the company designed and made by hand an edition that was waterproof as well as sinkable.

The actual components of the set were taken off the normal production line. The board label was laminated between several sheets of cellophane to give a glass-like quality. Each of the 240 pieces was laminated. The Deed, Community Chest and Chance cards were also laminated, but with a piece of metal sandwiched in. Each playing piece was attached to a small magnet. The houses and hotels were filled in with lead wool and capped with magnets to serve as weights, and also to hold the pieces to the board. Beneath the laminated board label were three layers of magnetic rubber strips which were followed by a quarter-inch steel plate.

Many problems were encountered in experimentation while making the set. At first the money was laquered, but fell apart after some use in Parker Brothers' test tank. The plastic and hotels were first filled with liquid solder, but it reacted with the plastic. The money was laminated with a sheet of steel, but after a while a stack of bills became too bulky to use. But finally, at a cost of more than $500, the set was completed.

Loaded with assorted underwater photography equipment and scuba gear, I descended to the bottom of the pool at the East Side Divers Club in Beverly to begin my duties as witness. In my earlier camp days, I had always been selected during color wars for my proficiencies in underwater swimming. Underwater sitting presented a new challenge. I had submerged wearing the same outfit as the other participants in the game—a face mask, weight belt and oxygen tank. The major difference was that I had never worn these pieces of equipment before. Within minutes, I surfaced to remove everything except my bathing suit. To avoid embarrassment, I made it appear that my ascent was for the purpose of taking some overhead views of the marathon in progress. My actual reason for surfacing, untold until now, was survival.

With that mission completed, I returned to the pool, and for the duration of the marathon, did my underwater witnessing in 30-60 second segments, interspersed with surfacing for air. The players changed every hour as the oxygen tanks emptied. But the witness had not bothered to change for an alternate. Because this was the world's first underwater marathon, the game could have lasted five minutes and been sanctioned as a world's record. But the event was also serving as a fund raiser for the educational television station in Boston, and the participants believed that the longer they played, the more money they would raise.

The 11-hour record established that night and next morning has since grown to 200 hours. But the 10 hour, 50 minute record for underwater Monopoly witnessing, set by the chairman of the Monopoly Marathon Records Documentation Committee, remains unchallenged.

—Mike Alber

Mike Alber is president of David O. Alber Associates, the New York public relations firm that has represented Parker Brothers, the famous game company, since 1953. He became chairman of the Monopoly Marathon Records Documentation Committee in 1965. The self-proclaimed "world's leading authority on Monopoly," is official historian for the game and is considered one of the most knowledgeable experts on the subject of table games in the United States.

For More Information

There are several magazines of interest: *The Gamesman,* 12315 Judson Rd., Wheaton, Md., 20906 and *The Gamesletter* at the same address. They give information about various aspects of gaming. *Nost-Algia*, Drawer G, Pittsford, N.Y. 14534 is mainly devoted to chess but covers all types of games that can be played by mail. Subscriptions are limited to member of NOST (Knights of the Square Table). *Europa,* published in Switzerland and their US agent is Edi Birsan, Apt. 302, 35-35 75th St., Jackson Heights, N.Y. 11372, is mainly devoted to war-gaming and Diplomacy but covers other types of board games. *Strategy & Tactics,* 44 East 23rd St., New York, N.Y. 10010 is primarily devoted to war-gaming but has a column of reviews of non-war games. The same company also publishes *Moves* which again is primarily devoted to war-gaming. The best publication is one from England called *Games & Puzzles,* 11 Tottenham Court Rd., London W1A 4XF, England. You can order copies from *The Gamesman* listed above. *Simulation Gaming News,* Box 3039, University Station, Moscow, Idaho 83843 is another good publication.

Some of the more active organizations: Scrabble Crossword Game Player, 200 Fifth Ave., New York, N.Y. 10010; International Games Association, 5820 John Ave., Long Beach, Calif. 90805; Monopoly Marathon Records Documentation Committee, c/o Dave Alber, 509 Madison Ave., New York, N.Y. 10022; and the American Games Association, 2837 Regent St., Berkeley, Calif. 94705. Gini Scott of the AGA works with several companies on new games and she has some interesting information available.

Here are some interesting table game books. All are available from World Publications, Box 366, Mountain View, Calif. 94040 at the price listed* plus 25 cents each postage.

The Monopoly Book, Maxine Brady. There is much more to Monopoly than chance. Some properties are more advantageous than others, some are landed on more often, some game strategies can win even if you don't own Boardwalk! Offers probabilities, strategies, and clarifications on rules. 1974 Hb., 144 pp., ill., $5.95, (McKay).

The Way to Play: The Illustrated Encyclopedia of the Games of the World. The only one-volume fully-illustrated encyclopedia that shows—and tells—how to play more than 2000 new and old games. Here are games for adults, games for the family, and even games to play by yourself! 1975 Hb., 320 (oversize) pp., ill., $15.95, (Two Continents).

The Domino Book, Frederick Berndt. A simple yet complete presentation of over 175 versions of the game of dominoes. Many of the games were created by the author. Numerous illustrations accompany explanations. 1974 Hb., 190 pp., ill., $5.95, (Thomas Nelson).

The Illustrated Book of Table Games, Peter Arnold, ed. Offers the games-player basic rules and well-tried strategies for the world's most popular board and table games, as well as such exotic diversions as Go (Japan) or Wari (West Africa). Also chess, checkers, bridge, poker, craps. 1975, color., ill., $12.95, (St. Martins).

A Player's Guide to Table Games, John Jackson. Those who are interested in Monopoly, Clue, Hearts, LeMans and many of the "war" games will find this book valuable and informative. 1975 Hb., 285 pp., ill., $8.95, (Stackpole).

Table Soccer Rules and Strategy, Robert & Steven Edgell. The only availabe guide on table soccer, or fussball available today. Covers basics, offense and defensive strategy and tactics, the psychology and physics of play. 1974 Ppb., 109 pp., ill., $1.95, (O'Sullivan, Woodside).

Table Tennis

If you play tennis and have ever come across an opponent with a good spin serve, then you might be able to imagine what it's like returning every stroke in top table tennis competition. Table tennis, at its best, is a game where the ball twists, slices, shoots suddenly up off the table, or deceptively takes a turn back toward your opposition. In table tennis it is possible to impart much more spin on the ball than in other racket sports because it weighs only 2½ grams and curves through the air very easily. Forward, backward, or sideward spins are all possible, but most skilled players concentrate on a very intense forward spin. The construction of the table tennis racket helps very much in this department.

This player uses the "shakehands" grip of the racket. This style allows an extended reach in all directions and many strokes and hitting angles.

Usually, casual players use a plywood racket covered with a layer of rubber pips, whereas the majority of tournament players prefer a "bat" that is covered with sponge rubber. This gives added spin and velocity to the small, white plastic ball.

This high-speed game is meant to be played indoors since winds can easily blow the ball off course, and the harsh elements can damage the rectangular, dark green table. But whether indoors or out, table tennis is a game that can be learned at an early age and enjoyed the rest of your life.

To begin play, the server throws the ball up and attempts to hit it so that it first bounces on his side of the table, goes over the net, and bounces on his opponent's side. If a doubles game is being played, the ball must bounce diagonally across the table to the receiver's quarter of the table. Service alternates every five points and a point may be scored either by the server or receiver if he forces his opponent into a failed return. Add a point to your score if your opponents's return goes into the net, or if it flies over the end or side of the table without hitting it. When you've scored 21 points, you've won, unless the score turns up 20-20 deuce, in which case you must win two points in a row in order to win.

For many years China dominated the sport of table tennis, mainly because of the government support which it received. Whereas China has always had a number of superior players, other countries have participated in table tennis as an amateur activity. Western countries, however, have quite recently given more attention to "ping-pong" and are improving in international competition.

The Long Point

Alex Ehrlich was the King of Chiselers, and the noblest aspirant to his throne was Paneth Farcas, Prinz of Sitzfleisch. When King Alex and Prinz Paneth finally tangled, it produced the most remarkable point of table tennis ever played. In table tennis a chiseler is not a cheat, but the term is an equally opprobrious epithet for a stubbornly defensive player who refuses to attack, pushing rather than smashing even the juiciest "meatball". In those leisurely days of the mid-'30s when King Alex reigned, if two good chiselers met only impatience or exhaustion prevented their pushing the ball back and forth forever. The King was a strapping Job, but the Prinz of Sitzfleisch was as patient as a penguin.

The King of Chiselers' long point is as famous in table tennis coteries as Tunney's long count is at *Ring* magazine. Quite literally that single point changed the game – changed it as much as the calamitous introduction of the sponge racket would 16 years later. The tale, however, through countless retellings, has collected an apocrypha not easily pruned, and King Alex himself had never told me the real story. So at the 28th World Table Tennis Championship at Ljubljana, Yugoslavia, I asked him about it. He began by deprecating the entire affair.

"Never believe it vaz three hours, Deek, like maybe you heered. I look at vatch ven first game begin, so I know exact. Vee play only two hours and tvelve minutes." (Alex speaks 15 languages – but he mutilates them.)

"Oh, I see, Alex," I said. "Well, how long was the second game?"

"Vee not play second game, Deek. It vaz first game."

"Ah! Now I see! It was the first game that took two hours and 12 minutes. Well, then, how long was the long point?"

"Nein! Nein! Deek. Es war die erste . . . le premier!" Alex was excited. Sputterings of Hungarian and Swedish came out. He rapped his forehead in exasperation. "Deek! Deek! Whole match only vun point!"

I knew if I asked one more stupid question Alex would have a fit, so I sat back and let him tell it.

A Prague arena, 1936, the World Championships, 3500 spectators. Rumania vs. Poland; a crucial match in the Swaythling Cup, the Davis Cup of table tennis. When the sealed team lineups were opened, Alex Ehrlich, Poland's King of Chiselers, and Paneth Farcas, Rumania's Prinz of Sitzfleisch, were brought together in the first match.

King Alex had one tactical advantage: a fair attacking forehand. Prinz Paneth had no driving stroke whatever. His haughty, professorial manner suggested that he thought hard hitting unbecoming conduct. "So much a pusher Paneth is," says Alex, "he not even attack ven he practice." Gamesmanship began even before the players came to the table. While Prinz Paneth laced his sneakers, Alex ostentatiously announced he'd lay four to one he'd win. He spoke in Roumanian. "I bet everything," he told me, "the food, hotel, train. If I lose whole team valk back to Varsaw. Ven vee come to table for varmup, I attack. Backhand! Forehand! Very hard. Paneth, he is clever. He pretend he cannot return."

Paneth won the umpire's toss. Just as he prepared to serve, however, King Alex turned his back on his opponent, walked dramatically to the Polish bench and returned with his special chiseling bat. "So big around it is," Alex explained, extending his enormous hands to watermelon length. "It is very heavy, but for pushing never do I miss." Prinz Paneth glanced coldly at Alex' perfectly legal outsized bat and served contemptuously. Alex returned to the forehand, and Paneth returned to the backhand. Alex returned to his opponent's forehand, and Paneth returned to the backhand. Alex again insisted on the forehand; Paneth again insisted on the backhand. And so it went . . . and went . . . and went.

Even a small-time chiseler knows that winning a pushing duel requires doggedness more than skill. The first few points are crucial. The burden of catching up must be put on one's opponent. Then, when his own passivity becomes unendurable and his chiseling determination cracks, he overreaches himself and he's lost. Alex therefore played the first point as though it were match point, but 35 minutes later the electric scoreboards still read 0-0. Alex was undisturbed: he had a plan. If the Rumania-Poland team encounter went the nine-match limit, Paneth, Rumania's hope, would have to play Alex' two other teammates. Said Alex, "I not vorry. Perhaps I not vin match. But Paneth absolutely play no more. He need rest for six months. I keel him for my team."

Elapsed time: 70 minutes. Score: 0-0, first game. The pattern of play had become hypnotic. Paneth Farcas had begun the match as erect as a Rumanian aristocrat, but he had shriveled with every return and now looked like a hunchbacked robot. Pools of perspiration had formed at the feet of both players, and Alex remembers wondering when Paneth would finally wear out. Alex himself had a problem. The extra weight of his chiseling bat had begun to tire his arm. His remedy was extraordinary. After one return, he deftly switched his bat and continued the point left-handed. Farcas didn't notice. He simply kept pushing the ball to that same spot on the table – except now Alex's switch had turned the match into a forehand-to-forehand struggle.

With a sudden twitch the umpire stopped following the ball and glared at Alex. The King was unnerved. "At first I think he is Rumanian. Then I see the trouble. His neck! Forth and back it had go for 85 minutes and now it lock in this position. So new umpire come in vile vee still play point. Now two Austrian players come back to hall. They are surprised vee still play. They had go to movies after vee begin, and now they think electric score machine must be kaput. It still say zero-zero! And soon also vee lose second umpire. His vife had make dinner and he must absolutely go home." Alex switched the bat back to his right hand. "And now I see Paneth seem veaker. Soon, I think, I attack and vin. But not yet. I had svore on my lips to my captain I attack not vun ball till Paneth is absolutely dead, and I see he still have forces."

Meanwhile, the tournament committee panicked. Alex and Paneth had started at seven p.m., and it was now 8:40. The angry hecklers had left and only a few dozers remained, but not a point had been scored, and the finals, scheduled for the following night, no longer seemed distant. So they called an on-the-spot emergency meeting of the International Table Tennis Federation. Through the loudspeakers the delegates were summoned, and they convened in a special room behind the stands. The first order of business was the roll call. "America?" "Here!" "Austria?" "Here!" And so it went until the chairman called, "Poland?" No reply. "Poland," he insisted. No reply. Suddenly everyone realized that the delegate from Poland was the King of the Chiselers himself! Since no decision could be legal without his vote, the delegates picked up their chairs, marched down to courtside and arranged themselves near the barrier on Alex' side of the table. Sometime during the second hour, to keep his man relaxed, Alex' captain, Jakob Gorski, had set a chessboard on a table near the sideline and had started a game with Alex. Between returns Alex would sneak a glance at the position and whisper his moves to Gorski. When the delegates arrived the chess game was necessarily abandoned. "But I have rook for knight and a vinning position," protested Alex. "Vile vee play, there is meeting," Alex went on. "Delegates ask first if vee agree to a draw. I say no. Paneth also say no. Then they ask if vee agree to five-point games. Paneth now say yes. But again I say no. I am stronger, I say. In five points perhaps I lose. But in tventy-vun points, never! I vill push him into ground! But vile I speak, Deek, I not take notice, and so it happen I push just vun ball to Paneth's backhand. Now you see, Deek, for two hours tvelve minutes had Paneth pushed forehands. Ball had crossed net more than tvelve thousand times – tvelve thousand times, Deek, and not vun ball had I give to backhand! So ven I give him backhand, Paneth scream! I look. He is helpless! He cannot move his arm to change! It push forehand by itself! But ball go right through backhand side! And so first point become mine. And now I give it to him, Deek. I say to him, in Rumanian, of course, 'Paneth, I am sorry this point over. I vaz just beginning to enjoy it. You are much better pusher than I thought, Paneth. Perhaps it is possible you vill even vin this match. But remember, Paneth, I am not best pusher on my team. Against the others you vill have to be more steady.' "

The match ended abruptly. When the second point had gone a mere 20 minutes, a member of the Polish bench behind Alex began to feel hungry. Without realizing the psychological effect it would have on Paneth, he reached down into an equipment bag and pulled out a knife, a long loaf of bread and a two-foot Polish sausage. He started slicing sandwiches. Another player filled cups from a huge coffee thermos. Paneth, who could see all this from his position at the table, must have assumed that the Poles were prepared for a winter siege. He began to mumble – soon Alex could pick up the words. "He vaz saying over and over, 'He not make me crazy, he not make me crazy, he not make me crazy.' " Then it happened. For the first time in his career the Prinz of Sitzfleisch attacked. Ferociously! His first drive, incredibly, went in. Alex returned it. Paneth smashed again, even harder. When that one came back too, something snapped. With one grotesque windup, a holler and a swat that sent ball and bat together sailing wildly over the King's head, the Prinz of Sitzfleisch ran screaming off the court.

—Dick Miles

At the age of 11, Dick Miles began playing table tennis on his mother's dining room table. Since then, he has won the US Men's Singles title an unprecedented 10 times, and in 1971 he visited China on the famous table tennis diplomatic trip. He is now a freelance writer, the author of **S.I. Table Tennis** *and* **The Game of Table Tennis.**

For More Information

The United States Table Tennis Association, Box 815, Orange, Conn. 06477 is the main organization. They do put out a newsletter called *Table Tennis Topics.* An excellent source for equipment and more information is TTO, Box 32111, 2601 N.W. Exp., Suite 444, Oklahoma City, Okla. 73132. In addition to offering top equipment mail-order they also have copies of the best table tennis magazine around called *Table Tennis Journal.* It is printed in Japan but they translate part of it. Ask them about this.

Here are some good table tennis books. All are available from World Publications, Box 366, Mountain View, Calif. 94040 at the price listed* plus 25 cents each postage. Write for a list.

Table Tennis Made Easy, Johnny Leach. Practical advice for those who want to improve their game by a former world champ. Over 150 illustrations of champion players in action. Covers the essentials of equipment, style, tactics, training, umpiring and rules. 1974 Ppb., 160 pp., ill., $2.00, (Wilshire).

Table Tennis, Varner and Harrison. A good introduction to the basic game that progresses into a presentation of the elements comprising the game. 1967 Ppb., 72 pp., ill., $2.50, (Brown).

Advanced Table Tennis, Jack Carr. The author comments that this book "was written to assist in developing the average player into a top-ranking tournament player." Covers all strategy and techniques with an emphasis on the finer points, and compares the currently popular styles of play. 1969 Hb., 122 pp., ill., $6.95, (Barnes).

Modern Table Tennis Tactics, Chester Barnes. The expert knowledge of one of England's greatest table tennis players is here presented from his amiable personal point of view. How to deal with pen holders and cope with spin shots, the loop drive, conditioning and more. 1972 Hb., 127 pp., ill., $5.95, (Barnes).

Table Tennis, Si Wasserman. Studying the illustrations with the text, you'll not only learn why the ball bounces or spins a certain way when you serve or return it, but also how you should stroke it or chop it to score points. 1963 (rev. 1973) Hb., 96 pp., ill., $3.95, (Sterling).

The Game of Table Tennis, Dick Miles. A 10-time US champion takes table tennis apart stroke by stroke, analyzing the form and technique of play. For the beginning and advanced player alike. 1968 Hb. & Ppb., 142 pp., ill., $7.95/$2.95, (Lippincott).

Sports Illustrated Table Tennis, Dick Miles. Combining sound theory with practical advice, the author describes the importance of equipment, the grip, spin, push strokes, the service and defense. 1974 Hb. & Ppb., 95 pp., ill., $4.95/$1.95, (Lippincott).

Table Tennis, David Philip & Joel Cohen. With the aid of action photos and illustrations, US table-tennis colligiate champ David Philip instructs beginners and advanced players in how to stand, stroke, and to produce loops, sidespins, chops, kills. Also covers defensive and offensive strategies in detail. 1975, 160 pp., ill., $6.95, (Atheneum).

Table Tennis, Jack Carrington. In this "Know the Game Series" booklet, the Coaching Adviser of the English Table Tennis Association provides a sound introduction to table tennis for the beginner. Covers the equipment, scoring, doubles, how to improve your game, stroke, attacking, and defensive play. 1951 Ppb., 36 pp., ill., $1.50, (E.P. Publishing).

Taichichuan

The reliable history of taichichuan can only be traced to a Chen family in Honan Province in central China. An essay expounding the theory is attributed to Wang Chung-yueh toward the second half of the 18th century. After the art had been kept exclusively in the Chen family for several generations, Yang Lu-chan (1799-1892) taught it to the Mandarin officials in Peking. Only then did the self-defense system become known to the public.

Over three generations in the Yang family, the emphasis of the art gradually changed from self-defense to maintaining and improving general health. The style of Yang Lu-chan's grandson, Yang Çheng-fu (1883-1936) is now the most popular in all China. The styles which are next in popularity are the Wu Chen-chuan style, which being derived from the Yang family style, and the Wu Yu-shiang/How Wei-chen/Sun Lutang style, which was derived from the Chen and Yang styles. The original Chen family style, being much more strenuous, is liked only by younger people. All these branches are based on the same principles, although the health benefits vary according to the aspects of the principles each style emphasizes. The most basic and popular form in the taichichuan exercise system is the slow taichichuan without equipment and without a partner. This form is suitable for people of both sexes at all ages with various physical constitutions. The movements are so sophisticated and refined that, although one can learn the external forms in a few months, it takes years of practice to perfect the skill of balancing, coordination, uninterrupted energy flow, etc., and to internalize the many intricacies. It is

John Chung Li reaches forward with the gentle pressure of t'ai chi chuan, beginning to shift the weight to his forward foot, carefully maintaining his center of balance.

the combination of achieving health benefits within a few months and the scope of a lifetime self-improvement that induced millions of people to indulge in this intriguing exercise.

The slow taichichuan trains you in mental tranquility, physical relaxation, concentration, body awareness and inward and outward harmony. It is often considered a meditation through movements. Your spirit should, however, be elevated with full alertness. The primary motive force being generated from your legs and waist, you keep your upper body supple and limber. This results in perfect coordination between your lower and upper body, as well as making all movements in circular or spherical forms. Continuity is achieved to such an extent that, in transforming from one posture to another, there is no break in the continuous, almost even energy flow. Techniques of achieving this are part of the training. When the exercise is well done, you will feel that energy fills your body and expands to all directions as if your whole body is a balloon. In addition to the practical, health aspects, all movements should be done with an aesthetic appeal.

There is a misconception that in the relaxed slow movements, one does not apply any strength. It is true that beginners are taught with techniques to remove all stiffness at their joints, and are warned against applying any stiff strength. The stiff strength is inefficient, requiring more efforts with less work done. After you can do the exercise relaxed and without stiffness, you will be taught how to apply the supple, integrated strength. In pressing out a palm, for example, the strength generated from the rear leg spirals up through the waist, the back and the arm. The forward pressing strength is not stopped on a palm's reaching its destination, but continuously flows out, as if you are doing isometrics against the air. The bent front leg serves as a brake to prevent you from tumbling forward. Your relaxed and bent arm, flexible waist and bent rear leg serve as shock absorbers in self-defense, if your opponent is stronger than you are. In contrast, hitting out a fist or palm with straightened arm may have a larger momentum, but the strength stops there. Against a very strong opponent, the impact may even be transmitted back to your body and you hurt yourself.

The relaxation taught in the exercise allows more blood to flow freely to all parts of your body, including the small capillaries. During the first lesson of instruction, all students find their palms and fingertips swollen with a tingling sensation responding to their heartbeats, even when they do the simple movements. After they are skillful in all the movements, they will get this feeling through the whole round of the exercise, continuing for 15, 20, 30 or 40 minutes, depending on their speed. This is so, even when they gradually increase the supple strength applied in the exercise. Only the advanced students can do the exercise at very slow speed.

The continuous rightward and leftward twisting of the waist for generating the primary movements gives very good exercise to the internal organs and improves the functioning of glands. The slow moving footsteps and the gradual, alternating shifting of your body weight between the two legs strengthens your leg joints and leg muscles. The prolonged, fuller contraction of the leg muscles pumps more blood to the rest of your body without overstraining your heart. Unless you are already an athlete, you will find your leg strength significantly improved after two months of daily practicing of the slow taichichuan, and can climb stairs and hills with greater ease. Even ballet dancers and skiiers find their balance and coordination improved after a few months of the exercise. The continuous movements with a tranquil mind and relaxed joints cultivate a habit of performing your daily activities similarly, whether during or after work. The application of supple strength trains you to use your energy efficiently and effectively. All these assume that you have learned the correct way of doing the exercise.

The main function of taichichuan is health promotion and prevention of diseases, but flexibility in the vigorousness and duration you may choose in the exercise makes it suitable for many patients under recuperation. Taichichuan exercise had been considered to have curative effects for many chronic ailments long before the western medical field recognized the value of exercise for many types of disease. The many varieties of movements and intricacies keep one fully interested in it without feeling bored. Its suitability indoors or outdoors in all weather enables you to continue it regularly every day without interruption. Western style hospitals in China are now using it as a physical therapy. Medical doctors in the United States are recommending it to their patients.

To meet the need of the cardiovascular stimulation now emphasized, the taichichuan exercise system includes the fast movements, the sword, and the falchion, all of which can be performed either slowly, or fast with vigor, or intermittently slow and fast. The slow-fast pattern has the similar heart-lung effect as the walk-jog exercise, but without its monotony, and is more balanced in exercising the various parts of the body. The fast movements are, of course, also done with a tranquil mind, a leisurely attitude, and relaxed joints. They train you to do your daily work efficiently without strain.

To use the exercise as a sport with a partner, there are several forms of joint hand operations or hand-pushing. These can be used as an exercise, as a sport, or as an introductory course to self-defense.

—Wu Ta-Yeh and Wu Teng Shu-hsien

Mr. and Mrs. Wu, both in their 60s, teach taichichuan at the Taichichuan Health Center in Palo Alto, Calif. Mr. Wu was an economics professor and has served as a United States advisor in several Asian countries. He has done social work in China and Thailand. This material is excerpted from their forthcoming book, **The Taichichuan Exercise System: A Self-Study Manual.**

For More Information

Taichichuan isn't covered exclusively in any one magazine, but has partial coverage in many of the general martial arts magazines (see Judo, Karate, etc) Major organizations to contact for information would be the National T'ai Chi Ch'uan Institute, Inc., 4621 Santa Monica Blvd., Los Angeles, Calif. 90029, and Tai Chi Chuan Association, 211 Canal Street, New York, N.Y. 10013.

Here are the books we have available on taichichuan. All are available from World Publications, Box 366, Mountain View, Calif. 94040 at the price listed* plus 25 cents each postage. Write for a complete list.

Embrace Tiger, Return to Mountain, Al Chung-liang Huang. Master Huang reveals the methods behind his T'ai-chi philosophies. An integrated work, blending the peaceful precepts with the all too grim realities of modern living. Color photos. 1973 Ppb., 188 pp., ill., $3.50, (Real People's Press).

T'ai Chi, Cheng Manch'ing and Robert W. Smith. This book introduces t'ai-chi as a means to a healthier life and as a method of self-defense. A great book fot the beginner, enabling him to master the sequence of 37 postures that make up the t'ai-chi solo exercise. 1967 Hb., 116 pp., ill., $10.00, (Tuttle).

T'ai Chi Handbook, Herman Kauz. T'ai Chi, the ancient Chinese art of rhythmic coordination, balance and harmony with nature, is treated as exercise, as a way of meditation, and as a form of self-defense. 1974 Ppb., 191 (oversize) pp., ill., $3.95, (Doubleday).

T'ai-Chi Chu'an, Yang Ming-shish. The eight simplest exercises have been selected so that the beginner can learn easily and well the slow ballet-like movements that bring about radiant good health. 1974 Ppb., 60 pp., ill., $2.50, (Japan).

Wave Hands Like Clouds, Ananda & Li Po. A "how-to-do-it" book of T'ai Chi, this contains basic information of general interest about T'ai Chi—what it is, its history examined, and how to perform it. This book is for everyone. Male or female, adult or child. 1975 Ppb., 140 (oversize) pp., ill., $6.95, (Harper & Row).

Team Handball

Team handball is played by three million athletes in over 50 countries. In Europe, it is second in popularity only to soccer, while in the United States it is rapidly gaining popularity due to its exciting brand of continuous action play.

The ancestry of modern team handball can be traced back more than 3000 years to ancient Greece. In the *Odyssey*, Homer described a handball game called urania. Shortly after the time of Christ, the Roman physician Claudius Galenus described harpastons, and during the Middle Ages, a third ancestral handball game named fangball was recorded by Walter von der Vogelweide. Each of these were played in an open field or courtyard, and were similar to team handball.

The modern game can be played outdoors on an open field very similar to that used for soccer, or indoors on a court about the same size as that used for basketball. Net goals are located at each end of the court or field, and are constructed like smaller versions of soccer goals. A leather covered ball seven inches in diameter is the other piece of equipment.

In international meets, team handball play is continuous for two 30-minute halves, punctuated by a 10-minute rest period. Teams of six field players and one goal keeper attempt to throw the ball into their opponents' net, while at the same time defending their own goal. The ball can be advanced an unlimited distance by dribbling it like a basketball, but once a dribble has been interrupted, only three steps can be taken. If a player stops his movement down the field, he must pass the ball within three seconds. Body contact is permitted, so that the game can occasionally be very punishing.

The rudiments of team handball can be learned both quickly and easily, but mastery of the game takes years. This is due to the myriad small nuances of team strategy and play. The ball, for example, is usually played with the hands, but it can be touched or played with any part of the body above and including the knees. Only the goal keeper can touch the ball with all parts of his body in an attempt to defend his net.

In addition to the stamina necessary for an hour of virtual non-stop running, several physical qualities are necessary for handball excellence. Running speed, agility, fast reaction time and dexterity are essential for success. These qualities are enhanced by doing gymnastics, running and throwing in each workout, as well as ball handling and strategy.

Team handball on the international level can be an elegant statement for team sports and the value of teamwork. It is easily equivalent to a championship basketball or soccer game. As a result, team handball is now permanently included on the Olympic Games program.

For More Information

The United States Team Handball Federation, 10 Nottingham Rd., Short Hills, New Jersey 07078, can provide additional information.

Tennis

The game of tennis, when played properly, has a certain aesthetic and picturesque quality that distinguishes it from other sports. The fluidity of motion and grace of execution that the players radiate, racket in hand, eye intent on the ball as it approaches them over the net, can truly be termed "art in motion". A subdued whispering among the spectators combined with the delicate "plop-plop" of the ball resounding against string adds to the general atmosphere. But don't let this tranquility fool you! At times the action can be fast and furious, and the suspense may grow to a breathless pitch during a long rally which can end with either a superbly executed drop-shot or a desperate lunge that, by luck, becomes a successful point-gain.

Besides its physical grace, tennis is often surrounded by an intellectual climate, due to the profound thought and strategy used by the players. Many of the early rackets used in France were covered with parchment, before the use of string, to the dismay of scores of collectors of precious manuscripts! Today, rackets are made from a number of different materials: wood, metal alloys, with some very expensive fiberglass models. According to historians, the mysterious counting of game points by 15 was borrowed from astronomy – a fitting fact for such a smoothly kinetic game.

While a game's scoring progresses 15, 30, 40 and game point, players may struggle quite a long time at the 40-all score, since here one player must win two points in a row to win the game. A player loses a point if he fails to return the cloth covered rubber ball after it has bounced one time. To win a set, one player must win six games, but if the game score is five-all, then two games in a row must be won in order to win the set. Finally, a tennis match is won by the competitor who first wins two sets (women's) or three sets (men's).

One of the world's heralded woman athletes, Billie Jean King reaches far for a backhand shot at the 1974 Wimbledon Championships. Ms. King won her first doubles title there at the age of 17, and has won many singles and doubles victories since then. (Duffy)

A Coach's Tips for Aspiring Champions

I think the biggest single trend in tennis in the last two or three years has been the phenomenal number of youngsters, especially teenagers, who have taken up the game. Not too long ago the public and school courts were deserted in the summer afternoons, but today, on most reasonably fair days, the kids jam the courts. Watching this upsurge has been a real source of pleasure for me. Not only can a youngster go out to the courts and find it easy to get involved in pick-up games, but he can practice by himself, hitting the ball against a wall, or practicing his serve, while waiting for someone else to arrive.

Tennis, no doubt, is one of the most difficult sports to learn how to play; it is a complex game as far as playing techniques are concerned, but still it can be enjoyed on any level. Despite the fact that strokes must be learned correctly in order to become proficient at them, many of the good players started out on their own. Quite a few of today's foreign players who are doing very well on the international circuits started out as ball boys at clubs. They would pick up balls all day, until a coach or player would notice that they had pretty good hand-eye coordination. Pretty soon the ball boys would be receiving expert instruction in return for help around the club. Tennis in the United States, however, is different in that it is a sport for the masses. With the many young, aspiring players, it is probably a good idea for the serious youngster to seek out good instruction. Of course, you don't have to have an instructor to enjoy tennis, but for the determined player it would be of great benefit.

It's amazing how many kids mow lawns, or babysit, just to earn money for a lesson – even if they can only afford instruction once a month. These are usually the boys and girls who make fast progress, and they grasp the basic fundamentals quickly.

Even with lots of instruction and practice, there comes a time in a tennis player's life when it takes a certain something inside him which allows him to become better than the other players. This is not necessarily the result of good athletic coordination, or fine coaching. There is a special quality that champions have – a drive, a certain outlook and attitude which makes them stand out. Over the years I have observed several special areas which I think contribute to the development of a champion – both on the court and off. I'd like to set them down, point-by-point, as pieces of advice for aspiring tennis players:

Be reasonable in setting goals: set attainable goals. Reach them and then set others. Have a purpose, but don't frustrate yourself. The rest will take care of itself. I've seen a lot of players on my own teams say, "I'm going to be number one this year," or "I'm going to win the National Junior Championship," or perhaps something similar. While these goals are important to the individual, I feel that it is much better to set several goals that are realistically obtainable. Once a player reaches these, he can reset them a little higher – rather than immediately setting the World Championship as a goal. An athlete that sets goals too high is often going to be tremendously frustrated, and fill himself with much undue tension. I have seen unrealistic attitudes hurt a lot of performances of the young men on my own teams. For this reason, I try to temper an athlete if I feel that the goals they have set are going to cause them grief and frustration.

Be proud of accomplishments: the greatest joy one can attain is to succeed in the face of failure. When this happens, hold your head up and be proud of what you did. Don't downplay success if you reach it; don't be embarrassed to show your pride. Often your pride will spur the team to perform even better, besides building your own sense of worth.

Be humble: no matter what you accomplish, keep it in perspective. Very few people on this earth, other than yourself and a few close friends, really care how you did. What you are striving for is relatively insignificant when considered in the full realm of things. Don't blow things out of perspective because when somebody comes along and knocks you off it is going to hurt – and somebody, eventually, will knock you off. That's a fact you have to face in tennis.

Prepare thoroughly: there is little good that comes easily. Most things are attained only through dedication and through hard work. When you practice, practice with a purpose. Learn your areas of weakness, both in tennis and all that you do in life, isolate them and work on their improvement. Tennis is the kind of sport where you don't have to have a coach around in order to practice. The important thing is that you don't want to waste time and energy during your practice sessions. You must practice to make strengths stronger, and even more importantly to improve on your weaknesses. Once your individual weaknesses are analyzed or pointed out, then you have to go about improving on them systematically. Some people say, "Let's go out and hit a few," and then they get out there and think about the birds, girls, or anything else except hitting the ball. No improvement will come this way. What a player has to do is take the mechanical motion involved and do it over and over again until it becomes so routine that under the pressure of a real game it is second nature.

Keep the emphasis on winning in perspective: a single match or a single tournament is not that important. Also, your success is measured less in winning an event or tournament than it is measured on improvement. Learn to appreciate certain moments within a match as much as the result of the match itself. The "Championship of the Street" can be as important to the winner as the "Championship of the World" is to the winner of the Wimbledon. Everybody has the capacity within themselves to be a "champion" of some degree – even in the popular sport of tennis.

Don't be afraid to lose: this is what causes "choking". Do your best but don't worry about it when it is over – whether it be an individual point, a set, match or tournament. No one can bat 1000. A .333 hitter in baseball fails 2/3 of the time.

Enjoy yourself: the important thing is to try – to attempt. In so doing, have fun with those around you. Even though playing against a friend, compete hard, but remember, he is a friend. The thing that I like about tennis, as far as my occupation is concerned, is that when I'm on the tennis court I'm out there with people who are having fun. They are there because they have some free time and they want to enjoy themselves. This makes it very easy for me to enjoy the relationships that I form with the people I am working with. Often we forget about this basic joy in a sport such as tennis. We look at the goal we have set in the game and take it as a life or death matter; we forget that it is an enjoyable game even though we can't always succeed or improve every day we play. No matter what the overall objective, tennis is a game meant to be fun.

Have something other than tennis: you are lucky to have tennis. It is one of the greatest of all games. But tennis is not life itself. Develop other interests, do something else as well.

Don't take for granted those who have helped you: this includes your parents, professionals, sporting goods companies, local tennis patrons groups, friends, and so on. When you become a top player in a sport, and even if you don't, it's too easy to forget that there are people who helped get you to where you are. Perhaps a coach, or an interested friend kept encouraging you along the way – whether you won or lost. Maybe a player gave you five minutes of advice that helped you overcome a difficult problem in play, or someone more experienced hit with you when you were younger. Then there are the organizers of tournaments, leagues, etc. They should not be forgotten. If a youngster goes to a well-run tournament, where he is housed and treated well, then I think it is appropriate that he send the tournament organizers a thank-you note. How many athletes who take part in well-organized track meets, for instance, actually take the time to send a letter saying, "Hey, the meet was really well run and I enjoyed participating!" Not too many athletes do this; we take it for granted that these things are just there. In reality, it takes a lot of people and a lot of organization to put on a good tennis tournament, or whatever. Of course, it is impossible to thank everybody, but I think the important thing is to realize that many people are making this opportunity for participation possible. I think too many times we forget this.

Have class: make this show in your dress, grooming, and manners. Make those whom you represent proud of you – whether you are losing or winning. In this way, you will eventually be the real winner. In competition, there are many instances where an athlete has to function under pressure, therefore, he must learn how to adjust to it and how to control it. Too many times it is very easy to simply get carried away in the heat of the game and do things that might be regretted later. I like to encourage my players to have pride in what they're doing and in what they represent. When they win, they win with class, and when they lose they are gracious. Most of the great athletes develop this ability. It's especially important for a person who is in the top ranks of his sport – who is under the public eye frequently – to exhibit the qualities that he would like his own children to exhibit. An athlete is a model in many ways, and he should remember that fact.

As a coach, I try to help develop the foregoing points whenever possible. I really hate to see things blown out of perspective in athletics, and I think it's part of a coach's job to give the guidance so they're not. There is more to the job of being a tennis coach than just teaching a youngster, or young man or woman how to execute a forehand or backhand. A

Martina Navratilova executes a hard service at Wimbledon. The ability to serve well is a great advantage for the tennis player, as it will immediately put the opponent on the defensive. A flat, straight serve, often referred to as a cannonball, may reach speeds of 130 m.p.h. In addition, a variety of spins can be put on the ball, causing it to slice and twist. (Duffy)

coach often plays a significant role in the personal development of young people – especially when they're away from home for the first time, as many of the players on my team are. I'm convinced that a coach can really help out, not only in athletics, but in the whole process of living. For me, it has been very rewarding.

–Dick Gould

An accomplished author, instructor and innovator, Stanford tennis coach Dick Gould has established himself as one of the nation's leading figures in tennis. He led his Stanford team to two consecutive NCAA Championships in 1973 and 1974. He is also the author of **Tennis Anyone?**

For More Information

Three magazines that deal with tennis thoroughly are *Tennis,* 297 Westport Ave., Norwalk, Conn. 06856, *World Tennis,* 383 Madison Ave., New York, N.Y. 10017, and *Tennis USA* (official publication of the USTA), Box 832, Radio City Station, New York, N.Y. 10019. Also available is *Tennis Week,* Box 1706, FDR Station, New York, N.Y. 10022, a weekly newspaper covering the sport.

The governing body for tennis in the USA is the United States Tennis Association, 51 East 42nd St., New York, N.Y. 10017. Not only does this body sanction hundreds of tournaments each year, but they are an excellent source for information, with an extensive publications list. For the professionals, or those people dreaming of becoming one, there is the Association of Tennis Professionals, for players, 10738 W. Pico Blvd., Los Angeles, Calif. 90064, and the United States Professional Tennis Association, for coaches and instructors, P.O. Box 145 Wakefield Station, New York, N.Y. 10466.

As far as equipment, there are many specialty tennis shops that cater especially to tennis players. Of course, the sporting goods stores all carry rackets, balls, etc. One bit of advice though: if you're a serious player, buy an unstrung racket and have it strung at the shop. In this way you're assured of tight, sound strings.

These books are some of the best that we've come across. All are available from World Publications, Box 366, Mountain View, Calif. 94040 at the price listed* plus 25 cents each postage.

Tennis Anyone? Dick Gould. The tennis coach of Stanford University's NCAA championship team directs this thorough guide to the tennis *player.* Features hundreds of photographs and drawings to help the player improve his game, with extensive treatment of singles and doubles strategy. 1964 (rev., 1971) Ppb., 80 pp., ill., $1.95, (Mayfield).

Sports Illustrated Tennis, Bill Talbert and the eds. of *Sports Illustrated.* Designed to give players a better understanding of not only the basics but the strategies and tactics of tennis. Analysis of singles, doubles, and mixed doubles play. Also covers grip, volley, forehand, backhand, and serves. 1972 Hb. & Ppb., 96 pp., ill., $4.95/$1.95, (Lippincott).

Courtside Companion, John Zweig. A practical tennis workbook to be used at the court to help perfect the style of the serious beginner and intermediate player. Covers each stroke, technique and strategy in clear, step-by-step photos and text that can be referred to during practice. 1973 Ppb., 93 (oversize) pp., ill., $4.95, (Chronical).

Tennis for Women, edited by Ford Hovis. A guide for women tennis players by 10 female tennis pros. With more than 400 photos, a large appealing format in which each pro tells you how she improved a certain technique, and easy-to-read prose, this is a great way for the aspiring woman tennis buff to develop a winning form. 1973 Hb., 256 (oversize) pp., ill., $12.95, (Doubleday).

Billie Jean King's Secrets of Winning Tennis, Billie Jean King and Joe Hyams. In a precise question-and-answer format, Ms. King covers every aspect of tennis playing–both singles and doubles, including special pointers for women. She also presents for the first time her radical "point of contact" method for developing an effective serve. 1974 Hb., 116 pp., ill., $6.95, (Holt, Rinehart, Winston).

The Inner Game of Tennis, Timothy Gallway. What goes on inside an expert tennis player's head can mean the difference between winning and losing. The author presents a revealing psychological study that shows you how to make the difference work for you. 1974 Hb., 141 pp., $7.95, (Random).

Arthur Ashe: Portrait in Motion, Arthur Ashe. An in-depth study of 12 months in the life of one of the world's best tennis players and one of the most articulate spokesmen of the game. Interesting insights into a black man living in a white world. 1975 Hb., 272 pp., ill., $8.85, (Crowell).

Mastering the Art of Winning Tennis: The Psychology Behind Successful Strategy, Dr. Claude Frazier. Mental attitude is crucial in tennis: psychological factors are very important–concentration is a must. Here's a book on how to "psych-out" your opponent. Hb., 160 pp., ill., $7.95, (Arco).

Use Your Head in Tennis, Bob Harman and Keith Monroe. A book for the once-a-week tennis player who wants to know how to improve his or her game, while still having fun. 1950 (rev. 1974), Hb., 230 pp., ill., $6.95, (Crowell).

Tennis to Win, Billie Jean King. The world's most famous female tennis player provides solid instruction in all facets of the game. An endorsement of the Big Game strategy used by most of today's championship players, men and women. 1970 Hb., 158 pp., ill., $6.95, (Harper & Row).

Rod Laver's Tennis Digest, Rod Laver & Bud Collins, eds. Instructions, and playing tips, personalities and their styles of play, questions and answers–everything about winning tennis from a superstar. Ppb. 288 (oversize) pp., ill., $7.95, (Digest Books).

The Education of a Tennis Player, Rod Laver. A highly readable account of how Laver became the world's top tennis player. Each chapter of memborable autobiography is followed by a game-improving lesson on the various strokes. Numerous illustrations show Laver's technique. 1971 Hb., 318 pp., ill., $8.95, (Simon & Schuster).

Net Results, Rick Devereux. A book of strategy aimed at the intermediate player, but written for players at all levels. Many diagrams and photos add to concise presentation of strokes, drills and play theory. 1974 Ppb., 182 pp., ill., $3.50, (Pathmark).

So You're Going to Take Tennis Seriously? Jack Roberts. A fun book for the hearty and enthusiastic player, as opposed to the skilled and victorious. Tells how to enjoy tennis even if you can't hack the game! 1974 Ppb., 142 pp., ill., $2.95, (Workman).

Speed, Strength, and Stamina: Conditioning for Tennis, Connie Haynes. A well-illustrated book describing an eight-week conditioning plan for players of all ages and abilities. Shows exercises that can be done both on the court and off. 1975 Hb. & Ppb., 94 pp., ill., $4.95/$2.50, (Doubleday).

Tennis Strokes & Strategy, Editors of *Tennis* Magazine. This book is a collection of the celebrated instruction series that Tennis Magazine includes in each issue, with photos of the great players and teachers in the game. 1975, ill., $9.95, (Simon & Schuster).

Tactics in Women's Singles, Doubles and Mixed Doubles, Rex Lardner. A book expressly written for women players. Basic exercises for the beginner as well as intricate tactics of the pro are described. All phases of singles and doubles competition are discussed, including serving, returning serve and pressuring your opponent. 1975 Hb. & Ppb., 135 pp., ill., $4.95/$2.50, (Doubleday).

Touch Football

If you know how regular tackle football is played then you don't have to alter your conceptions too much in order to understand touch football. The main difference – which is a big one – is that in touch football you are not allowed to tackle the player carrying the ball. Instead you "touch" him with two hands in order to halt his progress. The touch must be made with both hands somewhere between the ballcarrier's knees and neck. Of course, players can block and run all they want, although rough physical contact is discouraged.

Various other rules distinguish touch football from its hard-hitting counterpart: the normal size of the touch football field is 40 yards by 60 or 80 yards. Any unobstructed, rectangular area will serve the same purpose, though. The lines which run across the field at 10-yard intervals indicate "first down" marks. Seven players make up a touch football team. While the quarterback is not allowed to run with the ball, he can pass it to any of his players, or hand it off.

One nice thing about touch football, however, is that rules are not steadfast and can be altered by general agreement between the two teams.

Few experiences in sports can compare to the thrill of throwing a perfect pass far downfield and watching the receiver catch it to score a touchdown. But often the quarterback has to struggle to view the last half of the play, as he is buried beneath two gargantuan defensive linemen. No such problem exists in touch football. The game can still contain all the basic skills and strategies of football, but most of the pain is eliminated.

You don't need much to put together a good touch football game. Just get a group of people and a football, find an area large enough, and play ball! The players need not weigh 200 pounds. You don't need pads and helmets; the risk of serious injury is minimal. A grass field is nice as it hurts less when you fall, but concrete will do just fine if necessary. You can even play in the street and incorporate parked cars into your pass pattern ("Cut left at the front of that white Chevy").

While the pros battle on this fall afternoon, touch football enthusiasts compete in their own way during a friendly game at Central Park. (Williamson).

But if you yearn for more serious and regimented competition, touch football can still be the game for you. You can play in a league, and you can devise strategies as intricate as those used by the professionals. You can even wear uniforms. You can't put a vicious tackle on someone, though. If this is what you wish for, you should play another game. The lack of constant collisions tends to keep tempers from flaring regularly.

A touch football game can be as casual or as serious as the players want it to be. It is a logical alternative for the great many people who love to play football but do not wish to play tackle football.

–Steve Skolnik

Steve Skolnik is involved in the intramural recreational sports program at the University of California at Berkeley.

For More Information

Organization: National Rules Committee, Chicago.
People to contact for information: The intramural or recreational sports department of any university or college; physical education offices at high schools and junior high schools.
Equipment needed: Football, cleats (optional; rubber cleats such as those used for soccer are preferable to metal cleats)
Manufacturers and distributors: All equipment should be available at most any sporting goods store. Major brand names include Wilson, Rawlings, and Spalding.

A book that will be of interest is available from World Publications, Box 366, Mountain View, Calif. 94040 at the price listed* plus 25 cents postage.

Touch and Flag Football, Louis M. Marciani. Kids play touch and flag football all the time, and here is that missing ingredient – a practical, thoughtful guide for players and officials. 1975, 160 pp., ill., $8.95 (Barnes).

Tournament Casting

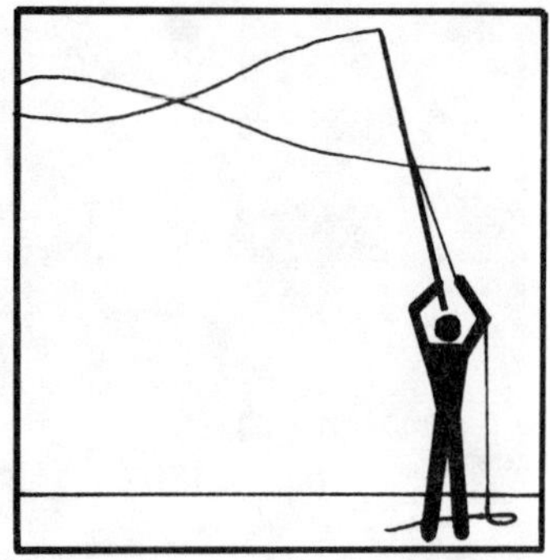

No one knows exactly where, when or how tournament casting began. It may have started with a wager between two or more fishermen, the object being to find who could cast the farthest or the most accurately. There are records, however, of competition dating back to 1887.

In 1906, five casting clubs organized the first national casting organization now called the American Casting Association. At present there are over 150 angling and/or casting clubs with more than 3000 members in the US and Canada. There are approximately 40 countries around the world that have forms of tournament casting and there is a world casting championship held annually.

Casting games are designed to encompass a variety of fishing equipment and different casting types. Eight of the 12 events comprising the US national tournament directly relate to fishing. The same tackle and casts used while fishing are used in competition. The other four events use highly specialized pieces of equipment, and serve as a proving ground for new innovations. Six events are judged for distance and six are for accuracy. The six distance events are split evenly between fly and plug casting, as are the six accuracy contests.

The 12 events in the US competition are: Anglers Fly Distance, Singlehand Fly Distance, Doublehand Fly Distance, 3/8 ounce Spinning Distance, 5/8 ounce Unrestricted Distance, 30 gram Doublehand Spinning Distance, Trout Fly Accuracy, Dry Fly Accuracy, Bass Plug Accuracy, ¼ ounce Accuracy Plug, 3/8 ounce Accuracy Plug, and 5/8 ounce Accuracy Plug. There is also a 5/8 ounce Accuracy Plug team event with five casters from the same club competing against five from another club.

In the fly accuracy events, six targets are placed from 20 to 70 feet away and, depending on which event, 10 to 15 casts are made. In the plug events, 10 casts are made at as many targets placed 40 to 80 feet away. The targets are 30 inches in diameter.

In scoring accuracy, either a demerit or an accumulative point basis is used. Under a demerit system, one point is deducted for every foot a cast misses the target. For example, if a caster misses by five feet, a five-demerit is scored. Using an accumulative point system, a caster gets points only when he or she hits the target. The accumulative point system is used in the world championships. Considering that casts in the fly distance events may exceed 250 feet, and in the plug distance, over 600 feet, the process of measuring a cast is much easier on grass as opposed to water. For this reason, some competitions are held on land – such as football or soccer fields.

Like any other sport, good casting comes from hours of diligent practice. It is true that one does not have to be a world casting champion to catch a fish, but good casting enhances the fisherman's chances of success in actual fishing. It is my opinion that the average fisherman is missing a great opportunity by not becoming a good caster through tournament competition.

—**Steve Rajeff**

Steve Rajeff is the best caster the United States has produced. Besides winning several national titles, he has also won the World Fly-Casting Championship.

For More Information

More information can be obtained from the American Casting Association, Box 158, Jackson, Ky. 41339. They also publish a newsletter that will be of interest. For books and magazines see the other fishing sports.

Track/Field: Field

"Field" is the forgotten half of track and field. When the proper name is shortened, it always comes down to "track." You never hear anyone say, "I'm going to a field meet this weekend," or that "the AAU field championships are on TV." It's always track.

The four jumps (high, long, triple and pole vault) and four throws (javelin, hammer, discus and shot put) are at least equal to the running events in skills required. But when the three-ring circus of competition starts, the field events almost always occupy the second and third rings—at the stadium's end zones or outside the gates.

That's a shame. Because to appreciate the subtleties of the field events, you must watch them closely. They take only an eye-blink. Runs are fairly drawn out and straightforward by comparison. The technique of getting from here to there doesn't leave much room for variation, so the races come down to matchs of trained-in and bred-in speed, strength and stamina. The running itself is natural enough to be instinctive.

Jumping and throwing require speed, strength and stamina, too—but of a different sort. The speed is a quick gathering of momentum to propel oneself or an implement into the air from a ring or runway, not the sustained speed of a sprinter. All strength centers on the explosive millisecond of takeoff or release, while a runner rations strength over a long series of powerful strides. While a track runner's stamina goes into no more than a half-hour's effort, a field eventer may have to endure an entire afternoon of throwing, waiting, jumping, worrying.

Field athletes train for speed, strength and stamina—but above all they work on technique. This, more than anything else, separates them from runners. The jumps and throws aren't as natural as running, so the field-eventers have to work harder at making their actions instinctive.

Athletes are constantly refining the techniques of hurling a body or a foreign object through thin air for height or distance. Most of the time, they polish existing styles, and only they and their coaches notice changes. Every few years, though, someone makes a change which revolutionizes an event.

This has happened recently in the high jump. In 1968, Dick Fosbury went over the bar backwards to win the Olympic title and electrify viewers in a way which seldom happens in a field event. Within a few years, the "Fosbury Flop" was a common enough style that it didn't rate special mention.

Last winter, Brian Oldfield spun around in the shot ring like a discus thrower. The ball finally plopped to earth three feet beyond the world record. We can now expect a mass switch to the Oldfield style, as there was to the Parry O'Brien technique 20 years ago.

Other innovations–such as the "flip" long jump and spinning javelin throw–have been tried and later outlawed as too dangerous. They show, however, that these events are a much more fertile field for experimentation than the runs. Technology has brought improved runways, pits and implements as well as more effective techniques on the one hand, and widespread drug use on the other. But it still hasn't given the field events an equal share in the sport's name.

Another Way

David Berman likes to throw weight around. And he is good at it. . .for his size. He has the square build of a weight-lifter, which he is. At 5'5", 150 pounds is about all his frame can safely and aesthetically carry.

David is best suited temperamentally and through training for the weight events in track and field. He's as strong as anyone his size–and in pickup competition he easily outputs oth-

As in many track and field events, shot put competition is an intensely personal one. When an athlete steps into the circle he is all alone. He knows what he has done in the past and what is possible on that particular day. Here, Ryszard Skowronek of Poland contemplates the task before him just before putting the shot. Months of preparation and practice culminate in a throw that will take only a few seconds to complete. (Horstmuller).

When the fiberglass pole was introduced into pole vaulting, vaulters found that they no longer had to use a pole which was equal, or greater in length than the height that they wished to vault. Here, a vaulter reaches 17 feet with a pole a foot shorter than that height. Notice the taped portion of the pole. This is where he actually grips it before he lets go and hurls himself over the crossbar. (Drennan)

er 150-pounders with the shot and outthrows them with the discus.

Yet because of his size, Berman competes–and not too well –in the sprints. He watches as men twice as large are launching their implements.

Another viewer comments, "You seem to enjoy these events more than your own."

Berman says, "You're right. But look at me. I couldn't any more be a competitive weightman than play defensive tackle with the Los Angeles Rams. I'm too small."

Size is only moderately important in other track and field events. Sprinters of 5'5" and 6'5" have set world records. Distance runners are usually rather short and lean–but occasionally we see a 6'7" Jack Bacheler or a 180-pound John Walker. Sometimes a high hurdler under six feet tall competes well, or a high jumper like Ron Livers who jumps a foot land a half above his head.

But weight throwing exludes average-sized people. Extra size equals extra power, and rarely does a man weighing less than 220 pounds have enough power to throw the shot, discus or hammer far enough to count in big meets. The entry lists are as beefy as pro football's rosters of linemen. And a David Berman would be laughed off the field if he signed up.

So here's what happens. The men of these events get bigger and bigger, and everyone who wasn't born to be big stays out. Most athletes can't ever hope to compete, which is bad enough. But worse are the practices of those who worship the scales they stand on.

Some of the weightmen, shot putters in particular, look almost grotesque as their event becomes as much a weight-gaining contest as an athletic one. Men built to carry 190 pounds balloon up to 250, wearing the extra muscle like an ill-proportioned Superman suit.

The weight race demands that they eat more than is wise for health, and lift more weights than is necessary to propel a 16-pound ball or a 4½-pound platter. And if the weight still isn't high enough, they seek help from a bottle.

Anabolic steroids. These powerful drugs are meant to restore the muscle tone of severly damaged medical patients. Healthy young athletes began taking them several years ago when they discovered that steroids gave a sudden jump in weight and strength.

Athletic rules outlaw the use of this drug. But there is no sure way to detect it, and steroids are now so widely used that a weightman can be presumed guilty until proven innocent. When one gains 20 to 30 pounds in a few months and improves five to 10 feet in the shot, you can bet he didn't do it on meat and potatoes and weight training alone.

The few athletes who admit to taking steroids argue, "Everyone else is dong it, so I am forced to take them too if I want to stay competitive." Even at the risk of frightening side effects.

There's no reason to think that weightmen will get together next week and agree to quit using steroids. And no pill or injection will build David Berman up to competitive weight. So an answer may be to remove the unhealthy emphasis from height weight and at the same to open up new opportunity in the throwing events.

The method is obvious. Set up the shot, discus, hammer and javelin by weight classes: 125 pounds, 150, 175, etc. Match the athletes only against others the same size, as is done in boxing. Keep separate records for each class, as in weight lifting. Encourage throwers to drop down to a lower–and presumably easier–weight division, as in wrestling.

If the idea of sport is to promote health and participation, the weight events are headed in the opposite direction. This change might help turn them around.

–Joe Henderson

Joe Henderson, author of seven books on running, edits **Runner's World** *Magazine and is a former staff writer for* **Track & Field News.**

For More Information

Track & Field News, Women's Track & Field World and *Track Technique* all cover the field events. Addresses for these magazines and other information can be found under track.

Here are a few good books. All are available from World Publications, Box 366, Mountain View, Calif. 94040 at the price listed* plus 25 cents each postage.

High Jump, Frank Ryan, 1969 Hb., 128 (oversize) pp., ill., $4.95.

Shot Put, Frank Ryan. 1973 Hb., 96 pp., ill., $5.95.

Discus, Frank Ryan. 1973 Hb., 56 pp., ill., $5.95.

A well-illustrated series of instructions from the most elementary steps to the advanced techniques, (Viking).

Track and Field, Harvey Greer. Part of the Sports Techniques series, this book will give the reader an understanding of the fundamentals of track and field. Written for the beginning coach. 1973 Ppb., 112 pp., ill., $1.50, (Athletic Institute).

Women's Track and Field. Part of the Sports Techniques series, this guide explains all the techniques of the events. 1974 Ppb., $1.50, (Athletic Institute).

The Jumps: Contemporary Theory, Technique & Training. Fred Wilt, ed. Modern technique and training for the four jumping events: pole vault, high jump, long jump and triple jump. Contains material never before published. 1972 Ppb., 160 (oversize) pp., ill., $6.00, (T & F News).

Track/Field: Track

Anyone who has tried to keep track of track running over the last 10 or 20 years knows there has been little chance to rest on comfortable assumptions.

Yesterday's "ultimates" are today's Olympic qualifying times. Yesterday's unthinkables are today's possibles, so we have to assume they'll be tomorrow's norms. In no other sport except perhaps swimming is change as regular, rapid and measurable as in track. Nowhere else is the talent so well distributed throughout the world.

In just over 20 years, the 100-yard dash record has gone down to 9.2, 9.1 and now 9.0. The milers have broken through the four-minute, 3:55 and 3:50 barriers. We've seen six-milers crack 28 and then 27 minutes.

The times keep going down. But individual runners blossom and wilt like spring flowers. A year is an eternity at the high levels of track, and the seasonal turnover at the top is swift and sure. We can't assume than that this year's world record-setter will be next year's Olympic champion.

National and continental balances of power are a little more predictable. But constant shifting is going on there, too. For instance, the United States has lost its monopoly in the sprints, notably to the Soviets and Cubans. The center of power in the longer track races has bounced from Eastern Europe to Australia, New Zealand, to the US, to Finland and East Africa.

We've been forced during these shifts to change several racial assumptions:

"White sprinters and hurdlers from Europe can't compete equally with American blacks." (Valeriy Borzov of the USSR won the two shortest men's races at the 1972 Olympic games, and East Germany's Renate Stecher took the two women's sprints. Guy Drut of France recently tied the world high hurdles record.)

"Blacks aren't built for distance running, and will never match whites in these events." (Black Africans almost swept the longest track races—1500 through 10,000 meters—at the 1968 Olympics. Tanzania's Filbert Bayi and Kenya's Ben Jipcho are two of the three best milers in the world.)

"Okay, so the Africans can run. But they're primitive people with no talent in events requiring technique." (Two of the most technical events on the track are the 400-meter hurdles and the steeplechase. John Akii-Bua of Uganda and Kip Keino of Kenya won these races against the world's best at the Munich Olympics.)

The Olympics, next year's world championships of track at Montreal, will provide the usual blows to the status quo: startling new world records. Gold medals for people whose names we hadn't known two months before. Expectations and prejudices withering in the heat of competition.

The excitement of all track racing—from Olympic to sandlot—comes equally from anticipating results which only can be decided here and now, and from comparing the results to those run by anyone, anywhere, anytime.

Maybe the Borzov Way?

It would be wrong to read too much into Valeriy Borzov's sprint victories at the 1972 Olympics. One man's 30 seconds of work—brilliant as it was—doesn't amount to a revolution. But Borzov did start changing a few assumptions about the nature of the short races. It had been assumed, for instance, that sprinters are born, not made; sprinters are American, not European; sprinters are black, not white.

It isn't as simple as that. Borzov in Munich was partial proof. He is from the Soviet Union, where the approach to sprint training contrasts sharply with the US system.

The US is sprint-rich. Natural talent oozes out of every high school. If a sprinter doesn't show 9.5 talent in the first few years of his career, he's likely to be pushed out of sprinting. Why bother? Nine-five barely qualifies for the nationals, and what else is there? Sprinting has no equivalent to distance runs-for-fun.

Alphonse Juilland calls this the "Roman Circus" approach. Juilland, a native of France who lives in the US, is one of the world's top over-50 sprinters. He says, "In this country, we throw these vast numbers of good sprinters together and let them fight it out. The survivors make the Olympic team."

Coaches have assumed sprinting is an in-born talent, and that Americans—particularly black Americans—have more of it than anyone else. They figure there's little need to do more than practice starts and "keep sharp." A lot of talent and a little training will win out. It almost always had—until Munich.

Imagine if Valeriy Borzov had been born an American. He would have been in junior high school when he began competing as a long jumper. Valeriy went a few inches over 16 feet his first year. His best 100 meters was 13-flat.

The next year, young Valeriy concentrated on the long jump and went over 20 feet. Good for a 14-year-old. If he had been an American entering high school, he probably would have stayed a long jumper because his sprint speed still wasn't great.

Soviets, however, measure their sprinters by different standards. The country's far-reaching intelligence network spotted Borzov's potential early. At 17, he was plucked from his home village in the Ukraine and placed in the Physical Education Institue in Kiev. Officials there tagged him as a sprinter, and Valentin Petrovski was assigned to head the Borzov project—"Borzov-70" they called it. Petrovski enlisted a team of scientists to help him, and the six-year plan began.

"Valeriy of course had enough natural speed to qualify him as an outstanding sprint prospect," Petrovski said. "And he had an excellent mind, great spirit and sufficient independence to provide the required self-reliance for competition."

Don't overlook this. Borzov was good "raw material"—both talented and intelligent, with the essential basic personality of an outstanding sprint competitor.

Borzov said, "I have the basic characgeristics of a sprinter. I like speed in cars, cycling, skating and skiing. Sometimes I can't even walk and I change automatically to a running stride before realizing that I am in no hurry. Fortunately, I am capable of switching off. A few years ago, I used to dream about the forthcoming race, but not any more. Now when I do dream about running it is running away from somebody."

Petrovski continued, "To turn Borzov into a 10.0 100-meter sprinter was the work of a whole team of scientists, not unlike the design of a motor car or airplane. University laboratories were responsible for deciding mathematically how model "Borzov 70" was going to function. Only after the completion of all research facts and figures did we begin to put the results into action. It was a delicate matter, similar to a ballet star who is aiming to establish the correct and complete movement."

Petrovski and team intentionally left Borzov out of the scientific programming discussions. They didn't want him bothered with trying to understand these details. "It would have only confused him," Petrovski said. "After all, the most important factor in sprinting is a natural and unrestricted action."

Borzov spoke up here to say, "Despite this, I was never just a mechanical toy in the hands of the coaches. On the contrary, I was given concrete tasks but without being bothered by minor background details. I am convinced that an athlete can only be successful if he doesn't blindly follow what he has been asked to perform."

Steve Williams, world record holder in the 100 and 200 meter races, is one of the few sprinters capable of turning on a noticeable "kick" late in a race. Here he demonstrates a tight turn. He wants to stay as close to the inside of the track as possible while still remaining in his lane, in order to cut down on the actual distance he has to run. (Lyons)

Initially, Borzov lacked speed. He worked on fast sprints with long recoveries—60-meter dashes with emphasis on complete rest between and high numbers of repetitions. He built endurance with 30-minute cross-country runs and repeat 800s.

Borzov said, "Petrovski is a scientist, and this is why I believe we make fewer errors in choosing the best possible training skills and methods. Like the repeat 800-meter runs I sometimes do. They help me develop will-power and endurance as well as helping polish running technique. So far there is no reason to believe such runs hurt my speed."

Petrovski thinks the day has passed when sprint coaches can rely on their "supernatural intuition." He said, "I regard sport to be an exact science and the coach a scientist. In the near future, success in sport will depend more on science laboratories than the athletes themselves."

The traditional hit-or-miss US system of producing sprinters has obvious faults, but the Borzov-70 project and the coach's last words also have chilling possibilities at two Olympiads away from 1984.

—Joe Henderson

Joe Henderson is a full-time track and field writer and editor who has covered the last two Olympic Games for **Runner's World** *and* **Track & Field News.**

For More Information

There are four major publications: *Runner's World,* Box 366, Mountain View, Calif. 94040. Published monthly at $9.50 per year. With over 40,000 circulation this magazine is the largest running publication in the world. *Track & Field News,* Box 296, Los Altos, Calif. 94022. Published monthly at $9.00. Centers on results of men's track and field. *Track Technique,* Box 296, Los Altos, Calif. 94022. Published quarterly at $4.00. Made up wholly of technical-practical articles. *Women's Track & Field World,* Box 371, Claremont, Calif. 91711. Competitive results from women's track and field. The major organization is the AAU (address in appendix).

Most people get started with track in school. If you are out of school and over 30 you might check into the master's program. The address is:
Robert Fine, Masters Sports Association, 11 Park Place, New York, N.Y. 10007.
A good source for equipment is Starting Line Sports, Box 8, Mountain View, Calif. 94040. They have a catalog. Also the editors at *Runner's World* can be very helpful in supplying information on equipment and general advice.
There are a lot of books and here's a sampling. All are available from World Publications, Box 366, Mountain View, Calif. 94040 at the price listed* plus 25 cents postage.

Track and Field Omnibook, J. Kenneth Doherty. All about coaching—sprints, relays and hurdles, field events, and endurance running—plus a section on the psychology of coaching. Sequence drawings of each event. 1971 Hb., 498 (oversize) pp., ill., $10.95, (TafMor).

The Complete Runner, *RW* staff. The only book in print to cover every aspect of running in such great detail. Articles by the experts on distance training, sprinting technique, diet, shoes, racing psychology and many more subjects—picked and assembled in one volume by the staff of *Runner's World* magazine. 1974 Hb., 398 pp., ill., $10.95, (World Publications).

Track in Theory and Technique, Rosandich, ed. A collection of excellent articles written by over 25 world-famous athletes. 1962 Ppb., 204 pp., ill., $5.95, (AAHPER).

Inside Track, Jim Bush. One of America's greatest coaches tells how to achieve the winning edge in track races by using the techniques that have brought his athletes unprecedented success. 1974 Hb. & Ppb., 75 (oversize) pp., ill., $7.95/$3.95, (Regnery).

The Complete Middle Distance Runner, Watts, Wilson & Horwill. British coaches have produced many fine runners in the years between Bannister and Bedford. Here, three of them get together to tell what you need to know to run the 880 or mile. 1972 Hb., 126 pp., ill., $6.95, (Stanley Paul).

Hurdling and Steeplechasing, Vern Gambetta. A beginner's guide to the special techniques necessary to meet the challenges of hurdling, with chapters on each of the events and sequence photos of top hurdlers in action. 1974 Ppb., 48 pp., ill., $1.75, (World Publications).

Guide to Distance Running, Anderson & Henderson, eds. Information on true distance running—over 2 miles—has traditionally been left out of t&f books. This was the first book published devoted entirely to the subject. Contains nearly 100 articles written for distance runners by other distance runners, plus 100 photos of great runners and races. 1971 Ppb., 108 (oversize) pp., ill., $5.95, (World Publications).

Trampoline/Tumbling

In 1936 George Nissen, diver and tumbling champion, developed a rebound bed designed after the springy safety net used by acrobats and trapeze artists. He called it a "trampoline" after several circus terms: the Italian *trampoli* means "performing on stilts;" the Spanish *trampolin* means spring-board. Dennis Horne in his book, **Trampolining,** even suggests that it was named after the French trapeze artist whose name was Du Trampoline.

After some experimentation in his father's garage, Nissen was finally satisfied with a canvas bed and metal frame. Today's apparatus is a webbed bed 12 feet by eight feet attached to a metal frame by steel coil springs. Safety pads lie on the outer edge of the farme to protect the temporarily misguided bouncer who falls too close to the edge.

Most high schools and colleges now include trampolines as a regular part of their gymnasium. Although trampoline is no longer an NCAA competitive event, each year a national competition is held under the auspices of the US Trampoline and Tumbling Association. Competitive trampoling is judged much the same as gymnastics or diving. Judges consider difficulty, form, continuity, and height of the skills. A competitor takes as many preliminary bounces as he wishes then begins a series of 10 skills that compose his routine. Competitors combine bounces, jumps, flips, and twists in varying patterns and difficulties for their routines.

Included in the championship is a synchronized trampoline contest in which two persons on two trampolines do the exact same routine at the exact same time! In mini-tramp competition competitors take a short run then one bounce onto a small trampoline which propels them into the air just long enough for one spectacular stunt before landing on soft crash pad.

Also at the USTA championships is the tumbling competition. Tumblers perform hand-to-foot stunts using flips and twists down a 60-foot by five-foot soft mat. Unlike gymnasts, they do not use a wide floor area nor dance and poses. Their routines are continuous motion—fast!

Tumbling is scored much the same as trampoline with points for difficulty and aesthetics, with the score doubling for any multiple somersault. Each competitor is judged on speed, height, form and power. The three passes show front, back, and mixed skills, and are often referred to as a "flipping" pass or "twisting" pass. Many trampolinists also tumble; some tumblers also participate in other gymnastic-related events. However, most are at their best bouncing and flipping along.

For More Information

The main organization is the United States Trampoline & Tumbling Association, c/o Jack Castle, 2340 Commonwealth Ave., Apt. 606, Chicago, Ill. 60614. They publish a newsletter called *USTA News,* 1301 Pyatt Rd., Algonquin, Ill. 60102. Also, *Gymnastics World* and *Gymnast* magazines (listed under gymnastics) cover these activities from time to time. A good source for equipment is the Nissen Corp., 930 27th Ave. S.W., Cedar Rapids, Iowa 52402.

There aren't too many books to be found at your local bookstore, but here are a few. All are available from World Publications, Box 366, Mountain View, Calif. 94040 at the price listed* plus 25 cents each postage. Write for a complete list.

Trampolining For All Ages, Know the Game Series. Here is the perfect beginners guide to trampolining which starts the enthusiast learning gradually with simple bouncing and working up to back somersaults and twists, all with safety spotting emphasized. 1972 Ppb., 48 pp., ill., $1.50, (E.P. Publishing).

The Tumbler's Manual, William LaPorte and Al Renner. Still one of the basic books on tumbling, with all the popular stints progressively illustrated and discussed. Both individual and group stunts. 1938 Hb., 128 pp., ill., $8.50, (Prentice-Hall).

Tumbling & Trampolining, Newton Loken. Every step in tumbling and trampolining stunts, from preparatory positions and mid air jumps to landing, is covered, in addition to the more difficult stunts. 1961 (rev. 1971) Hb., 128 pp., ill., $3.95, (Sterling).

Tumbling, Vannie M. Edwards. A primer which progresses from the forward roll through 82 other skills all the way to advanced aerial combinations. 1969 Ppb., 113 pp., ill., $3.95, (Saunders).

Trapping

Traps were among the earliest inventions of man used to improve his standard of living. Among primitive people traps were originally a means of survival by removing dangerous animals and a way of securing food. Many tribes of the world still use traps for these purposes.

In the pioneer days of North America trappers played an important role in opening up the country. Long before missionaries, gold miners, and cattlemen, trappers were paving routes into previously unexplored territories. These rough, coarse-haired men dressed in their beaverskin hats and buckskin garments soon gave way, however, to our more modern trapper.

Today, trapping serves a variety of functions and ends. The simple net trap, perhaps inspired by a web-spinning spider, has evolved into the elaborate trap systems often used in the modern commercial trapping industry. These operations supply a mass market with necessary edible goods, as well as luxury items like fur coats and rugs. Scientists involved in research and study of animals and their habitats obtain live specimens with traps. Pests and predators such as rats, fleas, and moths are kept in check almost entirely by trapping methods. Finally, trapping, today, can be classified as a type of sport related to hunting, fishing, wilderness living, etc.

Its Role in Life

Trapping is an art, a tool and also can be termed a recreational outdoor endeavor. Trapping is also used in furthering our knowledge in scientific research. It has taught us how to properly manage wilderness areas so that wildlife may survive the inroads of civilization. It has been a valuable tool in the study of disease which may affect both man and animal. Throughout the world a great many research projects are underway which involve the study of wildlife communities and their relation to man. By trapping animals, marking them, releasing them, and either monitoring them by radio telemetry or recapturing them, it can be determined how great their territory may be. This also may be done with birds and various other creatures.

Trapping is an art, practiced by many people, in much the same manner it was many years ago. To learn the habits of various wildlife communities one must make a study of the animal or bird he is interested in. It takes many years to learn the complete habits of various birds and animals. To capture an animal or bird one must know what it eats, how it lives, and what will attract it. In some cases this may be a scent or lure while in other cases it might be a particular food or color. A lure or scent may be composed of oils, of various musks, plants, and other attractants. Some birds and animals are attracted by various colors while others may be repelled by the same color. A study of the animal is necessary if one is to know what food odors are attractive to that particular animal. Colors are the most valuable tool in the capture of birds. Studies in this field have provided some background for biological control. Without such study much valuable research would have not come about.

Since time began, animals were trapped for food and clothing, valuable to the survival of man. This has taught man how to survive the rigors of life. Trapping, as a tool, is an invaluable piece of knowledge to those who live in the wilderness and mountains of our Northern-most remote areas. It also would be most valuable if some catastrophe would strike without warning. Those with the knowledge of trapping of animals and birds, in all probability, would be a valuable asset in the survival of our society.

Trapping also provides a recreation by encouraging one to keep his body in excellent physical condition. By walking the streams, hills, and woods a man or woman will use muscles which they would not while working in a factory or business. These people spend thousands of hours following the trails. Trapping teaches one how to live with nature and his fellow man, to appreciate everything in nature, plants, animals, birds, waters and the very air he breathes. Trapping has taught man many things which he would not otherwise learn—how to survive. It has brought many medicines out of the wilderness which have made life easier for those who have been ill, another priceless asset.

Trapping is a way of life, valuable in many ways to mankind, and wildlife as well. It's benefits are far reaching.

—**Gerald Walkup**

Gerald Walkup is the president of the National Trappers Association and editor of **The Voice of the Trapper.**

For More Information

Fur-Fish-Game, 2878 E. Main, Columbus, Ohio 43209 offers good coverage on trapping. Also the National Trappers Association, 529 Spring St., Teaneck, N.J. 07666 publishes a quarterly at $5.00 per year called *Voice of the Trapper.* The Fur Takers of America, 3057 Nettie Dr., St., Louis, Mo. 63129 also publishes a quarterly. Other sources of information: Robert Bailey, 432 E. High St., Elizabethtown, Pa. 17022 and Gerald Walkup, Rt. 2, Iowa City, Iowa 52240. Carr's Trading Post, 2868 Elm St., Dighton, Mass. 02175 has a catalog that lists lures, pack baskets, animal calls, fur forms, etc. The cost is 50 cents. Northwest Trappers Supply, Box 408, Owatonna, Minn. 55060 is another good source for supplies. And there are many listed in the Fur-Fish-Game classified advertising section.

Trapping books are few but here are a couple that are available from World Publications, Box 366, Mountain View, Calif. 94040 at the price listed* plus 25 cents each postage.

Science of Trapping, E. Kreps. Describes the fur bearing animals, their nature, habits and distribution, with practical methods for their capture. Good illustrations of each animal. 1944 Ppb., 229 pp., ill., $2.50, (Harding).

Animal Traps and Trapping, James Bateman. All the fine points of trapping big and small game. All kinds of snares, construction, history. 1971 Hb., 270 pp., ill., $8.50, (Stackpole).

Trapping, Harold McCracken and Harry Van Cleve. This fine book of instruction (one of a very few in the field) covers every North American fur-bearing animal having commercial value—habits, proper traps to use, and how to take care of yourself while on the hunt. 1947 Hb., 196 pp., ill., $6.95, (Barnes).

Treasure Hunting

Treasure hunting is probably one of the more demanding activities you'll come across. It's more involved than stamp collecting for fun or digging for arrowheads at an old Indian campground. It requires heavy library research to know where to look for treasure and to know what you're looking for; it necessitates special equipment such as metal detectors to maximize the find while minimizing digging or any other physical destruction; it demands much time and effort, patience and tenacity to make your efforts worthwhile.

Treasure hunting is definitely painstaking—but the returns are worth every back-breaking moment of it! Whether you dive to find undersea relics of the past century or unearth a miner's hoard of the last decade, treasure hunting provides adventure and excitement from the first inkling of discovery. After that, you're hooked!

Treasure hunters—or treasure finders—should be credited as that secret society responsible for unearthing everything from coins and firearms to relics and documents. They are our historian-archaeologists—researchers—antique collectors rolled into one, for they contribute much to historical sites and museums. And although many items are sold to clients, unclaimed treasures have made more than one treasure hunter's fortune! So if you are fond of adventure and the mystery of the past, the activity of treasure hunting is exactly for you.

Treasure Hunting for Fun or Profit

Treasure hunting has been a fascinating and sometmes profitable avocation for centuries, but it is within the last 50 years that it has become a profitable profession for so many people. The advent of *Treasure Hunter's News* magazine in Phoenix shortly after World War II stimulated considerable interest in the field and when it was absorbed by the *National Prospector's Gazette* in 1954 considerable new interest was stimulated in the small mining, prospecting, and lapidary fields. How-to-do-it books, such as my **Treasure Hunter's Manuals** (seven different volumes) and Nesmith and Potter's **How and Where to Find It**, appeared in the late 1960s and early 1970s, provided inexperienced treasure enthusiasts with step-by-step instructions on the successful pursuit of treasure, and the rush was on.

The fact that considerably more treasure is being hidden today than is being found has provided an added stimulus to the professional and semi-professional treasure hunter, and this fact has been an added inducement for the casual enthusiast. Newspaper reports of occasional recovery of huge amounts of money usually provide a new impetus to the field. Not mentioned at all are the frequent recoveries of appreciable amounts of money not reported because of tax problems and fear of legal action by claimants who have no vested interest in the trove. Despite all of this, treasure hunting is one of the

Treasure hunters line up for an annual hunt. They each hold their own metal detectors which aid them in locating their treasure. This attracted people from 42 states and Canada.

most fascinating, challenging, and profitable hobbies or avocations that a person can indulge in at relatively small cost.

Practically all treasure hunters use a conventional metal locator to help them in their search for treasure caches, but a locator is not necessary; it is merely a helpful tool that can reduce the final search period from hours to minutes. Most of the hard work in treasure hunting is done in libraries where adequate research of local treasure stories can often reduce the search area to a single building or a few square feet. The locator, or detector as some prefer to call it, can usually indicate the location of a cache in a matter of minutes when properly used.

Clues and leads to treasure caches usually come from history books, memoirs, newspaper articles, and even from barbershop and beauty parlor gossip. They are often derived from outlaw stories, articles or books dealing with local eccentrics and misers, and local or national scandals. One of the major "treasure rushes" today involves the search for huge amounts of cash that was allegedly hidden by CREEP (Committee to Re-elect the President). It is known that some caches have been recovered that amount to $30,000 and $40,000 each in California and Virginia.

Full-time and successful treasure hunters do not search for money alone. They look for artifacts, relics, and items for the antique trade and this can be a very profitable activity in itself. Some of them devote as much time as possible to prospecting and small mining and it is not unusual for these activities to become more certain and considerably more profitable than the treasure activity. All of these are, nevertheless, a true form of treasure hunting and they all lead to financial independence for those who succeed.

The art of "coinshooting" (the search for coins, jewelry, and other valuable objects) has become a popular and usually profitable activity for the treasure enthusiast who does not have the time nor inclination to indulge in treasure hunting as a full-time vocation. The coinshooter customarily uses a metal locator to search playgrounds, school and church yards, rest areas, carnival and fair grounds, parking lots, beaches, and other areas where people congregate. He may find, in an hour's time, several dollars worth of coins and a few pieces of jewelry. It is not uncommon, nor is it unusual, for a coinshooter to find a jewelry item that has been lost and receive a reward of several hundred dollars to as much as 1000 dollars or more.

The beachcomber has, in recent years, become the elite of the treasure fraternity because of his extremely high recovery rate. It is not unusual for an experienced beachcomber to recover several pounds of silver, gold, and platinum jewelry in a few hours. This is not particularly difficult, if you know how. Warren Merkitch, in his **Beachcomber's Handbook**, has used his extensive and successful experience to explain how to operate successfully and he has illustrated the tools he uses.

A relatively new and often highly-profitable activity in the treasure field is the contract treasure hunter who finds lost money, jewelry, and property for others. His customary modus operandi is to place business cards on shopping center bulletin boards that announce his profession. The most successful operators in this field distribute their cards to police departments, banks, loan agencies, and recreation centers and then find lost items on either a fixed fee or percentage basis.

A strange phenomenon that is taking place involves the fact that more and more business and professional people are leaving their normal professional activities and engaging in the treasure and small mining activities on a full-time basis. Most of them report that political suppression in the form of increasing inspections, bewildering laws, and an avalanche of paperwork cause them to lose interest in their professions, but then the excitement of treasure hunting along with the profit- and health-provoking opportunities is the deciding factor.

Treasure hunting and its surrounding activities can be a very profitable profession and a relatively safe but very exciting one, too. You can become a world-traveler, a local celebrity, or a relatively wealthy phantom of the adventure world solely from your own efforts. If you are not adventure-bent, the regular use of a metal detector in your parks, playgrounds and in old buildings can add years to your life, alleviate a lot of health problems before they have a chance to develop, and provide you with a meager additional income that can often be greatly increased by the finding of a rare coin. At the very least, this is one sport, activity, or avocation that deserves investigation and age is no deterent.

—Karl von Muller

Karl von Muller has done a lot of treasure hunting and has written many books on the subject including, **Treasure Hunter's Manual.**

For More Information

We were surprised to find out that there were at least six magazines on treasure hunting. The ones we like are: *Treasure,* 7950 Deering Ave., Canoga Park, Calif. 91304 and *Treasure Search* at the same address; *Treasure World,* Box 328, Conroe, Texas 77301; *True Treasure,* Drawer L, Conroe, Texas 77301. There are many regional groups but the national organization is the National Treasure Hunting Bureau, 806 North Ave., Battle Creek, Mich. 49017. The magazines listed above are just filled with sources for equipment.

Here are some books of interest. All are available from World Publications, Box 366, Mountain View, Calif. 94040 at the price listed* plus 25 cents each postage.

Treasure Hunter's Manual No. 7, Karl von Mueller. Treasure hunters foremost authority covers every possible aspect of treasure hunting, all in a easy-going vein. This book has everything: tools, where to look, how to look, equipment, the law, taxes, buried and sunken treasure, and much more. 1972 Ppb., 295 pp., ill., $6.50, (Ram Publications).

Treasure Hunter's Digest, Jack Lewis. How to go about finding your "pot of gold.' everywhere from mountain streams to antique shops. Tips and methods for beginner to pro. . .including a list of current treasure books and equipment guides. Ppb., 288 (Oversize) pp., ill., $7.95, (Digest Books).

Treasure Hunter's Guide: How and Where to Find It, Nesmith and Potter. If you are in search of treasure this book will tell you how to go about finding riches on land and sea. Equipment, adventure stories, and six maps of the US coastline showing the location of sunken ships. Hb., 160 pp., ill., $5.95, (Arco).

Tug of War

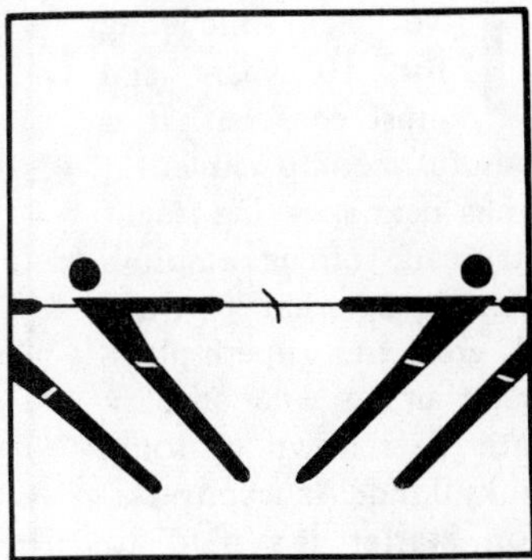

Men have been pulling heavy objects with ropes for thousands of years, but it is impossible to ascertain when teams might have begun pulling against each other for sport. Romantic historians occasionally trace tug-of-war to ancient China or to Pharaonic Egypt, where slaves were supposedly pitted against each other as a training exercise to build strength for pulling the heavy blocks used to build pyramids. These accounts are pure speculation, though, as written records of tug-of-war do not appear until the 18th century in England.

By the 19th century, tug-of-war had become such a popular rural pastime in England that it was sanctioned in 1880 by the British Amateur Athletic Association. The sport was also very popular in the 19th century American frontier, where it was usually practiced with one team on each side of a creek or muddy bog, the losers being readily recognized at the conclusion of a contest. By 1900, tug-of-war had become popular enough throughout Europe to be included in the Olympic Games, where it remained an event through 1920. British, Swedish and American teams consistently won all the Olympic tug-of-war contests.

The sport has gradually waned in popularity until today it is contested primarily in the British Isles. England, South Africa, Switzerland, Wales, Ireland, Sweden and Holland currently belong to the International Tug-of-War Federation headquartered in Surrey, England. Americans treat tug-of-war largely as an activity suitable for boy scout camps and factory picnics, but it is possible that recent television exposure via the ABC Superstars competition might cause a resurgence in popularity.

As contested in Great Britain, tug-of-war involves teams of eight that compete in firmly established weight classes. A team that can pull its opponents a distance of two meters for two out of three pulls is declared winner. Victorious teams are consistently those possessing great thigh and arm strength. They must be able to both withstand a heave from their opponents and be able to time their own heaving pull to catch the opposing team momentarily relaxed.

From 1900 through 1920 tug of war was an Olympic sport, with the best teams coming from Britain, Sweden, and the US. Although "pure" athletes have long regarded it as something of a joke, tug of war enthusiasts tend to be very strong and the teams well coordinated to pull at just the right moment to catch their opponents off guard. (Shearman)

Unicycling

I've been unicycling for 10 years and must confess that as a useful accomplishment it ranks near speaking fluent Etruscan, circus employment being what it is, but it's great fun, superb physical training, and an easy path to renown of some kinky kind. As a conversation starter it's hard to beat. You bump into all kinds of people and to start the ball rolling you can always say you're buying a Raleigh on the installment plan, or you want to get the knack with one wheel before you take on two. You can deadpan about the energy crisis and an imminent shortage of raw materials; look at all things you're doing without—even brakes—to save the world from its parlous condition, adding that just as you cut your wheel allotment in half, others might at least come down from four wheels to two.

All these inducements, the quirky glory and the scope for quips and comic lectures are strictly by the way. The main thing is what the Germans call *Funktionslust*—the sheer pleasure of functioning. Like body surfing and Zen archery, unicyling justifies itself. It's a neat thing to do.

I think people don't try unicycling because they assume only natural acrobats have the reflexes. Perhaps they tried once and fell right off, oof, which proves they "couldn't ever ride it." Of course it does no such thing; no one drives a unicycle out of the showroom. We forget our childhood experience with a two-wheeler, the kiddie wheels, the preliminary years of pedaling a trike, all the progressive learning until we rode no-hands and a bicycle was part of us. For practical purposes our bodies and reflexes are four years old when it comes to unicyling, and just as four-year-olds learn, so can we.

Unicycling *is* more challenging than bicycling because you can fall in four directions instead of two; also there is no gyroscopic stability from spinning wheels because it's nearly impossible to go that fast. Balance consists in keeping the wheel under your body. If you're falling forward, you pedal faster to make the wheel catch up; if falling back, you force the wheel to go slower to stop altogether. To prevent a sideways fall you steer the wheel towards the direction of fall. As in bicycling, a turn is a controlled fall, but instead of turning the handlebars you steer the wheel with your trunk and leg muscles, rarely banking more than a degree or two. All this is done unconsciously with reflexes built up over a short period of time, out of stock reflexes already developed since childhood.

Your chief requirements for unicycling are strength and endurance developed in normal cycling, not some magic sense of balance. If you can stand without falling over you already have all the balance you need! The rest is strength only. If you're patient, your body will learn the reflexes in a week or two of daily one-hour sessions. I believe this routine gives the brain time to strengthen the new connections it made during practice, and aside from getting enough sleep there's nothing you can do to hurry the process. It's wise to quit when you're tired because your chances of making mistakes and perhaps injuring yourself increase.

Don't worry about falling. In all my years of riding and learning I've always landed on my feet. If the balance gets too precarious, you must jump off and the unicycle falls out under you. Except at the beginning, most falls are forward, which is easier to handle.

Except for jockey shorts and trouser clips (or better, shorts), the only protective clothing you need is ankle length shoes or boots to protect your ankle bone when it rubs the crank. These shoes should have heels to hook behind the pedal; your feet tend to slip forward on the upstroke, so the securest position for them is heels hooked, arch over the pedal, preventing slippage in both directions. Toe clips which might keep the foot in a more advantageous position would hinder a quick dismount (*all* dismounts are quick) and lead to injury. So although you lose most of the strength of your calf, and your ankle rubs the crank, the best position for starting is the one you abandoned in third grade.

"Steve McPeak holds the world record for riding the tallest unicycle, a 20-footer. Danny Haynes, age 17, rode the tallest unicycle ever, 34 feet 5 inches, and Takafumi of Japan recently established a distance record by completing an around-the-world ride." (Staley)

As for equipment, you should have no trouble. Any cycle shop can get you one. Aside from strength of construction the only significant variable is seating. Some cycles have curved platforms for seats, which may be useful for stunt riding but aren't more comfortable or easy to stay aboard. My own has a Brooks leather seat which I thought would kill me but has never caused more pain than routine chafing on a long ride. Set the seat so your leg is slightly bent at the bottom of the stroke, and forego the temptation to set it low where you can touch the ground when riding. In low position the legs flex more and tire faster. High up you gain strength and keep your balance easier (since it takes longer to fall, you have more time to recover). Fasten the seat firmly, since you steer with it, and it takes a beating every time you jump off. Finally, inflate the tire to rated capacity. A soft tire is slightly more comfortable but sluggish and hard to control.

Now you're all set to learn. Choose a smooth, level, unobstructed stretch of concrete, blacktop, or a gym floor if nobody minds when it gets scarred by the pedals and seat hitting it. Stay away from corridors (too confined) and lawns or dirt paths which are too uneven to start on. And be sure there's room to keep going when you suddenly get the hang of it, meaning also space to fall. Don't worry about the hard surface since when you fall you'll instinctively come down on your feet. Probably the best place would be behind a supermarket where the loading platforms and dumpsters provide something to cling to. A long driveway next to a wall also fits the bill.

For the first attempts you need two friends to walk on each side. Have them stand at arm's length facing the same direction. Place the wheel between them with the left pedal at bottom point, hook your foot on the pedal, and grab your left friend's shoulder. Grab the seat with your right hand to keep it under you and stand on the pedal, hauling yourself up over the wheel, hooking your right foot on the pedal, grabbing your right friend's shoulder. Equilibrate, then start forward very slowly with your assistants, keeping the wheel under you at all costs. Continue this exercise for as many practice sessions as your friends will put up with, say three, until your legs get the hang of it and the wheel stops shooting out from under you.

After the basic reflexes are set up, assistants will hinder you. Graduate to a pavement with a wall beside it high enough to touch when you ride alongside. Find something to grab so you can mount the cycle, then lean on the wall and ride parallel to it, jumping your hand along the wall to maintain your balance. Keep at this, in both directions, until one day you push off and ride free of the wall. It took me 10 days.

Once you've achieved lift-off, develop your skill by riding on the level, then try bumpy surfaces like lawns, and gradually add slopes. When you've become proficient you'll be able to mount without holding on to anything.

If you're interested in riding backwards, you'll need two assistants again, or two ropes stretched parallel for you to hold while you ride. Unless you habitually walk backwards there's nothing in your experience to prepare you for this stunt, so it should take correspndingly longer, but in time you'll learn. Such a spectacular achievement may console you for being unable to move one step further on the spectrum, to no wheels at all, and flying.

—Jon Staley

Jon Staley is an avid unicyclist form Newton, Massachusetts.

One Wheel for Me

When I was in the seventh grade I purchased the remains of a unicycle that had been in a garage fire. It had once belonged to a professional performer. With the help of a man at a bicycle shop, the unicycle was restored. By trial and error (as I recall, a lot of error) I learned to ride it. A friend learned too. We worked up an act and performed in many shows, including the annual Fresno YMCA Circuses.

Through the years I built and learned to ride all types of cycles, including midget unicycles, tall chain-driven unicycles, and circus bicycles that could be ridden backwards and on one wheel like a unicycle.

I searched for information on unicycling and discovered that there wasn't a single book on the subject. I decided to someday write one, and finally a few years ago I did (*The Unicycle Book).* However, by the time I started writing the book unicycling was fast becoming a popular recreational activity and sport. Much of this was through the efforts of William M. Jenack of Westbury, N.Y., a long time promoter of the activity. There were a number of clubs and parade riding groups in various parts of the United States, but they were largely isolated until Bill Jenack and other unicycling enthusiasts started the Unicycling Society of America, Inc. There is now a quarterly newsletter and National Unicycle Championships.

Unicycling is a natural recreational activity and sport for our times. All ages, male and female, have learned to unicycle. Three-year olds have learned; senior citizens have picked up the skill, including one 66-year-old man who had never mastered the bicycle. Several blind persons have picked up the skill.

There are now many unicycle clubs and groups across the country, including Jenack Cyclists, the Paul Fox Unicycle Club, the Concord Club, the M.I.T. Unicycle Club, the San Diego Unicycle Club, and the Pontiac Unicyclists. These groups give demonstrations and rides in parades.

The first competition on a national scale was held in 1971 The competition is now sponsored by the Unicycling Society of America and held annually. There are racing events from 100 yards to a mile and individual and team trick riding.

A number of world records have been established. Steve McPeak holds the record for riding the tallest unicycle, a 20-footer, across a high tightwire. Danny Haynes, age 17, rode the tallest unicycle ever, 34 feet 5 inches, on August 22, 1974. Takafumi of Japan recently established a distance record by completing an around-the-world ride on a unicycle with a 20-inch wheel.

—Jack Wiley

Jack Wiley is not only a unicylist and show performer, but he is also the author of **The Unicycle Book.**

For More Information

The main organization is the Unicycling Society of America, 67 Lion Lane, Westbury, New York 11590. They publish a quarterly newsletter which is included with the $3 yearly membership dues. There are many clubs around the country and the Society can tell you about the one nearest you. Unicycles can be purchased by mail order from Jenack Cycles, 67 Lion Lane, Westbury, New York 11590. Custom built unicycles are available from The Hamilton's Bicycle Store, 1622

South Parkwood Lane, Wichita, Kansas 67218. Other good contacts: Bernard Crandall, 124 So. Josephine, Pontiac, Mich. 48053 and Paul Fox, 983 E. Center St., Marion, Ohio 43302. For more related material see juggling and circus skills. There is only one book available. It is available from World Publications, Box 366, Mountain View, Calif. 94040 at the price listed* plus 25 cents postage.

The Unicycle Book, Jack Wiley. The author, a lifelong unicycle fanatic, introduces the sport in this, the first book of its kind. Every facet of the unicycle and how to enjoy it is presented in loving detail. Discover another side of the bicycling scene. 1973 Hb., 224 pp., ill., $7.95, (Stackpole).

Volleyball

The exciting game of volleyball is one of the most diverse and widespread sports played in the US. You'll find nets set up on California beaches, company parking lots, and in elaborate gymnasiums. School children punch the ball up and over on schoolgrounds, and people in their 50s "spike" and "block" at the neighborhood YMCA. In fact, it was William G. Morgan, a YMCA Physical Director, who introduced a game that he called *mintonette* in 1895. Little did he know that by knocking a basketball back and forth with his hands he would pave the way to the modern international sport that can be both fiercely competitive and also a cordial leisure activity.

Part of the attractiveness of volleyball is that it requires little equipment, the number of players can vary from two to even nine on a team, and basic rules and skills are easy enough to grasp quickly. It is a sport that couples team play and co-operation with the performance of individual skills in a way that brings the spectator to his feet as a competitor dives to the floor to make a sensational recovery. . .and few team sports offer such an excellent opportunity for co-ed participation as volleyball.

In its official form, volleyball is played six players on a team, on a 60- by 30-foot court, with a net suspended across it. The ball used is light, made of rubber, and inflated. Each team sets up with three players in the front line and three players in the back, while the right-rear player steps out of bounds behind the court to begin service. The server strikes the ball across the net and the defensive team tries to return it using no more than three hits. Rallies progress in this manner, back and forth, until a team fails to return the ball over the net within fair bounds. A team continues to serve, and to score one point, as long as it wins rallies—with points allowed only to the serving team. After each winning point the team rotates, each player rotating one position to the right. The team that first scores 15 points wins the game, except for a 14-14 tie, when one team has to gain a two point advantage in order to win.

Modern power volleyball demands tremendous athletic skills, especially the ability to jump a great vertical distance. Spiking is the name of the game, as this action from the Cuba-United States series attests. (Courtesy ABC Sports)

The Modern Game

The status of volleyball has increased tremendously since it was adopted as an Olympic sport in 1964. The sensational performance of the 1964 Gold Medalist Japanese women's team opened the door to mass exposure of the sport via television, film, and tours of foreign teams throughout the world.

Japanese men and women use the greatest individual and team defenses known to the game. Japanese women have perfected the *rolling dig,* which enables them to go to the floor, and retrieve a hard-hit spike and then roll to their feet in time for the next play. Japanese men have perfected the spectacular *diving save,* which provides even greater court coverage and makes their defense almost impenetrable.

Volleyball was slow to develop in this country because of its image as a game that was not strenuous in which a ball was lobbed back and forth across a low net. Today the game of "power" volleyball demands a player who can dive or roll to the floor to recover his opponent's attack and jump high above the net to block or spike a moving ball into his opponent's court. Power volleyball requires more organization and team strategy than recreational volleyball. The athlete playing power volleyball must master the individual skills of the game in order to perform with quickness, alertness, coordination, and stamina in complex playing situations.

During the past few years, new standards of volleyball training and performance have emerged to test the speed, strength, endurance, and coordination of the best athletes. The sport has begun to assume a position of importance in the eyes of students and athletic departments throughout the country.

A majority of the better teams are using a three-hitter offense, which features a variety of sets and spikes designed around fast patterns of attack. There is increased emphasis on the defensive techniques of diving and rolling to the floor to dig or retrieve balls; these tactics, in turn, have led to longer rallies. Recent rule changes and interpretations have allowed officials to silence their whistles and let the players determine the outcome of the game.

Volleyball is a universal game easily adapted to the needs and abilities of all participants. For younger players, the net can be lowered, and for recreational and coeducational play, rules can be modified. Volleyball appeals to people of all ages at different levels of skill.

Volleyball is played in 120 countries and about 30 countries recognize the game as a major sport. In the United States, volleyball is the most popular participant sport and is fast becoming a popular spectator sport as well. The game is very popular in East Europe and the Far East. In the last decade, the USSR and Japan dominated men's and women's international competition. Young players from these countries participate in 100 to 150 international matches before they become a starter on the national team. Japan and the USSR host 60 to 70 international matches a year.

In America today, college teams are stronger than open or club teams. Our 1972 USA men's team consisted of 12 players who were recent graduates of Southern California colleges. Eleven of the 12 played on college teams that participated in the NCAA Volleyball Championships finals. To improve our national program we must broaden the base of participation throughout the United States. More club level participation must be encouraged, and I think the emergence of professional volleyball is going to help popularize the power aspects of the sport throughout the country.

—Al Scates

As varsity volleyball coach at UCLA, Al Scates has produced seven National Champion teams, five of them between 1970 and 1975. Al was the coach of the 1972 men's Olympic team, and was selected as a USVA All-American five times and USA international player three times. He is the author of **Winning**

Women have also adopted power volleyball tactics and play on the Olympic Games level with ferocity and elan. In the American professional league, female athletes play on the court at the same time as men. (Duffy)

Volleyball *(Allyn and Bacon, copyright 1972), from which portions of this article are adapted.*

For More Information

The major organization is the United States Volleyball Association, 557 Fourth St., San Francisco, Calif. 94107 and they do publish a bi-monthly newsletter called the *Volleyball Review.* A good source for equipment is Paul Barnes, Volleyball Equipment, 1859 South Madison St., Denver, Colo. 80210.

Here are some good books on volleyball. All are available from World Publications, Box 366, Mountain View, Calif. 94040 at the price listed* plus 25 cents each postage.

Volleyball, Know the Game Series. Good beginner's guide to this exciting sport. Details everything you need to know about the game and its rules, how to serve, teams and players, scoring, and the officials and their duties. 1958 (rev. 1970) Ppb., 36 pp., ill., $1.50, (E.P. Publishing).

Volleyball, Wilbur Peck. An illustrated book to help the beginner learn the basic skills he needs to play and enjoy the game. All the do's and don'ts, plus chapters on officiating, history, rules, and a glossary are included. 1970 Ppb., 128 pp., ill., $2.95, (MacMillan).

Volleyball, Egstrom and Schaefsma. The skills presented in this book are considered fundamental to effective play. Strategy and play patterns are represented in clear, concise language —a guide appropriate for any novice player who wishes to improve his level of play. 1972 Ppb., 58 pp., ill., $2.50, (Brown).

Power Volleyball for Girls and Women, Janet Thigpen. A presentation of this popular sport specifically for the female athlete. Includes a brief history, analysis of technique and skills, coaching suggestions, drills for training and court strategy. 1973 Ppb., 144 pp., ill., $3.95, (Brown).

Sports Illustrated Volleyball, Bonnie Robison and the eds. of *Sports Illustrated.* The universal American game is explained with the fundamental skills emphasized. Sections on training, rules and strategy benefit the advanced player. 1972 Hb. & Ppb., 96 pp., ill., $4.95/$1.95, (Lippincott).

Volleyball, Allen E. Scates, and Jane Ward. A brief analysis of the increasingly standardized basic skills. Beginners profit from the basics of passing, spiking and blocking, and advanced players will find dozens of finer points to improve their games. 1969 Ppb., 88 pp., $1.75, (Allyn & Bacon).

Inside Volleyball, Gene Selznick. A guide to the winning techniques by a 14-time All-American, and coach of US teams. Every element of the game is thoroughly covered. Especially important is the author's own 6-0 offense system. 1973 Hb. & Ppb., 96 (oversize) pp., ill., $7.95/$3.95, (Regnery).

Volleyball, Shondell & McManama. An innovative manual which is perfect for beginner and advanced participant alike. Not only presents in a clear, concise fashion the basic techniques, economics, facilities, psychology of the sport, but also covers the advanced techniques, ideas and hints that only an expert can provide. 1971 Ppb., 99 pp., ill., $3.00, (Prentice Hall).

Volleyball, Randy Sandefur. Presents a comprehensive analysis of the fundamental techniques, rules and strategies of this fast and challenging game. The author brings to the student much of the knowledge and skill he has gained from being an expert volleyball player and head volleyball coach at Cal State at Long Beach. 1970 Ppb., 80 pp., ill., $3.95, (Goodyear).

Water Polo

The sport of water polo developed in England in the late 1860s as a reaction against the boredom of just plain swimming. It combined teamwork and tactics with powerful movement in the water. The game was introduced to the United States in 1888 and first played in the Olympics in 1908. It was a very rough game, with few limitations on tackling or holding opponents who had possession of the ball.

During the 1920s, Hungary introduced a style of play which featured passing over the water and sprint swimming This was readily accepted in Europe, along with a restructuring of rules to prohibit ducking, holding the ball underwater, and most rough tactics. Unfortunately, the United States did not adopt these new rules and the game in this country evolved into a contest of brute strength. Much of the "action" went on under water, with many wild attempts to gain possession of the ball. This gave water polo a bad name among the public and among the swimming community, who could see only danger in it for their athletes.

In the late 1940s, Americans finally turned to the modern world-accepted style of play which, with refinements, is still played today. Water polo has become extremely popular for swimming conditioning, as well as for the game itself.

Water polo is basically simple. It can be played in almost any standard pool with a goal (frame and net) at each end and a ball. The net is defended by a goalie, and there are three defenders and three forwards. Players wear colored numbered caps, which serve to identify them and their team. The game is controlled by a referee, who is in charge of calling rule infractions and awarding penalties. Fouls include holding onto or pushing off the sides or bottom of the pool, taking the ball underwater, touching the ball with both hands at the same time, holding an opponent who does not have the ball, and interfering with a free throw or goal throw. Penalties result in a free throw or penalty throw for the opposing team, depending on the severity of the foul. A game consists of four five-minute quarters, with overtimes to play off a tie.

Many basic swimming skills are required in water polo, as well as ball handling skills. The front crawl stroke is the most frequently used, but with a deeper kick and the head up in order to follow the progress of the game. Players also use back crawl to see the whole pool better, the egg beater kick is used to gain height, and a player must be able to pivot and start suddenly. Ball handling skills include passing, shooting and dribbling (in which the ball is kept on the surface of the water between the stroking arms of the swimmer).

The variety of skills required, the teamwork needed and the tactics employed make water polo an excellent game for those who want something a bit more challenging that just swimming.

"Water polo is played in pools deep enough to keep players from standing on the bottom. A player's body mobility is directly related to his swimming skill. Good leg action allows one to tred water and launch his body high enough above the surface to block passes or shots." (Duffy)

The Making of a Championship Player

The qualities that make a champion water polo player are virtually the same as those required of a fine basketball player. Obviously the ability to swim is important, but adaptability to water is even more so. To be able to control and balance the body in water is as essential to being a superior player as those qualities are to a pro basketballer on a court.

Water polo is played in pools deep enough to keep players from standing on the bottom. A player's body mobility is directly related to his swimming skill. Good leg action allows one to tred water and launch his body high enough above the surface to block passes or shots. The ability to shoot and pass well also depends on leg position and body balance in the water. Sprint swimming speed is important, but I look for quick reactions more than raw speed.

Handling and shooting a water polo ball are very similar to handling and shooting a basketball. The same qualities of feel, touch and hand-eye coordination are required, and many of the shots are similar – we even have tip-ins. Shooting and passing accuracy are high on the list when I look for a good prospect.

Physical size occasionally becomes a factor, but I've seen a number of fine smaller international players. Doug Arth of our American team, for example, is only 5'6" or 5'7" and weighs about 140 in hard training. On the other hand, there's a guy on the Hungarian team who's 6'10" or 6'11". Essentially size only becomes a factor when comparing two players of exactly similar skill and conditioning. In this case, the bigger man would have an edge.

Overall body strength is extremely important to water polo players, especially in the leg and triceps muscles. The triceps are vital in getting any sort of speed on a shot. My teams, the University of California at Berkeley and the Concord Swim Club, are 100 percent weight trained and work out regularly with resistance exercises to attain strength levels that will give them an edge in tight games.

Certain experience factors also go into making a good player. I place a lot of value in guys who can adapt to the fluid movement of a world class water polo game. If he can anticipate well and be in the right place at the right time, a player can always make up for slightly inferior skills.

Unfortunately, a great many players are of almost equal ability when the above qualities are taken into consideration. In this case, the tiebreaker is mental attitude. He has to have a good positive approach to the game, as this and desire make a winner. I look for aggressiveness, intensity and emotional maturity. When everyone has equal skills, the difference becomes mental discipline and the maturity to stay consistent.

Right now on the international level, consistency seems to be the factor that sets the United States back from the traditionally good teams. Maybe we lack the killer instinct that they have, because Russia will pour it on when they are ahead of a mediocre team, while we would tend to let up. This is a mistake, because if we tied Russia 3-3 in a tournament and neither of us lost to any other teams, it would come down to a goals against average for the tourney and they'd win.

The final factor in manufacturing a world class water polo player is conditioning. Basically this involves starting easy and gradually building up to peak condition. I believe in training intensities very like those of world class swimmers. Thus, we use longer and longer workouts for skill building and endurance during the off season. Then for in-season workouts, we try to peak by shortening training sessions and going for more intensity.

If you want a specific type of program, I can outline the pattern I followed with my recent NCAA champion squads here at the University of California. Most of the players come in fairly good physical condition for the first workout, either from individual programs, international competition, or participating over the summer with my Concord Swim Club team.

For a month before classes start, we go with two a day workouts. Besides actual water polo drills and scrimmages, this includes running and weight training to improve conditioning. We probably do more scrimmaging than anything else during this phase.

Once classes start, we cut back to a single daily practice session, but that lasts for three hours. It's broken up here and there with chalk talks, strategy meetings and the like, but it's mostly good old country work. Weights are done on a player's own time during the morning. This lasts for most of the season, but about two weeks before the national, we will jump into a week of two-a-days to sort of shake up the conditioning index. The final week features single daily workouts, concentrating on quickness and sharpness. This is more or less a tapering period.

To any youngster contemplating a career in water polo, I would advise a heavy dose of competitive swimming until about 15 years of age. At that point, you just have to hope you live in a good water polo area, and most of those are here in California. The game can then be learned on the high school or club level, polished in college, and culminated on the national team. Sounds easy doesn't it? Well, don't bet on it, because water polo is one of the world's toughest sports.

—**Pete Cutino**

Pete Cutino is the 1975 Pan American Games and 1976 Olympic Games Coach. He has coached three National AAU champion and two NCAA champion teams within the last five years. His authoritative manual on water polo is currently in preparation and will soon be available.

For More Information

There is a good magazine covering water polo called *Water Polo Scoreboard,* 7 Sundance Dr., Newport Beach, Calif. 92660. Published 10 times per year at $6.00. Also *Aquatic World* and *Swimming World* offer coverage.

Here is one good book on water polo. It is available from World Publications, Box 366, Mountain View, Calif. 94040 at the price listed* plus 25 cents postage.

Water Polo, Hamilton Bland. Part of the Know the Game Series, this is an excellent beginners guide to one of the most strenuous sports, offering instruction on all the elementary skills, equipment, the idea of the game, fouling, free throws, and much more. 1972 Ppb., 39 pp., ill., $1.50, (E. P. Publishing).

Water Skiing

While water skiing is a comparatively new sport, there are many stories and rumors that surround its origin. If you meet an older water skiing enthusiast you're very likely to hear a story about how he skied in 1925 on two old planks with old shoes nailed to them. One popular story tells that somewhere in the Alps in the early 1900s a snow skier shussing into a gorge found himself heading into a small lake of melted snow at its bottom. To his surprise, instead of drowning he "water skied" right across it. Another slightly-fantastic legend describes a group of French alpine troops who were on leave somewhere along the Riviera and had their snow skis with them. Once they were bored with swimming and sunbathing they hauled out their skis and had a "speedboat" tow them around the Mediterranean!

It is probable, however, that water skiing wasn't too widespread until boats that could reach a speed of 20 miles per hour were developed. The sport probably began as "aquaplaning" in the 1920s. The real father of water skiing is generally acknowledged to be Ralph W. Samuelson who made and skied upon his own water skies on a Minnesota lake in 1922. For 15 years after, he put on one-man exhibitions in several states.

Actually there are several different types of water skiing practiced today. The first, which is the easiest to learn, is standard skiing with a standard ski attached to each foot. In riding a single ski a broader, heavier ski is usually used with bindings attached to fit both feet. In competition *slalom skiing* a skier riding one ski negotiates a series of buoys making sharp turns around each one. Many people prefer *trick skiing* to the other forms while getting a kick—and at first a spill or two—from jumping the wake, skiing backwards, and barefoot skiing. Perhaps the most exciting part of waterskiing is *jumping,* where participants approach a ramp, set in the water, at high speeds, are jettisoned into the air, land in the water, and hopefully continue on.

Trick Skiing

Trick skiing is the figure skating or the gymnastics in the sport of water skiing. Like doing tricks on the parallel bar or the rings, this type of skiing develops every muscle in the arms, neck, back and low back. For this reason trick skiing is the most body building of the water skiing activities. Also, it is open to more people since you don't need as powerful a boat as for slalom or jumping. Anybody with at least a 14 foot boat with a 35 horsepower motor can actually trick ski!

Other than a pair of trick skis, no special equipment is needed to get started. These skis, however, can be expensive—anywhere from $50 to $200—but a good slalom ski is in the same price range. In picking a pair of trick skis, you should make sure that they have good binders that hold you snug and are comfortable. Trick skis are short—usually 40 to 44 inches in length and nine to 10 inches wide—and it is important that you pick the right size. Anybody weighing up to 150 pounds should pick a pair of trick skis no longer than 40 inches. If you're over 150 pounds you should use a longer ski, 42 to 44 inches.

Before you try trick skiing it is beneficial to get out on a pair of standard skis and jump the wakes, cut across the wakes, etc. You should have anywhere between 25 and 35 rides on standard skis before you switch to trick skis. Once you feel comfortable and sure on regular skis, are able to cross the wakes easily and jump them occasionally, and can lift one ski out of the water and ride along in that position for a couple of hundred yards, then you're ready for tricks on the short skis.

When you first get up on trick skis don't be surprised if they feel very slippery over the water. Remember, they have no fin and have less surface area than regular skis. At first, it is very important that you merely take five or six rides on your new trick skis to get used to them—without doing any real tricks. You can cut back and forth across the wake and jump, but don't do anything more complicated at first. When you feel that you can handle them pretty well, then you can go ahead to the first trick.

The first trick that you should learn as a new trick skier is the *side slide.* In this trick you're actually sliding the skis sideways through the water. For this first trick, as for *all* tricks, you should adopt what I have coined the *vertical crouch.* You bend your knees and get down in sort of a semi-crouch position, but not bending forwards or backwards. In other words, while keeping your head erect and looking toward the horizon just lower your body about two-thirds of its height. When you're skiing on trick skis your weight should be right on the binders at all times.

Actually, the vertical crouch is only one of several important positions in trick skiing. Another thing that you should keep in mind is to keep the rope in close to your body. You should have a half-bend in your arms at all times when you're riding trick skis. Also keep in mind that when you're in the backwards position you should keep your knuckles almost touching your back. Say you're doing a *180* and you're riding backwards—pull your hands in and keep your knuckles close to your back. The last important point is that as you're turning to get your skis into the 90 degree position you should sort of *unweight* your skis. For instance, let's assume you're going straight with the boat, your skis are pointing towards the boat and you decide you want to do a side slide. In order to bring your skis around to the 90 degree position you have to unweight the skis by beginning the trick when your skis are bounching upward, all the time keeping the tow handle in close.

After you learn the side slide you can go on to the next trick, the *front to back*, often called simply the *back*. Then, of course, when you're in the backwards position you have to return to the front position. This trick is called the *front,* meaning you turn from back to front. After these tricks are done successfully then you can attempt the *360*, which means you start from the front position, make a turn, and come all the way around to the front position again. The next trick would be the *wake back:* You glide easily towards the wake and as your skis hit the wake you jump into the air just slightly, make a quick little hop and turn and land backwards. Of course, after this you'll want to attempt the *wake front.* In this trick you come at the wake backwards, jump into the air, and land forwards. Once the beginner learns the very basics then more and more tricks come quickly. You go on to *toehold turns, stepovers,* etc. These tricks are mostly problems of balance and how to hold yourself.

Carlos Suarez of Venezuela possesses the type of athletic ability typical of trick skiing champions as he wins his world title. Trick skiing is basically the figure skating or gymnastics of the sport of water skiing. (Duffy)

As for me, water skiing has probably been the most satisfying thing I've ever done in my life. It's a real challenge and I seem to have a real talent for it. I became interested in skiing because I was sort of a landlubber and was never near any lakes as a kid. Really, I started skiing for the first time when I was 22 years old. By the time I was 30 years old I had had won my first Nationals. I think that was quite an accomplishment. This was doubly so since I had only three months of the year to practice while the Southerners and Californians had all year. It was very satisfying for me to win over these fellows. The Californians and Floridians didn't hold this against me though and they were always in wonderment as to how I could achieve such a thing with only three months for practice. Some of them did admit, though, that they also would quit skiing after October, just like we did in the North. I couldn't believe it. It got a little chilly and they wouldn't go out. Fifty degrees was cold to me, but for them it was 70.

Of course, the nice part about water skiing is that anybody can do it for 15 minutes and get the same thrill out of it as I still do after 20 years of skiing. You can take about anybody and teach them in a few minutes how to get up on a pair of standard skis. After that he can have a nice ride and a heck of a lot of fun. If you want to go farther you can go for 25 years

With each trip through the slalom course, the tow rope is shortened to make negotiating the buoys more difficult. This gradually eliminates the field and provides very spectacular action on each turn. (Duffy)

and not learn all the tricks. This is what makes it a challenge.

Water skiing is one of the safest sports there is, too, because when you fall you fall into water.

Before I stop, I'd like to give one or two bits of personal advice to the beginning skier. As you're sitting in the water waiting to be pulled up you should keep your arms straight, your knees bent into your chest, and your skis parallel, about a foot apart. These are the most important things to remember. Also, when you're up, skiing along, and you feel yourself falling—hopelessly off balance—you should *let go of the line.* A lot of beginners, when they first start water skiing, have a tendency to hold onto the line and get dragged through the water. It's a normal reaction to try and hold onto something when you're falling. This, however, is a very unsafe practice. In water skiing you should get rid of the tow handle as soon as you start falling. Let go of the line. Of course, you shouldn't let go the minute that you get a little off balance because you can recover.

Another tip for *all* water skiers: most people who water ski don't have the correct propeller on their boat. Usually, boat manufacturers prop their boats for speed and not for pulling. For this reason you should get one with less pitch. A lot of people don't get as much fun out of water skiing as they could because they don't have their boats rigged up for it. All they need to do is buy another prop or have their original prop repitched with one or two inches less pitch. This will give you more power for pulling and maybe just a mile or two less top speed, but that doesn't matter. While you're skiing you probably won't even miss this slight speed loss.

—**Al Tyll**

Besides winning the National Men's Trick Skiing Championships in 1962, 1963, 1964, and 1965, Al Tyll has won over 100 tournaments. Needless to say, he is the greatest trick skier the sport has ever known. Mr. Tyll is also the author of **The Complete Beginner's Guide to Water Skiing** *and* **Water Skiing.**

For More Information

For those who are enthusiastic about water skiing, or those who are beginning to be, the American Water Ski Association, Seventh St. and G Ave., S.W., Winter Haven, Fla. 33880 not only sponsors tournaments, but also issue recognition for various levels of achievement by recreational skiers. Their magazine, which is the only one that we know of in the US that deals exclusively with the sport, is *The Water Skier.* This publication gives good advice, coverage of competitions, etc. Occasionally, there is water skiing coverage in the boating magazines, especially *Powerboat.*

Water skiing equipment is available in most sports stores, and through many boat dealers, but in the winter (off-season) goods are not readily available through stores. One hint: buy equipment at the end of the summer when many dealers have clearance sales. You can save yourself a heap of money. For the proficient skier who wants a custom-made ski, he might do well to contact one of the manufacturers: Maherajah Water Skis, 226 Healdsburg Ave., Healdsburg, Calif. 95448 and O'Brien Water Skis in Washington are two top names. Custom Dynamics, Inc., 119 River St., Waltham, Mass. 02154, makes an interesting device that lets you ski along, three feet above the water.

Although water skiing books are available, sometimes they are hard to come by. Here are a few. All are available from World Publications, Box 366, Mountain View, Calif. 94040 at the price listed* plus 25 cents each postage.

Complete Beginner's Guide to Water Skiing, Al Tyll. An instructional guide for all ages on how to get up on skis in the water. A perfect companion. 1970 Hb., 302 pp., ill., $6.95, (Doubleday).

Water Skiing, Al Tyll. An all-time great of the sport has written this very enjoyable "how-to-do-it" book for the expert as well as the beginner. Adequate coverage of the basics, and special coverage of trick and stunt skiing. Well-illustrated with step-by-step photos. 1966 Hb., 118 pp., ill., $4.95, (Arco).
Water Skiing Skill, Glen E. Anderson. A self-instruction guide to teach you how to ski. Once upright on the water you'll go on to turning, crossing wakes, riding single ski, etc. Sections on jumping, stunts and tournament competition are included. 1971 Ppb., 127 pp., ill., $1.95, (MacMillan).
Waterskiing, Kenneth Stephens. Provides sound, progressive introduction to all aspects of waterskiing from elementary techniques to trick skiing and kite flying. Safety, proper equipment, correct boating, and preliminary dry-land practice are stressed. 1974 Hb., 141 pp., ill., $6.95, (McGraw-Hill).
Waterskiing, George Athans, Jr. This book's profusion of photos clearly delineate the do's and don'ts of waterskiing. Begins with the fundamentals, then offers sections on equipment, safety, slalom skiing, figure skiing, and jumping, and skiing backwards. 1975 Ppb., 120 (oversize) pp., ill., $4.95, (St. Martins).

Weight Lifting

Competitions in what the uninitiated call weightlifting are divided by the true afficionado into Olympic lifting, powerlifting and bodybuilding championships. In each of these three divisions meets are held on local, state, district, national and international levels. Although competitions are held under AAU (and other) auspices in each of these sports year round, the peak season in the United States runs from November or December through the middle of June.

Olympic style weightlifting is the oldest of the three Iron Game sports, the first national championships having been held in 1928 at Philadelphia. Five different lifts were contested; the one hand snatch, one hand clean and jerk, two hands military press, two hands snatch and two hands clean and jerk. Since only the three two hand lifts were contested at the Olympic Games, the one hand exercises were soon dropped and the press, snatch and clean and jerk were contested in the United States through the 1972 Olympics. At that point the international federation for Olympic lifting voted to drop the press movement because it had become difficult to officiate. Thus the current biathon of snatch and clean and jerk are contested both domestically and internationally at this time.

World supremacy in Olympic lifting has shifted many times. During the 1920s athletes from Egypt and Germany alternated winning team titles at the World Championships. During World War II, there were no international meets, but American athletes were able to forge ahead because they were far from the war and able to train while their European and Asian counterparts were not. As a result, the United States was on top of world rankings from about 1946 to 1960. From the Rome Olympics until today, the Soviet Union has ruled international Olympic lifting despite challenges from Poland, Japan and lately Bulgaria.

Olympic style weightlifting demands every quality of an outstanding athlete: speed, flexibility, coordination, exceptional strength and, to some extent, endurance. So in addition to long workouts with barbells, weightlifters train in a variety of other sports including running, gymnastics, soccer, volleyball and basketball. Such an eclectic approach to training has produced some incredible lifts. Soviet super-heavyweight Vasili Alexeev, for example, snatches nearly 420 pounds and jerks about 540. The average person could not lift one end of a 540-pound barbell from the floor.

Weightlifting meets are held in nine weight classes. Due to international affiliations, the class limits are in kilos, but to the nearest pound, they are 114, 123, 132, 148, 165, 181, 198, 242 and unlimited or super-heavyweight. National and some lesser meets lift on kilo barbell sets, but most commonly American competitions are held on sets graduated in pounds.

The snatch is the first lift contested each meet. It consists of lifting a barbell from the floor to locked arms length overhead in one motion with no stops enroute. Usually a wide

Vasili Alexeev of the Soviet team is the current strongest man in the world. He has lifted nearly 540 pounds from the floor to arms length overhead, and has set in excess of 50 world records. (Duffy)

The key to lifting a very heavy weight from the floor is to dip the hips and initiate the pull with leg strength. Follow through with back and then arm power and you'll have it made . . . well, maybe if you are the GDR's Gerd Bonk. (Duffy)

grip is used and the lifter can either squat or split his legs fore and aft suddenly to lower the body once the barbell has reached its peak altitude. The athlete must then stand up with the weight still overhead and hold it with feet on a line for a period of about two seconds. Finally the referee signals down and the lift is complete.

The clean and jerk consists of hoisting the barbell from floor to the same finish position as for the snatch, but in two movements and with a narrower grip. The clean portion is from floor to shoulders in one motion while squatting or splitting under the weight. The lifter then comes erect, gathers his psych, dips his body slightly, rams the bar overhead with leg strength and splits to fix the weight. He recovers, waits for the count and lowers the bar back to the floor. The barbell can be dropped at the completion of the lift, but both hands must remain on the handle to guide it evenly back to the platform. It should be noted that many lifters consider psychological preparation to be 75 percent of the battle in weightlifting and powerlifting.

Three graduated attempts are allowed in each of the two exercises. Between first attempt and second, a minimum jump of 10 pounds (five kilos) must be taken, while between second and third attempts the jump is five pounds (2½ kilos). The winner of the competition is determined by adding up the best successful attempt of each exercise. In the event of a tie, the lighter individual wins, as he has lifted more efficiently than his heavier opponent. Often one's body weight will determine strategy as a meet goes down to the last two or three lifts.

The AAU holds a Junior National Championships in May of each year and a Senior Nationals in June. The World Championships are held in September or October, or in August during Olympic years. Each of these competitions also includes a team title computed by assigning graduated points for each of the first six finishers.

Powerlifters compete in three exercises: the squat, bench press and deadlift. The sport became popular in the United States during the 1950s, but was not organized on a national level until about 10 years ago. Junior and Senior Nationals are held annually, as well as a World Championships. The sport is still in its infancy, however, and international meets are not yet truly representative.

Power lifts are held in 10 bodyweight classes (they add 100 kilos or 220 pounds to the nine Olympic classes) and rules for scoring and number of attempts are the same as for Olympic lifts. Monstrous poundages are lifted, 900-pound squats, 650 bench presses and 850 deadlifts becoming common.

The squat is the first lift to be contested. The athlete approaches a loaded barbell which rests on a pair of stands. Shouldering the weight behind his head, he steps back and does a deep knee bend. At the bottom of this movement, the upper thigh line must go below a point parallel to the floor before the athlete recovers to starting position and places the bar back on its stands.

When doing a competitive bench press, the athlete lies back

on a bench and starts with the barbell at straight arms over the chest. The weight is lowered to mid-chest and held for one second. As soon as the referee claps, the bar is pressed back to starting position. A grip width limit of slightly over 30 inches has been imposed, and hips or feet cannot be shifted from bench or floor during the progress of the lift.

The deadlift is the simplest of the three, in that a barbell is lifted from the floor to a position across the upper thighs with the legs locked, torso upright and shoulders pulled back. The main causes for disqualification are either stopping the bar somewhere along its upward path or "hitching" it up the thighs.

Well, if you are still reading at this point, you can now take your friends to a meet and bluff through it enough to impress them with your great knowledge of the sport. I'll see you there!

—Bill Reynolds

Bill Reynolds is a veteran commentator on the Iron Game and a former competitive lifter. His articles regularly appear under his own and several pen names in **Strength & Health, Iron Man, Muscle Training Illustrated, Muscle Man International** *and* **Muscular Development.** *He is the author of* **The Complete Weight Training Book.**

Getting Started In Weight Training

Future physical fitness nuts, bodybuilders, powerlifters, Olympic style weightlifters and athletes all usually begin with a fairly common program that all can follow for the first four to six weeks. The place to work out, though, can come in many forms, as can the source of initial training advice.

There are basically five types of facilities available for weight training. The first of these and the least recommended is the commercial health spa. These are well equipped, but are very expensive. And since they cater to a monied businessman/woman clientel, managers tend to discourage hard training in the belief that such will frighten away paying customers.

Home training has both advantages and disadvantages. While it allows for workouts at any time during the day and costs nothing after an initial investment, it does present a danger to new trainees of forming bad habits. It must be noted, though, that this problem can be minimized if a weight training friend can be persuaded to sit in for the first two or three workouts. Any of the weight training magazines available on big news stands will advertize barbell-dumbell sets, but freight must be paid on these and ordering one by this means will many times entail a long wait. Large department and sporting goods stores also sell sets and are probably your best bet if you want to buy a new equipment package. Personally, I would recommend offering 12 cents to 15 cents for a used set through the want ads. Vinyl covered plates will not scratch floors, but the cast iron version is far more durable (the vinyl plates are filled with sand or concrete and often split open under heavy use). Take these factors into consideration in making your choice.

YMCA/YWCA's and commercial gyms are next in order of preference. They ask yearly dues, but are usually quite well equipped. Commercial gyms additionally offer quality instruction to new members. The primary disadvantages include a periodic cost and the requirement in many cases to fit one's exercise schedule to the hours that the "Y" or gym is open.

High school or college weight rooms are the best bet in the event that a new trainee is a student. The quality and variety of equipment is highly variable, but will always be sufficient for a beginning trainee. Instruction in the activity is offered at both high school and college levels and is generally of high quality. In colleges ask around first to see who teaches the best weight training activity classes and arrange to take that section.

Basic training advice also comes from several sources. Probably the worst is a quick article like this, because proper detail simply cannot be included due to space limitations. Weight training magazines are also pretty bad because they seldom run stories aimed at any but advanced trainees. Both of these sources can be upgraded, it might be noted, by utilizing additional hints from a weight wise friend.

As mentioned above, gym instructors are a good source of instruction, but they are inclined to lose interest in a beginner rather quickly. The many instruction manuals noted in the bibliography with this presentation can prove valuable, as they go into detail and usually include photos or drawings. There is latitude for error, however, in interpreting instructions. And finally we come to what I consider to be the best source of advice in any big gym. That's the experienced man or woman who works out there. In many cases he will appear as hulking as a big bear, but when asked he is invariably a font of readily given and authoritative information. All that a beginning person need do is ask! Experienced women can usually be recognized by the confident and speedy way they move from exercise to exercise and not by their appearance.

And now if all else fails, I will give a few hints on getting started and two programs you can try. As soon as a training facility is found, dress for the occasion. Sweat pants, a T-shirt and athletic shoes are the most appropriate for both men and women, but any costume that allows complete freedom of movement will do. Spend about five or 10 minutes at warming up. Stretching, jogging in place or a light run will do the trick. Warm muscles are less susceptible to injury and are also stronger.

Try one of the following two programs, depending on what equipment you have available (both are suitable for men or women):

Barbell Program – 1) Clean & Press (for added warmup). 2) Bench Press. 3) Bent Over Rowing. 4) Upright Rowing. 5) Military Press. 6) Curl. 7) Wrist Curl. 8) Squat. 9) Calf Raise. 10) Stiff Leg Deadlift. 11) Situps.

Universal Gym Program – 1) Leg Press. 2) Calf Press. 3) Bench Press. 4) Military Press. 5) Lat Pressdown. 6) Lat Pull-down. 7) Curl. 8) Back Hyperextension. 9) Situps.

In order to break in slowly and prevent muscle soreness, start with one set of each exercise and slowly work up to two or three sets of each movement. Begin with weights that feel very light and slowly work them upward as the body grows stronger. Do situps in repetitions of 20 to 100 per set, but keep reps in other exercises between six and 10 for power, 15 and 20 for endurance and 10 and 15 for a combination of the two.

Progression is accomplished by adding one or two repetitions each workout from the lower guide number for reps.

Once the upper guide number has been reached, add five or 10 pounds to the bar or machine, drop back to the lower guide number, and begin working up again.

You will definitely need a friend to help you learn the exercises (try the experts in the gym), as it would take ten more pages to adequately explain them. Then after a few weeks of training you will be ready to specialize on whichever branch of the sport you might like. That's where the bibliographies in this directory come into play. Good luck and good training.

—**Bill Reynolds**

For More Information

Two national magazines present good solid information on Olympic and Power lifting. *Iron Man,* listed in the Bodybuilding section also carries meet results and an occasional article on lifting. *Strength & Health,* Box 1707, York, Penn. Published bimonthly at $4.00 per year. This mag has been giving the best Olympic lifting advice and news reports since 1932. It's published by Bob Hoffman, a former Olympic coach, and it even includes a few family fitness articles. *Muscular Development,* Box 1707, York, Penn. 17405. Published bimonthly at $4.00 per year (you can get a combined year's subscription to both of these magazines at a money saving $7.00 per year). Powerlifting is the bag here, with complete contest coverage and many good training advice articles.

The AAU (address listed in the Appendix) administers weightlifting in the United States. For further help, you can contact Bill Reynolds, author of **The Complete Weight Training Book,** c/o World Publications, Box 366, Mountain View, Calif. 94040.

Many sources of equipment exist for weight sets. Any sporting goods store or large department store can sell you an exercise set, but the best Olympic sets are marketed by only a few manufacturers. Here are two of the best. You can write for brochures and catalogs. York Barbell Company, Box 1707, York, Pa. 17405. They have manufactured the York Olympic Standard Barbell for nearly 50 years. They also sell squat stands, bench press racks and training courses. Iron Man Industries, Box 10, Alliance, Neb. 69301. Distribute fine Swedish Eleiko sets, as well as many other varieties of equipment. Eleikos are the smoothest operating sets we've seen.

Here are some books worthy of your interest. All are available from World Publications, Box 366, Mountain View, Calif. 94040 at the price listed* plus 25 cents each postage.

The World's Strongest Man, Paul Anderson with Jerry Jenkins. The autobiography of the world heavyweight weightlifting champion. Paul Anderson raised the greatest weight ever lifted by a human being, according to the Guinness Book of World Records. 1975, Ppb., 136 pp., ill., $2.95, (Victor).

The Complete Weight Training Book, Bill Reynolds. Has an excellent chapter on competitive lifts and how to train for them. Available in February 1976, Hb., ill., $5.95, (World Publications).

Weight Lifting & Weight Training, George Kirkley. One of the foremost competitive weightlifting coaches offers sage instruction in Olympic style lifting. 1966, Ppb., 160 pp., ill., $1.25, (Arco).

For good books on weight training, see the section on Bodybuilding in this directory.

Wilderness Living

Wilderness living might be defined as the art of living in a remote and uninhabited area for a more-or-less extended period of time, while relying solely (or in great part) upon the natural resources available. Wilderness living is, in fact, a mode of existence where one is living in complete harmony with the earth, playing an intricate role in the ecological niche one inhabits. In comparison to camping, backpacking, motorhoming, and other activities where implements associated with modern lifestyle are carried, or transported, into wilderness area, wilderness living implies a great dependence upon natural materials immediately available. Gathering, shaping, and putting together these materials, without upsetting the delicate balance of the land is the essence of natural living. Unfortunately, with today's growing depletion of resources, it is often impossible, or unwise, to take all necessities for existence from the land. Providing oneself with basic tools such as axes, hammers, and knives is necessary, and often a special prefabricated shelter in kit form is preferable in an area where building materials are scarce.

Today, many individuals are returning to a lifestyle reminiscent of the early days of Daniel Boone and the tranquil settings of Henry David Thoreau. The fact that there lies a definite alternative in our wilderness to the mechanized, crowded, every-day problematic life that confronts one in our nation's cities, suburbs, and even less populated areas, has spurred mankind to take to the woods, deserts, and plains in search of the harmony and quietude that he desperately needs. Despite the huge onslaught of fraternalized men, a great part of the earth is still in a wild state. Sooner or later, many of us will come in contact with these often unfamiliar, areas; perhaps several will choose to make their home here permanently. But whether or not a person chooses to relocate himself temporarily, or permanently, the ability to live in the wilderness will be a real source of enjoyment if he learns to use his resources wisely and with sensible forethought to environmental impact.

Successful wilderness living does take quite a bit of essential knowledge and know-how. Despite the fact that our early ancestors could sustain themselves with gathered edibles, and find shelter in natural caves, it took many years for them to discover, and successfully adapt, fire for their uses. Just as in any other area of endeavor, perhaps the best teacher is discovery by force of necessity. Nevertheless, all wilderness dwellers can profit from the experiences of others.

Not all of us have the opportunity for spending a few months in the company of an experienced mountain man, but there are various means for learning the ways of the wilderness. Many organizations and local clubs offer courses in survival, canoe travel, making wilderness equipment, etc., and often these are the best bets for starting a gradual move into a remote area. Many of the tasks of wilderness life can be

learned before starting out on a journey into the wilds. For example, cooking can be learned in your own kitchen, and once you can prepare a substantial meal over a stove, then the only thing you have to learn is how to build and control a campfire. Similarly, this method applies to all other tasks. Learn them in advance, at least in part, and use them later, first on a short trek or two into the wilderness, and then on longer ones. After you have tried a few preliminary processions back to the land, and still find yourself undecided whether you'd like to make a longer stay, you might remind yourself of the old Indian saying, "Yesterday is ashes, tomorrow wood. Only today does the fire burn brightly."

Tipi Life

People of all ages are realizing that a higher quality, more personally rewarding lifestyle can be found by shucking unnecessary material possessions, changing unecological habits, and escaping to the quiet solitude of wilderness living. How far you go from a socially acceptable existence towards an alternative way of life, so different from the flush-toilet society, depends on you. Unlike any other physical activity, living outdoors will open your eyes to what is truly necessary to life.

If you have seriously considered an alternative lifestyle, the necessary mental changes have already begun. The reasons for a change in living pattern can be many, such as ecological awakening to the earth, its richness and resources which are over-used so greatly in the suburban atmosphere. You gain control of your physical impact on a specific area, and no longer contribute to gross quantities of waste.

Another reason for living outdoors is to save money, in our case toward the purchase of land. Paying monthly rent and utility bills affected our choice to live outdoors without unnecessary luxuries. Improved mental and physical health contribute more positive causes for making the change, and the security of feeling safe away from a concentrated population of people.

Shelter: of course, you really can't live completely outdoors – you must have shelter from the inclement periods of weather. Our decision in favor of a tipi came from learning of its strength and portability, along with low expense. Through my job at a sail loft, we obtained the 70-plus yards of marine canvas for the cover, door, and ozan (similar to a canopy over a bed).

We made our own tipi cover, mainly for having the personal satisfaction of completing such a project by ourselves. Covers, liners, and doors can be purchased ready-made or in kit form with directions for sewing, at reasonable prices considering the hours of labor involved.

We reinforced the cover more than was necessary to get maximum life out of the canvas – about 10 years with one waterproofing job.

As in any project, your confidence and practical mechanical ability will determine the end result. More important is experience with the use of a power-sewing machine. A standard, electric home sewing machine simply does not have the strength to produce a quality cover. We double-stitched each seam with a zig-zag and used extra layers of machine-sewn canvas and hand-sewn leather at stress points: pole pocket corners, top tie point to lifting pole, and front tie above door. It also helps to have a large layout area – outdoors would work in the summer. Rulers, pencils, scissors, wax thread, No. 2 grommet hole punch, sailmaker's needles and a hand palm are needed for sewing. About 60 feet of one-inch nylon webbing is needed for the hem.

Another improvement we have to "winterize" our tipi is a tin wood heater with 16 feet of stove pipe going straight up through the flaps. We secured a cage of wire around the stove pipe where it passes from inside to out, then brought the canvas in close around this cage. (We originally had a campfire in the center, as is sometimes highly praised, but got smoked out.) With advanced planning, you can put an asbestos patch on your cover for the stove pipe to fit through. We have a canvas "raincatcher", a four-foot square with ropes at the corners, tied up on the inside to the piles underneath the rope cluster.

On the floor, we used plastic as a ground cloth at first, with cedar sawdust over it. Sawdust got in everything! We now have a board floor, laid over logs, with the tipi cover pitched high on the poles, about a foot off the ground. You don't want the canvas to sit in water or it will rot. The weather where you settle will lead you to improvise accordingly.

Our poles are cedar, a wood of abundance here in western Washington. They are slightly larger than called for, but saved us recently when the top of a large big-leaf maple tree fell on us in a summer storm. Five poles broke off above the rope cluster, but the cover remained perfect!

The attitudes of our friends and relatives ranged from wonder to disbelief as we raised the poles into place on Thanksgiving Day. Few people realize that it is possible to winter-over in anything but a conventional house. With trial and error, we have lived within our cloth cone through all four seasons of the year, and will continue until our wood cabin is completed. For most people, living outdoors is only a temporary arrangement – a way to reach a particular goal or, perhaps, to experience another lifestyle for a summer. But even to live outdoors for a short while, you need to become a "professional" in the sport to survive.

Clothing: everyone is born with their fair-weather clothes – nothing! You have to put on a "hide", though, to survive the bad weather. The clothes we wear reflect our close relationship with the earth – dirt, to some people. They must be practical and comfortable, not stylish, for in the woods life there is no place for light-duty dress. Rain gear is necessary for us – boots, long coats, or pants and jacket, and hats. We each have two pairs of hiking/work boots.

While it may be abhorrent to city folks, we only do laundry once a month. We have just enough clothing to get it all good and dirty within that time. Our values have changed by our new way of life, and like children in play clothes, we no longer feel ourselves in tight, clean confining dress.

Tools: for basic survival, you can get by with an ax, knife, rope and matches. Other tools you need depend on your trip. We spent a year getting the tools and equipment necessary to clear land and build a log-frame cabin. If you are really green to this trip, there are lots of do-it-yourself homesteading books available now. Whenever possible, go to a library instead of buying books. Remember, the trip is not to consume so much.

Everyday Life: along with other mental changes, your concept of work and fun become different from a city person's. When your energy is spent on various self-satisfying projects, then it feels good to be exhausted by the end of a day. For us, work and fun are often combined in our daily activities. We have no typical day or mandatory routine schedule to follow, but rather, the weather, mood and the seasons determine our activities, just as it was in more self-sufficient times. We devote our energy to positive actions and thoughts, and try to better our awareness of our place in the circle of life.

Cooking: where you're at with what you eat will determine your kitchen trip. We are vegetarians for many reasons, and therefore have little worry of attracting wild animals into camp, particularly bears. If you eat meat, you need to consider your storage spot carefully.

Our kitchen is outside – a table lashed between trees with a temporary roof laid overhead, and fir bark laid on the ground to keep down the mud. Having the kitchen outside allows for greater spaciousness both inside the tipi and in the kitchen area. I cook over a campfire outside, or on the tin stove, depending on the weather. Campfire cooking is time-consuming as you have to wait for coals, then watch everything carefully while it cooks. A wood cook stove in our cabin will be a luxury! At night, everything in the kitchen must be put away, secure from mice.

Sanitation: the unasked question in the back of everyone's mind concerns sanitation. We live without running water, and prefer to bring water up from a stream that runs through the valley below, rather than drink piped city water. We also bathe in the same creek, but use non-polluting soap in the cold rushing water. This is too primitive for most people, with their hang-ups on cleanliness, but at least we know where our water comes from, where it goes, and how we affect its flow. We use a hole in the ground for "sewage" disposal, but will have a formal outhouse soon. In this way, our waste becomes humus and enriches the soil, with insignificant impact on the earth.

Dangers: fear is not a positive thought, so we hardly consider the dangers of living outdoors. Nevertheless, the possible natural dangers would be from animals and falling trees, although neither can be protected from, or is really a serious threat. Fortunately, the city-syndrome of everyone's fears being of everyone else, seldom affects woods people in remote places. If anything, country people have too much trust in other folks, but if you live according to good karma then you should be without fear.

Money and Working: greater independence is a common goal among back-to-the-landers. It's easy to break away from T.V., which runs your life deviously, and then you can take command of your own existence. This is often the case when working away from home – your umbilical cord is tied to the mother system, everyday. So unless you have a mellow job which you truly like – not just for the paycheck – it's easier to make do with less money, and trade or earn your own bread independently. This is an individual decision though, often dependent upon your own creativity and abilities.

If you long for a calm, rewarding life, let your spirit guide you toward a saner, safer existence that can be your true reality. Take to the outdoors!

—Julie Winn

Julie Winn has had a life-long interest in Indian life and the outdoors. After spending seven years at **The Signpost** *magazine, she moved to an area outside Fall City, Wash. where she now lives with her husband. They live on 11 acres, their tipi serving as their shelter.*

For More Information

Mother Earth News, Box 70, Hendersonville, N.C. 28739 has a lot of good articles on wilderness living. Anyone interested should be getting this magazine. A couple of organizations of interest: American Forest Institute, 1619 Massachusetts Ave., N.W., Washington D.C. 20036; American Forestry Association, 1319 18th St. N.W., Washington, D.C., 20036; and the US Dept. of Agriculture, Office of Information, Washington, D.C., 20250. It is important to be well read in this area. Here are some books that can be of help. All are available from World Publications, Box 366, Mountain View, Calif. 94040 at the price listed* plus 25 cents each postage. Write for a complete list.

The Manual of Practical Homesteading, John Vivian. Up-to-date manual drawn from the experiences of a contemporary pioneer who quit civilization for a quieter, more self-reliant life. Gets down to the nitty gritty details. 1975 Hb., 340 pp., ill., $8.95, (Rodale).

The Wilderness Life, Calvin Rutstrum. "Every armchair outdoorsman will sense the appeal of true wilderness through Rutstrum's charming accounts."–says the Library Journal about Rutstrum's last wilderness book. Here is another volume of his fine writing as he conveys–with his typical sense of joy of the glories of nature–thoughts on wilderness in relation to man and his planet. 1975, 288 pp., ill., $6.95, (MacMillan).

Outdoorsman's Fix-it Book, Monte Burch. The care and repair of equipment is an important area of knowledge for the outdoorsman and this book delves into a variety of sporting gear. Easy step-by-step instructions for fixing camping and fishing equipment, boats, guns, bows and arrows, snowmobiles and chainsaws. 1971 Hb., 274 pp., ill., $6.95, (Olson).

How to Build Your Home in the Woods, Bradford Angier. A useful volume which shows how to build log cabins, camping shelters, cabins without logs, and furniture stressing economy and simplicity. Includes many working drawings and practical plans. 1952 Ppb., 310 pp., ill., $3.95, (Hart).

The Foxfire Book, Elliot Wigginton, ed. The arts and crafts of southern Appalachia are presented in a format extremely interesting to the new outdoorsman who wants new insights into wilderness life. An extensive section of the book deals with log cabin building, while other sections discuss quilting, remedies and folklore. 1972 Hb. & Ppb., 384 pp., ill., $8.95/$3.95, (Doubleday).

The Wilderness Cabin, Calvin Rutstrum. Step-by-step instructions for building auxiliary and one-room log, frame and adobe cabins. Written with such detail and clarity that even the inexperienced do-it-yourselfer is assured of success. 1972 Hb. & Ppb., 194 pp., ill., $5.95/$1.95, (MacMillan).

Wilderness Gear You Can Make Yourself, Bradford Angier. This guidebook will save the outdoorsman many dollars in camping equipment. Instructions and illustrations for making packsacks, tents, sleeping bags, moccasins and camp furniture. 1973 Ppb., 115 pp., ill., $2.95, (MacMillan).

How to Build and Furnish a Log Cabin, W. Ben Hunt. The only manual available that shows you how to build and furnish an authentic pioneer cabin using only handtools and the woods around you. Step-by-step directions for building three different cabins, and all you need to know to build tables, chairs and beds. 1974 Ppb., 166 pp., ill., $3.95, (MacMillan).

The New Way of the Wilderness, Calvin Rutstrum. An authoritative guide for the woodsman–a far-reaching and diverse exploration on surviving, living in and enjoying the woods, written by a master outdoorsman. 1973 Hb. & Ppb., 280 pp., ill., $4.95/$2.95, (MacMillan).

Build a Yurt: The Low-Cost Mongolian Round House, Len Charney. Tired of living in a tract house? So was Len Charney, until he discovered the yurt, a sturdy, well-designed and attractive dwelling with a skylight used by Mongolian herdsmen for centuries. Less expensive and easier to build than domes or A-frames. 1974 Ppb., 134 pp., ill., $3.95, (MacMillan).

The Wilderness Route Finder, Calvin Rutstrum. Information on ways of finding your direction in the wilderness. The author begins by clearing up some popular myths on navigation, goes ahead to explain why people get lost, and then provides a variety of techniques and tips for making one's way confidently and safely on land and water. 1969 Hb. & 1967 Ppb., 214 pp., ill., $4.95/$1.50, (MacMillan).

Reading the Woods, Vinson Brown. A guide for recognizing the historical and geological development of wilderness areas. This unusual book tells you about the effects of climate, weather, animals and man on the terrain and discusses the variety of clues they leave behind. 1969 Hb., 160 pp., ill., $7.95, (Stackpole).

Windsurfing

Windsurfing is a sport with a misleading name. It is very concerned with the wind, but is almost totally unrelated to surfing. Windsurfing is a sailing art, but the experience is much like snow skiing.

A skiing sensation was the goal of the inventors, Hoyle Schweitzer and Jim Drake. Schweitzer and Drake assigned themselves the task of creating a sailboat that would not try to be the fastest, or able to go the greatest distance, but rather one that would yield the best personal sensation.

Since all of the most exciting individual sports, such as running, jumping, surfing and skiing are done standing, that position had to be the one principally used for sailing the craft. Also, the final machine had to be simple and free of gimmicks. In 1968, the pair of inventors patented a device which was propelled by what they named the "free sail system", a sail held in shape by double booms and universally pivoted on the surface of the craft that carries it.

In practice a free sail craft is operated by angling the sail around so that it is somewhat tipped toward the wind and supports itself on the breeze like a kite. Since one lower corner is attached to the deck through a universal joint, it supplies a push without making the craft tip. Supporting part of his weight on the deck and part on the sail, the rider flies the sail like a wing to raise or lower himself.

Because of the use of the lifting power of the sail, this system is much more efficient than that of a conventional

Windsurfing is a lot harder to learn than it looks. It's an unnatural act that sometimes takes more than 50 hours of instruction and practice to master. (Taylor)

sailboat, for as the wind rises in strength the craft lifts higher.

And the sensation? It is fantastic!

The Windsurfer Species

Windsurfing is an unnatural act. A person just doesn't jump onto a windsurfer and take off. Instead, he/she practices in ever increasing winds until the ability to hold oneself above the water using only the wind in the sail has become innate. It is very similar to the art of a snow skier in deep powder snow. He learns the unnatural act of going fast in order to keep moving at all, and leaning down the hill instead of up, as his instincts command.

Because of the apparent ease with which a person can maneuver a windsurfer after about 50 hours of experience, tales of the great difficulty of getting one to move at all in the first hour are legendary and are, in general, humorous. You have to be a pretty good sport to make it through the learning phase!

The fact that learning to windsurf looks ignoble has been a blessing to the sport. Few egotists make it through that phase and become owners of windsurfers! This weeding out has left only the most well-adjusted individuals as members of the windsurfing fraternity, a quality on which several yacht clubs have voluntarily commented after hosting a windsurfer regatta.

Windsurfing regattas are identical to those sailed in any other type of boat. Although the courses sailed tend to be shorter, the same qualities that are tested in other dinghy races are tested on the windsurfer. There is a mental challenge to make good tactical decisions, and qualities like familiarity with the craft, "boat handling", and physical conditioning are tested.

Unlike many other small boats, however, great size and strength are not required to sail a windsurfer. In general, lighter and smaller people, with their more efficient strength-to-weight ratio, do better in windsurfer races. The national and world champions are usually under 130 pounds, and women are prominent in the sport because of their lighter physiques.

In stronger winds of 30 m.p.h. or better, strength and endurance become important. It is only then that the heavyweight windsurfer sailors begin to show their stuff.

Because of the bias toward light weight, however, windsurfer regatta contestants are usually divided into groupings by their weights so that people of similar size race against one another.

It is after the races are over for the day that windsurfer sailors have the biggest advantage over sailors on other boats. A windsurfer takes about as much time to clean up as a pair of skis, so the apres windsurfing is immediately available! Most windsurfer regatta calendars show the usual races out of yacht clubs but they also are filled with races out of restaurants, campgrounds, or good picnic spots. A windsurfer can be launched through surf or off rocks, so if the social aspect of a site is good, a regatta will be held there no matter what the launching facilities are. Since the craft is so mechanically simple, it has attracted more female owners than other boat classes. That definitely improves the quality of windsurfer social affairs!

Windsurfers tend to be people who think for themselves and practice their not very well-known sport for the personal satisfaction it gives, rather than for any sort of wide recognition. They are people who like to stay exercised and who enjoy the outdoors, and they are as much fun as their rather unusual boat.

—Glenn Taylor

Glenn Taylor studied physics at Reed College and at the University of California, Santa Barbara, where he received a B.A. in 1968. Six years later he quit work as a scientific computer programmer for Stanford Research Institute in order to open the first windsurfing school in North America.

For More Information

There's only one windsurfing magazine, but it's a beauty, *Windsurfing News,* 1038 Princeton Drive, Marina Del Rey, California 90291. It costs $1.00 per issue.

The Windsurfing Association (same address as above) administers windsurfing in America. A good contact is Glenn Taylor, 940 Cotton Street, Menlo Park, Calif. 94025. Glenn runs a great windsurfing school and is a font of ready information on the subject.

There is only one book available that covers windsurfing. It is available from World Publications, Box 366, Mountain View, Calif. 94040 at the price listed* plus 25 cents postage.

Windsurfing Manual, Windsurfing Association. This basic how-to manual leads the newcomer step-by-step and day-by-day through all the fundamentals starting with training sails, preparing for the first day, paddling, rigging, and leading up to sailing downwind, storage and maintenance. Question and answer section after each chapter for self-test. 1975 Ppb., 26 (oversize) pp., ill., $4.00, (Windsurfing Association).

Wrestling-Freestyle

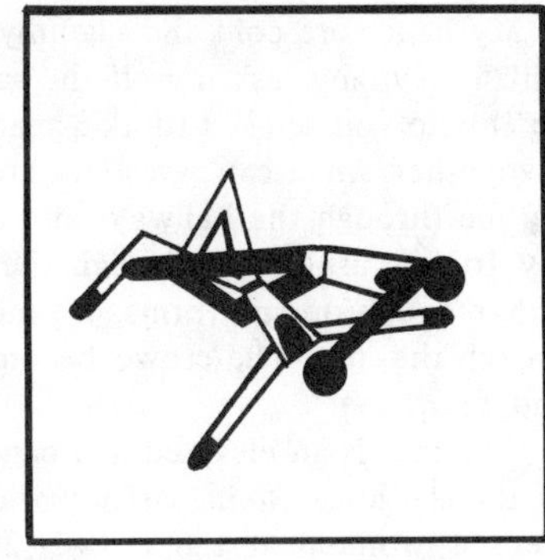

In the body contact sport of wrestling two opponents try to pin each other to the mat by using various holds and body maneuvers. Where two youngsters may roughly grapple with each other until one "gives," competitive wrestlers utilize polished combinations and techniques to win. Modern wrestling on the high school, collegiate, or international levels is a stylized and methodical but exciting sport that requires strength, quickness, balance, coordination and timing.

Nearly every civilization on earth developed a form of wrestling, and the modern Olympic sport can be traced 500 years to the ancient Sumerians, then to the Greeks and Romans. The Greek form, which became part of the Olympic Games in 704 B.C., was quite rough and probably looked similar to the professional "wrestlers" of today. Unimpressed by the Greek wrestling, the Romans cut down on the roughness by limiting the use of the legs to balance and allowed no holds below the waist. Today we call this Greco-Roman wrestling and use almost exactly the same moves and holds as ancient wrestlers employed.

Freestyle wrestling is derived from Roman grappling, English Renaissance wrestling and American Catch-as-Catch Can, and utilizes the entire body, not just the upper body. The legs are used for balance, bracing, holding, levering, and lifting. They are as important as the arms for throwing, pulling, and controlling.

Both forms, Greco-Roman and freestyle,require good conditioning and good daily habits for proper physical and mental development. Daily workouts that involve mental discipline

"For me this draw was a victory. I passed my own intensely personal test, the same kind of experience that is happening on wrestling mats at all ages and all levels nearly every day. I'm talking about something that athletes call "heart." Finding the "heart" to try harder than I had ever tried before was my greatest victory. This most important victory, the personal victory, often has nothing to do with the public scoreboard." (Duffy)

and competitive spirit along with drills, running, and calisthenics are needed to build a solid, intelligent, aggressive wrestler. Since the sport is highly individualized, each competitor must look to himself alone for success: his dedication and training will determine the degree of success.

Wrestlers compete against others in their own size. There is no "big man" in wrestling as there is in other sports–other than in the heavyweight class! The lower weight classes are composed of smaller and quicker men who employ dazzling maneuvers that others in the higher weight classes cannot perform as well. The higher weight class wrestlers display power and control.

High school and college wrestling are governed by collegiate rules which differ from international rules set by the International Amateur Wrestling Federation (FILA). Since this creates problems in international, continental, and Olympic competitions, the US is gradually moving toward consistency with the international rules. The major problem is that the US practices "control" wrestling and rewards wrestlers who maintain control over an opponent in a match by designating "riding time" and awarding points for time as well as specific skills displayed. Escapes from a "controlled" position are also rewarded by a point in the escapee's favor. FILA does not recognize riding time or escapes and requires progression toward a pin in the matches.

Seniors (open) and juniors (ages 15 to 19) compete in 10 weight classifications in international competition. The match lasts a total of nine minutes, divided into three three-minute periods with one minute of rest between periods. Victory for one of the competitors may occur in any one of the periods when a fall or pin takes place: the winner must force his opponent's shoulders flat to the wrestling mat for one full second.

In collegiate competition only enrolled college or university students may participate and their matches last eight minutes. The opening period is two minutes with second and third periods of three minutes each. Collegiate scoring is much more complex than international. A takedown (from a neutral position one wrestler achieves a position of control) is two points instead of one and escapes are rewarded by one point. A reversal (from "controlled" to a "position of control") merits two points and a predicament (close to a pin, maintained for a specific time) is two points. A near fall or near pin (shoulders inches from but not touching mat, position maintained) gets three points. A wrestler may score a maximum of two points for riding time, one point per minute of time in control. He may also score when his opponent violates a rule of conduct, uses an illegal hold or stalls: the referee will award a point to the other wrestler. High school wrestlers contest for three two-minute periods under collegiate rules.

My Most Important Victory

The loudspeaker has a loose wire and the Bulgarian voice is garbled. The crackling speaker is the only sound in the large cold room, deep in the bowels of the Sofia Stadium. Expressionless athletes, with glazed eyes are moving quietly stretching their tight muscles while listening carefully to the noise speaker.

This is the warm-up room for the 1970 World Wrestling Championships. A dozen of us are "on deck" waiting to recognize our names, listening and psychologically preparing to test ourselves against the best another nation can offer. We've all been national champions and we're still striving, striving for a moment of perfection, to become for just one instant the best in the world.

My hands are cold and clammy, my ears ring and I can't sit still. I inevitably ask myself the same question. "Why do you do this to yourself?" I think I hear my name, "Bak Deetrach." Two other American wrestlers are suddenly beside me, guiding me through the hallways and out into the bright sunlight. My friends usher me through the thick crowds; people reach out to touch our uniforms. We move past the barriers and approach the mat. The crowd becomes a passionate sea of noise and color.

The mat is an elevated and canopied platform in the center of the stadium. Taking off my warm-up suit and climbing the steps I wonder at the crowd–20,000 or 30,000? I'm surrounded by thousands and thousands of people and I feel absolutely alone. As I walk to the center of the mat I can see only my approaching opponent. I don't see a man, I see an abstract, a target. The ritual begins. We shake hands and step back. The referee blows his whistle and I move forward, simultaneously looking for an opening and protecting myself.

The cyclone of emotion is at its peak. I know that with the first contact I will either harness the energy and be propelled to a great match or I'll find myself in the face of the gale, crushed in an emotional torrent.

I am facing the Bulgarian heavyweight and the rabid crowd is very much behind him. He outweighs me by close to 100 pounds and they expect their hero to crush me easily. But there is much more to wrestling than size and strength. Wrestling is a sophisticated art. It's a multi-dimensional chess game employing speed, stamina, leverage and innovation.

The Bulgarian champion seems clumsy and awkward. I've been training steadily for two months, often twice a day. This moment is the culmination of all that I've worked for. The huge man reaches out for my head and shoulder as we circle together. This is the moment. I focus all of my experience, my energy, and my training on this instant. Ducking under his outstretched hand, my body follows a pattern of motion it has been through thousands of times before. As my chest collides with his massive thigh I stand and lift his leg to my full height. The mammoth Bulgarian hops on his other foot trying to keep his balance. Circling, I sweep the leg out from under him and follow him down to the mat. Executing a takedown on a first rate opponent, I always feet the grace, the power, the mastery of my discipline. I now have a one point lead but the action is continuous. There are moves and counter moves. The rhythms of motion become so pure that I can only feel action and reaction. My attention is absolute. The concentration is so intense and the timing so precise that the slightest distraction can mean defeat.

In the third and final period the Bulgarian is now ahead 2-1. I've lost two points, being penalized for passivity. He's using his massive weight to push me backward while maintaining an impenetrable defense. His home crowd is jeering at him. They've come to see their champion wrestle, not to push his way to victory over an opponent 100 pounds lighter. I wonder what role politics is playing as the referee ignores the Bulgarian's stalling tactics.

The big man seems to have run out of gas. I step up my attack and in an effort to survive the final minute, the giant feigns an injury. He rolls around the mat holding his knee and sucking up all the air he can. With seven seconds remaining in the bout and the crowd now solidly behind me the referee makes the Bulgarian stand and verbally warns him against passivity. I can see the score 2-1 and the clock, :07. Energy courses through my body like a great jolt of electricity. Instantly I fire deeply for the behemoths' legs. As he kicks his legs back I can sense his body falling toward me like some giant redwood tree. Coiled below him I concentrate on his falling mass. My timing must be perfect. I sit out to one side and his tremendous body crashes to the mat beside me. Quickly pivoting over the top of the fallen giant I can see the referee signaling my one point takedown as I hear the gong signifying the conclusion of the bout.

I reached down and helped the proud man to his feet. He hung his head as the referee raised our arms to indicate a draw. Exhausted we threw our arms around each other in a feeling of camaraderie. There was no competition left in us. We had given everything we had in the bout. The draw gave me fifth place and eliminated me from the tournament. The tie was all the Bulgarian needed to make the round robin final and ultimately win the silver medal.

For me, this draw was a victory. I passed my own intensely personal test. The same kind of experience that is happening on wrestling mats at all ages and all levels nearly everyday. I'm talking about something that athletes call "heart." Finding the "heart" to try harder than I had ever tried before was my greatest victory. This most important victory, the personal victory, often has nothing to do with the public scoreboard.

—Buck Deadrich

Buck Deadrich has won five AAU and USWF national freestyle titles. He wrestled on the United States team as a 220 pounder in the 1972 Olympics and was a silver medalist at the 1973 World University Games.

For More Information

There are two amateur wrestling magazines available: *Amateur Wrestling News,* Box 60387, Oklahoma City, Okla. 73106. Published 16 times a year at $5.00, very timely coverage of wrestling throughout the United States. Published weekly during the season. *The Young Wrestler,* published bi-monthly by Amateur Wrestling News, address above. Subscriptions are $3.00 per year. Covers news and techniques for high school and Junior Olympics competitors.

There are many national and international associations and federations for wrestling. Here are some of the basic addresses for these. US Wrestling Assoc. (AAU), c/o John Dustin, AAU House, 3400 W. 86th St., Indianapolis, Ind. 46268. US Wrestling Federation, c/o Steve Combs, Box 1016, Stillwater, Okla. 74074. United States Amateur Wrestling Foundation, c/o Charles A. Powers, Powers Chemco, Charles St., Glen Cove, NY 11542. Furnishes financial aid for the betterment of amateur wrestling.

With literally hundreds of wrestling equipment manufacturers and distributors it is difficult to make a choice, but here are two that offer mail order service. National Wrestling Equipment Co., Box 1102, Stillwater, Okla. 74074. They say that they supply everything for wrestling but the wrestlers. Cliff Keen Wrestling Products, Inc., Box 1224, Ann Arbor, Mich. 48104. Send for their free catalog. Sells everything a wrestler would need from training through tournament.

Here are some good books that should help you get started. All are available from World Publications, Box 366, Mountain View, Calif. 94040 at the price listed* plus 25 cents each postage. Write for a complete list.

Inside Wrestling, Tom Valentine. A scientific guide to winning techniques as they are practiced on national and international levels. Explains the rules governing amateur competition and tournaments, with illustrated instructions on the basic holds, etc. A very good basic guide. 1972 Hb. & Ppb., 96 (oversize) pp., ill., $7.95/$3.95, (Regnery).

Wrestling Physical Conditioning Encyclopedia, John Jesse. A complete and well-illustrated physical conditioning guide for wrestling. Designed for the athlete who wishes to improve his physique and for the coach and trainer who wish to improve team effectiveness. 1970 Ppb., 416 pp., ill., $6.95, (Athletic Press).

Wrestling, Umbach and Johnson. Prepared to introduce young men and women to the sport of amateur wrestling. All the basic information needed to prepare the beginner for the competitive sport. Equipment, rules, training methods and the skills are presented with illustrations. 1966 Ppb., 62 pp., ill., $2.95, (Brown).

Wrestling Techniques: Takedown, Richard C. Maertz. Successful wrestlers are those who get the takedown and gain the advantage quickly. The author has analyzed more than 50 different takedown moves and arranged them in easy-to-follow sequential order. 1970 Hb., 133 pp., ill., $7.95, (Barnes).

Action Drilling in Wrestling, George Gianakaris. Written for the wrestling coach, this is a manual of drills designed to supplement more general texts. Photos and clear instruction show the sequence of each drill. 1969 Hb., 79 pp., ill., $5.95, (Barnes).

Wrestling for Fun, Thompson Clayton. Emphasizing that wrestling can be fun if winning is removed as the objective, the author presents detailed instruction in the various styles of wrestling, including Greco-Roman and freestyle, AAU, collegiate, and interscholastic. All the techniques are explicitly explained and completely illustrated. 1973 Hb., 87 pp., ill., $6.95, (Barnes).

Principles of Championship Wrestling, Ray Carson and Buel Patterson. Presents the sport from a philosophical and scientific point of view. The authors explain why particular techniques must be executed in a certain manner, and psychological and physiological factors that affect the athlete are discussed. 1972 Hb., 192 pp., ill., $7.95, (Barnes).

Systematic Championship Wrestling, Ray F. Carson, Jr. A scholarly approach to wrestling that presents the philosophy, coaching methodology, training physiology and tactical methods used. Bridges the existing gap between how wrestling skills are put into action and why they are. 1973 Hb., 328 pp., ill., $9.95, (Barnes).

The Science and Skills of Wrestling, Warren Boring. A well-balanced representation that deals with the academic, scientific aspects and skills and techniques of wrestling. 1975 Hb., 330 pp., ill., $15.95, (Mosby).

An Introduction to Wrestling, Thompson Clayton. Designed especially for the wrestler with a noncompetitive interest. Discusses the rules and history of the sport, and explains the numerous throws, pins, counters and takedowns. Each move is illustrated step-by-step. 1970 Ppb., 88 pp., ill., $1.45, (Barnes).

Wrestling-Greco-Roman

Wrestling dates back at least 5000 years. The oldest wrestling artifacts are several hundred tomb paintings found at Beni Hasan on the banks of the Nile River in Upper Egypt. These paintings clearly depict virtually every hold used in modern freestyle and Greco-Roman wrestling, so it would be safe to assume that wrestling had evolved for many centuries before these were painted about 2500 BC. Indeed, when you read the words "girded their loins" in the Bible, this refers to a very ancient Hebrew form of belt wrestling in which holds were made by grasping a belt tightly girdled around each athlete's middle.

In classic times, the Greeks wrestled at each of their Crown Games—at Olympia, Nemea, Corrinth and Delphi. Few holds were barred and only the use of eye gouging and fisticuffs were forbidden. Both of these tactics, were allowed in the pancration, a bone crushing and extremely brutal event combining the worst of both wrestling and boxing. After the Roman conquest of Greece, wrestling was changed and made less violent by eliminating all leg holds. This classic style survives today in the Olympic sport of Greco-Roman wrestling.

Modern Greco-Roman wrestling has survived practically unchanged for many centuries. Even the rules formulated by the French in the middle 1800s have remained virtually the same for a century. The main feature of the Greco-Roman style is that a wrestler can not grasp his opponent below the hips and is forbidden to use his own legs for grasping or holding. This exclusive use of upper body holds results in somewhat less fluid wrestling than with freestyle, but neck bridging becomes more important and spectacular head spinning maneuvers will dot many Greco-Roman matches.

Wrestlers tend to specialize in either freestyle or Greco-Roman, but adherents to either style are usually able to wrestle well in the other. This situation results from the very similar training undergone for each style.

For More Information

For additional information on wrestling, see Wrestling–Freestyle. Here is one book covering this subject. It is available from World Publications, Box 366, Mountain View, Calif. 94040 at the price listed* plus 25 cents postage.

Greco-Roman Wrestling, M. Briggs Hunt. An illustrated guide to the international championship techniques, which can also be applied to scholastic and college freestyle wrestling. Well-illustrated and graded to guide the beginner or coach to mastery of these different wrestling holds. 1970 Ppb., 168 pp., ill., $3.95, (Athletic Press).

Greco-Roman wrestling (Left-Hoke) differs from freestyle (Above-Duke) in that no leg holds are allowed. Wrestlers tend to specialize in one style or another, but can usually give a good account of themselves in either style, especially on lower levels of competition. Greco-Roman wrestling today is virtually the same as it was at the time of Christ.

Wristwrestling

A wristwrestling match at a Petaluma saloon 24 years ago started something phenomenal for a little town 40 miles north of San Francisco. The World Championship Wristwrestling Tournament held annually in Petaluma, California, has produced some extraordinary encounters, humorous episodes, and some mighty battles of strength and courage.

How does a competitor prepare for such an event? What is it that makes a wristwrestling champion? First of all, a competitor must develop his strength with specialized weight and pulley training working the wrists, forearms, biceps, triceps, shoulders, chest and upper back, since they are all involved in wristwrestling. But strength must not be overemphasized as many strong "weightlifters" have tasted the agony of defeat over the years.

Second, one must develop a "technique" and practice wristwrestling on a regulation table with various opponents for months prior to the championship. Included in one's technique must be a knowledge of where to put your elbow in the cup, how to situate your feet and legs, what type of grip to assume, and how to react if you begin to win or lose. Believe it or not, the sport has developed more and more into a scientific art.

The next area of importance is that of building proper stamina and endurance. This is best done by running or bicycling every other day to improve your overall conditioning and wind. It's also helpful to apply pressure on opponents' arms for long periods of time to increase endurance. Many times a participant may have five to seven matches during an evening and must be prepared to make it through the long, strenuous night.

Next, practicing a fast start or what is referred to as getting the "pop" is extremely important. One should continually work on his timing to be able to react as quickly as possible once the referee gives the signal "Ready, Go!" This helps to catch your opponent off-guard and immediately put you in an offensive position as opposed to the strenuous, defensive position of your opponent.

The final and most important characteristic of a wristwrestling champion is what we like to term the "will to win", or in other words, the mental training involved. You must develop your concentration so that your whole being is in your right hand when the referee says "Ready, Go!" You must picture yourself as a winner and visualize your opponent's arms going down for many days prior to the championships. Part of this means being totally convinced in your own mind that you cannot be beaten. And all champions will say, you must train your mind so that it will function perfectly under the tension of competition.

The Petaluma contest has been a World Championship since 1962. Since that time, wristwrestlers with the best records are Jim Dolcini and Jim Pollock, who have won five titles; Jim Payne, who has won four titles; and Duane Benedix, Ted Pollock and Mickie Novis, who have all won three titles.

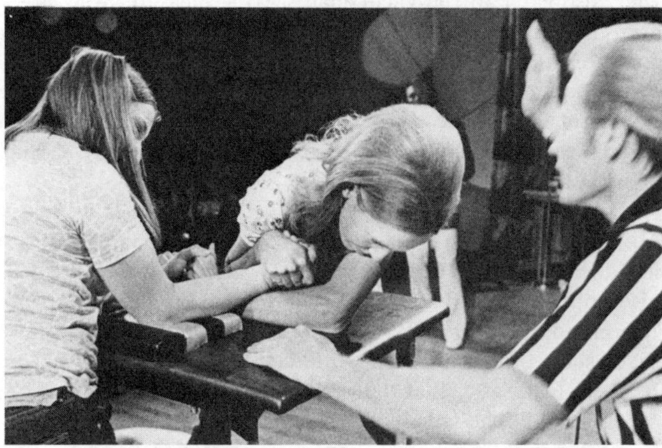

Competition for both men and women is held at the annual world championships in Petaluma, California. Solid technique, strength, and competitiveness are keys to winning in wrist wrestling. Competitors spend many hours honing their concentration for that penultimate moment in each match when pure courage and a steel arm combine to win a match. (Glusker)

The ABC Wide World of Sports has televised the Wristwrestling Championships many times and they claim it is one of their most popular events. It has been popular since Roman times and will probably continue forever, for it puts one man against another in arm to arm combat.

—Jim Pollock and Ted Pollock

Jim Pollock is a five-time middleweight wristwrestling champion. His brother, Ted, has won the lightweight division three times.

Yachting

While yachting can be a term applied to activities of both pleasure boating and sailboat racing, the early yachtsmen – ancient Greeks, Romans, and Egyptians – maintained vessels of various sorts largely for their ease. Cleopatra's Barge, named in tribute to its early Egyptian predecessor, was an 83-foot luxury vessel built in 1816 for a wealthy ship owner from Salem, Mass. This craft is generally regarded as the first American yacht, although well-financed Americans kept boats for pleasure as far back as the early 1700s. As early as 1811 yacht and boat clubs appeared in America, but no organizations really lasted until the 1840's, when clubs were organized on the Atlantic and Gulf coasts, and on the Great Lakes.

In 1966, it was estimated that there existed at least 800 yacht clubs in the United States.

While these clubs often hold races (see Sailboat Racing), they also cater to the yachtsman seeking pleasure, who either owns or charters boats. Many yachtsmen live aboard their craft for months at a time, either cruising upon the earth's ample waters, or merely idling in-port. Parties and gay festivities are not rare aboard the yacht. In fact, many skippers have an event every weekend. Yachts are also used for day sailing, sport fishing and racing.

Basically, yachts fall into two groups: power and sail. Motor yachts that are not used for competition can be any size and type, and they can be used for a variety of activities. This also applies for sailing yachts. Afternoon sailing parties are not uncommon in 100-footers, and yachts of under 40 feet have made successful around the world jaunts. The most remarkable of these feats, as well as the first, was made by Joshua Slocum, when, in 1890, he sailed around the globe, alone.

A combination power and sailing craft is known as an auxiliary yacht. Sailing yachts over 25 feet in length, used for cruising, carry engines as auxiliaries to their sails. Other types have engines as their main source of power, and small auxiliary sailing rigs.

Today, with rising inflation and untouchable yacht costs, many boatmen are turning to the charter boat. By chartering a craft, they can avoid many of the pitfalls and inconveniences that affect the yacht owners.

The Oceans Are Your Oyster

The past century has seen yachting change from a sport of kings to a king of sports enjoyed by millions. More subtle changes have included a trend away from large power yachts to sailing yachts and, recently, the abandonment of competitive yacht racing for leisurely cruising. You need not wet your feet to observe the trends; they can be illustrated just by looking at the covers of the nation's better boating magazines:

It used to be *Motor Boating*. In recent years that monthly publication changed its face to read *Motor Boating and Sailing*. Now each issue carries the reminder: "The Cruising Skipper's Magazine." *Yachting* adds to its nameplate, "Power and Sail."

The trend to cruising under sail is interesting to one who has been doing that, watching the past catch up to him. Why would the millions of Americans who go boating take up an archaic sport like yacht sailing? Like Latin in the Catholic church, sailing should have died out decades ago. Alvin Toffler in his **Future Shock** suggests that stressed persons will want to drop out of the present and go back in time. Hence the interest in the nation's bicentennial celebration. Sailing does just that; like skiing, you're on your own using Mother Nature to stay alive.

Other reasons why more people set sail for cruising include more leisure time available, earlier retirement, climbing gasoline prices, and perhaps women's lib. Take the latter. The modern woman has been climbing out of the galley and onto the deck, in case you haven't noticed – she wants to sail comfortably, and not on her ear. And what's the hurry, anyway? Many people are becoming less interested in blood-and-guts racing, also. So the ads in boating magazines now show replicas of cruising designs from 50 and more years ago.

Cruising sailing captures more landlubbers each year. They come to the sport tired of racing yachts or speedboats. Just as there are ski enthusiasts whose entire lives are spent on the slopes, so there is a growing body of yachtsmen who exist on and about the oceans of the world.

Tomorrow for yachting? I see less private ownership of yachts as the ability to purchase them disappears, with less spendable income, and as prices rise out of sight. But there'll be more people going boating. They'll rent or charter a sailing yacht for their vacation. After all, why pay for storage and maintainance for a boat you can use but four weeks a year? That's why many people already have turned to yacht chartering as their way afloat.

For a relatively modest fee – less than you'd spend at a plush resort – you can buy two weeks of high adventure. The scenery moves past you without your needing to turn your head or put down your drink.

The oceans of the world are your oyster, because someone, somewhere, has a boat you'd like at a reasonable price. If the engine fails to start, just get on the horn to the owner or his agent and he'd better fix it fast or you get an extra day of his time. On the other hand, if you run the boat aground on a reef, sink, and survive, insurance pays for adventure you couldn't come by in any other way.

For the man who doesn't own a boat, chartering can be heaven. After two weeks afloat, you leave the boat, knowing that you'll never have to see her again. When it comes time to haul to scrape for barnacles, you won't be there. Her sails looked old and about to rip. Someone else will replace them.

Pleasure yachts should be rigged to run as fast as possible, even though they may never enter a race; because it is easier to navigate a fast moving craft, because tides and vagrant winds have less chance to work against a straight course than with slower traveling boats. The basic difference between cruising craft and racing vessels is the capacity for food and supply storage. Cruisers have larger capacities for stores sufficient to sail around the world.

901
901
ALYSINA

There are three basic ways to go afloat without ownership. Least expensive – and least private – is group charter aboard a large yacht that usually makes stops at regular ports. An example is the fleet of Maine schooners plying the eastern seaboard. You will also find these boats in the Bahamas, the Caribbean, in a few California ports, and in the classified ad columns of boating magazines, where someone is always "looking for a paying crew" to sail around the world.

For the unskilled amateur sailor who has money, a captained yacht is another way to vacation afloat. Often the paying guest must do no more than lift his own drink, though he can, if he wishes, hoist sails, and learn navigation and piloting from the captain, who either owns or operates the yacht. It's the plush way to go, never less than $1000 per week for two, but the ultimate in personalized travel.

Skilled sailors can elect the third route, the bareboat. Usually you must demonstrate your ability to handle the boat, power or sail, and provide written references in advance before a bareboat operator will let you sail away with his investment. And you must put down a hefty insurance and damage deposit. Bareboating is available all over the world. It offers the ultimate in privacy, for you go where you want, when you want – within the insurance limitations of the yacht. Since you're the skipper, you're also the cook and bilge pumper, but there's no one else aboard whom you must pay. So bareboating is less expensive than chartering with a captain but more costly than group chartering.

There you have it. You can enjoy the sport of kings without being one.

—**Jack Weller-Grenard**

Jack Weller-Grenard lives on an island in Detroit, Mich. He has been involved in writing and publishing all his life, and is the publisher of the **Worldwide Yacht Charter and Boat Rental Guide** *and has an extensive knowledge of pleasure yachting.*

For More Information

The Worldwide Yacht Charter & Boat Rental Guide, 18226 Mack, Grosse Pointe, Mich. 48236 is an annual guide that lists more than 2000 yachts and fleets available in most of the areas of the world. These yachts are available for charter to yachtsmen or with captains. The price is $2.95. The Yachting Club of America, 700 S. Federal Hwy., Hdqtrs. & Yacht Basin, Pompano Beach, Fla. 33062 can supply information. For additional organizations and related magazines see sail boat racing. Here are some great books. All are available from World Publications, Box 366, Mountain View, Calif. 94040 at the price listed* plus 25 cents each postage.

Sea Survival, Dougal Robertson. If disaster strikes, you're going to want to know this one. This essential practical guide covers how to equip a survival craft, send distress signals, abandon skip, offer first aid, preserve morale, navigate and forecast weather, collect rainwater, detect the approach of land and identify marine birds. A special section offers four fold-out color charts of the world's oceans. 1975 Hb., 148 pp., ill., $15.00, (Praeger).

Yachting World Handbook, Peter Johnson. Everything on yachting—celestial navigation, racing rules, medical knowledge, and yachtsman's equipment. A thorough, well-done treatise on both racing and cruising. 1972 Hb., 368 pp., ill., $12.95, (St. Martins).

The Longest Race, Cook & Fisher. The complete story of the most adventurous yacht race of all time—a round-the-world race by 14 ocean-sailing yachts in 1973. Includes technical information to satisfy the most demanding nautical buff, and a great book for all lovers of an adventure story. 1975 Hb., ill., $14.95, (McKay).

Tactics and Strategy in Yacht Racing, Joachim Schult. Racing sailors find the greatest part of their pleasure is derived from the cut and thrust of tactical battles. This book covers the basics of the subject. 1971 Hb., ill., $9.85, (Dodd, Mead).

The Yachtman's Vade Mecum, Peter Heaton. An indispensible guide to every aspect of boats and boating, both sail and power. Drawings, charts and photographs highlight this fine book. 1970 Hb., ill., $8.95, (Dodd, Mead).

Yoga

"Who? Me? Stand on my head? Make like a human pretzel? Are you kidding?" Just a few years ago these feelings would have been the typical response of a westerner to yoga. At that time, yoga was on the fringes of respectability. A few fashion models might dabble in it, and some housewives who wanted to look like fashion models, but to most people it was just a senseless system of body contortions, a useless cultural import from India.

Attitudes have been changing, though. More and more people have discovered in yoga an ideal antidote to the stresses and strains of our jet-age society. The old standbys – our traditional sports and recreations – sometimes leave us more tense and tired than refreshed and centered. This is inevitable as long as we bring our habits of work and worry from school and office to the places we reserve for play.

What we need is a playful attitude, a renewing, childlike enjoyment of being alive. And this, surprisingly, is what yoga can offer us.

The yoga we are most familiar with, the yoga of headstands, cross-legged postures, and eye-boggling contortions, is only one of a whole range of mind/body disciplines designed to bring the practioner to a state of total ecstatic integration known as samadhi. Depending on his personality type, a yogi will choose to devote himself to some vision of God, to the path of self-knowledge, to the perfection of the body, or to some other path. The yoga of the body, or hatha yoga, seems to appeal to those who find the more traditional forms of meditation too nebulous or too difficult.

A hatha yogi, as he moves his body through pose after pose, getting progressively more tuned in to the sensuous qualities of stretching muscles and skin, is essentially engaged in a meditation of the body. He doesn't have to worry about falling asleep or fighting to keep his mind one-pointed. The intense

"There is no need to try to talk yourself into accepting stretch sensations: they are smooth and harmonious in comparison. Watch animals stretch—your pet cat, for instance. If you look closely you will see sensuous luxuriating, not pain. Animals instinctively avoid pain, and they instinctively stretch all through the day. Pain is bad, stretch is good." (OMPhoto)

feelings in the muscles automatically keep him alert and focused. Yet there is no need to strive to maintain this quality of awareness; it comes with simple, calm attention to the body sensations.

This rare state of mind has to be experienced to be fully appreciated, but the other benefits of the hatha yoga postures are easy to understand. The systematic and regular stretching of the body makes it extraordinarily supple and limber, so that all movements are easy and freeswinging.

Besides feeling weightless and full of energy, the hatha yogi enjoys freedom from injury, since his loose muscles won't tear readily, the way tight and hard muscles will. And loose muscles are the basis of increased accuracy and speed of response. They bring agility and increased levels of performance.

In developing the loose muscles through the hatha yoga poses, the yogi also develops the ability to concentrate, which is so important to the full enjoyment of any sport or game. Being still and receptive while in the poses seems to increase general openness and alertness, almost as if it re-establishes the primitive, instinctive response mechanisms of the body.

Without a doubt, it is a powerful tool for improving performance in almost anything; it's well worth the attention of people concerned with expanding and refining the ways in which they play.

Playing The Edges

A famous Japanese master of zen archery, Kenran Uneji, used a bow so powerful that none but himself was able to draw it. He was fond of teasing his students by asking them to test his arm muscles when the bow was drawn to its fullest extent. The muscles were always completely relaxed. Kenran Uneji would smile and laugh. "Only beginners use muscle power," he would say, "I draw simply with the spirit."

This story is difficult to accept. The typical westerner would probably dismiss it as nonsense. After all, we are filled from early childhood with beliefs about the virtue of striving and straining for our goals. Our Puritan heritage has taught us that honorable achievements come from hard exertion, and from "sweat of the brow." It stings to have someone from another culture suggest that we can perform better without all that draining effort. All of a sudden, the clenched jaw and the trembling muscles lose their glamor. It's like struggling vainly with a balky jar top only to have a child come by and spin it off with a gentle flick of the wrist.

So I was highly skeptical about the Uneji story, until I saw for myself something very much like it. This incident occurred during a yoga seminar given by the world famous master, B.K.S. Iyengar, of Poona, India. Mr. Iyengar was demonstrating one of the very strenuous standing poses. We students were having difficulties, so he called us up to the front of the hall to demonstrate what we were doing wrong.

"The forward leg must form a right angle," he said. "If the angle is too great or too small, then the body weight will not be supported by the vertical shin bone. The muscles will have to make compensation and counter-compensations. Watch carefully."

He smoothed the hair on the top of his thigh, and then went down into the pose, bending the forward leg too much. The hairs stood on end. The muscles were bulging. He smoothed the hair again and executed the pose incorrectly again, this time not bending the forward leg enough. Just as before, the hairs stood on end. Finally, he smoothed the hairs and executed the pose perfectly. This time, the hairs remained smooth.

Iyengar's dark face cracked into a broad grin as our eyes widened in surprise.

"This is a strenuous pose. Is it not?" he said. "And yet my muscles are at ease. This is the art of true laziness in yoga."

The one master says it is a matter of using spirit power instead of muscle power. The other says it is a matter of becoming truly lazy. Both explanations are inadequate since we don't know what to do with them. They both refer to a remarkably relaxed form of muscle function, but neither gives practical directions on how to achieve it.

Luckily, even the simplest hatha yoga poses can give us a hint of the right feeling, provided we go about them with the appropriate attitude. Take the simple forward bending pose, for instance. Unless we are remarkably limber, we will find it absolutely impossible to get into this position. If we managed to force ourselves into it, we would have to suffer excruciating agony. But true yoga is not a matter of attaining the classical positions, but rather an attitude of calm attentiveness in moving towards them.

Joel Kramer, an outstanding teacher of hatha yoga, uses the concept of "playing with the edges." As we put more and more stretch on a muscle, the intensity of the stretch sensation increases, and with it, the degree of body awareness. But at a certain point, the stretch sensation turns into pain, and the high awareness becomes a harsh, jangling, intolerable confusion. The mind tries to escape from this chaotic situation, by trying to see it as good or necessary. "If it doesn't hurt, it's not doing you any good. Pain equals gain."

But there is no need to try to talk yourself into accepting stretch sensations: they are smooth and harmonious in comparison. Watch animals stretch – your pet cat, for instance. If you look closely you will see sensuous luxuriating, not pain. Animals instinctively avoid pain, and they instinctively stretch, all through the day. Pain is bad, stretch is good.

The edge, then, is that point where the stretch sensation turns into pain sensation, from smooth and pleasurable to harsh and distressing. In the forward bend, or in any pose for that matter, you can experience this edge regardless of how limber or stiff you happen to be. If you put a stretch on the muscle, calmly and attentively, it will relax and lengthen. And if you wait patiently, it will keep relaxing and lengthening so that eventually, without pain or effort, you will find that you have gone far beyond what you thought were the limits of your stretch.

It's possible to push yourself just as far, and quicker, if you are prepared to suffer a lot of pain, and to risk pulling your muscle. But this is not yoga.

An adept yogi will tell you that the secret of getting into the advanced poses is learning how to relax the muscles totally. And he'll also tell you that the degree of relaxation he attains shows up in all his other activities. He can run with fluid floating ease. He can swim smoothly. He can jump and twist and throw with graceful ease.

He may not be as completely relaxed as Kenran Uneji or B.K.S. Iyengar, but he is far more so than most others who, with their striving and straining, waste most of their energy in fighting against themselves.

–Ian Jackson

Besides being a yoga teacher, Ian Jackson has written many articles on yoga and is the author of **Yoga and the Athlete.**

For More Information

3HO Foundation, 1620 Preuss Rd., Los Angeles, Calif. 90035 has over 150,000 members and can be of help. They also publish several publications. Another helpful group is the Self-Realization Fellowship, 2880 San Rafael Ave., Los Angeles, Calif. 90065. Here are some additional reading suggestions. All are available from World Publications, Box 366, Mountain View, Calif. 94040 at the price listed* plus 25 cents postage.

Light on Yoga, B.K.S. Iyengar. The most complete treatment of hatha yoga available. Each of 200 asanas is described simply and clearly, and demonstrated by the author in the 592 photos that accompany the text. A comprehensive reference work for the intermediate or advanced student. 1972 Ppb., 398 pp., ill., $4.95, (Schocken).

Yoga & The Athlete, Ian Jackson. "I want this book to be liberating in many ways . . . " The author discusses yoga and sports from a uniquely personal point of view. 1975 Ppb., 100 pp., ill., $2.50, (World Publications).

A Book of Yoga, Joann & David Weinrib. A new, visually dramatic presentation of this timeless material. The yoga postures are taught through photographs of the authors and their students, most of them in the nude. Illustrations demonstrate the connections between the exercises and their sources in the movements of animals and how they relate to mythology. 1975, 128 (oversize) pp., ill., $9.95, (Harper & Row).

Yoga and Sex, Pandit Shiv Sharma. A study of yoga exercise and how it can positively add to a fullfilling sexual life. Ppb., $1.95, (Simon & Schuster).

Yoga for All Ages, Rachel Carr. Easy-to-follow guide contains a six-stage yoga course, each stage lasting about one week progressing from the simple movements to the more complex. Also special children's section. 1975 Ppb., 160 (oversize) pp., ill., $3.95, (Simon & Schuster).

Illustrated Yoga, William Zorn. An abundance of easy yoga postures which can be practiced without any previous experience. A practical answer to fitness and health lies in the chapters which cover postures, exercises and routines, nutrition and reducing. Easy to read and follow. 1974 Ppb., 172 pp., ill., $2.00, (Wilshire).

The Complete Illustrated Book of Yoga, Swami Vishnudevananda. A training program for beginners as well as advanced students. Leads to remarkable joint flexibility and muscle tone, emotional balance and increased powers of concentration. 1974 Ppb., 411 pp., ill., $1.95, (Simon & Schuster).

Yoga and Health, Selvarajan Yesudian and Elizabeth Haich. Besides presenting detailed and fascinating information on the effects of hatha yoga in terms of Western physiology, this book contains a 21-week course to lead the student, step-by-step, into a balanced program of development. 1965 Ppb., 184 pp., ill., $1.25, (Harper & Row).

Yoga Self-Taught, Andre Van Lysebeth. By far the best book for beginners. Abundant photos which indicate clearly both correct practice and mistakes to be avoided. Those already doing yoga will find this book useful for identifying and correcting bad habits. 1973 Ppb., 264 pp., ill., $2.95, (Harper & Row).

Yoga 28 Day Exercise Plan, Richard Hittleman. Exercise to relieve tension and restore energy, nutrition and discipline information. A Book-of-the-Month Club and Cosmopolitan Book Club selection. 1975 Hb. & Ppb., 224 pp., ill., $8.95/$4.95, (Workman's).

Appendices

Appendix A: Organizations and Ruling Groups For Sports in General

Regardless of the sport in which an athlete competes, often he comes under the influence of one or more general sports bodies. Here are details of some of these organizations:

Amateur Athletic Union (AAU)—The AAU is the United States' representative for the International Amateur Athletic Federation (IAAF), the major international governing body. The address of the AAU is 3400 W. 86th St., Indianapolis, Ind. 46268. The IAAF is located at 162 Upper Richmond Rd., Putney, London S.W. 15, England. The AAU establishes rules and accepts American records. AAU-sponsored events include bobsled, boxing, track and field, swimming, diving, water polo, synchronized swimming, wrestling, weightlifting, luge, trampoline and tumbling, judo and karate.

United States Olympic Committee (USOC)—This is the US member organization of the International Olympic Committee. Its job is to select and prepare US men's and women's teams for the Olympics and Pan-American Games. See Appendix E for a list of the sports included in the Olympics. The USOC is located at 57 Park Avenue, New York, N.Y. 10016, and the address of the IOC is: Mon Repos, Lausanne, Switzerland.

National Collegiate Athletic Association (NCAA)—The NCAA, located at Midland Building, 1221 Baltimore, Kansas City, Mo. 64105, controls competition in various sports at most four-year college and universities in the country. It establishes rules, accepts collegiate records, and promotes competition for events in the following areas: baseball, basketball, cross-country running, fencing, football, golf, gymnastics, ice hockey, lacrosse, skiing, soccer, swimming, tennis, track and field, volleyball, water polo, wrestling. The NCAA has over 600 member schools. They are divided into the University Division for the major ones, and the College Division for the smaller ones.

National Association of Intercollegiate Athletics (NAIA)—This body has its headquarters at 106 W. 12th St., Kansas City, Mo. 64056. The NAIA is similar to the NCAA in that it caters to the needs of four-year college athletes. The schools—over 500 of them—belonging to the NAIA are generally smaller than those in the NCAA. Many of them belong to both organizations. The sports in which they sponsor events are cross-country running, soccer, football, ice hockey, swimming, gymnastics, basketball, wrestling, bowling, volleyball, baseball, golf, tennis and track.

National Junior College Athletic Association (NJCAA)—This group operates along the lines of the NCAA and the NAIA, but its members are two-year colleges. Just about every sport you can think of which takes place at the junior-college level is sanctioned by this organization. Their address is: Hilton Inn, Hilton Place, Hutchinson, Kans. 67501.

National Federation of State High School Athletic Associations—This body, as the name implies, is made up of individual state associations. The national group sets guidelines for the conduct of competitions in various high school sports throughout the country. Contact them at 7 S. Dearborn, Suite 1240, Chicago, Ill. 60603.

Appendix B: General Sports Magazines

Sports Illustrated—Time & Life Building, Chicago, Ill. 60611. Most sports enthusiasts are familiar with this staple publication for sport. Not only does it cover, in depth, the old familiar sports, but also sports, games, and other activities which the average sportsman may never have heard of—Over the Line, for instance. The magazine also prints anecdotal articles and special interest features, as well as excellent reportage of athletic events.

Sport—Mcfadden-Bartell Corporation, P.O. Box 5016, Des Moines, Ia. 50306. Now in existence for three decades, this publication provides excellent information on the more popular team sports, with an occasional piece on the smaller ones. Rather than concentrate on reporting the events, **Sport** prefers to provide close glimpses of the teams and the players.

WomenSports—1600 S. Amphlett Blvd., San Mateo, Calif. 94402. This is Billie Jean and Larry King's own presentation to the female sports enthusiast—and others who are interested in women's athletics. This substantial publication carries a variety of articles on a large sphere of sports subjects and personalities, from drag racing to figure skating, Olga Korbut to Howard Cosell.

Appendix C: Manufacturers of General Sports Equipment

Before listing the actual manufacturers, it might be beneficial to mention the National Sporting Goods Association, 717 N. Michigan Ave., Chicago, Illinois 60611. This is the national association of the sporting goods industry. If you have any questions at all about athletic equipment that your local dealer can't answer, this is the group to contact. Their publication, *Selling Sporting Goods,* is also an excellent source of information. The following is a list of the larger sporting goods manufacturers who produce a variety of sports equipment:

- AMF Voit Inc. —3801 S. Harbor Blvd., Santa Ana, Calif. 92704. Athletic, exercise, bowling, baseball, water sports.
- Bancroft Sporting Goods—Bancroft Court, Woonsocket, R.I. 02895. Tennis, squash, badminton, paddle rackets, tennis apparel.
- Browning—Route 1, Morgan, Utah 06469. Sporting arms, fishing rods and reels, archery, sportsman's boots and apparel, hunting knives, gun cases, camping, bicycles, golf carts.
- Dunlop Sports Div—P.O. Box 1109, Buffalo, N.Y. 14240. Golf, tennis, table tennis, and racket sports accessories.
- Macgregor Co.—One Brunswick Plaza, Skokie, Ill. 60076. Golf, tennis, and baseball equipment.
- Rawlings-Adirondack-Fred Perry—2300 Delmar, St. Louis, Mo. 63166. Equipment for a variety of sports.
- Wilson Sporting Goods—2233 West St., River Grove, Ill. 60171. Equipment for multitudes of sports.
- Spalding Division of Questor—Meadow St., Chicopee, Mass. 01014. Golf, tennis, baseball, basketball, football and hockey products.

Appendix D: Radio and Television Networks

- American Broadcasting Corporation–1330 Avenue of the Americas, New York, N.Y. 10019.
- National Broadcasting Corporation–30 Rockefeller Plaza, New York, N.Y. 10020.
- Columbia Broadcasting System–51 W. 52nd St., New York, N.Y. 10019.

Appendix E: List of Olympic Sports and Games

Summer Games

Archery
Basketball
Boxing
Canoeing and Kayaking
Cycling
Diving
Equestrian Sports
Fencing
Field Hockey
Gymnastics
Judo
Modern Pentathlon
Rowing
Shooting
Soccer
Swimming
Team Handball
Track and Field
Volleyball
Water Polo
Weight Lifting
Wrestling
Yachting

Winter Games

Alpine Skiing
Biathlon
Bobsled
Figure Skating
Ice Hockey
Luge
Nordic Combined
Nordic Skiing
Ski Jumping
Speed Skating

The SportSource Update

The **SportSource** will be periodically updated by means of the **SportSource Update.** We plan to include address changes, new books, additions and corrections to the original; new interviews from leading athletes, information on new sports and other important information will make up each edition of the **Update** published quarterly. If you like the **SportSource,** you'll want to get the **Update.** Just send a dollar and the coupon below to **SportSource Update,** Box 366, Mountain View, Calif. 94040.

SportSource Update, Box 366, Mountain View, CA 94040

[ ] Enclosed is $1.00 to cover the cost of the **SportSource Update** for one year.

Name________________________________

Address________________________________

List your five favorite sports and recreational activities (List your most favorite first):

Do you compete?________________ **In what sport?**__________

How many hours a week do you participate?__________ **Train?**__________

Do you follow a special diet?________________________

Do you use any other outside disciplines (yoga, meditation, etc.) to help improve your performance?____________________

Please enclose payment, we cannot bill you.

Also, ask for our free **Sport Book Catalog** listing over 1400 sport books.